P9-DDW-774

The World Book Encyclopedia

D Volume 5

Field Enterprises Educational Corporation
Chicago Frankfurt London Paris Rome Sydney Tokyo Toronto

The World Book Encyclopedia

Printed in the United States of America

ISBN 0-7166-0076-5

Library of Congress Catalog Card Number 75-1722

Dd

Dd is the fourth letter of our alphabet. It was also the fourth letter in the alphabet used by the Semites, who once lived in Syria and Palestine. They named it *daleth*, a word that meant *door*. It is believed that this word came from one of the *hieroglyphs* (picture writings) the ancient Egyptians used. They drew a picture of a door with panels. See ALPHABET.

Uses. *D* or *d* ranks as about the tenth most frequently used letter in books, newspapers, and other printed material in English. When used on a report card, *D* usually means poor work or near failure in a school subject. In music, it names one note of the scale. As an abbreviation, *D* stands for the isotope *deuterium* in chemistry, for *electric displacement* in electronics, and for *500* in the Roman numeral system. The symbol *d* denotes *drag* in aeronautics, and the fourth known quantity in algebra. The symbol *D* or *d* stands for *diameter* in mathematics and physics, or a wider-than-average shoe.

Pronunciation. In English, a person pronounces *d* with his tongue touching the roof of his mouth just back of his teeth. In French, Dutch, and Italian, the tongue touches the upper front teeth. In German, a *d* at the beginning of a word, followed by a vowel, resembles the English *d* sound. Otherwise, it usually has a *t* sound. The Spanish *d* is expressed more softly than in English when it is at the beginning of a word. Elsewhere, it has a *th* sound, similar to *the* in English, not the *th* of *thin*. See PRONUNCIATION.

I. J. GELB and JAMES M. WELLS

The fourth letter took its shape from an ancient Egyptian symbol used to show a door. Its sound came from the Semitic word *daleth*, which means *door.*

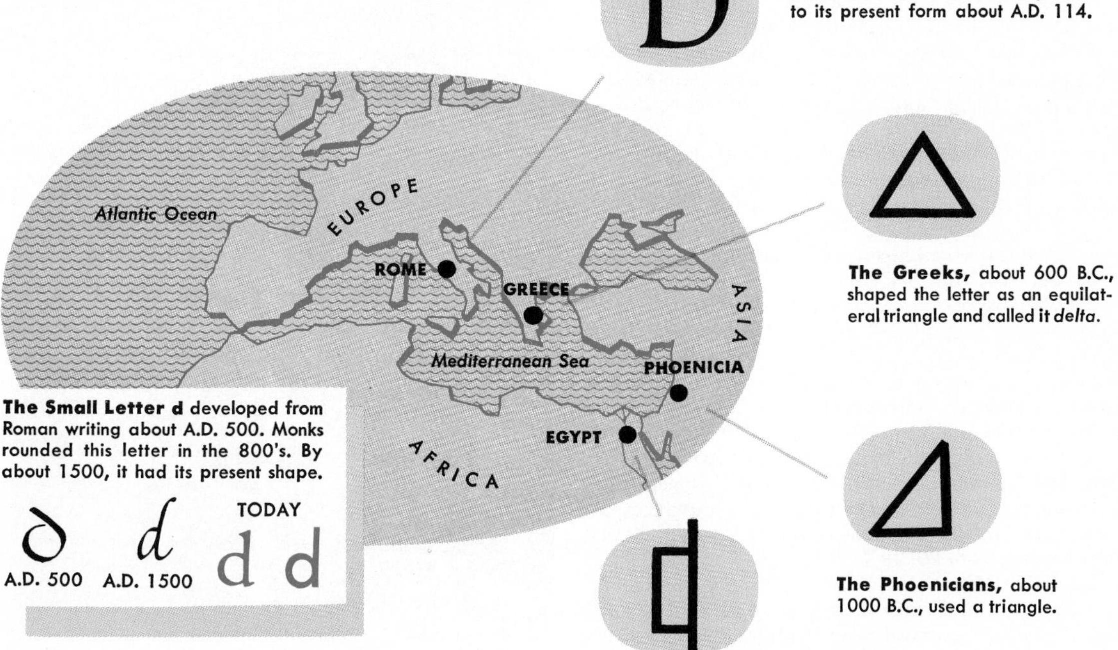

The Romans rounded the capital D to its present form about A.D. 114.

The Greeks, about 600 B.C., shaped the letter as an equilateral triangle and called it *delta*.

The Phoenicians, about 1000 B.C., used a triangle.

The Egyptians, about 3000 B.C., wrote with a symbol that represented a door with panels.

The Small Letter d developed from Roman writing about A.D. 500. Monks rounded this letter in the 800's. By about 1500, it had its present shape.

D-DAY is the term for a secret date on which a military operation is to begin. Peacetime planning of military operations is also based on hypothetical D-Days. Terms such as *D-plus-3* (three days after initial attack) are used to plan the sequence of operations. The expression *D-Day* became current in World War II when it defined the dates set for Allied landings on enemy-held coasts. The most famous D-Day is June 6, 1944, when the Allies invaded Normandy. STEFAN T. POSSONY

See also WORLD WAR II (The Invasion of Europe).

DA NANG, *dah NAHNG,* or TOURANE (pop. 427,834), is the second largest city in South Vietnam. Only Saigon, the capital, is larger. Da Nang's location on the South China Sea has made it an important trading center since the 1600's. For location, see VIETNAM (map). The city produces soap and textiles.

Da Nang became a key city in the Vietnam War because it lies only about 100 miles (160 kilometers) south of North Vietnam. United States military forces established bases in Da Nang, and it became a favorite target of the North Vietnamese. Vietnamese Communists gained control of the city in 1975. See VIETNAM WAR. DENNIS J. DUNCANSON

DABCHICK. See GREBE.

DACCA, *DAK uh* (pop. 556,712), is the capital and largest city of Bangladesh. It lies along the Burhi Ganga River in the central part of the country. For location, see BANGLADESH (political map).

Dacca has been a center of Moslem culture for more than 300 years. Many of the city's *mosques* (Moslem houses of worship) and other buildings were built during the 1600's. The city has three universities and several technical schools. The processing of jute ranks as a leading economic activity in the Dacca area. Factories in the city and its suburbs also manufacture leather goods, textiles, and other products.

From 1608 to 1704, Dacca was the capital of East Bengal province in the Mogul Empire (see MOGUL EMPIRE). Later, the city came under British control as part of British India. In 1947, India was divided into two nations—India and Pakistan. Dacca became the capital of the province of East Pakistan. In 1971, civil war in Pakistan led to the establishment of East Pakistan as the independent nation of Bangladesh. Dacca then became the capital of the new nation. ROBERT I. CRANE

DACE, HORNED. See CHUB.

DACHAU, *DAH kow,* was one of the first concentration camps set up in Germany by the Nazis. It stood near the town of Dachau, 10 miles (16 kilometers) from Munich. Dachau was built in 1933 as an extermination camp for Jews and political prisoners. After 1943, many prisoners worked in arms factories that were built there. The Nazis performed brutal medical experiments on over 3,500 persons. Almost all of these prisoners died. Thousands more were executed or died of starvation and epidemics. United States forces liberated about 32,000 prisoners on April 29, 1945. WILLIAM A. JENKS

DACHSHUND, *DAHKS hund,* is a dog known for its long body and short legs. It is considered the national dog of Germany. The dachshund has a cone-shaped head, a slim, tapering muzzle, and long, drooping ears. Its front legs are slightly curved. It has a large chest and a long pointed tail. Its glossy coat usually is black or tan, but it may be red, yellow, gray, spotted, or striped. Most dachshunds have short smooth hair. Two other varieties are the long-coated, with long, silky hair; and the wire-haired, with a rough coat.

The dachshund is a strong, hardy, alert dog with a good sense of smell. In central Europe, it was once used to hunt badgers. Dachshund is German for *badger hound.* A dachshund makes a good pet. OLGA DAKAN

See also DOG (color picture: Hounds).

DACIA. See TRAJAN; ROMAN EMPIRE (map).

DACRON is the Du Pont Company's trademark for a synthetic fiber used in clothing, home furnishings, and industry. Dacron resists fading and wrinkling. It is used to make such products as curtains, drapes, fire hoses, and filters. Dacron is made from coal, water, petroleum, limestone, and natural gases. British and Du Pont scientists developed it in the early 1940's. The British called it *Terylene.* Du Pont bought the exclusive right to U.S. production. It first appeared on the U.S. market in 1951. CHARLES H. RUTLEDGE

DACTYLIC METER. See POETRY (Metrical Patterns).

DADAISM, a protest movement in the arts, was formed in 1916 by a group of artists and poets in Zurich, Switzerland. The Dadaists reacted to what they believed were outworn traditions in art, and the evils they saw in society. They tried to shock and provoke the public with outrageous pieces of writing, cabaret skits, poetry recitals, and art exhibitions. Much Dada art was playful and highly experimental. The name

Third version (1951) after lost original of 1913; the Museum of Modern Art, New York City, Sidney and Harriet Janis Collection.

Dada Ready-Mades, such as Marcel Duchamp's *Bicycle Wheel,* were exhibited as art to discredit the idea that art was profound.

Dada, a French word meaning *hobbyhorse*, was deliberately chosen because it was nonsensical.

The founders of the movement included the French poet Tristan Tzara, the German artist Jean Arp, and the German poet Hugo Ball. Later members included the French artist Francis Picabia, the French poets Louis Aragon and André Breton, and the German artist Max Ernst. Perhaps the best-known Dadaist was the French artist Marcel Duchamp. He was not a member of the Zurich group, but was working in the Dada spirit as early as 1913. About that year, he completed his first *ready-made*. Ready-mades were common objects, such as bicycle wheels, exhibited as though they were works of art. In this way, Duchamp ridiculed the idea that art was something profound. MARCEL FRANCISCONO

See also ARP, JEAN; BRETON, ANDRÉ; DUCHAMP, MARCEL; ERNST, MAX; PAINTING (Dadaism).

DADDY LONGLEGS is a popular name in America for a harmless, long-legged creature related to the spider. Its legs are bent and its body hangs close to the ground. It is not an insect, but an *arachnid* (see ARACHNID). Another name for it is *harvestman*. In England, the *crane fly* is called *daddy longlegs*. The crane fly is an insect which has wings and looks much like a large mosquito.

Scientific Classification. The harvestman belongs to the class *Arachnida*. It makes up the order *Phalangida*. The crane fly belongs to the class *Insecta*, order *Diptera*, and family *Tipulidae*. EDWARD A. CHAPIN

DADE, FRANCIS L. See FLORIDA (Territorial Days).

DAEDALUS, *DEHD uh luhs*, was an architect and sculptor in Greek mythology. According to the myth, he was jealous of one of his pupils named Talos, and killed him. Because of this he had to escape from Athens to Crete. There he built the labyrinth (see LABYRINTH).

Daedalus and his son Icarus offended the king of Crete and were imprisoned. In order to escape, Daedalus made two pairs of large wings out of feathers and wax. He and Icarus flew away with these fastened on their shoulders, but Icarus fell into the sea. PADRAIC COLUM

See also AIRPLANE (History [picture]); MINOTAUR.

DAFFODIL, *DAF uh dihl*, is a yellow flower that blooms in the early spring. It is a kind of *narcissus*, and comes from Europe, where it grows wild in the woods. It is also grown in gardens in America and other regions.

There are many kinds of daffodils. The best-known daffodil is also called the *trumpet narcissus*. It has one blossom at the end of each stalk. The daffodil has a large flower and five or six bluish-green leaves about 15 inches (38 centimeters) long. Daffodil bulbs should be planted in autumn. They should be planted about 4 inches (10 centimeters) deep and about 5 inches (13 centimeters) apart.

Ferry-Morse Seed Co.

Daffodil Blossoms

Scientific Classification. Daffodils belong to the amaryllis family, *Amaryllidaceae*. They are classified as genus *Narcissus*, species *N. pseudo-narcissus*. DONALD WYMAN

See also BULB; FLOWER (color picture: Spring Garden Flowers); NARCISSUS; OREGON (picture).

DA GAMA, *duh GA muh*, **VASCO,** *VAS koh* (1469?-1524), a Portuguese explorer, was the first European to sail around the Cape of Good Hope to India. King John II of Portugal originally chose Da Gama's father to command the expedition. But both the king and the elder Da Gama died before their plans were completed. The new king, Manuel I, gave the command to Vasco. His four-ship expedition left Portugal on July 8, 1497. The fleet rounded the Cape of Good Hope in November, and arrived at Calicut (Kozhikode), India, in May, 1498.

Detail of an engraving by Broegg, Lisbon Geographical Society

Vasco da Gama

The Indian ruler received Da Gama coolly. Arab traders, resenting Da Gama's presence, set the Hindus against him, and the Portuguese were in constant danger. When he returned to Portugal with a cargo of spice, the king rewarded him with the title of Admiral of the Sea of the Indies. Later, the king made Da Gama Count of Vidigueira and helped him become wealthy.

Da Gama made another voyage to India in 1502 and 1503, to avenge Indian violence against Portuguese sailors and to establish colonies. He retired after that voyage, but during the next 20 years he acted as adviser to King Manuel and Manuel's successor, King John III.

In 1524, the king sent Da Gama to India to serve as viceroy. Da Gama died in Cochin, India, later that year. He was born in Sines. CHARLES EDWARD NOWELL

See also EXPLORATION AND DISCOVERY (map).

DAGGER is a short-bladed sword. It is divided into three parts. These are the *blade*, which may be from 6 to 18 inches (15 to 46 centimeters) long, the *guard*, and the *handle*, or *hilt*. Daggers are ordinarily worn at the belt and placed in a sheath or a scabbard. In Scotland, a dagger is called a *dirk;* in France, a *poniard;* and in Italy, a *stiletto*. Pioneers in America carried a dagger called the *bowie knife*. The earliest form of bayonet was a dagger with a tapered handle which would fit into the muzzle of a musket. Stone Age men used daggers made of flint or of horn from animals such as reindeer. See also BAYONET; BOWIE KNIFE. JACK O'CONNOR

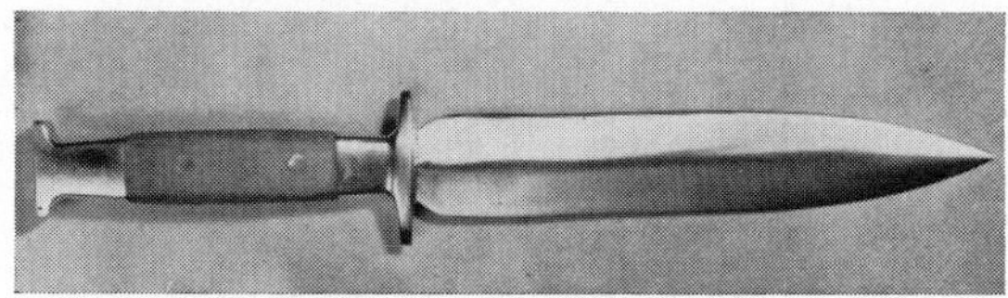

Press Syndicate

Razor-Sharp Daggers were carried by commandos and paratroops in daring raids and assaults during World War II.

DAGHESTAN, *DAH gih STAHN*, or DAGESTAN, is a state, or autonomous republic, in the Russian Soviet Federated Socialist Republic. It lies on the west shore of the Caspian Sea. It has a population of about 1,457,000 and an area of 19,421 square miles (50,300 square kilometers). The capital is Makhachkala.

DAGON was a god of the Philistines. See SAMSON.

DAGUERRE, *DAH GAIR*, **LOUIS JACQUES MANDÉ** (1787-1851), was a French inventor and painter. He perfected the daguerreotype process of making permanent pictures. He opened the Diorama, a theater without actors, in 1822, in Paris. In it, he produced effects of moonlight and other lights by illuminating transparent canvas scenery painted on both sides. In 1829, he began working with Joseph Niépce, a French physicist. Daguerre perfected the daguerreotype process after Niépce's death. See also DAGUERREOTYPE; PHOTOGRAPHY (History). BEAUMONT NEWHALL

DAGUERREOTYPE, *duh GEHR uh typ*, is one of the first forms of photographic print. It was named for its inventor Louis J. M. Daguerre. Daguerre first described the technique of making daguerreotypes in 1839. He made a polished, silvered copper plate light-sensitive by subjecting it to iodine fumes. He then exposed it from 3 to 30 minutes in a camera. He developed the image with mercury vapor, and "fixed" it with sodium thiosulfate (*hypo*). Improvements made in 1840 increased the sensitivity of the plate by bromine fuming, and enriched the image by toning it with gold chloride. The highlights of a daguerreotype are whitish. The shadows are bare, mirrorlike areas which appear dark when the plate is held to reflect a dark field. The permanency of the process and its ability to record minute details are its outstanding characteristics. After 1851, the wet collodion process gradually took the place of the daguerreotype. In the 1800's, Americans used daguerreotypes a great deal, especially for portraits. BEAUMONT NEWHALL

See also DAGUERRE, LOUIS J. M.; TALBOTYPE.

DAHLEM DISTRICT. See BERLIN (A New City).

DAHLGREN, *DAL gruhn*, **JOHN ADOLPHUS BERNARD** (1809-1870), an American naval officer and inventor, developed the Dahlgren gun that became famous during the Civil War. He served as chief of the U.S. Navy Bureau of Ordnance, and built a gun factory, where he made and tested his naval cannon.

He became an unofficial aid to President Abraham Lincoln in 1861, and directed the defense of Washington. Later, he served as commander of the Union Navy's South Atlantic Blockading Squadron. Dahlgren was born in Philadelphia. RICHARD S. WEST, JR.

DAHLIA, *DAL yuh*, is the name of a popular group of flowers cultivated from the original dahlia of Mexico. Some are shaped like balls; others have long, flat petals. *Cactus dahlias* have double blossoms with long, twisted petals. Dahlias are now grown throughout the United States, in southern Canada, and in Europe. They are named for the Swedish botanist, Anders Dahl.

Dahlias grow from *tuberous*, or thick, fleshy roots that look somewhat like bulbs. They should be planted in rich, well-drained soil, and in full sun after all danger of frost has passed. Dahlia stalks are brittle; the taller kinds should be tied to stakes. After the first frost, the roots should be dug up and stored for the winter in a dry place, at a temperature of 40° F. to 55° F. (4° C to 13° C). Storing the root clump with soil attached will stop shriveling. At planting time, the roots should be separated carefully and planted about 6 inches (15 centimeters) deep. Dahlias flower in the late summer.

Scientific Classification. Dahlias belong to the composite family, *Compositae*. Garden dahlias are genus *Dahlia*, species *D. pinnata*. GEORGE A. BEACH

See also FLOWER (color picture: Fall Garden Flowers).

A Daguerreotype Was Printed on a Copper Plate.
Eastman Historical Photographic Collection

The Fairy Dahlia Is Also Called the Pompon.
J. Horace McFarland

Capital
Other City or Town
Road
Rail Line
Highest Known Elevation
River

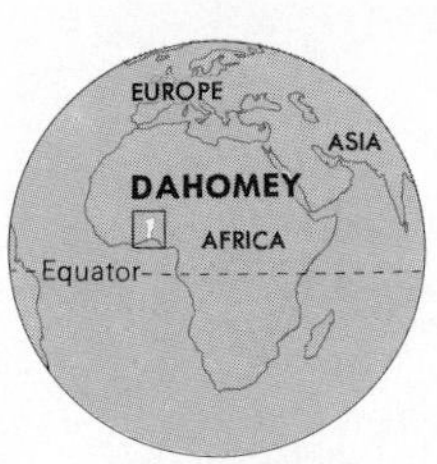

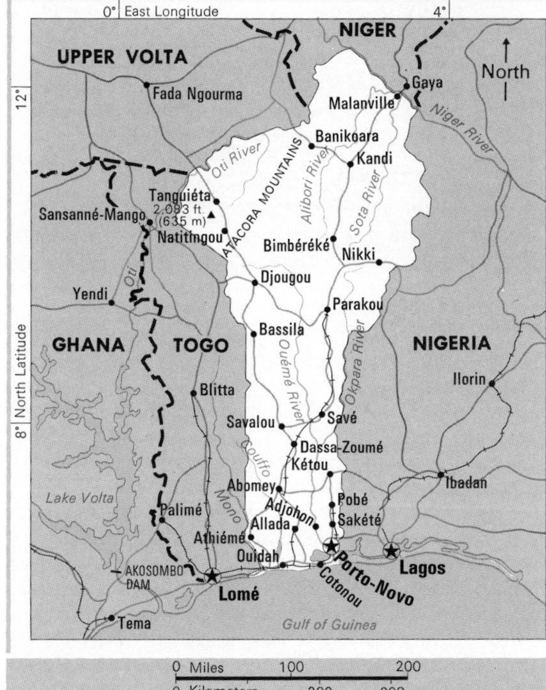

WORLD BOOK map

DAHOMEY, *duh HOH mee*, is a country on the west coast of Africa. It is a little larger than Tennessee and, like that state, is long and narrow. Dahomey extends 415 miles (668 kilometers) inland from the Gulf of Guinea. Most of the people of Dahomey are Negroes, and the majority of them farm the land.

Dahomey was formerly a territory in French West Africa. It became independent in 1960. The country's name in French, the official language, is RÉPUBLIQUE DU DAHOMEY. Porto-Novo is the capital. Cotonou is the largest city, main port, and commercial center.

Government of Dahomey has been unstable since the country became independent. Military and political leaders have overthrown the government several times, and the country has had a number of constitutions. In 1972, a military group took control of Dahomey's government. Mathieu Kerekou, the leader of the group, became president of the country.

People. Dahomey's population consists of about 60 groups of people. The largest groups are the Fons, who number about 700,000, and the Adjas, with about 220,000 members. Both these groups live in the southern part of Dahomey. The population includes about 5,500 Europeans.

Most of Dahomey's people live in simple houses built by hand. However, some people, particularly in the cities, live in concrete homes. In the lagoon areas, behind the coast, bamboo huts are perched on stakes to protect people from the water. In the Atacora Mountains in the northwest, people live in round houses that have mud walls and thatched roofs.

The women of Dahomey wear brightly colored dresses. A popular garment for men is the *agbade*, which includes trousers, short jacket, and full robe. Many people, particularly in southern Dahomey, wear clothing similar to that worn in the United States and Canada.

About 65 per cent of Dahomey's people practice *animism*, the belief that all things in nature have spirits. About 15 per cent of the people are Christians, and 13 per cent are Moslems. Most of the Christians live in the south. The Moslems live in the northern part of the country.

More than 30 per cent of the children go to school. Dahomey has elementary schools, high schools, and technical schools.

Land and Climate. The coast of Dahomey is flat and sandy, and has no natural harbors. Ships must anchor offshore, except at the man-made port of Cotonou. Beyond the lagoons that lie behind the coastal strip, the country is flat and forested. About 50 miles (80 kilometers) inland is a great marsh. Dahomey's highest elevation, about 2,000 feet (610 meters), is in the Atacora Mountains in the northwest. The Ouémé River, the country's longest river, flows 280 miles (451 kilometers) into the Gulf of Guinea.

Southern Dahomey has a hot, humid climate. Rainy seasons occur in the south from April to July and from September to November. Northern Dahomey has less humidity and greater changes in daily temperatures. In the north, the rainy season lasts from April to October. Rainfall averages 20 inches (51 centimeters) a year in the southeast, 50 inches (130 centimeters) in the central section, and 35 inches (89 centimeters) in the north.

FACTS IN BRIEF

Capital: Porto-Novo.

Official Language: French.

Form of Government: Republic.

Area: 43,484 sq. mi. (112,622 km²). *Greatest Distances*—north-south, 415 mi. (668 km); east-west, 202 mi. (325 km). *Coastline*—77 mi. (124 km).

Elevation: *Highest*—Atacora Mountains, about 2,000 ft. (610 m) above sea level. *Lowest*—sea level.

Population: *Estimated 1976 Population*—3,192,000; distribution, 84 per cent rural, 16 per cent urban; density, 73 persons per sq. mi. (28 persons per km²). *1961 Census*—2,106,000. *Estimated 1981 Population*—3,646,000.

Chief Products: *Agriculture*—coffee, cotton, palm oil and kernels, peanuts, shea nuts, tobacco.

National Anthem: "L'Aube Nouvelle" ("The New Dawn").

Flag: A green vertical stripe stands to the left of two horizontal stripes. The top stripe is gold and the bottom one is red. See FLAG (color picture: Flags of Africa).

Money: *Basic Unit*—franc. For the value of the franc in dollars, see MONEY (table: Values).

Marc and Evelyne Bernheim, Rapho Guillumette

Off to School! Children living in Ganvié, a lagoon village in Dahomey, ride to school in dugout canoes instead of in buses. The children study as they ride. They live in thatch-roofed huts that are built on *piles* (poles) in the water.

Economy. Dahomey is mainly an agricultural country. Palm trees in the south are the nation's chief source of wealth. Palm oil and palm kernels are the leading exports. The oil from the kernels is used in making soap and margarine. Other exports of the country include coffee, cotton, peanuts, tobacco, and shea nuts, from which butter is made. Most of Dahomey's trade is with France.

Dahomey produces all its own food, except meat and rice, which it imports. Food crops include beans, corn, manioc, millet, sorghum, sweet potatoes, and some rice. The people raise cattle, goats, pigs, and sheep.

Industry is at an early stage of development in Dahomey. The south has a few industrial plants, including palm oil refineries, industrial bakeries, and cotton mills. Some minerals—diamonds, gold, marble, petroleum, phosphate, and potash—have been discovered in Dahomey.

Dahomey provides an outlet to the sea for Niger by rail and road. It is a crossroads for coastal road traffic from Nigeria to Ghana. There are about 400 miles (640 kilometers) of railroad. The country has five airports.

History. During the 1100's or 1200's, several African kingdoms were founded in the region that is now Dahomey. By the 1600's, the kingdom of Dahomey, with Abomey its capital, controlled the area. Europeans began to establish slave-trading posts along the coast at about this time. The power of the king of Dahomey was based largely on the slave trade.

The palm oil trade replaced the slave trade during the 1800's. In 1851, France signed a trade agreement with Dahomey. Soldiers of the kingdom attacked French trading posts in 1892, and were defeated. France took over Dahomey and made it a territory of French West Africa in 1904. The French built railroads and roads, and encouraged coffee growing. Under the 1946 French constitution, Dahomey became an overseas territory of France. The French gave Dahomey self-government in 1958. Dahomey became fully independent in August, 1960, and joined the United Nations later that year.

Social unrest and political rivalries have led to frequent changes in Dahomey's government since the country's independence in 1960. Military leaders overthrew the government several times during the 1960's and 1970's. In May, 1970, a civilian government was formed, headed by a three-man presidential council. In October, 1972, a military government again took control of the country. It was headed by army leader Mathieu Kerekou. IMMANUEL WALLERSTEIN

See also PORTO-NOVO.

DAIKON. See RADISH.

DÁIL ÉIREANN. See IRELAND (History).

DAIMLER, *DYM lur*, **GOTTLIEB** (1834-1900), a German engineer, developed an internal-combustion engine light enough to power an automobile. He and Wilhelm Maybach worked with motors for years, and produced a motor-bicycle in 1885. They made a four-wheeled car in 1886. The Daimler Company was founded in 1890, and produced the Mercedes car. The Daimler and Benz companies merged to make the Mercedes-Benz car in 1926. SMITH HEMPSTONE OLIVER

See also AUTOMOBILE (The Gasoline Car); BENZ, KARL; MANUFACTURING (table: 25 Leading Manufacturers); MOTORCYCLE (picture); MAYBACH, WILHELM.

DAIMYO. See SAMURAI; JAPAN (Return of the Emperor's Power).

DAIREN, *DY REHN*, also called TALIEN and LÜ-TA, is the leading seaport of Manchuria. It stands on the southern coast of the Liaotung Peninsula (see CHINA [political map]). Dairen and Port Arthur form a municipality that has a population of 4,000,000 (see PORT ARTHUR). Dairen is about 100 feet (30 meters) above sea level. It has an excellent harbor, free from ice most of the winter. Russia leased the peninsula in 1898. Japan gained control of the city after the Russo-Japanese War. China took control in 1955. THEODORE H. E. CHEN

DAIRY BELT. See MILK (From Farm to Table).

DAIRYING is that branch of agriculture which is concerned with producing milk, butter, evaporated milk, ice cream, cheese, and dried milk products. It includes the care and feeding of the cattle which give the milk. Dairy farming is one of the leading farm activities in the United States, with an annual cash return of $6,815,-000,000 from the sale of milk. More than 560,000 farm families earn all or part of their living from dairying.

Each person in the United States consumes an average of about 560 pounds (254 kilograms) of dairy products every year. In the United States, dairy goods account for 14 cents of each dollar most families spend for food. These items make up their second largest food expense, ranking behind only the combined expenses for meat, fish, poultry, and eggs. Fluid milk and cream make up about half of the dairy goods used in the country, and butter accounts for about a fifth. The remainder includes cheese, ice cream, evaporated and condensed milk, and dried skim milk.

There are about 11,700,000 milk cows on farms in the United States today. These cows produce about 120 billion pounds (54 billion kilograms) of milk each year, and $4\frac{1}{3}$ billion pounds (2 billion kilograms) of butterfat. The average yearly milk production per cow is about 10,270 pounds (4,658 kilograms), an increase of about 2,525 pounds (1,145 kilograms) per cow during the past 10 years. Butterfat production per cow during this period has increased from 275 to 380 pounds (125 to 172 kilograms). About 62 billion pounds (28 billion kilograms) of milk a year are used for manufactured dairy products. The largest amount of this milk—about 40 per cent—is used to make butter. About 34 per cent is made into cheese, about 21 per cent is used for ice cream and other frozen dairy products, and about 5 per cent is used for evaporated and dried milk products. About 3 per cent is used on farms, mainly for feeding calves.

Dairy Farms

There is some dairy farming in every state, but the industry is concentrated in a group of states running from New York and Pennsylvania to Wisconsin and Minnesota. Dairy farming also is important on the Pacific Coast, particularly in California. Wisconsin leads the states in milk production. It produces about 19 billion pounds (9 billion kilograms) of milk annually. California, Minnesota, New York, and Pennsylvania are other leading dairy states.

Most dairy farms are near large cities. But with today's processing equipment and refrigerated tank trucks, dairymen can also ship milk long distances easily and safely. The average size of U.S. dairy herds is about 25 cows. Large commercial dairy farms may have more than 1,000 cows.

Dairy Cattle. The five most important breeds of dairy cattle in the United States are the Holstein-Friesian, Jersey, Guernsey, Ayrshire, and Brown Swiss. The various breeds of dairy cattle differ in their size and appearance. The composition of their milk and the amount of milk they produce also vary.

Holstein-Friesian cattle, often called merely Holsteins, produce the most milk. Their milk, however, does not contain as high a percentage of the natural fat called *butterfat* as does the milk of the other breeds. The Brown Swiss is second in the amount of milk produced, while the Ayrshire is third and the Guernsey fourth. The milk of Jersey and Guernsey cows is yellower in color than the milk of Holstein cows, because it contains a higher percentage of butterfat. Jersey milk contains about 5 per cent butterfat, Guernsey milk contains about 4.7 per cent, and Holstein milk contains about 3.7 per cent. Brown Swiss and Ayrshire cows produce milk with about 4 per cent butterfat.

The breed of cattle kept on a dairy farm will depend upon the farmer's breed preference and the market for milk. Sometimes it will be more advantageous to keep

Grant Heilman

Holstein Cows, *above,* produce more milk per cow than any other breed. About 85 per cent of U.S. dairy cows are Holsteins.

C. L. Norton, the contributor of this article, is Head of the Dairy and Poultry Science Department at Kansas State University.

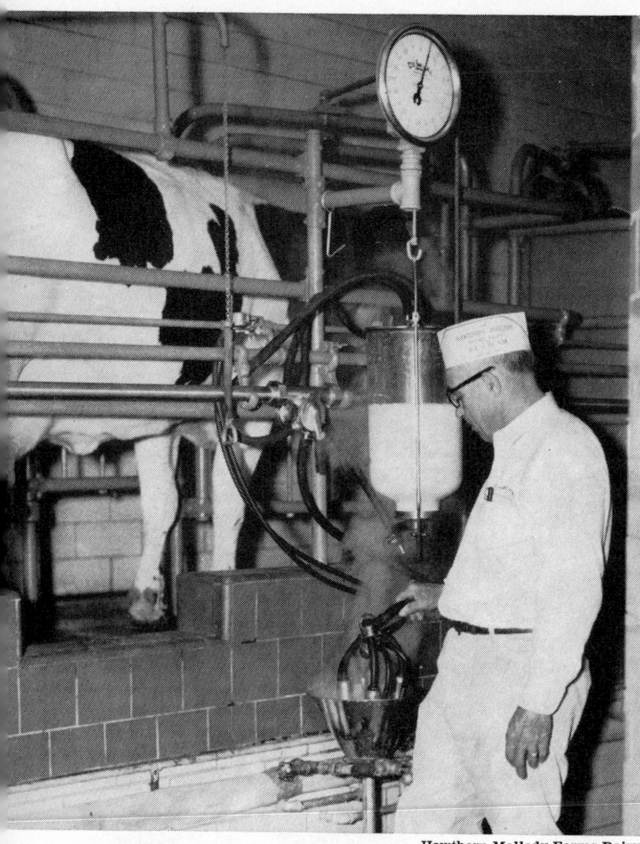

Hawthorn-Mellody Farms Dairy

The Milking Parlor of a Dairy Farm is a special room kept spotlessly clean. After machines milk the cows, the milk is weighed and piped by vacuum to refrigerated tanks for storage until it can be delivered to a processing plant.

Holsteins because of the quantity of milk they produce. In other regions, it may be more profitable for dairy farmers to raise Guernseys and Jerseys, because these breeds are efficient in the production of butterfat.

Dairy cattle whose history can be traced to the original animals of a breed are called *purebred.* A *registered* animal is one whose history has been recorded with a breed association. Most dairy cattle are not registered with a breed association. Such cattle are called *grade* cows. Some grade cows are the offspring of unregistered parents of the same breed. However, many are born of unregistered cows and registered purebred bulls.

Improvements in Dairy Farming. Today's farmers have increased milk production efficiency greatly through improved methods of breeding, feeding, and managing dairy cattle. In the United States, the average yearly production of milk per cow has risen to about 10,270 pounds (4,658 kilograms). Many of the better dairy herds average from 12,000 to 15,000 pounds (5,440 to 6,800 kilograms) of milk per dairy cow every year. One Holstein cow produced more than 44,000 pounds (20,000 kilograms) of milk and 1,505 pounds (683 kilograms) of butterfat in one year—a world record. She produced an average of about 60 quarts (57 liters) of milk per day.

Such improvement has resulted from better breeding methods and the work of dairy herd improvement (DHI) associations; the United States Department of Agriculture; colleges of agriculture; and the Purebred Dairy Cattle Association. DHI associations are cooperative organizations of about 25 dairy farmers each. Each association employs a trained supervisor to keep monthly milk and butterfat production records on association herds. The supervisor advises members on how to feed and care for the cattle, and which cows to remove from the herds because they are not good producers. Cows in these herds produce an average of 13,226 pounds (5,999 kilograms) of milk and 496 pounds (225 kilograms) of butterfat annually.

More than half of all dairy cows in the United States are now bred by *artificial insemination* (artificial breeding). This method enables dairy farmers to increase their use of outstanding purebred bulls. The average bull used by artificial insemination organizations is now mated to more than 3,000 cows in a year.

Milking usually is done at regular times, once each morning and once each evening. On a good dairy farm, the cows are carefully brushed and washed before they are milked. This keeps the milk clean. Many farmers who own only a few cows do their milking by hand. Most of the milk marketed as *Grade A* fluid milk comes from larger dairy farms that use milking machines.

On many farms, the milk is pumped directly from the cow through a glass pipeline into a separate milk house where it is cooled immediately. The milk may also be pumped into a closed pail and carried to a milk house for cooling. The milk's flavor is improved if it is not exposed to the air in the barn. The machines and pipelines are washed and sterilized after each milking.

Housing. During the summer, the cows may go out to the pasture between milkings. In the winter, they may run loose in a *loafing barn,* a large shed that is open on one side, or they may be confined to a closed barn for nearly the entire day.

A modern dairy barn is kept very clean. Each cow has a separate stall. Metal pipes called *stanchions* are placed around the cow's neck to see that she keeps her place in the stall. A well-trained cow entering the barn will go to her own stall and put her head through the open stanchions. When all the cows have taken their places, the stanchions are closed by pulling a lever at the end of the row of stalls. Each stanchion may be opened or closed separately. The cows have separate feeding troughs and drinking cups. A *gutter* runs behind the stalls. Manure from the cattle falls into the gutter. Many gutters are equipped with mechanical devices called *barn cleaners.* A barn cleaner is a chain with paddles attached that pulls the manure into a *manure spreader*. The spreader is used to scatter manure onto the land to make the soil more productive.

On many farms, the barns are washed from time to time with a disinfectant to kill germs and protect the health of the herd. In some barns, workers step into a pan of disinfectant before entering the milking barn. The barn must also be well ventilated to protect the health of the cows and the flavor of the milk.

Hay is usually stored in the barn loft, or in a hay shed. *Silage,* the chopped-up stalks of corn or other crops which cattle eat, is stored in a silo, where it is allowed to ferment. Most dairy farms have a milk house where the milk is refrigerated in tanks until it can be shipped. Milking machines and other equipment are usually washed and sterilized in the milk house. The dairy laws of many communities require that farms selling milk to their market maintain milk houses.

Feeding. A good dairy cow may weigh up to 1,700 pounds (770 kilograms) and produce 12,000 pounds (5,440 kilograms) or more of milk during a year. In order to do this, the cow eats large amounts of *concentrates* (grains and by-product feeds) and *roughages* (pasture, hay, and silage). A large cow eats many pounds of feed a day, including about 15 pounds (6.8 kilograms) of grain. This amounts to about $2\frac{1}{2}$ short tons (2.3 metric tons) of grain each year. She will drink about $11\frac{1}{2}$ short tons (10.4 metric tons) of water during a year, or about 8 gallons (30 liters) per day.

Cows that produce a large amount of milk need feed that provides energy, protein, and such essential minerals as calcium. A dairy farmer tries to balance a cow's ration and provide all food nutrients in the proper amounts and proportions. For example, if the farmer feeds the cow a low-protein roughage, such as corn silage, he increases the amount of protein in the concentrate mixture. Typical energy feeds include barley, corn, grain sorghums, oats, and wheat. Cottonseed and soybean meal are typical protein supplements. Roughages that supply both protein and energy include alfalfa, clover, corn silage, mixed hays, sorghum silage, and many varieties of pasture. Important by-product feeds include corn gluten feed and meal, dried beet pulp, molasses, and wheat millfeeds. Most high-producing herds are kept in *dry lots*. Feed is brought to the lots and fed to the cows in troughs called *feed bunks*.

Dairy Farming Regulations

Many states and local governments have laws regulating the conditions under which milk can be produced and sold. This is essential because of the many ways in which milk can become contaminated. All the various containers to which the milk is transferred as it passes from the cow to the consumer must be clean, sterilized, and dry. Some diseases of cattle can be given to human beings through impure milk. Tuberculosis was spread in this way, until tubercular cows were removed from dairy herds. *Brucellosis* is a disease found in a few herds. Ways of controlling this disease include cattle testing, vaccination of calves, and killing of infected cattle.

Most laws regulating dairies require that the operator of a dairy must have a license. Dairy barns are inspected to make sure that sanitary regulations are being met. Workers in both dairies and milk plants are given periodic physical examinations to make sure that they are healthy. The milk itself is tested, to make sure that its composition meets the legal standard and it contains no impurities or disease-causing bacteria.

Most communities have regulations dealing with *Grade A* milk. These laws cover the health of cows and the sanitary conditions under which milk is produced and handled. About three-fourths of all milk sold is Grade A. Slightly less than half of all milk sold is used as fluid milk and cream. The remainder is processed and eaten in the form of butter, cheese, ice cream, and other dairy products.

Dairying Around the World

Dairying is carried on in many countries of the world. Denmark, New Zealand, and Switzerland are famed for their dairy products. In Norway and Switzerland the cattle are taken up to meadows in the mountains where they are pastured all summer. In the fall they are brought down to the lowlands and kept in barns during the winter.

In many countries, goats are an important dairy animal. In the United States, goats produce only a small proportion of the milk supply. In some countries the milk of other animals is used. Sheep milk is used in making certain cheeses. In Arab lands, camel's milk is drunk, and in other places the milk of mares. The Laplanders drink reindeer milk, and the people of Egypt and India use the milk of the water buffalo.

History of Dairying

Years ago, cows gave milk only during the spring, summer, and fall when they could be fed in open pastures. What little milk the cows gave was used by the farmer and his family as milk or butter. Only small amounts of it could be sold.

Norwegian Vikings may have brought the first cattle to the Americas in the early 1000's. Historians are certain that Columbus brought cattle on his second voyage to America in 1493. Englishmen brought cows to the Jamestown settlement in the early 1600's. Later, they brought them to Plymouth and other New England settlements. Cattle raising spread quickly. An important advance in caring for dairy cattle came from colonial Massachusetts. In the late 1600's, the colonists began feeding grain and hay to cattle during the winter. The cows gave milk all winter. This method of feeding cattle, called *stall-feeding*, made possible the year-round production of milk.

When the pioneers moved westward, butter, cheese, and milk helped feed their families. It was discovered that cattle manure helped keep the soil productive. More cattle were kept, and the surplus milk was sold.

The biggest development in the growth of dairying in the United States came after 1840, when the large cities began to develop. Before that time it had not been difficult to supply the cities, because farm and city were close together. After the cities grew, came the problem of shipping milk to the consumer. Milk was first shipped into New York City by train in 1841. In a few years the large cities in the United States were receiving milk from farms 50 miles (80 kilometers) away.

For many years, dairy products were manufactured on the farm. In 1850 almost 315 million pounds (143 million kilograms) of butter were made on farms in the United States. But as city markets increased it became necessary to process milk on a larger scale. The first butter factory, or creamery, was set up in New York about 1856. Soon there were many creameries scattered throughout the Eastern and Midwestern states. The manufacture of milk products has become highly industrialized, and creameries are found throughout the country. The amount of butter produced on farms is small compared to that made commercially. C. L. NORTON

Related Articles in WORLD BOOK include:

Agriculture	Cooperative	Milking Machine
Barn	Disease (Animal Diseases)	Pasteurization
Butter		Pasture
Cattle	Hay	Separator
Cheese	Milk	Silo

DAISY, *DAY zee,* is a name given to many flowers. It means *day's eye,* because the daisy looks somewhat like an eye, with its round yellow center. Its petals grow around the center like rays of the sun. The daisy opens its blossoms in the morning and closes them at night.

Ferry-Morse Seed Co.

The Large Shasta Daisy has four-inch blossoms and saw-toothed leaves. It was named by Luther Burbank.

The American daisy is actually a wild chrysanthemum, and has several other names. Some people call it the *oxeye daisy* because of its yellow center. Farmers are troubled by daisies that grow in their fields. They call that flower the *whiteweed.* Some people give it the name of *marguerite,* because of its slender beauty. The American daisy has been improved by breeders, and there are many varieties. The daisy is a flower for the month of April.

Scientific Classification. Daisies belong to the composite family, *Compositae.* The English daisy is genus *Bellis,* species *B. perennis.* The common white American daisy is *Chrysanthemum leucanthemum.* Most of the new, larger daisies are *C. maximum.* GEORGE A. BEACH

See also BLACK-EYED SUSAN; BURBANK, LUTHER; COMPOSITE FAMILY; FLOWER (color picture: Fall Garden).

DAKAR, *dah KAHR* (pop. 581,000), is the capital of Senegal and the westernmost city in Africa. Dakar is an important transportation and commercial center. For location, see SENEGAL (map). The city has a hot climate, with a rainy season from the middle of June until late September.

Docks in Dakar usually are piled high with peanuts awaiting export. The city's industries include food processing, printing, and the manufacture of bricks, soap, and cigarettes. In 1941, an airline established a route between Dakar and Natal, Brazil. This is the shortest route across the South Atlantic. About 16,000 Europeans live in Dakar. ALAN P. MERRIAM

DAKOTA. See NORTH DAKOTA; SOUTH DAKOTA.

DAKOTA INDIANS. See SIOUX INDIANS.

DAKOTA STATE COLLEGE. See UNIVERSITIES AND COLLEGES (table).

DAKOTA WESLEYAN UNIVERSITY. See UNIVERSITIES AND COLLEGES (table).

DALADIER, *DAH LAH DYAY,* **ÉDOUARD** (1884-1970), served as French premier in 1933, 1934, and from 1938 to 1940. He agreed at Munich in 1938 to let Hitler partition Czechoslovakia (see MUNICH AGREEMENT). He served as a Radical Socialist deputy from 1919 to 1940. After France fell to Germany, he was imprisoned from 1941 until 1945. He testified against Marshal Henri Philippe Pétain in 1945, accusing him of collaborating with Germany. Daladier was born in Carpentras, in Vaucluse, France. ERNEST JOHN KNAPTON

DALAI LAMA, *dah LIE LAH muh,* was the supreme ruler of Tibet until Chinese Communist forces invaded his country in 1950. Tibet became an autonomous region within China, but is actually ruled by the Chinese government. They brought back the Panchen Lama, who had been exiled in China, to share nominal political power and spiritual rule with the Dalai Lama. Tibetans revolted unsuccessfully against Chinese rule in 1959, and the Dalai Lama fled to India. The Panchen Lama became the nominal ruler of Tibet, until he was stripped of his powers by the Communists in 1965.

Lamaists believe that the Dalai Lama is the *reincarnation* (reborn soul) of the man who ruled the people before him. The wise men of Tibet consult oracles and watch a sacred lake for the appearance of a face or some other clue to the identity of the new Dalai Lama. They then search among the children of Tibet to find the reincarnation of the ruler. THEODORE H. E. CHEN

See also LAMAISTS; LHASA; TIBET.

Eastfoto

The Dalai Lama, dressed in embroidered robes, burned incense at an altar in the Kwang Chi Temple during a visit to Peking.

DALEY, RICHARD JOSEPH (1902-), a Democrat, is mayor of Chicago and one of the most powerful political leaders in the United States. He was elected to his first four-year term as mayor in 1955, and was re-elected in 1959, 1963, 1967, 1971, and 1975.

Daley heads the Cook County Democratic organization, perhaps the strongest political machine in the United States. One of the most powerful Democrats, he became an adviser to President John F. Kennedy and to President Lyndon B. Johnson. Under Daley's leadership, Chicago reorganized its police department, encouraged the construction of many major downtown buildings, and pushed an urban renewal and rebuilding program that removed many slums.

During the early 1970's, Daley's administration was rocked by several scandals and trials involving corruption. None of the cases involved Daley himself. But many high officials—including seven aldermen, a former county clerk, and the mayor's former press secretary—were found guilty. More than 50 policemen, including some high-ranking officers, were convicted of taking bribes from tavern owners.

Daley suffered a political setback in 1972 when the city's regular Democratic delegates were barred from the party's national convention in a fight over delegate selection procedures. But he won renewed national prestige with a decisive re-election victory in 1975.

Daley was born in Chicago, and received his undergraduate and law degrees from DePaul University. He was elected to the Illinois House of Representatives in 1936, and later served in the Illinois Senate and as state revenue director. He was elected Cook County clerk in 1950. CHARLES E. NICODEMUS, JR.

DALHOUSIE UNIVERSITY, *dal HOW zee,* is a private, coeducational university in Halifax, N.S. It accepts students of all faiths. Dalhousie offers courses in arts, business administration, commerce, dentistry, education, engineering physics, law, library science, medicine, nursing, pharmacy, physical education, and science. It grants bachelor's, master's, and doctor's degrees, and offers diplomas in clinical psychology, dental hygiene, education, nursing, and physiotherapy.

The university was founded in 1818 through the efforts of George Ramsay, earl of Dalhousie, then lieutenant governor of Nova Scotia. The original funds came from customs duties collected in Castine, a town now in Maine. In 1923, the University of King's College associated with Dalhousie University. King's College grants degrees in divinity. For enrollment at the university, see CANADA (table: Universities and Colleges). HENRY D. HICKS

DALI, *DAH lee,* **SALVADOR** (1904-), is a famous surrealist painter. His unusual pictures have made him one of the most publicized figures in modern art.

Dali calls his surrealist paintings "hand-painted dream photographs." The pictures show strange, often nightmarish combinations of precisely detailed figures and objects. Many of his paintings have strong sexual associations. The barren landscapes and fantastic rock formations of the Spanish region of Catalonia, where Dali was born, appear in a number of his works. Dali's *Gala and the Angelus of Millet Immediately Preceding the Arrival of the Conic Anamorphoses* illustrates his realistic technique and his use of complicated, puzzling symbols. This painting is reproduced in color in the PAINTING article. Dali has also created many etchings and lithographs. He designed many of these prints to illustrate books.

United Press Int.

Salvador Dali

Salvador Felipe Jacinto Dali was born in Figueras, Spain. He is also a sculptor and jewelry designer. Dali collaborated with the Spanish film director Luis Buñuel on two famous surrealist motion pictures—*An Andalusian Dog* (1929) and *The Golden Age* (1930). WILLARD E. MISFELDT

See also SURREALISM.

DALL SHEEP. See BIGHORN (with picture).

DALLAPICCOLA, *dahl lah PEEK koh lah,* **LUIGI** (1904-1975), was an Italian composer. In much of his music, he used a 12-tone system derived from that of Arnold Schönberg. His important works include an opera, *The Prisoner* (1948), and the *Songs of Imprisonment* (1955), from texts by Boethius, Savonarola, and Mary, Queen of Scots. Dallapiccola was born in Pazin, Istria (now in Yugoslavia). HALSEY STEVENS

Collection of Julien Levy, Bridgewater, Conn., WORLD BOOK photo by Robert Crandall

Dali's *Accommodations of Desire* was completed about 1929. This oil and collage painting shows the mysterious combination of realistic figures and objects typical of the artist's style.

WORLD BOOK photo by Shel Hershorn

An Evening View of Dallas shows several skyscrapers towering above the main business district. The 52-story First National Bank Building, *right center,* is the city's tallest structure.

DALLAS, *DAL uhs,* is the second largest city in Texas and the eighth largest in the United States. Among Texas cities, only Houston is bigger. Dallas ranks as one of the nation's major centers of banking, fashion, manufacturing, trade, and transportation. Dallasites often call their city "Big D."

Dallas lies on the rolling prairies of north-central Texas, about 30 miles (48 kilometers) east of Fort Worth. It is the county seat of Dallas County. Historians believe the city may have been named for George M. Dallas, who served as Vice-President of the United States from 1845 to 1849 under President James K. Polk.

John Neely Bryan, a lawyer and trader, founded Dallas in 1841, when he built a trading post on the Trinity River. Trade and transportation accounted for much of Dallas' early development. Rapid industrial expansion since 1945 has made Dallas one of the fastest-growing cities in the nation. Major urban renewal projects in Dallas indicate continued growth.

President John F. Kennedy was assassinated in Dallas on Nov. 22, 1963 (see KENNEDY, JOHN F. [pictures]). Vice-President Lyndon B. Johnson took the oath of office as President aboard the presidential plane at Love Field in the city (see JOHNSON, LYNDON B. [picture]).

The City. Dallas covers about 301 square miles (780 square kilometers), or about a third of Dallas County. The city's metropolitan area covers 8,567 square miles (21,188 square kilometers) and includes 11 counties—Collin, Dallas, Denton, Ellis, Hood, Johnson, Kaufman, Parker, Rockwall, Tarrant, and Wise. About a fifth of Texas' people live in this area. The Dallas-Fort Worth metropolitan area makes up one of the most highly populated regions in the United States.

Three separate towns, each with its own government, lie within the city limits of Dallas. They are Cockrell Hill, Highland Park, and University Park. Suburbs with populations of over 40,000 include Garland, Grand Prairie, Irving, Mesquite, and Richardson.

A network of freeways links Dallas with its suburbs and forms a loop around the city. The Trinity River divides Dallas into two sections. The main business district lies north and east of the river. Oak Cliff, a residential area, is south and west of the Trinity.

The 52-story First National Bank Building on downtown Elm Street is the tallest structure in Dallas. The famous Neiman-Marcus department store on Main and Ervay streets attracts crowds of shoppers. At the south end of downtown Dallas, the Memorial Auditorium Convention Center provides a meeting place for businessmen and organizations from throughout the country. The county government center at the west end of the downtown area includes a restored version of the log

FACTS IN BRIEF

Population: 844,401; metropolitan area, 2,378,353.
Area: 301 sq. mi. (780 km²); metropolitan area, 8,567 sq. mi. (21,188 km²).
Altitude: 512 ft. (156 m) above sea level.
Climate: Average temp., Jan., 46° F. (8° C); July, 85° F. (29° C). Average annual precipitation (rainfall, melted snow, and other forms of moisture), 34½ in. (88 cm). For the monthly weather in Dallas, see TEXAS (Climate).
Government: Council-manager (councilmen elected to two-year terms; manager appointed).
Founded: 1841. Incorporated as a town, 1856; as a city, 1871.

cabin built by John Neely Bryan, who founded Dallas. City Hall stands between Commerce and Main streets at the east end of downtown Dallas.

Warehouses, light industries, and office buildings occupy the Trinity Industrial District, which adjoins downtown Dallas. The Dallas Market Center, off Stemmons Freeway, provides facilities for trade shows.

The People. About 98 per cent of the people of Dallas were born in the United States. Although many of Dallas' first residents were Southerners, people from all parts of the country have settled there. The city's population includes people of Canadian, English, German, Mexican, and Russian ancestry. American Indians of many tribes live in the city. Negroes make up about a fourth of the population.

Dallas has had relatively few racial disturbances, though there have been some sit-ins, picketings, and other incidents. A citizens' group, called the Interracial Council for Business Opportunity, has been an important factor in the peaceful integration of public facilities.

Baptists form the largest religious group in Dallas. Other major groups, in order of size, are Methodists, Roman Catholics, and Presbyterians.

Symbols of Dallas. The red, white, and blue in the flag of Dallas, *left,* represent the United States and Texas, which use these colors in their flags. The star is the chief symbol of Texas, the Lone Star State. The flag, adopted in 1967, also bears the city seal, *right.*

Economy. Dallas is one of the nation's major centers for the manufacture of electronics and electrical equipment, aircraft and missile parts, and women's clothing. Other important industries include nonelectrical machinery, food and food products, and printing and publishing. More than a fifth of the city's workers are employed in manufacturing. The city has about 2,500 factories.

Texas ranks as the nation's top cotton-producing state, and Dallas is one of the world's leading cotton

CITY OF DALLAS

Dallas is the second largest city in Texas and the county seat of Dallas County. The map below shows the Greater Dallas-Fort Worth area. The map at the right shows the boundaries of Dallas and of the built-up areas in and near the city.

City boundary
County boundary
Built-up area
Main road
Other road
Point of interest

GREATER DALLAS-FORT WORTH area

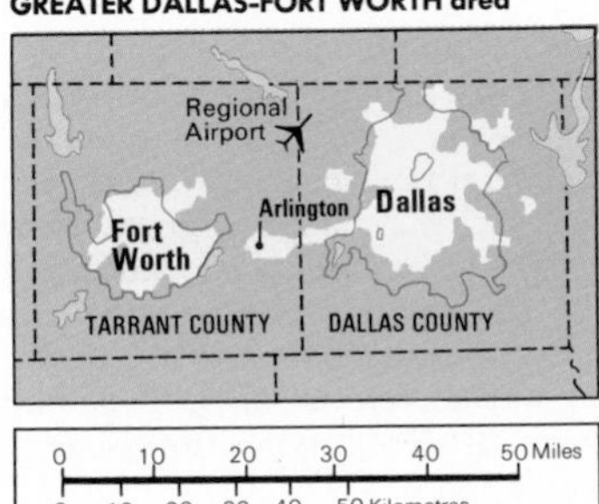

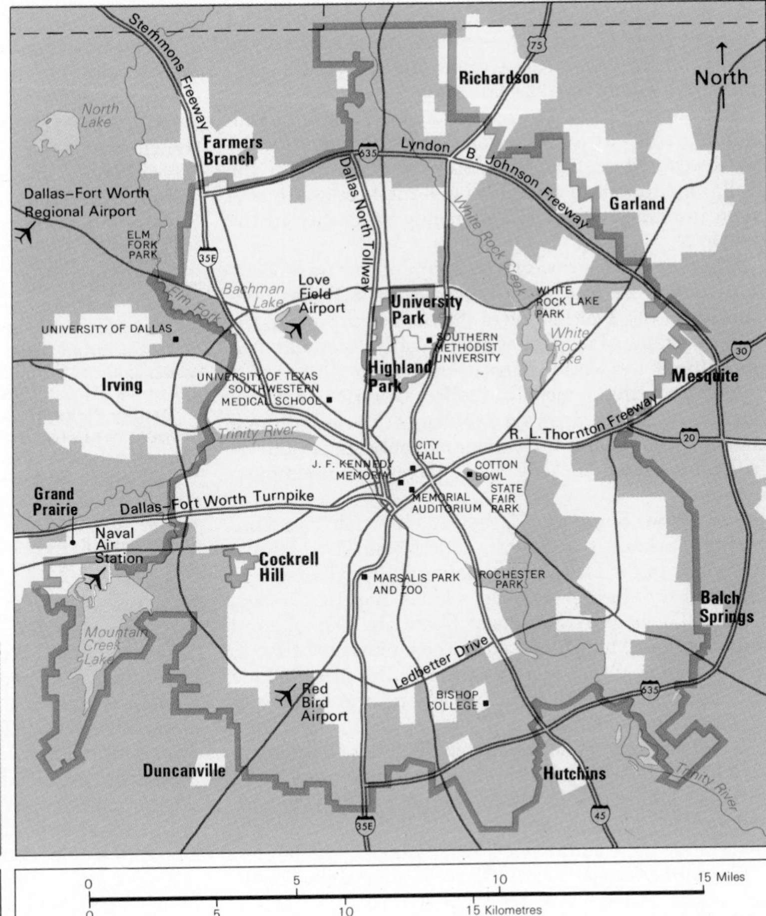

WORLD BOOK map

LTV Aerospace Corporation

Airplane Manufacturing is one of Dallas' chief industries. Most of the planes go to the United States armed forces.

markets. Dallas is the headquarters of more oil firms than any other U.S. city. More than three-fourths of the known oil reserves in the United States lie within 500 miles (805 kilometers) of Dallas.

The Eleventh District Federal Reserve Bank in Dallas makes the city an important financial center for the Southwest. More than 100 banks are located in the Dallas metropolitan area. Dallas is the headquarters of more insurance companies than any other city in the South.

Dallas is the Southwest's most important transportation center. Six interstate highways serve Dallas, and the city's Love Field is one of the busiest airports in the United States. The Dallas-Fort Worth Regional Airport, one of the world's largest, opened in 1974.

Reduced employment in Dallas' defense-related industries became a growing problem in the city during the early 1970's. But the wide range of business activity in Dallas helped the city avoid large-scale unemployment.

Education. Southern Methodist University, in University Park, is the largest, oldest, and best-known university in the Dallas area. Baylor University College of Dentistry, Bishop College, Dallas Baptist College, Dallas Theological Seminary Graduate School, and Southwestern Medical School of the University of Texas are in Dallas. Other schools in the Dallas area include the University of Dallas, in Irving, and the University of Texas, in Richardson.

The Dallas public school system includes 182 elementary and high schools, with a total enrollment of about 170,000. Dallas has 38 church-supported schools, with more than 12,000 students. Greenhill, Hockaday, and St. Mark's are well-known private schools.

Cultural Life. Dallas is a cultural center of the Southwest. The Dallas Civic Opera performs in the Music Hall of State Fair Park, and the New York Metropolitan Opera Company makes a yearly visit. The Dallas Symphony Orchestra performs in McFarlin Memorial Auditorium at Southern Methodist University. The city also has a Civic Ballet Society, a Metropolitan Ballet, a Civic Chorus, and a Chamber Music Society. The Dallas Theater Center is the only theater designed by the famous American architect Frank Lloyd Wright. Summer musicals at State Fair Park attract many theatergoers.

The Dallas Museum of Fine Arts exhibits American and European paintings and sculpture. Displays at the Dallas Health and Science Museum include transparent models of the human body. The Southwestern Historical Wax Museum features over 100 figures from Texas history. The Dallas Museum of Natural History exhibits wildlife and fossils from the Texas area. The Dallas Historical Society operates the Texas Hall of State, a museum that was built for the 1936 Texas Centennial Exposition.

The Dallas Public Library System includes a downtown unit and 15 branches throughout the city. The library system at Southern Methodist University is one of the largest college libraries in Texas.

Dallas has about 20 radio stations and 6 television stations. The city's two daily newspapers are the *Morning News* and the *Times Herald*.

Recreation. The Dallas park system covers about 14,000 acres (5,670 hectares). The Marsalis Park Zoo has more than 2,000 animals. The Dallas Cowboys of the National Football League play in Texas Stadium, which holds about 65,000 persons. The Texas Rangers of the American League play baseball in Vandergriff Stadium in Arlington. Dallas is the home of the Cotton Bowl, one of the most famous stadiums in the nation. Every New Year's Day, the Cotton Bowl football game features two of the nation's outstanding college teams.

Other Interesting Places to Visit include:

State Fair Park, about 2 miles (3 kilometers) east of downtown Dallas. It includes picnic grounds, concession stands, rides, the Cotton Bowl, and most of Dallas' museums. The State Fair of Texas attracts about 3 million persons to the park during its 16 days every October.

Observation Deck, at the First National Bank in downtown Dallas. On clear days, viewers can see Fort Worth, 30 miles (48 kilometers) away.

Dealey Plaza, in downtown Dallas. A memorial plaque stands near the site of President John F. Kennedy's assassination.

The World of Animals, in suburban Mesquite. Visitors can drive through a wild game preserve and see more than 2,500 wild animals in a natural setting.

Summer Rodeo, in suburban Mesquite. Rodeo events are held on weekends, from April through September.

Six Flags Over Texas, in Arlington, between Dallas and Fort Worth. This amusement park offers a variety of exhibits and rides.

Government. Dallas has a council-manager form of government. The voters elect a mayor and 10 other city council members to two-year terms. The mayor and councilmen establish general policies for governing the city. The council hires a city manager who serves as administrative head of the government. He carries out the policies set up by the council, prepares the city budget, and appoints and dismisses department heads. The city's chief sources of income are fees, fines, and property and sales taxes. Revenue bonds and federal grants have also provided funds.

The Dallas city government faces a number of problems, including air and water pollution and a rising crime rate. Dallas leaders are also working to prevent a large shift of retail trade from the city to the suburbs.

History. In 1841, John Neely Bryan built a home and trading post along the Trinity River, near what is now the county government center. Bryan traded with westward-bound wagon trains, Indians, and buffalo hunters. Soon he began selling lots in a town a half-mile (0.8 kilometer) square. The town became the county seat in 1846, when Dallas County was created.

In 1855, a group of French scientists, writers, artists, and musicians settled near Dallas to form a cooperative community. The community failed and many of its residents moved to Dallas.

Dallas was incorporated as a town in 1856. It became a stop for stagecoaches and for cowboys driving Longhorn cattle to markets in Missouri and Kansas. During the Civil War (1861-1865), Dallas served as an administrative center of the Confederate Army. Two railroad lines—the Houston and Texas Central, and the Texas and Pacific—reached Dallas in the early 1870's. Soon afterward, farm tool manufacturers began opening branches in Dallas. Hunters brought buffalo hides, and small factories started to produce leather goods. Wholesalers began to supply retail stores around Dallas.

Dallas was incorporated as a city in 1871. The growth of transportation and trade caused the population of Dallas to increase by more than 12 times between 1870 and 1890, when it reached 38,067. In 1890, Dallas replaced Galveston as the largest city in Texas. But by 1930, Houston had become the largest city. Discovery of the great East Texas oil field southeast of Dallas in 1930 helped boost Dallas' economy and growth.

World War II (1939-1945) brought aircraft plants and other defense industries to Dallas. After the war, Dallas became a leading U.S. center for the manufacture of electrical and electronics equipment and aircraft and missile parts. Many large companies, including Chance Vought Aircraft, moved to Dallas. In 1961, Chance Vought became part of the Ling-Temco-Vought corporation (now LTV Corporation), then the largest business firm in Dallas. Other companies that had been founded in Dallas, such as Texas Instruments, also expanded rapidly. This industrial growth helped the city's population increase by more than half a million persons from 1940 to 1970.

During the 1960's, population and retail trade grew at a faster rate in the suburbs of Dallas than in the city itself. To reverse this trend, Mayor Erik Jonsson helped form a "Goals for Dallas" program. In 1967, Dallas voters passed a $175-million bond issue—the largest in the city's history—to fulfill some of the goals. The plans led to construction of the Dallas-Fort Worth Airport and other improvements.

Also during the 1960's, work began on the privately financed Main Place project in downtown Dallas. This project, built on several levels above and below ground, includes office buildings, shops, and a hotel. It was completed in 1974. That same year, construction began on a downtown project called Reunion. The first part of the project, which will include a hotel, 50-story office building, and transportation center, is scheduled for completion in the late 1970's. WALTER B. MOORE

See also RADAR (picture: A Radar Map of Dallas); TEXAS (pictures).

DALLAS, GEORGE MIFFLIN (1792-1864), served as Vice-President of the United States from 1845 to 1849 under President James K. Polk. He was a loyal supporter of Polk's policies. His tie-breaking vote in favor of a low tariff bill Polk favored in 1846 destroyed him politically in Pennsylvania, his home state.

Library of Congress

George M. Dallas

He served as a Democratic U.S. senator from Pennsylvania from 1831 to 1833, as minister to Russia from 1837 to 1839, and as minister to England from 1856 to 1861. While in England, he helped settle disputes over the Clayton-Bulwer Treaty (see CLAYTON-BULWER TREATY).

Dallas also held office as mayor of Philadelphia, U.S. district attorney, and attorney general of Pennsylvania. He also served as secretary to Albert Gallatin, who helped negotiate an end to the War of 1812. Dallas was born in Philadelphia. IRVING G. WILLIAMS

See also VICE-PRESIDENT OF THE UNITED STATES (picture).

DALLAS, UNIVERSITY OF. See UNIVERSITIES AND COLLEGES (table).

DALLAS BAPTIST COLLEGE. See UNIVERSITIES AND COLLEGES (table).

DALLAS THEOLOGICAL SEMINARY. See UNIVERSITIES AND COLLEGES (table).

DALLES, *dalz,* are deep gorges in which rivers flow rapidly over basaltic rocks or slabs. The name comes from the French *dalle,* meaning *slab* or *tile.* The singular form

Minnesota Department of Economic Development

The St. Croix River Dalles on the Minnesota-Wisconsin border include some of the most scenic gorges in the United States.

of dalles in English is *dell*, and in many parts of the country these gorges are called *dells* instead of *dalles*. French explorers gave the name *dalles* to scenic gorges of North American rivers, especially those located in the northern part of the United States. Notable dalles in the United States include the *Wisconsin Dells* on the Wisconsin River, near Wisconsin Dells, Wis.; the *Saint Louis River Dalles* near Duluth, Minn.; and the *Saint Croix River Dalles* between Wisconsin and Minnesota. See also WISCONSIN (Places to Visit; picture); WISCONSIN RIVER. F. G. WALTON SMITH

DALLIN, *DAL ihn,* **CYRUS EDWIN** (1861-1944), an American sculptor, used American Indian life as the theme for many of his greatest works. *The Appeal to the Great Spirit,* at the entrance to Boston's Museum of Fine Arts, is typical of his realistic and dramatic style. His other works include *Signal of Peace* in Lincoln Park, Chicago; *Pioneer Monument* in Salt Lake City; and *Sir Isaac Newton* in the Library of Congress in Washington, D.C. Dallin was born in Springville, Utah. He studied at the École des Beaux-Arts and Julian Academy in Paris. He taught in Boston. JEAN LIPMAN

See also MASSASOIT (picture).

Life-sized bronze sculpture (1908); Museum of Fine Arts, Boston

Dallin's *The Appeal to the Great Spirit* was one of several works by the sculptor portraying Indians on horseback.

DALMATIA, *dal MAY shih uh,* a district of Yugoslavia, is a long, narrow strip of land which extends for more than 200 miles (320 kilometers) along the eastern shore of the Adriatic Sea. The Dalmatian coast is deeply indented and fringed with many islands.

Dalmatia lies in the Dinaric Alps. The chief rivers are the Neretva and the Krka. They flow into the Adriatic Sea. The most important cities are Split, Dubrovnik, Šibenik, and Zadar.

Most of the people are Croatians, but a few Italians also live there. The most important industry is fishing. Olives, grapes, cherries, and other fruits are grown in the valleys near the coast.

Dalmatia was once part of ancient Illyria. Both Dalmatia and Illyria were conquered by the Romans in the 200's B.C. Later, between the A.D. 600's and 1400's, the Slavs invaded Dalmatia. After the defeat of Napoleon in 1815, the Great Powers gave Dalmatia to Austria. The province declared its independence of Austria in 1918 and became part of Yugoslavia after World War I. During World War II, Italian forces occupied most of Dalmatia. In 1949, Dalmatia became an *oblast* (region) of Croatia, one of the Yugoslav republics. Its capital is Split. JOSEPH S. ROUCEK

DALMATIAN is a medium-sized dog that looks like a pointer. It is usually white, covered with many black or liver-colored spots. Dalmatian puppies are pure white when they are born. The spots appear after about three or four weeks. Dalmatians make good watchdogs. They are alert, curious, clean, and useful. They also can be taught to hunt. Another name for the Dalmatian is the *coach dog*. These dogs used to run along between the wheels of coaches or carriages, and were companions to the horses. The breed was named for Dalmatia, an area on the Adriatic Sea, but experts are not sure where the dogs were first raised. See also DOG (color picture: Nonsporting Dogs). JOSEPHINE Z. RINE

DALTON, JOHN (1766-1844), an English chemist, formulated the *law of partial pressures in gases* in 1802. The law states that for an ideal gas the total pressure of a confined gas mixture equals the sum of the pressures each gas would exert alone in the same volume. In 1803, Dalton proposed an *atomic theory of matter* that became one of the foundations of chemistry. From it, Dalton determined chemical formulas that showed the atomic composition of molecules. Dalton made the first, although inaccurate, table of atomic weights. He also investigated color blindness (called *Daltonism*), which he had. Dalton was born in Eaglesfield. See also ATOM (Dalton's Theory). SIDNEY ROSEN

DALTONISM. See COLOR BLINDNESS.

DALY, MARCUS (1841-1900), helped establish Montana's copper-mining industry. Daly developed mines near Butte and built a copper refining plant in Anaconda. He founded the Anaconda Copper Mining Company in 1895. Daly, Henry Rogers, and William Rockefeller founded the Amalgamated Copper Mining Company in 1899. Daly was a leader of the Democratic Party in Montana. Born in Ireland, he came to the United States in 1856, when he was a boy. See also MONTANA (Statehood). THOMAS A. CLINCH

DAM

Bureau of Reclamation

The Shasta Dam in Northern California Creates a Huge Reservoir on the Sacramento River.

DAM is a barrier placed across a river to stop the flow of water. Dams vary in size from small earth or rock barriers to concrete structures that rise as high as a skyscraper. Man has always had to gather water during wet seasons to have enough for himself, his animals, and his crops in dry spells. Ruins of ancient dams exist in the Tigris and Nile river valleys. Some Roman dams built in Italy, Spain, and North Africa are still being used today.

Throughout man's history, wherever people settled, an important first concern was to locate an adequate water supply. In many regions, streams full of water during certain seasons of the year become dry at other times, perhaps when water is most needed. At first, men built small dams of brush, earth, and rock that would store enough water for immediate needs. But floods frequently washed these small dams away. As communities grew and populations increased, men learned to construct larger dams that would provide a more permanent and abundant water supply. These dams could store enough water to meet man's needs not only during seasonal drops in the water supply, but also during drought periods covering several years. Later, men learned how to harness the energy of falling waters and use it to produce electric power for homes and industries.

What Does a Dam Do?

As a barrier across a river or stream, a dam stops the flow of water. It then stores the water, creating a lake or reservoir, and raises the level of the water as high as the dam itself. The stored water is available for many uses. The dam also raises the water surface from the level of the original riverbed to a higher level. This permits water to be diverted by the natural flow of gravity to adjacent lands. The stored water also flows through hydraulic turbines, producing electric power that is used in homes and industries. Water released from the dam in uniform quantities assures water for fish and other wildlife in the stream below the dam. Otherwise, the stream would go dry there. Water released in larger quantities permits river navigation throughout the year. Where dams create large reservoirs, floodwaters can be held back and released gradually over longer periods of time without overflowing riverbanks.

Reservoirs or lakes created by dams provide recreational areas for boating and swimming. They give refuge to fish and wildlife. They help preserve farmlands by reducing soil erosion. Much soil erosion occurs when rivers flood their valleys, and swift floodwaters carry off the rich topsoils.

Kinds of Dams

Man builds many kinds of dams. Each dam is built to suit the character of the damsite and the materials available for its construction. *Rock-fill* or *stone masonry dams* may be most economical where rock is abundant. *Timber dams* are built where lumber is plentiful. Concrete is a common construction material for dams, but cement and gravel are not always available without heavy transportation costs. *Earth dams* prove most economical in many locations. In some locations, building

---

T. W. Mermel, the contributor of this article, is Assistant to the Commissioner for Scientific Affairs, Bureau of Reclamation. He is also the author of Register of Dams in the United States.

Largest Dam in the United States is the Fort Peck Dam. It stretches about 4 miles (6 kilometers) across the Missouri River in northeastern Montana. Completed in 1940, the dam contains about 125 million cubic yards (96 million cubic meters) of earth, stone, and steel.

hollow dams saves materials. In narrow canyons, thin *arch dams* may prove most suitable. But in wide river valleys, where the length of the dam would be very great, multiple-arch dams, flat-slab dams, and dams built of earth, steel, or timber may be less costly.

Masonry Dams. Several types of dams qualify as masonry dams. But, in general, these are dams built of solid, substantial materials. Structures made of stone cut in shapes, or of concrete poured into interlocking blocks or segments to form a solid mass, are called *masonry dams*. A *gravity dam* is generally made of concrete or cut-stone blocks. It depends for stability primarily on the weight of materials used in its construction.

In order to conserve materials, and where the weight required for the stability of the dam can be reduced, men have designed modifications of the gravity dam. A *hollow dam* has a hollow portion inside its main body. If the face of the dam is held up by supporting walls or buttresses, the dam is called a *buttress dam*. A *flat-slab dam* is a dam which has a flat slab placed across buttress supports at an angle of about 45°. The weight of the water holds down the slab. In some cases, the slab can be formed into an arch that is supported by the buttresses. The arch is located between each pair of buttresses. This type is called a *multiple-arch dam*.

But many variations in these types of dams occur. Dams constructed in narrow canyons to form an arch are called *arch dams*. Some dams use a very thin arch. The arches of some dams almost form a dome. The arches in others are thickened to include the principles of the gravity dam, where the weight adds to the dam's stability. In the latter case, the principles of the arch dam and the gravity dam are combined in the design, and the structure is called an *arch-gravity dam*.

Embankment Dams. The *earth-fill dam* is the most common type of embankment dam. This dam is constructed by hauling selected earth materials into place, and compacting layer upon layer with heavy rollers to form a watertight mass. Materials placed in the dam are graded according to density, with the fine materials

WORLD'S HIGHEST AND LARGEST DAMS

TEN HIGHEST DAMS

Dam	Location	Type	Height In feet	Height In meters
Nurek†	U.S.S.R.	Earth-fill	1,040	317
Grand Dixence	Switzerland	Gravity	935	285
Inguri†	U.S.S.R.	Arch	892	272
Vaiont	Italy	Arch	858	262
Mica	Canada	Earth-fill	794	242
Sayansk†	U.S.S.R.	Arch	794	242
Chivor†	Colombia	Earth-fill	778	237
Mauvoisin	Switzerland	Arch	778	237
Oroville	U.S.	Earth-fill	770	235
Chirkey†	U.S.S.R.	Arch	764	233

TEN LARGEST DAMS*

Dam	Location	Type	Volume In cubic yards	Volume In cubic meters
Tarbela†	Pakistan	Earth-fill	186,000,000	142,000,000
Fort Peck	U.S.	Earth-fill	125,612,000	96,034,000
Oahe	U.S.	Earth-fill	92,008,000	70,343,000
Mangla	Pakistan	Earth-fill	85,872,000	65,651,000
Gardiner	Canada	Earth-fill	85,743,000	65,553,000
Oroville	U.S.	Earth-fill	78,008,000	59,639,000
San Luis	U.S.	Earth-fill	77,666,000	59,378,000
Nurek†	U.S.S.R.	Earth-fill	75,864,000	58,000,000
Nagarjuna Sagar†	India	Earth-fill	73,575,000	56,250,000
Garrison	U.S.	Earth-fill	66,506,000	50,846,000

*Based on volume of dam structure †Under construction

U.S. Army Corps of Engineers

Powerhouse of the dam generates electricity for farms and cities in Montana and North and South Dakota.

Mile-Long Spillway of the dam carries excess water from the reservoir to the Missouri River. It drops 215 feet (66 meters).

Fort Peck Lake, created by the dam, is 189 miles (304 kilometers) long and 16 miles (26 kilometers) wide.

located in the center. Coarser materials are placed in outside zones, blanketed with a cover of rock, called *riprap*. This serves as an outside protection against the wave action of the reservoir and against wind, rain, and ice. Walls made of reinforced concrete to cut off water passage are frequently used in the center section. These cut-off walls may be made of sheet-metal piling driven deep below the excavated foundation level. Frequently, thinned-out cement, called *grout*, is pumped under great pressure into the foundation. It fills cracks and fissures, thus supplementing the cut-off walls and making the foundation watertight.

Semihydraulic-fill and *hydraulic-fill dams* are other modifications of the embankment dam. These dams are constructed by pumping wet, fine materials into their central sections, and allowing the water to drain off. Where rock is available, it may prove most economical to build a *rock-fill dam*. Most dams of this type are constructed of coarse, heavy rock and boulders. These are graded in size to permit them to fit together more compactly. Such dams, however, must have other means of preventing water from passing through them. Many of them have a blanket of concrete, steel, clay, or asphalt on the side facing the water. This blanket makes the dam watertight. Combinations of rock and earth result in a type of dam called an *earth-and-rock-fill dam*.

Other Types of Dams. *Timber dams* are built where lumber is available and the dam is relatively small. The timber is weighted down with rock. Planking or other watertight material forms the facing. *Metal dams* have watertight facings and supports of steel.

Dams with movable gates are built where it is necessary to let large quantities of water, ice, or driftwood pass by the dam. A *roller dam* has a large roller located horizontally between piers. It can be raised and lowered. When the roller is raised, ice and other materials pass

A WORLD BOOK SCIENCE PROJECT

BUILDING A MODEL DAM

The purpose of this project is to show how a dam can turn a nearly useless river into a valuable asset. One part of the model represents a shallow, almost useless, stream. The other part shows how a dam can make the stream a source of power, irrigation, and recreation.

Assembling the Base. Cut pieces of ¼-inch plywood according to the pattern and dimensions given, *above*. Nail the front, back, and sides together as shown, *left*. Then nail on the four top pieces as shown. Be sure to let the top pieces overhang the front of the base by 1 inch.

Waterproofing the Model. After assembling the base, smooth off all rough edges with sandpaper. Use caulking compound to seal the joints in the two troughs. Prepare the dam as shown in the detailed illustration on the opposite page, and nail it in place in the trough. Caulk these joints, also. Then paint the whole model with a waterproof paint.

Making the Dam. Drill three holes in the triangular wooden piece as shown, *below.* Use a drill the same size as the diameter of the plastic straws. Push the straws through the holes, and put caulking compound around each to make a watertight seal.

Preparing the Irrigation Pipes. With a straight pin, punch holes about ½ inch apart along one side of each of two of the plastic straws, *right.* Plug one end of each straw with clay. Push the other end through the dam as shown, *above.*

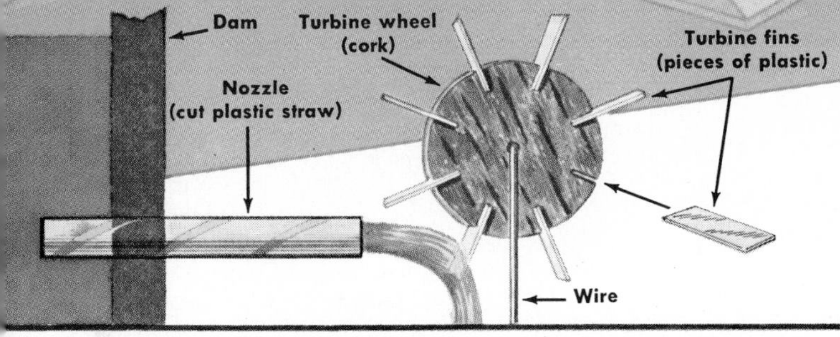

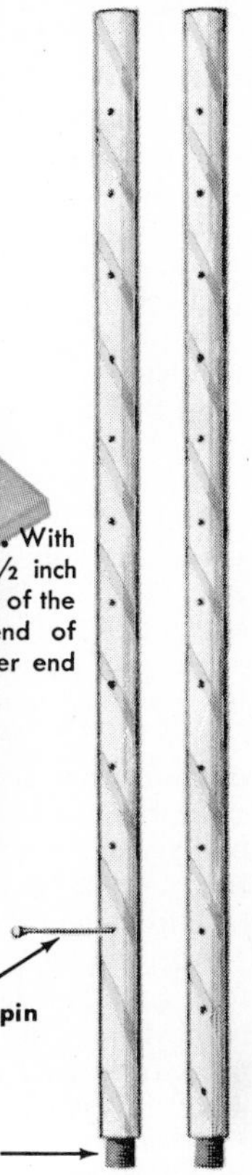

Building the Turbine. Drill a hole through the center of a large cork as shown, *below.* Make notches around the cork and insert the turbine fins, which may be pieces of tin, or thin, stiff plastic. Cut a piece of wire from a coat hanger and push the wire through the hole. Bend the wire and fasten it to the base near the dam. Be sure the cork can turn freely on the wire.

HOW THE MODEL WORKS

Demonstrating the Project. Glue small pieces of green sponge to represent trees in each of the troughs as shown, *below.* Place catch pans under the overhang at the front of each trough. Set a pail of water on a platform behind the model. Put two flexible tubes in the pail, and let water run slowly into the troughs. The water will flow right out of the trough without a dam. But in the other trough, a lake will form behind the dam. The "irrigation pipes" will take water to areas away from the dam. The jet of water coming through the tube at the base of the dam will cause the turbine to turn.

Illustrated by Art Lutz for WORLD BOOK

through the dam without much loss of reservoir water level. Many kinds of gates or wickets are used in these dams. Common types include the *taintor-gate dam, bear-trap dam,* and *wicket-gate dam.*

In 1966, France completed a dam on the Rance River at St. Malo for the world's first tidal power plant. St. Malo has some of the world's highest tides. Tides average 37 feet (11 meters) and rise to a maximum of about 44 feet (13 meters). Water fills the dam during high tide and flows through turbines during low tide.

How Men Build Dams

In order to construct a dam, the builders must first gather and study much information. The site where the dam is to be erected must be examined for its formation, quality of foundation, and the availability of suitable construction materials. A careful analysis must be made of the stream-flow characteristics. The area to be covered by the reservoir that the dam creates must be outlined when determining the height of the dam at any given site. This requires detailed topographic mapping and geologic studies. Subsurface drillings are necessary to determine the condition, quality, and location of the rock formation under the damsite.

All property in the reservoir area must be bought or relocated. This occasionally requires the relocation of entire towns, highways, railroads, and utilities. Engineers must also determine the amount of mud, silt, and debris which the dam will stop. This will determine the useful life of the reservoir, because when the reservoir becomes filled with this material it can no longer store water. If the dam is to be used for generating power, outlets must be provided which will connect to generating equipment. If the water is to be used for irrigation or municipal supply, outlets to control its release to canals or aqueducts must be built.

When the damsite has been selected, means must be found to remove or bypass the flow of the stream from the riverbed so that the foundation can be excavated and the concrete, earth, or rock placed. To divert the flow of the river from the area, frequently half of the riverbed is excavated at one time. The other half is used for the flow of the river. In some cases, it is more economical to bore a tunnel through an adjacent canyon wall, permitting the entire flow of the river to pass around the damsite. To accomplish this, *cofferdams* (small dams placed temporarily across a stream) are built upstream to divert the river into the tunnel. After the dam has been built high enough, the diversion tunnel is closed with gates, and permanently plugged.

A Hand-Operated Dam is used by a Bantu tribesman in South Africa to release water to irrigate his crops and fields.
Authenticated News

In designing the dam, provision must be made to bypass water when the reservoir is full, without overtopping the dam. For this purpose, a *spillway* is built.

In order to release water from behind the dam when the reservoir is not full, dams are equipped with reservoir outlets. These outlets consist of specially designed valves which can be opened and closed under high water pressure. Some of the many kinds of valves used for this purpose are called *needle valves, gate valves, slide valves,* and *cylinder gates.*

T. W. MERMEL

Related Articles. See also the Electric Power sections of certain state, province, and country articles, such as ALABAMA (Electric Power), and the following articles.

DAMS OF THE UNITED STATES

Alder
Anderson Ranch
Arrowrock
Bagnell
Bartlett
Belle Fourche
Bonneville
Buffalo Bill
Cherry Creek
Clearwater
Detroit
Diablo
Elephant Butte
Exchequer
Falcon
Fontana
Fort Peck
Fort Randall
Fort Supply
Friant
Garrison
Glen Canyon
Grand Coulee
Hansen
Hoover
Hungry Horse
John Martin
Kanopolis
Kensico
Keokuk
Kingsley
Marshall Ford
Merwin
Mud Mountain
New Croton
Oahe
Oroville
O'Shaughnessy
Owyhee
Pardee
Parker
Pensacola
Pine Flat
Reagan
Roosevelt
Ross
Salt Springs
Saluda
San Gabriel
San Luis
Santa Fe
Santee-Cooper Project
Sardis
Shadow Mountain
Shasta
Watauga
Winsor
Wolf Creek

FOREIGN DAMS

Aswan
Cárdenas
Castillon
Dneproges
Gatun Lake
Grand Dixence

OTHER RELATED ARTICLES

Arizona (color picture: Glen Canyon Dam)
Central Valley Project
Electric Power
Flood
Irrigation
Kentucky Lake
Missouri River Basin Project
Reservoir
Rio Grande Project
Saint Lawrence Seaway
Snowy Mountains Scheme
Tennessee Valley Authority
Water Power

Outline

I. What Does a Dam Do?

II. Kinds of Dams

A. Masonry Dams
B. Embankment Dams
C. Other Types of Dams

III. How Men Build Dams

Questions

Why do we need dams?
What is the highest dam in the world? The largest?
How do dams help farmers?
What materials are commonly used in building a dam?
How do builders decide where to construct a dam?
What is a *cofferdam?* A *spillway?*
Under what circumstances are *roller dams* necessary?
What determines the useful life of a dam?
How is an *earth-fill* dam built?
What is the purpose of a *spillway?*

DAMAGES, in law, means money that a court orders one person to pay to another person for violation of his rights. To collect damages, a victim ordinarily must show that he suffered loss or injury because of the other person's fault or carelessness.

The main types of damages include *compensatory*, *general*, *nominal*, and *punitive* damages. Compensatory damages are recovered only for actual damage, such as the cost of repairing an automobile damaged in an accident. Most damages are compensatory. General damages are based on indications of harm. They are awarded most often in *libel* and *slander* cases where it may be hard to show how one's reputation was harmed by a person making false statements. Nominal damages are small token awards given in cases where a person's rights have been violated, but where no harm has occurred. Suits fought on principle are often settled in this way. Punitive damages are in effect a fine levied against the wrongdoer. They are given in addition to other damages, when the wrongdoer has purposely harmed the other person.

There are few rules of law on how to measure damages. Damages may vary with each case, because the circumstances of each case may be different. Also, many lawsuits that seek damages today are tried before juries, and each jury may award different damages. Damages may often include elements that are hard to measure in money, such as pain and suffering. Some damages may have to be measured for harm that will occur only in the future. HARRY KALVEN, JR.

See also MALICE; NEGLIGENCE; TORT.

DAMÃO. See GOA.

DAMASCUS, *duh MAS kus* (pop. 618,457), the capital of Syria, is one of the oldest and most important caravan cities in the Middle East. For hundreds of years, Damascus has been famous for its craftsmen, who have made excellent inlaid metalwork, silk brocades, steel sword blades, and wooden mosaics.

Location and Appearance. Damascus lies in a beautiful oasis, or fertile area in the desert. The Barada River and several canals supply it with water. The oasis spreads eastward from the foothills of the Anti-Lebanon Mountains into the Syrian Desert. It lies at an altitude of about 2,250 feet (686 meters). Damascus enjoys a pleasant climate most of the year, but the *khamsin*, a desert wind, sometimes makes the city hot and dusty.

Damascus combines the old and the new. The new sections of the city are spacious, and contain many modern buildings. But some ancient streets are narrow and crowded. The *bazaars* (open shops and markets) are usually roofed with tin. Some old stone houses look like prisons from the outside. But they are beautifully decorated inside, and often have enclosed gardens.

Damascus contains many *mosques* (Moslem houses of worship). The Great Mosque of the Omayyad *caliphs* (rulers) is the most famous in the city. It was originally a Byzantine church. Artists covered the inside walls with beautiful *mosaics* (see MOSAIC). Pilgrims still visit the tomb of Saladin, one of the city's most famous rulers.

History. Damascus was probably founded before 2000 B.C. Aramaeans from the Syrian Desert first lived there. The city grew in importance until it became the caravan center of Syria after about 1000 B.C. Since the A.D. 600's, many Moslems who make the *hajj* (pilgrimage to Mecca) have begun their long journey from Damascus. Suleiman I, the Turkish ruler of Damascus in the 1500's, built a beautiful mosque and inn called the *Tekkiya*. Turkish pilgrims lived there while they waited for the hajj. Today it is used as a college mosque.

For a brief time after World War I, Damascus was the

N.E.N.A., Black Star

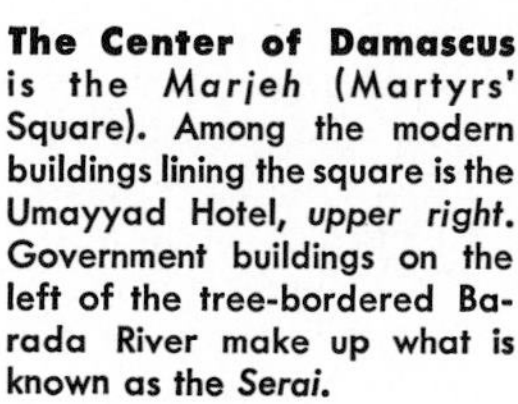

The Center of Damascus is the *Marjeh* (Martyrs' Square). Among the modern buildings lining the square is the Umayyad Hotel, *upper right*. Government buildings on the left of the tree-bordered Barada River make up what is known as the *Serai*.

capital of an Arab kingdom. When Syria became a French mandate of the League of Nations in 1920, French troops occupied Damascus. The Syrians clashed violently with the French for many years. In 1925 and 1926, French forces shelled the city. At the end of World War II, Damascus became the capital of the Republic of Syria. Damascus became the provincial capital of Syria in 1958, when Syria became a province of the United Arab Republic. In 1961, Syria withdrew from the United Arab Republic in a bloodless rebellion. Damascus became the capital of the Republic of Syria once again. CHRISTINA PHELPS HARRIS

See also SYRIA (pictures).

DAMASK is a firm, lustrous fabric that may be woven from any fiber. Its flat, woven design appears on both sides of the fabric.

In table damask, the design may be sateen weave with *floats* (longer, raised threads) in the *filling* (crosswise) threads. The background may be a satin weave with floats in the *warp* (lengthwise) threads. Single table damask has a four-float construction, and double damask has a seven-float construction. The double damask has more yarn, and the floats may pass over 18 to 20 yarns in an elaborate design. Damask's luster depends on length of floats, length of fibers used, closeness of weave, and uniformity of yarns. HAZEL B. STRAHAN

DAMASUS is the name of two popes.

Saint Damasus I served as pope from 366 to 384. He became famous for building churches and repairing the catacombs in Rome (see CATACOMBS). He also ornamented the tombs of martyrs. Damasus was deeply interested in the Bible and decided which books should make it up. He and Saint Jerome corrected the Latin translations, and the result was the Latin Vulgate, the standard version of the Bible in the Roman Catholic Church. Damasus was born in Rome.

Damasus II, a Bavarian, was elected pope on July 17, 1048. He had held office for less than a month when he died. GUSTAVE WEIGEL and FULTON J. SHEEN

D'AMBOISE, *d' am BOISE,* **JACQUES** (1934-), is an American dancer and a leading member of the New York City Ballet. He is particularly noted for roles featuring his high-spirited leaps.

D'Amboise was born in Dedham, Mass. He was trained by George Balanchine at the School of American Ballet and joined the New York City Ballet in 1950. He had major roles in such Balanchine ballets as *Western Symphony* (1954) and *Stars and Stripes* (1958). D'Amboise danced frequently on television and in motion pictures and Broadway musicals. As a *choreographer* (composer of dances), he created such ballets as *Irish Fantasy* (1964). He was interested in developing young American male dancers and taught classes for boys for the School of American Ballet. SELMA JEANNE COHEN

DAME SCHOOL. See COLONIAL LIFE IN AMERICA (The School).

DAMIEN DE VEUSTER, *DAH MYAN duh VUS TAR,* **JOSEPH** (1840-1889), was a Roman Catholic priest who gave his life to the care of lepers in a colony at Molokai, Hawaii. Father Damien was born in Belgium and became a member of the Fathers of the Sacred Hearts of Jesus and Mary. He was sent to Molokai as resident priest (see HAWAII [Molokai]). But because of the difficulty in getting doctors, Father Damien was obliged to serve as a doctor as well. He was stricken with leprosy himself in 1885. Hawaii has placed a statue of him in the Capitol in Washington, D.C. FULTON J. SHEEN

DAMOCLES, *DAM oh kleez,* was a member of the court of Dionysius II, who ruled Syracuse, Sicily, from 367 to 344 B.C. Damocles was an excessive flatterer. The Roman orator Cicero said that Damocles once talked too much about the happiness and good fortune of Dionysius. To teach Damocles a lesson, Dionysius invited him to a big feast. When he was seated, Damocles found a sword, suspended by a single hair, dangling over his head. This represented the constant danger that went with the wealth and material happiness of Dionysius. The *sword of Damocles* has become a byword for the threat of danger. DONALD W. BRADEEN

DAMON AND PYTHIAS, *DAY mun, PITH ih us,* were two noble Greek youths of Syracuse. Their friendship and loyalty to each other made them famous. According to a popular legend, Pythias, or Phintias, had been condemned to death by Dionysius of Syracuse. He was allowed to leave the city to put his affairs in order when Damon promised to die in place of Pythias if Pythias failed to keep his promise. Pythias was delayed, and arrived just in time to save Damon from death. Dionysius so admired this display of friendship that he pardoned Pythias and asked the two to become his friends. C. BRADFORD WELLES

DAMP is a dangerous gas found in mines. It is most often found in coal mines, where it is a hazard to miners. *Firedamp* is the most common kind of damp. It is chiefly *methane,* a tasteless, odorless gas. Firedamp forms when decaying plant matter produces coal. It is trapped in seams or cracks in rock. When miners cut into the seams or cracks, the gas is released. The gas burns readily and can explode when mixed with air in certain proportions. Exploded firedamp leaves *afterdamp,* a deadly gas that contains poisonous carbon monoxide and nonpoisonous nitrogen and carbon dioxide.

Chokedamp and *blackdamp* are common names for carbon dioxide, CO_2, a gas that is denser than air. This gas gathers at the bottom of pits and low places in mines, where it reduces the amount of oxygen in the air. If too much CO_2 is present, miners will suffocate.

Miners once carried canaries into the mines to test for gases. They knew gas was present if the birds collapsed. Today, various mechanical, chemical, and electrical devices are used to test for the presence of gases. GEORGE B. CLARK

See also COAL (Mine Safety Measures); METHANE.

DAMPIER, WILLIAM (1652?-1715), was an English seaman and pirate. He explored Australia and the far South Pacific, and wrote one of the first English accounts of the region. His journal, *A New Voyage Around the World* (1697), helped increase English interest in the Pacific. Dampier also strengthened racial prejudices when he wrote that the people then living in Australia were "the miserablest People" in the world.

Dampier was born in East Coker, England. He went to sea as a boy, and joined the navy in 1672. In 1688, he sailed to Australia (then called New Holland) on a pirate ship. In 1699, he reached Australia again in a voyage financed by the British Admiralty. Dampier also discovered New Britain and reached New Ireland, islands off the coast of New Guinea. ROBIN W. WINKS

DAMPING-OFF is a plant disease caused by fungi that live near the surface of the soil (see FUNGI). It affects all kinds of plants. Damping-off kills *seedlings* (young plants) before they grow above the ground, or destroys the stems of seedlings just above the surface of the soil. Damping-off cannot be cured. But farmers can prevent it by planting seeds in soil free from fungi, or by treating seeds with a protective dust. WILLIAM F. HANNA

DAMROSCH, *DAM rahsh,* was the family name of a father and son who spent their lives educating Americans to serious music. They came from a family of German musicians.

Leopold Damrosch (1832-1885), violinist and conductor, founded the New York Symphony Society in 1878, and conducted its orchestra until his death. Damrosch was born in Posen, Prussia (now Poznan, Poland). After receiving his degree in medicine from the University of Berlin in 1854, he joined the Weimar court orchestra as violinist under Franz Liszt. Damrosch came to the United States in 1871 to become conductor of the German Male Choral Society. He introduced German opera at the Metropolitan Opera House.

Walter Johannes Damrosch (1862-1950), son of Leopold, conducted the New York Symphony Orchestra in 1925 in the first symphonic program ever broadcast on radio. From 1928 to 1947, Damrosch served as musical counsel for the National Broadcasting Company. Children throughout the nation learned about great music by listening to the Music Appreciation Hour he directed. The music of such composers as Wagner, Stravinsky, Gershwin, Ravel, and Elgar became popular, in part, through Damrosch's efforts.

Damrosch was born in Breslau, Silesia, and came to the United States with his father in 1871. He succeeded his father as director of the Oratorio and Symphony societies of New York City in 1885. Later he founded the Damrosch Opera Company to present Wagnerian operas. Damrosch reorganized the New York Symphony Society in 1903, and then served as its conductor until 1927.

In addition to his conducting and educational work, Damrosch composed such operas as *The Scarlet Letter, Cyrano de Bergerac, The Man Without a Country,* and *Manila Te Deum,* celebrating Admiral George Dewey's victory. He wrote several songs, including "Danny Deever" and "Mandalay." IRVING KOLODIN

DAMSEL FLY. See DRAGONFLY.

DANA, *DAY nuh,* **CHARLES ANDERSON** (1819-1897), editor and part owner of the New York *Sun,* built it into one of the most important newspapers of its time. Dana and his associates paid $175,000 for the *Sun* in 1868. Under his management its value rose to an estimated $5 million. He made the *Sun* a witty, terse, and outspoken newspaper.

Dana was born on Aug. 8, 1819, in Hinsdale, N.H. He studied at Harvard University. In 1842, he became a member of the Brook Farm Association, an experimental social community at West Roxbury, Mass., and wrote for its publications, *The Harbinger* and *The Dial* (see BROOK FARM). He joined the staff of the New York *Tribune* in 1847, and later became its managing editor. He resigned in 1862 because he disagreed with *Tribune* owner Horace Greeley about the newspaper's stand on the Civil War. Dana served as an assistant secretary of war from 1863 to 1865. JOHN ELDRIDGE DREWRY

DANA, JAMES DWIGHT (1813-1895), was an American geologist, mineralogist, and zoologist. He was mineralogist and geologist of a government exploring expedition in the Pacific Ocean under Captain Charles Wilkes from 1838 to 1842. He also collected and studied corals and *crustaceans* (hard-shelled water creatures). He served as a professor at Yale from 1856 to 1890.

Later, he became editor in chief of the *American Journal of Science.* His most important books were *System of Mineralogy, Manual of Geology,* and *On Corals and Coral Islands.* He was born in Utica, N.Y., and was graduated from Yale University. CARROLL LANE FENTON

DANA, JOHN COTTON (1856-1929), was an American librarian. After he became head of the Denver Public Library in 1889, he started the first children's library and was the first to open all bookshelves to readers. He later worked in the Springfield (Mass.) Public Library, then became director of the Newark (N.J.) Public Library from 1902 to 1929. He made the Newark library famous by extending its services to everyone. Dana was born in Woodstock, Vt. R. B. DOWNS

DANA, RICHARD HENRY, JR. (1815-1882), a maritime lawyer and author, wrote *Two Years Before the Mast* (1840). The book was a best seller that was widely imitated. He also wrote *A Seaman's Friend* (1841) to help seamen know their rights and secure justice.

An attack of measles damaged his eyesight after his sophomore year at Harvard College. He became an ordinary seaman in 1834 to improve his health, and sailed around Cape Horn to California on the brig *Pilgrim.* He returned in 1836 aboard the *Alert,* and was graduated from Harvard Law School in 1840.

Dana wanted to serve his country in a high office, but he was defeated, because he put honor and justice above self-interest. Congress failed to confirm Dana's appointment as minister to England in 1876 when Dana refused to defend himself against false testimony. He worked for the Free Soil Party and fought for freedom for fugitive slaves (see FREE SOIL PARTY). He was born in Cambridge, Mass. WILLIAM H. GILMAN

DANA COLLEGE. See UNIVERSITIES AND COLLEGES (table).

DANAË was a Greek goddess. See PERSEUS.

DANBURY, Conn. (pop. 50,781; met. area 78,405), the *Hat City,* once made more hats than any other American city. At one time, over 35 factories made hats and related products in Danbury. By the mid-1960's, only one factory remained. Danbury still makes other products, including electrical, metal, and surgical products; furniture; paper; and textiles. Each fall, the Danbury State Fair attracts many visitors.

Danbury lies on the Still River, in southwestern Connecticut (see CONNECTICUT [political map]). Eight Norwalk families founded Danbury in 1685. In 1777, during the Revolutionary War, the British burned the city, then an army supply center. Zadoc Benedict started the nation's first beaver-hat factory there in 1780.

Danbury was incorporated as a city in 1889. In 1965, the city limits were extended to include the surrounding township. Danbury has a mayor-council government. ALBERT E. VAN DUSEN

DANCE MUSIC. See POPULAR MUSIC.

DANCING

From Kate Seredy's *The Good Master*, courtesy The Viking Press

DANCING is the oldest and liveliest of the arts. Men in all countries and in all times have expressed their feelings in rhythm and body movement. Our ancestors left pictures or writings which told of their dances. Men who study these records have found out why these people of ancient times danced, and how they danced.

The dance is the language of the body. It draws people together in their thoughts and feelings. A dancer can communicate any subject and any idea to his audience. His movements may interpret religious history or beliefs, or they may interpret things in our everyday life.

A dance may be social, so that everyone may take part in it. Or it may be entirely personal to the dancer. And, as in poetry and song, the dance may be in any style or form. It may be funny or sad. It may tell a story or merely describe an idea.

There are many reasons for dancing. Children dance because of the joy they feel. Their healthy little bodies will not remain quiet. Some primitive peoples believe dances will bring them magic powers. They dance to bring victory, health, or life. Much of our social dancing today is for the sake of companionship. And there are persons who dance to find relief from the sameness of everyday life. The dance reaches its most beautiful form with those who treat it as an art. These artists dance to give beauty and inspiration to others.

Dancing has been called the mother of the other arts. Throughout the ages, the dancing body has inspired the musician, the sculptor, and the painter. The drama of most countries started in their dances. The beginnings of music have been traced to the dance. The first music was merely a rhythm for the early dances. Perhaps it was only a chanting voice, the beat of a drum, the sound of two sticks struck together, or the clapping of hands. The dance has given richly to the other arts, and has in turn received much from the other arts.

Primitive Dance

The earliest records of people dancing are cave paintings in northern Spain. Scientists believe that these pictures were drawn about 50,000 years ago. The cave men could not write. The only records they left were such pictures. We can tell a great deal about their way of life from studying these pictures.

Probably the most important activity in the life of primitive peoples and ancient civilizations is the dance. From the dim past until today, primitive man has danced when his children were born, when they were old enough to be accepted as adult members of the tribe, when they were married, and when they died. He has danced to gain courage for battle. When the enemy was beaten, he has danced to celebrate the victory and to pray to his gods. Primitive medicine men have danced to drive away evil spirits which were thought to bring disease and misfortune. Primitive farmers had special ceremonial dances to bring rain and make crops grow. The primitive hunter and fisherman imitated in their dances the movements of the animals and fish they hoped to bring home.

Even among primitive dancers, there were special artists. All young men had to learn their own tribal dances. Some were better dancers than the others. These were sent away to be trained by tribes that were especially famous for dancing. After the training, the young men returned to their own tribes to teach others.

Primitive tribes held dance festivals. For weeks, months, and even years they practiced the dance steps. When festival time came, the dancers did not miss a step. They felt the whole purpose of the dance was lost if a single dancer moved out of turn. In some tribes in the New Hebrides, the older men stood by with bow and arrow and shot any dancer who made a mistake.

Primitive tribes today are just as serious about the dance as they were hundreds of years ago. Expeditions have brought back motion pictures of the primitive dances among the peoples of Africa, Australia, and the Pacific islands. Anyone who sees these movies will realize that the dance is a ruling part of primitive life.

Development of the Dance

Egypt got its dances from the peasant, or working, class. This is shown from records made as long ago as 2200 B.C. The Egyptians believed that their gods danced. Thus, magic and religion inspired the early dances. Often the priests performed them. One interesting dance which the priests did was an astronomical dance. In this the priests expressed symbolically the harmony of the universe, with every star and planet in its place and moving in rhythm with the others.

Egyptian kings must have danced. Ancient writings (hieroglyphics) and carvings on tombs show kings dancing before their gods. But the proud Egyptians had no social dance, and they did not dance for joy.

Some of the religious dances had acrobatic movements. In time these dances lost their meaning and were performed only for exhibition. The Egyptians brought dancers in from other countries and put them on exhibition. The dwarfs from Ethiopia were especially famous. The Egyptian dance was changed after 1500 B.C., when Egypt conquered the Near East. Lovely Asiatic girl dancers were brought into Egypt. The old dance had been masculine and severe, with open movements. But the Asiatic dancers were light and feminine, and the dance became gentler under their influence.

Greek Dancing also came from religion. Most of the Greek writings about dancing have been lost. We have

The Hoop Dance is one of the several dances performed as religious ceremonies by the Pueblo Indians of Taos, New Mexico.

Folk Dances such as this are a gay and important feature at the midsummer festival of the Norwegians.

The Sword Dance is a feature of the Highland games of Scotland.

Bolivian Indians take part in one of their lively traditional dances at the mountain village of Sorata. The women wear derby hats as a part of their everyday costumes.

Maori Men of New Zealand perform an age-old ceremonial dance. Such dances are among the customs the Maoris have retained for thousands of years.

U.S. Indian Service; Sawders; Black Star; Chicago Board of Ed.

A Ukrainian Folk Dance features dancers in colorful red boots and embroidered costumes.

learned about their ancient dances from sculpture and vase-paintings. There were special dances for each god.

Dances in honor of the god Dionysus were the beginning of the drama in Greece. The earliest drama was performed by principal actors and a chorus. The principal actors were speaker-actors. They wore heavy costumes, masks, and thick-soled shoes. The chorus was made up of dancer-actors. They wore light, flowing garments. The chorus danced, spoke, and sang, using their hands chiefly for expression. Among the stage dances were the slow and worshipful *Emmeleia* of the tragedy; the frolicsome *Kordax* of the comedy; and the vivid jumping and turning *Sikinnis* of the satirical drama.

The Greeks had other forms of dancing. Specially trained performers gave educational and acrobatic dances. Public festivals featured ball games in dance form. A thrilling weapon dance, the *Pyrrhic*, was performed by warriors. In this dance, the warriors prepared for battle by practicing movements of attack and defense. It was popular in Sparta. All strong Spartan lads from the age of five had to learn it. There was a Greek saying that the best dancer was the best fighter.

Even the philosophers danced in ancient Greece. Great men such as Plato and Socrates admired the dance. It is said that Socrates himself danced to celebrate the siege of Crete.

Romans added little new material to the dance. Like the Greeks, they had religious ceremonial dances. But even these came from the Etruscans, who held power in Italy before the Romans. The Romans in time spread their power throughout the Mediterranean world. Thus, Rome became important as a place where the dances of other nations were combined. The Romans were the first to appreciate the beauty of the Spanish dances.

The Roman theater was copied from the Greek theater. The Romans had wild dances for the god Bacchus, much like the dances the Greeks performed for Dionysus. But Romans themselves did little dancing. They brought in dancers from all the lands they conquered.

In Asia Minor and Egypt the Romans founded the art of *pantomime*. Pantomime is acting without speech. Rome developed the pantomime dance to a high degree. The dancers acted out stories through movements of their bodies. The most famous dancers of pantomime were Pylades and Bathyllus.

The Middle Ages saw the growth of social dancing and the rise of the dancing master, or teacher. There was little stage dancing. The Church controlled the theater, and only religious plays were presented. But the common people had a wonderful time in their folk dances. On holidays they danced for fun alone. Then they forgot the religious meanings of their dances, and out of these dances developed the so-called *social dances*.

In time the nobles also began to dance. They changed the simple dances of the common people into elaborate affairs. They wore brilliant and expensive costumes, and danced at court before the king and queen. The country folk had twirled happily in the *carol*, a circular dance. At court the noblemen danced a slow and stately carol with much stiff and elegant posturing. The nobles also started new creations, called *danza*. These were danced in couples or by men or ladies alone.

The growth of cities brought a new class of rich merchants and tradesmen. They wished to show off their wealth and social position, so they took up the stately dancing of the nobles. Social dances became more intricate and difficult. Soon dancing masters were needed to teach the new difficult steps.

The Renaissance (about 1500) brought again the refreshing influence of the common people. A new liveliness took the place of the stately dances of the Middle Ages. This influence was felt in all the countries of Europe. Italy danced the *pavan*, a stately ceremonial dance, and the *galliard*, a vivacious leaping dance. France presented the *courante*, with its quick running steps. Germany had the sprightly *allemande*, and Spain the passionate *saraband* and the *chaconne*. The most lively dance of all was the *volte* of southern France. The volte was the favorite dance of England's Queen Elizabeth I, and was popular throughout Great Britain.

During the 1600's, dancing lost much of its grace and charm. Gone was the gay mood of the Renaissance dances. The once light and hurried courante became stately and formal. The passionate saraband changed into a stiff and heavy dance. After 1650 the style changed again. Elegance and gracefulness became the new tone. Gentlemen bowed and ladies curtsied politely. Toes were pointed "just so," and steps were small and light. Lully, the French composer, arranged dances at the French court. He introduced the *minuet*, the *bourrée*, and the *passepied*. Another newcomer to the ballroom was the *gavotte*. All showed great elegance.

Late in the 1600's England's country dances came into style. Of these, the *contredanse* and the *square dances* are still popular. In the contredanse, partners arranged themselves in lines facing each other. For square dances, the dancers formed a square. The minuet was also very popular in England from 1650 to 1750.

The 1700's brought the new German *waltz*. This is still today one of the most popular of all dance steps. People had become tired of the difficult steps of older dances. The waltz has only one simple step. The dancers may move anywhere they wish on the floor. The waltz brought democracy, simplicity, and naturalness to ballroom dancing. And because it was so simple to learn, dancing masters lost their popularity.

The 1800's featured new dances which were taken from the common people. The *galop* and the *polka* were of Czech origin, and the *mazurka* was Polish. Early in the 1800's, there developed dances for couples. One of these was the *quadrille*. It was like the old English square dances and was popular for over a hundred years.

The 1900's have seen a great change in ballroom dancing. The young people found the waltz tiresome. They turned to the group dances, to the dances of the North American Creole or Negro, or to the dances of the South American countries.

The Brazilian *maxixe* in 1890 broke up the waltz pattern of turns and glides. The Negro influence showed in new rhythms which took the world by storm. In 1900 people danced the *one-step* and the *turkey trot*. The *cakewalk* (ancestor of *swing* music) was followed by the *fox trot*, the *shimmy*, the *Charleston*, and the *black bottom*.

Latin America contributed the Cuban *habanera*. The Argentines turned the habanera into a new dance, the *tango*. This gained wide popularity before World War I. After it came the *paso doble*, the *rhumba*, and the *conga*. These gave way to the *mambo*, *cha cha*, and *merengue*.

United Press Int.

High School Students Enjoyed Dancing the "Big Apple," a dance which was very popular in America in the 1930's.

Popular dancing reached its highest point of frenzy as the *jitterbugs* danced to *swing* music in the 1930's and 1940's. Some boys would even swing their girl partner over their head. Since the mid-1950's, *rock music* has dominated popular music and strongly influenced dancing. The first important dance based on rock music was the *twist* in the early 1960's. A succession of rock-related dances became popular during the 1960's and 1970's.

In the United States, clubs have sprung up which teach the folk dances of all nations. People from other lands try to keep alive the traditions of their homelands. One of the first traditions is the dance. The airplane and international education have brought us closer to other countries. Learning the dances of other peoples is one way of learning more about them.

Stage Dancing

The dance became clearly divided into two types. In the 1600's, one type was the dance as a social enjoyment. The other was the dance as a show, with performers dancing for an audience.

Ballet reached its first artistic peak under Louis XIV of France. Ballets were given as early as the late Middle Ages, and this kind of dancing flourished in Italy in the 1500's. Louis XIV, who ruled from 1643 to 1715, was the leading dancer of the realm. He was seriously interested in the dance as an art, and spent a great deal of money on elaborate ballets. Besides this, he started the Royal Academy of Dance and Music.

Women came onto the stage in the early 1700's. Mlle. Camargo was the first to use a short skirt for the ballet. This was to show her footwork better. She was also the first woman dancer to use certain jumps—among them the *entrechat*. Another ballerina, Mlle. Sallé, invented her own movements.

One of the greatest names of the period in ballet is Jean-Georges Noverre (1727-1810). He put new life in the dance. His first dramatic ballet was produced in 1761. Another great ballet dancer was Gaetano Vestris. He was called the king of dancers because of his skill.

In the 1800's, Salvatore Vigano originated the romantic ballet. Another new idea was toe dancing. Marie Taglioni was one of the first to perform on her toes. Fanny Elssler made popular the folk dances of Spain and other countries.

Russia has taken a great place in the ballet. Anna Pavlova and Vaslav Nijinsky, who performed in the early 1900's, represent ballet at its best. Pavlova will always be remembered for her dance *The Swan*, and Nijinsky for his *Spectre de la Rose*, *The Afternoon of a Faun*, and *Petrouchka*. See BALLET.

Exhibition Dancing is another kind of theater dance. There are many types of exhibition dances. Among them are the *acrobatic* and *adagio* dances, and the dances taken from the Orient and Spain. The Negro minstrel made America's greatest contribution to the exhibition dance. In the middle of the 1800's, "Jim Crow" Rice started the rage for a song and dance number called *Jim Crow*. Other early American dances were the *essence*, performed in soft shoes, and the *clog*, danced in wooden shoes. *Hand dancing*, introduced by Eddie Foy, was a great novelty.

All these types of dancing, including the *soft shoe*, *buck and wing*, *sand*, *stair*, and *pedestal* dancing, were the beginning of a great tradition, from Ed Christy to George M. Cohan and such masters of tap dancing as Bill Robinson, Paul Draper, Fred Astaire, and Gene Kelly. Tap dancers wear metal taps on their shoes to make the unusual rhythms clearly heard. Astaire and Kelly put ballet steps into their tap dancing.

Exhibition ballroom dancing became famous with

The Jitterbug Dance Was Popular in the 1940's.

Ruohomaa, Black Star

Don Cornelius Productions

Teen-Agers Dance to Rock Music.

Irene and Vernon Castle, who originated the *Castle walk*. The Castles danced all over the United States and in Europe in the *cakewalk*, *one-step*, *fox trot*, and *tango*.

Some colorful dances of other countries have been used on the stage. The Russian *Cossack* dances and the Spanish *flamenco* are popular.

Modern Dance

The 1900's brought new life and new forms to the dance. This new life started with the ideas of Isadora Duncan. She was tired of artificial forms, and fought for a simple and natural dance. She was inspired by the art of ancient Greece, and she preached the natural use of the body clothed in easy flowing garments. Her feet were bare as she danced. There was no scenery on the stage to draw attention from the dancing body. The entire Western world felt Isadora Duncan's influence on the dance.

Much has been done with the modern dance since the time of Isadora Duncan. Now the entire body is used to express anything that can be danced. The dance comes from within the performer. He follows no set patterns, but creates his own movements and style according to the idea for the dance. The themes of the modern dance are taken from the ups and downs of real life in its tragic as well as its humorous aspects.

The first great "modern dancer" was Mary Wigman. She used the new and different ideas of Rudolf von Laban of Germany, and founded her own school. Soon dancers from the Von Laban and Wigman schools were performing throughout Europe.

At the time of Isadora Duncan, there was also a famous new dancer in America. This was Ruth St. Denis, who turned to the Oriental countries for her inspiration. She, too, looked to the deeper realities of life. In her case these deeper realities were of a religious nature. She won fame during a two-year tour in Germany. Afterward, she and her husband, Ted Shawn, opened the Denishawn school of dancing in America.

But Denishawn students struck out on their own lines after leaving the school. This happened almost ten years later than the European movement which changed Isadora Duncan's dance. The three leaders of the revolt were Martha Graham, Doris Humphrey, and Charles Weidman. They dropped the elaborate staging and developed the dance as a personal and simple art.

Hanya Holm brought the ideas of Mary Wigman to America. She opened a school in New York in 1931, thus bringing together the American and German dance.

The modern dance reached its peak in America toward the end of the 1930's. Martha Graham, Doris Humphrey, Charles Weidman, and Hanya Holm danced, composed, taught, and traveled. In a very short time they spread the new dance across the country.

The modern dance has influenced other kinds of dancing too. Michel Fokine was greatly impressed after seeing Isadora Duncan in Russia. As a result, he brought many fresh ideas into ballet. Musical comedy, also, has borrowed much from the modern dance. The modern dance has also become a favorite with persons from all walks of life who dance for their own pleasure.

Oriental Dance

The Middle East gave full importance to song and dance. But there the dance was usually concerned with religion or ceremony. Ancient Semitic shepherds had their shepherd dances. Semitic farmers had special dances for the wheat harvest and for the grape harvest.

The Bible often mentions dancing. The Hebrew of the Old Testament danced at festivals. During the fall

George Gatts

Exhibition Ballroom Dancing and Ballet. Veloz and Yolanda, a team of exhibition ballroom dancers, were especially noted for their performances of Latin-American dance forms.

festival, men in Jerusalem tossed burning torches into the air and caught them while dancing. David in the Bible whirled and skipped before the Ark of the Covenant. The women danced when he returned after slaying Goliath. After the Jews passed through the Red Sea, Miriam and the maidens danced in chorus, with singing and beating of the timbrel. Hebrew dancing expressed happiness, for we read in the Bible of "a time to mourn and a time to dance."

The Arabs had a great many dances. Some are closely related to Hebrew dances. One of the early Arab dances is like the sword dance of the bride described in the Hebrew "Song of Songs." In the Arab world we find the religious sect of the whirling dervish. The dervishes twisted and turned to imitate the movements of the planets. Their movements called for aid from the good stars and appeased the evil stars.

The Persians had a classic dance which had seven basic steps which were supposed to be related to the planets. In Persia as in Arabia we find the religious cult of the whirling dervishes. But Persia was best known for its muscle dances. In these the dancer showed perfect control of muscles which many people hardly used at all. Ancient Persian records show that dancers traveled with the armies in 300 B.C.

Arabia and Persia both enjoyed acrobatic dancing. The juggler, the contortionist, and rope and acrobatic dancers amazed the crowds at bazaars and private parties. Most of the dances were done by young men, sometimes in women's costumes. They clacked castanets and jingled tambourines to add sparkle to the dance.

Hanya Holm Co.

The Dance May Be a Personal and Simple Art.

Dance Magazine

Fred Astaire, a world-famous tap dancer, added ballet movements to his dance steps.

The Far East is best known for its gesture dances, which were perfected thousands of years ago in India. In these dances, every gesture, every movement, has a meaning. The dancer can tell a wonderful story merely by placing certain parts of his body in certain positions. Only by hard work could a student learn the language of gesture. Dancing in India is not for entertainment. It has a higher purpose. Dance is supposed to be a gift of the god Shiva. Every dance contains a prayer. The dance may be dramatic or it may be humorous. But its movements tell the legends of the Hindu gods and heroes. Every audience understands the complicated language of the dance. The *Nautch* dance, a survival of old Indian culture, is part of all festivities.

As the Hindu religion spread, so did the mythical legends and dances of the Hindus. From India the dances traveled to Thailand, Indonesia, Cambodia, and Burma. In each country they took on the special characteristics of the people.

Tibet is a part of China, but its dances came from India, rather than China. We know that some dances of the Tibetan monasteries have not changed since about A.D. 900. The best known of these is the Tibetan Black Hat Devil Dance. Another dance is like a play. Monks act the parts.

China's ceremonial dances are as old as the country's history. The Chinese dances of today can be traced directly back to six ancient dances of the Chou dynasty (1027-256 B.C.). These were the *split-feather* dance, to drive away evil spirits; the *whole-feather*, used in worship; the *regulating* dance, to drive away ill winds; the *tail* dance, featuring an ox's tail, the symbol of agriculture; the *shield* dance, showing a defensive battle attitude; and the *battle-ax* dance, showing preparedness to strike if necessary. To these was added a seventh, the *humanity* dance. Here battle-axes, whole feathers, and oxtails were used merely as ornaments. The purpose of the dance was acted out by gestures. Chinese dancing takes place at funerals, sacrifices, and big festivals.

The Chinese theater was well begun in the 700's. Performances combined dancing, singing, and acting. There was no scenery or special lighting. The only attempt at realism was in the elaborate costumes. The audience was not the people, but the emperor and the priests. Performances, then as now, lasted for hours. The greatest name from this art is that of Mei Lan-fang.

DANCING

Among the Chinese, acrobatic dancing holds a high place. One of the reasons military plays are so popular is that they feature very fine acrobatic dancing.

Japan's people built their first dances around religion. They were greatly influenced by China. The stern but popular *no* plays were based on dancelike movements and gestures. The first no plays were written in the 1300's by a father and son, Kan-ami and Zeami. The dramas followed definite forms. A chorus would chant the story while the actors, wearing masks, danced and used pantomime. Simple gestures often were used to convey complicated meanings. Most no plays were short, and several were given on the same program. Often a brief dance-drama called a *kyogen* was presented between the no plays. These types of dramas have been passed down from father to son for many generations. In the last 600 years, the actors have been descendants of the original actors.

In the 1600's a new and livelier form of dance-drama arose in Japan. This was the *Kabuki*. The Kabuki took many movements and gestures from the older no dramas. Kabuki plays often lasted from morning to night, in contrast to the shorter no dramas.

Another old dance still appears on very special occasions. This is the *Bugaku*, an ancient court dance.

Japan has its popular dances, too. Among the favorite folk dances are the *Bon and Catfish*, the religious *Kagura*, and the lion-mask dances. The people also have country dances, such as the beautiful cherry blossom dances. Much of the dancing is done by lovely geisha girls.

Careers in Dancing

Dancing is a highly competitive field with limited opportunities. There are many more dancers seeking positions than there are positions available for them. Only the most capable reach the top.

Requirements. A person who wishes to be a dancer must be physically strong. In addition to great talent, he must have charm, grace, and physical attractiveness. He must love to dance so much that he will be able to continue his career in spite of many obstacles.

Training for a career in dancing begins at an early age. Some children start dancing lessons when they are as young as seven or eight. Almost all dancing, except ballroom, requires a knowledge of ballet. Students spend many hours practicing basic ballet movements and exercises. After years of technical training, a student is ready to enter a professional dance school or to study professionally with a private teacher. A dancer never really finishes his training. He must continue to take lessons and practice throughout his career. Dancers who wish to teach in a high school or college must have a bachelor's or master's degree.

Working Conditions. Successful dancers find great satisfaction in their careers. They often travel to perform in many different countries. But anyone entering the field must be prepared to spend long hours looking for openings, to accept part-time positions in related fields, and to face many hardships. Many dancers must support themselves by teaching in dance studios or offering private lessons.

Several organizations serve dancers in various fields. Ballet dancers belong to the American Guild of Musical Artists; dancers in Broadway plays belong to Chorus Equity; and television performers belong to the American Federation of Television and Radio Artists. These organizations assure minimum wages and notify members of job openings.

Dancers find the most opportunities in the entertainment centers of New York City and Los Angeles, and in other large cities such as Chicago, Detroit, Boston, Philadelphia, and San Francisco. HANYA HOLM

Related Articles in WORLD BOOK include:

BIOGRAPHIES

For biographies of ballet dancers, see the *Related Articles* at the end of the BALLET article. See also:

Astaire, Fred
Castle (family)
Duncan, Isadora
Dunham, Katherine
Graham, Martha
Greco, José
Robinson, Bill
Saint Denis, Ruth
Shawn, Ted

KINDS OF DANCES

Allemande
Ballet
Bolero
Charleston
Cotillion
Flamenco
Folk Dancing
Fox Trot
Gigue
Hornpipe
Minuet
Rhumba
Schottische
Square Dance
Tango
Tarantella
Two-Step
Waltz

PICTURES OF DANCERS

The following articles have pictures of dancers:

Africa
Alaska
Arizona
Australia
Bolivia
Chile
France
Gypsy
Indian, American
Indonesia
Iowa
Jews
Latin America
Pacific Islands
Pygmy
South Dakota
Spain

OTHER RELATED ARTICLES

Buffalo Ceremonials
Castanets
Japanese Literature (Drama)
Mask
Musical Comedy
Pantomime
Rain Dance
Rhythm

Outline

I. Primitive Dance

II. Development of the Dance

A. Egypt
B. Greek Dancing
C. Romans
D. The Middle Ages
E. The Renaissance
F. During the 1600's
G. The 1700's
H. The 1800's
I. The 1900's

III. Stage Dancing

A. Ballet
B. Exhibition Dancing

IV. Modern Dance

V. Oriental Dance

A. The Middle East
B. The Bible
C. The Arabs
D. The Persians
E. The Far East

VI. Careers in Dancing

Questions

Why were dancers in the New Hebrides sometimes shot?

What kind of Japanese dance-dramas often lasted from morning to night?

What character in the Bible danced before the Ark of the Covenant?

What new ideas and forms did Isadora Duncan introduce to the dance?

What people imitated the movements of the planets in their dances?

What people dance at funerals?

In what country do monks still dance?

What people danced while flinging burning torches into the air?

What is the name of the famous ballet dance for which Pavlova is remembered?

DANDELION, *DAN duh* LY *un,* is a bright-yellow wild flower that grows in lawns and meadows. Throughout the temperate regions of the world, gardeners usually consider it a troublesome weed that is difficult to control.

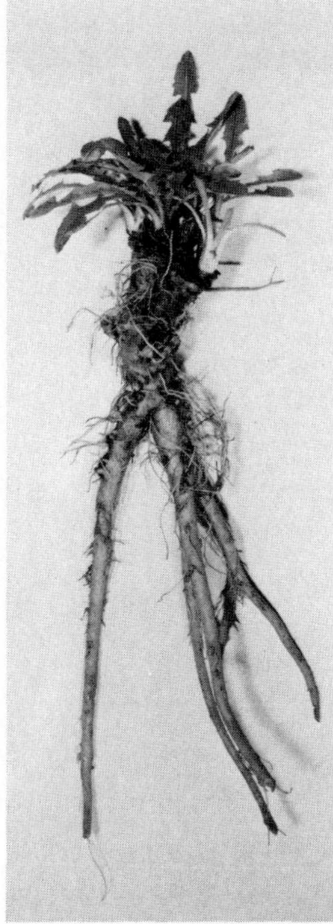

John H. Gerard

The Long Dandelion Root is called a *taproot.* Small *branch roots* grow out from its sides.

The early colonists brought the dandelion to America from Europe. Its name comes from the French words *dent de lion,* meaning lion's tooth. It has smooth leaves with coarse notches, which look like teeth. The golden-yellow head is really a cluster of flowers. The dandelion has a smooth, straight, and hollow stem, and the entire plant contains a white, milky juice. The root is long, thick, and pointed, with hairlike root branches growing from it. The dandelion differs from most other plants in the manner in which it reproduces. Its ovaries form fertile seeds without having to be pollinated (see POLLEN AND POLLINATION).

Young dandelion leaves can be used in salads or they can be cooked. They taste best when they are young, before the plant has blossomed. Wine sometimes is made from the dandelion flowers.

In order to keep dandelion plants from growing on lawns, gardeners must cut deep into their roots. The roots grow to about 3 feet (91 centimeters) long in soft, rich earth. Slicing close under the surface only encourages the plants to grow. Gardeners sometimes spray dandelions with chemicals that destroy the dandelions but do not harm grass.

Scientific Classification. The dandelion is a member of the composite family, *Compositae.* The common dandelion is genus *Taraxacum,* species *T. officinale.* ARTHUR CRONQUIST

See also FLOWER (picture: Bright Yellow Dandelions).

The Dandelion Blossoms open in the morning and close in the evening. The flowers, when they ripen, form feathered, cottony seeds which the wind carries far and wide.

J. Horace McFarland

DANDIE DINMONT TERRIER is a dog that got its name from a book. In Sir Walter Scott's novel *Guy Mannering,* a farmer named Dandie Dinmont raised an unusual pack of terriers that were all the color of either pepper or mustard. In the book, the dogs were famous as hunters of foxes, badgers, and otters. A new breed was later called Dandie Dinmont for the farmer in the book. This terrier has a big head and large, soft brown eyes. Its forehead is covered by a topknot, and its ears hang low. It has a crisp, shaggy coat and a long, slim body. For dog shows, the American Kennel Club requires that Dandies weigh from 18 to 24 pounds (8 to 11 kilograms). Because its hind legs are longer than its front legs, the Dandie seems tipped up from behind. See also DOG (picture: Terriers). JOSEPHINE Z. RINE

DANDRUFF is made up of flakes of skin thrown off by the scalp. The flakes are mixed with grease from the oil glands. Some scaling of the skin of the scalp is normal. But when the scalp loses many scales, the product is called *dandruff.* Some dandruff can be prevented by proper washing, brushing, and occasional oiling of the hair and scalp. Dandruff does not cause baldness.

The condition called *seborrhea* sometimes causes dandruff. Many authorities consider seborrhea a mild bacterial disease. In seborrhea, the scalp is red and itchy, and the dandruff is more greasy than usual. Keeping the head clean helps prevent seborrhea. It is wise to see a doctor for treatment. SIDNEY OLANSKY

DANE. See DENMARK; ENGLAND (The Anglo-Saxon Period).

DANELAW. See ALFRED THE GREAT.

DANFORTH FOUNDATION makes grants to schools, colleges, universities, and other public and private agencies, and also administers educational programs. The foundation, set up by Mr. and Mrs. William H. Danforth, was incorporated in Missouri in 1927. Its offices are at 222 S. Central Avenue, St. Louis, Mo. 63105. For assets, see FOUNDATIONS (table).

DANIEL is a well-known Biblical character. The Book of Daniel, chapter I, dramatically tells the story of his rise from the position of captive slave in the royal palace to that of a trusted adviser to the king.

Some scholars believe that the book was written about 165 B.C. Others believe that it was written earlier. Its purpose was to encourage persecuted Jews in their desperate struggle against the oppression of Antiochus IV, King of Syria from 176 to 164 B.C.

Nebuchadnezzar, King of Babylon, captured a group of people from Jerusalem in about the year 600 B.C., among them several young people of royal descent. Daniel was one of these. The captives were well fed, but Daniel refused to eat the food, which by Jewish law was impure. Instead he ate a simple diet of cereal. This drew the king's notice. Daniel won favor when he interpreted a dream that had puzzled the wise men. The king then made Daniel ruler of Babylon.

The Bible also tells how Daniel foretold the madness

National Gallery, Washington, D.C., Ailsa Mellon Bruce Fund

Daniel in the Lions' Den **was painted by the Flemish artist Peter Paul Rubens. The picture shows Daniel praying at dawn after safely spending the night in the lions' den. Completed in 1615, it is one of the few large works Rubens painted without assistants.**

of Nebuchadnezzar, how he remained safe when thrown into a den of lions, and how he told Belshazzar the meaning of the mysterious handwriting on the wall (see HANDWRITING ON THE WALL).

The last part of the Book of Daniel tells of the eventual triumph of right and of truth, and predicts the destruction of evil. WALTER G. WILLIAMS

See also BELSHAZZAR; NEBUCHADNEZZAR.

DANIEL-ROPS, HENRI (1901-1965), was the pen name of HENRI-JULES PERIOT, a French author and religious historian. He gained his greatest recognition for *Jesus in His Times* (1945), a brief and readable history of the life of Jesus Christ. His 10-volume *History of the Church of Christ* (1948-1965) traces the history of the Christian church.

Daniel-Rops was born in Epinal, France, and studied at the universities of Grenoble and Lyons. In the 1920's and 1930's, he wrote novels and essays that radiated religious devotion and concern for man's loss of genuine religion. During World War II, the Nazis tried to destroy his *Sacred History* (1943), a history of the Jews. But a few copies survived, and the book was reissued after the war. In 1955, Daniel-Rops was elected to the French Academy. ROLAND N. STROMBERG

DANIELL CELL. See BATTERY (Closed-Circuit Cells).

DANIELS is the family name of two American editors and statesmen, father and son.

Josephus Daniels (1862-1948), the father, served as secretary of the Navy from 1913 to 1921, and as ambassador to Mexico from 1933 to 1942. Daniels was born in Washington, N.C., and was educated at the University of North Carolina. He entered newspaper work in Wilson, N.C. Daniels consolidated the *State Chronicle* and the *North Carolinian* in 1894 to form the Raleigh *News and Observer*, which he edited until his death. ALVIN E. AUSTIN

Jonathan Worth Daniels (1902-), the son, first became known for *A Southerner Discovers the South* (1938). He later wrote *The Man of Independence* (1950), a biography of Harry S. Truman. *The End of Innocence* (1954) tells of Washington, D.C., during World War I. Daniels was born in Raleigh, N.C. He became editor of the Raleigh *News and Observer* in 1948. CARL NIEMEYER

DANILOVA, ALEXANDRA (1904?-), was a great Russian ballerina. She won international fame for her warmth, intelligence, and radiant dance style. Her roles included the leads in *Le Beau Danube*, *Gaîté Parisienne*, the second act of *Swan Lake*, *Coppélia*, *Danses Concertantes*, *Night Shadow*, and *Firebird*.

Alexandra Danilova was born in Peterhof. She became a soloist with the Maryinsky (now Kirov) Ballet in Leningrad in 1922. In 1924, she joined Sergei Diaghilev's ballet company in Paris and became an immediate favorite with audiences. She was prima ballerina with Col. W. de Basil's Ballets Russes in 1933 and then with the Ballet Russe de Monte Carlo from 1938 to 1952. She became a great favorite with American audiences when those companies toured the United States. She retired in the late 1950's. P. W. MANCHESTER

DANISH WEST INDIES was the name of the Virgin Islands in the Caribbean Sea when they were ruled by Denmark. See VIRGIN ISLANDS (History).

D'ANNUNZIO, GABRIELE (1863-1938), was an Italian author and political figure. His poetry deals with nature, the sea, and his own hunger for happiness. The poems show an unusual sensitivity for colors, moods, and feelings. His style is imaginative and melodious, but often flowery. D'Annunzio wrote many novels, several based on his scandalous personal life. *The Flame of Life* (1900) is based on his love affair with actress Eleonora Duse (see DUSE, ELEONORA). His plays include *La Gioconda* (1898) and *The Daughter of Jorio* (1904).

D'Annunzio was born in Pescara. In 1910, his extravagant living forced him to declare bankruptcy, and he moved to Paris. He returned to Italy to campaign for his country's entry into World War I. In 1919 and 1920, he served as the self-appointed ruler of the city of Fiume (now Rijeka) after seizing the city with a military force (see RIJEKA). SERGIO PACIFICI

DANTE ALIGHIERI, *DAN tay ah lee GYAY ree* (1265-1321), an Italian author, was one of the greatest poets of the Middle Ages. His epic poem the *Divine Comedy* ranks among the finest works of world literature. Critics have praised it not only as magnificent poetry, but also for its wisdom and scholarly learning.

Portrait by Giotto, Museo Nazionale, Florence (Alinari)

Dante Alighieri

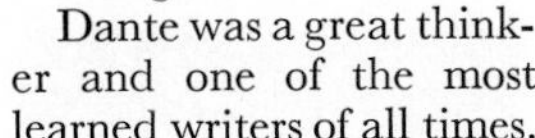

Dante was a great thinker and one of the most learned writers of all times. Many scholars consider the *Divine Comedy* a summary of medieval thought. Dante had a tremendous influence on later writers and scholars. Geoffrey Chaucer and John Milton imitated his works. Dante influenced such writers of the 1800's as Henry Wadsworth Longfellow, Percy Bysshe Shelley, Lord Byron, Lord Tennyson, Victor Hugo, and Friedrich Schlegel.

His Life. Dante was born in Florence. His mother died when he was a child, and his father died when Dante was about 18 years old. Dante received a rich education in classical and religious subjects. He may have studied at Bologna, Padua, and Paris.

Dante's idealized love for a beautiful girl, Beatrice Portinari (1266-1290), provided much inspiration for his literary works. He saw her only twice, once when he was 9 and again nine years later. Although grief-stricken after Beatrice's death, Dante married Gemma Donati before 1294. They had at least three children.

Dante was active in the political and military life of Florence. He entered the army as a youth and held several important positions in the Florentine government during the 1290's. Dante became involved in a political dispute between two groups, the Guelphs and the Ghibellines, who were fighting for control of Tuscany. A political group within the Guelphs gained control of Florence about 1300. This group was hostile to the poet and banished him in 1302, condemning him to death if he returned to Florence. Dante spent the last few years of his exile in Ravenna, and was buried there.

Dante Visited Hell, Purgatory, and Heaven in his poem, *The Divine Comedy.* This etching by Gustave Doré shows Dante being led by Virgil, the Roman poet.

Brown Bros.

His Works. Among Dante's early writings, the best known is *La Vita Nuova* (*The New Life*), written about 1293. This work is a collection of 31 poems with prose comments describing his love for Beatrice. *The New Life* shows the influence of troubadour poetry that flourished in southern France during the 1100's and 1200's.

Dante began the *Divine Comedy* about 1300. The poem relates his spiritual development and focuses the reader's attention on life after death. For more information about this work, see Divine Comedy.

Dante also wrote several nonfiction works. About 1303 and 1304 he wrote *De Vulgari Eloquentia* (*On Writing in the Italian Language*). This work in Latin prose stresses the importance of writing in a common Italian language, rather than in Latin or a minor dialect. Dante hoped that the Italians would develop a national literary language to help unite the country.

Il Convivo (*The Banquet*, 1304 1307) is an unfinished work written in Italian, consisting of three odes, with long, detailed comments on each. The work is filled with Dante's wide knowledge of philosophy and science. *De Monarchia* (*On Monarchy*, 1313?) is a long essay in Latin prose. Dante called for the state, in the form of the Holy Roman Empire, to join with the church in guiding man to a better life on earth and joy in heaven. Other works include a group of miscellaneous poems and several letters. Patricia M. Gathercole

DANTON, *DAHN TAWN,* **GEORGES JACQUES** (1759-1794), was a great leader of the French Revolution. His policy was "boldness, and more boldness, and ever more boldness, and France is saved!" He perhaps did more to create and defend the French Republic than any other person. Danton was partly responsible for the massacres of the Reign of Terror, which he considered necessary for the safety of his country. When he believed that safety was assured, he advocated more humane policies. He wished to restore, rather than to destroy, the normal life of France.

Danton was born in Arcissur-Aube, of middle-class parents. At the beginning of the revolution he was a successful lawyer in Paris, and a leader of the Cordeliers Club, one of the militant factions of the extreme Republicans. This group favored ridding France of the monarchy. They achieved their purpose on Aug. 10, 1792, when they forced the legislative assembly to imprison Louis XVI. Danton, who is called "the Man of August 10th" because of his leadership in the movement to imprison Louis XVI, became minister of justice.

Danton and his associates, Camille Desmoulins, Maximilien Robespierre, and Jean Paul Marat, established a national convention of revolutionary leaders and a revolutionary tribunal. These two bodies ruled France for the next three years. Almost anyone could be brought before the jury of the tribunal. Their victims were not only traitors, but also persons suspected of being too mild in their political views. Danton and Desmoulins soon recognized the need for stamping out this violence. They felt that the convention should relax its policy and prepare a workable republican constitution for an orderly government. Danton suggested halting the violence.

Robespierre was jealous of Danton's success. He ordered that Danton be arrested for disloyalty and brought before the tribunal. Danton's fiery and eloquent denunciation alarmed the members of the tribunal, who feared the loss of their power. Danton was condemned and executed. His execution climaxed the Reign of Terror. André Maurois

See also French Revolution; Marat, Jean Paul; Robespierre.

DANUBE RIVER is one of the great waterways of Europe. The Danube drains nearly one-tenth the area of the whole of Europe. The river basin covers 315,000 square miles (815,800 square kilometers), and includes southern Germany, Austria, Hungary, Yugoslavia, Bulgaria, Romania, and part of Czechoslovakia.

The Danube River is formed by two small mountain streams which join in the Black Forest near Schwenningen, Germany. The river runs east and south, winding for 1,776 miles (2,858 kilometers) to its mouth in the Black Sea. In length, the Danube ranks second only to the Volga among the rivers of Europe. For the location of the Danube, see Europe (physical map).

The Danube has been deepened by canals and channels to make it the chief water route for the commerce of central Europe. A canal makes it possible for boats to travel through the Iron Gate, a gorge with rapids where the Danube breaks through the Transylvanian Alps at the border of Romania and Yugoslavia. At Ulm in Bavaria, the Danube is connected to the Rhine River by the Ludwigs Canal. Large cities are located on the banks of the Danube River, including Vienna, Budapest, and Belgrade.

The "beautiful blue Danube" is famous in song and history. Roman colonies were established in the valley of the Danube. The Huns, Magyars, and Turks made their conquests through this valley. James K. Pollock

See also Budapest (picture); River (chart: Longest Rivers).

DANZIG. See Gdańsk.

DAPHNE, *DAF nee*, was the daughter of the river-god Peneus in Greek mythology. She wanted to be a huntress and to remain unmarried like her patron, Artemis (see Artemis). Eros shot her with a leaden arrow to keep her from loving anyone. But at the same time he wounded Apollo with a golden arrow to make him love Daphne (see Apollo). Apollo pursued Daphne everywhere. One day, when he was about to catch her, Daphne called on her father to protect her from her handsome lover. Peneus changed her into a laurel tree. Apollo then made the laurel his sacred tree and he wore a wreath of laurel leaves for his crown. For this reason, the laurel wreath has been a symbol of honor since that time. Padraic Colum

Alinari

Apollo and Daphne, a statue by Gian Bernini, stands in the Villa Borghese in Rome.

DAPHNIA. See Water Flea.

Leon, Pix

The Danube River flows through fertile valleys, dotted with ancient castles and terraced vineyards. The Huns, Magyars, and Turks led their armies into Europe through the Danube valley.

DAR. See DAUGHTERS OF THE AMERICAN REVOLUTION.

DAR ES SALAAM, *DAHR ess suh LAHM* (pop. 272,821), is the capital of Tanzania and one of the most important ports in eastern Africa. The city lies on a long, landlocked harbor about 40 miles (64 kilometers) southwest of Zanzibar. A railroad connects it with the interior. British forces captured Dar es Salaam during World War I. See also TANZANIA. HIBBERD V. B. KLINE, JR.

DARAZI. See DRUSES.

DARDANELLES, *DAHR d'n ELZ,* is a strait which joins the Aegean Sea with the Sea of Marmara. The strait is part of a waterway which leads from the landlocked Black Sea to the Mediterranean. Also part of this waterway is the Bosporus, a second strait which joins the Black Sea and the Sea of Marmara.

The word *Dardanelles* comes from the ancient Greek city of Dardanus, on Asia's side of the strait. The ancient Greeks called this strait the *Hellespont.*

At its narrowest point, the Dardanelles is about 1 mile (1.6 kilometers) wide from the European shore to the Asiatic. The average width of the strait is 3 to 4 miles (5 to 6 kilometers). It is about 37 miles (60 kilometers) long, and the average depth is 200 feet (61 meters). The Dardanelles usually has a strong surface current in the direction of the Aegean Sea, but a powerful undercurrent flows east and carries salty water through the Sea of Marmara and the Bosporus into the Black Sea. This undercurrent keeps the Black Sea from becoming a fresh-water body.

WORLD BOOK map

The Dardanelles Lies Between Europe and Asia.

About 480 B.C., Xerxes led an army across the Dardanelles near Abydos and invaded Europe. In 334 B.C., Alexander led his army over a bridge of boats across the Dardanelles into Asia. Hundreds of years later, the strait was important to the defense of the Byzantine Empire. After that empire fell, the Ottoman Turks ruled the Dardanelles. See BYZANTINE EMPIRE.

In 1841, the great powers of Europe—Great Britain, France, Prussia, and Austria—agreed to give Turkey control of the passage of ships through the Dardanelles. This agreement was renewed in 1856 and again in 1871 and 1878. The Treaty of Lausanne in 1923 opened the Dardanelles to all nations. In 1936, the Montreux convention gave Turkey permission to remilitarize the strait.

Early in World War II, the strait was closed to all ships except those with special permission from Turkey. Although the possession of the Dardanelles was threatened during the war, Turkey kept control of this important waterway. After World War II, Russia unsuccessfully attempted to gain control of the Dardanelles. The Western Powers supported Turkey's rights to the strategic strait. ROBERT O. REID

Related Articles in WORLD BOOK include:

Aegean Sea	Hellespont	Turkey
Black Sea	Lausanne, Treaty of	World War I (The Dardanelles)
Bosporus	Marmara, Sea of	

DARE, VIRGINIA (1587- ?), was the first English child born in America. Her parents were members of a band of 117 colonists who settled on Roanoke Island in 1587. Virginia Dare was the daughter of Ananias Dare and Ellinor White. She was born on August 18, and was named Virginia in what is believed to have been the first English christening ceremony in America. See also LOST COLONY. JOSEPH CARLYLE SITTERSON

Courtesy of North Carolina Department of Archives & History

The Christening of Virginia Dare, **a painting by William Steen, shows a historic christening in early America.**

DARIEN is a gulf of the Caribbean Sea on the north coast of South America, between Colombia and Panama. A small inlet at the southern end of the gulf is called the *Gulf of Urabá.* The name *Darien* formerly was given to the Isthmus of Panama. See also PANAMA, ISTHMUS OF. BOSTWICK H. KETCHUM

DARÍO, *dah REE oh,* **RUBÉN** (1867-1916), was the pen name of Félix Rubén García-Sarmiento, one of the most important poets in the Spanish language. Darío was the leader of the Modernist movement in Spanish poetry. In *Azul* (1888), he rejected sentimentality and moralizing in literature, proclaiming the doctrine of "art for art's sake." The elegant, sensual grace of *Profane Prose* (1896), *Songs of Life and Hope* (1905), and *Wandering Song* (1907) set a new tone for literary expression, as did his experiments in verse forms and his aristocratic language. Darío's impact was so great that many critics today can tell whether a poem in Spanish was written before or after him.

Darío was born in Metapa (now Ciudad Darío), Nicaragua. He rose from poverty to become a diplomat and foreign correspondent, but his wild living hastened his death. Darío served as Nicaraguan consul in Paris, and as minister to Brazil and Spain. MARSHALL R. NASON

DARIUS, *duh RY uhs,* was the name of three kings of ancient Persia (now Iran).

Darius I (558?-486 B.C.) was one of the most distinguished of eastern rulers. A record of his early achievements is carved in cuneiform writing on a high cliff known as Behistun Rock, in western Persia (see CUNEIFORM). Darius became king in 521 B.C. He put down widespread revolts and, later, added northwestern India and parts of central Asia and southeastern Europe to his empire. Darius is credited with organizing the empire into efficient administrative units called *satrapies.* He reorganized the tax system and encouraged trade with other countries. His army invaded Greece after conflicts with Greeks in Asia Minor and a campaign against the Scythians in Europe. It was defeated at Marathon in 490 B.C. (see MARATHON). Darius I died while preparing for a new attack on Greece. Darius' son, Xerxes, succeeded him.

Darius II ruled the Persian Empire from 424 to 404 B.C. Court intrigues and declining strength in the empire marked his reign.

Darius III, the last king of Persia, ruled from 336 to 330 B.C. He inherited a corrupt empire that was about to collapse. Alexander became king of Macedon in 336, and swept through western Asia in a great attack on Persia. Darius III was defeated at Issus in 333 B.C., and was crushed two years later at Gaugamela, near Arbela. He fled to his eastern provinces, and was murdered by his own men. RICHARD NELSON FRYE

See also PERSIA, ANCIENT.

DARJEELING, *dahr JEE lihng* (pop. 42,873), is the summer capital of the state of West Bengal in eastern India. It lies on the lower slopes of the Himalaya, north of Calcutta, about 7,100 feet (2,160 meters) above sea level. The high altitude makes the city cool and pleasant the year round. Persons who live in the Indian lowlands seek relief from the heat by going up to Darjeeling in September and October. Mount Kanchenjunga can be seen from the city. Mount Everest is visible from just outside the city. The well-known Darjeeling tea grows on hillsides near the city. A small railway climbs to the city over steep slopes and through tea plantations and teakwood forests. A wide square serves as an open-air bazaar for trading. ROBERT I. CRANE

See also INDIA (City Life [picture: Market Place]).

Joe Rychetnik, Van Cleve Photography

Darjeeling lies on the slopes of the Himalaya in northern India. Darjeeling tea is grown on nearby plantations.

DARK AGES is a term once used to describe the Middle Ages. The word *dark* referred to a supposed lack of learning during the period. We know now that the Middle Ages cannot be described as completely "dark." The period only seemed dark to scholars of the more advanced Renaissance and to historians who were later influenced by them.

The early centuries of the Middle Ages, from the A.D. 400's to the late 900's, came closest to being dark. Civilization sank low in Western Europe. Knowledge from the ancient Romans survived only in a few monastery, cathedral, and palace schools. Knowledge acquired from ancient Greece almost disappeared. Few persons

The Oriental Institute, University of Chicago

The Court of King Darius is shown on a carved stone panel that stands in the entrance of the Treasury building in Persepolis, Iran. The monarch is seated on the throne and his son Xerxes stands behind him, with members of his court.

received schooling. Many of the art skills and craftsmanship of the ancient world were lost. Writers had little sense of style. In their ignorance, they accepted popular stories and rumors as true.

While such darkness existed in Western Europe, life was brighter in other parts of the world. The Byzantine Empire preserved many features of Greek and Roman life (see BYZANTINE EMPIRE). The Arabs spread a splendid civilization from Spain to the borders of China (see MOSLEMS).

In the early 1000's, economic and political life began to revive in western Europe. This revival led to a remarkable improvement of culture during the 1100's. BRYCE LYON

For a description of life and culture of the Dark Ages, see MIDDLE AGES; FEUDALISM; RENAISSANCE.

DARK AND BLOODY GROUND was a name given to Kentucky because of Indian wars fought there. See INDIAN WARS (Lord Dunmore's War); KENTUCKY.

DARK CONTINENT. See AFRICA.

DARLING, DING (1876-1962), born JAY NORWOOD DARLING, was an American cartoonist whose drawings portray national events and human weaknesses. At the height of his career, probably more than a million persons enjoyed his cartoons daily. Darling won the Pulitzer prize for editorial cartooning in 1924 and in 1943.

Darling became a cartoonist for the *Sioux City Journal* in 1901, and joined the staff of *The Des Moines Register* in 1906. After 1917, his cartoons were syndicated through *The New York Tribune.* He wrote and illustrated *Ding Goes to Russia* (1932). He was interested in wildlife, and served as director of the United States Biological Survey in 1934 and 1935. He also was honorary president of the National Wildlife Federation. Darling was born in Norwood, Mich. DICK SPENCER III

DARLING, GRACE HORSLEY (1815-1842), became a famous English heroine by helping save nine survivors of a shipwreck. She lived at Longstone Lighthouse on one of the Farne Islands, off the English coast. Her father was keeper of the lighthouse. The steamer *Forfarshire* was wrecked on Sept. 7, 1838. Through a telescope, she saw several persons clinging to a rock. During a storm, she rowed to the rescue with her father. The Humane Society awarded Grace Darling and her father gold medals. She was born in Bamborough, Northumberland. HELEN E. MARSHALL

DARLING RIVER. See MURRAY RIVER.

DARMSTADT. See HESSE.

DARNEL grows as a weed in grain fields. This plant is thought to be the *tares* mentioned in the Bible (Matt. 13: 24-30).

DARNLEY, LORD. See MARY, QUEEN OF SCOTS (Her Reign).

DARROW, CLARENCE SEWARD (1857-1938), was a famous American criminal lawyer. He also was one of the first to be called a "labor lawyer." This was because of his enthusiasm in fighting legal battles for organized labor. He became known as the legal champion of the unfortunate and oppressed. Darrow defended Eugene V. Debs in an 1894 labor strike case. One of his best-known trials was the 1925 John T. Scopes case, in which he defended the right to teach evolution in Tennessee schools. Darrow also defended Loeb and Leopold in their 1924 trial for the murder of Bobby Franks. In later years, Darrow toured the country debating social issues with noted opponents.

Darrow was born in Kinsman, Ohio, and lived in Chicago where he practiced after 1888. His books include *Crime, Its Cause and Treatment; Resist Not Evil; Eye for an Eye;* and *Farmington.* H. G. REUSCHLEIN

See also IDAHO (Early Statehood).

N. Y. Herald Tribune and Des Moines Register

"Why Call Them Sportsmen?" Through his cartoons, Ding Darling fought for the conservation of wildlife in America.

Clarence Darrow, *left,* opposed William Jennings Bryan, *right,* during the famous John Scopes trial at Dayton, Tenn., in 1925.

Wide World

DART. See Blowgun; Darts.

DARTER is a name for several kinds of dwarf fresh-water fishes of the perch family found in eastern North America. The smallest is the *least darter*, about 1 inch (2.5 centimeters) long. The largest, the *log perch*, may reach 8 inches (20 centimeters). The breeding males of most darters have brilliant colors. Their markings are generally metallic green and bright red. The *rainbow darter* is the best known of the species with bright colors. The *Johnny darter* is plainer, but more common. Almost all darters live under and around stones in rapids. There they catch insects and other small animals. They swim in spurts from one resting place to another.

The Johnny Darter, like other darter fish, has no air bladder. It has to flap its chest fins to keep afloat in the water.

Scientific Classification. The darter belongs to the fresh-water perch family, *Percidae*. The least darter is genus *Etheostoma*, species *E. microperca*. The log perch is *Percina caprodes*. The rainbow darter is *Etheostoma caeruleum*. The Johnny darter is *Etheostoma nigrum*. Carl L. Hubbs

DARTER, a large tropical bird, lives in swamps, ponds, and rivers in nearly all the warm regions of the world. The American darter is about 3 feet (91 centimeters) long, with a long thin neck, small head, and pointed bill. It has glossy black plumage, silvery markings on the back of the neck and wings, and a broad brown-tipped tail. The bill is olive above and yellow below. The feet are olive with yellow webs. The darter feeds on fish and other water life. It is an excellent swimmer and a strong flier. It is sometimes called the *snakebird* because it occasionally swims half submerged, with only its snakelike neck visible above the water. The American darter is also called the *anhinga* or the *water turkey*.

Arthur H. Fisher

The Darter, or Snakebird

Scientific Classification. Darters make up the darter family, *Anhingidae*. The American darter is classified as genus *Anhinga*, species *A. anhinga*. Alexander Wetmore

DARTMOOR is a rocky plateau covering about 350 square miles (906 square kilometers) in south Devonshire, England. High Willhays (2,039 feet, or 621 meters), is its highest point and one of its many granite peaks. Dartmoor Prison, scene of the Dartmoor Massacre of 1815, is at Prince Town. In the massacre, the British killed 7 and wounded 60 American prisoners of the War of 1812 as they tried to escape. John W. Webb

DARTMOUTH, N.S. (pop. 64,770), lies on the eastern shore of Halifax harbor, opposite Halifax. Its chief industries are oil refining, electronics, wire manufacture, and ship maintenance and repair. A naval arms depot and the Shearwater naval air station are located there. Dartmouth's population increased 50 per cent between 1941 and 1961. The town was founded in 1750. It incorporated as a city in 1961. For location, see Nova Scotia (political map). Thomas H. Raddall

DARTMOUTH COLLEGE is a privately endowed coeducational liberal arts school in Hanover, N.H. Associated with it are three graduate schools: Dartmouth Medical School, Thayer School of Engineering, and the Amos Tuck School of Business Administration. Courses lead to A.B., B.S., M.A., M.S., and M.B.A. degrees. The college also awards Ph.D. degrees in mathematics, engineering, and in molecular biology. Baker Library is one of the largest college libraries in the United States. It is noted for its Stefansson Arctic collection (see Stefansson, Vilhjalmur).

Dartmouth was founded at Hanover in 1769 under a charter granted to Eleazar Wheelock by King George III of England. The college developed from Moor's Indian Charity School, founded by Wheelock about 1750 in Lebanon, Conn. In 1819, Daniel Webster, a Dartmouth alumnus, won the Dartmouth College Case before the Supreme Court (see Dartmouth College Case). For enrollment, see Universities and Colleges (table). George O'Connell

See also Painting (picture: Fresco Painting).

DARTMOUTH COLLEGE CASE, or Dartmouth College v. Woodward, upheld the constitutional freedom from unreasonable government interference with contracts. The Supreme Court of the United States decided this case in 1819. The decision helped protect the rights of private property and encouraged the development of the free-enterprise system.

In 1769, King George III of Great Britain granted Dartmouth College a charter as a private school. This charter was to last "forever." The various states succeeded to the rights and obligations of such charters when they became independent. But in 1816, New Hampshire tried to make Dartmouth College the state university by canceling the charter. Former trustees of the college claimed that the royal charter was still valid. They brought suit to recover the school seal and records from William H. Woodward, the college secretary. Daniel Webster, a graduate of Dartmouth, presented the trustees' case before the Supreme Court in one of his greatest arguments. The court held for the trustees. It ruled that the state had "impaired the obligation" of the charter in violation of Article I, Section 10 of the Constitution. Because of this case, legislatures today put time limitations in charters or include provisions allowing cancellation by the government under proper circumstances. Jerre S. Williams

DARTS is a game in which players try to hit the *bull's-eye* (center of a target) by throwing darts. A *dart* is a small arrowlike object with stiff guiding feathers at one end and a sharp metal point at the other. Darts for children have rubber suction cups instead of points. The target is usually made of cork or Beaverboard.

In tournament competition, players throw darts at a target 8 feet (2.4 meters) away. If a player hits the bull's-eye, he scores the highest number of points possible for

WORLD BOOK photo

Darts is a popular indoor game. The players toss darts at a target a few feet or meters away. A player scores the highest number of points by hitting the bull's-eye.

one throw. If he hits the first circle outside the bull's-eye, he scores the next highest number, and so on. The players decide on the number of points for each circle.

Each player in turn throws his darts at the target. The players then add up the points for their throws, and the one who has the highest number of points wins. Before starting the game, players sometimes choose a certain number as a winning score. ELMER D. MITCHELL

DARWIN (pop. 35,281) is the administrative center and largest city of the Northern Territory of Australia. It is an air gateway to Australia and the chief port in the Northern Territory. For location, see AUSTRALIA (color map). The discovery of uranium south of Darwin in 1949 stimulated its growth.

Darwin was planned in 1869 as the first station in Australia on a telegraph line connecting Australia with Europe. It was named for Charles Darwin. In 1974, a cyclone struck Darwin and destroyed most of the city. The Australian government appointed a commission to manage the reconstruction of Darwin. C. M. H. CLARK

DARWIN is the name of two noted biologists, father and son.

Charles Robert Darwin (1809-1882) was a British naturalist whose theory of evolution through natural selection caused a revolution in biological science. His book, *On the Origin of Species by Means of Natural Selection, or the Preservation of Favoured Races in the Struggle for Life* (1859), gave facts on which he based his concept of gradual changes of plants and animals.

His Books. Before *The Origin of Species* was published, several scientists, including Darwin's grandfather, Erasmus Darwin, had proposed evolutionary theories. Charles Darwin is famous for the theory because he was the first to collect factual evidence for it, through experimentation and observation. Alfred Russel Wallace, an English naturalist, worked out a statement of evolution similar to Darwin's shortly before Darwin's book was published (see WALLACE, ALFRED RUSSEL).

Wallace's paper and an abstract of Darwin's book were presented together at a meeting of the Linnean Society in London in 1858. The next year, Darwin published *The Origin of Species.* Such noted scientists as Thomas Henry Huxley, Sir Charles Lyell, and Asa Gray supported Darwin's disputed work. Its principles and facts, with some modifications, have since been accepted by many groups as a part of biological science.

The storm of debate following the publication of *The Origin of Species* increased in 1871 when Darwin published *The Descent of Man.* This book outlines his theory that man came from the same group of animals as the chimpanzee and other apes. He also wrote *The Variation of Animals and Plants under Domestication* (1868), *Insectivorous Plants* (1875), and *The Power of Movement in Plants* (1880).

His Life. Darwin was born on Feb. 12, 1809, in Shrewsbury, and was educated at the universities of Edinburgh and Cambridge. Soon after he was graduated, he sailed as a naturalist with a British expedition aboard the H.M.S. *Beagle* in December, 1831.

Brown Bros.

Charles R. Darwin

During this five-year exploratory voyage along the coast of South America and to the Galapagos and other islands in the Pacific, Darwin searched for fossils, and studied plants, animals, and geology.

Darwin returned from the voyage in poor health, and illness hampered him during the remainder of his life. He settled in London in 1836, and began writing the first of his books. In 1839, Darwin married his cousin, Emma Wedgwood. They had five sons. In 1842, Darwin moved from London to Down. He was buried in Westminster Abbey. ROGERS MCVAUGH

See also EVOLUTION; NATURAL SELECTION. For a *Reading and Study Guide*, see *Darwin, Charles*, in the RESEARCH GUIDE/INDEX, Volume 22.

Sir Francis Darwin (1848-1925) was an English botanist, the son of Charles R. Darwin. He assisted his father, and later became a reader in botany at Trinity College, Cambridge. His major works included *Life and Letters of Charles Darwin* (1887), *The Power of Movement in Plants*, which he wrote with his father (1880), and *Foundations of the Origin of Species* (1913). Darwin was born in Down. LORUS J. and MARGERY MILNE

DARWIN, ERASMUS. See EVOLUTION (History).

DASH. See PUNCTUATION.

DASHEEN. See TARO.

DASHT-I-KAVIR. See IRAN (Land Regions).

DASHT-I-LUT. See IRAN (Land Regions).

DASYURE, *DASS ih yoor*, is a small, catlike animal that lives in Australia. It has short legs, a long bushy tail, and a pouch in which it carries its young (see MARSUPIAL). Dasyures climb trees and eat meat.

Scientific Classification. Dasyures belong to the family *Dasyuridae*. The common dasyure is genus *Dasyurus*, species *D. viverrinus.* HAROLD E. ANTHONY

DATA PROCESSING. See AUTOMATION (Principles); COMPUTER (Careers).

Caterpillar Tractor Co.

Cultivating a Date Orchard in southern California helps prepare the ground for irrigation. To conserve space, date palms and grapefruit trees are planted alternately.

USDA

Clusters of Dates that have as many as 200 dates each and weigh up to 25 pounds (11 kilograms) grow on palm trees. The dates have a rich red or golden color while hanging on the tree.

DATE AND DATE PALM are the fruit and tree that supply one of the chief articles of food in north Africa and the Middle East. The Bible speaks of the date palm as the palm tree, and the poetry and proverbs of the East often mention it. Men probably cultivated the date palm before any other tree known to history. Sun-baked bricks, made more than 5,000 years ago in Mesopotamia, record directions for growing the tree.

Egypt and Iraq rank as the world's leading producers of dates. Other important date-growing regions include Saudi Arabia, Iran, Algeria, Pakistan, and Morocco. Growers in California and Arizona cultivate most of the date palm trees in the United States. In California, the date palm grows in the Salton Basin and some hot valleys in the interior. Arizona has good date-growing areas in the lower Salt River Valley and in the Colorado River Valley near Yuma. It has other date palm groves, scattered mostly in the Gila Valley and the upper Colorado River Valley. Texas grows date palms in the lower Rio Grande Valley and certain areas between Laredo and San Antonio.

The Tree. Next to the coconut palm, the date palm is the most interesting and useful of the palm family. The stem stands tall and straight, about the same thickness all the way up. Offshoots grow from the base, but they are removed except when used for growing new plants. A crown of large leaves shaped like feathers grows on top. Pagans, Jews, and Christians have used these leaves in their religious services from earliest times. The flowers growing among the leaves attract little attention. Male and female flowers grow on separate trees. In orchards, cultivators carry the pollen by hand to the female flowers. The fruit grows and ripens after the flowers have received the pollen.

Date palms begin to bear fruit four to ten years after planting. They need a hot dry climate. They grow best in a temperature that stays around 90° F. (32° C) for three months of the year. The trees grow well in a sandy, alkaline soil. Growers often rely on irrigation to supply the water needed by the roots. During the ripening season, rain harms the fruits, and growers protect them by covering them with paper bags. Algerian date trees grow in deep pits dug in the soil of an oasis. The roots of the trees reach moisture far below the surface.

Date palms grow 40 to 100 feet (12 to 30 meters) high. Growers consider a yearly yield of 100 to 200 pounds (45 to 91 kilograms) of dates for a tree as very good, but some trees produce more.

The Fruit. On the trees, dates have a rich red or golden color. Most people know them best when they are dried. Then they are sweet, fleshy, oblong fruit, a deep russet or brown, over 1 inch (2.5 centimeters) long. The long tough seed has a furrow along one side. People eat dates fresh or dried, and use them in cooking. The Arabs pound and mix them together to make cakes.

Other Uses. The date palm supplies us with other things besides fruit. The tree trunk and other parts provide fuel and building materials for fences. The large leaves can be used to weave matting, baskets, and bags. Rope is made from the fiber. The buds can be eaten as a vegetable. A liquor, called *arrack*, may be made from dates. The fruit seeds can be roasted as a substitute for coffee, or ground to yield oil.

Scientific Classification. The date palm belongs to the palm family, *Palmae*. It is classified as genus *Phoenix*, species *P. dactylifera*. HAROLD E. MOORE, JR.

See also PALM.

DATE LINE. See NEWSPAPER (Newspaper Terms).

DATE LINE, INTERNATIONAL. See INTERNATIONAL DATE LINE.

DATING. See SEX; TEEN AGE.

DATURA, *duh TYOO ruh*, is a group of poisonous shrubs and trees, including jimson weed and angel's-trumpet. These large bushy plants, also called *thorn apple*, have toothed, ill-smelling leaves, prickly fruit, and white to lavender trumpet-shaped flowers. Daturas are native to the tropics, but now grow in eastern North America as well.

Scientific Classification. Daturas make up a genus in the nightshade family, *Solanaceae*. The jimson weed is genus *Datura*, species *D. stramonium*. J. J. LEVISON

See also JIMSON WEED; NIGHTSHADE.

DAUDET, *doh DAY*, **ALPHONSE** (1840-1897), is sometimes called the *French Dickens*. Like the English author Charles Dickens, Daudet wrote about poor and suffering persons and the outcasts of society. Both writers often softened their pictures of the cruelty of reality with a sympathy that occasionally became too sentimental. Daudet had a clear, graceful style. His simple observations of society and his humor and fantasy have made him a favorite with young readers.

Daudet is best known for his humorous short stories in *Letters from My Mill* (1869) and the patriotic stories in *Monday's Tales* (1873). The comic adventures of his boastful character Tartarin appear in two novels, *Tartarin of Tarascon* (1872) and *Tartarin over the Alps* (1895). Daudet also wrote serious realistic novels that contain excellent pictures of his time. These books include *The Nabob* (1877) and *Sapho* (1884).

Daudet was born in Nîmes. His parents were poor and he was bullied in school by his classmates and teachers. He described his unhappy youth in *Little What's Your Name* (1868), his first novel. ROBERT J. NIESS

DAUGHERTY, HARRY M. See HARDING, WARREN G. (Political and Public Activities; Government Scandals); COOLIDGE, CALVIN (Vice-President; Corruption).

DAUGHERTY, JAMES HENRY (1889-1974), was an American artist and author of children's books. He won the 1940 Newbery medal for *Daniel Boone*, which he wrote and illustrated. He also wrote and illustrated *Andy and the Lion* (1938), *Poor Richard* (1941), *Abraham Lincoln* (1943), *Of Courage Undaunted* (1951), and *Magna Charta* (1956). Daugherty was born in Asheville, N.C. See also LITERATURE FOR CHILDREN (picture: A Biography of Daniel Boone). GEORGE E. BUTLER

DAUGHTERS OF THE AMERICAN REVOLUTION (DAR) is an organization of women directly descended from persons who aided in establishing American independence. Women over 18 years of age who can prove such descent are eligible for membership. The chief goal of the DAR is to teach and promote good citizenship among youths, adults, and immigrants. Its programs promote appreciation of the past, patriotic service in the present, and educational training for the future. The DAR helps preserve shrines that keep alive the memory of persons who won American independence. It encourages the study of American history, and maintains relics and records of early America.

The organization owns and operates two schools in remote mountain areas of Alabama and South Carolina that are cut off from regular school systems. It also aids six other schools and colleges. It publishes a *Manual for Citizenship* to help foreign-born residents of the United States in becoming citizens. The DAR sponsors Junior American Citizens Clubs for schoolchildren, provides scholarships for American Indians, and runs an annual Good Citizenship contest in U.S. high schools. The organization's official publication is *The Daughters of the American Revolution Magazine*.

The DAR, officially the NATIONAL SOCIETY OF THE DAUGHTERS OF THE AMERICAN REVOLUTION, was founded in Washington, D.C., in 1890. It was chartered by Congress in 1896 and must report to Congress each year. It has about 187,000 members in about 3,000 chapters in the United States and other countries.

Headquarters of the DAR consist of three adjoining buildings at 1776 D St. NW, Washington, D.C. 20006. Memorial Continental Hall houses one of the largest genealogical libraries in the United States. The building also contains 28 State Rooms that are furnished in historic American styles. The Administration Building houses the society's business offices and a museum. Constitution Hall is an auditorium where the society holds its annual Continental Congress, and where many of Washington's cultural events are held.

DAR

Memorial Continental Hall in Washington, D.C., is the original headquarters building of the Daughters of the American Revolution. Its cornerstone was laid in 1904.

Critically reviewed by the DAUGHTERS OF THE AMERICAN REVOLUTION

DAUGHTERS OF THE CONFEDERACY, UNITED, is an organization of women directly descended from members of the army and navy of the Confederacy. The organization was founded in 1894 at Nashville, Tenn., by the widows, wives, mothers, and sisters of Confederate fighting men. The original purposes of the group were to honor the memory of the Confederacy and to help needy Confederate soldiers and sailors and their families. The organization has about 35,000 members. There are about 900 chapters in the United States, and one chapter in Paris, France. The group engages in educational and philanthropic activities, and preserves records and data of the Confederacy. The national office is in the Memorial Building to the Women of the South, 328 North Boulevard, Richmond, Va. 23220.

Critically reviewed by the UNITED DAUGHTERS OF THE CONFEDERACY

DAUGHTERS OF THE NILE. See MASONRY (Organization).

DAUGHTERS OF UNION VETERANS OF THE CIVIL WAR. See SONS OF UNION VETERANS OF THE CIVIL WAR.

D'AULAIRE, *doh LAIR*, is the family name of a husband and wife who are writers and illustrators of children's books.

Edgar Parin d'Aulaire (1898-) and his wife, **Ingri Mortenson d'Aulaire** (1904-), won the Caldecott medal in 1940 for their picture-book biography, *Abraham Lincoln*. The couple also won the Regina Medal in 1970. They draw directly on lithographic stone in making their illustrations. Their career as book collaborators began in 1931 with *The Magic Rug*.

Their books include *Ola*, *Ola and Blakken*, *Children of the North Lights*, *Conquest of the Atlantic*, *George Washington*, *Benjamin Franklin*, and *Pocahontas*. They also illustrated *The Lord's Prayer*, *East of the Sun and West of the Moon*, and *Johnny Blossom*.

Edgar was born in Campoblenio, Switzerland, and Ingri in Kongsberg, Norway. They met in Munich, Germany, and were married in 1925. They have lived in the United States since 1929. RUTH HILL VIGUERS

DAUMIER, *DOH MYAY*, **HONORÉ,** *oh noh RAY*, (1808-1879), was a French lithographer, caricaturist, and painter. He made lithographic caricatures of legal and political leaders for newspapers. He was imprisoned for six months in 1832 for a caricature he drew of King Louis Philippe, which was entitled *Gargantua*.

Daumier's lithographs won fame for their biting satire. Many of his paintings are of traditional subjects. He painted people and places as he saw them. He pioneered realism in his paintings, but they did not gain recognition until after his death. One of his best-known realistic paintings is *The Third Class Carriage* (about 1862). During his career, Daumier produced about 3,950 lithographs and about 200 paintings. His painting *The Uprising* is reproduced in the PAINTING article. For pictures of his satirical lithographs, see the CARICATURE and CARTOON articles.

Daumier was born in Marseille, the son of a glazier. He was reared in Paris, and became a bookseller's clerk and a process server to a lawyer. He studied painting with Alexandre Lenoir, but his real training as an artist came from what he observed on the streets and in the courts. His father tried to discourage him from becoming an artist. In 1877, Daumier became blind. He died at Valmondois, near Paris. S. W. HAYTER

DAUPHIN, *DAW fin*, was the official title of the oldest son of the king of France from 1349 to 1830. The title was similar to that of "Prince of Wales" in England. The lords of Viennois and Auvergne, whose lands were known as Dauphiné, first used the title. The last lord of Viennois had no heir. He gave his lands to Philip VI, on condition that either the king or the heir to the throne should be lord of Dauphiné and should have the title "Dauphin of France."

At first the dauphin had many privileges as ruler of his lands. But the title became merely honorary after Dauphiné was put under the same rule as all the other provinces of France. J. SALWYN SCHAPIRO

Daumier ridiculed "realists" in his lithograph *The Rejected Painter* (1859). His caption said, "They refused my work . . . The idiots."
Bibliothèque Nationale, Paris

D.A.V. See DISABLED AMERICAN VETERANS.

DAVAINE, CASIMIR. See ANTHRAX.

DAVAO, *DAH vow* (pop. 438,769; met. area 591,500), is the chief port of southern Mindanao Island in the Philippines. For location, see PHILIPPINES (color map). Davao overlooks Davao Gulf on the southeastern shore of the island. The highest Philippine mountain, 9,690-foot (2,954-meter) Mount Apo, is 25 miles (40 kilometers) west of Davao.

Most of the people of Davao live in bamboo and wooden houses. This prosperous city has a busy, modern business district. Davao serves as the center of the abacá industry of the southern Philippine islands. Factories in Davao process the fibers of the abacá plant, also known as Manila hemp. The fibers are used to make rope. Davao also ships lumber and copra, the dried meat of the coconut. RUSSELL H. FIFIELD and CARLOS P. ROMULO

DAVENANT, SIR WILLIAM (1606-1668), was an English playwright. The popularity of his romantic plays and elaborate spectacles called *masques* gained him an appointment as poet laureate in 1638. But his reputation now rests on his techniques in staging plays.

Davenant trained the first actresses to replace the boy actors who had played all female roles in plays in England. In place of the bare open-air Elizabethan stages, he introduced to the English theater the painted scenery and artificial lighting used in continental Europe. Davenant wrote the words for what is generally considered the first English opera, *The Siege of Rhodes* (1656). He is generally blamed for cutting and rewriting some of Shakespeare's plays to fit new theatrical conditions and the changing taste of the audience. Davenant was born in Oxford. ALAN S. DOWNER

DAVENPORT, Iowa (pop. 98,469), is part of a metropolitan area that includes three Illinois cities—Rock Island, Moline, and East Moline. These cities, called the *Quad-Cities*, have a metropolitan area population of 362,638. Davenport is on the west bank of the Mississippi River (see IOWA [political map]).

The principal industries of Davenport include the manufacture of aluminum, cement, flour, locomotives, electronic equipment, men's clothing, and iron and steel products.

The first railroad from the East reached the Mississippi opposite Davenport in 1854. At this point, the first bridge across the river was erected in 1856. The city now has excellent rail, motor, river, and air transport services. Davenport is the home of St. Ambrose College, the Palmer College of Chiropractic, and the Annie Wittenmyer Orphans' Home.

George Davenport, a fur trader, and Antoine LeClaire, a half-breed interpreter, helped to found Davenport in 1836. LeClaire received the land from the Indians in 1832. The town was incorporated in 1839, and received its city charter in 1851. Davenport has a mayor-council government. WILLIAM J. PETERSEN

DAVENPORT, THOMAS. See ELECTRIC RAILROAD (History).

DAVID (1000? B.C.) was the second king of Israel and the successor of Saul. A humble shepherd lad of Bethlehem, he became the best-loved national figure in Israel's political life. He was a great warrior. As a boy, armed only with five stones and a sling, he killed Goliath, the giant Philistine warrior. He built an empire for his son, Solomon, and founded a famous line of kings. They ruled the Kingdom of Judah for more than 400 years, until Jerusalem was destroyed in 587 B.C.

Marble statue (1504) by Michelangelo; Academy of Fine Arts, Florence, Italy (Alinari)

David

The Bible tells of David's skill as a performer on the harp and as a poet. He wrote one of his most famous poems (II Sam. 1:19-27) as a tribute to King Saul and his son, Jonathan, after they lost their lives in battle against the Philistines. Tradition says David wrote many of the Psalms (see PSALMS). He moved the tabernacle to Jerusalem and made his capital the religious as well as political center of the Hebrew state.

His Youth. David was the youngest of eight brothers. He was handsome, and had a ruddy complexion. As a boy, he distinguished himself for bravery by slaying a lion and a bear that attacked his flock. The prophet Samuel anointed him for the kingship after it became apparent that Saul was not proving himself worthy of the crown. As a member of Saul's court, David played his harp and sang in Saul's palace at Gibeah. His friendship with Saul's son, Jonathan, is one of the most touching tales in the Old Testament. But David became a victim of Saul's jealous rage. He had to flee for his life and was hunted like an outlaw until Saul's death (see SAUL). David had a remarkable personality. He was exceptionally gentle and charming, and attracted many friends. In his dealings with Saul, he displayed great character that contrasted sharply with Saul's weakness. His tact, patience, and moderation in his youth fitted him for the high office he held later.

His Early Rule. He ruled as king of the tribe of Judah at Hebron for 7½ years until he was elected king of all the tribes. Then he conquered the Jebusite stronghold of Jerusalem and made it his capital. This was important, because Jerusalem's central location made possible his complete control of the 12 tribes. David's capital, called the City of David, offered a fortification that could hardly be taken by an enemy.

His Conquests. The Philistines tried to crush David when he became king of united Israel (see PHILISTINE). He beat back their attacks, and conquered them. This was the greatest victory of his career. David also defeated the Moabites, Aramaeans, Ammonites, Edomites, and Amalekites. He carved out an empire that extended from the region of Homs, bordering Hamath, on the north, to Ezion-geber on the Gulf of Akabah (now Aqaba), in the south.

His Administration of the kingdom was effective. This is clearly shown by the strong kingdom he left behind him. He was much more efficient than Saul. David patterned his administration in part after Egyptian models. His important officers included the recorder and scribe, or secretary, and the Council of Thirty. His army became an efficient fighting machine. It included a personal bodyguard called Cherethites and Pelethites.

His Later Life. David's successes had a weakening effect on his character. He left the fighting of his wars to his generals, and remained in Jerusalem. Prosperity and luxury robbed him of his early self-control. He was a true worshiper and lover of the God of Israel. But David sinned seriously by committing adultery with the beautiful Bathsheba and having her husband killed so that he could marry her (see HITTITE). David repented, but was punished for the rest of his life. His son, Absalom, rebelled against him and was killed (see ABSALOM). The revolt brought trouble between North and South Israel. Many people feel that David's sufferings were designed by God to purify David's character. After David's death, his son Solomon became king (see SOLOMON). Trouble between the regions of Israel increased during his reign. The regions split into the kingdoms of Israel and Judah during the reign of David's grandson, Rehoboam.

MERRILL F. UNGER

DAVID was the name of two kings of Scotland.

David I (1084-1153), the youngest son of Malcolm III Canmore, became king of Scotland in 1124. He invaded England twice, once to support his niece Matilda's claim to the English throne, and again to gain the earldom of Northumbria for his son, Henry. David won the support of the many Anglo-Norman barons in Scotland.

David II (1324-1371), the son of Robert Bruce, was married to Joanna, daughter of King Edward II of England, at the age of 4. He became king in 1329.

Alinari (Art Reference Bureau)

David and Goliath **is a detail from a fresco by Michelangelo which decorates the ceiling of the Sistine Chapel in the Vatican.**

David fled to France when England invaded Scotland. He later fought with France against England in 1346. The English captured him. They released him 11 years later, and he returned to Scotland. ROBERT S. HOYT

DAVID, HOUSE OF. See HOUSE OF DAVID.

DAVID, *dah VEED,* **JACQUES LOUIS** (1748-1825), was the leading French painter during the French Revolution and Napoleonic era. His painting, *The Oath of the Horatii,* became a great success in 1785. It greatly aroused revolutionary feelings in France. This and the paintings, *The Tennis Court Oath* and *The Death of Marat,* became important symbols of the French Revolution. David's style is sculptural and severe. It shows fine color and design, and is realistic.

David was born in Paris. He mastered the classical style of history painting in Rome (for an explanation of *neoclassicism,* see PAINTING [The 1800's]). David was a member of the Jacobin political party during the French Revolution, and voted for the death of King Louis XVI. Under Napoleon, he painted the great events of the Emperor's life. JOSEPH C. SLOANE

See also CLOTHING (picture: Women's Clothing); FRENCH REVOLUTION (picture: The Death of Marat); NAPOLEON I (picture); SOCRATES (picture).

DAVID, SAINT (520?-589?), is the patron saint of Wales and one of the most popular British saints. He was born into a royal family, and studied under the Welsh monk, Saint Paulinus. Later, David founded monasteries, including St. David's at Mynyw, or Menevia, in southwest Wales. When he was elected primate of the Welsh Church, he moved its see to St. David's. In art, David is shown standing on a mound with a dove on one shoulder. JAMES A. CORBETT and FULTON J. SHEEN

DAVID, STAR OF, or SHIELD OF DAVID, is the universal symbol of Judaism. It appears on the flag of the State of Israel, in synagogues, on Jewish ritual objects and on emblems of organizations. It is made up of two triangles that interlace to form a six-pointed star. The figure itself is an ancient one. Scholars do not know when it became widespread as a Jewish symbol. As far as is known, it first appeared on a Jewish holy seal in Sidon in the 600's B.C. (?). The name *shield of David* is found in a Hebrew manuscript of the 1500's. LEONARD C. MISHKIN

The Star of David

DAVID, SIR T. W. EDGEWORTH. See EXPLORATION AND DISCOVERY (table: Polar Explorers).

DAVID COPPERFIELD, a novel by Charles Dickens, vividly portrays the life of an orphan. David's stepfather, Mr. Murdstone, tries to harm him. So does the "humble" Uriah Heep. But his aunt, Miss Betsey Trotwood, and the cheerful ne'er-do-well, Mr. Micawber, befriend him. He finally becomes a famous author and marries Agnes Wickfield. The novel first appeared in serial form in 1849 and 1850. See also DICKENS, CHARLES.

DAVID LIPSCOMB COLLEGE. See UNIVERSITIES AND COLLEGES (table).

DAVIDSON, JO (1883-1952), an American portrait sculptor, created heads of many famous people. His work is direct and lifelike. He has been called a "biographer in bronze." Davidson worked chiefly in terra cotta and bronze. His best-known works include portraits of General Pershing and Franklin D. Roosevelt.

Davidson was born in New York City. He studied for three years at the Art Students' League there, but then decided on a medical career. While at Yale Medical School, he saw work done by art students in a modeling class, and chose to become a sculptor. He went to Paris in 1907 to work and study. Davidson served as a war correspondent in World War I. WILLIAM L. MACDONALD

See also UNITED STATES (The Arts in the United States [picture]).

DAVIDSON COLLEGE is a coeducational liberal arts school in Davidson, N.C. It is controlled by the Presbyterian Church. Davidson grants bachelor's degrees and has an ROTC unit. The school was founded in 1836. Woodrow Wilson studied at Davidson College. For enrollment, see UNIVERSITIES AND COLLEGES (table).

DAVIES, ARTHUR BOWEN (1862-1928), was an American painter and illustrator. He painted idealized figures in a lyrical style that reflects a highly intellectual and poetic personal vision. However, he was keenly aware of the changing artistic ideas of his time. Davies saw value in the more down-to-earth style of painter Robert Henri and his group. He joined Henri's group, known as "The Eight," or the Ashcan School (see HENRI, ROBERT). Davies also helped organize the famous Armory show of 1913. Held in New York City, this exhibition is generally considered the artistic event that did most to awaken Americans to developments in modern art abroad. Davies was born in Utica, N.Y. He first worked as an illustrator in New York, but soon turned exclusively to painting. E. MAURICE BLOCH

DAVIES, SIR LOUIS HENRY (1845-1924), served as chief justice of the Supreme Court of Canada from 1918 until his death. Born in Charlottetown, Prince Edward Island, he was the first "Islander" to hold this post. He had been prime minister and attorney-general of his home province from 1876 to 1879. He served in the Canadian Parliament as a Liberal from 1882 to 1901, when he was appointed a *puisne* (associate) justice of the Supreme Court. J. E. HODGETTS

DAVIES, ROBERTSON (1913-), is a Canadian novelist, playwright, and journalist. He sets most of his novels in small Ontario towns. Davies' early novels mock people of various fields, including ministers, journalists, and college teachers and students. In *A Mixture of Frailties* (1958), Davies described the artistic development of a gifted young Canadian singer. In *Fifth Business* (1970), he explored the relationship between religion and magic.

William Robertson Davies was born in Thamesville, Ont., and was educated in Canada and England. He worked in England as an actor, stage manager, director, and drama teacher. He later wrote critical studies in drama history and several plays.

In 1942, Davies became editor of the *Peterborough* (Ont.) *Examiner*. He wrote a syndicated column of witty observations on small-town American and Canadian life. Selections from this column were collected in *The Diary of Samuel Marchbanks* (1947) and *The Table Talk of Samuel Marchbanks* (1949). In 1963, Davies became master of Massey College for graduate students at the University of Toronto. CLAUDE T. BISSELL

Oil painting on wood (about 1503); The Louvre, Paris

Unfinished oil painting on wood (early 1500's); The Louvre, Paris

Leonardo da Vinci's Works include the *Mona Lisa, left,* probably the most famous portrait ever painted. *The Virgin and Child with Saint Anne, right,* illustrates how Leonardo organized his paintings in a pyramid design. Both pictures represent the artist's style in their blurred outlines, graceful figures, overall feeling of calm, and dramatic contrasts of dark and light.

DA VINCI, *duh VIHN chee,* **LEONARDO** (1452-1519), was one of the greatest painters of the Italian Renaissance. His portrait *Mona Lisa* and his religious scene *The Last Supper* rank among the most famous pictures ever painted.

Leonardo, as he is almost always called, was trained to be a painter. But he became one of the most versatile geniuses in history. His interests and achievements spread into an astonishing variety of fields that are usually considered scientific specialties. Leonardo studied anatomy, astronomy, botany, and geology, and he designed machines and drew plans for hundreds of inventions.

Leonardo recorded his scientific observations and his ideas for inventions in notebooks. Until the early 1900's, the notebooks remained generally unknown. Many of Leonardo's ideas and designs were far ahead of their time. For example, he drew plans for a flying machine and a parachute. Leonardo also stated that the sun does not move, though scientists of his day believed that the sun revolved around the earth. By the time Leonardo's scientific and technical investigations became widely known, other men had come up with many of the same ideas.

Although Leonardo explored an amazing number of areas of human knowledge, he was not a universal genius. For example, he had no interest in history, literature, or religion. He never developed his ideas systematically, and he did not formulate scientific laws or principles. But Leonardo was an excellent observer. He concerned himself with what the eye could see, rather than with abstract thoughts.

Early Career. Leonardo was born about 10 miles from the village of Vinci, near Florence in central Italy. At that time, Florence was an independent republic and a commercial center. Leonardo was the illegitimate son of Ser Piero da Vinci, a legal specialist, and a peasant girl. Ser Piero raised the boy.

About 1466, Leonardo became an apprentice to Andrea del Verrocchio, a leading painter and sculptor in Florence. He remained with Verrocchio as an assistant after completing his apprenticeship.

Verrocchio and Leonardo collaborated on the painting *The Baptism of Christ,* which is reproduced in the WORLD BOOK article on JOHN THE BAPTIST. Leonardo painted the head of the left angel, the distant landscape, and probably the skin of Christ. His parts of the painting have soft shadings, with shadows concealing the

Red chalk drawing on paper; Reale Library, Turin, Italy (SCALA)

A Self-Portrait is the only authentic likeness of Leonardo that has been preserved. The artist drew it about 1512.

In Milan, Leonardo painted the *Madonna of the Rocks* (about 1485), the first of his major completed paintings that has been preserved. It is reproduced in the PAINTING article.

Leonardo painted *The Last Supper* about 1495. He created the famous scene on a wall of the dining hall in the monastery of Santa Maria delle Grazie. The painting appears in the article on JESUS CHRIST. It shows Christ and His 12 apostles just after Jesus has announced that one of them will betray Him. Leonardo changed the traditional arrangement of the figures from a line of 13 figures to several small groups. Each apostle responds in a different way to Christ's announcement. Jesus sits in the center of the scene, apart from the other figures. Leonardo's composition creates a more active and centralized design than earlier artists had achieved.

When painting *The Last Supper*, Leonardo rejected the *fresco* technique normally used for wall paintings (see FRESCO). An artist who uses this fresco method must work quickly. But Leonardo wanted to paint slowly, revise his work, and use shadows—all of which would have been impossible in fresco painting. He developed a new technique that involved coating the monastery wall with a compound he had created. But the compound, which was supposed to hold the paint in place and protect it from moisture, did not work. Soon after Leonardo completed the picture, the paint began to flake away. *The Last Supper* still exists, but in poor condition.

edges. The figures are shown in the act of moving from one position to another. Verrocchio's figures and objects in this work are sharply defined. They reflect the style called Early Renaissance. Leonardo's more graceful approach marked the beginning of the High Renaissance style. However, this style did not become popular in Italy for another 25 years.

From about 1478 to 1482, Leonardo had his own studio in Florence. During this period he received an important commission to paint a church altarpiece now known as the *Adoration of the Three Kings*. It exists today in an unfinished form, with the figures and the light and dark areas visible only as outlines.

The *Adoration of the Three Kings* shows three kings worshiping the Christ child. Leonardo abandoned the traditional treatment of this subject. Earlier versions had shown the figures in profile, with the Virgin Mary and Jesus on one side of the painting and the kings on the other. To give the Holy Family more emphasis, Leonardo placed them in the center, facing the viewer. The kings and other figures form a semicircle around Mary and Jesus. This arrangement resulted in a livelier scene and greater unity among the figures.

Years in Milan. Leonardo never finished the *Adoration of the Three Kings* because he left Florence about 1482 to become court artist for Lodovico Sforza, the duke of Milan. Leonardo lived in Milan for 17 years.

Leonardo had a variety of duties in the duke's court. As a military engineer, he designed artillery and planned the diversion of rivers. As a civil engineer, he designed revolving stages for pageants. As a sculptor, he planned a huge monument of the duke's father mounted on a leaping horse.

During his years in Milan, Leonardo made many scientific drawings, especially of the human body. He studied anatomy by dissecting 30 corpses. Leonardo's drawings clarify not only the appearance of bones, tendons, and other parts of the body, but also their function. The drawings are considered the first accurate portrayals of human anatomy.

Return to Florence. In 1499, the French overthrew Lodovico Sforza and forced him to flee Milan. Leonardo also left the city. He visited Mantua, where he made a famous drawing of Isabella d'Este, the wife of the duke of Mantua. He also visited Venice briefly before returning to Florence.

Leonardo's paintings during his stay in Milan had made him famous, and the people of Florence welcomed him as a returning hero. The early work that he did there had strongly influenced the young men who had become the leaders of the next generation of Florentine painters. These artists included Sandro Botticelli and Piero di Cosimo. The work Leonardo was to create in Florence also inspired a third generation of artists, including Andrea Del Sarto, Michelangelo, and Raphael.

When Leonardo returned, Florence was building a new hall for the city council. The Florentine government hired Leonardo and Michelangelo to decorate the walls of the hall with scenes of the city's military victories. Leonardo chose the Battle of Anghiari, in which Florence had defeated Milan in 1440. His painting showed a cavalry battle, with tense soldiers, leaping horses, and clouds of dust.

In painting the *Battle of Anghiari*, Leonardo again rejected fresco and tried an experimental technique called *encaustic*. As in the case of *The Last Supper*, the experiment did not work. Leonardo left the painting unfinished when he went on a trip. The paint began to run while he was away, and he never finished the project. The painting no longer exists. Its general appearance is known from Leonardo's sketches and from copies made by other artists.

While working on the *Battle of Anghiari*, Leonardo painted the *Mona Lisa*, which appears with this article. The *Mona Lisa* is a portrait of Lisa del Giocondo, the young wife of a Florentine merchant. It is often called *La Gioconda*.

The *Mona Lisa* became famous because of the mysterious smile of the subject. Actually, Leonardo showed the woman's face moving into or out of a smile. He arranged her folded hands so that the figure formed a pyramid design. Leonardo's technique with the *Mona Lisa* solved a problem that had faced earlier portrait painters. These artists had shown only the head and upper part of the body, and the picture seemed to cut off the subject at the chest. Leonardo's placement of the hands of the *Mona Lisa* gave the woman a more complete, natural appearance.

Last Years. Leonardo did little painting during his later years, but he produced many drawings of machines and of experimental inventions. These drawings rank among Leonardo's greatest masterpieces, especially in their delicate use of shadow and their sense of motion.

In 1517, Leonardo settled in France at the invitation of King Francis I. The king wanted to surround himself with famous representatives of Renaissance culture. Leonardo spent his final two years near Tours in a large house provided by the king.

Good introductions to Leonardo's life and work include *Leonardo da Vinci* by Kenneth Clark, *Leonardo da Vinci* by Ludwig H. Heydenreich, and *The Drawings of Leonardo da Vinci* by A. E. Popham. CREIGHTON GILBERT

See also AIRPLANE (History and Development [picture]); HUMAN BODY (picture); PARACHUTE (picture). For a *Reading and Study Guide*, see *Da Vinci, Leonardo*, in the RESEARCH GUIDE/INDEX, Volume 22.

LEONARDO'S NOTEBOOKS Leonardo recorded his ideas about art, engineering, and science in several notebooks. About 4,200 pages still exist. Many pages include brilliant drawings that reveal Leonardo's powers of observation and skill as a draftsman. He wrote his notes backward, and so they can be read only with a mirror.

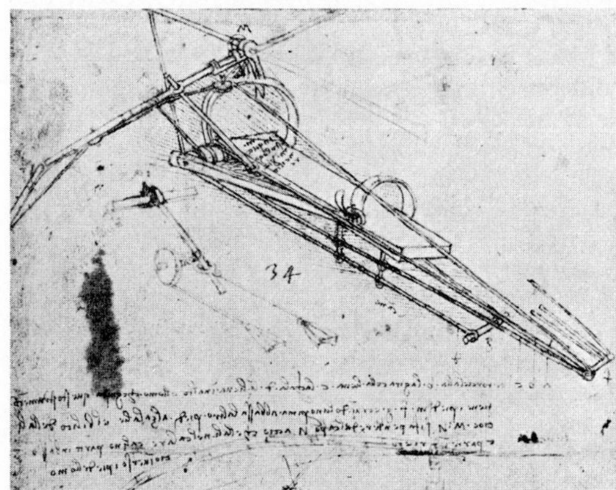

Detail of an ink drawing; Ambrosian Library, Milan, Italy

A Sketch of an Experimental Flying Machine

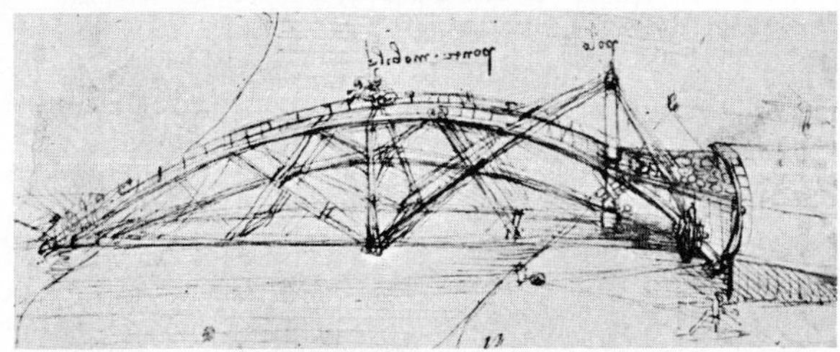

Detail of an ink drawing; Ambrosian Library, Milan, Italy

A Design for a Movable Bridge

A Drawing of a Rock Formation

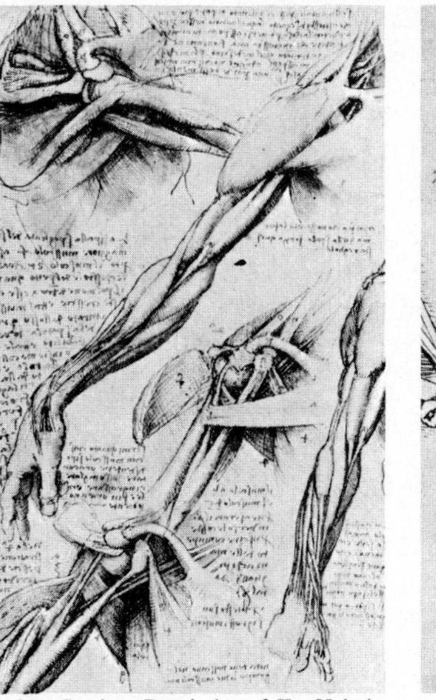

Details of drawings; reproduced by Gracious Permission of Her Majesty Queen Elizabeth II (Royal Library, Windsor Castle, Windsor, England)

A Study of the Human Shoulder

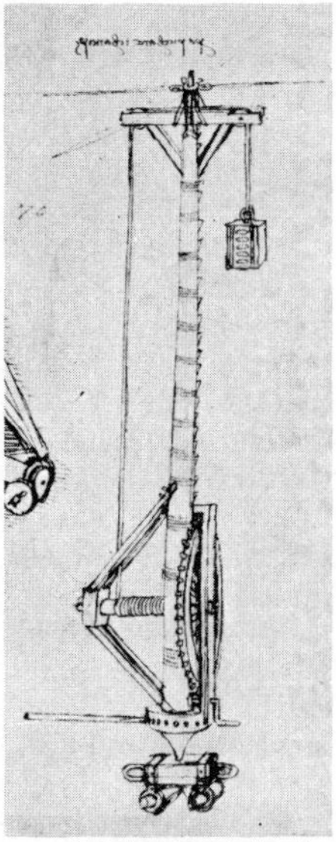

Ink drawing; Ambrosian Library, Milan, Italy

A Construction Crane

DAVIS, BENJAMIN OLIVER, JR. (1912-), was a United States Air Force officer. He became the highest ranking Negro U.S. officer in history when he was made a major general in 1959. He became a lieutenant general in 1965.

U.S. Air Force
Benjamin O. Davis, Jr.

Davis was born in Washington, D.C. His father, Benjamin O. Davis, rose from private to brigadier general in the U.S. Army. In 1936, the younger Davis became the first Negro graduate of the U.S. Military Academy in nearly 50 years. In World War II, he earned the Distinguished Flying Cross. He became director of Manpower and Organization of the U.S. Air Force in 1961. Davis was made Air Force chief of staff in South Korea in 1965, and commander of the 13th Air Force at Clark Base in the Philippines in 1967. In 1968, he became deputy commander in chief of U.S. Strike Command at MacDill Air Force Base in Tampa, Fla. Davis retired from the Air Force in 1970. He was named an assistant secretary of the Department of Transportation in 1971.
RICHARD BARDOLPH

DAVIS, BETTE (1908-), an American motion-picture actress, won Academy awards for her performances in *Dangerous* (1935) and *Jezebel* (1938). She was born Ruth Elizabeth Davis in Lowell, Mass. She studied acting in New York City, and first starred in the play *The Solid South.* She made her first motion picture, *Bad Sister,* in 1931. Her major films include *Of Human Bondage* (1934), *The Little Foxes* (1941), and *All About Eve* (1950). BOSLEY CROWTHER

A.S.P. from Tom Stack & Assoc.
Bette Davis

DAVIS, DAVID (1815-1886), an American judge and statesman, helped his close friend Abraham Lincoln obtain the nomination for President in 1860. Lincoln appointed Davis to the Supreme Court of the United States in 1862. Davis was nominated for President by the National Labor Reform Party in 1872, but he withdrew the nomination. He resigned from the Supreme Court in 1877, and was elected to the U.S. Senate from Illinois as an independent. His election prevented him from serving on the Electoral Commission in the disputed presidential election of 1876. Davis' vote as a member of the commission might have elected Democrat Samuel J. Tilden (see ELECTORAL COMMISSION). Davis was born in Cecil County, Maryland. He graduated from Kenyon College. ARTHUR A. EKIRCH, JR.

DAVIS, DWIGHT FILLEY. See DAVIS CUP.

DAVIS, EDWARD WILSON (1888-), is known as the *father of taconite,* because he discovered how to get iron ore from taconite rocks (see TACONITE). Davis was born in Cambridge City, Ind., and was graduated from Purdue University. He taught mining engineering at the University of Minnesota. IRA M. FREEMAN

DAVIS, HENRY GASSAWAY (1823-1916), was the Democratic candidate for Vice-President of the United States in 1904. He and presidential candidate Alton B. Parker lost to President Theodore Roosevelt and Charles W. Fairbanks. Davis, at 80, was the oldest man ever chosen to run for Vice-President. Davis served as a U.S. senator from West Virginia from 1871 to 1883. He was a member of the Permanent Pan American Railroad Committee from 1901 until his death. He was born in Woodstock, Md. IRVING G. WILLIAMS

DAVIS, JEFFERSON (1808-1889), served as president of the Confederate States of America during the Civil War. He has been called the man who "symbolized the solemn convictions and tragic fortunes of millions of men." He was not popular with the people of the South during the war, but he won their respect and affection after the war through his suffering in prison and also through his lifelong defense of the Southern cause.

Davis was a statesman with wide experience. He served in the United States House of Representatives and the Senate, and as a Cabinet member. He also won distinction as a soldier. He was a thoughtful student of the Constitution and of political philosophy.

Early Life. Davis was born on June 3, 1808, in Christian (later Todd) County, Kentucky. His father, Sam Davis, was a veteran of the Revolutionary War. His older brother, Joseph, moved to Mississippi and became a successful planter. The Davis family moved there while Jefferson was still an infant, and he grew up in Wilkinson County. He attended the county academy, then entered Transylvania University in Kentucky. At the age of 16, he entered the U.S. Military Academy, and graduated with comparatively low grades in 1828.

Davis' Army career took him to Forts Howard and Crawford on the Wisconsin frontier. He fought in campaigns against the Indians, and took charge of Indian prisoner removal after the Black Hawk War. After he resigned from the Army in 1835, he married the daughter of his commander, Colonel Zachary Taylor, who later became a general and President of the United States. He took his bride to Mississippi, and settled down to live as a cotton planter. But within three months, both he and his wife became ill with fever, and Mrs. Davis died. Davis traveled for a year, while he regained his strength. For several years after his return to his plantation "Brierfield," on the Mississippi River, he studied history, economics, political philosophy, and the Constitution of the United States. He managed his plantation successfully, and became wealthy.

His Political Career. Davis became interested in politics in 1843, and won a seat as a Democrat in the U.S. House of Representatives in 1845. He resigned from Congress in June, 1846, to become a colonel in a regiment of Mississippi volunteers in the Mexican War. He served under General Zachary Taylor in northern Mexico, and distinguished himself for bravery in the battles of Monterrey and Buena Vista. His deployment of his men in a V shape gave him credit for winning the battle of Buena Vista (see MEXICAN WAR). During the battle, Davis fought all day with a bullet in his foot.

The governor of Mississippi appointed Davis in 1847 to fill out the term of a United States senator who had died. The next year the state legislature elected him for the rest of the term, and in 1850 for a full term. Henry Clay's famous compromise measures came before the Senate in 1850, and Davis took an active part in opposing them in debate (see COMPROMISE OF 1850). He believed in a strict interpretation of the Constitution, and loyally supported Senator John C. Calhoun, a Southern states' rights leader (see CALHOUN, JOHN C.).

Davis believed that Mississippi should not accept the Compromise of 1850, and resigned from the Senate to become the candidate of the States' Rights Democrats for governor. He lost the election, and retired to his plantation in Wilkinson County.

Secretary of War. President Franklin Pierce appointed Davis secretary of war in 1853. Davis improved the Army during his term. He introduced an improved system of infantry tactics, and brought in new and better weapons. During his term the Army was enlarged. He organized engineer companies to explore routes for railroads from the Mississippi River to the Pacific Coast. He even tried the experiment of importing camels for army use in the western deserts. At the close of the Pierce Administration in 1857, Davis was re-elected to the Senate from Mississippi. In the Senate, Davis no longer advocated secession, but he defended the rights of the South and slavery. He opposed Stephen A. Douglas' "Freeport Doctrine," which held that the people of a territory could exclude slavery by refusing to protect it. Davis also opposed Douglas' ambition to be the Democratic presidential candidate in 1860 (see DOUGLAS, STEPHEN ARNOLD).

Spokesman for the South. Davis became the champion of the constitutional right of a state to choose and maintain its own institutions. He demanded that Congress protect slavery in the territories. In the positions he took, he considered himself the heir of Calhoun.

Photograph by Mathew Brady. National Archives, Washington, D.C.

Jefferson Davis became the provisional president of the Confederate States of America on Feb. 18, 1861.

After Abraham Lincoln was elected President of the United States, Mississippi passed an Ordinance of Secession, and Davis resigned from the Senate. Davis hoped to become head of the Army of the Confederate States. But shortly after his return to Mississippi, the convention at Montgomery, Ala., named him provisional president of the Confederacy. He took the oath of office on Feb. 18, 1861. He was inaugurated as regular president of the Confederacy on Feb. 22, 1862.

Leader of the Confederacy. Davis was probably not the wisest choice for president. His health was poor. Although he was a good administrator, he proved to be a poor planner. He had difficulties with his Congress, and bitter critics condemned his management of the war. Yet he acted with dignity, sincerity, and strict devotion to constitutional principle.

Soon after General Robert E. Lee surrendered, Davis was taken prisoner, and imprisoned at Fort Monroe. A grand jury indicted him for treason, and he was held in prison two years awaiting trial. Horace Greeley and other Northern men became his bondsmen in 1867, and he was released on bail. He was never tried.

His Last Years. Davis spent his last years writing and studying at "Beauvoir," his home at Biloxi, Miss., near the Gulf of Mexico. He published *The Rise and Fall of the Confederate Government* in 1881 as a defense against his critics. He appeared often at Confederate reunions, and eventually won the admiration of his fellow Southerners. He died on Dec. 6, 1889, and was buried in New Orleans. His body was moved to Richmond, Va., in 1893, and a monument was built there to his memory. The state of Mississippi presented a statue of Davis to Statuary Hall in 1931. There is also a monument in Richmond for his daughter, Winnie, who was known as the *Daughter of the Confederacy*. Davis' birthday, June 3, is a legal holiday in seven Southern states. One of them, Louisiana, celebrates it as Confederate Memorial Day. Kentucky celebrates it both as Confederate Memorial Day and as Davis' birthday.

Varina Howell Davis (1826-1906) became the second wife of Jefferson Davis in 1845. She came from a well-to-do Mississippi plantation family. Mrs. Davis became known as a brilliant and witty hostess, and is credited with helping advance her husband's political career. After the war, she assisted her husband in writing *The Rise and Fall of the Confederate Government.* After his death, she wrote a biography of Davis. W. B. HESSELTINE

See also CIVIL WAR; CONFEDERATE STATES OF AMERICA; RICHMOND; ALABAMA (picture).

DAVIS, JOHN (1543-1605), or DAVYS, was an English explorer. He became the first European to discover what is now Davis Strait, between Greenland and Canada. Davis' discoveries led the way for such explorers of northeast Canada as Henry Hudson and William Baffin. Davis was also one of the most skilled navigators of the late 1500's. He invented a type of *quadrant*, a device used in navigation.

From 1585 to 1587, Davis headed three expeditions in search of the Northwest Passage, a route through Canada between Europe and Asia (see NORTHWEST

PASSAGE). He discovered Davis Strait on his first trip. During his voyages, Davis explored the east coast of Baffin Island and the west coast of Greenland but did not find a route west. From 1591 to 1593, he tried to find a passage to Asia via the Strait of Magellan in South America. He failed to do so but sighted the Falkland Islands, off the southeast coast of South America.

Davis published two books on navigation, *The Seamans Secrets* (1594) and *The Worldes Hydrographical Discription* (1595). He was born in Sandridge in the county of Devon in England. MORRIS ZASLOW

DAVIS, JOHN WILLIAM (1873-1955), a famous American constitutional lawyer, was the unsuccessful Democratic candidate for the presidency of the United States in 1924, losing to Calvin Coolidge.

Davis represented a wide range of clients as a constitutional lawyer. He argued 140 cases before the Supreme Court of the United States, more than anyone had argued up to that time. Many considered him the most distinguished constitutional lawyer in the United States. But he lost his last and most famous case, his Supreme Court defense of South Carolina's public school segregation laws, in 1954.

Davis was born in Clarksburg, W. Va., and graduated from Washington and Lee University. He represented West Virginia in the U.S. House of Representatives from 1911 to 1913. He served as U.S. solicitor general from 1913 to 1918 and as ambassador to Great Britain from 1918 to 1921. ERIC F. GOLDMAN

DAVIS, MILES DEWEY, JR. (1926-), is a trumpet player and composer. He gained fame in the 1940's as a pioneer of the complex rhythmic, melodic, and harmonic movement in jazz called "bebop." Later, he developed a more personal moody trumpet style and became one of the most imitated soloists of the 1960's. In the 1970's, Davis added strong elements of rock music to his performances.

Davis was born in Alton, Ill. From 1948 to 1950, he led a small band that is credited with launching the more relaxed "cool" school of jazz. Davis also played the flügelhorn, similar to the trumpet but with a larger sound. LEONARD FEATHER

DAVIS, OWEN (1874-1956), an American playwright, wrote realistic dramas that rank close to the plays of Eugene O'Neill in portraying stern New England farm life. Davis' *The Family Cupboard* (1913) was one of America's first realistic plays. He also wrote the serious domestic drama *Detour* (1921). *Icebound* (1923) is a stark account of a cold-hearted family struggling over an inheritance. It won the 1923 Pulitzer drama prize. Davis adapted several novels into plays, including *Ethan Frome* (1936), a brilliant adaption of novelist Edith Wharton's story of disappointed love.

Davis was born in Portland, Me. For years, starting in 1899, he turned out a new melodrama every four to six weeks. His most famous melodrama is *Nellie, the Beautiful Cloak Model* (1906). THOMAS A. ERHARD

DAVIS, PAULINA WRIGHT (1813-1876), was an American social reformer. She worked for the right of women to own property and to vote.

In 1840, Davis joined a women's campaign against the property laws of the day. These laws made a man the owner of his wife's possessions. The campaign led to a New York law of 1848 that gave wives control of property they had owned before marriage.

National Portrait Gallery, Smithsonian Institution
Paulina Davis

From 1845 to 1849, Davis lectured to women's groups on the female anatomy. These talks encouraged some of her listeners to join the small number of women who became physicians.

Davis also helped organize the first and second national women's rights conventions. She presided at these meetings, held in 1850 and 1851 in Worcester, Mass. From 1853 to 1855, she published a women's rights magazine called *Una*. Davis was born in Bloomfield, N.Y. MIRIAM SCHNEIR

DAVIS, RICHARD HARDING (1864-1916), a war correspondent and writer, became the best-known reporter of his time. He covered six wars for New York and London newspapers. They included the revolution in Cuba and the Spanish-American War that followed it; the Greco-Turkish, Boer, and Russo-Japanese wars; and the early years of World War I. He toured and wrote for magazines about the western United States, the Mediterranean, Central America, and the Congo. He was sensational and dramatic, both in his personality and his writing for publication. Davis was born in Philadelphia. He began newspaper work in 1886. He wrote 25 plays, including *The Dictator;* 7 novels, including *Ranson's Folly;* and more than 80 short stories. JOHN TEBBEL

DAVIS, SAMUEL (1842-1863), a Confederate spy, was called the *Boy Hero of the Confederacy*. Union troops hanged him near Pulaski, Tenn., because he would not tell who gave him secret military information. Davis's last words were, "I would rather die a thousand deaths than betray a friend or be false to duty." Tennessee erected a statue to his memory on the Capitol grounds in Nashville. Davis's birthplace, near Smyrna, Tenn., is kept as a shrine. J. MILTON HENRY

DAVIS, STUART (1894-1964), was an American painter and illustrator. His bright, lively paintings deal with everyday life. Bold areas of intense, pure color and rugged written lines characterize his work. He received his inspiration from such things as jazz, motion pictures, gas stations, billboards, and store fronts. He included words from street signs and billboards in many of his works. His semi-abstract style emphasized the distinctly American flavor of his paintings.

Davis was born in Philadelphia. He studied at the Robert Henri School of Art in New York City, and in Paris. At 19, he exhibited in the famous Armory Show of 1913. The works of Vincent van Gogh, Paul Gauguin, and Henri Matisse deeply impressed him at this exhibition. He did murals for Radio City Music Hall and Rockefeller Center in New York City. GEORGE D. CULLER

See also PAINTING (picture: *The Barber Shop*); UNITED STATES (Arts [color picture]).

DAVIS AND ELKINS COLLEGE. See UNIVERSITIES AND COLLEGES (table).

DAVIS CUP is a silver bowl trophy awarded each year to the nation that wins the world's men's tennis championship. Dwight F. Davis, a leading American

DAVIS CUP TOURNAMENT

Year	Winner	Runner-Up	Score	Year	Winner	Runner-Up	Score
1900	United States	Great Britain	3-0	**1931**	France	Great Britain	3-2
1901	No competition			**1932**	France	United States	3-2
1902	United States	Great Britain	3-2	**1933**	Great Britain	France	3-2
1903	Great Britain	United States	4-1	**1934**	Great Britain	United States	4-1
1904	Great Britain	Belgium	5-0	**1935**	Great Britain	United States	5-0
1905	Great Britain	United States	5-0	**1936**	Great Britain	Australia	3-2
1906	Great Britain	United States	5-0	**1937**	United States	Great Britain	4-1
1907	Australia and New Zealand	Great Britain	3-2	**1938**	United States	Australia	3-2
				1939	Australia	United States	3-2
1908	Australia and New Zealand	United States	3-2	**1940-1945**	No competition		
				1946	United States	Australia	5-0
1909	Australia and New Zealand	United States	5-0	**1947**	United States	Australia	4-1
				1948	United States	Australia	5-0
1910	No competition			**1949**	United States	Australia	4-1
1911	Australia and New Zealand	United States	5-0	**1950**	Australia	United States	4-1
				1951	Australia	United States	3-2
1912	Great Britain	Australia and New Zealand	3-2	**1952**	Australia	United States	4-1
				1953	Australia	United States	3-2
1913	United States	Great Britain	3-2	**1954**	United States	Australia	3-2
1914	Australia and New Zealand	United States	3-2	**1955**	Australia	United States	5-0
				1956	Australia	United States	5-0
1915-1918	No competition			**1957**	Australia	United States	3-2
1919	Australia and New Zealand	Great Britain	4-1	**1958**	United States	Australia	3-2
				1959	Australia	United States	3-2
1920	United States	Australia and New Zealand	5-0	**1960**	Australia	Italy	4-1
				1961	Australia	Italy	5-0
1921	United States	Japan	5-0	**1962**	Australia	Mexico	5-0
1922	United States	Australia and New Zealand	4-1	**1963**	United States	Australia	3-2
				1964	Australia	United States	3-2
1923	United States	Australia and New Zealand	4-1	**1965**	Australia	Spain	4-1
				1966	Australia	India	4-1
1924	United States	Australia and New Zealand	5-0	**1967**	Australia	Spain	4-1
				1968	United States	Australia	4-1
1925	United States	France	5-0	**1969**	United States	Romania	5-0
1926	United States	France	4-1	**1970**	United States	West Germany	5-0
1927	France	United States	3-2	**1971**	United States	Romania	3-2
1928	France	United States	4-1	**1972**	United States	Romania	3-2
1929	France	United States	3-2	**1973**	Australia	United States	5-0
1930	France	United States	4-1	**1974**	South Africa	India	*

Source: United States Lawn Tennis Association. *Won by default.

tennis player, donated the cup in 1900, and competition began that year. The Davis Cup tournament features a series of dual meets between nations. Each meet consists of one doubles and four singles matches. Competition is organized by geographical zones. Teams play in European, American, and Eastern zone tournaments. The zone winners then play each other. Finalists compete for the trophy. FRED RUSSELL

DAVIS STRAIT. See NORTHWEST PASSAGE.

DAVISSON, CLINTON JOSEPH (1881-1958), was an American physicist. He and Lester H. Germer discovered *electron diffraction*. He found that when electrons are directed at a piece of metal, they are reflected only in certain directions by the layers of atoms inside the metal. For his work, Davisson shared the 1937 Nobel prize in physics with George P. Thomson of Great Britain. Thomson made a similar discovery by directing an electron beam at a paper-thin sheet of metal.

Davisson was born in Bloomington, Ill. He graduated from the University of Chicago and received a Ph.D. from Princeton University. He taught at the Carnegie Institute of Technology. Davisson also did research at the Bell Telephone Laboratories. R. T. ELLICKSON

DAVY, EDMUND. See ACETYLENE.

DAVY, SIR HUMPHRY (1778-1829), an English chemist, rose to fame as inventor of the miner's safety lamp. The Davy lamp, perfected in 1815, greatly reduced the risks of coal mine explosions. At the age of 20, Davy experimented with the use of nitrous oxide, or laughing gas, as an anesthetic. When he was 29, he became the first person to isolate the chemical elements sodium and potassium. He did this by passing an electric current through the fused hydroxides of these elements. He was also first to isolate barium, calcium, magnesium, and strontium.

Davy was born in Penzance, England. In 1802, he became professor of chemistry at the Royal Institution in London. His experiments and lectures made him famous. During the Napoleonic wars between England and France, Davy was given safe passage to Paris so he could accept an award from Napoleon. He was knighted in 1812. SIDNEY ROSEN

See also ALUMINUM (History); ELECTRIC ARC; MAGNESIUM (History); SAFETY LAMP; FARADAY, MICHAEL; CHLORINE; HEAT (Man's Understanding of Heat).

DAVY JONES is a humorous name for the spirit of the ocean deep, in sailors' folklore. He is known chiefly through the proverbial term for the bottom of the sea, Davy Jones' locker. Davy Jones is also a common Welsh name. Some have attempted to trace Jones to Jonah, the Hebrew prophet who lived three days in the belly of a large fish. While the bodies of drowned sailors and those buried at sea go to Davy Jones' locker, the souls of good sailors go to Fiddler's Green. B. A. BOTKIN

DAVY LAMP. See DAVY, SIR HUMPHRY.

DAWES, CHARLES GATES (1865-1951), served as Vice-President of the United States from 1925 to 1929 under President Calvin Coolidge. He shared the 1925 Nobel peace prize for arranging a plan for German reparations after World War I (see DAWES PLAN). Dawes entered national politics when he handled Republican Party finances in the 1896 campaign.

He served on the Allied General Purchasing Board during World War I, and became the first director of the federal budget in 1921. He served as ambassador to Great Britain from 1929 to 1932, and as the first chairman of the Reconstruction Finance Corporation in 1932. Dawes was chairman of the board of the City National Bank & Trust Company of Chicago from 1932 until his death in 1951. He was born in Marietta, Ohio, on Aug. 27, 1865. IRVING G. WILLIAMS

See also VICE-PRESIDENT OF THE U.S. (picture).

DAWES, WILLIAM. See REVERE, PAUL.

DAWES ACT. See INDIAN TERRITORY; INDIAN, AMERICAN (The Fall of Indian America).

DAWES PLAN was a program designed to help Germany pay its World War I *reparations* (payments for damages). The plan resulted from an international conference held in London in 1924. Charles G. Dawes, a banker who later became Vice-President of the United States, led the committee that formed the plan.

In 1921, the Allies had set Germany's debt at $33 billion. The Dawes Plan did not reduce this total, but it did ease Germany's payment schedule. The plan also provided for an international loan to help Germany pay its debt. Germany accepted the plan in 1924. In 1929, the Dawes Plan was replaced by the Young Plan. But Germany defaulted on its payments during the Great Depression. ROBERT HUGH FERRELL

See also WAR DEBT; RUHR (History).

DAWSON was the family name of a father and son who were early Canadian geologists.

Sir John William Dawson (1820-1899), the father, worked in eastern Canada, especially Nova Scotia. He and Sir Charles Lyell discovered bones of amphibians in Coal Age trees. *Acadian Geology* was his most important book. His *Relics of Primeval Life* described ancient fossils called *Eozoon*, some of which now seem to be sea plants. Dawson was born in Pictou, Nova Scotia, and was graduated from the University of Edinburgh in Scotland. He became professor of geology and principal of McGill University in Montreal in 1855.

George Mercer Dawson (1849-1901), the son, became a geologist and naturalist for the North American Boundary Commission in 1873. He joined the Geological Survey of Canada in 1875, and became its director in 1895. He helped settle disputes between the United States and Great Britain over Bering Sea seal fisheries in 1893 (see BERING SEA CONTROVERSY). Dawson was born in Pictou. He attended McGill University, and the Royal School of Mines in London, England. He became president of the Royal Society of Canada in Ottawa in 1893. CARROLL LANE FENTON

DAY. While the earth travels through space around the sun, it also spins on its own axis. A *solar* day is the length of time it takes the earth to turn around once with respect to the sun. We usually say *day* for the time the sun is shining on our part of the earth, and *night* for the time when our part of the earth is dark, or turned away from the sun. But the night is really a part of the whole day. We also say *business day* sometimes to mean the hours of business in any one day.

Each day begins at midnight. In most countries, the day is divided into two parts of 12 hours each. The hours from midnight to noon are the A.M. (before noon) hours. The hours from noon to midnight are the P.M. (after noon) hours. The military services often designate the time of day on a 24-hour basis, such as 0100 for one o'clock in the morning, 1200 for noon, and 2400 for midnight.

The Babylonians began their day at sunrise. The ancient Jews began the day at sunset. The Egyptians and the Romans were the first to begin the day at midnight.

The length of daylight changes during the year in all parts of the world because the earth tips first one pole toward the sun and then the other while it travels on its orbit. The longest day in the Northern Hemisphere usually is June 21. It has 13 hours and 13 minutes of daylight at 20° latitude. The same day has 14 hours and 30 minutes at 40° latitude. At 60°, it has 18 hours and 30 minutes of daylight. The shortest day usually is December 21. It has only 10 hours and 47 minutes of daylight at 20° latitude, and 9 hours, 9 minutes at 40°. At 60°, there are only 5 hours and 30 minutes of daylight on that day (see SEASON [table]). The length of daylight changes very little during the year at the equator.

When the earth tips so that the North Pole faces the sun, the South Pole is continuously dark and the North Pole is always in daylight. Then the North Pole tips away from the sun, and it becomes dark there while the South Pole has constant daylight. These long periods of darkness and daylight last about six months.

Astronomers use a day called a *sidereal day*. It is based on the period of the earth's rotation as measured by fixed stars. This day equals 23 hours, 56 minutes, and 4.09054 seconds of mean solar time. DONALD H. MENZEL

See also articles on the days of the week; DAYLIGHT SAVING; SIDEREAL TIME; TIME; TWILIGHT.

DAY, BENJAMIN HENRY (1810-1889), founded the first successful "penny paper," the *New York Sun*, in 1833. Day priced his little newspaper at one cent a copy, and sent newsboys onto the streets to sell it. This made the *Sun* a novelty in American journalism. Day also attracted readers by emphasizing the human and dramatic element in the news. By 1836, the *Sun* claimed a circulation of 30,000, the largest in the world at the time. Day sold the newspaper in 1837. Day was born in West Springfield, Mass. JOHN ELDRIDGE DREWRY

DAY, CLARENCE SHEPARD, JR. (1874-1935), an American author, wrote the humorous books, *Life with Father* (1935) and *Life with Mother* (1937). Both were produced as plays, and *Life with Father* became one of the most popular plays in the 1940's. He also wrote *This Simian World* (1920), *God and My Father* (1932), and verses called *Scenes from the Mesozoic* (1935).

Day was born in New York City. He joined the Navy during the Spanish-American War. After the war, he suffered from arthritis and had to stay in bed for the rest of his life. BERNARD DUFFEY

DAY-CARE CENTER is an institution that cares for the children of working mothers. A mother employed outside her home can leave her children at such a center while she works. Most day-care centers operate from 10 to 12 hours each weekday. A majority of the children are less than 6 years old. The centers also care for school-age children before and after school and during school vacations.

Children at a day-care center learn to play together. Some centers have instructors who teach them games and show them how to work with clay, crayons, paints, paper, and paste. The youngsters receive lunch at the center and take a nap after eating.

Many communities throughout the world have day-care centers. The centers include private homes in which an adult cares for 1 to 9 children. Larger centers look after as many as 150 youngsters. Day-care centers in the United States care for a total of about 700,000 children daily. Some companies and universities maintain a day-care center for the children of their employees.

The U.S. government operates many day-care centers for children of low-income families as part of the Head Start program. The government also provides day-care service for some mothers who receive welfare payments and are enrolled in a job-training program. Such programs teach them vocational skills so they eventually can support themselves and their children.

The United States has no national standards for day-care centers. But in the 1970's, efforts were made to establish such standards and to train more child-care workers for careers in day care. EDWARD ZIGLER

DAY-LEWIS, CECIL (1904-1972), was an Irish-born English poet and novelist. In 1968, Queen Elizabeth II appointed him poet laureate of England.

Day-Lewis was born in Ballintogher, near Sligo, and attended Oxford University in England. During the 1930's, along with W. H. Auden, Louis MacNeice, and Stephen Spender—all friends from Oxford—he gained fame for his poems expressing discontent with society. These poets influenced English verse by writing about modern political and social forces in a direct, informal, and often deliberately vulgar manner. Much of Day-Lewis' later poetry deals with his Irish heritage and memories of his childhood in Ireland.

Day-Lewis' *Collected Poems* were published in 1954. His novels include *The Friendly Tree* (1936) and *Starting Point* (1937). His autobiography, *The Buried Day*, was published in 1960. Day-Lewis wrote detective stories under the pen name of Nicholas Blake. DARCY O'BRIEN

DAY LILY is a lily plant whose beautiful blossoms, usually yellow or orange, live only from sunrise to sunset. The flowers grow in loose clusters at the top of a leafless stalk 3 to 5 feet (91 to 150 centimeters) high. Six to twelve flowers make up a cluster, and two or three open each day. The plant's long smooth leaves, 1 to 2 feet (30 to 61 centimeters) long, spring from the fleshy, fibrous root. These hardy plants can be cultivated easily in rich soil and a moist, shady area. They bloom from June to September. The related *plantain lily* resembles the day lily, but it has white and blue flowers.

Hugh Spencer

Day Lily

Scientific Classification. Day lilies belong to the lily family, *Liliaceae*. The tawny-orange day lily is genus *Hemerocallis*, species *H. fulva*. The fragrant, or lemon, day lily is *H. flava*. ALFRED C. HOTTES

DAY NURSERY. See NURSERY SCHOOL.

DAY OF ATONEMENT. See YOM KIPPUR.

DAYAK. See DYAK.

DAYAN, *dy AHN,* **MOSHE,** *MOY shuh* (1915-), is an Israeli military hero and political leader. He commanded the Israeli forces that won the Arab-Israeli war of 1956, and directed the Israeli victory in the six-day war against Egypt, Jordan, and Syria in June, 1967. Dayan served as Israel's minister of defense from 1967 to 1974. He had served as minister of agriculture from 1959 to 1964, and chief of staff from 1953 to 1958.

Israel Information Services

Moshe Dayan

In 1939, the British who ruled Palestine imprisoned Dayan for his work with the outlawed *Haganah*, a Jewish militia group. He was released in 1941 to fight with the British against the Vichy French. He was wounded during a battle in Lebanon, and lost his left eye. Dayan also fought in the first Arab-Israeli war of 1948. He was born in Deganiya, Palestine. ELLIS RIVKIN

See also ISRAEL (History).

DAYDREAM. See IMAGINATION.

DAYE, STEPHEN, also spelled DAY (1594?-1668), with his son Matthew, set up and operated the first printing office in what is now the United States. The Dayes arrived in Cambridge, Mass., in 1638. The Rev. Jose Glover financed their passage from England and supplied them with a press, type, and paper. The first book that came from the press was *The Bay Psalm Book* in 1640. Eleven copies of it survive. See BAY PSALM BOOK.

Stephen Daye was born in Cambridge, England, and first worked as a locksmith. He prospected for iron ore in New England. Matthew was evidently in charge of the press. The young printer began his career in the late 1630's by issuing a sheet that contained *The Freeman's Oath.* RAY NASH

DAYFLY. See MAYFLY.

DAYLIGHT. See DAY.

DAYLIGHT SAVING is a plan in which clocks are set one hour ahead of standard time for a certain period. As a result, darkness comes one hour later than on standard time. The advantages of this plan include an additional daylight hour for recreation in the evening. Great Britain adopted daylight time as an economy measure during World War I. The United States adopted it in 1918. The U.S. Congress repealed the law in 1919, but many cities continued to use daylight time.

After World War II began, daylight saving was again used in the United States, depending on the wishes of individual states or cities. An act of Congress, which became effective in 1967, established daylight time from the last Sunday in April to the last Sunday in October. A state may remain on standard time if its legislature votes to do so. An amendment to the law in 1972 allows states that lie in more than one time zone to use daylight time in one zone and not in the other. In 1973, Congress passed a year-round daylight saving law in an effort to conserve energy. The law went into effect on Jan. 6, 1974, and daylight time was scheduled to continue until Oct. 26, 1975. However, Congress later voted to return the nation to standard time for a four-month period—from Oct. 27, 1974, to Feb. 23, 1975. WILLIAM MARKOWITZ

DAYTON, Ohio (pop. 242,917; met. area 852,531), is one of the leading manufacturing centers of the state. It is called the *Birthplace of Aviation* because Orville and Wilbur Wright, who invented the first successful airplane, lived there. Dayton lies in the Miami River Valley in southwestern Ohio (see OHIO [political map]).

Settlers from Cincinnati founded Dayton in 1796. They chose the site because three major rivers—the Mad, the Miami, and the Stillwater—flow together there. This location makes Dayton a natural center of water transportation. The settlers named their town for Jonathan Dayton, the youngest signer of the United States Constitution, who owned land nearby.

Description. Dayton, the county seat of Montgomery County, covers about 38 square miles (98 square kilometers). The Dayton metropolitan area occupies 1,720 square miles (4,455 square kilometers) and consists of Greene, Miami, Montgomery, and Preble counties.

Nearly a third of Dayton's workers are employed in its more than 800 manufacturing plants. Major products, in order of value, include nonelectrical machinery, rubber and plastic goods, transportation equipment, electrical equipment, and printed materials. Wright-Patterson Air Force Base, just outside Dayton, is the city's single largest employer. The NCR Corporation, the world's chief producer of cash registers, has its headquarters in Dayton.

A major tourist attraction in the Dayton area is the U.S. Air Force Museum at the air base. The museum features more than 150 planes and missiles. Dayton also has an art institute and a museum of natural history. Educational institutions in the city include the University of Dayton and Wright State University.

Government and History. Dayton has a council-manager form of government. The council is called the City Commission. Dayton's voters elect the five commission members to four-year terms. The commission hires a city manager to carry out its policies.

Miami and Shawnee Indians lived in the Dayton area before white settlers first arrived in 1796. During the 1800's, the city grew into a market and transportation center. Many factories were built in the 1800's, creating new jobs. The city's population rose from 38,678 in 1880 to 116,577 in 1910.

In March, 1913, heavy rains caused the Mad, Miami, and Stillwater rivers to rise and flood the city. The flood killed more than 300 persons and caused about $100 million damage. Later that year, the city adopted the council-manager form of government, with a professional city manager hired to handle the problems caused by the flood. The new system of government took effect in 1914, and Dayton became the first U.S. city with more than 100,000 persons to adopt it.

The flood also led to the formation of the Miami Conservancy District in 1915. This agency built five dams upstream from Dayton between 1918 and 1922. Today, Dayton and the Miami River Valley have one of the most effective flood control systems in the world.

The Dayton Convention and Exhibition Center opened in 1973. The center, located in the city's downtown Dave Hall Plaza, includes an exhibition hall and a theater. JACK FOSTER

See also WRIGHT-PATTERSON AIR FORCE BASE.

DAYTON, JONATHAN (1760-1824), at the age of 26 was the youngest signer of the United States Constitution. He served in the Revolutionary War and in the New Jersey Assembly. Dayton was a member of the U.S. Congress from 1791 to 1799 and was the speaker of the House of Representatives from 1795 to 1799. He served as a U.S. senator from New Jersey from 1799 to 1805. Dayton was born in Elizabethtown, N.J. He speculated in lands near Dayton, Ohio, which was named for him. ROBERT J. TAYLOR

DAYTON, UNIVERSITY OF. See UNIVERSITIES AND COLLEGES (table).

DAYTON, WILLIAM LEWIS (1807-1864), was the Republican candidate for Vice-President of the United States in 1856. He and presidential candidate John C. Frémont were defeated by Democratic candidates James Buchanan (President) and John C. Breckinridge. As a member of the Whig Party, Dayton served as a U.S. senator from New Jersey from 1842 to 1851. He was attorney general of New Jersey from 1857 to 1861 and minister to France from 1861 to his death. Dayton was born in Basking Ridge, N.J. RICHARD P. McCORMICK

DAYTONA BEACH, Fla. (pop. 45,327; met. area 169,487), a year-round resort city, lies on the Atlantic Ocean and the Halifax River (see FLORIDA [political map]). Its hard-packed sand beach extends 23 miles (37 kilometers) and is 500 feet (150 meters) wide at low tide.

Docks, harbors for yachts and other small boats, and shipping piers lie in the Halifax River. Bridges connect the two sections of the city, one built on the mainland and the other on the peninsula. Hotels, motels, and apartment houses line its ocean front and river banks. The city offers many outdoor recreational facilities. Many championship automobile and motorcycle races are held at the Daytona International Speedway (see AUTOMOBILE RACING [color picture]).

Daytona Beach's industrial activities include citrus-fruit packing and shipping, fishing, and the manufacture of clothing, electronics components, cement, furniture, and boats.

The city was founded in 1870, and incorporated as Daytona in 1876. In 1926, it consolidated with the peninsula towns of Daytona Beach and Seabreeze, and was chartered as Daytona Beach. It has a council-manager form of government. KATHRYN ABBEY HANNA

D.C. See DISTRICT OF COLUMBIA.

DC. See ELECTRIC CURRENT (Direct and Alternating Current).

DDT is an insecticide that has been widely used on crops for pest control. The three letters come from its chemical name, *d*ichloro-*d*iphenyl-*t*richloroethane. DDT is a grayish-white powder that, when used for pest control, is mixed with other substances.

DDT kills insects by affecting the nervous system, though some insects have developed immunity to it. It differs from most other insecticides because it lasts a long time. DDT decays slowly and appears in plants and in animals that eat the plants. It also appears in human beings because it is absorbed into the body tissues from the animals and plants that people eat.

Large-scale application of DDT kills useful insects as well as harmful ones, and it may endanger other animal life, including birds and fish. It may also contaminate the food that humans eat. The use of DDT in the United States and other temperate areas has declined since the early 1960's. In 1972, the U.S. Environmental Protection Agency took steps to stop almost all uses of DDT. But the use of DDT in the tropics increased steadily during the late 1960's and early 1970's.

DDT was first prepared as an insecticide by Paul Mueller, a Swiss chemist, in 1939 (see MUELLER, PAUL). It became well known during World War II (1939-1945), when the United States Army used it to fight an epidemic of typhus fever in Naples, Italy. The Army used DDT as a means of destroying body lice, which carry the disease. PAUL A. DAHM

DE FACTO GOVERNMENT. The government of a country can change quickly as a result of invasion or revolution. Other countries may refuse to recognize such a new government officially, but they may find it necessary to deal with it informally. These countries recognize the new government as a *de facto government* (government in fact). Later, the countries may recognize the new government as a *government de jure* (legal and official government). ROBERT G. NEUMANN

DE FACTO SEGREGATION. See SEGREGATION (De Facto Segregation).

DE JURE SEGREGATION. See SEGREGATION (Jim Crow Laws).

DEAD-MAIL OFFICE is a division of the United States Postal Service. Letters and parcels that cannot be delivered or returned to the sender are sent to this office and its branches. There are two kinds of branches. Most large post offices have *dead-letter* branches to handle letters. Railroad mail division headquarters maintain *dead parcel post* branches in many cities.

About 23 million letters and 1½ million packages end up at dead-mail offices every year. This dead mail includes: (1) mail that has no return address; (2) letters and parcels containing materials which are not allowed in the mails; (3) mail that is wrongly addressed, or poorly wrapped; and (4) mail addressed to persons who have moved away and cannot be located.

The Postal Service returns more than $100,000 to senders each year. Money contained in letters that cannot be delivered or returned within one year is claimed by the Postal Service. This amounts to over $180,000 every year. A sale of the contents of unclaimed parcels is held every three months, adding more than $575,000 to postal receipts each year.

Critically reviewed by the UNITED STATES POSTAL SERVICE

See also FRANKLIN, BENJAMIN (Civic Leader).

DEAD RECKONING is a way of finding a ship's location on the seas without using the position of the stars. The officers keep a record of the direction in which the ship sails, and how fast it travels. They multiply the ship's speed by the length of time to get the number of miles or kilometers traveled. They then trace the ship's course on a map. Dead reckoning has been useful when clouds hide the stars, but ships now usually receive positions by radio. See also NAVIGATION.

DEAD SEA, the saltiest body of water in the world, is located at the mouth of the River Jordan and forms part of the border between Israel and Jordan. The Dead Sea is nine times as salty as the ocean. It lies at the bottom of the deepest *fault* (break) in the earth's crust, 1,299 feet (396 meters) below the level of the Mediterranean Sea. In the Middle Ages, travelers reported that no birds flew over the Dead Sea because the air there was poisonous. But today we know that birds avoid the Dead Sea because no fish are in it, and little plant life can grow in it because of the saltiness of the water.

The greatest depth of the Dead Sea is 1,297 feet (395 meters). It is about 50 miles (80 kilometers) long and 10 miles (16 kilometers) wide, and covers 405 square miles (1,049 square kilometers). The River Jordan flows into it from the north through a rapidly descending valley. Smaller streams also empty into the sea. These rivers pour 4,740,000 short tons (4,300,000 metric tons) of fresh water into the Dead Sea daily. This fresh water

DEAD SEA

Area: 405 sq. mi. (1,049 km²)

Elevation: 1,299 ft. (396 m) below sea level

Deepest point: 1,297 ft. (395 m)

Area occupied by Israel in 1967

o Historic site

Road **Railroad**

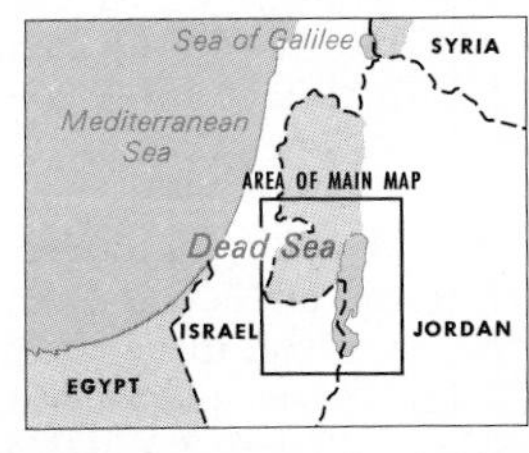

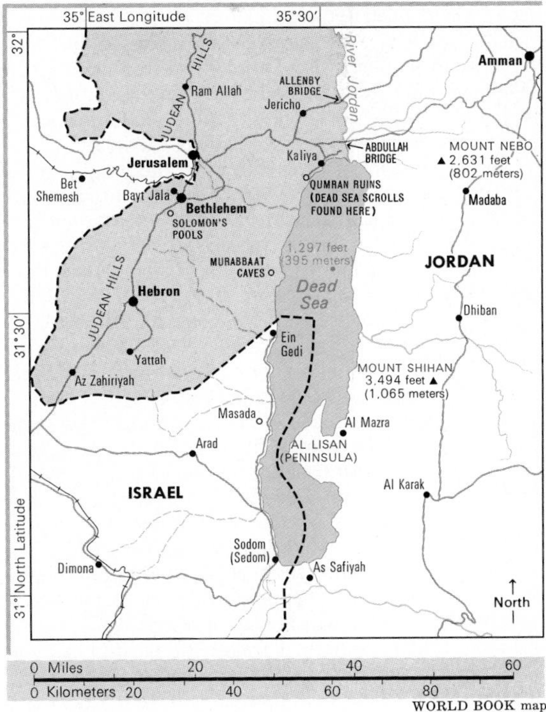

WORLD BOOK map

evaporates in the extreme heat in the Dead Sea basin. Thus, the level of the water changes very little and the sea never grows less salty. It contains about 24 per cent solid matter, mostly common salt.

The Dead Sea contains large quantities of minerals. Besides common salt (sodium chloride), the sea contains magnesium chloride, potassium chloride, calcium chloride, and magnesium bromide. These minerals are sources for potash, bromine, table salt, gypsum, and other chemical products. The shores around the Dead Sea are covered with lava, sulfur, and rock salt, because the sea lies near a volcanic zone stretching from Syria through Jordan to northwestern Arabia. Gases rising from the water give it an unpleasant odor. Some persons believe the water can cure certain diseases. A health resort is located in Kāliyā. The white limestone walls of the Plain of Moab rise sharply as high as 4,400 feet (1,340 meters) on the east side of the sea. The Plateau of Judea towers 3,000 feet (910 meters) on the west.

The smooth, sparkling water of the Dead Sea presents an attractive appearance. Spring-fed lagoons lie around the shores. Water and wind have worn away the mountainsides, making them brightly colored.

The Dead Sea was first mentioned as the *Salt Sea* in the Bible (Gen. 14:3). CHRISTINA PHELPS HARRIS

See also ISRAEL (Mining; picture); ASIA (picture).

DEAD SEA SCROLLS are ancient manuscripts from Palestine. The scrolls were found in caves near the northwestern shore of the Dead Sea (see DEAD SEA [map]). The scrolls have been called the "greatest manuscript discovery of modern times." They include all of the books of the Old Testament except Esther. A few of the books are in nearly complete form. They are the oldest known manuscripts of any books of the Bible. The scrolls are kept in the *Shrine of the Book*, part of the Israel Museum in Jerusalem.

The first group of scrolls was discovered in 1947. A Bedouin shepherd boy found them in a cave in the *Wādī Qumrān* (Qumran Valley). During the late 1940's and early 1950's, archaeologists and Bedouins found 10 additional caves containing ancient writings.

The discoveries consist of scrolls and fragments of hundreds of documents. Most of the manuscripts are made of leather and papyrus. These were part of a library that many scholars believe belonged to the Essenes, a Jewish religious sect. The Essenes may have lived in the Qumran area from about 100 B.C. to about A.D. 70 (see ESSENES). In 1951, archaeologists began excavating the ruins of a building called Khirbat Qumrān. There they found a room containing a table and materials used to write the manuscripts.

In addition to the Old Testament books, the Dead Sea Scrolls include some fragments of the *Septuagint* (the earliest Greek translation of the Old Testament), and parts of the book of Job written in Aramaic. They also include parts of some books of the Apocrypha, such as Tobit and the Wisdom of Solomon, written in Hebrew, Aramaic, and Greek. Scholars also found theological writings and some commentaries to the Bible. Caves in the Wādī Murabb'āt, a valley south of the Wādī Qumrān, contained fragments of Biblical and other documents, including some written in the Nabataean dialect. These texts date largely from a later historical period preceding and including the Jewish revolt against the Romans in A.D. 132-135. NELSON GLUECK

DEADLINE. See NEWSPAPER (Newspaper Terms).

DEADLY NIGHTSHADE. See BELLADONNA.

DEADWOOD. See BLACK HILLS; SOUTH DAKOTA (picture: Boom Town).

DEADWOOD DICK was a popular dime novel hero of the 1880's. He was created by Edward L. Wheeler, of Titusville, Pa. The original man who inspired the character is said to have been Richard W. Clark, a colorful prospector and gambler of Deadwood, S.Dak., who became an Indian fighter, Pony Express rider, and one of General George Custer's scouts. B. A. BOTKIN

DEAF-MUTE. See DEAFNESS.

DEAFNESS is the partial or complete inability to hear. About 7 out of 100 children in the public schools cannot hear as well as they should. Ability to hear grows less with age. It has been said that one person out of every four in the United States cannot hear normally.

If a person hears normally, the ear receives sound waves through a tube in the head called the *ear canal.* They strike on a thin membrane, the *eardrum,* which is stretched across a chamber in the ear called the *middle ear.* The eardrum vibrates very sensitively and is delicately connected with the hearing nerve, called the *auditory nerve,* by a very special apparatus in the *inner ear.* The sound sensation travels over this nerve to the brain. The middle ear is connected with the throat by a canal, the *Eustachian tube,* near the inner opening of the nose. Anything which interferes with any one of these parts may cause deafness of varying degrees.

Ordinarily the human ear can hear—or at least the human brain recognizes—sounds which have vibrations of from 20 to 20,000 cycles a second. The ordinary tones in conversation range from 200 to 3,000 vibrations per second in pitch. Some animals seem to hear vibrations of higher pitch. Sound is measured in decibels, a technical unit. A whisper is about 20 decibels in intensity; ordinary conversation, about 50 or 60 decibels (see SOUND [Hearing Sound]).

Hearing is considered good if all the sounds between 64 and 8,192 vibrations at 20 decibels are heard. Deafness which handicaps the person begins when the tones in ordinary speech cannot be heard at a whisper. Sometimes only part of the tone range is interfered with. Deafness can increase until it is almost impossible to hear any sound, but it has been found that most deaf persons can hear at least one sound.

Causes of Deafness. Some persons are born deaf. Others lose their hearing from disease or other causes. Injury to the auditory nerve by accident or disease will cause deafness. Meningitis may destroy the nerve, and syphilis is responsible for some cases of deafness in newborn infants. Deafness may be caused by epilepsy or other diseases affecting the parts of the brain which register sound.

Sudden tremendous noise or prolonged loud noise may cause permanent injury to the hearing. Workers in very noisy industries, such as steel mills or foundries, may eventually be affected.

Unequal air pressure on the sensitive eardrum may be a cause of deafness. This deafness is usually temporary unless the pressure on one side is so great as to burst the drum. Sometimes, when a person is going up in a very fast elevator in a very tall building, the hearing

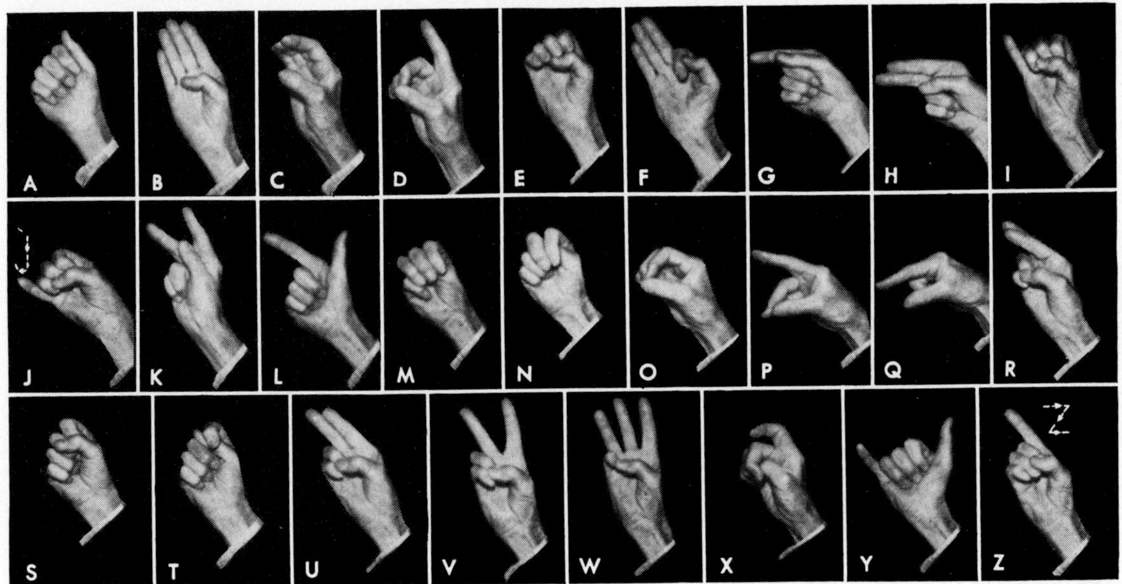

Harley D. Drake

A Hand Alphabet for Deaf Persons allows them to carry on conversations. Special positions of the fingers and hands stand for certain letters of the alphabet. A person uses this alphabet to spell out the words in his conversation. This may be a very slow process in the beginning, but soon the person can develop great facility and speed.

will be temporarily lessened and the ears "pop." Passengers in airplanes experience this difficulty, but it soon wears off. A hard blow on the side of the head may cause such unequal pressure that the eardrum is ruptured. A heavy explosion may also rupture the eardrum.

When the eardrum has a hole in it, it does not vibrate properly. The hole may heal over but the scar tissue thus formed is thicker and stiffer than the normal drum. As a result the eardrum vibrates less.

Most hearing troubles are caused by disease. This disease does not start within the ear but reaches the ear from other parts of the body, usually the nose and throat. Such diseases are particularly important during childhood, when hearing may be injured permanently. The common cold, tonsillitis, scarlet fever, measles, and some other diseases are often causes of such deafness.

Infection in the throat and nose may move up the Eustachian tube to the middle ear and cause inflammation and thickening of the eardrum. Often an abscess is formed in the inner ear and presses inside on the eardrum. Earache is the symptom of this pressure by an abscess. If the drum bursts, the pressure is relieved and the pain is gone, but the eardrum is damaged. If the drum can be pierced by a physician before it bursts, the hole will be small and sharply cut, and will heal sooner with less scar tissue than if it ruptures.

Often contaminated or infected fluids are forced up the Eustachian tube. This results in infection of the middle ear. Pressure of deep swimming and diving may force impure water into the middle ear. Severe nose blowing during throat and nose infections may result in a similar condition.

Infected adenoids may spread infection through the Eustachian tube to the middle ear. Occasionally adenoidal tissue will completely close the Eustachian tube. The blockage causes lowered air pressure on the inside of the eardrum. This change in pressure interferes with the proper vibration of the drum. Sometimes the swelling of the throat in "sore throat" or tonsillitis will produce a similar result.

Rarely does infection enter the middle ear from outside to affect the eardrum. But anything closing the ear canal will cut off the sound vibrations. Boils in the outer ear or in the canal may cause enough swelling to affect hearing. Excess wax, dirt, or foreign objects in the canal may cut off sound. Scar tissue caused by burns or scalds, or by other accidents, may also affect hearing.

Occasionally the delicate mechanism in the middle and inner ears becomes bony, so that the parts cannot vibrate. This is called *otosclerosis*, and usually appears to be hereditary.

Sometimes "deafness" is not due to any physical change in the ear, but to faulty mental processes. Some patients may be able to hear sounds but do not under-

Chicago Board of Education

Deaf Pupils in a special classroom at a public school receive instruction with a microphone and hearing aids.

stand words. Sudden or severe shock may produce this condition. In modern war, concussions from exploding shells sometimes puncture soldiers' eardrums. The eardrums usually heal in a few days, but the soldier may continue to think he is deaf. This is not true deafness, and must be treated as a mental problem.

Treatment. It is essential that any deafness or condition tending to cause deafness should be remedied at once. Infectious diseases should be treated by a competent physician. Middle ear infections can usually be prevented and possible deafness avoided if the causes are treated in time. Some drugs, such as penicillin and sulfa compounds, may be used in curing such infections. Proper lancing of abscesses of the middle ear by a physician does much to relieve the pain and prevent excessive formation of scar tissue. Accumulation of wax or anything else in the ear canal should be removed by a physician. Injury to the eardrum as well as to the canal is often the result of home treatment. Ear surgeons may treat otosclerosis by an operation called *fenestration*, in which they cut a tiny window in the inner ear.

Detection and prevention of deafness is particularly important in the public schools. Pupils have their hearing tested at regular intervals with an *audiometer*, an instrument which gives out sounds of known controlled intensity. Pupils not able to hear the normal range of sounds are sent to ear specialists for further examination. Removing the adenoids or tonsils may be advised. Cleaning of the ear canal will sometimes help. Advice may be given to use care in swimming and diving to avoid forcing infection into the middle ear.

Not much can be done to prevent congenital deafness from hereditary causes, but proper care of the mother during pregnancy will do much to prevent some such cases. In cases in which the hearing has already been affected, little can be done to bring it back to normal.

Deaf persons who do not speak are sometimes called *deaf-mutes*. Most such persons are not truly mute—they can learn to speak. Persons who are born deaf or who lose their hearing in infancy experience difficulty in learning to talk because they cannot hear others speak. When such a person learns to talk, his speech may be difficult for others to understand because he cannot hear himself and correct his tone. A person who knew how to speak before he became deaf retains the power of speech. But his voice may become harsh and unnatural.

In many cases, deaf persons learn to communicate by using their hands to form letters and words. Teachers of the deaf use special methods to show deaf persons how to speak correctly. Deaf students watch photographs of the vocal organs in operation and motion pictures of the pattern of sound waves produced by their voices.

Various techniques aid the deaf to understand the speech of others. Some deaf persons can read lips. Some partially deaf persons benefit from using powerful hearing aids.

GEORGE W. BEADLE

Related Articles in WORLD BOOK include:

Adenoids	Gallaudet	Keller, Helen A.
Bell, Alexander G.	Gallaudet College	Lip Reading
Ear	Handicapped	Mastoid
Education (picture: Special Education Programs)	Hearing Aids	Sign Language

DEAN, DIZZY (1911-1974), was one of baseball's greatest pitchers and most colorful personalities. He pitched for the St. Louis Cardinals and the Chicago Cubs from 1932 to 1941. He won 30 games in 1934. He and his brother Paul (Daffy) each pitched two victories for St. Louis over the Detroit Tigers in the 1934 World Series. St. Louis won this series, four games to three.

Dean loved to brag about his great pitching ability. One day in 1934, he walked into the Brooklyn Dodgers' clubhouse and told each Brooklyn player exactly how he would pitch to him. He beat Brooklyn that day, 13 to 0. Dean developed a sore arm in 1937 and was traded to the Chicago Cubs in 1938. His arm never returned to normal and in 1941 he retired from baseball to become a sports announcer.

Dean was born in Lucas, Ark. His real name was Jay Hanna Dean, but he also used the name of Jerome Herman Dean. He attended school in Chickalah, Ark., but he quit after the second grade. He picked cotton until he was 16, and then he served in the Army for three years. Dean became a professional baseball player in 1930.

As a radio and television sports announcer, Dean became famous for his quaint announcing style. He often used such expressions as "The runner *slud* into third," and "He *throwed* the ball." Dean was elected to baseball's Hall of Fame in 1953.

JOSEPH P. SPOHN

DEAN, JOHN W., III. See WATERGATE.

DEANE, SILAS (1737-1789), was an American patriot and diplomat. He was prominent in movements leading to the Revolutionary War. In March, 1776, the Continental Congress sent him to France to buy war supplies. After the Declaration of Independence, Benjamin Franklin and Arthur Lee were sent to join Deane in arranging treaties with France. Deane was recalled in 1778 to account for his financial transactions, but no evidence of dishonesty was found. He was born in Groton, Conn.

KENNETH R. ROSSMAN

DE ANGELI, *dee AN juh lih,* **MARGUERITE LOFFT** (1889-), is an American author and illustrator of children's books. She became best known for her stories about American minority groups, particularly people born in Europe, Quakers, and Negroes. She won the 1950 Newbery medal for *The Door in the Wall*, a story of England in the 1300's. In 1968, she was awarded the Regina medal. She wrote and illustrated *Henner's Lydia* (1936), *Thee, Hannah!* (1940), *Elin's Amerika* (1941), *Yonie Wondernose* (1944), and *Black Fox of Lorne* (1956). Born in Lapeer, Mich., she lived most of her life in Pennsylvania and New Jersey.

GEORGE E. BUTLER

See also LITERATURE FOR CHILDREN (Poetry; picture: Nursery Rhymes).

DEARBORN, Mich. (pop. 104,199), is the home of the main plant of the Ford Motor Company. Ford industries employ more than one of every four workers in Dearborn. The city's chief products include automobiles, steel, and heating and air-conditioning equipment. The city lies along the River Rouge on the western outskirts of Detroit (see MICHIGAN [political map]).

The city maintains Camp Dearborn, a 626-acre (253-hectare) recreational area, 35 miles (56 kilometers) to the northeast. Greenfield Village and the Henry Ford Museum attract over 1 million visitors yearly (see GREENFIELD VILLAGE). Within Dearborn lies Fairlane, Henry Ford's estate, which was presented to the University of Michigan in 1956. The city is the home of a campus of the University of Michigan. Dearborn also has a junior college, the McFadden-Ross Museum, and the Dearborn Historical Museum.

Dearborn was incorporated as a city in 1927. In the following year it united with Fordson, where Henry Ford had built his Rouge plant in 1919. Dearborn has a mayor-council government. WILLIS F. DUNBAR

See also FORD (Henry Ford); FORD MOTOR COMPANY; MICHIGAN (color picture: Greenfield Village Store in Dearborn).

DEARBORN, HENRY (1751-1829), was an American soldier and political leader. Fort Dearborn in Chicago was named for him (see FORT DEARBORN). He was born in North Hampton, N.H., and served as a captain in the Revolutionary War. He fought at Bunker Hill, went with Benedict Arnold to Quebec, and was serving as a major with General Horatio Gates when the British general John Burgoyne surrendered. Dearborn served twice in the U.S. Congress, and was secretary of war in Thomas Jefferson's Cabinet from 1801 to 1809. Dearborn was a major general during the War of 1812. He served as minister to Portugal from 1822 to 1824. RICHARD N. CURRENT

DEARDEN, JOHN FRANCIS CARDINAL (1907-), archbishop of Detroit, was appointed a cardinal of the Roman Catholic Church in 1969 by Pope Paul VI. In 1966, Dearden had been elected the first president of the National Conference of Catholic Bishops.

Cardinal Dearden was born in Valley Falls, R.I., and was ordained a priest in 1932. He was a professor of philosophy at St. Mary's Seminary in Cleveland from 1937 to 1944, and served as rector of the seminary from 1944 to 1948. Dearden was installed as archbishop of Detroit in 1959. THOMAS P. NEILL

DEATH means the ending of life. People usually die because the heart stops, and blood no longer circulates to bring oxygen and nourishment to body cells. But all the cells of the human body do not die at once. The hair may continue to grow for several hours after death. The cells of the cortex of the brain are very susceptible to lack of oxygen. They usually die first when the blood ceases to circulate. If the cells of the brain are completely deprived of oxygen for 5 or 10 minutes they can no longer completely regain their ability to function. The cells of the part of the brain called the *medulla oblongata* usually die next. Then the cells of the body's glands and the cells in the muscles which move the bones of the skeleton die. Cells in the skin and bones may live for several hours. The smooth muscles in the intestines may be stimulated and contract 12 hours after the heart has stopped beating. In some animals, certain cells have been kept alive for years in the laboratory in solutions containing nourishment.

Scientists have reported experiments in which they apparently have restored life to dead human beings. Electrical shock (countershock) applied to the heart can restore its pumping action when it has stopped. Restoration would not be possible if death had affected the tissues of the brain. In any case, the person's heart could not have stopped beating for more than a few minutes.

The death of some cells and structures in the body begins even before birth. Certain structures grow during life and then decay and are replaced by new structures. The thymus gland is an example of an organ that tends to disappear before adulthood. Death is also part of the processes of nature. When too many animals or plants live in a certain environment, many must die for lack of food, from disease, or because of poisons produced by their own bodies. Nature provides a cycle of experiences including birth, growth, and reproduction. Death is the way in which nature concludes the cycle.

Death, while feared by many, may be relatively calm and peaceful. The famous surgeon, Sir William Osler, found that many of his patients were unaware that they were dying, and that few died in the midst of mental torment. Several years before he died, Heywood Broun, American newspaperman, wrote: "He who dies a thousand deaths meets the final hour with the calmness of one who approaches a well-remembered door."

Death, in literature and myth, has often been portrayed as one of the great enemies of mankind. Many legends tell of man's desire to annihilate death. Death has been the subject for many poems. William Cullen Bryant's "Thanatopsis," Alfred Tennyson's "Crossing the Bar," and Robert Louis Stevenson's "Requiem" show a calm acceptance of death. EWALD E. SELKURT

Related Articles in WORLD BOOK include:

Autopsy	Funeral Customs	Necrology
Embalming	Immortality	Transmigration of the Soul
Euthanasia	Life	

DEATH, CIVIL, was a term used in English common law. It described the legal status of a living person who had lost his civil rights. Under the old law, a person lost all his civil rights if he entered a religious order, if he was banished from the country, or if he was convicted of a serious crime. The law then considered the man "as if he were dead." Therefore, the law spoke of *natural death* and *civil death*. The term *civil death* is not used in modern law, and is of interest today chiefly as a reminder of the harshness of past law. In some U.S. states today, men convicted of serious crimes may lose some rights. Penalties include the loss of the right to vote, to hold public office, or to receive certain licenses. Comparisons are sometimes made between these laws and civil death. HARRY KALVEN, JR.

DEATH CUP. See MUSHROOM (Poisonous Mushrooms).

DEATH OF A SALESMAN. See MILLER, ARTHUR.

DEATH PENALTY. See CAPITAL PUNISHMENT.

DEATH RATE. See BIRTH AND DEATH RATES.

DEATH VALLEY lies in east-central California, near the Nevada border. A group of pioneers named the valley for its desolate desert environment after they crossed it in 1849. It became part of the Death Valley National Monument, set up in 1933.

Death Valley is a deep trough, about 130 miles (209 kilometers) long and from 6 to 14 miles (10 to 23 kilometers) wide. The lowest elevation in the Western Hemisphere is near Badwater in Death Valley. It lies 282 feet (86 meters) below sea level. The Panamint Mountains stand west of the valley. Telescope Peak in the Panamint range is 11,049 feet (3,368 meters) high. The Amargosa Range, composed of the Grapevine, Funeral, and Black mountains, rises to the east.

The valley is a block in the earth's surface, dropped down by faults which form its east and west walls. *Faults* occur when the earth's crust breaks and slips into

DEATH VALLEY

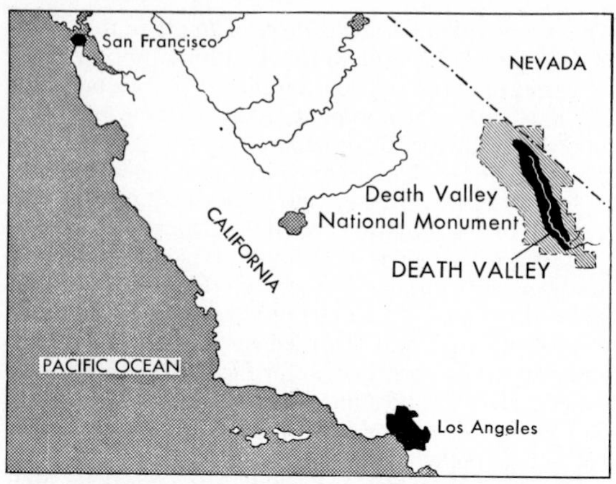

Death Valley lies in east-central California. Its Badwater area, *below,* includes the lowest land in the Western Hemisphere.

National Park Service

various positions. Erosion of the steep cliffs has formed beautiful canyons. In the northern part of the Valley is Ubehebe Crater, a small volcano on the west side fault. Flows of lava issue from the faults in the southern part of Death Valley.

During glacial times, the climate was moister, and a large lake occupied Death Valley. Today, rainfall averages about 2 inches (5 centimeters) a year there. The highest temperature ever recorded in the United States, 134° F. (57° C), was reported there on July 10, 1913. Summer temperatures of 125° F. (52° C) are common. The valley's geological attractions and warm winter sunshine have made it a popular winter-resort area. Plants include the creosote bush, desert holly, and mesquite. Wildlife includes bobcats, coyotes, foxes, rats, rabbits, reptiles, and squirrels.

Borax deposits were discovered in Death Valley in 1873. Actual mining began in the early 1880's, and famous 20-mule teams hauled the borax out of the valley. Prospectors also discovered copper, gold, lead, and silver in the nearby mountains. Mining towns sprang up around Death Valley, with such colorful names as Bullfrog, Greenwater, Rhyolite, and Skidoo. The towns died when the ores were exhausted. Today only cluttered debris remains.

JOHN W. REITH

DEATH VALLEY NATIONAL MONUMENT is in California and Nevada. It is a desert of scenic, scientific, and historical interest. The valley contains the lowest point in the Western Hemisphere (282 feet, or 86 meters, below sea level) near Badwater. The 2,067,790-acre (836,800-hectare) monument was established in 1933.

See also DEATH VALLEY (map).

DEATH'S-HEAD MOTH is a large *hawk*, or *sphinx*, moth with a thick, hairy body. Many superstitions arose because of the skull-like pattern on its body. The moth lives in Africa and southern Europe, and adults often migrate to northern Europe. They enter beehives to eat honey and may squeak loudly when disturbed. The caterpillar is bright-yellow with violet stripes and blue spots. It feeds on the leaves of potato plants.

Scientific Classification. The death's-head moth belongs to the family *Sphingidae*. It is genus *Acherontia*, species *A. atropos.*

ALEXANDER B. KLOTS

See also HAWK MOTH.

DEATHWATCH is a name given to several kinds of small brownish beetles that have the odd habit of knocking their heads against wood. This action produces a peculiar ticking or rapping sound. Superstitious people sometimes believe that the rapping, heard in the quiet of the night, foretells death in the house. The beetles burrow into furniture and woodwork and are often very destructive. The "drugstore beetle," which feasts on drugs stored in shops, is also called deathwatch.

Scientific Classification. The deathwatch is in the order *Coleoptera*. It belongs to the family *Anobiidae*. It is genus *Xestobium*, species *X. rufovillosum.*

H. H. ROSS

DE BAKEY, MICHAEL ELLIS (1908-), an American surgeon, won fame for his work with the heart and for his development of techniques to replace damaged blood vessels. He pioneered in giving a patient an *assisting heart*. This machine is inserted into the chest. It helps a weak heart pump blood until either the heart recovers or surgeons transplant another person's heart. De Bakey has also worked on the development of an artificial heart.

Wide World Photos, Inc.

Michael E. De Bakey

De Bakey became the first person to surgically repair an *aneurysm*, a condition in which the wall of a blood vessel weakens and balloons out. He replaced the weakened part of the vessel with another blood vessel (see ANEURYSM). He later developed artificial blood vessels made of Dacron.

De Bakey was born in Lake Charles, La., and earned an M.D. from Tulane University in 1932. He became head of the Department of Surgery at Baylor University in 1948 and president of the Baylor College of Medicine in 1969.

ISAAC ASIMOV

DEBATE is a series of formal spoken arguments for and against a definite proposal.

A debate differs from a discussion, though both are fundamental activities in a democracy. *Discussion* is the process by which a problem is recognized and investigated and then solutions explored. *Debate* is the process by which the best solution (in propositions of policy) or appraisal (in propositions of fact) is approved and adopted. Discussion begins with a problem, but debate begins with a proposed solution to a problem. A typical discussion might be, "What is wrong with student activities at Main High School?" Suppose this discussion were held, and the decision was that student activities were not properly guided. A debate could then be held. To select the best solution to the problem of guidance, a logical subject for the debate might be, "Resolved, that a combined student-faculty board should be established to control all student activities of Main High School."

The Formal Debate. In formal debating, the same number of persons speak for each side. They have the opportunity to reply directly to opposing speakers. Affirmative and negative speakers usually alternate, and all the speeches are limited in time. In informal (as in conversation) and in legislative debating, though there is the same opportunity to reply to opposing speakers, the speeches are not necessarily limited in time. There may be no attempt to alternate opposing speakers, and there may not be the same number of speakers on each side.

Propositions. Subjects for debates are expressed in the form of propositions. A proposition is a carefully worded statement that makes clear the positions of both the affirmative and negative sides.

Propositions should be:

(1) Appropriate to the knowledge, experience, and interests of both speakers and audience.

(2) Debatable—that is, not obviously true or false. The statements should involve an honest difference of opinion, with arguments and evidence on both sides.

(3) Phrased in the affirmative. Positive statements prevent confusion by making the issue clear-cut.

(4) Restricted to set forth only one idea. This policy keeps the debate within narrow limits.

(5) Worded clearly. The words should be ones that can be defined exactly, so the debate does not become a mere quibble over the meaning of words.

(6) Worded in such a way that they do not assume to be true. The following would be a proposition to avoid, "Resolved, that the inefficient committee system of Congress should be reorganized." The word *inefficient* would bring on a flood of arguments that could confuse the real debate issue.

There are two kinds of propositions: (1) those involving fact and (2) those involving policy.

Propositions of fact try to answer the question, "Is this true?" Examples are:

"Resolved, that the expenditures of the advertising department of the XYZ Manufacturing Company during the last year were wasteful."

"Resolved, that television soap operas have beneficial effects on listeners."

"Resolved, that John Jones did a good job as president of the student council."

Propositions of policy attempt to answer the question, "Should we change?" Examples of such propositions are:

"Resolved, that treaties should be ratified by a majority vote in both houses of Congress."

"Resolved, that uniform marriage and divorce laws should be adopted by the federal government."

"Resolved, that the United States should abolish the Electoral College and adopt a system that would provide for the election of the President by direct popular vote."

Other Good Debate Subjects might be:

(1) The President of the United States should be elected for one term of six years and should be ineligible for re-election.

(2) The President of the United States should have the power to veto items in appropriation bills.

(3) Trial by jury should be abolished in criminal cases.

(4) The city of ------ should adopt the city-manager form of government.

(5) States should adopt single-house legislatures.

(6) The federal government should be in charge of the total financing of elementary and secondary education.

(7) The United Nations should be granted more power to settle international problems.

(8) Labor unions should be required to incorporate.

(9) Social fraternities in high schools should be abolished.

(10) The federal government should own and operate all radio and television broadcasting stations.

(11) The city of ------ should own and operate its electric light and power plant.

(12) The state of ------ should provide 1,000 college scholarships each year for promising high school graduates.

(13) Capital punishment should be abolished.

(14) The United States and the British Commonwealth should establish joint citizenship for their citizens.

(15) The members of the Cabinet should be required to defend their departments on the floors of Congress.

(16) National governments should be replaced by membership in a world government.

(17) Spectator sports in high school and college should be abolished.

(18) All high schools should require a four-year course in the basic sciences.

Analysis. After a subject has been selected and the proposition carefully worded, the next step is analysis of the proposition by both debating teams. Analysis of the proposition begins with a broad understanding of it. Each member of a team should know as much about the opponents' case as he knows about his own side. Good debaters study the origin and history of a proposition, define its terms, and survey carefully all the arguments and evidence for and against it. After a broad understanding is gained, the debaters have to decide which arguments are *pertinent* (closely related and worthy of being included) and which are *irrelevant* (not closely related, and should be excluded). The areas of agreement and disagreement in the proposition are located by this process. The arguments are narrowed down to points on which the affirmative says "yes" and the negative says "no." This argumentative process is called *finding the issues.*

The Issues. The chief points of difference between the affirmative and the negative are the *main issues.* These may have divisions called *subordinate issues.* There must be a clash of opinion on both the main and the subordinate issues. A good way to help find the issues is to list the opposing arguments in parallel columns. In the subject, "Resolved, that the United States should abolish the Electoral College and adopt a system that would provide for the election of the President by direct popular vote," this process might lead to the following main and subordinate issues:

I. Would electing the President by direct popular vote correct flaws in the present system?
  A. Would it be more democratic and give each voter an equal voice in choosing the winner?
  B. Would it assure that the candidate with the most votes is elected?
  C. If no candidate receives a majority of the votes, would this system reduce the chances of political deals and an electoral crisis?

II. Would electing the President by direct popular vote have disadvantages?
  A. Would it weaken the power of the small states and threaten the federal system?
  B. Would it encourage the formation of small political parties and make it difficult for the winner to receive a majority of the votes?
  C. Would it reduce the power of minority groups to influence an election?

The Evidence. After the issues have been determined, the next step for the debaters is to find the evidence that will prove the issue true or false. Evidence can be in the form of either facts or opinions. *Facts* are actual occurrences or things that can be proved to exist. They may be made plain by means of comparisons, description, examples, narration, statistics, testimony, and visual aids. *Opinions* are interpretations of facts, and appraisals of the views of others. Only the opinions of experts on the particular subject should be given in a debate.

Rebuttal. After the issues have been determined and the evidence selected, the next step is to prepare to answer the arguments and evidence of the other team. The debaters must select the arguments and evidence of their opponents that they believe can be successfully attacked. Then they must prepare their own arguments and their own evidence that will make up the attack.

Several Types of Debates are used in high schools and colleges. In the *traditional* form of debate, there are two or three speakers on each side, each of whom makes both a *constructive* speech and a *rebuttal* speech. With two speakers on each side, the order of speaking is:

Constructive Speeches (eight minutes each)
1. First affirmative
2. First negative
3. Second affirmative
4. Second negative

Rebuttal Speeches (four minutes each)
1. First negative
2. First affirmative
3. Second negative
4. Second affirmative

Another type of debate is the *cross-examination* form, which was developed at the University of Oregon. Each constructive speaker is cross-examined by an opposing speaker. Then each side presents a rebuttal and a *summary*. Most teams consist of two speakers. However, a third speaker is sometimes used on each team to present the rebuttal and summary. With three speakers on each side, the order of speaking is:

Constructive Speeches (eight minutes) and **Cross-Examinations** (four minutes)
1. First affirmative
2. Cross-examination by second negative
3. First negative
4. Cross-examination by first affirmative
5. Second affirmative
6. Cross-examination by first negative
7. Second negative
8. Cross-examination by second affirmative

Rebuttal and Summary Speeches (eight minutes)
1. Third negative
2. Third affirmative

The Decision. If a decision is to be given in a debate, one or more judges listen to the speakers on both sides. Then each judge decides which team has presented the most convincing argument and votes for that team. The team with the most votes wins. W. HAYES YEAGER

See also ORATORS AND ORATORY; PARLIAMENTARY PROCEDURE; PUBLIC SPEAKING; LOGIC; LINCOLN, ABRAHAM (picture: Lincoln-Douglas Debates).

DEBENTURE BOND. See BOND.

DEBORAH was a Biblical prophetess of Israel in the period of the Judges, the 1100's B.C. She was the wife of Lapidoth. She acted as an adviser to her people, and as a judge in their disputes. She was admired for her wisdom, and rose to a position of leadership.

When she heard of the cruel treatment her people had received from the Canaanites, Deborah summoned Barak, the Israelite leader. Together they worked out a plan of action for the army of Israel. They hoped to defeat the Canaanite army under Sisera. They fought near Mount Tabor, on the plain of Esdraelon. A rainstorm aided Israel, turning the plain into mud and trapping the enemy chariots. Sisera fled on foot, and was later murdered in his sleep. The victory was important in Israel's struggle with the Canaanites. One of the most notable victory odes of the Bible is the *Song of Deborah* in Judges 5. WALTER G. WILLIAMS

DEBRÉ, *deh BRAY,* **MICHEL JEAN PIERRE** (1912-), served as prime minister of France from 1959 to 1962. In 1963, he was elected to the National Assembly, a branch of Parliament. Debré was appointed minister of economy and finances in 1966, and held that office until 1968. He was minister of foreign affairs in 1968 and 1969. He was named defense minister in 1969.

Debré served under French President Charles de Gaulle in the temporary government that was set up during World War II. Debré was a member of the Senate from 1948 to 1958. After De Gaulle came to power in 1958, he appointed Debré minister of justice. Debré helped write a constitution which provided for a strong presidency. Debré was born in Paris.

DEBRECEN, *DEH breh tsen* (pop. 155,122), is a commercial and industrial city in eastern Hungary. It serves as a market for nearby farming areas. For location, see HUNGARY (map). Debrecen became a major center of Protestantism in the 1500's and was called the *Calvinist Rome*. Lajos Kossuth proclaimed Hungarian independence there in 1849. In 1944, during World War II, Hungary's provisional government met in Debrecen. Places of interest in the city include an art gallery, a museum, and a university. GEORGE BARANY

DE BROGLIE, *duh BROH glih,* **LOUIS VICTOR** (1892-), PRINCE DE BROGLIE, is a French theoretical physicist, famous for his wave theory. He received the Nobel prize in physics in 1929 for his discovery of the wave nature of the electron. Arthur Compton showed that X rays might behave as waves or particles. De Broglie suggested in 1923 that any material particle should have wave properties. He related the wave length of a particle to its mass in an important equation.

Born in Dieppe, France, De Broglie was educated in Paris and became professor of physics at the Faculté des Sciences, Paris, in 1932. In 1944, he became a member of the French Academy. RALPH E. LAPP

See also COMPTON; QUANTUM THEORY; WAVES.

DEBS, EUGENE VICTOR (1855-1926), was a colorful and eloquent spokesman for the American labor movement and for socialism. He formed the American Railway Union (A.R.U.) in 1893 as an industrial union for all railroad workers regardless of their craft. The A.R.U. ordered its members not to move Pullman cars in 1894, in support of a strike by the workers making Pullman cars. President Grover Cleveland used federal troops to break the strike, charging that it interfered with the mails. Debs went to prison for six months when he refused to comply with a federal court injunction. He came out of jail a confirmed socialist.

Debs made a speech condemning war during World War I. He was convicted under the Espionage Law and went to prison in 1918, on a 10-year sentence. President Warren G. Harding commuted his sentence on Christmas Day in 1921.

Debs ran for the presidency as a socialist candidate five times. He was the nominee of the Social Democratic Party in 1900, and of the Socialist Party in 1904, 1908, 1912, and 1920. Debs ran his 1920 campaign while still in prison, and received nearly 1 million votes. He wrote *Walls and Bars,* a book dealing with prison conditions and problems.

U&U
Eugene V. Debs

Debs was born in Terre Haute, Ind., and went to work in the railroad shops at the age of 15. Later he became a locomotive fireman, and was active in the Brotherhood of Locomotive Firemen. He served as national secretary and treasurer of the Brotherhood from 1880 to 1893. Debs served in the Indiana legislature from 1885 to 1892. JACK BARBASH

DEBT, *det,* is anything owed, especially a sum of money which one person owes to another. The law states that a debt is *all that is due a man under any form of obligation or promise.* A person who owes a debt is called a *debtor,* and the one to whom it is owed is the *creditor.* If the debtor is unwilling or unable to pay the debt, the creditor may bring suit to recover his money. Such a suit brought by one citizen against another is a *civil suit.* If the court finds that the debt is owed, the creditor obtains a *judgment* against the debtor. Then if the debtor fails to pay, the creditor may appeal to the sheriff for an *execution* of judgment. This gives the creditor the right to seize enough property of the debtor to pay the debt and the costs of the process. But there are exceptions as to what may be seized by the creditor. This law varies in different states, provinces, and territories.

Time Limits on Collection of Debts. The courts ordinarily state that a debtor should pay his debts, even though the creditor does not demand payment. But if the creditor makes no effort to collect the money within a certain number of years, the debt becomes *outlawed* by a *statute of limitations.*

Penalties for Debts. In ancient times, a debtor was handed over to the mercy of his creditors to become a slave. This was true in Greece and Rome, among the Hebrews, and among the Saxons in England. During feudal times, however, every man was first of all a soldier, and armies would have broken up if overlords jailed their men for the debts they owed.

As feudalism declined, and trade and industry rose, harsh treatment of debtors was revived. Prison terms were the usual punishment, and thus no money was recovered. Early American settlers included many fugitives from debtors' prisons. JAMES B. LUDTKE

Related Articles in WORLD BOOK include:

Attachment	Encumbrance	Guaranty	Moratorium
Bankrupt	Garnishment	I.O.U.	National Debt
Bond			

DEBT, NATIONAL. See NATIONAL DEBT.

DEBUSSY, *dehb yoo SEE,* **CLAUDE** (1862-1918), was an important French composer. His revolutionary treatment of musical form and harmony helped change the direction of music in the 1900's.

Culver
Claude Debussy

Debussy felt closer to painters and poets than to other musicians, and he acknowledged the influence of literature and painting on his music. He based one of his best-known orchestral works, *Prelude to the Afternoon of a Faun,* on a poem by the French symbolist poet Stéphane Mallarmé. Debussy also wrote such vividly descriptive works as *La Mer* (*The Sea*). His *Suite Bergamasque* for piano includes the famous piece "Clair de Lune" ("Moonlight").

Achille Claude Debussy was born in St.-Germain-en-Laye. He entered the Paris Conservatory at the age of 11 and studied there for 11 years. In 1884, Debussy won the Rome Prize, the highest award a young French composer can receive. During the next several years, he established himself in the musical life of Paris as a composer and music critic. His best-known works of the late 1800's include *String Quartet in G minor* (1893), *Prelude to the Afternoon of a Faun* (1894), and three *Nocturnes* (1899) for orchestra.

The turning point in Debussy's career came in 1902 with the première of his opera *Pelléas and Mélisande.* This work caused much controversy because of its unconventional style and mysterious atmosphere. Debussy wrote the opera as a series of short scenes that end without climaxes. He eliminated opportunities for brilliant singing and instead closely followed patterns of natural speech.

The immediate success of *Pélleas and Mélisande* began a productive period for Debussy. His works during the next 15 years introduced new ideas in musical structure and *tonality*, the relationships among various notes. During this period, Debussy composed such masterpieces as *La Mer* (1905) and *Images* (1912) for orchestra, two books of *Preludes* (1910, 1913) for piano, and several sets of songs.

In 1909, Debussy suffered the first symptoms of cancer. He died of the disease nine years later. Probably because of his illness, he began working at a much slower pace. He started some operas and other large-scale projects but could not finish them.

From 1913 to 1917, Debussy wrote in a severe classical style. These later compositions include music for the ballet *Games* (1912), 12 Études for piano (1915), and 3 sonatas (1915, 1917). For many years, critics ranked these later works below Debussy's previous compositions. Today, however, Debussy's final works are widely admired and have had a great influence on later composers. JOSEPH BLOCH

DEBYE, *duh BY*, **PETER JOSEPH WILLIAM** (1884-1966), a Dutch physicist and chemist, won the 1936 Nobel prize in chemistry for his studies of molecular structure. He was born in Maastricht, The Netherlands, and attended engineering school at Aachen, Germany. He served as chairman of the Cornell University chemistry department from 1940 to 1950. CARL T. CHASE

DECAGRAM. See METRIC SYSTEM (table).

DECAL, or DECALCOMANIA, *dee KAL koh MAY nih uh*, is the process of transferring words, pictures, and designs from specially prepared paper to glass, metal, plastics, wood, or other surfaces. The word *decal* is also used for the item transferred. Many decals have an adhesive surface that is exposed after their paper backing is removed. They can be applied directly to an object. Some decals are coated with an adhesive that loosens in water. They are dipped in water and then slid from the paper onto the desired surface. The adhesive dries and makes them stick.

Decals were developed in Germany in the 1800's, and first used on dinnerware. With them, an artist could draw his design and have a printing press produce copies of it, instead of painting it by hand on every dish.

Today, manufacturers of toys and dishes put decals on their products. Decals are used as tax stamps and for automobile-licensing stickers, because they are difficult to remove and use again. Many products have decal signs and trademarks. Decals also are used to mark instrument dials in airplanes. JOHN B. CALKIN

DECALITER. See METRIC SYSTEM (table).

DECALOGUE. See TEN COMMANDMENTS.

DECAMERON. See BOCCACCIO, GIOVANNI.

DECAMETER. See METRIC SYSTEM (table).

DECATHLON, *dee KATH lahn*, is a two-day contest in 10 events to determine an all-around track and field champion. Athletes compete in the 100-meter dash, long jump, 16-pound (7.26-kilogram) shot-put, high jump, and 400-meter run, in that order, on the first day. They try the 110-meter hurdles, discus throw, pole vault, javelin throw, and 1,500-meter run on the second day. The athletes compete against established time and distance standards, instead of against each other. Up to 1,000 points can be won for each event. The athlete winning the most points in all 10 events wins the decathlon.

The Amateur Athletic Union (AAU) holds an annual decathlon event. The decathlon became a part of the Olympic Games in 1912.

Seven U.S. athletes have won the Olympic decathlon title. Harold Osborn won in 1924; James Bausch in 1932; Glenn Morris in 1936; Bob Mathias in 1948 and 1952; Milton Campbell in 1956; Rafer Johnson in 1960; and Bill Toomey in 1968. FRED RUSSELL

See also TRACK AND FIELD (The Decathlon; table).

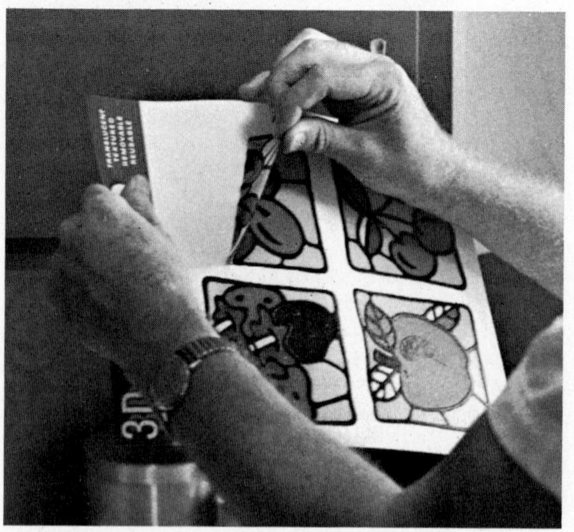

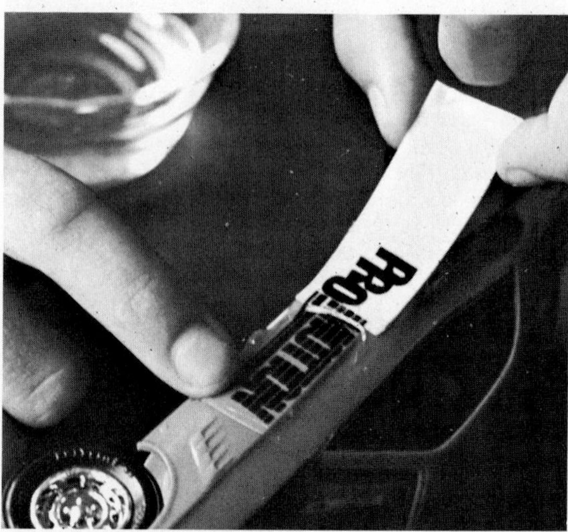

WORLD BOOK photos

Decals provide an easy way to decorate many items in the home. Some decals have a sticky coating, *left*, and can be applied directly to a surface. Other decals must first be soaked in water. Then the backing is slid off while the decal is pressed into place, *right*.

DECATUR, Ill. (pop. 90,397; met. area 125,010), is an industrial city located in a rich farming region. Decatur lies about 40 miles (64 kilometers) east of Springfield and about 170 miles (274 kilometers) southwest of Chicago (see ILLINOIS [political map]). Its major industries process soybeans, make corn products, and build tractors and motor graders. It also has the repair shops of the Norfolk and Western Railway, and iron and brass foundries. Other factories make carburetors, compressors, kites, pharmaceuticals, phonographs, pumps, store and restaurant fixtures, and water and gas systems. Decatur was settled about 1830. The Grand Army of the Republic was founded there in 1866. The city is the home of Millikin University. Decatur has a council-manager government. PAUL M. ANGLE

DECATUR, STEPHEN (1779-1820), was one of the most daring officers in the United States Navy during its early years. He is remembered for his toast: "Our country: In her intercourse with foreign nations may she always be right; but our country, right or wrong." Handsome, brave, and honorable, Decatur enjoyed great popularity with his men and with the public. He was one of a group of men who established the naval traditions of the United States. Others were John Barry, John Paul Jones, David Porter, Oliver Hazard Perry, Thomas Macdonough, and Isaac Hull.

Decatur was born in a log cabin in Sinepuxent, Md., on Jan. 5, 1779. He made his first long voyage at the age of 8, when he went to France on a ship commanded by his father, a merchant captain. He became a midshipman in 1798 during the naval war with France, and rose to lieutenant in 1799. Given command of the *Enterprise* during the war with Tripoli, he captured an enemy vessel that was renamed the *Intrepid.* In this ship he led a picked band into Tripoli Harbor on the night of Feb. 16, 1804, and set fire to the frigate *Philadelphia,* once commanded by his father, which the Tripoli pirates had captured. Not a man was killed and only one was wounded. The English Admiral Horatio Nelson called this exploit, "the most bold and daring act of the age." Because of it, Decatur won a sword from Congress and a captaincy when he was only 25.

Stephen Decatur stands victoriously on the deck of a man-of-war after successfully forcing Algiers to sign a peace treaty.

Portrait by Alonzo Chappel, Chicago Historical Society

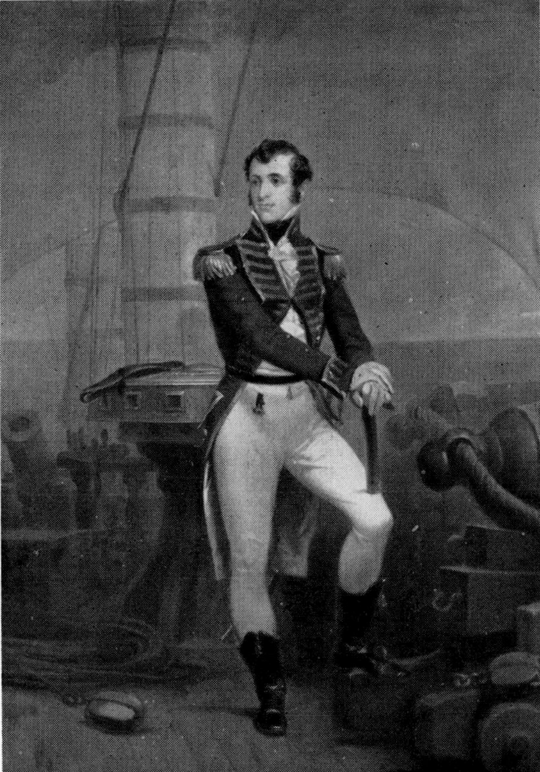

Commanding a squadron of three ships in the War of 1812, he captured the British frigate *Macedonian* after a desperate struggle. He became a commodore in 1813, and took command of a squadron in New York Harbor. He attempted to run the British blockade early in 1815, but his flagship, the *President,* struck the bar at Sandy Hook and was damaged. He was forced into a fight against heavy odds. Wounded, he had to surrender. The British sent him to Bermuda as a prisoner of war, but he was soon released.

He next sailed against Algiers, Tunis, and Tripoli, where he forced the rulers to release United States ships and prisoners and to stop molesting U.S. vessels. On his return he became a navy commissioner. Suspended Commodore James Barron, at whose court-martial Decatur had presided, challenged him to a duel in 1820. Decatur was killed by the commodore near Bladensburg, Md. Barron had accused certain officers, headed by Decatur, of persecuting him. BRADFORD SMITH

See also BARRON, JAMES.

DECAY may be understood by what happens to a piece of raw meat left on a dish in a warm room for a week or more. Bacteria, molds, and yeasts grow in and on the meat and *decompose,* or digest, it. The waste products of their growth remain as "decayed meat." Fruits and vegetables may also decay in the same manner.

When the decomposing substances are proteins, such as meat, fish, eggs, and cheese, bad-smelling gases are produced. *Hydrogen sulfide,* for example, is a bad-smelling gas of rotten eggs. Decay is aided by warmth and moisture, because bacteria grow well under these conditions. Decay sometimes is called *putrefaction.*

The bacteria causing decay are found in soil, air, water, manure, milk, and many other places. They are usually harmless and do good by decomposing manure and dead animals and plants. The waste products (products of decay) are of value as fertilizers.

If bacteria in foods are killed, as by baking or stewing, decay is prevented. Refrigeration retards the growth of bacteria. Decay and food spoilage by bacteria does not take place rapidly in refrigerators. Disinfectants such as carbolic acid stop the progress of decay because they destroy bacteria. MARTIN FROBISHER, JR.

Related Articles in WORLD BOOK include:

Antiseptic	Decomposition	Pasteur, Louis
Bacteria	Fermentation	Ptomaine Poisoning
Biochemistry	Food Preservation	Teeth

DECAY SERIES. See ISOTOPE (Radioactive Isotopes).

DECCAN. See INDIA (Land Regions; picture).

DECELERATION. See ACCELERATION; MOTION (Velocity and Acceleration).

DECEMBER

DECEMBER is the twelfth and last month of the year. It was the tenth month in the ancient Roman calendar. The first part of its name, *decem*, means *ten* in Latin. December once had 29 days, but Julius Caesar added two more, making it one of the longest months.

Winter begins in December in the northern half of the world. Some people call it "the frosty month." But winter does not begin until December 21 or 22, and most of December is usually warmer than other winter months. On the first day of winter, the sun reaches the solstice, when it appears to have gone farthest south. In the Northern Hemisphere, it is the shortest day of the year. But it is the longest day in the southern half of the world. The latter part of December has long been a holiday season. The Romans honored Saturn, the god of harvest, with a festival called *Saturnalia*. Today, Christmas is the chief holiday of the month in many countries. Christians celebrate it as the birthday of Jesus Christ, and its color and good feeling shed a glow of good will over the rest of the month. The Druids of northern Europe used mistletoe in a December festival. We still use mistletoe at Christmas.

Activities. In the Northern Hemisphere, most birds have gone to warmer climates. But many animals are active. Mink, ermine, beavers, and foxes grow beautiful coats of fur. Muskrats make their domed homes of ice in frozen streams and ponds. Nature finishes preparing for the long winter ahead. Many people make feeding places for birds and squirrels.

Special Days. People celebrate many holidays in December. They prepare for New Year's Eve parties on the last day of December. Some people in New England observe December 21 as Forefathers' Day in honor of the landing of the Pilgrims at Plymouth on Dec. 21, 1620. People in several European countries celebrate December 6 as the Feast of Saint Nicholas. Many of them exchange gifts on that day. Saint Nicholas is also a patron saint in Greece, Russia, and some other countries.

After Christmas day on December 25, some Christian

IMPORTANT DECEMBER EVENTS

2 Battle of Austerlitz fought between France and the combined forces of Austria and Russia, 1805.
—President Monroe proclaimed the Monroe Doctrine in his message to Congress, 1823.
—Georges Seurat, French painter, born 1859.
—John Brown, American abolitionist, hanged at Charles Town, Va. (now W. Va.), 1859.
—Scientists achieved the first controlled atomic chain reaction, in Chicago, 1942.

VAN BUREN

JOHNSON

WILSON

3 Gilbert Stuart, American painter, born 1755.
—Illinois admitted to the Union, 1818.
—George B. McClellan, Union general, born 1826.
—Novelist Joseph Conrad born 1857.
—First human heart transplant performed by Christiaan Barnard, South African surgeon, 1967.
4 Thomas Carlyle, Scottish author, born 1795.
5 Phi Beta Kappa, honorary scholastic fraternity, founded at the College of William and Mary, 1776.
—Martin Van Buren, eighth President of the United States, born at Kinderhook, N.Y., 1782.
—Walt Disney, American producer of animated cartoons and other motion pictures, born 1901.
—Amendment 21 to the United States Constitution, repealing prohibition, proclaimed, 1933.
—The AFL and CIO merged, 1955.
6 Families in Europe celebrate the Feast of St. Nicholas, often exchanging gifts.
—Columbus discovered Hispaniola, 1492.
—Warren Hastings, leader in India, born 1732.
—Dave Brubeck, American jazz pianist, born 1920.
7 Delaware ratified the Constitution, 1787.
—Japanese forces attacked Pearl Harbor, 1941. ▶
8 Horace, Roman poet, born 65 B.C.
—Eli Whitney, inventor of cotton gin, born 1765.
—Jan Sibelius, Finnish composer, born 1865.
—The American Federation of Labor organized, 1886.
9 John Milton, English poet, born 1608.
9 Joel Chandler Harris, American author of the "Uncle Remus" stories, born 1848.
—The British captured Jerusalem, 1917.
10 William Lloyd Garrison, American journalist and abolitionist, born 1805.
—Mississippi admitted to the Union, 1817.
—Composer César Franck born 1822.
—Emily Dickinson, American poet, born 1830.
—The Territory of Wyoming authorized women to vote and hold office, 1869.
—Spain ceded Philippines to the United States, 1898.
—President Theodore Roosevelt awarded Nobel peace prize for mediation in the Russo-Japanese War, 1906.
11 Hector Berlioz, French composer, born 1803.
—Indiana admitted to the Union, 1816.
—Robert Koch, German bacteriologist, born 1843.
—Edward VIII of Great Britain abdicated, 1936.
12 John Jay, American diplomat, born 1745.
—Pennsylvania ratified the Constitution, 1787.
—Gustave Flaubert, French novelist, born 1821.
—Guglielmo Marconi received the first radio signal sent across the Atlantic Ocean, from England to Newfoundland, 1901.
13 The Council of Trent opened, 1545.
—Sir Francis Drake left England to sail around the world, attacking Spanish possessions, 1577.
—Heinrich Heine, German poet, born 1797.
14 Tycho Brahe, Danish astronomer, born 1546.
—George Washington died at Mt. Vernon, 1799.
—Alabama admitted to the Union, 1819.
—James Doolittle, American air pioneer and air force general, born 1896.
—Roald Amundsen, Norwegian explorer, reached the South Pole, 1911.
15 The first 10 amendments to the Constitution, including the Bill of Rights, ratified, 1791. ▼

churches observe the Feast of Saint Stephen on December 26, the Feast of Saint John the Evangelist on December 27, and Holy Innocents' Day on December 28.

Popular Beliefs. A beautiful Bible story tells how the star of Bethlehem guided the wise men to the place where they found the Christ child. The star at the top of a Christmas tree symbolizes this star.

Symbols. Holly, narcissus, and poinsettia are regarded as special December flowers. People in many parts of the world use holly at Christmas celebrations. The turquoise and the zircon are the birthstones for December.

GRACE HUMPHREY

Quotations

'Twas the night before Christmas, when all through the house
Not a creature was stirring, not even a mouse;
The stockings were hung by the chimney with care,
In hopes that St. Nicholas soon would be there;
The children were nestled all snug in their beds,
While visions of sugar-plums danced in their heads.
Clement Clarke Moore

Heap on more wood! The wind is chill;
But let it whistle as it will,
We'll keep our Christmas merry still.
Sir Walter Scott

The sun that brief December day
Rose cheerless over hills of gray,
And, darkly circled, gave at noon
A sadder sight than waning moon.
John Greenleaf Whittier

I heard the bells on Christmas Day
Their old, familiar carols play,
And wild and sweet
The words repeat
Of peace on earth, good will to men.
Henry Wadsworth Longfellow

Related Articles in WORLD BOOK include:

Calendar	Holly	Solstice
Christmas	Nicholas, Saint	Turquoise
Feasts and Festivals	Santa Claus	

IMPORTANT DECEMBER EVENTS

15 Maxwell Anderson, American playwright, born 1888.
15 or 16 Composer Ludwig van Beethoven born 1770.
16 English Parliament passed Bill of Rights, 1689.
—Boston Tea Party, 1773.
—Novelist Jane Austen born 1775.
—Actor-playwright Sir Noel Coward born 1899.
—The Germans began the Battle of the Bulge, 1944.
17 Sir Humphry Davy, English chemist, born 1778.
—John Greenleaf Whittier, American poet, born 1807.
—William Lyon Mackenzie King, three times prime minister of Canada, born 1874.
—Orville Wright made first heavier-than-air flight at Kitty Hawk, N.C., 1903.

U.S. National Museum

—Willard Libby, American chemist, born 1908.
18 Charles Wesley, English clergyman and author of many hymns, born 1707.
—New Jersey ratified the Constitution, 1787.
—Edward Alexander MacDowell, American composer and pianist, born 1861.
—Amendment 13 to the U.S. Constitution, ending slavery, proclaimed, 1865.
—Christopher Fry, British playwright, born 1907.
19 Continental Army camped for the winter at Valley Forge, Pa., 1777.

Newberry Library

—Physicist Albert Michelson born 1852.
20 The United States took over Louisiana, 1803.
—Harvey Firestone, American industrial leader, born 1868.
21 The Pilgrims landed at Plymouth, Mass., 1620.
—Playwright Jean Baptiste Racine born 1639.
—Benjamin Disraeli, twice prime minister of Great Britain, born 1804.
—Joseph Stalin, Russian dictator, born 1879.
22 James Oglethorpe, founder of Georgia, born 1696.
—Opera composer Giacomo Puccini born 1858.
22 Poet Edwin Arlington Robinson born 1869.
23 Richard Arkwright, British inventor, born 1732.
—U.S. Federal Reserve System established, 1913.
24 "Kit" Carson, American frontier scout, born 1809.
—United States and Great Britain signed the Treaty of Ghent, ending the War of 1812, 1814.
—Matthew Arnold, British critic, born 1822.
25 Christmas, celebrated in Christian countries as the birthday of Jesus Christ.

H. Armstrong Roberts

—Isaac Newton, English mathematician who discovered laws of gravitation, born 1642.
—Washington and his men started across the Delaware River to Trenton, N.J., 1776.
—Clara Barton, "Angel of the Battlefield" and founder of the American Red Cross, born 1821.
26 Battle of Trenton, 1776.
—George Dewey, American admiral, born 1837.
27 Johannes Kepler, German astronomer, born 1571.
—Louis Pasteur, French chemist, born 1822.
—Sir Mackenzie Bowell, prime minister of Canada from 1894 to 1896, born 1823.
28 Iowa admitted to the Union, 1846.
29 Woodrow Wilson, 28th President of the United States, born at Staunton, Va., 1856.
—Charles Goodyear, American inventor, born 1800.
—Andrew Johnson, 17th President of the United States, born at Raleigh, N.C., 1808.
—William E. Gladstone, four-time prime minister of Great Britain, born 1809.
—Texas admitted to the Union, 1845.
—American aviator Billy Mitchell born 1879.

Visual Education Service

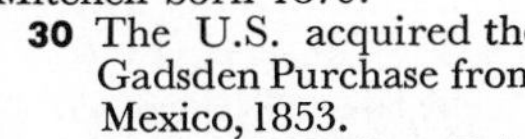

30 The U.S. acquired the Gadsden Purchase from Mexico, 1853.
—Rudyard Kipling, British poet and storyteller, born 1865.
—Andreas Vesalius, the first anatomist to describe the human body completely, born 1514.
—Henri Matisse, French painter, born 1869.

DECEMBRIST UPRISING. See RUSSIA (Alexander I).

DECEMVIRS, *dee SEHM vurz,* means a commission of 10 members. The term usually refers to the group set up in 451 B.C. to write out the laws of the Roman Republic. These laws were arranged and recorded in the Ten Tables. Two more tables were added by another commission in 450 B.C. Members of the second commission refused to resign when their one-year term was completed. They were overthrown by the army and the people of Rome in 449 B.C. HERBERT M. HOWE

See also TWELVE TABLES, LAWS OF THE.

DECENTRALIZATION. See CENTRALIZATION.

DECIBEL, *DEHS ih bell,* is the unit used to measure the intensity of a sound. A decibel is a tenth of a larger unit, the *bel,* which was named for Alexander Graham Bell, the inventor of the telephone.

The decibel is not the unit of loudness. Loudness is often measured in *phons,* which depend on both the intensity and the *frequency* (number of vibrations per second) of sound (see PHON).

The intensity of a sound depends on the energy it produces. The energy of sound is usually given in watts per square centimeter (see WATT). A sound of 0 decibels transmits 10^{-16} watts to each square centimeter of the ear. As a decimal fraction, this energy is written 0.0000000000000001 watts. Zero decibels is about the least intensity of sound that the normal ear can hear. A sound of 10 decibels (1 bel) transmits ten times as much energy as a 0 decibel sound. A sound of 20 decibels transmits a hundred times as much energy as a 0 decibel sound and ten times as much as a 10 decibel sound. Ordinary speech measures approximately 60 decibels. JOHN W. RENNER

See also SOUND (Measuring Sound).

DECIDUOUS TREE, *dee SID yoo us,* is the name for any tree which loses its leaves at a certain time each year and later grows new leaves. In northern temperate regions, most deciduous trees lose their leaves in the autumn. The twigs and branches stay bare all winter. The following spring the trees grow a new set of green leaves. Before the leaves die, some of the food material they contain is drawn back into the twigs and branches. There it is stored and used the following spring. Deciduous trees usually have broad leaves. Such trees include ash, beech, birch, chestnut, maple, and oak.

Dried leaves continue to hang on the branches of some deciduous trees until the new leaves come out. In warmer climates, deciduous trees leaf out earlier and retain their leaves later in the season.

Scientists think that losing the leaves helps some trees to conserve water in the winter. Water normally passes into the air from tree leaves by a process called *transpiration* (see TRANSPIRATION).

Scientific Classification. Deciduous trees belong to phylum *Tracheophyta.* They are in both class *Gymnospermae* and class *Angiospermae.* THEODORE W. BRETZ

See also TREE (Broadleaf Trees).

DECILLION, *dee SILL yun,* is a thousand nonillions, or a unit with 33 zeros, in the United States and France. One decillion is written 1,000,000,000,000,000,000,000,000,000,000,000. A decillion is a unit with 60 zeros in Great Britain and Germany.

DECIMAL NUMERAL SYSTEM is the way we express numbers. The name *decimal* comes from the Latin word for *ten.* In this system, we use single number symbols called *numerals,* such as 1, 2, and 3, to express the numbers from one to nine. Then we use two numerals—1 and 0—and two places to express ten. The number 10 is the base of the system. We also write fractions with the decimal numeral system. For example, .6 is $\frac{6}{10}$.

The decimal numeral system is one of the world's most useful ways of expressing numbers. It uses only 10 numerals. A child can learn to write these numerals easily. In ancient Egypt, a child had to learn ∩ for ten, 𓍢 for one hundred, and 𓆼 for one thousand. It is much easier to write 10, 100, and 1,000. We can use the system to express numbers as large or as small as we want. Some Australian tribes count from one to five, and use a word meaning plenty for any number larger than five. We can count in thousands, millions, billions, and larger numbers. And we can express tiny parts of numbers with decimal fraction numerals.

Prehistoric men counted on their fingers. This practice provided a natural base for a number system based on 10. Most civilizations of the ancient world—Egypt, Greece, and Rome—had separate symbols for 10 and 100. The Roman system, which used letters to stand for numbers, remained in use in Europe for many centuries. See ROMAN NUMERALS.

Mathematicians in India invented and developed the zero and the place system probably about A.D. 600. The Arabs borrowed this new decimal system from India in the 700's. European merchants adopted the system from the Arabs, and it began to spread through Europe in the 1200's. Most European countries now use the decimal system in all parts of their arithmetic. The English-speaking countries continue to use some measurements that are not based on a decimal system. For example, the foot is divided into 12 inches.

Learning the Decimal System

Place Value. The decimal numeral system has only nine *digits* (numerals) and *zero* [0]. However, you can express numbers larger than nine with these numerals. For example, you can express the numeral fourteen by using a system of *place value.* You do not need to invent a new symbol for fourteen. You use two digits you already know, 1 and 4.

By counting, you can see that fourteen consists of a group of ten things and a group of four things. You can use 1 to stand for the group of ten things and 4 to stand for the group of four things. You can see that a digit occupies a space or *place* on the page. Two digits together, for example, 25, occupy two places. *You use the first place on the right for single things. You use the second place to the left for groups of ten things.* Here is the way you express sixteen: 16. When you see the numeral 16, you know that it means six single things and one group of ten things. The first place on the right is called *the 1's place.* It is for the numerals from one to nine. The second place to the left is called *the 10's place.* It is for the groups of ten from ten to ninety.

Suppose you want to express the numeral twenty-four. Twenty-four consists of two groups of ten things and four single things. So you must write a 2 in the 10's place and a 4 in the 1's place: 24. When you see the numeral 24, you know that it stands for two groups of

WORLD BOOK photo

The Decimal Numeral System is the most common method of expressing numbers. This student is learning how to add a column of decimal numerals.

ten (or two 10's) and four single things (or four 1's).

Place value means that the *value*, or the number of things for which a digit stands, depends on the place it occupies. In the first place on the right, a 2 means two 1's. In the second place to the left, it means two 10's. Number systems based on numbers other than 10 often help a beginner to understand place value. For example, the binary system uses only two symbols, 0 and 1, and the duodecimal system has a base of 12 (see BINARY ARITHMETIC; DUODECIMAL NUMERALS).

Zero. Most people learn that 10 stands for a group of ten things before they understand place value. Look at the number 10. Zero means *no thing* or *no number*. So zero in the first place on the right means no 1's. The 1 in the second place to the left means one 10, or one group of ten things. Look at the numeral 30. It means three 10's and no 1's. Zero does more than show no thing or no number. *Zero holds a numeral in place*. Without zero, you might mistake 10 for 1 or 30 for 3. This explains why zero is so important in making the decimal numeral system work. See ZERO.

Larger Numbers. Using two places, you can write the numerals from 10 to 99. To write one hundred, you must use the *third* place to the left. Look at the numeral 100. It stands for one group of a hundred things. Because there are no 1's or 10's, you must write zeros in the 1's and 10's places. The 1 in the third place to the left means one group of a hundred things. The two zeros mean no 10's and no 1's. Here are two more examples of three-place numerals:

617 = six 100's, one 10, and seven 1's
403 = four 100's, no 10's and three 1's

You use the fourth place to the left for thousands, the fifth for ten-thousands, and so on. The chart at the top of the next column will help you learn the place values from one to one billion.

Look at the numeral 6,527,308,642. The chart shows you that this numeral means six billions, five hundred-millions, two ten-millions, seven millions, three hundred-thousands, no ten-thousands, eight thousands, six hundreds, four tens, and two ones. When you write such large numerals, set off every three digits with a comma starting at the right and counting to the left. For example, there are three commas within 6,527,308,642. These groups of three digits set off by commas are called *periods*. The names of the periods are shown in the table below. There are no standard names for numbers with periods to the left of vigintillion.

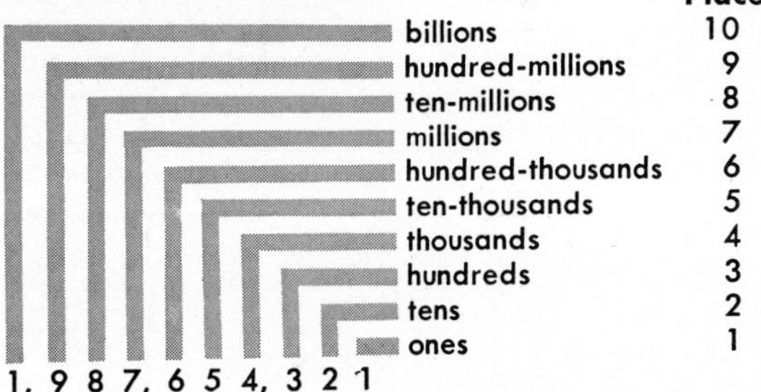

Zeros After Numeral	Name of Numeral	Zeros After Numeral	Name of Numeral
0	———	33	Decillion
3	Thousand	36	Undecillion
6	Million	39	Duodecillion
9	Billion	42	Tredecillion
12	Trillion	45	Quattuordecillion
15	Quadrillion	48	Quindecillion
18	Quintillion	51	Sexdecillion
21	Sextillion	54	Septendecillion
24	Septillion	57	Octodecillion
27	Octillion	60	Novemdecillion
30	Nonillion	63	Vigintillion

DECIMAL NUMERAL SYSTEM

Operations. You should always remember place value when you add, subtract, multiply, or divide numbers. For example, suppose you want to add 32, 18, and 21. First, you write the numerals so there is a column for 1's and a column for 10's.

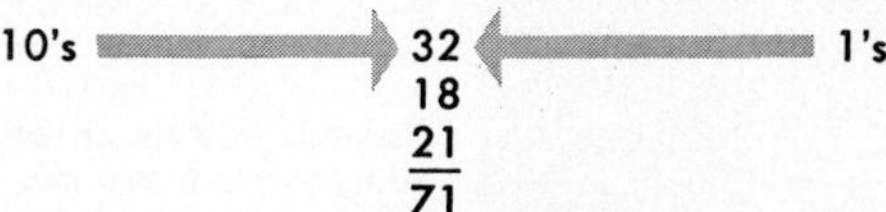

To be correct in arithmetic, you should always keep columns of numerals straight. If you are careless, you may forget whether the numeral with which you are working is a 10, a 100, or a 1,000. If you add the 1's column in the example above, you will find there are eleven 1's and that you must transfer ten 1's to the 10's column. Each operation in arithmetic has a regular method you can learn for transferring numerals from one place to another. See ADDITION (How to Carry); SUBTRACTION (How to Borrow); MULTIPLICATION (How to Carry); DIVISION (Short Division).

Decimal Fractions

Decimal fractions are fractions such as $\frac{1}{10}$, $\frac{1}{100}$, and $\frac{1}{1,000}$ (see FRACTION). You always express decimal fractions *without a denominator* as part of the decimal numeral system. For example, $\frac{25}{100}$ is written .25. In the United States and Canada, everyone deals with decimal fractions when using the system of dollars and cents. The amount $1.25 includes a decimal fraction, because .25 means $\frac{25}{100}$ of a dollar, or 25 cents.

Decimal Places. Look at the fraction $\frac{1}{10}$. Ten $\frac{1}{10}$'s are 1, a whole number. To write $\frac{1}{10}$ as part of the decimal system, place a *decimal point* [.] to the right of the 1's place. The decimal point means that anything to the right of the point is a fraction of 1. *Then the first place to the right of the decimal point is for* $\frac{1}{10}$*'s. Suppose you want to* express $6\frac{2}{10}$, using the decimal system. You write 6 in the 1's place and place a decimal point on its right. Then you write a 2 in the tenths place to the right: 6.2 . Here is the way you express $\frac{9}{10}$: .9 . Places to the right of the decimal point are called *decimal places.*

The second place to the right of the decimal point is for hundredths. Here is the way you express $1\frac{34}{100}$: 1.34 . If you add a dollar sign, 1.34 becomes a dollar and thirty-four cents: $1.34. You will find decimal fractions easier to learn if you think of decimal places in terms of money. Each dime or ten cents is a tenth of one dollar. The dimes are the first place to the right of the decimal point. Each cent, or penny, is a hundredth of one dollar. The cents are the second place to the right of the decimal point.

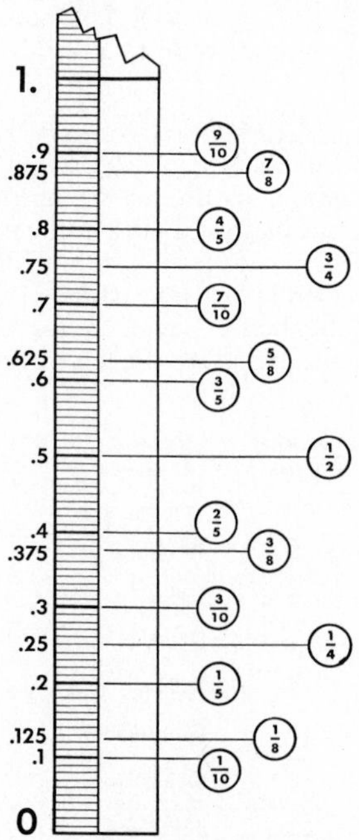

Common Fractions can be written as decimal fractions. The scale shows decimal and common fraction equivalents.

You use zero as a place holder. For example, suppose you want to express $\frac{6}{100}$ as a decimal fraction. The decimal fraction .6 means $\frac{6}{10}$, so you must use a zero to show there are no tenths when you express $\frac{6}{100}$: .06 . Here is the way you express $3\frac{7}{100}$: 3.07 .

You use the third decimal place to the right for thousandths, the fourth for ten-thousandths, and so on. Here is a chart that will help you learn the decimal places from tenths to billionths. Notice that the chart is for fractions, such as tenths and hundredths, and *not* for whole numbers, such as tens and hundreds.

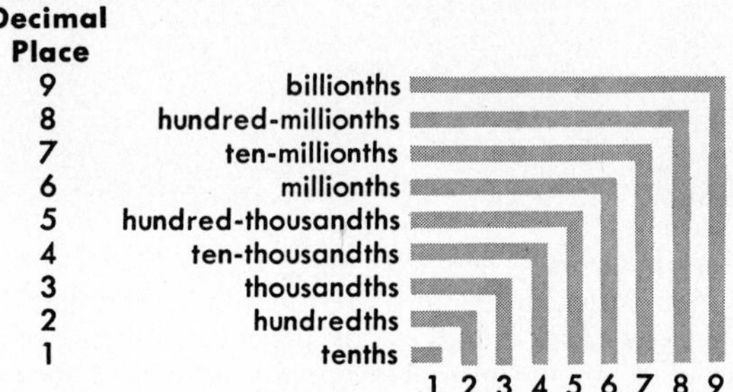

Look at the decimal fraction .0007 . The chart shows you that this is seven ten-thousandths, or $\frac{7}{10,000}$. The zeros in the decimal fraction show that there are no tenths, hundredths, or thousandths.

Changing Fractions. People call fractions such as $\frac{1}{4}$, $\frac{5}{6}$, and $\frac{7}{8}$ *common fractions.* Suppose you want to change $\frac{7}{8}$ to a decimal fraction expressed in thousandths. *To change a common fraction to a decimal fraction, divide the numerator by the denominator.* To change $\frac{7}{8}$ to a decimal fraction, divide 7, the numerator, by 8, the denominator:

$$\begin{array}{r} .875 \\ 8\overline{)7.000} \end{array}$$

First, add a decimal point and as many decimal places (zeros) as necessary to 7, the number being divided. Second, place the decimal point in the *quotient,* or answer, directly above the decimal point in the number being divided. Then complete the division. The common fraction $\frac{7}{8}$ becomes the decimal fraction .875 .

Some common fractions produce *repeating decimal fractions.* Suppose you want to change $\frac{1}{3}$ to a decimal fraction:

$$\begin{array}{r} .333333 \\ 3\overline{)1.000000} \end{array}$$

In a repeating decimal fraction, one digit or a group of digits repeats itself indefinitely. For practical purposes, this means you cannot complete the division. Most people use as many decimal places as necessary for their particular problem and attach a common fraction to the decimal fraction. For example, one choice you can use for $\frac{1}{3}$ is $.33\frac{1}{3}$.

To change a decimal fraction to a common fraction, remove the decimal point and write in the proper denominator. For example, .005 is $\frac{5}{1,000}$, .67 is $\frac{67}{100}$, and .1004 is $\frac{1,004}{10,000}$.

Then, if possible, reduce the fraction. For example, .75 becomes $\frac{75}{100}$, which can be reduced to $\frac{3}{4}$. See FRACTION (Converting and Reducing Fractions).

Rounding Off. When you work with decimal fractions, you must often *round off* your answer. For example, .354 rounded off to the nearest hundredth is .35, because .354 is nearer to .35 than to .36. Similarly, .354 rounded off to the nearest tenth is .4, because .354 is nearer to .4 than to .3. But .365 rounded off to the nearest hundredth is .37. *A number halfway between two values is usually rounded off to the greater value.*

Rounding off is useful in practical problems, particularly in measuring things. But you must be careful about attaching zeros to decimal fractions. When workmen measure things, they often do not make the most precise measurement. Instead, they use the most practical unit. For example, the measurement of a piece of wood might be recorded as .6 of a foot. This does not mean that the piece of wood is .60 or $\frac{60}{100}$ of a foot. It might be .59 or .61 of a foot. So if you wanted to add .6 and, for example, .29, you must either change .29 to .3 or find a more precise measurement for .6.

Operations with Decimal Fractions. You add and subtract decimal fractions just as you do whole numbers. Suppose you want to add 4.63, 5.02, and 4.80. Arrange the numerals so that there are columns for tenths and hundredths as well as for whole numbers.

$$\begin{array}{r} 4.63 \\ 5.02 \\ 4.80 \\ \hline 14.45 \end{array}$$

The decimal point in the answer is placed directly below its position in the columns of numerals for the numbers to be added or subtracted. The decimal point makes no difference in "carrying" or "borrowing" numbers from one place to another. In the example above, the sum of the tenths column is 14 tenths. Fourteen tenths is the same as 1.4, so you write a 4 in the tenths column and "carry" the 1 to the 1's column. The decimal point stays unchanged.

When you multiply exact decimal fractions, the operation itself is the same as the multiplication of whole numbers. But you must learn where to place the decimal point in the product, or answer. *The number of decimal places in the product is the sum of the decimal places in the two numbers multiplied.* Here are two examples:

$$\begin{array}{r} 234.62 \\ \times 2 \\ \hline 469.24 \end{array} \qquad \begin{array}{r} 18.972 \\ \times 3.13 \\ \hline 56916 \\ 1\ 8972 \\ 56\ 916 \\ \hline 59.38236 \end{array}$$

In the example on the left, count the decimal places in the multipliers. There are two: tenths and hundredths in 234.62, and no decimal places in 2. So the product will have two decimal places. Count two places from the right in the product and place the decimal point between the 2 and the 9. Use the same method in the example on the right. In this case, both multipliers include decimal fractions. They contain a total of five decimal places. So the decimal point in the answer appears five places from the right.

There is a regular method for dividing decimal fractions, but you must learn its steps in detail. See DIVISION (Division of Decimal Fractions). LEE E. BOYER

Related Articles in WORLD BOOK include:

Abacus	Division	Multiplication
Addition	Duodecimal Numerals	Numeration Systems
Arithmetic	Fraction	Percentage
Binary Arithmetic	Metric System	Subtraction
Dewey Decimal System		

Practice Decimal Examples

Express the following numbers and decimal fractions.

(1) One hundred, no tens, and six ones.

(2) Three ten-thousands, one thousand, no hundreds, four tens, and four ones.

(3) Seven thousands, no hundreds, two tens, and no ones.

(4) One million, three hundred-thousands, no ten-thousands, six thousands, two hundreds, no tens, and two ones.

(5) Six tenths and two hundredths.

(6) No tenths, no hundredths, and nine thousandths.

(7) No tenths, three hundredths, and two thousandths.

(8) No tenths, no hundredths, no thousandths, four ten-thousandths, and four hundred-thousandths.

Change into decimal fractions.

(9) $\frac{4}{5}$ (10) $\frac{3}{8}$ (11) $\frac{2}{3}$ (12) $\frac{1}{2}$ (13) $\frac{1}{16}$ (14) $\frac{5}{8}$

Change into common fractions.

(15) .40 (16) .02 (17) .125 (18) .875
(19) .175 (20) .003

Place the decimal point in the answer.

(21) $\begin{array}{r} 8.67 \\ +3.22 \\ \hline 1\,1\,8\,9 \end{array}$ (22) $\begin{array}{r} 6.45 \\ -3.31 \\ \hline 3\,1\,4 \end{array}$ (23) $\begin{array}{r} 7.28 \\ \times .3 \\ \hline 2\,1\,8\,4 \end{array}$ (24) $\begin{array}{r} 4\,3\,2 \\ 10\overline{)4\,3\,2.0} \end{array}$

Answers to the Practice Examples

(1) 106	(7) .032	(13) .0625	(19) $\frac{7}{40}$
(2) 31,044	(8) .00044	(14) .625	(20) $\frac{3}{1,000}$
(3) 7,020	(9) .8 or .80	(15) $\frac{2}{5}$	(21) 11.89
(4) 1,306,202	(10) .375	(16) $\frac{1}{50}$	(22) 3.14
(5) .62	(11) $.66\frac{2}{3}$	(17) $\frac{1}{8}$	(23) 2.184
(6) .009	(12) .5 or .50	(18) $\frac{7}{8}$	(24) 43.2

DECIMAL SYSTEM. See DECIMAL NUMERAL SYSTEM.

DECIMETER. See METRIC SYSTEM.

DECIPHER. See CODES AND CIPHERS.

DECK TENNIS is a game similar to tennis, in which the players use a 6-inch (15-centimeter) rope or rubber ring instead of racket and ball. They toss the ring back and forth over a net that is 4 feet 8 inches (1.4 meters) high. There is a 3-foot (0.91-meter) neutral zone on each side of the net. The court is 40 feet (12 meters) long and 18 feet (5.5 meters) wide. Inside alley lines narrow the singles court to 12 feet (3.7 meters) in width.

To serve, a player tosses the ring underhand over the net into the service court. The receiver must catch the ring in the air with one hand, and immediately return it over the net beyond the neutral zone. Only one serve is allowed, but serves that touch the top of the net are made again. Only the server scores. He receives points if an opponent fails to catch the ring or fails to return it to the server's court. The server continues to serve as long as he makes points. The game is usually 15 points. If a tie of 14-all occurs, a player must make two consecutive points to win. Two out of three games make up a match. Sometimes tennis scoring is used (see TENNIS). HELEN I. DRIVER

DECLARATION OF HUMAN RIGHTS. See HUMAN RIGHTS, UNIVERSAL DECLARATION OF.

DECLARATION OF INDEPENDENCE is the historic document in which the American Colonies declared their freedom from British rule. The Second Continental Congress, a meeting of delegates from the colonies, adopted the Declaration on July 4, 1776. This date has been celebrated ever since as the birthday of the United States.

The Declaration of Independence ranks as one of the greatest documents in human history. It eloquently expressed the colonies' reasons for proclaiming their freedom. The document blamed the British government for many abuses. But it also stated that all people have certain rights, including the right to change or overthrow any government that denies them their rights. The ideas expressed so majestically in the Declaration have long inspired freedom-loving people everywhere.

Events Leading to the Declaration. Friction between the American Colonies and Britain had been building for more than 10 years before the Declaration was adopted. During that period, the colonies had asked Britain for a larger role in making decisions that affected them, especially in the area of taxation. In 1765, the British Parliament passed the Stamp Act, which required the colonists to pay a tax on newspapers, legal and business documents, and various other items. The colonists protested so strongly against this "taxation without representation" that Parliament repealed the act in 1766.

Parliament then passed a law stating it had the right to legislate for the colonies in all matters. In 1767, it placed a tax on certain goods imported into the colonies. But colonial opposition led Parliament to remove these taxes in 1770—except for the tax on tea. In 1773, angry colonists boarded British ships in Boston Harbor and dumped their cargoes of tea overboard. Parliament then passed a series of laws to punish Massachusetts. These laws led the colonies to unite against what they called the Intolerable Acts.

The Continental Congress. In 1774, delegates from all the colonies except Georgia met in Philadelphia at the First Continental Congress. The delegates adopted an agreement that bound the colonies not to trade with Britain or to use British goods. They also proposed another meeting the next year if Britain did not change its policies before that time.

But Britain held to its policies, and the Second Continental Congress was called. The delegates met in Philadelphia's State House (now Independence Hall) on May 10, 1775. By that time, the Revolutionary War in America had already begun, with battles between Massachusetts colonists and British troops. Congress acted swiftly. It voted to organize an army and a navy and to issue money to pay for the war. Many delegates now believed that independence from Britain was the only solution. But others disagreed. Early in July, Congress therefore sent a final, useless appeal to Britain's King George III to remedy the colonies' grievances.

The independence movement grew rapidly early in 1776. The English writer Thomas Paine spurred the movement with his electrifying pamphlet *Common Sense.* This work presented brilliant arguments for the colonies' freedom. More and more Americans came to agree with the patriot Samuel Adams, who asked, "Is not America already independent? Why not then declare it?"

On June 7, 1776, Richard Henry Lee of Virginia introduced the resolution in Congress "That these United Colonies are, and of right ought to be, free and independent States. . . ." On June 10, Congress voted to name a committee to write a declaration of independence for the delegates to consider in case they adopted Lee's resolution. The committee, appointed the next day, consisted of John Adams, Benjamin Franklin, Thomas Jefferson, Robert R. Livingston, and Roger Sherman. Jefferson's committee associates asked him to draft the declaration, and he completed the task in about two weeks. Franklin and Adams made a few minor literary changes.

Adoption of the Declaration. On July 2, Congress approved the Lee resolution. The delegates then began to debate Jefferson's draft. A few passages, including one condemning King George for encouraging the slave trade, were removed. Most other changes dealt with style. On July 4, Congress adopted the final draft of the Declaration of Independence.

The Declaration, signed by John Hancock as presi-

Richard B. Morris, the contributor of this article and of the explanatory notes with the Declaration, is Gouverneur Morris Professor of History at Columbia University. He is the author of The American Revolution: A Brief History.

Signers of the Declaration of Independence

Fifty-six members of the Continental Congress signed the engrossed parchment copy of the Declaration. Most members signed on Aug. 2, 1776. The rest signed on later dates. WORLD BOOK has a biography of each signer. The signers, in alphabetical order, were:

John Adams (Mass.)
Samuel Adams (Mass.)
Josiah Bartlett (N.H.)
Carter Braxton (Va.)
Charles Carroll (Md.)
Samuel Chase (Md.)
Abraham Clark (N.J.)
George Clymer (Pa.)
William Ellery (R.I.)
William Floyd (N.Y.)
Benjamin Franklin (Pa.)
Elbridge Gerry (Mass.)
Button Gwinnett (Ga.)
Lyman Hall (Ga.)
John Hancock (Mass.)
Benjamin Harrison (Va.)
John Hart (N.J.)
Joseph Hewes (N.C.)
Thomas Heyward, Jr. (S.C.)
William Hooper (N.C.)
Stephen Hopkins (R.I.)
Francis Hopkinson (N.J.)
Samuel Huntington (Conn.)
Thomas Jefferson (Va.)
Francis Lightfoot Lee (Va.)
Richard Henry Lee (Va.)
Francis Lewis (N.Y.)
Philip Livingston (N.Y.)
Thomas Lynch, Jr. (S.C.)
Thomas McKean (Del.)
Arthur Middleton (S.C.)
Lewis Morris (N.Y.)
Robert Morris (Pa.)
John Morton (Pa.)
Thomas Nelson, Jr. (Va.)
William Paca (Md.)
Robert T. Paine (Mass.)
John Penn (N.C.)
George Read (Del.)
Caesar Rodney (Del.)
George Ross (Pa.)
Benjamin Rush (Pa.)
Edward Rutledge (S.C.)
Roger Sherman (Conn.)
James Smith (Pa.)
Richard Stockton (N.J.)
Thomas Stone (Md.)
George Taylor (Pa.)
Matthew Thornton (N.H.)
George Walton (Ga.)
William Whipple (N.H.)
William Williams (Conn.)
James Wilson (Pa.)
John Witherspoon (N.J.)
Oliver Wolcott (Conn.)
George Wythe (Va.)

IN CONGRESS, JULY 4, 1776.

The unanimous Declaration of the thirteen united States of America,

When in the Course of human events it becomes necessary for one people to dissolve the political bands which have connected them with another, and to assume among the powers of the earth, the separate and equal station to which the Laws of Nature and of Nature's God entitle them, a decent respect to the opinions of mankind requires that they should declare the causes which impel them to the separation. —— We hold these truths to be self-evident, that all men are created equal, that they are endowed by their Creator with certain unalienable Rights, that among these are Life, Liberty and the pursuit of Happiness. — That to secure these rights, Governments are instituted among Men, deriving their just powers from the consent of the governed, — That whenever any Form of Government becomes destructive of these ends, it is the Right of the People to alter or to abolish it, and to institute new Government, laying its foundation on such principles and organizing its powers in such form, as to them shall seem most likely to effect their Safety and Happiness. Prudence, indeed, will dictate that Governments long established should not be changed for light and transient causes; and accordingly all experience hath shewn, that mankind are more disposed to suffer, while evils are sufferable, than to right themselves by abolishing the forms to which they are accustomed. But when a long train of abuses and usurpations, pursuing invariably the same Object evinces a design to reduce them under absolute Despotism, it is their right, it is their duty, to throw off such Government, and to provide new Guards for their future security. — Such has been the patient sufferance of these Colonies; and such is now the necessity which constrains them to alter their former Systems of Government. The history of the present King of Great Britain is a history of repeated injuries and usurpations, all having in direct object the establishment of an absolute Tyranny over these States. To prove this, let Facts be submitted to a candid world. —— He has refused his Assent to Laws, the most wholesome and necessary for the public good. —— He has forbidden his Governors to pass Laws of immediate and pressing importance, unless suspended in their operation till his Assent should be obtained; and when so suspended, he has utterly neglected to attend to them. —— He has refused to pass other Laws for the accommodation of large districts of people, unless those people would relinquish the right of Representation in the Legislature, a right inestimable to them and formidable to tyrants only. —— He has called together legislative bodies at places unusual, uncomfortable, and distant from the depository of their Public Records, for the sole purpose of fatiguing them into compliance with his measures. —— He has dissolved Representative Houses repeatedly, for opposing with manly firmness his invasions on the rights of the people. —— He has refused for a long time, after such dissolutions, to cause others to be elected; whereby the Legislative powers, incapable of Annihilation, have returned to the People at large for their exercise; the State remaining in the mean time exposed to all the dangers of invasion from without, and convulsions within. —— He has endeavoured to prevent the population of these States; for that purpose obstructing the Laws for Naturalization of Foreigners; refusing to pass others to encourage their migrations hither, and raising the conditions of new Appropriations of Lands. —— He has obstructed the Administration of Justice, by refusing his Assent to Laws for establishing Judiciary powers. —— He has made Judges dependent on his Will alone, for the tenure of their offices, and the amount and payment of their salaries. —— He has erected a multitude of New Offices, and sent hither swarms of Officers to harrass our people, and eat out their substance. —— He has kept among us, in times of peace, Standing Armies without the Consent of our legislatures. —— He has affected to render the Military independent of and superior to the Civil power. —— He has combined with others to subject us to a jurisdiction foreign to our constitution, and unacknowledged by our laws; giving his Assent to their Acts of pretended Legislation: — For Quartering large bodies of armed troops among us: — For protecting them, by a mock Trial, from punishment for any Murders which they should commit on the Inhabitants of these States: — For cutting off our Trade with all parts of the world: — For imposing Taxes on us without our Consent: — For depriving us in many cases, of the benefits of Trial by Jury: — For transporting us beyond Seas to be tried for pretended offences: — For abolishing the free System of English Laws in a neighbouring Province, establishing therein an Arbitrary government, and enlarging its Boundaries so as to render it at once an example and fit instrument for introducing the same absolute rule into these Colonies: — For taking away our Charters, abolishing our most valuable Laws, and altering fundamentally the Forms of our Governments: — For suspending our own Legislatures, and declaring themselves invested with power to legislate for us in all cases whatsoever. — He has abdicated Government here, by declaring us out of his Protection and waging War against us. —— He has plundered our seas, ravaged our Coasts, burnt our towns, and destroyed the lives

death, desolation and tyranny, already begun with circumstances of Cruelty & perfidy
has constrained our fellow Citizens taken Captive on the high Seas to bear Arms against
He has excited domestic insurrections amongst us, and has endeavoured to bring on the
truction of all ages, sexes and conditions. In every stage of these Oppressions We
A Prince, whose character is thus marked by every act which may define a Tyrant,
have warned them from time to time of attempts by their legislature to extend an unwarrant-
We have appealed to their native justice and magnanimity, and we have conjured them
nections and correspondence. They too have been deaf to the voice of justice and of
them, as we hold the rest of mankind, Enemies in War, in Peace Friends.
ss, Assembled, appealing to the Supreme Judge of the world for the rectitude of our in-
That these United Colonies are, and of Right ought to be Free and Independent
ween them and the State of Great Britain, is and ought to be totally dissolved; and
establish Commerce, and to do all other Acts and Things which Independent
tection of divine Providence, we mutually pledge to each other our Lives, our Fortunes

Historical Documents Co.—Frank H. Fleer Corp.

WORLD BOOK photo

The Original Declaration of Independence is displayed in an upright case in the National Archives Building in Washington, D.C. The Declaration stands above the United States Constitution and Bill of Rights. All these historic documents are sealed under glass.

dent of Congress, was promptly printed. It was read to a large crowd in the State House yard on July 8. On July 19, Congress ordered the Declaration to be *engrossed* (written in beautiful script) on parchment. Congress also ordered that all its members sign the engrossed copy. Eventually, 56 members of Congress signed.

The Importance of the Declaration was that it magnificently expressed the thoughts of all patriots. It thus did not contain new ideas. The Declaration actually reflected ideas on social and political justice held by various philosophers of the time, especially the English philosopher John Locke. Yet the eloquent language of the document stirred the hearts of the American people. It also aroused people in Europe to make their governments more democratic. Over the years, many newly emerging nations have looked to the Declaration's expressive language in giving their reasons for seeking freedom from foreign control.

The original parchment copy of the Declaration is housed in the National Archives Building in Washington, D.C. It is displayed with two other historic American documents—the United States Constitution and the Bill of Rights. RICHARD B. MORRIS

See also CONTINENTAL CONGRESS; INDEPENDENCE DAY; LOCKE, JOHN; REVOLUTIONARY WAR IN AMERICA; UNITED STATES, HISTORY OF THE. For a *Reading and Study Guide*, see *Declaration of Independence* in the RESEARCH GUIDE/INDEX, Volume 22.

The Declaration of Independence

The Declaration of Independence can be divided into four parts: (1) The Preamble; (2) A Declaration of Rights; (3) A Bill of Indictment; and (4) A Statement of Independence. The text of the Declaration is printed in boldface. It follows the spelling and punctuation of the parchment copy. But unlike the parchment copy, each paragraph begins on a new line and is indented. The paragraphs printed in lightface are not part of the Declaration. They explain the meaning of various passages or give examples of injustices that a passage mentions.

In Congress, July 4, 1776. The unanimous Declaration of the thirteen united States of America,

[THE PREAMBLE]

When in the Course of human events, it becomes necessary for one people to dissolve the political bands which have connected them with another, and to assume among the powers of the earth, the separate and equal station to which the Laws of Nature and of Nature's God entitle them, a decent respect to the opinions of mankind requires that they should declare the causes which impel them to the separation.—

This paragraph tells why the Continental Congress drew up the Declaration. The members felt that when a people must break their ties with the mother country and become independent, they should explain their reasons to the world.

[A DECLARATION OF RIGHTS]

We hold these truths to be self-evident, that all men are created equal, that they are endowed by their Creator with certain unalienable Rights, that among these are Life, Liberty and the pursuit of Happiness.—

The signers of the Declaration believed it was obvious that "all men" are created equal and have rights that cannot be taken away. By "all men," they meant people of every race and of both sexes. The right to "Life" included the right to defend oneself against physical attack and unjust government. The right to "Liberty" included the right to criticize the government, to worship freely, and to form a government that protects liberty. The "pursuit of Happiness" meant the right to own property and to have it safeguarded. It also meant the right to strive for the good of all people, not only for one's personal happiness.

That to secure these rights, Governments are instituted among Men, deriving their just powers from the consent of the governed,—

The Declaration states that governments exist to protect the rights of the people. Governments receive their power to rule only through agreement of the people.

That whenever any Form of Government becomes destructive of these ends, it is the Right of the People to alter or to abolish it, and to institute new Government, laying its foundation on such principles and organizing its powers in such form, as to them shall seem most likely to effect their Safety and Happiness. Prudence, indeed, will dictate that Governments long established should not be changed for light and transient causes; and accordingly all experience hath shewn, that mankind are more disposed to suffer, while evils are sufferable, than to right themselves by abolishing the forms to which they are accustomed. But when a long train of abuses and usurpations, pursuing invariably the same Object evinces a design to reduce them under absolute Despotism, it is their right, it is their duty, to throw off such Government, and to provide new Guards for their future security.—

This paragraph declares that people may alter their government if it fails in its purpose. Or they may set up a new government. People should not, however, make a revolutionary change in long-established governments for unimportant reasons. But they have the right to overthrow a government that has committed many abuses and seeks complete control over the people.

[A BILL OF INDICTMENT]

Such has been the patient sufferance of these Colonies; and such is now the necessity which constrains them to alter their former Systems of Government. The history of the present King of Great Britain is a history of repeated injuries and usurpations, all having in direct object the establishment of an absolute Tyranny over these States. To prove this, let Facts be submitted to a candid world.—

The Declaration states that the colonists could no longer endure the abuses of their government and so must change it. It accuses King George III of inflicting the abuses to gain total power over the colonies. The document then lists the charges against him.

He has refused his Assent to Laws, the most wholesome and necessary for the public good.—

All laws passed by the colonial legislatures had to be sent to Great Britain for approval. George rejected many of the laws as harmful to Britain or its empire.

He has forbidden his Governors to pass Laws of immediate and pressing importance, unless suspended in

The Continental Congress adopted the Declaration of Independence on July 4, 1776. In this famous painting by the American artist John Trumbull, the president of the Congress, John Hancock, sits at the right. Before him stand the five committee members named to draft the Declaration. They are, *left to right,* John Adams, Roger Sherman, Robert R. Livingston, Thomas Jefferson, and Benjamin Franklin.

Yale University Art Gallery

their operation till his Assent should be obtained; and when so suspended, he has utterly neglected to attend to them.—

Royal governors could not approve any colonial law that did not have a clause suspending its operation until the king approved the law. Yet it took much time, sometimes years, for laws to be approved or rejected.

He has refused to pass other Laws for the accommodation of large districts of people, unless those people would relinquish the right of Representation in the Legislature, a right inestimable to them and formidable to tyrants only.—

The royal government failed to redraw the boundaries of legislative districts so that people in newly settled areas would be fairly represented in the legislatures.

He has called together legislative bodies at places unusual, uncomfortable, and distant from the depository of their public Records, for the sole purpose of fatiguing them into compliance with his measures.—

Royal governors sometimes had the members of colonial assemblies meet at inconvenient places.

He has dissolved Representative Houses repeatedly, for opposing with manly firmness his invasions on the rights of the people.—

Royal governors often dissolved colonial assemblies for disobeying their orders or for passing resolutions against the law.

He has refused for a long time, after such dissolutions, to cause others to be elected; whereby the Legislative powers, incapable of Annihilation, have returned to the People at large for their exercise; the State remaining in the mean time exposed to all the dangers of invasion from without, and convulsions within.—

After dissolving colonial legislatures, royal governors sometimes took a long time before allowing new assemblies to be elected.

He has endeavoured to prevent the population of these States; for that purpose obstructing the Laws for Naturalization of Foreigners; refusing to pass others to encourage their migrations hither, and raising the conditions of new Appropriations of Lands.—

The colonies wanted immigrants to settle in undeveloped lands in the west. For this reason, their laws made it easy for settlers to buy land and to become citizens. But in 1763, King George claimed the western lands and began to reject most new *naturalization* (citizenship) laws. In 1773, he prohibited the naturalization of foreigners. In 1774, he sharply raised the purchase prices for the western lands.

He has obstructed the Administration of Justice, by refusing his Assent to Laws for establishing Judiciary powers—

The North Carolina legislature passed a law setting up a court system. But Britain objected to a clause in the law, which the legislature refused to remove. As a result, the colony had no courts for several years.

He has made Judges dependent on his Will alone, for the tenure of their offices, and the amount and payment of their salaries.—

The royal government insisted that judges should serve as long as the king was pleased with them and that they should be paid by him. The colonies felt that judges should serve only as long as they proved to be competent and honest. They also wanted to pay the judges' salaries.

He has erected a multitude of New Offices, and sent hither swarms of Officers to harrass our people, and eat out their substance.—

In 1767, Great Britain passed the Townshend Acts, which taxed various products imported into the colonies. Britain also set up new agencies to enforce the laws and appointed tax commissioners. The commissioners, in turn, hired a large number of agents to aid them in collecting the taxes.

He has kept among us, in times of peace, Standing Armies without the Consent of our legislatures.—

British armies arrived in North America to fight the French in the French and Indian War (1754-1763). The colonists resented the fact that Britain kept troops in the colonies after the war.

He has affected to render the Military independent of and superior to the Civil power.—

The British altered the civil government in Massachusetts and named as governor General Thomas Gage, commander of Britain's military forces in America.

He has combined with others to subject us to a jurisdiction foreign to our constitution, and unacknowledged by our laws; giving his Assent to their Acts of pretended Legislation:—

The Declaratory Act, passed by Britain in 1766, claimed that the king and Parliament had full authority to make laws for the colonies. But the Declaration of Independence maintained that the colonies' own laws did not give the British that authority.

For quartering large bodies of armed troops among us:—

The royal government passed various quartering acts, which required the colonies to provide lodging and certain supplies to British troops stationed in America.

For protecting them, by a mock Trial, from punishment for any Murders which they should commit on the Inhabitants of these States:—

In 1774, Britain passed the Impartial Administration of Justice Act. Under this act, British soldiers and officials accused of murder while performing their duties in Massachusetts could be tried in Britain.

For cutting off our Trade with all parts of the world:—

Britain passed many laws to control colonial trade. The Restraining Acts of 1775, for example, severely limited the foreign trade that several colonies could engage in. One of these acts provided that American ships which violated the law could be seized.

For imposing Taxes on us without our Consent:—

This charge referred to all taxes levied on the colonies by the British, beginning with the Sugar Act of 1764.

For depriving us in many cases, of the benefits of Trial by Jury:—

British naval courts, which had no juries, dealt with smuggling and other violations of the trade laws.

For transporting us beyond Seas to be tried for pretended offences:—

This charge referred to a 1769 resolution by Parliament that colonists accused of treason could be brought to Britain for trial.

For abolishing the free System of English Laws in a neighbouring Province, establishing therein an Arbitrary government, and enlarging its Boundaries so as to render it at once an example and fit instrument for introducing the same absolute rule into these Colonies:—

In 1774, the Quebec Act provided for French civil law and an appointed governor and council in the province of Quebec. The act also extended the province's borders south to the Ohio River.

For taking away our Charters, abolishing our most valuable Laws, and altering fundamentally the Forms of our Governments:—

The Massachusetts Government Act of 1774 drastically changed the Massachusetts charter. It provided that councilors would no longer be elected but would be appointed by the king. The act also restricted the holding of town meetings and gave the governor control over all lower court judges.

For suspending our own Legislatures, and declaring themselves invested with power to legislate for us in all cases whatsoever.—

In 1767, Parliament passed an act suspending the New York Assembly for failing to fulfill all the requirements of the Quartering Act of 1765.

He has abdicated Government here, by declaring us out of his Protection and waging War against us.—

Early in 1775, Britain authorized General Gage to use force if necessary to make the colonists obey the laws of Parliament. Battles were fought at Lexington, Concord, and Breed's Hill. George declared the colonies to be in revolt and stated they would be crushed.

He has plundered our seas, ravaged our Coasts, burnt our towns, and destroyed the lives of our people.—

The British seized ships that violated the Restraining Act of December, 1775. They also bombarded such seaport towns as Falmouth (now Portland), Me.; Bristol, R.I.; and Norfolk, Va.

He is at this time transporting large Armies of foreign Mercenaries to compleat the works of death, desolation and tyranny, already begun with circumstances of Cruelty & perfidy scarcely paralleled in the most barbarous ages, and totally unworthy the Head of a civilized nation.—

The British used German *mercenaries* (hired soldiers) to help fight the colonists.

He has constrained our fellow Citizens taken Captive on the high Seas to bear Arms against their Country, to become the executioners of their friends and Brethren, or to fall themselves by their Hands.—

The British forced American seamen on ships seized under the Restraining Act to join the British navy.

He has excited domestic insurrections amongst us, and has endeavoured to bring on the inhabitants of our frontiers, the merciless Indian Savages, whose known rule of warfare, is an undistinguished destruction of all ages, sexes and conditions.

On Nov. 7, 1775, Virginia's royal governor proclaimed freedom for all Negro slaves who would join the British forces. British military plans included using Indians to fight colonists in frontier areas.

[A STATEMENT OF INDEPENDENCE]

In every stage of these Oppressions We have Petitioned for Redress in the most humble terms: Our repeated Petitions have been answered only by repeated injury. A Prince, whose character is thus marked by every act which may define a Tyrant, is unfit to be the ruler of a free people.

The Continental Congress had asked the king to correct many abuses stated in the Declaration. These appeals were ignored or followed by even worse abuses.

Nor have We been wanting in attentions to our Brittish brethren. We have warned them from time to time of attempts by their legislature to extend an unwarrantable jurisdiction over us. We have reminded them of the circumstances of our emigration and settlement here. We have appealed to their native justice and magnanimity, and we have conjured them by the ties of our common kindred to disavow these usurpations, which, would inevitably interrupt our connections and correspondence They too have been deaf to the voice of justice and of consanguinity. We must, therefore, acquiesce in the necessity, which denounces our Separation, and hold them, as we hold the rest of mankind, Enemies in War, in Peace Friends.—

Congress had also appealed without success to the British people themselves.

We, therefore, the Representatives of the united States of America, in General Congress, Assembled, appealing to the Supreme Judge of the world for the rectitude of our intentions, do, in the Name, and by Authority of the good People of these Colonies, solemnly publish and declare, That these United Colonies are, and of Right ought to be Free and Independent States; that they are Absolved from all Allegiance to the British Crown, and that all political connection between them and the State of Great Britain, is and ought to be totally dissolved; and that as Free and Independent States, they have full Power to levy War, conclude Peace, contract Alliances, establish Commerce, and to do all other Acts and Things which Independent States may of right do.—

And for the support of this Declaration, with a firm reliance on the protection of divine Providence, we mutually pledge to each other our Lives, our Fortunes and our sacred Honor.

Because all appeals had failed, the signers of the Declaration, as representatives of the American people, felt only one course of action remained. They thus declared the colonies independent, with all ties to Britain ended.

DECLARATION OF LONDON. See BLOCKADE.

DECLARATION OF PARIS. See BLOCKADE.

DECLARATION OF RIGHTS. See BILL OF RIGHTS; CONTINENTAL CONGRESS; RIGHTS OF MAN, DECLARATION OF THE.

DECLARATORY ACT. See REVOLUTIONARY WAR IN AMERICA (The Quartering and Stamp Acts).

DECLENSION is a listing of the different case forms of a noun or pronoun. Some languages, such as Latin, Greek, and Russian, have complicated case systems. They have many forms for each noun or pronoun, varying with the way the words are used in sentences.

In English, the declension of nouns is extremely simple. English nouns have only two case forms: a *common* case, used for both subject and object, and a *possessive* case. For example, in "The scoutmaster instructed the young boy," *scoutmaster* is the subject and *boy* is the object, but the common case is used for both. The possessive form is marked by the inflection *-'s*, as in the sentence "The *scoutmaster's* instructions helped the *boy's* progress."

The pronouns *I*, *he*, *she*, *we*, *they*, and *who* show three case forms—subjective (sometimes called nominative), objective, and possessive. The following declension shows the differences among the forms. It also includes a variation in the possessive form in four of the pronouns:

Subjective	I	he	she	we	they	who
Objective	me	him	her	us	them	whom
Possessive	my	his	her	our	their	whose
Variation	mine		hers	ours	theirs	

The pronouns *it* and *you* show only two case forms, common and possessive. WILLIAM F. IRMSCHER

See also CASE; PRONOUN; INFLECTION.

DECLINATION. See COMPASS (Variation).

DECODING. See CODES AND CIPHERS.

DECOMPOSITION, in chemistry, is the breaking down of a substance into simpler products, or into the elements of which it is composed. Decomposition may be brought about in several ways. Heat decomposes red mercuric oxide into its elements of oxygen and bright metallic mercury. Heat breaks down limestone to form lime and carbon dioxide. Heat also decomposes many organic compounds. An electric current decomposes water into its elements hydrogen and oxygen. Many substances are decomposed by chemical action. Sodium carbonate is used to decompose silicate rocks. Starch is broken down into a simple sugar, called *glucose*, by the action of a boiling, dilute acid. Decomposition may also be caused by the action of light, bacteria, or enzymes. The enzymes in yeast ferment sugar into simple products.

A distinction is sometimes made between decomposition caused by man, as in chemistry, and decomposition that occurs in nature. For example, animal and vegetable matter, when attacked by certain microorganisms, are said to *decompose*, or decay. Such natural decay is also called *putrefaction*. The decomposition of animals and plants is important in geology. For example, coal and petroleum are formed from marsh plants that became buried in swamps and decayed. JAMES S. FRITZ

DECOMPRESSION SICKNESS. See BENDS.

DECORATION, INTERIOR. See INTERIOR DECORATION.

DECORATION DAY. See MEMORIAL DAY.

DECORATIONS AND MEDALS honor persons who have performed deeds of bravery or distinguished service. The terms *decoration* and *medal* often refer to the same thing.

Almost every nation awards military decorations and medals. Many countries also have decorations that honor civilians. Nations often present decorations to members of military forces of friendly countries, and to statesmen and distinguished citizens of other countries. Some *orders* are actually decorations. For example, an English military leader may be knighted to honor his contribution to the security of his country (see KNIGHTHOOD, ORDERS OF).

Persons receive decorations for deeds that meet certain standards required by law or by order of a government or ruler. A person must be recommended individually for a decoration. Decorations differ from *service medals*, which are given only to military personnel and need no special recommendation. Military personnel receive service medals for long service with good conduct, or for service in wars or emergencies.

Most decorations are in the form of a star or cross, but some are round. Service medals are usually round. Most decorations and service medals are made of silver or bronze. They hang from ribbons of different color combinations. Each award has its own design and motto.

Persons wear decorations in rows on the left breast, before or above service medals. A few high decorations hang from ribbons or chains worn around the neck. People usually wear decorations only on formal occasions. At other times, military personnel wear rows of *service ribbons*. These ribbons have the same color combination as the ribbon of the decoration. Civilians wear a small emblem in the lapel to represent the medal.

Most decorations are awarded only once to the same person. If a person earns the award a second time, he receives a small emblem to pin on the decoration or service ribbon.

United States Decorations and Medals

Military Awards. In 1782, General George Washington established the first U.S. military decoration, the *Badge of Military Merit*. It became the *Purple Heart* in 1932. The heart-shaped badge was made of purple cloth. Washington created it to honor his soldiers for extraordinary bravery during the Revolutionary War.

After the Revolutionary War, the United States had no decorations until Congress approved the *Medal of Honor* in 1861, during the Civil War. Decorations were unpopular in the United States during the nation's early years because many people considered them symbols of European monarchies. Even the establishment of the Medal of Honor caused much debate. But more than 1,900 U.S. servicemen received it during the Civil War and the Indian Wars. The medal was the only U.S. decoration until World War I. In 1918, Congress restricted the Medal of Honor to persons who perform the most extraordinary acts of heroism. Today, this decoration, often called the *Congressional Medal of Honor*, is the highest U.S. military award.

James W. Peterson, the contributor of this article, is treasurer of the Orders and Medals Society of America.

MEDAL OF HONOR
(ARMY)

MEDAL OF HONOR
(AIR FORCE)

MEDAL OF HONOR
(NAVY)

DECORATIONS AND MEDALS OF THE UNITED STATES

WORLD BOOK photos

DISTINGUISHED SERVICE CROSS (ARMY)

AIR FORCE CROSS

NAVY CROSS

DISTINGUISHED SERVICE MEDAL (ARMY) (AIR FORCE) (NAVY)

DISTINGUISHED FLYING CROSS

PURPLE HEART

SILVER STAR

LEGION OF MERIT
(CHIEF COMMANDER)

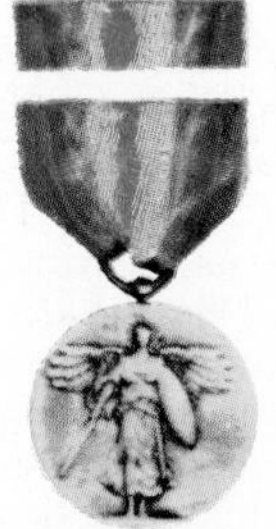

VICTORY MEDAL
(WORLD WAR I)

VICTORY MEDAL
(WORLD WAR II)

NASA
DISTINGUISHED
SERVICE MEDAL

PRESIDENTIAL MEDAL OF FREEDOM

YOUNG AMERICAN
MEDAL FOR BRAVERY

After the United States entered World War I in 1917, General John J. Pershing, commander of the U.S. forces, suggested the creation of additional decorations. In 1918, Congress established the *Distinguished Service Cross* for heroism in the army. In 1919, Congress established a similar award, the *Navy Cross*, for the U.S. Navy. In 1918, Congress created the *Distinguished Service Medal* to honor achievement by high-ranking army officers. A small silver star emblem on the Service Medal represented awards for bravery.

Congress established the *Distinguished Flying Cross* for military personnel and some civilians in 1926. Congress authorized the *Soldier's Medal* in 1926 to honor army troops for noncombat bravery.

In 1932, the President changed the small silver star emblem for bravery to a full-sized decoration on a ribbon, the *Silver Star*. Also in 1932, on the 200th anniversary of George Washington's birth, the President revived the Badge of Military Merit as the Purple Heart. At first, only the army awarded the Purple Heart. Soldiers could claim the award if they had been wounded in any earlier war or had received a special commendation certificate in World War I. In 1941, the War Department reserved the award for wounds in action. In 1942, the navy adopted the award for wounds in action.

Several new decorations appeared during World War II. In 1942, Congress gave the navy permission to award the Silver Star. That same year, Congress established the *Navy and Marine Corps Medal* for noncombat heroism, and the President created the *Air Medal* to honor distinguished service in flight. In 1942, Congress created the *Legion of Merit* for outstanding service by officers and enlisted men of the United States and other countries. In 1944, the army and navy began to award the *Bronze Star* for special bravery or merit.

The marine corps uses navy decorations. Until the

UNITED STATES MILITARY DECORATIONS AND MEDALS

(Listed in order of importance)

Name of Medal	Year Established	Persons Eligible	Awarded For
Medal of Honor	1861 (Navy) 1862 (Army, Air Force*)	All ranks of the U.S. armed forces only	Gallantry in action
Distinguished Service Cross (Army) **Navy Cross** **Air Force Cross**	1918 1919 1960	All ranks of the armed forces	Exceptional heroism in combat
Distinguished Service Medal	1918 (Army, Air Force*) 1919 (Navy) 1951 (Coast Guard)	Usually, only high-ranking officers	Exceptional meritorious service in a duty of great responsibility
Silver Star	1932	All ranks of the armed forces	Gallantry in action
Legion of Merit	1942	Normally to officers	Exceptionally meritorious service in peace or war
Distinguished Flying Cross	1926	All ranks of the armed forces	Heroism or extraordinary achievement in flight
Soldier's Medal **Navy and Marine Corps Medal** **Airman's Medal** **Coast Guard Medal**	1926 1942 1960 1951	All ranks of the armed forces	Heroism not involving conflict with the enemy
Bronze Star	1944	All ranks of the armed forces	Heroic or meritorious achievement during military operations
Air Medal	1942	All ranks of the armed forces	Meritorious achievement in flight
Commendation Medal	1944 (Navy) 1945 (Army) 1947 (Coast Guard) 1958 (Air Force)	All members of the armed forces	Meritorious service in war or peace
Purple Heart	1932 (Army) 1942 (Navy)	All ranks of the armed forces	Wounds or death in combat

UNITED STATES CIVILIAN DECORATIONS AND MEDALS

Name of Medal	Year Established	Persons Eligible	Awarded For
Presidential Medal of Freedom	1963	Any person	Service connected with U.S. or national interest, or cultural or public service
Gold and Silver Lifesaving Medals	1874	Any person	Lifesaving in maritime waters at personal risk of life
National Security Medal	1953	Any person	Distinguished achievement in the field of national security
President's Award for Distinguished Federal Civilian Service	1957	Federal employees	Outstanding service
Young American Medals for Bravery and for Service	1950	U.S. residents under 19	Courage or public service
National Aeronautics and Space Administration Distinguished Service Medal	1959	Astronauts and NASA personnel	Heroism or distinguished service

*A separate Air Force medal was designed in 1965.

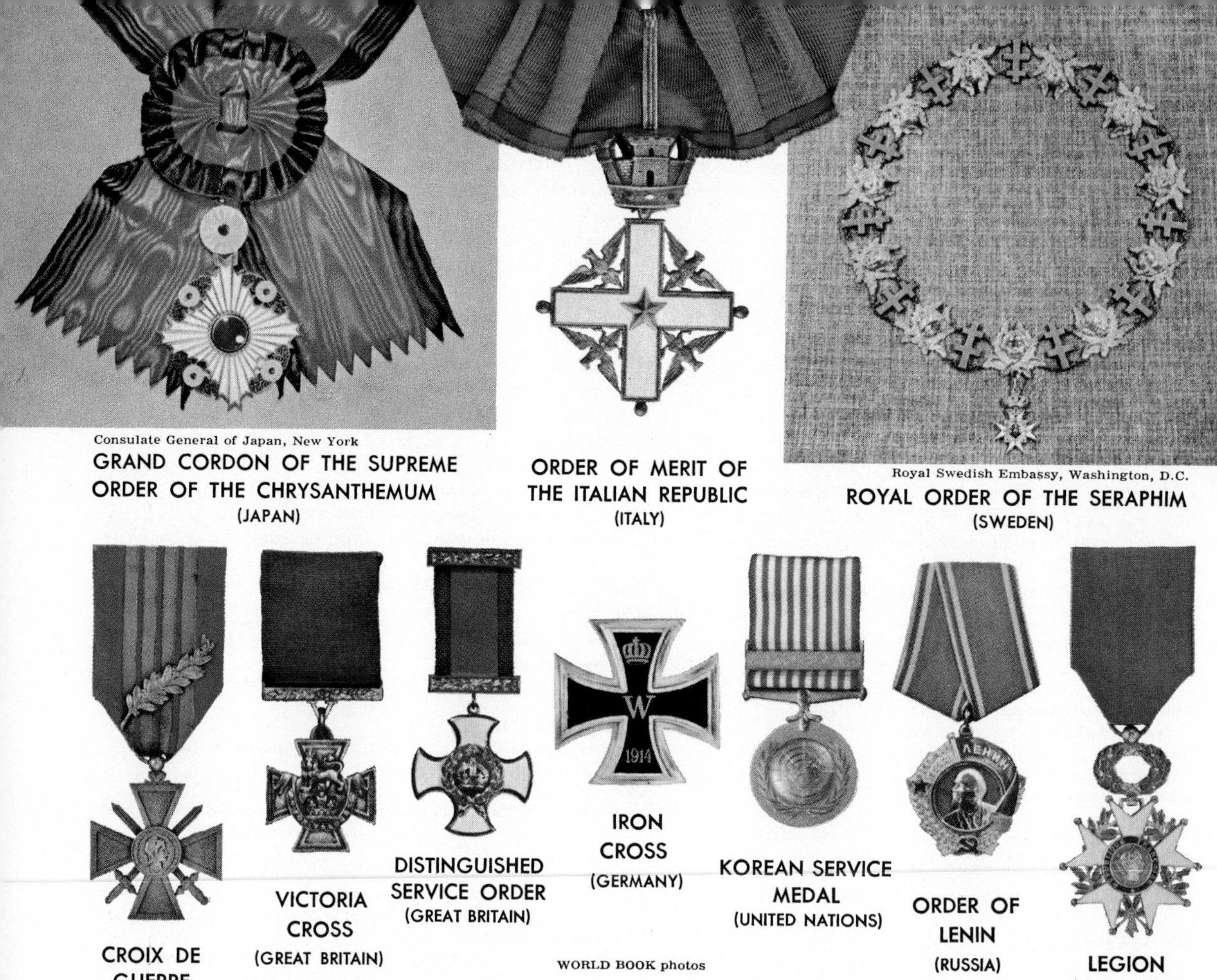

Consulate General of Japan, New York

GRAND CORDON OF THE SUPREME ORDER OF THE CHRYSANTHEMUM (JAPAN)

ORDER OF MERIT OF THE ITALIAN REPUBLIC (ITALY)

Royal Swedish Embassy, Washington, D.C.

ROYAL ORDER OF THE SERAPHIM (SWEDEN)

CROIX DE GUERRE (FRANCE)

VICTORIA CROSS (GREAT BRITAIN)

DISTINGUISHED SERVICE ORDER (GREAT BRITAIN)

IRON CROSS (GERMANY)

KOREAN SERVICE MEDAL (UNITED NATIONS)

ORDER OF LENIN (RUSSIA)

LEGION OF HONOR (FRANCE)

WORLD BOOK photos

DECORATIONS AND MEDALS OF OTHER COUNTRIES

air force became a separate service in 1947, it used army decorations. Since then, the air force has gradually established its own awards. The coast guard uses navy decorations in wartime, but has its own peacetime awards.

The army and air force use Bronze Oak Leaf Clusters to represent additional awards of the same decoration. The navy uses Gold Stars. Five clusters or stars may be represented by one silver emblem.

Campaign Medals have been awarded for every war fought by the United States from the Civil War to the Vietnam War, including Cold War actions. The first campaign medals, the *Dewey Medal* and the *Sampson Medal*, were awarded in 1905. The Dewey Medal went to personnel who took part in the Battle of Manila Bay during the Spanish-American War. The Sampson Medal was worn by men who served in various naval battles in the West Indies during the Spanish-American War.

Army and navy medals for the same campaign differ in design. But since 1913, both services have used the same ribbons. Bronze stars on the ribbons represent the number of campaigns in which the wearer served.

Unit Emblems, in the form of service ribbons, are worn by members of military units. These emblems honor outstanding achievement.

Badges are emblem pins awarded for specific skills, such as rifle marksmanship.

Civilian Awards. Since 1874, the Department of the Treasury has awarded gold and silver lifesaving medals for deeds of lifesaving at sea. During World War II, several decorations and service ribbons were created for the Merchant Marine. Congress also established the *Medal for Merit* in 1942. The President created the *Medal of Freedom* in 1945. Both honor civilians for war services. In 1963, President John F. Kennedy changed the Medal of Freedom to the *Presidential Medal of Freedom*. The President or a committee selects its winners.

The Department of Justice awards the *Young American Medal for Bravery* and the *Young American Medal for Service*. Not more than two boys or girls under the age of 19 can win either of these medals in one year. The National Aeronautics and Space Administration awards a *Distinguished Service Medal* to astronauts. Various federal agencies give decorations to their employees and to other citizens. Congress occasionally awards a special medal to distinguished citizens, such as composer Irving Berlin or comedian Bob Hope. This large gold medal has no ribbon, and is not worn.

Other Awards. Most of the states give their National Guardsmen decorations and medals that resemble federal military awards. Some cities, schools, associations, and foundations also award decorations.

The Constitution forbids U.S. citizens who work for the government to accept decorations from other gov-

DECORATIONS AND MEDALS OF OTHER COUNTRIES

(Listed in order of importance)

Country	Name of Medal	Year Established	Persons Eligible	Awarded For
British Commonwealth	**Victoria Cross**	1856	All ranks of the armed forces	Conspicuous bravery in action
	George Cross	1940	Civilians and military	Conspicuous bravery
	Order of Merit	1902	Civilians and military	Distinguished service
	Distinguished Service Order	1886	All officers	Distinguished service in combat
	Military Cross	1914	Army officers	Distinguished service in action
	Distinguished Flying Cross	1918	All officers	Bravery in combat flying
Canada	**Canada Medal**	1943	All Canadians and citizens of other countries	Meritorious service beyond the call of duty
	Canadian Forces Decoration	1951	All armed forces	12 years' service
Russia	**Order of Lenin**	1930	Russian individuals and organizations	General merit
	Gold Star Medal	1939	Russians	General merit
France	**Legion of Honor**	1802	Frenchmen and citizens of other countries	General merit
	Croix de Guerre	1915	All ranks of the armed forces	Bravery in combat
West Germany	**Iron Cross**	1813	All ranks of the armed forces	Bravery or general merit in combat
Japan	**Order of the Chrysanthemum**	1877	Japanese men and men of other countries	Great service to Japan
Sweden	**Order of the Seraphim**	1748	Royalty and heads of state	Service to humanity
Denmark	**Order of the Dannebrog**	1671	Danes and citizens of other countries	General merit
Belgium	**Order of Leopold**	1832	Belgians and citizens of other countries	General civilian and military merit
The Vatican	**Order of Pius**	1847	Any person	Personal merit
Israel	**Hero of Israel**	1949	Military personnel	Gallantry in combat
Greece	**Order of the Redeemer**	1829	Greeks and citizens of other countries	General merit
United Nations	**Korean Service Medal**	1951	Personnel of UN forces	Service in Korean War
	United Nations Medal	1959	Personnel of UN forces	Service in UN police actions

ernments without the consent of Congress. Congress has passed special laws authorizing specified persons to accept decorations awarded by another country. Congress usually does this when the decorated person retires from active government service. Congress also passed laws permitting U.S. military personnel to accept any award from another government during World War I, World War II, and the Korean War. All U.S. decorations except the Medal of Honor may be awarded to citizens of other countries.

Decorations and Medals of Other Countries

Canada, Great Britain, and Other Commonwealth Nations. The British monarch awards decorations and medals to citizens of Commonwealth countries that recognize the monarch as head of the British Commonwealth. These decorations may be awarded in any Commonwealth nation that recommends its citizens for the awards. Each Commonwealth nation also has its own decorations. A person who receives a high award is permitted to add the initials of the award after his name. For example, John Smith G. C. shows that Smith has received the *George Cross.*

Since the Battle of Waterloo in 1815, soldiers of the British Commonwealth have received silver war medals for military operations. In 1856, during the Crimean War, Queen Victoria created the *Victoria Cross,* the highest Commonwealth decoration for heroism in combat. In 1940, King George VI established the George Cross to honor extraordinary acts of bravery by military or civilian personnel in noncombat situations. The acts may be performed in wartime or in peacetime.

Other Commonwealth decorations for bravery are usually awarded in different forms for officers and enlisted men, and for different military branches.

The *Order of Merit,* established by King Edward VII in 1902, represents excellence in military, scientific, artistic, or professional work.

Second awards of Commonwealth decorations are represented by a bar on a ribbon, or a silver rose on a service ribbon.

Canada established the *Canada Medal* for extraordinary service by a Canadian or a citizen of another country. This medal was authorized in 1943, but has never been awarded. Canada established a *Voluntary Service Medal* for military service during World War II. The *Memorial Cross* goes to mothers and widows of servicemen killed during wartime.

Denmark awards the *Order of the Dannebrog* to Danes and citizens of other countries for deeds of civilian or military merit.

France. Napoleon I founded the *Legion of Honor* in 1802 as an honor society similar to the orders of knighthood. France awards the Legion of Honor for bravery and merit without regard to rank. Beginning in 1964, the government awarded this decoration for only the most distinguished merit. At that time, France created the *Order of Merit* to serve as a more general award.

France also awards the *Medaille Militaire* (Military Medal) to enlisted men for bravery and long service, and the *Croix de Guerre* (War Cross) for bravery.

Germany. In 1813, King Friedrich Wilhelm III created the *Iron Cross,* Germany's first and highest decoration for military valor. Germany awarded the

Iron Cross to all ranks of qualified enlisted men and officers through World War II. Today, West Germany gives the *Order of Merit* to civilians.

Italy awards the *Order of Merit* in five classes for merit in any field.

The Netherlands honors military bravery with *Willem's Order*, created in 1813.

Norway awards the *Order of St. Olaf*, created in 1847, for distinction in all military and civilian fields.

Russia. The highest Russian decorations are the *Order of Lenin* and the *Gold Star Medal*. The Order of Lenin is awarded to both individuals and organizations for exceptional achievement. It also goes to persons who receive the titles of "Hero of Socialist Labor" and "Hero of the Soviet Union" for outstanding peacetime or military service.

Sweden gives the *Order of the Seraphim* to royalty and heads of governments. It gives the *Order of the Sword* to military personnel.

United Nations. In 1951, the United Nations established the *Korean Service Medal* for troops of member nations who served in the Korean War. The UN established the *Emergency Forces Medal* for its soldiers stationed along the border between Israel and Egypt. The *United Nations Medal* honors UN forces who have served in any other area.

History

Since ancient times, people have worn decorations of honor. Records dating back to the Egyptian pharaohs about 1500 B.C. mention golden flies awarded as decorations of honor. In imperial China, people wore hat badges, peacock feathers, and robes as decorations.

Early European kings awarded medals as signs of royal favor. Formal military decorations and service medals generally appeared during the Napoleonic Wars, between 1796 and 1815. Later in the 1800's, many decorations were created for merit in civilian fields.

World Wars I and II brought an increase in the number and variety of military and civilian medals. During the 1950's and 1960's, the newly independent nations of Africa and Asia established many awards. Switzerland and Yemen (Sana) are among the few nations that have no national decorations. JAMES W. PETERSON

DECORATIVE ARTS is a term applied to objects used in decoration. It includes furniture, ceramics, silver, rugs, hangings, glass, small bronzes, carved woodwork, panels painted for decoration, and incidental objects for tables or cabinets. Decorative arts also include those often associated with churches, such as work in enamel, ivory, glass, gold, silver, bronze, and stained glass.

Decorative arts are often referred to as the *minor arts*. But this term does not mean they are inferior. The term *fine arts* usually refers to major works of painters, sculptors, and architects (see FINE ARTS). The *useful arts*, in combining beauty and practicality, are more closely related to the decorative arts (see ART AND THE ARTS).

Decorative arts have always played an important part in people's lives. Prehistoric man decorated his utensils, weapons, and clothing. The ancient Egyptians often buried decorative objects with their dead. The Greeks and Romans decorated such sacred objects as their temples and such ordinary objects as wine jugs. In the Middle Ages, men decorated their churches with ivory, enamel, and gold. The Renaissance produced many fine examples of the minor arts. Today many decorative arts are simple and useful. WILLIAM M. MILLIKEN

Related Articles in WORLD BOOK include:

Beadwork	Glassware	Mosaic
Carving	Inlay	Paperwork, Decorative
Ceramics	Interior Decoration	Pottery
Decoupage	Ironwork, Decorative	Pyrography
Enamel	Ivory	Stained Glass
Furniture	Jewelry	Tapestry
Gilding	Lace	

DECORATOR. See INTERIOR DECORATION (Careers).

DECOUPAGE, *DAY koo PAHZH*, is the art of using paper cutouts to decorate furniture and such accessories as boxes, lamps, plaques, and trays. The finished object looks and feels like fine enamel. Cutouts can be made from such articles as calendars, greeting cards, magazine and newspaper illustrations, photographs, and wrapping paper. The word *decoupage* comes from the French word *decouper*, meaning *to cut out*.

Decoupage usually involves four steps. First, the surface of the object to be decorated must be sanded and, if wood, painted or stained. Then a protective sealer is applied to the cutout, which is glued to the object. Next, the decorated surface is covered with many coats of varnish until the edge of the cutout cannot be felt. Last, the final coat of varnish is smoothed, polished, and waxed. DONA Z. MEILACH

WORLD BOOK photo

Decoupage is the art of decorating furniture and accessories with paper cutouts. The cutout is glued to a surface and covered with many coats of varnish. The final coat is waxed and polished.

DECRESCENDO. See MUSIC (Terms).

DEDUCTIVE METHOD is the process of reasoning by which we draw conclusions by logical inference from given premises. If we begin by accepting the propositions that "All Greeks have beards" and that "Zeno is a Greek," we may validly conclude that "Zeno has a beard." We refer to the conclusions of deductive reasoning as *valid*, rather than *true*, because we must distinguish clearly between *that which follows logically* from other statements and *that which is the case*.

Starting premises may be articles of faith or assumptions. Before we can consider the conclusions drawn from these premises as valid, we must show that they are consistent with each other and with the original premise. Mathematics and logic are examples of disciplines that make extensive use of the deductive method. The scientific method requires a combination of induction and deduction. S. I. HAYAKAWA

See also INDUCTIVE METHOD; LOGIC; SCIENCE (The Scientific Method; Logic and Organization).

DEED is a written agreement to transfer the ownership of real estate, either by sale or by gift. It must be signed by the persons directly involved in the agreement, and must be delivered. A deed also must give an adequate description of the real estate, and show an intent to transfer the property.

There are two main kinds of deeds, *quitclaim* and *warranty*. In a quitclaim deed, the buyer acquires only the seller's rights to a piece of property. The buyer bears the loss if someone has a claim against the property, or if the seller is mistaken in the amount of property he owned. A warranty deed guarantees the buyer that no claims exist against the *title* (legal evidence of ownership) to the property. If any claims arise later, the seller must protect the buyer from loss.

The buyer has the deed recorded, usually in the office of the registrar of deeds for the county in which the property is located. Before a deed can be recorded, it must be *acknowledged* by a public official who has power to give an oath. The seller acknowledges a deed when he swears he is selling the property of his own free will. An acknowledgment is not necessary to make the deed legal. But the buyer has maximum protection against possible claims of other persons if the deed has been acknowledged and recorded.

Before buying property, a person should obtain an *abstract of title* from the seller, and hire a lawyer to examine it. An abstract is a brief history of the title, and lists the individuals who have owned an interest in the property. Title insurance protects the owner against some defects in the deed or title. ROBERT E. SULLIVAN

DEEP refers to any ocean area with a depth of more than 18,000 feet (5,490 meters). More than 100 deeps have been found in ocean floors. Contrary to popular belief, they are not found in the center of the ocean. Most of them occur close to mountainous islands where steep shores plunge down to the bottom of the sea.

Challenger Deep, in the Mariana Trench 200 miles (320 kilometers) southwest of Guam, is the deepest known ocean deep. There, the ocean floor is 36,198 feet (11,033 meters) below the surface. Puerto Rico Trench, north of Puerto Rico, has the greatest recorded depth in the Atlantic. It was found in 1939, and has a depth of 28,374 feet (8,648 meters). ROBERT O. REID

See also ATLANTIC OCEAN (The Ocean Bed); OCEAN (The World Ocean; The Land Beneath the Sea); PACIFIC OCEAN (Location and Size).

DEEP-SEA ANIMALS. See FISH (pictures: Fish of the Deep Ocean); OCEAN (pictures).

DEEP-SEA DIVING. See DIVING, UNDERWATER.

DEEP SEA DRILLING PROJECT is a scientific program involving studies of the ocean bottom. These studies provide information about ocean currents, prehistoric life in the ocean, and the composition of the ocean floor. The project also has helped scientists understand the forces that formed the continents. Geologists use knowledge of the ocean bottom to find oil and other minerals beneath the sea.

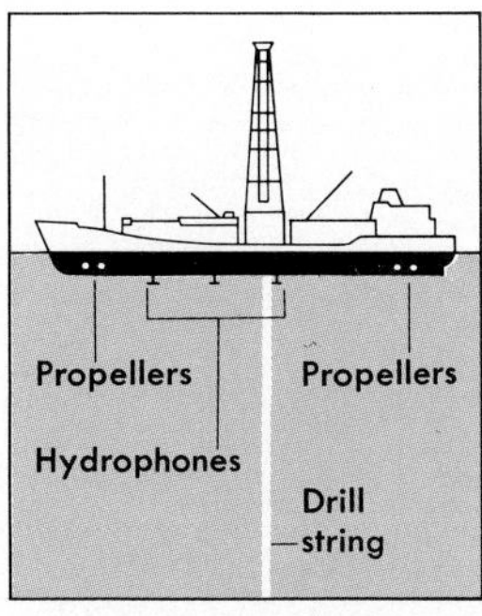

A Deep-Sea Drilling Ship, *above,* uses propellers to stay in place despite wind and waves. Devices called *hydrophones* help maintain its position. They receive signals from a sonar beacon on the sea floor.

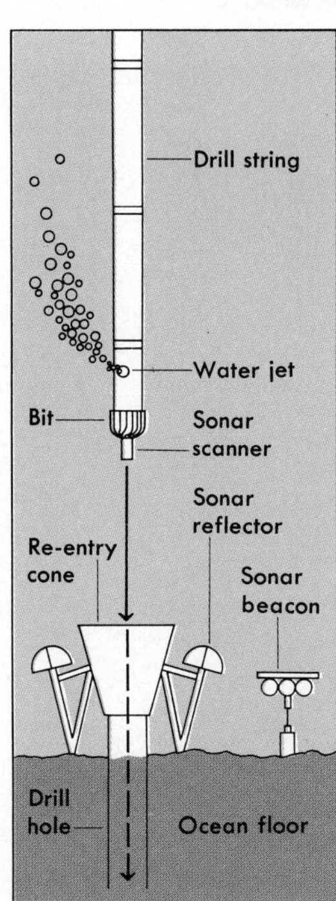

A Drill String of pipe may be put back in a drill hole, *right,* after removal for repairs. A sonar scanner and reflectors guide the pipe to a re-entry cone, which leads to the hole. A water jet maneuvers the pipe.

WORLD BOOK diagrams

The Deep Sea Drilling Project operates from a special ship called the *Glomar Challenger*. This ship has drilling gear and scientific laboratories. Advanced navigation and steering controls keep the vessel steady during drilling. A tall *derrick* (tower) lowers a long pipe straight down from the ship. The pipe may measure as long as 20,000 feet (6,100 meters). It consists of sections 90 feet (27 meters) long that are screwed together. The entire pipe turns so that a bit on the end of the pipe drills into the ocean floor. A motor pumps sea water through the pipe to wash out *cuttings* (waste) made by the bit. The *Glomar Challenger* has drilled as far as 3,900 feet (1,190 meters) into the ocean floor.

Equipment inside the pipe brings up *cores* (samples) from the bottom. Each core measures 30 feet (9 meters) long and about 3 inches (8 centimeters) wide. The cores contain deposits of fossils and minerals that have settled to the bottom through the centuries. Scientists study the cores to trace the development of the ocean. The cores also provide evidence that supports the theory of *continental drift*. According to this theory, changes in the ocean floor result in movements of the continents. Many scientists believe the continents once formed one land mass that began to break apart about 200 million years ago. See CONTINENTAL DRIFT.

The Scripps Institution of Oceanography in La Jolla, Calif., directs the Deep Sea Drilling Project. The National Science Foundation provides most of the funds for the project, in which scientists of many nations have taken part. The *Glomar Challenger* began operations in 1968. N. TERENCE EDGAR

DEEP-SEA FISHING. See FISHING; FISHING INDUSTRY.

Fritz Prenzel, Pix from Publix

A Mother White-Tailed Deer Guards Her Fawns while they search for food. Fawns may stay with their mothers for more than a year.

Stephen Collins, N.A.S.

New Antlers of a white-tailed deer, *above*, and moose, *below*, have a furry cover called *velvet* which the animals soon rub off.

D. Lichtenberg, N.A.S.

DEER are the only animals with bones called *antlers* on their heads. Antlers are true bones, unlike horns, which are strong, hard layers of skin.

There are more than 60 kinds of deer, including caribou, elk, moose, musk deer, reindeer, and white-tailed deer. Deer live in many parts of the world. Some kinds live in the hot, dry deserts. Others live in the cold lands above the Arctic Circle. Still others live in prairies, swamps, or woodlands, where the climate is mild.

Deer are among the largest wild animals of North America. The North American moose is the largest deer in the world. Some moose grow $7\frac{1}{2}$ feet (2.3 meters) tall and weigh over 1,800 pounds (820 kilograms). The smallest deer is the pudu of western South America. It is about 1 foot (30 centimeters) high and weighs about 20 pounds (9 kilograms).

Most male deer are called *bucks*. But male caribou, elk, and moose are called *bulls*, and male red deer are *stags* or *harts*. Most female deer are called *does*. But female caribou, elk, and moose are *cows*, and female red deer are *hinds*. Most young deer are called *fawns*, but young caribou, elk, and moose are *calves*.

For hundreds of years, man has used deer meat for food, and deer skins for clothing. In North America, deer were second only to beavers in supplying the pioneers with meat and clothing. The Indians taught the pioneers how to dry *venison* (deer meat) in the sun or over a campfire. This way of drying venison, called *jerking*, made the meat light in weight. Men could carry large amounts of the meat easily, and keep it for later use.

Hunters killed so many deer for food and for sport that the animals had to be protected by law. Massachusetts passed its first deer law in 1698. Today, most national and local governments have game laws. Special areas called game refuges or game preserves have been set aside to protect deer and other wildlife.

Charles M. Kirkpatrick, the contributor of this article, is Professor of Wildlife Biology at Purdue University.

DEER / The Body of a Deer

Some deer, including caribou, moose, and red deer, have large, powerful bodies. Other deer look somewhat like small horses with slender legs. Among them are fallow deer, swamp deer, and white-tailed deer. Most kinds of deer have short, shiny hair that lies flat so that the animal's coat looks smooth. The pudu and huemul of South America have rough, brittle hair that gives their coats a shaggy appearance.

Legs and Hoofs. All deer have long, thin legs. Powerful muscles in the upper part of the legs allow the animals to run swiftly and to take long jumps. A frightened white-tailed deer can run as fast as 40 miles (64 kilometers) per hour, and can leap 15 to 20 feet (4.6 to 6.1 meters). Even the huge, clumsy-looking moose can run about 20 miles (32 kilometers) per hour.

A deer runs on tiptoe. Its "foot" is really its two center toes. Each center toe is protected by a strong, curved hoof. Only the tips of these toes touch the ground. The other two toes, called *dewclaws*, grow higher on the leg and have no use when the animal runs. The dewclaws often leave dots at the back of a deer's track in the snow.

Head. Deer have narrower heads and somewhat smaller noses and mouths than do cattle. The deer's lips move easily, and the animal uses them to grasp food. Most kinds of deer have only bottom teeth in the front of the mouth. A thick pad of rough skin takes the place of upper front teeth. The lower teeth press against this pad of skin when the deer tears off leaves and twigs to eat. The upper and lower back teeth have many sharp-pointed tips. The animal uses these teeth for chewing.

A deer has large eyes at the sides of its head, but the animal depends on its ears and its nose to catch the first warnings of danger. The deer has keen hearing and smell. Its large ears are always erect, and can be moved to catch sounds from any direction. A deer usually faces into the wind when it eats or rests. The wind carries sounds and smells of approaching enemies.

Antlers grow from permanent knoblike bones on the deer's skull. Deer use their antlers chiefly to fight for mates or for leadership of the herd. Among most species of deer, only the males have antlers, but both male and female reindeer and caribou have them. The musk deer of Asia and the Chinese water deer do not have antlers.

Deer that live in mild or cold climates lose their antlers each winter. New ones begin to grow early the next summer. Deer that live in warm or hot climates may lose their antlers and grow new ones at other times of the year.

New antlers are soft and tender. Thin skin grows over the antlers as they develop. Short, fine hairs on this skin make it look like velvet. Full-grown antlers are hard and strong. The velvety skin dries up, and the deer rubs the dry skin off by scraping its antlers on the ground, or against trees or bushes. The antlers fall off several months later. They usually decay on the ground or are gnawed by small animals.

The size and shape of a deer's antlers depend on the animal's age and its health. The first set grows when the deer is 1 or 2 years old. On most deer, these first antlers are short and somewhat straight. The antlers grow longer and larger, and form branches.

THE SKELETON OF A DEER

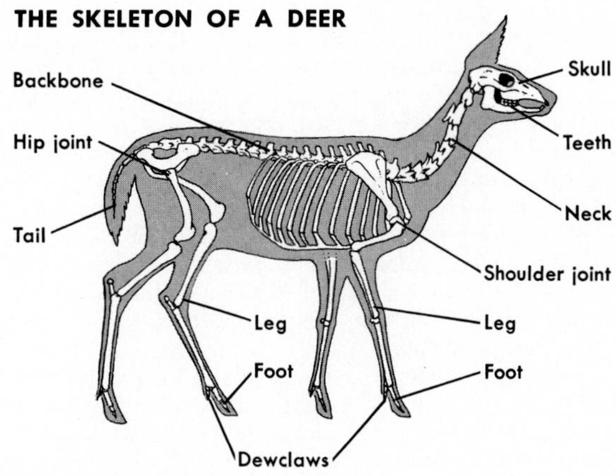

THE TRACKS OF A DEER

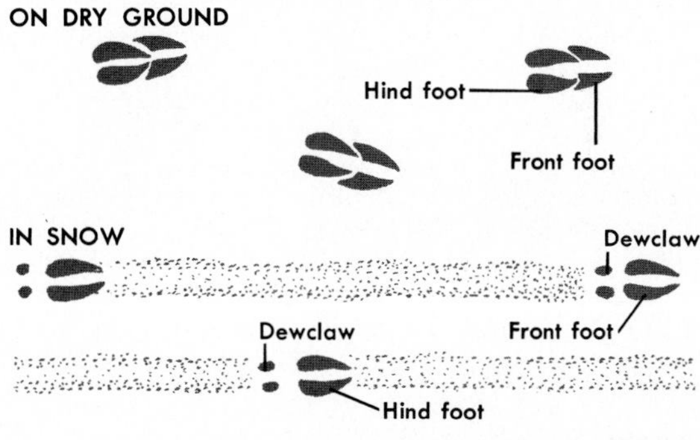

WORLD BOOK illustration by Tom Dolan

HOW A DEER'S ANTLERS GROW

Deer lose their antlers each winter and grow new ones during spring and summer. The new antlers are soft and tender. Thin skin with short, fine hairs called *velvet* covers the growing antlers. Full-grown antlers are hard and strong, and have no velvet.

WORLD BOOK illustration by Tom Dolan

DEER / *The Life of a Deer*

Deer have no permanent homes. They may spend their lives moving about in an area called a *home range*. They roam this area to search for food, to find mates, and to avoid enemies. Deer may live in groups or alone, depending on their age, sex, and species.

Some kinds of deer travel long distances each year. Caribou may make round trips of as long as 1,000 miles (1,600 kilometers) to reach feeding grounds. They spend the summer in the flat, marshy lands of the Arctic Circle. In late summer, they gather in herds of hundreds of animals and travel to warmer climates for the winter. In early spring, the caribou return to the cold lands of the far north.

Most species of deer do not make long migrations. Deer that live in the mountains may move down to lower altitudes for the winter. These mountain deer, and deer that live on flat land, usually stay near the edges of forests. There, trees and grasses supply food, and bushes serve as a place to sleep, to hide from enemies, or to give birth.

Young. A female deer chooses a hidden spot away from other deer to give birth to her young. The young deer remain in their hiding place until they can walk well enough to follow the mother.

Fawns of white-tailed deer weigh from 3½ to 6 pounds (1.6 to 2.7 kilograms) at birth. They stay hidden for four to five weeks. Newborn moose calves weigh about 25 to 35 pounds (11 to 16 kilograms). They can follow their mother when they are about 10 days old. Caribou calves, most of which are born during the herd's spring migration, weigh about 10 pounds (4.5 kilograms) at birth. They can walk with the herd several hours later.

Most kinds of deer have only one or two young at a time. Chinese water deer, which live along the Yangtze River, give birth to the most young—four to seven fawns at a time.

Food. Deer eat grass, leaves, bark, twigs, and the tender sprouts of trees and other plants. They also eat moss and plants called lichens. Some kinds of deer like particular foods. Chital, the graceful deer of Asia, eat blossoms and fruits that fall from forest trees. White-tailed deer eat various plants, including mushrooms and other types of fungi. Moose and swamp deer search streams and swamps for water plants. Caribou and reindeer like reindeer moss, a kind of lichen.

Deer do not chew their food well before swallowing it. A deer's stomach has four sections. One section serves as a storage place for the poorly chewed food. Food stored here is later returned to the mouth in a ball-like glob. The deer then chews this food, called *cud*. After the chewed food has been swallowed, it goes to other parts of the stomach. Animals that digest their food in this way are called *ruminants* (see RUMINANT).

Habits. Deer usually run away from danger. Their swiftness helps them escape such enemies as bears, cougars, coyotes, wolves, and human beings. Sometimes, instead of running, a deer stands motionless and lets an enemy pass by.

Wild deer live 10 to 20 years. In captivity, some deer live longer. However, the roe deer of Europe lives 10 to 12 years in the wild, but only 3 to 7 years in a zoo.

DEER / *Kinds of Deer*

There are more than 60 kinds of deer. They live in North America, Central and South America, and Asia and Europe. Deer also have been brought into places where they did not live naturally, including Australia, Hawaii, New Guinea, and New Zealand.

North American Deer. The best known deer of North America include (1) white-tailed deer, (2) mule deer, (3) caribou, (4) elk, and (5) moose.

White-Tailed Deer, also called *Virginia deer*, are the most common large game animals of North America. A white-tailed deer may stand 3½ feet (1.1 meters) tall and weigh 200 pounds (91 kilograms). The deer's tail, for which it is named, grows about 1 foot (30 centimeters) long. The tail has brown hair on top, and white hair underneath. When the deer is frightened and begins to run, its tail stands straight up, showing the white part. This deer has a reddish-brown coat in summer, and a gray or bluish-gray coat in winter.

THE SHAPES AND SIZES OF DEER

These drawings show the differences in size, body shape, and antlers of the five chief kinds of North American deer. The sizes given with each drawing are the average shoulder height of the adult deer.

WORLD BOOK illustration by Tom Dolan

Moose 6 feet (1.8 meters)

Elk (Wapiti) 5 feet (1.5 meters)

Caribou 4 feet (1.2 meters)

Mule Deer 3½ feet (1.1 meters)

White-Tailed Deer 3½ feet (1.1 meters)

Harry Engels, N.A.S.

An American Elk stands alert for danger in the grassy high mountain meadow that is its summer feeding area.

Frederick Baldwin, Photo Researchers

A Herd of Reindeer scrambles over the rocky ground of the Arctic regions to find grass and moss to eat.

Mule Deer are much like white-tailed deer. They are named for their large, furry ears, which look somewhat like those of a mule. Leather manufacturers make buckskin from the hides of mule and white-tailed deer.

Caribou are the reindeer of North America. Unlike all other deer except reindeer, both males and females have antlers. Caribou grow about 4 feet (1.2 meters) high and vary in color from white to brown. Arctic Eskimos and Indians eat caribou meat, carve the bones into utensils, and make the hide into clothing and tents.

Elk, also called *wapiti*, were once widely hunted for their teeth and for their antlers, which people used for ornaments. These deer stand about 5 feet (1.5 meters) tall. Their antlers may spread more than 5 feet (1.5 meters) at the widest part. Elk are the second largest deer in the world. Only moose are larger.

Moose are the largest of all deer. Some males stand $7\frac{1}{2}$ feet (2.3 meters) high and weigh about 1,800 pounds (816 kilograms). Their legs may be 4 feet (1.2 meters) long, and their antlers may weigh 60 pounds (27 kilograms). In spite of its size, a moose can move quickly and quietly through the forest. Like other deer, the moose avoids trouble. But it is a strong fighter when such enemies as bears or wolves attack. Its huge antlers and sharp hoofs are dangerous weapons.

Central and South American Deer include (1) pudu, (2) marsh deer, (3) brocket deer, (4) pampas deer, and (5) huemul.

Pudu, sometimes called *rabbit deer*, are the smallest of all deer. They live in the forests of western South America from sea level to altitudes of about 10,000 feet (3,000 meters) in the Andes Mountains. Pudu grow only about 1 foot (30 centimeters) high and weigh about 20 pounds (9 kilograms). They have short, spikelike antlers. Their rough, brittle hair is brown or gray. Pudu are probably the shyest deer, and little is known about their habits.

Marsh Deer, also called *swamp deer*, are the largest South American deer. They grow about 4 feet (1.2 meters) high. These deer live in the swampy plains and forests of Brazil, Paraguay, and Uruguay. They can spread each hoof wide to help them walk on the soft ground. Indians hunt these animals for their skins, but the meat has a poor flavor.

SOME MEMBERS OF THE DEER FAMILY

Common Name	Scientific Name	Where Found
Brocket Deer	*Mazama*	Central America
***Caribou and *Reindeer**	*Rangifer*	Asia, Europe, and North America
Chinese Water Deer	*Hydropotes inermis*	Asia
Chital (Axis Deer)	*Axis axis*	Asia
***Elk (Wapiti)**	*Cervus canadensis*	North America
Fallow Deer	*Dama dama*	Asia and Europe
Huemul (Andean Deer)	*Hippocamelus*	South America
Marsh Deer	*Blastocerus dichotomus*	South America
***Moose**	*Alces*	Asia, Europe, and North America
***Mule Deer**	*Odocoileus hemionus*	North America
Muntjac (Barking Deer)	*Muntiacus muntjak*	Asia
***Musk Deer**	*Moschus moschiferus*	Asia
Pampas Deer	*Blastoceros campestris*	South America
Père David's Deer	*Elaphurus davidianus*	Asia
Pudu	*Pudu*	South America
***Red Deer**	*Cervus elaphus*	Europe
Roe Deer	*Capreolus capreolus*	Asia and Europe
White-tailed Deer (Virginia Deer)	*Odocoileus virginianus*	North America

*Has a separate article in WORLD BOOK.

DEER

Brocket Deer are found from southern Mexico to Paraguay. They live in wooded areas from sea level to altitudes of 16,000 feet (4,880 meters). These deer grow about 20 inches (51 centimeters) high, and their antlers look somewhat like spikes. Brocket deer are so shy that they are rarely seen.

Pampas Deer are named for the tall pampas grasses of the South American plains in which they live. These deer grow about 3 feet (91 centimeters) high, and have reddish-brown or yellowish-brown hair. The male has glands in its back hoofs that give off a strong odor.

Huemul, or *Andean deer*, are found in the Andes Mountains from Ecuador southward to Patagonia. They live in thick forests and grassy plateaus at altitudes of about 16,000 feet (4,880 meters). Huemul grow about 3 feet (91 centimeters) high and have speckled coats of gray, yellow, and brown. The hair is rough and brittle, and grows longest on the forehead and tail.

Asian and European Deer include (1) musk deer; (2) muntjac; (3) chital, or axis deer; (4) fallow deer; (5) red deer; (6) reindeer; and (7) Père David's deer.

Musk Deer roam the forests of the mountains and high plateaus of central and northeastern Asia. These deer grow about 22 inches (56 centimeters) high and weigh about 25 pounds (11 kilograms). They have no antlers. Two tusklike teeth grow downward from the top jaw of the male. The deer are named for an oily substance called *musk*, which is produced by a gland in the skin of the male's abdomen. Musk is used in perfume.

WHERE DEER LIVE

The black areas of the map show the parts of the world in which deer live. Deer live on every continent except Antarctica.

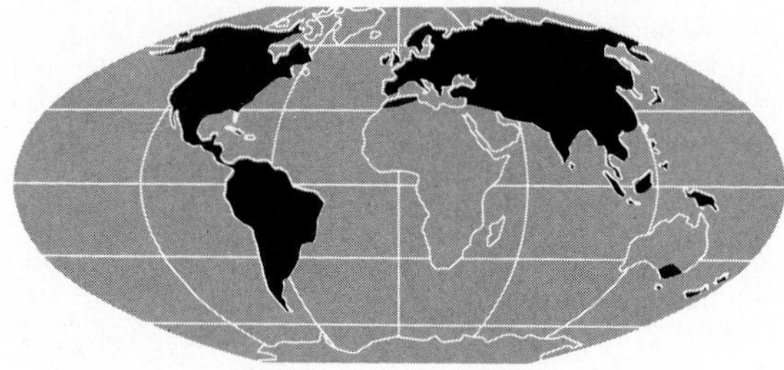

Muntjac live in the jungles of Borneo, India, Java, Nepal, southern China, Sri Lanka, and Taiwan. They stand about 20 inches (51 centimeters) high and weigh about 40 pounds (18 kilograms). These deer make a barking noise when they are frightened, and are sometimes called *barking deer*.

Chital, or *Axis deer*, are found in the grasslands and open forests of India and Sri Lanka. Some people consider them the most beautiful and graceful of all deer. Chital grow about 3 feet (91 centimeters) high and weigh 60 to 100 pounds (27 to 45 kilograms). Their sleek reddish-brown coats are spotted with white. Their antlers, which grow about 3 feet (91 centimeters) long, curve gracefully back from their heads. Like the male musk deer, male chital have two tusklike teeth that grow from the upper jaw. These deer are found in zoos in many parts of the world.

Fallow Deer originally lived only in lands along the Mediterranean Sea. Today, they may be found in most parts of Europe. Many are kept in herds on estates or in parks. Fallow deer are about as large as chital. Unlike most European deer, they have broad, flat antlers shaped somewhat like those of the moose.

Red Deer are the elk of Europe and Asia. They are smaller than American elk, and have reddish-brown hair. Red deer are famous for their courage and beauty.

Reindeer, which live in the Arctic and in the northern regions of Europe and Asia, look like caribou. The male and female both have antlers. Reindeer are among the most important animals of the far north. People eat reindeer meat, make clothing and tents from the hide, and carve utensils from the antlers and bones.

Père David's Deer once roamed the plains and marshes of northern China. They are named for a French priest who first saw the deer in 1865. Today, only about 400 of these deer are still alive. They live in private parks and zoos in many parts of the world. All are related to deer that were brought to England about 1900 from a herd kept by the Chinese emperor in Peking. The original herd in China died out in 1920, but the English herd did well. Père David's deer stand about $3\frac{1}{2}$ feet (1.1 meters) high, and have a grayish-tan coat in winter and a reddish-tan coat in summer.

Scientific Classification. Deer are members of the class *Mammalia*, and belong to the order of even-toed hoofed animals, *Artiodactyla*. They make up the deer family, *Cervidae*.

CHARLES M. KIRKPATRICK

DEER / Study Aids

Related Articles in WORLD BOOK include:

Animal (color pictures)	Hunting	Musk Deer
Buckskin	Moose	Red Deer
Caribou	Mule Deer	Reindeer
Elk	Musk	

Outline

I. The Body of a Deer
- A. Legs and Hoofs
- B. Head
- C. Antlers

II. The Life of a Deer
- A. Young
- B. Food
- C. Habits

III. Kinds of Deer
- A. North American Deer
- B. Central and South American Deer
- C. Asian and European Deer

Questions

How many kinds of deer are there?
What does *jerking* mean? What is venison?
How far can a deer jump?
Which is the largest deer? The smallest?
How many toes does a deer have?
What happens to a deer's antlers when they fall off?
What are young caribou called?
Why does a deer face the wind when it eats or rests?
What do deer eat?
Which kinds of deer have no antlers?

DEER FLY is an insect related to the horseflies. It has blotched or banded wings, some of them beautifully colored. Only the females bite man. In the western part of the United States, the name *deer fly* is given also to the *snipe fly*. These flies have two wings and six long legs. Some have long beaks shaped like the bill of the bird called a snipe. Snipe flies and deer flies suck blood from men and animals. Several botflies and ticks that attack deer are also called deer flies. Sometimes they carry diseases. A person may use mosquito repellents to avoid deer fly bites.

USDA

The Deer Fly bites both deer and men. Deer flies often carry a serious blood disease.

Scientific Classification. The deer fly is a member of the horsefly family, *Tabanidae*. It is classified as genus *Chrysops*. Snipe flies make up the snipe fly family, *Rhagionidae*. ROBERT L. USINGER

DEER MOUSE. See MOUSE (Deer Mice).

DEERE, JOHN (1804-1886), was an American inventor and manufacturer. In 1837, he invented the first steel plow that efficiently turned the heavy American prairie sod. He became one of the world's greatest plowmakers.

Deere was born in Rutland, Vt. He became a blacksmith's apprentice at the age of 17. In 1836, he opened a blacksmith shop in Grand Detour, Ill. He soon learned that nearby farmers were dissatisfied with their plows. The heavy, gummy prairie sod stuck to the rough surface of the wood or iron moldboard that was used to turn the soil.

Deere built a smooth, hard moldboard out of an old circular steel saw in 1837. The new moldboard worked just as he had hoped. The soil fell away cleanly in furrows and polished the surface of the moldboard as it turned. Deere and a partner, Leonard Andruss, began making quantities of steel plows. Within 10 years, they were producing 1,000 plows annually. In 1847, Deere sold his interests to Andruss and started a new company in Moline, Ill. To improve the quality of his plows, Deere ordered a special type of hard steel from England. He then had a similar type of steel made in Pittsburgh. This project resulted in the first plow steel ever manufactured in the United States. By 1857, Deere was producing 10,000 plows a year. The business was incorporated as Deere and Company in 1868. Today the company ranks as one of the largest industrial corporations in the United States. RICHARD D. HUMPHREY

See also PLOW (The Sulky Plow).

DEERHOUND is a Scottish breed of dog, close to the Irish wolfhound in ancestry. It was named for its skill at deer hunting, but it is now seldom used for hunting. The deerhound is a member of the hound class of dogs. It is a rugged, but graceful, dog with a keen sense of smell. It measures from 28 to 32 inches (71 to 81 centimeters) tall at the shoulder, and weighs from 75 to 110 pounds (34 to 50 kilograms). The coat of the deerhound is 3 to 4 inches (8 to 10 centimeters) long, and is coarse and wiry. It may be gray, brindle, or wheaten in color. The deerhound makes an excellent pet. JOSEPHINE Z. RINE

DE FALLA, MANUEL. See FALLA, MANUEL DE.

DEFAMATION. See LIBEL.

DEFENDANT. See COURT (How a Court Works).

DEFENESTRATION OF PRAGUE. See THIRTY YEARS' WAR (The Bohemian Period).

DEFENSE, CIVIL. See CIVIL DEFENSE.

John Deere Co., Moline, Ill.

John Deere, *above,* **produced the first riding plow, the Gilpin Sulky, at Moline, Ill., in 1875. The invention saved farmers from many back-breaking hours of work guiding walking plows.**

DEFENSE, DEPARTMENT OF

THE PRESIDENT

SECRETARY OF DEFENSE

The Pentagon—Wide World

The Department of Defense administers United States policies related to national security. It directs the activities of the Army, Navy, and Air Force and coordinates their plans and operations. The headquarters of the Department of Defense are in the Pentagon Building in Arlington, Va., across the Potomac River from Washington, D.C.

Armed Forces Policy Council

DEPUTY SECRETARY OF DEFENSE

- Director of Defense Research and Engineering
- Assistant Secretary of Defense (Comptroller)
- Assistant Secretary of Defense (International Security Affairs)
- Assistant Secretary of Defense (Legislative Affairs)
- General Counsel
- Assistant Secretary of Defense (Health and Environment)
- Assistant Secretary of Defense (Installations and Logistics)
- Assistant Secretary of Defense (Intelligence)
- Assistant Secretary of Defense (Manpower and Reserve Affairs)
- Assistant Secretary of Defense (Public Affairs)
- Director of Defense Telecommunications and Command and Control Systems
- Assistant Secretary of Defense (Program Analysis and Evaluation)
- Assistant to the Secretary (Atomic Energy)

- Defense Advanced Research Projects Agency
- Defense Civil Preparedness Agency
- Defense Security Assistance Agency
- Defense Contract Audit Agency
- Defense Supply Agency
- Defense Investigative Service

- The Joint Staff
- Joint Chiefs of Staff
- Department of the Army
- Department of the Navy
- Department of the Air Force

- Defense Communications Agency
- Defense Intelligence Agency
- Defense Mapping Agency
- Defense Nuclear Agency

- Alaskan Command
- Atlantic Command
- Continental Air Defense Command
- European Command
- Pacific Command
- Readiness Command
- Southern Command
- Strategic Air Command

DEFENSE, DEPARTMENT OF, is an executive department of the United States government. It directs the operations of the nation's armed forces, including the Army, Navy, and Air Force. The government maintains armed forces to ensure the security of the United States and to support the nation's policies and interests.

The Secretary of Defense, a member of the President's Cabinet, heads the Department of Defense. He is a civilian and is appointed by the President with the approval of the Senate. All the department's functions are carried out under his authority and control. The secretary is a member of the National Security Council and the North Atlantic Council. He maintains close contact with various governmental bodies, especially the Department of State.

Organization. The Department of Defense includes (1) the Office of the Secretary, (2) the Organization of the Joint Chiefs of Staff, (3) the military departments, (4) unified and specified commands, and (5) defense agencies.

The Office of the Secretary is made up of the secretary and his staff. The deputy secretary of defense is the secretary's chief assistant. He serves as acting secretary in the secretary's absence. The next senior official is the director of defense research and engineering. He is the secretary's principal adviser and assistant in scientific and technical matters.

Nine assistant secretaries of defense have responsibilities in other specific areas. They deal with (1) budgeting and fiscal affairs, (2) health and environment, (3) installations and logistics, (4) intelligence, (5) international security affairs, (6) legislative affairs, (7) manpower and reserve affairs, (8) public affairs, and (9) program analysis and evaluation. Other leading officials are the general counsel, the director for telecommunications and command and control systems, and the assistant to the secretary for atomic energy.

The Joint Chiefs of Staff consists of a chairman and the chiefs of the Army, Navy, and Air Force. The commandant of the Marine Corps also serves as a member on matters concerning the Marine Corps. Members of the Joint Chiefs of Staff are the principal military advisers to the President, the National Security Council, and the secretary of defense. They also direct the strategy of the unified and specified commands.

The Military Departments are the departments of the Army, Navy, and Air Force. The Marine Corps is included in the Department of the Navy. Each military department is headed by a civilian secretary who administers the department under the direction, control, and authority of the secretary of defense. The military departments organize, train, equip, and maintain the readiness of their forces.

Unified and Specified Commands perform continuing military missions. The military departments assign combat forces to unified or specified commanders, who have operational authority over these forces. Unified commands consist of large forces from more than one branch of service. Specified commands are made up of forces from only one branch of service. The unified commands are the Alaskan, Atlantic, Continental Air Defense, European, Pacific, Readiness, and Southern commands. The Strategic Air Command consists entirely of Air Force units and is the only specified command of the Department of Defense.

Defense Agencies meet specific defense requirements. These agencies include the Defense Advanced Research Projects, Defense Civil Preparedness, Defense Communications, Defense Contract Audit, Defense Intelligence, Defense Mapping, Defense Nuclear, Defense Security Assistance, and Defense Supply agencies; and the Defense Investigative Service.

History. In 1789, Congress established the Department of War to administer and conduct military affairs. In 1798, Congress separated the naval forces from the land forces, creating the Department of the Navy. For the next 149 years, the Department of War and the Department of the Navy were the only two military departments. Their secretaries were members of the Cabinet and reported directly to the President.

During World War II (1939-1945), President Franklin D. Roosevelt directed U.S. combat forces through the Joint Chiefs of Staff, which functioned without a formal charter. The armed services cooperated with one another through unified commands in overseas theaters of operation. On the home front, however, the Army and Navy competed for scarce manpower and materials. The Army Air Forces also pressed for equal status with the Army and Navy.

The National Security Act of 1947 created the *National Military Establishment.* It was headed by a secretary of defense and had three military departments. The Department of War became the Department of the Army. The Army Air Forces became a separate service under a new Department of the Air Force. The Navy and Marine Corps continued under the Department of the Navy. The secretary of defense became a member of the Cabinet, along with the secretaries of the military departments. He formulated general policies and programs for the National Military Establishment. The 1947 law also formally chartered the Joint Chiefs of Staff and provided for a separate Joint Staff to assist the Joint Chiefs.

In 1949, Congress set up the Department of Defense to replace the National Military Establishment. It also increased the powers of the secretary of defense. Congress withdrew executive status from the military departments and provided that they be administered separately under the direction, authority, and control of the secretary of defense. At the same time, Congress also

SECRETARIES OF DEFENSE

Name	Year Appointed	Under President
*James V. Forrestal	1947	Truman
Louis A. Johnson	1949	Truman
*George C. Marshall	1950	Truman
Robert A. Lovett	1951	Truman
Charles E. Wilson	1953	Eisenhower
Neil H. McElroy	1957	Eisenhower
Thomas S. Gates, Jr.	1959	Eisenhower
*Robert S. McNamara	1961	Kennedy, Johnson
*Clark M. Clifford	1968	Johnson
*Melvin R. Laird	1969	Nixon
*Elliot L. Richardson	1973	Nixon
*James R. Schlesinger	1973	Nixon, Ford

*Has a separate biography in WORLD BOOK.

created the post of deputy secretary of defense.

In 1953, Congress passed a reorganization plan for the department, authorizing a general counsel. In 1958, it established the post of director of defense research and engineering. In the mid-1970's, the Department of Defense had a total of about 3 million military and civilian personnel.

Critically reviewed by the DEPARTMENT OF DEFENSE

Related Articles in WORLD BOOK include:

Air Force, United States	Marine Corps, U.S.
Army, United States	National Defense
Flag (color picture: Flags of the United States Government)	National Security Agency
Joint Chiefs of Staff	Navy, United States
	Pentagon Building

DEFENSE, NATIONAL. See NATIONAL DEFENSE.

DEFENSE COMMAND. See AIR FORCE, U.S. (Combat Commands); ARMY, U.S. (Organization); NAVY, U.S. (Organization).

DEFENSE MECHANISM. See EMOTION; NEUROSIS.

DEFERRED PAYMENT. See INSTALLMENT PLAN.

DEFIANCE COLLEGE. See UNIVERSITIES AND COLLEGES (table).

DEFICIENCY DISEASE. See NUTRITION (Results of Malnutrition); DISEASE (Nutritional Diseases).

DEFLATION. See INFLATION AND DEFLATION.

DEFOE, DANIEL (1660-1731), was an English novelist and journalist. He wrote *Robinson Crusoe*, one of the first English novels and one of the most popular adventure stories in Western literature. Some critics have called Defoe the father of the English novel. Others rate him as much less important. But he was one of the great masters of realistic narrative long before such writers as Theodore Dreiser and Ernest Hemingway.

His Life. Defoe was born in London, the son of a butcher and candle merchant. He started a business career, but he went bankrupt and turned to writing. His earliest writings dealt with such controversial subjects as politics and religion. A political pamphlet led to his imprisonment in 1703 for about 4 months.

For about 25 years, Defoe earned his living writing for newspapers. He produced his own periodical, *The Review*, single-handedly from 1704 to 1713. Many politicians hired him to write for newspapers. At times he was secretly writing for the Whig Party in one paper and the Tories in another. Not much is known about his last years, but he continued to write much political journalism, as well as other kinds of work.

His Writings. Defoe is unique in the quantity and variety of his works. It is difficult to tell how many he produced, because most of them were published anonymously. The latest estimate is almost 550, including works of poetry, theology, economics, and geography.

For most readers today, Defoe is known primarily as a novelist. However, this was really a minor part of his writing, and not the part that gave him the most pride. Defoe's two most famous novels are *Robinson Crusoe* (1719) and *Moll Flanders* (1722).

Defoe's novels reflect the growing power and wealth the new English middle class developed through new business opportunities at home and abroad. Many of this new class were Puritans and they tended to believe in the glory of hard work and getting ahead through one's own efforts. The Puritans also stressed education, and therefore became a large part of the reading public. So for the first time, Defoe and other writers treated trade, capitalism, and individualism favorably.

Robinson Crusoe is the story of a man marooned on an island. It is a memorable adventure story and a study of what it is like to be truly alone. It is also a success story, because Crusoe's hard work, inventiveness, and ability to take advantage of others turns his island into a successful little colony. See ROBINSON CRUSOE.

Moll Flanders has been generally accepted as Defoe's best example of a genuine novel. Moll Flanders, the heroine, is a thief and a prostitute. Although her surroundings differ from those of Robinson Crusoe, there are basic similarities between the two characters. They both seem like real persons determined to get ahead and gain security. And eventually they both repent of their sins, and end very prosperously.

Defoe's novels marked an important break with the fiction of the past. He offered the ordinary lives of real people who were the normal products of their social and economic surroundings. Defoe makes us believe in the reality of what we are reading as we are hurried from scene to scene by his breathless prose. Only after we have finished do we realize that we have not really been given much psychological insight into the characters.

IAN WATT

DE FOREST, JOHN WILLIAM (1826-1906), was an American novelist. He was born in Seymour, Conn., but lived in Charleston, S.C., from 1856 until the outbreak of the Civil War in 1861. He then returned to Connecticut to serve as a captain in the Union army.

De Forest wrote about his war experiences and showed his knowledge of the South in his best novel, *Miss Ravenel's Conversion from Secession to Loyalty* (1867). This work and *Kate Beaumont* (1872) established him as one of the earliest realists in American fiction. De Forest's descriptions of war and of small-town Southern life before the war foreshadowed later antiromantic descriptions of the South. But they kept him from gaining a wide audience in his day.

De Forest also wrote novels that exposed political corruption and satirized many customs of his time. These works are inferior to his realistic portrayals of the South.

DEAN DONER

DE FOREST, LEE (1873-1961), an American inventor, pioneered in wireless telegraphy and radio broadcasting. He obtained patents on more than 300 inventions. He patented a vacuum tube called a *triode*, or *audion*, in 1907. It often is described as an invention as great as radio itself (see VACUUM TUBE). The tube, which amplifies weak sounds, is basic to long-distance radio and television communication.

De Forest staged the first musical radio broadcast in history from the Metropolitan Opera House in New York City in 1910. He designed and supervised construction of the United States government's first high-powered naval radio stations.

De Forest moved to the Pacific Coast in 1911. He became interested in sound pictures and diathermy machines. He worked on methods for photographing sound waves on motion picture films.

He was born on Aug. 26, 1873, in Council Bluffs, Iowa. He was graduated from Sheffield Scientific School of Yale University in 1896.

W. RUPERT MACLAURIN

DEGAS, *duh GAH,* **EDGAR** (1834-1917), was a French impressionist painter. Like the other impressionists, he wanted to portray situations from modern life. However, he did not share his fellow impressionists' enthusiasm for light and color. Degas emphasized composition, drawing, and form more than did the other members of the movement. See IMPRESSIONISM.

Degas is best known for his paintings of people in both public and unguarded private moments. He showed his figures in awkward or informal positions to free himself from what he felt were outmoded styles of portraying the human body. But he composed his pictures carefully to achieve formal balance.

Hilaire Germain Edgar Degas was born in Paris of wealthy parents. From 1854 to 1859, he spent much time in Italy studying the great Italian Renaissance painters to perfect his draftsmanship and sense of style. Degas intended to become a painter of historical scenes, but he abandoned this career because he felt a need to paint modern subjects. Probably under the influence of the painters Gustave Courbet and Edouard Manet, Degas began to paint scenes from everyday life. He especially enjoyed painting pictures of race-track and theatrical life.

During the 1870's, Degas began to use daring compositional techniques, partly influenced by Japanese prints. He placed his figures at unusual angles and used odd visual viewpoints. For example, he tilted his perspective to emphasize a sudden or informal movement by a figure. He even cut off parts of the subjects at the edge of the picture. In the 1880's, Degas started to concentrate on intimate scenes, such as women bathing, shopping, or drying or combing their hair.

Degas painted many pictures in oil, but he also excelled in pastel. His pastel *At the Milliner's* is reproduced in color in the PAINTING article. Degas was a fine sculptor as well and produced many figurines of clay or wax.

ALBERT BOIME

DE GASPERI, *GAHS pay ree,* **ALCIDE** (1881-1954), leader of the Italian Christian Democratic Party, was premier of Italy from 1945 to 1953. His leadership saved Italy from falling under control of the Communists in the years after World War II. He served in the Austrian Parliament from 1911 to 1918. After his home city of Trento became part of Italy in 1919, De Gasperi led the Popular Party in the Italian Chamber of Deputies. He was imprisoned by Benito Mussolini in 1926. He was foreign minister in 1944 and 1945.

R. JOHN RATH

Bronze statue, 39 inches (1 meter) high; the Tate Gallery, London

Degas' *Young Dancer* was completed in 1881. The artist now ranks as an important sculptor, but he created statues only to study movements of the body, not to be exhibited.

Oil painting on canvas (1874); The Louvre, Paris

The Dancing Class illustrates how Degas portrayed figures in informal poses. The picture's careful composition and unusual visual viewpoint are typical of Degas' style.

Wide World

CHARLES DE GAULLE

DE GAULLE, *duh GOHL*, **CHARLES ANDRÉ JOSEPH MARIE** (1890-1970), became the outstanding French patriot, soldier, and statesman of the 1900's. He led French resistance against Germany in World War II, and restored order in France after the war. He guided the formation of France's Fifth Republic in 1958, and served as its president until his resignation in 1969.

As president of France, De Gaulle led his country through a difficult period in which Algeria and other parts of France's overseas empire won independence. He fashioned a new role in Europe for France based on close association with a former enemy, Germany. His leadership restored French political and economic stability, and again made the nation one of Europe's leading powers.

Charles de Gaulle became a symbol of France to Frenchmen and to people in other parts of the world. Even his name suggested *Gaul*, the ancient Roman name for France. An imposing figure 6 feet 4 inches (193 centimeters) tall, De Gaulle was stern and aloof. Some thought him rude, stubborn, and arrogant. But De Gaulle had a deep love for France and great confidence in himself. He firmly believed that he was the one man who could make France a world power again.

Early Life. Charles de Gaulle was born Nov. 22, 1890, in Lille. His father, Henri, was an officer in the Franco-Prussian War, then taught philosophy, literature, and mathematics. His mother, Jeanne Maillot de Gaulle, came from a literary and military family.

With his sister and three brothers, Charles grew up in an atmosphere that was both military and religious. As a boy, he enjoyed reading stories of famous French battles. When he played soldiers with his friends, Charles always had to be "France."

After studying at the College Stanislas in Paris, De Gaulle served a year in the infantry. There his height won him the nicknames *Big Charles* and *Asparagus*. He was graduated with honors in 1911 from the famous French military school, St. Cyr.

During World War I, De Gaulle was wounded four times. He was captured at Verdun in 1916. After the war, he served with the French Army in Poland, then taught military history at St. Cyr for a year.

In 1921, he married Yvonne Vendroux. They had a son and two daughters. Yvonne de Gaulle followed her husband wherever his duties took him, but she rarely appeared in public.

Between World Wars I and II, De Gaulle held various military commands and taught at the French War College. His book *The Edge of the Sword* (1932) stressed the importance of powerful leadership in war. In *The Army of the Future* (1934), he outlined the theory of a war of movement, in which tanks and other mechanized forces would be used. Most French military leaders ignored this theory. But the Germans studied it carefully and used it in World War II.

Leader of the Free French. After the Germans invaded France in May, 1940, De Gaulle was put in charge of one of France's four armored divisions. He became undersecretary for war in June. But just days later, on June 22, France surrendered to Germany.

De Gaulle, now a general, escaped to London. He refused to accept the surrender. Nor would he recognize the authority of Marshal Pétain, his old regimental commander, who headed the Vichy government that cooperated with the Germans (see PÉTAIN, HENRI PHILIPPE). For this, a French military court sentenced De Gaulle to death. De Gaulle declared that France had lost a battle but not the war. He broadcast such messages to France as: "Soldiers of France, wherever you may be, arise!" His broadcasts stirred French patriotism and kept French resistance alive.

De Gaulle organized the Free French forces in Great Britain and in some of the French colonies. In September, 1941, he became president of the French National Committee in London. By 1943, the Allies accepted him as the unquestioned leader of the "Fighting French."

Peacetime Leader. De Gaulle triumphantly entered Paris with the Allies in August, 1944. In September, he became head of the provisional government.

De Gaulle got the machinery of government working again during the next 14 months. But France's left-wing parties did not support him, and he resigned in January, 1946. He bitterly opposed the constitution of 1946 because it did not provide a strong executive power. In 1947, he organized a new party, the Rally of the French People (R.P.F.) to reform the constitution. But it lost strength after the elections of 1951 and 1956.

He lived at his country home during his retirement. He wrote his World War II memoirs and watched the political situation in France go from bad to worse. In 1957, though he was 67, De Gaulle still hoped that France would recall him. But early in 1958 he admitted, "Now I begin to fear that it is too late."

The Fifth Republic. Finally, in May, 1958, the call came. France stood on the verge of civil war. Dissatisfied French officers, afraid they would lose the government's support against the Algerian rebels, seized power in Algiers. They demanded that De Gaulle head a new government. In June, De Gaulle accepted President René Coty's request to form a government on the condition that he have full powers for six months.

De Gaulle drew up a new constitution establishing

Wide World

the Fifth Republic. It provided broad powers for the president, who was to be elected for seven years by an electoral college of 80,000 public figures. French voters approved the plan, and the electoral college chose De Gaulle as president in December, 1958.

As president, De Gaulle acted with great firmness. After another revolt in Algeria in 1960, he arrested French officers there who had formerly supported him. He negotiated with Algerian nationalist leaders for a cease-fire agreement. The agreement they reached in March, 1962, ended more than seven years of bloody war. At De Gaulle's urging, the French people voted almost 10 to 1 in April, 1962, for Algerian independence.

The French Assembly ousted the De Gaulle-sponsored government in October, 1962. But De Gaulle dissolved the Assembly. The election that followed made history. For the first time in France, one party—De Gaulle's Union for a New Republic—won an absolute majority. In a separate referendum, the voters also approved De Gaulle's proposal to elect future French presidents by direct popular vote.

In January, 1963, De Gaulle and Chancellor Konrad Adenauer of West Germany signed a treaty providing for political, scientific, cultural, and military cooperation. At the same time, De Gaulle blocked Great Britain's entry into the European Community (Common Market). In 1964, France became the first Western power to recognize Communist China. De Gaulle narrowly won a second seven-year term as president in 1965. In 1966, De Gaulle announced his decision to withdraw French forces from the North Atlantic Treaty Organization (NATO) and remove the NATO headquarters from France. In 1967, he again blocked Britain's entry into the Common Market.

In 1968, French students and workers staged strikes and demonstrations. The economy suffered from inflation and currency problems, but De Gaulle maintained popular support. In April, 1969, however, his proposals for constitutional changes were defeated in a referendum, and he resigned. De Gaulle died on Nov. 9, 1970, after suffering a heart attack. ERNEST JOHN KNAPTON

De Gaulle, Leader of the Free French, led a triumphant parade down the Champs Élysées in August, 1944, to mark the liberation of Paris after the German occupation of World War II.

Wide World

De Gaulle, President of France, ended the seven-year Algerian war in 1962. He supported Algerian demands for freedom, and was warmly greeted during a 1959 tour of the country.

De Gaulle, European Statesman, promoted friendship and cooperation between France and Germany. He and West German Chancellor Konrad Adenauer signed an alliance in 1963.

Wide World

DEGAUSSING. See MINE, MILITARY (Naval Mines).

DEGENERATION, *dih JEHN uh RAY shuhn*, means the state of falling below a normal condition or quality. Any living thing may suffer from degeneration. In man, degeneration may be caused by old age, by lack of sufficient nourishment, by inactivity, by poisons, and by infectious diseases. These conditions cause changes in body tissues and organs and make it impossible for the affected parts to work properly. The accumulation of fat in or around the heart, arteries, and liver interferes with the work of these organs. Doctors call such conditions *fatty degeneration*. In some kinds of degeneration, such as *osteoarthritis*, a disease of the bones, the body tissues themselves may change. See ARTHRITIS.

In plants and animals, poor environment and improper breeding may cause degeneration. Plants that grow for many years in poor soil or an unsuitable climate show signs of degeneration. After several years, new plants will be smaller than the original ones. Seeds from these smaller plants will produce inferior plants.

Man has used degeneration in animals to advantage. He sacrificed speed in the horse to develop a strong draft horse. He reduced the beef-producing qualities of cattle to obtain the dairy cow. BENJAMIN F. MILLER

DEGREE is a name given to various small units of measure. In mathematics, degrees are used to measure angles and also arcs of circles. An angle of 1 degree (1°) is $\frac{1}{90}$ of a right angle. An arc of 1° is $\frac{1}{360}$ of a whole circle. Because longitude and latitude lines are circles, they are also measured in degrees. Degrees in geometry are divided into 60 units called *minutes*. See ANGLE; CIRCLE; LATITUDE; LONGITUDE; MINUTE.

In science, 1 degree of temperature on the Fahrenheit scale is $\frac{1}{180}$ of the difference between the temperatures of melting ice and boiling water. One degree on the Celsius scale of temperature is $\frac{1}{100}$ of the same difference. See THERMOMETER. HOLMES BOYNTON

DEGREE, COLLEGE. A university or college awards a *degree* to a person who has completed a required course of study. The institution presents the degree in the form of a *diploma*, a document which certifies the award. The four basic kinds of degrees are called *associate*, *bachelor*, *master*, and *doctor*. An honorary degree may be awarded for an outstanding contribution in a certain field.

The Associate Degree is awarded by many colleges and universities in the United States and most junior colleges (see JUNIOR COLLEGE). It usually indicates successful completion of two years of college work. The most commonly awarded associate degrees are the *Associate in Arts* and the *Associate in Science*.

The Bachelor's Degree. In the United States, a college student normally receives a bachelor's degree after four years of study in a university or college. He usually specializes in a field of study called his *major subject*. The institution often requires other types of study outside his major field in order to ensure a liberal education. There are many kinds of bachelor's degrees, but the two most common are the *Bachelor of Arts* (*B.A.*) and the *Bachelor of Science* (*B.S.*). The B.A. usually includes majors in such subjects as history, literature, and fine arts, and, in certain cases, science and mathematics. The B.S. usually includes majors in the physical and natural sciences. Most engineering students receive B.S. degrees. Many colleges offer specialized degrees, such as the *Bachelor of Education* or *Bachelor of Architecture*. Law students obtain the *Bachelor of Laws* or *Juris Doctor* after more training. Outstanding achievement in a bachelor's degree may be designated by the Latin phrases *cum laude* (*with praise*), *magna cum laude* (*with great praise*), or *summa cum laude* (*with the highest praise*).

British colleges and universities offer two types of bachelor's degrees, an ordinary, or *pass*, degree and an *honors* degree which requires more extensive and more advanced work. Canadian colleges and universities usually follow British or French tradition in their systems of degrees. See CANADA (Education).

ABBREVIATIONS USED FOR COLLEGE DEGREES

A.A. Associate in Arts
A.S. Associate in Science
B.A., A.B. Bachelor of Arts
B.A. in Ed. Bachelor of Arts in Education
B.Arch. Bachelor of Architecture
B.B.A. Bachelor of Business Administration
B.Ed. Bachelor of Education
B.E.E. Bachelor of Electrical Engineering
B.D. Bachelor of Divinity
B.F.A. Bachelor of Fine Arts
B.M., B.Mus. Bachelor of Music
B.M.E., B.Mus.Ed. Bachelor of Music Education
B.S. Bachelor of Science
B.S. in B.A., B.S.B.A. Bachelor of Science in Business Administration
B.S. in C.E., B.S.C.E. Bachelor of Science in Civil Engineering
B.S. in Ch.E., B.S.Ch.E. Bachelor of Science in Chemical Engineering
B.S. in Chemistry, B.S.Chem. Bachelor of Science in Chemistry
B.S. in Ed., B.S.Ed. Bachelor of Science in Education
B.S. in E.E., B.S.E.E. Bachelor of Science in Electrical Engineering
B.S. in Elem.Ed. Bachelor of Science in Elementary Education
B.S. in H.E., B.S. in H.Ec. Bachelor of Science in Home Economics
B.S. in M.E., B.S.M.E. Bachelor of Science in Mechanical Engineering
B.S. in Med.Tech. Bachelor of Science in Medical Technology
B.S.N. Bachelor of Science in Nursing
B.S.Pharm. Bachelor of Science in Pharmacy
D.B.A. Doctor of Business Administration
D.C. Doctor of Chiropractic
***D.D.** Doctor of Divinity
D.D.S. Doctor of Dental Surgery
D.M.D. Doctor of Dental Medicine
***D.Mus., Mus.D.** Doctor of Music
D.O. Doctor of Osteopathy
D.V.M. Doctor of Veterinary Medicine
Ed.D., D.Ed. Doctor of Education
J.D. Juris Doctor
***L.H.D.** Doctor of Humane Letters
***Lit.D., D.Lit.** Doctor of Literature
***Litt.D.** Doctor of Letters
LL.B. Bachelor of Laws
***LL.D.** Doctor of Laws
LL.M. Master of Laws
M.A., A.M. Master of Arts
M.A. in Ed. Master of Arts in Education
M.A.T. Master of Arts in Teaching
M.B.A. Master of Business Administration
M.D. Doctor of Medicine
M.Ed. Master of Education
M.F.A. Master of Fine Arts
M.M., M.Mus. Master of Music
M.M.Ed., M.Mus.Ed. Master of Music Education
M.R.E. Master of Religious Education
M.S. Master of Science
M.S. in C.E., M.S.C.E. Master of Science in Civil Engineering
M.S. in Ch.E. Master of Science in Chemical Engineering
M.S. in Ed. Master of Science in Education
M.S. in E.E., M.S.E.E. Master of Science in Electrical Engineering
M.S. in M.E. Master of Science in Mechanical Engineering
M.S.W. Master of Social Work
Ph.D. Doctor of Philosophy
†**Sc.D., D.Sc., D.S.** Doctor of Science
S.T.M. Master of Sacred Theology
Th.M. Master of Theology

*Honorary Degree Only
†Usually honorary

The Master's Degree. In the United States, students who desire a master's degree must complete one or two years of advanced study beyond the bachelor's degree. Many institutions require a *thesis*, a written report of a special investigation in the student's major field. The two most common master's degrees are the *Master of Arts* and the *Master of Science*.

In Great Britain, the master's degree is usually considered the highest requirement for an academic career, but a number of British universities also offer the doctorate. In Scotland, a student proceeds directly to the master's degree without taking a bachelor's degree.

The Doctor's Degree is the highest earned degree in the United States, France, Germany, and many other countries. There are two distinct types of doctor's degrees. One is a professional degree required to practice in certain professions, such as medicine. The other is a research degree that indicates the candidate has acquired mastery of a broad field of knowledge and the technique of scholarly research.

In the United States, the research doctorate requires at least two or three additional years of study beyond the master's degree. Most doctoral students are expected to have a reading knowledge in two foreign languages. The candidate must also complete a series of examinations and present a written thesis or *dissertation*. The doctoral thesis represents an original contribution to knowledge, and is a more detailed study of a research problem than that required for the master's degree.

The *Doctor of Philosophy* degree is the most important research doctorate and may include specialization in almost any academic subject. The *Doctor of Education*, *Doctor of Medicine*, and *Doctor of Dental Surgery* degrees represent advanced professional training. Students in such professions as medicine and dentistry can obtain a doctor's degree without first receiving a bachelor's or master's degree. But most acquire a bachelor of science degree before entering medical training.

Honorary Degrees. Many colleges and universities have adopted the custom of awarding honorary degrees to persons for achievement in their chosen fields. Chief among these are the *Doctor of Letters* and the *Doctor of Laws*. These are often given to prominent authors, scholars, and leaders in the professions, business, government, and industry.

History. College degrees date from the 1200's when schools in Europe won the right to examine and license their graduates. The system of degrees, which took form by the 1300's, was modeled on the guild system. A student spent a sort of apprenticeship as a candidate for a bachelor's degree. Receiving the bachelor's degree resembled becoming a journeyman in a craft. The master's degree represented the status of a master craftsman, and served as a license to teach. The student's thesis was his "masterpiece," just as a journeyman submitted an example of his work to become a master craftsman. If the student continued to study and teach in law, medicine, or theology, he might earn the title of doctor. The medieval system remained largely unchanged until the impact of science on education in the 1700's and 1800's. During the last hundred years, college degrees in the United States have been extended to include many new fields of knowledge. HAROLD A. HASWELL

See also CAPS AND GOWNS; GRADUATION.

DE GROOT, HUIG. See GROTIUS, HUGO.

DE HOOCH, *duh hoke,* **PIETER** (1629-1684?), a Dutch artist, made noted paintings of middle-class subjects. They include housewives with maids or children, ladies and gentlemen in conversation or playing games, and soldiers in camp. He liked to show open doors which permitted glimpses of other rooms or of streets and gardens. His pictures were done in warm colors, and he was especially skillful in painting sunlight. His best pictures come close to those of Jan Vermeer in quiet charm and technical perfection. De Hooch was born in Rotterdam, and became a member of the Guild of Painters at Delft in 1655. JULIUS S. HELD

DEHYDRATION, *dee hy DRAY shun,* is a way of preserving foods by drying them. Adding water to dehydrated food makes it ready for eating or for cooking. Dried milk and milk products, soups, coffee, tea, spices, gelatin, dessert mixes, and macaroni are sold in most stores. Other common dehydrated foods include yeast, eggs, and egg products.

Important features of dehydrated foods are their lightness in weight and their compactness. More than 90 per cent of the water is removed during drying. When adequately packaged, most dehydrated foods can be kept for several months if stored below 75° F. (24° C).

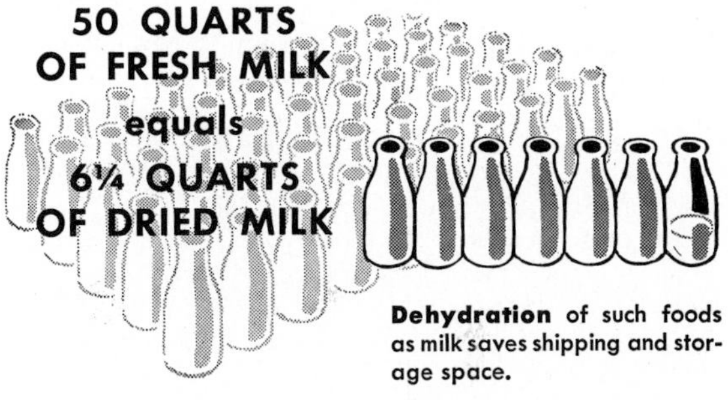

Dehydration of such foods as milk saves shipping and storage space.

Foods selected for drying must be fresh, clean, and at the proper stage of ripeness. Vegetables are usually *blanched* (briefly heated and cooled) to destroy enzymes before drying. Biological products such as serums and vaccines and such foods as chickens and mushrooms are freeze-dried. In the freeze-drying process, the product is frozen and held under conditions of low heat and a nearly perfect vacuum. As a result, the ice in the frozen food is vaporized without melting.

Exposing food to the sun's rays was the earliest known drying method. People have dried fish and meat in the sun for thousands of years. But dehydration did not become commercially important until the middle 1880's. Dried foods were sent to army camps during the Civil War, but they had a bad taste and smell.

World War II brought an increased need for dried foods. By the early 1970's, about 85 million pounds (39 million kilograms) of dried eggs were produced annually in the United States. About 324 million pounds (147 million kilograms) of dried milk were also packaged for consumer use. JOHN T. R. NICKERSON

See also FOOD PRESERVATION (Drying).

DEIANIRA. See HERCULES.

DEIMOS. See MARS (Satellites; picture: Mars Has Two Satellites).

DEISM is a theory about the nature and existence of God. It asserts that God exists, and that He created the world, but that He has no present relation to the world. The deist makes this assertion to harmonize science and free will with the existence of such a being as God. He feels that there is no real conflict between the idea of an all-powerful God and the idea of science studying a law-abiding world, or the idea of a person who makes real choices. The deist does not have to believe that no miracles are possible. Instead, he believes that God, being apart from the world, performs no miracles. The deist usually proves the existence of God from the order and harmony that exist in the universe. The deist also tends to reject revelation as the test of religious truth, accepting reason instead. LOUIS O. KATTSOFF

See also GOD; PANTHEISM.

DEJONG, *deh YAHNG,* **MEINDERT** (1906-), is an author of children's books. He won the 1955 Newbery medal for *The Wheel on the School* (1954), a story about life in a Dutch seashore village. DeJong won the 1969 National Book Award for *Journey from Peppermint Street* (1968), a story about everyday life in The Netherlands around the turn of the century.

DeJong was born in Wierum, The Netherlands, and came to the United States at the age of 8. In 1962, DeJong was awarded the Hans Christian Andersen medal, an international children's book award. DeJong won the Regina medal in 1972. GEORGE E. BUTLER

DE KALB, *duh KAHLP,* **JOHANN** (1721-1780), BARON DE KALB, was a German soldier who won distinction in the American Revolutionary War. He added *Baron* to his original name. He joined the French Army in 1743, and became a brigadier general in 1761. He came to America with the Marquis de Lafayette in 1777, and the Continental Congress appointed him a major general. He served under General George Washington at Brandywine, Germantown, Valley Forge, and Monmouth. He fought under General Horatio Gates in the Carolinas, and died in the battle of Camden, S.C. Lafayette laid the cornerstone of the De Kalb monument at Camden in 1825. De Kalb was born in Bavaria, Germany. ROBERT G. L. WAITE

DEKKER, THOMAS (1572?-1632?), brought to Elizabethan popular literature a fresh emphasis on the life of his day. Dekker's best-known play is *The Shoemaker's Holiday* (1599). It is a zestful picture of Elizabethan life that combines patriotism and romance with a favorable portrayal of the rising merchant class. Dekker's other plays include the romance *Old Fortunatus* (1599) and the comedy *The Honest Whore* (1604-1605).

Dekker wrote many dramas and pamphlets. Between 1598 and 1602 alone, he wrote all or part of over 40 plays, most of them now lost. Yet he usually had no money and apparently spent several years in prison for debt. From about 1604, Dekker turned increasingly to writing popular pamphlets, mainly satires of the London underworld. *The Gull's Hornbook* (1609) ranks among the liveliest records of London life of the time. LAWRENCE J. ROSS

DE KOONING, WILLEM (1904-), is a leading abstract expressionist artist. He is best known for his hectic and violent paintings dominated by lunging brush strokes, swirling paint patterns, and a strong emphasis on line. These works typify the abstract expressionist style. But the mood of De Kooning's paintings and drawings is not always explosive. In his early tender portraits, his studies of women in the 1960's, and other works, he has shown skill with refined, delicate compositions and colors.

Collection Mr. and Mrs. Earle Ludgin, Chicago
An Untitled Painting by Willem de Kooning has bold, strong lines. De Kooning painted this picture in black and white.

De Kooning was born in Rotterdam, The Netherlands, and moved to the United States in 1926. He gained his first critical acclaim for his abstract paintings of the late 1940's. Painted largely in black and white enamel, these pictures are composed of rhythmic curved lines mixed with oddly-shaped flat planes. In 1953, De Kooning exhibited a series of oils and pastels titled *Woman* in which he appeared to present a savage vision of woman as siren or dark goddess. *Woman, I,* a work from this series, is reproduced in color in the PAINTING article. The exhibition inspired many younger artists to attempt to find new ways of representing the human figure. Many of the pictures De Kooning painted in the 1960's contain landscape elements and suggest huge spaces and outdoor light. DORE ASHTON

DE KOVEN, REGINALD (1859-1920), an American composer, became known for his light operas. He wrote more than 400 songs. His greatest success was his light opera *Robin Hood.* It includes his most popular songs, "Brown October Ale" and "Oh, Promise Me." He wrote a grand opera, *The Canterbury Pilgrims,* and a folk opera, *Rip Van Winkle.* Henry Louis Reginald de Koven was born in Middletown, Conn. GILBERT CHASE

DE KRUIF, *duh KRIFE,* **PAUL** (1890-1971), an American writer, specialized in scientific and medical subjects. He publicized many medical discoveries and background facts about medical scientists at work. His books include such works as *Microbe Hunters, Hunger Fighters, Men Against Death,* and *Life Among the Doctors.*

Paul de Kruif
Don Wallace, Harcourt Brace

The Bark of Dante **was the first success achieved by Eugène Delacroix. The painting is based on an episode in Dante's poem *Inferno*. It shows Dante and the Roman poet Virgil crossing a lake in hell as the drowning damned clutch at their boat.**

The Louvre, Paris, Art Reference Bureau

De Kruif was born in Zeeland, Mich. He received a Ph.D. in bacteriology from the University of Michigan in 1916. He was a bacteriologist there from 1912 to 1917, and at the Rockefeller Institute (now Rockefeller University) from 1920 to 1922. De Kruif served as an officer in the Army Sanitary Corps during World War I. CARL NIEMEYER

DELACROIX, *duh lah KRWAH,* **EUGÈNE** (1798-1863), was the leader of the Romantic movement in French painting. The writings of William Shakespeare, Lord Byron, and Sir Walter Scott inspired many of his pictures. Dante's *Inferno* provided the subject for his first successful painting, *The Bark of Dante*, exhibited in the Salon of 1822, and now in the Louvre in Paris.

The colorist tradition of the Venetian painters and the dynamic baroque art of the painter Peter Paul Rubens influenced Delacroix's style of painting. He used dashing brushwork, emotional line, and bold color. He was a master of tragic subjects, and his paintings show an intense feeling unknown in works of his day. The classical painters of his time condemned his paintings because he disregarded established traditions. Delacroix's highly individual style and independence as an artist made him a forerunner of modern art.

After his visit to Morocco in 1832, Delacroix's canvases often dealt with harem subjects, lion hunts, and other scenes from Arab life. His paintings include *Women of Algiers*, *Jewish Wedding in Morocco*, *Christ on the Cross*, and *The Murder of the Bishop of Liège*. Ferdinand Victor Eugène Delacroix was born at Charenton, near Paris, on April 26, 1798. JOSEPH C. SLOANE

See also MILTON, JOHN (picture); GREECE (picture).

DELAGOA BAY, *DEL uh GO uh,* is an inlet of the Indian Ocean which cuts into the coast of Mozambique. The port of Lourenço Marques is located on Delagoa Bay. For location, see MOZAMBIQUE (map).

DE LA MARE, *DEL uh MAIR,* **WALTER** (1873-1956), a British writer, became famous for his poetry of childhood and for his novel, *Memoirs of a Midget*. Much of his poetry and prose is dreamlike and full of fantasy. His works include *Songs of Childhood* (which he wrote under the pen name of Walter Ramal); *Crossings*, a play; *The Burning-Glass;* and *Collected Stories for Children*.

De la Mare was born in Charlton, Kent. He attended St. Paul's School, and then worked for an oil company. King George VI of Great Britain made him a Companion of Honor in 1948, and Queen Elizabeth II appointed him to the Order of Merit in 1953. JOSEPH E. BAKER

See also REGINA MEDAL.

DELANY, MARTIN ROBINSON (1812-1885), was an American Negro army officer, physician, journalist, and social reformer. He was trained as a physician at Harvard University. He practiced medicine occasionally in Pittsburgh, but spent most of his time fighting against slavery. He worked for the *Underground Railroad*, a system for helping Negro slaves escape to the North in the days before the Civil War. He also wrote for an abolitionist newspaper owned by the Negro crusader Frederick Douglass. In the 1850's, Delany joined a movement that urged free Negroes to move to Africa. But Delany later lost his enthusiasm for this "back-to-Africa" movement. Delany served as a Union army surgeon during the Civil War. He became the first Negro to earn the rank of major. He was born in Charleston, W.Va. (then Virginia). RICHARD BARDOLPH

DE LA ROCHE, *rawsh,* **MAZO** (1879-1961), a Canadian novelist, was best known for her long series of books about the Whiteoak family. *Jalna*, first of the series, won the *Atlantic Monthly*'s $10,000 prize in 1927. She also wrote *Portrait of a Dog*, *The Master of Jalna*, *Young Renny*, *Whiteoak Harvest*, *Whiteoak Heritage*, and *Whiteoaks of Jalna*. Her books are noted for their description of simple and ordinary people. She was born in Toronto, Ont. GEORGE J. BECKER

DE LAVAL, CARL GUSTAF. See MILKING MACHINE; SEPARATOR; TURBINE (History).

H. Armstrong Roberts

Getty Oil Company Docks South of Wilmington

DELAWARE

THE FIRST STATE

Delaware (blue) ranks 49th in size among all the states, and is the smallest of the Southern States (gray).

DELAWARE is the second smallest state. Only Rhode Island has a smaller area. And only four states—Nevada, Vermont, Wyoming, and Alaska—have fewer people. Delaware, a Southern State, lies at the northeastern corner of the southern region. It is close to many of the nation's largest industrial cities. The Delaware River, and networks of canals, highways, and railroads, carry products from Delaware to Baltimore, New York City, Philadelphia, and Washington, D.C.

Delaware lies along the Atlantic coastline. It shares the Delmarva Peninsula with parts of Maryland and Virginia. Most of Delaware is a low, flat plain. Rolling hills and valleys cover the northern tip of the state.

Some of the largest corporations in the United States have their home offices in Delaware. This is because a Delaware state law allows companies to incorporate in Delaware even if they do much of their business elsewhere. It is easier and less expensive to incorporate in Delaware than in most other states. Several of the nation's biggest chemical companies have headquarters and research laboratories in or near Wilmington, the

Delaware River and Bay Authority

The Delaware Memorial Bridge near New Castle

FACTS IN BRIEF

Capital: Dover.

Government: *Congress*—U.S. senators, 2; U.S. representatives, 1. *Electoral Votes*—3. *State Legislature*—senators, 21; representatives, 41. *Counties*—3.

Area: 2,057 sq. mi. (5,328 km²), including 75 sq. mi. (194 km²) of inland water but excluding 350 sq. mi. (906 km²) of Delaware Bay; 49th in size among the states. *Greatest Distances*—north-south, 96 mi. (154 km); east-west, 35 mi. (56 km). *Coastline*—general coastline, 28 mi. (45 km); tidal shoreline, 381 mi. (613 km).

Elevation: *Highest*—442 ft. (135 m) above sea level on Ebright Road in New Castle County; *Lowest*—sea level along the coast.

Population: *Estimated 1975 Population*—601,000; 46th among the states; distribution, 72 per cent urban, 28 per cent rural; density, 292 persons per sq. mi. (113 persons per km²). *1970 Census*—548,104.

Chief Products: *Agriculture*—broilers, corn, dairy products, eggs, hogs, soybeans. *Fishing Industry*—clams, crabs, oysters. *Manufacturing and Processing*—chemicals, food and food products, metals and metal products, machinery. *Mining*—clays, sand and gravel.

Statehood: Dec. 7, 1787, the first state.

State Motto: *Liberty and Independence.*

State Song: "Our Delaware." Words by George B. Hynson; music by William M. S. Brown.

state's only large city. These firms include E. I. du Pont de Nemours & Company, the world's largest chemical manufacturer. Wilmington is sometimes called the *Chemical Capital of the World.* Dover is the capital of Delaware.

Delaware ranks among the leading states in the raising of *broilers* (chickens from 9 to 12 weeks old). Broiler raising has made Sussex County in southern Delaware one of the richest farm regions in the United States.

In 1610, a ship from the Virginia colony sailed into what is now called Delaware Bay. The captain named the bay *De La Warr Bay* for Lord De La Warr, the governor of Virginia. Delaware is known as the *First State*, because on Dec. 7, 1787, it became the first state to approve the United States Constitution.

Delaware is the only state with counties divided into areas called *hundreds.* It is also the only state in which the legislature can amend the state constitution without the approval of the voters. For Delaware's relationship to other states in its region, see SOUTHERN STATES.

Hagley Museum Historic Site near Wilmington

Hagley Museum

The contributors of this article are Johan J. Groot, Project Manager for the United Nations, and former Professor and State Geologist at the University of Delaware; John A. Munroe, H. Rodney Sharp Professor of History at the University of Delaware; and Bernard J. Smyth, Editor in Chief, Independent Newspapers, Inc., and former Editor and Publisher of the Delaware State News.

Constitution of Delaware dates from 1897. Earlier constitutions were adopted in 1776, 1792, and 1831. An *amendment* (change) to the constitution may be proposed by the state legislature or by a constitutional convention. Legislative amendments must be approved by two-thirds of the members of both houses of the legislature. They must then be approved in a similar manner after the next legislature is elected. Delaware is the only state in which legislative amendments do not need approval by the voters. Before a constitutional convention can meet, it must be approved by two-thirds of both houses of two successive legislatures. Then it must be approved by a majority of the voters who cast ballots for or against the convention.

Executive. Delaware's governor serves a four-year term. He may succeed himself, but he can serve only two terms. He receives a yearly salary of $35,000. For a list of Delaware's governors, see the *History* section of this article. The lieutenant governor, attorney general, and insurance commissioner are elected to four-year terms. The state treasurer and the auditor of accounts are elected to two-year terms.

The governor appoints the secretary of state, various officials who make up an executive department cabinet, judges, and members of the state board of education. Major appointed officials serve terms that range from 3 to 10 years.

Legislature is also called the *General Assembly.* It consists of a 21-member Senate and a 41-member House of Representatives. State senators are elected to four-year terms, and representatives to two-year terms. Regular legislative sessions begin on the second Tuesday in January each year. Regular sessions may not extend beyond June 30. The governor or the presiding officers of both houses may call for special sessions. Special sessions have no time limit.

Delaware's constitution was adopted in 1897, when the state was shifting toward an industrial economy. It tried to protect farmers by giving them greater representation than city areas in the legislature. In 1964, Delaware changed its legislative districts to give better representation to the state's city areas. But in 1967, a federal court ruled that the change did not give enough representation to city areas. Delaware redrew its districts in 1968 and again in 1971.

Courts. All Delaware judges are appointed by the governor, with the approval of the state Senate. The highest court in Delaware is the state Supreme Court. It has a chief justice and two associate justices. The governor selects the chief justice. The Superior Court has nine judges. It meets in all three counties of the state. Other Delaware courts include a Court of Chancery, the Wilmington Municipal Court, family courts and common pleas courts in each county, and justice of the peace courts. Justices of the peace serve four-year terms. All other judges serve 12-year terms.

Local Government. Delaware has only three counties —Kent, New Castle, and Sussex. New Castle, the largest Delaware county, is governed by a six-member council headed by an elected president. Sussex County has a five-member council, with one councilman serving as president. An elected *levy court* (county commission) governs Kent County. The levy court has seven members. All members of the three county governing bodies serve four-year terms. Other elected county officials in Delaware include a comptroller, sheriff, and recorder of deeds.

Delaware is the only state in which counties are divided into *hundreds.* A hundred has no government of its own, but it serves as a basis for property and zoning location. See HUNDRED.

A state law permits Delaware municipalities of 1,000 or more persons to have *home rule* (self-government) to the extent that they may amend their own charters. By

Delaware Bureau of Travel Development

The Governor's House, a restored home in Dover, was built about 1790. The historic house, known as *Woodburn* for many years, became the official residence of Delaware's governors in 1966. Previous governors had lived in houses rented by the state.

The State Seal

Symbols of Delaware. On the seal, a sheaf of wheat, an ear of corn, and an ox symbolize Delaware's early farms. A farmer and rifleman represent the duties of the people of Delaware both as productive workers and as defenders of their rights. The seal was adopted in 1911. The flag, adopted in 1912, has an adaptation of the seal. Below the seal, the date "December 7, 1787," shows that Delaware was the first state to ratify the U.S. Constitution.

Flag and bird illustrations, courtesy of Eli Lilly and Company

The State Flag

the early 1970's, about 10 municipalities had taken advantage of this law. Most Delaware cities and towns have either a mayor-council or a council-manager form of government.

Taxation. Individual income taxes account for about 30 per cent of the state government's income. Licenses provide another 18 per cent. Other sources of income include a corporate income tax, estate and gift taxes, excise taxes, and property taxes. About 12 per cent of the state's income comes from federal grants and other U.S. government programs.

Politics. Since 1900, only six Democratic presidential candidates have won Delaware's electoral votes. During that period, Democrats have been elected governor of the state only five times. However, Democrats in Delaware made major gains during the 1960's and 1970's. Democratic candidates for President and governor carried the state in the 1960 and 1964 elections. For Delaware's electoral votes and voting record in presidential elections, see ELECTORAL COLLEGE (table).

Delaware Division of Economic Development

Legislative Hall, the state capitol, is in Dover. The main part of the building was completed in 1933, and wings were added at each end in 1970. Dover became the capital of Delaware in 1777. New Castle had been the capital since 1704.

The State Flower
Peach Blossom

The State Bird
Blue Hen Chicken

The State Tree
American Holly

DELAWARE/People

The 1970 United States census reported that Delaware had a population of 548,104. This figure was an increase of about 23 per cent over the 1960 figure, 446,292. The U.S. Bureau of the Census estimated that by 1975 the state's population had reached about 601,000.

About three-fourths of the people in Delaware live in urban areas. That is, they live in or near cities and towns of 2,500 or more persons. More than two-thirds of the people live in the Wilmington metropolitan area. This is the state's only Standard Metropolitan Statistical Area (see METROPOLITAN AREA). For its population, see the *Index* to the political map of Delaware with this article.

Wilmington is the only large city in the state. None of the other cities has a population of over 25,000. Dover is the state capital. See the separate articles on the cities of Delaware listed in the *Related Articles* at the end of this article.

About 97 per cent of the persons who live in Delaware were born in the United States. Of the few persons born in other countries who live in the state, the largest groups came from Canada, Germany, Great Britain, Italy, and Poland.

Roman Catholics and Methodists make up the largest religious groups in Delaware. Other large church groups include Episcopalians, Lutherans, and Presbyterians.

DELAWARE MAP INDEX

Population

548,104 ...Census..1970
446,292 ......"....1960
318,085 ......"....1950
266,505 ......"....1940
238,380 ......"....1930
223,003 ......"....1920
202,322 ......"....1910
184,735 ......"....1900
168,493 ......"....1890
146,608 ......"....1880
125,015 ......"....1870
112,216 ......"....1860
91,532 ......"....1850
78,085 ......"....1840
76,748 ......"....1830
72,749 ......"....1820
72,674 ......"....1810
64,273 ......"....1800
59,096 ......"....1790

Counties

Kent ......81,892..F 3
New Castle 385,856..C 3
Sussex .....80,356..I 4

Metropolitan Area

Wilmington 499,493
(385,856 in Del.; 60,346 in N.J.; 53,291 in Md.)

Cities and Towns

Andrewsville ....H 3
Angola ....I 6
Arden ....555..A 4
Armstrong ....C 2
Atlanta ....I 3
Bacons ....K 3
Basin Corner ......B 3
Bay View Beach ...C 3
Bayard ....K 6
Bayville ....K 6
Bear ....B 3
Bellefonte ...1,442..A 4
Bennetts Pier ......G 5
Berrytown ....G 3
Bethany Beach 189..J 6
Bethel ....E 3
Bethel ....219..J 3
Biddles Corner .....C 3
Big Oak Corner ....E 3
Big Stone
Beach ....G 5
Bishops Corner .....E 3
Blackbird ....D 3
Blackiston ....E 3
Blades ....632..J 3
Bowers ....268..G 4
Bowers Beach ......G 4
Boyds Corner ......C 3
Brandywine ....A 3
Brenford ....E 3
Bridgeville ..1,317..I 3
Broad Creek ....J 3
Broadkill Beach ....H 6
Brookside ...7,856..B 2
Brownsville ....H 3
Camden .....1,241..F 4
Cannon ....I 3
Canterbury ....G 4
Centerville ....A 3
Chapeltown ....F 3
Cheswold .....286..E 3
Christiana ....B 3
Clarksville ....J 6
Claymont ...6,584..A 4
Clayton .....1,015..E 3
Cokesbury Church ..I 4
Coldwell Corner ....D 2
Collins Park ....B 3
Columbia ....K 3
Concord ....J 4
Coochs Bridge .....B 2
Cool Spring ....I 5
Coverdales
Crossroad ....I 4
Cowgill Corner .....F 4
Dagsboro .....375..J 5
Davis Corner ....F 3
Delaneys Corner ...E 2
Delaware
City ......2,024..C 3
Delmar ....943..K 3
Dewey Beach ....I 6
Dover* ....17,488.°F 4
Dover Base ..8,106..F 4
Downs Chapel ......E 3
Dublin Hill ....I 3
Dupont
Manor* ...1,256..F 4
Dutch Neck
Crossroad ....E 4
Edwardsville ....G 3
Ellendale .....399..H 4
Elsmere .....8,415..A 3
Everetts Corner .....F 2
Fairfax ....A 4
Fairmount ....J 6
Farmington ...109..H 3
Felton ....495..G 3
Fenwick Island 56..K 7
Fieldsboro ....D 3
Five Points ....I 6
Flemings Corner ...H 3
Flemings Landing ..D 4
Flower Station .....J 3
Fords Corner ......F 3
Forest ....D 3
Fowler Beach ....H 5
Frankford ....635..K 5
Frederica .....878..G 4
Georgetown .1,844.°I 4
Ginns Corner ......D 3
Glasgow ....B 2
Granogue ....A 3
Gravel Hill ....I 5
Green Spring ....E 3
Greenwood ....654..H 3
Gumboro ....K 5
Guyencourt ....A 3
Hanby Corner ......A 4
Harbeson ....I 5
Hardscrabble ....J 4
Hares Corner ....B 3
Harmons School ....J 6
Harrington ..2,407..H 3
Hartly ....180..F 3
Hazlettville ....F 3
Hickman ....H 3
Highland
Acres* ....1,471..F 4
Hockessin ....A 3
Hollandsville ....G 3
Holly Oak ....A 4
Hollyville ....I 5
Horseys Grove
Church ....J 3
Houston ......317..H 4
Hughes Crossroad ..G 3
Indian Mission .....I 5
Johnson ....K 6
Jones Crossroad ....J 4
Kent Acres-
South Dover
Manor* ...1,573..F 4
Kenton ....205..E 3
Kirkwood ....C 3
Kitts Hummock ....F 4
Laurel ......2,408..J 3
Leipsic ....247..E 4
Lewes ....2,563..I 6
Lincoln ....H 4
Little Creek ..215..F 4
Little Heaven ......G 4
Lowes Crossroad ...K 4
Lynch Heights .....G 4
Magnolia .....319..F 4
Marshallton ....B 3
Marvels Crossroad ..H 4
Marydel ....F 2
Masseys Landing ...J 6
Mastens Corner .....G 3
Mathews Corner ...D 3
McClellandville ....B 2
McDonough ....C 3
Mechanicsville .....B 2
Middleford ....I 3
Middletown .2,644..D 3
Midvale ....B 3
Midway ....I 6
Milford .....5,314..H 4
Millsboro ...1,073..J 5
Milltown ....A 3
Millville ......224..J 6
Milton ......1,490..I 5
Mission ....J 5
Montchanin ....A 3
Mount Pleasant ....C 3
Mount Pleasant
Church ....K 3
Naamans Corner ...A 4
Nassau ....I 6
New Castle ..4,814..B 3
Newark ....21,298..B 2
Newport ....1,366..B 3
Oak Grove ....F 4
Oak Orchard ....J 6
Oakley ....H 4
Ocean View ...411..J 6
Odessa ....547..D 3
Ogletown ....B 3
Omar ....K 6
Overbrook ....I 6
Owens ....H 4
Pearsons Corner ....F 3
Pepper ....J 4
Pepperbox ....K 4
Petersburg ....G 3
Pickering Beach ....F 4
Pine Tree Corner ...D 3
Pleasant Hill ......A 2
Plymouth ....G 4
Port Mahon ....F 4
Port Penn ....C 3
Porter ....C 3
Postles Corner .....F 4
Prices Corner ......A 3
Red Lion ....B 3
Rehoboth
Beach ....1,614..I 6
Reliance ....J 3
Rising Sun ....F 4
Rockland ....A 3
Rodney* ....2,127..F 4
Rogers Corner ......B 3
Roseville Park .....B 3
Roxana ....K 6
St. Georges ....C 3
Sandtown ....G 3
Scotts Corner ......I 3
Seaford .....5,537..J 3
Selbyville ...1,099..K 6
Seven Hickories ....E 3
Shaft Ox Corner ...K 5
Shorts Beach ......H 5
Slaughter
Beach ....84..H 5
Smyrna .....4,243..E 3
Southwood ....A 2
Stanton ....B 3
State Road ....B 3
Staytonville ....H 4
Stockley ....J 5
Stumps Corner .....D 3
Summit Bridge .....C 2
Talleyville ....A 3
Taylors Bridge .....D 3
Thomas Corner .....D 3
Thompsonville ......G 5
Townsend .....505..D 3
Tybouts Corner .....B 3
Underwoods Corner .E 3
Vandyke ....D 2
Vernon ....H 3
Viola ....154..G 3
Walker ....D 3
Warwick ....J 6
Westover Hills .....A 3
Whaleys ....K 4
Whiteleysburg ......G 3
Whitesville ....K 4
Williamsville ....H 4
Willow Grove ......F 3
Wilmington 80,386.°A 4
Wilmington Manor
[-Chelsea-
Leedom] .10,134..B 3
Winterthur ....A 3
Woodenhawk ....I 3
Woodland ....J 3
Woodland Beach ...E 4
Woodside .....223..G 4
Wrangle Hill ......C 3
Wrights
Crossroad ....F 2
Wyoming ...1,062..F 4
Yorklyn ....A 3

*Does not appear on map; key shows general location.
°County seat.
Source: Latest census figures (1970). Places without population figures are unincorporated areas and are not listed in census reports.

POPULATION

This map shows the *population density* of Delaware, and how it varies in different parts of the state. Population density means the average number of persons who live in a given area.

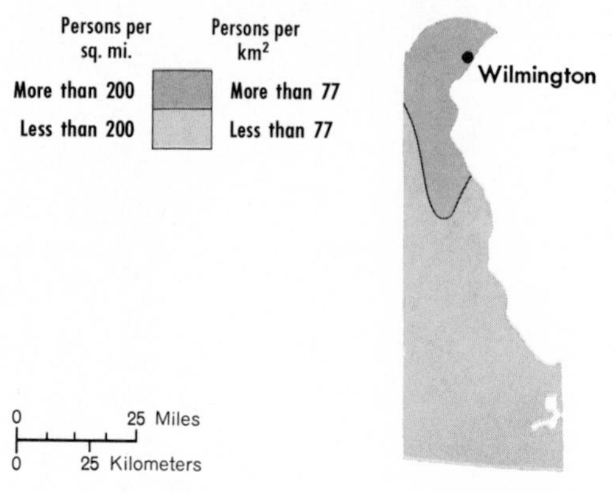

WORLD BOOK map

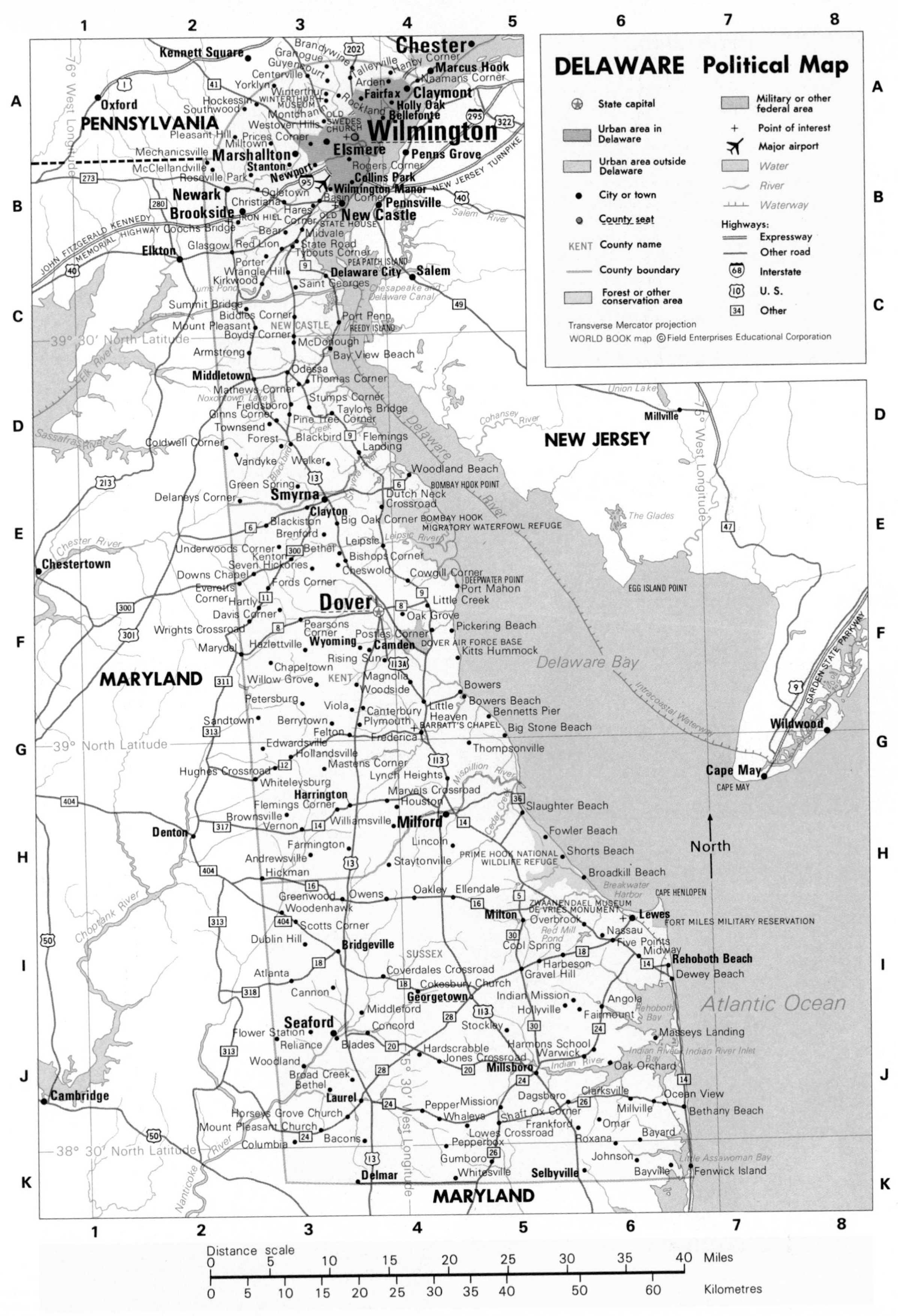

DELAWARE Political Map
State capital
Urban area in Delaware
Urban area outside Delaware
City or town
County seat
KENT County name
County boundary
Forest or other conservation area
Military or other federal area
Point of interest
Major airport
Water
River
Waterway
Highways:
Expressway
Other road
Interstate
U. S.
Other
Transverse Mercator projection
WORLD BOOK map © Field Enterprises Educational Corporation
1
2
3
4
5
6
7
8
A
B
C
D
E
F
G
H
I
J
K
PENNSYLVANIA
NEW JERSEY
MARYLAND
Delaware Bay
Atlantic Ocean
North
76° West Longitude
75° 30′ West Longitude
39° 30′ North Latitude
39° North Latitude
38° 30′ North Latitude
Kennett Square
Oxford
Chester
Marcus Hook
Claymont
Holly Oak
Bellefonte
Naamans Corner
Hanby Corner
Talleyville
Arden
Fairfax
Brandywine
Granogue
Guyencourt
Centerville
Yorklyn
Hockessin
Southwood
Winterthur
Winterthur Museum
Montchanin
Rockland
Old Swedes Church
Westover Hills
Wilmington
Pleasant Hill
Prices Corner
Milltown
Elsmere
Mechanicsville
Marshallton
McClellandville
Stanton
Newport
Rogers Corner
Penns Grove
Roseville Park
Collins Park
Newark
Ogletown
Wilmington Manor
Christiana
Basin Corner
Pennsville
New Jersey Turnpike
Salem River
Brookside
Iron Hill
Hares Corner
Old State House
New Castle
John Fitzgerald Kennedy Memorial Highway
Coochs Bridge
Bear
Midvale
Elkton
Glasgow
Red Lion
State Road
Tybouts Corner
Porter
Pea Patch Island
Wrangle Hill
Delaware City
Salem
Kirkwood
Lums Pond
Saint Georges
Chesapeake and Delaware Canal
Summit Bridge
Biddles Corner
Port Penn
Reedy Island
Mount Pleasant
Boyds Corner
New Castle
McDonough
Armstrong
Bay View Beach
Elk River
Middletown
Odessa
Thomas Corner
Mathews Corner
Noxontown Lake
Fieldsboro
Stumps Corner
Taylors Bridge
Ginns Corner
Pine Tree Corner
Townsend
Union Lake
Millville
Cohansey River
Sassafras River
Coldwell Corner
Forest
Blackbird
Blackbird Creek
Flemings Landing
Delaware River
Vandyke
Walker
Smyrna River
Woodland Beach
Green Spring
Bombay Hook Point
Delaneys Corner
Smyrna
Dutch Neck Crossroad
Clayton
Big Oak Corner
Bombay Hook Migratory Waterfowl Refuge
The Glades
Blackiston
Brenford
Leipsic
Leipsic River
Chester River
Underwoods Corner
Kenton
Bethel
Bishops Corner
Chestertown
Seven Hickories
Cheswold
Downs Chapel
Cowgill Corner
Deepwater Point
Port Mahon
Egg Island Point
Everetts Corner
Hartly
Fords Corner
Dover
Little Creek
Davis Corner
Oak Grove
Pickering Beach
Wrights Crossroad
Pearsons Corner
Postles Corner
Dover Air Force Base
Marydel
Hazlettville
Wyoming
Camden
Kitts Hummock
Rising Sun
Chapeltown
MARYLAND
Willow Grove
Kent
Magnolia
Woodside
Bowers
Intracoastal Waterway
Garden State Parkway
Petersburg
Viola
Canterbury
Bowers Beach
Bennetts Pier
Little Heaven
Sandtown
Berrytown
Plymouth
Barratt's Chapel
Big Stone Beach
Wildwood
Felton
Frederica
Edwardsville
Thompsonville
Hollandsville
Hughes Crossroad
Mastens Corner
Lynch Heights
Mispillion River
Cape May
Whiteleysburg
Harrington
Marvels Crossroad
Flemings Corner
Houston
Slaughter Beach
Brownsville
Vernon
Williamsville
Milford
Denton
Fowler Beach
Cedar Creek
Farmington
Lincoln
Shorts Beach
Andrewsville
Prime Hook National Wildlife Refuge
Staytonville
Hickman
Broadkill Beach
Breakwater Harbor
Cape Henlopen
Choptank River
Greenwood
Owens
Oakley
Ellendale
Zwaanendael Museum
De Vries Monument
Woodenhawk
Milton
Lewes
Overbrook
Scotts Corner
Red Mill Pond
Fort Miles Military Reservation
Nassau
Dublin Hill
Bridgeville
Cool Spring
Five Points
Midway
Sussex
Rehoboth Beach
Harbeson
Dewey Beach
Atlanta
Coverdales Crossroad
Gravel Hill
Cokesbury Church
Cannon
Georgetown
Indian Mission
Angola
Middleford
Hollyville
Fairmount
Rehoboth Bay
Seaford
Stockley
Flower Station
Concord
Masseys Landing
Reliance
Blades
Harmons School
Hardscrabble
Warwick
Indian River Bay
Indian River Inlet
Woodland
Jones Crossroad
Millsboro
Indian River
Oak Orchard
Broad Creek
Bethel
Cambridge
Laurel
Clarksville
Dagsboro
Ocean View
Pepper
Mission
Millville
Horseys Grove Church
Whaleys
Shaft Ox Corner
Bethany Beach
Mount Pleasant Church
Frankford
Omar
Lowes Crossroad
Bayard
Columbia
Bacons
Pepperbox
Roxana
Nanticoke River
Johnson
Little Assawoman Bay
Gumboro
Whitesville
Selbyville
Bayville
Fenwick Island
Delmar
Distance scale
0
5
10
15
20
25
30
35
40
Miles
0
5
10
15
20
25
30
35
40
50
60
Kilometres

DELAWARE/*Education*

Schools. The Dutch and Swedish colonists who settled the Delaware region in the 1600's made education an important part of their lives. Most of their early schools were run by churches. The English gained control of the region in the 1660's, and English churchmen built schools of their own. But many wealthy English sent their children to schools outside the region. Poorer children were taught in church schools or by friends.

Public education began in the Delaware region after the Revolutionary War. A public school fund was set up by the state legislature in 1792. The legislature established a system of public education in 1829. But education remained under local control until the 1920's.

Today, the state board of education is the policy-making agency for the public school system. The board has seven members who serve six-year terms. The governor appoints the members, but the state Senate must confirm the appointments. The department of public instruction, headed by the superintendent of public instruction, administers the public school system. The state board of education appoints the superintendent to a one-year term. A state law requires children between the ages of 6 and 16 to attend school. For the number of students and teachers in Delaware, see EDUCATION (table).

Universities and Colleges. The University of Delaware in Newark is the state's only university (see DELAWARE, UNIVERSITY OF). It was founded in 1833. Delaware State College, a state-supported school in Dover, was founded in 1891. Both institutions are accredited

University of Delaware's Morris Library in Newark was opened for use in 1963. The building faces a parklike mall near the center of the university's 200-acre (81-hectare) campus.

University of Delaware

Barratt's Chapel near Frederica

Robert J. Bennett

DELAWARE/*A Visitor's Guide*

Delaware's many fresh-water lakes and ponds, its ocean beaches, and its rivers and streams provide excellent fishing, swimming, and boating. Cultural and historic attractions also bring visitors to the state. Hunters search the salt marshes for small animals and birds. Each autumn, fox hunters follow their hounds across the countryside in the Middletown region.

PLACES TO VISIT

Amstel House, in New Castle, is the home of the New Castle Historical Society. The house was built in the early 1700's. Its colonial exhibits include arts, handicrafts, and furnishings for the kitchen and music room.

De Vries Monument, in Lewes, marks the site of a fort built in 1631 by Dutch colonists. The monument is named for David Pietersen de Vries, a Dutch navigator and adventurer who sent these colonists to America. Indians destroyed their colony.

Hagley Museum Historic Site and Museum Area, near Wilmington, covers 185 acres (75 hectares) on Brandywine Creek. Éleuthère Irénée du Pont built his first powder mill there. The site has several exhibit buildings and 21 mills. It uses old displays as well as modern

Henry Francis du Pont Winterthur Museum

The Henry Francis du Pont Winterthur Museum

by the Middle States Association of Colleges and Secondary Schools. For enrollments and further information, see UNIVERSITIES AND COLLEGES (table).

Libraries. The first library in the region was established in Wilmington in 1754, when Delaware was still a British colony. In 1788, after Delaware became a state, the Library Company of Wilmington was incorporated. This library still exists as the Wilmington Institute Free Library.

The state has about 20 smaller city and town libraries. Many rural communities are served by bookmobiles. The Historical Society of Delaware in Wilmington and the state archives in Dover have excellent collections on Delaware history. The Morris Library of the University of Delaware and the Eleutherian Mills Historical Library are the state's chief research libraries.

Museums. The Corbit-Sharp House and the Wilson-Warner House, both in Odessa, display American antiques. The John Dickinson Mansion, near Dover, stands as a historic shrine to John Dickinson, who helped draft the U.S. Constitution. The Hagley Museum, near Wilmington, has exhibits that show the activities of early industries. The Henry Francis du Pont Winterthur Museum, near Wilmington, owns a magnificent collection of Early American household furnishings. These are presented in over a hundred rooms. The Old Dutch House, built in New Castle in the 1600's, offers a glimpse into the lives of early Dutch colonists. Wilmington's Old Town Hall, built in 1798, displays material of the Historical Society of Delaware.

---

push-button exhibits to show the activities of early industries.

Henry Francis du Pont Winterthur Museum, near Wilmington, has a magnificent collection of Early American furniture. More than a hundred rooms are furnished in the styles of periods from 1640 to 1840.

Houses of Worship rank among Delaware's most interesting places to visit. *Barratt's Chapel*, near Frederica, has been called the *Cradle of Methodism in America.* The Methodist leaders Francis Asbury and Thomas Coke met in this chapel on Nov. 14, 1784. Their meeting led to the organization of the Methodist Episcopal Church in America. *Immanuel Church*, an Episcopal church in New Castle, was completed about 1710. In its churchyard are the graves of many men famous in Delaware's early days. These men include such early governors as Gunning Bedford, Thomas Stockton, and Nicholas Van Dyke. Other famous Delaware church buildings, with their completion dates, include *Christ Church* in Dover (Episcopal, 1734), *Christ Episcopal Church* on Chipman Pond near Laurel (1771), *Old Drawyer's Presbyterian Church* near Odessa (1770's), *Old Swedes Church* in Wilmington (now Episcopal, built as a Swedish Lutheran church in 1698), and *Welsh Tract Baptist Church* near Newark (1746).

Iron Hill, near Newark, is one of the highest and most scenic points in Delaware. The Delaware River and Chesapeake Bay can be seen on clear days from its summit, 334 feet (102 meters) above sea level.

Old Court House, in New Castle, became Delaware's first Capitol in 1704. Historians believe that there, in 1682, William Penn took possession of all his lands in Delaware.

State House, in Dover, is one of America's oldest state capitols. This colonial brick building was built in 1792. It houses several state administrative agencies.

Zwaanendael Museum, in Lewes, is modeled after a wing of the town hall in Hoorn, The Netherlands. The museum's exhibits include historic documents, Indian relics, and mementos of seafaring days in southern Delaware.

State Parks and Forests. Delaware has nine state parks and four state forests. For information on Delaware's recreational areas, write to the Delaware Bureau of Travel Development, 45 The Green, Dover, Del. 19901.

ANNUAL EVENTS

One of Delaware's most exciting annual events is the Delaware State Fair, held in Harrington during the third week in July. Other annual events in Delaware include the following.

January-April: Swedish Colonial Day in Wilmington (March 29); Delaware Kite Festival at Cape Henlopen State Park in Lewes (Good Friday); Boardwalk Fashion Promenade at Rehoboth Beach (Easter Sunday); Spring Garden Tour at Henry Francis du Pont Winterthur Museum near Wilmington (last week in April, first three weeks in May).

May-August: A Day in Old New Castle (third Saturday in May); Milford Go-Kart Races (Memorial Day); Old Dover Days (first weekend in May); Wilmington Garden Day (first Saturday in May); Delaware Scottish Games and Highland Gathering near Newark (first weekend in June); Cottage Tour of Art in Henlopen Acres (middle of July); Picnic on the Broadkill River in Milton (August).

September-December: Autumn and Christmas tours at Hagley Museum, near Wilmington (October and December); Brandywine Arts Festival in Wilmington (second Saturday in September); Delaware "500" stock car race in Dover (third Sunday in September); Autumn Garden Tour at Winterthur Museum near Wilmington (October); Delaware Day, honoring Delaware's ratification of the United States Constitution, statewide (December 7).

Land Regions. Delaware has two main land regions: (1) the Atlantic Coastal Plain and (2) the Piedmont.

The Atlantic Coastal Plain stretches along the east coast of the United States from New Jersey to southern Florida. The coastal plain covers all of Delaware but the northern tip. This region is a low, flat plain that seldom rises over 80 feet (24 meters) above sea level. Some sections have good farmland. A 30,000-acre (12,000-hectare) swamp lies along Delaware's southern boundary.

The Piedmont extends from New Jersey to Alabama. This region crosses the northern edge of Delaware and is about 10 miles (16 kilometers) wide at its widest point in the state. Rolling hills and fertile valleys cover the region. The highest point in Delaware, 442 feet (135 meters), is near the northern border of the state. Farms and estates occupy much of the Piedmont region.

Coastline of Delaware is 28 miles (45 kilometers) long from Maryland to the mouth of Delaware Bay. If bays, creeks, rivers, and sounds are included, it measures 381 miles (613 kilometers). A long sand reef forms the Atlantic coastline. This dune-covered strip is a popular vacation region. An inlet divides the reef near its center, leading into Rehoboth and Indian River bays.

Rivers, Bays, and Lakes. The broad Delaware River is the state's largest and most important river. It links the Atlantic Ocean with the northern part of Delaware and with parts of New York, Pennsylvania, and New Jersey. The mouth of the Christina River forms Wilmington Harbor. Barges carry cargo up the Christina from Wilmington as far west as Newport. Brandywine Creek is the Christina's chief tributary. Other streams that flow into the Delaware River include Appoquinimink Creek and the Smyrna River.

Many streams in southeastern Delaware empty into Delaware Bay and the Atlantic Ocean. The most important ones include the Broadkill, Indian, Mispillion, Murderkill, and St. Jones rivers. Most of Delaware's streams flow eastward from a long, low ridge near the western boundary. But most of the rivers in southwestern Delaware flow southward and westward across Maryland and into Chesapeake Bay. The Nanticoke is the most important of these rivers.

Ocean ships sail across Delaware Bay to reach the Delaware River. Rehoboth and Indian River bays lie within the great sand reef in southeastern Delaware. Many of the state's more than 50 small lakes and ponds have good beaches and excellent fresh-water fishing.

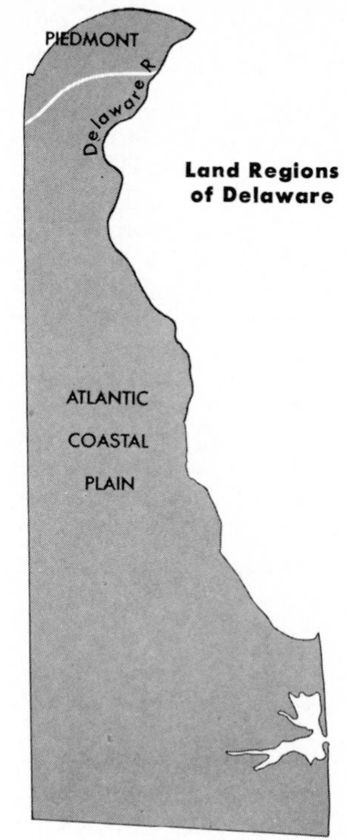

Map Index

Place	Key
Appoquinimink Creek	B 1
Bombay Hook Isl.	B 2
Bombay Hook Pt.	B 2
Brandywine Creek	A 1
Breakwater Harbor	C 2
Broad Creek	C 1
Broadkill R.	C 2
Cape Henlopen	C 2
Chesapeake and Delaware Canal	A 1
Christina R.	A 1
Deepwater Pt.	B 2
Delaware Bay	B 2
Delaware R.	B 2
Duck Creek	B 2
Ebright Road (Highest Point in Delaware)	A 1
Gravelly Brook	C 1
Great Pocomoke Swamp	D 2
Indian River Bay	C 2
Kelly Isl.	B 2
Kent Isl.	B 2
Leipsic R.	B 1
Little Assawoman Bay	D 2
Marshyhope Creek	C 1
Mispillion R.	C 2
Murderkill R.	B 2
Nanticoke R.	D 1
Noxontown Pond	B 1
Pea Patch Isl.	A 1
Pocomoke R.	C 2
Reedy Isl.	A 1
Refuge, Harbor of	C 2
Rehoboth Bay	C 2
St. Jones R.	B 1
Smyrna R.	B 1
White Clay Creek	A 1

William Henry

Dover, the State Capital, lies in central Delaware on the low, flat lands of the Atlantic Coastal Plain. This plain includes all Delaware except the northern tip of the state.

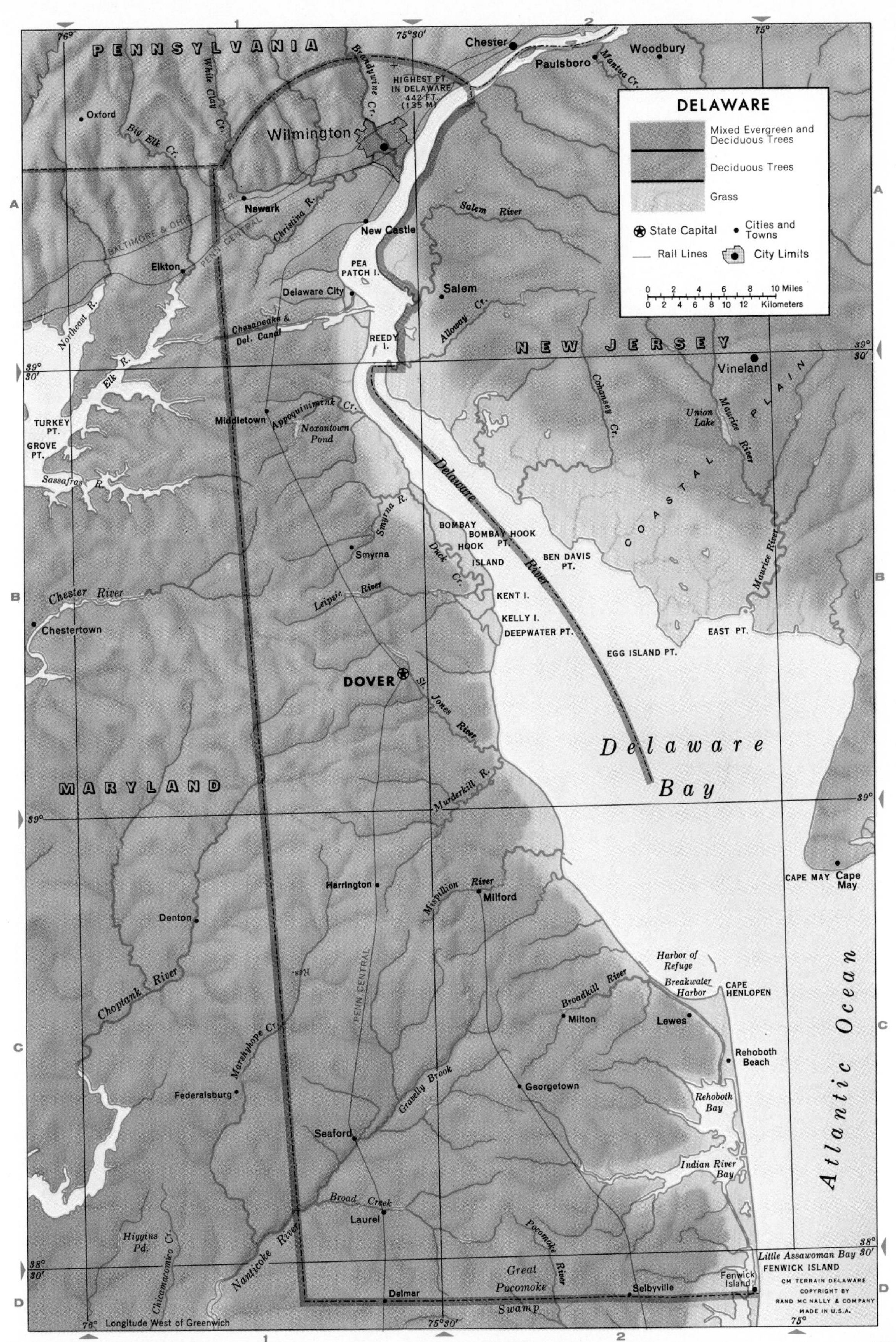

Specially created for **World Book Encyclopedia** by Rand McNally and World Book editors

DELAWARE/*Climate*

Delaware has a humid climate with hot summers and generally mild winters. On hot summer days, Atlantic breezes keep the beaches cooler than the inland towns by about 10° F. (6° C). Mountains in Pennsylvania protect Delaware from the northwest winds of winter. Temperatures away from the coast vary across the state by about 4° F. (2° C) in summer and 2° F. (1° C) in winter. Temperatures in the state average 76° F. (24° C) in July and 36° F. (2° C) in January. Millsboro had both the highest and lowest temperatures ever recorded in Delaware. On July 21, 1930, the temperature there reached 110° F. (43° C). On Jan. 17, 1893, the temperature there fell to −17° F. (−27° C).

The state averages about 45 inches (114 centimeters) of *precipitation* (rain, melted snow, and other forms of moisture) a year. The average annual snowfall varies from about 18 inches (46 centimeters) in the north to about 14 inches (36 centimeters) in the south. The Atlantic Coast receives about 12 inches (30 centimeters) of snow a year.

Delaware State Development Dept.

Rehoboth Beach attracts many visitors during the hot, humid weather typical of Delaware's summer. Vacationers enjoy the cool, salt-tanged ocean breezes that sweep over the white sand beach.

SEASONAL TEMPERATURES

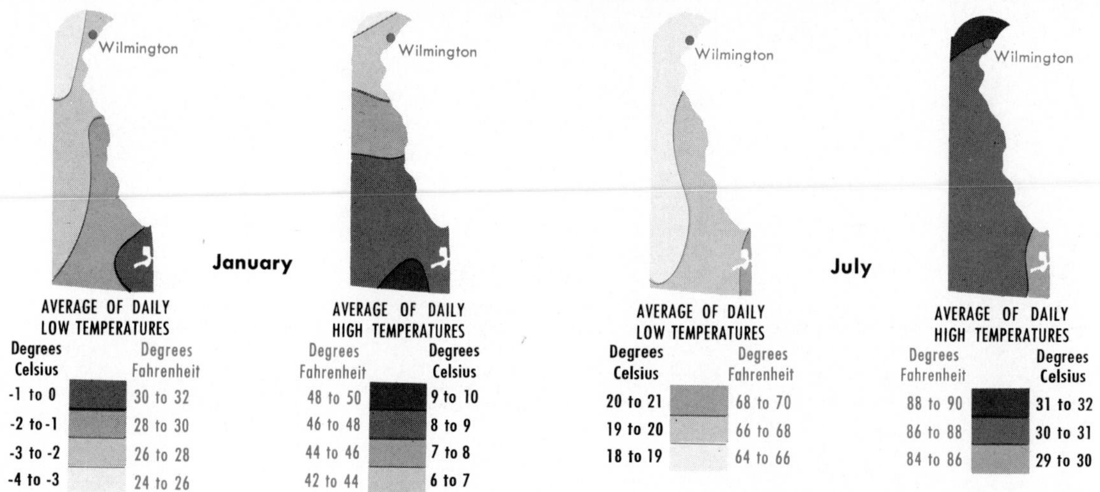

AVERAGE YEARLY PRECIPITATION

(Rain, Melted Snow and Other Moisture)

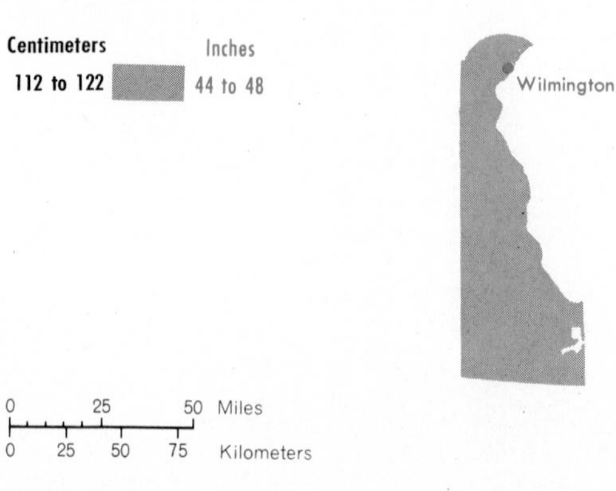

WORLD BOOK maps

AVERAGE MONTHLY WEATHER

WILMINGTON

	Temperatures F° High	F° Low	C° High	C° Low	Days of Rain or Snow
JAN.	42	25	6	-4	13
FEB.	43	25	6	-4	10
MAR.	53	32	12	0	13
APR.	63	40	17	4	12
MAY	75	51	24	11	13
JUNE	83	60	28	16	10
JULY	87	65	31	18	9
AUG.	85	63	29	17	9
SEPT.	79	57	26	14	9
OCT.	67	45	19	7	8
NOV.	55	36	13	2	10
DEC.	44	26	7	-3	11

Wilmington is the most important manufacturing center in Delaware. Farmland is generally good throughout the state. Sussex County, in southern Delaware, is one of the richest agricultural counties in the United States.

A state law permits businesses to incorporate in Delaware even if they have nothing but a mailing address in the state. Companies find it easy and inexpensive to incorporate in Delaware. Also, corporate tax rates are lower in Delaware than they are in most other states. For these reasons, many companies incorporate in Delaware even though they do much of their business outside the state.

Natural Resources of Delaware include fertile soil, large mineral deposits, thick forests, and a wealth of plant and animal life.

Soil. Most of the state is covered by soils that are generally fertile but somewhat sandy. Some of the rocky hills of the Piedmont in northern Delaware are covered by patches of gravel and coarse, red sand and silt. A mixture of clay and loam soils covers the region just south of the Piedmont.

Minerals. Delaware has deposits of clays, sand and gravel, and stone. Brandywine blue granite, a building material used for decorative purposes, is also found in the state.

Forests cover about a third of Delaware. The state's most common trees include beech, black tupelo, hickory, holly, loblolly pine, oak, shortleaf pine, and sweet gum. Smaller trees such as magnolia, sassafras, wild cherry, and willow are also common in the state. Bald cypress and red cedar trees thrive in the southern swamps.

Plant Life. A variety of wild flowers grows in the state. Floating hearts and water lilies dot the ponds and lakes. Pink and white hibiscus flourish in the sea marshes. Magnolias and pink lady's-slippers bloom in the swamps. In some places, blueberries and cranberries form almost impassable thickets.

Animal Life. Deer, mink, otter, rabbits, and red and gray foxes live in Delaware's fields and forests. Muskrats are found in the marshes and swamps. Common birds include bald eagles, blue herons, cardinals, ducks, hawks, orioles, ruby-throated hummingbirds, sandpipers, snowy egrets, and wrens. More than 300 species of birds have been identified in the Bombay Hook National Wildlife Refuge, a 16,000-acre (6,470-hectare) area on Delaware Bay. Hunters seek such game birds as partridge, pheasant, quail, and woodcocks.

Fishermen find bass, carp, catfish, eels, pike, trout, and white perch in the state's lakes, ponds, and streams. Coastal waters have clams, crabs, menhaden, oysters, sea trout, shad, and striped bass. Some diamondback terrapins live along the coast. Snapping turtles are found in the swamps.

Manufacturing accounts for about 89 per cent of the value of goods produced in Delaware. Manufactured goods have a *value added by manufacture* of about $1,281,000,000 annually. This figure represents the value created in products by Delaware's industries, not counting such costs as materials, supplies, and fuels. The leading industries in the state, in order of importance, are (1) chemicals and related products and (2) food and food products.

Chemicals and Related Products in Delaware have an annual value added of about $313 million. Wilmington is sometimes called the *Chemical Capital of the World.* The world's largest chemical manufacturer, E. I. du Pont de Nemours & Company, has its headquarters there. The Du Pont Company has many plants in the United States and in other countries. Several of them are in Delaware. Du Pont's research center, near Wilmington, is one of the largest in the world. Other important chemical companies also have factories, offices, and research laboratories in Delaware. Although Delaware does not rank among the leading chemical manufacturing states, it is among the leaders in chemical management and research.

Food and Food Products have a yearly value added of about $187 million. The state has several fruit-packing plants. Dover has large plants for canning gelatin and other desserts and chickens. Millsboro and Seaford plants pack cucumbers. Lewes is a clam-packing center.

Other Leading Industries. Wilmington factories produce many leather products, including glazed kid for kid gloves. Wilmington has been the center of Delaware's shipbuilding industry since early colonial days. Newark and Wilmington have automobile assembly plants.

PRODUCTION OF GOODS IN DELAWARE

Total value of goods produced in 1971—$1,432,231,000

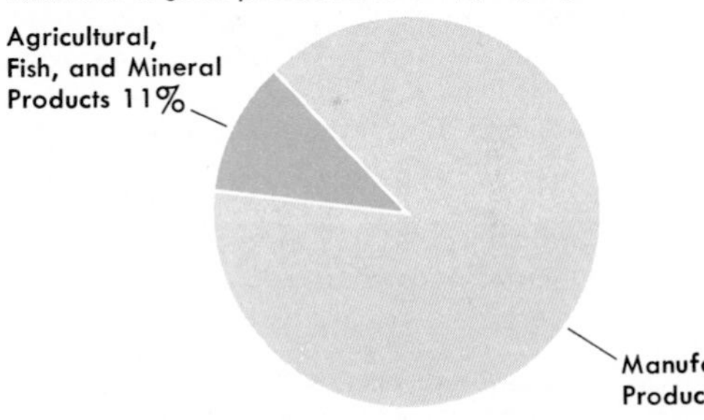

Note: Percentages are based on farm income, value added by manufacture, and value of fish and mineral production. Fish and mineral products are each less than 1 per cent.

Sources: U.S. government publications, 1971-1973.

EMPLOYMENT IN DELAWARE

Total number of persons employed in 1972—238,100

		Number of Employees
Manufacturing	🚶🚶🚶🚶🚶🚶🚶🚶🚶🚶	72,300
Wholesale & Retail Trade	🚶🚶🚶🚶🚶🚶🚶	48,300
Mining & Community, Business, & Personal Services	🚶🚶🚶🚶🚶🚶	39,700
Government	🚶🚶🚶🚶🚶	34,400
Construction	🚶🚶🚶	15,500
Transportation & Public Utilities	🚶🚶	11,000
Finance, Insurance, & Real Estate	🚶🚶	10,400
Agriculture	🚶	6,500

Sources: *Employment and Earnings*, May, 1973, U.S. Bureau of Labor Statistics; U.S. Bureau of Employment Security.

ILC Industries in Dover manufactures space suits for United States astronauts. Other important industries in the state manufacture furniture, machinery, metal products, paper products, petroleum products, plumbing supplies, vulcanized rubber, and wallpaper and drapery material.

Agriculture supplies about 10 per cent of the value of goods produced in Delaware. It earns a yearly income of about $148 million. Farmland covers about half of the state. Delaware's 3,700 farms have an average size of about 180 acres (73 hectares).

Livestock and Related Products have a value of about $93 million a year. *Broilers* (chickens between 9 and 12 weeks old) are Delaware's leading cash farm product. They provide a yearly income of about $72 million. Delaware ranks as one of the leading broiler-raising states. Most of the broilers come from Sussex County. Farms in Kent and New Castle counties produce the largest amounts of milk in the state. Southern Delaware farms raise most of the state's hogs. Beef cattle are raised in all three counties. Other leading livestock products include chickens, eggs, and turkeys.

Crops in Delaware have an annual value of about $52 million. Most farmers in the state raise corn, Delaware's leading cash crop. Corn earns over $14 million yearly. Soybeans, the second leading cash crop, are raised on about a third of the cultivated land in the state. Delaware's farmers also grow barley and wheat. New Castle County has an important mushroom industry. Potatoes and tomatoes grow especially well in Kent County. Sussex County farmers raise apples, beans, cantaloupes, cucumbers, peas, and watermelons. Other leading Delaware crops include hay, peaches, and rye.

Fishing Industry in Delaware has an annual fish catch of about $1½ million. Clams are the most valuable catch. Fishermen also bring in quantities of cod, crabs, oysters, shad, and striped bass. The most valuable fresh-water fish include eels and white perch.

Du Pont Experimental Plant near Wilmington is one of the largest and most productive chemical research centers in the world.
Delaware State Development Dept.

Delaware State Development Dept.
Processing Young Chickens for the market is a chief industry in Delaware. Within several hours after processing, these broilers will be on the counters of markets in major eastern cities.

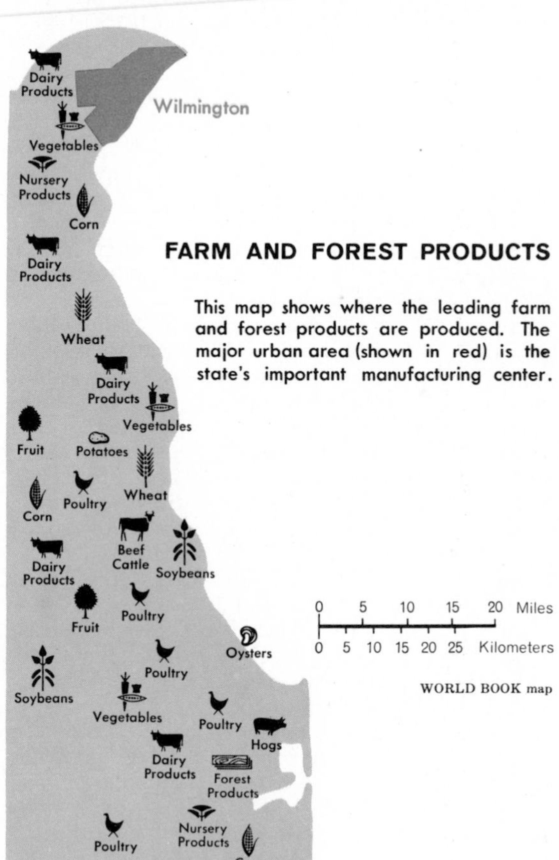

FARM AND FOREST PRODUCTS

This map shows where the leading farm and forest products are produced. The major urban area (shown in red) is the state's important manufacturing center.

WORLD BOOK map

Mining has an annual value of about $2 million. Delaware's mineral deposits have little commercial importance. The state produces clays, gemstones, and sand and gravel. Delaware also has deposits of Brandywine blue granite, which is occasionally used as decorative building stone.

Electric Power. Most of Delaware's electric power is produced by oil-burning steam generators. Private companies produce most of the power. A few Delaware cities operate their own power plants. But even most of these plants receive additional power from private sources.

Transportation. The Delaware River and its tributaries formed the first transportation system in the Delaware region. Most early roads in the region were cattle paths and Indian trails. The state's first railroad, the New Castle and Frenchtown Railroad, was completed in 1831. Delaware's modern highway system began in 1911, when Thomas Coleman du Pont built a paved highway between Wilmington and the Maryland border.

New Castle and Wilmington are Delaware's chief ports for foreign shipping. The Chesapeake and Delaware Canal crosses northern Delaware. Ships traveling between Baltimore, Md., and Philadelphia, Pa., can save about 285 miles (459 kilometers) by using the canal. The Lewes and Rehoboth Canal connects Lewes with Rehoboth Bay.

Nearly all of Delaware's 4,800 miles (7,720 kilometers) of roads and highways are surfaced. The Delaware Memorial Bridge, which crosses the Delaware River near New Castle, connects northern Delaware with New Jersey. The Delaware Turnpike John F. Kennedy Memorial Highway links northern Delaware and northeastern Maryland. It forms part of a major nonstop highway between Boston, Mass., and Washington, D.C. The Cape May-Lewes Ferry crosses Delaware Bay and connects southern Delaware with New Jersey.

Delaware has 22 airports. Greater Wilmington Airport near New Castle is the state's chief commercial air terminal. Railroads operate on about 300 miles (480 kilometers) of track in Delaware. Three rail lines provide freight service. Newark and Wilmington are the only Delaware cities served by passenger trains.

Communication. The *Delaware Gazette* was the first successful newspaper published in the Delaware region. Jacob A. Killen began publishing it in Wilmington in 1785. Delaware's first radio station, WDEL, began broadcasting in Wilmington in 1922. The first television station in Delaware opened in Wilmington in 1949.

Today, the state has 3 daily newspapers and 14 weeklies. The dailies are Dover's *Delaware State News* and Wilmington's *Evening Journal* and *Morning News*. Among the weekly papers, the *Milford Chronicle* has the largest circulation. Ten periodicals are published in the state. Delaware has 15 radio stations and an educational television station.

DELAWARE/*History*

Indian Days. Two tribes of Algonkian Indians lived in the Delaware region when white men first arrived. The Leni-Lenape tribe lived along the banks of the Delaware River. The Nanticoke lived along the Nanticoke River in the southwestern part of the region. By the mid-1700's, white settlers had forced most of the Indians out of the region.

Exploration and Early Settlement. Henry Hudson, an English explorer, was probably the first white man to visit the Delaware region. He sailed into present-day Delaware Bay in 1609. Hudson was trying to find a trade route to the Far East for the Dutch East India Company. Seeing that the bay led to a river, Hudson left the region and sailed northward. In 1610, Captain Samuel Argall of the Virginia colony sailed into the bay, seeking shelter from a storm. Argall named the bay De La Warr Bay, for Lord De La Warr, the governor of Virginia. The Dutch established the first settlement in the region at Zwaanendael (present-day Lewes) in 1631. But trouble developed between the Dutch settlers and the Indians. Within a year, the Indians massacred the settlers and burned their fort.

Swedish settlers came to the Delaware region in 1638. They founded the colony of New Sweden, the first permanent settlement in the region. The Swedes also built Fort Christina at present-day Wilmington. The Swedish government appointed Peter Minuit as the first governor of New Sweden. New settlers came from Sweden and Finland, and expanded the colony northward.

The Dutch government believed that New Sweden was in Dutch territory. In 1651, Peter Stuyvesant, governor of the Dutch colony of New Netherland, established Fort Casimir at present-day New Castle. The Swedish colonists captured Fort Casimir in 1654. But the following year, the Dutch captured all New Sweden and made it part of New Netherland.

English Rule. In 1664, England captured all New Netherland, including the Delaware region. The English ruled the Delaware settlements as part of the colony of New York. The Dutch recaptured the region in 1673, but returned it peacefully to the English the following year.

William Penn of England founded the colony of Pennsylvania in 1681. He wanted to establish a connection between his colony and the Atlantic Ocean. In 1682, the Duke of York gave the Delaware region to Penn as a territory of his Pennsylvania colony. That same year, Penn established representative government for both the colony and the territory. Both the Pennsylvania and Delaware regions had the same number of delegates in Pennsylvania's legislature.

The Delaware region became known as the *Three Lower Counties*, because it was down the Delaware River from Pennsylvania. Pennsylvania continued to grow in the late 1600's and added new counties. Colonists in the Three Lower Counties began to fear that they would soon have a minority voice in the government. In 1701, delegates from the Three Lower Counties refused to meet with those from Pennsylvania. They asked Penn to give them a separate legislature, and Penn consented. The first separate legislature of the Three Lower Counties met in 1704. Pennsylvania governors continued to govern those counties until the Revolutionary War.

The Revolutionary War. England imposed severe taxes on the American colonies during the 1760's. Colonists in the Three Lower Counties resented these taxes. They sent delegates to Philadelphia to attend the First Continental Congress in 1774.

The Revolutionary War began in 1775. On July 2, 1776, the Three Lower Counties joined other American colonies in voting for independence at the Second Continental Congress. Later that year, the region became the *Delaware State.* It adopted its first constitution and elected John McKinly as its first president (governor). New Castle was made the capital.

Delaware soldiers fought throughout the Revolutionary War. Only one small battle took place on Delaware soil. In August, 1777, British troops landed in Maryland and marched across Delaware toward Philadelphia. American troops met the British at Coochs Bridge near Newark on Sept. 3, 1777. The outnumbered Americans retreated, and the British went on to Pennsylvania. There they defeated General George Washington's forces in the Battle of Brandywine, just north of the Delaware border, on September 11. On September 12, the British occupied Wilmington. Delaware moved its capital from New Castle to Dover because of the closeness of British troops. The British stayed for about a month in Wilmington, where they treated their wounded. Then they moved on.

Statehood. On Feb. 22, 1779, Delaware signed the Articles of Confederation (the forerunner to the U.S. Constitution). But leaders from Delaware and other colonies were dissatisfied with the Articles of Confederation. They urged the adoption of a stronger body of rules. John Dickinson of Delaware helped draft a constitution. On Dec. 7, 1787, Delaware voted unanimously to *ratify* (approve) the United States Constitution. It was the first state to do so. Delaware adopted a new state constitution in 1792. At the same time, it changed its name from the Delaware State to the State of Delaware.

During and after the Revolutionary War, the Wilmington area became the center of the nation's flour-milling industry. In 1802, Éleuthère Irénée du Pont, a French immigrant, established a powder mill on Brandywine Creek near Wilmington. This mill was the beginning of Delaware's great chemical industry.

During the War of 1812, British ships stopped carrying goods to the United States. As a result, new industries sprang up in Delaware and in other states to provide needed goods. British ships bombarded Lewes in 1813, but they caused little damage.

The Civil War and Industrial Expansion. Delaware was a slave state, but it also was one of the original 13 states of the Union. Delawareans had strong ties with both the Union and the Confederate states. Delaware fought on the Union side during the Civil War (1861-1865). But many Delawareans felt that the Confederate States should have been allowed to *secede* (withdraw) peacefully from the Union.

President Abraham Lincoln issued the Emancipation Proclamation in 1863, freeing the slaves in all areas of the Confederate States still in rebellion. But the Emancipation Proclamation did not affect slave states that had remained loyal to the Union. The few slaves left in Delaware were not freed until 1865. That year, Amendment 13 to the U.S. Constitution abolished all slavery in the United States.

Delaware's farms and industries prospered during and after the Civil War. The growth of railroads in the 1850's helped farmers move their crops to market. As a result, the value of farmland in southern Delaware increased. During the late 1800's, Wilmington grew rapidly as an industrial city. Thousands of persons worked in the city's shipyards, iron foundries, machine shops, and manufacturing plants. Delaware's present constitution was adopted in 1897.

The Early 1900's brought improvements in education, public welfare, and road building in Delaware. By 1920, the state legislature had established an industrial-accident board, a state board of charities (now the state

IMPORTANT DATES IN DELAWARE

1609 English explorer Henry Hudson, sailing for the Dutch, visited Delaware Bay.

1610 A ship commissioned by Lord De La Warr, governor of Virginia, entered Delaware Bay.

1631 The Dutch founded Zwaanendael at present-day Lewes.

1638 Swedish colonists founded the colony of New Sweden. They established Fort Christina, Delaware's first permanent settlement, at present-day Wilmington.

1655 The Dutch captured New Sweden.

1664 The English seized Dutch territory on the Delaware River.

1682 William Penn took over the Delaware counties.

1704 Delaware's first separate legislature met in New Castle.

1777 The British invaded Delaware and won a small battle at Coochs Bridge.

1779 Delaware signed the Articles of Confederation.

1787 (Dec. 7) Delaware became the first state of the Union.

1802 Éleuthère Irénée du Pont founded a powder mill on the banks of Brandywine Creek.

1861-1865 Delaware fought on the Union side during the Civil War.

1897 Delaware adopted its present constitution.

1917 Delaware established a state highway department.

1951 The Delaware Memorial Bridge opened, connecting Delaware with New Jersey.

1957 The state began providing funds for needy students to attend the University of Delaware.

1963 The Delaware Turnpike John F. Kennedy Memorial Highway was opened, completing a nonstop highway between Boston and Washington, D.C.

1968 Delaware redrew its legislative districts.

1971 The Delaware Coastal Zone Act prohibited construction of industrial plants in Delaware coastal areas.

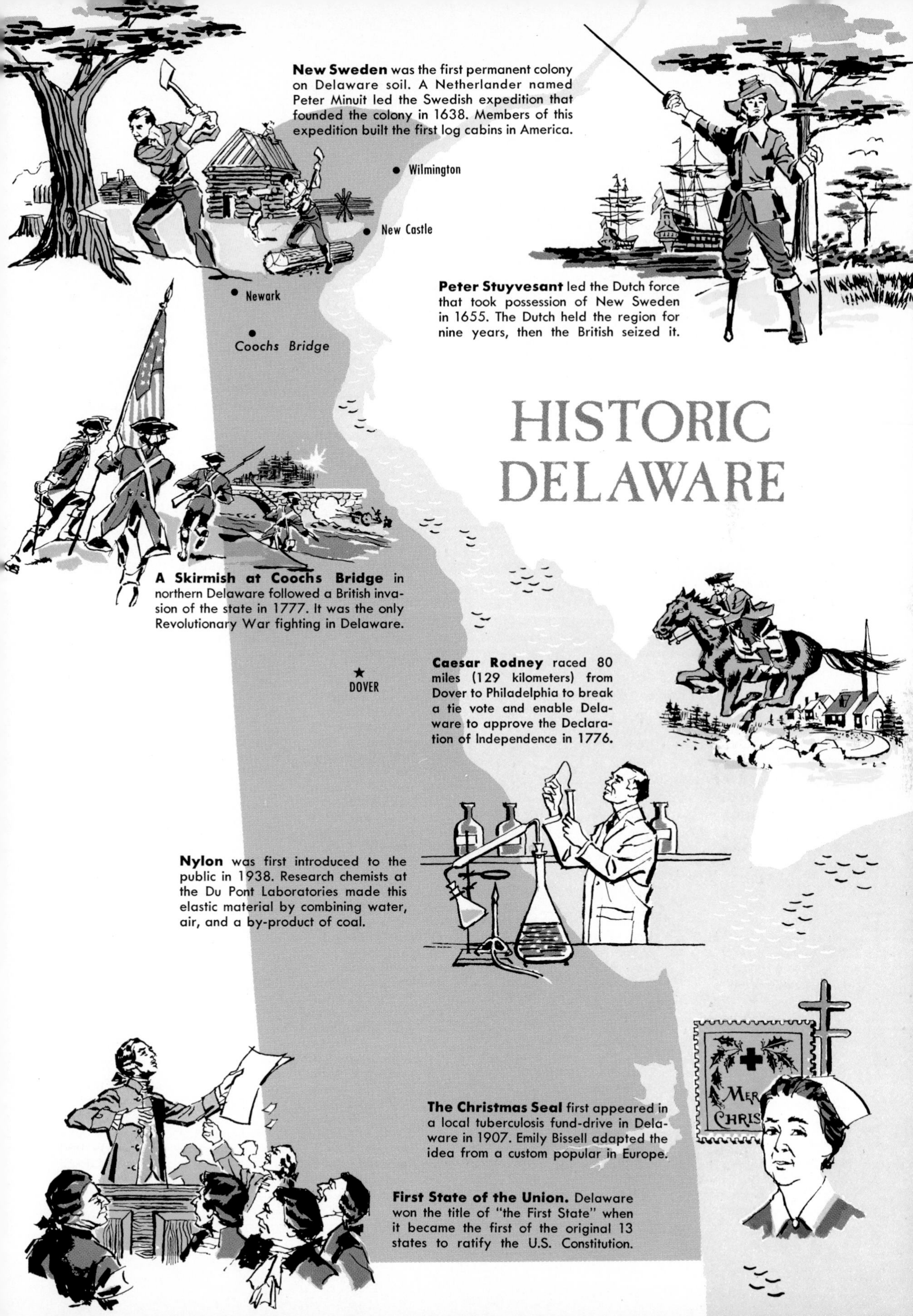

HISTORIC DELAWARE

New Sweden was the first permanent colony on Delaware soil. A Netherlander named Peter Minuit led the Swedish expedition that founded the colony in 1638. Members of this expedition built the first log cabins in America.

Peter Stuyvesant led the Dutch force that took possession of New Sweden in 1655. The Dutch held the region for nine years, then the British seized it.

A Skirmish at Coochs Bridge in northern Delaware followed a British invasion of the state in 1777. It was the only Revolutionary War fighting in Delaware.

Caesar Rodney raced 80 miles (129 kilometers) from Dover to Philadelphia to break a tie vote and enable Delaware to approve the Declaration of Independence in 1776.

Nylon was first introduced to the public in 1938. Research chemists at the Du Pont Laboratories made this elastic material by combining water, air, and a by-product of coal.

The Christmas Seal first appeared in a local tuberculosis fund-drive in Delaware in 1907. Emily Bissell adapted the idea from a custom popular in Europe.

First State of the Union. Delaware won the title of "the First State" when it became the first of the original 13 states to ratify the U.S. Constitution.

board of welfare), and a state highway department. The legislature also set up a state income tax, and a pension system to help mothers of needy children. In the 1920's, Pierre S. du Pont gave several million dollars to build new schools and to aid public education in the state. Du Pont also served as state tax commissioner.

The Great Depression of the 1930's put thousands of Delawareans out of work. Richard C. McMullen was elected governor in 1936. He was the state's first Democratic governor since 1901. In 1941, the state legislature changed its Sunday blue laws, placing fewer restrictions on Sunday activities (see BLUE LAWS).

The Mid-1900's. During World War II (1939-1945), many Delaware factories and mills produced materials for the armed services. The state's economy grew rapidly in the 1950's and 1960's. The Delaware Memorial Bridge across the Delaware River opened in 1951, connecting Delaware with New Jersey. New industries came into Delaware, including such giant corporations as Chrysler, General Foods, and General Motors. Many other companies expanded their facilities, and Du Pont became Delaware's largest employer.

Delaware's population increased about 40 per cent during the 1950's and rose another 20 per cent in the 1960's. This growth took place chiefly in cities and suburbs. However, the state constitution of 1897 favored representation of rural areas in the state legislature. By the 1960's, a minority of the voters was electing a majority of the legislators. Delaware's legislative districts were redrawn in 1964, 1968, and 1971 in an attempt to give voters equal representation.

Delaware State Development Dept.

Fort Christina Monument in Wilmington marks the founding of the first permanent settlement in the Delaware Valley. The monument was given by the children of Sweden in 1938.

Like many other states, Delaware faced racial problems in the 1950's and 1960's. Negro groups challenged the state's system of separate schools for white and Negro children. In 1954, the Supreme Court of the

THE GOVERNORS OF DELAWARE

	Party	Term
Under the Articles of Confederation		
1. Caesar Rodney	None	1778-1781
2. John Dickinson	None	1781-1782
3. John Cook	None	1782-1783
4. Nicholas Van Dyke	None	1783-1786
5. Thomas Collins	None	1786-1789
Under the United States Constitution		
1. Thomas Collins	None	1786-1789
2. Jehu Davis	None	1789
3. Joshua Clayton	Federalist	1789-1796
4. Gunning Bedford, Sr.	Federalist	1796-1797
5. Daniel Rogers	Federalist	1797-1799
6. Richard Bassett	Federalist	1799-1801
7. James Sykes	Federalist	1801-1802
8. David Hall	*Dem.-Rep.	1802-1805
9. Nathaniel Mitchell	Federalist	1805-1808
10. George Truitt	Federalist	1808-1811
11. Joseph Haslet	*Dem.-Rep.	1811-1814
12. Daniel Rodney	Federalist	1814-1817
13. John Clark	Federalist	1817-1820
14. Jacob Stout	Federalist	1820-1821
15. John Collins	*Dem.-Rep.	1821-1822
16. Caleb Rodney	Federalist	1822-1823
17. Joseph Haslet	*Dem.-Rep.	1823
18. Charles Thomas	*Dem.-Rep.	1823-1824
19. Samuel Paynter	Federalist	1824-1827
20. Charles Polk	Federalist	1827-1830
21. David Hazzard	American Republican	1830-1833
22. Caleb P. Bennett	Democratic	1833-1836
23. Charles Polk	Whig	1836-1837
24. Cornelius P. Comegys	Whig	1837-1841
25. William B. Cooper	Whig	1841-1845
26. Thomas Stockton	Whig	1845-1846
27. Joseph Maull	Whig	1846
28. William Temple	Whig	1846-1847
29. William Tharp	Democratic	1847-1851
30. William H. Ross	Democratic	1851-1855
31. Peter F. Causey	†American	1855-1859
32. William Burton	Democratic	1859-1863
33. William Cannon	Union	1863-1865
34. Gove Saulsbury	Democratic	1865-1871
35. James Ponder	Democratic	1871-1875
36. John P. Cochran	Democratic	1875-1879
37. John W. Hall	Democratic	1879-1883
38. Charles C. Stockley	Democratic	1883-1887
39. Benjamin T. Biggs	Democratic	1887-1891
40. Robert J. Reynolds	Democratic	1891-1895
41. Joshua H. Marvel	Republican	1895
42. William T. Watson	Democratic	1895-1897
43. Ebe W. Tunnell	Democratic	1897-1901
44. John Hunn	Republican	1901-1905
45. Preston Lea	Republican	1905-1909
46. Simeon S. Pennewill	Republican	1909-1913
47. Charles R. Miller	Republican	1913-1917
48. John G. Townsend, Jr.	Republican	1917-1921
49. William D. Denney	Republican	1921-1925
50. Robert P. Robinson	Republican	1925-1929
51. C. Douglass Buck	Republican	1929-1937
52. Richard C. McMullen	Democratic	1937-1941
53. Walter W. Bacon	Republican	1941-1949
54. Elbert N. Carvel	Democratic	1949-1953
55. J. Caleb Boggs	Republican	1953-1960
56. David P. Buckson	Republican	1960-1961
57. Elbert N. Carvel	Democratic	1961-1965
58. Charles L. Terry, Jr.	Democratic	1965-1969
59. Russell W. Peterson	Republican	1969-1973
60. Sherman W. Tribbitt	Democratic	1973-

*Democratic-Republican †Know-Nothing

United States ruled that compulsory segregation in public schools was unconstitutional. By the mid-1960's, all of Delaware's public school districts were integrated. In 1963, the state legislature passed a bill banning segregation in public eating and drinking places. In 1969, the legislature approved a bill ending discrimination in the rental or sale of housing in Delaware.

Delaware Today is one of the most prosperous states in the United States. But the rapid growth that began in Delaware during the 1950's has also brought challenges for the state. Expanded highways for increased traffic are another necessity. Air and water pollution have become serious in New Castle County, the most heavily populated and industrialized county in the state.

In 1969, the Delaware legislature authorized the state to borrow $49 million to finance construction of schools, highways, and other facilities. A new state agency, the Department of Natural Resources and Environmental Control, was set up that year to promote conservation and to control air and water pollution. In 1971, the legislature passed the Coastal Zone Act, which bans construction of industrial plants along the state's coastline.

JOHAN J. GROOT, JOHN A. MUNROE, and BERNARD J. SMYTH

DELAWARE / *Study Aids*

Related Articles in WORLD BOOK include:

BIOGRAPHIES

Bassett, Richard
Bayard (family)
Bedford, Gunning, Jr.
Broom, Jacob
Canby, Henry S.
Cannon, Annie J.
Carothers, Wallace H.
Clayton, John M.
Delaware, Lord
Dickinson, John
Du Pont de Nemours
Evans, Oliver
Hudson, Henry
Marquand, John P.
McKean, Thomas
Penn, William
Pyle, Howard
Read, George
Rodney, Caesar
Stuyvesant, Peter
Williams, John J.

CITIES

Dover
Newark
Wilmington

HISTORY

Colonial Life in America
Delaware Indians
Mason and Dixon's Line
New Netherland
New Sweden
Revolutionary War in America

PHYSICAL FEATURES

Delaware Bay
Delaware River
Delmarva Peninsula
Piedmont Region

OTHER RELATED ARTICLES

Chicken (table)
Delaware, University of
Du Pont Company
Log Cabin
Southern States

Outline

I. Government
- A. Constitution
- B. Executive
- C. Legislature
- D. Courts
- E. Local Government
- F. Taxation
- G. Politics

II. People

III. Education
- A. Schools
- B. Universities and Colleges
- C. Libraries
- D. Museums

IV. A Visitor's Guide
- A. Places to Visit
- B. Annual Events

V. The Land
- A. Land Regions
- B. Coastline
- C. Rivers, Bays, and Lakes

VI. Climate

VII. Economy
- A. Natural Resources
- B. Manufacturing
- C. Agriculture
- D. Fishing Industry
- E. Mining
- F. Electric Power
- G. Transportation
- H. Communication

VIII. History

Questions

Why do so many large corporations have their headquarters in Delaware?

What is a *hundred?*

With what other state did Delaware once share its governor and General Assembly? Why?

Why did the Emancipation Proclamation have no effect in Delaware, a slave state?

How does the Delaware constitution differ from all other state constitutions?

Why is Delaware often called the *First State?*

What name was given the Delaware region after it became a territory of Pennsylvania? Why?

When and why was Delaware's capital moved from New Castle to Dover?

How has Delaware tried to promote conservation and to control air and water pollution?

What is Delaware's leading agricultural product?

Books for Young Readers

BLEEKER, SONIA. *The Delaware Indians: Eastern Fishermen and Farmers.* Morrow, 1953.

CARPENTER, ALLAN. *Enchantment of Delaware.* Childrens Press, 1967.

MOTHER GOOSE. *To Market, To Market!* Illus. by Peter Spier. Doubleday, 1967. Colonial New Castle, Delaware, is the setting for these Mother Goose rhymes.

Books for Older Readers

Delaware: A Guide to the First State. Somerset Publishers. A reprint of the 1938 Federal Writers' Project guide.

GRAY, RALPH D. *The National Waterway: A History of the Chesapeake and Delaware Canal, 1769-1965.* Univ. of Illinois Press, 1967.

LIBERMAN, CY, and others. *The Delaware Citizen: The Guide to Active Citizenship in the First State.* 3rd ed. rev. Taplinger, 1967.

LUNT, DUDLEY C. *Taylors Gut in the Delaware State.* Knopf, 1968. The author describes his experiences with animal and bird life in Delaware.

MUNROE, JOHN A. *Delaware: A Students' Guide to Localized History.* Teachers College Press, 1965.

REED, HENRY C. *The Delaware Colony.* Macmillan, 1970.

TOWNSEND, GEORGE A. *The Entailed Hat.* Cornell Maritime Press, 1955. Fiction. A reissue of an 1884 novel concerning the Negro before the Civil War.

WESLAGER, CLINTON A. *Delaware's Buried Past: A Story of Archaeological Adventure.* Rutgers Univ. Press, 1968.

DELAWARE, LORD, or DE LA WARR (1577-1618), THOMAS WEST, became the first governor of the Virginia colony. Delaware River, Delaware Bay, the colony of Delaware, and the state of Delaware were named for him. He became a member of the Privy Council of Queen Elizabeth I. He also served as a member of the Virginia Company Council.

He arrived with supplies at Jamestown in June, 1610, in time to prevent the discouraged settlers from deserting the colony. He returned to England in 1611 and died on a trip to America in 1618. JOSEPH CARLYLE SITTERSON

See also DELAWARE; JAMESTOWN.

DELAWARE, UNIVERSITY OF, is a coeducational, land-grant state university at Newark, Del. It has colleges of arts and science, agricultural sciences, business and economics, education, engineering, graduate studies, home economics, marine studies, and nursing. The university grants bachelor's, master's, and doctor's degrees. In cooperation with three museums, it offers graduate programs in early American decorative arts, industrial history, and ornamental horticulture.

The university was founded as an academy in 1743. It became Newark College in 1833, and a university in 1921. For enrollment, see UNIVERSITIES AND COLLEGES (table). E. A. TRABANT

DELAWARE BAY is a large inlet of the Atlantic Ocean. It separates New Jersey and Delaware. The deep channel of the bay connects with the Delaware River, making it possible for ocean-going vessels to reach Philadelphia. Delaware Bay is about 50 miles (80 kilometers) long and about 35 miles (56 kilometers) wide at its widest point. The channel is from 30 to 60 feet (9 to 18 meters) deep through its entire length. At Cape Henlopen near the bay entrance, the federal government has built a breakwater to provide shelter for ships. Lighthouses have been built in the bay to warn vessels of shallow water. See also DELAWARE (physical map); DELAWARE RIVER. GEORGE MACINKO

DELAWARE INDIANS, also called LENI-LENAPE, were one of the most advanced and civilized tribes of the eastern United States. Other members of the Algonkian language family respectfully called them "grandfathers." Their villages once occupied the whole Delaware River Basin. Delaware Indians near the present site of Philadelphia signed several treaties with William Penn. A famous political organization in New York City was named for Tamenend, or Tammany, a Delaware chief.

The Delaware lived in rectangular, bark-covered houses. They ate wild game, and raised corn and other vegetables. The Delaware had a tribal chronicle called the *Walam Olum.* It consists of picture stories painted on wood that tell of their traditions and wanderings.

The Delaware began very early to take on the ways of white men, and many became Christians. But they preferred to live by themselves, and their story is one long history of flight from the whites and the warlike Iroquois Indians. They moved from Pennsylvania to Indiana under pressure from the whites. Part of one band called *Munsee* settled there permanently, and gave their name to the town of Muncie, Ind. (see MUNSEE INDIANS). The rest fled to Missouri, to Texas, and then to Kansas. Finally they settled in Oklahoma. Many became scouts for white pioneers. "Kit" Carson considered them among his best helpers in his travels through the western United States. WILLIAM H. GILBERT

See also INDIAN, AMERICAN (Table of Tribes).

DELAWARE RIVER rises in southern New York and flows southward for about 300 miles (480 kilometers) before emptying into Delaware Bay. It passes through the Delaware Water Gap near Stroudsburg, Pa. (see DELAWARE WATER GAP). The Delaware forms the boundary between New York and Pennsylvania, Pennsylvania and New Jersey, and New Jersey and Delaware. The Schuylkill and Lehigh rivers are its main *tributaries* (branches).

The Delaware serves as a water transportation route for Philadelphia, Trenton and Camden, N.J., and Wilmington, Del., which lie in one of the great industrial areas of the United States. The Chesapeake and Delaware Canal connects the river with Chesapeake Bay. In 1961, the Delaware Basin Compact created a regional administrative agency to develop and control the water resources of the Delaware River Basin. GEORGE MACINKO

See also DELAWARE BAY; PENNSYLVANIA (picture).

The Delaware River Is Pennsylvania's Eastern Boundary.

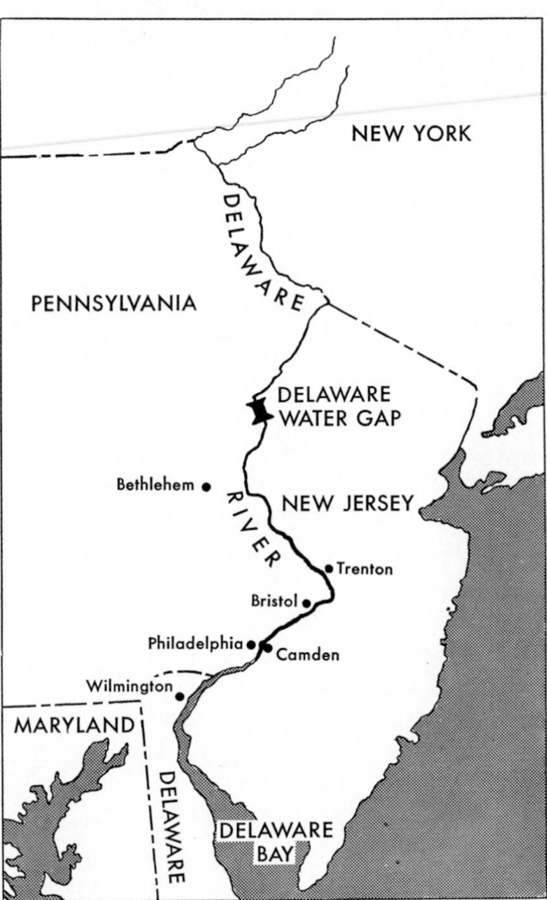

DELAWARE STATE COLLEGE. See UNIVERSITIES AND COLLEGES (table).

DELAWARE VALLEY COLLEGE OF SCIENCE AND AGRICULTURE. See UNIVERSITIES AND COLLEGES (table).

DELAWARE WATER GAP is a deep, narrow *gorge* (valley) cut through the Kittatinny Mountains east of Stroudsburg, Pa. The Delaware River carved the winding path out of solid rock millions of years ago. The gap is about 3 miles (5 kilometers) long and has steep rocky walls that rise as high as 1,400 feet (427 meters) on each side. Highways and a railroad follow the Delaware River's path through the gorge.

Mount Tammany stands on the New Jersey side of the Delaware Water Gap, and Mount Minsi is on the Pennsylvania side. Beautiful scenery around the gap makes it a popular summer resort area. George Macinko

See also Delaware River.

Gendreau

The Delaware Water Gap is a scenic gorge that separates New Jersey from Pennsylvania. The Delaware River carved this gorge in the Kittatinny Mountains millions of years ago.

DELBRÜCK, MAX. See Nobel Prizes (table: Nobel Prizes for Physiology and Medicine—1969).

DE LEE, JOSEPH BOLIVAR (1869-1942), an American obstetrician and gynecologist, was noted for his work in improving obstetrical methods. He devised 40 instruments to help the obstetrician, including an incubator for premature infants. De Lee founded the Chicago Lying-in Hospital in 1895 and the Maternity Center in 1932. His films on obstetrics have been shown all over the world. De Lee taught obstetrics at Northwestern University and the University of Chicago. He was born in Cold Springs, N.Y. Noah D. Fabricant

DELEGATE is a representative chosen by a group to speak or act in its interests. National governments send delegates to international meetings. A delegate to a national political convention is chosen by the state he represents. The states determine the method of selection. They generally use either the primary (popular election) or the state party convention. More delegates may be chosen than the state has votes, in which case there are fractional votes. David Fellman

DE LEÓN, JUAN PONCE. See Ponce de León, Juan.

DE LESSEPS, FERDINAND MARIE (1805-1894), was a French canal builder and diplomat. In 1854, Said Pasha, Viceroy of Egypt, invited him to start preparatory work on the Suez Canal. De Lesseps' plans provided for a canal without locks, extending from Port Said to Port Tewfik, connecting the Mediterranean Sea with the Gulf of Suez and the Red Sea. The company De Lesseps organized started work on the Canal in 1859, and completed it 10 years later (see Suez Canal).

De Lesseps was born in Versailles. From 1825 until his resignation in 1849, he worked in the French consular and diplomatic service. He was a member of the French Academy and the Academy of Science. At 74, De Lesseps reluctantly agreed to head the French company formed to build the Panama Canal (see Panama Canal [The French Failure]). Robert W. Abbett

DELFT (pop. 80,545) is a Dutch town located near The Hague. For location, see Netherlands (color map). It is a crossing point for many canals, and has about 70 bridges. One of its famous buildings, the Prinsehof, now a museum, is the place where William I of Orange was assassinated in 1584. The Nieuwe Kerk (New Church), built in the 1400's, contains the tombs of William I and other rulers of the House of Orange. Jan Vermeer, the Dutch painter, lived and worked in Delft.

The city once was famous for the manufacture of blue pottery. The industry declined in the late 1700's because less care was put into its production. The art has since been revived by pottery makers. They call the new product "New Delft" pottery. Benjamin Hunningher

The Corcoran Gallery of Art, W. A. Clark Collection, Washington, D.C.

A Delft Vase by Jacobus Rynaker. The beautiful design in this octagonal vase is typical of world-famous Delft pottery.

DELGADO, *dehl GAH doh,* **JOSÉ MATÍAS** (1767-1832), a Salvadoran priest and patriot, is called the father of his country. He led the people of El Salvador in three revolutions for their freedom, and became the nation's hero.

Many Latin-American countries revolted against Spain in 1810. Father Delgado directed the revolt in El Salvador in 1811. The Spaniards quickly put it down. The Central American countries finally won their independence from Spain in 1821. When Mexico tried to include them in its empire in 1822, Father Delgado headed the resistance movement in El Salvador. He was president of the congress that drew up a constitution for the Republic of the United States of Central America (1823-1838). Disappointed in the Republic, Father Delgado began a campaign against neighboring countries, but died before the battle ended. He was born in San Salvador. Harvey L. Johnson

DELHI, *DEHL ee* (pop. 3,287,883; met. area 3,647,-023), was once the capital of India. It lies on the Jumna River in the territory of Delhi. For location, see INDIA (political map).

Delhi has marble towers and domes, and the sunlight gleams on carved stone and silverwork. But it also has dirt and poverty, with narrow dark streets never touched by the sun.

The poor people of Delhi live in tiny, dark houses crowded into streets so narrow a person can almost reach from one side to the other. Sometimes as many as 20 persons live in one room, with no windows and no light. Many low-caste Indians work in the city's mills and factories. The wealthy people of Delhi live in large homes on wide streets. Gardens often surround the houses, which may also have an inner courtyard.

Industry and Trade. Delhi is a center of manufacturing and trade. Railroads and caravan routes cross in the city, and merchants on camels sell their wares to traders from other countries. Flour mills grind the grain brought in from the farms of Haryana, a state to the north. Cotton is woven into cloth in Delhi's cotton mills. Handcraftsmen make jewelry and other lovely objects of gold and silver, embroidered silk shawls, and wood carvings.

Many of the products of Delhi's hand industry are sold in the shops of the city's famous *Silver Street,* the Chandni Chauk. It stretches a mile through the center of Delhi and is the busiest street in India. Open-face shops line the sides of the street, and a *bazaar* (open trading place) runs down the center.

History. Other cities rose and fell in ruins on this site for hundreds of years before Delhi was built. Their ruins cover an area of about 45 square miles (117 square kilometers) around the city. Some of these earlier cities were built by Moslem emperors. The present city was started by Shah Jahan, a Mogul emperor, in 1639 (see SHAH JAHAN). A wall surrounds the palaces and temples built for the Shah in the eastern part of the city.

Many of the buildings of old Delhi, surrounded by a stone wall, were built at the direction of Shah Jahan during the middle 1600's. The Pearl Mosque is a small temple where the emperor worshiped. It is made of white and gray marble, and covered with delicate carving. The Halls of Public and Private Audience are marble buildings where the emperor greeted his guests of state in all the jeweled splendor of an Eastern court. Over the city towers the Great Mosque, built from 1644 to 1658 by order of Shah Jahan. It is made of white marble and red sandstone. Three domes of white marble rise above the building. Many other mosques and minarets are scattered throughout Delhi.

Delhi was the scene of great ceremonies in 1877, when Queen Victoria was declared Empress of India. There were many days of great celebration again after Edward VII became Emperor in 1901, and in 1911, when George V assumed the title. Delhi was made the capital of India in 1912, when the seat of government was moved from Calcutta. Then the capital was moved to New Delhi, a suburb of Delhi, where the seat of government was established in 1931. In 1947, New Delhi became the capital of independent India (see NEW DELHI). ROBERT I. CRANE

Fritz Henle, Black Star

The Kutab Minar, a red sandstone and white marble tower of victory, stands in Delhi, India. It rises 238 feet (73 meters) and is over 500 years old. Much of old Delhi was built at the direction of Shah Jahan, a Mogul emperor, in the 1600's.

DELHI SULTANATE was a Moslem empire that controlled much of what is now Bangladesh, India, and Pakistan from 1206 to 1526. The sultanate's boundaries shifted, depending on its military strength, but it centered in the Ganges Valley and Punjab. Delhi was the capital. The sultans brought many sections of India under Moslem rule for the first time. Trade routes opened and commerce flourished.

In the late 1100's, Mohammed of Ghor, a Turkish Moslem king, seized much of northern India. In 1206, a sultanate was established at Delhi. During the 1200's, the sultans successfully defended their territory from the remaining Hindu and Buddhist kings. They also prevented the Mongols, who had already conquered China and the Middle East, from conquering India.

During the 1300's, the sultanate temporarily extended its power far into southern India. In 1398, the conqueror Tamerlane looted and destroyed Delhi and massacred most of its people. Although the sultans regained Delhi after Tamerlane left that same year, their former territory was split into regional kingdoms. Babar, a descendant of Tamerlane, defeated the last sultan in 1526 and established the Mogul Empire.

During the sultanate, many Moslems migrated to India to serve as soldiers, government officials, priests, or merchants. Moslem holy men converted many Indians to Islam, the Moslem religion. Other Indians switched religions to improve their economic position. Most of the converts lived in the northwest and northeast, now Pakistan and Bangladesh. J. F. RICHARDS

DELIAN LEAGUE. See ARISTIDES; PERICLES.

DELIBES, *duh LEEB,* **LÉO** (1836-1891), a French composer, became known for his opera *Lakmé* and two ballets, *Coppélia* and *Sylvia.* He saw the ballet as a blending of symphonic music, dramatic action, and pantomime, instead of its being simply a series of conventional dance movements. He opened the path for an important revival of that form. His ballets inspired such composers as Peter Tchaikovsky and Maurice Ravel. He was born in St. Germain du Val and went to Paris as a chorus singer and student at the Conservatory. He composed music for the theater from the age of 19 until his death. THEODORE M. FINNEY

DELILAH, *dih LY luh*, was the Philistine mistress of the Israelite hero, Samson, a man famed for his tremendous strength. The Philistines bribed her to find out the secret of his power so that they might take him prisoner. After much coaxing, Samson told her that his strength lay in his long, thick hair which, because of a vow, he had never cut. Delilah had his head shaved while he was asleep. He became weak and helpless. His enemies easily captured him, blinded him, and made him work as a slave. This story is told in Judges 16. See also SAMSON. JOHN BRIGHT

DELINQUENCY, JUVENILE. See JUVENILE DELINQUENCY.

DELIRIUM TREMENS, *dih LIHR ee uhm TREE muhnz*, is a nervous and mental disturbance that results from acute alcoholism. A person often becomes markedly disturbed after unusually prolonged or heavy drinking of alcoholic beverages. He develops insomnia and a dislike for food, and becomes irritable and restless. He may then have visual illusions and hallucinations that are brief but terrifying. The condition itself may last from 3 to 10 days. Death sometimes results, often because pneumonia or heart failure develops. Doctors usually treat delirium tremens by taking alcohol away from the patient and giving him sedative and tranquilizing drugs. LOUIS D. BOSHES

See also ALCOHOLISM.

DELIUS, *DEE lih uhs*, **FREDERICK** (1862-1934), was an English composer whose works reflect the influences and color of the places in which he lived. *Over the Hills and Far Away* (1895), *Brigg Fair* (1907), and *On Hearing the First Cuckoo in Spring* (1912) are orchestral landscapes describing England. *Appalachia* (1902) sings of American mountains and forests, and *Sea Drift* (1903), of the Atlantic Ocean. He subtitled an orchestral nocturne *Paris: the Song of a Great City* (1899). He was born in Bradford, England. WILLIAM FLEMING

DELLA FRANCESCA, PIERO. See PIERO DELLA FRANCESCA.

DELLA ROBBIA, *dehl uh ROH bee uh*, was the family name of an uncle and his nephew who were Italian sculptors of the early Renaissance.

Luca Della Robbia (1400?-1482) made the famous marble sculpture, the *Singing Gallery*, for the Cathedral of Florence. He is better known for his work in terra cotta, a type of hard, durable earthenware. Della Robbia covered his terra cottas with glazes in white and brilliant colors. These terra cottas were less expensive than marble, and the glazed colors more durable than paint. Born in Florence, Della Robbia began his career as a goldsmith.

Andrea Della Robbia (1435-1525), the nephew, carried on the process of glazing terra cottas successfully. His uncle's will left the secret to him. He made a wider use of terra cotta than his uncle. One of his outstanding works is the infants on the Hospital of the Innocents in Florence. Della Robbia's work can be seen in the

Museo Nazionale, Florence. (Alinari)

***Madonna and Child Jesus* Is by Luca Della Robbia.**

National Gallery of Art in Washington, D.C. He was born in Florence. MARVIN C. ROSS

See also TERRA COTTA (picture: Enameled Terra-Cotta Sculpture).

DELLO JOIO, *JOY oh*, **NORMAN** (1913-), an American composer and pianist, won the Pulitzer prize in 1957 for his *Meditations on Ecclesiastes* for orchestra. He has produced musical compositions in many forms: ballets; operas; chamber, choral, and orchestral music. His opera about Joan of Arc, *The Trial at Rouen*, was produced on television in 1956. He won the 1949 Music Critics Circle award for his *Variations, Chaconne, and Finale* for orchestra. Dello Joio also composed *Psalm of David*, for chorus and small orchestra; and *Lamentation of Saul*, for baritone and orchestra.

Dello Joio was born in New York City. While still in his teens, he became an organist and choirmaster. He has taught at Sarah Lawrence College and at Mannes College of Music, New York City. HOMER ULRICH

DELLS. See DALLES.

DELMARVA PENINSULA is in the eastern United States, between the Chesapeake and Delaware bays. The name is derived from *Del*aware, *Mar*yland, and Virginia (*Va*). Most of the state of Delaware, and parts of Maryland and Virginia, are on the peninsula. For location, see MARYLAND (physical map).

DELOS. See CYCLADES.

DELPHI, *DEHL fy*, was a town situated on the southern slope of Mount Parnassus. The town had the oldest and most influential religious sanctuary in ancient Greece. It was in the district of Phocis.

The ancient Greeks believed that the site of Delphi was sacred to the god Apollo. It gained importance as early as the 1100's B.C. Later, it became an international Greek shrine. Its sanctuary contained the main temple of Apollo, a stadium, a theater, and many small buildings and monuments. The ancient Greeks held the

Pythian Games in Delphi (see Pythian Games).

The temple contained the famous *oracle*, or prophet (see Oracles). A woman oracle, called Pythia, would utter weird sounds while in a frenzy. People believed these were the words of Apollo. Temple priests interpreted these to the public. Cities, as well as private individuals, sought her advice. As a result, the oracle greatly influenced Greek religion, economics, and politics. This influence gradually waned in later Greek and Roman times. The Christian Roman emperor Theodosius closed the sanctuary in A.D. 390.

French scholars began excavations in 1880. The present-day village of Delphi, formerly called Kastri, is near the site of ancient Delphi. John H. Kent

See also Drama (color picture: Ancient Greek Theaters); Greece (color picture: Temple of Apollo); Greece, Ancient (picture: The Ruins of Delphi); Python (mythology).

DELPHINIUM. See Larkspur; Flower (color picture: Summer Garden Flowers).

DEL SARTO, ANDREA (1486-1531), was an outstanding painter of the Italian Renaissance. He worked in his home city of Florence. During his time, Florence was declining in power, and the greatest artists who had been trained there, such as Leonardo da Vinci and Raphael, lived elsewhere. Del Sarto worked in the style that they had developed. It is marked by balanced designs with easy movements, and by gradual shadows and soft colors. Though not original, his work maintained the great Florentine tradition. Andrea Del Sarto is the subject of a famous poem by the British writer Robert Browning. Creighton Gilbert

DELTA is a stretch of land, usually shaped like a rough triangle, built up by mud and sand at the mouth of a river. It is so named because it is shaped like *delta* (△), the fourth letter of the Greek alphabet. The name is applied to the mouths of rivers where they empty into gulfs, inland seas, bays, or lakes, and where one river joins another.

The main stream of a river usually divides into two or more branches near its mouth. Each of these branches often divides again. The strength of current in the river determines the size of the delta. A swiftly flowing current carries off the silt and sand to form sand bars or coastal islands. But a current that flows slowly will generally build up a much larger delta.

The delta area of the Mississippi River covers about 35,000 square miles (91,000 square kilometers). The Nile Delta covers an area of 10,000 square miles (26,000 square kilometers). Both the Nile and Mississippi deltas consist of rich, fertile land. They produce valuable crops of high-grade cotton. Ernest L. Thurston

See also River (Estuaries and Deltas); Erosion; Alluvial Fan; Alluvium.

DELTA AIR LINES. See Airline (Major Airlines of the World).

DELTA RAY. When a heavy cosmic ray particle, such as an alpha ray, falls on matter, the atoms of matter may give off slow electrons from their nuclei. These electrons, called *delta particles*, show up on a detecting medium such as photographic film. They appear as thin, wavy tracks, called *delta rays*, that branch off the track of the alpha particle. Scientists can measure the charge on the alpha particle from the number of delta rays in the track. See also Alpha Ray; Cosmic Rays; Wilson Cloud Chamber.

DELTA STATE COLLEGE. See Universities and Colleges (table).

DELTA WING. See Airplane (The Wing).

DELTIOLOGY is the hobby of collecting post cards. See Hobby (table: Fifty Popular Collection Hobbies).

DELTOID MUSCLE. See Human Body (Trans-Vision three-dimensional color picture).

DELUGE, *DEL yooj*, according to the Bible, was a great flood that covered all the earth with water thousands of years before Christ. All living things were destroyed except those that had been permitted to go into the ark which Noah had built.

The story is one of the most familiar of all Biblical tales (Gen. 6-8). The Deluge was sent to punish the wickedness of men, according to the account. Only Noah and his family were thought to be worth saving. They took with them at least one male and one female

Fairchild Aerial Surveys, Inc.

The Mississippi Delta, *above,* grows into the Gulf of Mexico at the rate of 1 mile (1.6 kilometers) every 16 years. The river's slow current continuously deposits fertile soil there. The delta has assumed the shape of a bird's foot, *below right.* The name *delta* was first given to deposits formed by the Nile River, *below left.*

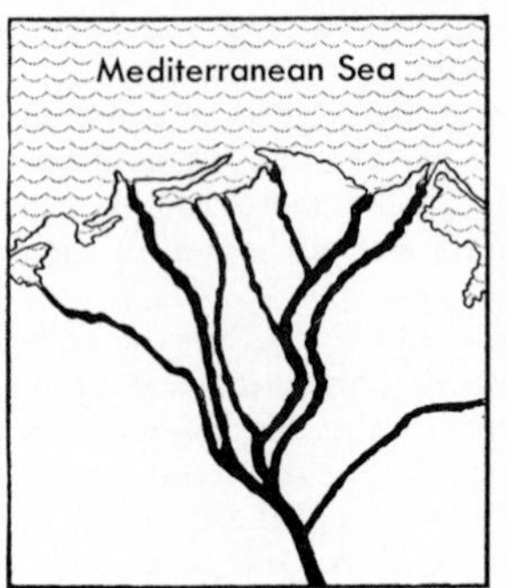

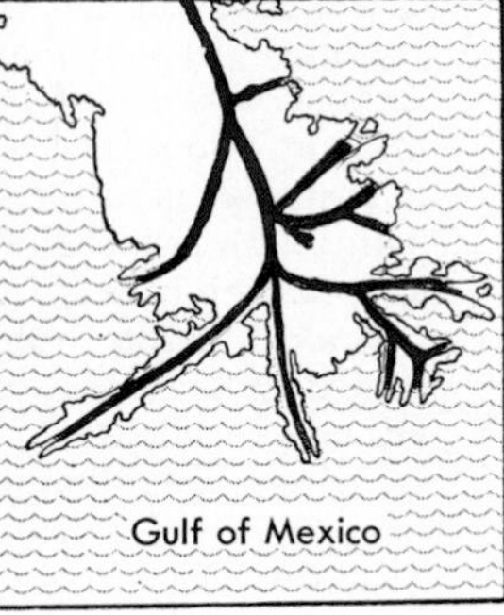

of each animal. The story of the Deluge resembles the flood story in the Babylonian epic of Gilgamesh. Many scholars believe that the Biblical story is simply a retelling of this poem. Flood legends occur in the tradition of many peoples. CYRUS H. GORDON

See also ARARAT; ARK; DEUCALION; NOAH.

DELUSION, *dee LYOO zhun,* is a false belief. Persons with mental illness often have delusions. A common delusion is that of *grandeur,* in which a person has an exaggerated idea of his importance. Other delusions include those of *persecution,* in which a person believes he is being mistreated, and of *reference,* in which he falsely believes he is being talked about.

DEMAND. See SUPPLY AND DEMAND.

DEMAND BILL. See BILL OF EXCHANGE.

DEMARCATION, LINE OF. See LINE OF DEMARCATION.

DEMARÇAY, EUGÈNE. See EUROPIUM.

DE MAUPASSANT, *du moh pah SAHN,* **GUY,** *GEE* (1850-1893), a French author, is considered one of the world's great short-story writers. De Maupassant wrote clearly and simply. His tales are realistic, and reflect his often brutally sarcastic and pessimistic attitude toward people. De Maupassant wrote with sympathy only about the poor and outcasts of society.

De Maupassant's stories deal with many subjects—the middle class, peasants, government officials, the Franco-Prussian War, outdoor life, animals, and ghosts. He wrote about 250 stories, most of them between 1880 and 1890. He published them in several collections. The best known include *The Tellier House* (1881), *Yvette* (1885), *Toine* (1886), and *The Horla* (1887). His most famous stories include "Ball-of-Fat," "The Diamond Necklace," "The Umbrella," and "The Piece of String."

De Maupassant's novels have the same qualities his short stories have. *A Woman's Life* (1883) is a portrait of an unhappy country wife. *Bel-Ami* (1885) describes the rise of an unprincipled journalist. *Peter and John* (1888) is a psychological study of two brothers.

De Maupassant was born in Normandy, in northern France. He learned much of his literary technique and philosophy of life from his godfather, the famous French novelist Gustave Flaubert. De Maupassant died in an insane asylum. ROBERT J. NIESS

DEME. See ATHENS (History).

DEMENTIA. See MENTAL ILLNESS (Schizophrenia).

DEMETER, *dih MEE tuhr,* in Greek mythology, was the goddess of the earth, agriculture, fertility, and grain. The ancient Romans had a similar goddess whom they called Ceres.

The most famous myth about Demeter tells of her search for her daughter Persephone, whom the Romans called Proserpina. The girl had been kidnaped by Hades, the god of the dead, and taken to his kingdom in the underworld. For details of this myth, see the WORLD BOOK article on PERSEPHONE.

The Greeks believed that man learned farming through Demeter. She gave Triptolemus, a Greek hero, a bag of seeds and sent him throughout the world in a magic chariot to teach man how to farm.

The most important center of Demeter's worship was in Eleusis, near Athens. There, the Greeks held secret rituals called the Eleusinian Mysteries in her honor. The ceremonies were based on Demeter's search for her daughter. The Greeks also based these ceremonies on a belief in the immortality of man's soul, and reward or punishment in a life after death. ROBERT J. LENARDON

See also MYSTERIES; CERES.

DE MILLE, AGNES (1909-), is an American *choreographer* (dance composer), dancer, and author. She began her career as a dancer in 1929, and gave concerts in the United States and Europe until 1940. She then began creating ballets based on American themes. The first was *Rodeo* (1942). In 1943, she created and staged the dances for the musical play *Oklahoma!* This landmark musical was one of the first to successfully blend dancing, story, and music into a unified work. Many of her ballets are regularly performed by the American Ballet Theatre, including *Fall River Legend* (1948).

Miss De Mille was born in New York City. In 1965, she became a member of the National Council on the Arts. She wrote the autobiographies *Dance to the Piper* (1952) and *And Promenade Home* (1958). SELMA JEANNE COHEN

Agnes De Mille danced in the 1942 première of her ballet *Rodeo* with Casimir Kokitch, *left,* and Frederic Franklin, *right.*

Fred Fehl

DE MILLE, CECIL BLOUNT (1881-1959), a motion-picture producer and director, became famous for his spectacular films based on the Bible. His first Biblical film was *The Ten Commandments* (1923). His final film was a remake of this picture in 1956. A shrewd showman, De Mille balanced religion with romance in such films as *The Sign of the Cross* (1932) and *Samson and Delilah* (1949). His striking drama of Christ *The King of Kings* (1927) was one of the few De Mille Biblical films to win praise from both critics and clergymen.

De Mille also made romantic adventures, including *The Plainsman* (1937), *Union Pacific* (1939), and *Unconquered* (1947). His circus spectacle *The Greatest Show on Earth* won the 1952 Academy Award as best picture of the year. De Mille received an Academy Award in 1949 honoring his 35 years of film-making.

De Mille was born in Ashfield, Mass., and went to Hollywood in 1913. His early silent films, including *Male and Female* (1919) and *Forbidden Fruit* (1921), generally dealt with romantic entanglements in high society. HOWARD THOMPSON

DEMOBILIZATION. See ARMY, UNITED STATES (World War II).

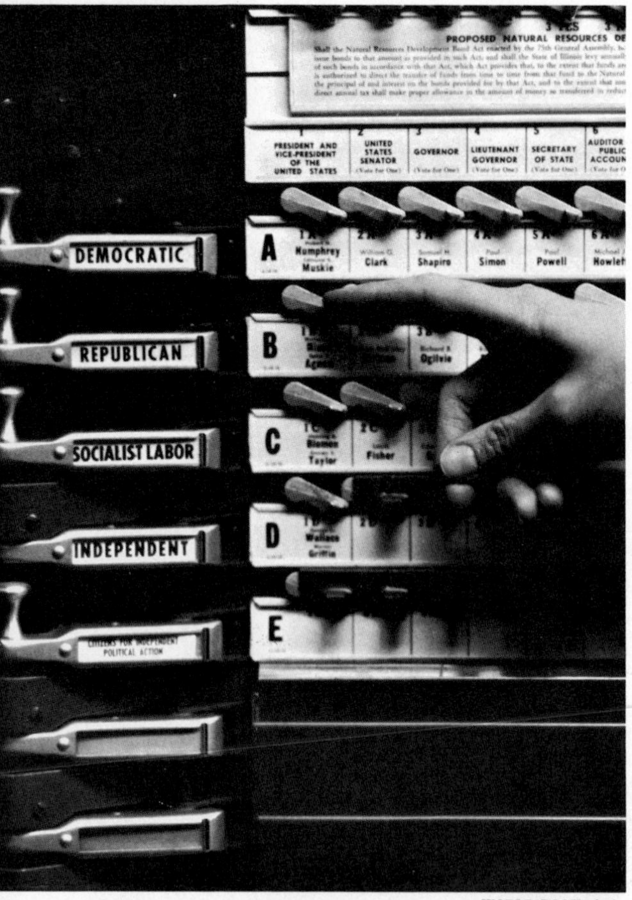

WORLD BOOK photo

The basis of a democratic state is liberty.

Aristotle

As I would not be a *slave,* so I would not be a *master.* This expresses my idea of democracy. Whatever differs from this, to the extent of the difference, is no democracy.

Abraham Lincoln

The measure of a democracy is the measure of the freedom of its humblest citizens.

John Galsworthy

I believe in democracy because it releases the energies of every human being.

Woodrow Wilson

Never in the history of the world has a nation lost its democracy by a successful struggle to defend its democracy.

Franklin D. Roosevelt

Government of the people, by the people, for the people, still remains the sovereign definition of democracy.

Winston Churchill

My political ideal is democracy. Everyone should be respected as an individual, but no one idolized.

Albert Einstein

Democracy is the recurrent suspicion that more than half of the people are right more than half of the time.

E. B. White

Democracy . . . is the only form of government that is founded on the dignity of man, not the dignity of some men, of rich men, of educated men or of white men, but of all men.

Robert Maynard Hutchins

Each person quoted above has a biography in WORLD BOOK.

DEMOCRACY

DEMOCRACY is a form of government, a way of life, and a goal or ideal. The term also refers to a country that has a democratic form of government. The word *democracy* means *rule by the people.* Abraham Lincoln described such self-government as "government of the people, by the people, for the people."

The citizens of a democracy take part in government either directly or indirectly. In a *direct,* or *pure,* democracy, the people meet in one place to make the laws for their community. Such democracy was practiced in ancient Athens, and still exists today in the form of the New England town meeting (see TOWN MEETING).

Most modern democracy is *representative* democracy. In large communities—cities, states, provinces, or countries—it is impossible for all the people to meet as a group. Instead, they elect a certain number of their fellow citizens to represent them in making decisions about laws and other matters that affect the people. An assembly of representatives may be called a council, a legislature, a parliament, or a congress. Government by the people through their freely elected representatives is sometimes called *republican government.*

The democratic way of life recognizes the equality and dignity of all persons regardless of race, religion, sex, or social standing. It holds that everyone is equal in court trials and other legal matters. It provides freedom of speech, freedom of the press, and freedom of religion. A goal of democratic society is to assure each person an opportunity to make full use of his abilities.

Democracy in practice often falls short of democracy as an ideal. Nations and governments are classified as being more or less democratic according to how close they come to the democratic ideal. Almost all governments claim to be democratic, but many are actually *totalitarian.* Totalitarian governments have almost complete control over the lives of the people. Communist governments operate largely on totalitarian principles.

This article presents a broad survey of democracy—what it is, how it works, and how it has developed. For

---

John H. Hallowell, the contributor of this article, is Professor of Political Science at Duke University and the author of The Moral Foundation of Democracy.

more information on democracy and other forms of government, see the WORLD BOOK article on GOVERNMENT.

Features of Democracy

The characteristics of democracy vary from one country to another. But certain basic features are more or less the same in all democratic nations.

Freedom of Expression. The citizens of a democracy select their leaders and influence the policies of their government. For this reason, discussion and understanding of public issues are necessary. To encourage the exchange of ideas, democracies guarantee freedom of speech, the press, assembly, and *petition* (giving a written request to a government official).

Citizens of a democracy have many opportunities to make their government truly representative. Chances for taking part are usually greatest at the local level. In many local school districts in the United States, for example, voters elect the school board members, and may run for office themselves. Citizens may attend school board meetings and meetings of city councils, and listen to debates on matters that affect them. The people may form groups to influence opinion on public issues and policies. School bond issues and other steps that involve the spending of large sums of money must be given to the voters for approval.

In a democratic society, it is important that politicians know how the people feel about public issues, if for no other reason than to be re-elected. Government officials are influenced by public opinion. They often can—and must—try to lead and change public opinion, but they are limited in the methods they can use. In seeking support for their own ideas, they must respect the rights of others to express different ideas.

Free Elections give the people a chance to choose their leaders and express their opinions on various issues. Elections are held periodically in democracies to ensure that elected officials truly represent the people. The possibility of being voted out of office helps assure that these officials pay attention to public opinion.

In most democracies, the only legal requirements for voting or for holding public office have to do with age, residence, and citizenship. The democratic process permits citizens to vote by secret ballot, free from force or bribes. It also requires that election results be protected against dishonesty. See ELECTION.

Majority Rule and Minority Rights. Decisions in a democracy are made according to *majority rule*. The people accept the choices made by the majority of voters in free elections. After legislatures pass laws, the people follow the will of the majority of representatives. Such majority rule is based on the idea that the judgment of the many is likely to be better than the judgment of the few.

Majority rule does not mean that the majority can do whatever it wants. The majority must keep in mind the rights and freedoms of the minority. Democratic countries guarantee that certain rights can never be taken from the people, even by extremely large majorities. These rights include the basic freedoms of speech, press, assembly, and religious worship. The majority must be willing to listen to the views of the minority. The majority also must recognize the right of the minority to try to become the majority by legal means.

Political Parties are a necessary part of democratic government. Rival parties make elections meaningful by giving voters a choice among candidates who represent different interests and points of view. Most political parties try to unite as many of these divided interests and opinions as possible through a broad party program. The United States and Great Britain have found that a two-party system works best in uniting various interests. In a system with more than two major parties, it is more difficult to get and keep majority rule.

In democratic countries, the party or parties that are out of power serve as the "loyal opposition." That is, they criticize the policies and actions of the party in power. In this way, the party in power is called on to justify its actions, and is made responsible to the people. In a totalitarian country, criticism of the party in power may be labeled as treason. Often, only the "government party" is allowed to exist. Elections mean little in these countries. The people have no real choice among candidates, and no opportunity to express dissatisfaction with the government. See POLITICAL PARTY.

Division of Power. Democratic societies believe it is important to divide and spread out political power. Democracies have various arrangements to prevent any person or branch of government from becoming too powerful. For example, the Constitution of the United States divides political power between the states and the federal government. Some powers belong only to the states, some only to the federal government, and some are shared by both.

The Constitution further divides the powers of the U.S. government among the President, Congress, and the federal courts. No person can serve in more than one of these branches of government at the same time. The power of each branch is designed to check or balance the power of the others. Powers not granted to governments by a constitution or charter are often reserved for the citizens. See GOVERNMENT (The Organization of Government).

Constitutional Government. Democratic government is government based on law, and in most cases is constitutional government. Constitutions state the powers and duties of government, and limit what the government may do. They also say how laws shall be made and enforced. Most constitutions include a detailed *bill of rights* that describes the basic liberties of the people and forbids the government to violate those rights. See BILL OF RIGHTS.

A constitution may be written or unwritten. The United States has a written constitution. The British constitution is unwritten. It consists of laws passed by Parliament, such documents as the Magna Carta, and common-law customs and beliefs. See CONSTITUTION.

Private Organizations. In a democracy, individuals and private organizations carry on many social and economic activities that are, for the most part, free of government control. For example, newspapers and magazines are privately owned and managed. Labor unions are run by and for the benefit of workers, not the state. Democratic governments generally do not interfere with religious worship. Private schools operate along with public schools. Most businesses in democratic societies are privately owned and managed. Great Britain, Sweden, and some other democracies have government ownership and control of certain basic industries and services.

In totalitarian societies, the government alone organizes and controls most associations. The people are not permitted to establish or join most groups without the permission of the state. In such countries as the Soviet Union, the economy is almost completely owned and managed by the state.

Why Democracy?

Preserving Human Rights. Democracies attempt to preserve individual freedom and to promote equality of opportunity. The U.S. Declaration of Independence expressed the belief that "all men are created equal, that they are endowed by their Creator with certain unalienable Rights, that among these are Life, Liberty and the pursuit of Happiness." The declaration added that the people may change or abolish the government if it interferes with those rights.

People once thought that the greatest obstacles to individual freedom and equality were political. They believed they could preserve freedom simply by changing the form of government from a monarchy to a republic. They claimed that the government that governs least governs best. But in time, many persons became convinced that some government regulation of society and the economy was necessary to preserve personal freedom and equality, as well as to improve the welfare of the nation.

In today's democracies, the government plays an active role in removing inequalities and promoting freedom for all. These nations have programs to provide economic security, to ease suffering, and to develop human potential. Such programs include unemployment insurance, minimum wage laws, old age pensions, health insurance, civil rights laws, and aid to education. Many democracies aim to provide a minimum standard of living and adequate medical care for all. Their goal is not perfect equality, because people differ in ability, and some work harder than others. The goal is equality of opportunity—sometimes called *social democracy*.

Ensuring Peaceful Change. Those who favor democracy believe that democratic procedures for bringing about change make violent revolutions unnecessary. They claim that democracy meets the just demands of the people more effectively than any other form of government. Supporters of democracy point to the sweeping economic and social changes that have occurred in the United States and Great Britain during the 1900's. Most of these changes have taken place peacefully, within the framework of existing political institutions.

Democracy also provides for the orderly change and succession of political leaders. Democratic constitutions call for periodic free elections of government leaders. Democracies have an order of succession in case a ruler dies in office or is unable to perform his duties.

Making Democracy Work

Citizen Participation. Democracy calls for widespread participation in politics by the people. It is the duty of all adult citizens to vote in local, state or provincial, and national elections. Qualified individuals should be willing to run for public office, to serve on juries, and to contribute to the welfare of their country to the best of their ability. Citizens should help shape public opinion by speaking out on important issues and by supporting the political party of their choice. An active citizenry is one of the best guarantees against corrupt and inefficient government.

Education and Democracy. Widespread participation in politics does not necessarily ensure good government. The quality of government depends on the quality of participation. Well-informed and well-educated citizens are able to participate more intelligently in their government. History shows that democracy is most likely to succeed in countries with high levels of literacy and good educational opportunities. For this reason, democratic governments strongly support education for all citizens.

A democracy needs educated citizens who can think for themselves. Citizens have a duty to take part in public affairs, to keep informed on public issues, and to vote intelligently. Democratic institutions must produce leaders worthy of public trust and responsibility.

In a modern industrial society, a person must have extensive technical knowledge to understand and solve many problems of government. Few voters have either the time or the specialized knowledge for the more difficult problems. Even elected officials are turning more and more to experts for advice. As a result, the voter's role is limited to determining general policy and directions. He does this by making his views known to his representatives, and by voting for candidates who share his views and in whom he has confidence.

Democracy and Economic Development. History shows that democracy has the best chance of success in countries that have a stable, growing economy, and few extremes of wealth and poverty. Some scholars believe that democracy works best in countries with a large middle class.

Many democratic governments have collapsed during periods of severe economic depression. When large numbers of persons cannot find jobs, they are more likely to support groups that want to overthrow the government. To a nation facing possible mass starvation, having enough food may be more important than having voting or other political rights.

Social Mobility is the movement of persons or groups from one class or social group to another. It is vital to democracy. For a person to have genuine equality of opportunity, he must be able to improve his income, occupation, or social position. A society with a strict class system cannot provide the opportunities for individual advancement which democracy calls for. Democracy cannot work, for example, if some persons are excluded from certain jobs because of their race, religion, or nationality.

Agreement on Fundamentals is basic to democracy. A majority of the people in a democracy must believe in the fundamental dignity and equality of all persons. Although democracy stresses the importance of the individual, citizens must be willing to place the welfare of their country ahead of their own personal interests. The people also must agree generally on the purposes of government. They will differ on how best to achieve these purposes. But if the purposes themselves are unclear, the democracy will be unstable.

The Development of Democracy

Origins of Democracy. Democracy began to develop in ancient Greece as early as the 600's B.C. The word *democracy* comes from the Greek words *demos*, meaning *people*, and *kratos*, which means *rule* or *authority*. Greek political thinkers stressed the idea of rule by law. They criticized dictatorship as the worst form of government. Athens and some other Greek city-states had democratic governments.

Democracy in ancient Athens differed in important ways from democracy today. Athenian democracy was a direct democracy rather than a representative one. Each male citizen had the duty to serve permanently in the assembly, which passed the laws and decided all important government policies. There was no division between legislative and executive branches of the government. Slaves made up a large part of the Athenian population, and did most of the work. Neither the slaves nor women could vote.

The ancient Romans experimented with democracy, but they never practiced it so fully as did the Athenians. Roman political thinkers taught that political power comes from the consent of the people. The Roman statesman Cicero contributed the idea of a universal law of reason that is binding on all men and governments everywhere. He suggested that men have natural rights which every state must respect.

The Middle Ages. Christianity taught that all men are equal before God. This teaching promoted the democratic ideal of brotherhood among men. Christianity also introduced the idea that Christians are citizens of two kingdoms—the kingdom of God and the kingdom of the world. It held that no state can demand absolute loyalty from its citizens because men must also obey God and His commandments. During the Middle Ages (A.D. 400's to the 1500's), the conflict between these two loyalties helped lay the foundation for constitutional government.

The Middle Ages produced a social system known as *feudalism*. Under feudalism, persons pledged their loyalty and services to one another. Individuals had certain rights which other persons were required to recognize. A feudal court system was established to protect these rights. Such courts later led to kings' councils, representative assemblies, and modern parliaments. See FEUDALISM.

The Renaissance and the Reformation. The great cultural reawakening called the Renaissance spread throughout Europe during the 1300's, 1400's, and 1500's. A new spirit of individual thought and independence developed. It influenced political thinking and hastened the growth of democracy. People began to demand greater freedom in all areas of life.

The new independence of the individual found religious expression in the Protestant Reformation. The Reformation emphasized the importance of individual conscience. During the early 1500's, Martin Luther, a leader of the Reformation, opposed the Roman Catholic Church as an intermediary between God and man. A number of Protestant churches were established during the period. Some of these churches practiced the congregational form of government, which had a democratic structure. During the 1500's, both Catholics and Protestants defended the right to oppose absolute monarchy. They argued that the political power of earthly rulers comes from the consent of the people.

Democracy in England. In 1215, English nobles forced King John to approve the Magna Carta. This historic document became a symbol of human liberty. It was used to support later demands for trial by jury, protection against unlawful arrest, and no taxation without representation.

English democracy developed slowly during the next several hundred years. In 1628, Parliament passed the Petition of Right. The petition called on King Charles I to stop collecting taxes without the consent of Parliament. It also provided that Parliament should meet at regular intervals. Charles refused to agree to limits on the royal power, and civil war broke out in 1642. The Puritans, led by Oliver Cromwell, fought the followers of the king. Charles was beheaded in 1649, and the Puritans established a short-lived *commonwealth* (republic). See ENGLAND (The Civil War).

The English revolution of 1688 finally established the supremacy of Parliament. John Locke, the philosopher of the revolution, declared that final authority in political matters belonged to the people. The government's main purpose, he said, was to protect the lives, liberties, and property of the people. Parliament passed the Bill of Rights in 1689, assuring the people basic civil rights.

Modern democracy was still far off. The larger factory towns were not represented in Parliament until after the adoption of the Reform Bill of 1832. Property qualifications for voting disappeared only gradually. In 1918, for the first time, all men were permitted to vote. Not until 1928 could all women vote.

French Contributions to Democracy were made in the 1700's by such political thinkers as Montesquieu, Voltaire, and Jean Jacques Rousseau. Their writings helped bring about the French Revolution, which began in 1789. Montesquieu argued that political freedom requires the separation of the executive, legislative, and judicial powers of government. Voltaire spoke out against government invasion of individual rights and freedoms. Rousseau declared in his book *The Social Contract* (1762) that people "have a duty to obey only legitimate powers." The only rightful rulers, he added, were those chosen freely by the people.

The French Revolution, an important event in the history of democracy, promoted the ideas of liberty and equality. It did not make France a democracy, but it did limit the king's powers. See FRENCH REVOLUTION.

American Democracy took root in traditions brought to North America by the first English colonists. The Pilgrims, who settled in Massachusetts in 1620, joined in signing the Mayflower Compact to obey "just and equal laws." The American Revolution began more than 150 years later, in 1775. The colonists wanted self-government and no taxation without representation. The Declaration of Independence, adopted by the Continental Congress in 1776, is a classic document of democracy. It established human rights as an ideal by which government must be guided.

Most of the Founding Fathers distrusted the Athenian version of direct democracy. They wanted to establish a republic because they feared that giving the people too much power would lead to mob rule. For this reason, the men who wrote the Constitution of the United States adopted a system of dividing power between the federal government and the states. They also provided that the federal powers be divided among the legislative, executive, and judicial branches. In addition, they provided that the President be elected by an electoral college rather than by the direct vote of the people (see ELECTORAL COLLEGE).

Thomas Jefferson favored a government that would pay more attention to the common man. After Jefferson became President in 1801, he spoke of his election as a "revolution." In 1828, the election of Andrew Jackson to the presidency further advanced American democracy. The pioneer spirit of the settlers in the West encouraged self-reliance, promoted individual liberty, and gave meaning to the promise of equal opportunity.

The long-term trend in the United States has been to give almost all adult citizens the right to vote. By 1850, white males could vote in all the states. The 15th Amendment to the Constitution, adopted in 1870, gave Negroes the right to vote. In 1920, the 19th Amendment gave women the vote. In 1964, the 24th Amendment prohibited poll taxes as voting requirements in national elections (see POLL TAX).

The Spread of Democracy. During the 1800's, democracy developed steadily. Many countries followed the American and British examples. Such democratic institutions as elections and legislatures became common. Where kings still ruled, they lost much of their power and performed mainly ceremonial duties.

The Industrial Revolution brought political changes of great importance. During the second half of the 1800's, the working classes demanded and received greater political rights. New laws gave more citizens the right to vote. The freedoms of speech, the press, assembly, and religion were extended and enlarged.

Democracy did not take root everywhere. Some countries that adopted constitutions modeled after that of the United States later became dictatorships. These nations found that a constitution alone did not guarantee democracy. In Russia, a group of revolutionists set up a Communist dictatorship in 1917 and halted Russia's progress toward democracy. Germany adopted a democratic government in 1919, but Adolf Hitler's rise to power brought a fascist dictatorship in 1933.

Democracy Today. Most governments today claim to be democratic, but many lack some essential freedoms usually associated with democracy. Many Communist governments call themselves "people's democracies." But the people of these countries are not permitted to criticize their government. Nor are they allowed certain basic freedoms, such as those of speech and of the press.

Many modern nations have a long history of democratic government. These countries include Australia, Belgium, Canada, Denmark, Great Britain, The Netherlands, New Zealand, Norway, Sweden, Switzerland, and the United States. Other nations—including India, Italy, Japan, and West Germany—have been democracies since the mid-1900's. The structure of French government has changed many times since the French Revolution. The present government is a democracy. Several newly independent nations in Africa and Asia are trying to develop democratic institutions. But inexperience with self-rule and other problems make democratic government difficult to achieve. JOHN H. HALLOWELL

Related Articles in WORLD BOOK include:

GREAT DOCUMENTS OF DEMOCRACY

Bill of Rights
Constitution of the United States
Declaration of Independence
Emancipation Proclamation
Gettysburg Address
Human Rights, Universal Declaration of
Magna Carta
Petition of Right
Rights of Man, Declaration of the

TOOLS OF DEMOCRACY

Absentee Voting
Assembly
Ballot
Citizenship
Civil Rights
Constitution
Due Process of Law
Election
Fifteenth Amendment
Freedom
Habeas Corpus
Initiative and Referendum
Jury and Trial by Jury
Majority Rule
Plebiscite
Political Party
Recall
Voting
Voting Machine
Woman Suffrage

OTHER RELATED ARTICLES

Aristocracy
Authority
Center for the Study of Democratic Institutions
Communism
Conservatism
Fascism
Federal Government
Liberalism
Monarchy
Power
Propaganda
Public Opinion
Republic
Socialism
Town Meeting

Outline

I. **Features of Democracy**
   A. Freedom of Expression
   B. Free Elections
   C. Majority Rule and Minority Rights
   D. Political Parties
   E. Division of Power
   F. Constitutional Government
   G. Private Organizations
II. **Why Democracy?**
   A. Preserving Human Rights
   B. Ensuring Peaceful Change
III. **Making Democracy Work**
   A. Citizen Participation
   B. Education and Democracy
   C. Democracy and Economic Development
   D. Social Mobility
   E. Agreement on Fundamentals
IV. **The Development of Democracy**

Questions

What does the word *democracy* mean?
How do political parties aid democratic government?
What is *representative* democracy? *Direct* democracy?
What part do private organizations play in a democracy?
Why did the framers of the U.S. Constitution distrust the Athenian model of direct democracy?
How are political decisions made in a democracy?
How do modern democratic governments attempt to promote equality of opportunity?
Why are Communist governments not true democracies?
What are some of the countries that have a long history of democratic government?
How do elections in a democracy differ from elections in a totalitarian country?

Reading and Study Guide

See *Democracy* in the RESEARCH GUIDE/INDEX, Volume 22, for a *Reading and Study Guide*.

DEMOCRATIC-FARMER-LABOR PARTY. See FARMER-LABOR PARTY.

DEMOCRATIC PARTY is one of the two major political parties of the United States. The Republican Party is the other.

The Democratic Party, the nation's oldest existing party, has played a vital role in the history and politics of the United States. From 1828 through 1968, Democrats won 17 of the 36 presidential elections. They dominated U.S. politics from 1828 through 1856, winning six of the eight presidential elections. From 1860 through 1928, they won only 4 of the 18 presidential elections. But the Democratic candidate won 7 of the 10 presidential elections held from 1932 through 1968. Traditionally, the Democratic Party has drawn support from several groups, including many immigrants, Southerners, wage earners, and—since the 1930's—Negroes.

The policies of the Democratic Party, like those of other parties, have changed with the flow of history. Until Wilson became President in 1913, the Democrats generally approved a strict interpretation of the U.S. Constitution and favored a limitation on government powers. As President, Wilson expanded the role of government and mobilized the nation to help defeat Germany in World War I (1914-1918). Roosevelt boldly took government action to pull the nation through the Great Depression of the 1930's. During World War II (1939-1945), Roosevelt again expanded government powers to fight Germany and Japan.

Some Democrats thought Roosevelt extended the government's powers too far. Others believed these powers had not been extended far enough. Ever since Roosevelt's presidency, Democrats have disagreed on how extensive the role of government should be.

This article chiefly describes the history of the Democratic Party. For information about the party's national convention and organization, see the articles on POLITICAL CONVENTION and POLITICAL PARTY.

Origin of the Democratic Party is uncertain. Some historians trace its beginnings to the Democratic-Republican Party that Thomas Jefferson created during the 1790's (see DEMOCRATIC-REPUBLICAN PARTY). Most historians, however, believe that the Democratic Party started as a campaign organization to win the presidency for Andrew Jackson in 1828.

Jefferson served as President from 1801 to 1809, and other Democratic-Republicans held the presidency from 1809 to 1825. After 1816, the Democratic-Republican Party began to split into several groups and fell apart as a national organization. Jackson became the favorite of one of these groups and gained tremendous popularity. He lost a bid for the presidency in 1824. But he easily won election in 1828 and swept to re-election in 1832. By about 1830, Jackson and his followers were called Democrats.

By the late 1830's, top Jacksonian Democrats had turned Jackson's loose organization into an effective national political party—the Democratic Party. One of these men, Martin Van Buren, became President in 1837. Other leading Jacksonians included newspaper editor Francis P. Blair, Sr.; presidential adviser Amos Kendall; and such state politicians as Thomas Hart Benton of Missouri and James Buchanan of Pennsylvania.

William Nisbet Chambers, the contributor of this article, is Edward Mallinckrodt Distinguished University Professor at Washington University and the author of The Democrats, 1789-1964.

"A LIVE JACKASS KICKING A DEAD LION"
And such a Lion! and such a Jackass!

From *Thomas Nast* by Albert Bigelow Paine, permission of Harper & Bros.

The Donkey was used as a political symbol by Andrew Jackson after his opponents called him a "jackass" during the 1828 election campaign. By the 1880's, such cartoons as the one above by Thomas Nast had caught the public eye and established the donkey as the symbol of the Democratic Party.

Jacksonian Policies appealed to a wide variety of voters. Small farmers, large plantation owners, city laborers, and state bankers joined in their support of the Democratic Party. They had in common a strong belief in states' rights and a firm faith in limited government (see STATES' RIGHTS). But Democrats also disagreed frequently. For example, they argued over banking policies, slavery, and tariff rates.

In spite of their differences, Democrats won the presidential election of 1844 with James K. Polk. In 1852, they won with Franklin Pierce and in 1856 with James Buchanan. They also controlled Congress during most of the 1840's and 1850's.

The Slavery Issue, more than any other, divided the Democrats. During Polk's Administration, from 1845 to 1849, vast new territories in the West became part of the United States. Southerners wanted to extend slavery into the new lands, but many Northerners urged Congress to prohibit it. Southerners replied that Congress had no authority to stop citizens of any state from taking slaves anywhere in the United States.

Fierce debates led to division within the party and to sectional hostility between North and South. Congressional leaders, such as Stephen A. Douglas of Illinois, worked for legislation that would satisfy both Northerners and Southerners. They favored the Compromise of 1850, which, for a time, quieted both party and sectional differences (see COMPROMISE OF 1850).

Hostility flared again after Congress passed the Kansas-Nebraska Act in 1854. In this act, Douglas had provided for "popular sovereignty," which let settlers decide for themselves whether a new state would permit slavery. The act pleased few people. It led to renewed hostility between North and South and caused the Democratic Party to split apart.

In 1860, Northern Democrats nominated Douglas for President. Southern Democrats chose John C. Breckinridge. Both Democratic candidates lost to Abraham Lincoln, the candidate of the new Republican Party. In 1860 and 1861, 11 Southern states took the idea of states' rights as far as it could go when they seceded from the Union. In April, 1861, shortly after the seventh state had withdrawn, the Civil War began.

During the Civil War, the Northern Democrats divided. The so-called "War Democrats" supported Lincoln and the war. The "Peace Democrats," especially those known as "Copperheads," opposed Lincoln and the war. In the election of 1864, many War Democrats supported Lincoln, and the Peace Democrats nominated General George B. McClellan. Lincoln won the election. Following Lincoln's assassination in April, 1865—just five days after the war ended—Vice-President Andrew Johnson, a War Democrat, became President.

After the Civil War. Republicans condemned the Democrats as disloyal to the Union during the Civil War. Unable to win the presidency or to gain control of Congress, the Democratic Party reached its lowest point.

Under Johnson's leadership, the Democrats attacked the Reconstruction plans of the Radical Republicans for the defeated South (see RECONSTRUCTION). Among other actions, the Republicans (1) denied the vote to Southerners who had fought against the Union and (2) gave the vote to Southern Negroes. Enraged white Southerners deprived Negroes of the vote after regaining power later. These white Southerners believed that the Republicans opposed most Southern beliefs. Thus, the Democratic "Solid South" was born. During the 1870's, meanwhile, Democrats demanded reforms to end dishonesty in business and in government.

A business depression swept the nation during the 1870's and helped change the party's fortunes. Many voters blamed the Republicans for the depression and

DEMOCRATIC PRESIDENTIAL AND VICE-PRESIDENTIAL CANDIDATES

Year	President	Vice-President
1828	*Andrew Jackson*	*John Calhoun*
1832	*Andrew Jackson*	*Martin Van Buren*
1836	*Martin Van Buren*	*Richard M. Johnson*
1840	Martin Van Buren	Richard M. Johnson
1844	*James K. Polk*	*George M. Dallas*
1848	Lewis Cass	William O. Butler
1852	*Franklin Pierce*	*William R. D. King*
1856	*James Buchanan*	*John C. Breckinridge*
1860	Stephen A. Douglas	Herschel V. Johnson
1864	George B. McClellan	George H. Pendleton
1868	Horatio Seymour	Francis P. Blair, Jr.
1872	Horace Greeley	B. Gratz Brown
1876	Samuel J. Tilden	Thomas A. Hendricks
1880	Winfield S. Hancock	William H. English
1884	*Grover Cleveland*	*Thomas A. Hendricks*
1888	Grover Cleveland	Allen G. Thurman
1892	*Grover Cleveland*	*Adlai E. Stevenson*
1896	William Jennings Bryan	Arthur Sewall
1900	William Jennings Bryan	Adlai E. Stevenson
1904	Alton B. Parker	Henry G. Davis
1908	William Jennings Bryan	John W. Kern
1912	*Woodrow Wilson*	*Thomas R. Marshall*
1916	*Woodrow Wilson*	*Thomas R. Marshall*
1920	James M. Cox	Franklin D. Roosevelt
1924	John W. Davis	Charles W. Bryan
1928	Alfred E. Smith	Joseph T. Robinson
1932	*Franklin D. Roosevelt*	*John Nance Garner*
1936	*Franklin D. Roosevelt*	*John Nance Garner*
1940	*Franklin D. Roosevelt*	*Henry A. Wallace*
1944	*Franklin D. Roosevelt*	*Harry S. Truman*
1948	*Harry S. Truman*	*Alben W. Barkley*
1952	Adlai E. Stevenson	John J. Sparkman
1956	Adlai E. Stevenson	Estes Kefauver
1960	*John F. Kennedy*	*Lyndon B. Johnson*
1964	*Lyndon B. Johnson*	*Hubert H. Humphrey*
1968	Hubert H. Humphrey	Edmund S. Muskie
1972	George S. McGovern	Sargent Shriver

Names of elected candidates are in italics.
Each candidate has a biography in WORLD BOOK.

ADMINISTRATIONS IN OFFICE

WORLD BOOK graph

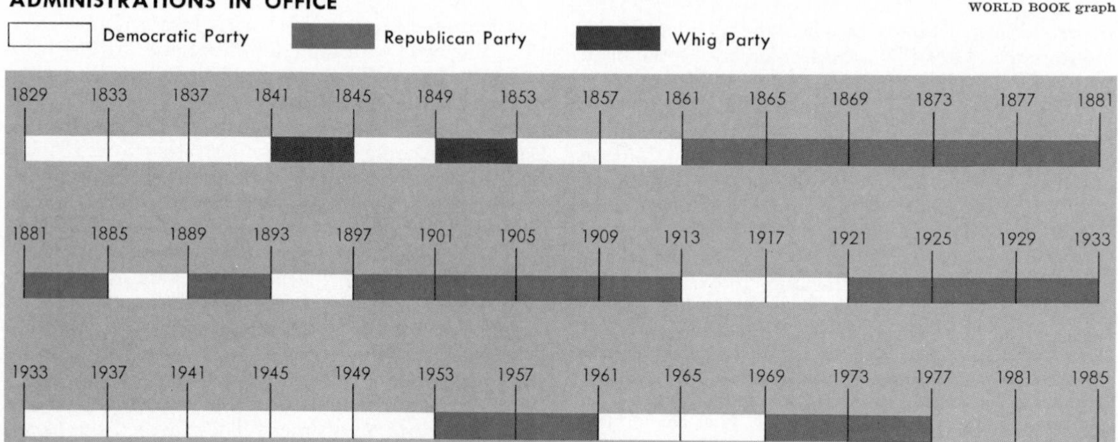

Library of Congress

Grover Cleveland, *above,* is shown "landing" the presidency for the Democratic Party in 1892. His Republican opponent, Benjamin Harrison, looks on after a narrow defeat for re-election.

San Francisco *Chronicle*

President Woodrow Wilson, *above,* lost political prestige when he tried desperately—and failed—to gain public support for U.S. membership in the League of Nations.

United Press Int.

Franklin D. Roosevelt shakes hands with a coal miner—one of the "forgotten" men for whom he promised a "new deal" during his successful campaign for the presidency in 1932.

voted Democratic in the congressional elections of 1874. As a result, the Democrats gained control of the House of Representatives. This victory brought hope to the Democrats. They worked hard to win the presidency in 1876 and made reform the central issue of their campaign. The Democratic candidate, Samuel J. Tilden, received more popular votes than did his Republican opponent, Rutherford B. Hayes. But Hayes won the election by a margin of one electoral vote.

During the 1880's and 1890's, the Democratic and Republican parties received almost equal popular support. There seemed to be little difference between the two, except that Democrats wanted lower tariffs and demanded reforms in the civil service. In 1884, Grover Cleveland became the first Democrat to be elected President since 1856. Cleveland narrowly lost the presidency to Benjamin Harrison in a close race in 1888, but regained it in another close race in 1892.

Tremendous changes had reshaped the nation's economy since the Civil War. Railroads had expanded to carry manufactured goods to farmers and farm products to city workers. Vast business and industrial empires had appeared.

Politicians knew little about business growth, depressions, or economic theories. The Democrats and the Republicans both favored a policy of *laissez faire* (nonregulation), and the government left business largely in the hands of businessmen. Neither party seemed aware of the hardships that industrialization brought to many farmers and city workers. These groups demanded reforms to gain a larger share of the nation's wealth.

In 1893, shortly after Cleveland began his second term as President, a major economic depression struck the nation. Farmers cried out against high railroad charges to send their goods to market. Many city workers demanded jobs, and others called for higher wages. Confused by the problems of an increasingly industrialized society, Cleveland hoped the economy would adjust itself. He followed a laissez-faire policy at the same time that farmers faced ruin, city workers went on strike, and the unemployment rate went up.

As President, Cleveland stood for a national currency

backed by gold. By the election of 1896, many Democrats favored government action to increase the supply of money in circulation by allowing the free coinage of silver. They believed that the free coinage of silver would help solve the nation's economic problems. The money question became the major campaign issue. Most Democrats supported silver, but most Republicans favored gold.

At the 1896 Democratic National Convention, William Jennings Bryan won the party's nomination with his famous "cross of gold" speech (see BRYAN). He campaigned energetically and won wide support in the South and West—but ran poorly in the East and lost the election. Bryan lost again in 1900 and, after another Democratic defeat in 1904, he lost for the third time in 1908.

Wilsonian Democracy. In 1912, a split in the Republican Party enabled the Democratic candidate, Woodrow Wilson, to win the presidency (see ROOSEVELT, THEODORE ["Bull Moose" Candidate]). And, for the first time in 20 years, the Democrats gained control of both houses of Congress. Wilson won re-election in 1916, and the Democrats retained control of Congress.

Wilson wanted the free-enterprise system to work for the benefit of all the people, not just the wealthy. He attacked monopolies as dangerous to free business competition and called for all people to have a "new freedom" to prosper. Wilson's first Administration featured such reform legislation as the Clayton Antitrust Act, the Federal Trade Commission Act, and the Underwood-Simmons Tariff.

During Wilson's second Administration, World War I (1914-1918) overshadowed his drive for reform legislation. Wilson directed the nation's energy to the defeat of Germany. After the war, he called for the United States to join the League of Nations. Wilson, the chief planner of the league, believed that the international organization would prevent future wars. Most Democrats supported the league, but some joined conservative Republicans and blocked American membership.

During the 1920's, the Democrats failed to win the presidency or to gain control of either house in Congress. In the 1928 election, however, the Democratic presidential candidate, Alfred E. Smith, won majorities in most of the largest cities.

The nation seemed prosperous during the Roaring 20's. Business boomed, industries expanded, and Americans looked forward confidently to an even brighter future. But beneath the surface of prosperity lay much economic disorder. Neither business nor government took action in spite of danger signals in 1927 and 1928.

In 1929, the worst business crash in United States history brought some government action. But the Republican government of Herbert Hoover did not do enough. During the Great Depression of the 1930's, banks closed, businesses failed, and millions of people lost their jobs.

The New Deal. The Great Depression brought a revolution in the fortunes of the Democratic Party. Democrats won every presidential election of the 1930's and 1940's and controlled Congress for most of that period. Franklin D. Roosevelt won the elections of 1932, 1936, 1940, and 1944 and became the only man to win the presidency four times. Vice-President Harry S. Truman became President after Roosevelt's death in 1945 and won the election of 1948.

Roosevelt was the dominating figure of the years of the Great Depression. During the 1932 campaign, he had promised Americans a "new deal" that included economic relief, recovery, and reform and a better life for what he called the "forgotten man." Roosevelt's personality and confidence made him a popular hero to millions as he carried through the promises of his New Deal program by greatly extending the role of government. See NEW DEAL.

Under the New Deal, the federal government imposed many business controls and regulations and passed laws to help the needy. For example, the government established work projects for the unemployed, insured bank deposits up to $5,000, wrote codes of "fair competition" for business, and introduced social security (see SOCIAL SECURITY).

Most farmers, intellectuals, unemployed workers, wage earners, and members of minority groups supported the New Deal and voted Democratic. During the 1930's, most Negroes dropped their Republican ties and turned to the Democrats. Most Southerners and residents of big cities also backed the party. But conservatives—both Democrats and Republicans—believed that the federal government was taking far too great a role in people's lives. The conservatives thought that many problems should be handled by the state governments or by individuals themselves.

During World War II (1939-1945), Roosevelt turned the nation's efforts to defeating Germany and Japan. Shortly before his death in 1945, he helped create the United Nations in the hope of ensuring future peace.

The Fair Deal. President Truman continued the policies of the New Deal, calling his program the Fair Deal. Truman fought for civil rights for black Americans and for a national medical insurance plan. Southern Democrats often joined Republicans to block his efforts.

In 1948, some Southern Democrats formed the States' Rights Democratic Party, or Dixiecrat Party, to oppose Truman. But Truman won a surprise victory over the Republican candidate, Thomas E. Dewey, even though the Dixiecrats carried four Southern states. During the next four years, Truman directed much of his attention to the Cold War with the Communist nations and to the Korean War (1950-1953).

In both 1952 and 1956, the Democratic presidential candidate, Adlai E. Stevenson, lost to Dwight D. Eisenhower, one of the nation's greatest heroes of World War II. Yet the Democrats controlled Congress for the last six of Eisenhower's eight years in office.

The New Frontier. The youthful John F. Kennedy won the presidency in 1960, defeating Republican Richard M. Nixon. Kennedy called for many reforms in his program, which he named the New Frontier. Democrats outnumbered Republicans in both houses of Congress, but conservative Southern Democrats frequently joined conservative Republicans to defeat bills supported by Kennedy. Congress did grant Kennedy's requests for funds to aid economically depressed areas and to increase the minimum hourly wage from $1 to $1.25.

The Great Society. Vice-President Lyndon B. Johnson succeeded Kennedy after the assassination of the chief executive in November, 1963. In 1964, Johnson won a full term as President with a landslide victory over his Republican opponent, Barry M. Goldwater.

Johnson, who as a young congressman had been one of Roosevelt's strongest supporters, took office with whirlwind vigor. A skillful politician, he worked hard for the program begun by Kennedy. Johnson called on the nation to join him in building what he termed the Great Society. In spite of opposition from conservatives, Congress approved Johnson's requests for aid to cities and education, stronger civil rights laws, greater social security benefits, and tax cuts.

Times of Trouble. By 1966, the Vietnam War—and the nationwide dispute about it—overshadowed Johnson's Great Society program. The war divided Americans into "hawks," who supported the nation's involvement in Vietnam, and "doves," who opposed it. Peace marches and campus demonstrations attacked U.S. policy in Vietnam.

In March, 1968, Johnson announced that he would not run for re-election. At a stormy national convention, the Democrats nominated Vice-President Hubert H. Humphrey for the presidency. George C. Wallace, a Southern Democrat, became the candidate of a third party, the American Independent Party. The Republican candidate, again Richard M. Nixon, won the presidency by a narrow margin in 1968, but the Democrats kept control of Congress. During Nixon's Administration, an economic recession brought rising prices and widespread unemployment to the United States.

At the 1968 convention, the Democrats called for reforms to ensure fairness in selecting convention delegates. In 1969, a commission chaired by Senator George S. McGovern of South Dakota adopted a set of rules for the states to follow. One rule required delegates to be chosen in the year of the convention so that they would reflect the voters' current wishes. Another rule called for adequate representation of minorities, women, and youth at the convention.

In 1972, the Democrats nominated McGovern for the presidency, and the Republicans nominated President Nixon. Nixon won a landslide victory over McGovern, but the Democratic Party again kept control of Congress.

WILLIAM NISBET CHAMBERS

Related Articles in WORLD BOOK include:

Dixiecrat Party	Political Party	United States, History of
Liberty League	President of the United States	
Political Convention		

DEMOCRATIC-REPUBLICAN PARTY was a political party that was established during the 1790's under the leadership of Thomas Jefferson and James Madison. It was generally called the Republican Party, but it had no relation to today's Republican Party, which was founded in 1854.

People from a variety of backgrounds formed the Democratic-Republican Party to oppose the policies of the Federalist Party, led by Alexander Hamilton. The Federalists wanted a strong national government controlled by the upper classes. The Democratic-Republicans favored a weak national government. They believed that all the people should take part in the process of government. See FEDERALIST PARTY.

Jefferson was President from 1801 to 1809. He reversed some Federalist policies that had been put into effect when Hamilton was secretary of the treasury. Madison succeeded Jefferson and served from 1809 to 1817. Another Democratic-Republican, James Monroe, held the presidency from 1817 to 1825.

By about 1816, the Federalist Party had broken up as a national organization. With its decline, the Democratic-Republican Party split into several groups. Andrew Jackson emerged as the candidate of one of these groups and was elected President in 1828. Most historians regard the campaign organization that was formed to work for Jackson's election as the beginning of today's Democratic Party. The Democratic Party itself traces its origin to Jefferson's Democratic-Republican Party.

WILLIAM NISBET CHAMBERS

DEMOCRITUS, *dee MAHK rih tuhs* (460?-370? B.C.), was a Greek philosopher. He believed that the basic elements of reality are the *void* (empty space) and *atoms*, solid particles of matter that cannot be divided. All existing things consist of atoms and differ from each other because of the shape, arrangement, and position of the atoms. Countless worlds are formed when atoms come together in large groups. But the atoms collide and rebound, then scatter after a time, instead of fitting together. Then worlds disappear into the void.

Democritus believed that all sensation is a form of touch resulting from atoms colliding with sense organs. But the senses do not provide a true knowledge of reality, because the senses reveal only a world of color, smells, and tastes. Only atoms and empty space exist. Genuine knowledge, such as that of the atoms and the void, comes from the intellect and not the senses.

Democritus' views on ethics seem unrelated to his theory about atoms. He believed in common sense, emphasized well-being based on cheerfulness and freedom from worry, and approved a way of life free from any excess.

JOSIAH B. GOULD

See also ATOMISM; CHEMISTRY (Early Times; picture); ATOM (Development of the Atomic Theory).

DEMOGRAPHY, *dih MAHG ruh fee*, is the study of human population. *Demographers* (population experts) study the composition, distribution, changes, and movements in the population. They analyze trends in population and the relationship of a country's population to its standard of living. Population changes may be measured by birth rates, death rates, and migration. Demographers study the characteristics of population, such as age, sex, life span, and life expectancy. See also SOCIOLOGY (Demography); VITAL STATISTICS.

DE MOLAY, *DEE moh LAY*, **ORDER OF,** is an international organization of young men between the ages of 13 and 21. Since its founding in 1919, De Molay has initiated more than 2½ million members. The Order has 2,200 local chapters in the United States and several other countries. De Molay has international headquarters at 201 E. Armour Blvd., Kansas City, Mo. 64111.

The organization is under the guidance of the Masonic Order. Each chapter must have at least 25 members and be sponsored by a group of Masons or a Masonic body. Membership is open to boys of good character and of any faith who are recommended by two chapter members or a senior De Molay or a master Mason.

The De Molay Order was founded in Kansas City in 1919 by Frank S. Land. Land asked a boy named Louis Lower to invite some of his friends to a meeting to discuss forming a club. When a name was needed, Land suggested some historical figures and the boys chose Jacques De Molay (1243?-1314?) as their namesake. De Molay was the last Grand Master of the Knights Templars, a famous group of French crusaders.

The ritual for the De Molay Order includes secret ceremonies and is based on seven points: filial love, reverence for God, courtesy, comradeship, fidelity, cleanness, and patriotism. RICHARD E. HARKINS

DEMON. See DEVIL; DEVIL WORSHIP.

DEMON STINGER. See FISH (picture: Fish Protected by Spines).

DEMOSTHENES, *dih MAHS thuh neez* (384?-322 B.C.), was a great Greek orator and patriot. He is best known for his *Philippics*, a series of speeches in which he violently attacked King Philip II of Macedon (see PHILIP II).

He was born in Attica. His father was a wealthy Athenian who, on his death, left his property and children to the care of three guardians. These men proved to be dishonest, and took the property. Demosthenes prosecuted them successfully when he came of age. He was so successful as a speaker in this lawsuit that he entered public life. He mastered Greek law and politics, and the art of oratory. Demosthenes had to overcome great difficulties to become an orator. He had a harsh, unpleasant voice, weak lungs, and an awkward manner. He is said to have trained himself by reciting as he climbed steep hills, and by shouting above the roar of ocean waves with his mouth full of pebbles.

A Statue of Demosthenes is a famous example of Greek Hellenistic sculpture. The sculptor is unknown.

The Vatican Museum, Rome, Alinari

Demosthenes worked unselfishly for Greek liberty from the age of 30 until he died. Philip of Macedon had gained a foothold at Delphi, in central Greece, by 346 B.C. Demosthenes created an alliance of the great Greek cities of Athens and Thebes. Philip defeated their combined armies in the battle of Chaeronea, 338 B.C. (see GREECE, ANCIENT [The End of the Classical Period]). Athens made peace, but Demosthenes kept up his opposition. Later he defended his policy in his greatest speech, *On the Crown*. Many critics consider this the most nearly perfect speech in history. He poisoned himself in 322 B.C. when the last Greek effort to win freedom was a failure. THOMAS W. AFRICA

DEMOTIC. See HIEROGLYPHIC; GREEK LANGUAGE.

United Press Int.

Jack Dempsey fought Gene Tunney in two heavyweight championship bouts. The famous "long count" occurred in Chicago in 1927 in their second fight. Dempsey knocked Tunney down, but did not go immediately to a neutral corner. The referee had to wave Dempsey away, *above*, before starting to count. Estimates on the length of the count vary from 14 to 21 seconds. Tunney won on a 10-round decision.

DEMPSEY, JACK (1895-), became one of the most popular heavyweight boxing champions of all time. He knocked out Jess Willard in 1919 to win the title. He lost it in 1926 to Gene Tunney. Their second fight, in 1927, was climaxed by the famous long count. Dempsey knocked Tunney down in the seventh round. But he did not go to a neutral corner immediately, so the referee delayed starting the count over Tunney. Tunney rose at the count of 9, but it was estimated this was equivalent to a count of 14. Tunney went on to win the fight. William Harrison Dempsey was born in Manassa, Colo. He started fighting in mining camps in 1912. He was called the *Manassa Mauler*. See also BOXING (picture); TUNNEY, GENE. FRED RUSSELL

DEMPSTER, ARTHUR JEFFREY (1886-1950), was an American physicist. In 1935, he discovered uranium 235 (U-235), the rare isotope of the element uranium. The U-235 isotope is a key substance in the production of the atomic bomb.

Arthur Dempster

University of Chicago Archives

Dempster's highly accurate determinations of the masses of many elements and isotopes are of fundamental importance in nuclear physics. They provide the means for measuring mass and energy transformations. He developed a *mass spectrograph*, an instrument for weighing and sorting out atoms by their mass. He made important contributions to the work of the Manhattan Project, a United States government agency that directed the development and production of the atomic bomb during World War II.

Dempster was born in Toronto, Ont., and was graduated from the University of Toronto. He moved to the United States in 1914, and was naturalized in 1918. In 1916, he took his doctor of philosophy degree at the University of Chicago. He became professor of physics there in 1927, and did pioneer work in discovering many isotopes. RALPH E. LAPP

See also ISOTOPE; U-235.

DEMURRER, in law, is a pleading that raises the question of whether the case being presented would win the lawsuit even if it were proved. For example, a man who had stored property in his neighbor's garage might sue the neighbor if his property was damaged by a lightning bolt. The garage owner could then reply with a *demurrer*, asking the court to consider whether the facts presented would entitle the man to win his case if they were proved. In meaning and in spirit, the demurrer is equivalent to the slang expression "So what!" When the court considers the demurrer, it must act as though the statements made by both parties in the case are true. But the demurrer does not admit that the statements are true. If the court rejects the demurrer, then it is still up to the property owner to prove his case. The demurrer has been abolished in many states of the United States. The same result is reached in other ways. THOMAS A. COWAN

DEMUTH, CHARLES (1883-1935), an American painter, is best known for his still lifes and flower pieces, principally in watercolor. He also used architectural and ship themes, painted figures, and made illustrations based on stories and novels that appealed to him.

Demuth's work before about 1918 has a sketchlike quality. He began to mix new cubist influences with realistic subject matter as early as 1917. His later work is more geometrical and precisely executed. In this later period, Demuth began to use tempera and oil in addition to watercolors. His best-known pictures include *My Egypt* (1927), at the Whitney Museum of American Art, and *I Saw a Figure 5 in Gold* (1928), at the Metropolitan Museum of Art.

Demuth was born in Lancaster, Pa. He received his art training at the Pennsylvania Academy of Fine Arts in Philadelphia, and in Paris. GEORGE EHRLICH

DEN. See LION (Cubs); WOLF; BEAR.

DEN, in scouting. See BOY SCOUTS (Cub Scouting).

DENARIUS, *dih NAIR ee uhs,* was a silver coin used by the Romans during the periods of the Republic and the Empire. The Romans first issued the coins about 269 B.C. with the introduction of a new silver currency. They disappeared from circulation in the A.D. 200's. The silver denarius by that time had been replaced by a copper one coated with silver. The value of the denarius first equaled 10, and later 16, of the coins called *asses*. The standard gold coin of the Roman Empire was the *aureus*. It was about the same size as the denarius and was worth 25 denarii. The denarius was the penny referred to in the New Testament. Its initial, *d*, was the English symbol for penny, or pence. FRED REINFELD

The Denarius of Tiberius Caesar, which was issued from A.D. 14 to 37, carried the portrait of Tiberius on its front side.

Chase Manhattan Bank Money Museum

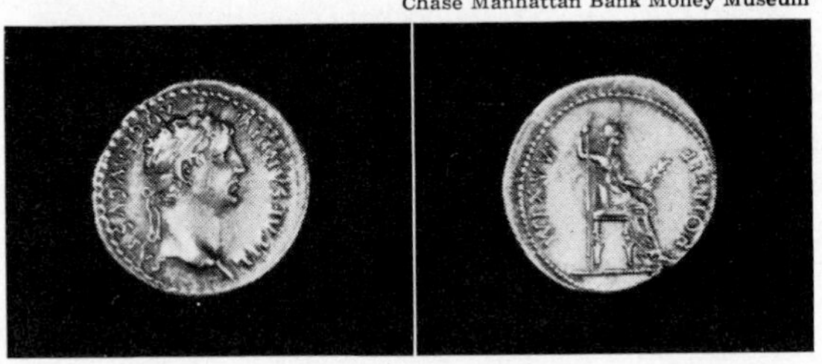

DENATURALIZATION. See NATURALIZATION (Denaturalization).

DENATURED ALCOHOL. See ALCOHOL (Ethyl Alcohol).

DENBY, EDWIN. See TEAPOT DOME.

DENDRITE. See NERVOUS SYSTEM; BRAIN (The Composition of the Brain).

DENDROCHRONOLOGY. See ARCHAEOLOGY (Absolute Chronology).

DENEB, *DEHN ehb,* is the brightest star in the constellation *Cygnus*. It is at the top of this crosslike constellation, so far from the earth that astronomers cannot accurately determine its distance. Deneb is 10,000 times as bright as the sun. Navigators use it as a guide.

DENEBOLA. See LEO (constellation).

DENGUE, *DEHNG gay,* is a fever that makes the head and eyes ache, and causes pain in muscles and joints. It may also cause a running nose and sore throat and make the skin break out in a rash. Dengue is caused by a *filtrable virus* that is carried by mosquitoes. Symptoms of the disease appear three to six days after a disease-bearing mosquito bites the victim. The rash breaks out on the fifth day of the illness. The fever subsides and then usually rises again. The disease is seldom fatal. Dengue occurs chiefly in Egypt, India, Iran, and the West Indies. BENJAMIN F. MILLER

See also VIRUS.

DENIER, *DEHN yuhr* or *duh NIHR,* is a unit of weight used to measure silk or synthetic threads. It is the weight in grams of 9,000 meters, or 9,842 yards, of yarn. The term is most often used to describe the fineness of yarn in women's nylon hosiery, which ranges from 7 to 70 denier. A 7-denier nylon is so sheer that the hosiery made from it is almost transparent. CHARLES H. RUTLEDGE

DENIM is a durable twill fabric made of coarse, single, hard-twisted cotton yarns. The standard white-back denim is made with indigo-blue dyed *warp* (lengthwise) yarns and unbleached *filling* (crosswise) yarns. Solid-color face denims are made from yarns that are a blend of black and white fibers.

Denim is used chiefly for work clothes. But it is also woven for use in sportswear, usually in white, pastel shades, and stripes. Most denims are preshrunk in a process called *Sanforizing*. HAZEL B. STRAHAN

DENIS, SAINT (A.D. 200's), is the patron saint of France. Saint Gregory of Tours reported that Denis was sent to preach the gospel in Gaul during the reign of Emperor Decius (249-251), became bishop of Paris, and died a martyr. His feast day is October 9. Denis was sometimes confused with Denis the Areopagite, who was a convert of Saint Paul. WALTER J. BURGHARDT

DENISON UNIVERSITY. See UNIVERSITIES AND COLLEGES (table).

Erich Lessing, Magnum

The Farms of Denmark are small but productive. The nation exports much bacon, ham, cheese, and butter.

WORLD BOOK photo

The Little Mermaid, **from a fairy tale by Hans Christian Andersen, greets ships arriving in the Copenhagen harbor.**

DENMARK

DENMARK is a small kingdom in northern Europe that is almost surrounded by water. It consists of a peninsula and 482 nearby islands. The peninsula, called Jutland, shares a 42-mile (68-kilometer) border with West Germany. Greenland, off the northeastern coast of Canada, is a province of Denmark even though it lies 1,300 miles (2,090 kilometers) away. Denmark, along with Norway and Sweden, is one of the Scandinavian countries.

More than half the people of Denmark live on the islands near the peninsula. Copenhagen, Denmark's capital and largest city, is on the largest of these islands. Over a fourth of the Danes live in the Copenhagen area, and almost half the country's industries are there.

The people of Denmark are prosperous, and they have one of the world's highest standards of living. The Danes have achieved prosperity even though their land is poor in natural resources. They sell their products to other countries to pay for the fuels and metals they must import for their industries. Denmark is famous for its butter, cheese, bacon, ham, and other processed foods. The Danes are also known for their beautifully designed manufactured goods, including furniture and silverware. Since the time of the Vikings, the Danes have been a seafaring people, and Denmark is still a great shipping and fishing nation.

Denmark is a land of small green farms, blue lakes, and white coastal beaches. The carefully tended farmlands make up about three-fourths of the country. In the farm areas, the roofs of most houses are made of red or blue tiles, or are thatched. Storks, which the Danes believe bring good luck, build nests on some rooftops. Castles and windmills rise above the rolling landscape. Visitors can enjoy Denmark's charm even in the busy, modern cities, with their well-preserved sections of colorful old buildings and cobblestone streets.

The contributors of this article are H. Peter Krosby, Associate Professor of History and Scandinavian Studies at the University of Wisconsin at Madison; Mark W. Leiserson, Associate Professor of Economics at Yale University; and William C. Wonders, Professor of Geography at the University of Alberta.

FACTS IN BRIEF

Capital: Copenhagen.

Official Language: Danish.

Official Name: *Kongeriget Danmark* (Kingdom of Denmark).

Form of Government: Constitutional monarchy. *Head of State*—King or Queen. *Head of Government*—Prime Minister. *Legislature*—Folketing (179 members, 4-year terms). *Political Divisions*—14 counties and the municipalities of Copenhagen and Frederiksberg.

Area: 16,629 sq. mi. (43,069 km^2). *Greatest Distances*—east-west, 250 mi. (402 km); north-south, 225 mi. (362 km). *Coastline*—1,057 mi. (1,701 km).

Elevation: *Highest*—Yding Skovhøj, 568 ft. (173 m) above sea level. *Lowest*—sea level along the coasts.

Population: *Estimated 1976 Population*—5,134,000; distribution, 83 per cent urban, 17 per cent rural; density, 308 persons per sq. mi. (119 persons per km^2). *1970 Census*—4,937,784. *Estimated 1981 Population*—5,316,000.

Chief Products: *Agriculture*—bacon, barley, beef and dairy cattle, beets, eggs, hogs, oats, potatoes, poultry, rye, wheat. *Fishing*—cod, haddock, herring, plaice, salmon, trout. *Manufacturing*—cement, diesel engines, electrical equipment, furniture, machinery, processed foods, ships, silverware.

National Holiday: Constitution Day, June 5.

National Anthem: "Der er et yndigt land" ("There Is a Lovely Land").

Money: *Basic Unit*—krone. One hundred öre equal one krone. For the value of the krone in dollars, see MONEY (table: Values). See also KRONE.

DENMARK / *Government*

Denmark is a constitutional monarchy with a king or queen, a prime minister, and a parliament. Its government is based on the Danish constitution of 1953. This constitution, like that of the United States, divides the government into three branches—executive, legislative, and judicial. All executive powers are carried out by the government in the monarch's name, but the monarch has little real power. Almost all appointed officials, including judges and governors, are named by the monarch on the advice of the cabinet. The parliament appoints an official called an *ombudsman*, who investigates complaints of citizens against actions or decisions by the government (see OMBUDSMAN).

Prime Minister of Denmark is the actual head of the government. The monarch appoints the leader of the majority party, or combination of parties, in the parliament to be prime minister. The prime minister forms a cabinet called the Council of State.

If the prime minister receives a vote of no confidence from the parliament, he has two choices. He must either (1) resign with all the other cabinet ministers, or (2) ask the monarch to order a new parliamentary election and dissolve the old parliament.

Parliament of Denmark, called the *Folketing*, consists of one house. It has 179 members, who are elected to four-year terms. Of these, 135 are elected from Denmark, 2 from Greenland, and 2 from the Faeroe Islands. The Faeroes lie north of Scotland and are part of the Danish kingdom. The other 40 seats are divided among the various political parties according to their share of the total votes in the latest election. Many kinds of bills that are passed by the parliament are subject to approval by the voters. A bill must be voted on by the people if a third of the members of parliament call for such action.

Courts. Denmark's highest court is the Supreme Court. It consists of 15 judges, at least 5 of whom must hear each case. There are also two High Courts, with a total of about 50 judges. At least 3 High Court judges and a jury of 12 persons hear serious criminal cases. A jury verdict of innocent is final, but the judges may reverse a verdict of guilty. The judges and jurors act together to set the length of prison sentences. There are more than 100 lower courts.

Local Government. Denmark is divided into 14 counties and 2 large municipalities—Copenhagen and Frederiksberg. The 14 counties are subdivided into almost 300 smaller municipalities. In most cases, a municipality consists of an urban center and a rural area. Each county and municipality in Denmark, including Copenhagen and Frederiksberg, has a council elected by the people. Each council selects a mayor to head the local government.

Politics. The strongest of Denmark's many political parties is the Social Democratic party. Other parties include the Agrarian, Conservative, Radical Liberal, and Socialist People's parties. Danes at least 20 years old may vote in national and local elections.

Armed Forces. A total of more than 50,000 men serve in Denmark's army, navy, and air force. Men from the age of 19 to 25 are required to serve from 14 to 16 months in the armed forces.

Politikens Presse Foto

Margrethe II became queen of Denmark in 1972. She and her husband, Prince Henrik, *far left*, are shown at an art exhibit.

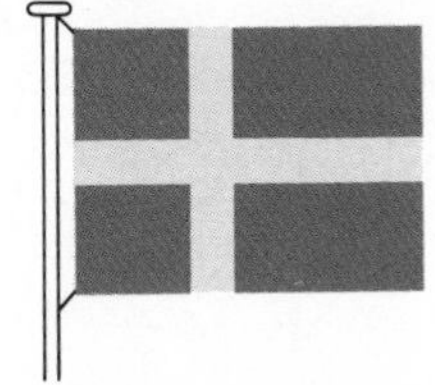

Symbols of Denmark. According to legend, the Danish flag came from the sky to King Valdemar II in 1219. It appeared as a sign of victory during a battle. The coat of arms shows the three lions that represented his family.

H. E. Harris & Co.

Bob Serating, Birnback

Christiansborg Palace is the home of Denmark's parliament, the *Folketing*. It also houses the Supreme Court.

Denmark is 0.6 per cent as large as the United States, not counting Alaska and Hawaii. Denmark lies just north of Germany.

WORLD BOOK map

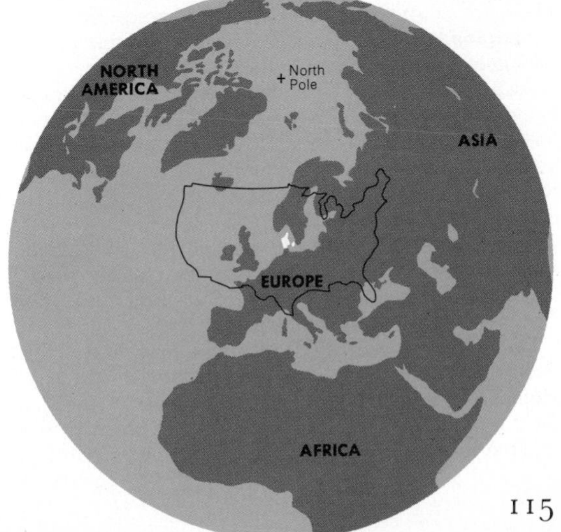

DENMARK/*People*

The Danes are closely related to the Norwegians and the Swedes. The Danish language is also much like those of the other two Scandinavian nations. Denmark's only minority nationality group consists of about 30,000 persons of German ancestry. They live in southern Jutland, along Denmark's border with West Germany.

About 350,000 Danes have migrated to the United States, most of them between 1870 and 1920. In 1911, a group of Danish-Americans bought the Rebild Hills area near Ålborg. The next year, they gave it to the Danish government as a national park. The gift was made under an agreement providing that the government celebrate the U.S. Independence Day there each year. Ever since, thousands of Danes have observed the Fourth of July in the park. The Danish royal family attends the celebration.

Population. In 1976, Denmark had a population of 5,134,000. The following table shows some official census figures for Denmark through the years:

Year	Population	Year	Population
1970	4,937,784	1921	3,267,831
1965	4,767,597	1901	2,449,540
1960	4,585,256	1850	1,414,648
1950	4,281,275	1801	929,001
1940	3,844,312	1769	797,584
1930	3,550,656		

Copenhagen, the largest city in Denmark, has about 626,000 persons. More than a fourth of all the Danish people live in Copenhagen or its suburbs. Four other cities have populations over 100,000. They are, in order of size, Århus, Odense, Ålborg, and Frederiksberg. Eleven cities have from 50,000 to 100,000 persons. About a fifth of the people live in rural villages or on farms. See the separate articles on the cities of Denmark listed in the *Related Articles* at the end of this article.

Food. Most Danes eat four meals a day—breakfast, lunch, dinner, and a late-evening supper. Breakfast generally consists of cereal, cheese, or eggs. Dinner, which includes fish or meat, is usually the only hot meal. People in the cities and towns eat dinner in the evening, and those in farm areas eat it at midday. The chief part of the other meals consists of open-faced sandwiches called *smørrebrød*. One sandwich may be a pyramid-shaped pile of about 20 small shrimps on thin bread. The Danes often prepare a plate of smørrebrød almost as a work of art, with many attractive sandwiches.

Religion. About 97 per cent of the Danish people belong to the Evangelical Lutheran Church, the official church of Denmark. The monarch is required by law to belong to the church, but the people have complete freedom to worship as they please. The church is supported largely by a national tax paid only by members. Roman Catholics form Denmark's second largest religious group.

The Evangelical Lutheran Church has no supreme spiritual leader. Ten bishops manage church affairs. The Danish parliament has control of the church, but does not interfere in its religious practices.

Education. Almost all Danes can read and write. Danish law requires children from the age of 7 to 14 to attend school. Elementary school consists of the first seven grades, and high school lasts from three to five years. A five-year high school education makes a student eligible to enter a university. Denmark has three universities. The University of Copenhagen is the oldest and largest. It was founded in 1479 and has about 16,000 students. The other universities are those of Århus and Odense.

The famous Danish folk high schools operate separately from the public educational system. They are private schools, but are supported largely by government funds. These schools provide young adults with a general education in Danish government, history, and literature. Courses last up to six months, and the students live at the schools. Denmark has about 70 folk high schools. The first ones were founded during the mid-1800's. They were set up to help young farmers take a more active part in Denmark's political and social life. Today, folk high schools also attract many young adults of the cities and towns.

Libraries and Museums. The Danish government supports a nationwide system of about 1,500 public libraries. They own more than 11 million books. The chief libraries include the Royal Library in Copenhagen, founded in the mid-1600's. It is Denmark's national library, and is similar to the Library of Congress in the United States. The Royal Library has more than 1,300,000 books. Other leading libraries include the University Library in Copenhagen, and the State and University Library in Århus.

Denmark also has nearly 200 museums, more than 50 of which are owned by the national or local governments. Among the most important are the National Museum and the State Museum of Art, both in Copenhagen, and the Natural History Museum in Århus.

Arts. Many Danes have won fame in the arts, especially in literature. Ludvig Holberg is known as the father of Danish literature. During the early 1700's, he wrote plays that poked fun at Danish society. Hans Christian Andersen won world fame for his fairy tales, and is probably Denmark's most famous writer. The books of Søren Kierkegaard led to the development of the modern philosophy called *existentialism*.

Denmark's greatest novelist of the 1900's has probably been Johannes V. Jensen, who also wrote fine poetry. Danish writers who won the Nobel prize for literature were Jensen, Karl Gjellerup, and Henrik Pontoppidan. Other outstanding Danish writers include Isak Dinesen, Johannes Ewald, Martin A. Hansen, and Martin Andersen Nexö. See the separate biographies of Danish writers listed in the *Related Articles* at the end of this article.

Carl A. Nielsen is considered Denmark's greatest composer. He wrote six symphonies and many other works, including the comic opera *Maskarade* (see NIELSEN, CARL A.). Well-known Danish painters include Michael Ancher and C. W. Eckersberg. Denmark's leading sculptor was Bertel Thorvaldsen. His statue of Christ is one of the most copied sculptures in the world. See THORVALDSEN, BERTEL.

Recreation. Soccer is the most popular sport in Denmark. Other favorite sports include bicycling, gymnastics, rowing, sailing, swimming, and tennis. Danes have won Olympic and other world championships in most of these sports, and also in archery, boxing,

Bob Serating, Birnback

Tivoli Gardens is one of the most famous amusement parks in the world. It covers about 20 acres (8 hectares) of Copenhagen.

John LaDue

Danish Porcelain Workers produce beautiful dishes, figures, and vases that are prized in all parts of the world.

diving, fencing, riding, weight lifting, and wrestling.

Copenhagen is world famous for its Tivoli Gardens amusement park, which opened in 1843 in the heart of the city. The park offers ballet and pantomime, rides and shooting galleries, restaurants, circus acts, concerts, and fireworks displays.

Social Welfare. Since the 1890's, Denmark has developed many social welfare programs. The country has social insurance plans that cover accidents, handicapping injuries, illness, old age, unemployment, and the death of husbands. Any person living in Denmark may join these programs. Most plans are managed by private, government-approved organizations, with costs shared by insured persons, employers, and the government. The government manages some plans, including aid for the aged and for widows, and pays the total cost.

H. Kurtz, Pix from Publix

Copenhagen, Denmark's capital and largest city, is the nation's chief commercial and industrial center. The older sections of Copenhagen have narrow streets that are closed to motor traffic.

Danish Fishermen generally hand down their skills from father to son. Most of the fishermen live in ports along the North Sea.

S. E. Hedin from Carl Östman

The Land

The peninsula of Jutland forms almost 70 per cent of Denmark. But most Danes live on about 100 nearby islands. No one lives on other islands in the area, which cover only 18 square miles (47 square kilometers).

The land is low throughout Denmark. The highest point, the hill of Yding Skovhøj, rises only 568 feet (173 meters) above sea level. The land is covered mainly by *moraine*, the earth and stone deposited by melting glaciers thousands of years ago. The underlying rock can be seen in only a few areas.

Land Regions. Denmark has five main land regions: (1) the Western Dune Coast, (2) the Western Sand Plains, (3) the East-Central Hills, (4) the Northern Flat Plains, and (5) Bornholm.

The Western Dune Coast consists chiefly of great sandy beaches that extend along almost the entire western coast. These beaches close off many long, narrow inlets called *fiords* that once were connected to the sea. In the southwest are marshes that the tide covers regularly.

The East-Central Hills. Kronborg Castle, in Helsingør, is the scene of Shakespeare's *Hamlet*, a play about a Danish prince.
Nordisk Pressefoto from Keystone

The Western Sand Plains are almost flat. Water from ancient melting glaciers flowed over this region and deposited much sand, forming the plains.

The East-Central Hills make up Denmark's largest land region. This gently rolling region includes much of Jutland and almost all the nearby islands. Long, narrow fiords form natural harbors along the coastlines. The largest inlet is Lim Fiord, which winds across northern Jutland for 112 miles (180 kilometers). This fiord forms an inland lagoon 15 miles (24 kilometers) wide. A beach on the Western Dune Coast closes off the fiord's outlet to the North Sea. Small vessels use the Thyborøn Canal to move between the fiord and the sea.

The islands in the region lie close together. Their deep moraine soils are the best farmlands in Denmark. The largest island, Sjælland, is 2,708 square miles (7,014 square kilometers). On this island stands Copenhagen, the capital and largest city of Denmark. Sjælland is the most thickly populated part of the country. Other major islands include Falster, Fyn, and Lolland.

The Northern Flat Plains were once a part of the sea bottom. The region rose from the water when the weight of ancient glaciers was removed by melting.

Bornholm and nearby small islands lie much closer to southern Sweden than to the rest of Denmark. Granite rock covers most of this region.

Lakes and Rivers. Denmark has many small lakes. They formed in small hollows left in the ground by melting ice from the glaciers. Lake Arresø, the largest lake, covers 16 square miles (41 square kilometers). Denmark also has many short rivers. The longest one, Guden River, is 98 miles (158 kilometers) long.

LAND REGIONS OF DENMARK

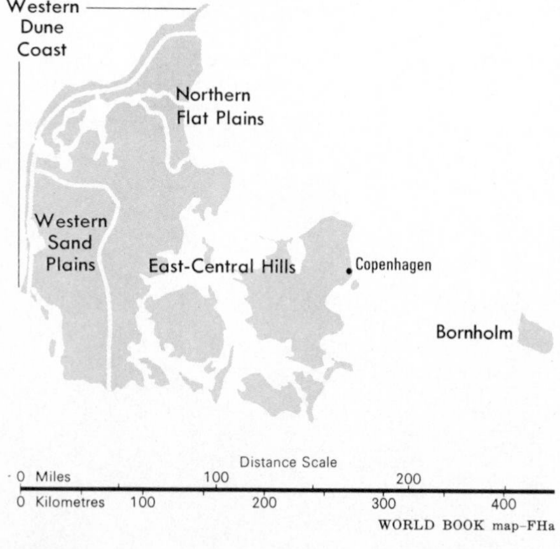

WORLD BOOK map-FHa

The Northern Flat Plains, leveled by ancient glaciers, are in northernmost Jutland. This region consists mostly of farmland.
John LaDue

CM TERRAIN DENMARK
COPYRIGHT BY
RAND MC NALLY & COMPANY
MADE IN U.S.A.
Longitude East of Greenwich
DENMARK
Mixed Evergreen and Deciduous Trees
Shrub
Grass
National Capital
Cities and Towns
Canals
Rail Lines
County Boundaries
0 5 10 15 20 25 30 Miles
0 10 20 30 40 Kilometers
Skagerrak
Kattegat
THE SKAW
Skagen
Tannis Bay
Ålbæk Bay
Hirtshals
Hjørring
Frederikshavn
Sæby
LÆSØ
Brønderslev
NORDJYLLAND
Jammer Bay
Vigsø Bay
Rye
Dronninglund
Nørresundby
Ålborg
Langerak
Lindenborg
Lim Fiord
Ålborg Bay
Thisted
Løgstør
Nibe
Nykøbing
MORS
Thyborøn Canal
Års
Mariager Fiord
Mariager
Hobro
Nissum Bay
VENØ
VIBORG
Skive
Lemvig
Struer
Randers
Viborg
Nissum Fiord
Stor
Holstebro
Bjerringbro
Guden
Grenå
ÅRHUS
Kjellerup
RINGKØBING
Silkeberg
Ebeltoft
Herning
Ikast
Århus
Århus Bay
Ringkøbing
Ringkøbing Fiord
Skanderborg
YDING SKOVHØJ 568 FT. (173 M)
Skjern
Odder
TUNØ
SAMSØ
Samsø Belt
Give
Horsens
Hedensted
VEJLE
ENDELAVE
Grinsted
Juelsminde
Vejle
Varde
ÆBELØ
BLÅVANDS POINT
Egtved
RIBE
Fredericia
Bogense
Esbjerg
Kolding
Middelfart
Kerteminde
FANØ
Fanø Bay
Konge
Vejen
Ribe
Flads
Christiansfeld
BÅGØ
Odense
Nyborg
MANØ
Assens
FYN
Ringe
Vojens
Haderslev
RØMØ
Åbenrå
HELNÆS
BARSØ
Fiord
Little Belt
SØNDERJYLLAND
Fåborg
Svendborg
Løgumkloster
Åbenrå
Nordborg
ALS
LYØ
TÅSINGE
THURØ
Arn
SYLT
Højer
Tønder
Augustenborg
Sønderborg
ÆRØ
Ærøskøbing
Marstal
Flensborg Fiord
Flensburg
FÖHR
AMRUM
PELLWORM
NORTH FRISIAN ISLANDS
Helgoland Bay
SCHARHÖRN
NEUWERK
ALTE MELLUM
Schlei
Eckernförder Bay
Kiel Bay
Kiel Canal
Kiel
Selent Lake
Hohwacht Bay
Grub Lake
WEST GERMANY
Grosser Plön Lake
Lübeck Bay
Lübeck
Trave
Ratzeburg Lake
Schaal Lake
Hamburg
Oste
Elbe
FEHMARN
FERRY
Fehmarn Belt
Kadet Channel
Mecklenburg Bay
Wismar Bay
POEL
EAST GERMANY
Schwerin
Schwerin Lake
ANHOLT (DENMARK)
HESSELØ
SJÆLLANDS POINT
SEJERØ
Sejerø Bay
Nykøbing
Frederiksværk
Ise Fiord
Lake Arresø
Kalundborg
Great Belt
Holbæk
FREDERIKSBORG
Frederikssund
ORØ
Hillerød
Søllerød
Hørsholm
Helsinge
Helsingør
IVEN
Gladsakse
Ballerup
Gentofte
KØBENHAVN
SALTHOLM
Hvidovre
Frederiksberg
Roskilde
AMAGER
VESTSJÆLLAND
COPENHAGEN (København)
ROSKILDE
Dragør
SJÆLLAND
Ringsted
Køge Bay
Køge
Slagelse
Sorø
Haslev
Store-Heddinge
Korsør
FY.
Skælskør
AGERSØ
Næstved
OMØ
Smålands Sound
STORSTRØM
Fakse Bay
Præstø
Baltic Sea
MØN
Vordingborg
STORSTRØM BRIDGE
Stege
FEJØ
FEMØ
LANGELAND
Rudkøbing
Langelands Belt
Nakskov
LOLLAND
Sakskøbing
FALSTER
Maribo
Nykøbing
Stubbekøbing
Nysted
Rødby
HÄLSÖ
ÖCKERÖ
HÖNÖ
Göteborg
Borås
Lygnern Lake
Viskan
SWEDEN
Fegen Lake
Ätran
Nissan
Halmstad
Laholm Bay
HALLANDS VÄDERÖ
Skälder Bay
Rönne
Hälsingborg
The Sound
Malmö
Karlskrona
Kristianstad
Hanö Bay
SWEDEN
CAPE SANDHAMMAREN
Allinge
Hasle
BORNHOLM
Bornholmsgat
Rønne
Svaneke
Åkirkeby
Neksø
BORNHOLM (DENMARK)
Baltic Sea
0 5 10 15 20 Miles
0 10 20 Kilometers
©RMCN.
8° 9° 10° 11° 12° 13° 15°
54° 55° 56° 57°
1 2 3 4 5 7 8
A B C D E
Specially created for World Book Encyclopedia by Rand McNally and World Book editors

DENMARK MAP INDEX

Counties

County	Population	Key
Århus	534,333	B 3
Bornholm	47,241	D 7
Frederiksborg	260,825	C 5
Fyn	433,765	C 3
København	616,571	C 5
Nordjylland	457,165	B 2
Ribe	198,153	C 1
Ringkøbing	242,006	B 1
Roskilde	154,314	C 5
Sønderjylland	238,502	C 2
Storstrem	252,780	C 2
Vejle	306,809	C 2
Vestsjælland	259,484	C 4
Viborg	221,002	B 2

Cities and Towns†

City or town	Population	Key
Åbenrå	20,472	C 2
Ålborg	154,737	A 2
Allerød*	15,089	C 5
Århus	238,138	B 3
Års	11,033	B 2
Ballerup-Måløv	50,965	C 5
Birkerød*	21,022	C 5
Bjerringbro	11,859	B 2
Brøndbyerne*	33,420	C 5
Brønderslev	19,511	A 2
Copenhagen (København)	625,678 *1,384,411	C 5
Dronninglund	13,719	A 3
Ebeltoft	11,006	B 3
Egtved	12,030	C 2
Esbjerg	76,488	C 1
Fåborg	17,300	C 3
Fredensborg-Humlebæk*	13,331	C 5
Fredericia	44,015	C 2
Frederiksberg	101,970	C 5
Frederikshavn	33,141	A 3
Frederikssund	12,988	C 5
Frederiksværk	14,692	C 5
Gentofte	77,683	C 5
Give	12,616	C 2
Gladsakse	74,841	C 5
Glostrup*	28,373	C 5
Græsted-Gilleleje*	11,296	C 5
Grenå	17,698	B 3
Greve*	21,943	C 5
Grinsted	16,342	C 1
Haderslev	29,733	C 2
Haslev	11,201	C 4
Hedensted	11,040	C 2
Helsinge	12,005	B 5
Helsingør	52,842	B 5
Herlev*	24,654	C 5
Herning	52,873	B 1
Herstederne*	23,646	C 5
Hillerød	30,172	C 5
Hirtshals	14,106	B 2
Hjørring	31,178	A 2
Hobro	13,532	B 2
Høje Tåstrup*	30,769	C 5
Holbæk	26,208	C 4
Holstebro	33,305	B 1
Horsens	52,164	C 2
Hørsholm	19,548	C 5
Hvidovre	45,264	C 5
Ikast	16,611	B 2
Juelsminde	14,423	C 3
Kalundborg	19,415	C 4
Kjellerup	13,116	B 2
Køge	30,718	C 5
Kolding	52,735	C 2
Korsør	19,921	C 4
Lemvig	19,931	B 1
Løgstør	11,066	B 2
Lyngby-Tårbæk*	61,446	C 5
Maribo	12,307	D 4
Middelfart	16,213	C 2
Møn*	12,250	C 4
Morsø*	25,027	B 2
Næstved	42,024	C 4
Nakskov	17,203	D 4
Nordborg	15,507	C 2
Nyborg	17,852	C 3
Nykøbing	25,907	D 4
Odder	16,053	C 3
Odense	165,520	C 3
Randers	64,351	B 3
Ribe	17,295	C 1
Ringe	11,089	C 3
Ringkøbing	15,228	B 1
Ringsted	25,544	C 4
Rødovre*	44,630	C 5
Rønne	15,479	C 7
Roskilde	50,433	C 5
Sæby	16,423	A 3
Silkeborg	43,243	B 2
Skagen	13,521	A 3
Skanderborg	15,324	B 2
Skive	25,597	B 2
Skjern	12,102	C 1
Slagelse	32,439	C 4
Søllerød	31,023	C 5
Sønderborg	29,645	D 2
Sorø	13,946	C 4
Struer	17,416	B 1
Svendborg	35,822	C 3
Sydthy*	12,641	B 2
Tårnby*	45,672	C 5
Thisted	28,947	B 1
Tønder	11,649	D 1
Værløse*	15,683	C 5
Varde	16,872	C 1
Vejen	14,446	C 2
Vejle	49,876	C 2
Viborg	36,304	B 2
Vojens	16,428	C 2
Vordingborg	19,036	C 4

†Populations of municipalities, which may include rural areas as well as the urban center.
*Population of metropolitan area, including suburbs.

Physical Features

Feature	Key
Åbenrå Fiord	C 2
Æbelo (Island)	C 3
Ærø (Island)	D 3
Agersø (Island)	C 4
Ålbæk Bay	A 3
Ålborg Bay	B 3
Als (Island)	C 2
Amager (Island)	C 5
Anholt (Island)	B 4
Århus Bay	B 3
Atn River	D 2
Bågø (Island)	C 2
Baltic Sea	C 5
Barsø (Island)	C 2
Blåvands Point	C 1
Bornholm (Island)	C 7
Bornholmsgat (Channel)	C 7
Endelave (Island)	C 3
Fakse Bay	C 5
Falster (Island)	D 5
Fanø (Island)	C 1
Fanø Bay	C 1
Fehmarn Belt (Strait)	D 4
Fejø (Island)	D 4
Femø (Island)	D 4
Flensborg Fiord	D 2
Fyn (Island)	C 3
Great Belt (Strait)	C 3
Guden River	B 2
Helnæs (Island)	C 2
Hesselø (Island)	B 4
Ise Fiord	C 4
Jammer Bay	A 2
Jutland (Peninsula)	C 2
Kadet Channel	D 4
Kattegat (Channel)	B 4
Køge Bay	C 5
Konge River	C 1
Læsø (Island)	A 3
Lake Arresø	C 5
Langeland (Island)	D 3
Langelands Belt (Strait)	D 3
Langerak River	A 3
Lim Fiord	B 2
Lindenborg River	B 2
Little Belt (Strait)	C 2
Lolland (Island)	D 4
Lyø (Island)	C 3
Manø (Island)	C 1
Mariager Fiord	B 3
Møn (Island)	C 5
Mors (Island)	B 1
Nissum Bay	B 1
Nissum Fiord	B 1
North Frisian Is.	C 1
Odense River	C 3
Omø (Island)	C 4
Orø (Island)	C 4
Ringkøbing Fiord	B 1
Rømø (Island)	C 1
Rye River	A 2
Saltholm (Island)	C 5
Samsø (Island)	C 3
Samsø Belt (Strait)	C 3
Sejerø (Island)	C 4
Sejerø Bay	C 4
Sjælland (Island)	C 4
Sjællands Point	B 4
Skaggerak (Channel)	A 1
Skive River	B 2
Skjern River	C 1
Smålands Sound	C 4
Stor River	B 1
Storstrøm Bridge	D 4
Tannis Bay	A 3
Tåsinge (Island)	C 3
The Skaw (Cape)	A 3
The Sound (Øresund)	C 5
Thurø (Island)	C 3
Thyborøn Canal	B 1
Tunø (Island)	C 3
Varde River	C 1
Venø (Island)	B 1
Vigsø Bay	A 1
Yding Skovhøj (Hill)	C 2

*Does not appear on map; key shows general location.
Source: Latest official estimates (1971).

DENMARK/*Climate*

Denmark has a mild, damp climate, chiefly because it is almost surrounded by water. In winter, seas are not so cold as land, and in summer they are not so warm. As a result, west winds from the seas warm Denmark in winter and cool it in summer. These winds affect Denmark's weather throughout the year. Also in winter, west winds bring some warmth from the North Atlantic Current of the Gulf Stream (see Gulf Stream). Denmark is small and has no mountains to block the wind, so the climate does not differ much from area to area.

Winter temperatures average about 32° F. (0° C) in Denmark, with the coldest days from 15° to 20° F. (−9° to −7° C). The waters on the east may freeze over during especially cold winters. At these times, the waters cannot warm the cold winds that occasionally blow in from the east, and the weather may become bitterly cold. Summer temperatures in Denmark average 63° F. (17° C). The warmest weather usually varies from 75° to 82° F. (24° to 28° C). Winds from eastern Europe may cause higher temperatures during especially hot summers.

Denmark receives a yearly average of about 24 inches (61 centimeters) of *precipitation* (rain, melted snow, and other forms of moisture). Western Denmark gets a little more precipitation than eastern Denmark because the moisture-bearing west winds reach it first. Rain falls throughout the year, with the most during August and October. Snow falls from 20 to 30 days a year, but usually melts quickly. Fog and mist occur frequently, especially on the west coast in winter.

Winds from the North Sea give Denmark a mild, damp climate. The western parts of the country have the mildest temperatures and get the most rain. Beautiful beaches make Fanø, an island off the western coast of Jutland, a popular summer resort.

J. Stage, Photo Researchers

DENMARK/*Economy*

Denmark has a thriving economy, even though the country is poor in natural resources. The few industrial minerals found in Denmark include clay, lignite, limestone, and peat. Coal, iron, petroleum, and most other industrial fuels and metals must be imported. Much of the soil is not too fertile, and requires heavy use of fertilizers. The land is flat or gently rolling, so the rivers cannot be used to generate hydroelectric power. Forests cover only about a tenth of the land, and supply less than half of Denmark's wood. The seas that almost surround the country provide a cheap means of transportation by which Denmark can import its industrial needs and export its products. The seas are also rich in fish.

Manufacturing in Denmark has expanded rapidly since the mid-1950's. Manufacturing more than doubled by the late 1960's and replaced agriculture as the nation's leading industry. Exports of manufactured goods more than tripled during the same period. The government has done much to promote industry by expanding educational programs to train engineers, technicians, and skilled workers.

Nearly half the industries of Denmark are in the Copenhagen area. The nation's factories produce beautifully designed, high-quality goods including radios, television sets, furniture, and silverware. Among Denmark's other products are cement, diesel engines, machinery, ships, and processed foods including bacon, butter, cheese, and ham.

Agriculture. Farmland makes up about three-fourths of Denmark's total land area. The farms are small and cover an average of 38 acres (15 hectares), compared with about 350 acres (142 hectares) in the United States.

Until the 1880's, wheat was Denmark's most important farm product. Then wheat prices fell, and Danish farmers began to stress the production of dairy products, eggs, and hogs. They organized cooperative dairies and slaughterhouses, and shared equipment and profits. Today, cooperatives cover all branches of farming.

Raising hogs and beef or dairy cattle is the major activity on most Danish farms. Most crops are used for livestock feed. They include barley, beets, oats, potatoes, and rye. Barley is grown on more farmland than any other crop, and Denmark is one of the world's leading barley producers. About 60 per cent of the country's farm production is exported.

Fishing. Danish commercial fishermen catch about $1\frac{1}{3}$ million short tons (1.2 million metric tons) of fish a year. Important fish are cod, haddock, herring, plaice, salmon, and trout. Over half the catch comes from the North Sea. Esbjerg is the major fishing port.

Transportation. Denmark has about 35,000 miles (56,300 kilometers) of roads and highways. About one-fifth of the people own automobiles. At least half of the people use bicycles for transportation, and many roads have separate bicycle lanes.

A government-owned railroad provides most of the service in Denmark, which has about 2,500 miles (4,020 kilometers) of track. Train-carrying ferries connect many Danish islands with each other and with the mainland. The islands of Sjælland and Falster are linked by the 10,535-foot (3,211-meter) Storstrøm Bridge, the longest bridge in Europe.

Denmark has many busy seaports, of which Copenhagen is the most important. The Danish merchant fleet includes about 1,260 ships of about 100 short tons (91 metric tons) each. Kastrup Airport, near Copenhagen, is one of Europe's largest air terminals. It handles about $7\frac{1}{2}$ million passengers a year.

Communication. Denmark has about 75 daily newspapers, with a total daily circulation of about 1,600,000 copies. The largest dailies include the *Aktuelt*, *Berlingske Tidende*, and *Politiken*, all of Copenhagen, and the *Jyllands-Posten* of Århus.

All radio and television broadcasting is handled by Radio Denmark, a public organization responsible to the Danish Ministry of Cultural Affairs. No advertising is allowed on the programs. The people pay a yearly license fee for each radio and television set.

The government owns and operates the Danish telegraph system and long-distance telephone service. Most local telephone service is privately owned.

DENMARK'S GROSS NATIONAL PRODUCT

Total gross national product in 1970—$16,971,000,000

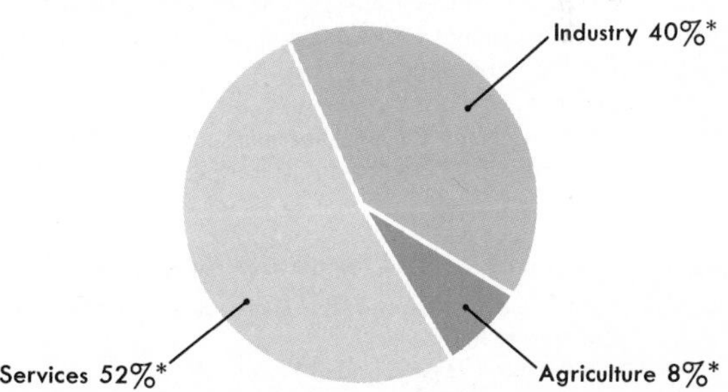

The Gross National Product (GNP) is the total value of goods and services produced by a country in a year. The GNP measures a nation's total annual economic performance. It can also be used to compare the economic output and growth of countries.

Production and Workers by Economic Activities

Economic Activities	Per Cent of GDP* Produced	Labor Force: Number of Persons	Labor Force: Per Cent of Total
Manufacturing	28	691,000	29
Government	16	†	†
Hotels, Restaurants & Trade	15	383,000	16
Construction	10	201,000	8
Transportation & Communication	9	158,000	7
Agriculture, Forestry & Fishing	8	268,000	11
Housing	6	—	—
Banking, Insurance & Real Estate	3	†	†
Community, Business & Personal Services	3	659,000	28
Mining & Utilities	2	**	**
Other	—	20,000	1
Total	100	2,380,000	100

*Gross domestic product. GDP is gross national product less net income sent abroad.
†Government and Banking, Insurance & Real Estate included in Community, Business & Personal Services.
**Mining & Utilities included in Manufacturing.
Source: Statistical Office, Copenhagen

Early Days. As long as 100,000 years ago, people lived in what is now Denmark. Great changes in the climate occurred, and the region became too cold for human life. The climate started to become warmer about 14,000 years ago, and continuous settlement began. Farming developed after 2500 B.C.

By the time of Christ, trade by sea had brought the people into close contact with leading civilizations. The contact expanded for hundreds of years. During this period, the Danes lived in small communities governed by local chieftains. About A.D. 950, all Denmark was united by King Harald Bluetooth. Harald introduced Christianity in Denmark.

About 800, Danish seamen began raiding European coastal towns and sailing away with slaves and treasure. The Danish Vikings spread terror throughout much of western Europe for about 300 years. They conquered England in 1013, and Danish kings ruled that country until 1042. See VIKING (The Danish Vikings).

A Great Power. During the late 1100's and early 1200's, Danish power expanded along the southern coast of the Baltic Sea to Estonia, which Denmark conquered in 1219. But a long period of civil wars and struggles with north German cities, beginning in the 1240's, greatly weakened the country.

Denmark regained its power under Queen Margrete, who became ruler in 1375. Margrete was also the wife of King Haakon VI of Norway. After he died in 1380, Margrete became ruler of Norway as well as Denmark. In 1388, during political confusion in Sweden, Swedish noblemen elected her ruler of Sweden, too. In 1397, Margrete united Denmark, Norway, and Sweden in the Union of Kalmar, with power centered in Denmark. Sweden broke away from the union in 1523.

In 1536, during the Reformation, King Christian III established Lutheranism as the official religion of Denmark. That same year, Christian made Norway a province of Denmark.

Wars with Sweden. During the 1600's and 1700's, Sweden defeated Denmark in several wars fought for control of the Baltic Sea. In the Danish-Swedish War (1657-1660), Sweden won much Danish and Norwegian territory in what is now Sweden. Only pressure from England, France, and The Netherlands prevented Sweden from dividing Denmark itself. During the Great Northern War (1700-1721), Denmark tried unsuccessfully to win back the territory it had lost to Sweden.

In 1788, Denmark began freeing its serfs. These peasants had been bound to the land on which they worked. Educational reforms were begun during the early 1800's. Denmark sided with France during the Napoleonic Wars of that period, and was again defeated by Sweden in 1813. In the Treaty of Kiel in 1814, Denmark gave Norway to Sweden, but kept Greenland and other Norwegian colonies.

The Schleswig Wars. In 1848, the pressure of public opinion forced King Frederik VII to accept a democratic constitution for Denmark. The constitution was adopted in 1849. It granted the highest power of government to an elected two-house parliament.

Also in 1848, a revolt broke out in Holstein and Schleswig, two German states just south of Denmark. These regions were ruled by the Danish king though they were not part of Denmark. A revolutionary government of Schleswig-Holstein was set up. It wanted to throw off Danish control and join the German Con-

IMPORTANT DATES IN DENMARK

c. 950 King Harald Bluetooth united Denmark and introduced Christianity in the country.

1013-1042 Denmark ruled England.

1380 Denmark and Norway were united under Queen Margrete.

1388 Queen Margrete was elected ruler of Sweden as well.

1397 Denmark, Norway, and Sweden were united in the Union of Kalmar.

1536 Lutheranism became the official Danish religion.

1657-1660 Denmark lost much territory to Sweden in the Danish-Swedish War.

1788 The government began freeing the Danish serfs.

1814 Denmark lost Norway to Sweden in the Napoleonic Wars.

1849 Denmark adopted its first democratic constitution.

1864 Denmark lost Schleswig and Holstein to Prussia and Austria.

1918 Denmark granted independence to Iceland, which remained under the Danish king until 1944.

1920 North Schleswig was returned to Denmark.

1940-1945 Germany occupied Denmark during World War II.

1944 Iceland ended its union with Denmark.

1949 Denmark and 11 other nations formed the North Atlantic Treaty Organization (NATO).

1953 Denmark adopted a new constitution that ended the upper house of parliament.

1959 Denmark and six other countries formed the European Free Trade Association (EFTA).

1966 Denmark began a $600-million development program in Greenland.

1973 Denmark became a member of the European Community.

The Seal of King Valdemar II was used to stamp official papers. Valdemar, called the Victorious, extended Danish power along the Baltic Sea to Estonia, which he conquered in 1219.

Rigsarkivet, Copenhagen

federation, of which Holstein was already a member. Danish troops defeated the rebels in 1850. In 1863, Schleswig was made a part of Denmark. Prussia and Austria, its ally, invaded Denmark in 1864. They won a quick victory and took over Schleswig and Holstein.

Social and Political Reforms. During the late 1800's, education, industry, and trade were expanded in Denmark. The Danes also developed cooperatives and improved their farming methods. At this time, the upper classes had special rights that gave them control of the upper house of the parliament. The small farmers and industrial workers formed political parties and struggled for political equality. A new constitution, adopted in 1915, ended the special rights of the upper classes in Denmark.

Denmark remained neutral during World War I (1914-1918). After the war, Denmark granted independence to Iceland, a Danish colony. However, Iceland stayed united with Denmark until 1944, when it became a republic. In 1920, the Allies transferred North Schleswig to Denmark from Germany. Most people of the region had voted for the transfer.

World War II began in 1939. On April 9, 1940, German forces invaded Denmark, and the Danes surrendered after a few hours of fighting. The Germans allowed the Danish government to continue as long as it met their demands. But resistance groups developed and blew up factories and transportation facilities. The Germans took over the government in August, 1943.

In September, 1943, the Danes organized the secret Freedom Council to lead the resistance movement. They also helped about 7,000 Danish Jews escape to Sweden. On May 5, 1945, after the fall of Germany, Allied troops entered Denmark and the Germans there surrendered. See WORLD WAR II.

Denmark became a charter member of the United Nations in 1945, and of the North Atlantic Treaty Organization (NATO) in 1949. During the late 1940's, the United States gave Denmark much aid. The Danes rebuilt industries that had been damaged during the war, and the nation's economy became strong again.

Denmark Today. Denmark continued its political reforms and economic expansion under King Frederik IX, who inherited the throne in 1947. In 1953, a new constitution ended the upper house of parliament. The constitution also made Greenland a province, rather than a colony, of Denmark. In 1959, Denmark and six other European countries formed the European Free Trade Association (EFTA), an economic union.

In 1966, Denmark began a $600-million development program in Greenland. This 10-year program includes expanding and modernizing Greenland's fishing and food-processing industries and its towns.

King Frederik IX died in 1972. His oldest daughter, Margrethe, succeeded him to the throne.

In 1972, Denmark signed a treaty to join the European Community, also called the European Common Market. The community is an economic association originally made up of six European nations. In October, 1972, Danish voters approved entry into the community. The treaty went into effect on Jan. 1, 1973.

H. PETER KROSBY, MARK W. LEISERSON, and WILLIAM C. WONDERS

DENMARK / *Study Aids*

Related Articles in WORLD BOOK include:

Outline

I. Government
- A. Prime Minister
- B. Parliament
- C. Courts
- D. Local Government
- E. Politics
- F. Armed Forces

II. People
- A. Population
- B. Food
- C. Religion
- D. Education
- E. Libraries and Museums
- F. Arts
- G. Recreation
- H. Social Welfare

III. The Land
- A. Land Regions
- B. Lakes and Rivers

IV. Climate

V. Economy
- A. Manufacturing
- B. Agriculture
- C. Fishing
- D. Transportation
- E. Communication

VI. History

Questions

What do Denmark's folk high schools offer students?

What is Denmark's official church?

What is the major farm activity in Denmark?

Which area has more than a fourth of Denmark's total population and almost half the country's industries?

Why does the Danish government celebrate the U.S. Independence Day?

How did Denmark, Norway, and Sweden become united during the late 1300's?

Why can Denmark's rivers not be used to generate hydroelectric power?

What is the longest bridge in Europe?

How is the Danish broadcasting system supported?

Who united Denmark? When?

DENOMINATE NUMBER, *dee NAHM uh nayt,* is a number with a name, such as 5 miles, 10 meters, 3 pounds, or 6 grams, rather than just 5, 10, 3, or 6. Denominate numbers are usually measurements. Parts of denominate numbers are sometimes indicated by decimals, such as $4.30, 8.14 inches, or 5.41 meters. When the numbers are written this way, they can be added, subtracted, multiplied, or divided, as any other decimals are.

Many denominate numbers contain irregular subdivisions. For example, 1 rod contains 5½ yards, 1 yard contains 3 feet, and 1 foot contains 12 inches. A denominate number which contains two or more irregular subdivisions is called a *compound denominate number.* 6 yards 4 feet 9 inches is an example. Such compounds are more difficult to add, subtract, multiply, or divide, because the subdivisions must first be *reduced* (changed) to the same *denomination* (unit of measurement) before the operations are performed. HOWARD F. FEHR

DENOMINATOR. See FRACTION (Writing Fractions with Numbers); ARITHMETIC (Working with Fractions).

DENSITY of a substance is the amount of *mass* (matter) it contains for each unit of its volume. The density of a substance is calculated by dividing its mass by its *volume* (amount of space it occupies). In the metric system, density is measured in either grams per cubic centimeter or kilograms per cubic meter. For example, a piece of iron with a mass of 780 grams and a volume of 100 cubic centimeters has a density of 7.8 grams per cubic centimeter (780 ÷ 100 = 7.8). In the customary system of measurement, density is measured in pounds per cubic inch or pounds per cubic foot. For example, a piece of iron with a mass of 28 pounds and a volume of 100 cubic inches has a density of 0.28 pounds per cubic inch (28 ÷ 100 = 0.28).

Most substances expand in volume when they are heated. Therefore, the density of most substances decreases when they are heated. Water is an exception. It *contracts* (takes up less volume) when heated from 0° C to 4° C (32° F. to 39° F.) and its density increases. Above 4° C, water expands when heated and its density decreases. Most substances contract when they freeze so that the density of the solid is higher than the density of the liquid. Again, water behaves differently. It expands when it freezes, and its density decreases. Ice floats on water because lower density substances float in liquids of higher density.

See also GRAVITY, SPECIFIC.

DENSITY OF POPULATION figures tell how many people, on the average, live on each unit of area in a certain place. For the density of population in countries, states, and provinces, see the *Facts in Brief* tables in the articles on various countries, states, and provinces. See also POPULATION; WORLD (People of the World).

DENT, JOHN CHARLES (1841-1888), was a Canadian journalist and historian. He is best known for *The Last Forty Years,* a history of Canada from 1841 to 1881. He also wrote *The Canadian Portrait Gallery* and *The Story of the Upper Canadian Rebellion.*

Dent was born at Kendal, England, but came to Canada as an infant with his parents. He became a lawyer, but practiced for only a short time. He returned to England and served as a journalist with the *London Daily Telegraph.* He became editor of the *Toronto Evening Telegraph* in 1876, and later joined the editorial staff of the *Toronto Globe.* DESMOND PACEY

DENT, JULIA. See GRANT, ULYSSES S. (Early Army Career; Grant's Family).

DENTAL ASSOCIATION, AMERICAN, is a national organization of dentists. Its purpose is to improve public health and promote the science and art of dentistry. It has 54 societies with over 450 branches in the United States and its possessions. It has about 116,000 members. The association was founded in 1859. Headquarters are at 211 E. Chicago Avenue, Chicago, Ill. 60611. Critically reviewed by the AMERICAN DENTAL ASSOCIATION

DENTAL EROSION. See TEETH (Defects and Diseases).

DENTAL HYGIENE is a science related to keeping the teeth, gums, and mouth healthy. A dental hygienist is a member of the dental health "team" that includes the dentist, dental assistant, and dental laboratory technician. But only the dentist and dental hygienist are licensed to work directly in a patient's mouth. Most dental hygienists are women.

Dental Hygienist's Duties include important services that help the dentist give complete dental service to his patients. Her chief duties are *dental prophylaxis* (cleaning and polishing the teeth) and dental health education, stressing the necessity for good home care of the teeth. She may take and develop X-ray pictures of the teeth and jaws, and apply solutions to the teeth to aid in reducing decay. When necessary, the dental hygienist may assist the dentist in other dental work.

Education. Accredited schools of dental hygiene require that applicants have at least a high-school education. Students are chosen on the basis of special aptitudes. This helps schools select students who probably have the best chance of completing their study.

Persons who enter schools of dental hygiene may choose either of two kinds of programs. They may take a two-year course, which leads to a certificate or diploma, or they may take a four-year course to earn a bachelor's degree. Several schools that offer the bachelor's degree admit students to the dental hygiene program only after they have completed two years of college. Subjects studied in both of the programs include anatomy, chemistry, and bacteriology. They also include such special subjects as dental anatomy, dental health education, and the clinical practice of dental hygiene skills.

All states require dental hygienists to have a license to practice. Applicants must pass state board examinations to get the license.

Career Opportunities. Most dental hygienists work in private dental offices. Other dental hygienists work in industrial and hospital clinics, do public health work in government and private health agencies, or teach in schools of dental hygiene. For information about a career in dental hygiene, write to the American Dental Hygienists' Association, 211 E. Chicago Avenue, Chicago, Ill. 60611. MARGARET E. SWANSON

See also TEETH (Care of the Teeth).

DENTAL PULP. See TEETH (picture: The Parts of a Tooth).

DENTAL SCHOOL. See DENTISTRY (Careers).

DENTIFRICE. See TEETH (Daily Care).

DENTIN. See TEETH (picture: The Parts of a Tooth).

DENTISTRY is the art and science of treating diseases of the teeth and of other parts of the mouth. Dentists help to keep people healthy in many ways. They correct deformities of the teeth and mouth. Some specialize in making replacements for teeth and other parts of the mouth. They prescribe medicines and may perform operations on the mouth and jaws.

Fields in Dentistry

General Dental Practice includes mouth examination, diagnosis, treatment planning, treatment, and prevention of disease. The dentist frequently uses X rays and other equipment to ensure correct diagnosis and treatment planning. Treatment may include filling cavities, removing the nerves of teeth, treating diseases of the gums, removing teeth, and replacing lost teeth with *bridges* and *dentures* (dental plates). Anesthesia is often used in any treatment that might cause pain. Teeth may be filled with gold, silver, amalgam, or cements, and with fused porcelain inlays. Dentists treat diseases of the mouth and gums such as trench mouth and pyorrhea. Perhaps one of the most important parts of a dentist's work is preventive dentistry. If a dentist examines a patient's teeth at regular intervals, he may find and treat a disease before it becomes serious. As part of this preventive work, a dentist may demonstrate the proper methods of brushing and flossing the teeth. He may also advise his patients about what foods to eat or to avoid for good dental health. In addition, a dentist may treat teeth with fluorides or other substances to prevent decay.

Oral Surgery includes treating diseases, injuries, and deformities of the mouth and teeth by surgery. Broken jaws, injuries caused by automobile accidents, and harelips are among the conditions treated by the oral surgeon. He removes tumors from the mouth. An oral surgeon also extracts teeth, including impacted wisdom teeth, which might prove too difficult for the general dentist.

Orthodontics is concerned with deformities that develop during the growth of the teeth and jaws. Such malformations often cause teeth to be crowded and irregularly placed. This results in *malocclusion*, or "bad bite." These deformities detract from personal appearance, tend to make the teeth decay more readily, and often make chewing difficult. The orthodontist corrects these conditions by mechanical devices such as braces, and by other means which stimulate the growth of bones and bring teeth into a correct position in the mouth. Orthodontic treatment is sometimes put off until the child has grown the second, or permanent, set of teeth. See ORTHODONTICS.

Prosthodontics is the branch of dentistry that specializes in replacing lost teeth. The three most common ways of replacing lost teeth are by *bridgework*, which replaces one or more missing teeth; *partial dentures*, which replace several lost teeth; and *full dentures*, or plates, which are used when all the teeth in either jaw or both jaws are missing. Lost teeth are sometimes replaced by implants—false teeth that are permanently anchored to the jawbone. The development of plastics and the use of various alloys have improved the function and appearance of artificial teeth.

Periodontics is concerned with treating the gums and the parts of the jaws that support the teeth. More teeth are extracted during adult life because of the periodontal disease *pyorrhea* than for all other reasons combined (see PYORRHEA). Periodontal diseases destroy gum tissue and the supporting bone around the teeth. Once these tissues are destroyed, they cannot be restored. But dentists can prevent further destruction through treatment.

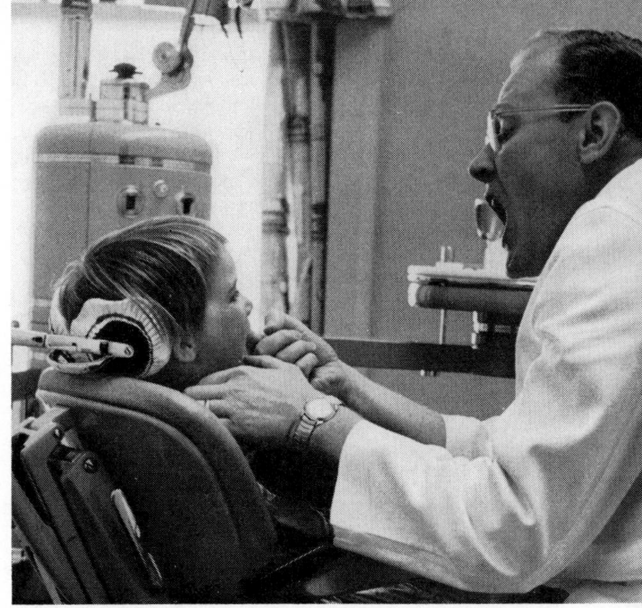

Dorothy Reed

A Visit to the Dentist becomes an interesting adventure to a child. Periodic trips to a dentist should begin when a child's first set of teeth have come in, and should continue throughout a person's life.

Pedodontics concentrates on the prevention and treatment of dental disease in children. Tooth decay is common during childhood. The pedodontist pays special attention to the diet of children, especially limiting the use of refined sugars.

Other Fields of dentistry are *public health dentistry*, which promotes dental health, and *oral pathology*, which deals with tumors and injuries of the mouth.

History of Dentistry

Prehistoric man used both magic and medicine to treat pain, including that caused by teeth. After writing was invented, both the Egyptians and the Babylonians recorded their methods of treatment.

Greek medical texts written in the 500's and 600's B.C. contain references to teething difficulties, oral symptoms found in such diseases as malaria, and to "pincers for pulling out teeth." But the first gold dental bridges are older than the Greek texts. These bridges, which show much technical skill, have been found in the ruins of the ancient Etruscan civilization in Italy.

Dentistry developed slowly. During the Middle Ages barbers served as doctors and dentists. Jewelers and other craftsmen made dentures. It was not until 1840 that dentistry became a profession. In that year the first dental school was organized in Baltimore.

Since 1840, dentistry has made important progress in the United States. Josiah Flagg of Boston was the first native-born American dentist. He began practicing after his discharge from the army in 1783. Flagg was one of the first to use gold foil in filling teeth. The discovery of the X ray in 1895 gave dentistry a way of looking inside teeth to discover their defects. In 1910 Sir William Hunter and Sir Kenneth Goodby of England pointed out that infected teeth could cause infection to spread throughout the entire body.

The discovery of anesthesia was one of the most important forward steps in the history of dentistry. On Dec. 11, 1844, Dr. Horace Wells (1815-1848), a dentist, took laughing gas before having a tooth extracted. The tooth was pulled without pain. Laughing gas, or nitrous oxide, combined with oxygen, is still used to make tooth extraction painless.

Two years after Wells' discovery, William Morton, also a dentist, gave a public demonstration of the use of ether as an anesthetic during a surgical operation. See MORTON, WILLIAM THOMAS GREEN.

Quieter, faster drilling equipment, aimed at taking discomfort out of drilling, was developed in the 1950's. These drills worked at such high speeds that they reduced pain caused by heat and pressure.

Careers in Dentistry

Because tooth decay is the most common disease of man, the field of dentistry is constantly expanding as the population grows. There are about 104,000 dentists in the United States. About 100,000 engage in active practice. Most of the remainder work in dental education and research, dental public health, or for other dentists' organizations. Dentistry ranks as one of the highest paid professions in the United States.

In Canada, dentistry also ranks as one of the best-paid professions. There are about 7,400 dentists in Canada. They must meet the same personal and professional qualifications as dentists in the United States. They must also pass examinations given by a board of examiners in their provinces before they receive a license to practice.

Personal Requirements. Dentistry requires manual skills and a high level of intelligence. All dental schools participate in an aptitude testing program. On the basis of these tests, dental educators can predict quite accurately whether a prospective student will successfully complete dental training.

Educational Requirements. Every student preparing to enter a dental school must have at least two years of college education. Professional education requires another four years of study at an accredited dental school.

The students in a dental school concentrate on three main areas of study: (1) academic, (2) dental sciences, and (3) professional matters. *Academic* work emphasizes the basic sciences. The study of *dental sciences* allows each student to learn and develop actual skills he needs to practice dentistry. The study of *professional matters* includes courses in the history of dentistry, management of a practice, professional ethics, and the legal aspects of dentistry. Students who successfully com-

FILLING A CAVITY

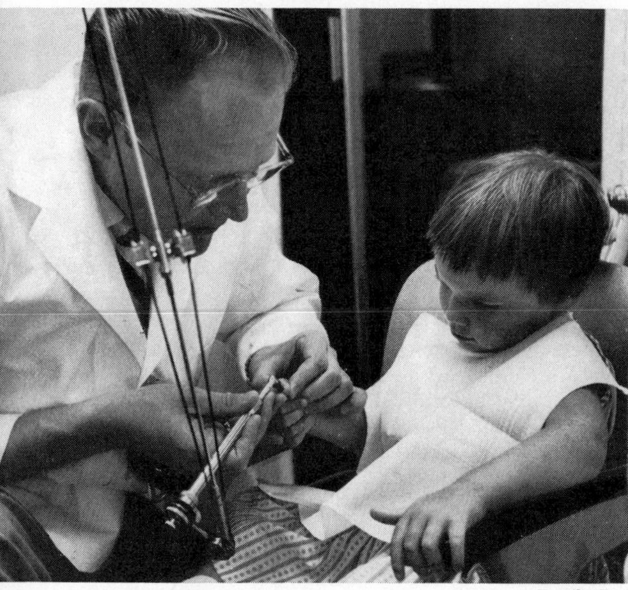

Dorothy Reed

The Dentist's Drill has many uses. The dentist explains to a young patient that a buffer attachment helps clean teeth.

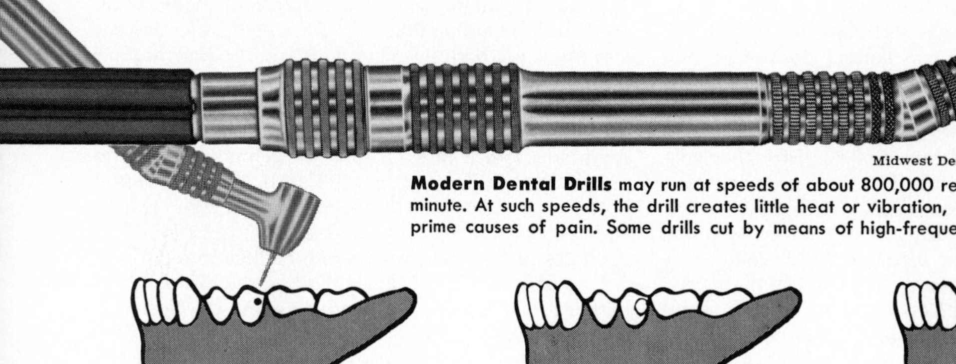

Midwest Dental Mfg. Co.

Modern Dental Drills may run at speeds of about 800,000 revolutions a minute. At such speeds, the drill creates little heat or vibration, two of the prime causes of pain. Some drills cut by means of high-frequency sound.

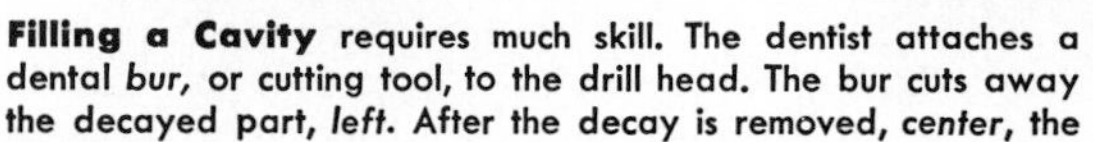

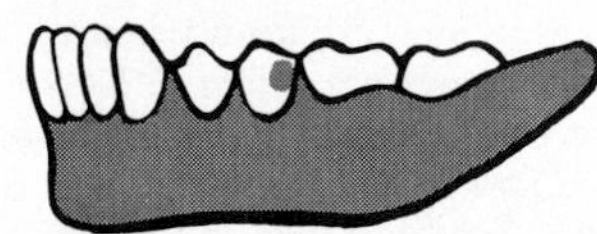

Filling a Cavity requires much skill. The dentist attaches a dental *bur,* or cutting tool, to the drill head. The bur cuts away the decayed part, *left.* After the decay is removed, *center,* the dentist fills the tooth by pressing gold, silver, or amalgams into the hole. He smooths the surface to remove rough spots and makes sure the finished filling, *right,* matches the shape of the tooth.

U.S. SCHOOLS

State	School	City
Alabama	Univ. of Alabama	Birmingham
California	Loma Linda Univ.	Loma Linda
	Univ. of California	Los Angeles
	Univ. of California	San Francisco
	Univ. of Southern California	Los Angeles
	Univ. of the Pacific	San Francisco
Colorado	Univ. of Colorado	Denver
Connecticut	Univ. of Connecticut	Farmington
District of Columbia	Georgetown Univ.	Washington
	Howard Univ.	Washington
Florida	Univ. of Florida	Gainesville
Georgia	Emory Univ.	Atlanta
	Medical Coll. of Georgia	Augusta
Illinois	Loyola Univ.	Maywood
	Northwestern Univ.	Chicago
	Southern Illinois Univ.	Edwardsville
	Univ. of Illinois	Chicago
Indiana	Indiana Univ.—Purdue Univ.	Indianapolis
Iowa	Univ. of Iowa	Iowa City
Kentucky	Univ. of Kentucky	Lexington
	Univ. of Louisville	Louisville
Louisiana	Louisiana State Univ.	New Orleans
Maryland	Univ. of Maryland	Baltimore
Massachusetts	Boston Univ.	Boston
	Harvard School of Dental Medicine	Boston
	Tufts Univ.	Boston
Michigan	Univ. of Detroit	Detroit
	Univ. of Michigan	Ann Arbor
Minnesota	Univ. of Minnesota	Minneapolis
Mississippi	Univ. of Mississippi	Jackson
Missouri	Univ. of Missouri	Kansas City
	Washington Univ.	St. Louis
Nebraska	Creighton Univ.	Omaha
	Univ. of Nebraska	Lincoln
New Jersey	College of Medicine and Dentistry of New Jersey	Jersey City
	Fairleigh Dickinson Univ.	Hackensack
New York	Columbia Univ.	New York
	New York Univ.	New York
	State Univ. of New York	Buffalo
	State Univ. of New York	Stony Brook
North Carolina	Univ. of North Carolina	Chapel Hill
Ohio	Case Western Reserve Univ.	Cleveland
	Ohio State Univ.	Columbus
Oklahoma	Univ. of Oklahoma	Oklahoma City
Oregon	Univ. of Oregon	Portland
Pennsylvania	Temple Univ.	Philadelphia
	Univ. of Pennsylvania	Philadelphia
	Univ. of Pittsburgh	Pittsburgh
South Carolina	Medical Univ. of South Carolina	Charleston
Tennessee	Meharry Medical Coll.	Nashville
	Univ. of Tennessee	Memphis
Texas	Baylor Coll. of Dentistry	Dallas
	Univ. of Texas	Houston
	Univ. of Texas	San Antonio
Virginia	Virginia Commonwealth Univ.	Richmond
Washington	Univ. of Washington	Seattle
West Virginia	West Virginia Univ.	Morgantown
Wisconsin	Marquette Univ.	Milwaukee
Puerto Rico	Univ. of Puerto Rico	San Juan

CANADIAN SCHOOLS

Province	School	City
Alberta	Univ. of Alberta	Edmonton
British Columbia	Univ. of British Columbia	Vancouver
Manitoba	Univ. of Manitoba	Winnipeg
Nova Scotia	Dalhousie Univ.	Halifax
Ontario	Univ. of Toronto	Toronto
	Univ. of Western Ontario	London
Quebec	Laval Univ.	Quebec
	McGill Univ.	Montreal
	Univ. of Montreal	Montreal
Saskatchewan	Univ. of Saskatchewan	Saskatoon

plete all these courses are awarded a degree of D.D.S. (Doctor of Dental Surgery), or D.M.D. (Doctor of Dental Medicine).

Postgraduate courses are offered for dentists who want to specialize, teach, or enter research, and for those who want to keep up with advances in dentistry.

Licensing. All states and Canadian provinces require that a dentist be licensed before he can practice. Applicants must be graduates of a school approved by the Council on Dental Education of the American Dental Association, or, in Canada, the Canadian Dental Association. Each must pass an examination given by a board of examiners. Most licenses allow dentists to practice as either general practitioners or specialists. But 13 states require additional examinations for specialists. Few states allow a dentist from another state to begin practice without taking another examination.

Organizations. The professional organization of dentists in the United States is the American Dental Association (see DENTAL ASSOCIATION, AMERICAN). In Canada, it is the Canadian Dental Association, which maintains headquarters at 234 St. George Street, Toronto 5, Ont.

ROBERT G. KESEL

See also TEETH; ORTHODONTICS; PROSTHETICS; HYPNOTISM (picture); DENTAL HYGIENE.

A DENTAL BRIDGE

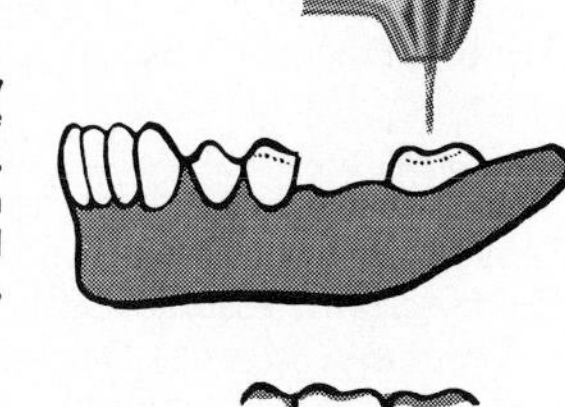

After a tooth has been pulled, the dentist may fill the space with a *bridge*, or false tooth. He prepares the teeth on each side to hold plates that will keep the new tooth in place.

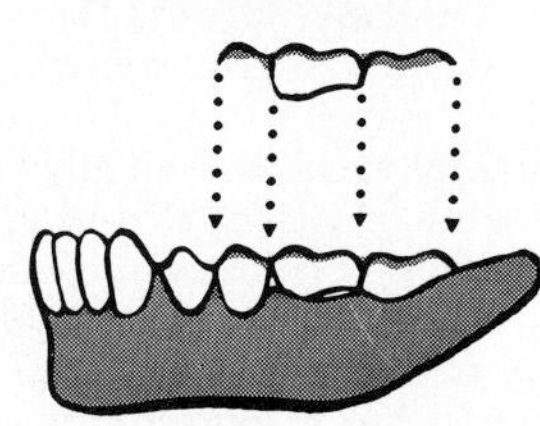

The dentist makes the new tooth the same shape as the one that was pulled. He fastens a plate in the false tooth. He puts the bridge in place, with a plate capping the teeth on each side.

D'ENTRECASTEAUX ISLANDS, *DAHN truh KAHS TOH,* lie in the Pacific Ocean, north of the eastern tip of New Guinea. Three large islands (Goodenough, Fergusson, and Normanby) and over a dozen small ones have a land area of 1,233 square miles (3,193 square kilometers). The islands are forested and mountainous. Evidence of their volcanic origin is seen in craters, geysers, and hot springs on Fergusson Island. They are governed as part of the Australian Territory of Papua. The 34,405 inhabitants are Melanesians. The island group is named for Bruni d'Entrecasteaux, a French explorer of the 1700's. See also NEW GUINEA.

EDWIN H. BRYAN, JR.

Roach Photos

Downtown Denver is the commercial center of the Rocky Mountain region. The Colorado Capitol, *left foreground,* stands near the business district. The Rocky Mountains rise in the background.

DENVER is the capital of Colorado, and the distribution, manufacturing, and transportation center for the Rocky Mountain region. The city is also a central point for snow sports and serves as a gateway to nearby mountain vacation spots. Denver lies on the South Platte River, 10 miles (16 kilometers) east of the Rocky Mountains. It is called the *Mile High City* because the state Capitol stands on land 1 mile (1.6 kilometers) above sea level.

When gold prospectors founded Denver in 1858, it formed part of the Kansas Territory. The town was named for James W. Denver, the governor of the territory. From 1860 to 1945, Denver was a mining and agricultural community. After World War II ended in 1945, the city became known for its industries. Denver's continued expansion in industry and population has made it one of the nation's fastest growing cities.

The City covers 118 square miles (306 square kilometers) and has the same boundaries as Denver County.

FACTS IN BRIEF

Population: 514,678. *Metropolitan Area Population*—1,239,477.

Area: 118 sq. mi. (306 km²). *Metropolitan Area*—4,677 sq. mi. (12,113 km²).

Altitude: 5,280 ft. (1,609 m) above sea level.

Climate: *Average Temperature*—January, 29° F. (−2° C); July, 73° F. (23° C). *Average Annual Precipitation* (rainfall, melted snow, and other forms of moisture)—15 in. (38 cm). For the monthly weather in Denver, see COLORADO (Climate).

Government: Mayor-council. *Terms*—4 years for the mayor and the 13 council members.

Founded: 1858. Incorporated as a city in 1861.

City Flag: The blue, red, white, and yellow design symbolizes the sky, soil, mountains, and sun.

City Seal: The black and gold circular seal has an eagle, a shield with a key, a smokestack, the state Capitol, the sun setting over the mountains, and the words *City and County of Denver Seal.*

Denver and nearby Boulder form a metropolitan area that extends over 4,677 square miles (12,113 square kilometers).

Broadway, Colfax Avenue, and Larimer Street form a triangle around Denver's main business district. Cherry Creek joins the South Platte River northwest of the triangle. Skyscrapers with banks and investment firms make 17th Street the "Wall Street of the West."

Southeast of the main business district, the Civic Center includes the City and County Building, the Colorado State Capitol, the Denver Art Museum, and the Denver Public Library. The City Auditorium and Theater, the Denver Coliseum, and the Currigan Exhibition Hall stand west of the business district.

Military installations in the Denver area include the Air Force Accounting and Finance Center, Fitzsimons General Hospital, and Lowry Air Force Base.

The People. More than 80 per cent of Denver's people were born in the United States. Almost 12 per cent of the people are of Mexican ancestry. Negroes form about 9 per cent. Denver has a small number of American Indians and people of Oriental descent.

Opposition to racial discrimination and a shortage of low-rent housing led a group of citizens to form the Metro Denver Fair Housing Center in 1965. The center helps families of all races and nationalities rent or buy homes in areas where they have not traditionally lived.

Methodists make up the largest religious group in Denver. Other denominations, in order of size, include Presbyterians, Roman Catholics, and Baptists.

Economy. More of Denver's people work for the federal and state governments than for any other employer. Denver is the national or regional headquarters of more federal agencies than any other U.S. city except Washington, D.C. The Denver mint, near the Capitol, makes millions of coins every year.

The Denver metropolitan area has more than 1,500 manufacturing plants. Food processing ranks as the city's chief manufacturing activity. Other Denver products include defense, space travel, and transportation equipment; luggage; sporting goods; tires; and toys. The Denver Union Stockyards are one of the nation's major livestock centers.

In 1964, to attract more industry, the city established an organization called Forward Metro Denver. This organization provides manufacturers throughout the country with information on Denver's available land, construction costs, and mild climate. New companies increased the number of people employed in manufacturing from about 63,500 in 1965 to 82,200 in 1969.

A large number of warehouses helps make Denver the distribution center of the Rocky Mountain region. The city also serves as the region's transportation center. Nine commercial airlines use Stapleton International Airport. Railroad passenger trains, six freight lines, and several highways also serve the city.

Five television stations and over 25 radio stations serve Denver. The city has three daily newspapers—the *Daily Journal*, the *Post*, and the *Rocky Mountain News*.

Education. Denver's public school system has about 100 elementary schools and 25 secondary schools. The city also has almost 60 church-supported schools. A seven-member board of education runs the public schools. Board members are elected to six-year terms.

More than 80 per cent of the public school students are white or of Mexican ancestry, and most of the rest are black. Several thousand children are bused to achieve a balance among these groups in certain Denver schools. The busing program began in 1974. A federal court ruled in 1970 that the schools had to be racially balanced by 1972, but court appeals delayed action on the program.

Colleges and universities in Denver include the University of Colorado Medical School, Colorado Women's College, the University of Denver, Iliff School of Theology, Loretto Heights College, Metropolitan State College, Regis College, and St. Thomas Seminary.

Cultural Life and Recreation. The Denver Art Museum owns one of the world's finest collections of West-

CITY OF DENVER

Denver, the "Mile High City," lies near the center of Colorado. It is the largest city and the commercial and industrial center of the Rocky Mountain Region. The map below shows the city and its main points of interest. Denver and Denver County have the same boundaries.

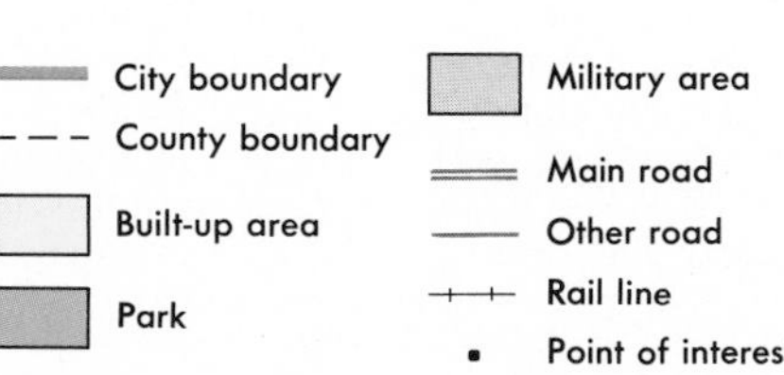

WORLD BOOK map

0 5 10 15 20 Miles
0 5 10 15 20 Kilometres

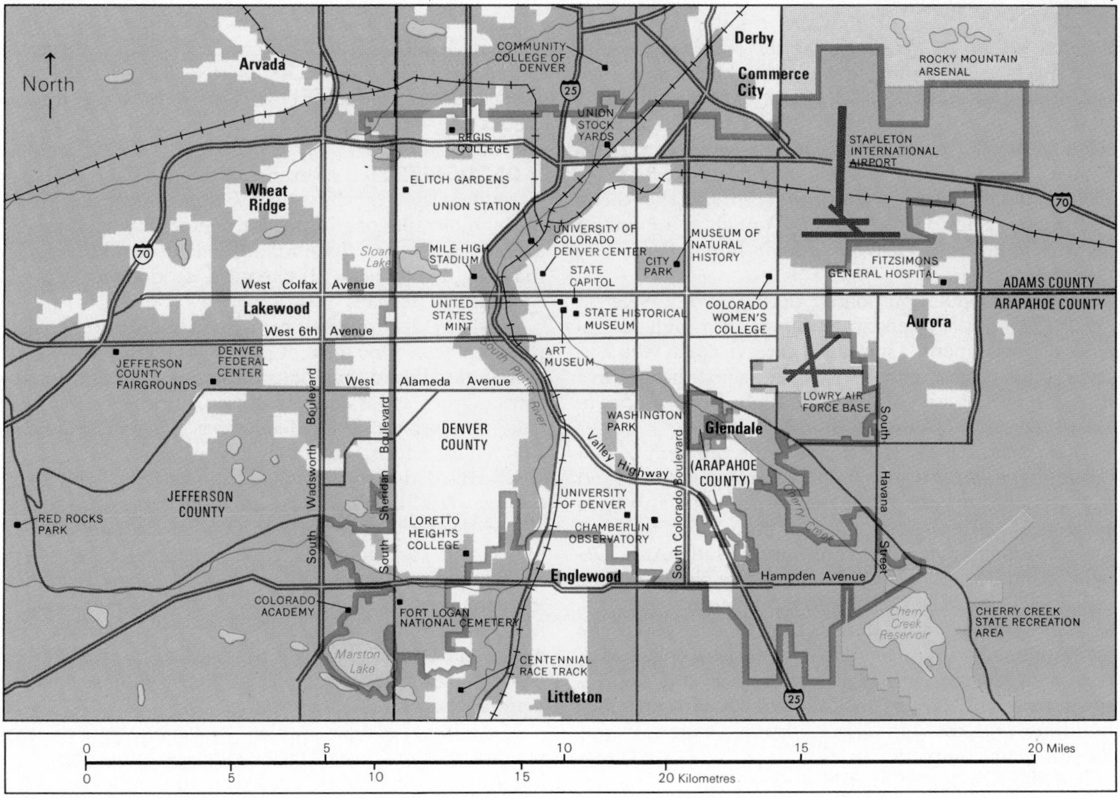

ern Indian art. The Colorado State Museum has articles that belonged to Colorado's early cliff dwellers.

The Denver Public Library, the largest in the Rocky Mountain region, operates 18 branches. The Denver Symphony Orchestra performs in the City Auditorium. The Elitch Summer Theater, the nation's oldest theater with a permanent group of performers, was established in Denver in 1891.

Denver maintains about 100 parks within the city and about 32 square miles (83 square kilometers) of parkland in the Rocky Mountains. The Denver Broncos of the National Football League play their home games in Mile High Stadium. The Denver Nuggets of the American Basketball Association play in the City Auditorium and the Denver Coliseum.

Government. Denver has a mayor-council form of government. The people elect a mayor and 13 city council members—all to four-year terms. In 1902, Denver led a home-rule movement among the cities of Colorado. As a result of this movement, an amendment to the state constitution made Denver both a city and a county. Denver gets most of its income from taxes on personal property, real estate, and general sales.

History. Denver was founded in 1858, after prospectors found gold at Cherry Creek. The community became a supply point for mining settlements during the "Pikes Peak or Bust" gold rush of 1859. Denver and nearby Auraria merged in April, 1860. The next year, Denver was incorporated as a city. The city became capital of the Colorado Territory in 1867 and the capital of Colorado when it became a state in 1876.

Denver expanded with completion of the Denver Pacific Railroad in 1870. A new mining boom gave the city additional wealth during the 1880's and 1890's after silver was discovered in the Rocky Mountains.

During the early 1900's, Denver changed from a prairie town to a beautiful city. It established many wide parkways, created the Denver Mountain Parks System, and planted trees throughout the city. By 1910, Denver had become the commercial center of the Rocky Mountain region. The Moffat Tunnel, a mountain railway route from Denver through James Peak, was completed in 1927.

Denver's population soared during World War II (1939-1945) and the postwar years with a high rate of federal employment. Thousands of servicemen who had been stationed in the Denver area returned there to live after the war. Between 1950 and 1960, Denver's population increased from 612,128 to 929,383.

During the 1970's, Denver faces the problem of preserving its natural beauty while continuing to expand the city's industry. In 1968, Denver prohibited all open burning of wastes by city agencies in an effort to lessen air pollution. Since 1968, the South Platte Area Development Council has worked with the city to reduce industrial pollution on the South Platte River.

The Denver Urban Renewal Authority began the $200-million Skyline Project in 1965 to replace old, run-down buildings in a large section of the city's downtown area. This project includes apartment and office buildings and the Japanese Cultural Center. It was scheduled for completion in 1985. CLARK SECREST

See also COLORADO (pictures).

DENVER, UNIVERSITY OF, is a private coeducational university in Denver, Colo. It has colleges of arts and sciences, business administration, engineering, and law; and schools of art, communication arts, education, hotel and restaurant management, international studies, librarianship, music, and social work. The university grants bachelor's, master's, and doctor's degrees. Its research facilities include the Denver Research Institute, the research division of the college of business administration, the Bureau of Educational Research, and the Social Science Foundation. Founded in 1864, the school became a university in 1880. For the enrollment of the University of Denver, see UNIVERSITIES AND COLLEGES (table). WILBUR C. MILLER

DEODAR. See CEDAR.

DEODORANT is a substance that is applied to the body to prevent unpleasant odors. Most body odor occurs when underarm perspiration reacts with bacteria on the skin. Perspiration itself has no odor. Most deodorants contain chemicals that reduce the growth of bacteria and have a fragrance that masks odor.

Some deodorants, called *antiperspirants*, also decrease the amount of perspiration. Deodorants and antiperspirants are manufactured in the form of creams, pads, roll-on liquids, and sprays. Deodorants are made for the feet and the genital area, as well as the underarms. Some soaps contain a deodorant.

Common antibacterial ingredients in deodorants and antiperspirants include a variety of zinc salts. Most antiperspirants also contain some type of aluminum salt that acts as an *astringent* to decrease perspiration (see ASTRINGENT). Some experts believe that excessive use of products containing antibacterial chemicals may destroy helpful bacteria.

Until 1972, the most common antibacterial ingredient in deodorants and antiperspirants was a chemical called *hexachlorophene*. The United States Food and Drug Administration (FDA) restricted its use in cosmetics after research showed that it could damage the nervous system. ROBERT F. KAUFMAN

DEODORIZER is a substance or device that eliminates or reduces disagreeable odors. Odors are carried in the air by molecules of gas that are released by various substances. There are three main kinds of deodorizers: (1) masking deodorizers, (2) chemical deodorizers, and (3) mechanical devices.

Masking deodorizers are used in many homes and public places. One form of masking deodorizer consists of a bottled liquid that soaks through a wick and evaporates. Other types include sprays, incense, and solid cake deodorizers. Solid deodorizers contain chemicals that release a scent when they evaporate.

Chemical deodorizers called *disinfectants*, which deodorize by killing bacteria, are often used in industry. These deodorizers include formaldehyde and phenol, also called carbolic acid. Other chemical deodorizers, such as potassium permanganate and hydrogen peroxide, destroy odors by *oxidation*. In this process, oxygen from the chemicals combines with the particles that cause odor. Some porous substances, such as activated charcoal and silica gel, collect odors on their surface by a process called *adsorption*.

Mechanical devices called *electrostatic precipitators*, which free the air and other gases of impurities, also eliminate odors that are caused by the impurities. In a process called *scrubbing*, the particles that cause odors in gases dissolve when forced through water or other liquids. ROBERT F. KAUFMAN

See also AIR CLEANER.

DE OÑATE, JUAN. See OÑATE, JUAN DE.

DEOXYRIBONUCLEIC ACID. See NUCLEIC ACID.

DE PALMA, *duh PAHL muh,* **RALPH** (1883-1956), was a pioneer American automobile race driver. He won the Indianapolis Speedway 500-mile (805-kilometer) race in 1915 and the national driving title in 1912 and 1914. De Palma set a world record of 149.875 mph (241.2 kph) in 1919. He claimed 2,557 victories in 2,889 races. Many of these were match races against another driver, rather than open competition. De Palma was born in Italy. FRED RUSSELL

DEPARTMENT is the largest administrative and territorial subdivision of France. It corresponds somewhat to a state in the United States or to a province in Canada. France, including Corsica, has 95 departments. French territories, such as Martinique, also have department governments.

A *prefect* is in charge of each department. Departments are divided into *arrondissements,* each under a *subprefect.* The central government appoints these officials. There are also electoral districts in each arrondissement called *cantons. Communes* are the smallest administrative units in the French government.

The French National Assembly created departments in February, 1790. They were based on population, area, and amount of taxes paid. Geographical features gave each department its name. Departments replaced provinces, which had been the chief territorial subdivisions of France until the French Revolution. ROBERT B. HOLTMAN

See also ARRONDISSEMENT; CANTON; COMMUNE.

DEPARTMENT OF ———. See the executive departments of the U.S. government listed under the key word in their name, such as LABOR, DEPARTMENT OF.

DEPARTMENT STORE is a store which sells many different kinds of goods, each arranged in a separate department. People can make all their purchases under one roof. Department stores need many customers in order to exist. Therefore, companies usually open them in large cities. Some companies open chain stores in different cities (see CHAIN STORE). Many department stores operate branch stores in suburban communities.

Arrangement of a Department Store. The typical department store occupies one large building, with separate departments located on a number of floors. Small articles, which people often request, are usually placed on the first floor. The stores often sell less expensive grades of merchandise in the basement. Sometimes stores have several levels of sub-basement sales floors. A number provide special services, such as that of a shopping adviser. Others have sewing centers where women learn to cut, fit, and sew clothing. Some department stores hold special exhibitions to attract new customers.

Department stores employ hundreds of people for different jobs. Many employees, under the merchandise manager, buy, price, and sell the goods. The sales promotion manager and his staff promote the sale of merchandise through advertising and other techniques. The comptroller heads the section that keeps records and manages store financial affairs. The personnel staff hires employees and handles employment problems.

Origin of the Department Store. Since the early 1800's, stores that handle a variety of merchandise have existed in the United States. These *general* stores still operate in many small towns. After 1870, several large American stores began to offer different types of merchandise arranged in separate departments.

Today, almost all American cities have department stores. Among the best-known are Marshall Field (Chicago), R. H. Macy (New York City), I. Magnin (San Francisco), Nieman-Marcus (Dallas), and John Wanamaker (Philadelphia). Several mail-order companies also operate department stores (see MAIL-ORDER BUSINESS). Department stores in the U.S. sell about $23½ billion worth of merchandise a year. FRED M. JONES

DE PAUL UNIVERSITY is a coeducational Roman Catholic university in Chicago. It was founded in 1898 by the Vincentian Fathers, and is now managed by a board of trustees composed of laymen and priests.

DePaul University grants bachelor's, master's, and doctor's degrees. It has colleges of commerce, education, law, music, and liberal arts and sciences. Another college, called DePaul College, offers a general educational program. Several of the colleges have evening divisions. For enrollment, see UNIVERSITIES AND COLLEGES (table). JOHN R. CORTELYOU

DEPAUW UNIVERSITY. See UNIVERSITIES AND COLLEGES (table).

DEPENDENCY. See COMMONWEALTH OF NATIONS.

DEPENDENT PENSION BILL. See HARRISON, BENJAMIN (Domestic Affairs).

DEPILATORY. See HAIR (Excess Hair).

DEPORTATION is the action a government takes when it forces an alien to leave the country and return to the place where he was born or had lived. It may deport him because he entered the country illegally, or because it is believed that he may harm the nation's interests in some way.

In the United States, the attorney general has the power to deport aliens as part of his responsibility to enforce immigration laws. Aliens may be deported if they become public charges, stay longer than their visas permit, or engage in subversive or criminal activities. A naturalized citizen who loses his citizenship may be deported by the Department of Justice.

Deportation also means banishing, or sending a convict to a penal settlement outside the country as punishment for a crime. ROBERT RIENOW

DEPOSIT, in banking. See BANKS AND BANKING (How Banks Receive and Lend Money).

DEPOSIT, in geology. See ROCK (Sedimentary Rock).

DEPOSITION, *DEP oh ZISH un,* in law, is the testimony of a witness who is unable to appear in court. The witness testifies under oath before a judicial officer. He makes a statement in answer to questions, either oral or written, asked by the officer. The second party in a lawsuit must also have a chance to question the witness. A deposition differs from an *affidavit,* which is a one-sided statement given voluntarily under oath (see AFFIDAVIT). THOMAS A. COWAN

DEPOT is a storehouse or a transportation station such as a bus or railroad depot.

DEPRECIATION, *dee PREE she AY shun,* is the loss of value. Buildings, machines, vehicles, and other property *depreciate* (lose value) through use or accident, because they grow older, or because a new, better product replaces them. In accounting, depreciation is figured as a normal cost of doing business. The term *depreciation* is also used to mean the loss of value or purchasing power resulting from an increase in the level of prices. If prices rise, the purchasing power of money falls, or depreciates. JAMES B. LUDTKE

DEPRESSANT is a drug that slows the activity of the nervous system. Physicians prescribe depressants to ease pain, cause sleep, or reduce tension. Many depressants are either habit-forming or addictive. If a person takes such a depressant daily for several weeks, he may develop a physical or psychological dependence on it. An overdose of a depressant can be fatal.

Major types of depressants include alcohol, anesthetics, sedatives, and tranquilizers. Alcohol decreases most brain functions. Anesthetics, the most powerful painkillers, are used during surgery. Sedatives calm a patient or put him to sleep. Such sedatives as barbiturates depress the central nervous system. Tranquilizers lessen tension without decreasing mental or physical activity. EDWARD F. DOMINO

See also ALCOHOLISM (Effects); ANESTHESIA; SEDATIVE; TRANQUILIZER.

DEPRESSION, in psychiatry. See MENTAL ILLNESS (Manic-Depressive Psychosis).

DEPRESSION is a condition in economic life in which a great many men have no work, machines stand idle, and the general level of economic activity is low, or *depressed.* A depression is the low part of the business cycle, or the opposite of *prosperity.* The *business cycle* refers to the waves of good and bad times that have plagued modern, industrialized economics.

The Seriousness of the Problem. Depression may well be the most serious problem facing our free enterprise economic system (see FREE ENTERPRISE SYSTEM). During a depression, people often follow any man who promises a change—the socialist, the communist, the fascist, or the crackpot with an impossible scheme to cure all the ills of society. Frequent depressions could be a danger to our way of life.

To one man, depression means standing in bread lines or walking the streets looking for work. To another, it means business failure and the necessity for a new start. To still another, it means the loss of his life's savings in a bank failure. To the nation, it means economic paralysis. To the world, it usually means a breakdown of friendly trade relations, as each nation tries to solve its own problems at the expense of other nations. In extreme cases, depression may set in motion the forces that lead to war. The effect of depression on Germany in the early 1930's made the German people more willing to follow Adolf Hitler into World War II as a fancied "cure" for their economic ills.

What Can Be Done to Avoid Depressions. In spite of the importance of the problem, economists cannot agree on what causes depression, or how to prevent it. A modern, highly industrialized economy is a very complex machine. When it breaks down, the causes of the trouble are difficult to identify. Each expert has his own diagnosis, and each diagnosis suggests a different cure. Some of the more widely-accepted explanations of the business cycle, and of the remedies associated with each explanation, are discussed below.

Underconsumption or Over-Saving Theories. Some men insist that depressions come because people spend too little of their incomes, which is the same as saying that they save too much. These men say such a practice leads to a lower demand for goods and services, and to unemployment. *The remedy they suggest:* redistribute income from the rich, who have high rates of saving, to the poor, who can be depended on to spend most of the dollars they receive. High taxes on the rich, to pay for a dole to the poor, would accomplish this.

Saving-Investment Theories. Another version of the theory presented above says depressions are caused by changes in the amount of spending for *capital goods,* such as tools, machinery, and buildings, which are used for producing other goods. Such spending is called *investment.* When people invest, they put their savings back into circulation. If there are not enough investment opportunities for all the dollars saved, the extra dollars do not get back into circulation. People hoard them. Hoarding reduces the number of dollars being spent for goods and services, and, in this way, leads to depression and unemployment.

Remedies the theorists suggest: (a) reduce the number of dollars saved, for instance, by redistributing income; and (b) increase the number of dollars invested by business firms. Most of the men who support this theory do not believe that these two remedies will be enough. They propose as well (c) that the government offset the hoarded dollars by borrowing money and spending it for such things as relief payments and public works projects. This remedy, and the saving-investment theory itself, is closely associated with the name of the English economist John Maynard Keynes. If it is thought that government spending will get the economy rolling and that deficit spending can then be stopped, proposal (c) is called "pump-priming." The Roosevelt administration acted on this idea in an attempt to lift the United States out of the depression of the 1930's.

Quantity-of-Money Theories. Other economists argue that "booms" and "busts" are caused by the violent *fluctuations* (changes) in the money supply of the economy, particularly in the supply of check money. Checks are drawn on demand deposits in banks. When the total of demand deposits changes, it is just as if the government had increased or decreased the amount of its own coins and currency in circulation. According to this theory, changes in the total of demand deposits are largely responsible for the business cycle. *The suggested remedy:* control or change the banking system so as to prevent violent fluctuations in the supply of check money.

Price-of-Progress Theories. Some economists believe that the business cycle is the price a modern economy pays for progress, particularly for technological progress. According to this theory, progress never comes about smoothly, but rather by a process of "three steps forward and two backward." The "two backward" take the form of depression. *The suggested remedy:* all that can be done is to soften the effects of the low part of the business cycle. To stop the cycle would be to stop progress.

Price "Stickiness" Theories. Other economists insist that the business cycle comes because prices and wages are not permitted to move up and down in free response to changes in supply and demand conditions. They argue that in a free market the price would always seek that level which would "clear the market." No goods would ever be unsold and no workers would ever be unemployed. Unemployment comes, they say, because markets are not free. *The proposed remedy:* restore free markets by curbing the activities of monopolists, trade unions, and all other groups which prevent the free movement of prices and wages.

Other Explanations. Some people say the business cycle is caused by changes in the *direction*, as distinguished from the *amount*, of spending. Others blame variations in farm crops, psychological waves of optimism and pessimism, and even sunspots.

The Outlook for the Future. The great number of explanations and remedies might seem to mean that nothing can be done about depressions. But most economists agree on the steps that should be taken to prevent a severe depression such as the one that occurred in the United States during the 1930's.

Most economists feel that in order to avoid serious depressions we must avoid extremes in the economic system during the prosperity periods. This usually means (1) that the quantity of check money should not be permitted to increase in a runaway fashion during prosperity; and (2) that the price-fixing activities of monopoly groups should be curbed to avoid upsetting the *price structure*, or the relationships among the prices for different types of goods.

Most economists—but certainly not all—agree that a depression can be held within reasonable limits by the use of government deficit spending to offset a drop in private spending, at least partially. How soon the government should do this and how far it should go are still hotly disputed questions. Actually, certain

U.S. PROSPERITY AND DEPRESSIONS SINCE 1790

The United States has gone through many periods of prosperity and depression. This graph shows how much business activity has been above or below the long-term economic trend each year. Since 1902, business activity has been measured by industrial production, including manufacturing and mining. Before 1902, such things as exports, government receipts, and canal freight were also used to measure business activity.

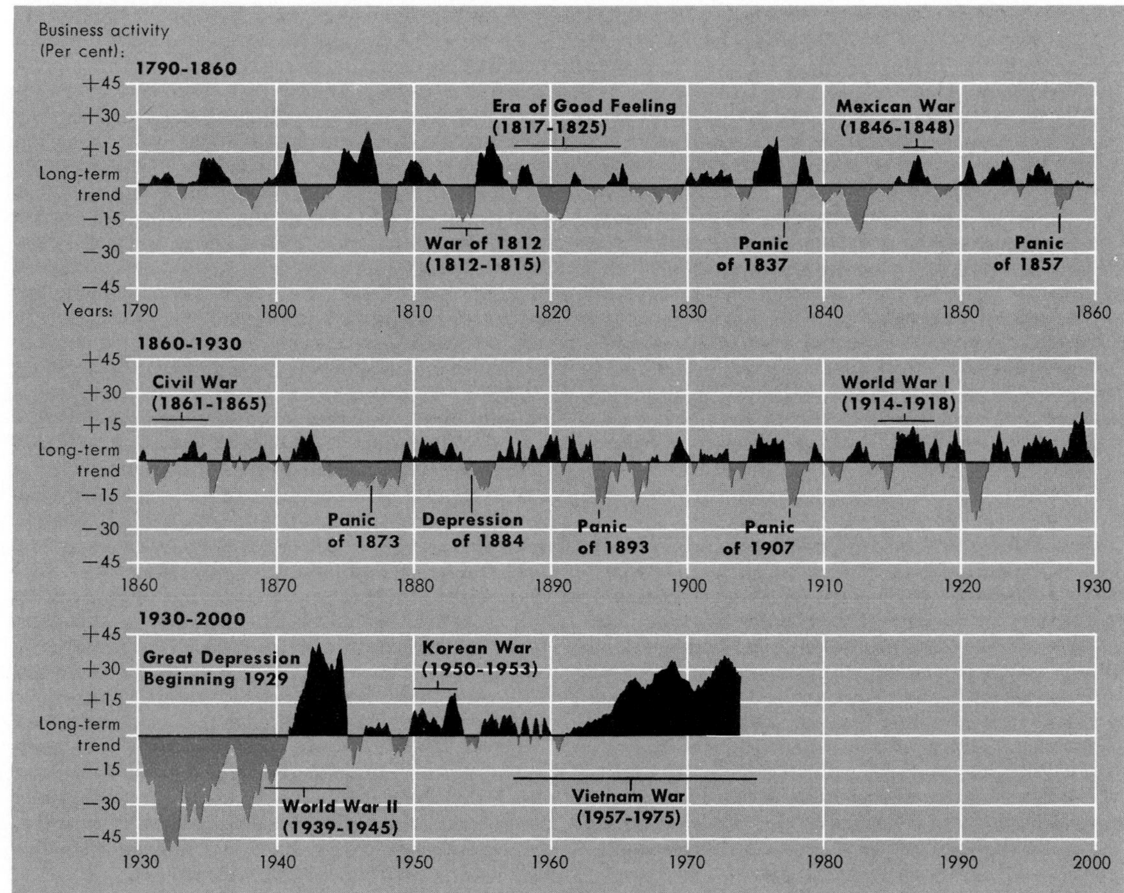

Source: The Cleveland Trust Company, Cleveland, Ohio.

features of our present economic system automatically produce government deficits during a depression. The social security system, including unemployment insurance, and the income-tax system both are set up so that government revenues fall off while government expenditures increase as a depression gets under way. These are called *built-in stabilizers*. Finally, there is now general agreement that the government must provide all citizens with basic necessities during a depression.

Many economists hesitate to recommend stronger action than that outlined. They fear that a stronger remedy might "cure the disease but kill the patient" (the free enterprise system). They fear also that severe remedies might bring other serious problems such as continuous inflation or slower economic progress (see INFLATION AND DEFLATION). BENJAMIN A. ROGGE

Critically reviewed by JAMES WASHINGTON BELL

Related Articles in WORLD BOOK include:

Grant, Ulysses S. (The Panic of 1873)
Great Depression
Hoover, Herbert Clark (The Great Depression)
Roosevelt, Franklin Delano (First Administration)
Roosevelt, Theodore (Domestic Problems)
Unemployment
United States, History of (The Great Depression)
Van Buren, Martin (The Panic of 1837)

See also *Depression* in the RESEARCH GUIDE/INDEX, Volume 22, for a *Reading and Study Guide*.

DEPTH CHARGE is a weapon designed to destroy submarines. It explodes under water and creates a shock wave that causes the submarine to collapse.

Depth charges during World War II consisted of light metal cases filled with an explosive such as TNT. Destroyers laid a pattern of charges over a submarine, rolling some off the deck and firing others to the side.

In 1957, the United States Navy announced the development of atomic depth charges, to be dropped by antisubmarine planes. These consist of a core of fissionable material surrounded by heavy casing (see FISSION [Nuclear]). The weapon has a mechanical time device to control its firing time and can be preset to explode at varying depths. The atomic depth charge eliminates the need for knowing the exact location of a submarine. It can destroy a target within 1 square mile (2.6 square kilometers), and is particularly effective against submarines located at great depths. PAUL D. STROOP

See also WARSHIP (picture).

DEPTH INDICATOR. See FATHOMETER; SONAR.

DEPTH OF FIELD. See PHOTOGRAPHY (Adjustable Cameras).

DEPTH PERCEPTION. See EYE (Stereoscopic Vision).

DEPTHS. See DEEP.

DE QUINCEY, *duh KWIHN sih,* **THOMAS** (1785-1859), was an English essayist. He wrote a rare kind of imaginative prose—highly ornate, full of subtle rhythms, and sensitive to the sound and arrangement of words.

At the age of 19, De Quincey started to take opium to ease the pain of severe neuralgic headaches. He was addicted to the drug until he died. He told the story of his opium addiction in his most famous work, *Confessions of an English Opium Eater* (1821). De Quincey is also known for his imaginative essays describing his visions under the influence of opium. The visions were gorgeous and lofty, as well as tortured and terrible. These fantasies have a sense of fearful reality, as in "Vision of Sudden Death" (part of the essay "The English Mail-Coach," 1849).

De Quincey wrote many critical works, but few are read today. Many readers believe that too many of his flashes of insight were buried by a tendency to wander from his subject. There are brilliant exceptions, including "On the Knocking at the Gate in *Macbeth*" (1823), "On Murder Considered as One of the Fine Arts" (1827), and "The Literature of Knowledge and the Literature of Power" (1848).

De Quincey was born in Manchester. He lived in Edinburgh from 1828 until his death. JOHN W. DODDS

DERAIN, ANDRÉ (1880-1954) was a French artist. He and his friends Henri Matisse and Maurice de Vlaminck were leaders of the fauves, a group of painters of the early 1900's.

Derain's fauve paintings, his most significant works, feature vivid colors, particularly blues, oranges, and reds. He applied paint with short, broken brushstrokes. Derain's paintings are flat in design, with little use of perspective. Many of them show the influence of the artists Paul Gauguin and Vincent Van Gogh. Derain's *London Bridge* is reproduced in color in the FAUVES article. His works after about 1913 are more traditional than his fauve paintings.

Derain was also noted for his book illustrations and his costume and set designs for ballets and plays. He was born in Chatou. WILLARD E. MISFELDT

DERBY, *DUR bee,* or (British) *DAHR bih,* is a stiff felt hat with a dome-shaped crown. The British usually call it a *bowler*. The name derby may come from England. The Earl of Derby, who established the Derby horse races in Epsom in 1780, often wore such hats. They were popular among men who attended the races. Derbies were first made in the U.S. in 1850 at South Norwalk, Conn. See also HAT (Felt Hats). WARREN S. SMITH

DERBY, *DAHR bee,* is a famous horse race begun in 1780 by the Earl of Derby in Epsom, England. The race, called "Epsom's Derby" in England, is known as "the English Derby" in other countries. The horse race at Churchill Downs, Louisville, Ky., was copied after the Derby (see KENTUCKY DERBY).

DERBY, or CROWN DERBY, is a famous china made in Derby, England.

DERBY, SOAP BOX. See SOAP BOX DERBY.

DERBYSHIRE. See ENGLAND (political map).

DERINGER, HENRY, JR. See PISTOL (Early Pistols).

DERMAPTERA. See INSECT (table); EARWIG.

DERMATITIS is an inflammation of the skin that itches or burns. It shows redness, swelling, blisters, oozing, crusting, or scaling. It may be produced by friction, heat, cold, or the sun's rays. However, chemical agents most frequently cause dermatitis. These may be strong poisons that affect anyone's skin, or chemicals that irritate the skin of a person especially sensitive to the chemicals. These chemicals may be found in certain plants, foods, fabrics, dyes, cosmetics, and medications. See also ALLERGY; ECZEMA. MARCUS R. CARO

DERMATOLOGY deals with diseases of the skin. Dermatologists are physicians trained to diagnose and treat these diseases. When a disease of the whole body also affects the skin, dermatologists may help diagnose the disease from clues the affected skin provides. See also SKIN with its list of *Related Articles*.

DERMIS. See SKIN.

DERRICK

A Huge Barge Derrick, *right,* raises a sunken oil-drilling barge.

Guy Derrick, *below,* has a long boom that can move heavy loads from side to side.

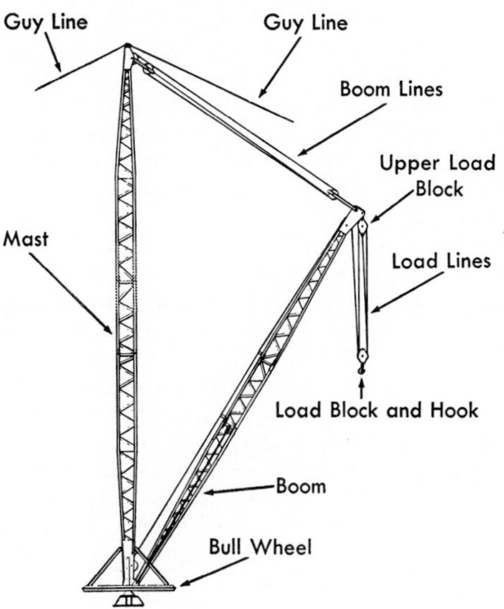

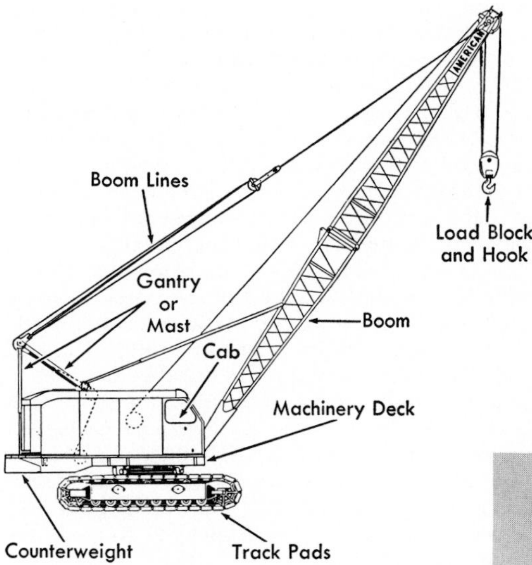

CRANE

Tractor-Mounted Crawler Crane, *above,* can carry loads from place to place. Track pads allow the crane to travel over rough or muddy ground.

Truck Crane, *right,* lowers a palm tree. The crane operator has controls to move the truck forward and backward.

DERRICKS AND CRANES are hoisting machines used to lift and move heavy loads in such places as shipyards, factories, and at construction sites. Most *cranes* can move from place to place under their own power, while most *derricks* are stationary. However, engineers sometimes use either name to describe the same machine.

Derricks. The *gin-pole* is the simplest form of derrick. It has a *mast,* or pole, supported by four *guys,* or cables, staked to the ground. A pulley at the top of the mast supports ropes to lift the weight. The *sheers derrick* has two crossed masts and two guys. Other derricks have a long *boom,* or pole. The boom slants out from the base of the mast and supports the hoisting cable that carries the load. A cable attached to the top of the mast supports the boom. *Oil derricks* are tall steel structures that raise and lower the equipment used to drill an oil well.

Cranes. The *hand-operated jib crane* is the simplest type of crane. It has a long *jib,* or arm, that extends several feet from a heavy base. The base keeps the crane from tipping over. The end of the jib has a pulley. A rope or a cable, with a lifting hook in the end, runs from this pulley to a *winch* (crank) in the foundation. The operator turns the winch to lift or lower the hook. The arm of the crane can be swung in a circle before the weight is lowered. Thus, a jib crane can move a weight to any point around the circumference of the circle its jib makes. The *pillar jib crane* has a pillar rising from its

Photos: American Hoist & Derrick Co.

base. A cable attached to the top of the pillar raises and lowers the end of the jib so the jib can be moved up and down as well as from side to side. When the jib moves up, it carries the load toward the base. When lowered, it moves the load away from the base.

Factories and foundries often use *bridge cranes*, sometimes called *overhead traveling cranes*. This type of crane moves back and forth on a bridge extending across the width of a factory room. The bridge travels the length of the roof on overhead rails. *Locomotive cranes* are mounted on railroad cars and have long, power-operated booms. *Crawler cranes* are mounted on tractors. *Truck cranes*, frequently used by building contractors, are mounted on trucks. *Tower cranes* are used to construct high-rise buildings. Most tower cranes, called *climbing cranes*, have built-in jacks that raise the cranes through openings in the floor as the building goes up. Workers take the cranes apart to lower them after the building's completion. ROBERT G. HENNES

See also BLOCK AND TACKLE; BUILDING AND WRECKING MACHINES (pictures); PETROLEUM (pictures).

DERRINGER. See PISTOL (Early Pistols; picture).

DERVISH, *DUR vihsh*, is a member of one of the mystical religious orders of the Islamic religion. Most dervishes lead wandering lives of self-denial. They live by begging. The word *dervish* comes from Persian, and means *beggar* or *religious mendicant*. In the A.D. 1000's and 1100's, Moslem mystics organized the first dervish orders. Each order lived in a center resembling a monastery and had its own ritual. One order is known commonly as the *whirling dervishes* because they whirl and dance to the music of a reed pipe as part of their worship. Other orders give special prayers or practice unusual forms of devotion, such as wearing rough clothing, fasting, and keeping vigils. Many Moslems look upon dervishes as holy men, and often think them capable of miracles or predicting the future. Dervishes are sometimes called *fakirs*. ALI HASSAN ABDEL-KADER

DERWENT, RIVER, is a beautiful stream in west Cumberland County, England. The River Derwent rises in the Cumbrian Mountains and flows for 33 miles (53 kilometers) through the Cumberland Lake district. Here it widens to form Derwentwater, a wooded lake with falls and isles. The river empties into Solway Firth, an Irish Sea inlet at Workington. Three other rivers—in Derbyshire, in Yorkshire, and between Durham and Northumberland—have the same name. JOHN D. ISAACS

DERZHAVIN, GAVRIIL. See RUSSIAN LITERATURE (The Classical Movement).

DESALINATION. See WATER (Fresh Water from the Sea).

DESCARTES, *day KAHRT*, **RENÉ** (1596-1650), was a French philosopher, mathematician, and scientist. Many scholars consider him the father of modern philosophy. Descartes's emphasis on the use of reason as the chief tool of philosophical inquiry greatly influenced later philosophy, mathematics, and science. His philosophy became known as *Cartesian philosophy*.

His Life. Descartes was born in the province of Touraine and was educated at a Jesuit college. He served in the armies of two noblemen and traveled widely. Money from an inheritance and from patrons enabled him to devote most of his life to study. From 1628 to 1649, Descartes led a quiet, scholarly life in The Netherlands and produced most of his philosophical writings. Late in 1649, he accepted an invitation from Queen Christina to visit Sweden. He became ill there and died in February, 1650.

His Philosophy. Descartes wanted to find truth through the use of reason alone. He sought knowledge by starting with a single proposition that reason could establish and no one could doubt. He hoped then to move systematically from this first proposition to others.

Descartes's basic proposition was "I think, therefore I am." Whenever a person thought, he was aware of his thinking and, thus, of his existence as a thinking being. From this starting point, Descartes offered a proof of the existence of God and of the physical world. He believed that he relied solely on the power of reason to establish his doctrines.

Descartes thought the world consisted of two kinds of substances: thinking substance (mind) and extended substance (matter). He struggled with the problem of how mind and matter interacted and decided that they did so in the pineal gland of the brain.

According to Descartes, the physical world was only a collection of microscopic, colorless extended substances. Men's minds interpreted the world as the collection of visible, colored physical objects that people were aware of in everyday life. The physical world was subject to the laws of science, and events could be scientifically predicted and explained. But Descartes declared that this concept did not apply to minds. He thus tried to preserve the doctrine of free will and to reconcile science and religion.

Descartes called the interpretations made by the mind *ideas*. He believed there were two kinds of true ideas, *clear* and *distinct*. A clear idea could be distinguished from other ideas. A distinct idea had parts that could be distinguished from one another. The chief task of philosophy was to analyze complex ideas into simpler ones, always striving for clear and distinct ideas. Descartes thought the only ideas that could be made perfectly clear and distinct originated in the mind. Ideas that resulted from the experience of living in the physical world could not be so clarified. Descartes did not believe that the idea of God originated in the mind or came from man's awareness of the physical world. He argued that the idea of God was perfect and could only have been put in man's mind by the perfect God Himself. To Descartes, this proved God's existence.

Descartes's most famous philosophical work was *Discourse on the Method of Rightly Conducting the Reason and Seeking for Truth in the Sciences*. His other major works included *Rules for the Direction of the Mind* and *Meditations on First Philosophy*. STEPHEN A. ERICKSON

See also PHILOSOPHY (The Appeal to Reason; picture); GEOMETRY (History).

DESCHUTES RIVER. See OREGON (Rivers).

DESCRIPTION. See LITERATURE (Kinds of Discourse).

DESEGREGATION. See SEGREGATION.

DESERET, *DEHZ uh reht*, is a word meaning *honeybee* in the Book of Mormon. The Mormons adopted the honeybee as the symbol of hard work necessary for the success of their Salt Lake Valley settlement. In 1849, they organized the State of Deseret. Congress refused to admit it as a state, and created instead the Territory of Utah. See also MORMONS. HAROLD W. BRADLEY

Ewing Galloway

Death Valley in Eastern California Has Sand Dunes Formed by the Wind.

DESERT is land that is so dry that few plants can grow on it. The term *desert* is applied to any region which has little water and vegetation. Deserts are seldom flat, featureless wastes of bare sand. They may be mountainous or rocky. Parts of them may be deeply cut by rushing streams of water that follow occasional bursts of rain. Some deserts, such as the Sahara, are extremely hot. Others, such as the Gobi, are hot in summer and very cold in winter. The term *cold desert* is sometimes applied to Siberia, and to the frozen arctic regions of Europe and North America. There is water in cold deserts, but it is usually frozen, so few plants can grow.

Location of Desert Regions. Deserts occupy nearly a fifth of the earth's land surface. All continents except Europe have large deserts. The greatest desert area in the world stretches across Africa and Asia. It extends from the Sahara across the Great Arabian Desert and the deserts of Iran and Afghanistan.

Other large deserts include the Atacama desert on the Pacific coast of South America; the Kalahari, in southern Africa; the Gobi, in China and Mongolia; and the desert in central and western Australia. Much of the southwestern United States and northern Mexico is desert.

Water in the Desert. Many deserts are almost totally without water. Winds may blow the sands of these deserts into *dunes* (sand hills), which shift and move endlessly across the desert's surface. Few plants can live in these dry, moving sands.

An *oasis* in the desert is a place where a spring, or irrigation from wells, gives plants the water they need to grow. Oases are like green islands in the middle of the desert. Travelers can see the palm trees in oases from far away. People living in oases can grow many kinds of fruits and cereals, including dates, peaches, apricots, oranges, grapes, wheat, barley, and corn.

Engineers have irrigated large areas of some deserts. They have built dams on rivers crossing desert regions, and made the river water flow into the deserts in canals. They have also dug artesian wells in desert regions (see ARTESIAN WELL). Many deserts have soil rich in the minerals that plants need for growth. When these deserts are irrigated, they grow abundant and useful crops where once nothing grew but cactuses and other desert plants. Large areas of desert around the Nile Delta in Egypt have been turned into valuable farming land by irrigation (see NILE RIVER). In India and Pakistan, water from the Indus River is carried in canals to irrigate huge areas of desert land (see INDUS RIVER). California's Imperial Valley is a desert region that was turned into farmland by irrigation (see IMPERIAL VALLEY).

Life in the Desert. Few men live in desert regions. Most of those who do, such as the Bedouin in the Sahara, live near oases, or wander between them so that they can obtain water (see BEDOUINS). Some desert mining settlements have water brought to them by tankers or pipelines.

The few plants and animals that live in deserts have become *adapted* (changed) so that they require less water than most plants and animals. Camels sweat very little

H. William Tetlow, Devaney

A Desert Water Hole in the Gaza Strip has water piped from a well. Travelers and their camels stop there to drink.

Statile, Black Star

The Mojave Desert Lies Northeast of Los Angeles.

and can keep for long periods the water they drink. The smaller desert animals do not drink water. Most of them burrow underground to get away from the hot sun during the day. They come out at night to eat. Some of them eat other animals, and get the water they need from the moisture in the meat. Others, such as the kangaroo rat, eat plants and seeds. These plant eaters get their water from plant juices.

Desert plants are also adapted to conditions in the desert. Cactuses and other *succulent* (juicy) plants store water in their thick leaves or stems. Their roots lie close to the surface of the ground, and quickly absorb water from the occasional rains. Most plants have thin, broad leaves that lose moisture into the air. Succulent plants have thick, waxy leaves or thornlike leaves that lose little water. Such plants are able to store water for long periods and resist long dry spells. Only specially adapted animals and plants are able to live in cold deserts. See Animal (Animals and Climate); Arctic (Plant Life).

Travel in the Desert. Roads and tracks cross many of the world's deserts. Some of these roads have been used for thousands of years. They connect towns on the edges of deserts, or are used as trade routes to oases. One desert route across the Sahara is 1,000 miles (1,600 kilometers) long. Travelers who leave the known desert routes and cross open desert seldom find any landmarks to guide them. They have to find their way by observing the stars, just as sailors do at sea (see Navigation).

Camels are used for transport by most people who live in the deserts of Africa and Asia. Camels may carry desert travelers from one place to another. Or they may carry food and other goods, such as cloth, carpets, and jewelry, to people who live in oases. Generally, camels and their riders travel in *caravans*, or groups (see Caravan). Camels were once the only means of transport across deserts. They are sometimes called *ships of the desert*.

Nowadays, buses and trucks cross many desert routes. Travelers on some routes even find small restaurants, which have been built in the desert hundreds of miles from any town. Railroads have been built in many desert regions. Airplanes now fly over deserts, sometimes soaring high above places where men have never walked.

R. Will Burnett

Related Articles in World Book include:

Deserts

Arabian Desert
Atacama Desert
Australian Desert
Colorado Desert
Death Valley
Gobi
Great Basin
Great Salt Lake Desert
Great Victoria Desert
High Desert
Kalahari Desert
Kara Kum
Kyzyl Kum
Libyan Desert
Mojave
Negev
Painted Desert
Qattara Depression
Sahara
Sechura Desert
Syrian Desert
Takla Makan Desert
Vizcaíno Desert

Desert Animal Life

Animal (color pictures: Animals of the Deserts)
Camel
Chuckwalla
Dromedary
Horned Toad
Kangaroo Rat
Lizard
Tortoise

Desert Plant Life

Cactus
Century Plant
Creosote Bush
Date and Date Palm
Flower (color pictures: Flowers of the Desert)
Mesquite
Sagebrush
Succulent

Other Related Articles

Arab
Bedouins
Caravan
Climate
Dune
Irrigation
Mirage
Nomad
Oasis
Rain
Sand
Sandstorm

DESERT FOX. See Rommel, Erwin.

DESERTED VILLAGE. See Goldsmith, Oliver.

DESERTION is the military crime of running away from the armed forces with the intention of staying away. A person who leaves the armed forces for only a short time to avoid hazardous duty or important work may also be treated as a deserter.

During wartime, the death penalty may be imposed on a deserter. In peacetime, the penalty may be any punishment except death. A person convicted of being Absent Without Leave (AWOL) is not a deserter, because he did not intend to stay away from his duty.

Desertion occurs in civil law when a married person intentionally leaves his spouse, and stays away for a certain length of time without consent or adequate reason. In many states in the United States, desertion is a ground for divorce. A person may also be treated as a deserter if he forces his spouse to run away by making their home unsafe or unbearable.

John W. Wade

See also Abandonment.

DE SEVERSKY, ALEXANDER PROCOFIEFF (1894-1974), was a pilot, aircraft designer, and military authority. His fighter plane designs were among the most advanced of the 1930's. He invented an automatic bombsight, skis for aircraft, amphibian landing gear, and hydraulic shock absorbers for aircraft. His theories about the use of air power attracted wide attention.

De Seversky was born in Tbilisi, Russia, and received his education at Russia's Imperial Naval Academy. He served in World War I, and lost a leg in aerial combat.

He came to the United States in 1918, after the Bolshevik revolution in

Seversky Electronatom Corporation

Alexander de Seversky

Russia. In 1927 he became a naturalized American citizen. De Seversky founded his own aircraft manufacturing firm, the Seversky Aero Corporation, in 1922. He operated the company in New York until 1931 when it was reorganized as the Seversky Aircraft Corporation. He headed this company until 1939 when it became Republic Aviation. Later, he lectured and wrote *Victory Through Air Power* (1942). Robert B. Hotz

DE SICA, VITTORIO (1902-1974), an Italian motion-picture director and actor, became noted for his realistic portrayals of life among the poor. His best films include *Shoeshine* (1946), about juvenile delinquency, and *The Bicycle Thief* (1949), about unemployment. In these and other motion pictures, he presented a grim view of life. De Sica's films won wide critical acclaim, but the hopelessness of their situations became unpopular with audiences. After *Umberto D* (1952), De Sica found it difficult to find backing for the type of film he wished to make.

De Sica was born in Sora, Italy. A popular actor, he turned to directing in 1939 and had his first success with *The Children Are Watching* (1942). His other films include *Miracle in Milan* (1951), *Two Women* (1961), *Marriage, Italian Style* (1964), and *The Garden of the Finzi-Continis* (1971). Harvey R. Deneroff

DESIDERIO DA SETTIGNANO. See Sculpture (Italian Renaissance; color picture: Julius Caesar).

DESIGN is the intended arrangement of materials to produce a certain result or effect. The principles of design can be seen most clearly in the visual arts of drawing, painting, sculpture, and architecture.

The painter works with *lines*, *shapes*, and *colors*. He is also concerned with the *direction* of lines, the *size* of the shapes, and the *shading* of the colors. He tries to arrange all these elements into a pattern that will seem emotionally satisfying to the spectator. If this effect is obtained, his design will have *unity*.

Repetition is an important principle of design. It consists in the repeating of lines or shapes. Japanese color prints are noted for their handling of repetition. Many of them have fine slanting lines of rain, or scenes with reflections on water repeated over and over again.

Harmony, or Balance, is as important as repetition. Harmony can be obtained in many ways in design. It may be either *symmetrical* (in balance) or *asymmetrical* (out of perfect balance, but still pleasing to the eye). Or a small area may balance a large area if the small area has an importance to the eye (because of treatment or color) that is equal to that of the larger area.

Contrast, or Discord, is the opposite of harmony. The colors red and orange harmonize, since orange contains red. A circle and an oval harmonize, because they both are made up of curved lines. But a short line does not harmonize with a long line. It is in contrast.

Rhythm and Movement are obtained by the use of wavy lines, or motifs placed in contrast to *static* (set) patterns which give interest to a design.

Unity occurs when all the elements in a design combine to form a consistent whole. Unity resembles balance. A design has unity if its masses are balanced, or if its tones and colors harmonize. But unity differs from balance because it implies that all these balanced

PRINCIPLES OF DESIGN

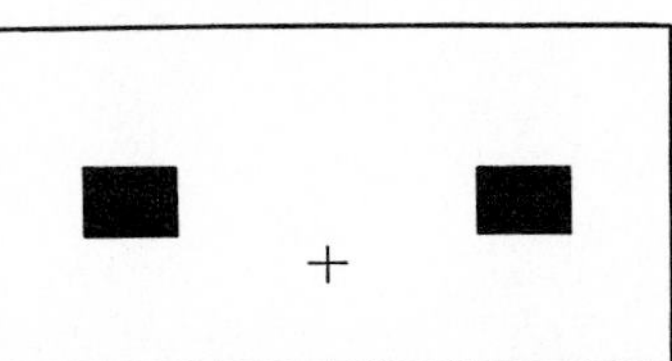

Symmetrical Balance is accomplished by placing two identical objects the same distance from the center.

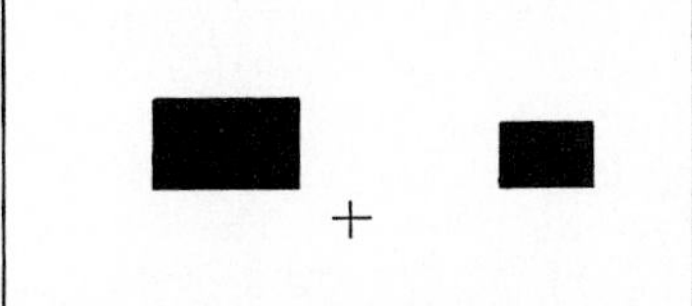

Asymmetrical Balance is possible because the smaller object is twice the distance from the center.

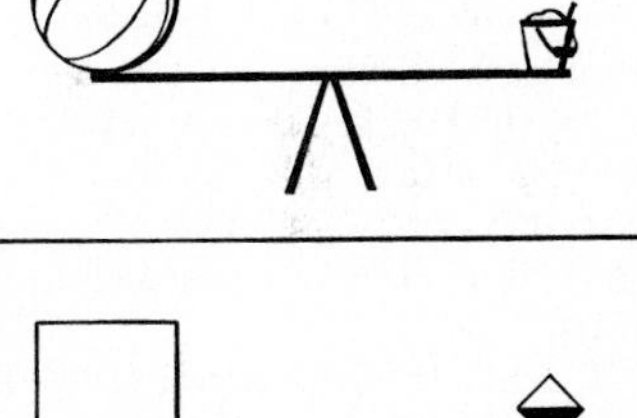

Visual Balance is gained when a design has a small important object opposite a big uninteresting object.

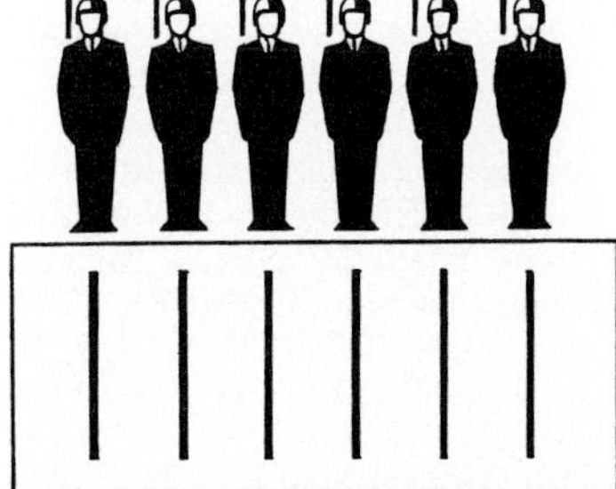

Unity of design may place stress on equally spaced straight lines, such as a row of identical soldiers.

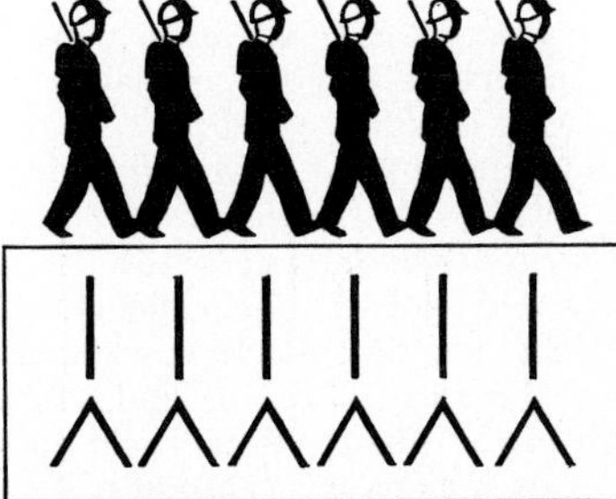

Movement gives interest to unity because it brings variation to the monotonous straight lines.

Rhythm is added to design by interrupted horizontal and vertical lines. The waving flags also add emphasis.

elements form harmony in the design as a whole.

Design in Other Arts is always present. In music, sounds heard in a sequence of time provide the design materials. A sonata follows a set pattern. A symphony consists of several themes which are repeated in changing forms throughout the composition. In poetry, words are heard or read in a designed time sequence. A sonnet has a fixed form, or design, of fourteen lines. In architecture and sculpture, the design is usually called *structural.* The size and shape of a statue are the chief design concern of the sculptor, just as the architect's concern is with the size and shape of his building. The surfaces of buildings are sometimes decorated. This design is known as *decorative,* in contrast to structural design.

Industrial design has become more and more important. The kind of industrial design called structural design is used in mass production of such commodities as cars and fountain pens. HARRY MUIR KURTZWORTH

Related Articles in WORLD BOOK include:

Airplane	Fashion	Motion Picture (The Designers; pictures)
Architecture	Furniture	Painting
Automobile (Design)	Geometric Style	Sculpture
Clothing	Industrial Arts	Theater (Scene Design)
Decorative Arts	Industrial Design	
Engineering (The Design Engineer)	Interior Decoration	
	Moiré Pattern	

DE SITTER, WILLEM (1872-1934), was a noted Dutch astronomer. From his studies of Jupiter's satellites and his calculation of their elements and masses, he contributed to the theoretical understanding of satellites. He is most famous for his work on the age, size, and structure of the universe, and for his early realization of the importance of the Einstein theory of relativity in cosmology. In 1917, he proposed an extension of the theory. He suggested that distant galaxies might be receding rapidly from us and that, as a result, space might be expanding. His ideas were later proved by observation. De Sitter was born in Sneek in The Netherlands. HELEN WRIGHT

DE SMET, PIERRE JEAN (1801-1873), was a Roman Catholic missionary who worked among the Indians of the United States for 50 years. De Smet was a Belgian who went to America at the age of 20. There he entered the Society of Jesus. In 1838 he went to the Potawatomi Indians, and succeeded in making peace between the Potawatomi and the Sioux. Later, he was sent west to the Flathead and Pend d'Oreille tribes. After a visit to the Blackfoot tribe in 1846, he returned to St. Louis and remained there to do other work. But he never lost interest in the Indians. The government asked him to go to the West Coast in 1851 and in 1858 to calm the Indians who were angered by the coming of white men to California and Oregon.

Father De Smet crossed the ocean many times and sought aid in European countries during the long years of his work. At the age of 67, he went alone into the camp of the Sioux, who had sworn to kill all white men. He was able to open the way to peace. His many writings give important facts about the American Indians. The Indians called De Smet "Blackrobe" because of his clerical dress. FULTON J. SHEEN

DES MOINES, *duh MOYN,* Iowa (pop. 201,404; met. area 313,562), is the capital, largest city, and chief manufacturing center of the state. The city lies in south-central Iowa, where the Des Moines and Raccoon rivers meet. For location, see IOWA (political map).

The city takes its name from the Des Moines River. According to tradition, the river had been called *Moingona,* meaning *river of the mounds,* because Indians had built mounds in the area. However, French explorers changed the name to *Moin* and called the stream *la rivière des moines.*

In 1843, the Army built Fort Des Moines on the site of what is now Des Moines. The government established the post to protect the Indians of the area. The Army viewed these Indians as "untaught children" and took charge of all their affairs. By 1845, the Indians had given up their rights to the territory.

Description. Des Moines, the county seat of Polk County, covers about 65 square miles (168 square kilometers). The State Capitol is the most famous landmark in downtown Des Moines. The city is the home of Drake University, the Des Moines Art Center, and the Center of Science and Industry.

Economy. Des Moines ranks as Iowa's main commercial center. About a fifth of the workers in the Des Moines metropolitan area are employed in wholesale and retail trade, the chief economic activity. The approximately 400 manufacturing plants in the area employ about 15 per cent of the work force.

More than 50 insurance companies have their headquarters in Des Moines. The great amount of printing required by these firms helps make printing and publishing the leading industrial activity in the area. Other industries, in order of importance, produce nonelectrical machinery, food products, fabricated metal goods, and glass products. Five freight railroads and the Des Moines Municipal Airport serve the city.

Government and History. Des Moines has a council-manager form of government. The council consists of seven members, including the mayor, all of whom serve four-year terms. The voters of the entire city elect the mayor and two other council members. The four remaining council members are elected from the city's various wards. The council hires a city manager to carry out its policies.

The Sauk and Fox Indians lived in the area before white settlers arrived. Fort Des Moines, built in 1843, was later abandoned, and the surrounding settlement was incorporated as a town in 1853. It was renamed Des Moines in 1857, and became the state capital that same year. The Iowa legislature chose the city as the capital because of its central location. A major period of growth occurred after Des Moines became the capital. Its population jumped from 3,965 in 1860 to 50,093 in 1890.

Des Moines later developed as a military training center. In 1898, during the Spanish-American War, the city had a National Guard camp. In 1902, a cavalry post called Fort Des Moines was established there. It served as a training camp during World War I (1914-1918) and World War II (1939-1945). By 1950, Des Moines had a population of 177,965.

During the early 1970's, Des Moines took part in a federal program established to help solve community problems in various cities. The program enabled Des

Moines to set up day care and mental health facilities, recreational areas, and other projects. John R. Fryar

For the monthly weather in Des Moines, see Iowa (Climate). See also Iowa (pictures).

DES MOINES RIVER. See Iowa (Rivers and Lakes).

DE SOTO, *dee SOH toh,* **HERNANDO** (1500?-1542), a Spanish explorer, was the first white man to cross the Mississippi River. He had become wealthy in the Spanish conquest of Peru. He arrived in Cuba as governor in 1538. He decided to explore Florida, which had been described to him as "a land of gold."

De Soto landed with 600 soldiers near Tampa Bay in May, 1539. He moved north to an Indian area called Apalache. A party he sent west from there reached Pensacola Bay. The explorers crossed Georgia to the Savannah River, and followed it to the Blue Ridge Mountains. Crossing them, De Soto descended the Alabama River to a place called Mabila. There he defeated an Indian tribe, but suffered heavy losses.

Unwilling to abandon his search for gold, De Soto turned northwest. In May, 1541, he sighted the Mississippi River in the northeastern part of what is now the state of Mississippi. Then De Soto crossed into Arkansas, traveled west and south, then returned to the Mississippi River, where he died of fever. His men weighted his body and buried it in the river.

De Soto's tour had taken him through territory that later became Florida, Georgia, South Carolina, North Carolina, Tennessee, Alabama, Mississippi, Arkansas, and Louisiana. After De Soto's death, his men traveled as far west as Texas.

The survivors, under the leadership of Luis de Moscoso, built crude boats and floated down the Mississippi River. Indians attacked them constantly. But they found refuge in Tampico, Mexico, then a Spanish settlement. De Soto was born in the Estremadura region of Spain. Historians disagree on his exact birthplace. During the 1520's, De Soto took part in the Spanish conquest of Central America. Charles Gibson

DE SOTO'S EXPEDITION 1539-1542

This map shows the explorations of Hernando de Soto in the American Southeast. While searching for gold he came upon the Mississippi River. De Soto died in 1542, and Luis de Moscoso completed the expedition.

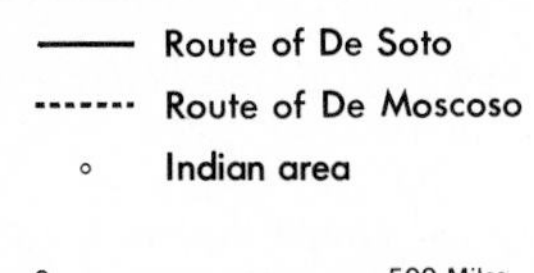

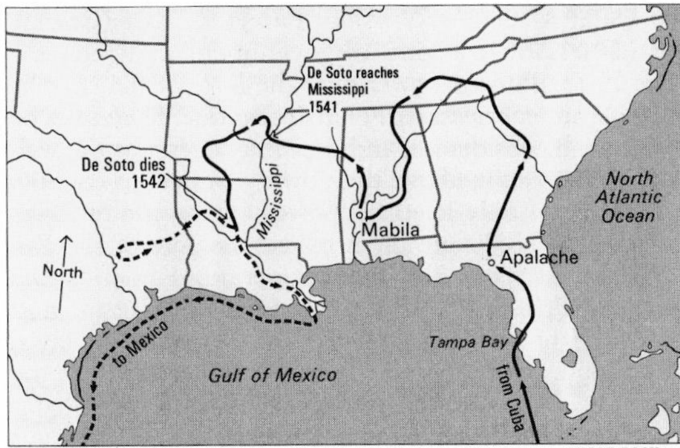

WORLD BOOK map

United States Capitol Historical Society, Washington, D.C.

Hernando de Soto Arrived at the Mississippi River on May 8, 1541. William H. Powell's painting, *Discovery of the Mississippi,* shows De Soto and his men approaching the river's edge.

DE SOTO NATIONAL MEMORIAL is a national memorial at Shaw's Point, four miles west of Bradenton, Fla. It covers an area of 30.00 acres (12.14 hectares). The memorial was established in 1948 to commemorate Hernando de Soto's landing place in his expedition of 1539 (see DE SOTO, HERNANDO).

DESPERADO. See WESTERN FRONTIER LIFE (Crime).

DESPOTISM is a form of government in which the ruler has unlimited power over the lives of the people. Despots are not necessarily harsh or cruel. They may be kindly and considerate, and they may even put the welfare of the people above their own wishes. But usually, a despot can only keep his power by the use of force.

The late 1700's are often called the Age of the Enlightened Despots. During this period, Frederick the Great of Prussia, Catherine the Great of Russia, and Joseph II of Austria did their best to reform the laws, to promote education and the arts, and to conduct the affairs of the country efficiently. Charles III of Spain, Leopold of Tuscany, Joseph of Portugal, and Gustavus III of Sweden also deserved the name of "enlightened despots." Some of these rulers learned that freedom and education make rebellious subjects, and gave up enlightenment. Nearly all were followed by weak rulers who undid whatever good the "enlightened despots" had accomplished. WILLIAM EBENSTEIN

See also CATHERINE (II); FREDERICK (II) of Prussia.

DESROCHES ISLAND. See BRITISH INDIAN OCEAN TERRITORY.

DESSALINES, *DAY SA LEEN,* **JEAN JACQUES** (1758?-1806), is the national hero of Haiti. He was an illiterate slave who freed Haiti from France and became the country's emperor. He was born on a plantation at Grande Rivière, Haiti, and took the name of his French master. He joined the 1791 Negro revolt that resulted in the abolition of slavery in 1793. He fought under Toussaint L'Ouverture against the invasion of the British, and became a general (see TOUSSAINT L'OUVERTURE).

After Toussaint was seized and sent to France, Dessalines led a successful rebellion against the French. This made Haiti the second independent nation in the Western Hemisphere, the United States being the first. Dessalines became president of Haiti on Jan. 1, 1804, but soon proclaimed himself emperor. He was murdered two years later. DONALD E. WORCESTER

See also HAITI (Independence); CHRISTOPHE, HENRI.

DESTROYER is the smallest seagoing combat ship. It is generally from 300 to 400 feet (90 to 120 meters) long, and displaces from 2,000 to 4,000 short tons (1,800 to 3,600 metric tons). Destroyers are used mainly to screen other ships, to picket certain areas, and to escort ships. Destroyers are long-range, high-speed, hard-hitting ships. For protection, they rely on watertight compartments and speed. Sailors call destroyers "tin cans" because of their light steel hulls.

The most common type of destroyer in the U.S. Navy is known as the *710 Class* or *long hull*, developed during World War II. They have two main engine groups of high-pressure steam turbines that total over 60,000 horsepower (45,000 kilowatts). A newer and larger version of the destroyer, the *Forrest Sherman* class, includes the most powerful craft of this size afloat. Engines, boilers, and other machinery for propulsion occupy nearly

U.S. Navy

A Guided Missile Destroyer, the U.S.S. *Waddell*, can launch two surface-to-air guided missiles at a time. It is one of several missile destroyers built in the early 1960's by the U.S. Navy.

three-fourths of their length below the main deck. The ships are capable of speeds above 35 knots. Some destroyers of other navies are able to steam at nearly 40 knots. However, these destroyers do not have the long cruising range that the United States Navy *Forrest Sherman* class destroyers have.

Destroyers are armed with torpedoes in tubes on deck, depth charges, and multipurpose five-inch (13-centimeter) guns. Torpedoes are a destroyer's main weapon against surface ships. The guns can be used against ships as well as against aircraft. On the newest destroyers, guided missile systems replace deck guns. The missiles make the destroyers even more versatile. Armed with missiles, the ships are capable of supporting invasion forces and striking land targets.

The *destroyer escort* is a smaller ship developed during World War II for slower speed convoy duties. These ships displace from 1,300 to 1,500 short tons (1,180 to 2,270 metric tons). They are armed with torpedoes, depth charges, and three-inch (8-centimeter) and five-inch (13-centimeter) guns. They are similar to small frigates in other navies. *Guided-missile escort ships* were developed from the destroyer escort. RAYMOND V. B. BLACKMAN

See also NAVY, UNITED STATES (table: Names of Naval Ships; picture: Warships of the Navy); WARSHIP.

DESTROYING ANGEL. See MUSHROOM (with pictures).

DESTRUCTIVE DISTILLATION. See DISTILLATION.

DE SUCRE, ANTONIO J. See SUCRE, A. J. DE.

DETECTIVE. See POLICE (The Detective Division).

DETECTIVE STORY is a work of fiction about a puzzling crime, a number of clues, and a detective who solves the mystery. In most detective stories, the crime is murder and the clues lead to or away from the solution.

The Pattern of most detective stories is the same, whether the tale is a novel, a novelette, or a short story. The author presents the crime, the detective, and several clues and suspects. The detective follows the clues and may even discover additional crimes. The climax of the story comes when the detective reveals the criminal and tells how he solved the mystery.

Certain conventions have developed from the detective story pattern. The author is expected to "play fair" with the reader. That is, he should give the reader exactly the same information that the detective uses to find the criminal. The reader can treat the story as a battle of wits between himself and the detective.

The detective in most of these stories is not a professional policeman but a private consultant. For example, G. K. Chesterton's Father Brown is a priest, Rex Stout's Nero Wolfe is a gourmet and intellectual, and S. S. Van Dine's Philo Vance is a sophisticated socialite. Fictional professional detectives include Wilkie Collins' Sgt. Cuff, John Creasey's Inspector Gideon (written under the name of J. J. Marric), and Dashiell Hammett's Sam Spade. Romance or financial gain may be a factor in the story, but the main theme is the mystery and its solution.

History of the detective story began with Edgar Allan Poe's "The Murders in the Rue Morgue" (1841). With this story and "The Mystery of Marie Rogêt" and "The Purloined Letter," Poe single-handedly created the literary tradition of detective fiction. His detective was C. Auguste Dupin, a brilliant amateur who uses logic to solve mysteries.

Charles Dickens tried the new form in *Bleak House* (1852-1853) and in his unfinished novel, *The Mystery of Edwin Drood.* Wilkie Collins' *The Moonstone* (1868) was one of the most important early detective novels. Mark Twain wrote a detective story, *Pudd'nhead Wilson* (1894). Sherlock Holmes and his comrade, Dr. John Watson, appeared in 1887 in Sir Arthur Conan Doyle's *A Study in Scarlet.* Holmes is the most famous character in detective fiction—and perhaps in all fiction.

The early 1900's were a period of excitement and originality in detective fiction. The English author R. Austin Freeman introduced the *inverted* detective story, in which the criminal is known from the beginning. The mystery is whether—and how—he will be uncovered. The American writer Jacques Futrelle created a character called the Thinking Machine, and the Hungarian-born Baroness Orczy introduced the Old Man in the Corner. The period from 1925 to 1935 brought the publication of the first or major works by such masters as Margery Allingham, Earl Derr Biggers, John Dickson Carr, Dame Agatha Christie, Mignon G. Eberhart, Erle Stanley Gardner, Dashiell Hammett, Msgr. Ronald Knox, Ngaio Marsh, Ellery Queen, Georges Simenon, Rex Stout, and S. S. Van Dine.

Because of many uninspired writers, the detective story has suffered from its own popularity. Such writers have flooded the market with stories featuring illogical motives, lifeless characters, needless sex and violence, and dull investigations. But detective fiction at its best has an international appeal that continues to grow. The detective story attracts readers throughout the world, particularly in England, France, Germany, Japan, and the South American countries. HERBERT BREAN

Related Articles in WORLD BOOK include:

Chandler, Raymond
Chesterton, Gilbert K.
Christie, Dame Agatha
Collins, Wilkie
Doyle, Sir Arthur Conan
Gardner, Erle Stanley
Hammett, Dashiell
Holmes, Sherlock
Poe, Edgar Allan
Queen, Ellery
Stout, Rex
Van Dine, S. S.

DETECTOR. See RADIO (Amplifiers); TRAFFIC (Signals, Signs, and Markings).

Brown Bros.

Making Soap in Early America. American colonists made soap outside their houses in huge iron kettles. The soap cleaned fairly well, but it often had a bad odor and harmed the skin.

DETERGENT AND SOAP. A detergent is any substance that cleans. Soap is a detergent. But the word detergent usually refers to *synthetic detergents,* which are like soap in many ways but have a completely different chemical makeup. Synthetic detergents are usually called simply *detergents.*

Detergents and soap have many everyday uses. People use soap for bathing. They wash clothes, dishes, floors, and walls with detergents and soaps. These cleaning materials are in the form of bars, *granules* (grains), flakes, liquid, and tablets. A person in the United States uses an average of 28 pounds (13 kilograms) of soap and detergents a year. Bar soaps are used most often for bathing. But detergents make up over 90 per cent of all home laundering and housecleaning products.

Detergents and soaps are made up of molecules that attach themselves to dirt particles in soiled material. The molecules pull the dirt particles out of the material and hold the particles in the wash water until they are rinsed away.

Although synthetic detergents and soaps are much alike, detergents have certain advantages soaps do not have. Detergents can penetrate soiled areas better than soaps. The most important characteristic of detergents, however, is their ability to clean effectively in all kinds of water. Soaps are often ineffective when used for laundering in hard water. Soaps react with minerals in hard water and form a substance that does not dissolve. This substance, called *lime soap deposit, soap curd,* or *scum*, is difficult to remove from fabrics and other surfaces. It also causes the familiar bathtub ring. Detergents do not leave this deposit.

Uses of Detergents and Soaps

People use soap for baths. They shampoo their hair with soaps or detergents. Good health depends in part on cleanliness. Regular bathing with soap prevents natural body oils and dirt from clogging the pores of the skin. Doctors wash sores and wounds with soap to help prevent infections. They use soap to destroy germs that can cause sickness and disease.

Detergents and soaps have many household and industrial uses. Housewives wash their dishes and laundry, scrub floors, wash windows and walls, and do other work with detergents and soaps. Industries use detergents and soaps as cleaners, lubricants, softeners, and polishers. In the rubber industry, for example, soap is used to keep hot rubber tires from sticking to the *vulcanizing* (hardening) molds. Some motor oils contain detergents that break down soot, dust, and other particles that can harm engine parts. Soap is used to polish jewelry, and to soften leather for shoes and handbags. Cotton, silk, and wool fabrics are washed with detergents before being made into clothing. Detergents, unlike soaps, do not leave a deposit that interferes with the dyeing of fabrics.

How Detergents and Soaps Work

Detergents and soaps clean soiled material in much the same way. The cleaning process consists of (1) wetting the soiled material thoroughly; (2) removing dirt particles from the soiled material; and (3) *suspending* (holding) the dirt particles in the water until they are rinsed away.

Wetting the Material. Detergents and soaps increase the wetting ability of water by lowering water's *surface tension.* Surface tension holds water molecules together, and causes the water to form in drops. Detergent and soap molecules gather at the water's surface and force the water to expand and spread out. With surface tension reduced, water can penetrate the soiled material more completely. Lowering the surface tension also helps detergents and soaps to form bubbles and suds.

Removing the Dirt. To understand how detergents and soaps remove soil, picture each detergent or soap molecule as a pencil. One end of each pencil (molecule) is *hydrophilic* (water-loving); the other end is *hydrophobic* (water-hating). Water repels the hydrophobic ends. These ends attach themselves to any surface other than water. Many grab onto and surround the tiny particles of dirt in the material to be cleaned. At the same time, the hydrophilic ends pull away from the soiled material and toward the wash water. The mechanical *agitation* (motion) of a washing machine, or the movement caused by rubbing by hand, helps the hydrophilic ends of the detergent or soap molecules pull the dirt particles from the material and into the water.

Suspending the Particles. After the tiny dirt particles are in the water, the thin layer of detergent or soap around them keeps the particles separated. It prevents them from settling again on the washed material. The dirt particles remain suspended in water until they are rinsed away.

How Soap Is Made

Fats and alkalis are the chief soapmaking ingredients. The fats are animal fats, such as tallow; or vegetable oils, such as coconut oil and olive oil. The alkali is usually sodium hydroxide (often called *lye*, or *caustic soda*). Potassium hydroxide is used as the alkali in liquid soaps and some bar soaps.

Kettle Method. Some soap is still made in kettles. The soap industry's "kettles" are steel tanks 3 stories high. Each kettle can hold over 100,000 pounds (45,000 kilograms) of ingredients. The mixture of fats and alkali is heated by steam through coils inside the kettle.

The mixture is boiled for several hours. The heat triggers a chemical reaction that causes a creamy soap to form. Salt is added to the mixture, causing the soap to rise to the top of the mixture. At this stage, the soap is called *neat soap.* A solution of excess alkali, salt, and glycerin is left beneath the layer of soap. Glycerin, a valuable by-product of soapmaking, is used to make cosmetics, drugs, explosives, and many other products (see GLYCERIN).

Other ingredients may then be added to the neat soap in a huge mixer called a *crutcher.* These ingredients include perfumes, colors, fabric brighteners, *germicides* (germ killers), and *builders* (substances that help remove dirt). After the ingredients have been added, the soap mixture may be hardened into bars, or changed into flakes or grains.

Continuous Processing is a more efficient method of making soap. Soapmakers using this method can make as much soap in a few hours as they can make in a few days by the kettle method.

A stainless-steel tube called a *hydrolyzer* is used in

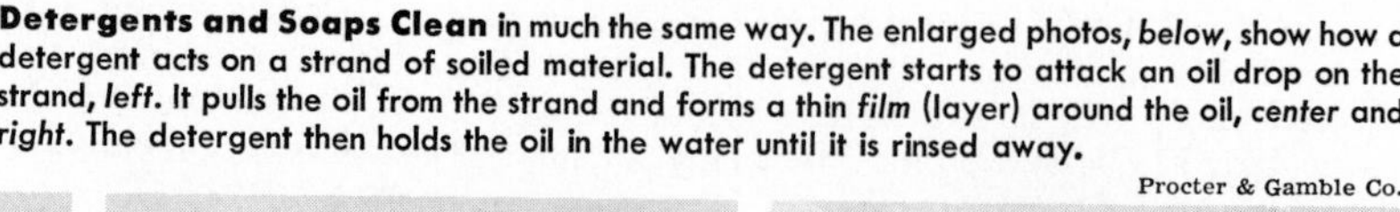

Detergents and Soaps Clean in much the same way. The enlarged photos, *below*, show how a detergent acts on a strand of soiled material. The detergent starts to attack an oil drop on the strand, *left.* It pulls the oil from the strand and forms a thin *film* (layer) around the oil, *center* and *right.* The detergent then holds the oil in the water until it is rinsed away.

Procter & Gamble Co.

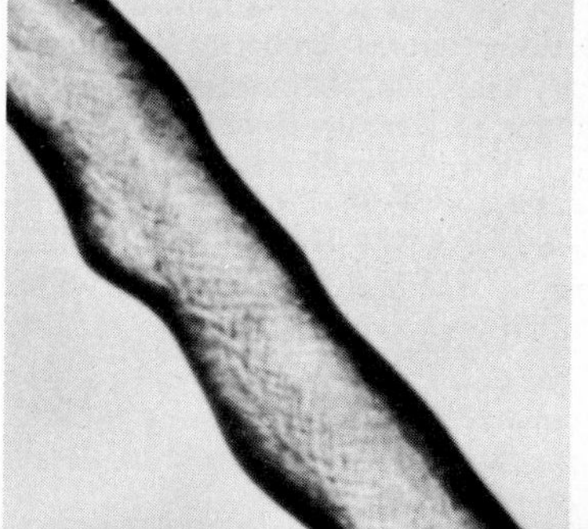

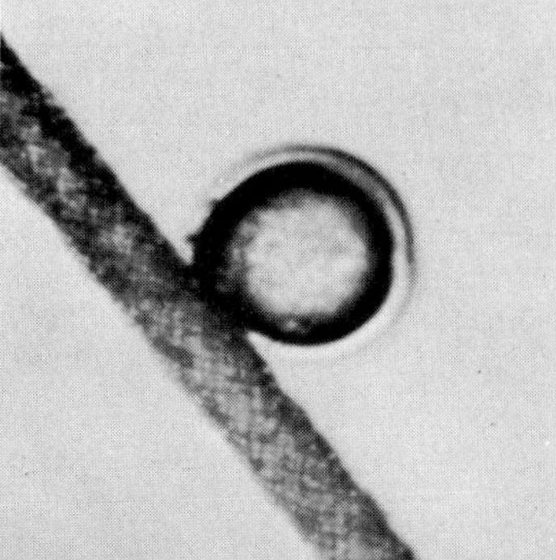

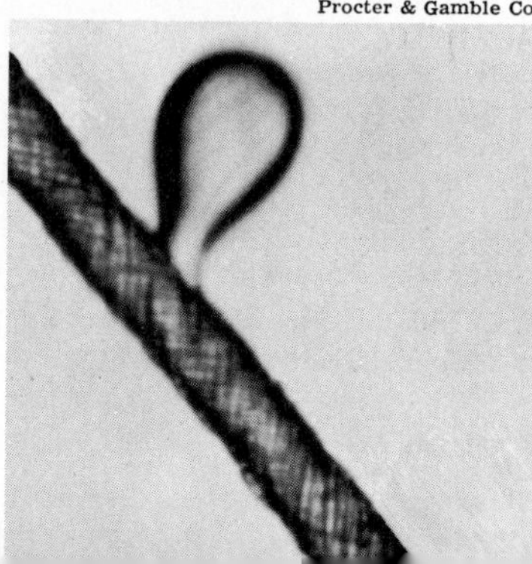

Procter & Gamble Co.

Long Bars of Soap are cut into smaller bars by a mechanical knife. The bars are then stamped and wrapped for shipment.

Procter & Gamble Co.

Liquid Detergent is poured into plastic bottles by machine. The bottles are inspected as they pass along a conveyor belt.

continuous soapmaking. The tube is about 3 feet (91 centimeters) in diameter and about 80 feet (24 meters) high. Water under high pressure and at a temperature of 500° F. (260° C) is pumped into the top of the hydrolyzer. At the same time, hot fat is pumped in at the bottom. Under these conditions, the fat splits into fatty acids and glycerin. The fatty acids rise to the top, and are removed. The glycerin dissolves in water, and is drawn off at the bottom. The fatty acids, either in this form or after further purification, are mixed with alkali to make soap. The soap is mixed with other ingredients in the crutcher, and is made into bars, flakes, or granules.

Granules and Flakes. Almost all soaps used for home laundering are either granules or flakes. Manufacturers make soap granules by pumping warm soap from the crutcher to the top of a tall drying tower. The warm soap mixture is sprayed into a stream of hot air that dries it into bubble-like granules. The granules fall to the bottom of the tower. There they are screened to remove any coarse or very fine particles.

Soap flakes are made by pouring soap from the crutcher between steel rollers. One roller is hot and the other is cold. A thin sheet of soap sticks to the cold roller. This soap is scraped off, cut into ribbons, and dried. During drying, the ribbons either break or are cut into flakes.

Bar Soaps used for bathing are commonly called *toilet soaps*. Some bar soaps are also used for washing clothes. Bars are made in various ways. Some bars are made by pouring melted soap into large steel frames with removable sides. The soap cools and hardens. Then workers remove the sides of the frame and cut the huge cake into bars. *Floating soaps* are made by mixing the warm soap mixture with air in a machine equipped with cooling coils. The soap is squeezed from an opening in the machine as a long continuous bar. Machines cut the bar into individual bars. *Milled soaps* are made by grinding soap flakes through *mills* (sets of rollers). The mills mix and squeeze the soap. The mixture is then placed in a machine, squeezed out as a continuous bar, and cut into smaller bars. The milling operation produces a hard soap with high lathering qualities.

How Detergents Are Made

Several complicated chemical processes are used in making detergents. First, workers make the *surfactant*, or *surface-active agent*. This is the basic cleaning agent in a detergent. The surfactant can be made from a variety of starting materials, including by-products of petroleum, as well as the same vegetable oils and animal fats used to make soap. Many processes may be necessary to make these materials into surfactants. Tallow, for example, may be made to react chemically with the following substances to make a surfactant: an alcohol, hydrogen gas, sulfuric acid, and an alkali.

Other ingredients are mixed with the surfactant in the crutcher. These include bleaches, builders, coloring agents, suds stabilizers, and *antiredeposition agents* (ingredients that help prevent dirt from returning to cleaned material). The detergent mixture is processed into granules, flakes, liquids, or tablets.

Detergent granules and flakes are produced in much the same way as soap granules and flakes. Liquid detergents are made by dissolving the surfactants and other ingredients in water. Detergent tablets are made by blending detergent granules with special ingredients, and then pressing them into tablet form.

History

Early Soapmaking. No one knows exactly when or where man first made soap. According to one legend, soapmaking began by accident about 3,000 years ago on Sapo Hill near Rome. Peasants offered animals as burnt sacrifices to their gods on Sapo Hill. Fat from the animals filled the altars and soaked down through the wood ashes into the clay soil. Women discovered that this soapy clay was a help in washing clothes. The word for *soap* in many languages, including English, comes from the Latin word *sapo*.

Historians report that a rough kind of soap was used in France about A.D. 100. By about 700, soapmaking was a craft in Italy. Spain was a leading soapmaker by 800. Soapmaking began in England about 1200.

In the late 1700's, a French scientist named Nicolas Leblanc found that caustic soda could be made from common table salt. This discovery meant that soap could be made and sold at prices most people could afford.

In North America, many early settlers made their own soap. They poured hot water over wood ashes to make an alkali called potash. Then they boiled the potash with animal fats to make soap. The soap did a fair cleaning job, but often was harsh and had a bad odor.

Soapmaking as an industry in North America began in the early 1800's. Some persons began collecting waste fats from villagers and making soap outdoors in huge iron kettles. They poured the soap into large wooden frames for hardening. Then they cut the hardened soap into bars and sold them from door to door.

Today, fats and alkalis are still the basic ingredients for soapmaking. But the quality of these materials has improved greatly. Since the early 1900's, manufacturers have made big improvements in the mildness, color, fragrance, and cleaning ability of soaps.

Development of Detergents. Fritz Gunther, a German scientist, is usually credited with developing the first synthetic detergent in 1916. His detergent was used by industry but was too harsh for household use. In 1933, Procter & Gamble, a U.S. soap company, introduced the world's first synthetic household detergents. Before long, other soap companies also began making detergents. A shortage of fats and chemicals during World War II (1939-1945) slowed the development of detergents. Since then, detergents have been developed for almost every cleaning job.

Before 1965, detergents sometimes caused surface foam on rivers and streams. Alkyl Benzene Sulfonate (ABS), the surfactant then used in most detergents, was composed of molecules grouped together as a branched chain, like a cluster of grapes. These molecules could not be broken down completely in sewage treatment systems. In 1965, after more than 10 years of research, the detergent industry developed a new type of surfactant called Linear Alkylate Sulfonate (LAS). LAS molecules are connected in a long, straight chain. These molecules can be broken down quickly by bacteria. As a result, detergents no longer cause foam after adequate sewage treatment. This new surfactant permits washing products to perform just as effectively as before.

In the early 1970's, some persons charged that the phosphates used as builders in detergents were contributing to water pollution. When phosphates and other nutrients enter rivers or lakes, they can fertilize aquatic plants called algae. Overproduction of these plants causes the water's oxygen supply to be used up (see ENVIRONMENTAL POLLUTION [Water Pollution]). Critics urged that phosphates be removed from detergents, and some local governments banned detergents that contained phosphates. Manufacturers worked to develop phosphate substitutes, and several companies reduced the phosphate level in their products.

Critically reviewed by THE PROCTER & GAMBLE COMPANY

DETERMINANT, in mathematics, is a single number related to a square *array* (arrangement) of numbers called *elements*. For example, the array

$$\begin{vmatrix} 3 & 1 \\ 2 & 6 \end{vmatrix}$$

is related to the single number 16. You can compute the value of this determinant in three steps. (1) Multiply the upper left element *3* by the lower right element *6*: $3 \times 6 = 18$. (2) Multiply the lower left element *2* by the upper right element *1*: $2 \times 1 = 2$. (3) Subtract the product of step 2 from the product of step 1: $18 - 2 = 16$. The word *determinant* is also used for the square array itself.

Mathematicians use determinants to state formulas for the solution of many problems. Such problems include the solution of equations and the calculation of certain areas and volumes.

Using 2 by 2 Determinants. The array above is called a *2 by 2* determinant because it has two *rows* (3,1 and 2,6) and two *columns* (3,2 and 1,6).

In general, the symbols a_1, b_1, a_2, b_2 can be used to represent the numbers of any 2 by 2 determinant. The value of the determinant is stated as follows:

$$\begin{vmatrix} a_1 & b_1 \\ a_2 & b_2 \end{vmatrix} = a_1b_2 - a_2b_1$$

The 2 by 2 determinant can be used to solve linear equations in two variables (see ALGEBRA [Solving Linear Equations in Two Variables]). For example, suppose you wanted to solve the following equations:

$$\begin{aligned} 3x + 1y &= 5 \\ 2x + 6y &= 14 \end{aligned}$$

To find the value of the variable x, eliminate the variable y by multiplying the first equation by 6, and then subtracting the second equation:

$$\begin{aligned} 18x + 6y &= 30 \\ -2x - 6y &= -14 \\ \hline 16x \quad &= 16 \\ x &= \frac{16}{16} = 1 \end{aligned}$$

The above operations could also be written as follows:

$$\begin{aligned} 6 \times 3x + 6 \times 1y &= 6 \times 5 \\ -2x - \quad 6y &= -14 \\ \hline (6 \times 3 - 1 \times 2)x &= 6 \times 5 - 1 \times 14 \\ x &= \frac{6 \times 5 - 1 \times 14}{6 \times 3 - 1 \times 2} \end{aligned}$$

The last expression can be written as the ratio of two determinants:

$$x = \frac{\begin{vmatrix} 5 & 1 \\ 14 & 6 \end{vmatrix}}{\begin{vmatrix} 3 & 1 \\ 2 & 6 \end{vmatrix}} = \frac{5 \times 6 - 14 \times 1}{3 \times 6 - 2 \times 1} = \frac{30 - 14}{18 - 2} = \frac{16}{16} = 1$$

You could solve the original equations in a similar way for y and get

$$y = \frac{\begin{vmatrix} 3 & 5 \\ 2 & 14 \end{vmatrix}}{\begin{vmatrix} 3 & 1 \\ 2 & 6 \end{vmatrix}} = \frac{3 \times 14 - 2 \times 5}{3 \times 6 - 2 \times 1} = \frac{42 - 10}{18 - 2} = \frac{32}{16} = 2$$

Note that the same determinant appears as the denominator in the formulas for both x and y. This determinant is called the *determinant of the system*. It is made up of the coefficients of x and y in the original equations

(3,1,2,6). The numerator in the formula for x is the determinant of the system with the coefficients of x replaced by the constants in the original equations (5,14). Similarly, these constants replace the coefficients of y in the numerator of the formula for y.

In general, equations in x and y can be written in the form

$$a_1x + b_1y = c_1$$
$$a_2x + b_2y = c_2$$

You can solve these equations for x as follows: (1) multiply the first equation by b_2; (2) multiply the second equation by b_1; (3) subtract the product of step 2 from the product of step 1. The result is:

$$(a_1b_2 - a_2b_1)x = c_1b_2 - c_2b_1$$

$$x = \frac{c_1b_2 - c_2b_1}{a_1b_2 - a_2b_1} = \frac{\begin{vmatrix} c_1 & b_1 \\ c_2 & b_2 \end{vmatrix}}{\begin{vmatrix} a_1 & b_1 \\ a_2 & b_2 \end{vmatrix}}$$

You could solve for y in a similar way and get:

$$y = \frac{a_1c_2 - a_2c_1}{a_1b_2 - a_2b_1} = \frac{\begin{vmatrix} a_1 & c_1 \\ a_2 & c_2 \end{vmatrix}}{\begin{vmatrix} a_1 & b_1 \\ a_2 & b_2 \end{vmatrix}}$$

Using Higher Order Determinants. The order of a determinant is the number of rows or columns it has. A 2 by 2 determinant is of the *second* order, a 3 by 3 of the *third*, and so on. Determinants of an order higher than the second appear, for example, in the solution of three or more simultaneous equations.

You can use third order determinants to solve the following three equations:

$$\begin{aligned} 3x + 2y + z &= 10 \\ 4y - z &= 5 \\ 5x + y - 2z &= 1 \end{aligned}$$

The formulas for x, y, and z are similar to the ones used to solve only two equations. The denominator of each formula is the determinant of the system. The numerators are the determinant of the system with the coefficients of x, y, or z replaced by the constants. For example, the formula for x is:

$$x = \frac{\begin{vmatrix} 10 & 2 & 1 \\ 5 & 4 & -1 \\ 1 & 1 & -2 \end{vmatrix}}{\begin{vmatrix} 3 & 2 & 1 \\ 0 & 4 & -1 \\ 5 & 1 & -2 \end{vmatrix}}$$

Third order determinants such as the one above can be computed in several ways. One method is to reduce the determinant to a series of 2 by 2 determinants. With this method, the denominator in the above formula can be reduced as follows:

$$\begin{vmatrix} 3 & 2 & 1 \\ 0 & 4 & -1 \\ 5 & 1 & -2 \end{vmatrix} = 3\begin{vmatrix} 4 & -1 \\ 1 & -2 \end{vmatrix} - 2\begin{vmatrix} 0 & -1 \\ 5 & -2 \end{vmatrix} + 1\begin{vmatrix} 0 & 4 \\ 5 & 1 \end{vmatrix}$$
$$= 3(-7) - 2(5) + 1(-20)$$
$$= -21 - 10 - 20 = -51$$

In this operation, each 2 by 2 determinant is multiplied by a number that appears in the first row of the 3 by 3 determinant (3,2,1). The 2 by 2 determinants are called *minors* of these first row elements. For example, the determinant

$$\begin{vmatrix} 4 & -1 \\ 1 & -2 \end{vmatrix}$$

is the minor of 3. It consists of the elements that remain in the 3 by 3 determinant after the row and column in which 3 appears are crossed out. Similarly, the minor of 2 includes the elements that remain after the first row and second column are crossed out.

This series of 2 by 2 determinants is called an *expansion in terms of the minors of the first row.* It consists of the products of the first row elements and their respective minors. The value of the 3 by 3 determinant is computed by alternately adding and subtracting these products. In general terms, the formula for expanding a 3 by 3 determinant in this way is

$$\begin{vmatrix} a_1 & b_1 & c_1 \\ a_2 & b_2 & c_2 \\ a_3 & b_3 & c_3 \end{vmatrix} = a_1\begin{vmatrix} b_2 & c_2 \\ b_3 & c_3 \end{vmatrix} - b_1\begin{vmatrix} a_2 & c_2 \\ a_3 & c_3 \end{vmatrix} + c_1\begin{vmatrix} a_2 & b_2 \\ a_3 & b_3 \end{vmatrix}$$

Determinants can be expanded similarly in terms of the minors of any row or column if the signs of the minors are properly chosen.

Determinants of orders higher than the third also can be computed by reducing them to 2 by 2 determinants. However, the minors of these determinants are not 2 by 2 determinants. (The order of a minor is always one less than the order of the determinant from which it is formed.) The minors themselves must be repeatedly expanded until 2 by 2 determinants are finally obtained. Mathematicians may use other methods to simplify high order determinants. PHILLIP S. JONES

DETERMINISM. See FREE WILL.

DETONATOR, *DET oh NAY tur,* is a small metal or plastic capsule that contains an easily explodable charge. It is used to *detonate* (set off) larger explosive charges, such as dynamite, mines, and bombs. It contains a heat-sensitive *priming charge,* such as lead azide, and a *base charge* of some more powerful explosive, such as RDX. Flame from a fuse or heat from an electric wire ignites the priming charge which ignites the base charge. The explosion of the base charge sets off the dynamite, mine, or bomb. Detonators for dynamite are called *blasting caps.* Blasting caps can cause serious injury. Police should be notified immediately if children find blasting caps. JULIUS ROTH

John Gajda, Publix

Downtown Detroit lies on the north bank of the Detroit River. The Civic Center, consisting of several public buildings, overlooks the river, one of the nation's busiest shipping routes.

DETROIT, *dee TROYT*, Mich., produces more automobiles and trucks than any other city in the world. It is called the *Automobile Capital of the World* or the *Motor City*. Automobile manufacturing helped Detroit become one of the world's greatest industrial centers.

Detroit, Michigan's largest city, lies on the southeastern border of the state, where the Detroit River separates the United States and Canada. Like a strait, the river connects Lakes Erie and St. Clair. The French word *Detroit* means *strait*. The river carries more shipping than almost any other river in North America, and Detroit ranks as one of the most important U.S. ports. The city is also a center of transportation.

Antoine de la Mothe Cadillac, a French colonist, founded Detroit in 1701. Much of the city's early development resulted from fur trading and agriculture.

FACTS IN BRIEF

Population: 1,513,601. *Metropolitan Area Population*—4,435,051.

Area: 142 sq. mi. (368 km²). *Metropolitan Area*—4,001 sq. mi. (10,363 km²).

Altitude: 581 ft. (177 m) above sea level.

Climate: *Average Temperature*—January, 26° F. (−3° C); July, 73° F. (23° C). *Average Annual Precipitation* (rainfall, melted snow, and other forms of moisture)—31 in. (79 cm). For the monthly weather in Detroit, see MICHIGAN (Climate).

Government: Mayor-council. *Terms*—4 years for the mayor and the nine council members.

Founded: 1701. Incorporated as a city in 1806.

The automobile industry grew rapidly during the 1900's, and Detroit's population boomed. During World War II (1939-1945), the city produced huge amounts of military equipment and became known as the *Arsenal of Democracy*.

The City

Detroit covers 142 square miles (368 square kilometers), or about a fourth of Wayne County. Downtown Detroit lies along the Detroit River. Because of a bend in the river, Detroit is directly north of the Canadian city of Windsor, Ont.

Detroit's Civic Center borders the river at the foot of Woodward Avenue. Gardens set off its handsome buildings. These structures include the Veterans Memorial Building, a meeting place for veterans and civic groups; the 20-story City-County Building, which houses gov-

Symbols of Detroit. The city flag shows French fleurs-de-lis, British lions, and American stars and stripes to represent the three nations that have controlled Detroit. The city seal symbolizes the Detroit fire of 1805 and the city's rebirth. It bears the city's mottoes, *Speramus Meliora* (We hope for better things) and *Resurget Cineribus* (It shall rise again from the ashes).

ernment offices and courtrooms; the Henry and Edsel Ford Auditorium, with a seating capacity of nearly 3,000; the circular Cobo Arena, which can seat about 12,000 persons; and Cobo Hall, which has more than 9 acres (3.6 hectares) of exhibition space. The arena and hall were named for Albert E. Cobo, who served as mayor of Detroit from 1950 to 1957.

Inland from the waterfront, downtown Detroit spreads over more than 40 square blocks. The J. L. Hudson Company, one of the nation's largest department stores, is on Woodward Avenue in the downtown section. The Penobscot Building, Detroit's tallest skyscraper, rises 557 feet (170 meters) on Fort Street.

Detroit's residential areas spread outward from the downtown section. About 70 per cent of the residential units are single-family homes. Like many other large industrial cities, Detroit has slums. These areas stand in sharp contrast to the clean, modern, and relatively wealthy suburbs that surround the city.

The Detroit metropolitan area covers 4,001 square miles (10,363 square kilometers) in Lapeer, Livingston, Macomb, Oakland, St. Clair, and Wayne counties. About half of Michigan's people live in this area. Three Detroit suburbs—Dearborn, Livonia, and Warren—have more than 100,000 persons each. Other suburbs include East Detroit, Ferndale, Lincoln Park, Pontiac, River Rouge, Roseville, Royal Oak, St. Clair Shores, Wyandotte, and five cities with Grosse Pointe as part of

CITY OF DETROIT

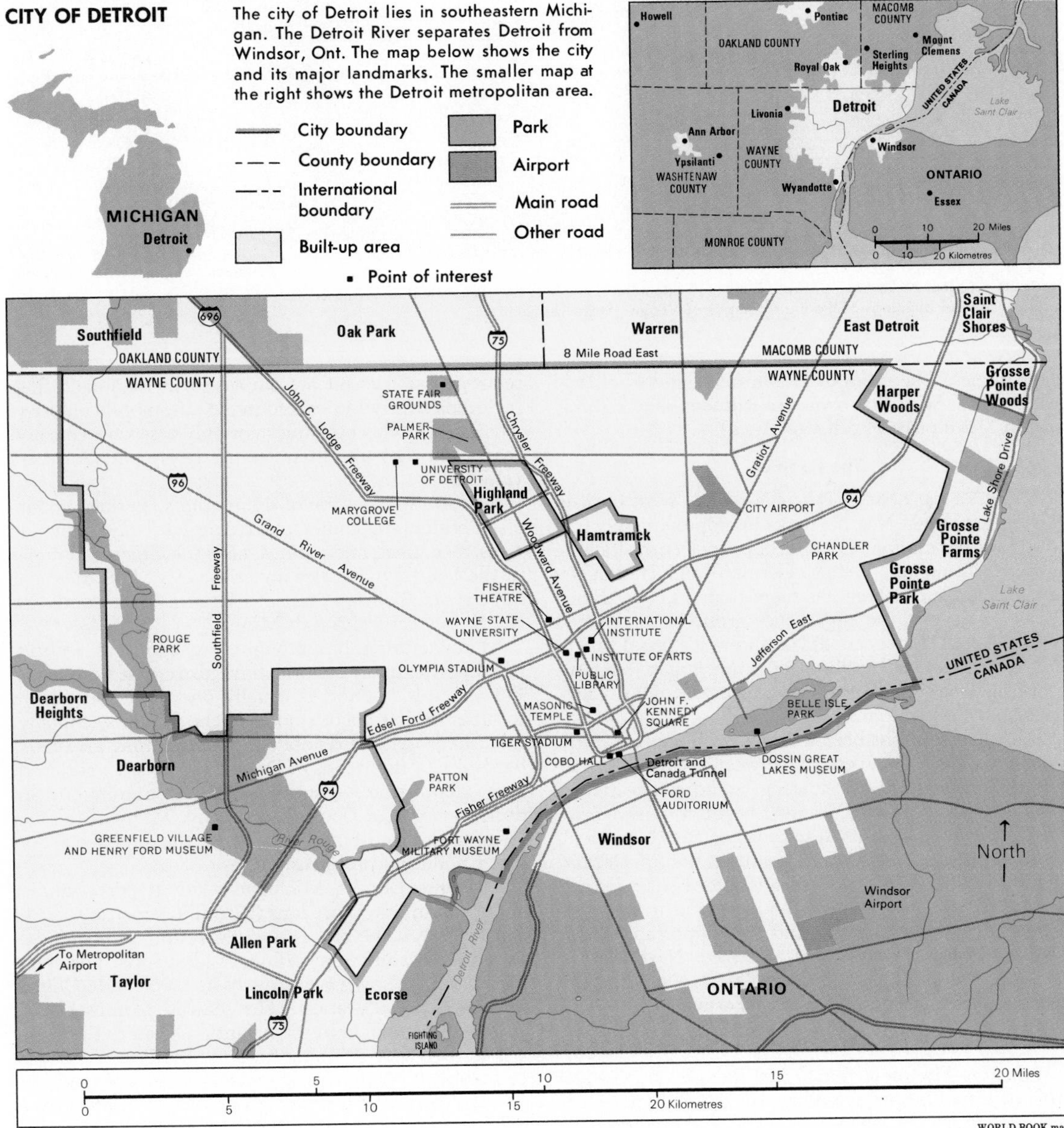

The city of Detroit lies in southeastern Michigan. The Detroit River separates Detroit from Windsor, Ont. The map below shows the city and its major landmarks. The smaller map at the right shows the Detroit metropolitan area.

Southeast Michigan Tourist Association

Detroit's Cultural Center is about 2 miles (3 kilometers) north of the downtown area. The center includes several buildings of the main campus of Wayne State University.

their names. The cities of Hamtramck and Highland Park—each with its own government—lie entirely within Detroit (see HIGHLAND PARK).

The People

About 90 per cent of Detroit's people were born in the United States. Negroes make up approximately half the city's population. Other groups in Detroit include those of Canadian, French, German, and Italian descent. The Detroit area has more than 17,000 Arabic-speaking persons, the largest such group in the United States. About 80 per cent of Hamtramck's people are of Polish ancestry. Methodists form the largest religious group in Detroit, followed by Baptists, Roman Catholics, and Presbyterians.

Racial tension has been a major problem in Detroit since the 1940's. Competition between the city's blacks and whites for jobs and housing led to a race riot in 1943. During the 1960's, Negroes began to push harder for equal rights, and racial tension increased. In 1967, a riot broke out in a largely Negro section of Detroit. After this riot, many civic organizations were formed to ease the tension between the races and to help improve education, housing, and job opportunities for blacks. These organizations included New Detroit Inc., the Economic Development Corporation, and the Inner City Business Improvement Forum.

Economy

Industry. The more than 7,000 factories in the Detroit metropolitan area produce over $8 billion worth of goods yearly. About 40 per cent of the workers in metropolitan Detroit are employed in manufacturing, including nearly 14 per cent in the automobile industry. The automobile companies not only assemble cars and trucks but they also manufacture many parts for these vehicles.

Detroit ranks as one of the nation's leading producers of business machines, chemicals, hardware, machine tools, medicines, and paint. One of the largest salt mines in the United States lies under the city. This mine has large rooms hollowed out of what was once solid salt. See SALT (picture: A Salt Mine).

Manufacturing has brought prosperity to Detroit, but the city's many factories have also created problems. For example, Detroit is usually one of the first cities to suffer during major slumps in the nation's economy. A sharp drop in automobile production may also cause hardship for thousands of Detroit workers. In addition, long labor strikes—especially in the automobile industry—can hurt Detroit's economy. Many of the factories also contribute heavily to the city's air and water pollution problems.

Shipping. Detroit, Michigan's largest port, handles about 30 million short tons (27 million metric tons) of cargo yearly. The city is a gateway for commerce between eastern and western Great Lakes ports. The opening of the St. Lawrence Seaway in 1959 made Detroit an international seaport. The seaway permits ocean-going ships to sail from the Atlantic Ocean to the Great Lakes. About 60 shipping lines use the Port of Detroit, and nearly 1,000 foreign ships dock there annually.

The Detroit River ranks as one of the busiest inland waterways in the world. Every year, ships carry more than 120 million short tons (109 million metric tons) of cargo on the Detroit River.

Transportation. The Detroit Metropolitan Airport, 21 miles (34 kilometers) west of the city, serves nearly 20 commercial airlines. Smaller, regional airlines use the Detroit City Airport in northeastern Detroit. Railroad passenger trains, seven freight rail lines, and 200 trucking lines also serve the city. Detroit has more than 50 miles (80 kilometers) of freeways that connect with major highways.

Communication. Detroit's two daily newspapers are the *Free Press* and the *News*. About 20 radio stations and 5 television stations serve the city. Radio station WWJ, which began operating in Detroit in 1920, made one of the nation's first regular commercial broadcasts.

Education

Detroit's public school system consists of about 300 elementary schools and 25 high schools. Approximately 300,000 students attend these schools, and Negroes make up more than 60 per cent of the enrollment. Property taxes and state aid provide the chief sources of income for the public schools. More than 150 parochial and private schools serve about 90,000 students.

In 1970, the Michigan legislature passed a law that gave Detroiters more control of the public schools in their communities. This law divided the city into eight districts and established a school board for each. The voters of each district elect five board members to three-year terms. The law also enlarged the Detroit Board of Education from 7 members to 13 members to improve the administration of the schools.

The city's public school system faces several problems. Efforts to preserve a racial balance in integrated schools have failed, and racial disturbances have increased. In addition, property taxes and other sources of income have often been unable to provide enough money to pay for sharply rising school costs.

Universities and colleges in Detroit include the Detroit College of Law, the Detroit Institute of Technology, Marygrove College, Mercy College of Detroit, Sacred Heart Seminary College, the University of Detroit, and Wayne State University. The University of Michigan is in nearby Ann Arbor.

The Detroit Public Library has almost 30 branches. The main library owns more than 2 million books.

Cultural Life

The Arts. The Detroit Symphony Orchestra presents concerts in the Henry and Edsel Ford Auditorium. The orchestra gives outdoor concerts every summer in downtown Detroit and in other sections of the city. The Metropolitan Opera Company performs annually in Detroit's Masonic Temple. The Detroit Institute of Arts owns a fine collection of sculptures and paintings, including murals by the Mexican artist Diego Rivera.

Museums. Detroit's Cultural Center includes three large museums. The Detroit Historical Museum has exhibits on the city as it looked during the 1800's. The Children's Museum of the Detroit Public Schools has a bird room and a planetarium. The International Institute displays arts and crafts from over 40 nations.

Other Detroit museums include the Dossin Great Lakes Museum, featuring models of historic ships, and the Fort Wayne Military Museum, one of the best-preserved forts in the United States.

Recreation

Parks. Detroit's park system covers about 6,000 acres (2,400 hectares) and includes more than 200 parks, playfields, and playgrounds. The largest park, 1,172-acre (474-hectare) River Rouge Park, has a golf course, swimming pools, and tennis courts. Belle Isle, a 982-acre (397-hectare) park in the Detroit River, features an aquarium, a beach, and a children's zoo. The Detroit Zoological Park covers 122 acres (49 hectares) in Royal Oak. This zoo has wide moats, rather than bars, between the animals and visitors. The Michigan State Fair is held every August and September at the State Fairgrounds in Detroit.

Sports. The Detroit Tigers of the American League play baseball in Tiger Stadium. The Detroit Red Wings skate against their National Hockey League opponents in Olympia Stadium. The Detroit Pistons of the National Basketball Association play in Cobo Arena. The Michigan Stags of the World Hockey Association also play there. The Detroit Lions of the National Football League were scheduled to play in Pontiac Metropolitan Stadium by 1975.

Other Interesting Places to Visit include:

Automobile Plants, in Detroit, Dearborn, and Warren. The Chrysler, Ford, and General Motors companies offer guided tours.

Cranbrook, in Bloomfield Hills. This 300-acre (120-hectare) educational center includes three private schools, an art museum, and a science institute.

Automobile Manufacturing is Detroit's chief industry. The city is one of the world's greatest manufacturing centers.

Ford Motor Company

DETROIT

Greenfield Village and Henry Ford Museum, in Dearborn. The village has nearly 100 restored early American homes, schools, and stores. The museum, which stands next to the village, features the world's largest collection of antique cars. See GREENFIELD VILLAGE.

Government

Detroit has a mayor-council form of government. The people elect the mayor and the nine members of the Common Council—all to four-year terms. These elections are nonpartisan. That is, party labels do not appear on the ballots.

Detroit's mayor has broad powers. For example, he can veto acts of the Common Council and can appoint many key officials, including the police commissioner. The council is the city's legislative body. It passes laws, holds public hearings, and provides money for city services. Detroit's main sources of income are a property tax and a city income tax. The income tax, adopted in 1962, applies to all Detroit residents and to suburbanites who work in the city.

History

Early Settlement. The Wyandot Indians lived in the Detroit region before the first white men arrived. In 1701, a group of French settlers led by Antoine de la Mothe Cadillac built Fort Pontchartrain on the north bank of the Detroit River. The fort became an important fur-trading post.

The British gained control of the fort in 1760, during the French and Indian War. Pontiac, an Ottawa chief, led an Indian attack on the fort in 1763 but could not capture it (see PONTIAC). The British began to build Fort Lernoult on the site in 1778, during the Revolutionary War in America. The war ended in 1783, but the British wanted to keep their valuable fur trade in the Michigan region and refused to surrender Fort Lernoult until 1796. Lieutenant Colonel John Francis Hamtramck became the fort's first American commander. Also in 1796, the surrounding area was named Wayne County, and Detroit became the county seat. The county was named after General "Mad Anthony" Wayne, who had won fame for his reckless courage during the Revolutionary War.

The 1800's. Detroit was incorporated as a town in 1802. Fire destroyed the entire settlement in 1805. In rebuilding their community, the people followed a street plan suggested by the layout of Washington, D.C. In 1806, Detroit was incorporated as a city.

British forces captured the city during the War of 1812 and held it briefly. Detroit served as Michigan's first capital from 1837 until 1847, when Lansing became the capital. The opening of the Erie Canal in 1825 provided a cheap water route between the East and Northwest. Thousands of settlers moved to Detroit from New York and New England, and the city became a commercial center.

In 1855, the Soo Canals were completed on the United States-Canadian border, and shipping on the Great Lakes increased. This traffic aided the growth of industry in Detroit, and the city's population climbed to 45,600 by 1860. At that time, Detroit served mainly as a marketing center for the farm products of the area. After the Civil War ended in 1865, manufacturing became the city's chief activity. By 1880, Detroit had 116,000 people and more than 900 factories.

The 1900's. During the early 1900's, a group of Detroit businessmen helped make the city the center of the nation's automobile industry. These men included Henry Ford, John and Horace Dodge, and Ransom E. Olds. The automobile industry grew rapidly in Detroit, partly because the city had a large labor supply. In addition, land and lake routes made it easy and cheap to bring raw materials to Detroit. Between 1900 and 1910, the city's population rose from 285,704 to 465,766.

During World War I (1914-1918), Detroit produced airplane motors, armored vehicles, and trucks for the Allies. Detroit's population soared and reached over $1\frac{1}{2}$ million by 1930. The city suffered widespread unemployment during the Great Depression of the 1930's. In 1935, the United Automobile Workers (UAW) was organized in Detroit. A UAW strike in 1937 caused General Motors to recognize the union and greatly strengthened the labor movement in the United States.

During World War II, the city's automobile plants switched to the manufacture of military products, including artillery, jeeps, and ships. The war created thousands of jobs in Detroit. Many persons from other parts of the United States, including great numbers of Negroes from the South, came to the city seeking work. In 1943, fighting between blacks and whites led to a riot. Thirty-four persons were killed and more than 1,000 were injured in the outbreak. By 1950, the city's population had reached 1,849,568.

Recent Developments. Detroit's rapid population growth created several problems. Schools became overcrowded, crime increased, and race relations grew more tense. Detroit began many urban renewal projects during the 1950's and 1960's. Slums were cleared in 17 areas, and the city erected nine large, low-rent housing developments and a medical center. The $106-million Civic Center was built along the waterfront.

A trend toward suburban living developed in the 1950's, and thousands of white middle-class families moved from Detroit to new developments outside the city. Detroit's population fell to 1,670,144 by 1960 and continued to drop during the 1960's.

In July, 1967, rioting broke out in a chiefly Negro section of Detroit. Rioters burned buildings, looted stores, and shot at policemen and firemen. National Guardsmen and U.S. Army troops helped restore order. The riot lasted a week and resulted in 43 deaths and property damage of $45 million.

Large renewal projects continued in Detroit during the 1970's. Construction of Elmwood Park, a housing development, started in 1961 on 500 acres (200 hectares) of a cleared slum area. Completion was scheduled for the late 1970's. In 1973, work began on a $500-million riverfront project. Plans call for the construction of apartment buildings, hotels, office buildings, and stores.

In 1973, Detroit voters elected Coleman A. Young mayor. Young, a Democrat, became the first black mayor of Detroit. The city's economy suffered in 1974 and 1975 because of a nationwide recession and a sharp decline in automobile production. WILLIAM C. TREMBLAY

See also CADILLAC, ANTOINE DE LA MOTHE; FORD (family); GENERAL MOTORS CORPORATION.

DETROIT, UNIVERSITY OF, is a private coeducational school in Detroit, Mich. It includes colleges of arts and sciences, architecture and environmental studies, business and administration, dentistry, engineering, and law. It also has a graduate division. It was founded by the Roman Catholic Society of Jesus in 1877 as Detroit College. It is managed by a board of trustees composed of laymen and priests. For the enrollment, see UNIVERSITIES AND COLLEGES (table). MALCOLM CARRON

DETROIT DAM stands on the North Santiam River about 45 miles (72 kilometers) southeast of Salem, Ore. It is a concrete gravity-type dam 454 feet (138 meters) high and 1,528 feet (466 meters) long. The reservoir holds 455,000 acre-feet (561 million cubic meters) of water. The dam's powerhouse has a capacity of 100,000 kilowatts. Completed in 1953, the dam is used for flood control, navigation, and power purposes. T. W. MERMEL

DETROIT INSTITUTE OF TECHNOLOGY. See UNIVERSITIES AND COLLEGES (table).

DETROIT RIVER connects Lake Saint Clair and Lake Erie. It carries more shipping than almost any other river in North America. This river forms part of the boundary between Michigan and the province of Ontario, Canada. The Detroit is sometimes called the *Dardanelles of America* because it serves the same purpose as the Dardanelles, which connects the Aegean Sea and Sea of Marmara. Boats passing through the Detroit River carry much of the grain shipped from the northwestern United States. They also carry iron ore shipped from Minnesota, Wisconsin, and northern Michigan. The Detroit River is 25 miles (40 kilometers) long, and from one-half mile to 3 miles (0.8 to 5 kilometers) wide. The upper section contains islands which have been used as summer resorts. The banks of the river are lined with warehouses and factories of Detroit, Mich., and Windsor, Ont. An international bridge spans the river at Detroit. GEORGE MACINKO

DEUCALION, *doo KAY lih un,* was the "Noah" of Greek mythology. He was the son of Prometheus, and, according to some authorities, his mother was Pandora (see PANDORA; PROMETHEUS). When Zeus decided to destroy mankind by floods because of its wickedness, Prometheus warned Deucalion and his wife Pyrrha. He told them to build a wooden ark. They floated in this ark for nine days, until they landed on the top of Mount Parnassus. When the water went down, they were the only living creatures left on the earth.

Deucalion and Pyrrha asked the oracle at Delphi how they might restore mankind. The Oracle told them to "throw the bones of their mother." They guessed this to mean stones, the bones of mother earth. The stones Deucalion threw became men, and those that Pyrrha threw became women. Deucalion became the ancestor of the Greeks through his son Hellen, for whom the Hellenes (Greeks) were named. The grave of Deucalion was said to be visible in the city of Athens in the ancient temple of Zeus. H. L. STOW

DEUTERIUM, *doo TIHR ee uhm,* or *dyoo TIHR ee uhm,* also called HEAVY HYDROGEN, is a stable isotope of hydrogen (see ISOTOPE). Its chemical symbol is D or H^2. Deuterium is an important part of the hydrogen bomb, and is used in research in biochemistry and atomic physics. About 1 part in 6,700 parts of all normal hydrogen is deuterium.

Properties. The mass of an atom of deuterium is about twice that of a normal hydrogen atom. The nucleus of an ordinary hydrogen atom contains only a proton. A hydrogen atom has the atomic weight, 1.007825. The nucleus of a deuterium atom, called a *deuteron,* contains a proton and a neutron. Deuterium has an atomic weight of 2.01410. Deuterium and ordinary hydrogen have one electron. Chemically, deuterium reacts in the same way as ordinary hydrogen. But it generally reacts more slowly and less completely. Deuterium combines with oxygen to form *deuterium oxide* (D_2O), commonly called *heavy water* (see HEAVY WATER). Deuterium oxide may be used as a *moderator* in atomic reactors to reduce the speed of neutrons in a nuclear chain reaction.

Uses. Scientists frequently use deuterium to study organic and biochemical reactions. The heavy hydrogen atom serves as an *isotopic tracer.* A carbon atom can be *tagged* (labeled) by substituting the deuterium isotope for one or more of the associated hydrogen atoms. After the organic or biochemical reaction is completed, the deuterium can be located by the density of water produced, or by spectroscopic studies. This enables scientists to tell exactly how the reaction took place.

Atomic scientists use deuterons as bombarding particles in atomic reactors. A cyclotron may accelerate their energy up to many millions, or even billions, of electron volts. When these particles hit the target material, they alter the composition of its atoms and form another element or a new isotope of the original element (see CYCLOTRON; TRANSMUTATION OF ELEMENTS).

Deuterium is an important ingredient in the hydrogen bomb. *Tritium,* an isotope of hydrogen with an atomic weight of 3, is unstable. When a mixture of deuterium and tritium is triggered by an atomic explosion, a *thermonuclear* (heat-induced) chain reaction takes place. The atoms of the hydrogen isotopes fuse with each other and release energy (see FUSION; HYDROGEN BOMB).

Discovery. Harold C. Urey, an American chemist, announced his discovery of deuterium in 1932. Urey applied Niels Bohr's theories of the atom to the hydrogen atom (see BOHR, NIELS). He distilled liquid hydrogen and detected deuterium in the liquid remaining. Urey received the Nobel prize in 1934 for his discovery. Gilbert N. Lewis, a chemist at the University of California, first separated deuterium oxide from ordinary water in 1932. HAROLD C. UREY

See also HYDROGEN; ISOTOPE; TRITIUM; UREY, HAROLD C.

DEUTERON. See DEUTERIUM.

DEUTERONOMY, *DYOO ter AHN oh mih,* is the fifth book of the Bible, and the last of the Pentateuch, or Five Books of Moses. Its name comes from a Greek word meaning *the second law.* The book contains Moses' last words to the Israelites as they prepared to enter the Promised Land. In this important hour, Moses repeated and added to many of the laws found in the earlier books of the Bible. The most famous example is the Ten Commandments, which appear in Exodus (20: 3-17) and in Deuteronomy (5: 7-21) with several changes.

Deuteronomy contains four main sections: (1) *The orations* (chapters 1 to 11) review the history of the Hebrew people in order to emphasize God's love for them and to urge them to be loyal to His Law. (2) *The laws* (12-25) deal with all areas of life. They range from rituals for religious festivals to regulations concerning family living. (3) *The great warning* (26-29) emphasizes that only obedience to God's Law can bring national well-being, and that disobedience brings disaster. A description of Moses' preparations for his death follows this section. (4) *The song of Moses* (32) stresses the relationship of love and loyalty between God and Israel, and *the blessing of Moses* (33) tells the future destiny of the tribes of Israel. The book ends with a moving account of Moses' death.

Many scholars believe that the book of Deuteronomy, or a part of it, was the book of the Law found in the Temple in Jerusalem in 621 B.C. The book of Kings tells how this book of law became the basis for a great religious reformation during the reign of King Josiah of Judah (about 639-608 B.C.). ROBERT GORDIS

See also PENTATEUCH; MOSES; JOSIAH.

DEUTSCHE MARK. See MARK.

DEUTSCHLAND. See GERMANY.

DEUTSCHLAND ÜBER ALLES, or *Germany Over All*, became Germany's national anthem in 1922. Germany was divided into west and east sections at the end of World War II. In 1952, the third stanza of *Deutschland über Alles* (*Das Deutschlandlied*) became West Germany's anthem. East Germany's anthem is an entirely different song (see GERMANY [Facts in Brief]). Hoffmann von Fallersleben wrote *Deutschland über Alles* in 1841.

DEUTZIA, *DYUT see uh*, is a shrub related to the hydrangea. It has clusters of white, pink, or purplish flowers. They bloom in spring or early summer, and usually have five petals. The leaves, which are new each year, have small teeth along the edges and are covered with a rough fuzz. Deutzias came from Asia, but grow well in North America and other northern regions. They make fine garden borders.

J. Horace McFarland

Deutzia Gracilis

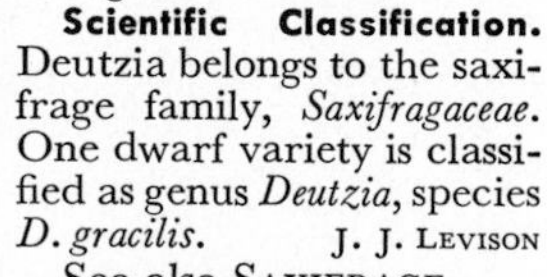

Scientific Classification. Deutzia belongs to the saxifrage family, *Saxifragaceae*. One dwarf variety is classified as genus *Deutzia*, species *D. gracilis*. J. J. LEVISON

See also SAXIFRAGE.

DE VACA. See CABEZA DE VACA, ÁLVAR NÚÑEZ.

DE VALERA, *DEV uh LAIR uh*, **EAMON** (1882-), a leader in Ireland's fight to win independence, served three times as prime minister after 1937, and was elected president of Ireland in 1959 and 1966. He was president of the Irish Free State from 1932 to 1937.

De Valera was born in New York City, of a Spanish father and an Irish mother. He spent his childhood in Ireland and became a leader in the unsuccessful Easter Rebellion in 1916. A British court sentenced him to death, but the sentence was changed to life imprisonment because he was American-born. He was released in 1917, and was elected to the British Parliament. The Sinn Féin convention in 1917 elected him "President of the Irish Republic," a paper organization. He was sent to prison in 1918. He escaped in 1919 and went to the United States.

In 1921, De Valera took part in negotiations with the British government that established the Irish Free State. But this settlement divided Ireland, and he opposed it. In 1926, De Valera quit as president of Sinn Féin because the party refused to recognize the *Dáil Éireann* (Assembly of Ireland), whose members had to take an oath of allegiance to the British Crown. He then formed the *Fianna Fáil* (Soldiers of Destiny) party, which won control of the government in 1932. He was prime minister of Ireland from 1937 to 1948, from 1951 to 1954, and from 1957 to 1959. ALFRED F. HAVIGHURST

Miller Services, Ltd.

Eamon de Valera

See also IRELAND (History); SINN FÉIN.

DE VALOIS, *d' val WAH*, **DAME NINETTE** (1898-), founded Great Britain's Royal Ballet and served as its director until her retirement in 1963. She was born in County Wicklow, Ireland, and trained to be a dancer. In 1926, she opened a school in London and began producing dances for the plays of Shakespeare. The group was first called the Vic-Wells, then the Sadler's Wells Ballet, after the theaters where the company danced. In 1956, the company became The Royal Ballet under a charter that was granted by Queen Elizabeth II.

Dame Ninette *choreographed* (composed) several dramatic ballets, including *The Rake's Progress* (1935) and *Checkmate* (1937). She was made a Dame of the British Empire in 1951. SELMA JEANNE COHEN

DEVALUATION is a method of reducing the value of a currency. Many countries have devalued their currencies in attempts to stop falling prices at home and to improve their competitive positions in world trade. Great Britain devalued the worth of the pound from $4.03 to $2.80 in 1949 and from $2.80 to $2.40 in 1967, thus cutting each time the price of British goods in other countries. Britain hoped to increase its sales to other countries and to earn enough money to pay for its imports. The United States devalued the dollar by 41 per cent in 1934. The United States also devalued the dollar in 1972—by about 8 per cent and again in 1973 by 10 per cent. Both devaluations were intended primarily to improve the U.S. balance of payments. See also BALANCE OF PAYMENTS; MONEY (International Reserves); GREAT BRITAIN (Devaluation). LEONARD C. R. LANGER

DEVELOPING. See PHOTOGRAPHY.

DEVELOPING COUNTRY. See UNDERDEVELOPED COUNTRY.

DEVELOPMENTAL PSYCHOLOGY is the study of changes in behavior as we grow from infancy to old age. Many developmental psychologists study only a part of the lifespan. Most of them are chiefly interested in childhood, the period between birth and the early 20's.

There are four main theories of child development that psychologists use in research on the behavior of children: (1) maturational theory, (2) psychoanalytic theory, (3) learning theory, and (4) cognitive theory.

Maturational Theory states that the chief principle of developmental change is *maturation*, which means physiological "ripening," especially of the nervous system. Arnold L. Gesell, the leading American supporter of this theory, found that the growing child's behavior seems to follow a set developmental pattern. He described in detail the ways in which behavior changes with age. Gesell believed that differences among people result more from heredity than from environment. See GESELL, ARNOLD L.

Psychoanalytic Theory is based on Sigmund Freud's theory of psychoanalysis. According to Freud, the child is driven by impulses of sex and aggression. The child develops through a complicated interaction between his needs, based on sexual impulses, and the demands of his environment. Environmental demands are represented first by loving and restricting parents, and later by the child's own version of his parents' demands. See LIBIDO; PSYCHOANALYSIS.

Anna Freud, Erik Erikson, and others have modified Freud's theory and applied it to child behavior. In the psychoanalytic view of development, the child changes through conflict, chiefly between his own impulses and the demands of reality. A successful solution of this conflict brings normal development, and an unsuccessful solution may lead to mental illness.

Learning Theory says a child's development depends mainly on his experience with reward and punishment. The child must learn certain responses—such as speech, manners, and attitudes—to adults. He learns these responses through their association with *reinforcement* (any condition that makes learning occur). If a child's mother smiles at him each time he is polite to adults, her smile reinforces his learning of manners. The task of the parent or teacher is to arrange the environment to provide suitable and effective reinforcements for desired behavior.

Learning theorists base their ideas on two basic learning experiments—studies of classical conditioning by Ivan P. Pavlov and studies of instrumental conditioning by E. L. Thorndike and B. F. Skinner (see LEARNING [How We Learn]; THORNDIKE, EDWARD L.). Maturation and heredity have relatively little importance in the learning theory of development.

Cognitive Theory regards the child as an active solver of problems. Cognitive theorists emphasize the role of a child's natural motivation as the key factor in his development. This motivation can include the child's desire to satisfy his curiosity, master challenging tasks, or reduce the inconsistencies and ambiguities he finds in the world about him. According to cognitive theory, the child forms his own theories about the world and the relationships among its different aspects. His theories are primitive at first, but after he tests them against his experience, the theories become more realistic.

Comprehensive cognitive theories of development have been proposed by Kurt Koffka, Heinz Werner, and Jean Piaget. Piaget described in detail how the growing child changes his ideas about number, cause, time, space, and morality. First, the child represents the world in terms of his own activities. Then he moves to a limited set of generalizations based on his knowledge of specific cases. Finally, he gains the ability to make valid and abstract generalizations about the nature of reality.

Maturity and Old Age. In general, the study of maturity and old age has been based on observation. There have been no clear theoretical principles to guide psychologists in the search for consistent patterns of development.

Scientists have established that sensory *acuity* (keenness), speed of response, productivity in art and science, and the ability to process new information decline with age, particularly after the late 50's. Less well documented are declines in memory and in the ability to solve familiar kinds of problems. Psychologists know little about the most remarkable fact of old age—that some persons go through a degrading decline with the passage of years, and others remain capable and active until the end of their lives. WILLIAM KESSEN

Related Articles in WORLD BOOK include:

Adolescence	Freud, Sigmund	Personality
Baby	Koffka, Kurt	Psychology
Behavior	Motivation	Teen Age
Child		

DEVIATION INDICATOR. See AIRCRAFT INSTRUMENTS.

DEVIATION OF THE COMPASS. See COMPASS.

DEVIL is an evil spirit. The word *devil* comes from the Greek, and means *slanderer* or *false accuser*. The ancient Hebrew word for *devil* was *Satan*. Early men believed that the harmful forces of nature were demons and evil spirits. They blamed demons for all their troubles.

In the Old Testament, Satan is not God's opponent. Instead, he searches out men's sins, and accuses mankind before God. In the Apocrypha, Satan is the author of all evil, and rules over a host of angels. In the New Testament, Satan's other names include devil, enemy, and Beelzebub. In the Middle Ages, he was usually represented with horns, a tail, and cloven hoofs.

Most religions have a devil or devils. Early Buddhists called the devil *Mara*. Zoroastrians first called the devil *Angra Mainyu*, or *lying mind*. Later, they personified him as *Ahriman*. They believe that Ahura-Mazda, their god, will defeat Ahriman at the end of history. The Moslem devil, *Iblis*, was an angel who rebelled when Adam was created, refusing to bow down to a creature made of earth. Moslems believe Iblis became the tempter and enemy of man. FLOYD H. ROSS

See also BEELZEBUB; DEVIL WORSHIP; LUCIFER; MEPHISTOPHELES.

DEVIL WORSHIP is part of the religion of certain tribes in Africa, Asia, and South America. Devil dances played a large part in demon worship in Tibet, both before and after the coming of Buddhism. Devil worshipers believe that the powers of evil are as great as the powers of good. They believe that the devil is an evil god and that he can harm those who refuse to worship him.

Devil worship seems to arise out of two human needs. One is for men to deal with the evil forces they believe are present in the world. The other is a desire to act out some of the evil forces that men vaguely sense in themselves but cannot deal with consciously.

People have often used the phrase *devil worshipers* to describe people who worship gods different from their own. The early Christians regarded most other religions as the worship of devils, indicating a lack of understanding of these religions. FLOYD H. ROSS

See also ANIMISM; DEVIL.

DEVILFISH. See OCTOPUS; OCEAN (color picture).

DEVILLE, HENRI ÉTIENNE SAINTE-CLAIRE. See ALUMINUM (Henri Étienne Sainte-Claire Deville).

DEVILS ISLAND. See FRENCH GUIANA.

DEVILS LAKE, N. Dak. (pop. 7,078), is a distribution and trade center for the north-central part of the state. It lies about 130 miles (209 kilometers) northeast of Bismarck. The State School for the Deaf is located in Devils Lake. The region contains the Fort Totten Indian Reservation, a state historic site. For location, see NORTH DAKOTA (political map). RUSSELL REID

DEVIL'S PAINTBRUSH is a wild flower also called *orange hawkweed.* A cluster of orange-red flower heads grows on a leafless stem, sometimes 28 inches (71 centimeters) high. Oblong leaves grow around the bottom of the stem. The paintbrush appearance comes from a row of bristles attached to the ripening seeds. Devil's paintbrush grows in Europe and eastern North America.

Scientific Classification. Devil's paintbrush belongs to the composite family, *Compositae.* It is genus *Hieracium,* species *H. aurantiacum.* JULIAN A. STEYERMARK

DEVILS POSTPILE NATIONAL MONUMENT is in the Sierra National Forest in east-central California. The monument contains a spectacular mass of blue-gray basalt columns. The columns resemble a pile of posts. They tower 60 feet (18 meters) above the San Joaquin River. The 798.46-acre (323.13-hectare) monument was established in 1911. See also BASALT (picture).

DEVILS TOWER NATIONAL MONUMENT is in northeastern Wyoming. It contains a tower of volcanic rock that rises 865 feet (264 meters) from the hills bordering the Belle Fourche River. The 1,347-acre (545-hectare) monument, established in 1906, was the first national monument in the United States. See also WYOMING (picture: Devils Tower).

DEVIL'S TRIANGLE. See BERMUDA TRIANGLE.

DEVLIN, BERNADETTE JOSEPHINE (1947-), is a civil rights leader of the Roman Catholic minority in Northern Ireland. She was elected to the British Parliament in 1969. At 21, Devlin became the youngest woman ever to be a member of Parliament. But she was defeated in her bid for reelection in 1974.

Wide World

Bernadette Devlin

Devlin was born in Cookstown and graduated from Queen's University in Belfast. As a college student, she helped organize a nonviolent civil rights group called People's Democracy. Catholics in Northern Ireland have long sought economic and political equality with Protestants, who control the government.

Devlin grew impatient for reforms. In 1969, she and other Catholic protesters fought policemen and Protestants during riots in Londonderry. She served four months in jail for her part in the riots. After her release, she announced that she would work to unite northern and southern Ireland under a socialist government. In 1973, Devlin married Michael McAlaskey, a schoolteacher. JOHN MAGEE

DEVOLUTION, WAR OF. See AIX-LA-CHAPELLE, TREATIES OF.

DEVON. See ENGLAND (political map).

DEVONIAN PERIOD, *duh VOH nee uhn,* in geology, is a period of the earth's history. It began approximately 405 million years ago and lasted for 60 million years. During this time, seas covered the continents, laying down thick sediment that became rock. The Devonian Period has been called *the age of fishes.* See also EARTH (table: Outline of Earth History).

DEVONSHIRE, DUKE OF (1868-1938), VICTOR CHRISTIAN WILLIAM CAVENDISH, served as governor general of Canada from 1916 to 1921. He was treasurer to the household of Queen Victoria in 1900, and of King Edward VII from 1901 to 1903. He served as British secretary of state for the colonies from 1922 to 1924. He was born in England. LUCIEN BRAULT

DE VOTO, BERNARD AUGUSTINE (1897-1955), an American editor and critic, became well known for his histories of the western frontier. He won the Pulitzer prize for *Across the Wide Missouri* in 1948. He also wrote a history, *The Year of Decision: 1846,* and *Literary Fallacy,* a criticism of fiction writing. He wrote fiction under the name John August. He wrote his books like a straight-talking frontiersman. De Voto promoted conservation in a column, "The Easy Chair," in *Harper's* magazine. He served as editor of *The Saturday Review of Literature* from 1936 to 1938. De Voto was born in Ogden, Utah, on Jan. 11, 1897. EDWIN H. CADY

DE VRIES, HUGO (1848-1935), a Dutch botanist and student of organic evolution, was known primarily as the author of the *mutation theory* (see MUTATION). This theory states that new species of plants and animals arise by *mutations* (sudden transformations) which might appear at any time and are then continued from generation to generation. De Vries' work stimulated research on heredity and evolution. However, mutations as conspicuous as those he described in the evening primrose were later proved to be the exception rather than the rule. Born in Haarlem, The Netherlands, De Vries became famous with the publication of *The Mutation Theory* (1900-1903). ROGERS MCVAUGH

DEW is the name given to the tiny, glistening drops of water that often appear on plants and blades of grass early on clear mornings.

Formation of Dew. Dew forms when moist air is cooled by direct contact with cold objects out in the open. This process is called *condensation.* Such things as blades of grass, leaves, or outside wires receive heat from the sun during the day by direct radiation (see RADIATION [How Radiation Affects Life on the Earth]). The heat also evaporates moisture into the air. These objects lose the heat again at night, also through radiation. Since radiation is most effective on clear nights, objects in the open cool down faster when the sky is clear than when it is cloudy. As the objects cool, the air next to them cools too. When this air reaches the *dew point,* it can no longer hold all the moisture present (see DEW POINT). It deposits this excess moisture as dew. When the temperature falls below the freezing point, *frost* forms instead of dew.

Dew forms best on still, clear nights. When the wind is blowing, the air cannot stay in contact with cool objects long enough to cool to the dew point. When the sky is cloudy, the earth and objects in exposed places lose heat more slowly than when the sky is clear.

Where Dew Forms. Dew forms better on dark objects than on light-colored ones because dark objects radiate heat best. Dew also forms more readily on materials that conduct heat well, such as metal car tops, than on poor heat conductors, such as wooden poles.

Importance of Dew. In some places where rainfall is light, dew is important to plant growth. In Lima, Peru, for example, dew supplies more water than rain. Dew is often heavy in tropical regions where the air is moist and the nights cool. GEORGE F. TAYLOR

See also AIR (Moisture in Air); FROST.

DEW LINE, or DISTANT EARLY WARNING LINE, protects the United States and Canada against air attack from the north. It has 64 radar stations and extends 4,500 miles (7,240 kilometers) from the Aleutian Islands, across Canada, to Iceland. The original 3,000 miles (4,800 kilometers) of the DEW line is operated by the United States and Canada from North American Air Defense (NORAD) headquarters at Colorado Springs, Colo. NORAD and Space Surveillance (SPASUR) control the rest. SPASUR tracks objects in earth orbit. See RADAR (Radar Warning Systems; map).

DEW POINT is the temperature at which moisture in the air begins to condense. The dew point is either lower than the air temperature, or the same as the air temperature, when the relative humidity is 100 per cent. Dew forms when a thin film of air, in contact with the surface, is cooled to below the dew point. Cooling the air below its dew point causes dew on the surface or fog in the air, when the dew point is above the freezing temperature. If the air temperature and dew point are below freezing, frost may form on the surface, or ice crystals may form in the air. Fog and clouds occur when large volumes of air are cooled to below the dew point. PHIL E. CHURCH

See also CONDENSATION; DEW; FOG; FROST; HUMIDITY.

DEWAR, SIR JAMES. See VACUUM BOTTLE.

DEWBERRY is a trailing blackberry. It is not an erect bush, like other blackberries, but a bramble of long and willowy branches that trail on the ground or climb over other shrubs and fences. The dewberry is also called *running blackberry* and *ground blackberry.* The fruit is similar to that of the erect blackberries. However, dewberries tend to ripen earlier than most erect ones. New plants are raised from the tips of branches, which grow roots when they come in contact with the soil. The roots grow for many years, but the tops live only two years. The fruit grows on branches during the second year. Both wild and cultivated varieties grow well in the Southern States, in parts of the North, Midwest, and East, and along the Pacific.

Dr. C. C. Zych

Dewberries

Scientific Classification. The dewberry belongs to the rose family, *Rosaceae.* The southern dewberry is genus *Rubus,* species *R. trivialis.* REID M. BROOKS

DEWEY, GEORGE (1837-1917), an American naval officer, won fame as the *hero of Manila.* He was the only American ever to become Admiral of the Navy.

Dewey was in Hong Kong in command of the Asiatic Squadron when war broke out between Spain and the United States in 1898. He received orders on April 25 to go to the Philippine Islands and capture or destroy the Spanish fleet. Late on April 30, Dewey's six ships, led by the U.S.S. *Olympia,* approached Manila Bay. Early the next day Dewey gave the captain of the *Olympia* the famous command, "You may fire when you are ready, Gridley," and attacked the Spanish fleet of 10 cruisers and gunboats. By noon Dewey's force had destroyed the Spanish fleet without the loss of a single American life. This victory made the United States an important power in the Pacific Ocean, and inspired the confidence of the American people in the U.S. Navy.

Brown Bros.

Admiral George Dewey

After his victory Dewey remained in Manila Bay until troops arrived to capture Manila. When Dewey returned to New York City in 1899, he received a great welcome. The people of the country donated funds to buy a home for him in Washington, D.C. The Congress presented Dewey with a sword, and all his men were awarded medals.

Dewey was born in Montpelier, Vt. He studied at Norwich Military Academy and at the United States Naval Academy at Annapolis. Dewey saw his first wartime naval service in the Civil War. As a lieutenant, he became the executive officer of the U.S.S. *Mississippi* in David Farragut's fleet in 1861. He took part in the famous run past the forts that guarded New Orleans. Later, Dewey served on Farragut's flagship (see FARRAGUT, DAVID G.).

Dewey became president of the newly created General Board of the Navy Department in 1900, and the next year he served as president of the Schley court of inquiry (see SCHLEY, WINFIELD SCOTT). He served as an honored adviser on all naval matters until his death. In 1925, Dewey's body was placed in the Washington Cathedral in Washington, D.C. DONALD W. MITCHELL

See also PHILIPPINES (War with Spain).

DEWEY, JOHN (1859-1952), was an American philosopher and educator. He helped lead a philosophical movement called *pragmatism* (see PRAGMATISM).

Dewey was strongly influenced by the then-new science of psychology and by the theory of evolution proposed by the English scientist Charles R. Darwin. Dewey came to regard intelligence as a power that man uses when he faces a conflict or challenge. He believed that man lives by custom and habit. In most situations, it is sufficient to think and act as we have done in the past, but some physical and social situations present problems calling for new responses. According to Dewey, man cannot solve such problems by habitual action and thought. He must use intelligence as an instrument for overcoming any obstacles. Dewey's philosophy is thus called *instrumentalism.*

Dewey believed that knowledge is a means of

controlling the environment, hopefully to improve the quality of human life. He wrote widely on art, democracy, education, philosophy, and science. In his writings, Dewey always focused on the same problem—how to close the gap between thought and action. Dewey's interpretation of science shows how thought and action are united. He considered science as a method for inquiring into the behavior of things. The results of such inquiry are the joint products of thought and activity. Dewey regarded *activity* as conducting experiments under controlled situations and *thought* as those theories that guide our experiments.

G. P. Putnam's Sons
John Dewey

In every area of life, Dewey called for experimenting and trying out new methods. As an educator, he opposed the traditional method of learning by memory under the authority of teachers. He believed that education should not be concerned only with the mind. Students should develop manual skills. Learning must be related to the interests of students and connected with current problems. Dewey declared that education must include a student's physical and moral well-being as well as his intellectual development.

In *Art as Experience* (1934), Dewey connected works of art with the experiences of everyday life. He wrote that daily experience can be glorious, joyous, sad, tedious, terrifying, and tragic. These, he said, are the qualities that architects, composers, painters, and writers seek to capture and express. Dewey regarded education as incomplete if it ignores these experiences.

Dewey was born in Burlington, Vt. He had a distinguished teaching career at several universities, especially at Columbia University from 1904 until his retirement in 1930. He was also active in humanitarian and social causes. Dewey's works include *Democracy and Education* (1916), *Reconstruction in Philosophy* (1920), and *Experience and Nature* (1925). JOHN E. SMITH

See also PROGRESSIVE EDUCATION.

DEWEY, MELVIL (1851-1931), an American librarian, began the decimal library-classification system (see DEWEY DECIMAL SYSTEM). He founded the American Library Association and the *Library Journal* in 1876 (see AMERICAN LIBRARY ASSOCIATION). He became chief librarian of Columbia University in 1883, and established the first library school there in 1887. He served as director of the New York State Library from 1889 to 1906. He was born in Adams Center, N.Y. R. B. DOWNS

DEWEY, NELSON. See WISCONSIN (Statehood).

DEWEY, THOMAS EDMUND (1902-1971), a prosecuting attorney and Republican politician, served as governor of New York from 1943 to 1954. He ran unsuccessfully for President of the United States on the Republican ticket in 1944 and 1948. His running mates for Vice-President were John Bricker and Earl Warren.

Dewey was born on March 24, 1902, in Owosso, Mich. He was graduated from the University of Michigan, and finished his law course at Columbia University in two years. In 1933, he became United States attorney for the southern district of New York state. Governor Herbert Lehman appointed him special prosecutor for vice and racket investigations in New York City in 1935. Dewey's vigorous and successful prosecution of organized crime brought him wide recognition.

United Press Int.
Thomas E. Dewey

He was defeated for the New York governorship in 1938, but was elected in 1942, the first Republican governor of the state in 20 years. He was re-elected in 1946 and 1950, but did not seek office in 1954. Dewey's defeat in the 1948 presidential election was considered a major political upset. Dewey returned to his private law practice in 1955. RICHARD L. WATSON, JR.

DEWEY DECIMAL SYSTEM is the most widely used method of classifying books in a library. It is named for Melvil Dewey, who developed it in 1876 (see DEWEY, MELVIL). This system classifies books by dividing them into 10 main groups. Each of these different classes is represented by figures, as in the following table:

000-099	Generalities (encyclopedias, bibliographies, periodicals, journalism)
100-199	Philosophy and Related Disciplines (conduct)
200-299	Religion
300-399	The Social Sciences (economics, sociology, civics, law, education, vocations, customs)
400-499	Language (language, dictionaries, grammar)
500-599	Pure Sciences (mathematics, astronomy, physics, chemistry, geology, paleontology, biology, zoology, botany)
600-699	Technology (medicine, engineering, agriculture, home economics, business, radio, television, aviation)
700-799	The Arts (architecture, sculpture, painting, music, photography, recreation)
800-899	Literature (novels, poetry, plays, criticism)
900-999	General Geography and History

Each of these 10 main classes is broken up into more specialized fields. For example, class 600-699, Technology, is subdivided into 10 special classes. Each of these divisions is further subdivided. The numbers 630-639, for example, represent Agriculture, and are subdivided into such classes as Field Crops, Garden Crops, and Dairy and Related Technologies. When the classification becomes very fine, decimals are used. For example, books on useful insects, such as bees and silkworms, would be grouped under 638. Books on beekeeping would be in 638.1, and those on silkworms in 638.2.

Some libraries, such as the Library of Congress, do not use the Dewey Decimal System. They have their own classifications. RALPH A. ULVELING

DEXEDRINE SULFATE. See AMPHETAMINE.

DEXTRIN, *DEKS trin,* is a sticky substance formed during the chemical breakdown of starch. Some dextrins are used in industry as a *mucilage* (glue) on postage stamps and envelopes. Manufacturers also use dextrins in *sizing* (stiffening) paper and textiles. These commercial dextrins are produced by treating starch with heat or acid or both.

Dextrins are also produced in the human body. During digestion, starch-containing foods are broken down into dextrins and other products. Starch is also converted into dextrins during the baking of foods. DEXTER FRENCH

See also STARCH.

DEXTROSE, *DEKS trohs,* is the name used in industry for pure, crystalline glucose sugar. It is usually sold in the form of fine, white *granules* (grains). Dextrose is produced commercially by putting starch in water mixed with dilute hydrochloric acid. When this mixture is heated to about 130° C under about 40 pounds of steam pressure per square inch (2.8 kilograms per square centimeter) in a converter, it changes to glucose. Glucose can be purified and dried to fine granules called dextrose. As a pure white sugar, dextrose is used mainly in candy, baked goods, and canned fruit. The taste of dextrose is not as sweet as that of the common table sugar called *sucrose*. See also GLUCOSE. DEXTER FRENCH

DHAULAGIRI. See HIMALAYA; MOUNTAIN (table).

DHOLE. See DOG (Wild Dogs).

DHOTI. See INDIA (Clothing).

DHOW. See TRANSPORTATION (Transportation in Other Lands); SHIP (Sailing Ships in the 1900's).

DIABASE. See BASALT.

DIABETES, *DY uh BEE tihs,* is the name of two diseases that have the same sign, excessive urination. *Diabetes mellitus,* the more common of the two, occurs when the pancreas does not produce enough of the hormone *insulin* (see PANCREAS). *Diabetes insipidus* results when the *posterior lobe* (rear portion) of the pituitary gland or the *hypothalamus,* a part of the brain, does not function normally.

Diabetes Mellitus is characterized by the presence of abnormal amounts of sugar in the blood and by sugar in the urine. Insulin enables the body to store and burn the sugar in food properly. When the pancreas does not produce enough insulin, the body cannot use or store sugar normally. Excess sugar accumulates in the blood. The kidneys give off some of this sugar into the urine. The way fat and protein are used is also abnormal in diabetes mellitus, and excessive amounts of the products of their breakdown appear in the blood and urine.

The Signs and Symptoms, besides the presence of too much sugar and other products in the blood and urine, may include great thirst, passing large amounts of urine, loss of weight, and loss of strength. Untreated diabetics have a tendency toward attacks of boils, carbuncles, and other infections. The disease also causes decreased blood circulation in the limbs. This may result in gangrene.

Treatment. Diabetes cannot be cured. But the disease can be controlled by injections of insulin and careful attention to diet. Many diabetics live almost as long as people of normal health. Every diabetic should be under a doctor's care. The patient should learn to test his urine for sugar, and keep a record of his diet, weight, and urine sugar.

Some mild cases of diabetes can be controlled by diet alone. The diabetic should not eat foods high in sugar, such as candy, cake, and jam. Special foods that contain little or no added sugar are available. The diet can be pleasing and varied if the patient is careful about the food he chooses. He should carefully select foods that contain needed vitamins and minerals.

Even when a diabetic uses insulin, he must watch his diet carefully. The amount of insulin given depends on weight, diet, amount of exercise, severity of the disease, and general health. Most diabetics, including small children, give themselves injections of insulin with hypodermic needles.

Insulin, the natural antidiabetic hormone, must be given by injection, because if taken by mouth it is destroyed in the digestive system. Scientists have developed several drugs that some diabetics can take by mouth. These drugs stimulate the pancreas to produce some insulin. They are taken if diet cannot control the blood sugar level and if injections are considered unnecessary. Some physicians believe the drugs are harmful.

Diabetes Insipidus is characterized by the excessive passing of urine. Because the patient loses so much water, he becomes very thirsty. This condition results when the body has insufficient amounts of the hormone *vasopressin,* also called *antidiuretic hormone.* This hormone is produced by the hypothalamus and stored in and released by the posterior pituitary. Damage to either of these organs can cause diabetes insipidus. Without vasopressin, the kidneys cannot hold back water that passes to them from the blood. Diabetes insipidus cannot be cured, but it can be controlled by injections of vasopressin.

The American Diabetes Association sponsors research and conducts public education primarily in the field of diabetes mellitus. The headquarters of the American Diabetes Association are at 1 West 48th Street, New York, N.Y. 10020. CHARLES H. BEST

See also INSULIN; CORI; DISEASE (table: U.S. Deaths from Major Diseases); FEHLING'S SOLUTION; GLAND (The Endocrine Glands).

DIABLO DAM is part of the Seattle power system on the Skagit River in northwestern Washington. This power project lies in the high, wooded slopes of Mount Baker National Forest near Pyramid Peak. Diablo is an arch dam, 389 feet (119 meters) high and 1,180 feet (360 meters) long. The reservoir holds 90,000 acre-feet (111 million cubic meters) of water. It was completed in 1930. The powerhouse was completed in 1936, and has a capacity of 122,400 kilowatts. T. W. MERMEL

See also DAM (Masonry Dams); ROSS DAM.

DIACRITICAL MARK, *DY uh KRIT ih kuhl,* is a sign used with letters of the alphabet to show pronunciation or meaning of words. Diacritical marks are a regular part of spelling in many foreign languages (see the Key to Pronunciation at front of the A volume). But in English, their use is almost entirely restricted to showing pronunciation in dictionaries. Diacritical marks in English include the *circumflex* (written as ^ as in ôrder); the *dieresis* (¨ as in fär, rüle); the *macron* (¯ as in āge, ēqual, īce, ōpen, ūse); the *tilde* (~ as in cãre); the *single dot* (˙ as in tėrm, pu̇t); and the *schwa* (ə as in əbout, takən, pencəl, lemən, circəs).

DIAGHILEV, *DYAH gih lef,* **SERGEI PAVLOVICH** (1872-1929), was probably the greatest director in ballet history. He directed his own company, *Les Ballets Russes de Diaghilev,* from its first performance in 1909 to its last in 1929. With his company, he won for ballet the status of a great contemporary art. Diaghilev persuaded great composers, *choreographers* (dance composers), dancers, and artists to collaborate on ballets. These included dancer Vaslav Nijinsky, composer Igor Stravinsky, artist Pablo Picasso, and choreographer Michel Fokine.

Diaghilev introduced several trends that greatly influenced modern ballet. For example, he began revivals of the ballets of the late 1800's with his production of *Sleeping Beauty* in 1921. One of his most famous productions was *The Rite of Spring*. The savage music of Stravinsky and choreography of Nijinsky caused the audience to riot at the opening of this ballet in 1913. Diaghilev was born in Perm, Russia. P. W. MANCHESTER

See also BALLET (Russian Ballet).

DIAGNOSIS, *DY uhg NOH sihs*, is the art by which doctors determine which diseases are affecting their patients. The X ray may be used to give a diagnosis of tuberculosis. A chemical analysis of the patient's urine is often taken to see if the patient has diabetes. Diagnosis is one of the most important branches of medicine.

There are many different types of diagnosis. A *biological* diagnosis is made by performing tests on animals with a sample of one of the patient's body fluids. A *clinical diagnosis* is made completely from symptoms. A *differential diagnosis* is one that compares symptoms of several diseases to see which one is most likely to be causing the trouble. One way of deciding what is wrong with a sick person is to decide what disease he does *not* have. The doctor compares the sick person's symptoms with the known symptoms of various diseases. All the diseases are weeded out until it is fairly certain that the patient could have only one disease. This is called *diagnosis by exclusion*. A *laboratory diagnosis* is made by studying the blood, urine, or other liquids of the body in a laboratory, as in the case of anemia and diabetes.

A *physical diagnosis* is made by looking at the patient for signs of disease apparent to the eye, such as rashes or broken bones, and examining the patient with the hands. Sometimes doctors will actually try to induce symptoms or make them worse, when they think a disease is present but cannot be sure because the symptoms are not definite enough. Another type of bacteriologic diagnosis involves the injection of sera and observing the change of appearance in the skin at the site of injection. For example, an injection of tuberculin is often given as a test for tuberculosis. The patient is susceptible to the disease if the injection makes him develop a local rash. A *tentative diagnosis* is sometimes made when the symptoms are not definite. The diagnosis is made, and the doctors give treatment for what they decide the disease to be, but they watch the patient closely for new symptoms.

When a patient is first seen, the doctor usually checks a few basic things immediately. He may look into the mouth to see if the patient's tongue is coated, or if his throat shows signs of an infection. He may listen to the patient's heart and lungs with a stethoscope, take his pulse, and examine his ears and eyes. All these things are part of a simple diagnosis. If the doctor hears something unusual in the heart action, for example, he may make further heart diagnosis with an electrocardiograph machine. Terminals of wire conducting very small amounts of electricity are fastened to the patient's arms and legs so that they register the way the heart functions and record the movement on a graph. Any irregular heart action will make an irregular line on the graph.

Modern methods of diagnosis have been aided by the invention of such devices as the stethoscope and the electrocardiograph, and by improvements in laboratory technique. If cancer is suspected, a small piece of tissue may be cut from the diseased part and examined in the laboratory to see if cancerous cells are present. Smears of body fluids can be examined underneath the microscope to identify the germ of a disease. AUSTIN SMITH

Related Articles in WORLD BOOK include:

Biopsy	Fluoroscope	Ophthalmoscope
Bronchoscope	Gastroscope	Spirometer
Electrocardiograph	Manometer	Stethoscope

DIAGRAMING, in grammar. See SENTENCE.

DIAL. See CLOCK; SUNDIAL.

DIAL, THE. See AMERICAN LITERATURE (The Transcendentalists).

DIALECT, *DY uh lehkt*, is the way people talk in a certain district of a country, or in a certain social class. Dialect differs from accepted speech patterns of the language. The people of New England will usually say "idear" instead of *idea*, "caah" instead of *car*, or "Bahstun" for *Boston*. This localized usage in pronunciation is part of the *dialect* of the people in that district. The use of certain words or expressions in a locality is also considered as part of the dialect.

Once it was not so easy to move about and talk with others as it is now. People living only a short distance apart spoke differently. Sometimes a group of people, such as cowboys, rivermen, or thieves, would develop a dialect as important as that of a region. Newspapers and the radio of today, by following standard usages, are helping to reduce these differences in speech.

Dialects have been preserved in literature for readers to enjoy and study. They are as much a part of local color as are geography and customs. Many authors have recognized this fact and become famous as a result. Among stories told in dialect are Mark Twain's stories of the Mississippi, Joel Chandler Harris' *Uncle Remus* stories of the Southern Negro, and Bret Harte's tales of the Western mining camps.

Dialects are even more marked in Great Britain. Some of them are London Cockney, Yorkshire, and Scottish. Rudyard Kipling immortalized the British soldiers' dialect in his stories and poems. Sir James Barrie was a master of Scottish dialect. The French language has several dialects, including Picard, Norman, Lorrain, and Walloon. CLARENCE STRATTON

See also IDIOM; LANGUAGE; SLANG.

DIALECTICAL MATERIALISM. See MATERIALISM; METAPHYSICS (Doctrines); PHILOSOPHY (Philosophy and Government).

DIAMETER, *dy AM uh tur*, in geometry, is the length of a straight line that crosses through the center of a circle or a sphere and touches its boundaries. *Diameter* is also the name of the line itself. The *radius* runs from the center to the boundary of a circle or sphere. It is half as long as a diameter.

When a microscope or telescope enlarges the apparent size of an object, the degree of magnification is expressed in *diameters*. HOLMES BOYNTON

See also CIRCLE; MICROSCOPE; SPHERE.

John Reader

Diamonds have been prized throughout history for their beauty and extreme hardness. Skilled cutters and polishers transform rough diamonds, such as those shown above, into brilliant jewels. Some of the world's most famous diamonds are pictured at the right. Each stone is shown about three-fourths its actual size.

DIAMOND is the hardest naturally occurring substance known to man, and also one of the most valuable. Because of its hardness, the diamond is the most enduring of all gem stones. In Europe and America the diamond is the traditional jewel for engagement and wedding rings. Diamonds are also used in industry for cutting, grinding, and boring. About 80 per cent of the world's diamonds are suitable only for industrial use.

What Diamonds Are. Diamonds are crystals formed almost entirely of carbon. Most diamonds have eight sides, which form a double pyramid. Some diamonds have as many as 12 sides. Others have six sides, forming a cube. Scientists believe diamonds were formed millions of years ago when carbon was subjected to great heat and pressure.

A diamond must be used to cut another diamond. But a diamond can be separated or broken with a severe blow because of its *cleavage*. Cleavage is a property some minerals have of splitting in certain directions and producing flat, even surfaces. A diamond will not dissolve in acid. But it can be destroyed when it is subjected to intense heat. If a diamond is heated in the presence of oxygen, it will burn and form carbon dioxide. If it is heated without oxygen, it will turn to graphite, a mineral so soft that it is used as a lubricant. Some diamonds glow when they are exposed to ultraviolet light.

Where Diamonds Are Found. Diamonds are among the most costly jewels in the world, partly because they are rare. Only four important diamond fields have been found—in Africa, India, Russia, and South America. Africa produces about 80 per cent of the world's supply. South Africa provides most of the diamonds used for jewelry. Zaire, in Central Africa, is a chief source of industrial diamonds. The earliest diamonds came from

The Louvre, Paris

Regent
The Louvre, Paris
140 carats
Found in India

Tiffany & Company

Tiffany
Tiffany & Company, New York City
128 carats
Found in South Africa

©By kind permission of the Controller of Her Majesty's Stationery Office, from Colorific

Cullinan I, or Star of Africa
British Crown Jewels, London
530 carats
Found in South Africa

Orloff
Diamond Treasury, Moscow
189 carats
Found in India

Arnaud de Rosnay from Peter Schub

Lee Boltin

Hope
Smithsonian Institution, Washington, D.C.
44 carats
Found in India

Baumgold Brothers

Earth Star
Baumgold Brothers, New York City
111 carats
Found in South Africa

Giraudon

Condé
Condé Museum, Chantilly, France
50 carats
Found in India

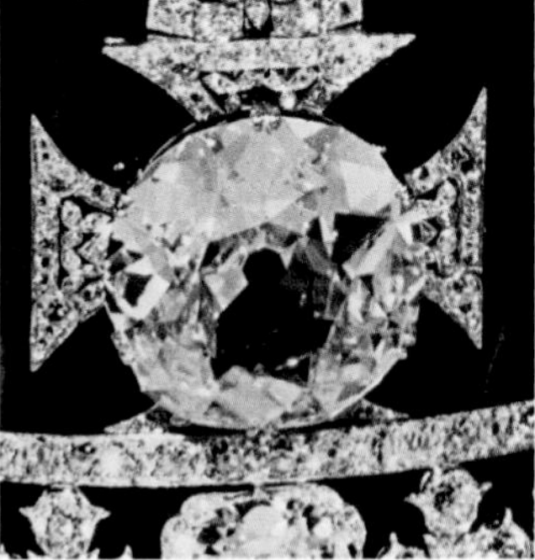
©By kind permission of the Controller of Her Majesty's Stationery Office, from Colorific

Koh-i-noor
British Crown Jewels, London
108 carats
Found in India

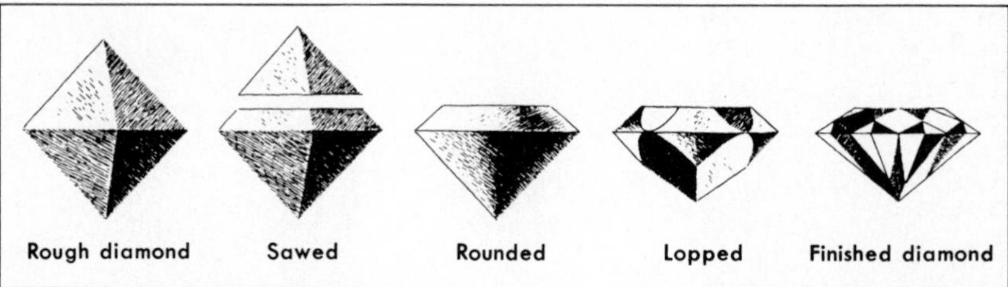

De Beers Consolidated Mines, Ltd.

N. W. Ayer & Son, Inc.

Diamond Cutting begins when skilled craftsmen saw a rough diamond in two. They use a thin circular saw that holds diamond dust. The corners are then rounded by rubbing together a spinning diamond and a stationary one. Later, cutters use the *lopping* process to grind *facets* (sides) on the stone. Lopping, *right,* involves carefully pressing the diamond against a rotating wheel coated with diamond dust. Most finished diamonds have 58 facets.

stream beds in India, but India produces few diamonds today. Russia supplies about 16 per cent of the world's diamonds. Its deposits lie in Siberia.

The first diamonds were found in the sand and gravel of stream beds. These are called *alluvial* diamonds. Later, diamonds were found deep in the earth, in rock formations, called *pipes*, thought to be the throats of extinct volcanoes. The rock in which diamonds are found is called *blue ground.* But even in the South African mines, the world's richest source of gem diamonds, many tons of blue ground must be taken from deep in the earth, crushed, and sorted to obtain one small diamond. Of the ore taken from these mines, only 1 *carat* (200 milligrams) out of 3 short tons (2.7 metric tons) of blue ground is diamond.

The diamond fields of South Africa were discovered in about 1866, when a Boer farmer's children found "a pretty pebble" in the sandy bed of the Vaal River. The "pebble" proved to be a diamond that was worth $2,500.

In the United States, single alluvial diamonds have been found in widely separated places. The only diamond mine in the United States is located near Murfreesboro, Ark. See ARKANSAS (color picture).

How Diamonds Are Cut to Make Jewels. Diamonds have great power to reflect light, bend rays of light, and to break light up into all the colors of the rainbow. But to produce the greatest possible brilliance in a diamond, many little sides, or *facets,* must be cut and polished on it, and each tiny facet must be exactly the right size and shape and must be placed at exactly the right angle.

During the 1400's, diamond cutters learned how to shape and polish a stone by use of an iron wheel coated with diamond dust. As man learned more about diamonds, he discovered the shapes which would give the greatest brilliance. The style of cut often seen today is the round shape with fifty-eight facets, which is called the *brilliant cut.* This style of cutting was begun in the 1600's. In recent years, diamond saws have been developed. They are used to saw the diamond crystals into parts. A stone is polished from each part. See LAPIDARY; GEM (illustration: Types of Gem Cuts).

How Diamonds Can Be Judged. Gem diamonds are graded according to weight, purity, color, and cut. The *weight* of a diamond is measured by the *carat,* one carat weighing 200 milligrams. The *purity* of a diamond can be lessened by various kinds of flaws. These flaws include the presence of foreign material, small bubbles, and small cracks, or *fissures,* which jewelers sometimes call *feathers.* The color of most diamonds used in jewelry consists of a faintly yellowish tint. A small percentage of gem diamonds are colorless, and a few possess a faint tinge of blue. There are also red, yellow, brown, green, and even black diamonds, although only yellow and brown diamonds are common. The *cut* of the diamond affects its value, because a stone that is not properly proportioned does not have as much brilliance as a stone that is well cut.

In buying a diamond, the buyer should have the advice of a reliable dealer. Terms used to describe gem diamonds vary considerably. A *flawless* diamond should have no physical defects, such as cracks, spots, scratches, blemishes, or cloudy texture. But a flawless diamond may not have the right color. Some dealers restrict the term *perfect* to describe a diamond that has no flaws, and also is the right color and cut.

Cutting and polishing the rough diamond is a slow

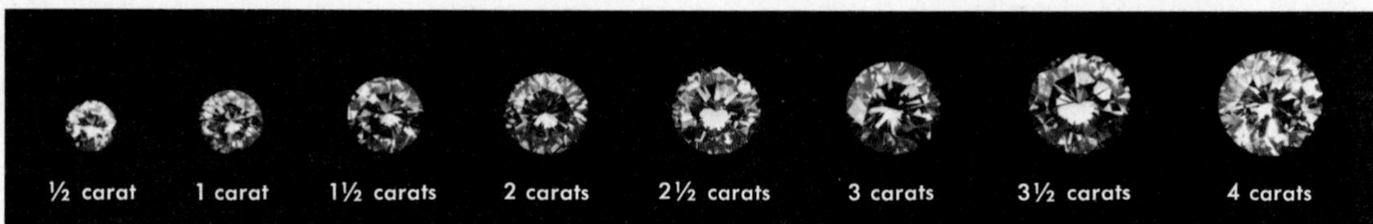

Marshall Field & Company (WORLD BOOK photo)

The Size of a Diamond is determined by its weight in carats. One carat equals 200 milligrams. The picture above shows round diamonds of different carats and the approximate difference in their diameters. However, not all diamonds of these weights would have exactly these diameters. For example, a 4-carat diamond deeper than the one shown would have a smaller diameter.

and costly process. It must be done by highly trained workers, who take many years to learn to do their work skillfully.

Famous Diamonds. Many large diamonds of rare quality are the property of royalty or of a government. The largest stone ever discovered was the *Cullinan.* This diamond, found in 1905 in the Premier mine of South Africa, weighed 3,106 carats, or about $1\frac{1}{3}$ pounds (0.6 kilogram). It was purchased by the Transvaal Government and presented to King Edward VII of England. Amsterdam cutters trimmed the Cullinan into 9 large stones and 96 smaller stones. The largest of these is the largest cut diamond in the world. In 1934 the *Jonker* diamond was found. It weighed 726 carats, and was said to be unequalled in purity. In 1935-1937 the Jonker was cut into 12 flawless stones. The *Orloff* is a magnificent Russian crown jewel which was bought by Prince Orloff for the Empress Catherine II. This huge diamond is said to have been stolen from the eye of an idol in a Hindu temple. The *Koh-i-noor,* now in the British crown jewels, was for many centuries in the possession of Indian and Persian rulers. It came into the possession of Great Britain when the British annexed the Punjab in 1849. The *Regent,* or *Pitt,* diamond is an Indian gem and is regarded as one of the most beautiful of the large stones. The Regent is owned by France and exhibited in the Louvre Museum. The most famous of Brazilian diamonds is the *Star of the South.* The blue, $44\frac{1}{2}$-carat *Hope* diamond became the property of the Smithsonian Institution in 1958.

Industrial Uses. Diamonds are widely used today for industrial work. Industrial diamonds include stones that are imperfectly formed, contain flaws, or have poor color. They are necessary because manufacturers of automobiles, airplanes, and other kinds of engines and machinery began to use harder metals and to design engines and motors which required greater accuracy in shaping the parts. Diamonds are used in such work because of their extreme hardness. They can cut, grind, and bore very hard metal quickly and accurately. Sometimes whole rough diamonds are set into industrial tools. Sometimes the diamonds are crushed and the diamond dust is baked into the industrial tools. Occasionally, the diamonds are cut to some special shape before they are set into tools. Diamonds are set in the ends of drills used in mining. Very fine wire is drawn to size through diamonds in which tapering holes have been cut. A permanent, indestructible diamond needle is used in almost all record players.

Man-Made Diamonds. The demand for industrial diamonds cannot be met by the supply of natural diamonds. For this reason, industry now depends on man-made diamonds. The first man-made diamonds were produced in 1955 by a team of scientists at the General Electric Research Laboratory. The scientists made tiny diamonds by compressing carbon under extreme pressure and heat. Today, several companies manufacture industrial diamonds. Most of the diamonds are no larger than a grain of sand.

In 1970, General Electric Company produced the first man-made diamonds of gem quality and size. Scientists use these gem-sized diamonds to research new uses for diamonds. For example, researchers found that adding boron to diamonds turns them into *semiconductors.* Semiconductors are materials with special electrical properties. They are used to make transistors and other electronic equipment. Man-made diamonds are not sold as jewelry because they cost so much to produce that they would cost even more than natural diamonds.

Imitation Diamonds are jewelry items that resemble genuine diamonds. Manufacturers make them from several substances and sell them under a variety of trade names. Some of the substances, such as spinel, are minerals. Other substances, such as glass strontium titanate and yttrium aluminate, do not exist in nature and are man-made. Imitation diamonds do not have the hardness of real diamonds, and so they soon show scratches and other signs of wear. FREDERICK H. POUGH

Related Articles in WORLD BOOK include:

Borazon	Carbon	Hardness
Carat	Gem	Lapidary

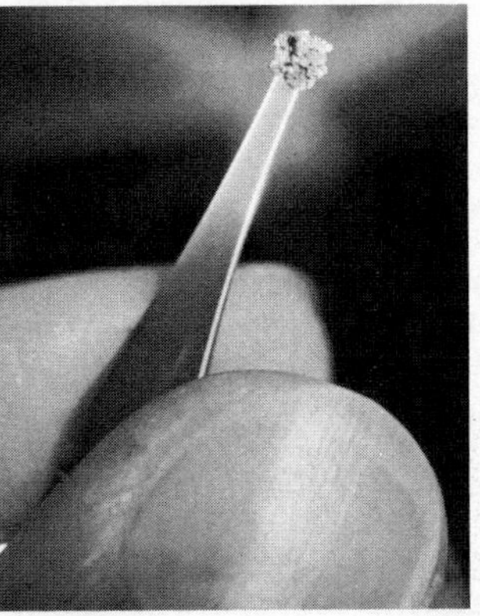

General Electric Research and Development Center

Man-Made Diamonds are produced in a press that squeezes carbon under extreme heat and pressure, *left.* Most of them are extremely small, *center,* and highly suitable for such industrial work as polishing and grinding. In 1970, scientists made diamonds of gem size, *right.* They used these stones to experiment on new uses for diamonds in industry.

DIAMOND HEAD is an extinct volcano, 760 feet (232 meters) high, on the Hawaiian island of Oahu, 5 miles (8 kilometers) southeast of Honolulu. The crater contains a National Guard base. See also HAWAII (picture: Punchbowl Crater).

DIANA was a goddess in Roman mythology. She was the daughter of Jupiter, the king of the gods, and the goddess Latona. Diana and the god Apollo were twins. She was born on the island of Delos, and so the ancient Romans sometimes called her the Delian goddess, or Delia. She closely resembled the Greek goddess Artemis.

The Louvre, Paris.
Alinari (Art Reference Bureau)

The Diana of Versailles was done by a Greek sculptor.

Diana was a moon goddess and the goddess of various aspects of women's life, including childbirth. She also was the goddess of young living things, particularly young animals, and of hunting. Diana symbolized chastity and modesty. She was a virgin and demanded that all her attendants be virgins. Artists showed the goddess wearing hunting clothes, carrying a bow and quiver of arrows, and accompanied by forest nymphs and hunting dogs. PAUL PASCAL

See also ARTEMIS; ACTAEON.

DIANTHUS. See PINK.

DIAPHRAGM, *DIE uh fram*, the large muscle attached to the lower ribs, separates the chest from the abdomen. Only man and the group of animals called *mammals* have complete diaphragms. The diaphragm is the chief muscle used in breathing. It is shaped like a dome. When you take a breath, the dome of the diaphragm moves downward. This increases the space in the chest. At the same time, the small muscles that are attached to the ribs cause these ribs to move outward, making the chest expand. This expansion creates a slight vacuum inside the chest, which causes air from the outside to rush in. When air rushes in, you are taking a breath. This action is called *inspiration*. Breathing out is *expiration*. In expiration, the diaphragm relaxes and curves up toward the chest, and air is forced out of the lungs. In hard breathing, the abdominal muscles squeeze the abdominal organs upward against the diaphragm during expiration, helping force air out.

The *phrenic nerve* carries to the diaphragm the stimuli which make it work. This nerve arises in the neck area of the spinal cord and extends through the chest down to the diaphragm.

In addition to its work in breathing, the diaphragm often helps an animal support itself. If a person wants to pull or lift a heavy object, he will usually take a deep breath and then hold it while he acts. This action "fixes" the ribs. It is important in doing heavy work, because many large muscles of the back and abdomen pull against the ribs with great force. The word *diaphragm* comes from two Greek words meaning *across* and *fence*. ARTHUR C. GUYTON

The Diaphragm, the great dome-shaped muscle separating the main cavities of the trunk, is used in breathing.

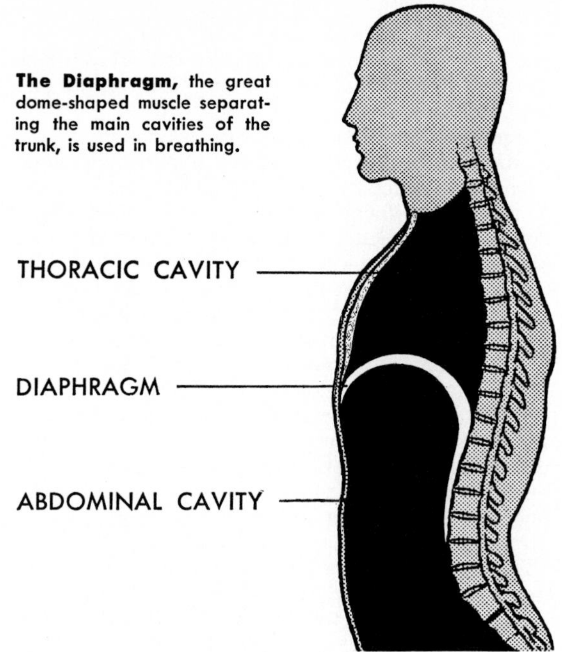

See also HUMAN BODY (Trans-Vision three-dimensional color picture); ABDOMEN; CHEST; RESPIRATION.

DIARRHEA, *DIE uh REE uh*, is an intestinal disorder suffered by people and animals. It is characterized by frequent bowel movements. The stools may be soft or watery, and may contain either mucus or pus. In severe cases the stools may contain blood. The victim of diarrhea often has cramping pains in the abdomen. In severe cases, the victim may have a constant thirst.

Diarrhea is often a symptom rather than a disease itself. It accompanies bacillary or amebic dysentery, and ulcerative colitis. It also occurs in regional enteritis and chronic pancreatic disease. Diarrhea is sometimes caused by infected food. It occurs when intestinal parasites infest the body. Poisons, such as arsenic, silver salts, and mercury, can cause an attack. Diarrhea may also come with emotional disturbances, such as fear and grief. E. CLINTON TEXTER

See also CHOLERA; COLITIS; DYSENTERY.

DIARY is a notebook containing a day-by-day account of personal experiences. Diaries are also known as *journals*. Keeping a diary is a valuable activity for young persons. It helps them learn to express their beliefs, their experiences, and their desires. The rereading of a diary which has been kept for several years helps the writer to realize how his attitudes may have changed and how his mind has grown. A diary also serves as a factual record of events that might otherwise be difficult for a person to recall.

Samuel Pepys, an Englishman, kept a diary over a period of nine years, from 1660 to 1669. Pepys' diary has become one of the most notable in the world. In it the author gives a full and realistic portrayal of his own character, as well as much valuable information about the society of his time, all in a chatty, delightfully informal manner. Later, Jonathan Swift, the English satirist, contributed his remarkable *Journal to Stella*. John Wesley, who founded the Methodist Church, wrote a set of journals. In the 1800's, diaries appeared more frequently. Sir Walter Scott's *Journal* and the diary of Henry Crabb Robinson (1775-1867) are among the best examples from this period.

France also produced a number of good diarists. The Marquis de Dangeau (1638-1720) kept a diary which is the source of a great deal of knowledge about the reign of Louis XIV. The *Mémoires Secrets* of Petit de Bachaumont is also valued for its historical information. Another famous French diary is that of the brothers Jules and Edmond de Goncourt, who recorded the doings of Parisian artistic circles in the 1800's. MARTHA F. SIMMONDS

See also PEPYS, SAMUEL; SWIFT, JONATHAN; WESLEY (John); FRANK, ANNE.

DIAS, *DE ush,* or **DIAZ, BARTOLOMEU** (1457?-1500), was a Portuguese sea captain who discovered the Cape of Good Hope in 1488 (see CAPE OF GOOD HOPE). He made several voyages to the west coast of Africa. In 1487, King John II of Portugal ordered him to try to sail around Africa. Dias, with a fleet of two ships, followed the African coast to the mouth of the Orange River. Heavy winds blew the fleet far to the south. He rounded the Cape of Good Hope without sighting it, and landed at Mossel Bay in South Africa.

Dias sailed on until the northward bend of the continent showed that he had entered the Indian Ocean. He would have sailed to India, but his weary crews staged a sit-down strike which forced him to return to Portugal. He discovered the Cape of Good Hope on the way home.

In 1497, Dias sailed as far as West Africa with Vasco da Gama, who was looking for a sea route to India by way of the Cape of Good Hope. In 1500, Dias commanded a ship in the fleet of Pedro Álvares Cabral, who discovered Brazil while trying to follow da Gama's route to India (see CABRAL, PEDRO ÁLVARES). Dias died when his ship went down in a storm. CHARLES EDWARD NOWELL

Bartolomeu Dias Discovered the Cape of Good Hope.
Courtesy of *Salvat* Editores, S.A.

DIASPORA. See JEWS (The Destruction of Jerusalem).

DIASTASE, *DY uh stace,* is an amylase, or enzyme, found in germinating seeds and in animal secretions and tissues. See ENZYME; DIGESTION; YEAST.

DIASTOLIC PRESSURE. See BLOOD PRESSURE.

DIASTROPHISM, *dy AS troh fiz'm,* is the uplifting of the earth's crust, forming continents, ocean basins, mountains, and *faults* (see FAULT). Most of the movements are very slow.

DIATHERMY, *DY uh THUR mee,* is a method of treating ailments by passing an electric current through the body. An oscillating current is used, with the very high frequency of 10 million to 100 million cycles per second. It changes direction so quickly that the nervous system does not have time to react as it would in low-frequency electric shock. The tissues grow warm because of their resistance as the high-frequency current passes through them. By using diathermy, doctors can warm parts inside the body. It would be difficult, if not impossible, to do this with baths or hot pads.

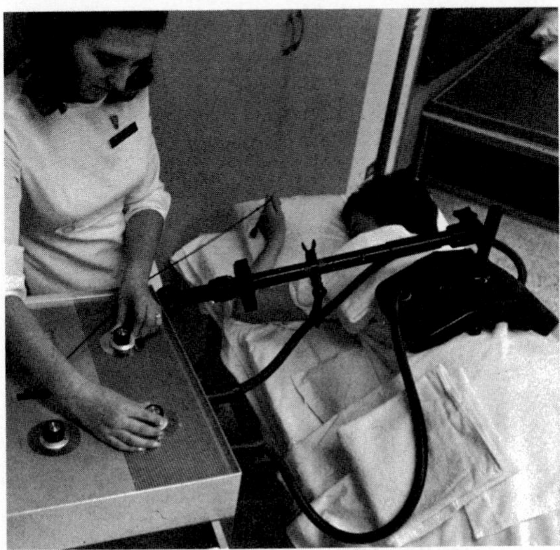

WORLD BOOK photo, courtesy St. Joseph's Hospital
Diathermy Machines produce heat by electromagnetic induction and treat patients by warming tissues inside the body.

In *medical diathermy,* the heat is kept low enough so it will not injure the tissues. In *long-wave diathermy,* the current flows between two metal conductors which fit against the patient's leg or any part of the body to be treated. When using *short-wave diathermy,* short-length radio waves are passed through the tissues from one rubber-covered electrode to the other. Diathermy is used for conditions which require heat, such as inflammation, muscle strain, neuritis, and arthritis.

In *surgical diathermy,* a point of wire takes the place of one of the electrodes. The electric current is concentrated at the point and sufficient heat is generated to destroy the tissues. The point can then be used to cut tissues or remove growths, such as warts and cancer. It can also be used inside the body to remove growths endangering internal organs. HOWARD A. CARTER

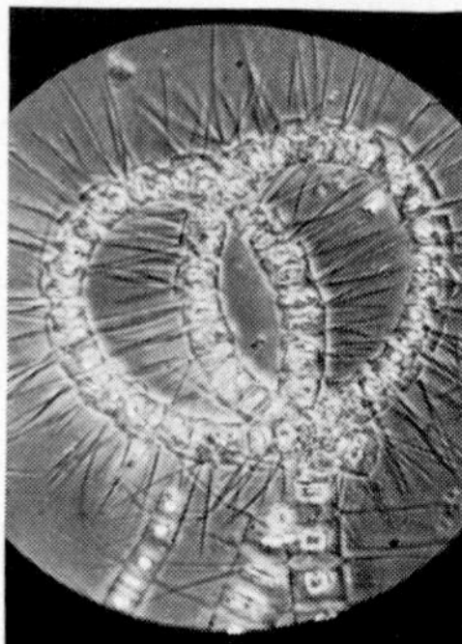

Chaetoceros Debilis, a diatom of the sea, forms these spiral chains.

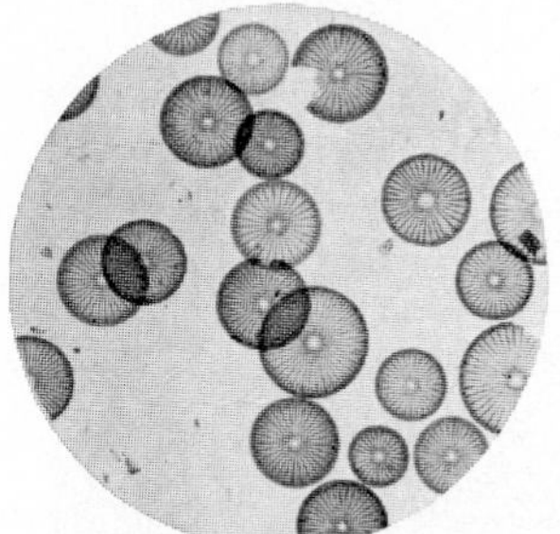

Roman Vishniac; Roy M. Allen

◀ **This Circular Pattern** is in an *Arachnodiscus* diatom.

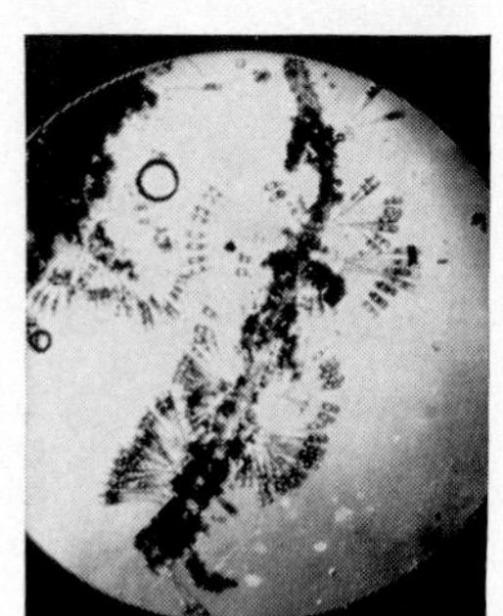

Fanlike Patterns of great beauty mark this fresh-water diatom of the *Pennatae* group.

DIATOM, *DIE uh tahm,* is a tiny water plant of the kind called algae. Unlike some of the other algae, which include large seaweeds, a diatom consists of only one golden-brown cell. There are several thousand species of diatoms, including both salt- and fresh-water types. Some appear as brown, slimy coatings on stones and piles in water. Many of these one-celled plants may hang together in chains, and in various other arrangements. Still others float free. Diatoms can move by themselves through the water with jerky, creeping, or pendulumlike motions. The cell wall of the individual diatom is made up of two nearly equal halves, called valves. They are joined together somewhat as the two halves of a pillbox. The "glassy" cell wall is largely made up of silica, and forms a shell. Often the shell is very beautiful. Silica will not dissolve in water, so large masses of the tiny shells may be found at the bottom of seas, lakes, and ponds. The free, floating diatoms which grow in midocean and in lakes are a very important food for small sea animals. These, in turn, are eaten by fishes. If there were no diatoms, most of the fish of the world would die.

An earthy material composed largely of diatom shells is called *diatomite.* It is mined in California, Oregon, Washington, Nevada, Arizona, and Florida. Diatomite is used as a polishing powder, abrasive, plastic filler, insulator, filter, and in manufacturing explosives.

Scientific Classification. Diatoms are in phylum *Chrysophyta.* The many kinds of diatoms make up the class *Bacillariophyceae.*

LEWIS HANFORD TIFFANY

See also ALGAE; WATER PLANT.

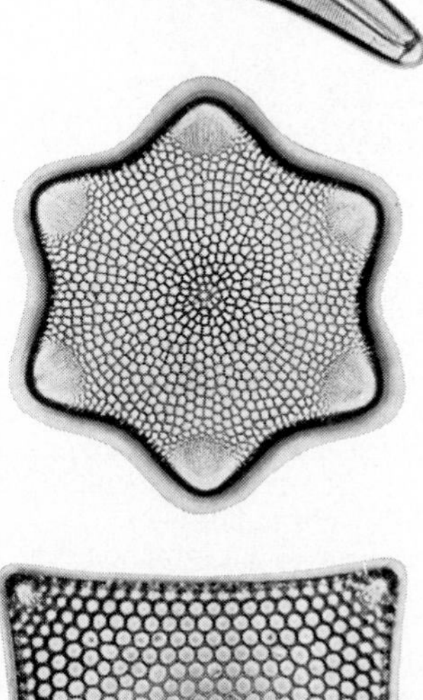

Bausch and Lomb

The Delicate Shells of Diatoms, *above left,* reveal only a few of the many different shapes of these one-celled plants. The top photograph, an edgewise view, shows how the two shells or "valves" of the diatom fit together. The lower two are flat views.

Johns-Manville

Diatomite, taken from diatom shells, has many industrial uses. Each load of this power shovel contains millions of tiny diatom shells. Each shell is from 12,000,000 to 28,000,000 years old. This huge deposit of diatom shells is located at Lompoc, Calif.

DIATONIC SCALE. See MUSIC (picture).

DIATRYMA, *DIE uh TRY muh*, was a large bird that lived about 60 million years ago. The bird stood about 7 feet (2.1 meters) high, and had a huge head, neck, and bill. It had small wings and could not fly. But the bird's strong legs probably made it a swift runner. It could easily have caught and killed *Hyracotherium*, the small horse that lived during that time (see HORSE [Origins of the Horse]). Fossils of *Diatryma* have been found in New Mexico and Wyoming. SAMUEL PAUL WELLES

DÍAZ, ARMANDO. See WORLD WAR I (War Leaders; The End of the Central Powers).

DIAZ, BARTOLOMEU. See DIAS, BARTOLOMEU.

DÍAZ, *DEE ahs*, **PORFIRIO,** *pawr FEE rih oh* (1830-1915), served as president of Mexico from 1877 to 1880 and from 1884 to 1911. He gained fame as a general in the war against French invaders that lasted from 1863 to 1867. Overthrowing President Lerdo de Tejada in 1876, he acted as provisional president until his election in 1877. His policies encouraged railroads, large-scale agriculture, banking, and industry. But conditions improved little for most people. A popular uprising in 1910 forced him into exile in France, where he died. Díaz was born in Oaxaca, Mexico. See also MEXICO (The Dictatorship of Porfirio Díaz). HAROLD E. DAVIS

DÍAZ ORDAZ, GUSTAVO (1911-), served as president of Mexico from 1964 to 1970. Díaz Ordaz served as secretary of the interior in the cabinet of his predecessor, Adolfo López Mateos. Díaz Ordaz became known as a political moderate and a capable and strict administrator. While he was interior secretary, Díaz Ordaz was criticized by some Mexicans because he gave the United States information on Mexicans who visited Communist Cuba. A lawyer, Díaz Ordaz first entered public service as a judge. He was born in Ciudad Serdán, Mexico.

DICE are small cubes that are used in such games of chance as craps, and in games involving both chance and skill, such as backgammon. (A single cube is a *die*.)

Frank Cassidy

Dice are used in gambling. They are also used in many children's games to determine the number of moves a player may make.

The six faces of a die are stamped with dots, ranging from one to six. Dice may be made of plastic, bone, ivory, wood, or other materials.

A player shakes the dice and tosses them on a level surface. The total number of dots showing on the top faces is a basis for deciding games. The number of times any total will turn up depends entirely on chance, so skill is not involved. Dice games played for money or other goods are considered gambling and are illegal in most parts of the United States. JOHN SCARNE

DICENTRA, *dy SEN truh*, is the name of a group of plants which include bleeding heart, Dutchman's-breeches, and squirrel corn. These plants produce a heart-shaped flower. They are abundant in Asia and America. Bleeding heart is a favorite garden plant. Squirrel corn and Dutchman's-breeches are early spring wild flowers.

Scientific Classification. Dicentras are in the fumitory family, *Fumariaceae*. They are genus *Dicentra*. DONALD WYMAN

See also BLEEDING HEART; DUTCHMAN'S-BREECHES.

DICHOTOMY, *die KAHT oh mih*, in biology, means a branching into two parts. In astronomy it describes that phase of the moon in which only half of its disk appears.

DICK, GEORGE FREDERICK and **GLADYS.** See DICK TEST; SCARLET FEVER.

DICK TEST is a test used to determine whether or not a person is immune to scarlet fever. A small amount of substance containing scarlet fever toxin is injected under the skin of one arm (see TOXIN). This substance is prepared from liquids filtered off a culture of scarlet fever bacteria. If the person is not immune to scarlet fever, tender, red, swollen spots will appear on the skin after 24 hours. Since the person's skin may be sensitive to other substances in the filtrate besides the toxin, a comparison, or control, injection is usually made on the other arm. This is done by injecting a small amount of filtrate in which the toxin has been neutralized. In this way a positive reaction to the Dick test can be seen immediately. The Dick test was developed by the American bacteriologists George and Gladys Dick in 1923. They also developed an antitoxin for the treatment of scarlet fever. See also SCARLET FEVER. AUSTIN SMITH

DICKCISSEL, *dik SISS ul*, is a bunting of the finch and sparrow family (see BUNTING). The dickcissel is a bird about 6 inches (15 centimeters) long. Its plumage is a streaked grayish-brown, varied by a yellow breast and bright chestnut wing patches. There is a conspicuous black crescent on the throat. Dickcissels are common in the central United States, and are sometimes seen in the eastern states. They live along railroads and roadsides. The birds eat insects and seeds. The female lays from 3 to 5 eggs. The nest is built of leaves, grass, and hair, and is on or near the ground.

Scientific Classification. The dickcissel belongs to the New World seedeater family, *Fringillidae*. The bird is genus *Spiza*, species *S. americana*. GEORGE J. WALLACE

The Dickcissel is named for its loud, persistent call. This suggests the syllables, "Dick, dick, dick, cis-cis-cis-cis." The last four notes of the bird's call are sounded rapidly.

The Dickens Fellowship, London

Charles Dickens, the most famous English writer of his time, enchanted audiences with dramatic readings from his novels.

DICKENS, CHARLES (1812-1870), was a great English novelist and one of the most popular writers of all time. His best-known books include *A Christmas Carol, David Copperfield, Great Expectations, Oliver Twist, The Pickwick Papers*, and *A Tale of Two Cities*. Dickens created some of the most famous characters in English literature. He also created scenes and descriptions of places that have delighted readers for more than a hundred years. Dickens was a keen observer of life, and had a great understanding of people. He showed sympathy for the poor and helpless, and mocked and criticized the selfish, the greedy, and the cruel.

Dickens was also a wonderfully inventive comic artist. The warmth and humor of his personality appear in all his works. Perhaps in no other large body of fiction does the reader receive so strong and agreeable an impression of the man behind the story. This may be the major reason for Dickens' lasting popularity.

Dickens' Life

Charles John Huffam Dickens was born in Portsmouth, on the southern coast of England, on Feb. 7, 1812. He moved with his family to London when he was about two years old. Many of the events and people in his books are based on events and people in his life. Dickens' father, John Dickens, was a poor and easygoing clerk who worked for the navy. John Dickens served in some respects as the model for Wilkins Micawber in *David Copperfield*. He spent time in prison for debt, an event Charles re-created in *Little Dorrit*.

Even when John was free, he lacked the money to support his family adequately. At the age of 12, Charles worked in a London factory pasting labels on bottles of shoe polish. He held the job only a short time, but the misery of that experience left lasting scars on his memory. He never spoke of it to his wife or children in later years.

Dickens attended school off and on until he was about 14, and then left for good. He enjoyed reading and was especially fond of adventure tales and novels. However, most of the knowledge he later used as an author came from his observation of life around him.

Dickens became a newspaper reporter in the late 1820's. He specialized in covering debates in Parliament, and also wrote feature articles. His work as a reporter sharpened his naturally keen ear for conversation and helped develop his skill in portraying his characters' speech realistically. It also increased his ability to observe and to write swiftly and clearly. Dickens' first book, *Sketches by Boz* (1836), consisted of articles he wrote for the London *Evening Chronicle*.

Literary Success. Dickens won his first literary fame with *The Posthumous Papers of the Pickwick Club*. Published in monthly parts in 1836 and 1837, the book describes the humorous adventures and misadventures of a group of slightly eccentric characters in London and the English countryside. After a slow start, *The Pickwick Papers*—as the book is usually called—gained a popularity seldom matched in the history of literature. At 24, Dickens suddenly found himself famous. He remained so until his death.

Dickens founded and edited two highly successful weekly magazines. He edited *Household Words* from 1850 to 1859 and *All the Year Round* from 1859 to his death. As a public figure, Dickens was constantly in the news, and was recognized and honored wherever he went. He was famous in America as well as in Britain, and he toured the United States in 1842 and in 1867 and 1868.

Personal Life. Personal unhappiness marred Dickens' public success. In 1836, he married Catherine Hogarth. Catherine had a sister Mary, who died in 1837. Dickens' grief at Mary's death has led some scholars to believe that he really loved Mary more than his wife. Catherine was a good woman, but lacked great intelligence. She and Dickens had 10 children. The couple separated in 1858.

Dickens had unusual mental and physical energy. He recorded his activities in letters, many of which make as delightful reading as the novels. He spent much of his crowded social life with friends from the worlds of art and literature. Dickens enjoyed drama, and went to the theater as often as he could. At one time, he thought of becoming an actor. When he was rich and famous, he made a hobby of producing and acting in amateur theatrical productions. He had great success giving public readings of his works. Dickens' gift for creating dramatic scenes in his novels can be traced to his love for the theater.

In addition to writing, editing, and touring as a dramatic reader, Dickens busied himself with various charities. The charities he promoted included schools for poor children and a loan society to enable the poor to move to Australia. Dickens often walked for hours to work off his remaining energy. He came to know the streets and alleys of London better, perhaps, than any

---

Richard D. Altick, the contributor of this article, is Regents' Professor of English at Ohio State University and author of Lives and Letters, *a history of literary biography in England and America.*

other person of his time. He sometimes walked as far as 30 miles (48 kilometers), into his favorite county of Kent.

Dickens' health began to decline about 1865 and he died of a stroke on June 9, 1870.

Dickens' Books

Dickens wrote 20 novels (including 5 short Christmas books), and many sketches, travel books, and other nonfiction works. Not all of his books were best sellers, but the most popular ones broke all sales records for the time. Most of his novels were published in separate parts.

The First Phase. After the success of *The Pickwick Papers,* Dickens turned to serious themes and plots. However, he always introduced enough humor to keep his books entertaining.

Oliver Twist (1837-1839) describes the adventures of a poor orphan boy. The book was noted for its sensational presentation of London's criminal world and for its attack on England's mistreatment of the poor.

In *Nicholas Nickleby* (1838-1839), Dickens criticized greedy proprietors of private schools, who treated students brutally and taught them nothing. However, as in *Oliver Twist,* the social criticism in *Nicholas Nickleby* is largely incidental to the plot.

The Old Curiosity Shop (1840-1841) today is considered by many critics to be the least important of Dickens' novels. It was admired when first published, but it seems inferior today, largely because of the sentimental death scene of Little Nell.

Barnaby Rudge (1841) is a historical novel that centers around a series of riots in London in 1780. *Martin Chuzzlewit* (1843-1844) is one of two books that Dickens based on his first trip to America. The other is the travel book *American Notes* (1842). Dickens intended *Martin Chuzzlewit* to be a study of many forms of selfishness. But the book is best remembered for its unflattering picture of the crudeness of American manners and for its comic characters. Two of its finest comic characters are the hypocrite Pecksniff and the chattering, alcoholic midwife Sairy Gamp.

Dickens wrote his five "Christmas books" during the 1840's. The first, *A Christmas Carol* (1843), is one of the most famous stories ever written. In the book, three ghosts show the old miser Ebenezer Scrooge his past, present, and future. Scrooge realizes that he has been living a life of greed, and he changes into a warm and unselfish person. The other Christmas books are *The Chimes* (1844), *The Cricket on the Hearth* (1845), *The Battle of Life* (1846), and *The Haunted Man* (1848).

The Second Phase. During the 1840's, Dickens' view of Victorian society, and perhaps of the world, grew darker. His humor became more bitter, often taking the form of biting satire. The characters and plots in his works seemed to emphasize the evil side of human experience.

At the same time, Dickens increasingly refined his art. The range of his tone widened and he paid more attention to structure and arrangement. He turned to symbolic themes to help express and expand his observations on topical political and social issues and on larger matters of morality and values. The unhealthy London fog in *Bleak House,* for example, symbolizes the illness of society, especially its lack of responsibility toward the downtrodden and the unfortunate.

Dombey and Son (1846-1848) deals primarily with a selfish egotist whose pride cuts him off from the warmth of human love. The book stresses the evils of the Victorian admiration for money. Dickens believed money

Oliver Twist and David Copperfield contain many popular Dickens characters. In *Oliver Twist, left,* an original illustration by the artist George Cruikshank shows Oliver watching in alarm as the Artful Dodger and Charley Bates pick Mr. Brownlow's pocket. In *David Copperfield, right,* David, Betsy Trotwood, and Mr. Dick watch the joyful reunion of Wilkins Micawber and his family. Hablot Knight Browne, popularly known as Phiz, drew this illustration for the first edition of the novel.

Collection of Mr. and Mrs. David Bradford, Chicago

had become the measure of all personal relations and the goal of all ambition.

With *David Copperfield* (1849-1850), Dickens temporarily abandoned social criticism for semiautobiography. The novel describes a young man's discovery of the realities of adult life. David's youth is clearly patterned after Dickens' own youth.

Bleak House (1852-1853) is in many respects Dickens' greatest novel. It has a complex structure and many levels of meaning, mixing melodrama with satire and social commentary. The book deals with many social evils, chiefly wasteful and cruel legal processes. It also attacks the neglect of the poor, false humanitarians and clergymen, and poor sanitation.

This long novel was followed by the much shorter and simpler *Hard Times* (1854). *Hard Times* attacks philosopher Jeremy Bentham's doctrine of *utilitarianism*. Bentham believed all human ideas, actions, and institutions should be judged by their usefulness. Dickens believed Bentham's philosophy reduced social relations to problems of cold, mechanical self-interest.

In *Little Dorrit* (1855-1857), Dickens continued his campaign against materialism and snobbery, which were represented by the rich Merdle family and their social-climbing friends. He also ridiculed government inefficiency in the form of the "Circumlocution Office."

A Tale of Two Cities (1859) was the second of Dickens' two historical novels. It is set in London and Paris and tells of the heroism of fictional Sidney Carton during the French Revolution. Critics do not rank it highly.

In *Great Expectations* (1860-1861), Dickens returned to the theme of a youth's discovery of the realities of life. An unknown person provides the young hero Pip with money so that Pip can live as a gentleman. Pip's pride is shattered when he learns that his "great expectations" come from a convict. Only by painfully revising his values does Pip re-establish his life on a foundation of human sympathy, rather than on vanity, possessions, and social position.

Our Mutual Friend (1864-1865) was Dickens' final novel of social criticism. Dickens again attacked the false values of the newly rich. He satirized greed, using the great garbage heaps of the London dumps as a symbol of filthy money.

Dickens had completed about one-third of his novel *The Mystery of Edwin Drood* when he died. Nobody knows how Dickens intended the mystery to end, and the problem still intrigues scholars and readers.

Dickens' Place in Literature

Dickens is now considered one of the major figures in English literature, but his position was not always so high. His reputation declined between 1880 and 1940. This was partly due to the increasing sophistication and psychological emphasis that became fashionable in novels after Dickens' death. Critics valued Dickens chiefly as an entertainer and, above all, as a creator of a huge gallery of comic, pleasant, and villainous characters. They recognized him as a master creator of plot and scene, and as a sharp-eyed observer of London life. But these critics considered Dickens' outlook too simple and unrealistic. They believed he lacked artistic taste and subtlety, and that he relied too much on broad comedy, cheap dramatic effects, sentimentality, and superficial psychology.

However, since 1940 a flood of books and essays have described Dickens as a writer of considerable depth and complexity and a sensitive and philosophical observer of "the condition of man." They have associated him in this sense with such writers as Fyodor Dostoevsky, Franz Kafka, and Herman Melville. They sometimes attribute to him purposes and ideas he never held, and credit him with effects he never sought. Recent criticism of Dickens may sometimes be extravagant, but it has demonstrated beyond doubt that Dickens can no longer be regarded as a mere teller of tales. And, whatever his other claims to greatness may be, Dickens certainly ranks as a superbly inventive comic artist. He was always aware of the evil in life but, in the last analysis, his art was sustained by an awareness and appreciation of the human comedy.

One of the best modern studies of Dickens' life and work is *Charles Dickens* (two volumes, 1952) by Edgar Johnson. RICHARD D. ALTICK

See also *Dickens, Charles* in the RESEARCH GUIDE/INDEX, Volume 22, for a *Reading and Study Guide*.

DICKEY, JAMES (1923-), is an American poet and novelist. He is known chiefly for works that portray people testing their survival instincts against other people and nature. Some of Dickey's writings explore man's animal instincts, which include killing for enjoyment. Dickey writes in a clear, matter-of-fact style that shows people learning about the brutal side of human nature.

Dickey's novel *Deliverance* (1970) tells about a middle-class businessman who must struggle to survive in the wilderness. In his fight to survive, he has to kill another man. This experience teaches him that cruelty is part of man's nature.

Many of Dickey's writings are based on episodes from his own life. Some of his works, particularly the poem "The Firebombing" (1964), reflect his experiences as a combat pilot. The pilot in "The Firebombing" feels a sense of power at killing, but no sorrow.

Dickey was born in Atlanta, Ga. He won the National Book Award for poetry in 1966 for his collection *Buckdancer's Choice* (1965). His other books include *Poems 1957-1967* (1967) and *Sorties: Journals and New Essays* (1971). MARCUS KLEIN

DICKINSON, EMILY (1830-1886), was one of the great American poets of the 1800's. Most critics rank her with Ralph Waldo Emerson, Edgar Allan Poe, and Walt Whitman as the finest American poets of the century.

Emily Dickinson wrote her poetry while living in seclusion. She saw only a few close friends in her family home in Amherst, Mass. Nevertheless, she gave universal significance to the most intimate experiences and feelings. Scholars have several theories to explain her withdrawal, but none really solve the mystery. Perhaps the best answer lies in the poems themselves. Her poetry indicates that before she could write about the world, she had to back away from it and contemplate it from a distance.

Her Poems. Emily Dickinson's most important poems concern the relationship between the inner self and the external world. Her poems were short and untitled, usually written in four-line stanzas. Although she could write in a playful or witty style, her outlook was basically tragic. She recorded loneliness and anxiety without making these topics seem morbid. She wrote, "The soul selects its own society,/Then shuts the door."

She analyzed emotions poetically, and tried to define and expose particular states of mind. For example:

For each ecstatic instant
We must an anguish pay
In keen and quivering ratio
To the ecstasy.

She wrote with great force about the ominousness and unfeeling qualities of nature:

There's a certain slant of light,
Winter afternoons
That oppresses, like the weight
Of Cathedral tunes.

She also expressed the soul's yearning for immortality and for communion with a remote and seemingly indifferent God:

I know that he exists;
Somewhere, in silence,
He has hid his rare life
From our gross eyes.

Her poem "Because I Could Not Stop for Death" describes with beauty and simplicity the inevitable passage of time and the certainty of death. This poem is reprinted in the POETRY article.

Her Life. Emily Dickinson was born in Amherst on Dec. 10, 1830, and died there on May 15, 1886. She wrote over 1,700 poems, but only 7 were published during her lifetime—and those without her consent. She wrote in secret; most of her work was discovered after her death by a sister. The first volume of her poetry was published four years after her death. CLARK GRIFFITH

See also AMERICAN LITERATURE (picture).

DICKINSON, JOHN (1732-1808), an American statesman, served in the Delaware and Pennsylvania assemblies, the Stamp Act Congress, and the Continental Congress. Dickinson favored conciliation with England. He expressed his calm political views in his *Letters from a Farmer in Pennsylvania to the Inhabitants of the British Colonies.* As a delegate from Delaware, he helped to draft the United States Constitution. He was not present when the Constitution was signed, but he asked another delegate to add his name.

Dickinson was born in Talbot County, Maryland, and became a lawyer. Dickinson College at Carlisle, Pa., was named for him. KENNETH R. ROSSMAN

DICKINSON COLLEGE. See UNIVERSITIES AND COLLEGES (table).

DICKSON MOUNDS. See ILLINOIS (Places to Visit).

DICOTYLEDON, *die CAHT uh LEE dun,* is a type of flowering plant that has two *cotyledons* (seed leaves). The cotyledons store reserve food for the embryo plant. Dicotyledon foliage leaves have netted veins. Their flower petals usually grow in multiples of 4 or 5. See also COTYLEDON.

DICTATING MACHINE records speech and then reproduces it, like a phonograph. The person who dictates speaks into a microphone. The microphone is connected to a recorder that makes a record. When the typist is ready for the record, she places it on a transcribing machine. Then she listens through a hearing device to the voice from the record. The records used include plastic belts, disks, and sheets; wax cylinders; wire; and tape.

Dictating machines save time because a person can dictate at any time without calling a stenographer.

WORLD BOOK photo

A Dictating Machine saves valuable time. The machine shown in the foreground above records a person's voice on a cassette. The typist places the cassette into a transcriber and puts on earphones before starting to type the recorded message.

After the stenographer has typed the letter, she can check it with the record to make sure the letter is correct. Some dictating machines are light enough in weight to be carried easily on business trips.

Electronic devices have made dictating machines extremely sensitive. No matter how rapidly a person dictates, the dictating machine can keep up with him. It can reproduce the dictation at any speed desired.

"Remote control" dictating systems carry dictation from several desks by telephone wire to a group of dictating machines in a central typing pool. There, several typists do the transcribing. WILLIAM H. FISH

DICTATOR is any ruler whose power is not limited either by law or by the acts of any official body. Dictators usually have come to power under conditions of turmoil and confusion. Governments, unable to provide their people with security, may turn to a dictator who promises to achieve it. Often the dictator seizes power by political trickery or revolutionary violence.

Once in control, the dictator and his followers retain their positions through force or threat of force. They abolish or closely control the legislature, and quickly suppress freedom of speech, assembly, and the press. They set up an elaborate secret-police system to detect opponents of the government. Persons who object to dictatorship are persecuted by the government.

Familiar examples of the dictator have included Benito Mussolini in Italy, Adolf Hitler in Germany, and Joseph Stalin in Russia.

In ancient Rome, the Senate often met national emergencies by appointing one consul to select a dictator. The Roman dictator held office for 6 months and could be reappointed if the emergency still existed. The dictator had power of life and death without appeal to the people or the Senate, but he could not leave the country and had no control of the treasury. Julius Caesar was appointed dictator by the Roman Senate on three different occasions. WILLIAM EBENSTEIN

See also AUTOCRACY; GOVERNMENT. For a *Reading and Study Guide,* see *Dictatorship* in the RESEARCH GUIDE/INDEX, Volume 22.

DICTIONARY is a book that contains a selected list of words arranged in alphabetical order. It explains their meanings and gives information about them. With a dictionary, a person can look up a word quickly, discover what it means, and learn how it is pronounced. A good dictionary puts down the facts of a language as educated speakers and writers use that language. A dictionary editor cannot change the facts of a language any more than a map maker can change the position of mountains, rivers, or cities when making a map.

What Dictionaries Contain

Dictionaries contain the meanings of many kinds of words. Most dictionaries include (1) the ordinary words of everyday life, such as *bread*, *run*, and *with;* (2) literary words used in formal writing, such as *aggregation*, *despoil*, and *incontrovertible;* (3) technical words, such as *starboard*, *gene*, and *ratio;* (4) words used chiefly on informal occasions, such as *gab* and *razz;* (5) words used in writing to give an old-fashioned flavor, such as *aweary* and *avaunt;* (6) words not used today but found in the writings of some authors, such as *plaister* for *plaster;* (7) words or phrases from other languages, such as *coup d'état* from French and *troika* from Russian; (8) *idioms* (groups of words with meanings different from their literal meanings), such as *split hairs* and *under the thumb of;* (9) abbreviations, such as *U.S.A.*, *Kans.*, and *p.;* and (10) important proper names, such as *Juno* and *Jupiter*.

No dictionary records all the words of our language. In fact, no one knows exactly how many English words there are. Besides ordinary words used in everyday speech, the English language includes thousands of geographical names. There are thousands of words that are no longer used. And there are hundreds of thousands of technical terms, including more than 750,000 names of insects alone. New words are coined for new scientific and technical discoveries, and slang words and special vocabularies constantly spring up. As nations draw closer together through trade and travel, languages tend to borrow more and more words from each other. That is why a dictionary editor must be selective in the words he decides to include.

Most dictionaries tell us much more than just the meanings of words. Many list pronunciations, derivations, illustrative quotations, synonyms and antonyms, and other information. The color illustration with this article shows in detail what dictionaries tell us.

Kinds of Dictionaries

Dictionaries may be classified as *general dictionaries* and *specialized dictionaries*. A general dictionary contains information on everyday words such as *it* and *the*. But it also defines many technical terms such as *chromatography* and *columella*. A specialized dictionary omits most everyday terms, and limits itself to information on words used in a particular field, such as biology.

General Dictionaries range in size from small pocket dictionaries to large multivolume or table dictionaries.

The number of entries in a general dictionary depends on its purpose. Each dictionary is designed to answer the questions of a certain type of reader. A sixth-grade student, for example, would not want all the information given in a dictionary a college professor would use. For this reason, dictionary editors work hard to design their products to suit the needs of their intended audiences. They know that the usefulness of any dictionary depends on the education of the user and the kind of information he wishes to find.

WORLD BOOK photo

A Dictionary, such as *The World Book Dictionary,* contains valuable information on thousands of words and phrases.

A general dictionary may be designed for use by elementary-school students, high-school students, or college students. It may also be designed for use by the general reader, or even by the entire family. *The World Book Dictionary* is an example of a dictionary designed for family use.

The largest general dictionaries may contain over 400,000 entries. When a dictionary has this many entries, many obsolete and technical terms must be included. Other general dictionaries may range in size from those with about 15,000 entries to those with about 200,000 entries.

Specialized Dictionaries are designed to give more information in particular fields than general dictionaries can. A *gazetteer* (geographical dictionary) lists the names of cities, countries, islands, lakes, and other places. It gives the pronunciation of each name and a brief description of the place. A *biographical dictionary* lists and gives the pronunciation of the names of famous people. Each entry includes the dates the person lived, his nationality, and why he is remembered. A *thesaurus* contains lists of synonyms and antonyms. Other specialized dictionaries are devoted exclusively to English usage; idioms; Old English; pronunciations; slang; spelling; and various aspects of science and technology. There are dictionaries of all the major languages of the world. *Bilingual* dictionaries translate the words of one language into another. They include French-English,

What a Dictionary Tells You

In addition to defining words, a dictionary provides much useful information about them. You can get the most out of a dictionary by learning what its abbreviations and symbols stand for. These examples come from THE WORLD BOOK DICTIONARY.

Word Entries begin in bold black type. Only proper nouns are capitalized. The first letter of the entry extends into the margin for easy location. This dictionary uses an asterisk to indicate that the entry is accompanied by an illustration.

Definitions give the precise meanings of words. If a word has more than one meaning, the definitions are numbered. This dictionary lists the most common meanings first. Some dictionaries present definitions in historical order, with the earliest meanings first.

Illustrations clarify the definitions. Labels show which meaning of the word is illustrated.

Pronunciations are given in phonetic symbols. This dictionary has a key to its phonetic symbols at the bottom of each right-hand page, with more detailed information at the front of the book.

Examples point out how the word is used in phrases or sentences.

Cross References show that the form consulted is less widely used than some other form, which has its own main entry.

Parts of Speech Labels show the word's grammatical use. Any word used as more than one part of speech is defined accordingly. The parts of speech are abbreviated, as in *adj.* for *adjective* and *n.* for *noun.* Verbs are shown as transitive (*v.t.*) or intransitive (*v.i.*).

Other Forms of the word include the principal parts of verbs, unusual plural forms, and comparative forms for adjectives.

Quotations from well-known authors or publications illustrate the meaning of the word. The sources of quotations are identified.

Levels of Usage Labels, such as *slang, informal, Archaic,* and *Obsolete,* indicate when and where the word is acceptable in current English usage. Each label is defined in a list at the front of the dictionary.

Phrases that include the key word but have special meanings of their own are explained separately.

Synonyms that have the same or nearly the same meaning as the defined words appear immediately after the definition.

Derivations tell what language or languages a word comes from, usually with its meaning in the original language. The symbol < means *comes from.*

Synonym Studies explain in detail the various shades of meaning of some synonyms. All these studies include examples.

Usage Notes explain points of spelling or grammar and advise how to use the word in speaking or writing.

Foreign Words and Phrases in common use in English have entries that give their pronunciation and translation, often with examples or illustrative quotations.

***ab|do|men** (ab′də mən, ab dō′-), *n.* **1a** the part of the body containing the stomach and the intestines; belly. In man and other mammals the abdomen is a large cavity between the chest (thorax) and the pelvis, and also contains the liver, pancreas, kidneys, and spleen. **b** a corresponding region in vertebrates below mammals. **2** the last of the three parts of the body of insects and many other arthropods, including spiders and crustaceans. [< Latin *abdōmen*]

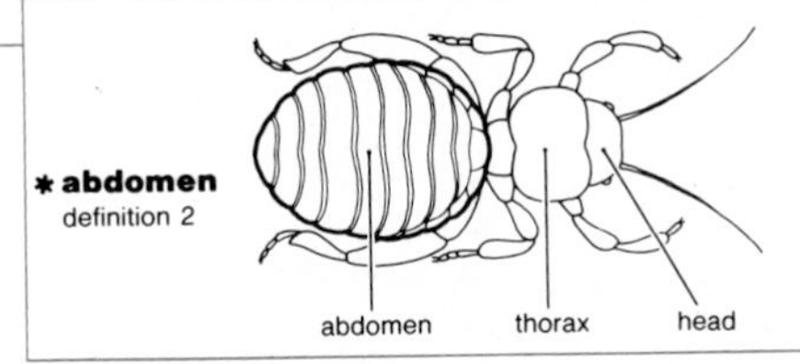

***abdomen** definition 2

ab|dom|i|nal (ab dom′ə nəl), *adj.* of the abdomen; in the abdomen; for the abdomen: *Bending the body exercises the abdominal muscles.* SYN: ventral, visceral. — **ab|dom′i|nal|ly**, *adv.*

abdominal brain, = solar plexus.

ab|dom|i|nous (ab dom′ə nəs), *adj.* = potbellied.

a|bide[1] (ə bīd′), *v.*, **a|bode** or **a|bid|ed, a|bid|ing.** — *v.t.* **1** to put up with; endure; tolerate: *A good housekeeper can't abide dust. She can't abide him.* SYN: bear, stand. **2** to await submissively; submit to; sustain: *He must abide his fatal doom* (Joanna Baillie). **3** to await defiantly; withstand: *He soon learned to abide ... terrors which most of my bolder companions shrank from encountering* (Hugh Miller). **4** *Archaic.* to wait for; await: *I will abide the coming of my lord* (Tennyson).
— *v.i.* **1** to stay; remain; wait: *Abide with me for a time. I'll call upon you straight: abide within* (Shakespeare). *He within his ships abode the while* (William Cowper). **2** to continue to live (in a place); reside; dwell: *No martin there in winter shall abide* (John Dryden). **3** to continue (in some state or action): *... ye shall abide in my love* (John 15:10). **4** to continue in existence; endure: *Thou hast established the earth, and it abideth* (Psalms 119:90). SYN: last. **5** *Archaic.* to be left. **6** *Obsolete.* to stay behind.

abide by, a to accept and follow out; be bound by: *Both teams will abide by the umpire's decision.* **b** to remain faithful to; stand firm by; be true to; fulfill: *Abide by your promise.*

a|bil|i|ty (ə bil′ə tē), *n., pl.* **-ties. 1** the power to do or act: *the ability to think clearly. The old horse still has the ability to work.* SYN: capability, capacity. **2** skill: *Washington had great ability as a general.* **3** power to do some special thing; natural gift; talent: *Musical ability often shows itself early in life.* [< Middle French *habilité*, learned borrowing from Latin *habilitās* aptness < *habilis* able]

—*Syn.* **2, 3 Ability, talent** mean special power to do or for doing something. **Ability** applies to a demonstrated physical or mental power to do a certain thing well: *She has developed unusual ability as a dancer.* **Talent** applies to an inborn capacity for doing a special thing: *a child with a remarkable talent for painting.*

▶ After **ability** the infinitive of a verb preceded by *to* is used, rather than the gerund preceded by *of: A lawyer needs the ability to think clearly,* not *of thinking clearly.* The preposition used after *ability* and before a noun is *in: ability in music.*

A|bim|e|lech (ə bim′ə lek), *n.* a son of Gideon who was set up as king of Israel by the people of Shechem (in the Bible, Judges 9).

ab init., ab initio.

ab in|i|ti|o (ab′ i nish′ē ō), *Latin.* from the beginning: *The decree was not a nullity in the sense of being void ab initio* (London Times).

English-German, Spanish-Italian, Italian-French, Greek-Latin, Russian-Polish, and Hebrew-Arabic dictionaries.

How To Use a Dictionary

Before you use a dictionary, try to become familiar with the methods, principles, and scope of the book. You will find that various dictionaries are arranged in different ways. Most American dictionaries arrange all entries in a single alphabetical list. Others put abbreviations, geographical names, and biographical names in separate lists, usually at the end of the book. All good dictionaries today have introductory sections that explain what the book contains and how the dictionary is arranged.

The first thing a dictionary entry shows you is how to spell a word and how to divide it into syllables. Accent marks and symbols that are explained in the book tell you how to pronounce the word. Many dictionaries also tell what part of speech the word is. For example, they list *boy* as a *noun*, and *speak* as a *verb*.

Definitions of the word usually follow. Some dictionaries list the most commonly used meaning of the word first. Others arrange the meanings historically, so that the first meaning listed is the one that occurred first in the language. Most dictionaries use the word in a sentence or quotation to help define it. Sometimes they add pictures or drawings to tell more about the entry.

After the definitions, many dictionaries include a list of *synonyms*, or words having about the same meaning as the word being defined. Sometimes a list of *antonyms*, words with opposite meanings, follows the synonyms.

History

The word *dictionary* comes from the medieval Latin word *dictionarium*, which in turn came from the Latin *dictio*, meaning *saying*. The ancient Greeks and Romans were the first to produce these works. But most Greek and Latin dictionaries were either lists of rare and difficult words or specialized lists of words.

During the Middle Ages, scholars made much use of Latin dictionaries which explained hard Latin words in easier Latin. Toward the end of the Middle Ages, as Latin began to lose ground to English, French, German, and other national languages of Europe, scholars began to rely on *glossaries* to understand Latin manuscripts. The glossaries usually gave the meanings of hard Latin words in the words of the national language. As these languages became accepted in each country, people needed new dictionaries to explain the hard words of their own language in terms of simpler words in the same language.

Early English Dictionaries. In 1604, Robert Cawdrey, a schoolmaster, prepared the first English dictionary. Called *The Table Alphabeticall of Hard Words*, it defined about 3,000 hard English words that had been taken from other languages. Larger dictionaries that offered more information about the words they contained were produced in the 1600's. In 1721, Nathan Bailey published a dictionary containing about 60,000 words. This was the first English dictionary that tried to include all English words instead of hard words only.

In the early 1700's, Jonathan Swift, Alexander Pope, Joseph Addison, Samuel Johnson, and other literary men of England wanted to prepare a dictionary that would set the standard for good usage in English. French and Italian scholars had already published dictionaries in their languages, and the success of those works influenced the literary men of England. Samuel Johnson undertook the task of preparing an English dictionary. He spent several years selecting quotations from the best writers to illustrate the meanings of words. He finally published his great work, *A Dictionary of the English Language*, in 1755. With John Walker's *Critical and Pronouncing Dictionary and Expositor of the English Language* (1791), it served as the standard for information about English words until the middle of the 1800's.

In 1806, Noah Webster published a small school dictionary in the United States. Webster wanted to set up an American standard of good usage to compare with the British standard set by Johnson and Walker. He had received encouragement from Benjamin Franklin, James Madison, and other American leaders. In 1828, he published a dictionary containing 70,000 entries. Since then, Webster's dictionaries have been frequently revised and are widely used today.

The period of national dictionaries gave way to scholarly dictionaries in the 1880's. The first scholarly dictionary was *A New English Dictionary on Historical Principles*. It appeared in parts from 1884 to 1928 and had almost 415,000 entries. In 1933, it was published in 12 volumes, with a one-volume supplement, as the *Oxford English Dictionary* (*O.E.D.*). This great dictionary gives a historical record of each meaning of a word. The *O.E.D.* tells the date the word first occurred in written English. It also lists other dates that show how the word was used through the years. No other dictionary in any language approaches the *O.E.D.* in wealth and authority of historical detail. In 1971, the *O.E.D.* was published in a two-volume compact edition, with all 13 volumes photographically reduced to a fourth of their original size. A three-volume supplement was scheduled to be published during the 1970's to replace the 13th volume of the 1933 edition. The first volume, covering letters A through G, appeared in 1972.

Current Dictionaries sold in the United States and Canada include *Webster's Third New International Dictionary*, with about 450,000 entries, the most complete modern dictionary of the English language, and *The Random House Dictionary*, which has about 260,000 entries. *The World Book Dictionary*, a Thorndike-Barnhart work that consists of more than 200,000 entries, is designed for family use. It was the first dictionary especially designed to be used with a specific encyclopedia. College dictionaries with about 150,000 entries include *The American Heritage Dictionary*, *The Random House College Dictionary*, the *Standard College Dictionary*, *Webster's New Collegiate Dictionary*, and *Webster's New World Dictionary*. Many dictionary publishers offer basic, intermediate, and high school dictionaries that contain from as few as 18,000 to as many as 100,000 entries.

CLARENCE L. BARNHART

Related Articles. See the separate articles in WORLD BOOK on each letter of the alphabet. See also:

Abbreviation	Grammar	Pronunciation
Antonym	Johnson, Samuel	Punctuation
Barnhart, Clarence L.	Language	Spelling
Capitalization	Lexicographer	Synonym
Etymology	Linguistics	Syntax
	Parts of Speech	Webster, Noah

DIDEROT, *DEE DROH,* **DENIS** (1713-1784), was one of the major philosophers of an intellectual movement called the Age of Reason. His work extended beyond philosophy and included writings in fiction, drama, and art and literary criticism. Diderot was also a satirist and a brilliant conversationalist. He spent much of his life compiling, editing, and writing the French *Encyclopedia*, a reference work that reflected revolutionary political views and antireligious sentiment. Diderot's major philosophical works include *Philosophical Thoughts* (1746) and *Thoughts on the Interpretation of Nature* (1754).

Diderot strongly supported experimental methods in philosophy and science. He believed that nature was in a state of constant change and no permanently adequate interpretation of it was possible. Diderot was also a philosophical materialist, believing that thought developed from the movements and changes of matter. His views on this subject were vague, as were his religious opinions. He was an atheist and also a deist, believing that God existed independently of the world and had no interest in it. But he later suggested that all of nature was God. Diderot was born in Langres, France, near Chaumont. STEPHEN A. ERICKSON

See also ENCYCLOPEDIA (An Age of Experiment); DRAMA (European Drama [France]).

DIDO, *DY doh*, or ELISSA, was the legendary founder and queen of Carthage. She was the daughter of King Belus of Tyre, and the wife of Acerbas, or Sychaeus. She fled to Africa with many devoted followers after her brother, Pygmalion, murdered her husband. There she was offered as much land as might be surrounded by a bull's hide. She cut a hide into thin strips, pieced them together, and laid them out to surround a large area. This area became Carthage (see CARTHAGE).

Hiarbas, or Iarbas, an African prince, wished to marry Dido and threatened war if she refused. Dido hated and feared him. She built a large funeral fire, threw herself upon it, and stabbed herself.

In his *Aeneid*, Virgil changed this story. He had Dido commit suicide because Aeneas, the Trojan hero, deserted her (see AENEID). VAN JOHNSON

DIDRIKSON, *DIHD rihk suhn*, **BABE** (1914-1956), was one of the greatest woman athletes in history. She won fame as an outstanding golfer. She set world records in the 1932 Olympic Games in the woman's 80-meter hurdles and javelin throw. The Amateur Athletic Union (AAU) named her to its All-America woman's basketball team in 1930 and 1931. She also played baseball, football, pocket billiards, and tennis, did some boxing, and competed in swimming events.

Babe Didrikson
Wide World

She began playing golf in the late 1930's. During the middle 1940's she set a record by winning 17 major women's golf tournaments in a row. She won every important title for women. In 1947, she became the first woman from the United States to win the British Women's Amateur golf tournament.

Babe Didrikson survived a 1953 cancer operation, and came back to win the National Women's Open and the Tam O'Shanter All-America tournaments in 1954. In 1950, the Associated Press named her the outstanding woman athlete of the first half of the 1900's. Mildred Ella Didrikson was born in Port Arthur, Tex., and married George Zaharias, a wrestler, in 1938. FRED RUSSELL

DIDYMUS. See THOMAS, SAINT.

DIE AND DIEMAKING. A die is a precision tool used to shape or cut metals or other materials. Diemaking is the process of producing dies. Diemakers, who are usually called *tool and diemakers*, rank among the most highly skilled industrial workers. The diemaker's product ranges from small diamond dies, used to draw metal into fine wire, to huge metal dies that form automobile parts from sheet metal.

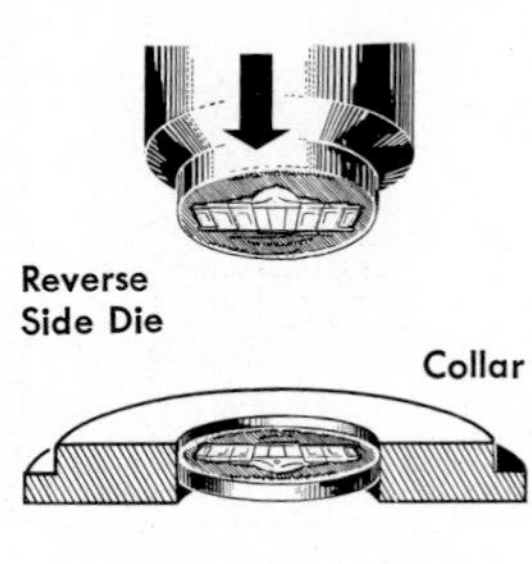

Coin-Stamping Dies are used to stamp both sides of a coin in a single operation. A collar holds the smooth disk of coin metal, called a *blank*, as it is fed into a power-driven stamping press.

Materials used for making dies include alloy steels, rubber, plastics, and certain combinations of materials. The die materials are shaped by basic machine tools or by newer methods, including the use of electricity (see MACHINE TOOL [New Developments]). After shaping, most dies are *heat treated* (carefully heated and cooled) to make them more resistant to wear.

When in use, certain dies must be lubricated. Common lubricants include oils and greases, soap solutions, and various chemical compounds. Dies used at high temperatures require such lubricants as graphite in oil or water, or molybdenum disulfide.

Dies play an important part in several industrial processes, including die casting, drawing, extrusion, forging, and stamping. Some of these processes use pairs of dies, one called a *male* die, or *punch*, and the other a *female* die.

In die casting, metals are melted in a machine that forces the liquid metal into steel dies. These dies replace the molds used in other casting. The metal hardens into the design of the die and comes out as a solid product. See CAST AND CASTING.

In drawing and extrusion, a hot or cold solid material, usually metal, is forced through an opening in a die (see EXTRUSION).

In forging, metal is often heated and put into two dies. The dies are pressed together and form the metal into the desired shape. See FORGING.

In stamping, a machine uses dies to stamp sheets, plates, or strips of metal or other materials, including plastics. Some stamping dies punch a hole in metal or cut it to a desired shape. Others form and shape the metal. Still others do both jobs. SEROPE KALPAKJIAN

See also TOOLMAKING; SILVER (pictures: How Silver Plate Tableware is Made).

JOHN G. DIEFENBAKER

Prime Minister of Canada
1957-1963

ST. LAURENT
1948-1957

DIEFENBAKER
1957-1963

PEARSON
1963-1968

John Evans

DIEFENBAKER, *DEE fen bayk ur,* **JOHN GEORGE** (1895-), served as prime minister of Canada from 1957 to 1963. One of the reasons for the defeat of Diefenbaker's Progressive Conservative government was his refusal to accept atomic warheads for defense missiles supplied by the United States. The Liberals won the election of April, 1963, and Liberal leader Lester B. Pearson became prime minister.

The Progressive Conservatives elected Diefenbaker as party leader in 1956. Diefenbaker led his party to victory in the 1957 election, and became the first Progressive Conservative prime minister in 22 years. In 1958, Canadians re-elected the party with the largest parliamentary majority in the nation's history. The party won again in the 1962 election, but did not have an absolute majority in Parliament. Diefenbaker's government stayed in power only with the support of the small Social Credit Party.

As prime minister, Diefenbaker increased Canada's social welfare programs and speeded development of the nation's rich northland. Canada faced serious economic problems in the early 1960's, and Diefenbaker adopted austerity measures to fight them. Under Diefenbaker, Canada increased its trade with Communist countries. The St. Lawrence Seaway was completed, and Georges P. Vanier became the first French-Canadian governor-general of Canada.

Tall and thin, with gray, curly hair and piercing blue eyes, Diefenbaker won friends and made enemies with his strong personality and fighting spirit. Diefenbaker made strong appeals to the national feeling of Canadians. "We are an independent country," he declared, "and we have the right to assert our rights and not have them determined by another country." Some persons called Diefenbaker's attitude "anti-American," but he disagreed. "The very thought is repugnant to me," Diefenbaker said. "I am strongly pro-Canadian."

Early Life

Boyhood and Education. John Diefenbaker was born on Sept. 18, 1895, in the village of Neustadt, Ont. The family of his father, William, had come to Canada from Germany. His mother, Mary Florence Bannerman Diefenbaker, was a granddaughter of George Bannerman, one of Lord Selkirk's Scottish settlers in the Red River Colony of Manitoba. John had a younger brother, Elmer.

John's father taught school for 20 years, then became a civil servant. As prime minister, Diefenbaker recalled: "My father was a person who had a dedicated devotion to the public service. Throughout the schools he taught, there were a great many who went into public life, because of his feeling that it was one field in which there was a need."

In 1903, when John was 8 years old, the family moved to a homestead in Saskatchewan. The boy loved stories of the early days on the prairie. He was particularly fascinated by tales about Gabriel Dumont, Louis Riel's right-hand man during the Saskatchewan Rebellion of 1885 (see SASKATCHEWAN REBELLION). John also studied the lives of such men as Abraham Lincoln, William Gladstone, and Napoleon.

John's interest later shifted to Canadian history. One night, according to a family legend, he looked up from reading a biography of Prime Minister Sir Wilfrid Laurier and announced: "I'm going to be premier (prime minister) of Canada." But John most admired former Prime Minister Sir John A. Macdonald.

In 1910, the Diefenbakers moved to Saskatoon, Sask., so John could attend high school there. John went on to the University of Saskatchewan, where he was active in campus politics. The college magazine predicted that someday he would lead the opposition in the House of Commons. He received his bachelor's degree in 1915 and a master's degree in 1916.

Diefenbaker was commissioned a lieutenant in the Canadian Army during World War I. He arrived in France in 1916, but was returned to Canada the next year after being injured in training camp.

Young Lawyer. Diefenbaker had always planned to be a lawyer. "There was no member of my family who was a lawyer," he said, "but I never deviated from that course from the time I was 8 or 9 years of age." He studied law at the University of Saskatchewan and received his law degree in 1919. That same year, he opened a small office in the nearby town of Wakaw.

Diefenbaker developed an outstanding reputation as a defense lawyer. Some persons who heard him in court claimed he could hold a jury spellbound with his oratory. "I just chat with the jury," said Diefenbaker.

In 1923, Diefenbaker moved to Prince Albert, Sask. He became a King's Counsel in 1929, and was a vice-president of the Canadian Bar Association from 1939 to 1942.

Diefenbaker married Edna May Brower in 1929. She died in 1951. Two years later, he married Mrs. Olive Freeman Palmer, an old friend from Wakaw. Mrs. Palmer, a widow with a grown daughter, was assistant director of the Ontario Department of Education.

Member of Parliament

In 1925 and 1926, Diefenbaker ran as a Conservative Party (called Progressive Conservative Party after 1942) candidate for the Canadian House of Commons. He lost both times. He ran for the Saskatchewan legislature in 1929 and 1938, and was defeated each time. He also ran for mayor of Prince Albert in 1934, and lost.

Diefenbaker's repeated defeats did not discourage him. He became leader of the Saskatchewan Conservative Party in 1936 and served until 1940. That year, he won election to the House of Commons from Lake Centre. Diefenbaker was re-elected to Parliament from Lake Centre in 1945 and 1949. He won election to the House of Commons from Prince Albert in 1953.

As a lawyer, Diefenbaker had made a reputation by defending individual civil rights. As a member of Parliament, he argued for a national bill of rights. Canada's first bill of rights was adopted in 1960 when Diefenbaker was prime minister.

The first bill Diefenbaker introduced in Parliament provided for Canadian citizenship for Canadians. They were then British subjects. Diefenbaker denounced what he called "hyphenated citizenship." He meant that every Canadian was listed in the census by the national origin of his father, such as French or Italian.

In 1948, the Progressive Conservative Party met to choose a leader to succeed John Bracken. Some members suggested Diefenbaker, but the party chose George Drew. In 1956, Drew became ill and gave up politics. Diefenbaker was chosen leader in December, 1956.

The Progressive Conservatives, discouraged after a long period of Liberal rule, held little hope for a victory in the 1957 election. But Diefenbaker waged a vigorous campaign. He charged that the Liberals had grown too powerful. Diefenbaker seemed to radiate vitality as

IMPORTANT DATES IN DIEFENBAKER'S LIFE

1895 (Sept. 18) Born in Neustadt, Ont.
1929 Married Edna May Brower.
1936 Became leader of Saskatchewan Conservative Party.
1940 Elected to Parliament.
1951 Mrs. Edna Diefenbaker died.
1953 Married Mrs. Olive Freeman Palmer.
1956 Chosen leader of Progressive Conservative Party.
1957 (June 21) Became prime minister of Canada.
1958 Progressive Conservatives won largest parliamentary majority in Canadian history.
1962 Progressive Conservatives won re-election.
1963 Liberals defeated Progressive Conservatives. Diefenbaker resigned as prime minister on April 22.
1967 Succeeded as leader of Progressive Conservative Party by Robert L. Stanfield.

IMPORTANT EVENTS DURING DIEFENBAKER'S ADMINISTRATION

Francis Miller for *Life* Magazine, © 1957 Time, Inc.

Campaigning in 1957, Diefenbaker visited his home town of Prince Albert, Sask.

Hospitalization Insurance for all Canadians was set up by the government in 1961.

Atomic Weapons Dispute with the United States led to the downfall of Diefenbaker's government in early 1963.

Canadian Dollar was devalued to 92.5 cents during the nation's economic crisis of 1962.

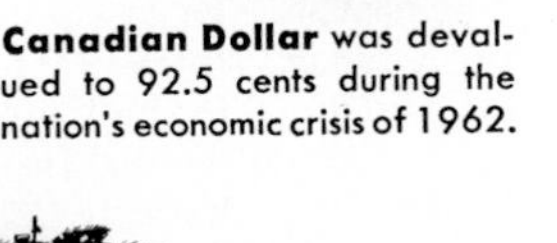
St. Lawrence Seaway was opened in 1959 by Queen Elizabeth II and President Dwight D. Eisenhower.

by Tom Doresett for WORLD BOOK

Queen Elizabeth II conferred with Diefenbaker and opened a new session of Parliament when she visited Canada in 1957.

United Press Int.

he told of his plans for developing northern Canada.

In the 1957 election, the Progressive Conservatives won more seats in Parliament than any other party, though they did not win an absolute majority. Diefenbaker became the first Progressive Conservative prime minister since Richard B. Bennett, who served from 1930 to 1935.

Prime Minister (1957-1963)

John G. Diefenbaker, the first prime minister of Canada to come from a prairie province, took office on June 21, 1957. He succeeded Louis S. St. Laurent.

Parliament passed several bills sponsored by Diefenbaker's government. One bill increased old-age pensions. Other legislation provided loans to economically depressed areas. Another bill gave financial aid to expand hydroelectric power in the Atlantic provinces.

In 1958, Diefenbaker asked for a new election. He wanted more supporters in Parliament to help him pass his legislative program. His party won 208 of the 265 seats in the House of Commons—the largest parliamentary majority in Canadian history.

Much of Diefenbaker's social legislation soon became law. Parliament increased pensions for the blind and disabled, and approved a program of federal hospital insurance. In 1958, the government began to build roads into Canada's rich but undeveloped northland.

Diefenbaker addressed the United Nations General Assembly in 1957 and 1960. He also attended the Commonwealth Prime Ministers' Conferences in London, England, in 1957, 1960, 1961, and 1962.

Economic Problems. During the early 1960's, Diefenbaker's government faced major economic problems. Canada had an unfavorable balance of trade with the United States. It imported far more from the United States than it sold there. In an effort to improve the trade balance, Diefenbaker urged Canadians to increase their trade with nations of the British Commonwealth. The government set up restrictions to discourage Canadians from investing abroad. It wanted such investment to take place in Canada, where it would aid the economy. But these measures did not solve the problem. Canada also faced major unemployment—up to 11 per cent of the work force in 1961 and 1962.

By the middle of 1962, Diefenbaker was forced to adopt austerity measures to boost the economy. The government lowered the value of the Canadian dollar. It reduced spending, raised tariffs on imports, and borrowed about $1 billion from foreign banks. In the election of June, 1962, the Progressive Conservatives won the most seats in Parliament, but not an absolute majority. Diefenbaker remained prime minister only because the Social Credit Party supported him.

Nuclear Controversy. In 1961, it was announced that the United States would supply Canada with missiles essential for the defense of North America. However, the Canadian government was not ready to accept atomic warheads for missiles received from the United States. By 1963, Canada had still not equipped the missiles with atomic warheads.

On Jan. 30, 1963, the United States charged that Canada had failed to propose a practical plan for arming its forces against a possible Russian attack. Diefenbaker angrily answered that the U.S. statement was "an unwarranted intrusion in Canadian affairs." He opposed acquiring nuclear warheads, saying that U.S. control of the missiles would threaten Canadian sovereignty. But Liberal leader Lester B. Pearson declared Canada should live up to its agreement and accept nuclear warheads. On Feb. 5, the House of Commons passed a motion of no-confidence in Diefenbaker's government, and the government fell from power.

In the election of April, 1963, the Liberals won 129 seats in the House of Commons. This was just short of an absolute majority of the 265 seats, but more than any other party won. The Progressive Conservatives won only 95 seats. Pearson succeeded Diefenbaker as prime minister on April 22, 1963. Diefenbaker led the opposition in Parliament until 1967, when the Progressive Conservatives chose Robert L. Stanfield to succeed him. Diefenbaker continued to represent Prince Albert in the Canadian House of Commons. G. F. G. Stanley

See also Canada, History of; Pearson, Lester B.

DIEFENBAKER LAKE. See Saskatchewan (Rivers and Lakes).

DIELECTRIC. See Electricity (Current Electricity).

DIELS, *deels,* **OTTO** (1876-1954), a German chemist, shared the 1950 Nobel prize for chemistry with his former pupil, Kurt Alder. They discovered and developed a process called *diene synthesis* for joining molecules containing carbon atoms. It yields complex natural molecules such as vitamins and hormones, and man-made materials such as synthetic rubber and fuels. Diels was born in Hamburg, Germany.

DIEM, NGO DINH. See Ngo Dinh Diem.

DIEMAKING. See Die and Diemaking.

DIEN BIEN PHU. See Indochina (Independence).

DIENCEPHALON. See Brain (The Diencephalon; picture).

DIEPPE, *dee EHP* (pop. 29,970), is a resort town on the north coast of France, 33 miles (53 kilometers) north of Rouen. For location, see France (political map). Tourists take over the town during the summer. They crowd the beaches and stay in the large hotels that stand along the waterfront. During the rest of the year, Dieppe is a quiet town where the people are busy with spinning, porcelain making, and shipbuilding. The town has a good harbor, bordered with white chalk cliffs. The English held Dieppe from 1420 to 1435. It was nearly destroyed by the bombardment of an Anglo-Dutch fleet in 1694. Dieppe became a fashionable resort for French society in the 1700's. Germans occupied the town during World War II. It was the scene of the largest commando raid of the war. Canadian and British troops landed at Dieppe on Aug. 19, 1942. They damaged German installations and emplacements in spite of heavy losses of men and equipment. Edward W. Fox

DIEPPE RAID. See World War II (The Invasion of Europe).

DIES, MARTIN (1900-1972), a lawyer, served as a Democrat from Texas in the United States House of Representatives from 1931 to 1945, and again from 1953 to 1959. Dies became a center of national controversy in the 1930's as chairman of the House Special Committee to Investigate Un-American Activities. He was born in Colorado City, Tex., and was graduated from National University, Washington, D.C. In 1940, Dies wrote *Trojan Horses in America.* Eric F. Goldman

DIESEL, *DEE zul,* **RUDOLF** (1858-1913), a German mechanical engineer, developed an internal-combustion machine that used oil as fuel. Because of its simplicity of design and the economy of its fuel, the diesel engine is frequently preferred to the gasoline engine. It has greatly increased the efficiency of industry and transportation. See DIESEL ENGINE.

Diesel was born in Paris of German parents, and received his technical education in Munich. He became interested in designing an engine more efficient than steam and gas engines. He based his work on the theory of heat engines and on the designs of other engineers. He patented his design in 1892, and had completed and operated the first successful diesel engine by 1897. He also founded a factory to make diesel engines. In 1913, Diesel mysteriously disappeared from a German ship bound for London. ROBERT E. SCHOFIELD

See also SHIP (Increasing Power and Speed).

DIESEL ENGINE is a type of internal-combustion engine used chiefly for heavy-duty work. Most of the locomotives in the United States are diesel powered. Diesel engines drive huge freight trucks, large buses, tractors, and heavy road-building equipment. They are also used to power submarines and ships, and the generators of electric-power stations in small cities.

How a Diesel Engine Works. There are two main types of internal-combustion engines. One type, found in most automobiles, is called a *spark-ignition* engine. It uses electricity and spark plugs to ignite the fuel in the engine's cylinders (see GASOLINE ENGINE). The other type, the diesel engine, is a *compression-ignition* engine. When air confined in a cylinder is suddenly compressed, the temperature of the air rises. In a diesel engine, each piston compresses air in a cylinder. Fuel is injected and the heat of the air makes it ignite.

Diesel engines burn fuel oils, which require less refining and are cheaper than higher-grade fuels such as gasoline. During the combustion process, the stored chemical energy in the fuel is converted to *thermal,* or heat, energy. The temperature in each cylinder rises as high as 4500° F. (2480° C) and creates pressures of 1,500 pounds per square inch (105 kilograms per square centimeter). The pressure pushes against the tops of the pistons, forcing them to the other end of their cylinders. The pistons are connected by a rod or other suitable connecting mechanism to a crankshaft which they turn. In this way, a diesel engine supplies rotary power to drive vehicles and other machines.

In order for the compressed air inside the cylinders to ignite the fuel, it must have a certain temperature. The degree to which the temperature of the air rises depends on the amount of work done by the piston in compressing it. This work is measured in terms of the ratio between the volume of uncompressed air and the volume of the air after it is compressed. The compression ratio necessary to ignite the fuel depends on the size of the engine's cylinders. In large cylinders, the compression ratio is about 13 to 1. For small cylinders, it may be as high as 20 to 1. The average is 14.5 to 1.

Near the end of the piston's compression stroke, the fuel is injected into a cylinder. In order to have the fuel and air mix well, the fuel is injected under high pressure as a spray. Combustion usually starts just before the piston ends its compression stroke. The power of diesel engines can be increased by *supercharging,* or forcing air under pressure into the cylinders. See FUEL INJECTION; SUPERCHARGER.

Diesel engines have a high *thermal efficiency,* or ability to convert the stored chemical energy in the fuel into *mechanical energy,* or work. They burn cheap fuel and can perform heavy work under highly overloaded conditions. This is why they are favored for heavy-duty work.

Kinds of Diesel Engines. There are two main types of diesel engines. They differ according to the number of piston strokes required to complete a cycle of air compression, exhaust, and intake of fresh air. A *stroke* is the distance a piston travels in one direction. These engines are (1) the four-stroke cycle engine and (2) the two-stroke cycle engine.

In a *four-stroke engine,* each piston moves down, up,

The Diesel Engine operates in two or four cycles. This diagram shows how a single cylinder in a four-cycle engine operates. On Stroke 1, the piston moves down, drawing air into the cylinder. On Stroke 2, the rising piston compresses the air in the cylinder, raising the air temperature to about 900° F. (480° C). When oil is sprayed into the cylinder, the heat causes it to burn explosively, forcing the piston down in Stroke 3. This is called the *power stroke.* On Stroke 4, the piston rises, emptying the cylinder.

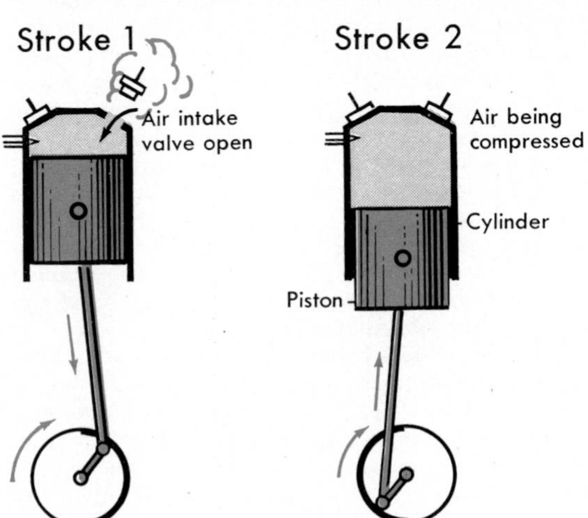

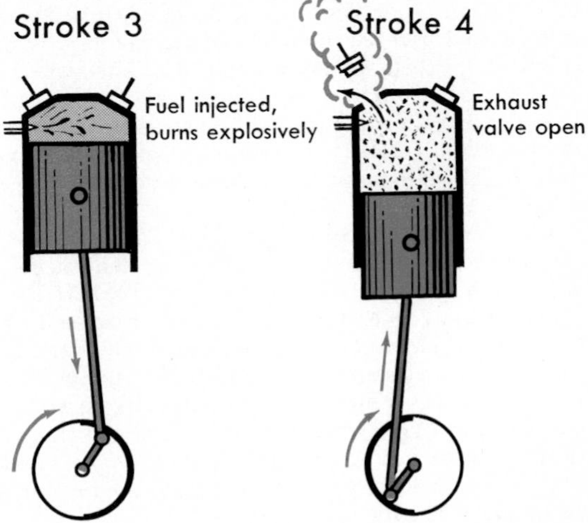

down, and up to complete a cycle. The first downstroke draws air into the cylinder. The first upstroke compresses the air. The second downstroke is the power stroke. The second upstroke exhausts the gases produced by combustion. A four-stroke engine requires exhaust and air-intake valves.

In a *two-stroke engine*, the exhaust and intake of fresh air occur through openings in the cylinder near the end of the down-, or power, stroke. The one upstroke is the compression stroke. A two-stroke engine does not need valves. These engines have twice as many power strokes per cycle as four-stroke engines, and are used where high power is needed in a small engine.

History. The diesel engine is named for Rudolf Diesel, the German engineer who invented it. Diesel built his first engine in 1893. It exploded and almost killed him, but it proved that fuel could be ignited without a spark. He operated his first successful engine in 1897. Later, Sir Dugald Clerk of Great Britain developed the two-stroke diesel. OTTO A. UYEHARA

See also DIESEL, RUDOLF; ENGINE ANALYZER; LOCOMOTIVE; STARTER.

DIET, *DIE ut*, is the name of the parliament of Japan. The parliament of the Holy Roman Empire in Europe also was called the Diet. The parliament of Hungary, now the national assembly, formerly was called the Diet. The word was long applied in Europe to religious assemblies. In 1521, Martin Luther was judged by the Diet of Worms. See also JAPAN (Government; picture); LUTHER, MARTIN. WILFRID DYSON HAMBLY

DIET is the food and drink that a person takes regularly day after day. The word *diet* also refers to the amounts or kinds of food needed under special circumstances, such as losing or gaining weight. Diet needs vary according to age, weight, condition of health, climate, and amount of activity. *Dietetics* is the science of feeding individuals or groups. The money available and health and nutritional needs affect the type of feeding prescribed.

Normal Diet, or *balanced diet*, contains all the food elements needed to keep a person healthy. To stay healthy, one needs *proteins* to build tissues, and *fats* and *carbohydrates* to provide energy and heat. *Minerals* and *vitamins* are needed for growth and to maintain tissues and regulate body functions. In the United States, calcium and iron are the minerals most often in short supply in the diet. Vitamins A and C are often eaten in smaller amounts than are recommended.

A diet that lacks any needed food element may cause certain *deficiency diseases*. For example, lack of vitamin A causes night blindness, and lack of vitamin C causes scurvy (see SCURVY).

Diets for Losing or Gaining Weight. Both the energy value of food and the energy spent in daily activity are measured in *Calories*, or units of heat (see CALORIE). Diets for gaining or losing weight are based on the amount of calories taken into the body in food and the amount of calories used up in activity. If a person takes in more calories than he uses up, he will gain weight. He will lose weight if he takes in less calories than he uses up. A diet aimed toward gaining weight should include all the food elements. A doctor's advice should be sought before dieting to lose weight.

Special Diets may be prescribed for persons suffering from certain diseases. For example, the healthy body needs sugar, but a person with diabetes must limit the use of sugar unless he takes insulin (see INSULIN). Doctors may prescribe low-salt diets for patients with certain heart or kidney diseases.

Some persons suffer allergic or skin reactions from certain food products, such as milk, tomatoes, strawberries, wheat, potatoes, eggs, fish, nuts, chocolate, or pork. These persons should avoid such foods and consult a physician.

Certain groups of people, such as young children or older people, have special dietary needs. Because children grow rapidly, they need food not only to replace worn-out tissues and provide energy, but also to build new tissue.

A child's diet should include milk and milk products, eggs, lean meat, poultry, fish, fruits, vegetables, and cereals.

A well-balanced diet is as important to the older person as it is to the child. Older people need as many nutrients as young adults. But if their activity is reduced, they need fewer calories. Expectant or nursing mothers and babies also need special diets (see BABY [The Expectant Mother; Feeding Procedures]). JANICE M. SMITH

Related Articles in WORLD BOOK include:

Allergy	Food	Milk (Food Values)
Calorie	Fruit (Food Value)	Nutrition
Carbohydrate	Health	Protein
Cooking	Lipid	Vitamin
Digestion	Metabolism	Weight Control
Fat		

DIETETICS. See DIET; DIETITIAN.

DIETITIAN is a person who uses the principles of nutrition to plan menus and supervise the preparation of food. Dietitians are educated in nutrition and *dietetics* (the science that deals with the relationship of food to health). Persons working in public health agencies are sometimes called *nutritionists* and usually have more advanced education than dietitians. Dietitians work in hospitals, universities, schools, restaurants, industrial food services, and many other areas.

Over half the professionally qualified dietitians work in hospitals. Their responsibilities include planning diets and supervising the preparation of food for patients and hospital employees. Dietitians also help patients plan and understand the diets prescribed for them. Others work in educational and research programs.

To become a dietitian, a student must complete a planned college or university course of study leading to a bachelor's degree. The curriculum should include such courses as biology, chemistry, foods, nutrition, and institution management. Then, the student gains practical knowledge by serving an internship at a medical center, university, or business firm. Additional information about careers in dietetics can be obtained from the American Dietetic Association, 620 N. Michigan Ave., Chicago, Ill. 60611.

Interest in dietetics began in the late 1800's. Dietitians were trained only in college *domestic science* (homemaking) courses. They prepared food only for hospital patients who were on special diets. During the early 1900's, dietitians began to supervise the diets of all patients. Following World War I, schools, industrial cafeterias, and restaurants began employing dietitians to supervise the planning of diets and of menus.

Critically reviewed by the AMERICAN DIETETIC ASSOCIATION

See also DIET; NUTRITION.

DIETRICH, MARLENE (1904-), a German-born actress and singer, became a famous Hollywood motion picture star. Her charm, famous figure, expressive eyes, and husky voice have made her an international favorite for over 40 years.

United Press Int.

Marlene Dietrich

Marlene Dietrich first attracted attention for her performance in the German film *The Blue Angel* (1930). Then she made such American films as *Morocco* (1930), *Shanghai Express* (1932), *The Garden of Allah* (1936), and *Destry Rides Again* (1939). Since World War II her films have included *A Foreign Affair* (1948), *Witness for the Prosecution* (1958), and *Judgment at Nuremberg* (1961). In 1950, she began touring internationally as the star of a cabaret show. Miss Dietrich was born MARIA MAGDALENE DIETRICH in Berlin. HOWARD THOMPSON

DIEZ, FRIEDRICH. See LINGUISTICS (The Comparativists).

DIFFERENTIAL is a system of gears mounted between the rear axles of a motor vehicle. These gears make it possible for one rear wheel to turn faster than the other when the vehicle goes around a corner.

The differential gears of an automobile are assembled inside a metal housing and are turned by the drive shaft from the engine. An axle extends from each side of the housing to a rear wheel. These axles are connected only by the gears of the differential.

When the vehicle moves straight ahead, the differential gears divide the driving force equally between the two axles. This keeps each of the rear wheels spinning at the same speed. But when the car turns a corner, the gears permit one axle to turn faster than the other. This makes it possible for the outer wheel, which has farther to go, to spin faster than the inner wheel. Therefore, the car does not skid. In the same way, when a car gets stuck in snow or mud, the differential gears allow one rear wheel to spin while the other does not move.

Racing cars are built without differentials because the gearing causes a loss in power on turns. That is why racing cars always skid around turns.

Charles S. Mott (1875-1973) and H. H. Timken (1831-1909) were pioneer developers of differential gearing in the United States. FRANKLIN M. RECK

See also AUTOMOBILE (The Drive Train); GEAR.

DIFFERENTIAL ANALYZER is a calculating machine that works by electronics. It can solve advanced mathematical problems of physics, electrical engineering, aerodynamics, and other sciences. The differential analyzer was invented in 1930 by the American scientist Vannevar Bush. See also COMPUTER (History); INVENTION (picture: Computers).

DIFFERENTIAL CALCULUS. See CALCULUS.

DIFFERENTIATION, in biology. See GROWTH (In Living Things); CELL (Growth and Specialization).

DIFFRACTION is the spreading out of waves—water, sound, light, or any other kind—as they pass by the edge of an obstacle or through an opening. Diffraction explains why water waves spread in all directions after passing through a narrow channel in a breakwater. It also explains why sound can be heard around a corner when no straight path exists from the source to the ear.

Diffraction of light differs from diffraction of sound because diffraction is most evident when the obstacle is about the same size as the wave length diffracted. The sound waves we hear have wave lengths of about a yard and are diffracted by ordinary objects. But visible light waves have wave lengths of less than $\frac{1}{35,000}$ of an inch (0.00007 centimeter). Thus, light waves can be diffracted noticeably only by very small objects.

How Diffraction Occurs. Diffraction takes place among all waves at all times. To understand why it becomes noticeable only when the obstacle is about the size of the diffracted wave length, one must understand both diffraction and *interference*.

Christian Huygens, a Dutch scientist, developed the principle that explains why diffraction occurs. This

Light Waves Diffracted at the Edge of a Small Disk produce a pattern of light and dark rings. The diagram shows how the photograph was taken. Some diffracted light spreads toward the center of the disk where it produces a bright spot surrounded by a series of rings. Other diffracted light spreads away from the center and produces a series of rings around the disk. A thin rod holding the disk also causes a diffraction pattern.

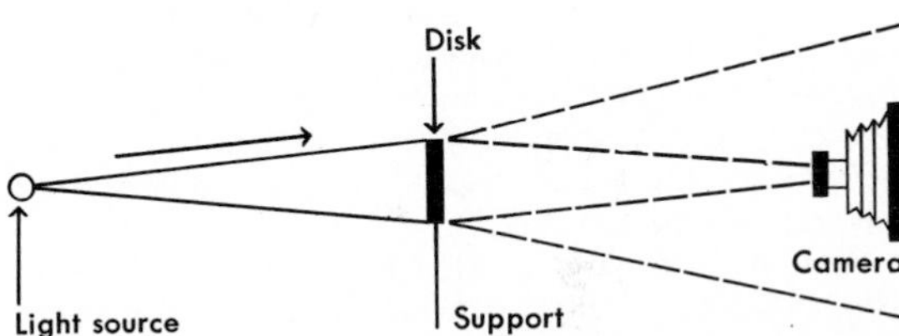

From *Fundamental University Physics, Volume II,* by Alonso and Finn, published by Addison-Wesley

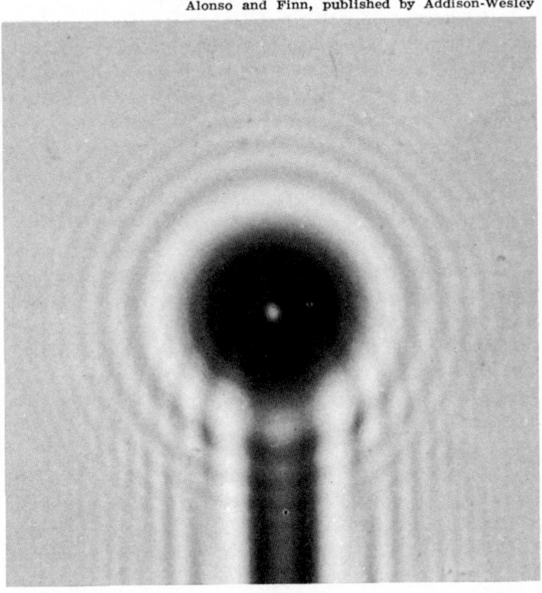

principle states that each point on the surface of a wave is the source of small waves. These wavelets move outward in all directions. To find the total wave reaching an area, all the wavelets that strike the area must be considered. If the crests of two wavelets reach a point at the same time, they reinforce one another. This condition is called *constructive interference*, and the resulting wave is large. If the crest of one wave reaches a point at the same time as the low point of another, the two waves cancel one another. This condition is called *destructive interference*, and the resulting wave is small or nonexistent. See INTERFERENCE.

A beam of light moves in a straight line because effects of diffraction along the beam are canceled by destructive interference. The wavelets at the edge of the beam spread, but most of the light travels in a straight line with the beam.

When light travels through a tiny opening, interference occurs only among the wavelets coming from the opening. These wavelets produce a diffraction pattern because most of the destructive interference has been eliminated.

Diffraction of light from a tiny source can likewise be observed if all other light—and thus all interference—is removed. A disk placed in the path of such a source blocks out the wavelets that originate behind the disk. At points beyond the disk, these eliminated wavelets are missing not only in the shadow of the disk but also outside of the shadow, where they would have interfered constructively. The shadow pattern on a screen beyond the disk consists of a series of rings, alternately light and dark, in and surrounding the shadow area. A bright spot occurs at the center of the shadow because at that point all waves interfere constructively. They do so because they have all traveled the same distance from the edge of the disk.

Uses of Diffraction. The occurrence of diffraction has been used as a test of whether various things are waves. For example, diffraction of X rays by crystals convinced scientists that X rays are waves.

The pattern of X-ray diffraction depends on the type and distribution of atoms in the diffracting substance. This fact has been used to study the structure of crystals by X-ray diffraction and to discover the structure of proteins and nucleic acids.

A *diffraction grating* is a glass plate with lines ruled on it at extremely small, equal intervals. Light can pass only between the lines, and the slits are about as wide as a wave length of light. If a parallel beam of white light strikes the grating, a pattern of light of various colors appears on a screen beyond the grating. The colors appear because white light consists of different colors. These colors have different wave lengths, and the longer wave lengths are diffracted at greater angles. Scientists can identify a substance by the pattern of colors that the substance produces through a diffraction grating. GERALD FEINBERG

See also LIGHT (How Light Behaves); MOLECULE (Studying Molecules; picture); SPECTROSCOPE; WAVES.

DIFFUSION, *dih FYOO zhuhn,* is said to occur when the molecules of one substance mix with those of another. All substances—gases, liquids, or solids—are made of tiny particles called *molecules*. The molecules constantly move. Substances mix when their molecules move among each other. They can move most easily if they bump into each other as little as possible. The farther apart they are, the less danger they have of colliding, and the more rapid is the diffusion. The molecules in gases, such as air, are farther apart than the molecules

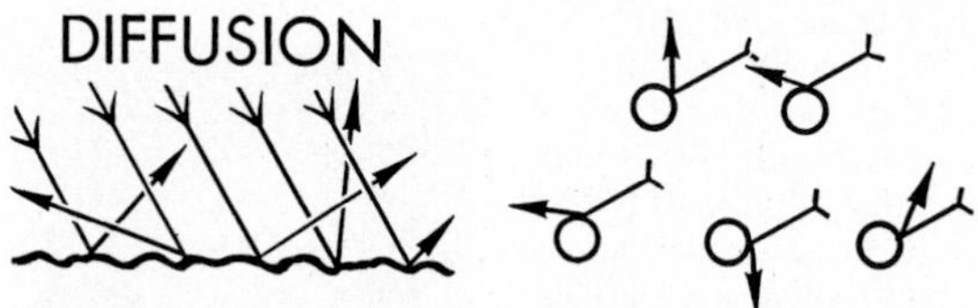

Light is scattered in all directions when it falls on an uneven surface.

The rays of the sun are spread by gas molecules and dust in the air.

in liquids and solids. Therefore, diffusion occurs more rapidly in gases than in liquids.

If you uncork a bottle of smelling salts in a room, you can soon smell the odor all through the room. The same thing is true of the fragrance of flowers. These odors come from gases whose molecules have mingled with the molecules of the other gases in the air. We say the molecules of gases have *diffused*.

If you pour a little red ink through a tube to the bottom of a glass jar of water, all the water will soon turn red. The ink has diffused all through the water. In ammonia water, the gas ammonia has diffused through the liquid water. When a lump of sugar sweetens a cup of coffee, the solid sugar has dissolved in the coffee and diffused through it.

In the plant world, diffusion takes place when sap passes through cell walls (see OSMOSIS).

When light shines on a rough surface, the rays are diffused, or reflected in many directions. Diffused light makes good reading light because it does not give off any glare. LOUIS MARICK

See also GAS; MOLECULE.

DIGESTION, *dih JEHS chuhn,* is the process by which food is broken down into smaller particles, or molecules, for use in the human body. This breakdown makes it possible for the smaller digested particles to pass through the intestinal wall into the blood stream. The simple digested food particles in the blood stream are distributed to nourish all parts of the body. Digestion takes place in almost all parts of the alimentary canal (see ALIMENTARY CANAL). In these parts, the food is mixed with substances called *enzymes*, which speed up chemical reactions of the food.

The fats, proteins, and carbohydrates (starches and sugars) in foods are made up of very complex molecules and must be digested, or broken down. When digestion is completed, starches and complex sugars are broken down into simple sugars, fats are digested to fatty acids and glycerin, and proteins are digested to amino acids. Simple sugars, fatty acids and glycerin, and amino acids are the digested foods which can be absorbed into the blood stream. Other foods such as vitamins, minerals, and water do not need digestion.

From Mouth to Stomach. Digestion begins in the mouth. Chewing is very important to good digestion for two reasons. When chewed food is ground into fine particles, the digestive juices, which contain enzymes, can

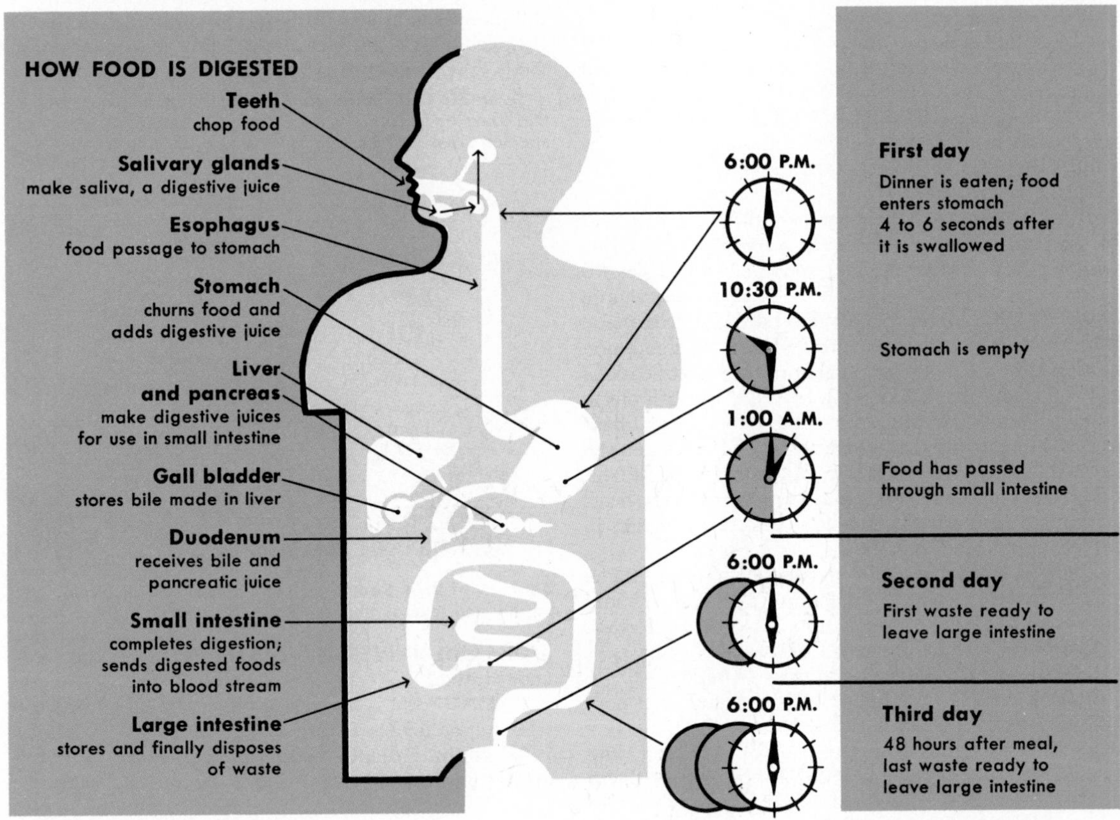

react more easily. As the food is chewed, it is moistened and mixed with saliva, which contains the enzyme *ptyalin*. Ptyalin changes some of the starches to sugar.

After the food is swallowed, it passes through the esophagus into the stomach. In the stomach it is thoroughly mixed with more digestive juices by a vigorous churning motion. This motion is caused by contraction of strong muscles in the stomach walls.

The digestive juice in the stomach is called *gastric juice*. It contains hydrochloric acid and the enzyme *pepsin*. This juice begins the digestion of protein foods such as meat, eggs, and milk. Starches, sugars, and fats are not digested by the gastric juice. The food remains in the stomach for two to five hours. Food that has been churned, partly digested, and changed to a thick liquid in the stomach is called *chyme*. Chyme passes from the stomach into the small intestine.

In the Small Intestine, the digestive process is completed on the partly digested food by pancreatic juice, intestinal juice, and bile. The pancreatic juice is produced by the pancreas and pours into the small intestine through a tube, or duct. The pancreatic juice contains the enzymes *trypsin*, *amylase*, and *lipase*. Trypsin breaks down the partly digested proteins, amylase changes starch into simple sugars, and lipase splits fats into fatty acids and glycerin. The intestinal juice is produced by the walls of the small intestine. It has milder digestive effects than the pancreatic juice, but carries out similar digestion. Bile is produced in the liver, stored in the gall bladder, and flows into the small intestine through the bile duct. Bile helps the body digest and absorb fats.

When the food is completely digested, it is absorbed by tiny blood and lymph vessels in the walls of the small intestine. It is then carried into the circulation for nourishment of the body. Food particles are small enough to pass through the walls of the intestine and blood vessels only when they are completely digested.

Almost no digestion takes place in the large intestine. The large intestine stores waste food products and absorbs small amounts of water and minerals. The waste materials that accumulate in the large intestine are roughage that cannot be digested in the body. Bacterial action produces the final waste product, the *feces*. Such waste materials are eliminated from the body from time to time.

Ewald E. Selkurt

Related Articles in World Book include:

Alimentary Canal
Amino Acid
Assimilation
Beaumont, William
Bile
Carbohydrate
Cellulose
Dyspepsia
Enzyme
Esophagus
Fat
Gland
Indigestion
Intestine
Liver
Lymphatic System
Mastication
Pancreas
Pepsin
Starch
Stomach
Sugar
Swallowing
Teeth

See also *Digestive System* in the Research Guide/Index, Volume 22, for a *Reading and Study Guide*.

DIGIT, *DIHJ iht,* means any one of the ten numerals from 0 to 9. The word *digit* comes from the Latin word *digitus* (finger). The digit was a measure used in ancient times. It was the breadth of a forefinger, about three-fourths of an inch (19 millimeters). We write numbers in the decimal number system by means of digits and place value. See ARABIC NUMERALS; DECIMAL NUMERAL SYSTEM.

In astronomy, a digit is one-twelfth of the diameter of the sun or moon. Astronomers measure an eclipse with digits. For example, they speak of an eclipse of 8 digits. HOWARD W. EVES

DIGITALIS, *DIHJ uh TAL ihs,* is a powerful drug made from the dried leaves of the purple foxglove, a common garden flower. It takes its name from the scientific name of the foxglove (see FOXGLOVE). In 1785, a British physician, William Withering, introduced it for the treatment of certain heart diseases. Doctors use digitalis when the action of the heart muscles is too weak to force blood out of the heart normally. They also use it to make the heart beat more regularly. It can be given as a powder, in tablets, as a liquid, or as a tincture.

Digitalis is very powerful and should never be taken except under a doctor's direction. The doses should always be small. A. K. REYNOLDS

DIGRAPH. See CODES AND CIPHERS (Cryptanalysis).

DIHEDRAL WINGS. See AIRPLANE (The Wing).

DIJON, *dee ZHAWN* (pop. 145,357; met. area pop. 183,989), a city in France, is the center of the Burgundy wine trade. It stands at the junction of the Ouche and Suzon rivers, about 160 miles (257 kilometers) southeast of Paris (see FRANCE [political map]). The city's industries produce chemical, metal, and food products. Dijon is famous for its restaurants and pastry shops. The University of Dijon is a leading French university.

Dijon has many old and interesting buildings. The palace of the dukes of Burgundy, started in the A.D. 1100's, now houses the town hall and a museum. Parts of Dijon's most historic church, the Cathedral of Saint Bénigne, date from A.D. 1001. From about 1100 to 1500, Dijon was the chief city of the independent and powerful Duchy of Burgundy. See BURGUNDY.

DIK-DIK is the smallest of the antelopes. It lives only in eastern Africa, except for one species in southwest Africa. The tallest dik-diks are about 15 inches (38 centimeters) high at the shoulder. Females are somewhat larger than males, but have no horns. The slightly curved horns of the male are more than half as long as the head. Dik-diks are very delicate, slender animals, with tiny hoofs, short tails, and long hairy muzzles. See also ANTELOPE, with picture.

Scientific Classification. Dik-diks are in the bovid family, *Bovidae.* The seven species of dik-diks are all in genus *Modoqua.* VICTOR H. CAHALANE

DIKE. See VEIN; RICE (The Rice Field); LEVEE; NETHERLANDS (introduction; pictures).

DILI, *DIHL ee* (pop. 6,730), is the capital, chief port, and commercial center of Portuguese Timor. It lies on the northern coast of the island (see INDONESIA [color map]; TIMOR). Ships reach Dili through a channel in the coral reef. Dili exports copra, tobacco, coffee, and sandalwood. Its factories process coffee and make soap and pottery. JUSTUS M. VAN DER KROEF

DILL is a small hardy plant related to parsley, anise, and caraway. It grows wild in southeastern Europe. The dill plant is light green and has an umbrellalike shape. People use the bitter seeds and tiny leaves to season foods. Useful medicines are made from dill.

Scientific Classification. The dill plant is a member of the parsley family, *Umbelliferae.* It is genus *Anethum,* species *A. graveolens.* HAROLD NORMAN MOLDENKE

J. Horace McFarland

Clusters of Ripe Seeds grow on stalks of dill. Dill is related to parsley and several other common herbs and vegetables.

DILLARD UNIVERSITY. See UNIVERSITIES AND COLLEGES (table).

DILLINGHAM is the family name of a father and son who helped develop Hawaii.

Benjamin Franklin Dillingham (1844-1918) developed railroad and sugar industries on the island of Oahu. He settled in Hawaii in 1865, and, by the 1890's, had become Oahu's pioneer railroad builder. He built railroads to carry harvested sugar cane from plantations to seaports. Later, Dillingham's railroad and sugar industries spread to the islands of Hawaii, Kauai, and Maui. He was born in West Brewster, Mass.

Walter Francis Dillingham (1875-1963) founded an engineering firm in 1903 that developed harbors and improved land in Hawaii. The firm widened Pearl Harbor and turned thousands of acres of waterfront swampland into valuable property. Dillingham was born in Honolulu. DONALD D. JOHNSON

DILLON, CLARENCE DOUGLAS (1909-), was appointed secretary of the treasury in 1961 by President John F. Kennedy. He served until 1965. An investment banker, Dillon served as President Dwight D. Eisenhower's undersecretary of state for economic affairs and later as undersecretary of state.

Dillon was graduated from Harvard University in 1931. He entered his father's Wall Street firm, Dillon, Read, & Co. Inc., and served as chairman of the board from 1946 to 1953. He was ambassador to France from 1953 to 1957. Dillon was born in Geneva, Switzerland. ERIC SEVAREID

DILLON, GEORGE (1906-1968), an American poet, published his first book, *Boy in the Wind,* in 1927. His second book of poems, *The Flowering Stone,* won the 1932 Pulitzer prize in poetry. With Edna St. Vincent Millay, he translated Charles Baudelaire's book of poems *The Flowers of Evil* from the French. He worked for 24 years on the staff of *Poetry* magazine. Dillon was born in Jacksonville, Fla. JOHN HOLMES

DIMAGGIO, *dee MAH jih oh,* **JOSEPH PAUL** (1914-), was one of the greatest outfielders in baseball history. He played with the New York Yankees from 1936 through 1951. DiMaggio hit safely in 56 straight games in 1941, to set a major league record. He had a lifetime batting average of .325 in 1,736 games, and played in 10 World Series and 11 major league All-Star games. In 1939, 1941, and 1947, DiMaggio was the American League's most valuable player. He was elected to the baseball Hall of Fame in 1955. He was born in Martinez, Calif. FRED RUSSELL

DIME is a United States coin worth 10 cents, or one-tenth of a dollar. The word dime comes from the Latin *decimus* (tenth). Until 1933, the dime was only legal as payment in amounts of $10 or less. Then, Congress made the dime legal tender in any amount. Dimes were made of silver until 1965. That year, Congress ruled that dimes should be made of a solid copper center between two layers of a copper-nickel alloy. The Canadian dime, worth 10 Canadian cents, is basically silver. It has an alloy for hardening. FRED REINFELD

See also FASCES; MONEY.

U.S. Dime pictures Franklin D. Roosevelt. On the reverse side, the torch of liberty appears between sprigs of laurel and oak.

Chase Manhattan Bank Money Museum

DIMENSION. See FOURTH DIMENSION.

DIMETER. See METER (poetry).

DIMINUENDO. See MUSIC (table: Terms Used in Music).

DIMITY, *DIM uh tih,* is a sheer, plain-weave, lightweight cotton fabric. It often has a corded or checked effect that is achieved by weaving two or more yarns together. The word *dimity* comes from the Greek *dimitos,* which means *double thread.* HAZEL B. STRAHAN

DINAR is the monetary unit of Yugoslavia, Iraq, Jordan, Kuwait, Algeria, and Tunisia. In Iraq, the dinar is a gold coin. In Yugoslavia, where 100 para equal one dinar, the dinar is a copper-and-nickel or aluminum-and-bronze coin. It was once the chief coin of the Moslems and the territory they controlled. Its name comes from a silver Roman coin, the *denarius* (see DENARIUS). For values of the dinar, see MONEY (table: Values of Monetary Units). FRED REINFELD

D'INDY, *dan DEE,* **VINCENT** (1851-1931), was a French composer, organist, and conductor. His compositions are noted for the way they express his love of nature. His works include *Poem of the Mountains,* a suite for piano and orchestra; *Istar Variations,* for orchestra; *Symphony on a French Mountain Air,* for orchestra and piano; and *Symphony No. 2 in B flat,* and several chamber music works.

D'Indy was born in Paris, and studied with the composer César Franck. He became widely known as a teacher of composition. In 1894, D'Indy helped found the *Schola Cantorum,* a school in Paris devoted to religious music. He directed the school from 1911 until his death. He also taught at the Paris Conservatory. His pupils included composers Georges Auric, Arthur Honegger, Erik Satie, and Albert Roussel. JOYCE MICHELL

DINESEN, *DEE nuh suhn,* **ISAK** (1885-1962), was the pen name of BARONESS KAREN BLIXEN-FINECKE, a Danish author who wrote in English and Danish. Her stories deal with fantastic, unreal, often grotesque people and situations. She had a deep concern for the supernatural, and she preferred to portray life in romantic settings of the past. Her volumes of short stories include *Seven Gothic Tales* (1934), *Winter's Tales* (1942), *Last Tales* (1957), *Anecdotes of Destiny* (1958), and *Ehrengard* (published in 1963, after her death). Her other works include a novel, *The Angelic Avengers* (1944); and two books of memoirs, *Out of Africa* (1937) and *Shadows on the Grass* (1961).

Born KAREN CHRISTENCE DINESEN in Rungsted, Denmark, she was married to Baron Bror Blixen-Finecke in 1914, and divorced in 1921. She owned a coffee plantation in eastern Africa, and lived there from 1914 to 1931. Then she returned to Denmark. EINAR HAUGEN

DINGO, *DING go,* is the wild dog of Australia. Dingoes are the only wild members of the dog family found in the country. Scientists believe that prehistoric men brought the first dingoes to Australia.

Dingoes are medium-sized dogs, about as large as English setters. They have alert faces; sharp, erect ears; and brushlike tails. Most dingoes have yellowish-brown fur. But the animal's colors range from yellowish-white to black. Dingoes rarely bark, but howl instead. If caught as puppies, they make good pets.

Dingoes hunt alone or in family groups. Their chief food is the *wallaby* (small kangaroo). Dingoes also kill sheep. For this reason, the Australian government has spent large sums of money to exterminate the dogs.

Scientific Classification. The dingo belongs to the dog family, *Canidae.* It is classified as genus *Canis,* species *C. dingo.* WILLIAM O. PRUITT, JR.

See also ANIMAL (picture: Animals of the Deserts).

DINMONT. See DANDIE DINMONT TERRIER.

The Dingo Is the Only Dog Native to Australia.

New York Zoological Society

Field Museum of Natural History

Mighty Dinosaurs Once Roamed North America. The monster *Tyrannosaurus, right,* ranks as the largest meat-eating animal that ever lived. A 45-foot (14-meter) giant, it often attacked plant-eating dinosaurs, such as the horned *Triceratops, left.*

DINOSAUR, *DY nuh sawr,* is the common name for two groups of reptiles that lived millions of years ago. Some of them were the largest, most terrifying animals that ever stalked the earth. The word *dinosaur* comes from the Greek words *dinos,* meaning *terrible,* and *sauros,* meaning *lizard.* Dinosaurs were not lizards, but the biggest flesh-eating dinosaurs were indeed "terrible." They stood as much as 20 feet (6 meters) high and had skulls 4 feet (1.2 meters) long, with huge, daggerlike teeth. The biggest plant eaters must have shaken the earth when they moved. Some were 90 feet (27 meters) long, and some weighed 85 short tons (77 metric tons). But not all dinosaurs were giants. One was only 2½ feet (76 centimeters) long.

Samuel Paul Welles, the contributor of this article, is Lecturer and Principal Museum Scientist at the University of California, Berkeley, and coauthor of From Bones to Bodies.

Dinosaurs dominated the world during the *Mesozoic era*—from about 225 million years ago to 65 million years ago. The Mesozoic is divided into three *periods.* The oldest period, the *Triassic,* was from 225 million to 180 million years ago. The middle period, the *Jurassic,* was from 180 million to 130 million years ago. The most recent period, the *Cretaceous,* covered the time from 130 million to 65 million years ago. Dinosaurs appeared in the middle of the Triassic period and died out at the end of the Cretaceous period.

Scientists learn about dinosaurs from *fossils,* the records and remains of ancient living things. *Paleontologists,* scientists who study fossils, search for dinosaur bones and tracks. They study them and try to reconstruct the appearance and habits of the animals. This work requires a thorough knowledge of the body structure of living animals, and of the relation of body structure to habits. See Fossil (Studying Fossils).

Kinds of Dinosaurs

Dinosaurs were as varied in appearance and habits as are land animals of today. Some dinosaurs were large, some small. Some walked on two feet, some on four. Some ate plants, others ate meat. Some had smooth skin, others had scaly skin. Still others had skin studded with bony plates. But all dinosaurs had tiny brains. The dinosaurs, like other reptiles, laid their eggs on land. Scientists believe that large dinosaurs lived to be more than 100 years old.

Dinosaurs made up two great *orders,* or groups, of reptiles. The two groups differed in the structure of the *pelvis,* or hip bone. The *Saurischia* (pronounced *saw RIHS kee uh*) had hips similar to those of modern lizards. The *Ornithischia* (*AWR nih THIS kee uh*) had birdlike hips.

Lizard-Hipped Dinosaurs were divided into two groups: the *sauropods,* the gigantic plant eaters, and the *theropods,* including all the meat eaters.

Sauropods were the largest of all land animals. One of these monsters was *Apatosaurus,* also called *Brontosaurus.* This swamp dweller grew up to 80 feet (24 meters) long, and stood on four big legs that resembled an elephant's legs. Another of these animals, *Diplodocus,* was almost 90 feet (27 meters) long, but was more slender than *Apatosaurus. Brachiosaurus* was the largest of all the dinosaurs, even though it had a rather short tail. This dinosaur was 70 feet (21 meters) long and weighed 85 short tons (77 metric tons).

All the sauropods had long necks and long tails. But their heads were only about 2 feet (61 centimeters) long. They had fragile teeth and must have eaten only tender plants. They probably spent most of their time in shallow water, which helped support their tremendous weight. Sauropods were fairly common in the late Jurassic period. They began to die out in the Cretaceous period. Scientists have found their fossils in Africa, Asia, Australia, Europe, Madagascar, and North and South America.

Theropods all walked on their hind legs and had small front legs that they used for grasping and tearing food.

DINOSAUR FAMILY TREE

Dinosaurs ruled the earth for about 145,000,000 years. They ranged in size from creatures no bigger than chickens to huge animals such as *Brachiosaurus.* This monster, shown compared in size to a man, could look over the top of a three-story building. The two main groups of dinosaurs were the *ornithischians,* or bird-hipped dinosaurs, and the *saurischians,* or lizard-hipped dinosaurs. The dinosaurs illustrated are not drawn to scale.

TRIASSIC 225,000,000 years ago

THECODONTS, ancestors of dinosaurs, grew to about 3 feet (91 centimeters) in length. They ran on their hind legs.

JURASSIC 180,000,000 years ago

SAUROPODS ate huge amounts of plants. The clumsy *Apatosaurus* was 80 feet (24 meters) long.

STEGOSAURS, the first of the armored dinosaurs, were protected by triangular bony plates standing up along their backs.

CRETACEOUS 130,000,000 years ago

ORNITHOPODS lived in shallow water along the shores of lakes and rivers. *Anatosaurus* grew to be about 40 feet (12 meters) long.

ANKYLOSAURS had spikes and bony plates that protected their bodies. *Palaeoscinus* could use its mighty tail as a club.

THEROPODS, such as the terrible *Tyrannosaurus,* were flesh-eating dinosaurs. They preyed on the plant-eating dinosaurs.

CERATOPSIANS had horns or bony frills to protect their heads. *Triceratops,* the last ceratopsian, was 25 feet (8 meters) long.

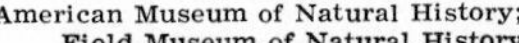

American Museum of Natural History;
Field Museum of Natural History

They had big heads with large, sharp teeth. The first theropod discovered, *Megalosaurus*, stood about 12 feet (3.7 meters) high. Its direct descendant, *Allosaurus*, was a 34-foot (10-meter) terror that preyed on the huge sauropods. The largest meat-eating animal that ever lived, *Tyrannosaurus*, measured about 45 feet (14 meters) from head to tail. It stood almost 20 feet (6 meters) high and had a 4-foot (1.2-meter) head. Its mouth was armed with 6-inch (15-centimeter), daggerlike teeth. It had ridiculously small, useless front legs. Theropods also include the smallest well-known dinosaur, *Compsognathus*, which measured only 2½ feet (76 centimeters), including its long tail.

Theropods lived from the middle Triassic through the Cretaceous periods. They lived in Africa, Asia, Australia, Europe, and North and South America.

Bird-Hipped Dinosaurs, the *Ornithischia*, were divided into four groups: (1) *stegosaurs*, armored dinosaurs of the Jurassic period; (2) *ankylosaurs*, armored dinosaurs of the Cretaceous period; (3) *ornithopods*, or duck-billed dinosaurs; and (4) *ceratopsians*, or horned dinosaurs. All these dinosaurs were plant eaters.

Stegosaurs were among the earliest of the *Ornithischia*. *Stegosaurus*, a typical member, was about 18 feet (5.5 meters) long and had a small head. Great bony plates set on edge protected its neck, back, and tail. It probably lashed out at attackers with these spikes. *Stegosaurus' brain* was about the size of a walnut. But near its hip it had a nerve center 20 times as large as the brain. This center controlled the action of its tail and hind legs. Stegosaurs lived until the early Cretaceous period, then died out. Their remains have been found in Africa, Asia, Europe, and North and South America.

Ankylosaurs generally resembled *Ankylosaurus*, a low, squat, powerful dinosaur. *Ankylosaurus* had almost solid armor, like an armadillo, with a row of large, sharp spikes down both its sides. Its tail was clublike, tipped with a heavy mass of bone. Ankylosaurs lived in Africa, Asia, Europe, and North and South America.

Ornithopods walked on two legs and had a long, balancing tail. They had no front teeth, and many of them had mouths that broadened into ducklike bills. Later ornithopods, such as *Anatosaurus*, had as many as 2,000 teeth. Preserved casts of the skin of a few of these dinosaurs show that they had webbed feet. This indicates that they were good swimmers. Ornithopods lived from the late Triassic period through the Cretaceous period in Asia, Europe, and North America.

Ceratopsians looked much like rhinoceroses, but many, including *Triceratops*, were larger. Some had one horn, some as many as five. They all had big fringes growing back from their skulls to protect their necks. Paleon-

RECONSTRUCTING A DINOSAUR SKELETON

Preparing the Skeleton may take months or even years of work. Scientists first clean the bones and glue together broken pieces. They make plaster substitutes for any missing parts. Then they drill holes in large bones and strengthen them with steel rods.

Chicago *Daily News*

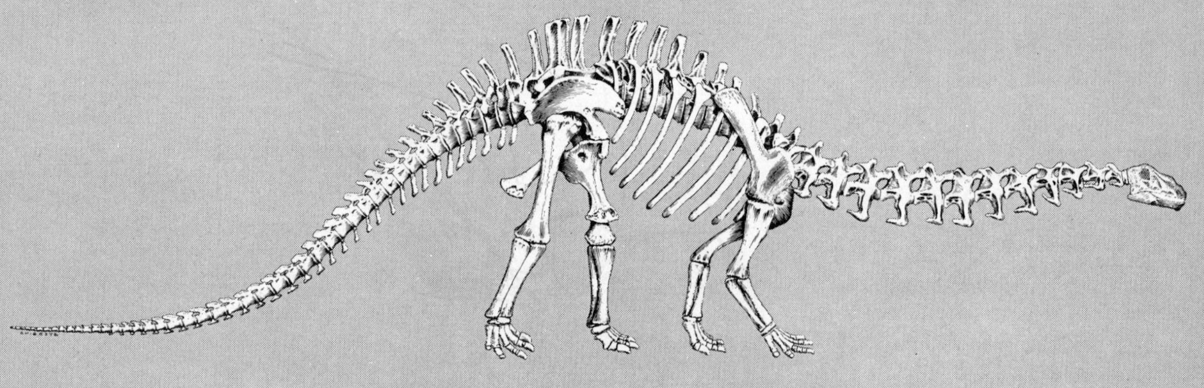

Field Museum of Natural History

An Assembled *Apatosaurus* Skeleton looks like this drawing prepared by the Field Museum of Natural History. The bones of the actual skeleton are supported and fastened together by steel rods. The scientists mount it in a natural position.

tologists have found many fossils of *Protoceratops*, a small ceratopsian. These fossils range from adult animals to eggs. The eggs are about 6 to 7 inches (15 to 18 centimeters) long and 3 inches (8 centimeters) across (see FOSSIL [picture: Dinosaur Egg]). Ceratopsians, the last dinosaurs to appear, lived during the late Cretaceous period in Asia, and in North and South America.

How Dinosaurs Lived

Surroundings. When dinosaurs first appeared, North America was a low-lying continent with a great sea bordered by swamps where the Rocky Mountains now rise. The climate was warm, and forests of pines, redwoods, and cycads (a subtropical plant) grew on land (see CYCAD). Flowering plants appeared in the Cretaceous period.

Dinosaurs shared the swamps with other animals. Snakes glided through the water. Crocodiles as much as 40 feet (12 meters) long lived along the shores. *Pterosaurs*, flying reptiles, flew overhead on leathery wings. Birds appeared during the Jurassic period. Small mammals became numerous and varied.

Getting Food. The lush vegetation of the steaming swamps furnished food for the great sauropods. They moved slowly through the swamps with their ridiculously small heads working all the time to gulp down enough food for their huge bodies. Ornithopods swam in river mouths feeding on floating water plants. The stegosaurs, land dinosaurs of the Jurassic period, ate ferns, cycads, and pines. Ankylosaurs and ceratopsians of the Cretaceous period also ate these plants, along with flowering plants. The flesh-eating theropods preyed upon all the other kinds of animals.

Protection. Plant eaters developed many kinds of protection against the theropods. Some, including the sauropods and ornithopods, retreated into the water where the theropods could not go. The theropods were land animals and probably could not swim. Land-dwelling ornithischians had horns or armor, or both. Bony armor and spiked or clubbed tails protected the stegosaurs and ankylosaurs. Ceratopsians, like the modern rhinoceros, developed a counterattack. The charge of an enraged *Triceratops* must have put many a *Tyrannosaurus* to flight.

Why Dinosaurs Died Out

Scientists have advanced many reasons to explain why the dinosaurs died out. Probably the basic cause was the rise of mountain ranges during the Cretaceous period. When the mountain ranges formed, the great seaways drained from the continents and the vast swamplands that were the homes of the dinosaurs dried up. This caused tremendous changes in climate and food supply. But the dinosaurs had become specially adapted to the old conditions. When these conditions changed rapidly, the dinosaurs could not adjust. New plants appeared, and old ones died out. The plant eaters could not live on the new plants. As the plant eaters died out, the meat eaters that depended on them for food also died. This long, slow process took from 10 million to 20 million years. By the end of the Cretaceous period, all the dinosaurs had disappeared from the earth.

Other factors, including disease, probably affected the dinosaurs. Many scientists believe that the development of mammals also ranked as an important factor in the extinction of the dinosaurs. Mammals have better brains than the dinosaurs and better protection against cold. Some of the mammals probably ate dinosaur eggs and young dinosaurs. Although they were not the only cause, they almost certainly helped in the extinction of the great reptiles. SAMUEL PAUL WELLES

Related Articles. For additional information and color pictures of dinosaurs, see PREHISTORIC ANIMAL. Other related articles in WORLD BOOK include:

American Museum of Natural History	Dinosaur National Monument
Andrews, Roy Chapman	Fossil
	Reptile

Painting by Charles R. Knight, from Field Museum of Natural History

Painted Restoration shows what *Apatosaurus* probably looked like when it lived. Scientists and artists work together to make the restoration as realistic as possible. They add plants and other animals that lived where the dinosaurs roamed.

DINOSAUR NATIONAL MONUMENT, located in Utah and Colorado, is a scenic region containing spectacular canyons cut by the Green and Yampa rivers. Its deposits of fossil remains of prehistoric reptiles are of scientific interest. The monument covers about 211,000 acres (85,000 hectares). It was established in 1915.

DINWIDDIE, *dihn WIHD ih,* **ROBERT** (1693-1770), was lieutenant governor of Virginia from 1751 to 1758. He served as the acting governor of the colony, because the governors usually lived in England. Greatly interested in the Ohio region, he decided to keep that area from the French. In 1753, he sent George Washington to demand that the French withdraw from western Pennsylvania, claimed by Virginia. In the war that followed, Dinwiddie urged the colonies to help the English drive the French from the Ohio Valley. He aided the expedition sent against Fort Duquesne in 1755. He quarreled with the Virginia Assembly because of its reluctance to vote funds for the war. He returned to England in 1758. He was born near Glasgow, Scotland. See also WASHINGTON, GEORGE (Early Military Career). JOSEPH CARLYLE SITTERSON

DIOCESE. See BISHOP.

DIOCLETIAN, *DY oh KLEE shuhn,* a Roman emperor, was born about A.D. 245 and died in 313. He divided the empire into four regions called *prefectures.* He shared the rule with three other men. Diocletian is remembered for his persecutions of Christians, beginning in 303.

Diocletian's official name was Gaius Aurelius Valerius Diocletian. He was born in Illyricum (now Yugoslavia). Diocletian became a general, and was proclaimed emperor by his troops in 284. In 286, he made Maximian his co-emperor. He gave two other men each authority over a prefecture, creating a four-man rule that lasted until 305. Diocletian and Maximian then gave up their power. The shared rule, though effective, was unpopular because it increased the size of government and raised taxes. RAMSAY MACMULLEN

Diogenes With His Lantern by Salvator Rosa, The Fine Arts Gallery of San Diego, Calif.

Diogenes went through the streets carrying a lantern. He held it up to strangers and said he was looking for an honest man.

DIODE. See ELECTRONICS (Rectification; The First Commercial Vacuum Tubes); VACUUM TUBE.

DIOECIOUS PLANT. See FLOWER (Variations).

DIOGENES, *dy AH juh neez* (412?-323 B.C.), a philosopher of ancient Greece, was called the *Cynic.* He belonged to the Cynic school of philosophy, which taught that a man ought to lead a life of self-control, and be free from all desire for material things and pleasures. Diogenes carried this view to extremes in his own life. According to tradition, he used a tub for shelter and walked the streets barefoot. Diogenes believed that good birth, riches, and honor were of little value because they did not help a man lead a virtuous life.

He was born at Sinope, in Asia Minor. Pirates captured him during a journey from Athens to Aegina and offered him for sale as a slave. He told his captors he knew no trade except how to govern men. Pointing to a wealthy Corinthian, he said: "Sell me to this man, he needs a master." The Corinthian bought Diogenes and made him tutor to his sons. When Alexander the Great came to see Diogenes, who was sunning himself, he said, "Ask any favor you wish." Legend says that Diogenes replied: "Please move out of my sunlight." To which Alexander commented: "If I were not Alexander, I would like to be Diogenes." LEWIS M. HAMMOND

See also CYNIC PHILOSOPHY.

DIOMEDE ISLANDS. See ALASKA (introduction).

DIOMEDES, king of Argos. See ULYSSES.

DIOMEDES, king of Thrace. See HERCULES.

DIONAEA. See VENUS'S-FLYTRAP.

DIONNE QUINTUPLETS. See MULTIPLE BIRTH.

DIONYSIA. See DRAMA (Greek Drama).

DIONYSIUS EXIGUUS. See CHRISTIAN ERA.

DIONYSIUS THE AREOPAGITE. See ANGEL.

DIONYSIUS THE ELDER, *DY oh NIHSH ih uhs* (430?-367 B.C.), was a Greek military leader who ruled ancient Sicily and southern Italy for a time. Dionysius used huge armies of paid foreign soldiers in his battles. He was a cruel ruler, and was hated by most Greeks. He liked writers and artists, and the Greek philosopher Plato stayed briefly in his palace. In 405 B.C., he became commander of the army of Syracuse, the largest Greek city on Sicily. He soon took over the government, and made Syracuse the strongest and richest city in Europe. Dionysius controlled the Greek cities in Sicily. He won wars against Carthage in 396 B.C. and 392 B.C., and later took control of southern Italy. In 378 B.C., he was defeated by Carthage and was forced to give up half of Sicily. THOMAS W. AFRICA

DIONYSUS, *DY uh NY suhs,* was the god of wine in Greek mythology. After coming into contact with Greek culture, the Romans adopted Dionysus as their god of wine, but they called him Bacchus.

The ancient Greeks associated Dionysus with violent and unpredictable behavior, especially actions caused by drinking too much wine. Most stories about Dionysus tell of his leading sessions of drunken merrymaking. Dionysus' followers at these gatherings included *nymphs* (maidens), creatures called *satyrs* that were half man and half horse or goat, and women at-

Detail of a painting (about 530 to 510 B.C.) from a Greek vase showing Dionysus with satyrs and a maenad; the Louvre, Paris (André Held)

Dionysus was the Greek god of wine. In the painting above, he holds a wine cup and grape vines. Dionysus presided over festivals known for drinking and wild behavior.

tendants called *maenads* (see NYMPH; SATYR). The merrymaking ended with religious ceremonies honoring Dionysus.

Dionysus' parents were Zeus, the king of the gods, and Semele, the mortal daughter of King Cadmus of Thebes. Dionysus married Ariadne, the daughter of King Minos of Crete.

Not all the stories about Dionysus concern drunkenness or violent behavior. Many Greeks believed that Dionysus taught man farming techniques, especially those related to growing grapes and making wine. The Greeks also dedicated the great theater in Athens to Dionysus. Their concept of tragedy in drama grew from a ceremony honoring Dionysus. The word *tragedy* comes from the Greek word *tragos*, meaning *goat*. The goat was sacred to and symbolic of Dionysus. C. SCOTT LITTLETON

See also BACCHUS; DRAMA (Greek Drama); SEMELE.

DIOPHANTUS. See ALGEBRA (History).

DIOPSIDE, *dy AHP syd*, is a hard, green mineral that is sometimes used as a gemstone. It belongs to the pyroxene group of rock minerals, which make up the dark parts of some granites and some lava rocks. It may be found in its nearly pure form ($CaMgSi_2O_6$) in marble. See also GEM (color picture). WILLIAM C. LUTH

DIOR, CHRISTIAN (1905-1957), a French fashion designer, created a "new look" in women's fashions in 1947. The "new look" featured long hemlines and full skirts. Dior was born in Granville, France, and became a fashion illustrator for the newspaper *Le Figaro Illustré*. He opened his own fashion salon, the House of Dior, in Paris in 1946, and became known as the leading designer in France.

DIORAMA, *DIE oh RAH muh*, is an exhibit showing modeled figures or objects in front of a painted or modeled background. The models become smaller toward the back of the exhibit and blend so skillfully with the background that the scene looks real. Dioramas showing outdoor scenes have curved backgrounds to help give a feeling of distance. Museums use dioramas to show historical events, industrial methods, and animals and plants in their natural settings. Schoolchildren sometimes make simple dioramas as projects.

The word *diorama* comes from Greek words meaning *a view through*. Louis Daguerre, a French inventor, first used the word about 1822 for transparent paintings he exhibited and for a theater he opened. RALPH H. LEWIS

For other examples of dioramas, see PURIM (picture: The Feast of Purim); LINCOLN, ABRAHAM (pictures); FREEDOM OF THE PRESS (picture).

DIOSCURI. See CASTOR AND POLLUX.

DIPHTHERIA, *dihf THEER ee uh*, is a severe contagious disease in which a false membrane grows over the mucous membrane, usually in the throat or nose. Most people can get diphtheria, but it is unusual in infants less than six months old. The disease most commonly occurs during autumn and winter. During the late 1800's, diphtheria epidemics swept Western Europe and the United States. Since 1890, the number of diphtheria cases in these regions has sharply declined.

How Diphtheria Spreads. Diphtheria is caused by a specific bacillus, *Corynebacterium diphtheriae*. The bacteria spread from one person to another. Because the bacteria usually live in the human nose and throat, doctors believe the most common method for spreading the disease is by coughing and sneezing. Persons called *carriers* may harbor the bacteria without showing any signs of the disease. Such persons may spread the disease to others.

Symptoms. The strong false membrane of diphtheria appears as a yellowish-gray patch on the mucous membrane of the victim's pharynx, tonsils, nose, or throat. In rare cases, the membrane may form over an open skin wound. When it forms in the throat, the membrane may obstruct the throat so that the victim cannot breathe. To save the patient's life, the doctor makes a temporary opening through the neck, directly into the windpipe.

In most cases of diphtheria, the microorganisms remain in the victim's throat and never enter the blood stream. But they produce a *toxin* (poison) which the blood carries to all parts of the body.

Treatment. Doctors treat diphtheria by injecting an *antitoxin* into the patient's muscles. The antitoxin is a substance that neutralizes the toxin produced by the germs. It is made by concentrating the blood serum of horses or sheep that have been inoculated repeatedly with diphtheria toxin (see ANTITOXIN). The first effective diphtheria antitoxin was developed in 1890 by Emil von Behring, a German bacteriologist.

Prevention. Diphtheria can be prevented. Doctors give three injections of diphtheria toxoid at weekly intervals. Diphtheria toxoid is made from diphtheria toxins that have been treated with chemicals to prevent harmful effects. The toxoid stimulates a person's body to produce immune antibodies (see ANTIBODY).

A test to determine a person's immunity to diphtheria was introduced by the physician Béla Schick in 1913 (see SCHICK TEST). Doctors use this test during outbreaks of diphtheria to determine which persons need inoculations. They also use the test after an inoculation to make sure that the toxoid has made the person immune. PAUL S. RHOADS

See also DISEASE (table: Communicable Diseases).

DIPHTHONG, *DIHF thawng,* is the sound produced by pronouncing two vowels as a single syllable. Examples are the *ou* in *out* and *oi* in *oil.* One sees readily how two sounds become a diphthong by pronouncing *ah* and *ee* together slowly, then more rapidly. They become the diphthong heard in *mine,* commonly described as *long i.* Diphthongs are often called *digraphs.*

DIPLODOCUS. See DINOSAUR (Lizard-Hipped Dinosaurs).

DIPLOMACY, *dih PLOH muh see,* is the means of conducting negotiations between nations. Most nations send representatives to live in other countries. There, they help carry on day-to-day relationships between their country and the country where they serve. These *diplomats* work to gain political or economic advantages for their country and to promote international cooperation. The diplomats follow strict rules of procedure in official discussions.

Diplomatic Representatives observe strict rules about rank and importance. The highest rank is ambassador extraordinary and plenipotentiary, followed by envoy extraordinary and minister plenipotentiary, minister resident, minister-counselor, counselor of embassy, secretary of embassy, and attaché. Most large nations send ambassadors to each other, and to many smaller nations. Smaller countries sometimes send and receive diplomats of lower rank. Most governments also send *consuls* to foreign cities to handle international business. The pope sends *nuncios, legates,* and *delegates* to many countries to represent him.

Each nation handles its diplomatic affairs through a foreign office. In the United States, the office that handles foreign relations is known as the Department of State. A foreign office usually forms the most important part of the executive branch of the government.

Diplomatic Duties. A diplomatic officer abroad is the accredited spokesman for his government. He gathers information on everything of value to his government and transmits it in formal reports, usually in code (see CODES AND CIPHERS). He protects the rights of his fellow citizens who are living or traveling abroad.

Diplomats maintain their headquarters in an embassy or legation. The only difference between an embassy and a legation is the rank of the diplomat in charge. An ambassador heads an embassy, and a minister heads a legation. A diplomat's staff may include attachés and other special advisers who report on economic, political, and social conditions.

Diplomatic Immunity. Diplomats enjoy several important privileges and immunities while serving abroad. These privileges arise partly because diplomats are the direct representatives of sovereign powers. Just as important, diplomats must have complete independence of action in order to perform their duties. A diplomat's privileges are based on the principle of *extraterritoriality.* This principle, used in international law, includes the guarantee that persons living in foreign countries remain under the authority of their own governments. Four important diplomatic privileges and immunities are:

1. A diplomat cannot be arrested for any reason. His family and staff usually share this exemption.
2. His residence, papers, and effects cannot be searched or seized.
3. His personal belongings cannot be taxed by the country in which he serves.
4. He, his family, and his staff enjoy complete freedom of worship.

History. Nations have not always used diplomacy to settle international problems. The ancient Romans used diplomatic representatives only for special purposes. But as relations among countries grew more complex, many nations found that they needed permanent representatives in other countries. Embassies first appeared in Italy during the 1200's and 1300's. At that time, they served as headquarters for spies and espionage agents, as well as for diplomats. Many historians believe that Cardinal Richelieu of France started the system of resident representatives during the 1600's.

Some scholars argue that diplomatic representatives are unnecessary today. They suggest that nations can take care of all diplomatic matters by letter, telegraph, or radio. They believe that diplomacy is kept alive only to satisfy the vanity of some governments. But personal diplomatic contact has many advantages. Diplomats take great care to make friends with government officials

COUNTRIES TO WHICH THE UNITED STATES SENDS AMBASSADORS

Afghanistan
Algeria
Argentina
Australia
Austria
Bahamas
Bahrain
Bangladesh
Barbados
Belgium
Bolivia
Botswana
Brazil
Bulgaria
Burma
Burundi
Cameroon
Canada
Central African Republic
Chad
Chile
Colombia
Costa Rica
Cyprus
Czechoslovakia
Dahomey
Denmark
Dominican Republic
Ecuador
Egypt
El Salvador
Equatorial Guinea
Ethiopia
Fiji
Finland
France
Gabon
Gambia
Germany, East
Germany, West
Ghana
Great Britain
Greece
Grenada
Guatemala
Guinea
Guyana
Haiti
Honduras
Hungary
Iceland
India
Indonesia
Iran
Ireland
Israel
Italy
Ivory Coast
Jamaica
Japan
Jordan
Kenya
Korea, South
Kuwait
Laos
Lebanon
Lesotho
Liberia
Libya
Luxembourg
Malagasy Republic
Malawi
Malaysia
Maldives
Mali
Malta
Mauritania
Mauritius
Mexico
Morocco
Nauru
Nepal
Netherlands
New Zealand
Nicaragua
Niger
Nigeria
Norway
Oman
Pakistan
Panama
Paraguay
Peru
Philippines
Poland
Portugal
Qatar
Romania
Russia
Rwanda
Saudi Arabia
Senegal
Sierra Leone
Singapore
Somalia
South Africa
Spain
Sri Lanka
Sudan
Swaziland
Sweden
Switzerland
Syria
Taiwan
Tanzania
Thailand
Togo
Tonga
Trinidad and Tobago
Tunisia
Turkey
United Arab Emirates
Upper Volta
Uruguay
Venezuela
Western Samoa
Yemen (Sana)
Yugoslavia
Zaire
Zambia

and influential citizens. When they present a formal proposal, they can count on these friendships to help them. A diplomat also can test reaction to ideas his government is considering by talking with acquaintances.

Sometimes heads of various governments feel that they need personal conferences with leaders of other governments. They bypass their own diplomats in such "summit meetings." CARTER L. DAVIDSON

Related Articles in WORLD BOOK include:

Ambassador	Foreign Policy	Minister
Attaché	Foreign Service	Nuncio
Cold War	International Relations	Protocol
Consul	Legate	State, Department of
Diplomatic Corps	Legation	
Extraterritoriality		

DIPLOMATIC CORPS consists of all the heads of diplomatic missions, such as ambassadors and ministers, who represent their governments in the capital of a nation. The term may also refer to all the diplomatic personnel of such missions. A diplomatic mission, generally an embassy or a legation, consists of an ambassador, a minister, or a chargé d'affairs; counselors and secretaries; and various attachés.

Diplomats conduct their government's official relations with the host government, including the negotiation of treaties. They also report to their government on economic, financial, military, and political conditions in the host country. PAYSON S. WILD

See also AMBASSADOR; DIPLOMACY; FOREIGN SERVICE.

DIPLURA is an order of insects that have no eyes and no wings. They have slender, whitish bodies, and live in rotten wood or under leaves or stones. These insects shun light and move quickly to find a hiding place whenever they are disturbed. See INSECT (table).

DIPOLE. See ANTENNA.

DIPPER. See WATER OUZEL.

DIPPERS, BIG AND LITTLE. See BIG AND LITTLE DIPPERS.

DIPPING NEEDLE is a magnetic needle suspended so that it will dip toward the earth. It points toward magnetic substances. It is somewhat like a compass, but it is held on edge so that it points vertically instead of horizontally. In a compass, the north-seeking end of the needle will swing *around* horizontally until it points toward the north magnetic pole. But the north-seeking end of a dipping needle will swing *down* until it points toward the north magnetic pole.

W. S. Darley and Co.

A Dipping Needle is used to locate water pipes and other underground magnetic objects. It points down when held directly over the metal object.

The north-seeking end would point straight down if a dipping needle were held over the north magnetic pole. The other end of the needle, the south-seeking end, would point straight down if the dipping needle were held over the south magnetic pole. The needle remains horizontal at the magnetic equator. At all other places on the earth, the needle points down at an angle from the horizontal. A scale marked on the case shows the angle of dip from the true horizontal (see MAGNETIC EQUATOR).

Dipping needles are used to study the earth's magnetism, to locate iron and other magnetic objects just under the earth's surface, and to locate underground meter boxes and water pipes. R. WILL BURNETT

DIPSOMANIA. See ALCOHOLISM.

DIPTERA, *DIP tur uh,* is the large order of insects that are true flies. *Diptera* means *two wings.* Diptera have only two wings and a pair of knobbed threads called *halteres* (balancers). Most other winged insects have four wings in two pairs. Diptera mouth parts usually consist of a tube, called a *proboscis,* for piercing and sucking juices from animals and plants. The Diptera include crane flies, gnats, midges, mosquitoes, houseflies, horseflies, black flies, and deer flies. Insects such as May flies and dragonflies are not true flies, and therefore are not Diptera. WILLIAM C. BEAVER

Related Articles in WORLD BOOK include:

Apple Maggot	Fly	Mediterranean Fruit Fly
Beefly	Fruit Fly	Mosquito
Blowfly	Gnat	Sand Fly
Botfly	Hessian Fly	Tachina Fly
Daddy Longlegs	Horsefly	Tsetse Fly
Deer Fly	Insect (table)	Warble Fly
Face Fly	Maggot	

DIRAC, *dih RACK,* **PAUL ADRIEN MAURICE** (1902-), is a British physicist noted for his prediction of the existence of the positive electron, or *positron,* and for other contributions to theoretical physics. He won the 1933 Nobel prize in physics with Erwin Schrödinger, an Austrian physicist, for his brilliant studies and research in the field of atomic physics.

United Press Int.

Paul Dirac

Dirac and Schrödinger developed the science of wave mechanics, a mathematical system based on the *energy states* in atoms. Dirac predicted, as a result of this theory, the presence of a positively charged electron. The negative electron had been known and observed for many years (see ELECTRON). Carl D. Anderson observed the positron in 1932, thus proving Dirac's theory (see ANDERSON, CARL D.; LAMB, WILLIS E., JR.).

Dirac was born in Bristol, England, and received degrees from Bristol and Cambridge universities. He became a fellow of the Royal Society in 1930, and won the society's Royal Medal in 1939 for the development of new quantum mechanics. Dirac joined the Cambridge University faculty in 1932. He wrote *Principles of Quantum Mechanics,* and papers on the quantum theory (see QUANTUM MECHANICS). CARL T. CHASE

DIRECT CURRENT. See ELECTRIC CURRENT; ELECTRIC GENERATOR.

DIRECT-MAIL ADVERTISING. See ADVERTISING (Ways of Advertising).

DIRECT PRIMARY. See PRIMARY ELECTION.

DIRECTION

HOW TO TELL DIRECTION

When telling direction in a neighborhood, people can use such landmarks as buildings and streets. In places without familiar landmarks, they use the geographic directions north, south, east, and west.

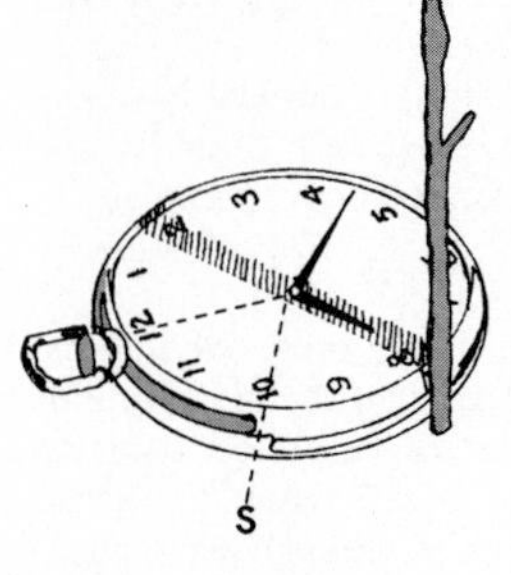

An easy way to find direction is by using a watch, a stick, and the sun. Hold the stick upright at the outer end of the hour hand of the watch. Turn the watch slowly until the shadow of the stick falls along the hour hand. South will be halfway between the shadow and the 12 o'clock numeral. With south established, it is easy to tell the other directions.

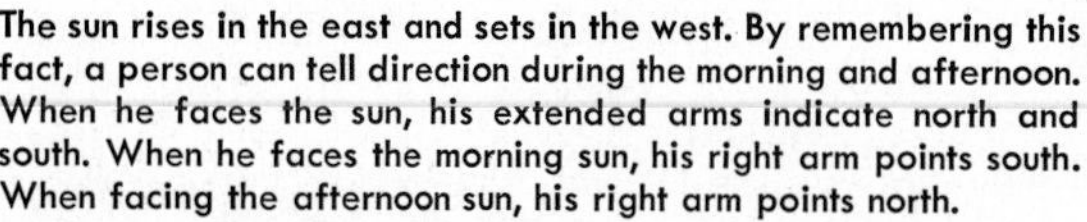

The sun rises in the east and sets in the west. By remembering this fact, a person can tell direction during the morning and afternoon. When he faces the sun, his extended arms indicate north and south. When he faces the morning sun, his right arm points south. When facing the afternoon sun, his right arm points north.

Giving accurate directions is not always easy. The best way to direct someone is to form a mental picture of the route he must follow to reach his destination. It helps to mention prominent landmarks, such as a stoplight, a store, or a church steeple, as well as the names of streets along the way.

DIRECTION. One of the first things a child must learn is how to find his way around his neighborhood. He first learns the direction of his home. Wherever he is, he knows if he is walking toward his home or away from it. This knowledge is called a *sense of direction.*

A child gains a sense of direction by comparing the location of things. He learns the direction of the school by locating it in relation to his home and to himself. All directions are learned this way. In a short while, the child can leave his home and walk many blocks. He may change his direction many times and always know the direction of his home and other places that he knew before. He learns how to use street signs and all the familiar landmarks in his town. He not only knows directions for himself, but he can give directions to others by calling attention to objects along the way.

If the child is in a strange area where there are no familiar objects, he will be lost. Grown men, even sailors and explorers, would also be lost in strange places if they depended on familiar landmarks, for there would not be any. Some other landmarks must be used.

Men long ago divided direction into four main parts —north, south, east, and west. At all points of the world, north is in the same direction, and so are east, west, and south. When a man enters a strange country going north, he knows that east is to his right, west to his left, and south behind him. If he knows the distance he travels in any direction, he can find his way back.

Direction can be told from the sun. In most parts of the northern half of the world, the sun is slightly to the south. It rises in the east and sets in the west. At noon, the sun is directly south. When a man faces the sun at noon, north is behind him, east is on his left, and west is on his right. At night, he can find north by looking at the group of stars called the Big Dipper. The last two stars on the dipper cup point to the North Star. When a man faces this star, he faces north.

Compasses tell the direction of north by magnetism (see COMPASS). With a compass and other instruments, sailors can tell exactly where they are and in which direction they are sailing even when the stars are not visible. Maps, compasses, and astronomy are all based on direction and distance. E. B. ESPENSHADE

See also NAVIGATION.

DIRECTION FINDER is a radio device that enables ships and airplanes to find their location. It is also used to determine the direction in which they are moving. It is simply a radio antenna wound in square or round form and arranged so that it can be turned on a pivot.

When the flat side of the finder faces the radio sending station, the radio wave strikes all four sides at the same time, and the volume of sound produced in the receiving set is reduced. When one of the edges is facing the sending station, the volume of sound response is loudest. The radio operator turns the antenna until his radio goes silent. Then he knows the flat side of the direction finder loop antenna is facing the sending station. When the signal is weakest, a line drawn through the antenna will be perpendicular to the direction of the broadcasting station heard. The operator may use a vertical *sense antenna* with the loop antenna to determine on which side of the antenna the sending station is located. To find his geographical position, the operator uses a direction finder to find the direction of two or more other stations. Then he draws lines along those directions on a map. The spot at which the lines intersect is the location of his ship or plane.

Most direction finders on ships and planes have been replaced by more accurate devices (see AIRCRAFT INSTRUMENTS; ANTENNA; RADAR [Ships]; LORAN). Government agencies use direction finders to locate illegal radio stations. Direction finders are sometimes known as radio compasses. RAYMOND F. YATES

DIRECTOIRE STYLE. See FURNITURE (French); CLOTHING (The 1700's).

DIRECTOR. See THEATER (The Director); MOTION PICTURE (The People Who Make a Motion Picture); DRAMA (Early Realism); also the list of Directors and Producers in the Related Articles of MOTION PICTURE.

DIRECTOR SYSTEM. See RANGE FINDER.

DIRECTORS, BOARD OF. See CORPORATION.

DIRECTORY (in French, *Directoire, dee rehk TWAHR*) was the conservative form of government established in France under the constitution of 1795. It was an executive body composed of five directors. One director retired each year. The Directory became unpopular because of its mismanagement of domestic and military affairs. It ended with Napoleon's seizure of power in November, 1799. ROBERT B. HOLTMAN

See also FRANCE (picture: The Directory).

DIRIGIBLE, *DIHR uh juh buhl*, is a lighter-than-air airship. It is a cigar-shaped balloon driven by an engine. It has a rudder and vertical fins to help control it. A dirigible contains hydrogen or helium gas bags to make it lighter than air. For more detailed information on dirigibles, see AIRSHIP.

DIRK. See DAGGER.

DIRKS, RUDOLPH. See CARTOON (Modern Cartooning).

DIRKSEN, EVERETT McKINLEY (1896-1969), a Republican from Illinois, served as minority leader of the United States Senate from 1959 until his death. A skilled legislator and powerful speaker, Dirksen was probably the most influential senator of the 1960's. He worked closely with every President from Dwight D. Eisenhower to Richard M. Nixon. His deep voice, tousled hair, and theatrical manner made him one of America's best-known public figures.

Dirksen was an isolationist before the United States entered World War II in 1941. He later defended the foreign policies of both Democratic and Republican administrations. Dirksen set his own course concerning problems in America. He opposed some social legislation but supported the civil rights law of 1964.

Gravemann, © 1967
Everett M. Dirksen

Dirksen was born in Pekin, Ill., and attended the University of Minnesota. From 1933 to 1949, he served in the United States House of Representatives. He then left Congress for two years because of an eye ailment. Dirksen was elected to the Senate in 1950 and was reelected in 1956, 1962, and 1968. DAVID S. BRODER

DIS. See PLUTO (mythology).

DISABLED. See HANDICAPPED.

DISABLED AMERICAN VETERANS (D.A.V.) is an organization of men and women who have been disabled in line of duty during time of war. It was founded in March, 1920, by a group of disabled veterans under the leadership of Judge Robert S. Marx of Cincinnati, Ohio.

The purpose of the organization is to care for disabled veterans and to help them return to a useful way of living. Money for rehabilitation work comes from a yearly campaign in which the D.A.V. manufactures and sends out millions of miniature automobile license plates for identifying key chains. The D.A.V. has about 250,000 members in over 1,900 chapters in the United States and other countries. Headquarters are at 3725 Alexandria Pike, Cold Spring, Ky. 41076. Critically reviewed by the DISABLED AMERICAN VETERANS

Disabled American Veterans
The D.A.V. Emblem

DISARMAMENT, also called ARMS CONTROL, means reducing, limiting, controlling, or eliminating a nation's armed forces and weapons. International agreements usually form the basis for disarmament. Types of disarmament include (1) general and complete, (2) limited or partial, and (3) regional.

General and complete disarmament would allow nations to keep only those forces and non-nuclear armaments necessary to protect their citizens and support United Nations peace forces. General and complete disarmament would be planned so that no nation would achieve a military advantage during the disarmament process. The plan would include stronger methods for peacefully settling disagreements between nations.

Limited or partial disarmament describes agreements between nations that apply only to one or more parts of their total armed forces and weapons. A treaty among nuclear powers to ban the testing of nuclear weapons is an example of limited disarmament.

Regional disarmament usually means limiting armed forces and weapons in a certain geographical area. Two or more nations may agree to limit their armed forces and weapons. Nations may also carry out regional disarmament by setting up *demilitarized zones* (areas in which there are no troops or weapons).

The Argument for Disarmament

Persons favoring disarmament use these arguments:

The need for disarmament agreements became more critical in the 1950's and 1960's as nations developed powerful weapons of mass destruction. One Polaris submarine with its missiles and nuclear warheads contains more destructive power than all of the weapons used in

World War II. Nations can no longer think of total war as a way to attain national goals. Even if a nation attacked another nation with nuclear weapons, it would probably be destroyed by a counterattack.

The high cost of missiles and nuclear weapons is another reason for disarmament. Any nation that tries to keep up in a nuclear armaments race must spend a large part of its resources to do so. In addition, countries in an arms race also must keep a large number of their scientists and engineers working on military projects.

As the number of nations that possess nuclear weapons increases, the chance increases that a nuclear war may begin. There can be no assurance of peace as long as large stocks of weapons exist in the world. Disarmament agreements would stop or slow down the arms buildup and reduce tension between nations.

The Argument Against Disarmament

Persons who oppose disarmament use these arguments: Armed forces and weapons in themselves do not cause international disputes or tension. They merely reflect political, economic, and other kinds of disputes. These disputes must be settled before nations can agree on disarmament. Nations that first try to agree on disarmament raise false hopes. False hopes may cause people to oppose spending the money necessary for defense. A false sense of security can do more to bring on war than having armed forces and weapons ready to deter war. Disarmament also may damage a nation's military defense, which has been worked out by military planners.

Without mutual inspection, disarmament agreements cannot work between an open, free society and a secret, totalitarian society. No one can be certain the closed society is keeping its part of the agreement.

History of Disarmament

Until the 1900's, there were only a few limited disarmament agreements. One of these, the Rush-Bagot Agreement of 1817 between the United States and Great Britain, limited their forces along the Great Lakes.

The armistice signed after World War I disarmed Germany and limited the size of its army. France, Italy, Japan, Great Britain, and the United States held a conference on arms limitation in Washington, D.C., in 1921 and 1922. They agreed to limit the number, size, and guns of their battleships for 15 years. In 1930, at the London Naval Conference, Japan, Great Britain, and the United States consented to limit the size and guns of their cruisers, destroyers, and submarines. But these agreements lasted only until 1936. The League of Nations called a disarmament conference in Geneva, Switzerland, in 1932, but it failed.

The peace treaties signed at the end of World War II provided for the disarmament of Germany and Japan. In the years following World War II, the United Nations tried to obtain a general agreement limiting armaments. A 12-nation Disarmament Commission, set up by the General Assembly, began meeting in February, 1952. In 1959, it was expanded to include all UN members. Great Britain, Russia, and the United States then set up a 10-nation committee, but it broke down in 1960.

In 1962, an 18-nation committee began disarmament talks. Russia and the United States made proposals for limited disarmament that differed greatly. Russia said that U.S. inspection provisions amounted to spying. The United States said inspection would help guarantee that nations were abiding by the agreement. More nations joined the committee in 1969, and its name became the Conference of the Committee on Disarmament. Nations also discussed ways to prevent accidental war and military use of outer space and the ocean bed.

In late 1963, the United States, Russia, and Great Britain signed a partial nuclear test ban treaty. They agreed not to test nuclear weapons in the atmosphere, in outer space, or under water. In 1968, the UN approved a treaty to stop the spread of nuclear weapons. It bars nuclear powers from giving nuclear weapons or knowledge to other nations. The treaty went into effect in 1970. It was ratified by the United States, Great Britain, Russia, and more than 40 other nations.

In 1969, Russia and the United States began a series of meetings to discuss the possibility of placing limitations on strategic nuclear weapons. In 1972, these meetings resulted in two agreements. The first agreement was a treaty limiting each nation's defensive missile strength. The U.S. Senate ratified the treaty in August, 1972. The other agreement limited U.S. and Russian production of certain offensive nuclear weapons for five years. This agreement was approved by a congressional resolution. In October, 1972, both agreements entered into force when Russia and the United States exchanged ratification documents and notices of acceptance. See STRATEGIC ARMS LIMITATION TALKS.

Also in 1972, a treaty prohibiting nuclear weapons on the ocean floor went into effect. The treaty bans the use or testing of nuclear weapons beyond a 12-nautical-mile coastal zone. A. S. FISHER

See also UNITED NATIONS (Arms Control); ARMS CONTROL AND DISARMAMENT AGENCY, UNITED STATES.

DISASTER is a sudden and extremely unfortunate event that affects many people. Some of the world's greatest disasters are listed in the table on the opposite page.

Related Articles in WORLD BOOK include:

Earthquake	Hurricane (Famous Hurricanes Since 1900)
Fire Fighting (Disastrous Fires in History)	Shipwreck
Flood	Volcano (Famous Eruptions)

DISASTER RELIEF. See CARE; CIVIL DEFENSE; COAST GUARD, UNITED STATES; NATIONAL GUARD; RED CROSS; SALVATION ARMY.

DISCHARGE, MILITARY. See MILITARY DISCHARGE.

DISCIPLE. See APOSTLE.

DISCIPLES OF CHRIST is a Protestant denomination that developed from several religious movements in the United States during the early 1800's. Its full name is the Christian Church (Disciples of Christ). Its founders included three men of Presbyterian background—Thomas Campbell and his son Alexander in Pennsylvania and Barton W. Stone in Kentucky. The church took its present name in 1968 as part of a general reorganization.

The church observes two ordinances—Communion or the Lord's Supper, and Baptism. Communion is observed every Sunday as the central part of the worship service. The denomination observes baptism for adults rather than for infants because it considers children too young to fulfill the requirements of a personal decision to follow Christ. Baptism is by *immersion* (submerging the person in water). Headquarters are at 221 Ohmer Ave., Indianapolis, Ind. 46219. For membership, see RELIGION (table [Christian Church]).

Critically reviewed by the DISCIPLES OF CHRIST

DISCOUNT is a term applied in business to a deduction from a stated price or from a payment due at some future date. The forms most commonly used in business include *bank discount*, *trade discount*, and *cash discount*.

Bank Discount is the deduction which a bank makes from the face value of a note. The bank does this when it cashes a note before it is due. Bank discount is determined in the same manner as simple interest. But it is taken in advance, by being deducted from the face value of the note. The difference between the face value of the note and the discount is called the *proceeds*. For example, the holder of a note may wish to turn it into cash, or have it *discounted*, before it becomes due. He may do so by presenting the note to the bank and receiving for it the amount of its face value, less the interest due during the term of discount. The *term of discount*, or *time to run*, is the period of time following the day the note is presented for payment through the day on which it matures. Bank discount creates a higher effective rate of interest than simple interest. The borrower pays the same amount in either case for the use of the money received, but with bank discount he receives only the proceeds instead of the face value of the note. Suppose a note for $5,000, dated February 26 and maturing on May 26, were presented to the bank on April 1. The number of days following April 1 through May 26 is 55. If the note bears interest at 6 per cent a year, the interest for this 55-day period would be $45.83 (based on a 360-day year). The bank *deducts* (discounts) this sum from the face value of the note as its charge for cashing it. Then the bank pays the balance, or $4,954.17, to the person who presents the note for payment. The bank collects the full sum of $5,000 on the date the note matures.

Trade Discount is a term used by manufacturers and wholesale merchants when they take off a certain percentage of the price given in a price list. This price is called the *list price*. The list price less the discount is known as the *net price*. Market values may change after price lists are issued. Changes in list prices are often made by varying the trade discount.

Cash Discount is a deduction of a percentage of a bill for goods sold on credit. A cash discount is given when the bill is paid within a specific period of time. Such a discount might be expressed as *2/10, n/30*, which is read as *two ten, net thirty*. This means that the buyer may deduct 2 per cent from the bill if he pays it within 10 days, or he may wait and pay the whole amount at the end of 30 days. Cash discounts may be used to increase the demand for a product or to speed up the collection of bills.

JAMES B. LUDTKE

DISCOUNT HOUSE is a retail store that sells products at prices lower than those usually charged by other retail stores. Discount houses sell in mass volume and make only a small profit on each item. They became an important form of mass distribution after World War II. Most discount houses operate on a self-service basis and their operating expenses are lower than those of other retail stores. Some specialize in certain products. Others carry a variety of products.

NATHANIEL SCHWARTZ

DISCOVERY. See EXPLORATION AND DISCOVERY; INVENTION.

DISCRIMINATION. See SEGREGATION.

MAJOR DISASTERS

Year	Location	Dead	Disaster
64	Rome	Unknown	City fire
79	Pompeii and Herculaneum	2,000	Vesuvius eruption
1556	Shensi, China	830,000	Earthquake
1666	London	Unknown	City fire
1669	Sicily	20,000	Mount Etna eruption
1737	Calcutta, India	300,000	Earthquake; tornado
1755	Lisbon, Portugal	60,000	Earthquake
1865	Mississippi River	1,653	Steamboat explosion
1871	Chicago	300	City fire
1871	Peshtigo, Wis.	800	Forest fire
1883	Indonesia	36,000	Krakatoa eruption; tidal wave
1887	Honan, China	900,000	Hwang Ho flood
1889	Johnstown, Pa.	2,200	Burst dam; flood
1900	Galveston, Tex.	6,000	Hurricane; storm tide
1902	Martinique	38,000	Mont Pélee eruption
1903	Chicago	575	Iroquois Theater fire
1904	New York City	1,030	Excursion boat fire
1906	San Francisco	700	Earthquake; fire
1907	Monongah, W. Va.	361	Coal mine explosion
1912	North Atlantic	1,500	Liner *Titanic* collision with iceberg
1913	Indiana; Ohio	467	Ohio River Basin flood
1914	Saint Lawrence R.	1,029	Ship collision
1917	Modane, France	550	Train derailment
1917	Halifax, N. S.	1,635	Ship explosion
1918	Nashville, Tenn.	101	Train collision
1920	Kansu, China	180,000	Earthquake; landslide
1923	Tokyo-Yokohama	143,000	Earthquake; fire
1925	Illinois; Indiana; Missouri	689	Tornadoes
1928	Florida	1,836	Hurricane
1934	Hakodate, Japan	2,015	Widespread fire
1937	New London, Tex.	296	Gas explosion in school
1938	New England	600	Hurricane
1942	Manchuria, China	1,572	Coal mine explosion
1942	Boston	499	Nightclub fire
1947	Texas City, Tex.	512	Ship explosion
1956	Off Nantucket Island, Mass.	51	Liner *Andrea Doria* collision
1960	New York City	134	Airliner collision
1962	Peru	3,500	Huascaran avalanche
1963	Bali	1,500	Mount Agung eruption
1963	Cuba; Haiti	6,000	Hurricane (Flora)
1964	Alaska	131	Earthquake
1966	Aberfan, Wales	144	Coal mine avalanche
1970	East Pakistan (now Bangladesh)	200,000	Cyclone; tidal wave
1971	Los Angeles	64	Earthquake
1971	Morioka, Japan	162	Airliner collision
1972	Managua, Nicaragua	10,000	Earthquake
1972	Moscow	176	Airliner crash
1972	Rapid City, S. Dak.	239	Burst dam; flood
1973	Kano, Nigeria	180	Airliner crash
1973	Mexico	539	Earthquake
1974	Near Paris	345	Airliner crash
1974	Honduras	8,000	Hurricane (Fifi)
1974	Pakistan	5,200	Earthquake

HOW TO THROW A DISCUS

The discus thrower stands in a circle measuring 8 ft. 2½ in. (2.5 meters) in diameter. He must not step outside this circle. He holds the discus flat against the palm of his hand, and swings within the circle with his arm outstretched. He releases the discus at the end of the second turn. The power comes from his body and the follow-through of his arm.

DISCUS THROW is one of the oldest individual sports. It was a popular event with the ancient Greeks in their Olympic Games. The Greeks considered the discus-throwing champion the greatest athlete. Myron, a Greek sculptor, made a remarkable bronze statue known as the *Discobolus*, or *Discus Thrower*. Only copies remain. The finest is in the Vatican in Rome.

Athletes in ancient times threw a discus made of stone or metal. The discus used today is a round wooden plate with a smooth metal rim. It is $8\frac{5}{8}$ inches (21.9 centimeters) in diameter and $1\frac{3}{4}$ inches (4.4 centimeters) thick at the center, tapering slightly at the edge. It weighs 4 pounds, $6\frac{2}{3}$ ounces (2 kilograms). The circular metal rim must be from $1\frac{31}{32}$ to $2\frac{7}{32}$ inches (5.0 to 5.7 centimeters) in diameter.

Athletes throw the discus from a circle that is 8 feet, $2\frac{1}{2}$ inches (2.5 meters) in diameter. The discus thrower holds the discus in the palm of one hand, the ends of his fingers curling around the metal rim. He whirls his body in a complete turn to gather speed and power, and hurls the discus at the end of his second turn. His fingertips spin the discus as it leaves his hand, and it flies through the air in a fairly flat position.

The thrower fouls if he touches the ground outside the circle before the discus strikes the ground, or if he steps on the circle. Judges measure the throw from the inside edge of the circle to the nearest point the discus struck the ground. Each competitor gets three throws, and his best mark counts. In big meets, the best seven competitors each receive three more throws.

Discus throwing requires less strain than shot-putting or the hammer throw. Good throwing is a matter of practice and form rather than great strength.

For the world discus-throwing record, see TRACK AND FIELD (table). FRED RUSSELL

DISCUSSION. See DEBATE; PANEL DISCUSSION; SYMPOSIUM.

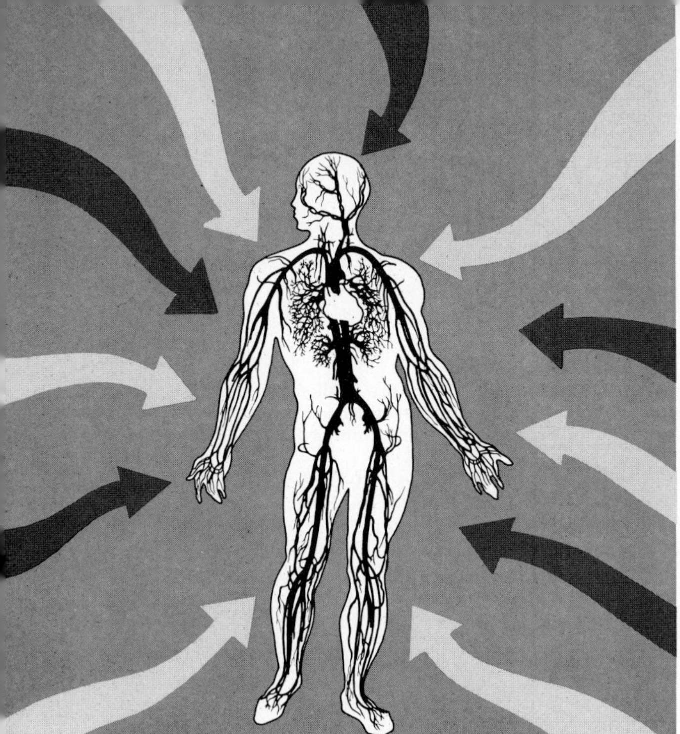

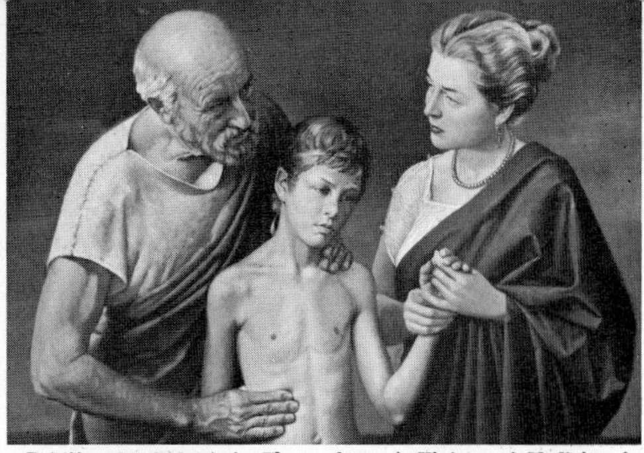

Painting by Robert A. Thom, from *A History of Medicine in Pictures* © 1958, Parke, Davis, & Co.

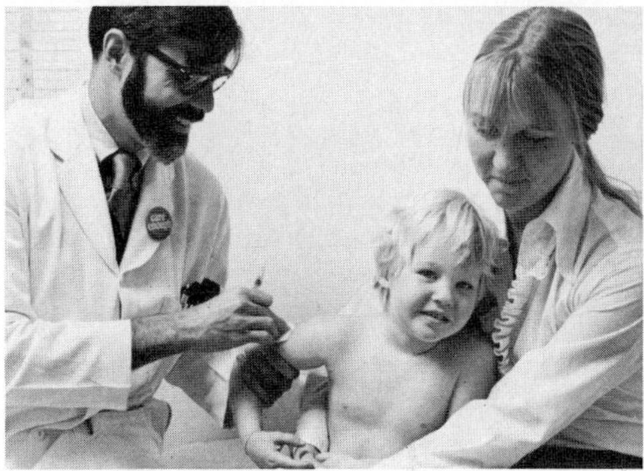

Suzanne Szasz

Throughout history, man has fought disease. In the 400's B.C., the Greek physician Hippocrates established rules of conduct that doctors still follow. Today, aided by modern instruments and increasing knowledge of the causes of disease, physicians achieve results impossible in Hippocrates' time.

DISEASE

DISEASE is one of man's greatest enemies. It has killed and crippled more persons than all the wars ever fought. It has even influenced the course of history. Man has conquered many diseases. But millions of persons in all parts of the world still become ill from diseases each day. All living things can get diseases—plants and animals as well as humans.

Human diseases include most conditions that interfere with the normal state of the body or of the mind. Originally, the word *disease* meant chiefly illnesses for which the cause was unknown. But scientists now know that diseases have many different causes. For example, some diseases, such as poliomyelitis, pneumonia, and scarlet fever, can be caused by germs. Other diseases, including scurvy and rickets, may result from poor diets. Still others may be caused by allergies, harmful fumes in the air, and even old age.

Some diseases, called *communicable* or *contagious* diseases, can spread from one person to another. An *epidemic* takes place when a communicable disease, such as diphtheria or typhoid fever, spreads widely through a community. Sometimes epidemics occur at the same time in many countries throughout the world, as did the influenza epidemic of 1957. Then they are called *pandemics*. In some countries, certain diseases are always present, as the bubonic plague in India and China. These are called *endemic* diseases.

North Americans are considered to be among the healthiest people in the world. But in Canada, experts have found that more than 10,000,000 persons have some kind of illness during a year. In the United States, a survey showed that two of every five persons has a *chronic*, or long-continued, disease. The survey also showed that the average person has two or more *acute*, or short and severe, illnesses each year.

Diseases affect the working efficiency of industries as well as of individuals. In the United States, persons absent because of the common cold cost industries about 120 million days of work every year.

Diseases Caused by Germs

Men once believed that evil spirits made people sick. It was not until the 1400's that scientists began to suspect that some diseases were caused by tiny, invisible particles called *germs*. Early researchers called these germs "living seeds of disease." They believed that germs developed out of nothing in the blood streams of man and of animals. In the 1500's, doctors began to suggest that some germs could be passed from one person to another and spread disease.

Bacteria and other germs were first seen under a microscope in the 1600's. But the *germ theory* of disease was not proved until the late 1800's. Robert Koch, a German physician, and Louis Pasteur, a French chemist, both experimented with anthrax, an infectious disease of man and animals. Koch showed that animals injected with anthrax germs soon got the disease. Pasteur developed a vaccine to slow down the multiplication of the germs.

Today, scientists know that infectious diseases are caused by many kinds of germs, including bacteria, viruses, and protozoa. These microorganisms cause disease by attacking living tissue. Some germs live in the tissue and multiply so rapidly that the tissue dies. Others produce *toxins* (poisons) that kill tissue.

TYPES OF DISEASE GERMS

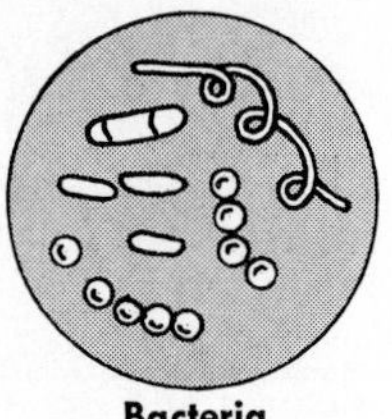

Bacteria

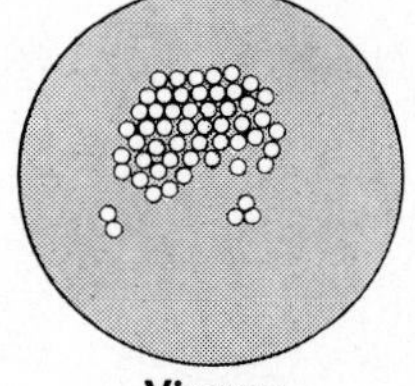

Viruses

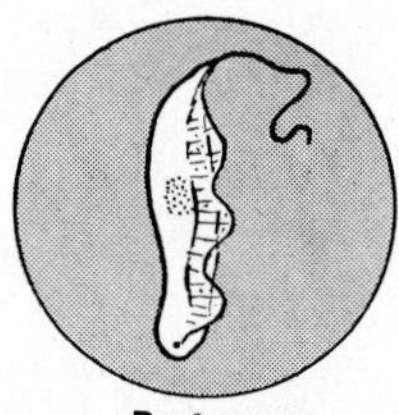

Protozoa

Three common kinds of disease germs are bacteria, viruses, and protozoa. *Bacteria* have different shapes. They may be round, rod-shaped, or coiled. They cause such diseases as diphtheria and tuberculosis. *Viruses* are smaller than bacteria and multiply very rapidly. They cause mumps and smallpox. *Protozoa* are one-celled animals. Some kinds cause malaria and sleeping sickness.

Bacterial Diseases are caused by *bacteria* (one-celled organisms that can be seen only through a microscope). Scientists do not know exactly how many kinds of bacteria exist. But they do know that a single grain of soil may hold more than 100 million bacteria of many different kinds. Fortunately, most bacteria do not cause disease, and many are useful. For example, bacteria cause milk to ferment so that dairies can use it to make buttermilk and cheese.

DISEASE TERMS

Bacteria are tiny one-celled organisms that may be shaped like spheres, rods, or spirals. Some cause diseases, but many do not.

Contagious Disease or **Communicable Disease** is a disease that can be passed from a sick person to a healthy person through direct or indirect contact.

Epidemic is the spread of disease throughout a community.

Germ, or **Microorganism,** is any tiny plant or animal that can only be seen through a microscope.

Incubation Period is the time between invasion of the body by a disease-producing germ and the appearance of the first symptoms of the disease.

Infectious Disease is a disease caused by organisms that destroy living cells. An infectious disease can be contagious. But the germs that cause it may also be carried in the air or in water.

Organism is any living thing.

Pandemic is a widespread epidemic, as in the spread of a disease through a whole region, or through many countries of the world.

Parasite is an organism that feeds and lives in or on another organism.

Period of Communicability is the time during which contagious diseases are most easily passed from sick persons to healthy persons.

Viruses are microorganisms smaller than bacteria. Most viruses can be seen only with the aid of an electron microscope. Many are called *filterable viruses* because they pass through filters that hold back bacteria.

MEANINGS OF DISEASE TERM ENDINGS

—itis means *inflammation.* It is usually associated with infection. Appendicitis is an inflammation of the appendix, and tonsillitis is an inflammation of the tonsils.

—emia refers to *blood.* Anemia is a deficiency in the blood. Septicemia, sometimes called blood poisoning, is the presence of disease germs in the blood.

—ism denotes *excess.* Morphinism means too much morphine in the body, and alcoholism too much alcohol.

—phobia means *fear.* Claustrophobia means fear of being confined, and hydrophobia is a fear of water.

—osis denotes a *diseased* or *abnormal condition.* Arteriosclerosis is a disease of the arteries. A psychosis is a severe mental illness.

Some bacteria always live in the bodies of man and animals. They may be found on the skin; in the nose, mouth, and throat; and in the lungs, stomach, and intestines. These bacteria normally do no harm. But they may cause disease when the body's resistance is low for any reason. For example, bacteria called *streptococci* are often present in a person's throat. Disease or fatigue may lower the body's resistance to these bacteria, allowing them to multiply so rapidly that they harm the throat tissue. The person then suffers a *sore throat.*

Bacteria that pass from person to person cause many diseases, including scarlet fever, whooping cough, diphtheria, and tuberculosis. Bacteria that live in the soil may produce *tetanus* (lockjaw). Other kinds of bacteria cause leprosy and undulant fever. See BACTERIA.

Protozoan Diseases. Protozoa are one-celled animals found in great numbers almost everywhere in nature. Some protozoa harm man. One of these, the *Plasmodium,* causes malaria. Other protozoa cause sleeping sickness and amebic dysentery. See PROTOZOAN.

Worm Diseases. Some worms can cause diseases. Certain kinds of *flatworms* spend part of their growing period in the bodies of humans or animals. Perhaps the best-known flatworm is the tapeworm, which causes an intestinal disease. *Roundworms* cause intestinal and respiratory diseases in man and animals. They also attack plants. See FLATWORM; ROUNDWORM.

Fungus Diseases. Fungi are tiny plants. They cause many skin diseases. Ringworm infections such as

U.S. DEATHS FROM MAJOR DISEASES

Number of deaths in 1973

Diseases of the Heart and Blood Vessels	1,037,460 deaths
Cancer	353,440 deaths
Influenza and Pneumonia	61,160 deaths
Diabetes Mellitus	36,450 deaths
Cirrhosis of the Liver	33,630 deaths
Diseases of Early Infancy	31,030 deaths

Source: U.S. Public Health Service.

HOW GERMS ENTER THE BODY

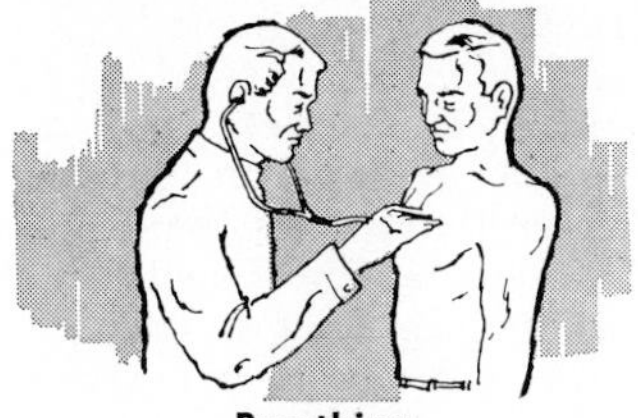

Breathing

Eating

Skin Breaks

Germs invade the body through the nose, the mouth, or breaks in the skin. The germs that cause the common cold "ride" on moisture in the air. They enter the nose and lungs when we breathe. Food carries the germs of dysentery and other diseases into the stomach and intestines. Germs that cause boils and blood poisoning can enter the body through a scratch or pin prick in the skin.

athlete's foot are caused by fungi, not by worms. Fungi also cause lung diseases such as histoplasmosis. See FUNGI; FUNGUS DISEASE; HISTOPLASMOSIS.

Virus Diseases are caused by germs called *viruses*, which are even smaller than bacteria. Most viruses are so small that scientists can see them only by means of a powerful electron microscope. There are hundreds of kinds of viruses. All are infectious and can cause diseases in most living things. Some even infect other germs. Scientists have found that viruses may sometimes remain inactive for years, but can quickly infect any defenseless cell. After they invade the cell, they multiply rapidly. For example, millions of polio viruses crowded together form only a speck. But a single one of these viruses can enter a human nerve cell and produce many more new viruses in a few hours. Each new virus is as dangerous as the original one.

Viruses cause many common diseases, including mumps, measles, smallpox, chicken pox, and influenza. Some kinds of viruses cause cells to multiply rapidly and produce cancer. Other kinds of viruses, or a combination of several different kinds, cause the common cold. See VIRUS.

Diseases Present at Birth

Some babies are born with a disease. For example, a *blue baby* is born with a heart defect that prevents the blood from flowing properly to the lungs. Doctors use the term *congenital* for a defect or disease present at birth.

MAIN CONTAGIOUS DISEASES IN THE U.S.

Cases reported in 1973

Venereal Diseases	931,725 cases
Scarlet Fever and Streptococcal Sore Throat	474,212 cases
Chicken Pox	182,927 cases
Mumps	69,612 cases
Hepatitis	59,200 cases

Source: U.S. Public Health Service.

Congenital defects may result when a mother gets a serious disease while pregnant. Babies can get syphilis from their mothers. If a woman has German measles during the first three months of pregnancy, there is an increased chance that her baby will be born with a defect. Certain types of malnutrition during the early months of pregnancy may have similar effects.

Perhaps the most important cause of congenital disease is heredity. Hemophilia, a disease in which the blood does not clot, is hereditary. Doctors believe that persons may inherit a tendency toward some diseases, such as diabetes. See HEREDITY.

Diseases Caused by Environment

Our *environment* (surroundings) contains several factors that may cause disease. Even the weather can be dangerous. Too much cold may result in frostbite. Excessive heat may produce heat exhaustion.

Sometimes man poisons his environment, producing a new source of disease. In many communities, factories and motor vehicles pollute the air with poisonous gas fumes that may cause lung diseases. Sometimes the poisonous fumes become so thick that they form a kind of fog called *smog*. In 1952, during a few days of smog in London, more than 5,000 persons died. Some doctors believe that air pollution may even cause cancer of the lungs and other parts of the body.

Our environment is filled with many forms of radiant energy which make life possible. Radiation from the sun provides us with heat, light, and food. But radiation from any source may be dangerous because it can destroy body tissues. Even the sun's rays which penetrate the atmosphere can cause serious burns. Most scientists believe that some effects of radiation may be delayed, and may later produce cancer. Experts also believe that radiation may cause unfavorable *mutations*, or hereditary changes (see MUTATION).

Man is learning to protect himself against damage from radiation. In atomic energy projects, thick concrete walls shield workers from the effects of radiation. In hospitals and laboratories, X-ray technicians stand out of the range of the radiation. When radium is used, lead shields protect workers from the rays. Scientists are seeking ways to protect man from the effects of radioactive fallout. See RADIATION (Learning to Live with High-Energy Radiation); RADIATION SICKNESS.

Nutritional Diseases

Improper diet can cause sickness and death. Diseases caused by not eating the right foods are called *nutri-*

tional diseases. A *deficiency*, or lack, of certain vitamins can cause rickets, scurvy, or pellagra. These deficiency diseases can be cured or prevented by eating foods containing the vitamins.

Poor nutrition remains a common cause of illness in spite of medical knowledge about proper diet. In some parts of the world, people do not get enough food, or can obtain food of only poor quality. Most difficult for them to obtain are the protein foods, such as meat, eggs, and milk. See NUTRITION.

Eating too much also can cause disease. Overweight may shorten a person's life by helping bring about heart disease, or by affecting the circulation of the blood. Overweight is usually caused by eating too much. See WEIGHT CONTROL.

Allergies

Some persons become sick when they eat certain foods, or when they come in contact with certain plants or animals. Such a sensitivity is called an *allergy*. Sometimes an allergy develops only after repeated exposure to a substance. Persons may develop allergies after exposure to almost any substance, such as cat hair, ragweed, or house dust. Doctors do not know why only some individuals develop allergies. See ALLERGY.

Functional Diseases

All parts of a healthy body work together in harmony. If anything disturbs the *function*, or work, of one part, other parts are usually disturbed, too. The nervous system and the hormones produced by glands act as a regulatory system. They control the development and function of all body parts. When this regulatory system operates properly, the composition of the body usually remains stable.

Diseases that affect the nervous system or the hormone glands may produce serious disturbances of the whole body. A nerve may be damaged in an accident or by a disease such as poliomyelitis. Then the body muscles that are controlled by that nerve may begin to *deteriorate*, or waste away. If glands that produce hormones, such as the thyroid and adrenal glands, do not work properly, disease also may result. When the thyroid gland is not active enough, a person may get *hypothyroidism*, a disease in which the mind and body suffer. See THYROID GLAND.

Doctors do not know exactly how all the regulating systems of the body work. One of the least known of these systems is the one that controls the production of cells and the growth of tissues. When this system is disturbed, one type of cell may grow unchecked and may destroy other cells. Such abnormal growths form *tumors*, including cancers. See CANCER.

Diseases of Children

Children in various parts of the world have different kinds of diseases. In regions where food and sanitation are poor, many children die during their first year from nutritional and infectious diseases. The most frequent ailments of American children are the common cold and other infections of the nose, throat, and lungs. Childhood diseases include whooping cough, measles, mumps, scarlet fever, and chicken pox. Adults also may get these diseases, particularly if they did not have them during childhood.

Some diseases, such as whooping cough and chicken pox, usually leave a child *immune*, or protected, for the rest of his life. A baby usually is protected from many diseases for a short time after birth by an immunity inherited from his mother. Antibodies pass from mother to baby before birth. These disease-fighting substances protect the infant for about three months. They give his body time to form its own *antibodies*, or protective substances, against some diseases. The doctor may vaccinate him for protection against others. See ANTIBODY; IMMUNITY.

Diseases of the Aged

Some doctors believe that the body organs gradually become weaker as a person grows older. *Geriatric diseases*, or diseases of old people, often result from the natural process of growing older. Common ailments of adults and the aged include cancer, high blood pressure, and damage to the blood vessels, heart, and brain. Mental illness usually strikes adults and the aged, but children may also suffer from it. Patients with mental illness occupy about half the hospital beds in the United States. See GERIATRICS; MENTAL ILLNESS.

Occupational Diseases

Persons who do certain kinds of work may get special kinds of diseases. Painters may suffer from lead poisoning as a result of exposure to the lead in paint. Coal miners and workers in the asbestos, iron, and cotton industries may breathe in dust, which can cause lung diseases. These workers often wear masks over their noses and mouths to keep the dust out. Silica dust causes a lung disease called silicosis. Glassmakers, grinders, granite cutters, and road builders may get silicosis. They wear nose filters, respirators, or masks to prevent the disease. In the chemical industry, workers' lungs may be irritated by gases, dust, or chemical fumes. Persons who handle insecticides may develop skin rashes. Most states have laws to provide safety measures for the prevention of industrial diseases.

Some occupational diseases result from physical causes. One of these diseases is called the bends. It results from rapidly lowering the air pressure surrounding the body. Bubbles of nitrogen form in the blood and body tissues, causing great pain. The bends may affect persons who must work in compressed air, as in constructing a tunnel under a river. Skin divers and deep-sea divers may also suffer from this illness.

How Diseases Spread

Diseases may spread from one person to another, from one animal to another, or from one plant to another. Some animal diseases also can be passed to humans. Occasionally, diseases may spread through whole communities and become epidemics. Scientists called *epidemiologists* study the spread of disease and search for ways to prevent it.

By Humans. Many infectious diseases pass from one person to another by direct contact. A healthy person can pick up the germs by touching infected areas on the sick person's body. Diseases that spread in this way include boils, abscesses, venereal diseases, and athlete's foot. Other diseases spread indirectly. When a person

SOME COMMON COMMUNICABLE DISEASES

DISEASE	SYMPTOMS	INCUBATION PERIOD	PERIOD OF COMMUNICABILITY	PREVENTIVE MEASURES
Chicken Pox	Headache, fever, recurrent skin rashes that form crusts.	14 to 21 days	From day before symptoms appear until 6 days after first rashes form.	None. Attack gives permanent immunity.
Diphtheria	Sore throat, hoarseness, fever.	2 to 5 days	About 2 to 4 weeks.	Diphtheria toxoid injections, started at 3 months of age. Repeated doses throughout childhood.
German Measles	Headache, enlarged lymph nodes, cough, sore throat, rash.	14 to 21 days, usually 18 days.	From about 7 days before rash appears until about 5 days after.	German measles (rubella) vaccine. Attack usually gives permanent immunity.
Influenza	Fever, chills, muscular aches and pains.	1 to 3 days	When symptoms appear until 7 days after.	Influenza vaccine protects for only a few months.
Measles	Fever, body aches, cough, rash, eyes sensitive to light.	10 to 14 days	From 4 days before rash appears until 5 days after.	Measles vaccines.
Mononucleosis (Glandular Fever)	Sore throat, enlarged lymph glands, fatigue.	4 to 14 days	Unknown	None
Mumps	Chills, headache, fever, swollen glands in neck and throat.	14 to 21 days, usually 18 days.	From 7 days before until 9 days after symptoms, or until swelling disappears.	Mumps vaccine. Gamma globulin protects after exposure.
Poliomyelitis	Fever, sore throat, muscle pain, stiff back, paralysis.	Paralytic, 9 to 13 days. Nonparalytic, 4 to 10 days.	Last part of incubation period and first week of acute illness.	Poliomyelitis vaccines.
Scarlet Fever	Sore throat, rash, high fever, chills.	2 to 5 days	Beginning of incubation period until 2 or 3 weeks after symptoms appear.	None. Attack usually gives permanent immunity.
Smallpox	Chills, fever, headache, backache, rash that forms scabs.	7 to 16 days, commonly 12; rarely up to 21 days.	When symptoms appear until 2 or 3 weeks after, when scabs disappear.	Smallpox vaccination between 1 and 2 years of age, and every 5 to 7 years thereafter. Attack gives permanent immunity.
Whooping Cough	Increased nose and throat secretion, violent cough, vomiting, fever.	7 to 10 days, rarely up to 21 days.	7 days after exposure to 3 weeks after coughing begins.	Whooping cough vaccine started at 3 months. Repeated doses during preschool years. Attack usually gives permanent immunity.

Each disease listed in this table has a separate article in WORLD BOOK.

with a cold sneezes or coughs, small drops of moisture containing germs are sprayed into the air. Another person may breathe in the droplets and catch a cold.

Humans and animals can spread disease even though they show no sign of illness themselves. These *carriers* have the disease germs within their bodies. Human carriers may spread such diseases as typhoid fever, diphtheria, syphilis, scarlet fever, and pneumonia. Public health laws require that certain known carriers have physical examinations and receive treatment. In addition, their activities are controlled by law. A carrier of typhoid fever, for example, would not be allowed to work in a restaurant. See PUBLIC HEALTH.

By Insects and Other Animals. Insects spread some of the most deadly diseases known to man. The germs that cause typhus and bubonic plague are carried by fleas and lice. These insects put the germs in a person's body when they bite. Certain mosquitoes spread malaria and yellow fever germs. They get the germs when they bite a person who has the disease. If they bite another person, they inject the disease germs into his blood stream. In the same way, the tsetse fly transmits the tiny organism that causes African sleeping sickness. The common housefly also spreads serious diseases. It may rest on human or animal wastes that contain typhoid and dysentery germs. Particles of the waste material cling to the fly's hairy legs and body, and may be brushed off on food.

Some animals, when infected with rabies, can pass the germs to a person whom they bite. These animals include dogs, cats, and bats. Other animals spread disease to humans by direct contact. For example, a hunter may get tularemia, or rabbit fever, when he handles an infected rabbit or squirrel. Even the pelts of infected animals can be dangerous. Tanners and wool sorters sometimes get anthrax, a serious infectious disease, when they handle the hides of sick animals. Parakeets, parrots, and pigeons may spread psittacosis, a disease similar to pneumonia.

Animals also pass diseases to humans indirectly, usually through meat and other foods. The small worms that cause trichinosis, a hog disease, may stay alive in pork that is not thoroughly cooked. The worms enter the intestines of a person who eats the undercooked pork, and multiply rapidly.

Cows may spread two serious diseases in milk. One is bovine tuberculosis. The other is called Bang's disease when it affects cows, and undulant fever when it invades the human body. Before the discovery of the process of pasteurization, these diseases killed thousands of persons every year.

How the Body Fights Disease

The skin is often called "the body's first line of defense." It acts as armor, resisting many germs that might harm the more delicate parts of the body. Any break in the skin, even a pin prick, provides an opening for dangerous germs. Some germs enter the body through the nose and mouth and other natural openings. These areas provide warmth and moisture, in which germs thrive. But mucous membrane, the thin tissue that lines the body openings, has a high resistance to germs. It also produces *mucus*, a sticky liquid, that catches many germs. When the membrane of the nose and throat becomes irritated, we cough or sneeze, blowing out the unwanted substances.

Other body liquids also provide a defense against disease. Tears, for example, wash bacteria from the eyes. Tears also contain substances that fight bacteria. Acid in the stomach kills many germs before they can reach other parts of the body.

The various kinds of *tissue cells*, or the cells that make up the tissues of the body, and the white blood cells, form a second line of defense. Germs may attack tissue cells anywhere in the body. Then the body produces new cells to replace those that are destroyed by the invaders. These new tissue cells try to form a "wall" around the germs. The blood supply to the area increases, and white blood cells devour the germs and the dead tissue cells. The white blood cells then form *pus*, which may drain out of the body through a break in the skin. Or the pus may be carried away by the lymph and gradually be destroyed in the body. See Blood (White Blood Cells); Lymphatic System; Pus.

Sometimes the invading germs cannot be killed where they enter the body. Then the body sets up a stronger defense that centers in the blood stream. The tissues and organs form different kinds of antibodies, each of which does a specific job. One kind, the *antitoxins*, neutralizes poisons produced by certain bacteria. Another type of antibody, the *agglutinins*, causes some bacteria to clump together in the blood. This clumping

HOW YOUR BODY FIGHTS GERMS

The body has many defenses against disease germs. The *skin* is the body's "first line of defense." *Tears* wash germs from the eyes. *Mucus*, a sticky fluid, and *cilia*, tiny hairs, catch germs in the nose. *Saliva* in the mouth and *acids* in the stomach kill germs. The *liver* also kills many kinds of germs.

White corpuscles in the blood help the body fight disease germs. If a germ enters the body, the white corpuscles attack it. They "swallow" the germs or poison them with powerful chemicals.

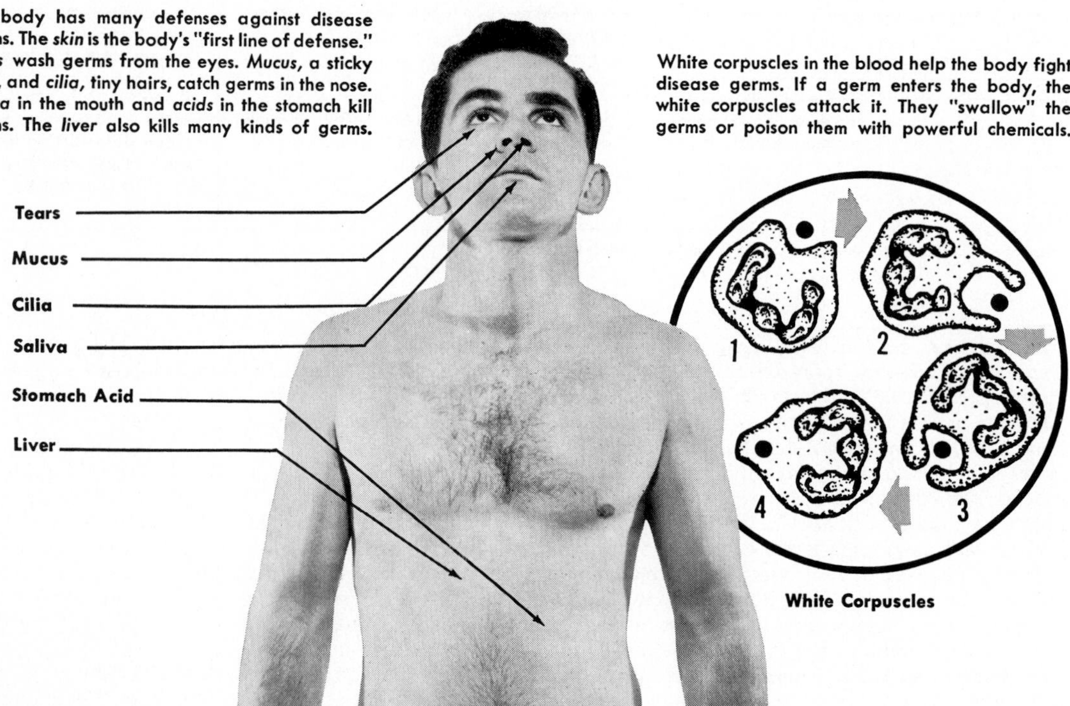

White Corpuscles

process allows white blood cells to surround the bacteria and devour them. Other kinds of antibodies kill or weaken germs in different ways.

Man's Battle Against Disease

An epidemic was responsible for some of the earliest public health laws in Europe. From 1347 to 1350, about one-fourth of Europe's population died as a result of a plague that swept in from Asia. Governments then began making laws regulating sanitary conditions.

Diseases have also affected the course of history. Smallpox, which European explorers brought with them, aided in the conquest of North and South America. The disease killed millions of Indians who had no immunity to smallpox. During the Civil War, more soldiers died of typhoid fever than were killed in battle. The influenza epidemic of 1918 and 1919 killed about 20 million persons throughout the world—more than died during four years of battle in World War I. During World War II, Allied armies in the Pacific theater had five times as many casualties from malaria as from combat.

Until about 1870, more than a third of the world's children died during their first few years of life. Infant death is still high in some underprivileged countries. But in the United States, Canada, and many other Western nations, every child has a good chance of living from 60 to 70 years. The remarkable increase in life expectancy has resulted from two factors: (1) a higher standard of living and (2) advances in medical science. An improved standard of living allows people to have good food and clean, comfortable homes, and to take care of their health. Advances in medical science make it possible to prevent and to treat many diseases that once caused death.

Detecting Disease. Only a hundred years ago, a doctor had little help in *diagnosing* (determining) a patient's disease. He had to rely on symptoms that he could observe or those that the patient could tell him about. If the patient's body was hot, the doctor knew he probably had a fever. The doctor put his ear to the patient's chest to hear the heart and other body sounds. He felt the patient's pulse, and examined his tongue. See DIAGNOSIS.

A doctor still uses most of these physical signs to diagnose illness. But he also has many instruments that help him. He can examine blood cells through a powerful microscope. He can use X rays to study the lungs, the heart, and bones, and other parts of the body. Chemical tests tell him much about the blood, urine, and other body fluids. With such tools, the physician can detect the exact cause and location of a disease.

Treating Disease. One of the most important medical achievements has been the discovery of drugs to treat diseases. Drugs that attack one kind of germ may be useless against another kind. Penicillin and the sulfa drugs, for example, attack the germs that cause pneumonia, gonorrhea, and syphilis. But they do not harm the common viruses. See DRUG.

Another advancement in the treatment of disease was the use of substances that occur naturally in the body. Some of these substances are *hormones*, such as insulin for the treatment of diabetes. Other substances come from certain tissues, such as liver extract for the treatment of pernicious anemia. See HORMONE.

The development of surgical techniques has been still another great achievement in fighting disease. Surgeons can remove all or part of a lung or kidney. They can repair the heart or stomach. Surgeons can even replace bones with metal or plastic parts. See SURGERY.

Preventing Disease. Many diseases, even serious ones, can be prevented. Nutritional diseases such as rickets, scurvy, and pellagra may be avoided by eating well-balanced meals. When a person's diet does not supply enough vitamins, a doctor may prescribe additional vitamins. Other diseases, including cholera and typhus, may be prevented by proper sanitation and adequate housing. Most countries have laws that regulate sanitation, the purity of water and food, and working conditions in factories. Quarantine laws prevent the sick from coming in contact with healthy persons (see QUARANTINE).

Vaccines and serums can help build up a person's resistance to disease. Doctors use *inoculations* (injections of killed or weakened disease germs) that cause the body to build up resistance to a disease. People are inoculated against many bacterial diseases, including diphtheria, whooping cough, typhoid fever, and cholera. See INOCULATION.

Vaccines cause the body to produce antibodies that fight certain diseases such as smallpox and poliomyelitis. Vaccines contain dead or weakened disease germs. When the doctor injects a vaccine, the body begins to form antibodies. The body continues to produce antibodies for several years. But just to make sure, doctors sometimes give "booster shots," or small additional doses of vaccine. See ANTIBODY; VACCINATION.

Doctors may give *serums* to persons who already have a disease, or to those who have been exposed to one. Serums injected into the body add antibodies to the blood. Unlike vaccines, serums do not cause the body to form antibodies. See SERUM.

Knowledge of the causes of disease enables scientists to find ways to prevent or control it. For example, swamps can be drained to prevent malaria mosquitoes from breeding. Insecticides are sprayed over infested areas to destroy flies and other insects that carry germs. Farmers inoculate cattle against Bang's disease. Milk is pasteurized to destroy germs it may contain.

Research. Throughout the world, research scientists seek ways to cure or prevent diseases. They also try to find what causes certain diseases. They may make thousands of experiments, and their findings must satisfy rigid tests. Chemists, biologists, physicists, and psychologists work with physicians in the study of disease.

Plant and Animal Diseases

Plant Diseases in the United States cause crop losses totaling about $3,000,000,000 every year. Some diseases kill plants, ruining entire orchards and fields of grain. Others weaken plants, causing them to produce poor quality crops and reducing the size of the crops. The greatest threat of plant diseases to man is that they destroy materials essential to life. Green plants manufacture *carbohydrates*, or starches and sugars, which all living things need for energy. Only plants, or animals that eat plants, can provide man with the carbohydrates he must have. Serious outbreaks of plant diseases can cause famine. During the 1840's, over 750,000 persons died in Ireland when a fungus blight destroyed the nation's potato crop, causing a famine.

Some plant diseases cause serious illness in humans. *Ergot*, a fungus that attacks wheat, barley, and rye, can produce *ergotism* in persons who eat bread made from infected grain. However, scientists use ergot from rye to make powerful drugs to help control bleeding. When ergot epidemics strike rye fields, the crop may become more valuable for drugs than for grain.

Plant diseases may also result from infection by other fungi, bacteria, and viruses. Rust fungi destroy many grains, fruits, and green plants. More than 170 kinds of bacteria can produce diseases in flowering plants. Viruses cause *mosaic disease*, which destroys many edible fruits and plants.

Scientists and farmers have developed various ways to control plant diseases. They breed new varieties of plants that resist disease. They also rotate their crops, and use chemicals in the soil and to spray their fields. See FUNGICIDE; INSECTICIDE; CROPPING SYSTEM.

Animal Diseases kill more than $2 billion worth of livestock annually in the United States. Sometimes a serious disease kills most of the animals in a herd. Then the farmer must destroy all animals that have come in contact with the herd. He kills these other animals in order to prevent an epidemic in the entire region. One of the most dreaded animal diseases is foot-and-mouth disease. It attacks cattle, hogs, sheep, and goats. The disease spreads rapidly, and many infected animals die.

Animals suffer from many diseases caused by bacteria, viruses, and protozoa. Bacteria cause white diarrhea, which is often fatal to chicks. Distemper and hog cholera result from virus infections. *Coccidiosis*, a protozoan infection, is a destructive disease of poultry. It also attacks cattle, hogs, and cats.

Humans can get some diseases from animals. A person who drinks unpasteurized milk from cows that have tuberculosis or brucellosis may develop these diseases.

Veterinarians (animal doctors) work with other scientists and farmers to keep animals healthy. They study diseases, develop ways to keep them from spreading, and conduct research programs to find new cures. See VETERINARY MEDICINE.

RENÉ J. DUBOS

Related Articles in WORLD BOOK include:

ALLERGIES

Allergy
Asthma
Conjunctivitis
Eczema
Hay Fever
Hives

BACTERIAL DISEASES

Anthrax
Bacteria
Bubonic Plague
Cholera
Chorea
Croup
Diphtheria
Dysentery (Bacillary Dysentery)
Erysipelas
Leprosy
Meningitis
Osteomyelitis
Paratyphoid Fever
Pneumonia
Rheumatic Fever
Scarlet Fever
Scrofula
Tetanus
Tuberculosis
Tularemia
Typhoid Fever
Undulant Fever
Whooping Cough
Yaws

ENVIRONMENTAL AND OCCUPATIONAL DISEASES

Airsickness
Altitude Sickness
Asphyxiation
Bends
Frostbite
Gangrene
Immersion Foot
Lead Poisoning
Radiation Sickness
Red-Out
Seasickness
Sunstroke

FUNGUS DISEASES

Athlete's Foot
Fungus Disease
Histoplasmosis
Jungle Rot
Lumpy Jaw
Ringworm
Thrush

NUTRITIONAL DISEASES

Beriberi
Malnutrition
Pellagra
Rickets
Scurvy

PARASITIC DISEASES

Dysentery (Amebic)
Elephantiasis
Hookworm
Kala-Azar
Malaria
Parasite
Pinworm
Roundworm
Schistosomiasis
Sleeping Sickness
Tapeworm

VIRUS DISEASES

Chicken Pox
Cold, Common
Dengue
Encephalitis
German Measles
Herpes
Influenza
Measles
Mononucleosis
Mumps
Poliomyelitis
Rabies
Smallpox
Virus
Yellow Fever

SYMPTOMS OF DISEASE

Abscess
Backache
Bleeding
Colic
Constipation
Convulsions
Cough
Cramp
Diarrhea
Dizziness
Dyspepsia
Edema
Fainting
Fatigue
Fever
Headache
Hemorrhage
Hiccup
Indigestion
Inflammation
Insomnia
Itch
Jaundice
Lumbago
Nausea
Neuralgia
Pain
Pus
Shock
Sneezing
Squint
Vomiting

OTHER RELATED ARTICLES

Appendicitis
Arthritis
Blindness (Diseases)
Brain (Brain Diseases)
Cancer
Cell (The Cell in Disease)
Colitis
Cystic Fibrosis
Diabetes
Diagnosis
Epidemic
Eye (Defects and Diseases)
Gland (Diseases of Glands)
Heart (Heart Diseases)
Kidney (Kidney Diseases)
Liver (Diseases of the Liver)
Lung (Diseases and Care of the Lungs)
Medic Alert Foundation
Mental Illness
Myelitis
Peritonitis
Quarantine
Relapsing Fever
Rheumatism
Rocky Mountain Spotted Fever
Senility
Sickle Cell Anemia
Skin
Stomach
Tick Fever
Trench Mouth
Typhus
Vaccination
Venereal Diseases

Outline

I. Diseases Caused by Germs
A. Bacterial Diseases
B. Protozoan Diseases
C. Worm Diseases
D. Fungus Diseases
E. Virus Diseases

II. Diseases Present at Birth

III. Diseases Caused by Environment

IV. Nutritional Diseases

V. Allergies

VI. Functional Diseases

VII. Diseases of Children

VIII. Diseases of the Aged

IX. Occupational Diseases

X. How Diseases Spread
A. By Humans
B. By Insects and Other Animals

XI. How the Body Fights Disease

XII. Man's Battle Against Disease
A. Detecting Disease
B. Treating Disease
C. Preventing Disease
D. Research

XIII. Plant and Animal Diseases
A. Plant Diseases
B. Animal Diseases

Questions

What is disease? What is an epidemic? A pandemic?
What is "the body's first line of defense"?

What are two reasons that people live longer than they did a hundred years ago?

What substances necessary for life can man get only from green plants or from animals that eat plants?

What two diseases can be caused by the weather?

Who proved the germ theory of disease?

How many bacteria have been found in a grain of soil?

What is the leading cause of congenital disease?

What disease do skin divers often get?

What is a carrier?

DISH. See PORCELAIN; POTTERY; STONEWARE.

DISINFECTANT, *DIHS in FECK tunt,* is a chemical substance used to kill bacteria and other organisms which cause disease. People use disinfectants to clean and sterilize instruments and utensils, clothes, and rooms. Disinfectants have a limited value in controlling the spread of epidemics of disease. They should not be confused with *antiseptics* which prevent or stop the growth of bacteria. Disinfectants are sometimes called *germicides* or *bactericides.* They sometimes include substances called *deodorants,* which neutralize odors.

Disinfectants are powerful chemicals which should be properly labeled. They should be carefully handled and always kept away from children.

Some of the most important disinfectants are the following:

Bleaching Powder, chloride of lime, or sodium hypochlorite, is widely used for purifying water. It also kills bacteria on contaminated objects which are scattered about an infected area.

Carbolic Acid, or phenol, disinfects body discharges and dirty rooms. Certain preparations of it can be used to sterilize clothing and utensils. Doctors once used carbolic acid to disinfect the skin, but this practice is no longer used. A disinfecting solution of carbolic acid should contain one part carbolic acid to 20 parts water.

Formaldehyde in water solution disinfects clothing and body discharges. In water solution it is called formalin. A 2 to 5 per cent solution of formaldehyde disinfects clothing. A 10 per cent solution kills germs in body discharges.

Mercuric Chloride, bichloride of mercury, or corrosive sublimate, is used to disinfect hands and other parts of the body which do not have cuts or openings. It should never touch a mucous membrane. Mercuric chloride is very poisonous and dangerous to use except under proper direction. It is used in a solution of one part of mercuric chloride to 2,000 parts of water.

Potassium Permanganate is used to disinfect sinks, drains, and water pipes. It can also destroy organic matter. Surgeons use water solutions of potassium permanganate to disinfect their hands. It should always be used greatly diluted in water. W. W. BAUER

Related Articles in WORLD BOOK include:

Antiseptic	Chlorine	Deodorizer
Bichloride of Mercury	Creosote	Formaldehyde
Carbolic Acid	Cresol	Lye

DISJOINT SET. See SET THEORY.

DISK JOCKEY. See RADIO (Kinds of Programs; picture: A Radio Broadcast).

DISLOCATION occurs when any part of the body moves from its normal position. The term usually refers to the movement out of normal position of the bones of a joint (see JOINT). When bones become dislocated, they do not meet properly at the joint. This usually results in pain and swelling.

Sometimes in dislocation the bones of a joint are pulled out of place only slightly. Physicians call this an *incomplete dislocation.* In other cases, the bones become completely separated from each other. This is a *complete dislocation.* A complete dislocation must be corrected immediately. In *simple dislocation,* the patient has no external wound. A *compound dislocation* is one accompanied by a wound opening from the body surface. When a dislocation occurs in the same joint many times, physicians say it is *habitual.*

Some types of dislocation are *congenital,* or present at birth. These may be hereditary, or may be caused by some factor before or during birth. An example is congenital dislocation of the hip. BENJAMIN F. MILLER

DISMAL SWAMP is a wild marshland covering about 750 square miles (1,940 square kilometers) in northeastern North Carolina and southeastern Virginia. For location, see NORTH CAROLINA (physical map). It is one of the largest swamps in the United States. It is a tangle of vines and bald cypress, black tupelo, juniper, and pine trees. Its wildlife includes bear, deer, opossum, raccoon, and snakes. Lake Drummond lies in Virginia in the center of the swamp. Part of the Dismal Swamp has been cleared for farming and drained. GEORGE MACINKO

DISMAS, SAINT, is a saint of the Roman Catholic Church. The Bible tells us that two thieves were crucified beside Christ (Luke 23: 39-43). One of them criticized the other for mocking Christ. He asked Jesus to remember him. Hearing this, Christ said: "Today thou shalt be with me in Paradise." The name of this "good thief" was Dismas. Dismas is considered a saint, and his feast day is March 25. The thief who mocked Christ is said to have been called Gestas. FULTON J. SHEEN

Dismal Swamp's tangled tree roots and shallow marshland make navigation difficult even for small boats.

Virginia Chamber of Commerce

© Walt Disney Productions

Disneyland and Walt Disney World are spectacular amusement parks that feature exhibits, rides, and shows based on movies by Walt Disney. There, visitors meet such Disney characters as, *left to right*, Pluto, Goofy, and Mickey Mouse.

DISNEY, WALT (1901-1966), was one of the most famous motion-picture producers in history. Disney first became known in the 1920's and 1930's for creating such cartoon film characters as Mickey Mouse and Donald Duck. He later produced feature-length cartoon films, movies about wild animals in their natural surroundings, and films starring human actors. The Disney studio has won more than 45 Academy Awards for its movies and for scientific and technical contributions to film making.

Disney achieved one of his greatest successes in 1955, when he opened Disneyland, a spectacular amusement park in Anaheim, Calif. A similar park, Walt Disney World, opened near Orlando, Fla., in 1971, after Disney's death. Most of the exhibits, rides, and shows at both parks are based on characters from Disney movies.

© Walt Disney Productions

Cartoon Characters made Walt Disney famous throughout the world. Donald Duck first appeared in a short cartoon in 1934. In 1942, the full-length cartoon motion picture *Bambi* starred Flower, the skunk; Thumper, the rabbit; and Bambi, the deer.

Early Life. Walter Elias Disney was born in Chicago. His family moved to Missouri when he was a child, and Disney spent much of his boyhood on a farm near Marceline. At the age of 16, Disney studied art in Chicago. In 1920, he joined the Kansas City Film Ad Company, where he helped make crude cartoon advertisements to be shown in movie theaters.

The First Disney Cartoons. In 1923, Disney moved to Los Angeles with the goal of becoming an *animator*, an artist who draws movie cartoons. He set up his first studio in a garage. For several years, Disney struggled just to pay his expenses. He finally gained success in 1928, when he released the first short Mickey Mouse cartoons. Earlier film makers had found that animals were easier to animate than people. Mickey Mouse, drawn with a series of circles, proved ideal for animation.

In 1927, sound had been added to motion pictures, and a process for making movies in color was developed a few years later. Disney and his assistants made imaginative use of both sound and color, and Disney himself provided Mickey Mouse's voice. His cartoon *Flowers and Trees* (1932) was the first film that was made in full Technicolor.

During the early 1930's, Disney produced a cartoon series called *Silly Symphonies.* Mickey Mouse appeared in these and later cartoons, along with such characters as Donald Duck, Goofy, and Pluto. Throughout his career, Disney actually drew few cartoons. His genius lay in creating, organizing, and directing the films.

Full-Length Movies. In 1937, Disney released the first full-length cartoon film ever made, *Snow White and the Seven Dwarfs.* It became one of the most popular movies in history. Disney's later full-length animated films included *Pinocchio* (1940), *Fantasia* (1940), *Dumbo* (1941), *Bambi* (1942), *Cinderella* (1950), *Lady and the Tramp* (1955), and *The Jungle Book*, which was issued in 1967, after his death.

During World War II (1939-1945), Disney's studio made educational films for the United States government. After the war, Disney created fewer animated movies. He concentrated on making films that starred real animals or human actors.

In 1948, Disney released *Seal Island.* This short movie was the first in a series of "True-Life Adventures" that show how animals live in nature. Disney released his first full-length nature film, *The Living Desert,* in 1953. All his nature movies include scenes of animal life rarely seen by human beings.

Disney released *Treasure Island,* his first full-length movie with human actors, in 1950. *Mary Poppins* (1964) probably ranks as the most successful of these Disney pictures.

After television became popular about 1950, many film makers either ignored TV or fought it as a threat to the movie industry. But Disney adjusted easily to the new form of entertainment. He produced a number of movies especially for television. Disney also served as the host of a weekly television show that presented Disney films.

Roy Paul Nelson

See also Motion Picture (pictures: *Snow White and the Seven Dwarfs;* A Documentary Film).

© Walt Disney Productions

© Walt Disney Productions

© Walt Disney Productions

Disney Movies have featured both cartoon characters and human actors. Mickey Mouse starred in *Steamboat Willie, upper left,* the first cartoon to use sound. *Mary Poppins, left,* combines human actors with cartoon scenes. The film describes the adventures of a nursemaid who can fly. *Pinocchio, above,* is a full-length cartoon about a puppet named Pinocchio. Near the story's end, a whale swallows Pinocchio and Geppetto, the puppet's father. They escape from the whale's stomach on a raft.

DISNEY WORLD. See DISNEY, WALT; FLORIDA (Places to Visit); ORLANDO.

DISNEYLAND. See DISNEY, WALT; ANAHEIM; CALIFORNIA (Places to Visit; picture).

DISORDERLY CONDUCT. See BREACH OF THE PEACE.

DISPERSION. See LIGHT (Dispersion).

DISPLACED PERSON (DP) is a person who is forced to leave his country because of war or political, religious, or racial persecution. Nazi Germany moved millions of persons to slave-labor and concentration camps. Others fled their homes. Western Europe had more than 8 million DP's at the end of World War II in 1945. About 1 million Russians refused to return home. Boundary changes and escape from Communist terrorism swelled the number of DP's after the war.

On Dec. 15, 1946, the United Nations established the International Refugee Organization to care for and settle DP's. Between 1948 and 1952, more than 440,000 DP's entered the United States. Canada received over 160,000. After 1956, the United States admitted Hungarian and other Eastern European DP's. Many North Koreans, North Vietnamese, and Chinese who escaped Communist rule were accepted by free Asian countries and Hong Kong. Many Cuban DP's settled in the United States during the 1950's and 1960's. STEFAN T. POSSONY

DISPLACEMENT means putting an object out of place. Rock formations may be *displaced* by faulting (see FAULT). A ship or other floating object will *displace* an amount of water equal to its own weight (see GRAVITY, SPECIFIC; SHIP [table: Nautical Measurements]).

DISPLACEMENT BEHAVIOR includes a variety of animal or human activities. Such activities seem to be out of place in the situation in which they occur. For example, songbirds may pause during fights to feed, or smooth their feathers. Many mammals scratch themselves or groom their fur when faced with a decision of whether to fight or run away. An embarrassed man may adjust his tie. Much displacement behavior occurs during emotional conflict. But scientists do not know exactly why such behavior takes place. JOHN A. WIENS

DISRAELI, *dihz RAY lih,* **BENJAMIN** (1804-1881), EARL OF BEACONSFIELD, was the only man to be born a Jew who became prime minister of Great Britain. The eldest son of a noted Jewish author, he became a member of the Church of England in 1817. He gave up the study of law as a young man, and created a sensation by writing *Vivian Grey* and other novels. He tried several times to win a seat in the House of Commons before being elected as a Tory in 1837.

National Portrait Gallery, London

Benjamin Disraeli

His extreme clothes and exaggerated speech made him stand out in the House of Commons. After almost 10 years he became the champion of high tariffs. He opposed Sir Robert Peel's bill to repeal the Corn Laws (see CORN LAWS). Disraeli became Chancellor of the Exchequer in 1852, and held that office three more times.

Disraeli was largely responsible for the 1867 Parliamentary Reform Act. He served as prime minister for about 10 months in 1868. In his second term, lasting from 1874 to 1880, he introduced laws to improve slum conditions, to protect the factory worker, and to help the farm laborer, who was in economic distress.

The Disraeli government was imperialistic in its policy outside Great Britain. It defended and advanced the country's colonial claims in India and Africa. Disraeli thwarted Russia's claim to Turkey and confined Russia to the Black Sea. He also obtained a major interest in the Suez Canal for Great Britain by purchasing a large number of shares.

Disraeli believed in progress within the limits of traditionalism. He deeply impressed his country by insisting that conservative policy must provide for progress and the improvement of working-class conditions. He thought that Tories would have to favor laws designed to make the lower classes more comfortable in Great Britain, and the country more respected and powerful abroad. He described himself as "a conservative to preserve all that is good in our constitution, and a radical to remove all that is bad." He was the political opponent of William E. Gladstone. Disraeli was born on Dec. 21, 1804, in London. JAMES L. GODFREY

See also CONSERVATIVE PARTY.

DISSECTION. See ANATOMY.

DISSENT. See RIOT; CIVIL DISOBEDIENCE.

DISSONANCE. See SOUND (Beats).

DISTANCE is the space between two points. It can be measured in miles, rods, feet, inches, meters, kilometers, centimeters, and many other units of measurement. The vast spaces between the stars and planets, or astronomical distances, are measured by the speed of light. Astronomers say, for example, that a star is six *light-years* away, which means that light reaches the earth six years after it leaves the star. Light travels at a speed of 299,792 kilometers, or 186,282 miles, per second. In one year, light travels about 9,500,000,000,000 kilometers. If a star is 6 light-years away, it is about 57,000,000,000,000 kilometers away.

Ordinary distances, such as a few miles, are too small to have meaning in astronomy. But these same distances are extremely large in other sciences. In biology and physics, men can measure the distance between two cells, or between atoms in a crystal. They measure such distances in *microns* (millionths of a meter), or in *millimicrons* (thousandths of a micron). PHILLIP S. JONES

Related Articles in WORLD BOOK include:

Astronomy (A Trip Through the Universe; Measuring Distances in Space)	Measurement (Length and Distance)
Aviation (World Air Mileage Chart)	Parallax
	Telemetry
	Visibility, Distances of
	Weights and Measures (Length)

DISTANT EARLY WARNING LINE. See DEW LINE.

DISTEMPER is a common contagious disease of young dogs. It usually begins with loss of appetite, chill, fever, reddened eyes, and dry muzzle. Later there may be infections in the lungs, intestines, or nervous system. If the infection is in the lung there is discharging through the nose, coughing, and heavy breathing. An intestinal infection usually results in frothy and bloody diarrhea. If the infection is in the nervous system, the dog may suffer from convulsions and may die, or it may suffer from a muscular twitching called *chorea.*

Distemper can be prevented by vaccination with specially prepared vaccines. It can be treated by giving the dog antiserum and other drugs. The dog should be under the care of a veterinarian. Dogs that have recovered from one attack of distemper are immune to later attacks. Distemper is caused by a virus discovered by Louis Carré of France in 1904.

Distemper of young horses is called *strangles.* It is caused by *Streptococcus equi* bacteria, and differs from distemper in dogs. The horse suffers from a sore throat, fever, and infection in the lymph glands. Strangles can be treated with antibiotics such as penicillin.

Cats also contract distemper, different from that of dogs (see CAT [Cat Diseases]). D. W. BRUNER

DISTILLATION, *DIHS tuh LAY shuhn,* is a process used to extract gas from a liquid or solid. The method employs heat and an apparatus called a *still.* When water is exposed to air it will dry up. When the water disappears, it has not been destroyed, but has changed to an invisible gas called *water vapor.* This water has *evaporated.* Boiling water forms the same gas, only more quickly. This water vapor is called *steam.* When steam is formed, the water *vaporizes.* The clear space just above the spout of a boiling kettle is filled with steam. The cloud above this clear space, which is often called "steam," is not really water vapor, but droplets of water formed again when the gas cooled. The formation of these water droplets is called *condensation.* Condensed steam can be collected by holding a cold vessel, such as an empty milk bottle, inverted above the spout of the kettle. This condensed steam is called *distilled water.* It contains almost no impurities.

Distillation is this process of boiling a liquid, such as water, and condensing the vapor which forms. So distillation really includes two processes, *vaporization* and *condensation.* The *distilled water* is purer than the original water, because the process leaves behind substances, such as salt, which do not evaporate at the boiling temperature of water. Water is constantly evaporating from sea, soil, and plants, and the naturally distilled water is rain or dew.

A still consists of a *boiler,* a *condenser,* and a *receiver.* The mixture to be distilled is heated in the boiler. Whichever substance in the mixture boils at the lowest temperature will be the first to turn to a vapor. The vapor enters the condenser, where it cools and becomes a liquid again. The distilled liquid, called the *distillate,* then collects in the receiver. Many liquids besides water are purified by distillation.

Fractional Distillation. When several liquids are mixed, it is usually impossible to separate them completely by simple distillation. For example, alcohol boils at 172° F. (78° C), and water boils at 212° F. (100° C). But even the water will evaporate fairly rapidly at the boiling point of alcohol. So the distillate from an alcohol-water mixture will contain some water. But the distillate collected at first will have a larger proportion of alcohol than the portions that condense later. So this first batch is removed before much water distillate has condensed. In the same way the remaining distillate is collected in *fractions,* and the whole process is called *fractional distillation.* Then each fraction can be redistilled, to get a much purer product. Fractional distillation is used to make distilled liquors, such as brandy and whiskey. These always contain much more alcohol than

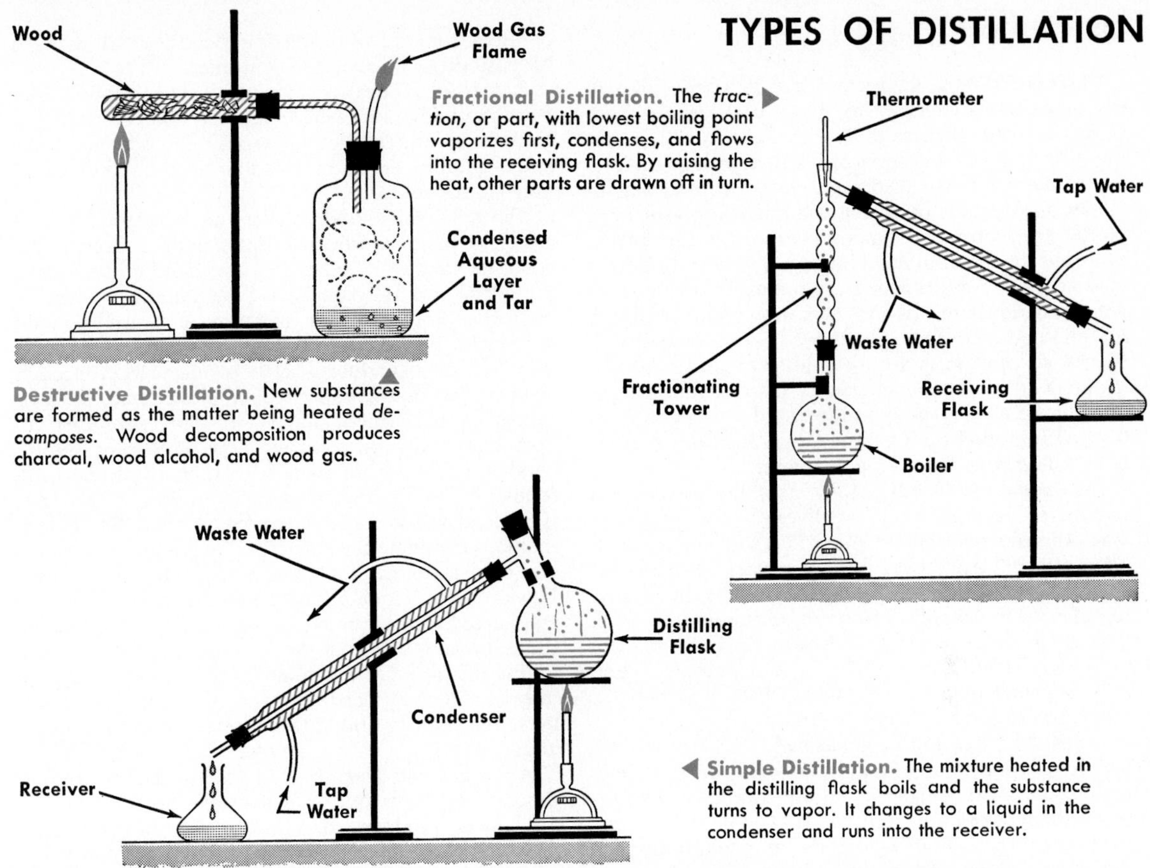

TYPES OF DISTILLATION

Fractional Distillation. The *fraction,* or part, with lowest boiling point vaporizes first, condenses, and flows into the receiving flask. By raising the heat, other parts are drawn off in turn.

Destructive Distillation. New substances are formed as the matter being heated *decomposes.* Wood decomposition produces charcoal, wood alcohol, and wood gas.

Simple Distillation. The mixture heated in the distilling flask boils and the substance turns to vapor. It changes to a liquid in the condenser and runs into the receiver.

wines and beers, which are not distilled. But fractional distillation of an alcohol-water mixture, no matter how far carried out, cannot yield alcohol which is more than about 95 per cent pure. The remaining 5 per cent of water must be removed with certain chemicals, such as metallic sodium or quicklime. Fractional distillation is also important in petroleum refining. Petroleum is a mixture of many substances which have to be separated to be useful. The earlier fractions give naphtha and benzine. Next comes gasoline, afterward kerosene, and then the heavier lubricating oils. Much of this separation is brought about in a single distillation by using huge *fractionating* towers. The substances which make up the earliest fractions are the ones that boil off at the lowest temperatures. Their vapors rise highest in the towers and are carried off by pipes high up. Separate pipes carry off the different fractions at different levels. Fractional distillation is also used to separate the different products obtained directly from coal tar.

Destructive Distillation. Neither simple nor fractional distillation forms new substances. Each merely separates substances that have been mixed together. But when a substance such as wood is heated in a closed vessel, it *decomposes,* and gives substances that were not there before. This is *destructive distillation,* and is a chemical process. GEORGE L. BUSH

Related Articles in WORLD BOOK include:

Acetic Acid	Condensation	Petroleum (Refining)
Alcohol	Distilling	Water (Distillation)
Alcoholic Drink	Evaporation	

DISTILLING is the process of manufacturing alcoholic beverages such as whisky, brandy, and rum. Manufacturers distill whisky from a fermented "mash" of corn, rye, wheat, or other small grains, malt, and water. They make brandy from the fermented juice of grapes and other fruits. Rum comes from fermented molasses and sugar-cane juices.

Liquors are first fermented, then put through several distillation processes (see FERMENTATION; DISTILLATION). This removes impurities such as fusel oil, aldehydes, and acids. By a process called *rectification,* some of the impurities remain in the beverage to add flavor. Liquors have no color when first made. Manufacturers add color to them either by storing them in charred wooden barrels, or by adding caramel coloring.

The distilling industry is one of the largest in the United States. People spend almost $4 billion a year for distilled liquors. The federal and state governments collect large sums from liquor taxes.

Leading companies in the distilling industry include Joseph E. Seagram & Sons; Schenley Industries, Inc.; National Distillers Products Corp.; Hiram Walker & Sons, Inc.; James B. Beam Distilling Co.; and Brown-Forman Distillers Corp. J. BERNARD ROBB

See also ALCOHOLIC DRINK (Distilled Liquors); INTERNAL REVENUE.

DISTINGUISHED. For medals beginning with the word *distinguished,* such as Distinguished Flying Cross, see DECORATIONS AND MEDALS.

DISTRIBUTARY. See RIVER (Parts).

DISTRIBUTION

DISTRIBUTION is the second step in a series of economic processes which bring goods and services from those who make them to those who use them. The making of such goods and services is called *production*. The use of the goods is called *consumption*. *Distribution* includes all methods by which the goods are sent from producers to consumers. Another part of this distribution process is the distribution of income. The distribution of income is the way in which the national income is divided among those who produce, those who distribute, and those who consume goods (see NATIONAL INCOME). Nearly all consumers are also either producers or distributors. Without the process of distribution, people would have no way of obtaining useful services or products, such as food from a farmer, clothing from a tailor, or an automobile from a manufacturer.

Distribution of Goods. Many steps lie between the making of a product and its delivery to the consumer. The process of distribution enters into the production of a loaf of bread long before the loaf is baked. Wheat that is grown on the plains of Nebraska may be distributed to mills at Minneapolis, Minn., to be ground into flour. This flour may be sent to a bakery at Chicago, Ill., where it is baked into bread, sliced, and wrapped. Then it is delivered to a grocery store, where it is bought, taken home, and consumed.

Methods of distributing goods vary with the particular product and its industry. In colonial times, a shoemaker sold his shoes directly to the consumer, who ordered them before they were made. Today, most of our food, clothing, and other products are made in quantities long before any individual consumer has any thought of buying them. Goods usually go from the producer to a *wholesaler*, who is a person or a company dealing in large quantities of goods.

A wholesaler of potatoes buys potatoes from farmers in carload lots. Few grocers could handle such large quantities of potatoes, since they would spoil before they could be sold. The wholesaler sells smaller quantities to *retailers*. The grocer can buy a dozen sacks of potatoes from the wholesaler's carload and sell them to his customers, who are the consumers.

Storage is another process involved in distribution. Foods and other products which may spoil are stored in cold-storage warehouses. Eggs, meat, seafood, and fruits and vegetables are often stored for several months until they can be sold.

The wholesalers and retailers are sometimes called *middlemen*. Each middleman tries to make a profit on the goods he handles. These profits are added to the costs of the goods and are paid for by the consumer when he buys the product. Some methods of distribution do away with one or more of these middlemen. Farmers often sell their produce directly to the market through co-operative associations, which return part of their profits to the farmers. There are many consumer co-operatives which do away with the wholesaler's profit. Mail-order houses do away with both wholesaler and retailer by selling directly to the consumer, who selects the merchandise from a catalog. Other distributing methods eliminate the expense of keeping up wholesale and retail stores by employing house-to-house salesmen. However, the elimination of middlemen does not always guarantee lower prices for the consumer. Sometimes it means only that the producer assumes the costs ordinarily paid by the middlemen. Occasionally, he may be able to reduce the costs of distributing his products, and thus be able to lower prices or even to make larger profits.

Advertising and *packaging* are parts of the distributing process which attempt to increase the flow of goods to consumers. Producers and distributors advertise their products in newspapers and magazines, over the radio, on television, and in outdoor advertising. By packaging their products in attractively designed and labeled boxes, wrappings, or other containers, they make the product more appealing to prospective buyers.

Distribution of Income. Money has been called the oil that makes the wheels of the distribution machine turn smoothly. The producer must have money to invest in plants, machinery, and labor to make his product. The wholesaler, retailer, and others involved in produc-

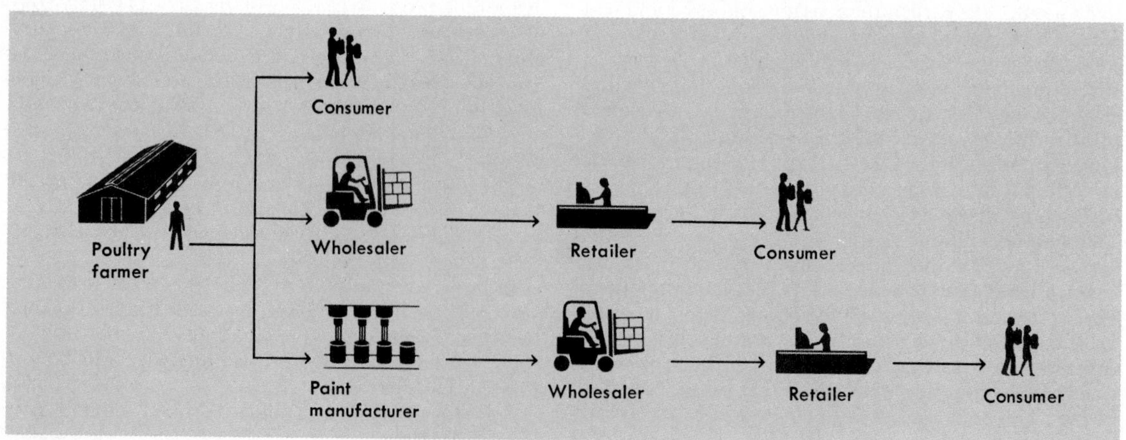

WORLD BOOK diagram by Mas Nakagawa

Distribution is the movement of goods and services from producer to consumer. A poultry farmer, for example, may sell eggs directly to consumers. He also may sell many crates of eggs to a *wholesaler*, a merchant who deals in large quantities of goods. The wholesaler sells smaller quantities to retailers—in this case, grocers—who then sell individual cartons to consumers. Or, a manufacturer may buy eggs to make paint and sell the paint to a wholesaler.

tion and in distribution must have money to engage in their part of the distribution process. The consumer must have money to buy the products. Most consumers obtain their money by working to produce goods.

The total of all the incomes received in the distribution process is called the *gross national income.* A fair distribution of the national income is necessary for an even distribution of goods. If the consumers do not have enough money to buy the goods produced, the wholesalers, retailers, and producers do not make a profit. So workers, who are also consumers, may have to be laid off, and many plants may have to close. If farmers do not get enough money for their produce, they cannot buy manufactured goods. An economic depression may take place if the distribution process breaks down.

The proper distribution of income is a complicated matter. It involves not only fair profits and wages, but also fair prices, rent, and interest. High wages do not help the consumer to buy more goods if the price of goods is too high. Low prices are of no value to the distribution process if many persons are unemployed and cannot afford to buy goods. See INCOME.

Distribution of Services. Too many gasoline stations in the same neighborhood means that most or all of them will be unable to make a fair profit. This is a problem of *distribution of services.* Sometimes a new machine does away with the jobs of thousands of workers. This happened when the automatic teletypewriter replaced the skill of many Morse-code telegraphers. These men had to learn a new occupation before they could again take their place in the distribution system.

Problems of Distribution. In an ideal society, production, distribution, and consumption would be balanced so as to meet the needs of all the people. Many economists believe that we now have enough factories, machinery, and tools to come nearer to producing all the things that people would like to consume than we have ever done. These economists believe that the fact that many persons do not receive all the goods they can consume is the fault of distribution. Other economists believe that the fault lies with improper production—that not enough goods can be produced at all times at a profit to satisfy the people's needs. The solution of the problem of distribution is one of the major tasks confronting modern society. ROBERT D. PATTON

Related Articles in WORLD BOOK include:

Advertising	Economics	Production
Banks and Banking	Investment	Profit
Black Market	Money	Rent
Business	Motion Picture	Retailing
Cold Storage	(Distribution	Stock Exchange
Consumption	and Exhibition)	Supermarket
Cooperative	Packaging	Trade
Credit	Parity	Wages and Hours

DISTRIBUTIVE EDUCATION. See HIGH SCHOOL (Activities and Services).

DISTRIBUTOR. See IGNITION; GASOLINE ENGINE (The Ignition System).

DISTRICT ATTORNEY is a public official whose chief duties are bringing charges against and prosecuting persons charged with a crime or offense. He is also called the county attorney, prosecuting attorney, or state's attorney. A district attorney is the attorney for the people in criminal trials. He may act as attorney for the government in civil suits to collect taxes or to take property for public use. He may appear for the defense in suits brought against the government. He is elected in some states and appointed in others.

United States district attorneys are officially called United States attorneys. They are appointed by the President and are responsible to the attorney general. A U.S. attorney is appointed for each federal judicial district. His term of office is four years. He serves as attorney for the government when it prosecutes for crimes, sues, or is sued. ERWIN N. GRISWOLD

DISTRICT COURT is the court in which most federal court cases are first heard in the United States. The district court ranks below the court of appeals. In a district court, questions of fact are decided by a jury, or, if the parties wish, by a judge. The first hearing of a case is called a trial, and the district court is called a *trial court.* The district court decides on the truth of contested events, and the court's decision is final. But the rules of law used by the district court may be reviewed by a higher court, on appeal. The appeal is usually to the Court of Appeals. The Supreme Court of the United States sometimes reviews a decision of the Court of Appeals.

There are about 90 district courts in the United States and its possessions. Each court has one or more judges, and a United States attorney. The courts hear most federal crime cases, as well as civil suits arising under postal, patent, copyright, internal revenue, and bankruptcy laws. ERWIN N. GRISWOLD

See also COURT OF APPEALS; COURT (Federal Courts).

DISTRICT OF COLUMBIA (D.C.) is the seat of the United States government. This federal district covers 68 square miles (176 square kilometers) along the Potomac River between Maryland and Virginia. It lies about 38 miles (61 kilometers) southwest of Baltimore. The city of Washington covers the entire District. For a history of the District of Columbia, see WASHINGTON, D.C. See also FEDERAL DISTRICT.

DISULFIRAM. See ANTABUSE.

DITMARS, *DIT mahrz,* **RAYMOND LEE** (1876-1942), was a noted American authority on reptiles. His popular books included *The Reptile Book, Reptiles of the World, Snakes of the World,* and *Strange Animals I Have Known.* He became curator of reptiles at the New York Zoological Park in 1899, and remained at the park until his death. He pioneered in developing snake-bite serums which have saved many lives. Ditmars was born in Newark, N.J., and was graduated from Barnard Military Academy in 1891. A. M. WINCHESTER

DIU. See GOA.

DIURETIC, *DIE yu REHT ick,* is a drug or other substance that increases the secretion of urine by the kidneys. Many substances such as water, glucose solution, tea, coffee, mineral waters, and beer have a diuretic effect on the kidneys. Diuretics are used to treat many diseases in which the secretion and flow of urine are greatly affected, such as when the kidneys are damaged by poisons. They are also used to rid the body of extra fluid, as in edema. AUSTIN SMITH

DIURNATION, or DIURNAL HIBERNATION. See HIBERNATION.

DIVE BOMBER. See BOMBER.

DIVER, a bird. See LOON.

DIVERSIFIED FARMING. See AGRICULTURE (Kinds).

DIVERTICULITIS, *DY vuhr TIHK yuh LY tihs,* is a common disease of the *colon* (large intestine). Its symptoms include pain in the lower left part of the abdomen and a fever. Treatment with certain medicines cures most cases of diverticulitis. The disease develops from *diverticulosis,* a disorder widespread among middle-aged and elderly people in North America and northern Europe.

Diverticulosis involves the presence of pouches called *diverticula* along the outside of the colon. Diverticula rarely form in people under the age of 30. Most diverticulosis patients have no symptoms.

For many years, physicians believed that a diet low in *roughage* (fruit and vegetable fibers) would help prevent diverticulosis. But today, evidence suggests that the opposite is true. A shortage of roughage in the diet makes the waste material in the colon extremely firm and compact. The waste cannot move easily through the colon, and high pressure results. This pressure can force the inner membrane of the colon to bulge out through several weak points in the lining of the organ. Such action forms small, permanent diverticula that may be seen with an X-ray examination.

In the United States, where most people eat relatively little roughage, nearly half of those over 60 have diverticulosis. The condition rarely occurs in underdeveloped countries, where the standard diet has a high fiber content.

Diverticulitis develops in many cases of diverticulosis. It results when one of the diverticula breaks open. The material that leaks out infects the outer surface of the colon. In most cases, the infection stays in a small area. But it may spread and develop into *peritonitis,* a severe illness that can cause death (see PERITONITIS).

Doctors treat diverticulitis with antibiotics to control infection, drugs to relax the muscle of the colon, and compounds to help empty the colon. A diet high in roughage may help prevent a recurrence of the disease. A. WILLIAM HOLMES

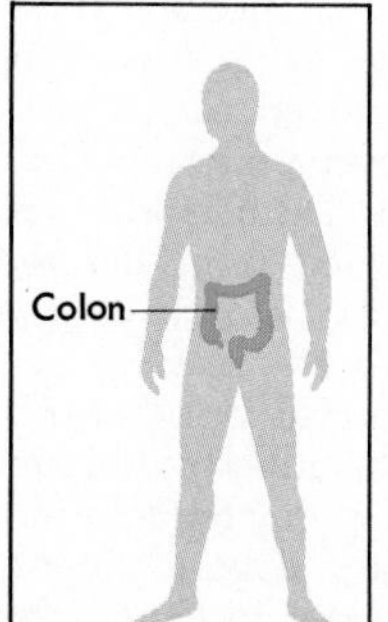

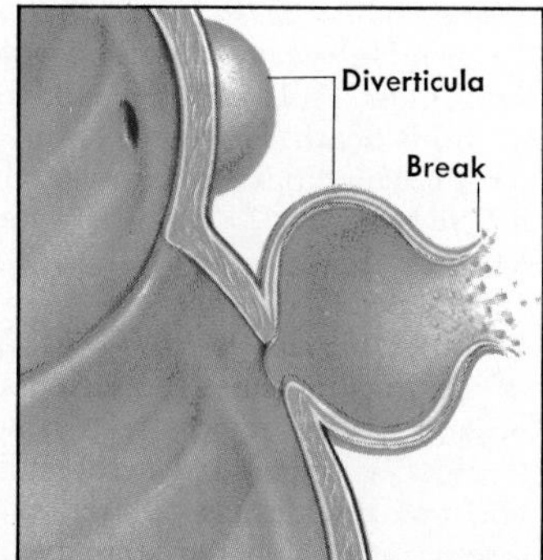

WORLD BOOK illustrations by Robert Demarest

Diverticulitis is a disease of the colon. It occurs when a *diverticulum,* an abnormal pouch on the surface of the colon, breaks open and infectious waste material spills out.

DIVIDE is a high place in the land, situated so that the streams on one side flow in the opposite direction to the streams on the other side. These streams then flow into different river systems, which may empty into different oceans. The little streams are called the *headwaters* of the river systems. The divide separates the headwaters of the systems. Another name for a divide is *watershed.* A divide may be rather low, like the height of land that runs from east to west across North America. This divide separates the rivers that flow generally northward into the Gulf of Saint Lawrence, Hudson Bay, and the Arctic Ocean from those that flow into the Mississippi basin. Some divides are very high with steep slopes, like the Rocky Mountains. This separates the rivers flowing into the Mississippi from those flowing into the Pacific Ocean. The watershed that runs north and south through the Rocky Mountains is called the *Continental Divide.* On Cutbank Pass in Glacier National Park, there are three brooks so close together that a person can pour water into all three. One brook carries water to Hudson Bay, another to the Pacific Ocean, and the third into the Gulf of Mexico. This point is actually the top of the North American continent. At several places, sources of streams flowing to the Pacific and to the Gulf lie only a short distance apart. ELDRED D. WILSON

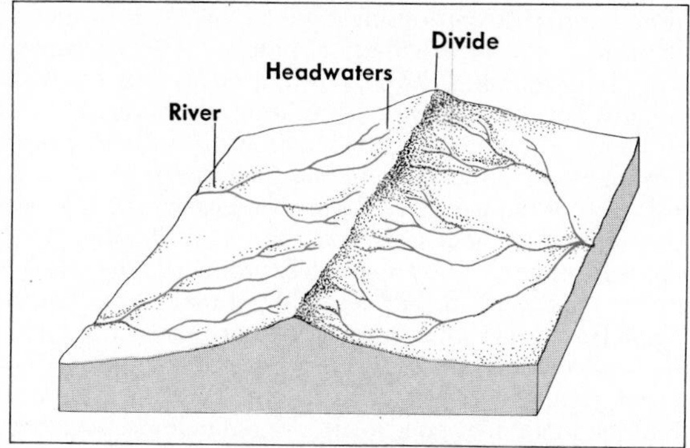

WORLD BOOK diagram by Marion Pahl

A Divide is a high area of land that separates river systems from one another. The headwaters of each system form near the top of the divide. The waters join and form streams and rivers.

See also CONTINENTAL DIVIDE; GREAT DIVIDE.

DIVIDEND, in arithmetic, see DIVISION (Learning to Divide; table: Division Terms). In insurance and securities, see INSURANCE (How Life Insurance Policies Pay Benefits); STOCK, CAPITAL.

DIVIDER is a drafting instrument used to divide lines into equal parts. It also transfers dimensions from a ruler to a map or a drawing. A divider measures and plots small distances between two points more accurately than a ruler. It can be used on maps to check the distance between two points against the distance scale.

A divider has two needle-pointed legs, joined together at the top. An adjusting screw changes the distance between the two legs. Dividers range in length from about 3 to 8 inches (8 to 20 centimeters). They are a type of caliper (see CALIPER). E. B. ESPENSHADE

DIVINATION, *DIHV uh NAY shuhn,* is the practice of trying to learn about the unknown by magical or supernatural means. A diviner supposedly can learn about the past, present, or future. Some diviners believe they can learn the causes of past events, such as a person's illness or death. Other diviners, called *dowsers,* claim they can find the location of underground water. Still others believe they can foretell events, such as when a person will die or whom a person will marry.

There are many kinds of divination. For example, *necromancy* involves communicating with the spirits of the dead. *Astrology* is an attempt to predict events by studying the positions of the sun, moon, stars, and planets. Some diviners interpret dreams to foretell events.

Another type of divination, called *palmistry*, involves the prediction of events by reading the lines and marks of the hand. Some fortunetellers claim to read messages in coffee grounds, tea leaves, dried mud, or crystal balls. Others use *tarot cards*, a special deck of pictured playing cards, to tell the future.

Throughout history, people have believed in the powers of divination. In ancient Greece and Rome, prophets known as *oracles* foretold events by interpreting messages from the gods.

At one time, courts used divination to determine the guilt or innocence of criminals. Divination in a trial was called an *ordeal*. For example, in many witch trials of the 1600's in Europe and colonial America, a suspected witch was tied up and thrown into water. If she sank, she was considered innocent. If she floated, she was considered a witch—and was burned at the stake or hanged. ALAN DUNDES

Related Articles in WORLD BOOK include:

Astrology	Magic	Ouija Board
Augur	Necromancy	Palmistry
Clairvoyance	Numerology	Superstition
Fortunetelling	Omen	Well (Locating Wells)
Graphology	Oracles	

DIVINE COMEDY is a beautiful, long epic poem by the Italian writer Dante Alighieri. Dante began the poem about 1300 and finished it just before his death in 1321. Its main theme is life after death, and Dante himself is the chief character. The *Divine Comedy* is divided into the *Inferno* (Hell); the *Purgatorio* (Purgatory); and the *Paradiso* (Paradise). Dante called the work simply *Commedia* (Comedy) because it ended happily. Later generations added the word *Divine*.

Dante divided each of the three parts of the poem into 33 sections called *cantos*. The cantos have a powerful rhythm because of their three-line *terza rima* stanzas. In such verses, the first and third lines of each stanza rhyme with the middle line of the preceding stanza.

The poem begins with Dante lost in a dark forest, symbolizing what he felt was his own unworthy life and the evil he saw in society. On Good Friday, after a night of painful wandering, he meets the Roman poet Virgil, who promises to lead him out of the forest. They reach Hell, a horrible pit shaped like a cone, deep in the earth. It has nine circles where Dante and Virgil visit crowds of suffering individuals tormented by monsters and devils. Some of the damned are from the past, and some are from Dante's time.

Dante and Virgil leave Hell and reach the mountain of Purgatory. From there they climb to bright terraces where men seek forgiveness for their misdeeds on earth. An atmosphere of peace and hope fills this place of purification, in contrast with Hell's hatred and despair.

On reaching Paradise, Virgil entrusts Dante to the poet's idealized woman Beatrice. This character was based on a real woman whom Dante loved. She guides the poet through heaven at the top of the mountain of Purgatory. Dante and Beatrice arrive at the throne of God, set among hosts of angels. Dante stands in rapture

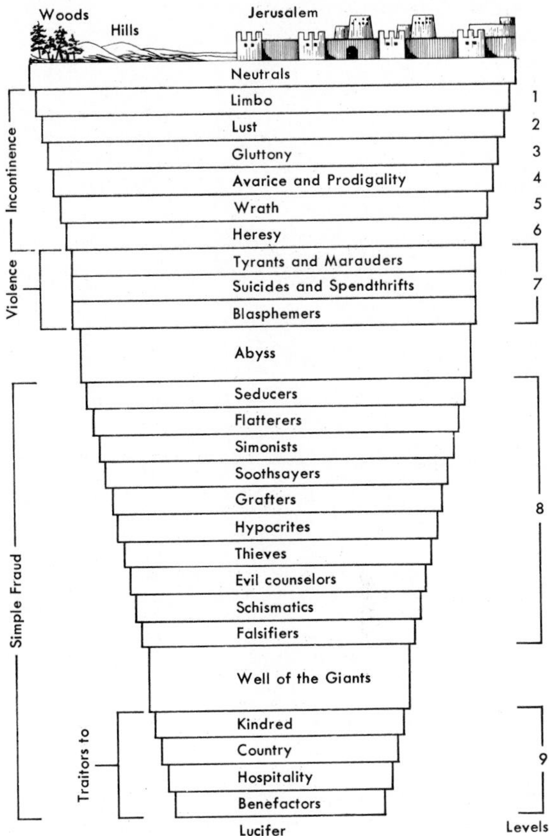

WORLD BOOK diagram

Hell in the *Divine Comedy* was pictured by Dante as nine levels descending into the earth. At the top is a place for neutrals —people who did neither good nor evil in life. Limbo is for those who did no wrong but died unbaptized. Dante reserved the greatest torments for the damned souls of the bottom three levels. Traitors, the worst of all, are frozen in ice at the ninth level.

but is struck blind by the radiance. The meaning of the *Divine Comedy* becomes apparent: Love for God will complement human love in the eternal search for happiness. PATRICIA M. GATHERCOLE

See also DANTE ALIGHIERI.

DIVINE RIGHT OF KINGS is the belief that monarchs get their right to rule directly from God, rather than from the consent or wish of their subjects. According to this belief, it is up to God to punish a wicked king. So far as the people are concerned, "the king can do no wrong." This idea was at its height in England during the reign of the Stuarts and in France during the reign of Louis XIV. The first blow at divine right was the execution of the English king, Charles I, in 1649. The French Revolution completely repudiated the belief, and asserted the doctrine that the right to rule came from the people. But the divine-right doctrine lasted long after that time. It was asserted in the early 1900's by the German emperor, Wilhelm II, as king of Prussia, and by Czar Nicholas II of Russia. J. SALWYN SCHAPIRO

DIVINE WORD COLLEGE. See UNIVERSITIES AND COLLEGES (table).

H. Armstrong Roberts

Diving Is a Popular, Healthful Water Sport.

DIVING is a water sport performed by plunging into water in various ways, usually head first. A diver needs long practice to become highly skilled. Diving techniques have become so varied and elaborate that competitive diving is known as *fancy diving*. Expert divers compete for world recognition in the Olympic Games every four years. The United States and many other nations choose national champions every year. But most swimmers learn diving only as a form of recreation.

Diving demands coordination, muscular control, and exact timing. The combination of relaxation and smooth execution of a properly performed dive makes it a thrilling sport to watch.

Forms of Diving

Dives are in five main groups. (1) The diver faces the water and enters it from a forward position in *forward dives*. (2) The diver stands with his back to the water and enters it from a backward position in *backward dives*. (3) The diver first faces the water but then turns in mid-air in *gainer dives*. (4) The diver stands with his back to the water but turns and enters it in a forward position in a *cutaway dive*, such as the back jackknife. (5) The diver twists before entering the water in a *twist dive*. Each dive is often combined with others.

Diving Positions. A diver may make a dive from a running or standing position. A diver may perform dives from three positions. (1) The body may be straight, or in *layout*. (2) The diver, when in the air, may bring his knees up close to or touching his chest in a *tuck*. (3) The diver may bend his body forward from the hips, keep his legs straight at the knees, and his toes pointed in a *pike*.

Styles of Fancy Diving. Three common styles of fancy diving are the *backward somersault*, the *half-gainer*, and the *swan dive*. These dives demand fine precision.

In the *backward somersault*, the diver starts the dive with his back to the water. His body makes one complete turn backwards, and he enters the water feet first, facing the springboard.

In the *half-gainer*, the diver faces the water and turns backward in the air. He enters the water head first, facing the springboard.

In the *swan dive*, the diver stretches his arms out sideways, in line with his shoulders in mid-air. He keeps his arms in this position until just before he enters the water. Then he brings them together above his head, in a straight line with his body.

Competitive Diving

Springboard Diving, in formal competition, is judged on four main points. (1) The diver's *approach* to the end of the springboard is important. In a running forward dive, for example, a diver takes three quick steps plus a jump, or *hurdle*, and finishes with both feet at the end of the board. From there, he springs into the air. (2) The *height of the spring* should be at least 3 feet (1 meter) above the board. (3) Judges rate the *execution* of the dive, or how smoothly it is performed, after it reaches full height. (4) They judge the diver's *entry into the water*.

OLYMPIC DIVING CHAMPIONS SINCE 1952

Year	Where Won	Springboard	High Platform
		MEN	
1952	Helsinki	**David Browning,** United States	**Sammy Lee,** United States
1956	Melbourne	**Bob Clotworthy,** United States	**Pepi Capilla,** Mexico
1960	Rome	**Gary Tobian,** United States	**Bob Webster,** United States
1964	Tokyo	**Ken Sitzberger,** United States	**Bob Webster,** United States
1968	Mexico City	**Bernie Wrightson,** United States	**Klaus DiBiasi,** Italy
1972	Munich	**Vladimir Vasin,** Russia	**Klaus DiBiasi,** Italy
		WOMEN	
1952	Helsinki	**Pat McCormick,** United States	**Pat McCormick,** United States
1956	Melbourne	**Pat McCormick,** United States	**Pat McCormick,** United States
1960	Rome	**Ingrid Kramer,** East Germany	**Ingrid Kramer,** East Germany
1964	Tokyo	**Ingrid Kramer Engel,** East Germany	**Lesley Bush,** United States
1968	Mexico City	**Sue Gossick,** United States	**Milena Duchkova,** Czechoslovakia
1972	Munich	**Micki King,** United States	**Ulrica Knape,** Sweden

Source: U.S. Olympic Committee

backward dive

The diver should enter the water nearly in line with the board, and his body should be almost at right angles to the surface of the water. The body should form a straight line, with arms and legs straight, toes pointed, and head in natural position. His arms should be straight above the head in headfirst dives, and at the sides in feet-first dives.

High-Platform Diving is judged in much the same way, but the judges do not consider the height of the spring to be so important. The firm surface of the platform permits little spring. The greater distance of the diver from the water also allows more time to complete the dive. Otherwise, such dives are the same as those from a high or low springboard. The diving rules of the Olympic Games are used as a guide for judging other springboard and platform diving contests.

Standard Springboard Equipment and Heights. The low board is 14 feet (4.3 meters) long and 20 inches (51 centimeters) wide. It is 1 meter, or 39 inches, above water level. The high board is 16 feet (4.8 meters) long and 20 inches (51 centimeters) wide. It is 3 meters, or 10 feet, above the water. Cocoa matting, or a suitable nonskid material, covers the board. The front edge of the board extends at least 5 feet (1.5 meters) beyond the edge of the pool. The degree of the board's slope should always be so that the forward edge is raised above the base end not more than 2 inches (5 centimeters). A diver makes a platform dive from a platform that stands 10 meters, or 33 feet, above the water.

Diving for Fun

Learning to dive can be a pleasant and challenging experience. But diving should be learned only from a qualified diver or diving instructor at a properly supervised swimming pool. Many deaths occur each year because divers have not learned how to protect themselves in diving, or because they dive into waters that are too shallow or cover submerged objects.

An experienced high diver avoids striking the water flatly with his stomach or back. Such a dive might force the air from his lungs and stun him long enough to permit drowning. He also clasps his hands together by joining his fingers just before entering the water. This prevents the force of the water from separating the diver's extended arms and injuring his head. When diving feet first, he keeps his legs together to avoid a groin injury. If the dive gets out of control, the experienced diver tucks himself into a compact knot. He thereby receives less impact when he strikes the water.

History

Diving in its present highly organized form dates from about 1895. In that year, the Royal Life Saving Society of Great Britain became interested in a "graceful diving competition." A similar interest swept the United States about 1900. It started with dives from fixed platforms. Springboards developed later, and more difficult dives were invented. Diving enthusiasts set up scoring systems, and standardized the diving boards in size and height.

FRED RUSSELL

See also SWIMMING; SKIN DIVING.

Jacques-Yves Cousteau, courtesy Jaspard, Polus, & Cie.

An Underwater Diver makes a final check on men who will spend several days in a submerged metal house. The building was anchored about 85 feet (26 meters) beneath the Red Sea's surface.

DIVING, UNDERWATER, is man's way of reaching the strange and beautiful world beneath the water's surface. Underwater divers risk their lives to recover valuable goods, find crime and disaster evidence, repair ships, build bridges and piers, and study underwater life. Military divers perform such important jobs as clearing obstacles ahead of landing craft and blowing up enemy ships. Many persons enjoy underwater diving as a sport. They dive to hunt for water animals or just to explore the bottom of a lake, river, or ocean.

Many divers, including some pearl divers and sponge divers, go under water while holding their breath. But this type of diving does not allow the diver to dive very deep or for very long. Until recently, long deep dives could be made only by using clumsy helmet diving suits. Today, most underwater work is done by divers who breathe compressed air from metal tanks that are strapped to their backs. Most deep underwater exploration is done by scientists who go under water in special kinds of submarines that provide them with working conditions similar to those above the water.

Kinds of Underwater Diving

The three kinds of underwater diving are (1) *helmet diving*, (2) *free diving*, and (3) *diving in oceanographic submarines*. The diver uses different equipment for each.

Helmet Diving. A helmet diver wears a big copper helmet attached to a waterproof canvas suit. The helmet, which has glass windows, fits over the diver's head and is bolted to the suit. The diver straps a weighted belt around his waist, and wears weighted shoes to keep him from floating to the surface. He breathes through a hose that runs from his helmet to pumps or tanks above the water.

Above the water, workmen called *tenders* operate the pumps or tanks that supply the diver with the compressed air or helium and oxygen that he breathes. The diver may have a telephone line clamped to his air hose so he can talk to the tenders. He also can communicate with them by tugging on a thick rope, called a *life line*, that leads from his waist to the surface.

The helmet diver must be careful to keep the pressure inside the suit equal to the pressure of the water surrounding him. If his suit pressure gets too low, the water pressure will squeeze the flexible suit and his body up into the helmet. If the pressure in the suit gets too high, his suit will *balloon* (swell up) and he will rise too quickly to the surface.

Free Diving, sometimes called *skin diving*, allows a diver to move freely under water. Free diving includes (1) *naked diving*, (2) *mask diving*, and (3) *diving with independent breathing devices*.

Naked Diving is done without any equipment, except a swim suit and perhaps a pair of rubber swim fins. A naked diver must hold his breath, so most naked divers make only shallow, short dives. But some naked divers can dive more than 100 feet (30 meters).

Mask Diving. The diver wears a glass plate mounted on rubber over his nose and eyes so he can see under water. A mask diver breathes through a *snorkel* (short tube) that extends above the water, and swims face down on the surface. When he sees an interesting object, he takes a deep breath and then dives toward the object. Mask divers and most other free divers wear rubber foot fins to help them swim.

Independent Breathing Devices allow free divers to go under water without holding their breath. These devices are popularly called *SCUBA* (Self-Contained

Underwater Breathing Apparatus). The *aqualung* is the best-known device. It releases compressed air from metal bottles that the diver wears on his back. The air passes through a hose to the diver's mouthpiece. A valve called a *demand regulator* opens and closes automatically as the diver breathes, feeding the exact volume of air he needs to withstand water pressure. The aqualung and similar devices are called *open circuit devices* because the air the diver exhales is released into the water. Experts who dive over 200 feet (61 meters) may use a mixture of helium and oxygen in such equipment. In *rebreathing devices*, the air exhaled by the diver is repurified so that the diver may breathe it again. Rebreathing devices are most commonly used in military missions. They do not release air, and therefore bubbles that would warn the enemy are not formed in the water.

Diving in Oceanographic Submarines permits exploration under water at surface air pressure. Oceanographic submarines, called *submarinos*, are metal hulls with windows. They carry their own air or gas supply. The bathysphere and the benthoscope were ball-shaped submarinos that were lowered on cables and dived down to 4,000 feet (1,200 meters).

Most of today's submarinos do not depend on cables. They use *buoyancy* (the ability to float) to control the depth of their dive. The U.S. Navy's submarinos use air to control buoyancy. Navy submarinos have *ballast* (air) tanks built into their hulls. In order to dive, air is let out of the tanks and water is let in. Water is heavier than air, so the incoming water pushes the submarino down. To rise, compressed air is released to force the water out of the ballast tanks. Most of today's submarinos have a motor so that they can move around under water.

The bathyscaph, a submarino now in use, consists of a ball-shaped hull attached to the bottom of a cigar-shaped hull. The ball-shaped hull holds the divers and the cigar-shaped hull holds gasoline. Water is heavier than gasoline. Therefore, when gasoline is let out of the hull and water is let in, the bathyscaph goes down. Bathyscaphs have descended more than 6 miles (10 kilometers). See BATHYSCAPH.

The *diving saucer* type of submarino has weights attached to make it sink. It goes deeper when water fills the ballast tanks. It rises when the weights are released. Saucers have dived 4,000 feet (1,200 meters).

Dangers in Underwater Diving

Pressure is greater under water than on land. For example, the water pressure 33 feet (10 meters) under water is twice that of the air at the surface. At 66 feet (20 meters) the pressure is three times greater than at the surface. A diver may be harmed if the pressure under water is not equal to the pressure in his lungs and the other air passages in his body.

Increased pressure causes *air embolism*. A diver breathes more molecules of air under water than he does on land, because the air under water is compressed. At 33 feet (10 meters), he breathes twice as much air to offset the doubled water pressure. When a diver rises to the surface, the air in his lungs expands because there is less pressure. If he cannot exhale the air, the air will burst the air sacs in his lungs and form air bubbles in his blood stream. The bubbles can block the flow of blood and cripple or kill the diver. A diver can prevent air embolism by breathing naturally while rising to the surface instead of holding his breath. By breathing while rising slowly, the pressure in the lungs decreases.

Bends, sometimes called *decompression sickness*, occurs when nitrogen bubbles form in the blood. Nitrogen gas makes up over three-fourths of the air we breathe. An increased number of air molecules in the lungs causes the blood and body tissue fluids to become *saturated* (soaked) with nitrogen. When the diver rises too quickly, nitrogen gas bubbles form. The bubbles can block the flow of blood and cripple or kill the diver. A diver can avoid the bends by stopping on the way to the surface to get rid of excess nitrogen.

A diver who is forced to rise quickly after becoming saturated with nitrogen should be put in a decompres-

Oceanographic Submarines such as the *Aluminaut* take scientists deeper than ever before to study the ocean's mysteries.
Reynolds Metals Co.

Divers Using Independent Breathing Devices can move about easily to set up cameras for a photographic assignment.
Jerry Greenberg

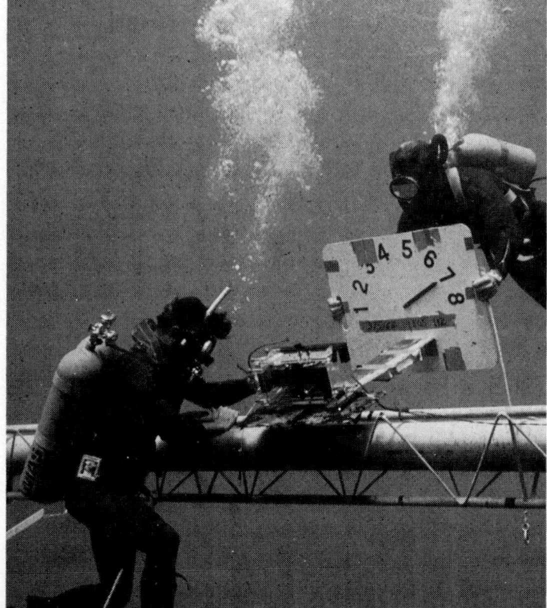

sion chamber immediately. In the chamber, the diver is returned to the pressure he experienced under water. The pressure is then reduced in stages. *Decompression tables* tell a diver how long he can stay at a given depth without gaining a dangerous amount of nitrogen. They also tell how slowly he must rise to avoid the bends.

A diver with too much nitrogen in his blood may also suffer *nitrogen narcosis*. In this condition, he loses his ability to reason and may do dangerous things. To avoid nitrogen narcosis, some divers breathe a mixture of helium and oxygen.

Divers who breathe pure oxygen too deep under water can get oxygen poisoning. Oxygen poisoning victims become dizzy, vomit, and may have *convulsions* (uncontrolled muscular activity). Gas mixtures with high oxygen content can also lead to oxygen poisoning.

How deep a diver can safely go depends upon his experience and the equipment he uses. For the limits of compressed-air, aqualung diving, see SKIN DIVING.

History

Naked divers dived for shells in the Mediterranean Sea as early as 4500 B.C. Naked divers in ancient Greece and Rome sought pearls, sponges, and shells.

Divers in the Persian Gulf used goggles made of polished clear tortoise shell as early as A.D. 1300. The goggles brought the blurred underwater scene into focus. Guy Gilpatric, an American diver, used rubber goggles with glass lenses in the 1930's. By the mid-1930's, the face mask, foot fins, and snorkels were used.

Diving bells were the first devices that allowed men to breathe under water. These bell-shaped hulls that are open to the water at the bottom have been used since ancient times. Bells are supplied with air through a hose from the surface. The greater air pressure within the bell keeps the water out of the bell.

In 1715, John Lethbridge of England designed a leather diving suit that was used in salvage work. The helmet diving suit used today is based on a suit that was introduced in 1837 by Augustus Siebe, a German engineer living in England.

A Helmet Diver, clinging to his life line, lowers himself to the ocean floor. He breathes through a hose that extends to the surface.
U.S. Navy

The first independent breathing devices were tested in the late 1800's and early 1900's. The aqualung, the first safe, simple, independent breathing device, was developed by Jacques-Yves Cousteau and Émile Gagnan of France. Cousteau successfully tested it in 1943.

The development of oceanographic submarines during the 1900's expanded man's range under water. Otis Barton of the United States made the first bathysphere. He and William Beebe dived in it in 1930. Auguste Piccard of Switzerland designed the first bathyscaph. It was successfully tested in 1948. Cousteau made the first diving saucer in 1959. In 1966, the Navy submarino U.S.S. *Alvin* was used to locate a nuclear bomb that had been lost in an airplane crash off the coast of Spain.

Experimental underwater laboratories were developed in the 1960's. These manned stations consist of one or more buildings set up on the ocean floor. They have been tested at depths ranging from 30 to 400 feet (9 to 120 meters). Compartments inside the buildings are filled with compressed gas. Divers may live there for weeks, going out each day to explore or work. By staying under water, they avoid the need to undergo decompression each day. The first underwater station was built off the coast of France in 1962. The U.S. Navy conducted a series of experiments in a station called *Sealab* during the late 1960's. Astronaut M. Scott Carpenter took part in several of these tests. JAMES DUGAN

Related Articles in WORLD BOOK include:

Bathyscaph	Ocean (Discovering the Secrets of the Deep)	Piccard, Auguste
Beebe, William		Skin Diving
Cousteau, Jacques-Yves		Spearfishing
Marine Biology		

DIVING BEETLE. See WATER BEETLE.

DIVING BELL. See DIVING, UNDERWATER (History).

DIVING SAUCER. See DIVING, UNDERWATER (Diving in Oceanographic Submarines).

DIVINING ROD. See WELL (Locating Wells).

DIVISION (military) is a unit in the armed forces. It is the major combat unit of the U.S. Army. The army has 17 divisions, each of which has about 15,000 men. There are five types of army divisions: (1) airborne, (2) airmobile, (3) armored, (4) infantry, and (5) mechanized. The army reorganized its divisions under the Reorganization Army Divisions (ROAD) program in 1962 to make them more flexible so each would be equipped for its location and mission. A division may have from 6 to 15 battalions, depending on its mission. Most divisions have 10 battalions, as well as control and supply units. In each division, the battalions and other units are organized into three brigades. See ARMY, U.S. (table: Army Levels of Command).

The division is also a basic ground-fighting unit in the U.S. Marine Corps (see MARINE CORPS, U.S.). A Marine Corps division has about 19,000 men, organized into three regiments and support troops. A U.S. Air Force air division includes two or more *wings* (see AIR FORCE, U.S.). A wing is a mobile unit that can operate independently. The U.S. Navy groups two or more ships within a fleet to form a division for administrative purposes (see NAVY, U.S.). In naval aviation, a division, such as a carrier division, includes two or more sections. Division organization is also used by the armed forces of other countries. MARK M. BOATNER III

WORLD BOOK photo

A Division Problem at the chalkboard tests a student's knowledge of one of the most basic processes of mathematics.

DIVISION, *duh VIZH un,* is a way of separating a group of things into equal parts.

Suppose you had 16¢ to spend on postage stamps. They cost 4¢ each. You want to know how many stamps you can buy for 16¢. If you have 16 pennies, you can count out the pennies into equal groups of 4. There are four equal groups of 4. So you can buy four four-cent stamps for 16¢, as shown below.

Separating a group of 16 things into four equal parts of 4 things is an example of division.

Division is one of the four basic operations in arithmetic. The others are addition, subtraction, and multiplication. You must learn how to add, subtract, and multiply before you begin to study division.

Learning to Divide

Once people learned division only by memorizing. Most teachers now agree that the best way to learn division is by understanding. You can learn to understand division without much difficulty.

Writing Division. One way of separating a group into equal parts is by counting it out into equal parts. But there is a much easier way to divide. To find how many groups of 3 there are in 12, you can subtract 3 from 12 until nothing is left:

$$\begin{array}{r}12\\-3\\\hline 9\end{array} \Rightarrow \begin{array}{r}9\\-3\\\hline 6\end{array} \Rightarrow \begin{array}{r}6\\-3\\\hline 3\end{array} \Rightarrow \begin{array}{r}3\\-3\\\hline 0\end{array}$$

This shows that there are four 3's in 12.

Each basic operation in arithmetic is indicated by a special symbol. The symbol for division is ÷. The statement $12 \div 3 = 4$ means that when 12 things are separated into groups of three, there are four such groups. Or, that there are four 3's in 12. People who know division usually read $12 \div 3 = 4$ as "12 divided by 3 is 4." When you actually work a problem in division, you will find it useful to write it this way:

$$\begin{array}{r}4\\3\overline{)12}\end{array}$$

The parts of a problem in division have special names. The number being divided is called the *dividend.* The number by which the dividend is divided is the *divisor.* The answer, or result, of the division is called the *quotient.*

$$\begin{array}{r}4\\3\overline{)12}\end{array}$$

Divisor → 3; 4 ← *Quotient*; 12 ← *Dividend*

Another way of writing a problem in division is the form used in writing fractions (see FRACTION):

$$\frac{12}{3}=4$$

Division Facts. By using subtraction, you discovered that there are three equal groups of 4 things in a group of 12. Or, $12 \div 3 = 4$. This is a *division fact.* You can find all the division facts by using subtraction.

The 64 Division Facts

2	3	4	5	6	7	8	9
2/4	2/6	2/8	2/10	2/12	2/14	2/16	2/18
2	3	4	5	6	7	8	9
3/6	3/9	3/12	3/15	3/18	3/21	3/24	3/27
2	3	4	5	6	7	8	9
4/8	4/12	4/16	4/20	4/24	4/28	4/32	4/36
2	3	4	5	6	7	8	9
5/10	5/15	5/20	5/25	5/30	5/35	5/40	5/45
2	3	4	5	6	7	8	9
6/12	6/18	6/24	6/30	6/36	6/42	6/48	6/54
2	3	4	5	6	7	8	9
7/14	7/21	7/28	7/35	7/42	7/49	7/56	7/63
2	3	4	5	6	7	8	9
8/16	8/24	8/32	8/40	8/48	8/56	8/64	8/72
2	3	4	5	6	7	8	9
9/18	9/27	9/36	9/45	9/54	9/63	9/72	9/81

DIVISION TERMS

Dividend. In $32 \div 8 = 4$, 32 is the dividend.

Division Fact is a division in which the divisor and quotient are whole numbers not larger than 9. For example, $42 \div 7 = 6$ is a division fact.

Divisor. In $32 \div 8 = 4$, 8 is the divisor.

Long Division is a method of dividing numbers in which the work is written out.

Quotient. In $32 \div 8 = 4$, 4 is the quotient.

Remainder is any amount left over after a division operation has been completed. The remainder is always less than the divisor.

Short Division is a method of dividing numbers in which much of the work is done mentally.

It is important to learn the division facts so well that you can use them automatically. The facts are useful themselves. They are also necessary in learning how to divide larger numbers quickly and accurately.

Long Division

Long division is a method that can be used to divide large numbers. In long division, you write out the work carefully.

Suppose you want to find out how many 3's there are in 79, or 79 ÷ 3. Instead of subtracting one 3 at a time, you can shorten your work by subtracting several 3's at once. To begin, you might subtract five 3's, or 15, each time:

```
 79     64     49     34     19     4
-15    -15    -15    -15    -15    -3
 64     49     34     19      4     1
```

All together, you subtracted 5 + 5 + 5 + 5 + 5 or twenty-five 3's from 79, leaving 4. You cannot take away five more 3's, but you can take away one more 3, leaving a *remainder* of 1. Thus, there are 25 + 1 or twenty-six 3's in 79 with 1 left over.

Subtracting five 3's at a time shortened your work. Next, you might try subtracting ten 3's, or 30, each time:

```
 79     49     19     4
-30    -30    -15    -3
 49     19      4     1
```

This time, you subtracted 10 + 10 + 5 + 1 or twenty-six 3's from 79, and had 1 left as a remainder. A better form to use is this:

```
           3/79
            -30     10   The number of 3's
             49
            -30     10   subtracted are re-
             19
            -15      5   corded in this column.
              4
             -3      1
Remainder     1     26   The total number
                         of 3's subtracted.
```

After some practice, you might subtract twenty 3's and then six 3's:

```
 26        The result is written
3/79
-60   20   above the dividend
 19
-18    6   to complete the form.
  1   26
```

To gain further practice in long division, you might now try to find out how many 21's there are in 891, or 891 ÷ 21. First, you must decide how many 21's you will subtract at a time. Ten 21's, or 210, might prove to be useful. Using 10's, 100's, or 1,000's in multiplying the divisor makes division much easier.

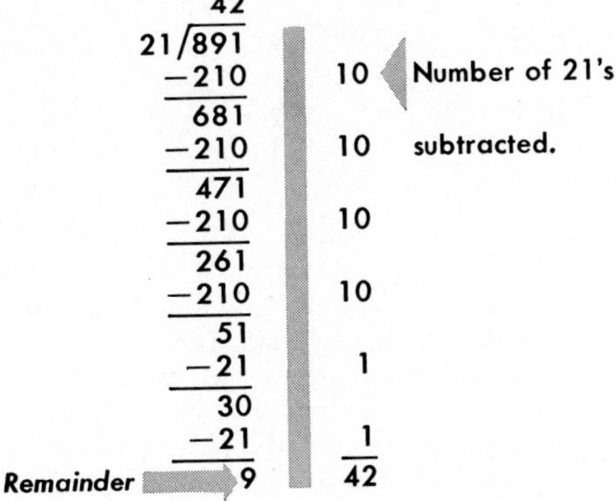

When you have subtracted four 210's or forty 21's, you find that the remainder, 51, is too small to subtract ten more 21's. You can, however, subtract one 21 at a time. This finally gives you 10 + 10 + 10 + 10 + 1 + 1 or forty-two 21's in 891, with a remainder of 9.

You could have used twenty 21's, or 420, as your first unit.

```
             42
          21/891
           -420     20   Number of 21's
            471
           -420     20   subtracted.
             51
            -42      2
Remainder     9     42
```

One last example will illustrate further the process of long division. Suppose you want to know how many 37's there are in 12,526, or 12,526 ÷ 37. Once again you must decide how many 37's to subtract at one time.

```
             338
        37/12526
          -7400    200   Number of 37's
           5126
          -3700    100   subtracted.
           1426
          -1110     30
            316
           -185      5
            131
           -111      3
Remainder    20    338
```

You may have to experiment on a sheet of scrap paper to find the units that you can use to solve the problem easily. You can use even larger units than 200.

```
             338
        37/12526
         -11100    300   Number of 37's
           1426
          -1110     30   subtracted.
            316
           -296      8
Remainder    20    338
```

DIVISION

Many persons use a form for long division even shorter than those outlined above. The three steps look like this:

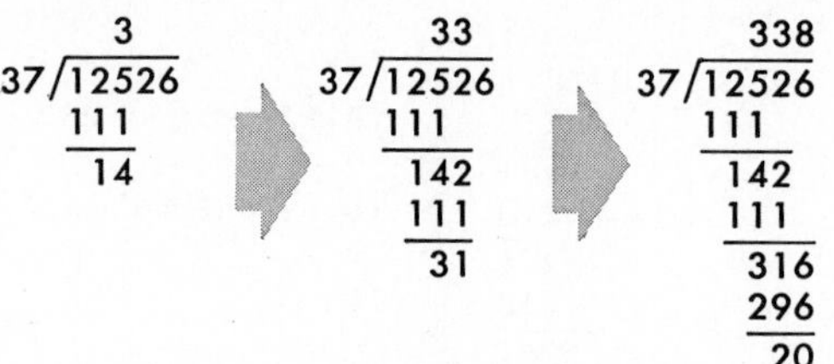

This form does the same things that have been discussed above, but by a different method. It does not illustrate the process of long division so well to a beginner.

When using this shorter form, it helps to notice that in all these examples you write the answer (quotient) above the proper places in the dividend. That is, when you subtract a unit of 100's, you record the number of 100's above the 100's place in the dividend.

Remainders in Division. There is often a remainder when you have completed a problem in division. What you do with this remainder depends on the kind of problem. If you want to know how many 3's there are in 79, you might have had 79¢ to spend on three-cent postage stamps. You would find that you could buy 26 stamps and have 1¢ left.

If you wanted to share 79 apples among three persons, you would also find that there are twenty-six 3's in 79 and a remainder of 1. This means that each person gets 26 apples and there is one left to share. If the sharing is to be absolutely equal, you would have to cut the remaining apple into three equal parts. Each person would receive $26\frac{1}{3}$ apples.

These examples show that what is done to a remainder depends on the problem. In some cases, further division into fractional parts is indicated. In other cases, the remainder merely tells how many are "left over."

Division of Decimal Fractions. You can also use long division to divide numbers that include decimal fractions. The statement 78.35 ÷ 3.6 is this kind of problem. In order to understand division of decimal fractions, you must learn an interesting feature of division.

You know that 15 ÷ 3 = 5 is a division fact. What would happen if both the 15 and 3 were multiplied by 10? That is, what is the result of dividing 150 by 30? Long division will show you that this quotient is also 5. Thus, 15 ÷ 3 = 5, and 150 ÷ 30 = 5. Similarly, 72 ÷ 6 = 12 and 720 ÷ 60 = 12. If the 72 and 6 are multiplied by 100, the quotient of 7,200 ÷ 600 is also 12. These examples illustrate a general rule: *multiplying both the dividend and divisor by 10, 100, 1,000, and so on, does not change the quotient.*

This rule can be used to divide 78.35 by 3.6. Both 78.35 and 3.6 can be multiplied by 10. Thus, 78.35 × 10 = 783.5 and 3.6 × 10 = 36. The quotient of 783.5 ÷ 36 will be the same as the quotient of 78.35 ÷ 3.6. But the decimal points now have new positions. A useful device is to use a caret mark (∧) to indicate the new position of the decimal points. The decimal point in the quotient will appear directly above the caret mark in the dividend.

3.6∧/78.3∧5

This shows that 78.35 and 3.6 have both been multiplied by 10. Sometimes it is necessary to multiply the dividend and divisor by 100, 1,000, or some larger multiple of 10. For example, 25.773 ÷ 17.94 should be multiplied by 100:

17.94∧/25.77∧3

You should multiply the dividend and divisor by a multiple of 10 large enough to change the divisor into a *whole number*, or a number that does not include a decimal fraction.

After you have learned to change the divisor into a whole number, you can solve problems in this new form, for example, 4.2 ÷ 3. Put in the form of a question, this is "how many 3's are there in 4.2?" The number 4.2 is the same as 42 tenths. You can restate the question as "how many 3's are there in 42 tenths?" You can find the answer by subtracting units of 3's:

```
      14 tenths
    3/42 tenths
     -30 tenths      10 tenths
      12 tenths
     -12 tenths       4 tenths
                     14 tenths
```

Thus, 14 tenths, or 1.4, is the answer. When you have learned this process, you will not have to write out the names. This form is better:

```
      1.4
    3/4.2
      3 0       10
      1 2
      1 2        4
                14
```

If the divisor is a whole number, you can disregard the decimal point in the dividend while you are working the problem. When you get a number for the quotient, put as many decimal places in the quotient as there are in the dividend.

In division problems, you often have to find the quotient to the nearest tenth, hundredth, and so on. You can do this easily. After you have placed the caret marks in the divisor and dividend, use just as many digits to the right of the dividend's caret mark as the number of decimal places wanted in the answer. Sometimes it is necessary to add zeros to the dividend. For example, you must first change 3.6/78.35 to 3.6∧/78.3∧5 to make the divisor a whole number. Suppose the quotient must be correct to the nearest hundredth. Then you must add a zero to the dividend, making it 78.3∧50.

```
          2 1.76
    3.6∧/78.3∧50
        -72 0 00        2000
          6 3 50
         -3 6 00         100
          2 7 50
         -2 5 20          70
            2 30
           -2 16           6
              14        2176
```

You do not have to do anything with the remainder, because the problem asked you to be accurate only to the nearest hundredth.

Short Division

When dividing by a one-digit number such as 7, you can do some of the work in long division without writing it down. Division of this kind, which is usually done in the mind rather than on paper, is called *short division*. The method is the same as in long division, but you do the work mentally.

Long Division		*Short Division*
212		212 R(emainder) 1
4/849		4/849
−800	200	
49		
−40	10	
9		
−8	2	
1	212	

The only difference between these two examples is that in short division you do the work mentally and indicate the remainder next to the quotient. The letter *R* is often used to mean *Remainder*. In this example, you first see that you can subtract two hundred 4's from 849. You write the 2 in the 100's place over the 8 in the dividend. Next, you can take away ten 4's from the remaining 49. You write the 1 in the 10's place over the 4 in the dividend. Finally, you can take away two 4's from the remaining 9. You write the 2 in the 1's place over the 9 in the dividend. You show the remainder to the right of the quotient.

In more difficult problems in short division, you must use a new device. The problem 415 ÷ 7 will show this.

$$7\overline{)415} \quad \text{quotient } 5$$

Your first step is to subtract fifty 7's or 350, which is thirty-five 10's. Write the 5 (for 50 or five 10's) over the 1 in the dividend. You do the subtraction mentally. Thirty-five 10's subtracted from forty-one 10's is six 10's. You write a little 6 to the left of the 5 in the dividend.

$$7\overline{)41\,{}^{6}5} \quad \text{quotient } 5$$

Now you are dividing six 10's and 5, or 65, by 7. You can subtract nine 7's or 63 from 65, leaving a remainder of 2.

$$7\overline{)41\,{}^{6}5} \quad \text{quotient } 5\ 9 \quad \text{R } 2 \quad \text{or } 59\tfrac{2}{7}$$

It is useful to see how this process is derived from long division.

59		5 9	R 2
7/415		7/41 ⁶5	
−350	50		
65			
− 63	9		
2			

Another example is 7,536 ÷ 9. As in the case of long division, you must decide how many 9's you can subtract at one time.

$$9\overline{)75\,{}^{3}3\,{}^{6}6} \quad \text{quotient } 8\ 3\ 7 \quad \text{R } 3 \quad \text{or } 837\tfrac{3}{9} \text{ or } 837\tfrac{1}{3}$$

First, you subtract eight hundred 9's, or 7,200. You write the 8 (for eight 100's or 800) over the 5 in the dividend. Mentally you subtract 72 (hundreds) from 75 (hundreds): 75—72=3. You write a little 3 to the left of the 3 in the dividend to keep the three 100's in the work. From this new figure of 336, you can subtract thirty 9's or 270. You write the 3 for the thirty 9's over the 3 in the dividend. Next, 33—27=6. You write a little 6 to the left of the 6 in the dividend to keep the six 10's in the work. From this new figure of 66, you can subtract seven 9's, or 63. You write the 7 for the seven 9's over the 6 in the dividend. Finally, 66 — 63 = 3. You indicate the remainder of 3 to the right of the quotient. After some practice, you will be able to leave out the little numbers as reminders of figures that must be included in the work. You will soon be able to remember these numbers in your head.

How to Check Division

You will be wise to check the answer to a division problem to be sure you have solved it correctly.

Rounding Off. One way to check is to see whether or not the quotient is a sensible answer. You can estimate a quotient by rounding off the dividend and divisor. To estimate the quotient of 158 ÷ 76, you can round off 158 to 160 and 76 to 80. Because 160 ÷ 80 = 2, the quotient of 158 ÷ 76 should be about 2. To estimate the quotient of 5,124 ÷ 36, you can round off 5,124 to 5,000 and 36 to 50. You can see that 5,000 ÷ 50 = 100, and 5,000 ÷ 25 = 200. Thus, the quotient of 5,124 ÷ 36 should be somewhere between 100 and 200. Estimating the quotient will help you decide if your answer is sensible.

Checking by Multiplication. Another way of checking a quotient is to multiply the quotient by the divisor to see if the product is the dividend. If you have multiplied correctly, this method will catch any error. This is because multiplication is the opposite of division.

13	13
24/312	×24
	52
	26
	312

The next example shows how to use the remainder in checking by multiplication:

42	R 7	42	
21/889		×21	
		42	
		84	
		882	
		+ 7	← R
		889	

DIVISION

The quotient is multiplied by the divisor, and the remainder is added to the product.

Four Key Division Ideas

Here are four important rules to remember for solving division problems.

1. Remember that division means breaking up a number into smaller equal groups. The divisor shows the size of these groups.
2. Learn the division facts so well that you do not have to stop and figure them out each time. You will use the division facts constantly in everyday arithmetic, and will need to know them to divide larger numbers.
3. Remember the method for dividing larger numbers used in long division. In long division, subtract the divisor from the dividend as many times as possible in a single step. In this way, you can reduce the number of steps in long division.
4. Always check the answer after finishing a division problem. You can do this by estimating or by multiplying the quotient by the divisor and adding any remainder.

Fun with Division

Space is a game played with cards much like those used in bingo. Each card has a square drawn on it. The square is subdivided into 25 smaller squares. The letters S P A C E are written across the top of the card. The squares are filled in with any arrangement of the numerals from 1 to 9. Each square has one number, except the one in the center which is marked *F* for "free." Each card should have a different pattern of numerals on it. Each player has a card and a set of small markers. The leader of the game calls out questions on the division facts, for example, "Under *A*, the 4's in 20." There are five 4's in 20. If the player has the number 5 under *A* on his card, he covers the number. The first player to completely cover all numbers in a row, a column, or a diagonal calls out "Space!" and wins the game. The leader keeps a record of the division facts as he calls them out. He uses this record to check the winner's card. For a new game, exchange the cards among the players.

S	P	A	C	E
2	1	3	4	5
3	4	5	5	3
5	6	F	6	4
6	8	6	7	6
8	9	8	9	8

Divide-Down is an arithmetic version of a spelldown. The players are divided into two teams. Each player is asked one of the division facts, such as "how many 6's in 42?" If he answers correctly, he stays in the game. If he misses, he must leave the game. When all the members of one team have missed, the other team is declared the winner.

HENRY VAN ENGEN

Related Articles in WORLD BOOK include:

Addition
Algebra (Division)
Arithmetic
Decimal Numeral System
Fraction
Multiplication
Numeration Systems
Subtraction

Outline

I. Learning to Divide
A. Writing Division
B. Division Facts
II. Long Division
A. Remainders in Division
B. Division of Decimal Fractions
III. Short Division
IV. How to Check Division
A. Rounding Off
B. Checking by Multiplication
V. Four Key Division Ideas
VI. Fun with Division

PRACTICE DIVISION EXAMPLES

1. 4/56
2. 7/105
3. 5/625
4. 6/522
5. 9/387
6. 2/1146
7. 3/1008
8. 8/984
9. 23/483
10. 47/6281
11. 326/10457
12. 29/1201
13. 3.14/25.60
14. .06/9.87
15. 1.26/.00882

16. Miss Smith's class at school is going to visit the local newspaper. Some of the mothers have offered to drive. There are 35 children in the class, and each car can take 5 children. How many cars will be needed for the trip?
17. A certain kind of candy bar costs 6¢ each. How many of these candy bars can Sue buy with 48¢?
18. There are 7 days in a week. How many weeks are there in one year (365 days)?
19. Four boys wish to share equally 64 pieces of candy. How many pieces should each boy get?
20. Tom rides his bicycle at a speed of 6 miles an hour. At this rate, how many hours will it take him to ride 15 miles?
21. Jane's class in school wants to buy some sketchbooks that cost 23¢ each. Her class has $5.85 to spend for books. How many sketchbooks can Jane's class buy?
22. An airplane travels at the rate of 565 kilometers an hour. How long will it take to fly 1,320 kilometers?
23. Bill and his father went on a trip in their car. They traveled 613.9 kilometers in 10 hours, 18 minutes. What was their average rate of speed?
24. Mary's mother rents a house for $2,520 a year. How much rent would she have to pay for one month?

ANSWERS TO THE DIVISION EXAMPLES

1. 14
2. 15
3. 125
4. 87
5. 43
6. 573
7. 336
8. 123
9. 21
10. 133 R 30
11. 32 R 25
12. 41 R 12
13. 8.15
14. 164.5
15. .007
16. 7 cars
17. 8 bars
18. 52 weeks and 1 day
19. 16 pieces
20. 2½ hours
21. 25 books and 10¢ left
22. 2 hrs. and about 20 min.
23. 59.6 kilometers an hour
24. $210 a month

DIVORCE is the legal ending of a marriage. The laws of most nations, including the United States and Canada, permit divorce only under certain circumstances. Divorce is restricted chiefly because it breaks up a family, the basic unit of society. Some countries, including Brazil and Spain, prohibit divorce.

Most men and women who seek a divorce do so because they cannot solve certain problems in their marriage. Such problems may include differences in goals, financial difficulties, or a poor sexual relationship.

In the United States, a person seeking a divorce generally must appear in court to explain why he wants to end his marriage. A judge then decides whether to grant a divorce. A few states prohibit remarriage for a certain period after a divorce. But in general, a man and woman may marry again—each other or someone else—after their divorce becomes final.

Divorce differs from *annulment*, in which a court declares that a marriage has been invalid from its beginning. A person whose marriage has been annulled may remarry. Divorce also differs from *legal separation*, in which a court authorizes a husband and wife to live apart. *Spouses* (a husband and wife) who are legally separated may not remarry.

Divorce is a sizable problem in the United States and many other countries. Experts estimate that from 25 to 30 per cent of all U.S. marriages end in divorce. In more than half these divorces, the couple has children under 18 years old. Divorce affects many young children deeply. But many experts believe that living with one parent is less harmful to a child than living with both parents in an unhappy environment.

The first written divorce regulations were incorporated in the ancient Babylonian *Code of Hammurabi*. Many early societies permitted only the husband to get a divorce. The early Christians taught that marriage was permanent until death, and they abolished divorce in the areas they governed. They also established special church courts to deal with marriage matters. Beginning in the A.D. 1500's, Protestant reformers successfully worked to have matters of marriage and divorce placed under government jurisdiction.

Divorce rarely occurred in the American Colonies. Some colonies made no provision for divorce at all. But by the mid-1800's, almost every state had a divorce law. Today, the U.S. divorce rate is about 14 times as high as it was in 1867, the first year for which the Bureau of the Census published divorce figures. This article deals mainly with divorce in the United States.

Kinds of Divorce

Each state of the United States has its own divorce laws. But all the states recognize a divorce granted by the state in which one or both of the spouses are legal residents. State laws set forth the *grounds for divorce*—that is, the reasons for which a divorce may be granted. Depending on the kind of grounds, a divorce can be classified as a *fault divorce* or a *no-fault divorce*.

The contributors of this article are Brigitte M. Bodenheimer, Professor of Law at the University of California at Davis; and William M. Kephart, Professor of Sociology at the University of Pennsylvania.

Fault Divorce. Courts traditionally have granted divorces chiefly on *fault grounds*. These grounds vary, but the most common ones are adultery, alcoholism, desertion, drug addiction, failure to support, imprisonment for felony, and mental or physical cruelty.

A person seeking a divorce on a fault ground must prove that his spouse committed the fault. For example, a woman seeking a divorce on the ground of desertion must prove that her husband deserted her. The husband may *contest* (argue against) the divorce action. Many divorces are uncontested. If the judge accepts the wife's proof, he grants her a divorce. But if the husband can prove that his wife consented to or encouraged his action, the judge may refuse to grant a divorce. The judge also may rule against the wife if the husband can prove that she committed a legal fault.

No-Fault Divorce. A person seeking a divorce on a *no-fault ground* does not try to prove that his spouse committed a wrong. The person simply testifies that their marriage has failed and should be legally ended. In many cases, the judge grants a divorce even if the person's spouse objects.

In 1969, California became the first state to enact a no-fault divorce law. The California law provides only two grounds for divorce. These grounds are (1) *irreconcilable differences*—that is, disagreements that cannot be settled and have led to the breakdown of the marriage; or (2) the incurable insanity of one spouse. Generally, a person may not tell the judge about any misconduct of his spouse.

Some states have replaced all traditional grounds for divorce with the single no-fault ground of marriage breakdown. Other states have added this ground to their traditional grounds. Several states allow a couple to obtain a divorce on the ground that they have been separated for a certain period. A number of states grant divorce on the ground of *incompatibility* (being unable to get along together).

Arguments For No-Fault Divorce. People who favor no-fault divorce argue that many marriage failures result from causes other than one spouse's misconduct. Therefore, they declare, a divorce should be granted for reasons other than a fault. In addition, these people believe that relations between spouses remain friendlier in no-fault cases than in fault cases.

Supporters of no-fault laws also point out that traditional divorce laws lead many couples to lie in court. For example, a couple may want a divorce because they cannot get along. But they live in a state that grants divorces only on a few fault grounds. To obtain a divorce, the couple might lie to the judge that one spouse has been physically cruel to the other.

A related argument for no-fault laws is that traditional divorce laws lead some people to seek a divorce in another state. For example, a person who lives in a traditional divorce state may go to a no-fault divorce state that has a short residency requirement. After living in this state for the required period, the person might falsely declare himself a permanent resident. He would then obtain a divorce and return to his own state. If his spouse disputes the validity of the divorce, a court may decide that residence was not truly established in the state that granted the divorce. As

Divorce Rate in the United States

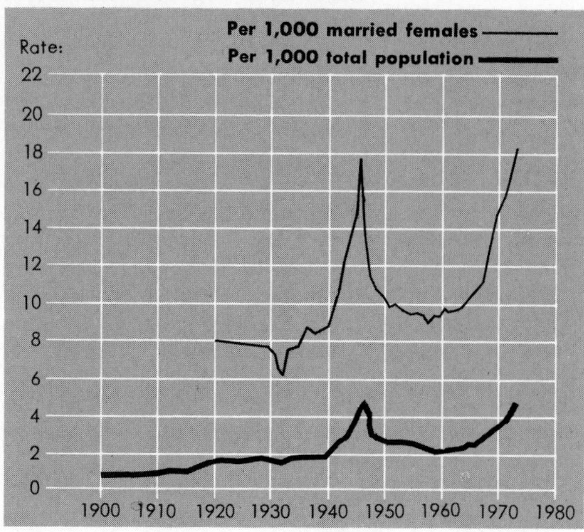

Year	Divorces	Per 1,000 total population	Per 1,000 married females
1900	56,000	0.7	—
1905	68,000	0.8	—
1910	83,000	0.9	—
1915	104,000	1.0	—
1920	171,000	1.6	8.0
1925	175,000	1.5	—
1930	196,000	1.6	7.5
1935	218,000	1.7	7.8
1940	264,000	2.0	8.8
1945	485,000	3.5	14.5
1950	385,000	2.6	10.3
1955	377,000	2.3	9.3
1960	393,000	2.2	9.2
1965	479,000	2.5	10.6
1970	715,000	3.5	15.0
1971	768,000	3.7	15.7
1973	913,000	4.4	18.2

Source: U.S. Public Health Service.

more states liberalize their laws, fewer people seek a divorce in such a state as Nevada, which has a residency requirement of only six weeks.

Arguments Against No-Fault Divorce. Some people oppose no-fault divorces because they believe such divorces can be obtained too easily. They fear that judges may grant a divorce to anyone who says his marriage has broken down, whether it actually has or not. Others believe restrictions should be added to no-fault laws to help prevent premature or unnecessary divorces. In some states, for example, courts direct couples planning divorce to consult a marriage counselor. Some states require a waiting period—either before the divorce hearing, or between the hearing and the date that the divorce becomes final. Such a period gives a couple time to reconsider their decision to get a divorce.

The divorce process may be simpler under no-fault laws than under fault laws. Therefore, in some no-fault states, some couples can obtain a divorce without hiring lawyers. This method of obtaining a divorce is sometimes called *do-it-yourself divorce*. Some judges oppose this type of divorce because they believe a lawyer is needed to protect the rights of spouses and children.

Divorce Provisions

A husband and wife planning a divorce must make arrangements for alimony, child custody and support, and division of their property. They may reach agreement on these arrangements through their lawyers. In some states, courts offer divorce counseling to help couples resolve any disagreements in a friendly way. If the judge considers the agreement fair, he approves it. If the spouses cannot reach an agreement, the judge decides on the arrangements.

Financial Arrangements. In the past, the judge ordered many divorced men to pay considerable alimony. They also had to give up some of their property and bear most of the responsibility for supporting their children. There were two chief reasons for this situation. First, large numbers of divorced women had no job outside the home and needed money to support themselves and their children. Second, traditional fault laws provided that the "guilty" spouse could not receive alimony. In many cases, the husband was the legally guilty spouse because his wife filed for the divorce, even though both might have wanted it.

Today, in a growing number of states, courts base their decisions on financial arrangements primarily on the financial condition of each spouse. Judges realize that many women have the qualifications to work outside the home and need not be fully supported by their former husband. Therefore, if both spouses can earn enough income to support themselves, the court may order that no alimony be paid. If the wife has a higher income than her husband, she may have to pay alimony to him. In addition, the judge may give both parents the responsibility for child support.

The court may also divide a couple's property on the basis of financial circumstances. Under the *community property* laws of a few states, property acquired during a marriage belongs equally to both spouses. This property is divided equally in most cases.

Child Custody Arrangements. In the early and mid-1900's, judges granted custody of the children to the wife almost automatically in the majority of divorce cases. They believed that children should not be separated from the mother. But today, many judges realize that some children might be better off living with the father. Therefore, the court may grant custody to either parent, depending on the circumstances. The judge also determines each parent's rights to visit the children. The judge may ask the children with which parent they would prefer to live.

Some divorced parents return to court several times because one or both of them wants to challenge the child custody decision. If the court changes its decision, the children may have to leave the home of one parent and move in with the other. Such a move can harm children emotionally. As a result, some courts have become reluctant to move children unless the children are in some kind of danger.

The U.S. Divorce Rate

The divorce rate is higher in the United States than in almost any other country. Experts have suggested many reasons for this high rate. (1) Divorce is more socially acceptable than ever before. (2) Many people expect more of marriage than earlier generations did, and so they may be more easily disappointed. (3) More and more high-paying jobs are now open to women. These opportunities have made wives much less dependent economically on their husbands than women used to be. (4) Changes in divorce laws have made divorce easier to obtain.

In general, cities have a higher divorce rate than rural areas. The rate also varies among the various states and regions. This difference in rates results partly from differences in divorce laws and in court practices. But the rate probably also differs because of variances in the cultural, economic, racial, and religious composition of the population. In general, for example, people who have a nonprofessional job and those who earn a low income have a high divorce rate. On the other hand, people who have a professional job and those who earn a high income have a generally lower divorce rate. One nonprofessional group—farmers—has an extremely low divorce rate, however.

Most studies show that black couples have a higher divorce rate than white couples. Mixed marriages involving a black and a white apparently have about the same divorce rate as other marriages.

Of the three major religious groups in the United States, Roman Catholics have the lowest divorce rate and Protestants the highest. The Roman Catholic Church generally does not recognize divorce. It holds that valid marriages can be ended only by death. However, the church grants annulments and permits the persons involved to remarry. Judaism and most Protestant groups permit divorce. Some divorce surveys show that Catholic-Protestant couples and Christian-Jewish couples have a higher divorce rate than couples of the same religion. However, one study showed no difference in the divorce rate of Catholic-Protestant couples. BRIGITTE M. BODENHEIMER and WILLIAM M. KEPHART

Related Articles in WORLD BOOK include:

Abandonment	Annulment	Desertion
Alienation of Affections	Collusion	Marriage
Alimony	Community Property	

See also *Marriage and Divorce* in the RESEARCH GUIDE/INDEX, Volume 22, for a *Reading and Study Guide.*

DIX, DOROTHEA LYNDE (1802-1887), led the drive to build state hospitals for the mentally ill in the United States. She also improved prison conditions. She traveled through the U.S. and Europe for this cause until she was 80. She gained the support of wealthy people, and of such distinguished educators and statesmen as Horace Mann and Charles Sumner.

Library of Congress

Dorothea Dix

Dorothea Dix was born in Hampden, Maine, but grew up in Massachusetts. She visited a Massachusetts house of correction in 1841, and was shocked by the treatment of mentally ill persons. She asked the legislature to provide better care for the mentally ill, and started the reform in that state. She was Superintendent of Women Nurses for the Union during the Civil War. LOUIS FILLER

DIXIE is the name of a famous song especially popular in the South. Daniel D. Emmett, member of a minstrel-show company, wrote the song in 1859 in New York City. He intended it to be a closing number because it permitted a parade of the entire company. The song became an immediate hit. Many publishers printed their own versions. The original first stanza was:

"I wish I was in de land ob cotton,
Old times dar am not forgotten,
Look away! Look away! Look away! Dixie Land."

When Abraham Lincoln ran for the presidency in 1860, "Dixie" was used as a campaign song against him. Five years later, after the Civil War, he asked a band at the White House to play "Dixie." CHARLES B. RIGHTER

DIXIE, or DIXIELAND, is a name often given to the southern part of the United States. There are different explanations for this name. A Louisiana bank once printed $10 bills bearing the French word *dix*, which means *ten.* According to one story, people called Louisiana "Dix's Land," and then shortened it to Dixie. In time, *Dixie* came to mean the entire South. In another story, a slaveowner named Dixie, or Dixy, was kind to his slaves. "Dixie's Land" became known as a happy, comfortable place to live. Gradually, the term came to refer to the South. RAY ALLEN BILLINGTON

DIXIE HIGHWAY is a series of scenic automobile roads that lead from the Straits of Mackinac, at the northern tip of Lake Michigan, to Miami, near the southern end of the peninsula of Florida. It has two main routes, an east route and a west route. The east route passes through Detroit, Mich., Cincinnati, Ohio, and Jacksonville, Fla. The west route passes through South Bend, Ind., Louisville, Ky., and Atlanta, Ga.

Carl G. Fisher, a pioneer automobile manufacturer, originated the idea of the Dixie Highway. The building of the highway began in 1915. MATTHEW C. SIELSKI

DIXIECRAT PARTY is the nickname for the States' Rights Democratic Party. In the national election of 1948, many Southern Democrats objected to their party's civil rights program. They formed the Dixiecrat Party and nominated Strom Thurmond for President and Fielding L. Wright for Vice-President. The party won the electoral votes of four Southern states (see ELECTORAL COLLEGE [table]). DONALD R. MCCOY

DIXON, JEREMIAH. See MASON AND DIXON'S LINE.

DIXON, JOSEPH (1799-1869), was an American inventor and manufacturer. He founded a factory to make lead pencils and stove polish from graphite at Salem, Mass., in 1827. In 1832, he patented a process of using colored inks to prevent counterfeiting. After moving his factory to Jersey City, N.J., Dixon patented and introduced graphite crucibles for making pottery and steel in 1850. He was born in Marblehead, Mass.

DIZZINESS is a condition in which a person feels that his surroundings are whirling about, or that he is falling. Dizziness also means lightheadedness, the sensation that comes before fainting. It causes a person to stagger or fall. Often there is nausea and vomiting. Dizziness is also called *vertigo.* Too large or too small a flow of blood to the brain may cause dizziness. It may also be caused by changes in the pressure of the fluid in the semicircular canals of the inner ear. Dizziness often accompanies such disorders as anemia, epilepsy, heart trouble, and diseases of the inner ear. Some people feel dizzy when they are whirled very rapidly or when they stand at great heights. R. B. CAPPS

DJAKARTA. See JAKARTA.

DJIBOUTI, *juh BOO tee,* also spelled JIBUTI (pop. 62,000), is the capital of the French Territory of Afars and Issas, in eastern Africa. The territory was formerly called French Somaliland. Djibouti is a port city on the Gulf of Aden. It lies on the northern end of a railroad that links Addis Ababa, the capital of Ethiopia, with the sea. The port was created in 1888. The city became the capital of the French colony in 1892.

DJILAS, MILOVAN. See YUGOSLAVIA (In the 1950's).

DJUGASHVILI, IOSIF. See STALIN, JOSEPH.

DNA. See NUCLEIC ACID; HEREDITY; CELL (The Nucleus; The 1900's; The Code of Life).

DNEPR RIVER, *DNYEH pur,* or DNIEPER, *NEE pur,* is the second longest waterway in European Russia. The Dnepr rises near Smolensk in central European Russia. It flows southward for 1,420 miles (2,285 kilometers) to empty into the Black Sea. The Dnepr drains an area of about 200,000 square miles (520,000 square kilometers) in one of Russia's most important economic regions. For location, see RUSSIA (physical map).

The Dnepr has been dredged so that boats can travel over almost the entire length of the river. Dams and reservoirs have deepened the Dnepr and removed obstacles caused by rapids. The Dneproges Dam is near Zaporozh'ye (see DNEPROGES DAM). Other dams on the Dnepr include those at Kiev, Kremenchug, Dneprodzerzhinsk, and Kakhovka. River vessels carry timber from the north and grain from the Ukraine along the lower course. Important tributaries of the Dnepr River are the Berezina, Desna, and Pripet rivers. The Pripet River and a canal connect the Dnepr with the Bug and Vistula rivers in Poland. THEODORE SHABAD

DNEPROGES DAM, *duhn yehp ruh GEHS,* one of the large concrete dams in Russia, is located 200 miles (320 kilometers) from the mouth of the Dnepr River. It provides hydroelectric power for most of the mines and industries in southern Russia. The dam is 5,000 feet (1,500 meters) long and 200 feet (61 meters) high, and was completed in 1932. When the Germans invaded the Ukraine in 1941, the Russians blew up the dam and hydroelectric power plant. They rebuilt them after the war. The dam holds back 1,600,000 cubic yards (1,220,000 cubic meters) of water. Its power plant can generate 650,000 kilowatts of electricity. T. W. MERMEL

DNEPROPETROVSK, *NEHP roh puh TRAWFSK* (pop. 882,000), formerly called *Ekaterinoslav,* ranks among the most important industrial cities of Russia. It lies on the Dnepr River about 250 miles (402 kilometers) northeast of Odessa in the Ukraine. The city is a steel and machinery center. THEODORE SHABAD

DNESTR RIVER, *DNYEHS tur,* or DNIESTER, *NEES tur,* rises in the Carpathian Mountains in the district of Galicia, in central Europe, and empties into the Black Sea. The Dnestr flows to the southeast for 875 miles (1,408 kilometers). For much of this distance, it passes through Russia along the border of Bessarabia. Boats travel the Dnestr to Khotin. M. KAMIL DZIEWANOWSKI

DO-IT-YOURSELF. See HOBBY (Do-It-Yourself and Handicraft; and the list of Related Articles).

DO-NOTHING KINGS. See MEROVINGIAN.

DOANE COLLEGE. See UNIVERSITIES AND COLLEGES (table).

DÖBEREINER, JOHANN. See FURFURAL.

DOBERMAN PINSCHER, *DOH ber muhn PIN sher,* is an intelligent breed of dogs that was developed for police work. The Doberman has short hair, usually black with rust-brown markings. Other colors are red or blue, with the same markings. It is a medium-sized dog, 24 to 28 inches (61 to 71 centimeters) high at the shoulder. It weighs 60 to 75 pounds (27 to 34 kilograms). The Doberman has long legs and a lean, long head. Its tail is cut short and its ears are trimmed to a taper. The Doberman, a swift runner, is the fastest of the police dogs. It is also a high jumper. In World War II, the Doberman served with U.S. troops in the Southwest Pacific. The breed is named after Louis Dobermann, a German watchman who first raised the dogs in the 1800's. The miniature pinscher weighs from 6 to 10 pounds (2.7 to 4.5 kilograms). OLGA DAKAN

See also DOG (color picture: Working Dogs).

DOBIE, JAMES FRANK (1888-1964), was an American author and professor, and a leading collector of Texas lore and folk tales. Dobie was born on a Texas ranch, was graduated from Southwestern University, and taught at the University of Texas. His books include *Coronado's Children, The Longhorns, Up the Trail from Texas, Tales of Old-Time Texas, The Mustangs,* and *A Texan in England.* E. HUDSON LONG

DOBRUJA. See ROMANIA (Land Regions).

DOBSON FLY. See HELLGRAMMITE.

DOCK is the water beside a wharf or pier (or between two wharves or piers) in which a ship floats. The term *dock* is often used incorrectly to mean a wharf or pier. The *wet* dock is a basin with gates to keep in or shut out water, and maintain the same water level while unloading and loading ships. Such docks are used in harbors where the tide rises and falls greatly. See also DRY DOCK; MARINA. ALVIN F. HARLOW

DOCK is the name of several kinds of plants belonging to the buckwheat family. Three common perennial weeds brought into the United States and Canada belong to this family. They are the *narrow-leaf,* or *yellow, dock* (from the color of the taproot), the *sour dock,* and the *broadleaf dock.* These weeds infest meadowland, gardens, lawns, and pastures, and are common wayside weeds. These plants grow from 2 to 4 feet (61 to 122 centimeters) high, and they have long, large leaves with wavy margins. Their thick, tapering roots are used medicinally for tonics, astringents, and skin remedies. The leaves of sour dock are eaten as potherbs, or greens, but they may poison animals that have a diet low in calcium. Dock may be controlled with amino triazole sprays.

Scientific Classification. The dock plants are members of the buckwheat family, *Polygonaceae.* The narrow-leaf dock is genus *Rumex,* species *R. crispus.* The broadleaf dock is *R. obtusifolius.* The sour dock is *R. acetosa.* LOUIS PYENSON

See also BUCKWHEAT.

J. Horace McFarland

Dock usually is considered a weed. But some varieties are used as herbs and to make dyes.

DOCTOR, in medicine. See MEDICINE.

Ewing Galloway

A Dock and Pier in the port of Baltimore clearly show the difference between the two. The dock is the water in which the ship rides. A warehouse is on the pier, which extends into the harbor. The railway cars are on floating piers.

DOCTOR is a degree awarded to a person by a college or university. Physicians have the *Doctor of Medicine* (*M.D.*) degree. Many scientists and teachers have the *Doctor of Philosophy* (*Ph.D.*) degree. Clergymen, dentists, lawyers, mathematicians, and other professional people may have doctors' degrees. See also CAPS AND GOWNS; DEGREE, COLLEGE. HOLLIS L. CASWELL

DOCTOR DOLITTLE. See LOFTING, HUGH.

DOCTORFISH, one of the surgeonfishes, is a tropical marine fish, found in the East Indies. The doctorfish is sometimes called the *tang*. It is a brilliant metallic blue on top and turquoise below. It has a black tail, and its fins are outlined with bright blue. The fish gets its name because it has a sharp erectile spine in a little groove on each side of the body near the tail. This spine is shaped like a *lancet* (surgeon's knife).

John G. Shedd Aquarium

The Doctorfish lives in the tropical ocean waters of the East Indies. It is also called the ***blue tang*** and ***blue max***.

Scientific Classification. The doctorfish is a member of the surgeonfish family, *Acanthuridae*. It is genus *Paracanthurus*, species *P. hepatus*. LEONARD P. SCHULTZ

See also FISH (picture: Fish of Coral Reefs).

DODD, THOMAS JOSEPH (1907-1971), a Connecticut Democrat, served in the U.S. Senate from 1959 to 1971. He served in the U.S. House of Representatives from 1953 to 1957. In 1967, the Senate censured Dodd on the charge that he used some donations that were intended for political use to pay his personal expenses.

A lawyer, Dodd served as a special agent for the Federal Bureau of Investigation in 1933 and 1934. As an assistant to the U.S. attorney general from 1938 to 1945, he helped create the first civil rights section of the Justice Department. He served as executive trial counsel for the United States at the Nuremberg trials in 1945 and 1946. He received a presidential citation for this work. Dodd was born in Norwich, Conn., and was graduated from Providence College and Yale University. ALBERT E. VAN DUSEN

DODD, WILLIAM EDWARD (1869-1940), a noted American historian, served as U.S. ambassador to Germany from 1933 to 1937. He resigned in protest against Adolf Hitler's policies, and published the widely read *Ambassador Dodd's Diary*.

He made lecture tours in the United States criticizing Nazi Germany. His works include the historical books—*Life of Jefferson Davis, Expansion and Conflict, Statesmen of the Old South*, and *Woodrow Wilson and His Work*.

Dodd was born in Clayton, N.C. He received his Ph.D. degree from the University of Leipzig, Germany. He taught history at Randolph-Macon College, and at the University of Chicago. ERIC F. GOLDMAN

Grosset & Dunlap

An Illustration from Mary Dodge's Book, ***Hans Brinker, or, The Silver Skates.*** **The burgomaster's daughter is shown persuading Hans to buy new skates for the important race.**

DODDER is a destructive weed found over most of the world. It is called a *parasite* because it takes its food from other plants. The dodder grows from seed in the spring, then attaches itself by little suckers to some nearby plant. The root and older part of the stem die, break off, and leave the dodder plant free. Dodder destroys much alfalfa, clover, and flax.

The stems of the dodder look like yellow, orange, white, and brown threads. The stems twine around other plants and sprawl from one plant to another, forming tangled masses. Dodder flowers are small and white, and they form in dense clusters.

Scientific Classification. The dodder plants are members of the morning-glory family, *Convolvulaceae.* They make up the genus *Cuscuta.* ARTHUR CRONQUIST

See also PLANT (picture: How Nongreen Plants Get Their Food).

DODDS, HAROLD WILLIS (1889-), an American educator, served as president of Princeton University from 1933 to 1957. He stated his educational philosophy in an essay: "We are not put into the world to sit still and know; we are put here to act." He served on the executive board of the United Nations Educational, Scientific, and Cultural Organization (UNESCO) in 1946. Dodds was born in Utica, Pa., and was graduated from Grove City (Pa.) College and received his Ph.D. from the University of Pennsylvania. He also taught at Purdue University and Western Reserve University (now Case Western Reserve University). JOHN S. BRUBACHER

DODECANESE ISLANDS, *doh DEK uh neece,* is a group of 16 islands in the Aegean Sea near Asia Minor. The islands cover 1,028 square miles (2,663 square kilometers) and have a population of 123,021. Only two of the islands, Rhodes and Kós, are really fertile. The islanders raise sheep and goats, and grow wheat, vegetables, tobacco, grapes, olives, oranges, figs, and almonds. They also dive for sponges. Italy acquired the islands from Turkey in 1912. They were given to Greece after World War II. HARRY N. HOWARD

See also PATMOS; RHODES; GREECE (map).

DODGE is the family name of two brothers who pioneered in automobile manufacturing. Both **John Francis Dodge** (1864-1920) and **Horace Elgin Dodge** (1868-1920) were born in Niles, Mich.

The Dodge brothers began their business careers making bicycles. In 1901, they opened a machine shop in Detroit. The brothers built parts for the Olds Motor Works and Ford Motor Company.

The Dodge brothers began making their own automobiles in 1914, and produced one of the first American automobiles with an all-steel body. Horace Dodge invented many improvements for automobiles, including an oven for baking enamel on steel bodies. The Dodge Company became part of Chrysler Corporation in 1928. SMITH HEMPSTONE OLIVER

DODGE, MARY ELIZABETH MAPES (1831-1905), an American author, wrote *Hans Brinker, or, The Silver Skates* (1865), a famous children's book about Holland. Within 30 years the book had appeared in more than 100 editions and was translated into six languages. Mrs. Dodge was recognized as a leader in the field of juvenile literature. She became editor of *St. Nicholas Magazine* when it was organized in 1873, and persuaded the best authors of the time to contribute to the magazine.

She was born in New York City, and grew up in a home that was a center for literary groups. William Cullen Bryant and Horace Greeley were frequent visitors. Her husband died when she was 27, leaving her with two small sons. Because she had to support them, she returned to her father's home in Newark, N.J., and started her literary career. EVELYN RAY SICKELS

DODGE CITY, Kans. (pop. 14,127), called the *Cowboy Capital of the World,* was a well-known "Wild West" frontier town. It lies on the Arkansas River, about 100 miles (160 kilometers) east of the Colorado border (see KANSAS [political map]). Dodge City is the chief commercial center of southwestern Kansas. It is the seat of Ford County, and has a commission form of government. The city is the home of St. Mary of the Plains College.

Traders on the Santa Fe Trail traveled through the area in the 1800's. The town was established when the Santa Fe Railroad came in 1872. For about 10 years after 1875, it was the largest cattle market in the world. Many gunmen lived here, and such famous peace officers as Wyatt Earp and "Bat" Masterson enforced the law. The city hall stands on Boot Hill. It was called *Boot Hill* because many gunmen in the 1870's were buried there, still wearing their boots. WILLIAM F. ZORNOW

See also KANSAS (picture: Restoration of Notorious Front Street).

DODGSON, CHARLES LUTWIDGE. See CARROLL, LEWIS.

DODO, *DOH doh,* is an extinct bird that could not fly. The dodo was about the size of a large turkey. It had short legs, an enormous beak, stubby wings, and a

American Museum of Natural History

The Dodo of Mauritius island had tiny wings that were so small the bird could not fly. This model of a dodo was constructed according to a painting made of a living bird.

tuftlike tail with curly feathers. The dodo lived on the island of Mauritius in the Indian Ocean. Two related species called *solitaires* lived on nearby Reunion and Rodrigues islands.

European seamen killed the birds for food. Hogs, rats, and dogs that the men brought with them destroyed the eggs. The dodo died out about 1681, the Rodrigues solitaire in the 1740's, and the Reunion solitaire in the 1790's. Several dodos, and possibly some solitaires, were exhibited alive in Europe and served as models for paintings. The heads and feet of a few dodos are preserved in museums, but the solitaires are known only from pictures, from accounts of travelers, and from bones that can be found on the islands.

Scientific Classification. The dodo and solitaires belong to the pigeon and dove order, *Columbiformes*. They are in the dodo and solitaire family, *Raphidae*. The dodo is genus *Raphus*, species *R. cucullatus*. The Reunion solitaire is classified as *Raphus solitarius*, and the Rodrigues solitaire as *Pezophaps solitaria*. R. A. PAYNTER, JR.

DODONA, *doh DOH nuh,* was an ancient sanctuary in northwestern Greece. It was located near the present-day city of Ioánnina. The sanctuary had an oracle of Zeus which was second in fame only to the oracle of Apollo at Delphi. People wrote their questions on lead tablets. They believed the rustling of the leaves of a sacred red oak tree answered them. Temple priests called *Selli* interpreted these rustlings. The Romans destroyed the sanctuary in 219 B.C. JOHN H. KENT

DOE. See DEER; GOAT.

DOE, JOHN, is the name used in legal documents to describe a person whose real name is unknown.

DOENITZ, *DUH nits,* **KARL** (1891-   ), a German admiral, became commander in chief of the German fleet in January, 1943, during World War II. Before this appointment, he directed development of the German submarine service. He invented the "wolf pack" technique of submarine warfare to penetrate convoy defenses. With the collapse of Germany in 1945, Adolf Hitler chose Doenitz to succeed him as head of the government. Doenitz concluded peace with the Allies. He was tried for war crimes in Nuremberg, and was sentenced to 10 years in prison. He was released in 1956. Doenitz was born in Berlin-Grünau. LESTER B. MASON

Thomas Gilcrease Institute of American History and Art, Tulsa, Okla.

Dodge City in the Late 1800's was the scene of many gunfights. Cowboy artist Charles Marion Russell portrayed one vividly in his painting *When Guns Speak, Death Settles Disputes.*

Kwiatkowski

dog

DOG has been "man's best friend" for thousands of years. These friendly, obedient animals serve people throughout the world in work, play, and sport. Dogs live near the Eskimo's igloo, in jungle villages, in farm homes, and in city apartments. About 25 million dogs live in the United States.

Dogs have earned man's love and respect with their faithfulness and devotion. Many dogs have given their own lives to save or protect their masters. Dogs guard the home, and herd cattle and sheep. Their keen sense of smell makes them fine hunting companions. Dogs like to be with people, especially children, and they often howl sadly when left alone. One of the happiest sights is a dog greeting a child with joyful barks and wagging tail.

A dog can be taught to obey commands because it is intelligent and wants to please. Dogs were the first animals to be tamed by man.

How Dogs Help Man

Most dogs can be trained to guard their masters' homes and property. Their barking and growling frighten burglars, and awaken sleeping families in case of fire. Fierce watchdogs protect stores and factories at night. Sometimes dogs accompany policemen on lonely beats. Bloodhounds track down criminals. Specially trained guide dogs lead blind persons (see GUIDE DOG). German shepherds and other dogs are trained to find people buried under avalanches in the Alps.

About 8,500 dogs served in the "K9 Corps" of the United States Army during World War II. They located wounded soldiers on battlefields, and carried messages and medical supplies under fire. Other dogs helped the Coast Guard patrol the shoreline of the United States.

Dogs tend cattle and sheep, and keep livestock from straying during the day. They drive the animals into the barn at night, and attack wolves and other wild beasts that might harm livestock. Dogs also kill rats and mice that eat grain.

In Belgium and some other countries, farmers use dogs to haul milk, vegetables, and other produce in small carts. Tribes that wander from place to place sometimes use dogs to drag or carry loads. A medium-sized dog can carry loads of 30 to 60 pounds (14 to 27 kilograms) on its back. In many Arctic regions, sleds pulled by dogs serve as the only means of transportation in winter (see DOG SLED).

Doctors try out new medicines and operations on dogs before using them on humans. Frederick G. Banting and Charles H. Best used dogs in experiments that led to the discovery of insulin (see INSULIN). Ivan P. Pavlov, a Russian doctor, discovered the conditioned reflex by experimenting with dogs (see REFLEX ACTION).

For hundreds of years, performing dogs have entertained audiences in circuses and theaters. The collies that played the role of Lassie, and the German shepherds that played the role of Rin-Tin-Tin, became famous motion-picture and television stars.

Breeds of Dogs

The American Kennel Club is the chief organization of dog breeders. It recognizes 121 breeds and varieties of purebreds. A *purebred* is a dog whose *sire* (father)

77 Breeds of Dogs are shown in color illustrations on the following pages. All color photographs are by Walter Chandoha, unless otherwise noted. All color paintings are by Edwin Megargee.

English Setter

Irish Setter

German Short-Haired Pointer

Brittany Spaniel

Weimaraner

Cocker Spaniel

Golden Retriever

Camera Clix

sporting dogs

Chesapeake Bay Retriever

English Springer Spaniel

Irish Water Spaniel

English Cocker Spaniel

Pointer

Labrador Retriever

Gordon Setter

and *dam* (mother) belong to the same breed. When the ancestors of a purebred are known and registered by a breed club, the dog has a *pedigree*. Dog clubs and associations register only proven purebreds in their *studbooks*. The AKC registers all 121 pure breeds. Other organizations that keep studbooks include the National Coursing Association, the American Coonhunters Association, and sporting publications such as *American Field*.

The AKC divides the 121 pure breeds into six groups: (1) sporting dogs, (2) hounds, (3) working dogs, (4) terriers, (5) toy dogs, and (6) nonsporting dogs.

Sporting Dogs hunt chiefly by smelling the air to locate game birds. The sporting group includes 24 breeds of pointers, setters, retrievers, and spaniels. Pointers and setters smell the game, then "point" their bodies and noses toward it to guide the hunter. Setters take their name from dogs that were once trained to *set* (crouch) after locating game birds hiding in grass or bushes. The hunters then cast nets over the birds. Retrievers pick up birds that have been shot, and bring them back to the hunters. When sportsmen began using guns for hunting, they trained certain dogs to *spring* (scare) game birds into the air. Such dogs are called *springers*. Most spaniels hunt in this way.

Hounds include 19 breeds of dogs that hunt by smell or sight. Bloodhounds and other *scent hounds* follow an odor on the ground by running with their noses to the earth. Coonhounds and other breeds *bay*, or *give tongue*, when trailing game. When hounds bay, their barks become deep and prolonged. The basenji, an African hound, is the only dog that cannot bark. Tall, slender *sight hounds*, or *gazehounds*, watch game as they run after it. Sportsmen use such gazehounds as whippets and greyhounds for dog racing (see Dog Racing). Hounds are among the oldest known dogs. See Hound.

Working Dogs serve man as herders, guards, sled dogs, and in other useful ways. The working group has the largest number of breeds, 30. Some of them, including Doberman pinschers and German shepherds, have become famous as war dogs. Collies, old English sheep dogs, Shetland sheep dogs, and Welsh corgis herd cattle and sheep. Siberian huskies, Alaskan malamutes, and Samoyeds pull sleds.

Terriers hunt rats, mice, and other vermin, chiefly by digging in the ground. These dogs kill their prey by crushing it with their powerful jaws. The terrier group includes 22 breeds. Most have wire-haired coats, and bushy whiskers and eyebrows. See Terrier.

Toy Dogs include 15 small breeds that are kept as pets. Breeders have developed some of the toys from much larger dogs. The pug, for example, might be called a small mastiff, and the miniature pinscher a pocket-size Doberman pinscher. See Toy Dog.

Nonsporting Dogs include 11 breeds kept chiefly as pets. The Boston terrier is the only nonsporting breed developed in the United States. This breed is classed as a nonsporting dog, although it is partly descended from crossbreeding with an English terrier. The Lhasa apso guarded the monasteries of Tibet 800 years ago. The Chinese raised chow chows, commonly called *chows*, as hunters. Poodles once served French hunters as retrievers.

Other Breeds of dogs are not registered by the American Kennel Club, because so few are raised in the United States. These breeds include the Australian kelpie, British border collie, Mexican hairless, Russian owtchah, and Italian spinone. Breeders occasionally exhibit these dogs at shows as *miscellaneous* breeds.

Crossbreds and Mongrels make up the largest number of dogs throughout the world. A *crossbred* has parents that belong to different breeds. *Mongrels* have such mixed parentage that no one breed can be recognized. Crossbreds and mongrels often are as good pets as pure-

THE SIZES OF DOGS

The Chihuahua is the smallest breed of dog. The St. Bernard is the heaviest breed and the Irish wolfhound is the tallest. Other breeds of dogs range in size between these extremes. The measurements below indicate average weight and shoulder height.

WORLD BOOK illustration by Mary Baker

Chihuahua
1-6 lb. (0.5-2.7 kg)
5 in. (13 cm)

Cocker Spaniel
22-28 lb. (10-13 kg)
14-15 in. (36-38 cm)

Collie
50-75 lb. (23-34 kg)
22-26 in. (56-66 cm)

St. Bernard
165-180 lb. (75-82 kg)
25½-30 in. (65-76 cm)

Irish Wolfhound
105-140 lb. (48-64 kg)
30-34 in. (76-86 cm)

breds. They vary greatly in size and appearance.

Wild Dogs still roam in hungry packs in many parts of the world. They include wolves, coyotes, foxes, jackals, the dholes of eastern India, the South American bush dogs, the African hunting dogs, and the dingoes of Australia. Many of these dogs have great natural hunting abilities. Wild dogs sometimes mate with tame dogs. The puppies of some wild dogs have been tamed.

The Body of the Dog

Dogs range in size from the Chihuahua, which is not much larger than a pigeon, to the Irish wolfhound, which may stand nearly 3 feet (91 centimeters) high at the shoulders. Saint Bernards, the heaviest dogs, may weigh more than 200 pounds (91 kilograms).

Coat. Some dogs have long coats and others have short coats. The hair may be curly as on the poodle, or straight as on the Pekingese. The collie's coat feels rough, and the Kerry blue terrier's coat is soft. Most dogs have two coats. The outer coat protects the dog's body from rain and snow, and the undercoat keeps the animal warm. In winter, a dog's undercoat grows thick and furry. Dogs shed their undercoats in summer and grow them back in autumn.

Bones. All dogs have the same number of bones, but the length, shape, and size differ from breed to breed. Long leg bones and sloping ribs make the greyhound tall and slim. Stockier dogs, such as the German rottweiler, have rounder ribs and heavier bones. A dog's front leg bones are usually straight.

Dogs, like cats, have five claws on their front feet and four on their hind feet. But dogs cannot pull their claws inside their paws as cats can.

Nose. Dogs recognize objects by smell, much as man recognizes them by sight. A dog can detect the scent of an object which its master has held in his hand for only a second. Avalanche shepherd dogs of Switzerland can smell men buried under 20 feet (6 meters) of snow. Moisture helps a dog detect odors, and most dogs have moist noses. Dogs lick their noses to keep them moist. However, a healthy dog can have a warm, dry nose.

Mouth. The mouths of dogs differ in shape according to the breed. For example, bulldogs have broad jaws and collies have narrow jaws. Puppies have 32 temporary teeth, which they shed when they are about 5 months old. Adult dogs have 42 permanent teeth, including four large teeth, two in each jaw, called *fangs*.

DOG TERMS

Bitch is an adult female dog.

Canine means a dog or doglike. It comes from *canis*, the Latin word for dog.

Crossbred is a dog whose parents belong to different breeds.

Dog is an adult male dog. However, the term is generally used for all dogs, regardless of age or sex.

Litter is a group of puppies born at one time.

Mongrel is a dog of such mixed ancestry that no one breed can be recognized.

Pack is a group of dogs.

Pedigree is a record of a purebred dog's ancestors.

Puppy is a dog less than 1 year old.

Purebred is a dog whose parents belong to the same breed.

Studbook is a book in which breeders register the pedigrees of dogs.

Whelp is an *unweaned* puppy, or one that still drinks its mother's milk.

PARTS OF A DOG

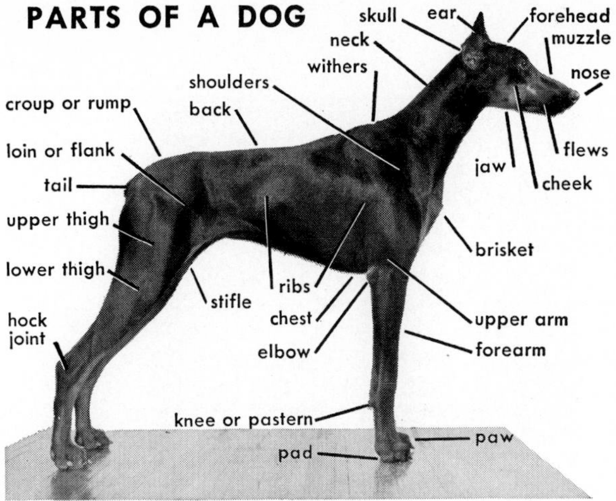

Walter Chandoha

Dogs tear meat with their fangs. A dog drinks by lapping liquids with its tongue, a few drops at a time.

Ears. A dog can hear sounds 250 yards (229 meters) away that most people cannot hear beyond 25 yards (23 meters). The human ear can detect sound waves that vibrate at frequencies up to 20,000 times a second. But dogs can hear sound waves that vibrate at frequencies of more than 30,000 times a second. Some persons signal to their dogs by blowing on high-pitched whistles that cannot be heard by humans. The outsides of a dog's ears have flaps of skin called *leathers*. These protect the dog's ears, and can be moved to help catch and locate sounds. Most small dogs hear better than large dogs.

Eyes. Dogs cannot see as well as men. They have difficulty telling colors apart, except by the degree of brightness, and are considered color blind. A dog sees objects first by their movement, second by their brightness, and third by their shape.

Body Functions of a dog differ only slightly from those of a human. For example, a dog's normal body temperature is about 101° F. (38° C), only a little higher than a human's normal temperature of 98.6° F. (37° C). A dog's heart beats between 70 and 120 times a minute. The human heart beats 70 to 80 times a minute. When a dog becomes excited or overheated, it sticks out its tongue and *pants* (breathes heavily). The extra air cools the inside of the animal's body. Dogs have sweat glands on their noses, foot pads, and hairy parts of the body. The glands on the hairy surfaces are not active in cooling the body, but protect the skin from an unusual increase in temperature.

Life History. A female carries its young 58 to 63 days before the puppies are born. A puppy is born blind and helpless. Its eyes open about 10 to 14 days after birth. Dogs usually give birth to litters of 1 to 12 puppies, though litters of 20 or more puppies have been reported. The mother provides milk for her puppies until they are 4 to 5 weeks old. Dogs become fully grown at 8 months to 2 years of age, depending on the size of the breed. Large dogs develop more slowly than small dogs.

The average dog lives for about 12 to 13 years. It is difficult to compare the age of a dog to that of a man because breeds of dogs develop at greatly different rates. A 6-month-old puppy may compare in development to a 10-year-old child, and a 2-year-old dog may compare to a 24-year-old man. After a dog's second

nonsporting dogs

Camera Clix
Dalmatian

Schipperke

Keeshond

Boston Terrier

Ira Haas, Photo Researchers
French Bulldog

Poodle

Chow Chow

Bulldog

Basset Hound

Greyhound

Camera Clix

Borzoi

hounds

American Foxhound

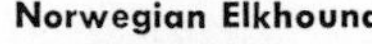

Norwegian Elkhound

Irish Wolfhound

Basenji

Rhodesian Ridgeback

Black and Tan Coonhound

Dachshund

Bloodhound

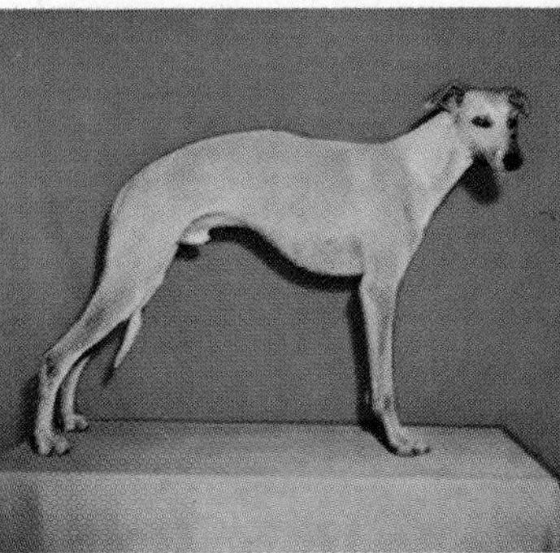
Whippet

Ira Haas, F.P.G.

Saluki

Hanks, F.P.G.

Afghan Hound

Beagle

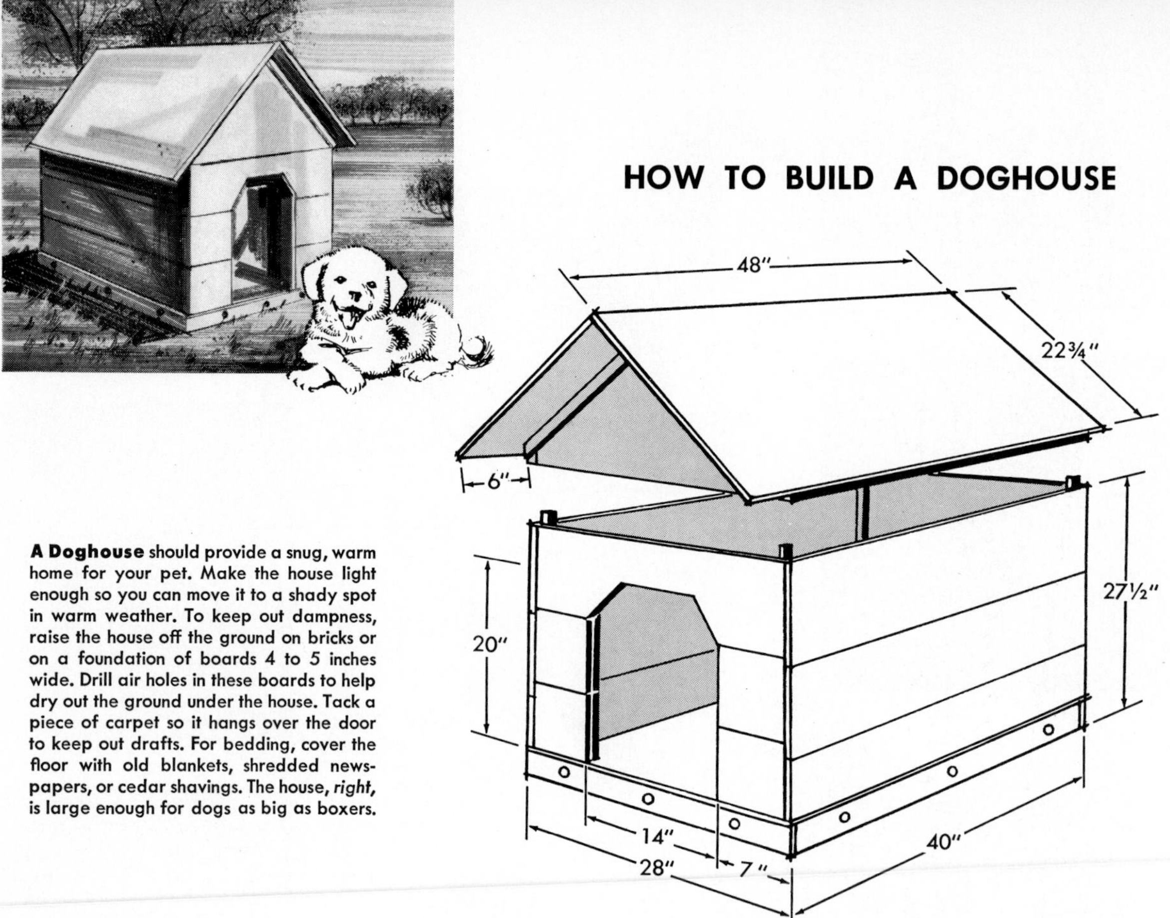

HOW TO BUILD A DOGHOUSE

A Doghouse should provide a snug, warm home for your pet. Make the house light enough so you can move it to a shady spot in warm weather. To keep out dampness, raise the house off the ground on bricks or on a foundation of boards 4 to 5 inches wide. Drill air holes in these boards to help dry out the ground under the house. Tack a piece of carpet so it hangs over the door to keep out drafts. For bedding, cover the floor with old blankets, shredded newspapers, or cedar shavings. The house, *right*, is large enough for dogs as big as boxers.

year, each year may be compared to about four years of a man's life. For example, a 16-year-old dog may be compared to an 80-year-old man.

Instincts and Intelligence. Dogs have many of the instincts of their wild ancestors. For example, all dogs gobble their food as though they were keeping other animals from grabbing it. They turn around several times before lying down, in much the same way that wild dogs trample grass to make a sheltered bed. A frightened dog curls its tail between its legs to keep it out of the reach of enemies. Male dogs urinate on trees to tell other dogs they have been there.

The ability of dogs to learn to obey commands is one mark of their intelligence. But for the first three weeks of a puppy's life, it knows nothing and needs only warmth and food. In the fourth week of life, the puppy can see, hear, and smell, and it begins to learn. From the fourth to the seventh week, the puppy starts playing and responds to humans. From the seventh to the twelfth week, the puppy can learn simple commands such as "Let's go for a walk." Such orders, if repeated several times, come to mean to the dog exactly what they mean to a person. Some dogs seem to have the power to reason, or solve problems such as how to get food from a box by pressing a lever.

How to Care for Your Dog

Before you buy a dog, consider the size of your house or apartment. Large dogs, such as great Danes and collies, need big yards in which to run and play. Smaller dogs can live in smaller homes. But even large dogs will be happy in small homes if you take them out regularly for long walks. All dogs need daily exercise.

Either a purebred or a mongrel makes a good pet. But you can tell in advance what a purebred will look like and how big it will be when fully grown. Breeders raise purebreds to have good health and good tempers. A puppy's disposition depends partly on the way you treat it. If you treat your puppy roughly, it will grow into a rough dog. Treat it gently, and it will become a gentle pet.

A puppy should be about 8 weeks old before you take it home. It should appear lively and playful. Its eyes should be bright and clear, its skin clean, and its coat shiny. Your puppy, like a baby, depends upon you for everything—food, shelter, and training.

Feeding. No one can tell exactly how much any dog should eat. If your dog becomes fat, feed it less food. If it appears thin, feed it more food. Dogs of all ages need meat every day. You may give a fully grown dog table scraps that contain at least one-third meat. Do not give your dog bones. Bone splinters can injure him if he swallows them. Serve your dog warm food in a clean dish. Throw uneaten food away after about 20 minutes. Wash the food dish thoroughly every day. Keep cool, fresh drinking water available at all times in a dish that the dog cannot tip over.

Small daily amounts of vitamin-rich cod-liver oil help fortify puppies and adult dogs in cold weather. A veterinarian can prescribe the correct doses of cod-liver oil and other vitamins and minerals that are necessary for your dog (see VETERINARY MEDICINE). Dog-food companies make a wide variety of dry meals and canned meat foods that supply most of the necessary vitamins and minerals.

Shelter. A dog that lives indoors needs a clean sleeping box lined with blankets or shredded paper. Short-haired dogs need more warmth than long-haired ones. A dog should not sleep next to a radiator or on a cement floor. A dog that lives outdoors needs a weatherproof kennel, or doghouse, with a dry, warm floor covered with cedar shavings, sawdust, or blankets.

Grooming. A daily brushing cleans the dog's coat and stimulates the skin. It also stops a dog from scratching itself to remove loose hair. A dog should be washed as seldom as possible. Too much washing can cause a dog's skin to dry out and crack. If your dog needs a bath, wash it with warm water and soap. Rinse and dry the animal thoroughly. Puppies should not be washed until they are 6 months old. Trim your dog's toenails about once every two months. Clean its teeth weekly with a damp cloth dipped in salt. If your dog's eyes run, wipe them gently with cotton moistened with a weak boric-acid solution. Clean your dog's ears with cotton if they look brown or dirty inside or are filled with wax.

Diseases. Dogs suffer many diseases that attack humans, including colds, tonsillitis, and pneumonia. A veterinarian should always treat a sick dog. Signs of illness include fever, coughing, running eyes and nose, and excessive water drinking.

Distemper and hepatitis are two common virus diseases that attack dogs. Veterinarians can vaccinate puppies against them. Chills, fever, reddened eyes, and loss of appetite may be signs of these diseases. Dogs also suffer from rabies if they are bitten by an animal that has this rare but serious disease. Some communities require that dogs be inoculated against rabies. See DISTEMPER; HEPATITIS; RABIES.

Most puppies suffer from worms. Signs of worms include vomiting, bloating, and general unfitness. A veterinarian can provide pills to rid the dog of worms. Fleas are common pests in summer, and transmit tapeworms to dogs. Comb fleas off your dog, or dust it with flea powder. Use only flea powders made for dogs, or the animal may become poisoned by licking its coat. Dogs also may suffer from skin diseases such as mange.

Puppies often suffer fits, or convulsions. If a puppy has a fit, it should be shut in a box so that it cannot injure itself. A fit is not a disease, but a sign that something is wrong. A veterinarian should examine the dog.

Laws. Most cities and states have laws that require a dog owner to buy a license for his dog. Many communities also have laws that require dogs to be leashed outdoors. Laws usually make the dog owner responsible for any damage caused by his pet.

Other laws protect dogs, and punish persons who beat, starve, or are otherwise cruel to them. These laws have been passed largely through the work of such groups as the Society for the Prevention of Cruelty to Animals and other humane societies.

How to Train Your Dog

Dogs need to be taught good manners just as children do. Training makes a dog easier to care for, cleaner in the house, and safer on the street. An untrained dog that roams outdoors and barks constantly can annoy an entire neighborhood.

Housebreaking a puppy should start as soon as you bring it home. Many animal experts recommend using the *den-bed* method to housebreak a puppy. This method is explained in detail in the WORLD BOOK article on PET (House Training).

Obedience Training begins with teaching your dog to walk on a leash, to come when called, to sit, to lie down, and to heel. Training should start when your puppy is 8 weeks old. Give a 15-minute lesson several times a day. Use kind words and pats, and reward your dog when it does something right. Do not begin a

WORLD BOOK photo

A Daily Brushing keeps a dog's coat clean and free of loose hair. Brushing also helps stimulate the animal's skin.

WORLD BOOK photo

An Obedient Dog is a pleasure to take for a walk. It sits on command and walks without straining or pulling on its leash.

working

Shetland Sheep Dog

Ira Haas, Photo Researchers

Welsh Corgi (Pembroke)

Siberian Husky

German Shepherd

Puli

Mastiff

Great Dane

Old English Sheep Dog

Saint Bernard

Three Lions

Samoyed

Boxer

dogs

Newfoundland

Collie

Doberman Pinscher

Standard Schnauzer

Alaskan Malamute

J. Julius Fanta, Photo Researchers

Great Pyrenees

COMMON SAYINGS ABOUT DOGS

Barking dogs never bite describes people who sound more dangerous than they really are.

Barking up the wrong tree means to look for something in the wrong place.

Dog in a manger describes a person who keeps others from using something that he himself cannot use. It comes from Aesop's fable of a dog that crawled into a manger of hay and prevented a horse from eating, even though dogs do not eat hay.

Every dog has his day is an expression used when something pleasant happens to a person, especially one who has been having bad luck.

Let sleeping dogs lie means to leave a situation undisturbed.

Tail wagging the dog means, for example, that an unimportant member of a group is actually directing everyone's activities.

You can't teach an old dog new tricks is often used to describe a person who refuses to change his ways, or to learn a new way of doing something.

second exercise until the first one has been learned. Be patient but firm. The dog must understand that a command means instant obedience.

Put a collar around your dog's neck before training it to walk on a leash. After the dog gets used to wearing a collar, take it out walking with a leash. Your dog will probably fight the leash at first. But it will soon learn that the leash means a walk. You may also want to teach your dog to *heel*, or walk by your side. To do this, hold the dog at your left side on a short leash. Then walk forward swiftly. Strike the dog lightly on the nose with a folded newspaper if it tries to run in front of you. At the same time give the command, "heel."

To teach your dog to come when called, fasten a light rope about 20 to 30 feet (6 to 9 meters) long to its collar. Let the dog romp at the full length of the cord for a while, and then call it. If your pet does not come, pull it toward you. Repeat this until the dog learns to come on command. To teach the dog to sit, hold it near you on a short leash and order it to sit. Hold the leash tightly to keep its head up. At the same time, push down on the animal's hindquarters until it is in a sitting position.

To break your dog of the habit of jumping up on people, bring your knee up against its chest when it leaps up to greet you. At the same time, repeat the order, "down." Your knee may knock the dog over, but this will teach it to stay down when told to do so. Puppies often howl and whine at night. A ticking clock placed next to a puppy's box will often keep him quiet.

Tricks. Many people enjoy teaching their pets to shake hands, play dead, roll over, sit up, and do other tricks. In general, follow the same methods to teach a dog tricks as you would to teach it obedience commands. For example, to teach a dog to shake hands, pick up one of its front paws, and at the same time say "shake hands." Keep repeating this until the dog learns to offer a paw when you ask it to shake hands.

Dog Shows. Hundreds of dog shows are held in the United States every year. The American Kennel Club licenses judges, and supervises most of these shows. They are usually called *bench shows*, because the dogs are exhibited in stalls mounted on benches. A dog must be registered with the AKC to be entered in such contests. The Westminster Kennel Club of New York City stages one of the most important shows on the second Monday and Tuesday in February at Madison Square Garden. This show, held every year since 1877, is one of the oldest regular sporting events in the United States.

The judges of a dog show pick the best dog of each breed. Next, the judges choose the best dog of its group

Grooming keeps a dog's coat clean and free of insects. The Dandie Dinmont terrier shown at the left is being brushed before being exhibited in a dog show. Dog shows, *below*, feature purebred dogs that are judged on appearance and behavior.

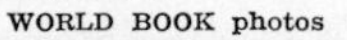
WORLD BOOK photos

RECOGNIZED BREEDS OF PUREBRED DOGS

SPORTING GROUP

Breed	Country and probable date of origin	Average weight in lbs.	in kg
American Water Spaniel	United States 1800's	25-45	11-20
Brittany Spaniel	France, 1800's	30-40	14-18
Chesapeake Bay Retriever	United States, 1800's	55-75	25-34
Clumber Spaniel	England, 1800's	35-65	15-29
Cocker Spaniel	England, 1800's	22-28	10-13
Curly-Coated Retriever	England, 1800's	60-70	27-32
English Cocker Spaniel	England, 1800's	26-34	12-15
English Setter	England, 1500's	50-70	23-32
English Springer Spaniel	England, 1800's	49-55	22-25
Field Spaniel	England, 1700's	35-50	16-23
Flat-Coated Retriever	England, 1800's	60-70	27-32
German Short-Haired Pointer	Germany, about 1900	45-70	20-32
German Wire-Haired Pointer	Germany, 1870	55-65	25-29
Golden Retriever	Scotland, 1870	60-75	27-34
Gordon Setter	Scotland, 1600's	45-80	20-36
Griffon (Wire-Haired Pointing)	The Netherlands and France, 1800's	50-60	23-27
Irish Setter	Ireland, 1700's	60-70	27-32
Irish Water Spaniel	Ireland, 1800's	45-65	20-29
Labrador Retriever	Newfoundland, 1800's	55-75	25-34
Pointer	Spain, Portugal, Eastern Europe, and England, about 1650	45-60	20-27
Sussex Spaniel	England, 1800's	35-45	16-20
Vizsla	Hungary, 1000's	50	23
Weimaraner	Germany, 1800's	55-85	25-39
Welsh Springer Spaniel	Wales, 1700's	40	18

HOUND GROUP

Breed	Country and probable date of origin	Average weight in lbs.	in kg
Afghan Hound	Sinai Peninsula, Egypt, 4000-3000 B.C.	50-60	23-27
American Foxhound	United States, 1600's	60-70	27-32
Basenji	Africa, 3400 B.C.	22-24	10-11
Basset Hound	France, 1600's	25-45	11-20
Beagle	England, Wales, 1600's	18-30	8-14
Bloodhound	The Middle East, 100 B.C.	80-110	36-50
Borzoi	Russia, 1600's	60-105	27-48
Coonhound (Black and Tan)	England, 1700's	50-60	23-27
Dachshund	Germany, 1700's	5-20	2-9
English Foxhound	England, 1600's	60-75	27-34
Greyhound	Egypt, 4000-3500 B.C.	60-70	27-32
Harrier	France, 1000's	40-50	18-23
Irish Wolfhound	Ireland, 400's	105-140	48-64
Norwegian Elkhound	Norway, 5000–4000 B.C.	50	23
Otter Hound	England, 1300's	65	29
Rhodesian Ridgeback	Africa, 1700's	65-75	29-34
Saluki	Egypt, 4000 B.C. or earlier	60	27
Scottish Deerhound	Scotland, 1500's	75-110	34-50
Whippet	England, 1800's	18-23	8-10

TOY GROUP

Breed	Country and probable date of origin	Average weight in lbs.	in kg
Affenpinscher	Europe, 1700's	7-8	3-4
Brussels Griffon	Belgium, 1600's	8-10	4-6
Chihuahua	Mexico, 1500's or earlier	1-6	0.5-3
English Toy Spaniel	Japan or China, Ancient Times	9-12	4-5
Italian Greyhound	Italy, 100 B.C.	6-10	3-5
Japanese Spaniel	China, Ancient Times	7	3
Maltese	Malta, 800 B.C. or earlier	4-6	2-3
Miniature Pinscher	Germany, 1700's	6-10	3-5
Papillon	Spain, 1500's	5-11	2-5
Pekingese	China, 700's	6-10	3-5
Pomeranian	Pomerania, Poland, 1800's	3-7	1-3
Pug	China, 1700's	14-18	6-8
Shih Tzu	China, Ancient Times	12-15	5-9
Silky Terrier	Australia, about 1900	8-10	4-5
Yorkshire Terrier	England, 1800's	4-8	2-4

Source: American Kennel Club.

WORKING GROUP

Breed	Country and probable date of origin	Average weight in lbs.	in kg
Akita	Japan, 1600's	80-120	36-54
Alaskan Malamute	Alaska, 1000 B.C. or earlier	75-85	34-39
Belgian Malinois	Belgium, 1800's	50-55	23-25
Belgian Sheep Dog	Belgium, 1800's	55-60	25-27
Belgian Tervuren	Belgium, about 1880	55	25
Bernese Mountain Dog	Switzerland, 100 B.C.	50-75	23-34
Bouvier des Flandres	Flanders, 1800's	70	32
Boxer	Germany, 1800's	60-75	27-34
Briard	France, 1100's	70-80	32-36
Bullmastiff	England, 1800's	100-130	45-59
Collie	Scotland, 1600's	50-75	23-34
Doberman Pinscher	Germany, 1800's	60-75	27-34
German Shepherd Dog	Germany, 1800's	60-85	27-39
Giant Schnauzer	Bavaria, 1600-1800	75	34
Great Dane	Germany, 1500's	120-150	54-68
Great Pyrenees	France, 1800-1000 B.C.	90-125	41-57
Komondor	Hungary, 900's	90	41
Kuvasz	Tibet, 1200's	70	32
Mastiff	England, 55 B.C. or earlier	165-185	75-84
Newfoundland	Newfoundland, 1600's	110-150	50-68
Old English Sheep Dog	England, 1800's	50-65	23-29
Puli	Hungary, 1000's	30-35	14-16
Rottweiler	Germany, about A.D. 50	80-90	36-41
Saint Bernard	Switzerland, 1600's	165-180	75-82
Samoyed	Northern Siberia, 1000 B.C. or earlier	35-60	16-27
Schnauzer (Standard)	Germany, before 1400	35-40	16-18
Shetland Sheep Dog	Shetland Islands, 1600's	16-24	7-11
Siberian Husky	Siberia, 1000 B.C. or earlier	35-60	16-27
Welsh Corgi (Cardigan)	Wales, 1200 B.C. or earlier	15-25	7-11
Welsh Corgi (Pembroke)	Wales, 1107	18-24	8-11

TERRIER GROUP

Breed	Country and probable date of origin	Average weight in lbs.	in kg
Airedale Terrier	England, 1800's	40-50	18-23
American Staffordshire Terrier	United States, early 1900's	35-50	16-23
Australian Terrier	Australia, 1885	12-14	5-6
Bedlington Terrier	England, 1800's	17-23	8-10
Border Terrier	Scottish-English border, 1700's	11½-15½	5-7
Bull Terrier	England, 1800's	30-60	14-27
Cairn Terrier	Scotland, 1700's	13-14	6
Dandie Dinmont Terrier	England and Scotland, about 1700	18-24	8-11
Fox Terrier	England, 1700's	15-19	7-9
Irish Terrier	Ireland, 1700's	25-27	11-12
Kerry Blue Terrier	Ireland, 1800's	30-40	14-18
Lakeland Terrier	England, 1800's	15-17	7-8
Manchester Terrier	England, 1800's	5-22	2-10
Norwich Terrier	England, 1880	10-15	5-7
Schnauzer (Miniature)	Germany, 1800's	15	7
Scottish Terrier	Scotland, 1800's	18-22	8-10
Sealyham Terrier	Wales, 1800's	20-21	9-10
Skye Terrier	Scotland, 1600's	25	11
Soft-Coated Wheaten Terrier	Ireland, 1900's	35-45	16-20
Staffordshire Bull Terrier	England, 1800's	35	16
Welsh Terrier	Wales, 1700's	20	9
West Highland White Terrier	Scotland, 1600's	13-19	6-9

NONSPORTING GROUP

Breed	Country and probable date of origin	Average weight in lbs.	in kg
Bichon Frise	Mediterranean, 200 B.C.	12-15	5-7
Boston Terrier	Boston, Mass., 1870	12-25	5-11
Bulldog	England, 1200's	40-50	18-23
Chow Chow	China, 150 B.C.	50-60	23-27
Dalmatian	Dalmatia, Austria, 1700's	40-50	18-23
French Bulldog	France, 1400's	18-28	8-13
Keeshond	Holland, 1500's	35-40	16-18
Lhasa Apso	Tibet, about 1100	15	7
Poodle	Germany, 1500's	7-55	3-25
Schipperke	Belgium, 1600's	15	7
Tibetan Terrier	Tibet, about 50 B.C.	22-23	10

Each breed listed in this table has a separate article in WORLD BOOK.

terriers

Bull Terrier

Airedale Terrier

American Staffordshire Terrier

Welsh Terrier

Kerry Blue Terrier

Miniature Schnauzer

Fox Terrier

Manchester Terrier

Scottish Terrier

Irish Terrier

Dandie Dinmont Terrier

Photo Library

Bedlington Terrier

Skye Terrier

Camera Clix

Sealyham Terrier

Cairn Terrier

Pug

Miniature Pinscher

Pekingese

Ylla, Rapho-Guillumette

Chihuahua

toy dogs

Maltese

Pomeranian

Brussels Griffon

Yorkshire Terrier

Camera Clix

in each of the six main groups of dogs. From these winners, the judges name the best dog in the show. Judges rate a dog on such points as color, posture, the condition of its coat and teeth, the shape and size of its body, and the way it moves about.

Field Trials test the hunting ability of sporting dogs and hounds. In bird-dog field trials, judges rate the dogs on such points as endurance, ability to scent game, obedience to a handler's commands, and the thoroughness with which the dogs cover the hunting area. In retriever field trials, judges rate the dogs on their ability to find quickly and return without damage the birds that hunters have shot.

Other events for dogs include sheep-dog trials, obedience trials, sled-dog racing, and coursing and racing contests. Sheep-dog trials test the ability of the animals to herd flocks of sheep. In obedience trials, judges rate dogs on their ability to obey commands. Coursing contests test how well greyhounds can run down rabbits.

History

All dogs are probably descended from an animal called *Tomarctus*. This animal lived about 15 million years ago. It probably looked much like a wolf. It had a wedge-shaped head; long, low body; thick coat; and long, furry tail. Descendants of Tomarctus developed into wolves, jackals, coyotes, foxes, and other wild dogs that spread throughout the world.

Stone Age people who lived in Europe 10,000 to 20,000 years ago tamed dogs to help them track game. About 8,000 years ago, the ancient Egyptians raised greyhoundlike dogs to hunt antelope. Several thousand years later, the Egyptians developed Saluki hunting dogs. These dogs are probably the oldest known breed (see SALUKI). North American Indians tamed dogs as early as 4,000 years ago. The ancient Greeks raised large lion-hunting dogs called mastiffs. The Romans kept dogs as pets, and also used them to hunt and to herd sheep. The ancient Chinese bred watchdogs and hunting dogs.

In the Middle Ages, from about A.D. 400 to 1400, knights kept hounds for hunting deer, elk, and other game. English sportsmen in the 1500's developed the bulldog for the sport of *baiting* (fighting) bulls. The various breeds of dogs gradually became fixed in size, color, and the ability to perform certain tasks. People named the breeds after the game they hunted, the work they performed, and the places where they developed.

Scientific Classification. All dogs belong to the dog family, *Canidae*. Tamed dogs are in the genus *Canis*, species *C. familiaris*.

JOSEPHINE Z. RINE

Related Articles in WORLD BOOK include:

RECOGNIZED BREEDS OF PUREBRED DOGS

There is a separate article for each breed listed in the *table* with this article.

OTHER DOGS

Eskimo Dog	Police Dog	Toy Manchester Terrier
Foxhound	Sheep Dog	Wire-Haired Fox Terrier
Guide Dog	Spitz	Wolfhound
Hound	Terrier	
Mexican Hairless	Toy Dog	

DOG FAMILY

Coyote | Dingo | Fox | Jackal | Wolf

OTHER RELATED ARTICLES

Breeding	Insurance (picture: Dogs Can Be Insured)	Pet
Dog Racing	Pedigree	Society for the Prevention of Cruelty to Animals
Dog Sled		Terhune, Albert P.
Humane Society		

Outline

I. How Dogs Help Man

II. Breeds of Dogs
- A. Sporting Dogs
- B. Hounds
- C. Working Dogs
- D. Terriers
- E. Toy Dogs
- F. Nonsporting Dogs
- G. Other Breeds
- H. Crossbreds and Mongrels
- I. Wild Dogs

III. The Body of the Dog
- A. Coat
- B. Bones
- C. Nose
- D. Mouth
- E. Ears
- F. Eyes
- G. Body Functions
- H. Life History
- I. Instincts and Intelligence

IV. How to Care for Your Dog
- A. Feeding
- B. Shelter
- C. Grooming
- D. Diseases
- E. Laws

V. How to Train Your Dog
- A. Housebreaking
- B. Obedience Training
- C. Tricks
- D. Dog Shows
- E. Field Trials

VI. History

Questions

What is the only dog that cannot bark?

What is probably the oldest known breed of dog? Where did this breed originate?

Why do dogs turn around before lying down? Why do they gobble their food?

What are the six main groups of purebred dogs?

What do you know in advance about a purebred dog that you do not know about a mongrel?

Why do most dogs have two coats?

How long does the average dog live?

Why does a dog *pant* when it is overheated?

FAMOUS DOGS IN HISTORY AND LEGEND

Aibe was a wolfhound famed for its hunting ability. The King of Connacht in Ireland offered 6,000 cows for Aibe in the 1100's.

Argos, or ARGUS, Ulysses' hunting dog, was the only creature to recognize the Greek hero when he returned home disguised as a beggar after 20 years of adventure.

Balto, an Eskimo dog, led a dog team that carried diphtheria serum 650 miles (1,050 kilometers) through an Alaskan blizzard from Nenana to Nome in 1925.

Barry, a Saint Bernard, rescued 40 persons when they became lost in the snows of Switzerland's Saint Bernard Pass about 1800.

Caesar, a terrier, was the pet of King Edward VII of Great Britain. He walked ahead of kings and princes in his master's funeral procession in 1910.

Cerberus, the three-headed dog of Greek mythology, guarded the gates to the underworld (see CERBERUS).

Fala, a Scottish terrier, became famous as the devoted pet of President Franklin Delano Roosevelt.

Greyfriars Bobby, a Skye terrier, accompanied his Scotch master to Edinburgh every market day. After the man died in 1858, Bobby lived about 10 years by his grave until he died at the age of 14.

Igloo, a fox terrier, was the special pet of Admiral Richard E. Byrd. He flew with Byrd on flights over the North and South poles. See also ANTARCTICA (picture).

Laika became the world's first space traveler. Russian scientists sent the small animal aloft in an artificial earth satellite in 1957. See also SPACE TRAVEL (picture).

DOG-DAY CICADA. See CICADA.

DOG DAYS are periods of hot, sticky, uncomfortable summer weather. In the middle latitudes and subtropics of the Northern Hemisphere, these periods occur most frequently between early July and late August. Exactly when they occur and how long they last varies somewhat from place to place and year to year.

The ancient Greeks named the dog days. The hot, dry Greek summer began about the same time that the dog star, Sirius, rose with the sun. JOHN E. KUTZBACH

DOG RACING is a sport in which dogs chase a mechanical rabbit that runs around a race track on an electric rail. The track is oval, and usually is about 550 yards (503 meters) long. An American, Oliver B. Smith, invented this type of dog racing in 1919.

Eight dogs usually compete in a dog race. The races usually feature two breeds of dogs. They are the greyhound and the whippet (see GREYHOUND; WHIPPET).

The sport is popular in Florida, Massachusetts, and other areas in the United States, as well as in Great Britain. The annual Waterloo Cup race, held in Liverpool, England, is perhaps the most important dog race.

In ancient times, dogs were trained to race after live game. This sport is called *coursing*. The Saluki, a popular racing dog in ancient Egypt, is still used in some European dog races (see SALUKI). FRED RUSSELL

DOG SHOW. See DOG (Dog Shows).

DOG SLED is used for transportation in such Arctic regions as Alaska, northern Canada, and Siberia. Dog sleds are often the only means of carrying supplies on the ground in these areas during winter. They are usually wooden and are from 6 to 13 feet (2 to 4 meters) long and from 12 to 24 inches (30 to 61 centimeters) wide. They have wooden or metal runners.

The stocky, hardy dogs harnessed to the sleds can move over ice and snow easily because of their size and agility. Dog teams generally include from 7 to 10 dogs. Each team has a lead dog that guides the others. It obeys the driver's commands. In an average day, a dog team can pull a load twice the team's weight about 25 miles (40 kilometers), at a speed of from 2 to 5 miles (3 to 8 kilometers) an hour. Sled dogs weigh from 50 to 100 pounds (23 to 45 kilograms). One team can haul more than 1,000 pounds (450 kilograms). ELMER HARP, JR.

See also ESKIMO (Transportation; pictures); ESKIMO DOG; MANITOBA (Annual Events); SLED.

DOG STAR. See SIRIUS.

Hugh Spencer

The Dogbane Blossoms grow on the ends of thin spreading branches. The flower has the shape of a tiny bell.

DOGBANE is the name of 11 closely related plants. They grow in the north temperate zone, mostly in the United States and Canada. All the dogbanes are poisonous green plants which contain a milky bitter juice. But they are not very dangerous because most grazing animals dislike the bitter juice and will not eat them.

A common dogbane called the *spreading dogbane*, or *honeybloom*, has light-green leaves and clusters of pale pink flowers. It has a bitter root which physicians sometimes use to cause vomiting. Another dogbane called the *Canada* or *Indian hemp* has greenish-white flowers that grow in clusters. These clusters are followed by long, slender pods. The bark of this dogbane produces a long, strong white fiber that is used to make nets.

Scientific Classification. Dogbanes belong to the dogbane family, *Apocynaceae*. The spreading dogbane is genus *Apocynum*, species *A. androsaemifolium*. The Indian hemp is *A. cannabinum*. HAROLD NORMAN MOLDENKE

DOGE, *dohj*, was the title of the rulers of Venice from 697 to 1797. *Doge* comes from the Latin word *dux*, meaning *leader*. Genoa also had doges.

The doges of Venice were elected for life from among the richest and most powerful families. They enjoyed almost absolute power in governmental, military, and church affairs until 1032. Then they tried unsuccess-

City of Miami News Bureau

Racing Greyhounds round a turn at one of the four dog tracks in Miami, Fla. Dog racing attracts many fans during the Miami racing season, which runs from November until summer.

May, Black Star

The Doges' Palace, built during the Middle Ages, was the home of medieval rulers of Venice. A striking example of early Italian architecture, it borders the Canale di San Marco.

fully to make the office hereditary. After this the doges were closely supervised. In 1310, the doge became subordinate to the Council of Ten, and from then on this *oligarchy* (small, powerful group) really ruled Venice. The Council ruled Venice until 1797, when Napoleon suppressed the Republic of Venice. He abolished the Council and the *dogate* (office of the doges) in the same year. WILLIAM H. MAEHL

See also GENOA; VENICE (History; picture: Venice).

DOGFISH are small sharks. They live in temperate and warm seas. The *spiny dogfish* has spines in front of the *dorsal* (back) fins, but the *smooth dogfish* lacks these spines. Dogfish have no bones. Their skeleton is made of cartilage. They seldom grow more than 3 feet (91 centimeters) long. Americans rarely eat dogfish, but Europeans consider the fish an important food. Dogfish skin can be dried and used to polish wood. Fishermen once caught dogfish for their vitamin-rich livers, but the manufacture of synthetic vitamins ended the need.

The *bowfin*, or *mudfish*, is sometimes called dogfish. It lives in the rivers of the United States and Canada, but it is not related to the salt-water dogfish. The bowfin lays its eggs in a nest. See BOWFIN.

Scientific Classification. Spiny dogfishes belong to the family *Squalidae*. The common spiny dogfish is classified in the genus *Squalus*, species *S. acanthias*. Smooth dogfishes belong to the family *Carcharhinidae*. They are classified as *Mustelus canis*. LEONARD P. SCHULTZ

State of Calif. Dept. of Fish and Game

The Spiny Dogfish Is a Member of the Shark Family.

See also LIFE (table: Length of Life of Animals).

DOGGER BANK is a large area of shallow water located in the middle of the North Sea between England and Denmark. It is a famous fishing ground, chiefly because the water is only 50 to 120 feet (15 to 37 meters) deep. In 1915, the British navy won an important battle against the German fleet off Dogger Bank. Undersea exploration in the area is expected to uncover reserves of petroleum and natural gas. JOHN W. WEBB

DOGTOOTH. See TEETH (Permanent Teeth).

DOGTOOTH VIOLET, or **ADDER'S-TONGUE,** is an attractive spring wildflower of the eastern United States and Canada. It is not really a violet, but belongs to the lily family. It breaks through the ground early, and catches the sunshine before leaves appear on the trees and darken the ground. Dogtooth violet has been oddly misnamed because it does not resemble a dog's tooth. The young shoots are sharply pointed. The two smooth, grayish-green leaves, mottled with brown, spring from the bulb. The yellow, white, or pink bell-shaped flower nods on a stem 6 to 12 inches (15 to 30 centimeters) long. The flower has a faint fragrance. Dogtooth violet may be found in early spring along the banks of brooks. It is sometimes called *trout lily*.

Scientific Classification. The common dogtooth violet belongs to the lily family, *Liliaceae*. It is genus *Erythronium*, species *E. dens-canis*. GEORGE H. M. LAWRENCE

DOGWOOD is the common name for a group of shrubs and small trees. About 40 kinds of dogwood exist. Fourteen kinds are native to the United States.

The best known is the *flowering dogwood*. It has four large whitish *bracts* (modified leaves) beneath its small, greenish-white flowers. The bright-red *drupes* (fruits) usually have two seeds. The leaves have parallel veins, and are quite rich in calcium. The neat bark pattern and the gray, urn-shaped flower buds make the dogwood an attractive winter tree.

Flowering dogwood rarely grows more than 40 feet (12 meters) high or 18 inches (46 centimeters) in diameter. Its wood is hard and heavy. The dogwood is the

J. Horace McFarland

The Flowering Dogwood blooms in early spring before the leaves appear. The blossom is really a tiny cluster of flowers surrounded by four white leaves that look like petals.

state flower of North Carolina and Virginia, and the provincial flower of British Columbia.

Scientific Classification. Dogwoods belong to the dogwood family, *Cornaceae*. Flowering dogwood is genus *Cornus*, species *C. florida*. T. EWALD MAKI

See also LEAF (picture: Kinds of Tree Leaves); TREE (Familiar Broadleaf and Needleleaf Trees [picture]).

DOHA, *DOH huh* (pop. 80,000), is the capital, largest city, and chief port of Qatar, a country on the Persian Gulf. Doha lies on the east coast of this Arab nation. For location, see QATAR (map).

Doha was a minor fishing port until the 1950's, when Qatar's rapidly developing oil wealth caused the city to change greatly. Doha became the commercial center of Qatar, and its population grew quickly. Many Arabs from nearby countries moved to Doha.

The city began a modernization program in the 1950's. This program included construction of an international airport and of a new harbor to serve ocean-going ships. Air-conditioned apartment and government buildings, hospitals, hotels, and schools replaced many of Doha's mud-walled houses. ROBERT GERAN LANDEN

DOHENY, EDWARD L. See TEAPOT DOME.

DOHNÁNYI, *DOH nahn yih,* **ERNST VON,** or ERNÖ (1877-1960), a Hungarian composer and conductor, became one of the outstanding pianists of his time. He was appointed director of the Budapest Conservatory in 1919, and director of Hungarian radio in 1931. He became noted for his piano compositions, including *Ruralia Hungarica*, *Four Rhapsodies*, and *Humoresques*. Dohnányi was born in Pressburg (now Bratislava in Czechoslovakia). In 1949, he moved to Tallahassee, Fla., where he became a professor of music at Florida State University. JOYCE MICHELL

DOISY, EDWARD ADELBERT (1893-), an American chemist, determined the nature of vitamin K, which helps the liver produce prothrombin, one of the clotting factors in blood. He isolated and synthesized pure vitamin K_1. Its use saves many lives each year. Doisy shared the 1943 Nobel prize for this work and for the isolation of the female sex hormone. He was born in Hume, Ill., and was graduated from the University of Illinois and Harvard University. HERBERT S. RHINESMITH

See also VITAMIN (Vitamin K).

DOLBEAR, *DOHL beer,* **AMOS E.** (1837-1910), an American physicist and inventor, might be known today as the inventor of the telephone and radio, if he had only had better luck. In 1864, he made a "talking machine" much like the telephone Alexander Graham Bell patented in 1876. Dolbear insisted the idea was his. After a long, bitter court fight, Bell was declared the true inventor. Dolbear produced radio waves in 1882, but the discovery is usually credited to the German scientist Heinrich R. Hertz in 1888. Dolbear was born in Norwich, Conn. IRA M. FREEMAN

DOLDRUMS, *DOLE drums,* is a belt of calms, light breezes, or sudden squalls near the equator, mainly over the oceans. Meteorologists call it the *intertropic convergence zone*. The name *doldrums* means *listlessness*. Seamen were the first to use this name for the region near the equator because their sailing ships often were *becalmed* (unable to sail) there.

In the doldrums, the air moves upward, causing sudden thunderstorms and gusty winds. The region is one of the rainiest in the world. It is also dangerous to airplanes because the turbulent clouds build up higher than most aircraft can fly. WALTER J. SAUCIER

See also CALMS, REGIONS OF; HORSE LATITUDES.

DOLE. See UNEMPLOYMENT INSURANCE.

DOLE is the family name of two cousins who helped develop Hawaii.

Sanford Ballard Dole (1844-1926) led a group that helped make Hawaii a United States territory. In 1893, he took part in a movement that deposed Queen Liliuokalani. He then headed the provisional government.

Dole became president of the Republic of Hawaii in 1894 when President Grover Cleveland opposed annexation. The United States annexed Hawaii in 1898, after Cleveland left office. Dole served as the first territorial governor from 1900 to 1903, and as U.S. district judge in Hawaii from 1903 to 1916. He was born in Honolulu.

James Drummond Dole (1877-1958) founded Hawaii's canned pineapple industry. Dole started the Hawaiian Pineapple Company which sold the first commercially canned pineapple in 1903. In 1932, he helped develop pineapple by-products, including pineapple juice. Born in Boston, Mass., he moved to Hawaii in 1899. DONALD D. JOHNSON

DOLE, VINCENT. See METHADONE.

DOLIN, ANTON (1904-), became the first internationally famous English male dancer. He was partner to many great ballerinas, particularly Alicia Markova. Together they were key figures in starting English ballet. Dolin helped form and develop many companies, including what is now The Royal Ballet, the London Festival Ballet, and the American Ballet Theatre. He also led his own touring companies.

Dolin was born Sydney Francis Patrick Chippendall Healey-Kay in Sussex, England. He became the only English-born male dancer to star with the famous Diaghilev ballet company. Dolin enjoyed his greatest triumphs with Alicia Markova in his version of *Giselle* in the United States. As a choreographer, Dolin composed his best-known ballet, *Le Pas de Quatre*, for Miss Markova. P. W. MANCHESTER

Anton Dolin danced in *Les Sylphides* with two famous ballerinas, Alicia Alonso, *left*, and Dame Alicia Markova, *right*.

Fred Fehl

DOLL

Ideal Toy Corp.

DOLL. In almost every part of the world, children play with dolls. Dolls are loved the world around. They may be made of anything from cooky dough and candy to cloth and rubber. They may be made in factories and bought in shops, or they may be made at home and cost nothing.

The doll is a favorite playmate of most girls. All the secrets of its owner are poured into its ears. Girls like to play grownup with the cuddly child dolls of today. They sew for their dolls and keep them neat and clean. Singing to them and rocking them to sleep is part of the fun of playing mother. Girls sometimes pretend their dolls are sick, so that they may nurse them.

Dolls are the playthings of rich and poor alike. They comfort the sick and amuse the well. They are the hobby of young and old. Even boys may like dolls that look like clowns, policemen, or Indians.

Costume dolls from foreign lands show how other peoples dress. From old dolls, we can find out how people of long ago lived and what they wore.

The word *doll* was first used about 1750. There was no such word in earlier days. The dolls of different lands were called by different names. In the American colonies they were called puppets, babes or babies, and "little ladies." Dolls at that time were usually made to look like women or girls. In an ancient language of India, the only word for dolls meant *little daughter*.

Dolls of Early Days

Nobody is sure who made the first doll. Perhaps somebody found a stone or root or piece of wood that looked like a human being. The first dolls were believed to bring good luck to their owners. No child was allowed to touch the dolls because they were thought to have magic powers.

Good-Luck Dolls were supposed to bring rain or food when they were needed, to make goats give more milk, or to help win wars. Some people thought dolls could even make sick people well. Some tribes who believed this made wooden dolls that looked like ugly elves. They were supposed to frighten people. Only the medicine men, or *witch doctors*, were allowed to handle them.

Paddle Dolls are perhaps the oldest dolls. They were made by the Egyptians three thousand years ago and may be seen today in the British Museum in London. They are called paddle dolls because they were made from thin pieces of board carved in the shape of canoe paddles. Lines were carved and painted on them to look like clothes. Hair was made of short strings of beads. The figures were made without legs so they could not run away. When an important person died in old Egypt, many such doll figures were buried with him. They looked like barbers, bakers, cooks, clowns, maids, actors, and musicians. They were supposed to be friends and servants for the dead person in the spirit world.

Doll-Size Figures have been found among old Roman and Greek tombs. Most of these are also believed to have been funeral figures. They were usually made of wood or clay of some kind. The oldest-known Greek play doll is a clay rattle in the form of a woman. The Greek or Roman girl often played with her dolls until shortly before her marriage. Then the Greek girl would

UNUSUAL DOLLS

SACRED INDIAN DOLL

The "Kachina" doll was used by the Hopi Indians who lived in the southwestern part of the United States. From it, and from the designs on its clothes, the Hopi children learned about the ancient spirits of the tribe.

EGGSHELL DOLLS

Eggshell dolls are often used as Easter favors. Cotton is stuck in the empty end of the eggshell for hair. The eyes, nose, and mouth are painted on, and the bottom end is glued.

CORNHUSK DOLL

Pioneer and Indian boys and girls were very clever in making cornhusk dolls. They braided the cornhusks for hair and for arms. They stuck bright bird feathers in the braids.

SPOOL DOLL

Big and little spools are strung together to make a loose-jointed doll. A face is drawn on the top spool, and other trimmings may also be added.

WITCH DOLL

The "Kalifa" doll is found in the Egyptian Sudan. Its body is made from the stalk of a plant. The head is of black wax and beads are used for eyes.

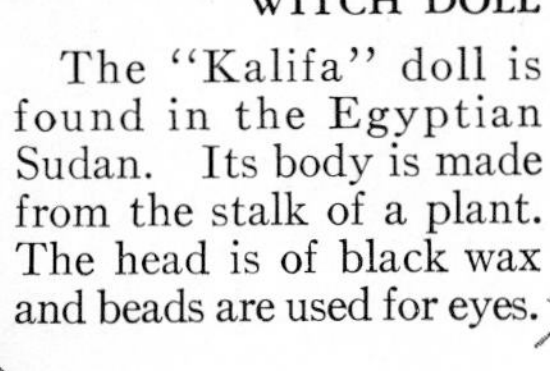

TUMBLE DOLL

A tumble doll is weighted at the bottom. Push this doll over and it bobs up again. The Chinese invented the tumble doll. The Chinese name for it means "struck, not falling."

CRAB-CLAW DOLL

A crab-claw doll is made from the claw of a hard crab. For a headdress, seagull or other bright bird feathers are put in the open end of the claw.

COSTUME DOLLS FROM MANY LANDS

Different countries, different dolls! Katrinka of Holland wears wooden shoes and a stiff-starched cap. Sandy of Scotland has kilts, a bonnet, a plaid over his shoulder, and a sporran (fur pouch). Greta of Sweden has long puffed sleeves and a striped apron. Sonia of Russia wears a bright tunic and hat. Dolores, the Spanish senorita, is very gay with shawl, high comb, and red rose. Little Butterfly of Japan has on her best silk kimono, ready for the Festival of Dolls.

The Eskimo doll is clothed in fur-lined parka. Heidi of Switzerland, in her flowered apron and puffy sleeves, is in holiday dress. Pedro, in his sombrero (hat) and sash is from Mexico. Nanette of France wears a dainty dress and wooden shoes. Little Eagle, the Indian doll, looks brave in beads and feathers. Ling Fu, the Chinese doll, is in holiday clothes of silk cap, trousers, and colorful tunic. Such dolls as these are loved the world around.

leave them on the altar of Artemis, the goddess of unmarried girls. The Roman girl took them to the altar of Diana. The girls did this to show that they were no longer interested in childish things. The best Roman dolls were made of clay. Strips of carved wood served for legs and arms. Even in these early times, the limbs of some dolls could be moved by pulling strings.

Dolls have also been used by the Christian church. Not so many years ago they were used to take the parts of saints in church plays. Even today, at Christmastime, dolls made to look like Mary, Joseph, and baby Jesus may be seen in the churches and homes of many lands.

Fashion Dolls were first used in France about six hundred years ago. These were large dolls dressed in the latest fashions. These "fashion babies" were sent to other lands to show what fine clothes the French could make. They took the place of fashion magazines. They had wardrobes complete even to hats, shoes, and undergarments. Only the rich could afford these dolls. But, strangely enough, these beautifully dressed dolls had the crudest kinds of bodies. Their legs were often no more than a pair of sticks.

Kings and queens sent these fashion dolls as gifts to one another. About 1390, the queen of England received a group of French dolls dressed in the rich costumes of court ladies. Two fashion dolls which were sent to King Gustavus Adolphus of Sweden about three hundred years ago may still be seen at the University of Uppsala in Sweden.

Later, fashion dolls 40 inches (100 centimeters) tall were sent to far-off India to show the women how to wear their English clothes. Before the dolls were sent, the people of India had been folding up their English-made wraps and wearing them as head coverings. Fashion dolls also made a great stir among the well-to-do in the American colonies. Newspapers announced their arrival and told what it would cost to see them.

Pantin Dolls were popular in France about two hundred years ago. These pasteboard dolls were somewhat like the jumping jacks or puppets of today. For years men and women played with them no matter where they were, in their homes, on the streets, in their shops, and at parties. By pulling strings, the French made their funny pantins dance and act.

Dolls in America

Indian Dolls were usually made from the skins of animals. The skins were sewed together with strong strips of leather. Then they were stuffed with moss, animal hair, or dried grass. Their clothes were made of soft deerskin, and they wore necklaces and bracelets of tiny beads, shells, or seeds. Wigs made from the hair of goats, buffaloes, or horses were sewed to the tops of their leather heads. Other Indian dolls were made from cornhusks, grass, or apples. As the funny apple-headed dolls grew older, their faces began to dry up. In only a few days they looked like old squaws, with dark, dry, and wrinkled faces.

Colonial Dolls were usually whittled from wood or cut from cloth and dressed like their owners. Others were made from pine cones, corncobs, or other materials at hand. Though crude, they were treasured friends.

The oldest doll in America is probably the one called *Letitia Penn*. William Penn brought it from England in 1699 for a friend of his little daughter, Letitia. Its gown has a tight waist and sleeves, and the skirt is wider than the doll is high. The doll has only one arm now, and its face seems to us to look somewhat unfriendly.

Another famous doll is *Mehitable Hodges*, sometimes called the *Salem Doll*. She was brought to America in 1724 by Captain Gamaliel Hodges as a gift for his daughter. Still another of the very old colonial dolls is a stumpy, homemade rag doll. Even her name sounds homemade. It is *Bangwell Putt*. Bangwell had no face. But for eighty years she did her rag-doll best to brighten the life of her blind mistress, Clarissa Field of Northfield, Mass.

Improvements in Dolls. For many years, little girls in America continued to play with dolls that had been brought from Europe. Little by little, better dolls began

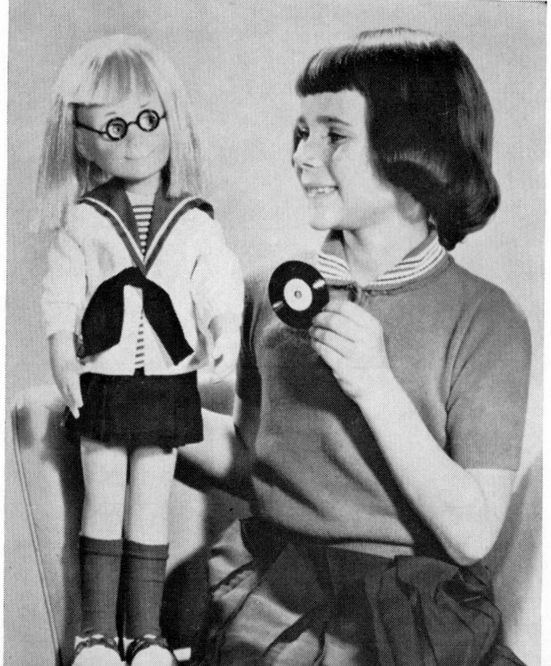

A Modern Talking Doll, *left,* can speak as many as 216 phrases in English and six other languages. To make the doll talk, the little girl puts a tiny record in a slot in the doll's side and pulls a string. Another doll, *below,* bubbles after feeding.

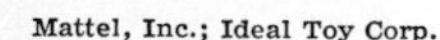

Mattel, Inc.; Ideal Toy Corp.

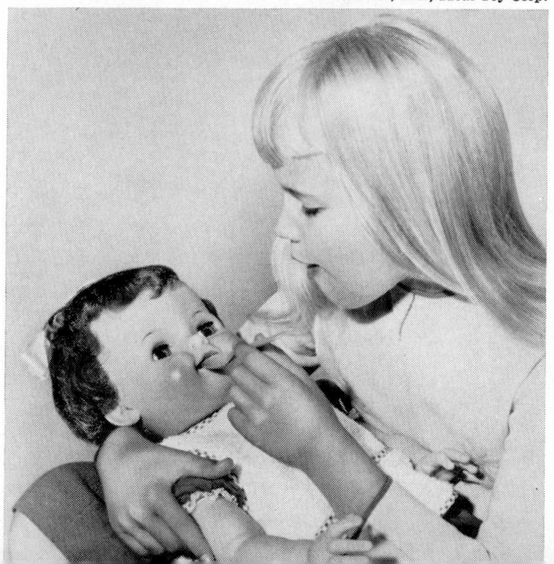

to be made. Soft kid was used for their bodies, and they took on a more lifelike shape. Stuffings improved. Bran and sawdust were common for many, many years. Later, hair, shavings, and seaweed were used.

At first most dolls belonged to grownups, not to children. But by 1800, dolls had become the child's own toy. Factories did not make enough dolls for all the little girls, so the homemade rag doll became popular. In order to get to an American girl from Europe, a factory-made doll had to travel by boat, stagecoach, and perhaps by saddlebag or covered wagon.

For a long time, doll heads were made of china. Their faces were round and rosy and were not supposed to look like real people. Penny china dolls about 2 inches (5 centimeters) high also became very popular. Many girls owned whole families of them.

Doll hands and feet were of leather, china, or wood. It was fashionable for women to have small feet, so doll feet were made much too small for their bodies. China heads, hands, and feet were sold in stores to those who wished to make dolls at home.

Until about 1870, American girls played with dolls that looked like serious, grown-up ladies. They wore bustles, jackets, and the quaint dresses of these days. Only a few dolls were made to look like children. Some had wax heads, which broke if the dolls were dropped. The wax cracked in cold weather and melted in hot weather. The finest wax dolls came from England. Other dolls had heads made of *papier-mâché*, a mixture of pulped paper and glue.

The best doll heads then were made of *bisque*, a kind of hard earthenware. Such dolls had kid bodies and jointed necks, arms, and legs. They also had real curls, and eyes which opened and closed. Most of them came dressed only in cotton slips and had to have their clothing made for them by their owners.

Modern Dolls

Beginning about 1900, new developments occurred in the world of dolls. Manufacturers made more dolls that looked like babies. Many of them, called *ma-ma dolls*, had built-in devices that made them seem to cry. Johann Maelzel of Germany had invented this mechanism about 1825, but few manufacturers used it until around 1900. Dolls that opened and shut their eyes became popular. Factories made remarkable mechanical dolls that could walk, do tricks, or play music.

Europe. Germany, especially the cities of Nuremberg and Sonnenberg, made most of the best dolls between 1870 and 1914. Käthe Kruse was one of the first to make dolls that looked like real children. Her husband did not want their children to play with the ugly dolls of the time, so she made new ones. The first ones had heads made of raw potatoes, with faces drawn on with a burnt match. Later ones were made of waterproof cloth stuffed with *kapok*, a light fiber. Madame Lenci of Italy became famous for her felt dolls, many dressed in gay costumes. France and England also made good dolls.

United States factories first began making dolls in the 1900's. They used unbreakable materials such as rubber and *composition*, a mixture of wood flour, starch, rosin, and water. The first really successful American doll, *Billiken*, became popular around 1910. Many American dolls appeared during World War I, when children could not get German dolls. The plump *Kewpie Doll* found a large audience. Other American dolls included the *Bye-Lo Baby*, which looked like a tiny baby; the little girl *Patsy;* and *Ginny*, with her many clothes. *Character Dolls* included Mickey and Minnie Mouse, Raggedy Anne and Raggedy Andy, and comic-strip figures. *Portrait Dolls* resembled real persons.

Zylstra

Out for a Stroll. These two dolls are modeled on the kind first made in Germany by the famous woman dollmaker, Käthe Kruse.

American dolls grew more and more lifelike. Dolls that cried followed the *Dy-Dee Doll* of the 1930's. Later dolls had nylon "hair," make-up kits, roller skates, and even mink coats. "Teen-age" dolls and giant "walking dolls" also became popular.

Homemade Dolls

Dolls can be made from almost anything. Forest dwellers use wood, bark, and roots. People of the plains wrap grasses, straws, or cornhusks into doll shapes. Those who live near the sea use shells and seaweed. In hot countries, palm leaves are woven into dolls.

Swedish girls make pretty dolls of rolled-up birchbark. Birchbark is fringed for hands, and clothes are scraps of neatly hemmed birchbark. Hungarian children make rag dolls with oats for eyes and a grain of corn for a nose. They also make poppy dolls by pulling down the flower petals and binding them with a blade of grass. The seed pod is the poppy doll's head. To the Russian girl, no doll is more dear than a painted woodsman cut from wood. Arms are pine cones, hair is moss, and dresses and shoes are woven from fibers.

In Bermuda, doll bodies are made from the heart of the banana stalk. Large round nuts are used as heads. In South Africa, children make their dolls from corncobs. A small home-woven blanket serves as clothing. In England and many other lands, dolls are baked from bread dough and dressed in long, white baby dresses.

Mexican children play with rag dolls or wooden ones covered with cloth. The potter's children model tiny dolls of clay and paint them with homemade colors.

Still other Mexican dolls are braided leaf fibers. Very sturdy dolls are made of straw, cornhusks, and pieces of cornstalk. These are painted in brilliant colors.

In Chile and Brazil, yarn is wrapped around pieces of wire to make dolls. Heads are of cork or wood. Odd little woven woolen dolls are made in Peru.

Eskimo play dolls have long been made from skins. They are dressed in fur scraps and stuffed with reindeer hair or fur. Many doll figures are carved from bone or walrus tusk.

In the United States, all kinds of materials may be used for making dolls. Scraps of cloth, old stockings, or pieces of felt or leather are excellent. Corncobs and cornhusks are good, and so are peanuts and acorns. A clever person can make a doll of a spool, clothespin, or tenpin. Other materials are paper, cardboard, hairpins, wires, raffia, string, and rubber from old inner tubes.

Stocking Dolls are about the easiest to make. The only materials needed are old stockings, stuffing, and thread. Stuffing can be cotton, old rags, or even some finely torn bits of newspaper. The best stockings are those of heavy silk or smooth cotton. Pert little faces can be made by stitching on eyes, mouth, and nose with colored thread. Buttons make good eyes.

Rag Dolls are the most popular of all homemade dolls. They are almost as old as history. One in Egypt was probably used about two thousand years ago. It is made of linen and stuffed with coarse grass. The features are embroidered on. Its hair is linen threads.

Two-in-One Dolls are rag dolls, each with a black face and a white face. They can be easily made by making two bodies that go only to the waist. One is of black material and the other of white material, and each has a matching pair of arms. A blue dress looks well on the white doll and a red dress on the black one. Each dress should be twice as long as the body. Paints or colored threads can be used to make the faces. Raveled yarn will do for hair, and soft caps or bonnets may be made for each head. When both dolls are finished, they should be sewn tightly together at the waist. When the white head is held up, the black one hangs beneath the full blue skirt. When the black head is up, the white one hangs under the red dress.

Cork Dolls are made with two corks, a large one for the body and a smaller one for the head. Matchsticks are stuck into the larger cork to serve as arms and legs and to hold head and body together. Thumbtacks in the leg-ends make these dolls stand up easily.

Making the Doll's Clothes is as much fun as making the doll itself. Soft, thin materials are best for small dolls. Scraps of old clothing may be used. A single tiny piece of cloth will make a whole outfit for a spool doll. If light bulbs are used for heads, the faces are painted on and crepe paper is often used for clothing.

Dollhouses

Even three hundred years ago, fine dollhouses were the fashion in Europe. Fancy Dutch houses were made in the form of cupboards. When the doors were open, one could peep into every room in the house, from basement to attic. The houses were sometimes 6 to 8 feet (1.8 to 2.4 meters) high, and were made for grownups. A few of these old dollhouses may still be seen in the museums of Europe.

One of the finest was the Utrecht (Holland) Dollhouse, made in 1670. It had 15 rooms. One of these was full of tiny vases and other small treasures. These great dollhouses were furnished exactly like the homes of wealthy persons. Anyone who studies them can learn a great deal about how people lived long ago.

A dollhouse usually had doll people in it, too. Doll lords and ladies sat in the drawing rooms. Cooks, butlers, maids, and laundresses were at work in other rooms. In one of these houses, a tiny nurse is seen holding a baby doll whose long dress almost sweeps the floor. In the best dollhouses, every tiny article is perfectly made. Kitchens are complete with pots and pans, knives, ladles, forks, dishes, candlesticks, baskets, brushes, and tiny brooms.

These houses cost so much that only the wealthy could own them. Peter the Great, the ruler of all Russia, once ordered one. When it was finished, he refused to pay for it, because he felt that it cost too much even for him. Mary of Teck, the wife of King George V of Great Britain, was also interested in dollhouses. She found enjoyment in an elaborate dollhouse that cost nearly a million dollars. In it are real pianos, and works of noted composers, authors, and painters. The 11-room dollhouse of the American actress Colleen Moore is 12 feet (3.7 meters) high and 9 feet (2.7 meters) square. It is valued at about $500,000. One drawing-room chandelier is decorated with real diamonds and other precious stones. But dollhouses for children are not so big or so costly. Some have six or seven rooms, and others only one. There are also one-room doll stores.

Homemade dollhouses are simple to make. A square hatbox or a grocery carton makes a cozy one-room apartment. A great favorite is an orange box stood on end. This becomes a two-story house with an upstairs. Fringed rugs for the floors may be cut from old cloth. Spools and pieces of cardboard make fine tables and benches. Chairs may be made from old salt boxes, round ice cream cartons, or other small boxes. A cracker carton becomes a davenport, a cigar box makes a bed, and a raisin box is a chest of drawers.

Gay furniture can be created by using colored paper or cloth, or paint. Leftover scraps of wallpaper will help to make the walls seem real. Oval cocoa-can lids become tiny, framed pictures when colored cutouts are pasted on them. Old purse mirrors are dollhouse size. The table may be set with bottle caps.

Doll Collections

Thousands of people, young and old, in all parts of the world, make a hobby of collecting dolls. Some collectors own a thousand or more dolls. Many persons collect antique dolls. Others specialize in costume dolls that represent all countries and times. Instead of buying dolls for their collections, some persons make their own. A few dolls stand as high as adults, while others can fit in a thimble. Doll collections are often exhibited in libraries, schools, clubs, and museums.

Famous Collectors include the Aztec emperor Montezuma. More than 400 years ago, Cortes, the Spanish conqueror of Mexico, found the emperor amusing himself with his doll collection. Before Victoria became queen of England, she owned dozens and dozens of dolls. She put her best needlework into their tiny silken gowns, and named them after the ladies and actresses

HOW DOLLS HAVE CHANGED

Ancient Egyptians and Greeks had dolls thousands of years ago. The painted wooden paddle doll, *left below,* dates from the Middle Kingdom in Egypt, 2050-1800 B.C. These dolls were often put in tombs to keep the dead company. The Greek terra cotta doll, *right below,* dates from the 500's B.C.

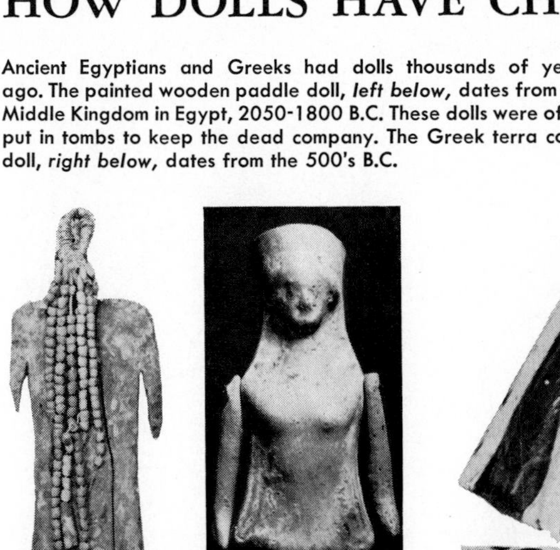

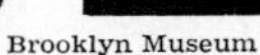

Brooklyn Museum

Smithsonian Institution

One of the Oldest American Dolls, "Letitia Penn," *above*, was probably brought to America by William Penn. The wooden doll has a brocade and velvet gown like those worn by ladies of the English court.

Thayer Museum of Art

Dolls of the Late 1800's had china heads. The body was made of leather or cloth that was stuffed with bran and sawdust.

Ideal Toy Corp.

"Dress-Up" Dolls captured the hearts of little girls in the 1960's. Such dolls have wardrobes, accessories, and even their own families of other dolls.

Brooklyn Museum

Fashion Dolls were once used to carry the latest dress and hair styles from one country to another. France used them 500 years ago. They came to the United States in Revolutionary War days.

HOW TO MAKE

PAPER DOLL

Pocahontas is a sitting doll made from paper. Cut out a newspaper pattern and outline it on stiff wrapping paper. Draw the eyes, nose, and mouth. Paste on the feathers, braids, and headband. Use crayon to put on the bright colors, as water colors might wrinkle the paper.

Little Miss Muffet, Goldilocks, and other dolls may be made in the same way. In making curly-headed dolls, cut the hair longer at the sides. Snip into the fringe and curl it by putting fringes across a blunt knife blade.

STOCKING DOLL

Cut the pieces as shown. Sew up the bottom of the body and stuff it with cotton, kapok, or rags. Then tie it at the neck. If the head seems too wide, gather it at the back.

Sew on the arms and legs and tie the body at the waistline. Use buttons for eyes and red chainstitching for the nose and mouth. Over-and-over stitches at the center of the mouth improve its shape. Sew on a stocking wig. Then braid it or leave it hanging. If you prefer, the doll may be dressed as Red Riding Hood, Little Bopeep, Cinderella, Little Miss Muffet, or anyone else.

HOMEMADE DOLLS

ACORN DOLLS

To make funny little acorn dolls, use acorns and matchsticks. With a nail, punch tiny holes in the acorns for the arms, legs, and neck. Then cement them into the holes. Punch holes for eyes, nose, and mouth, or draw them. For hair, use the fuzzy-edged acorn cup of a burr oak. The top of the cup makes a fine cap.

CORNCOB DOLL

For hair, use the silk on the corncob. The arms, skirt, and kerchief are made of cornhusks. Draw the eyes, nose, and mouth.

CORNSTARCH DOLL

The head of this 9-inch wire doll is made of cornstarch, salt, and water. Mix 2 tablespoonfuls of salt, 1 tablespoonful of cornstarch with 1 tablespoonful of boiling water. Heat over the fire for a moment. When cool, knead it into a ball the size of a walnut and press it over the head wire. Model the head and hair. Shape the hands and feet out of the leftovers. Let these dry for two days, and then color with water colors.

Wire for body and legs, 18 inches long. Arm wire, 9 inches. Stuff body slightly and wrap with cloth.

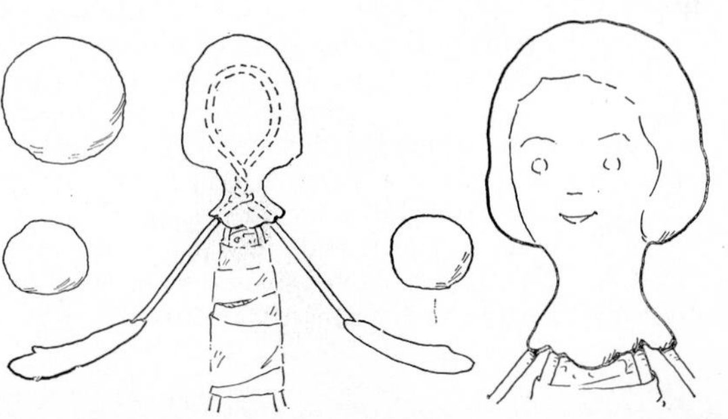

whose costumes she copied. She especially liked small wooden dolls with jointed limbs. Queen Marie of Romania had a collection of more than a thousand dolls, most of them dressed in various costumes. The people of The Netherlands gave their queen, Wilhelmina, a large collection of costume dolls. Another famous doll collection belonged to Eugene Field, the poet who wrote "Little Boy Blue" and "Wynken, Blynken, and Nod."

Noted Collections of dolls include a large one at the Metropolitan Museum in New York City. Another fine collection, dressed in various European costumes, is found in the New York Children's Museum. Noted collections may also be seen in the Smithsonian Institution in Washington, D.C.; Essex Institute at Salem, Mass.; the Museum of Art in Toledo, Ohio; the children's library in Hartford, Conn.; Pennsylvania Museum at Philadelphia, Pa.; children's museums at Detroit, Mich., and Boston, Mass.; Plymouth Antiquarian Society at Plymouth, Mass.; and in museums at Cleveland, Ohio, and Brooklyn, N.Y. Another large exhibit of dolls is at the State Historical Society of Wisconsin, in Madison. It includes the famous Trimpey and Fairchild collections.

Doll Festivals and Customs

For hundreds of years, the Japanese have paid the highest honor to their dolls. They hold a three-day Festival of Dolls on the third day of the third month of each year. Sometimes the celebration is called the Girls' Festival, because all Japanese girls celebrate their birthday at that time, even if it falls on some other day.

The festival dolls are not playthings. They are brought out only on this special day. During the year they are packed away carefully in the family treasure chest. Every family has these special dolls, which are passed on from parents to children. During the festival, five shelves are set up in the best room in the house. The dolls are arranged on these shelves. Richly dressed emperor and empress dolls are placed on the highest shelf, where none can look down on them. The other dolls are placed on the lower shelves in the order of their importance. The children's play dolls are not allowed on the shelves. But the children take care of the festival dolls, and entertain friends who come to visit them. Tea is served to the dolls, the family, and the guests. Japanese children cherish the dolls as living things, and look forward to this charming holiday.

Various peoples held their own beliefs about dolls. The Hopi Indians of the Southwestern United States carve wooden dolls called *kachinas* for use in their religious ceremonies. Each color and design has its own meaning for the Hopi. After medicine men have used these dolls, they give them to the children to play with. See INDIAN, AMERICAN (picture: Kachina Dolls).

In some parts of England, dolls take part in the harvest thanksgiving festivals. Each autumn the smallest ears of corn are bound up as a doll and hung in the farmer's house. There the doll stays until next harvest time. Then a new one is made and hung with great ceremony. The old doll is carefully burned.

In Belgium, a special doll is given to each baby to help the child cut its teeth with less pain. This doll is dressed in white and has a tooth pinned to its dress. Nearly everyone believes that it brings good luck. In Africa, fishermen on the Congo River carry dolls which they believe will keep them from drowning. The Eskimos of the Far North carve dolls from bone to hang in their *kayaks* (canoes). They believe that these dolls keep the kayaks from turning over. In Korea, in the Far East, a straw doll is thought to bring good luck.

Making Dolls

Today, most of the world's dolls come from the United States. American manufacturers sell more than 40 million dolls every year. Skilled craftsmen design new dolls, and often create complete wardrobes and elaborate accessories for them.

Manufacturers often use washable cloth to make dolls for very young children. Various types of plastics furnish the best material for most other dolls. In the first step, an artist makes a model in clay or wax. A metal mold is then formed around the model. Workmen pour liquid vinyl plastic into the molds and let it solidify. The plastic is soft and durable, and seems like real skin. The workmen usually cast the doll's body in one piece and its head in another. Then other workers put together a whole doll, attaching its head, arms, and legs to the body. Artists paint faces on the heads. As finishing touches, they add the doll's clothes, its eyes, and a nylon wig. The dolls are inspected to make sure they are perfect. Then they are tagged and packed, and they are ready for shipment.

NINA R. JORDAN

Related Articles in WORLD BOOK include:

Child (picture: The Child's World)	Hobby	Kachina
Conveyor Belt (picture)	Hopi Indians	Puppet
		Toy

Outline

I. Dolls of Early Days
- A. Good-Luck Dolls
- B. Paddle Dolls
- C. Doll-Size Figures
- D. Fashion Dolls
- E. Pantin Dolls

II. Dolls in America
- A. Indian Dolls
- B. Colonial Dolls
- C. Improvements in Dolls

III. Modern Dolls
- A. Europe
- B. United States

IV. Homemade Dolls
- A. Stocking Dolls
- B. Rag Dolls
- C. Two-in-One Dolls
- D. Cork Dolls
- E. Making the Doll's Clothes

V. Dollhouses

VI. Doll Collections
- A. Famous Collectors
- B. Noted Collections

VII. Doll Festivals and Customs

VIII. Making Dolls

Questions

Why did Roman girls take their dolls to the altar of Diana?

Why did the paddle dolls of the Egyptians have no legs?

Why were English "fashion dolls" sent to India?

What were dolls called in the colonial days of America?

What is the name of the oldest doll in America? How old is she?

Why did early American dolls have tiny feet?

What children made dolls that could be seen to grow older? Of what were they made?

When was the *ma-ma* doll invented?

What famous queen of England had a large collection of dolls?

Why do the Eskimos carry dolls in their kayaks?

DOLLAR is one of several units of money used in various countries. The name comes from the old German word *thal*, meaning *valley*. This name was adopted because one of the earliest coins of this type was made in 1519 in the valley of St. Joachim in Bohemia. These coins were called *Joachimsthaler*, then *thaler*, which in English became *dollar*. The dollars of the United States and Canada are paper bills or coins equal to 100 cents.

The dollar became the basic unit of money in the United States through the Coinage Act of 1792. It was copied after the Spanish dollar then being widely circulated in America. United States paper dollars were printed as early as 1775. The first United States silver dollars were coined in 1794, and nearly 900,000,000 were made from that time to 1935, when the Treasury stopped minting them. Silver dollars circulated mainly in the West, Southwest, and Northwest. People in the East objected to their weight and demanded paper dollars. The silver dollar weighed 416 grains (27 grams) at first, but its weight was changed to $412\frac{1}{2}$ grains (26.7 grams) in 1837 by Congress.

In 1971, the United States resumed minting of dollar coins. The new coins for circulation contained no silver. They had a solid copper center between two layers of a copper-nickel alloy. In addition, a large number of silver dollars were scheduled to be specially minted and sold at higher prices to coin collectors. These coins contained 40 per cent silver.

From 1873 to 1885, a special dollar weighing 420 grains (27.2 grams) was issued. This was called the *trade dollar* and was intended to help American trade in the Orient, where the Mexican dollar was being used. At various times the U.S. government issued gold pieces with values of $1, $2.50, $3, $5, $10, and $20. The one-dollar gold piece was issued from 1849 through 1889. Coinage of gold ceased in the United States and all gold coins were taken out of circulation in 1933.

The first paper dollars issued by the Dominion of Canada appeared in 1870. Canada issued its first silver dollars in 1935. Australia changed its chief monetary unit from the pound to the dollar in 1966.

A form of the dollar is found in Mexico, where it is known as the *peso*. Another form, called the *yuan*, has been used in China. The British government issued a

Chase Manhattan Bank Money Museum

The First U.S. Silver Dollar, *above,* was minted in 1794. It had an eagle on the back and a liberty head on the front.

U.S. Treasury

The Eisenhower Dollar, *above,* first minted in 1971, honors Dwight D. Eisenhower, the 34th President of the United States.

Chase Manhattan Bank Money Museum

The Peace Dollar, *above,* was issued in the United States from 1921 to 1935. The word *Peace* appeared on the back of the coin.

Chase Manhattan Bank Money Museum

The Canadian Silver Dollar, *above,* honors Queen Elizabeth II on the front and agents of the fur trade on the back.

A $100,000 Bill, *left,* passes only between the Treasury Department and Federal Reserve Banks. It is not for public circulation.

By special permission of the Chief, U.S. Secret Service, Treasury Dept. Further reproduction, in whole or in part, is strictly prohibited.

coin called the *Hong Kong dollar*, for use in Hong Kong. Other countries issue silver coins resembling dollars. The coins have other names, but are often called dollars.

The origin of the dollar sign is not certain. Several theories explain it, the main one being that the S in the sign is a broken 8. That figure was on the old Spanish pieces of eight, meaning 8 *reals*. The two bars appeared as the Pillars of Hercules on pieces of eight minted in Mexico City as early as 1732. FRED REINFELD

See also MONEY (pictures); EURODOLLAR; CENT; DIME; HALF DOLLAR; NICKEL; QUARTER.

DOLLAR DIPLOMACY seeks to extend a nation's business interests in other countries by any means except war. The term was first applied to United States policy in the Caribbean and other areas during President William Howard Taft's Administration. The period from 1909 to 1913 is generally considered to be the era of dollar diplomacy. See also TAFT, WILLIAM HOWARD (Foreign Affairs).

DOLLARFISH. See BUTTERFISH.

DOLLFUS, AUDOUIN. See SATURN (Satellites).

DOLLFUSS, *DAWL foos,* **ENGELBERT** (1892-1934), became chancellor of Austria in 1932, at a time of political and economic trouble. He adjourned Austria's parliament in 1933, and then ruled the country as a dictator. Nazi revolutionaries assassinated him on July 25, 1934, because he tried to prevent Adolf Hitler from taking over Austria. Dollfuss was born near Vienna. He was graduated from the University of Vienna. See also AUSTRIA (After World War I). GABRIEL A. ALMOND

DOLLHOUSE. See DOLL (Dollhouses).

DOLMEN. See MEGALITHIC MONUMENTS.

DOLOMITE, *DAHL oh mite,* is a mineral composed of carbonates of calcium and magnesium. Dolomite is moderately soft, and is colored milky-white, brownish, or pink. Impurities sometimes give it other colors. Geologists call crystals of the purest varieties *pearl spar*. The crystals have curved surfaces with a pearly luster.

Some dolomite is so much like calcite that a chemical test must be made to tell them apart. When the mineral dolomite is in large masses, it forms the kind of rock also called dolomite. There are great mountain ranges of dolomite in Europe. Dolomite is found in most parts of the United States.

Many limestones, and some of the finest statuary marbles, are made up of dolomite. The mineral is also used in making Epsom salts. WILLIAM C. LUTH

See also CALCITE; DOLOMITES; LIMESTONE; MARBLE.

DOLOMITES, or DOLOMITE ALPS, are a part of the Alps mountain system in northeastern Italy and in the Austrian Tyrol. They were named for the French geologist Déodat Dolomieu, who discovered the magnesium-calcium rock called *dolomite* in these mountains.

The Dolomite area covers about 200 square miles (520 square kilometers). The highest peak of the Dolomites is Marmolada (10,965 feet, or 3,342 meters). Minerals color some of the mountainsides a brilliant red or produce blue-black and yellow splotches. Pieve di Cadore, a town on the southern slope of the Dolomites, was the birthplace of Titian, a famous painter of the Renaissance. SHEPARD B. CLOUGH

See also DOLOMITE; ITALY (physical map).

DOLORES MISSION. See SAN FRANCISCO (History).

Jim Annan

Aquariums and Zoos Train Dolphins to leap high out of the water and snatch an object from a trainer's hand. A dolphin can jump through a hoop and use its mouth to catch and throw a ball.

DOLPHIN, *DAHL fin,* is a small, whalelike mammal whose snout forms a "beak." The dolphin is often confused with the porpoise, which has no beak. Dolphins are swift and graceful swimmers. Their sharp turns, sudden stops, and high leaps make them entertaining to watch. Dolphins are found in all the oceans of the world and in some rivers. They feed mainly on fish and octopuslike animals called *squids*. Two of the commonest kinds of dolphins are (1) bottle-nosed dolphins and (2) common dolphins.

The Bottle-Nosed Dolphin is a star performer in many aquariums. Almost all the "porpoises" that delight audiences with their tricks are really bottle-nosed dolphins. This dolphin can be trained to leap high into the air to grab a fish from its keeper's hand. It also can be taught to jump through a hoop and to fetch a thrown ball or stick.

Scientists consider the bottle-nosed dolphin one of the most intelligent animals. Some think its intelligence ranks between that of the chimpanzee—the most intelligent animal—and the dog. A few believe it outranks even the chimpanzee. The bottle-nosed dolphin has keen eyesight and hearing and an excellent sense of taste. But it has no sense of smell.

Dolphins communicate with one another by making sounds that include barks, clicks, and whistles. Bottle-nosed dolphins can even imitate some sounds of human speech. A dolphin produces sounds by blowing air through the air passages it uses for breathing. These passages lead to the *blowhole*, an opening at the top of the

WORLD BOOK illustrations by Tom Dolan

dolphin's head. The air passages and the blowhole have flaps of muscle that move to help make different sounds.

Because of the dolphin's high intelligence, some persons have believed that man could learn how to communicate with the animal. An American physician, John C. Lilly, conducted communications experiments with dolphins during the 1950's and 1960's. But he failed to develop a system of communication with them.

Dolphins have a natural sonar system called *echolocation* that helps them locate underwater objects. A dolphin locates an object by making sounds and listening for echoes the sounds make when reflected by the object. Scientists believe these sounds originate in the animal's breathing system. The sounds are sent out of the dolphin's body through an organ called the *melon*. This organ lies within a bulge at the top of the animal's head. The U.S. Navy is conducting research to learn more about the dolphin's use of echolocation.

The bottle-nosed dolphin is found in coastal waters. It grows up to 12 feet (3.7 meters) long and weighs as much as 800 pounds (360 kilograms), but most are smaller. Its beak is about 3 inches (8 centimeters) long, and it has from 80 to 88 teeth. This dolphin has a grayish color, and its back is darker than its underside. In the early days, men captured bottle-nosed dolphins with nets. They used the oil from the animal's head for lubrication, and oil from the blubber for cooking. The meat was dried for use as human food.

The Common Dolphin is found in warm ocean waters. It grows to a length of 7 feet (2.1 meters) and weighs up to 150 pounds (68 kilograms). Its beak is about 6 inches (15 centimeters) long, and it has from 80 to 100 teeth. This dolphin has a black back and a white underside, and prominent gray and brown stripes on its sides.

Large *schools* (groups) of common dolphins often leap around ships in apparent joy. For hundreds of years, many seamen have regarded these dolphins as a sign

Tom Stack

Many Sharp Teeth line the dolphin's jaws. A fatty organ called the *melon* causes a bulge on top of the animal's head.

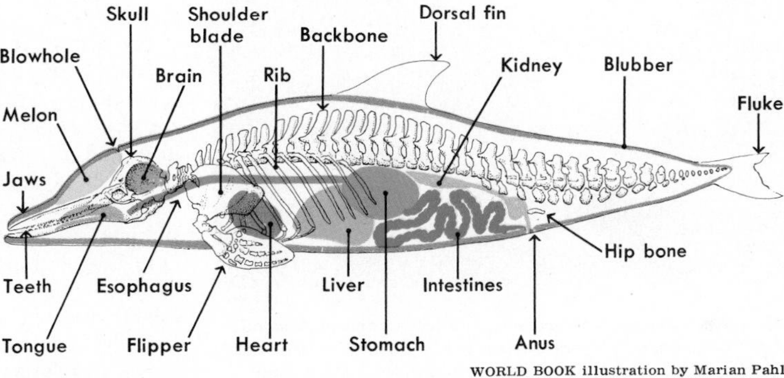

WORLD BOOK illustration by Marian Pahl

Lewis Wayne Walker

Dolphins Swim in Groups Called *Schools*. The animals try to aid an injured or sick member. A dolphin swims by moving its tail and the rear part of its body up and down. The dolphin's streamlined shape and smooth skin reduce friction with the water.

Wometco Miami Seaquarium

Baby Dolphins are born in the water. The mother and other female dolphins push the infant to the surface for its first breath of air. The mother nurses its baby with milk for about a year. Dolphins breathe through a *blowhole* on top of the head.

Flip Schulke, Black Star

Scientists Conduct Experiments to learn more about how dolphins communicate. This researcher is holding a microphone near a dolphin's blowhole to record the sounds made by the animal.

that their voyage will be smooth and happy. For this reason, sailors frequently refuse to kill the dolphin, even though its meat is delicious.

The common dolphin appeared in ancient Greek and Roman mythology. The Greeks considered it sacred to the god Apollo.

Scientific Classification. Dolphins, porpoises, and toothed whales make up the suborder *Odontoceti* of the order *Cetacea*. RAYMOND M. GILMORE

See also PORPOISE; WHALE.

DOLPHIN, DORADO, or CORYPHENE, is a large game fish that lives in warm salt waters. The largest dolphins are about 6 feet (1.8 meters) long and weigh 75 to 100 pounds (34 to 45 kilograms). They live in all tropical oceans. The dolphin's long body tapers toward a V-shaped tail. A fast swimmer, it sometimes chases flying fishes at sea for food. The dolphin is good to eat. It is blue and silver gray and sometimes changes into many colors when first removed from the sea.

Scientific Classification. The dolphin is a member of the family *Coryphaenidae*. It is genus *Coryphaena*, species *C. hippurus*. LEONARD P. SCHULTZ

See also FISH (picture: Fish of Coastal Waters).

DOMAGK, *DOH mahk*, **GERHARD** (1895-1964), a German physician, discovered the first of the sulfa drugs, the drug *prontosil*. He is best known for his work on a group of chemicals that included prontosil, a powerful destroyer of streptococcic bacteria. Domagk won the 1939 Nobel prize for this discovery. Domagk's early publications dealt chiefly with the search for a cancer cure. He also worked on drugs for tuberculosis, and in 1952 described the drug *isonicotinic acid hydrazide* (INH), used in the treatment of tuberculosis. He was born in Lagow, Brandenburg, Germany. K. L. KAUFMAN

See also SULFA DRUGS (Development of Sulfa Drugs).

DOME is a kind of roof shaped like a bowl turned upside down. The word comes from the Latin *doma*, meaning *roof* or *house*, which in turn came from the Greek word *doma*, meaning *housetop*. The ancient Assyrians, Persians, and Romans used domes on their buildings. But until the A.D. 500's, builders placed most domes on round or equal-sided buildings. The church of Hagia Sophia in Constantinople (now Istanbul) was the first large rectangular building to be covered by a dome. It has a 107-foot (33-meter) dome. Later Byzantine and Russian churches usually had domes.

Most Arabian tombs and mosques are roofed with a dome. Builders in India copied the Arabs. An especially beautiful dome tops the Taj Mahal at Agra, India. The Pantheon in Rome has the world's largest masonry dome. Both its height and its diameter measure 142 feet (43 meters). One of the largest domes in the world covers the Astrodome in Houston, Tex. This steel and plastic dome rises 208 feet (63 meters) and has a span of 642 feet (196 meters) between supports. The United Nations General Assembly Building in New York City has a stainless steel dome. Other notable domes top Saint Peter's in Rome, Saint Paul's Cathedral in London, the *Église du Dôme* (Church of the Dome) in Paris, the Capitol in Washington, D.C., and the cathedral in Florence, Italy. KENNETH J. CONANT

See also CUPOLA; PANTHEON; HAGIA SOPHIA; HOUSTON (picture); TAJ MAHAL.

DOME OF THE ROCK. See JERUSALEM (Holy Places; picture).

DOMEI. See KYODO.

DOMESDAY BOOK, or DOOMSDAY BOOK, was the first official record of the property owners living in England and the amount of land they owned. The information was collected and published at the command of William of Normandy. He ordered the territory to be taken from the nobility and large landowners and divided among his followers. William wanted to know how much land he owned, how the rest was divided, and how the land was peopled. The survey was ordered in 1085 and completed in 1086.

The country was divided into districts. Each district supplied census takers who knew the territory. The census and the land survey covered all the territory William controlled. No survey was held in either London or Winchester, and the king's authority did not

Bosshard, Black Star

Hagia Sophia in Istanbul, Turkey

Keystone

The Pantheon in Rome

Sawders

The Taj Mahal in Agra, India

Italian Government Travel Bureau

Saint Peter's Church in Vatican City

Public Records Office, London

The Domesday Book, which consists of two volumes, was the first official census of the English people and their possessions.

include Northumberland, Cumberland, Durham, or Westmorland. Information in the book was considered final and authoritative. Copies of the original Domesday Book were published between 1861 and 1863.

See also NORMAN CONQUEST.

DOMESTIC ANIMAL. See ANIMAL (The Importance of Animals).

DOMESTIC COUNCIL is an agency of the United States government that advises the President on domestic policies and programs. It is part of the Executive Office of the President. The President serves as chairman and the Vice-President as vice-chairman. Other members include the attorney general, the director of the Office of Management and Budget, the chairman of the Council of Economic Advisers, the administrator of Veterans Affairs, and the secretaries of agriculture; commerce; health, education, and welfare; housing and urban development; the interior; labor; transportation; and the treasury.

The Domestic Council estimates the needs of the nation and establishes priorities to meet them. When the President wants policy advice on some domestic issue or problem, the council can provide it. The council also reviews policies of programs already in operation. Much of the council's work is done by committees. The council deals with such issues as the environment, economic and social trends, and urban and rural life.

The Domestic Council was established in 1970 under President Richard M. Nixon. Its creation was part of a reorganization of a number of government agencies. It replaced the Council on Rural Affairs and the Council for Urban Affairs. Critically reviewed by the DOMESTIC COUNCIL

See also PRESIDENT OF THE UNITED STATES (Executive Office of the President).

DOMESTIC RELATIONS COURT. See COURT OF DOMESTIC RELATIONS.

DOMESTIC SHORTHAIR CAT. See CAT (Breeds).

DOMESTIC SYSTEM. See COTTAGE INDUSTRY; INDUSTRIAL REVOLUTION (The Textile Industry).

DOMESTICATION. See PREHISTORIC MAN (The First Steps to Farming).

DOMICILIARY. See VETERANS ADMINISTRATION.

DOMINANCE is animal behavior that reflects the relative importance of the members of a group. Dominance may be observed easily among a flock of hens that have never seen one another before. The birds quarrel at first, and the winner of a series of quarrels becomes dominant over the losers. Thereafter, a threatening movement or an aggressive peck by a dominant bird forces other birds to get out of the way. Such relationships develop among all members of the flock. The result is a ranking called a *pecking order* or *dominance hierarchy*.

The animals that rank high in the pecking order are called *dominants*. They have first choice of food, mates, shelter, and other necessities. Animals of low rank, called *subordinates*, must wait their turn and take what is left. Dominance reduces fighting within a group because a subordinate rarely attacks a dominant, and a dominant need not attack a subordinate.

Among higher animals, dominance determines most social organization. For example, monkey troops and wolf packs are organized on the basis of dominance. Animals that claim and defend territories as their own are always dominant in their own territory and subordinate in the territory of another (see TERRITORIALITY). Few invertebrates show dominance behavior.

Among some species of animals, dominance may prevent the population from growing beyond what the environment can support. If a necessity, such as food, becomes scarce, the most dominant individuals still get their normal amount. The lowest-ranking subordinates must either go elsewhere or starve. JOHN A. WIENS

DOMINANT. See HARMONICS.

DOMINANT GENE. See HEREDITY (Genes).

DOMINIC, SAINT, is a saint of the Roman Catholic Church. He founded the Order of Preachers, also called the *Dominican Order*. He was born at Calaroga in Old Castile about 1170, the son of Felix Guzman and Joanna of Aza. From 1184 to 1194 he studied at the University of Palencia. He became a canon of Osma, where he remained for some years. Later he entered the struggle against the Albigenses. He wanted to establish a new religious order for the purpose of preaching against heresy (see HERESY). After some difficulties, he finally got permission to do so from Pope Honorius III in 1216. When Dominic died in 1221, the Dominican Order he founded had spread over Europe. He was canonized in 1234. Saint Dominic's feast day is August 4. See also ALBIGENSES; DOMINICANS. FULTON J. SHEEN

DOMINICA. See WEST INDIES ASSOCIATED STATES; LEEWARD ISLANDS.

DOMINICAN. See DOMINICANS.

DOMINICAN COLLEGE OF BLAUVELT. See UNIVERSITIES AND COLLEGES (table).

DOMINICAN COLLEGE OF PHILOSOPHY AND THEOLOGY is a coeducational institution in Ottawa, Ont. It is operated by the Friars Preachers order of the Roman Catholic Church. The college has departments of pastoral studies, philosophy, and theology. Courses are conducted chiefly in French. The college grants bachelor's, master's, and doctor's degrees.

The college was founded in 1900. It became a degree-granting institution in 1967. For enrollment, see CANADA (table: Universities and Colleges). GILLES D. MAILHIOT

DOMINICAN COLLEGE OF SAN RAFAEL. See UNIVERSITIES AND COLLEGES (table).

DOMINICAN REPUBLIC

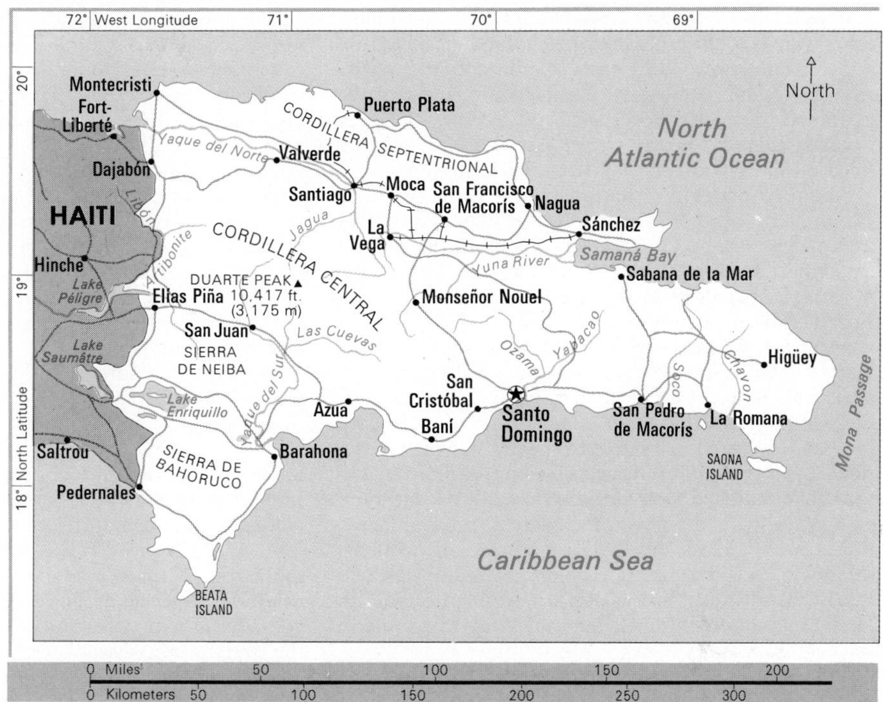

WORLD BOOK map

- ⊛ Capital
- • Other City or Town
- —— Road
- +—+ Rail Line
- ▲ MOUNTAIN
- ~ River

Haiti and the Dominican Republic occupy the island of Hispaniola.

DOMINICAN REPUBLIC is the country that makes up the eastern two-thirds of the island of Hispaniola. Haiti covers the western end of the island. The Dominican Republic is in the West Indies island group, about 575 miles (925 kilometers) southeast of Miami, Fla. It is a land of fertile valleys and forested mountain ranges.

Most Dominicans live on small farms or large plantations. Santo Domingo, a busy port city of about 650,000, is the capital and largest city. The country's name in Spanish, the official language, is REPÚBLICA DOMINICANA.

Christopher Columbus landed on Hispaniola in 1492. Some historians believe he is buried in the Cathedral of Santo Domingo there. The country's capital, Santo Domingo, was the first city in the Western Hemisphere founded by Europeans. The University of Santo Domingo, established in 1538, is the oldest university in the Western Hemisphere.

During much of its history, the Dominican Republic has been ruled by dictators and other countries. United States troops occupied the Dominican Republic twice in the 1900's to halt fighting between rival political groups.

Government. A president heads the Dominican Republic and appoints a Cabinet to assist him. The national legislature consists of a 27-member Senate and a 74-member Chamber of Deputies. The people elect the president and legislators to four-year terms. Only civilians over 18 can vote.

Thomas G. Mathews, the contributor of this article, is Research Professor at the Institute of Caribbean Studies of the University of Puerto Rico.

The Dominican Republic is divided into 26 provinces and one national district—the capital and its surrounding area. Provincial governors and *commune* (county) leaders are appointed by the president. In 1966, after receiving a heavy vote from the women of the country, President Joaquín Balaguer appointed women to all 26 provincial governorships. The people elect the leaders of the country's 100 *municipios* (townships).

FACTS IN BRIEF

Capital: Santo Domingo.

Official Language: Spanish.

Form of Government: Republic. *Head of State*—President.

Area: 18,816 sq. mi. (48,734 km²). *Greatest Distances*—east-west, 240 mi. (388 km); north-south, 170 mi. (274 km). *Coastline*—604 mi. (972 km).

Elevation: *Highest*—Duarte Peak, 10,417 ft. (3,175 m) above sea level. *Lowest*—Lake Enriquillo, 150 ft. (46 m) below sea level.

Population: *Estimated 1976 Population*—4,825,000; distribution, 57 per cent rural, 43 per cent urban; density, 256 persons per sq. mi. (99 persons per km²). *1970 Census*—4,006,405. *Estimated 1981 Population*—5,567,000.

Chief Products: *Agriculture*—bananas, cacao, cassava, coffee, peanuts, pineapples, rice, sugar cane, tobacco. *Mining*—bauxite, clay, gold, gypsum, marble, salt. *Manufacturing*—animal feed, beer, cement, chocolate, glass, molasses, rum, sugar, textiles, vegetable oil.

National Anthem: "Himno Nacional."

Flag: A white cross divides the flag into quarters which are alternately red and blue. The Dominican coat of arms is centered on the cross. Blue stands for liberty, white for salvation, and red for the blood of heroes. See FLAG (color picture: Flags of the Americas).

Money: *Basic Unit*—peso. See MONEY (table: Values).

DOMINICAN REPUBLIC

People. Most Dominicans speak Spanish and follow other ways of life brought to their land from Spain. African influence, which came to the country chiefly by way of Haiti, also is strong. In Haiti, most of the people are descendants of slaves from Africa. The early Spanish colonists nearly wiped out the Indians who lived on the island before the Spaniards arrived.

About 65 per cent of the people are of mixed Caucasian-Negro descent. About 20 per cent are Negro, and about 15 per cent white. Some descendants of ex-slaves from the United States live near Samaná Bay in the northeast. A small group of European Jews settled near Puerto Plata in the north about 1940.

Most Dominicans live in rural areas and work on farms. Some own small farms and raise their own food. They sell some of what they raise to buy clothing, household goods, and other items. Other farmers work for wages on large plantations, especially sugar plantations. Many Dominican farmers live in two-room shacks that have thatched roofs and dirt floors. But small bungalows built by the government are slowly replacing these shacks. Most city dwellers are factory workers, fishermen, or government employees. Many of them live in crowded, old Spanish-style apartment buildings. Dominicans dress in much the same way as people in the United States.

Dominicans love music that mixes the rhythmic pounding of African drums with the rattle of Spanish *maracas* (dried gourd shells with seeds and lead inside). They enjoy dancing the *merengue*, the national dance.

Most Dominicans are Roman Catholic. Some people who live near the Haitian border practice voodoo religions (see VOODOO).

Children between the ages of 7 and 14 must attend school. The government supplies most of the funds for most schools.

Land. The West Indies lie between the Atlantic Ocean and the Caribbean Sea. Hispaniola is formed by the peaks of two undersea mountain chains, one coming from Cuba and the other from Jamaica.

The Dominican Republic is a mountainous land. The *Cordillera Central* (Central Mountain Range) runs from northwest to southeast through the center of the country. Duarte Peak, which rises 10,417 feet (3,175 meters) above sea level in the Cordillera Central, is the highest point in the West Indies. The land west of the Cordillera Central is mostly dry and desertlike. Mountains in the west include Sierra de Neiba and the Sierra de Bahoruco. Lake Enriquillo, the lowest point in the West Indies at 150 feet (46 meters) below sea level, lies between these mountains.

The *Cibao* lies north of the Cordillera Central. The *Cibao* is an area of pine-covered slopes and a fertile plain called the *Vega Real* (Royal Plain). It is the country's chief agricultural area. The *Cordillera Septentrional* (northerly range) is in the far north.

The eastern end of the Dominican Republic is less mountainous. Most of the country's sugar cane is grown along the southern coast east of Santo Domingo and in other eastern areas.

The Dominican Republic has a warm, tropical climate all year. Temperatures vary little and seldom go below 60° F. (16° C) or above 90° F. (32° C). The country averages about 60 inches (150 centimeters) of rainfall a year. The rainy season lasts from May to November in the south and from December to April in the north. Hurricanes sometimes strike the country.

Economy. The Dominican Republic is an agricultural country. About 65 per cent of the working people are farmers. About 78 per cent of the farmers work on their own small farms, or as sharecroppers for large landowners. Others rent land from large landowners. About 22 per cent work on large plantations, most of them owned by wealthy Dominicans and the government. The broad, fertile plains are heavily farmed to produce sugar, tropical fruits (especially bananas), tobacco, and rice. In the forest-covered mountain foothills, coffee and cacao beans grow in the shade of fruit and mahogany trees.

Most manufacturing in the Dominican Republic is related to the refining of farm products, especially sugar. Refineries process about 1 million short tons (910,000 metric tons) of sugar annually, and about three-fourths of it goes to the United States. The people consume most of the rest or turn it into molasses and rum.

Miners take bauxite, from which aluminum is made, from a rich deposit in the Barahona Peninsula in the southwest. Most of the bauxite goes to the United States for processing. The Dominicans also mine clay, gold, gypsum, marble, and salt. Salt is also produced by the evaporation of seawater.

The country has 11 seaports. Four airlines from other countries stop there. Two Dominican airlines fly

Santo Domingo, the Nation's Capital, has been largely rebuilt since a severe hurricane destroyed most of it in 1930.

Norman Thomas

to 15 local airports. There are about 3,000 miles (4,800 kilometers) of paved roads, and a few railroads, most of which are owned by sugar companies. The Dominican Republic has four television transmitter stations and about 70 radio stations.

History. Christopher Columbus landed on Hispaniola on Dec. 6, 1492, on his first voyage to the New World. He ordered Fort La Navidad built on the north coast from the ruins of his flagship, the *Santa Maria*. He returned in 1493 with about 1,300 men to seek the island's gold. Columbus found that the Indians had destroyed the fort and killed the men he had left behind. Thousands of Spanish colonists soon came to Hispaniola. They conquered the Indians and established towns on the north coast. In 1496, they founded La Nueva Isabela (now Santo Domingo).

By the mid-1500's, the scarcity of gold in Hispaniola sent Spaniards in search of more promising lands. They moved on to Cuba, Mexico, and Peru. Hispaniola had barely 30,000 inhabitants and produced little of value. It was neglected by Spanish trading vessels. Pirates and Dutch, English, and French merchants began trading with the people in the small ports on the northern and western coasts.

In 1606, Spain ordered all Spanish settlers to move to the Santo Domingo area to strengthen the defense of Santo Domingo and increase trade for Spanish merchants there. This plan backfired when non-Spanish settlers moved into the abandoned lands in the interior and on the northern coast. By the Treaty of Ryswick of 1697, Spain turned over the western third of the island (now Haiti) to France.

The Sugar Cane Crop is the Dominican Republic's most important product. Plantation workers cut most of the crop by hand.
Paul Popper

The French section prospered, but the Spanish section suffered from neglect. Negro slaves in Haiti, led by Toussaint L'Ouverture, rebelled against their French masters and conquered the whole island by 1801. France and Spain recovered their colonies for brief periods after 1801, but the Haitians gained control of the island again in 1822.

Dominican heroes Juan Pablo Duarte, Francisco del Rosario Sánchez, and Ramón Mella led a successful revolt against the Haitians in 1844. From 1861 to 1865, at the Dominicans' request, Spain governed the country to protect it from the Haitians. Dictator Ulises (Lilis) Heureaux, who ruled the country from 1882 to 1899, left it in debt to several European nations. The United States took over the collection of customs duties in the Dominican Republic from 1905 to 1941 and used the money to pay the debts. From 1916 to 1924, U.S. Marines occupied the Dominican Republic to keep peace between rival political groups and to prevent *anarchy* (complete disorder) in the Caribbean area during a critical time in world affairs.

Rafael Leonidas Trujillo Molina seized power in a military revolt in 1930. He ruled harshly for 30 years, allowing little freedom and imprisoning or killing many of his opponents. Trujillo carried out some beneficial projects, such as rebuilding Santo Domingo after a destructive hurricane in 1930. He ruled efficiently, and the country prospered economically. But the people gained little or no benefits, because all the profits were channeled to members of the Trujillo family.

Conspirators shot and killed Trujillo in 1961. A power struggle then began among the military, the upper class, the people who wanted a democracy, and those who favored Communism. Juan Bosch, a writer and popular foe of Trujillo who had been exiled, promised land and economic aid to the people. He was elected president in December, 1962, but military and upper class leaders ousted him in September, 1963. They charged him with allowing too many Communists in the government. Military leaders then formed a three-man *junta* (council) to govern.

Rebels tried to seize power in 1965. They captured parts of Santo Domingo, but met strong military opposition. President Lyndon B. Johnson sent U.S. troops to the Dominican Republic in April, 1965, to maintain order. He said he acted to protect U.S. citizens there and to keep Communists from taking over the country. Some members of the Organization of American States also sent troops. A truce was arranged in May, 1965. The last foreign troops left in September, 1966.

In June, 1966, Dominican voters elected Joaquín Balaguer president over Juan Bosch. Balaguer had previously served as president from 1960 to 1962, chiefly during the Trujillo dictatorship. Balaguer was re-elected in 1970 and 1974. THOMAS G. MATHEWS

Related Articles in WORLD BOOK include:

Chocolate (graph)
Grant, Ulysses S. (Foreign Relations)
Haiti
Puerto Plata
Santiago
Santo Domingo
Santo Domingo, University of
Trujillo Molina, Rafael L.
West Indies

DOMINICANS, *duh MIHN uh kuhnz,* are members of a Roman Catholic order of friars. The order was founded in 1215 by Saint Dominic, to oppose the teachings of the Albigenses. The first house was established in France. In 1216, under the rule of Saint Augustine, the order received the approval of Pope Honorius III and the right to preach. The members are officially known as the *Order of Friars Preachers.* The order took shape in 1220. It soon became a power in the great universities, as well as a preaching order. To these universities it contributed many learned men, including Albertus Magnus and Thomas Aquinas. Four Dominicans became popes. Dominicans Fra Angelico and Fra Bartolommeo were important painters.

The members take the usual vows of obedience, poverty, and chastity. Many features of monastic life, such as fasting and penitential exercises, are combined with the Dominicans' preaching ministry.

Saint Dominic also established an order of nuns in 1206. From the beginning it served as a shelter for the women of districts overrun by heresy, and later as a medium for the education of children. FULTON J. SHEEN

See also DOMINIC, SAINT; ECKHARDT, JOHANNES; FRIAR.

DOMINION, *doh MIN yun,* is a self-governing country associated with Great Britain in the British Commonwealth of Nations. A dominion owes allegiance to the British Crown. Otherwise, it is independent, with its own constitution, cabinet, parliament, and military forces. Dominions in the Commonwealth include Australia and New Zealand. Canada became the first dominion in 1867, but dropped the title in 1949. The Union of South Africa became a dominion in 1910, but left the Commonwealth in 1961. ROBERT G. NEUMANN

DOMINION DAY is one of Canada's most important national holidays. It is often popularly called *Canada Day.* It is celebrated on July 1 of each year to honor the day the provinces of Canada were united in one government called the Dominion of Canada. On July 1, 1867, the Dominion of Canada was created by the terms of the British North America Act. The day is a time for patriotic programs and events. ELIZABETH HOUGH SECHRIST

DOMINION OBSERVATORY is a Canadian government research institute in Ottawa, Ont. Scientists there study astronomy, seismology, gravity, and terrestrial magnetism. Founded in 1902, it now includes two other observatories, and over 30 outlying stations. One of the other observatories, the Dominion Astrophysical Observatory in Victoria, B.C., has 72-inch (183-centimeter) and 48-inch (122-centimeter) reflecting optical telescopes. The other, the Dominion Radio Astrophysical Observatory in Penticton, B.C., makes radio observations of space with an 84-inch (213-centimeter) parabolic reflector and two 4,500-foot (1,370-meter) antennas. The observatories study time, stars, materials in space, and the earth's crust and atmosphere.

Critically reviewed by DOMINION OBSERVATORY

DOMINO THEORY. See VIETNAM WAR.

DOMINOES, *DAHM uh nohz,* is the name of several games played with small, flat, oblong pieces called dominoes. Most sets of dominoes are made of bone, ivory, plastic, or wood. A regular set consists of 28 dominoes. A line divides each domino into two sections. Each section of 21 of the 28 dominoes is marked with from one to six dots. Both sections on one domino are blank, and six have one blank section and one with dots.

WORLD BOOK photo

In Playing Dominoes, each person matches a section of one of his dominoes with an identical section of an opponent's domino.

The simplest domino game is called the *block* game. In this game, the players first place all the pieces face down and mix them well. Then each chooses a certain number, usually seven if there are two playing, or five if there are three or four. The player with the highest *double domino* (piece with matching sections of dots) usually plays first. Suppose it is the 4-4. The player at the left plays next by matching any domino with four dots in one section to the 4-4 domino. For example, the matching domino may be the 4-6. The following player may then match a section with six dots to the 4-6 domino, or a section with four dots to the 4-4 domino. *Single dominoes* (pieces with different sections of dots) are placed end to end. Double dominoes are placed at right angles to the line of pieces. Plays can be made on either end of a single domino. In block dominoes, plays can be made on both sides of a double, but not on the ends.

If a player cannot match from the dominoes he has chosen, he draws from the pile that remains until he finds a domino that will match. After the pile is used, a player who cannot match must miss his turn, or *pass.*

The game ends when one player plays off all his dominoes or when no player can match any of the remaining dominoes with those he still holds. The player who goes out or has the fewest dots on his remaining dominoes scores points equal to the number of dots on his opponents' pieces. In most games, the first player to reach 100 points wins. LILLIAN FRANKEL

DOMITIAN, *doh MISH ee un* (A.D. 51-96), succeeded his brother Titus as Roman emperor in A.D. 81. His father Vespasian had been emperor from A.D. 69 to 79. Domitian spent his youth studying Roman history. When he became emperor, he tried to restore old standards of conduct and religion. He settled a war with Dacia (now Hungary and Romania) by compromise. To improve agriculture, he cut down on grape production to raise bigger grain and food crops. During his reign, people of other religions, such as Christians and Jews, were executed. His absolute rule made him unpopular. He was assassinated, with his wife's help. See also VESPASIAN; TITUS. MARY FRANCIS GYLES

DON BOSCO COLLEGE. See UNIVERSITIES AND COLLEGES (table).

DON COSSACKS. See COSSACKS, DON.

DON GIOVANNI. See OPERA (The Libretto; The Opera Repertoire).

DON JUAN, *dahn JOO un*, or, in Spanish, *dohn HWAHN*, is the hero of one of the most famous legends in literature. The legend originated in Europe during the Middle Ages. Its form became established in *The Deceiver of Seville* (1630), a play by the Spanish author Tirso de Molina. In this work, the handsome nobleman Don Juan Tenorio tries to seduce the daughter of Don Gonzalo, the knight commander. Don Gonzalo challenges Don Juan to a duel, and is killed by the hero. Don Juan visits the commander's tomb and scornfully invites the statue of his victim to dinner. The statue appears at the feast and returns the invitation, which Don Juan accepts. In the graveyard, the statue takes Don Juan's hand and drags him down into hell.

The complex personality of Don Juan has fascinated writers and composers for centuries. He has appeared in plays by Molière and George Bernard Shaw, an opera by Mozart, and a poem by Lord Byron. José Zorrilla's *Don Juan Tenorio* (1844) is the most popular treatment of the theme in modern Spanish literature. Each interprets Don Juan's personality differently. PETER G. EARLE

DON QUIXOTE, *kee HO tay*, a novel by Miguel de Cervantes of Spain, is one of the world's great works of literature. Cervantes published the novel in two parts, in 1605 and 1615. Until the 1800's, *Don Quixote* was thought of as a humorous story of a madman's adventures. Then, it became a model for a new type of fiction with heroes who do not conform to their times.

The hero of *Don Quixote* is a Spanish landowner who enlivens his monotonous life by reading fictional tales about knights of old. Wishing to live like the knights, he takes the name Don Quixote of La Mancha, dresses in armor, and sets out to gain fame by performing heroic deeds. The hero attacks windmills he thinks are giants and flocks of sheep he mistakes for armies. He chooses the peasant Sancho Panza to serve as his *squire* (attendant). Small, round Sancho riding his donkey contrasts with tall, thin Don Quixote on his scrawny horse Rocinante. Sancho stands for the real in life, Don Quixote for the ideal.

Although beaten and scorned, Don Quixote still believes in his heroic destiny. When part two of the novel begins, Quixote is enjoying his imagined fame. Then, he loses his faith in his destiny, but he becomes a prisoner of his imagined reputation and is forced to behave as if he really believed in himself as a hero. He finally regains his senses before he dies. GERMÁN BLEIBERG

See also SPANISH LITERATURE (Prose).

Drawing by Honoré Daumier. The Metropolitan Museum of Art, New York

Don Quixote and Sancho Panza, one of them lanky and the other squat, have been popular subjects in art for centuries.

DON RIVER is an important waterway in the southern part of Russia. The Don rises from a small lake near Tula. It flows south for 1,220 miles (1,963 kilometers) and empties into the Sea of Azov. Large ships can sail on the Don for about 800 miles (1,300 kilometers). A canal connects the Don and Volga rivers at a point where the rivers are only 37 miles (60 kilometers) apart. The northern part of the Don River flows through wooded, swampy land. But most of the river course is through rich farm and timber lands. The river carries shipments of lumber, grain, and cattle. The Don also has valuable fish, especially sturgeon. The city of Rostov is near the mouth of the Don. The chief branch of the Don is the Donets. THEODORE SHABAD

DONATELLO, *DAHN uh TEHL oh* (1386?-1466), was a great Italian sculptor. He was a master of all the techniques and materials of sculpture, and seemed able to handle any subject in the most striking manner.

Donatello was born in Florence, and served as assistant to sculptor Lorenzo Ghiberti. About 1415, he carved the marble statue of *St. George* and the relief below it, *St. George Killing the Dragon*. The saint stands relaxed, as if he is in deep thought—an ideal example of the Christian knight. The relief is remarkably flat, although it shows an extensive landscape.

Museo Nazionale, Florence, Italy. Alinari (Art Reference Bureau)

Donatello's *Saint George*

Donatello's effective use of realism appears in the statue of a prophet, known as *Lo Zuccone* (*The Pumpkinhead*), which he created about 1425. Late in life, Donatello began using distortion as he tried to show even more realistic emotional expression.

Donatello did three well-known statues of *David*. One of the statues is reproduced in the SCULPTURE article. His bronze *David* from the 1430's shows the influence of classical Greek sculpture on his own personal style. Donatello's other famous works include the bronze *equestrian monument* (man on horseback) of the Italian general *Gattamelata*. It was done in Padua between 1443 and 1453. G. HAYDN HUNTLEY

See also SCULPTURE (Early Renaissance).

DONATI'S COMET. See COMET (table).

DONELSON, JOHN. See TENNESSEE (History).

DONETSK, *dah NEHTSK* (pop. 891,000), is the largest city in the Donets River Basin of Russia. It lies in the Ukrainian Soviet Socialist Republic, about 80 miles (130 kilometers) northwest of Rostov (see RUSSIA [political map]). Donetsk is in the center of the rich

Donets coal fields. The coal is used in the huge iron and steel mills that make Donetsk one of the most important Russian industrial cities. Machinery and food products are also produced there.

The city was founded in the 1870's under the name Yuzovka. After the Russian Revolution, its name was changed to Stalin. In 1935, it became Stalino. The name was changed to Donetsk in 1961 as part of Russian Premier Nikita Khrushchev's drive to downgrade Joseph Stalin. THEODORE SHABAD

DONIZETTI, *DAHN ih ZEHT ih,* **GAETANO** (1797-1848), was an Italian opera composer. During his lifetime, he ranked second only to Gioacchino Rossini among Italian opera composers of his day. Donizetti wrote about 70 operas, and became famous for his ability to compose an opera in an astonishingly short time. He established his reputation with *Anna Bolena* (1830).

Of Donizetti's tragic works, only *Lucia di Lammermoor* (1835), with its famous sextet and "mad scene," is still popular. His finest work is perhaps the comic *Don Pasquale* (1843). This and several of his other operas are still occasionally produced, especially in Europe. They include *L'Elisir d'amore* (1832), *Lucrezia Borgia* (1833), *The Daughter of the Regiment* (1840), *La Favorite* (1840), and *Linda di Chamounix* (1842). Donizetti was born in Bergamo. HERBERT WEINSTOCK

DONJON. See CASTLE.

DONKEY, or BURRO, is the name of several animals which are relatives of horses, but are smaller and sturdier. Donkeys have huge ears. The wild ass of Ethiopia and northern Africa is the ancestor of the common domestic donkey. This wild ass looks like a zebra with no stripes. It stands about 4 feet (1.2 meters) high at the shoulders. Its coat of hair is gray, with a darker line along its back. This animal can run swiftly.

Thousands of years ago, men tamed the African wild ass and raised it for their own use. The domestic donkey is most common in southern Asia, southern Europe, and northern Africa. There are several varieties of the domestic donkey. People use light, speedy donkeys for riding. Those of a larger, heavier breed draw carts or carry loads on their backs. The hardy donkeys do not require as much or as good food as horses do. But they become stubborn and dull if badly treated. Female donkeys give good milk. In Northern Africa, they were once kept in large herds for this purpose. A female donkey is called a *jenny* or a *jennet*. The young donkey is called a *colt*. If a *jack* (male donkey) is mated with a *mare* (female horse), the animal that is born is a *mule* (see MULE). A cross between a female donkey and a *stallion* (male horse) is called a *hinny* (see HINNY). Small donkeys called *burros* are often used as pack animals, because they are sure-footed. Other kinds of wild asses are found in the dry plains of Asia. They include the *onager* and the *kiang* (see ONAGER).

J. C. Allen & Son

The Donkey, one of the first animals to be tamed by man, makes a gentle pet. Many donkeys, or *burros*, are exported from Mexico.

Scientific Classification. Donkeys are in the horse family, *Equidae*. The domestic donkey and the African wild ass are genus *Equus*, species *E. asinus*. E. LENDELL COCKRUM

DONNE, *duhn,* **JOHN** (1571?-1631), was one of the greatest English poets and preachers of the 1600's. He was an intellectual man, but he was also deeply emotional and had a fiery personality. These qualities are evident in his poems and sermons.

During his own time, Donne influenced several other poets including Abraham Cowley, George Herbert, Andrew Marvell, and Henry Vaughan. Donne and these men, called the *metaphysical poets*, wrote complex and dramatic verse in irregular meters. Donne's work was generally ignored during the 1700's and 1800's, but interest in his poetry revived in the 1900's. Modern poets, including T. S. Eliot, have praised and imitated his works. See METAPHYSICAL POETS.

His Life. Donne was born in London. A descendant of Saint Thomas More, he was raised as a Roman Catholic. Sometime during the 1590's, however, he became an Anglican. In 1597, he became secretary to Sir Thomas Egerton. He secretly married Egerton's niece, Ann More, in 1601. Ann's father resented the marriage and caused Egerton to dismiss Donne from his job.

For many years, Donne struggled to support himself and his growing family. He became an Anglican priest in 1615. Through his powers as a preacher and his influence with King James I, Donne became dean of St. Paul's Cathedral in 1621, a position he held until his death. Donne preached many sermons at the cathedral and at the royal court. Only four of his poems were published in his lifetime. The most important were the *elegies* (poems lamenting a death) *The First Anniversary* (1611) and *The Second Anniversary* (1612).

His Poetry. Donne wrote poetry about a wide range of subjects. He also used many poetic styles. His *Satires* and *Elegies*, written early in his career, mingle classical forms with a distinctly modern flavor. In *Songs and Sonnets*, his best-known group of poems, Donne wrote both tenderly and cynically of love and death. Donne's major lyric poems include "The Canonization" and "The Extasie." In later life, Donne turned to religious poetry. He produced a superb series called *Holy Sonnets*, which includes "Death be not proud" and "Batter my heart, three personed God"; a great meditative poem called "Good Friday, 1613"; and three personal hymns.

Donne's language is forceful and has the quality of everyday speech. At times, his meaning seems obscure, but he was always logical. Donne was a master at blending thought and emotion. He had a genius for creating extended poetic metaphors called *conceits*. In the metaphysical conceit, the poet developed a lengthy, complex image to express his involved, but subtly controlled, view of a person, object, or feeling. In his lyric "A Valediction: Forbidding Mourning," Donne compared the souls of lovers to the legs of a compass:

If they be two, they are two so
As stiff twin compasses are two;
Thy soul the fixed foot, makes no show
To move, but doth, if th' other do.

Donne's *Devotions upon Emergent Occasions* (1624) contains the famous line ". . . never send to know for whom the bell tolls; it tolls for thee." RICHARD S. SYLVESTER

DONNELLY, IGNATIUS (1831-1901), was an American politician, reformer, and author who helped form the Populist Party. He served in the U.S. House of Representatives from 1863 to 1869 as a Republican congressman from Minnesota, then later quit the party.

Donnelly wrote part of the Populist Party platform in 1892 (see POPULIST PARTY). This platform called for a federal income tax, government ownership of railroads, an eight-hour work day, and unlimited coinage of silver (see FREE SILVER).

Donnelly was born in Philadelphia, and moved to Minnesota in 1857. He wrote several books, including one on his own theory of the earth's collision with a comet and one on Francis Bacon's supposed writing of Shakespeare's plays. CHARLES FORCEY and LINDA FORCEY

DONNER PASS cuts through the Sierra Nevada, a mountain range in eastern California. The pass was the scene of a great tragedy in the severe winter of 1846-1847. A party of 82 settlers from Illinois and adjoining states, led by George and Jacob Donner, became snowbound there, and only 47 survived. They built crude shelters of logs, rocks, and hides, and ate twigs, mice, their animals, their shoes, and finally their own dead.

The party reached the High Sierras in late October, but a snowstorm had already closed the pass. In December, 15 persons tried to get through the snow-blocked pass. Eight of them died, but seven got through and sent back rescue workers. The rescue workers brought the other 40 survivors through the pass.

Donner Pass lies 7,088 feet (2,160 meters) above sea level, about 35 miles (56 kilometers) southwest of Reno, Nev. The first transcontinental railroad system, completed in 1869, went through the pass. Donner Pass is a national historical landmark. The area is now a summer resort and ski resort. RICHARD A. BARTLETT

"DON'T GIVE UP THE SHIP." See LAWRENCE, JAMES.

DOODLEBUG. See ANT LION.

DOOLEY, THOMAS ANTHONY, III (1927-1961), an American physician, became famous in the 1950's as the *jungle doctor of Laos.* He helped found MEDICO (Medical International Cooperation Organization) in 1957. Through it, he established two hospitals in Laos, and one each in Vietnam, Cambodia, and Malaya. He helped finance MEDICO with funds from lecture tours and books he wrote.

Dooley's first book, *Deliver Us from Evil* (1956), described his experiences as a U.S. Navy doctor in Vietnam in 1954. There, he helped refugees fleeing from Communist North Vietnam. He left the Navy in 1956 and started his medical work in Laos. At the age of 34, Dooley died of cancer. After his death, Congress awarded him a gold medal for his humanitarian work. Dooley was born in St. Louis. L. T. COGGESHALL

DOOLITTLE, HILDA (1886-1961), an American poet, became a leader of the imagist poets. The *imagists* tried to present direct impressions by a careful use of words, rhythms, and other poetic devices. During World War I, Miss Doolittle edited the *Egoist*, the imagist magazine. Her books of verse include *Sea Garden* (1916), *Hymen* (1921), *Collected Poems* (1940), and *Flowering of the Rod* (1946). She signed her poems "H.D." She was born in Bethlehem, Pa., and lived in Europe after 1911.

DOOLITTLE, JAMES HAROLD (1896-), a noted American flier, led the first bombing raid on Tokyo in World War II. He led 16 B-25 twin-engine bombers, normally land-based planes, from the deck of the aircraft carrier U.S.S. *Hornet* in the surprise attack on Tokyo on April 18, 1942. Congress awarded him the Medal of Honor for this daring raid.

A lieutenant colonel when he led his raid, Doolittle rose to lieutenant general during World War II. He commanded the 12th Air Force in the North African invasion in 1942, and later the 15th Air Force in the Mediterranean area. In 1944 and 1945, he was commander of the 8th Air Force, which bombed western Europe. He also commanded the 8th Air Force on Okinawa after Germany surrendered.

U.S. Army
James H. Doolittle

Doolittle was born in Alameda, Calif., and was graduated from the University of California. He was an Army aviator during World War I. Doolittle left the Army in 1930 to work for the Shell Petroleum Corporation. He returned to military duty in 1940.

Doolittle was chairman of the National Advisory Committee for Aeronautics from 1956 to 1958. In 1962, he became director of the Space Technology Laboratories, which designs and tests spacecraft. ALFRED GOLDBERG

See also AIRPLANE (table: Speed Records).

DOOM PALM. See DOUM PALM.

DOOMSDAY BOOK. See DOMESDAY BOOK.

DOON, RIVER, is a stream in Ayr County of southern Scotland which was made famous by the poetry of Robert Burns. The River Doon rises in the Kells Range and flows northwest to empty into the Firth of Clyde near the town of Ayr. Burns was born 2 miles (3.2 kilometers) from Ayr. Also nearby is the bridge Burns made famous as the "Auld Brig o' Doon" in the poem "Tam o'Shanter." JOHN W. WEBB

DOOR is an opening through which people enter and leave a room or building. A door is also the movable frame used to open and close such an opening. This frame may be hung on hinges. It may slide in a groove, turn on a pivot like a vertical axle, or fold like an accordion. Some doors have an upper half and a lower half that open separately. A revolving door consists of four panels that turn on a central axle.

Some doors are made of rare woods decorated with carvings and precious metals. Many church doors are made of or covered with bronze and decorated with designs and figures. Such doors include the bronze door made in the 1400's by the Italian sculptor Lorenzo Ghiberti for the baptistery in Florence. Kenneth J. Conant

See also Ghiberti, Lorenzo.

DOORBELL. See Electric Bell.

DOORWEED. See Knotgrass.

DOPPLER EFFECT is the apparent change in frequency of sound, light, or radio waves caused by motion. For example, the *pitch* (frequency) of a train whistle seems higher when the train approaches and lower after it passes and begins to move away. The actual pitch of the whistle remains constant. Astronomers study the speed of a star by measuring the apparent change in the frequency of its light waves due to motion. Christian Doppler, a German physicist, described the effect in 1842. See also Sound (Pitch); Radar (Other Radars); Relativity (General Relativity Theory). Rawson Bennett

DORADO. See Dolphin (fish).

DORCHESTER, BARON. See Carleton (Sir Guy).

DORDOGNE RIVER. See Garonne River.

DORDT COLLEGE. See Universities and Colleges (table).

DORÉ, *daw RAY*, **GUSTAVE** (1832-1883), a French painter and sculptor, illustrated a large number of literary masterpieces. These include the Bible, the works of Rabelais and Balzac, Dante's *Divine Comedy*, LaFontaine's *Fables*, Tennyson's *Idylls of the King*, Cervantes' *Don Quixote*, Coleridge's "The Rime of the Ancient Mariner" and Poe's "The Raven." His style is dramatic and imaginative, but sometimes repetitious.

Doré was born Paul Gustave Doré in Strasbourg, Alsace-Lorraine. As a boy, he showed a remarkable talent for drawing. His work was in great demand while he was still quite young. His fame outside of France rests chiefly on his illustrations. Norman L. Rice

For reproductions of several of Doré's works, see Charon; Dante Alighieri; Ezra; Peter, Saint; see also City (pictures: The Industrial Revolution, An Early Traffic Jam).

From *The Terrible Gustave Doré* by Lehmann-Haupt.
© 1943 by Marchbanks Press

Gustave Doré illustrated the fairy tales of Charles Perrault. This heavily detailed scene shows Tom Thumb entering the forest.

DORIANS were a group of ancient Greeks. They lived in the northwestern part of the Greek mainland before 1150 B.C. Toward the end of the 1100's, they overran most of the *Peloponnesus* (the southern peninsula of Greece). The invasion helped end the Mycenaean civilization which flourished there. The best known Greeks of Dorian descent were the Spartans. In addition to Sparta, Dorian cities included Argos, Corinth, Megara, and Rhodes. Dorians also settled in Crete, Sicily, southern Italy, the Sporades Islands, and southwestern Asia Minor (present-day Turkey). See also Achaean; Aeolians; Corinth; Greece, Ancient (History); Ionians; Mycenae; Sparta. Norman A. Doenges

DORIC COLUMN. See Column.

DORIS was a Greek goddess. See Nereid.

DORMER. See Architecture (Architectural Terms).

DORMOUSE, *DAWR mous*, is a tiny animal that looks like a small squirrel. Dormice are well known for their sleepy ways. When cold weather arrives, they stock a nest with food and *hibernate* (sleep through the winter). They may wake up on warm winter days and eat some of their food. In *Alice's Adventures in Wonderland*, author Lewis Carroll described a humorous dormouse that could not be kept awake at a tea party.

Stephan Dalton, FRPS-NAS

A Dormouse Hunts for Food at Night.

The dormouse has fine, silky fur, a pointed nose, and big black eyes. Its body is about 3 inches (8 centimeters) long, and so is its tail. Dormice are rodents, and are closely related to mice and rats. They live in trees and bushes in Africa, Asia, and Europe. They hunt for food at night, and eat berries, grains, and nuts.

Scientific Classification. Dormice belong to the dormouse family, *Gliridae*. There are several genera of dormice. Daniel Brant

See also Animal (picture: Hibernating Animals).

DÖRPFELD, WILHELM. See Troy (Archaeological Troy).

DORR, THOMAS WILSON. See Dorr's Rebellion.

DORR'S REBELLION. Before 1843, factory workers and city dwellers in Rhode Island were not generally allowed to vote. Rhode Island was still operating under its old charter of 1663, which restricted voting to landholders or their eldest sons. This charter deprived over half of Rhode Island's adult males of the right to vote.

Thomas Dorr, a member of the state legislature from 1833 to 1837, became head of a party that sought to grant the vote to all men of legal age. In 1841, the party held a convention and drafted a constitution. The state government, realizing that affairs were drifting toward revolution, drafted a new constitution, but it was voted down by the people. Dorr's reform constitution received a decisive majority in a separate election, but the government ruled that it had been illegally adopted. Dorr's party then held its own election and chose Dorr to be governor, but state troops put down the rebellion. Dorr was convicted of treason and sentenced to life imprisonment, but was released after one year.

Partly as a result of Dorr's Rebellion, Rhode Island obtained a new constitution in 1842. It gave native-born citizens the right to vote if they paid taxes of $1 a year or served in the militia. RAY ALLEN BILLINGTON

DORSET. See ENGLAND (political map).

DORTMUND, *DAWRT moont* (pop. 648,900), is a major German industrial city. An iron, steel, and heavy machinery center, Dortmund stands in the heart of Germany's famous coal-bearing Ruhr district. Canals link the city with the North Sea and the Rhine and Weser rivers. Dortmund was founded in the 800's and was one of the cities of the Hanseatic League. It grew rapidly after 1870. During World War II, Dortmund was heavily bombed. Since then it has recovered rapidly, and is again famous for its brewing industry and its Westfalenhalle, one of the largest sports arenas in western Europe. For location, see GERMANY (political map). JAMES K. POLLOCK

DOSHISHA UNIVERSITY. See JAPAN (Education).

DOS PASSOS, JOHN (1896-1970), was an American novelist whose work is dominated by social and political themes. His experiments in fiction writing earned him distinction as a novelist in the 1920's and 1930's.

Dos Passos first achieved fame with his World War I novels, *One Man's Initiation* (1917) and *Three Soldiers* (1921). *Three Soldiers* is a protest against the impact of war on civilization and art. *Manhattan Transfer* (1925) reveals Dos Passos' disillusioned response to postwar urban America. This novel led to his most famous work, the *U.S.A.* trilogy, which pessimistically surveys the disintegration of U.S. culture that Dos Passos believed took place during the first three decades of the 1900's. The trilogy consists of *The 42nd Parallel* (1930), *1919* (1932), and *The Big Money* (1936).

U.S.A. brings together many characters in a wide variety of episodes. Dos Passos featured a technique called the Newsreel, which used newspaper headlines, words from popular songs, and advertisements to surround the action and characters. Another technique, called The Camera's Eye, gives the author's view of his subject. Dos Passos regarded his style as providing a social and historical background in which individual actions reflected larger patterns in U.S. society.

Houghton Mifflin
John Dos Passos

John Roderigo Dos Passos was born in Chicago and attended Harvard University. He was a political liberal in his early years, but moved sharply toward conservatism by the 1940's. His *District of Columbia* trilogy—*Adventures of a Young Man* (1939), *Number One* (1943), and *The Grand Design* (1949)—reveals his conservative attitudes. Dos Passos also wrote *Mr. Wilson's War* (1962), a history of World War I. JOSEPH N. RIDDEL

DOSTOEVSKY, *DAHS tuh YEHF skee,* **FYODOR MIKHAILOVICH** (1821-1881), must be regarded as one of the two or three greatest novelists Russia has produced. His works are widely read throughout the world.

Dostoevsky's novels are essentially novels of ideas embodied in his great characters. His characters are intensely individual, vital, and complex. They are usually caught up in tremendous dramatic situations as they struggle between good and evil in an effort to achieve salvation through suffering.

Dostoevsky was born in Moscow. By the time he had finished his education, he had already decided to make literature his career. His first story, *Poor Folk* (1846), won the enthusiastic praise of the critics because it added something new to Russian literature at that time—a deep psychological study of poor, unhappy people. Throughout his life, he wrote about the poor and unhappy, the insulted and injured, and the strange, abnormal people who defied conventional society.

While still a young man, Dostoevsky was arrested for taking part in a political conspiracy, and was sentenced to death. When he was on the scaffold waiting for his execution, the czar's courier brought a reprieve. Dostoevsky, instead, was sent to prison for four years to work at hard labor in Siberia. He then served four more years of punishment as a common soldier. In his *Memoirs from the House of the Dead* (1861-1862), he told in realistic detail of his prison life.

Years of bitter, poverty-stricken existence followed for Dostoevsky. He published periodicals, and always had to write against time to keep his creditors from sending him to a debtors' prison. After his *Memoirs from Underground* (1864), an extraordinary psychological study of a spiritual and intellectual misfit, he once again won popularity with his famous novel *Crime and Punishment* (1866). It tells of a student who commits murder to fulfill a theory that would enable him to be one of the strong men of the earth.

Despite his success, Dostoevsky remained poor, largely because he was generous and could not take care of his money. He went abroad, and wrote two great novels, *The Idiot* (1868) and *The Possessed* (1871-1872). Dostoevsky later returned to Russia, and completed his last, and, in many respects, his greatest novel, *The Brothers Karamazov* (1879-1880). ERNEST J. SIMMONS

See also BROTHERS KARAMAZOV; RUSSIAN LITERATURE (The 1860's and 1870's).

Pictorial Parade
Fyodor Dostoevsky

DOTY, JAMES D. See MADISON (Government).

DOUAY, or **DOUAI, BIBLE.** See BIBLE (The Vulgate and the Douay).

DOUBLE BASS. See BASS (musical instrument).

DOUBLE-ENTRY BOOKKEEPING. See BOOKKEEPING.

DOUBLE INDEMNITY. See INSURANCE (Terms).

DOUBLE JEOPARDY. See CONSTITUTION OF THE UNITED STATES (Amendment 5).

DOUBLE STAR is a pair of stars that revolve around a center of gravity between them. Double stars are also called *binaries.* The term *binary star* was probably used for the first time by Sir William Herschel in 1802. There are three kinds of double stars—visual, spectroscopic, and eclipsing. Many times double stars are so close together that even the largest telescope shows them as a single star. Sometimes two stars appear close together only because they are in nearly the same direction in space. One such star may be much closer to us than the other. Astronomers call such cases *optical pairs.*

Most double stars appear as one to the unaided eye. If they can be seen as two stars, or if a telescope reveals them as two stars, they are called *visual doubles* or *visual binaries.* Mizar, the next to the last star in the handle of the Big Dipper, is the first visual binary ever discovered. John Baptist Riccioli discovered it in 1650. The smaller partner of Mizar is Alcor. Mizar and Alcor are *spectroscopic binaries.* So what may appear as a single star in the handle of the Big Dipper is four stars: a visual binary, each star of which is a spectroscopic binary.

Astronomers detect spectroscopic binaries by an instrument called the *spectroscope* (see SPECTROSCOPE). At regular intervals, the lines in the spectra of such double stars appear alternately single and double, showing two stars are present, revolving around each other.

Some spectroscopic binaries revolve in such a way that one star *eclipses,* or passes in front of, its companion star at regular intervals. The light we see becomes less for a short period. Such double stars are called *eclipsing binaries,* and are discovered by their regular variations in brightness. An example of an eclipsing binary is the star Algol (see ALGOL). CHARLES A. FEDERER, JR.

DOUBLEDAY, ABNER (1819-1893), was a United States Army officer who was once considered the inventor of baseball. A commission established by major league baseball officials in 1906 credited Doubleday with inventing baseball in Cooperstown, N.Y., in 1839. In honor of Doubleday, Cooperstown residents established the National Baseball Hall of Fame and Museum in the town. The baseball field there is called Doubleday Field. The Hall of Fame operates under the jurisdiction of professional baseball. Most historians today claim that Doubleday had little, if anything, to do with baseball. They believe the sport probably developed from an English game called *rounders.* See BASEBALL (History [The Abner Doubleday Theory]).

Doubleday was born in Ballston Spa, N.Y. He graduated from the United States Military Academy in 1842, and he served in the Mexican War (1846-1848). Doubleday became a major general in the Union Army during the Civil War (1861-1865). He commanded the troops at Fort Sumter that fired the first shots by the North in the Civil War. Doubleday also fought heroically at the Battle of Gettysburg. ED FITZGERALD

DOUBLET, in clothing, see CLOTHING (Renaissance); in jewelry, see GEM (Imitation and Artificial Gems).

DOUBLOON is a Spanish and Spanish-American gold coin that was widely used in America until the 1800's. The name comes from the Latin *duplus,* meaning *double.* The doubloon was equal to four *pistoles*

Chase Manhattan Bank Money Museum

The Spanish Doubloon shows the face of Charles IV, King of Spain. The other side bears his royal coat of arms.

(16 silver dollars). It was also called *doblón de a ocho* meaning *doubloon of eight,* because it was worth eight gold escudos. It weighed about 27 grams (slightly less than one ounce). BURTON H. HOBSON

DOUBTING THOMAS. See THOMAS, SAINT.

DOUC LANGUR. See MONKEY (picture).

DOUGHNUT is a round, fried cake with a hole in the center. Dutch settlers brought the fried cake (*olykoeck*) to colonial America. A legend suggests that Captain Hanson Gregory, a sea captain, invented the doughnut hole in 1847. According to this legend, he cut holes in the dough before frying to make the cakes more digestible. A bronze plaque marks his birthplace in Camden township (now Rockport), in Maine.

DOUGLAS. See MAN, ISLE OF.

DOUGLAS, DONALD WILLS (1892-), an American aircraft manufacturer, organized the Douglas Company in 1921. It became the Douglas Aircraft Company, Inc., in 1928 and the McDonnell Douglas Corporation in 1967. He designed the army planes that made the first flight around the world in 1924. His firm has made widely used commercial airliners. Douglas was born in Brooklyn, N.Y. See also AVIATION (History of the Aviation Industry). V. E. CANGELOSI and R. E. WESTMEYER

DOUGLAS, SIR JAMES (1803-1877), served as the first governor of the colony of British Columbia, in what is now Canada. He held the office from 1858 to 1864.

Douglas was born in Demerara, British Guiana (now Guyana), and was educated in Great Britain. In 1820, he went to Quebec as an employee of the North West Company, a British fur-trading firm. The Hudson's Bay Company, a rival organization, took over the North West Company in 1821.

From 1839 to 1858, Douglas served as chief officer in the Columbia territory for the Hudson's Bay Company. In 1843, he founded Fort Victoria (now Victoria) as headquarters for the company. The fort stood on Vancouver Island, which today forms part of British Columbia. Vancouver Island became a British colony in 1849, and Douglas served as governor from 1851 to 1863. He was knighted in 1863. P. B. WAITE

DOUGLAS, SIR JOHN SHOLTO. See QUEENSBERRY, MARQUIS OF.

DOUGLAS, LLOYD CASSEL (1877-1951), a Protestant minister, wrote the best-selling novels *Magnificent Obsession* (1929), *The Robe* (1942), and *The Big Fisherman* (1948). He also wrote *Forgive Us Our Trespasses* (1932), *Green Light* (1935), and *Invitation to Live* (1940). *A Time to Remember* (1951) is his autobiography. As a novelist, his chief interest was to inspire religious teaching, but, to his surprise, his books won great popularity.

Douglas was born in Columbia City, Ind. He graduated from Wittenberg College. He began to preach in Indiana, and then became a pastor in Washington, D.C. Later, he directed religious work at the University of Illinois, and served as a pastor in Ann Arbor, Mich.; Akron, Ohio; and Los Angeles, Calif. BERNARD DUFFEY

DOUGLAS, NORMAN (1868-1952), a British writer, is best known for his witty and satirical novel *South Wind* (1917). The book is set on an imaginary island called Nepenthe, based on the island of Capri. The word *nepenthe* means a drug capable of banishing sorrow and fear. The central theme is the nature of truth. Thomas Heard, an Anglican bishop, receives an education in the complexity of truth and a doctrine of individualism. Douglas' books about the Mediterranean region, include *Siren Land* (1911) and *Old Calabria* (1915). He wrote two other novels, *They Went* (1921) and *In the Beginning* (1928). George Norman Douglas was born near Aberdeen, Scotland. JOHN ESPEY

DOUGLAS, PAUL HOWARD (1892-), a noted economist, served as a United States senator from Illinois. A Democrat, Douglas was a senator from 1949 to 1967. He was a leading liberal in the Senate.

Douglas was an economics professor at the University of Chicago from 1925 to 1948. He helped revise the Federal Social Security Act in 1939, wrote the first Illinois Old Age Pension Act of 1935, and helped write the first Unemployment Insurance Act of Illinois in 1937. He served as a Chicago alderman from 1939 to 1942. During World War II, Douglas enlisted as a private in the First Marine Division at the age of 50. He was wounded twice in the South Pacific, and received the Bronze Star for "heroic achievement in action." He was born in Salem, Mass. PAUL M. ANGLE

DOUGLAS, STEPHEN ARNOLD (1813-1861), was a popular and skillful American orator and political leader just before the Civil War. He became especially well known for his debates with Abraham Lincoln on the question of slavery. These debates ranked as noteworthy events in American history. See LINCOLN, ABRAHAM (The Debates with Douglas).

Douglas was born on a farm near Brandon, Vt. Politics interested him and he wanted to become a lawyer. When he was twenty, he went to Illinois. He was admitted to the bar at Jacksonville, Ill. Douglas, a Democrat, was elected prosecuting attorney for his district in 1835. The next year he was elected to the state legislature. He was judge of the Supreme Court of Illinois from 1841 to 1843. He was elected to the United States House of Representatives in 1843, and became a member of the United States Senate in 1847.

Photograph by Mathew Brady. National Archives, Washington, D.C.
Stephen A. Douglas

Douglas was a short man, with a large head and broad shoulders. Because of his appearance, he received the nickname the *Little Giant*. He won respect in the Senate for his ability, energy, sincerity, and fearlessness, and became chairman of the Senate committee on territories.

The slavery controversy was the great issue of that period. As each territory applied for admission to the Union, a storm of debate arose in Congress as to whether the new state should be free or slaveholding. Douglas would not own slaves himself, but he was not opposed to slavery and did not believe that the Union should be sacrificed for it. He thought that the problem could be settled by peaceable means. He warmly favored westward expansion, but believed that the people of the territories should decide for themselves whether they wanted slavery. He called this principle *popular sovereignty*. It was also called *squatter sovereignty* (see SQUATTER SOVEREIGNTY). Douglas' committee reported the famous Kansas-Nebraska Bill in 1854. It included the principle of popular sovereignty (see KANSAS-NEBRASKA ACT). Douglas' brilliant leadership was responsible for the passage of this much disputed bill.

When Douglas ran for re-election to the Senate in 1858, his Republican opponent was Abraham Lincoln, a man then almost unknown outside Illinois. The two men held a series of public meetings in which they debated the problem of slavery and its extension. These meetings attracted the attention of the entire country.

Douglas argued that the people must have the right to control slavery. Lincoln said that a nation half-slave and half-free could not exist. Douglas won his re-election to the Senate, but some of his speeches in the debates displeased Southern Democrats. He was nominated for President by Northern Democrats in 1860, but the South refused to support him. The Democratic party split its votes among three candidates. Douglas received only 12 electoral votes. The Republican candidate, Abraham Lincoln, won the election.

Douglas offered his services to President Lincoln when the Civil War broke out. At Lincoln's request, he started on a tour of the border states to arouse enthusiasm for the Union cause. But two months after the fall of Fort Sumter, he died. He was buried in a small park at the foot of Thirty-Sixth Street in Chicago. JEANNETTE C. NOLAN

See also COMPROMISE OF 1850.

DOUGLAS, WILLIAM ORVILLE (1898-), has served on the Supreme Court of the United States longer than any other justice. He gained renown not only because of his work as a member of the Supreme Court, but also because of his wide travels and his books on vital problems in America's national and international life.

Douglas, a Democrat, became an associate justice in 1939. On the Supreme Court, he strongly supported government protection of civil liberties and civil rights. His books include *Of Men and Mountains* (1950), *Strange Lands and Friendly People* (1951), *An Almanac of Liberty* (1954), *The Anatomy of Liberty* (1963), and *Points of Rebellion* (1970).

Douglas was born in Maine, Minn., and was

graduated from Whitman College. He received his law degree from Columbia University. He was chairman of the Securities and Exchange Commission, 1937 to 1939. H. G. REUSCHLEIN

See also SUPREME COURT OF THE U.S. (picture).

DOUGLAS FIR is one of the largest and most valuable timber trees in the world. This *softwood* (cone-bearing) tree is the source of more lumber than any other single tree in North America. It is common in the Western United States and Canada, both in the Pacific Coast region and the Rocky Mountains. This tree grows about 200 feet (61 meters) tall and 3 to 4 feet (91 to 120 centimeters) thick through the trunk. Its flat needles are about 1 inch (2.5 centimeters) long. Its egg-shaped cones have odd, three-pointed *bracts* (leaflike structures). The Douglas fir is the state tree of Oregon.

Scientific Classification. The Douglas fir belongs to the pine family, *Pinaceae*. It is genus *Pseudotsuga*, species *P. menziesii*. ELBERT L. LITTLE, JR.

See also CONE-BEARING PLANT; PINE; SPRUCE; TREE (picture: Familiar Broadleaf and Needleleaf Trees).

DOUGLAS-HOME, ALEXANDER FREDERICK. See HOME, LORD.

DOUGLASS, FREDERICK (1817-1895), was the leading spokesman of American Negroes in the 1800's. Born a slave, Douglass became a noted author and speaker. He devoted his life to the abolition of slavery and the fight for Negro rights.

Frederick Augustus Washington Bailey was born in Tuckahoe, Md., near Easton. At the age of 8, he was sent to Baltimore to work for one of his master's relatives. There, helped by his new master's wife, he began to educate himself. He later worked in a shipyard, where he *calked* ships, making them watertight.

In 1838, the young man fled from his master and went to New Bedford, Mass. To avoid capture, he dropped his two middle names and changed his last name to Douglass. He got a job as a calker, but the other men refused to work with him because he was black. Douglass then held a number of jobs, among them collecting rubbish and digging cellars.

In 1841, at a meeting of the Massachusetts Antislavery Society, Douglass told what freedom meant to him. The audience was so impressed that the society hired him to lecture about his experiences as a slave. During the early 1840's, Douglass protested against segregated seating on trains by sitting in cars reserved for whites. He had to be dragged from the white cars. Douglass also protested against religious discrimination. He walked out of a church that kept blacks from taking part in a service until the whites had finished participating.

J. W. Hurn, Library of Congress
Frederick Douglass

In 1845, Douglass published his autobiography, *Narrative of the Life of Frederick Douglass*. He feared that his identity as a runaway slave would be revealed when the book was published, so he went to England that same year. In England, Douglass continued to speak against slavery. He also found friends who raised enough money to buy his freedom.

Douglass returned to the United States in 1847 and founded an antislavery newspaper, the *North Star*, in Rochester, N.Y. In the 1850's, Douglass charged that employers hired white immigrants ahead of black Americans. He once declared: "Every hour sees the black man elbowed out of employment by some newly arrived emigrant whose hunger and whose color are thought to give him a better title to the place." He accused even some abolitionist businessmen of job discrimination against Negroes.

Douglass also led a successful attack against segregated schools in Rochester. His home was a station on the underground railroad, which helped runaway slaves reach freedom (see UNDERGROUND RAILROAD).

During the Civil War (1861-1865), Douglass helped recruit blacks for the Union Army. He discussed the problems of slavery with President Abraham Lincoln several times. Douglass served as Recorder of Deeds in the District of Columbia from 1881 to 1886 and as U.S. minister to Haiti from 1889 to 1891. He wrote two expanded versions of his autobiography—*My Bondage and My Freedom* (1855) and *Life and Times of Frederick Douglass* (1881). ELLIOTT RUDWICK

DOUKHOBORS, *DOO kuh bawrz*, also spelled DUKHOBORS, belong to a Christian sect in western Canada. *Doukhobors* is a Russian word meaning *spirit wrestlers*. They believe the "voice within" each person is his guide. Therefore, they see no need for churches or governments. Doukhobors are pacifists.

Peasants founded the sect in Russia in the mid-1700's. The Doukhobors adopted many of the ideas of the Russian author Leo Tolstoy in the late 1800's, under the leadership of Peter Verigin. In 1899, Tolstoy and English and American Quakers helped more than 7,000 Doukhobors emigrate to western Canada. There they established communal farms. The group still survives, but its communal life has largely died out. A small group of Doukhobors called the *Sons of Freedom* wishes to restore the communal communities in Canada or in any country that would welcome them. H. B. HAWTHORN

See also TOLSTOY, LEO (New Ideas).

DOUM PALM, or DOOM PALM, grows in Arabia, Upper Egypt, and Central Africa. Each branch of the doum palm ends in a tuft of deeply lobed, fan-shaped leaves. The tree bears an irregularly oval fruit about the size of an apple. The fruit has a red outer skin and a thick, spongy, and rather sweet inner substance that tastes like gingerbread. The palm has often been called the *gingerbread tree*. Large quantities of these fruits have been found in the tombs of the Egyptian pharaohs. The seeds are a source of *vegetable ivory*.

Scientific Classification. Doum palms belong to the palm family, *Palmae*. They are classified as genus *Hyphaene*, species *H. thebaica*. HAROLD E. MOORE, JR.

DOUPPIONI. See SILK (Douppioni).

DOURO RIVER, *DOH roo*, rises in the central plateau of Spain and flows west through Portugal to the Atlantic Ocean. It is 485 miles (781 kilometers) long and drains about 37,000 square miles (95,800 square kilometers). Porto, the chief seaport of Portugal, lies about 3 miles (5 kilometers) from the mouth of the river. Large vessels cannot travel on the Douro because of its rapids. In Spain, the river is called the DUERO; in Portugal, the DOURO. WALTER C. LANGSAM

DOVE is the name of some birds in the pigeon and dove family. The term *dove* generally refers to the smaller members of the family, and *pigeon* to the larger ones.

Doves live throughout the world. They grow from 6 to 12 inches (15 to 30 centimeters) long and weigh from 1 to 9 ounces (28 to 255 grams). Doves eat a wide variety of fruits, grains, and nuts. For more specific information, see the WORLD BOOK article on PIGEON.

Scientific Classification. Doves belong to the pigeon and dove family, *Columbidae*. RICHARD F. JOHNSTON

See also MOURNING DOVE; TURTLEDOVE.

DOVE, ARTHUR GARFIELD (1880-1946), was one of the earliest abstract painters in the United States. He painted his first symbolic abstract pictures of nature in 1910, long before abstract painting was common in America. His compositions, which are usually rather small, emphasize areas of solid color and lines and edges. Dove made constructions similar to collages in the 1920's (see COLLAGE).

Dove was born in Canandaigua, N.Y., and gained early success as a magazine illustrator. He lived in Paris for 18 months during 1908 and 1909, and absorbed the influence of the new abstract art movements there. When he returned to New York, he began painting in a manner similar to that of the abstract expressionists of the 1940's. Dove was never a popular success. Alfred Stieglitz, a photographer and art dealer, helped support him and exhibited his work. GEORGE EHRLICH

DOVEKIE. See AUK.

DOVER, Del. (pop. 17,488), is the state capital, and commercial center of a rich farm area. Dover is on the St. Jones River, about 45 miles (72 kilometers) south of Wilmington. The main industries include canning, and the manufacture of latex products. Delaware State College and Wesley College are in the city. Dover was founded in 1717 and became the capital of Delaware in 1777. It was incorporated as a town in 1829 and as a city in 1929. It has a council-manager government. Dover is the seat of Kent County. In 1776, Caesar Rodney, a planter living near Dover, rode horseback to Philadelphia, where he cast a vote for the adoption of the Declaration of Independence. His vote broke a tie between the Delaware delegates to the Continental Congress. JOHN A. MUNROE

See also DELAWARE; RODNEY, CAESAR.

DOVER (pop. 34,030) is a British town located on the Strait of Dover about 65 miles (105 kilometers) southeast of London. It is the chief port for travel between England and France. On clear days, persons 24 miles (39 kilometers) away in Calais, France, can see the white chalk cliffs of Dover. The remains of Dover castle overlook the town from one of the chalk hills 320 feet (98 meters) above the water. During World War II, German guns and planes shelled and bombed Dover. See also ENGLAND (picture). FRANCIS H. HERRICK

DOVER, STRAIT OF, is a narrow channel which connects the North Sea with the English Channel and separates England and France at their closest points. The Strait of Dover is only about 21 miles (34 kilometers) wide and is very shallow, with an average depth of less than 100 feet (30 meters). Chalk cliffs rise high on either side of the Strait. The ports of Dover, England, and Calais, France, are located opposite each other on the Strait of Dover. In 1964, Great Britain and France agreed to build a railroad tunnel under the English Channel.

Many athletes have set records by swimming the Channel, usually from Calais to Dover (see ENGLISH CHANNEL [Swimming the Channel]). JOHN W. WEBB

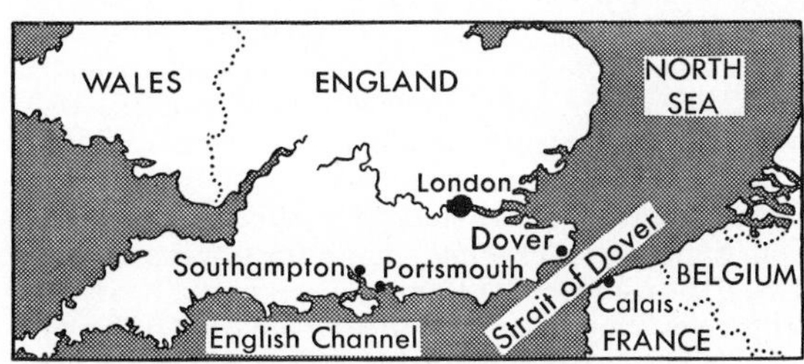

Location Map of the City and Strait of Dover

DOW, HERBERT HENRY (1866-1930), was an early leader in the U.S. chemical industry. In 1897, he founded the Dow Chemical Company. Through research, which Dow emphasized, the company has manufactured a variety of products. It mass-produced industrial chemicals, led in developing carbon tetrachloride, introduced a cheap *phenol* (carbolic acid),

Grant Heilman

The Mourning Dove was named for the sad cooing sound made by the male. Its range includes the entire United States except Alaska and Hawaii.

and developed uses for bromine extracted from sea water (see BROMINE; CARBON TETRACHLORIDE). Dow was born in Belleville, Ont., Canada. J. R. CRAF

DOW CHEMICAL COMPANY. See DOW, HERBERT HENRY; CHEMICAL INDUSTRY (Leading U.S. Companies in Chemical Sales).

DOW JONES AVERAGES are statistics that show the trend of prices of stocks and bonds. They are averages of selected stocks and bonds traded on the New York Stock Exchange. Dow Jones & Company, a financial publishing firm, computes averages for each trading hour of every business day. There are four kinds of these averages: (1) an average of the common stock prices of 30 industrial firms, (2) an average of the common stocks of 20 transportation companies, (3) an average of the common stocks of 15 utility companies, and (4) an average of these 65 stocks. Public interest is centered on these stock averages.

The industrial stock average is the one most frequently used by investors. Its advances and declines, like those of the other averages, are given in *points*. For example, suppose the industrial average at the close of trading on one day is 879.32, and on the following day the average goes up to 882.56. The average has then risen 3.24 points.

In 1897, Dow Jones began to publish an industrial average, using the stocks of 12 companies. The average was a simple total of the prices of these stocks, divided by 12. However, some companies whose stocks were used in the average began *splitting* their stocks. That is, they issued two or more shares of stock for each existing share. The price of the stock then dropped in proportion. Suppose, for example, that a stock was selling for $18. If the company *split it two for one* (issued two shares for each existing share), the price would drop to $9. The investor would lose nothing, because he still would have $18 worth of stock. But the Dow Jones average, if the $9 price were used, would take into account an artificial decline from $18.

Stock averages can be distorted by other causes besides splits. To provide a correction for all these causes, Dow Jones uses a flexible divisor. After a stock split, the total of the prices of all the stocks used in the average is not divided by the number of stocks. Instead, a divisor is used that will make the average equal to what it was before the split. The first flexible divisor, introduced in 1928, was 16.67. Because of corrections made through the years, the divisor for industrials had dropped to about 1.6 by the mid-1970's. The divisor is changed only to correct a distortion of five or more points in the average. LEONARD S. SILK

DOWER is a wife's right to a share of her deceased husband's *real property* (real estate). It is sometimes called the *widow's share*. Under English and American common law, the widow is entitled to one-third of her husband's property during her lifetime. The common law bars a husband from transferring ownership of his real property during his lifetime without his wife's consent. This protects the wife's dower right. A husband may also claim a share of his deceased wife's property. This right is called *estate by curtesy*.

Most states in the United States have passed legislation substantially altering the common-law dower right, frequently making the widow's share larger. Some states have *community property* laws, rather than the law of dower. These laws provide that the husband and wife share the ownership of property gained during the marriage. JOHN W. WADE

See also COMMON LAW; COMMUNITY PROPERTY.

DOWIE, JOHN ALEXANDER (1847-1907), founded a sect that stressed divine healing, the Christian Catholic Apostolic Church in Zion. He formed the sect in 1896 at Chicago, and founded Zion City, Ill., north of Chicago in 1901 as a home for his church. He banned doctors, drugstores, liquor, tobacco, dancing, and card playing from Zion. He was deposed in 1906 for unwise use of funds. Dowie was born in Edinburgh, Scotland. He came to Chicago in 1890. EARLE E. CAIRNS

DOWLAND, JOHN (1563-1626), was an English composer of church, instrumental, and secular vocal music. He attained his greatest fame, however, by his excellent lute playing. His works include *Lachrymae, or Seven Teares*, and four books of *Ayres*.

Dowland was probably born in London. He traveled widely, and studied European music. He became a lute player to Christian IV of Denmark and to Charles I of England. He was a leader in composition during the Elizabethan period, and did more to advance the art-song form than any other early composer. WARREN S. FREEMAN

DOWLING COLLEGE. See UNIVERSITIES AND COLLEGES (table).

DOWN EAST. See MAINE.

DOWNING STREET. See LONDON (Central London; picture: No. 10 Downing Street).

DOWN'S SYNDROME. See MONGOLISM.

DOWNSTATE MEDICAL CENTER. See UNIVERSITIES AND COLLEGES (table [New York, State University of]).

DOWNY MILDEW. See MILDEW.

DOWRY. See MARRIAGE (Marriage Customs).

DOWSER. See DIVINATION.

DOYLE, SIR ARTHUR CONAN (1859-1930), a British writer, created Sherlock Holmes, the world's best-known detective. Millions of readers have followed Holmes' adventures and delighted in his ability to solve crimes by an amazing use of reason and observation. Doyle wrote a story in 1893 in which Holmes was killed. But public demand forced Doyle to bring Holmes back to life in another story. Critic Christopher Morley said of Holmes, "Perhaps no fiction character ever created has become so charmingly real to his readers."

Doyle was born in Edinburgh, Scotland. He began practicing medicine in 1882, but his practice was not a success. He started writing while waiting for the patients that never came. His early stories earned him little money, but he won great success with his first Holmes novel, *A Study in Scarlet* (1887).

Holmes eventually appeared in 56 short stories and three other novels—*The Sign of Four* (1890), *The Hound of the Baskervilles* (1902), and *The Valley of Fear* (1915). Doyle may have been the most highly paid short-story

Brown Bros.

Sir Arthur Conan Doyle

writer of his time. He also wrote historical novels, romances, and plays. He eventually abandoned fiction to devote himself to studying and lecturing on *spiritualism* (communication with spirits). PHILIP DURHAM

See also HOLMES, SHERLOCK.

D'OYLY CARTE, RICHARD (1844-1901), an English theater manager, produced all but the first of the 14 operettas written by Sir William S. Gilbert and Sir Arthur S. Sullivan. D'Oyly Carte's production of Gilbert and Sullivan's second work, *Trial by Jury* (1875), established the team as a success.

D'Oyly Carte used the profits from his productions of Gilbert and Sullivan's early operettas to build the Savoy Theatre in London in 1881. Gilbert and Sullivan's last eight operettas had their premières at the Savoy. Their works became known as *Savoy operas*, and performers and other persons associated with them became known as *Savoyards*. In the 1880's, D'Oyly Carte founded the D'Oyly Carte Opera Company, which still performs Gilbert and Sullivan operettas. D'Oyly Carte was born in London. JAMES SYKES

See also GILBERT AND SULLIVAN.

DOZEN. See WEIGHTS AND MEASURES (Counting).

DP. See DISPLACED PERSON; REFUGEE.

DRACHMA, *DRAK muh*, is a copper-nickel coin that is the monetary unit of Greece. It is divided into 100 *lepta*. The drachma was formerly made of silver. The drachma was a standard coin of ancient Greece, and one drachma equaled six *obols*. For the value of the drachma, see MONEY (table: Values). FRED REINFELD

Chase Manhattan Bank Money Museum

Drachma Is a Coin Used in Greece.

DRACO, *DRAY koh*, a lawmaker in ancient Athens, introduced the first written code of law in Athens in 621 B.C. The code was designed to reduce widespread discontent. It allowed the common people to appeal to written law, rather than to upper-class judges.

The code was said to be "written in blood," because it contained severe punishments for crimes. Murder was an important crime treated by the code. Previously, punishment for murder was left to the relatives of the victim, and bloody feuds were common. Draco's laws placed legal responsibility in the hands of the government and helped to create a true city-state. DONALD KAGAN

DRACO, *DRAY koh*, the Dragon, is a constellation near Polaris (the North Star). Four stars make up its head. Its tail winds around the Big and Little dippers.

DRACULA. See STOKER, BRAM.

DRAFT is a written order drawn by one person, directing a second person to pay a definite amount of money to a third person at a stated time. If desired, the draft may be drawn payable to the person who draws it. A draft is the same as a *bill of exchange*, except that the term *draft* usually means a transfer of money between persons in the same country. A draft drawn on a bank is a *check*. Checks originate with the buyer, but trade drafts originate with the seller.

A draft may read *pay at sight* or *on demand*. Then a debtor must either pay the amount of the draft at once or reject it. If it is payable within a stated period, he may *accept* it, in which case he agrees to pay it within the period set. He indicates his acceptance by writing the word *accepted* above his signature on the face of the draft. After he accepts it, he becomes legally responsible for its amount. It is then, in effect, a *note*. Sellers often use drafts when they do not wish to take the credit risk of open book accounts. JAMES B. LUDTKE

See also BILL OF EXCHANGE; NEGOTIABLE INSTRUMENT; NOTE; TRADE ACCEPTANCE.

DRAFT, MILITARY, also called *conscription*, is a system of selecting men for required military service. A nation's needs for military manpower determine (1) how long a man must serve and (2) the branch of the armed forces in which he serves.

Since ancient times, governments have conscripted men whenever they needed larger military forces than they felt they could get through voluntary enlistments. Many countries use a draft during wartime. Some nations also draft men—and women in a few countries—in peacetime. Other countries have never had a draft.

The United States used a draft during the Civil War (1861-1865), World War I (1914-1918), and World War II (1939-1945). The government also drafted men from 1948 through 1972 because of its deep involvement in world affairs, the tensions created by the Cold War, and U.S. commitments in the Vietnam War. In 1973, the U.S. government stopped drafting men, except doctors and dentists, and established nearly all-volunteer armed services. The government also created a *standby draft* that allowed for eligible men to be called up in case of national emergency. This article discusses the standby draft system in the United States.

Canada conscripted troops during World War I and World War II. After each war, Canada returned to all-volunteer armed forces.

The U.S. Draft System

The Selective Service System, a federal agency, administers the standby draft in the United States. The system's national headquarters in Washington, D.C., issues rules and guidelines for placing men into the draft classification set up by Congress. About 3,700 local boards in the United States determine draft classifications for the men in their jurisdiction. Each board consists of three to seven unpaid local residents and a paid clerk. The President appoints the board members on the recommendation of the state governor. Local board members meet at least once a month to determine classifications and to hear special claims or requests of men in their jurisdiction.

Registration. After reaching the age of 18 years, every male United States citizen and almost every male *alien* (noncitizen) who lives in the United States must register with his local board. This local board keeps jurisdiction over the registrant even if he moves out of the state. The registrant must notify the board of any change in his address. In almost all cases, a man registering at the time of his 18th birthday receives a 1-H classification, indicating that he is not eligible for induction. The registrant participates in the annual lottery held in the year of his 19th birthday.

The Lottery helps determine which men will be classified 1-A or 1-A-O and therefore become liable for induction in case of a national emergency. In the lottery system, a registrant receives a number that has been matched by chance with his birth date. Lottery numbers range from 1 through 366 and include a *cutoff number* set by the government. This number represents the number of men needed to fill the country's troop needs. Registrants with numbers higher than the cutoff number remain ineligible for the draft with a 1-H classification. Those who receive numbers lower than or equal to the cutoff number fill out a classification questionnaire.

DRAFT CLASSIFICATIONS

Class	Description
1-A	Available for induction.
1-AM	Member of a medical profession; available for induction.
1-A-O	Conscientious objector available for noncombatant military service.
1-C	Member of the armed forces, the National Oceanic and Atmospheric Administration, or the Public Health Service (serving certain assignments).
1-D	Member of the reserves or a student taking military training.
1-H	Registrant not currently subject to induction.
1-O	Conscientious objector available for civilian service.
1-W	Conscientious objector serving his term of civilian service.
2-A*	Engaged in an occupation considered essential to the national or community interest. (Many scientific researchers, skilled engineers, industrial technicians, teachers, and students in trade and technical courses obtain this deferment.)
2-C*	Farmworker engaged in work vital to the national or community interest.
2-D	Man studying for the ministry.
2-M	Medical student.
2-S*	Full-time college student.
3-A*	Father of a natural or adopted child (applies only if the father did not previously have a student deferment); or a man whose dependents would suffer extreme hardship if he were inducted.
4-A	Man who has completed military duty.
4-B	Certain public officials.
4-C	Certain aliens exempted from military obligations.
4-D	Minister of religion.
4-F	Not qualified for military service because of failure to pass physical or mental tests, or for administrative reasons.
4-G	Surviving son.
4-W	Conscientious objector who has completed his term of civilian service.
5-A	Over the age of liability for induction. (A registrant is liable to the age of 26. But if he was previously deferred or is a medical specialist, he is liable until 35.)

*No new requests for 2-A, 2-C, or 3-A (fatherhood) deferments accepted after April 23, 1970. Requests for 3-A (extreme hardship on dependents) deferments are still accepted. No new 2-S deferments granted after the 1970-1971 school year.

Local boards then reclassify these men on the basis of the questionnaire. The men reclassified 1-A or 1-A-O become the standby force. See the *table* with this article for classifications.

Doctors and other medical specialists are eligible for a special draft of medical personnel. Their eligibility lasts for 365 days after they earn their first professional degree, or after they complete internship or a year of equivalent training. They are eligible for induction until they reach age 26.

Deferments. A man may request a reclassification from his local board if he believes his personal circumstances warrant it. Such a reclassification is often called a *deferment.* A deferment postpones a man's eligibility for induction. If the local board rejects his request, he may ask his state appeal board to review his case. If that board rejects his request, he may request a hearing from the national appeal board, but only if the state board's decision was not unanimous.

Deferment standards vary, depending on the country's military situation. In peacetime, many men receive deferments. Fewer men receive them during a national emergency. A deferment may be renewed as long as a man qualifies for it. Men who receive a deferment are eligible for induction in case of a national emergency until age 35.

Enlistment in the all-volunteer armed services is open to young men 17 years of age or older. Men who enlist before they become 19 do not participate in the lottery. For more information on enlisting in a particular branch of service, see the separate article on that service, such as NAVY, UNITED STATES. Men may also enlist in the Coast Guard, National Guard, or Armed Forces Reserves. Reserve forces usually require only short annual periods of active duty. See COAST GUARD, UNITED STATES; NATIONAL GUARD.

The History of Conscription

In Europe and Asia. Ancient Greece and Rome conscripted men into their armies at times, but they generally relied on professional troops. In Europe during the Middle Ages, warfare was not part of the ordinary man's life. To bear arms was considered a privilege of the nobility. In addition, rulers often employed *mercenaries* (soldiers who offered their services for hire).

King Gustavus Adolphus of Sweden conscripted men in the 1600's, and France practiced conscription in the 1700's. In the 1800's, Prussia produced a large, skilled army by calling up small groups of conscripts for a year's training and then placing them in the reserves. From the early 1900's to the 1950's, most major European countries staffed their armies through conscription. But since the 1950's, a number of countries have abandoned the draft because of the high cost of maintaining a large army and because modern methods of warfare have generally reduced the need for large ground forces. The British Army is made up of volunteers. India and many other non-Communist Asian countries also rely on volunteer forces.

In the United States, conscription dates back to colonial times, when the colonies drafted men to serve in their militias. Most of the colonies sent militia troops to fight in the Revolutionary War (1775-1783). In 1790, Secretary of War Henry Knox and President George Washington proposed a universal military service plan, but Congress rejected it. Until 1940, the United States maintained only volunteer military forces in peacetime. During the Civil War, both the Union and the Confederacy drafted men.

During World War I, the United States drafted about 2½ million men. About 10 million were drafted during World War II, and about 2 million were drafted at the time of the Korean War (1950-1953). During the Vietnam War, from 1965 to 1973, about 1,700,000 were drafted.

Criticism of the Draft. During the 1960's, many Americans began to criticize the Selective Service System. Some charged that the draft favored the middle and upper classes. They said that too high a proportion of poor men were being drafted because they could not afford to go to college and so obtain student deferments. Some people also charged that the draft was not being run uniformly by the local boards. Other Americans complained that the policy of drafting the oldest men ahead of the youngest ones resulted in a long period of uncertainty for some men classified 1-A. During that period, such men had trouble finding jobs and getting loans.

Also at this time, many Americans began to challenge the morality of the draft itself. A number of them believed that the United States was involved in an immoral war in Vietnam. Some viewed the draft as an unjust and unnecessary restriction of individual liberties. Some persons also believed that the rules governing conscientious objector deferments were too narrow (see CONSCIENTIOUS OBJECTOR). Opposition to the draft system or to the Vietnam War led some men to burn their draft cards and refuse to be inducted. Some left the United States and moved to other countries. A number of draft resisters were imprisoned.

In 1969, the United States adopted a draft lottery to ease some of the problems associated with the draft system. In the lottery system, the order of induction of 1-A men depended on a chance drawing of birth dates. Inductions started with undeferred men whose birth date was paired with the number 1 and ended with the men whose birth date was paired with the highest number needed to fill the draft call.

The Standby Draft. In 1970, a presidential commission recommended that the United States develop all-volunteer armed forces, which would attract men by offering high pay and improved benefits. In January, 1973, after the signing of a cease-fire agreement ending the Vietnam War, the U.S. armed services became volunteer forces and the standby draft system took effect. KENNETH M. DOLBEARE

See also ARMY (Conscription); RECRUITING; SELECTIVE SERVICE SYSTEM; WORLD WAR I (The United States Enters the War); WORLD WAR II (Expanding the Armed Forces).

DRAFTSMAN. See MECHANICAL DRAWING.

DRAG. See AERODYNAMICS (Drag); STREAMLINING.

DRAG, a means of transportation. See TRAVOIS.

DRAG RACING. See AUTOMOBILE RACING (Drag Races; picture); HOT ROD.

DRAGLINE. See BUILDING AND WRECKING MACHINES.

DRAGO, *DRAH goh,* **LUIS MARÍA** (1859-1921), an Argentine statesman and jurist, supported the principle that became known as the *Drago Doctrine.* He was minister of foreign affairs in 1902, when Great Britain, Germany, and Italy aroused Latin America by blockading Venezuelan ports. Drago argued that no European power could use public debt as an excuse for armed intervention or occupation of American territory. The Hague Conference of 1907 accepted his doctrine.

Drago was born in Buenos Aires. He studied law, and became a judge of both the civil and criminal courts. Great Britain and the United States asked him to arbitrate the Atlantic fisheries dispute in 1909 and 1910. The Carnegie Endowment of International Peace invited him to visit the United States. It described Drago as the "most eminent exponent of intellectual culture in South America." DONALD E. WORCESTER

DRAGON, *DRAG uhn,* was the name given to the most terrible monsters of the ancient world. Dragons did not really exist, but most people believed in them. They were huge fire-breathing serpents with wings like those of a great bat, and they could swallow ships and men at one gulp. Maps of early times represent unknown parts of the world as being the homes of these mythical creatures. The dragons of legend are much like the great reptiles which inhabited the earth long before man is supposed to have appeared on earth.

Dragons were generally evil and destructive. Every country had them in its mythology. In Greece, dragons were slain by Hercules, Apollo, and Perseus. Sigurd, Siegfried, and Beowulf killed them in Norse, German, and early English legend.

The Louvre, Paris, France. Alinari (Art Reference Bureau)

Fighting a Dragon **is a pen-and-ink drawing done on parchment by the famous Venetian Renaissance artist Jacopo Bellini.**

The dragon was a symbol of sin in early Christian times. Saint Michael and Saint George both had to fight these beasts, according to legend. The dragon represents evil in the book of Revelation in the Bible. But the Chinese took the dragon as a kingly emblem and thought of it as a god. KNOX WILSON

See also GEORGE, SAINT; MICHAEL, SAINT.

DRAGON OF KOMODO is the largest living lizard. It grows to be 10 feet (3 meters) long, and belongs to the most ancient group of lizards still alive. It is found on the island of Komodo and on other small islands of Indonesia. It has a long tail and rough skin. It is covered with small dull-colored scales. When the lizard opens its wide red mouth, it shows rows of teeth like the edge of a saw. The dragon of Komodo hunts other animals

New York Zoological Society

The Dragon of Komodo, an Indonesian lizard, may grow to be 10 feet (3 meters) long. It resembles legendary dragons.

during the day. It digs a cave with its strong claws and hides in it at night.

Scientific Classification. Dragon of Komodo is a member of the monitor family, *Varanidae*. It is genus *Varanus*, species *V. komodoensis*. CLIFFORD H. POPE

See also MONITOR.

DRAGONFLY is a beautiful water insect. It has four large, fragile wings which look like fine gauze. The wings shimmer and gleam in the sunlight when the insect flies. The dragonfly's long slender body is colored either green, blue, or brown. Large compound eyes, which look like beads, cover most of the head. The dragonfly can see motionless objects almost 6 feet (1.8 meters) away, and moving objects two or three times that distance. The insect has six legs covered with spines. It can use its legs to perch on a limb, but it cannot walk. As it flies through the air, it holds its legs together to form a basket in which to capture insects. The dragonfly grasps its prey with its legs or jaws, and eats it while flying. Dragonflies have been known to fly 50 to 60 miles (80 to 97 kilometers) an hour. They fly so swiftly that they usually escape from birds or other animals. Some extinct species of dragonflies had wingspreads of 2½ feet (76 centimeters).

The dragonfly mates while in flight. The female often drops her eggs from the air into the water, or inside the stem of water plants. The *nymph* (young dragonfly) hatches from the egg in 5 to 15 days. It has a thick body, big head and mouth, and no wings. It has a folding lower lip which is half as long as its body. The lip has jawlike hooks at the end and can move out to catch victims. The nymph breathes by means of gills.

The dragonfly nymph remains in the water for 1 to 5 years. It eats water insects and other small water animals. Some large dragonfly nymphs feed on young fish. While developing into an adult dragonfly, the nymph

Ralph Buchsbaum

A Dragonfly Clings to a Stem. This insect can see moving objects, such as flies and mosquitoes, 18 feet (6 meters) away.

molts (sheds its skin) about 12 times. For its final molt, the nymph leaves the water and climbs onto a reed or rock. It then sheds its skin for the last time and emerges as an adult that soon can fly. Adult dragonflies live for only a few weeks to a few months.

Dragonflies are sometimes called *devil's-darning-needles*, *snake doctors*, *snake feeders*, *horse stingers*, and *mule killers*. They help man by feeding on harmful insects such as mosquitoes. Small, graceful *damsel flies* look like dragonflies, but have more slender bodies. Damsel flies have narrow, transparent wings.

Scientific Classification. Dragonflies and damsel flies belong to the class *Insecta*. They make up the order *Odonata*. E. G. LINSLEY

DRAGOON. See PIGEON (Domestic Breeds).

DRAGSTER. See AUTOMOBILE RACING (Drag Races).

DRAINAGE. In all soil there is a point not far below the surface where it is *saturated* (soaked) with water. This point is called the *water table*. In clay soil, the moisture often rises about 4 feet (1.2 meters) above the water table by capillary action, in the same way that ink will "climb" in a piece of blotting paper. In sand, mois-

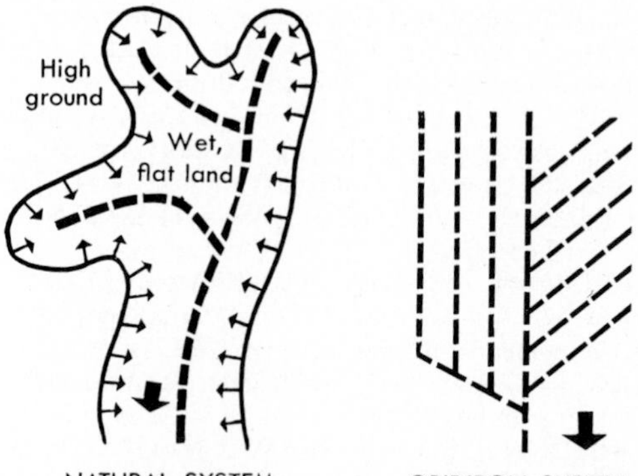

Drainage Tile Systems are designed to lower the water table in wet land. Water enters the buried tiles through spaces left between them and flows in the direction indicated by the arrows.

ture rises about 2 feet (61 centimeters) above the water table.

To provide ideal growing conditions for farm crops, the water table should be 4 feet (1.2 meters) or more below the surface. This is because plant roots stop growing when they reach the water table. If the water table is low, the roots of normally long-rooted plants will grow to be long enough to obtain their full share of nourishment from the soil above the water table.

By natural drainage, excess water above the water table seeps into the soil, is taken up by plants, or evaporates. In many areas, however, rain falls more rapidly than it can drain off naturally. In these areas, artificial drainage is needed to lower the water table.

Methods of Artificial Drainage. There are two chief methods of artificial drainage, the open-surface ditch and the underground drain. The *underground drain*, usually built of hollow tile, is the more useful and convenient method. The *open-surface ditch* takes up farmland and limits the movement of men, animals, and machines in working the land. These ditches often fill with weeds and make breeding places for mosquitoes.

Tile Drains are built to suit the particular kind of soil to be drained, the surface of the land, and the amount of water to be carried by the drain pipes. The main drain usually follows low places in the land where rain water runs off naturally. Branch drains enter the main drain from 2½ to 5 feet (76 to 152 centimeters) below the surface at angles of less than a right angle. Drains can be 30 feet (9 meters) apart in wet clay, or up to 150 feet (46 meters) apart in sandy soil. Drains laid near the surface should be closer together than deeper ones. The hollow tiles used in these drainage systems vary from 4 to 12 inches (10 to 30 centimeters) in diameter. The tiles are laid with their ends close together, but the ends are not sealed. This loose connection allows water to enter the drain but keeps out dirt. Branch drains should slope slightly downward toward the main drain. Two branch drains should not enter the main drain opposite each other. If the mouth of the main drain empties into a stream, it must be above the average high level of the water in the stream. Strong, durable tile must be used. *Breathers* (air vents) often run from the surface of the ground to the tile drains. They let trapped air escape and thus improve the flow of water.

Effects of Drainage. Artificial drainage has created some of the best farming soil in the world from lands that were once under water. It has also made some lands more healthful for man. Outstanding examples of land drained for farming include the lands back of the Holland dikes, the marshy *fen* lands of eastern England, the Po Valley of Italy, the Nile River Delta, and the Yazoo Delta of Mississippi. The draining of swamps in many parts of the world has destroyed breeding places of disease-carrying mosquitoes. Drainage systems must be kept in good repair, or they may wash out and create gullies that ruin good farmland. Systems that drain water too fast may increase erosion. GLENN K. RULE

See also CAPILLARITY; EROSION.

DRAISINE. See BICYCLE (History).

DRAKE is the male duck. See DUCK.

DRAKE, EDWIN LAURENTINE. See PETROLEUM (The Birth of the Oil Industry; picture: Drake's Well).

DRAKE, SIR FRANCIS (1540?-1596), an explorer and military commander, was the first Englishman to sail around the world. His naval warfare against the Spaniards, the chief rivals of the English, helped England become a major sea power.

Drake was the most famous of the sea captains who roved the oceans during the rule of Queen Elizabeth I. The queen encouraged the "sea dogs," as the captains were called, to raid Spanish shipping. She gave them money and ships for such voyages, and she shared in the treasure they brought back. Drake lived in the great age of piracy and became one of the most feared pirates of his time.

Drake had no formal education, but he had great self-confidence and ambition. In battle, he was courageous, quick, and sometimes merciless. He treated his crewmen kindly but demanded loyalty and respect.

Early Life. Drake was born near Plymouth in Devonshire. In 1549, his family moved to Rochester, an English seaport. Francis' father became a minister at nearby naval shipyards, and the boy grew up among ships and seamen. As a youth, Drake sailed on short commercial voyages along the English coast.

From 1566 to 1569, Drake sailed on two slave-trading voyages organized by his cousin, Sir John Hawkins, a famous sea dog. Hawkins obtained slaves in Africa and sold them to West Indian plantation owners. These voyages brought protests from both Portugal and Spain. Portugal did not want English competition in the slave

Oil painting by an unknown artist; National Maritime Museum, Greenwich, England

Sir Francis Drake, a daring English seaman and pirate, helped England become a mighty sea power. Queen Elizabeth I knighted Drake in 1581 after he had sailed around the world.

trade, and Spain objected to English ships sailing in Caribbean waters. The slave-trading voyages gave Drake valuable sailing experience.

In 1567, Drake commanded the *Judith* on Hawkins' second expedition. On the return trip, the ships stopped at the Mexican port of San Juan de Ulúa, near Veracruz. A fleet of Spanish ships approached the harbor, pretending to be friendly. But the Spaniards attacked the English, killing many English sailors and sinking several English vessels. Only the *Judith* and Hawkins' ship, the *Minion*, escaped. Drake returned to England hating the Spaniards and vowing revenge.

From 1570 to 1572, Queen Elizabeth sent Drake on looting missions to the West Indies. In 1572, Drake seized several Spanish ships off the coast of Panama. He landed on the coast and captured the port of Nombre de Dios, near Colón. Drake then looted the town and ambushed a mule train carrying Peruvian silver across the Isthmus of Panama. From then on, the Spaniards called Drake *El Draque*, meaning *The Dragon*.

Voyage Around the World. Drake's most famous voyage began on Dec. 13, 1577. He and more than 160 men sailed from Plymouth in the *Pelican*, the *Elizabeth*, and the *Marigold*. Two smaller ships, the *Swan* and the *Benedict*, carried supplies. The crewmen did not know the real destination or reasons for the voyage. Drake planned to explore the possibilities of trade and colonial settlement in the Pacific Ocean. He hoped to

Water color by Gregory Robinson; National Maritime Museum, Greenwich, England

The *Golden Hind* was Sir Francis Drake's ship during his voyage around the world from 1577 to 1580. It was about 75 feet (23 meters) long and had 18 guns. Approximately 50 men finished the famous voyage with Drake.

DRAKE'S VOYAGE AROUND THE WORLD, 1577-1580

This map shows the route Drake followed on his voyage around the world. After passing the Straits of Magellan, Drake raided Spanish ships along the western coast of South America. The voyage made Drake the first Englishman to sail around the world.

WORLD BOOK map

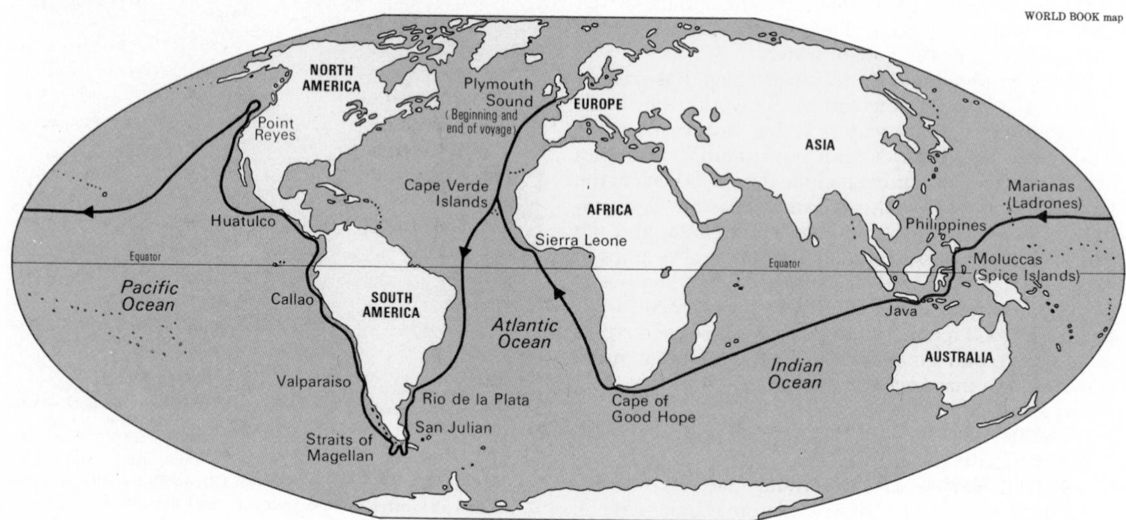

explore Australia, then known only as *Terra Australis Incognita* (the Unknown Land of Australia). Drake also wanted to find the western outlet of the Northwest Passage (see NORTHWEST PASSAGE). In addition, Drake and the queen secretly planned that he would loot Spanish ships and colonies along the Pacific coast of South America.

After leaving São Tiago in the Cape Verde Islands, Drake's expedition met two Portuguese ships. Drake captured one of the vessels and gave its command to a friend, Thomas Doughty. The ships sailed south along the Atlantic coast of South America and ran into violent storms. The expedition then stopped at San Julián for supplies. There, Drake had Doughty beheaded because he suspected him of planning a mutiny.

Before leaving San Julián, Drake destroyed the supply ships and the captured Portuguese ship because they were in poor condition and he did not think they could complete the voyage. The three remaining ships sailed through the Strait of Magellan. Shortly afterward, violent storms wrecked the *Marigold*. The storms also blew the *Elizabeth* off course and forced it to return to England. Drake continued in the last ship, the *Pelican*, which he renamed the *Golden Hind*. He headed north along the Pacific coast of South America. The Spaniards had left their coastal ports unguarded because until then, only Spanish ships had sailed the Pacific. After raiding several Spanish settlements, Drake captured a Spanish ship, the *Cacafuego*, and stole its cargo of gold, silver, and jewels.

Loaded with treasure, the *Golden Hind* sailed north to what is now San Francisco Bay. Drake stopped for supplies and named the area New Albion. He found the people there so friendly that he nailed to a post a brass plate claiming the land for England. A plate believed to be this one was found in 1936 and is on exhibit at the University of California.

Drake had planned to return to England through the Strait of Magellan, not to sail around the world. But he feared an attack by the Spaniards if he sailed south again. So he decided to sail home by way of the Pacific and Indian oceans.

Drake stopped for water at the Philippine Islands and for spices at the Molucca Islands. He also visited the Celebes Islands and Java. After crossing the Indian Ocean, he sailed around the Cape of Good Hope. Drake reached Plymouth on Sept. 26, 1580. He had been gone almost three years, and the voyage made him a national hero.

Drake's voyage also increased British interest in the Pacific Ocean and led to many trading ventures in the Far East. It broadened English knowledge about the world and paved the way for later exploration. Drake's raids on Spanish possessions angered King Philip II of Spain, and he demanded that Drake be punished. Elizabeth responded by going aboard the *Golden Hind* in 1581 and making Drake a knight.

From 1580 to 1585, Drake lived at Buckland Abbey, his country home near Plymouth. He bought the home with his share of the wealth from the voyage. In 1581 and 1582, Drake served as mayor of Plymouth. In 1584 and 1585, he represented the town of Bossiney in the House of Commons.

Expeditions Against Spain. In May, 1585, King Philip ordered an embargo on English goods in Spain and on English ships in Spanish ports. His action angered Elizabeth. In September, she put Drake in command of a fleet of 25 ships and 2,000 men. He left that fall with orders to capture Spanish treasure ships in the West Indies.

On his way, Drake looted the Spanish port of Vigo and burned São Tiago. After landing on the island of Hispaniola, Drake's men burned Santo Domingo. They later occupied the town of Cartagena for six weeks and held it for ransom. On the return voyage, Drake looted and burned St. Augustine. He then sailed north to the Virginia Colony and took some colonists back to England.

Meanwhile, Philip had begun to gather Spain's warships into a fleet called the *Invincible Armada*. The Spaniards gave their fleet this name because they thought it could not be defeated. Philip planned a great attack on England, but Elizabeth learned of his intention. She sent Drake to the Spanish port of Cádiz, where he sank about 30 ships and seized a large amount of supplies.

Yet, Drake could not prevent the Armada from sailing in May, 1588. He proposed a plan to attack the Armada along the coast of Portugal, but the plan was not approved in time. The queen appointed Drake vice-admiral of the English fleet.

In the summer of 1588, in the English Channel, the English and Spanish fleets fought one of history's greatest naval battles. Drake commanded a large group of warships from his ship, the *Revenge*. He played an important part in the Battle of Gravelines, in which the English sank or captured many Spanish ships. The surviving ships of the Armada fled into the North Sea, hoping to find a friendly port in Ireland. But storms wrecked many of the ships and the Irish killed several Spaniards who landed. See ARMADA.

Later Life. In 1589, Drake led a fleet in a raid on Lisbon, which was then a Spanish port. He seized much treasure, but a storm destroyed many of his ships. Thousands of English sailors died on the voyage, and Elizabeth called it a failure. Drake lost her approval and received no commands for almost six years. He retired to Buckland Abbey and, in 1593, he represented Plymouth in the House of Commons.

Drake's last voyage took place in 1595, when he and Sir John Hawkins again sailed to the West Indies. Hawkins died as the fleet reached the islands. Drake went on and destroyed many towns, including Nombre de Dios. While returning with treasure, he died of dysentery. His crew buried him at sea. VERNON F. SNOW

DRAKE UNIVERSITY is a private, coeducational university in Des Moines, Iowa. The university has colleges of business administration, education, fine arts, liberal arts, and pharmacy; and journalism and law schools. The graduate school offers master's degrees and the specialist in education degree. The University College offers evening and extension courses.

Drake was founded in 1881. The Drake Relays, an annual intercollegiate track and field meet, is held there. For Drake's enrollment, see UNIVERSITIES AND COLLEGES (table). PAUL F. SHARP

DRAKENSBERG. See AFRICA (Mountains).

DRAM. See APOTHECARIES' WEIGHT.

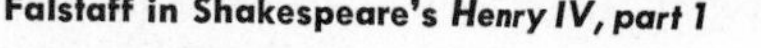

Tony Van Bridge as Falstaff (De Wys)

Falstaff in Shakespeare's *Henry IV, part 1*

William Hutt as Tartuffe, Stratford Festival Theatre

Tartuffe in Molière's *Tartuffe*

Lee J. Cobb as Willy Loman (Fred Fehl)

Willy Loman in Arthur Miller's *Death of a Salesman*

DRAMA

DRAMA is an art form that tells a story through the speech and actions of the characters in the story. Most drama is performed by actors who impersonate the characters before an audience in a theater.

Although drama is a form of literature, it differs from other literary forms in the way it is presented. For example, a novel also tells a story involving characters. But a novel tells its story through a combination of dialogue and narrative, and is complete on the printed page. Most drama achieves its greatest effect when it is performed. Some critics believe that a written script is not really a play until it has been acted on a stage before an audience.

Drama probably gets most of its effectiveness from its ability to give order and clarity to human experience. The basic elements of drama—feelings, desires, conflicts, and reconciliations—are the major ingredients of human experience. In real life, these emotional experiences often seem to be a jumble of unrelated impressions. In drama, however, the playwright can organize these experiences into understandable patterns. The audience sees the material of real life presented in meaningful form—with the unimportant omitted and the significant emphasized.

No one knows exactly how or when drama originated, but nearly every civilization has had some form of it. Drama may have developed from primitive religious ceremonies that were performed to win favor from the gods. These ceremonies contained many seeds of drama. Priests often impersonated supernatural beings or animals, and sometimes imitated such actions as hunting. Stories grew up around some rites and lasted even after the ceremonies themselves had died out. These myths later formed the basis of much drama.

Another theory suggests that drama originated in choral hymns of praise sung at the tomb of a dead hero. At some point, a speaker separated himself from the chorus and began to act out deeds in the hero's life. This acted part gradually became more elaborate, and the role of the chorus diminished. Eventually, the stories were performed as plays, their origins forgotten.

According to a third theory, drama grew out of man's natural love of storytelling. Stories told around campfires re-created victories in the hunt or in battle, or the feats of dead heroes. These stories developed into dramatic retellings of the events.

This article describes the history of drama. For a discussion of modern theater arts, see THEATER.

The contributors of this article are Oscar G. Brockett, Professor of Theatre and Drama at Indiana University, and Lenyth Brockett, a copywriter for the Indiana University Press. The critical reviewer, Hubert C. Heffner, is Distinguished Professor Emeritus of Dramatic Literature at Indiana University.

DRAMA / *Forms of Drama*

Most plays reflect a dominant emotional tone, which may be serious, comic, or a combination of the two. These qualities are found in the three most common dramatic forms: (1) tragedy, (2) comedy, and (3) melodrama. Many plays combine more than one form.

Tragedy maintains a mood throughout that emphasizes the play's serious intention, though there may be moments of comic relief. Tragedy raises important questions about the meaning of man's existence, his moral nature, and his social or psychological relationships. Aristotle identified the emotional effect of tragedy as "the arousal of pity and fear." However, these basic emotions include a wide range of responses—for example, understanding, pity, admiration, dread, and terror.

Comedy is based on some exaggerated or eccentric occurrence or behavior. This departure from the normal must not threaten the normal characters, who have the audience's sympathy. Comedy can be both critical and playful, and it tries to arouse responses that range between scorn and joy. Comedy seldom raises the moral or philosophical issues found in tragedy, but shows man in social relationships. Sometimes *farce* is considered a distinct dramatic form, but it is essentially a type of comedy. Farce uses ridiculous situations and broad physical clowning for its humorous effects.

Melodrama involves a villain who initiates actions that threaten characters with whom the audience is sympathetic. Melodrama portrays a world in which good and evil are clearly distinguished. As a result, almost all melodramas have a sharply defined, oversimplified moral conflict.

Douglas Campbell as Oedipus, Stratford Festival Theatre

Oedipus in Sophocles' *Oedipus Rex*

DRAMA / *The Structure of Drama*

A well-written play consists of dramatic action—a sequence of incidents organized to accomplish a purpose, such as arousing laughter. The action is unified. Every part of the play advances the central purpose, and nothing in it should be unrelated to that purpose.

Aristotle, a Greek philosopher of the 300's B.C., wrote the earliest surviving and most influential essay on drama, called *Poetics*. He identified the parts of a tragedy as (1) plot, (2) character, (3) thought, (4) diction, (5) music, and (6) spectacle.

Plot is a term sometimes used to mean a summary of a play's story. More properly, it means the overall structure of the play. In this sense, it is the most important element of drama. The beginning of a play includes *exposition*, which gives the audience necessary information about earlier events, the present situation, or the characters. Early in most plays, the author focuses on a question or a potential conflict. He brings out this question or conflict through an *inciting incident* which sets the action in motion. The inciting incident makes the audience aware of a *major dramatic question*, the thread that holds the events of the play together.

Most of the play involves a series of *complications*—discoveries and decisions that change the course of action. The complication leads to a *crisis*, a turning point when previously concealed information is at least partly revealed and the major dramatic question may be answered. The final part of the play, often called the *resolution*, extends from the crisis to the final curtain. It pulls together the various strands of action and brings the situation to a new balance, thus satisfying the expectations of the audience.

Character is the principal material from which a plot is created. Incidents develop mainly through the speech and behavior of dramatic characters. The characters must be shaped to fit the needs of the plot, and all parts of each characterization must fit together.

Thought. Every play, even the most light-hearted comedy, involves thought in its broadest sense. In dramatic structure, thought includes the ideas and emotions implied by the words of all the characters. Thought also includes the overall meaning of the play, sometimes called the *theme*. Not all plays explore significant ideas. But every play makes some comment on human experience, either through direct statement or, more commonly, by implication.

Other Parts of Drama. *Diction*, or *dialogue*, is the use of language to create thought, character, and incident. *Music* involves either musical accompaniment or, more commonly today, the arranged pattern of sound that makes up human speech. *Spectacle* deals with the visual aspects of a play, especially the physical actions of the characters. Spectacle also refers to scenery, costumes, makeup, stage lighting, and props.

IMPORTANT MOVEMENTS IN WORLD DRAMA

This table lists the major playwrights, traditions, and movements in the history of world drama. The table begins, *right*, with the first great period of drama, the classical age in Greece, Rome, and India.

	GREECE		
500 B.C. to 200 B.C.	**Tragedy** Aeschylus Sophocles Euripides	**Old Comedy** Aristophanes **New Comedy** Menander	
	ROME		**INDIA**
200 B.C. to A.D. 400	**Tragedy** Seneca	**Comedy** Plautus Terence	*Natyasastra* *The Little Clay Cart* Kalidasa

Drama almost disappeared for several hundred years during the Middle Ages. Drama revived in the 900's after brief religious plays were introduced in Europe by the church.

DATES	ENGLAND	FRANCE	GERMANY	ITALY	SPAIN	OTHERS
900 to 1500	Development of liturgical drama, cycle plays, miracle and morality plays, and secular farces in Europe.					Beginnings of Chinese drama
1500's	**Elizabethan Drama** *The Spanish Tragedy* Marlowe Lyly Shakespeare Jonson	Establishment of first professional acting companies in Paris	Crude popular theater	Ariosto Intermezzi Commedia dell' arte Serlio scenic designs	**Golden Age** *Autos sacramentales* Lope de Rueda Lope de Vega	The no theater originates in Japan in the 1300's
1600's	**Stuart Drama** Jonson, Webster Beaumont, Fletcher Theaters closed, 1642 **Restoration Drama** Theaters reopen, 1660 **Comedy** Etherege, Congreve **Tragedy** Otway, Dryden	**Neoclassical Drama** **Tragedy** Corneille Racine **Comedy** Molière		Rise of opera Commedia flourishes	Lope de Vega Calderón Decline of Spanish national drama after the death of Calderón in 1681	The no theater achieves present form Development of doll and kabuki theater in Japan
1700's	**Comedy** Steele Gay Goldsmith Sheridan **Tragedy** Lillo	**Tragedy** Voltaire Diderot **Comedy** Marivaux Beaumarchais	**Development of a national German drama** Neuber Gottsched Lessing Goethe Schiller	**Comedy** Gozzi Goldoni **Tragedy** Alfieri		
1800 to 1850	Melodrama Bulwer-Lytton	**Romanticism** Hugo's *Hernani* Musset	Goethe Schiller Kleist Büchner	Opera dominates Italian stage		Development of Peking opera in China
1850 to 1900	The rise of realism Shaw Wilde	**Realism and Naturalism** Dumas the Younger Augier Zola	Duke of Saxe-Meiningen Freie Bühne Theatre			**RUSSIA** Gogol, Ostrovsky Turgenev, Chekhov **SCANDINAVIA** Ibsen (Norway) Strindberg (Sweden)

During the 1900's, drama in Western Europe and America lost many of its national characteristics and became identified with several literary, political, and philosophical movements.

1900's	**Symbolism** Maeterlinck (Belgium) **Expressionism** Kaiser (Germany) Strindberg (Sweden) O'Neill (U.S.), Rice (U.S.)	**Epic Theater** Brecht (Germany) **The Realistic Tradition** O'Casey (Ireland), O'Neill Galsworthy (England), Williams (U.S.) Miller (U.S.), Osborne (England)	**Theater of the Absurd** Sartre (France), Ionesco (France) Genêt (France), Beckett (France) Pinter (England)

Drama as we know it was born in ancient Greece. Much of our knowledge of Greek theater comes from archaeological studies and historical writings of the time. By the 600's B.C., the Greeks were giving choral performances of dancing and singing at festivals honoring Dionysus, their god of wine and fertility. Later, they held drama contests to honor Dionysus. The earliest record of Greek drama dates from 534 B.C., when a contest for tragedy was started in Athens. Thespis, who won the first competition, was the earliest known actor and dramatist. The word *thespian* comes from his name.

The most important period of ancient Greek drama was the 400's B.C. Tragedies were performed as part of an important yearly religious and civic celebration called the *City Dionysia*. This festival, which lasted several days, included contests for tragedy, comedy, acting, and choral singing.

The Greeks staged performances in the Theater of Dionysus, on the slope below the Acropolis in Athens. The theater seated about 14,000 persons. It consisted of rows of stadiumlike seats that curved about halfway around a circular acting area called the *orchestra*. Beyond the circle and facing the audience was the *skene* (stage house), originally used as a dressing area and later as a background for the action. This structure eventually developed into a long building with side wings called *paraskenia* projecting toward the audience. The skene probably had three doors. The action may have taken place on a raised platform, or perhaps entirely in the orchestra.

Tragedy. Greek tragedy, perhaps because it originally was associated with religious celebrations, was solemn, poetic, and philosophic. Nearly all the surviving tragedies were based on myths. The typical hero was an admirable, but not perfect, man confronted by a difficult moral choice. His struggle against hostile forces ended in his defeat and, in most Greek tragedies, his death.

Greek tragedies consisted of a series of dramatic episodes separated by choral odes (see ODE). The episodes were performed by a few actors, never more than three on stage at one time during the 400's B.C. A chorus danced and sang and chanted the odes to musical accompaniment.

The actors wore masks to indicate the nature of the characters they played. Men played women's roles, and the same actor appeared in several parts. The acting style, by modern standards, was probably far from realistic. The poetic language and the idealized characters suggest that Greek acting was dignified and formal. The dramatist usually staged his own plays. A wealthy citizen called the *choregus* provided the money to train and costume the chorus.

Of the hundreds of Greek tragedies written, fewer than 35 survive. All but one were written by three dramatists—Aeschylus, Sophocles, and Euripides.

Aeschylus, the earliest of the three, won 13 contests for tragedy. His plays are noted for their lofty tone and majestic language. His trilogy, a group of three plays called the *Oresteia*, tells the myth of Orestes, who slays his mother. The trilogy traces the development

Ruins of the theater at Delphi (Erich Lessing, Magnum)

Ancient Greek Theaters were outdoor amphitheaters that seated thousands of spectators for annual contests in acting, choral singing, and writing comedy and tragedy. Scholars are not sure what the stages looked like. These drawings show possible reconstructions of the stage of the theater of Dionysus.

Illustration from *Antike Grieschische Theaterbauten* by Robert Fiechter, courtesy University of Chicago Library

Roman copy of a Greek marble bas-relief of 100's or 200's B.C., courtesy Vatican Museums (Raymond Schoder, S.J.)

Menander was the most popular Greek playwright of his time. This bas-relief shows him with masks worn by actors in comedy. The woman at the right may represent Thalia, the goddess of comedy.

of the idea of justice from primitive vengeance to enlightened, impersonal justice administered by the state. This development is portrayed in a powerful story of murder, revenge, remorse, and divine mercy. The chorus is important in Aeschylus' plays.

Sophocles is considered by many experts to have been the best of the Greek tragic playwrights. His plays have much of Aeschylus' philosophic concern, but his characters are more fully drawn and his plots are better constructed. He was also more skillful in building climaxes and developing episodes. Aeschylus used only two characters on stage at a time until Sophocles introduced a third actor. This technique increased the dramatic complexity of Greek drama. Sophocles also reduced the importance of the chorus. His most famous play, *Oedipus Rex*, is a masterpiece of suspenseful storytelling and perhaps the greatest Greek tragedy.

Euripides was not widely appreciated in his own day, but his plays later became extremely popular. Euripides is often praised for his realism. His treatment of traditional gods and myths shows considerable doubt about religion, and he questioned moral standards of his time. Euripides showed his interest in psychology in his many understanding portraits of women. His *Medea* describes how a mother kills her children to gain revenge against their father. This play is probably the most frequently produced Greek tragedy today.

Euripides used a chorus, but did not always blend it well with the episodes of his tragedies. He is sometimes criticized for his dramatic structure. Many of his plays begin with a prologue summarizing past events and end with the appearance of a god who resolves a seemingly impossible situation.

Satyr Plays. Each playwright who competed in the contests at the City Dionysia had to present three tragedies and then a satyr play. The satyr play, a short comic parody of a Greek myth, served as a kind of humorous afterpiece to the three tragedies. It may be even older than tragedy. The satyr play used a chorus performing as *satyrs* (mythical creatures that were half human and half animal). The actors and chorus in the tragedies also appeared in the satyr play.

Only one complete satyr play still exists—Euripides' *Cyclops*. It is a parody of Odysseus' encounter with the monster Cyclops. The satyr play was a regular part of the Athenian theater during the 400's B.C., but disappeared when Greek drama declined after the 200's B.C.

Old Comedy. Greek playwrights did not mix tragedy and comedy in the same play. Greek Old Comedy, as the comic plays of the 400's are called, was outspoken and bawdy. The word *comedy* comes from the Greek word *komoidia*, which means *merrymaking*.

In the first scene of a typical Old Comedy, a character suggests the adoption of a *happy idea*—for example, making peace to end a war. After a debate called an *agon*, the proposal is adopted. The rest of the play shows the humorous results. Most of these plays end with a *komos* (an exit to feasting and merrymaking).

The only surviving examples of Old Comedy are by Aristophanes, one of the most original and inventive comic drama writers. Aristophanes combined social and political satire with fantasy, robust farce, obscenity, personal abuse, and beautiful lyric poetry. He was a conservative moral philosopher who objected to the social and political changes occurring in Athenian society. In each of his plays, he ridiculed and criticized some aspect of the life of his day.

New Comedy. Tragedy declined after 400 B.C., but comedy remained vigorous. Comedy changed so drastically, however, that most comedies written after 338 B.C. are called New Comedy. In spite of its popularity, only numerous fragments and a single play have survived. The play is *The Grouch* by Menander, the most popular playwright of his time. Most New Comedy dealt with the domestic affairs of middle-class Athenians. Private intrigues replaced the political and social satire and fantasy of Old Comedy. In New Comedy, most plots depended on concealed identities, coincidences, and recognitions. The chorus provided little more than interludes between episodes.

After the 200's B.C., Greek drama declined and leadership in the art began to pass to Rome. Most critics agree that surviving Roman plays were inferior to the Greek works they imitated. Roman drama was important chiefly because it influenced later playwrights, particularly during the Renaissance. William Shakespeare and the dramatists of his day knew Greek drama almost entirely through Latin imitations.

In Rome, serious drama was less popular than comedy, short farces, pantomime, or such nondramatic spectacles as battles between gladiators. Roman theaters were adaptations of Greek theaters. The government supported performances as part of the many Roman religious festivals, but wealthy citizens financed some performances. Admission was free and audiences were unruly in the brawling, holiday atmosphere.

The Roman Stage was about 100 feet (30 meters) long and was about 5 feet (1.5 meters) above the level of the orchestra. The back wall represented a *façade* (building front) and probably had three openings. In comedies, these openings were treated as entrances to houses, and the stage became a street. Scholars disagree on whether the back wall was flat or three-dimensional.

Tragedy was introduced in Rome by Livius Andronicus in 240 B.C. But the works of only one Roman tragedian, Lucius Annaeus Seneca, still exist, and they probably were never performed. Seneca's nine surviving plays were based on Greek originals. They are not admired today, but were extremely influential during the Renaissance. Later dramatists borrowed a number of techniques from Seneca. These techniques included the five-act form; the use of elaborate, flowery language; the theme of revenge; the use of magic rites and ghosts; and the device of the *confidant*, a trusted companion in whom the leading character confides.

Comedy. The only surviving Roman comedies are the works of Plautus and Terence. All their plays were adaptations of Greek New Comedy. Typical plots revolved around misunderstandings based on mistaken identity, free-spending sons deceiving their fathers, and humorous intrigues invented by clever slaves. Although the chorus was eliminated, the authors added many songs and much musical accompaniment. Plautus' humor was robust, and his plays were filled with farcical comic action. Terence's plays were more sentimental and more sophisticated.

Minor Forms of drama were popular in Rome, but no examples exist today. The most important were short farces; *mimes* (short plays about events of current interest); and *pantomimes*, in which a single performer silently acted out stories to the accompaniment of choral narration and orchestra music.

The Roman theater gradually declined after the empire replaced the republic in 27 B.C. The minor dramatic forms and spectacles became more popular than regular comedy and tragedy. Most of these performances were sensational and indecent, and offended the early Christians. In the A.D. 400's, actors were excommunicated. The rising power of the church, combined with invasions by barbarian tribes, brought an end to the Roman theater. The last known performances in ancient Rome took place in A.D. 533.

Illustration from *Stadte Pamphyliens und Pisidiens* by G. Niemann and E. Petersen, courtesy Library of Congress

The Roman Stage represented a public street in most comedy productions. The architectural background represented building fronts, doorways, and other scene effects.

Minor Dramatic Forms surpassed comedy and tragedy in popularity with Roman audiences after the birth of the empire in 27 B.C. This mosaic shows mimes, musicians, and dancers.

WORLD BOOK photo courtesy Vatican Museums

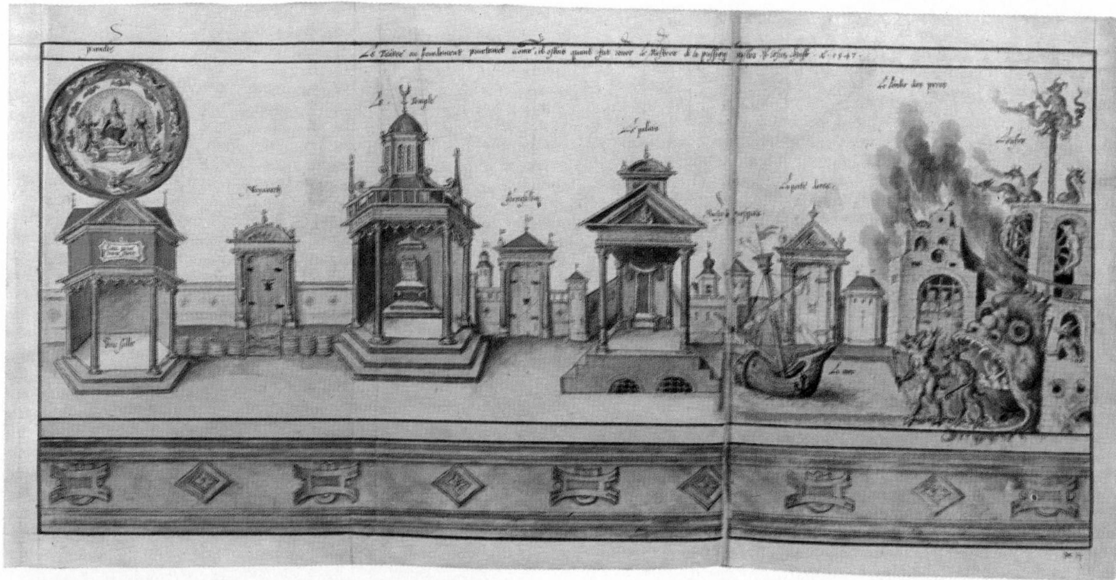

Manuscript illustration by Hubert Cailleau, courtesy Bibliotheque Nationale, Paris

Mansion Stages were popular in medieval Europe. They consisted of separate settings on a long platform. The actors moved from one setting to another, following the action of the play.

Pageant Wagons were traveling stages used to present drama in medieval England. Audiences stood in the street or saw the plays from nearby houses. The actors were townspeople.

Illustration from *A Dissertation on the Pageants or Dramatic Mysteries Anciently Performed at Coventry* by Thomas Sharp, courtesy Oscar G. Brockett

Although state-supported drama ended in the A.D. 500's, scattered performances by traveling mimes and troubadours probably continued throughout the Middle Ages. The plays of Plautus, Terence, and Seneca were preserved by religious orders which studied them not as plays but as models of Latin style.

Medieval drama flourished from the 900's to the 1500's, and became increasingly diverse. It was gradually suppressed, however, because of the religious strife of the Reformation. By 1600, religious drama had almost disappeared in every European country except Spain.

Liturgical Drama. The rebirth of drama began in the 900's with brief playlets acted by priests as part of the *liturgy* (worship service) of the church. The Resurrection was the first event to receive dramatic treatment. A large body of plays also grew up around the Christmas story, and a smaller number around other Biblical events. In the church, the plays were performed in Latin by priests and choirboys.

Beginning in the 1200's, the plays were moved outdoors. During the 1300's, they were taken over by such *secular* (nonreligious) organizations as trade guilds. The *vernacular* (local language) replaced Latin. The short plays had been presented throughout the year. But by the 1300's, the plays were given as a group called a *cycle*, usually during the summer.

Cycle Plays were based on the Bible and other religious writings. They were loosely organized, with no sense of history, and combined Biblical scenes with references to events of the day. Written in verse, they used sketchily-drawn characters and generally few settings. The cycles were essentially religious, but many included comic scenes, often involving the Devil or fools.

Texts of cycles from four English towns—York, Chester, Wakefield, and Lincoln—have been preserved. All date from the 1300's. Plays from France, Italy, Germany, Spain, and elsewhere have also survived.

In England, the setting for each play was mounted on a *pageant wagon*. This wagon was drawn through a city to various places where audiences gathered. Because of the limited space, the actors probably performed on a platform alongside the wagon. The audience usually stood in the street or watched from surrounding houses. The actors were townspeople, and most of them belonged to the trade guilds that financed and produced the plays.

In cities on the European continent, several *mansions* (miniature settings) were erected on a long platform. The actors moved from one setting to another, according to the action of the play.

Miracle and Morality Plays. Miracle plays dramatized events from the lives of the saints or the Virgin Mary. The action in most of these plays reached a climax in a miracle performed by the saint. Morality plays were more fully developed. These dramas developed from fairly simple religious plays into secular entertainments performed by professional acting companies. The famous English play *Everyman* was typical of the form. See MIRACLE PLAY; MORALITY PLAY.

Farces and Interludes. Purely secular drama achieved its greatest development in two short forms of drama—the farce and the interlude. Farces were almost entirely comic, and many were based on folk tales. Interludes originally were entertaining skits, probably acted between courses during banquets or at other events. The interlude was especially associated with the coming of professional actors who became regular parts of many noble households.

Even before the development of the theater in England and Spain, the Renaissance had begun to transform Italian drama. A new interest in ancient Greece and Rome extended to the drama, and classical plays were studied for the first time as drama, not just as literature. Italian critics of the 1500's wrote essays based on Aristotle's *Poetics* and Horace's *Art of Poetry*. From these essays grew a movement in the arts known later as *neoclassicism*.

The centers of Italian theatrical activity were the royal courts and the academies, where men wrote plays that imitated classical drama. These plays were produced in small private theaters for the aristocracy. Most of the actors were courtiers, and most performances were a part of court festivities.

There were three types of plays—comedy, tragedy, and *pastoral*. Pastoral drama dealt with love stories about woodland goddesses and shepherds in idealized rural settings. All three types had little artistic value. But they are important historically because they departed from the shapelessness of medieval drama and moved toward greater control of the plot. Ludovico Ariosto was the first important comic writer. His *Cassaria* (1508) and *I Suppositi* (1509) are considered the beginning of Italian drama. The first important tragedy was *Sofonisba* (1515), by Giangiorgio Trissino, who followed the Greeks rather than Seneca.

Intermezzi and Operas. To satisfy the Italian love of spectacle, the *intermezzo*, a new form, developed from the court entertainments. The intermezzi were performed between acts of regular plays. They drew flattering parallels between mythological figures and people of the day, and provided opportunities for imag-

Commedia dell' arte was a loosely-constructed form of comedy that dominated Italian drama from the 1500's through the 1700's. A stock group of characters appeared in all the commedia plays.

Pantalone Serenading His Mistress, a painting by an unknown artist of the early 1600's showing, *left to right*, the heroine, Harlequin, Pantalone, and Zanni. Drottningholms Teatermuseum, Stockholm

Serlio's design for comedy from *The First Book of Architecture,* courtesy Newberry Library, Chicago

Scenic Designs by Sebastiano Serlio popularized perspective settings in Renaissance drama. His influential designs for comedy, tragedy, and satire were based on the classical Roman stage.

inative costumes and scenery. After 1600, the intermezzi were absorbed into opera, which originated in the 1590's from attempts to reproduce Greek tragedy. By 1650, opera was Italy's favorite dramatic form.

The Italian Stage. More important than the plays was the new type of theater developed in Italian courts and academies. Italian scenic designers were influenced by two traditions—the Roman façade theaters and the newly acquired knowledge of perspective painting. In 1545, Sebastiano Serlio published the first Italian essay on staging. He summarized contemporary methods of adapting the Roman theater for use indoors. Serlio's designs show semicircular seating in a rectangular hall and a wide, shallow stage. Behind the shallow stage was a *raked* (tilted) stage on which painted sets created a perspective setting. Serlio's three designs—for comedy, tragedy, and pastoral dramas—were widely imitated.

The Roman façade was recreated in the Teatro Olimpico, Italy's first important permanent theater, which opened in 1585. A *perspective alley* showing a view down a city street was placed behind each of seven openings in the façade. A more significant development of the façade appeared in the Teatro Farnese, built in 1618. This theater had the first permanent *proscenium* arch, a kind of large frame that enclosed the action on stage. It was especially suited for perspective settings. In 1637, the first public opera house opened in Venice. There, earlier developments helped create the proscenium stage that dominated theater until the 1900's.

Commedia dell' arte (pronounced *kawm ME dyah del LAHR tay*) was the name given to boisterous Italian plays in which the actors *improvised* (made up) the dialogue as they went along. Commedia was a truly popular form in Italian, as opposed to the literary drama of the court and academies. Commedia was performed by professional actors who worked as easily on simple platforms in a market square as on elaborate court stages.

The commedia script consisted of a *scenario* (outline of the basic plot). Characters included such basic types as Harlequin the clown and Pantalone the old man. The same actor always played the same role. Most of the lively, farcical plots dealt with love affairs, but the main interest lay in the comic characters. We do not know how commedia originated, but by 1575 the companies that performed it had become extremely popular in Italy. Commedia soon was appearing throughout Europe. It remained a vigorous force in drama until the mid-1600's, and continued to be performed until the end of the 1700's. Commedia had an important influence on nearly all comedy written during the 1600's.

DRAMA/*Elizabethan and Stuart Drama*

The Reformation directly affected the history of drama by promoting the use of national languages rather than Latin. The use of these languages led to the development of national drama. The first such drama to reach a high level of excellence appeared in England between 1580 and 1642. Elizabethan drama was written during the last half of the reign of Queen Elizabeth I, from about 1580 to 1603. William Shakespeare was the greatest Elizabethan dramatist. Stuart drama was written during the reigns of James I and Charles I in the 1600's.

Elizabethan Theaters. The first public theater in England, called the Theatre, was built in London in 1576. By 1642, there had been at least nine others in the city, including the Globe, Rose, and Fortune.

All Elizabethan public theaters had the same basic design. A large unroofed area called the *yard* was enclosed by a three-storied, gallery-type structure that was round, square, or octagonal. A large, elevated platform stage projected into the yard and served as the theater's principal acting area. The audience stood in the yard or sat in the galleries, watching from three sides.

At the rear of the platform stood a two- or three-story façade. On the stage level, the façade had two doors that served as the principal entrances. Another acting area on the second level was used to represent balconies, walls, or other high places. Some theaters had a façade with a third level where the musicians sat. The specific place of the dramatic action was indicated primarily through descriptive passages in the play's dialogue. A few pieces of scenery were used. This theater design was ideal for Elizabethan plays, which moved at a rapid pace and had many scenes.

Performances began in the early afternoon and lasted until just before dusk. No women appeared on the stage. Boys played women's roles, and some acting companies consisted entirely of boys. All classes of society attended the theater, and refreshments were sold during performances. The audience watched in a boisterous, holiday mood.

Elizabethan Playwrights. Elizabethan plays developed from the interludes performed by wandering

Illustration from the 1615 edition of *The Spanish Tragedy*, courtesy the Folger Shakespeare Library, Washington, D.C.

The Spanish Tragedy **by Thomas Kyd was the most influential tragedy in Elizabethan drama. It brought classical elements into English tragedy and established blank verse as the writing style.**

Masques were elaborate, colorful spectacles that combined music, dancing, vivid costumes, and symbolic drama. English masques were strongly influenced by Italian court entertainments.

Detail from a painting (about 1597) by an unknown artist of a wedding masque during a banquet at the house of Sir Henry Unton, National Portrait Gallery, London

actors, and the classically-inspired plays of schools and universities. These two traditions merged in the 1580's when a group of university-educated men began writing for professional actors of the public theater. The greatest figure of Elizabethan drama was Shakespeare, but several earlier dramatists prepared his way.

Thomas Kyd is important in the history of drama because he brought classical influence to popular drama. Kyd wrote the most popular play of the 1500's, *The Spanish Tragedy* (1580's). This play established the fashion for tragedy in the theater. It moved freely in place and time, as did medieval drama, but it also used devices taken from Seneca. These included a ghost, the revenge theme, the chorus, the lofty poetic style, and the division of the play into five acts. Most of all, Kyd demonstrated how to construct a clear, absorbing story. He wrote *The Spanish Tragedy* in blank verse and established this poetic form as the style for English tragedy (see Blank Verse). *The Spanish Tragedy* may seem crude today, but it was a remarkable advance over earlier drama and had great influence on later drama.

Christopher Marlowe perfected blank verse in English tragedy. Marlowe wrote a series of tragedies that centered on a strong *protagonist* (main character). His work was filled with sensationalism and cruelty, but it included splendid poetry and scenes of sweeping passion.

John Lyly wrote primarily for companies of boy actors that specialized in performing before aristocratic audiences. Most of Lyly's plays were pastoral comedies. He mixed classical mythology with English subjects, and wrote in a refined, artificial style.

Robert Greene also wrote pastoral and romantic comedies. His *Friar Bacon and Friar Bungay* and *James IV* combined love stories and rural adventures with historical incidents. Greene's heroines are noted for their cleverness and charm.

Thus, by 1590, several dramatists had bridged the gap between the learned and popular audiences. Their blending of classical and medieval devices with absorbing stories established the foundations upon which Shakespeare built. William Shakespeare, like other writers of his time, borrowed from fiction, histories, myths, and earlier plays. Shakespeare contributed little that was new, but he perfected the dramatic techniques of earlier playwrights. His dramatic poetry is unequaled, and he had a genius for probing character, producing emotion, and relating human experience to broad philosophical issues.

Ben Jonson was the most influential of Shakespeare's fellow playwrights. Jonson's comedies are sometimes called *corrective* because he tried to improve human behavior by ridiculing foolishness and vice. He popularized the *comedy of humours*. According to a Renaissance medical concept, everyone had four *humours* (fluids) in his body. Good health depended on a proper balance among them. An excess of one humour might dominate a person's disposition. An excess of bile, for example, supposedly made a person melancholy. Jonson also wrote two tragedies on classical subjects, and many elaborate spectacles called *masques*.

The most important Elizabethan playwrights after Shakespeare and Jonson included George Chapman,

Thomas Dekker, Thomas Heywood, John Marston, Thomas Middleton, and Cyril Tourneur.

Stuart Drama. A significant change in English drama began about 1610, during the reign of James I. Playwrights became less interested in moral problems and more concerned with telling a thrilling story for its own sake. The *tragicomedy*, a serious play with a happy ending, increased in popularity. Many plots were artificially arranged, and sensational or pathetic elements replaced the genuinely tragic. A number of plays of this period had passages of magnificent poetry, but their emphasis on sensationalism has brought much criticism. The most important Stuart playwrights included Francis Beaumont, John Fletcher, John Ford, Philip Massinger, and John Webster.

After Charles I was deposed in the 1640's and the Puritans gained control of Parliament, theatrical performances were prohibited. The Puritan government closed the theaters in 1642, ending the richest and most varied era of English drama.

DRAMA / *The Golden Age of Spanish Drama*

The late 1500's brought a burst of theatrical activity in Spain as well as in England. The period between the mid-1500's and late 1600's was so productive that it is called the Golden Age of Spanish drama.

During the Middle Ages, religious drama developed only in northwestern Spain. The rest of the country was occupied by the Moors. After the Moors were driven out in the late 1400's, Spanish rulers began to re-Christianize the country. Drama became an important means of religious teaching. Religious drama, perhaps because of church control, grew in importance in Spain while being banned in other countries during the Reformation. Until the 1550's, Spanish religious plays resembled those of other European nations. After 1550, they assumed traits of their own.

Religious Plays in Spain were called *autos sacramentales*. They combined features of the cycle play and the morality play. Human and supernatural characters were mingled with such symbolic figures as Sin, Grace, and Pleasure. Dramatists took stories from secular as well as religious sources, and adapted them to uphold church teachings. In Madrid, trade guilds staged the plays until the city council took over the job in the 1550's. The council engaged Spain's finest dramatists to write plays and hired professional companies to perform them. The public and religious stages closely resembled each other after 1550, and the same dramatists wrote for both.

Production of the plays varied from community to community, but the staging in Madrid was typical. The autos sacramentales were performed on *carros* (two-storied wagons) that resembled the pageant wagons of the English cycle plays. Carros carrying scenery were drawn through the streets to various points where audiences gathered. A second wagon served as a stage when placed in front of the carro. The second wagons eventually became permanent acting areas at various places, and the carros were drawn up to them. The autos were performed by professionals, but they retained their religious content and their close association with the church. They were performed annually during the Feast of Corpus Christi.

In addition to the autos, the actors performed short farces in the form of interludes and dances. These grew in importance, and gradually the secular elements began to dominate the performances. In 1765, church authorities forbade autos because of their content and the carnival spirit of farce and dancing.

Carros, the Spanish traveling stages, brought religious drama to town audiences during the annual Feast of Corpus Christi.

Illustration by Juan Comba from *El Corral de la Pacheca* by Ricardo Sepúlveda, courtesy University of Chicago Library

Secular Drama. The first permanent theater in Spain opened in Madrid in 1579. Spanish theaters generally resembled Elizabethan theaters in design. Lope de Rueda, a dramatist, actor, and producer, established the professional theater in Spain in the mid-1500's, but it did not flourish until after 1580. The two great playwrights of the Golden Age were Lope de Vega and Pedro Calderón.

Lope de Vega may have written as many as 1,800 plays. More than 400 surviving plays are attributed to him. Lope took his subjects from the Bible, the lives of the saints, mythology, history, romances, and other sources. He was inventive and skillful, but his plays lack the depth of Shakespeare's. Like Shakespeare, he often used song and dance and mixed the comic with the serious. Lope influenced almost all future Spanish drama.

Calderón wrote many kinds of plays, but is best known for works exploring religious and philosophical ideas. Most of his works were autos written for the Corpus Christi festivals of Madrid. After Calderón's death in 1681, Spanish drama declined rapidly and never fully recovered its early vitality.

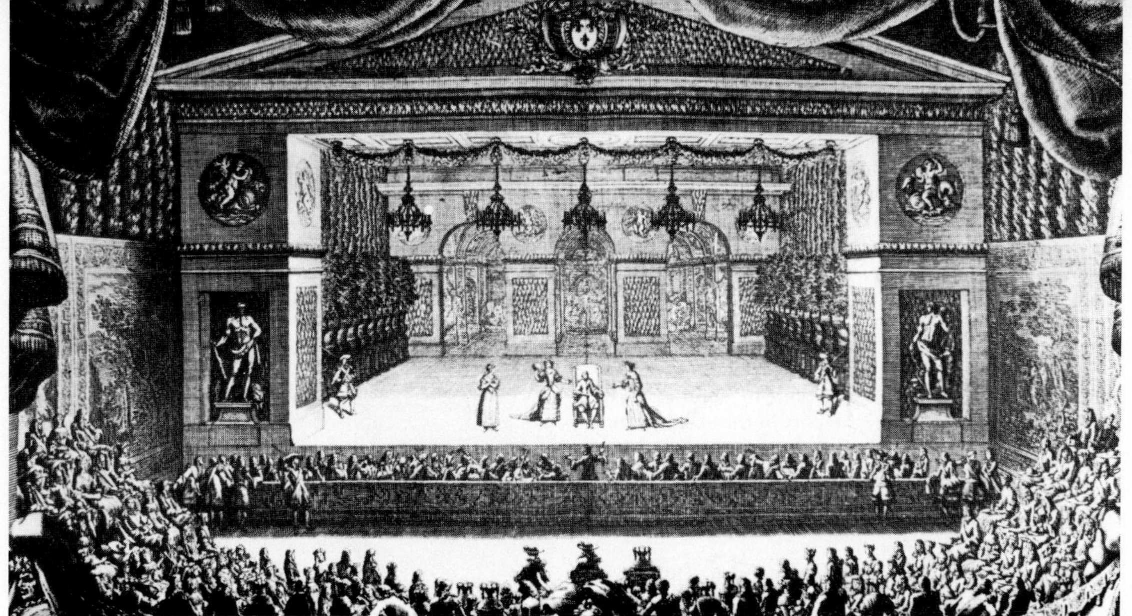

Scene from Molière's *The Imaginary Invalid* performed before Louis XIV and the French court at Versailles; School of Drama Library, Yale University

Molière was the greatest comic dramatist of French neoclassicism. King Louis XIV admired his satiric plays and often protected Molière from victims of the playwright's wit.

DRAMA / *French Neoclassical Drama*

The French Theater had its roots in the medieval religious plays produced by trade guilds. The most important of these amateur groups, the Confrérie de la Passion, established a permanent theater in Paris in the early 1400's. It eventually received a royal monopoly, making it the city's only play-producing organization.

During the late 1500's and 1600's, the Confrérie's theater, called the Hôtel de Bourgogne, was rented to visiting professional companies. The first of these groups to establish itself was Les Comédiens du Roi, sometime after 1598. Alexandre Hardy, the most popular dramatist of the early 1600's, wrote many plays for this company. Hardy mostly wrote loosely constructed tragicomedies filled with adventures of chivalry.

The French theater changed significantly after the neoclassic theories were imported from Italy. In France, these theories took firmer root and were followed more rigidly than elsewhere. The basic beliefs of neoclassicism can be summarized in four parts. (1) Only two types of drama, tragedy and comedy, were legitimate forms, and tragic and comic elements should not be mixed. (2) Drama should be written to teach a moral lesson by presenting the lesson in a pleasant form. (3) Characters should be universal types rather than eccentric individuals. This principle became known as the doctrine of *decorum*. (4) The unities of time, place, and action should be observed. This rule usually meant that a plot should cover no more than 24 hours, take place in a single locality, and deal with a single action.

Neoclassical Playwrights. Although neoclassical ideas were accepted among educated Frenchmen in the late 1500's, they made little impression in public theaters until the 1630's. The playwright most closely associated with the change to neoclassic drama in France was Pierre Corneille. His play *The Cid* set off a stormy dispute that ended with the triumph of neoclassicism. *The Cid* is a tragicomedy based on a Spanish story. It follows many neoclassical rules, but violates the doctrine of decorum because the heroine marries her father's murderer. In later plays, Corneille observed the neoclassic rules and helped establish neoclassicism as the standard for French drama. The distinguishing characteristic of Corneille's drama is the hero of unyielding will. The hero gains steadily in power, but his character does not become more complex. Corneille wrote in a form of verse called Alexandrine, which became standard for French neoclassic drama.

The plays of Jean Racine marked the peak of French neoclassic tragedy. His first dramas in the 1660's established his reputation, and he soon surpassed Corneille. Racine used neoclassical rules to concentrate and intensify the dramatic power of his stories. His tragedies contained little outward action. Their drama came from internal conflicts centering on a single fully developed personality. This character usually wants to act ethically, but is prevented by other forces—often by conflicting desires. Racine created simple plots, but he revealed his characters with remarkable truth.

Molière raised French comedy to a level comparable with French tragedy. He also was the finest comic actor of his age, and a theater manager and a director. Molière borrowed freely from many sources, including Roman comedy, medieval farce, and Spanish and Italian stories. His most famous plays were comedies that centered around such humorous eccentrics as misers. The ridiculous excesses of the protagonists were exposed by characters of "good sense." Molière's comedies offered much biting social and moral criticism, but were amusing and good-natured. He has achieved wider and more lasting appeal than Corneille or Racine.

By 1680, the three major French dramatists were either dead or had given up writing. Most of their successors merely repeated the old formulas, and French drama declined.

England. With the restoration of Charles II to the throne in 1660, the English theater regained vitality. But it took a form much different from the drama that had flourished before the Puritans closed the theaters. From 1660 to 1800, the character of the audience changed. The English theater lost the broad popular appeal it had enjoyed in Shakespeare's day, and became the pastime of the middle and upper classes.

Soon after the theaters reopened in 1660, new playhouses in the Italian style were built in London. These theaters had a large *apron* (the part of the stage in front of the proscenium arch). Permanent doors opened onto the apron. The auditorium had tiered galleries with some private boxes. Cheaper seats were in a roughly U-shaped flat area called the *pit*. Until 1762, spectators often sat on the stage itself.

Settings closely resembled those used in Italy, with scenes painted in perspective. Because of the neoclassic demand for universal themes, most settings were generalized—a palace or a garden, for example. During the later 1700's, settings began to show specific places.

Actresses first appeared on the English stage in the 1660's, and male actors soon stopped playing women's roles. Actors became increasingly important during the 1700's, and audiences often went to see outstanding performers rather than a particular play. Actors apparently based their style on real life, but their acting was undoubtedly more exaggerated than today's audiences would approve. During the 1740's, David Garrick brought greater realism to English acting.

The Restoration period is known especially for the *comedy of manners* and the *heroic drama*. The comedy of manners was the form most identified with the Restora-

David Garrick and Mrs. Pritchard in *Macbeth*, detail from a painting (about 1770) by Johann Zoffany; Garrick Club, London

David Garrick was the leading English actor of his day. His realistic style of acting and faithful productions of Shakespeare's plays had a great influence on the English theater.

The School for Scandal by Richard Brinsley Sheridan is one of the greatest English comedies. This print shows a scene from the play at the famous Drury Lane Theatre in London in 1778.

School of Drama Library, Yale University

tion. It *satirized* (poked fun at) the faults of upper-class society in witty prose. Some of these satires tolerated immorality, but the ideal behind them was self-knowledge. Characters were ridiculed for deceiving themselves or trying to deceive others. The most common characters included the old woman trying to appear young, and the jealous old man married to a young wife. The ideal characters—the hero and heroine—were worldly, intelligent, and undeceived.

The comedy of manners originated largely in the plays of George Etherege. The form was perfected in the dramas of William Congreve, whose *The Way of the World* (1700) is often called the finest example of the form. In the works of William Wycherley, the tone was coarser and the humor more robust.

English comedy enjoyed a period of extreme liberty during the reign of Charles II. But Puritan elements reappeared in the early 1700's as the merchant class grew more powerful. Middle-class disapproval of the comic tone was reflected in the change from the mocking Restoration plays to the more sentimental comedies of George Farquhar. Farquhar put emphasis on emotion and traditional standards of behavior.

The heroic play flourished from about 1660 to 1680. It was written in rhymed couplets and dealt with the conflict between love and honor. These plays featured elaborate rhetoric, many shifts in plot, and violent action. Such dramas seem absurd today, but they were popular in their time.

A more vital strain of tragedy developed alongside heroic drama. These tragedies were written in blank verse that imitated Shakespeare's. A notable example was Thomas Otway's *Venice Preserv'd* (1682). John Dryden's *All for Love* (1677) helped establish tragedy with simpler dialogue.

The term *sentimental* is often applied to most drama of the 1700's. It indicates an overemphasis on arousing sympathy for the misfortunes of others. Increasingly, plots dealt with the ordeals of characters with whom the audience sympathized. The humorous portions of plays featured such minor characters as servants. Today, the characters seem too noble and the situations too artificial to be convincing. But audiences of the 1700's liked them, believing that emotional displays were spiritually uplifting.

Sentimental comedy had its first full expression in *The Conscious Lovers* (1722) by Sir Richard Steele. In the 1770's, when this type of comedy dominated the English stage, two dramatists tried to reform public taste with comedies that avoided excessive sentimentality. Oliver Goldsmith attempted to re-establish what he called *laughing comedy* in the tradition of Ben Jonson. The plays of Richard Brinsley Sheridan have the satire of Restoration comedy, but lack its questionable moral tone.

Domestic tragedy substituted middle-class characters for the kings and nobles of earlier tragedy. It showed the horrifying results of yielding to sin, while sentimental comedy showed the rewards of resisting sin. George Lillo's *The London Merchant* (1731) established the popularity of domestic tragedy. It became a model for playwrights in France and Germany as well as England.

Several minor dramatic forms also developed. The *ballad opera* was a prose comedy with lyrics sung to popular tunes. The most famous one was John Gay's *The Beggar's Opera* (1728). The *burlesque* was a parody of well-known dramas or literary practices. The *pantomime* combined dance, music, acting without dialogue, and elaborate scenery and special effects.

France. By the end of the 1600's, France had become the cultural center of Europe. The standard for European drama was set by the neoclassic tragedies of Corneille and Racine and the comedies of Molière. The effort to obey the rules of neoclassicism tended to freeze dramatic invention during the 1700's. Voltaire was the only notable French tragic dramatist. The first important French writer of domestic tragedy was Denis Diderot. His plays enjoyed little popularity during his lifetime. However, his proposed reforms in staging, acting, and playwriting—all designed for greater realism—greatly influenced dramatists of the 1800's.

For most of the 1700's, the French government permitted only one theatrical company, the Comédie-Française, to produce regular comedy and tragedy. Minor forms, including comic opera, short plays, and burlesques, were staged by the Comédie-Italienne, an Italian group, and at Paris fairs.

Pierre Marivaux wrote comedies in a sophisticated style that had some sentimental touches but were primarily revelations of human psychology. Sentimental comedy appeared in the works of Pierre de La Chaussée. His play *The False Antipathy* (1733) established the popularity of *comédie larmoyante* (tearful comedy). True comedy in the form of brilliant social satire appeared in the plays of Pierre Beaumarchais.

Italy. During the 1700's, Italian dramatists worked to keep commedia dell' arte a vital form. Carlo Goldoni was the greatest Italian dramatist of the period. He wrote sentimental versions of commedia, as well as many excellent comedies. Carlo Gozzi opposed Goldoni's changes in commedia, and attempted reforms of his own by writing imaginative fantasies with some improvised scenes. In spite of the efforts of Goldoni and Gozzi, commedia dell' arte declined in popularity. By the end of the 1700's, it was no longer a significant form. The only important Italian tragic dramatist was Vittorio Alfieri.

Germany. A crude type of drama developed in various German states during the 1500's and 1600's. German theater had a low reputation until about 1725. At that time, the actress-manager Caroline Neuber and the dramatist Johann Gottsched made serious efforts to reform both production and playwriting. Their work marked a turning point in German theater.

The dramatist and critic Gotthold Ephraim Lessing also made important contributions. His plays and his influential critical work *The Hamburg Dramaturgy* turned attention from French neoclassicism to English dramatic models. By the end of the 1700's, the German theater had been revolutionized. All major German states supported theaters modeled on the Comédie-Française, and German playwrights were soon recognized as the finest in Europe. The neoclassical ideal was giving way to the romantic movement.

Drama in Asia developed independently of European drama. Not until the 1800's did Western playwrights generally become aware of Oriental drama and begin to borrow from its rich heritage.

India. Indian drama is one of the oldest in the world. Its exact origins are uncertain, but sometime between 200 B.C. and A.D. 200, the wise man Bharata wrote the *Natyasastra*, an essay which established traditions of dance, drama, makeup, costume, and acting.

By the mid-A.D. 300's, flourishing drama in the Sanskrit language had developed. In technique, Sanskrit plays resembled epic poems. Each play was organized around one of nine *rasas* (moods). The goal was to produce harmony, so authors avoided clashing moods and all these plays ended happily. The most important of the surviving plays are *The Little Clay Cart* (probably A.D. 300's) and *Shakuntala* by Kalidasa (late 300's or early 400's).

Edward B. Harper, University of Washington, Seattle

Indian Folk Theater, *above,* dramatizes in a colorful, vigorous style legends from the great Indian epics and the sacred writings of Hindu mythology.

Scene from *The White Serpent;* Prof. Josephine Huang Hung, National Taiwan University, Taipei, Taiwan

Peking Opera, *above,* is the leading dramatic tradition of China. The action in Peking opera is highly symbolic. In this scene, the characters indicate they are in a boat by carrying an oar and moving in rhythm with the imaginary waves.

Japanese Kabuki Plays, *below,* are violent and melodramatic. These plays, traditionally performed by male casts, dramatize historical or domestic events.

Woodcut (1800-1803) by Utagawa Toyokuni, The British Museum, London

China. The drama of China probably originated in ancient ceremonies performed in song, dance, and mime by priests at Buddhist shrines. Professional storytellers became common by the A.D. 700's, but not until the 1200's did performances become truly dramatic.

The first formal Chinese drama appeared during the Yüan dynasty (1280-1368). Since the 1800's, *Peking opera* has been the major form. The plays of the Peking opera are based on traditional stories, history, mythology, folklore, and popular romances. All these stories end happily. The play is merely an outline for a performance. Actors often make changes in the script.

The Chinese stage is simple, permitting rapid changes of location. These changes are indicated by speech, actions, or symbolic props. A whip, for example, indicates that an actor is on horseback. Musicians, and assistants who help the actors with their costumes and props, remain on stage during the performance. But by tradition they are considered invisible. The actor is the heart of Chinese theater. Richly and colorfully costumed, he moves, sings, and speaks according to rigid conventions. Each type of role has a definite vocal tone and pitch, and delivery follows fixed rhythmic patterns.

Japan. The *no* plays are the oldest of the three traditional forms of Japanese drama. They developed during the 1300's from dances performed at religious shrines. The no theater reached its present form in the 1600's and has remained practically unchanged.

No plays are poetic treatments of history and legend, influenced by the religious beliefs of Buddhism and Shintoism. Many of these plays are shorter than Western one-act plays, and they may seem undramatic. Like ancient Greek tragedy, a no drama is performed by masked actors and is accompanied by music, dance, and choral speaking. The no performance is probably the most carefully controlled in the world. Every detail of the traditional stage, every movement of the hands and feet, every vocal intonation, and every detail of costume and makeup follows a rule.

Japanese *doll* or *puppet* theater enjoyed great popularity in the 1600's and 1700's. Today, only one theatrical company performs these plays. Like the no plays, the puppet dramas originally were religious. The puppets stand 3 to 4 feet (0.9 to 1.2 meters) high and look realistic, with flexible joints and movable eyes, mouth, and eyebrows. The puppet handlers remain in view of the audience. A narrator recites the story to musical accompaniment and expresses each puppet's emotions.

The *kabuki* play is the most popular form in Japan today, and the most sensitive to changing times. It is also the least pure of the three traditional forms, having borrowed freely from other types of theater. Kabuki, the last of the forms to develop, appeared about 1600. It not only surpassed the puppet theater in popularity during the late 1700's, but also took over many puppet theater plays and techniques.

The earliest kabuki were performed by a single female dancer. An all-male cast later became traditional. Although kabuki borrowed much from the no drama, it differs greatly from the formality of the no plays. Kabuki theater is violently melodramatic. It features colorful costumes and makeup, spectacular scenery, and a lively and exaggerated acting style. See JAPAN (Arts [Theater; color picture]).

DRAMA / *Romanticism*

Many elements made up romanticism, a European literary movement of the late 1700's and early 1800's. The most important was a growing distrust of reason and a new belief that man should be guided by his feelings and emotions. The romantics tended to rebel against traditional social and political institutions. Variety and richness became the standard for judging drama, replacing the unity and simplicity admired by the classicists. See ROMANTICISM.

By 1800, a productive romantic movement had become established in Germany. Two important dramatists of the period, Johann Wolfgang von Goethe and Friedrich von Schiller, wrote plays in the romantic style, but both denied being romantics. In many ways, Goethe's *Faust* showed the romantic outlook in the protagonist's unending search for fulfillment. Many of Schiller's plays dramatized moments of crisis in history.

After Germany's defeat by Napoleon's armies in 1806, Germans became increasingly interested in their national past and less hopeful about human nature. This skeptical attitude appeared in the work of two of the best German dramatists of the day, Heinrich von Kleist and Georg Büchner.

The aims of French romantics were clearly established with the publication of Victor Hugo's preface to his play *Cromwell* in 1827. Romanticism triumphed in the French theater with the production of Hugo's *Hernani* in 1830. *Hernani* dealt with the conflict between love and honor, and was filled with exciting episodes, suspense, and powerful verse.

French romantic plays were less philosophical than German ones, and depended more on such devices as disguises and narrow escapes. Probably the best French romantic dramatist was Alfred de Musset, who explored the psychological motives of his protagonists.

Many leading English romantic poets, including Lord Byron, Samuel Taylor Coleridge, and Percy Bysshe Shelley, wrote plays. But their works were not well suited to the stage, and few were produced. The best known English romantic playwrights of the 1800's were James Sheridan Knowles and Edward Bulwer-Lytton.

Melodrama appeared along with romantic drama at the beginning of the 1800's. It helped stimulate the development of realistic scenery. Many melodramatic scenes of breathtaking escapes and such natural disasters as floods required clever, detailed settings. Melodrama appealed to a much wider audience than romantic drama, and remained popular long after the romantic movement had ended.

DRAMA / *Early Realism*

By the mid-1800's, Europe was being transformed by the development of an industrial society creating new and complex social conditions. Many people believed that these conditions should be studied to determine their effect on human behavior. They also felt that literature should reflect real life. As these attitudes spread throughout literature and the theater, they were reflected in the style known as realism. The realistic playwright tried to portray the real world, which he studied by direct observation. He found his subjects in daily life and wrote dialogue in conversational prose.

Realism first developed in France during the 1850's, where the *well-made play* advanced the movement. The well-made play was a form perfected by dramatist Eugène Scribe. Its characters and ideas were superficial, but its plot was constructed carefully. The story had mounting suspense, unexpected reversals, and a surprising but logical outcome. Alexandre Dumas the younger and Émile Augier were among the first to use this form to dramatize such serious social problems as divorce and illegitimacy. See REALISM.

The popularity of melodrama stimulated the development of realistic settings and elaborate special effects. The gradual development of the *box set* was an important step toward stage realism in the 1800's. Scenery enclosed the acting area at the back and sides, imitating the shape of a room with one wall removed. Developments in stage lighting aided the progress of realism. A style of acting developed in which the actors tried to create the illusion of real people in a real room.

Realism was soon followed by *naturalism*, a more extreme but less influential movement. The naturalists believed that drama should become scientific in its methods. They argued that drama should either demonstrate scientific laws of human behavior or record case histories. Naturalists also placed greater emphasis on heredity and environment in determining behavior. The chief spokesman for naturalism was Émile Zola. Naturalism declined rapidly after 1900, but by emphasizing the need for copying the details of daily life, it strengthened the realist movement. See NATURALISM.

Directors appeared in the late 1800's, partly as a result of the growing complexity in staging. In earlier periods, a leading actor took the responsibility of staging most plays. As the demand for greater realism increased, so did the need for more careful rehearsals and better coordination of all elements. The history of the modern director is usually traced from the work of Georg II, Duke of Saxe-Meiningen. His well-rehearsed German acting company toured Europe between 1874 and 1890. This group demonstrated the value of integrating all aspects of a theatrical production into an artistic whole.

The independent theater movement developed in most European countries because commercial theaters refused to present realistic drama. Commercial theater managers feared the controversy it aroused, leading to the possibility of government opposition. Independent theaters began to appear in the 1880's. They were private organizations open only to members and could perform works that otherwise would not have been presented. The first important independent theater was the Théâtre Libre, founded in Paris in 1887 by André Antoine. The Freie Bühne was established in Berlin by Otto Brahm in 1889. The Independent Theatre Society, founded by Jacob T. Grein in London in 1891, introduced the witty plays of George Bernard Shaw to audiences in England.

DRAMA / *Modern Drama*

Ibsen. The strongest influence in the development of realistic drama came from Henrik Ibsen, Norway's first important dramatist. Ibsen is often called the founder of modern drama. His plays were both the high point of realism and the forerunner of movements away from realism. Ibsen broke with tradition not only in technique but also in his fearless treatment of human problems. He portrayed the environment in his plays realistically. His characters reveal themselves as they would in real life—through their words and actions rather than by a statement by the author.

Ibsen's *The League of Youth* (1869) was the first of a series of plays that handled social problems realistically. Beginning with *The Wild Duck* (1884), Ibsen expanded his realistic style to include elements of symbolism. In *Hedda Gabler* (1890) and *The Master Builder* (1892), he shifted his interest from society to the individual. In his late plays, especially in *When We Dead Awaken* (1899), Ibsen increased his stress on symbols and mysterious forces beyond man's control.

Russian Drama and Chekhov. The realistic plays of the Russian writer Anton Chekhov became nearly as influential as those of Ibsen. The principal playwrights in Russia before Chekhov included Nikolai Gogol, Alexander Ostrovsky, and Ivan Turgenev. Gogol's farce *The Inspector-General* (1836) satirized small town officials. Ostrovsky drew heavily on everyday life in his portraits of the merchant class in such plays as *The Storm* (1860). Turgenev's play *A Month in the Country* (1850) was a realistic study of boredom, jealousy, and compromise, elements that appear in Chekhov's plays.

Chekhov took his subjects from Russian society of his day. They show how an unrewarding daily life can drain a person's willpower. Chekhov skillfully created action that reflects the apparent aimlessness of life itself. As in life, comic incidents often intermingle with pathetic or tragic ones.

English Drama. The realistic spirit gradually influenced dramatists throughout Europe. Until the last quarter of the 1800's, the British theater was dominated by sentimental romances and melodrama. Henry Arthur Jones and Arthur Wing Pinero, the most popular British dramatists of the late 1800's, moved toward realism.

The plays of Sir James M. Barrie have some realism, but they are basically romantic and many are overly sentimental. Oscar Wilde is remembered chiefly for his brilliant comedy *The Importance of Being Earnest* (1895). Novelist John Galsworthy wrote powerful realistic plays,

Maxim Gorki's *The Lower Depths* staged by the Moscow Art Theater, courtesy of the Theatre Collection, New York Public Library at Lincoln Center

Realism and Naturalism dominated drama in the late 1800's through the productions of such organizations as the Moscow Art Theater, under the direction of Konstantin Stanislavski.

including *Strife* (1909), a drama about labor strikes.

George Bernard Shaw was an influential critic as well as dramatist. He supported the social and artistic ideals of Ibsen, and was chiefly responsible for their spread in England. Most of Shaw's plays are examples of the comedy of ideas, in which the theater is used as a forum for social, political, and moral criticism.

Irish Drama. A remarkable period of theatrical activity developed in Ireland during the late 1800's and extended into the 1900's. It was part of a general nationalistic revival of Irish literature known as the Irish Renaissance. Irish drama centered around the Abbey Theatre in Dublin. It staged the plays of most major Irish dramatists, including Padraic Colum, Lady Gregory, Sean O'Casey, John Millington Synge, and William Butler Yeats.

French Drama. Jean Giraudoux was probably the leading French playwright between World War I and World War II. He often used Greek myths, Biblical stories, and fantasy to make sympathetic and witty comments about humanity. Jean Cocteau also used Greek myths as the basis of his plays, but he was much more experimental in his style. Paul Claudel became famous for his religious verse plays. Jean Anouilh's many plays vary in tone, but they usually take the side of youthful purity against the corrupting forces of age and greed.

United States Drama. From its origin in the 1700's until the early 1900's, American drama closely followed the European theater. Few American dramatists of distinction appeared until the 1800's, and none gained international recognition until Eugene O'Neill began writing about 1914. O'Neill's plays are a record of persistent experimentation with various styles and dramatic devices. His power is probably best revealed in his drama of tortured family relationships, *Long Day's Journey into Night*, which won the 1957 Pulitzer prize.

O'Neill's greatest rival was Maxwell Anderson, remembered chiefly for his effort to revive poetic drama. The outstanding comic dramatists of the period between 1915 and 1945 were Philip Barry and S. N. Behrman, both noted for their comedies of manners. Thornton Wilder earned great respect in the United States and abroad with his simply written plays showing faith in man's basic goodness.

Italian Drama. Since the late 1700's, the best Italian dramatic writers have concentrated on opera, and few important dramatists have appeared. A noteworthy exception is Luigi Pirandello, the leading Italian playwright of the 1900's. His plays are based on the idea that there is no single truth—only the conflicting views of individuals. Another dramatist, Ugo Betti, became famous for his tragedies about guilt and justice.

Symbolism in drama developed in France during the 1880's. The symbolists believed that appearance is only a minor aspect of reality. They believed that reality could be found in mysterious, unknowable forces that control human destiny. They argued that truth could not be portrayed by logical thought, but could only be suggested by symbols. Their plays tended to be vague and puzzling. The settings and the performers' movements and speaking style were deliberately unrealistic in an attempt to stimulate the audience to look for deeper meanings in the action. The most celebrated symbolist dramatist was Maurice Maeterlinck. See MAETERLINCK, MAURICE.

Symbolism had little immediate effect on the popular theater. But its influence still exists in almost all attempts to substitute suggestion for direct statement, and in the use of simplified settings and nonrealistic styles.

Expressionism is difficult to define because the term was used in Germany between 1910 and 1925 to describe almost any departure from realism. Most German expressionists believed that the human spirit was the basic shaper of reality. Surface appearance, therefore, was important only as it reflected an inner vision. To portray this view, expressionist playwrights used distorted sets, lighting, and costumes; short, jerky speeches; and machinelike movements. Expressionistic techniques can be seen in Georg Kaiser's *From Morn to Midnight* (1916), a symbolic story of humanity's misguided search for happiness through wealth.

Expressionism appeared in Germany about 1910. Its dramatic techniques owed much to the Swedish dramatist August Strindberg. In such plays as *A Dream Play* (1902) and *The Spook Sonata* (1907), Strindberg concentrated the dramatic action in the mind of a person dreaming. In these plays, time and place shift freely, characters multiply or merge, and objects change in appearance. See EXPRESSIONISM.

Courtesy of the Theatre Collection, New York Public Library at Lincoln Center, Astor, Lenox and Tilden Foundation

Expressionism distorts the outside world to reveal the tortured minds of the characters in the grip of fear or other violent emotions. This scene is from *The Adding Machine* by Elmer Rice.

Epic Theater. The discontent of the post-World War I era appeared in much drama of the 1920's. Dramatists of this period believed that the theater should focus attention on political and social evils. The most fruitful of the experiments to focus this attention was epic theater, developed by the German dramatist Bertolt Brecht. Brecht retained some techniques of expressionism. But he replaced the emphasis on the inner spirit with economic and political goals.

Brecht adopted the name *epic* to distinguish his aims from those of the traditional *dramatic* theater. He used many techniques of the epic poem, especially condensing the action and mixing narrative with dialogue. He tried to make his audience think critically, so that the spectators could relate what they saw to real-life conditions. Brecht wrote all his major works before 1945, but his greatest influence came after World War II.

Theater of the Absurd was the most influential movement in postwar drama. It developed in France about 1950. This movement owed much to the work of Jean-Paul Sartre, a French philosopher. He denied the value of fixed moral codes and argued that each person must choose his own set of values. Sartre dramatized this view in such plays as *The Flies* (1943).

The absurdists learned much from Sartre. But they tended to emphasize the illogical and confusing elements in life, rather than any positive points. Most absurdist drama is concerned with the anxieties of individuals trying to survive in an essentially hostile world. The structure of most of these plays consists of strange episodes deliberately placed in odd relationships.

Absurdism first caught public attention with Samuel Beckett's play *Waiting for Godot* (1952). In this play, two bums pass the time while waiting for the unidentified Godot, who never arrives. Eugène Ionesco pointed out the absurdities he saw in modern life. Jean Genet portrayed human behavior as a series of ceremonies by

Epic Theater is largely the work of one playwright, Bertolt Brecht. Social and political issues dominate Brecht's plays, including *The Threepenny Opera,* his most popular drama, *below.*

Courtesy of the Theatre Collection, New York Public Library at Lincoln Center, Astor, Lenox and Tilden Foundation

Bert Lahr, *left,* and E. G. Marshall, *right,* in a scene from *Waiting for Godot* by Samuel Beckett; Elliot Erwitt, Magnum

Theater of the Absurd was a broad movement that included many important new playwrights of the 1950's. Samuel Beckett wrote about helpless characters who lead meaningless lives.

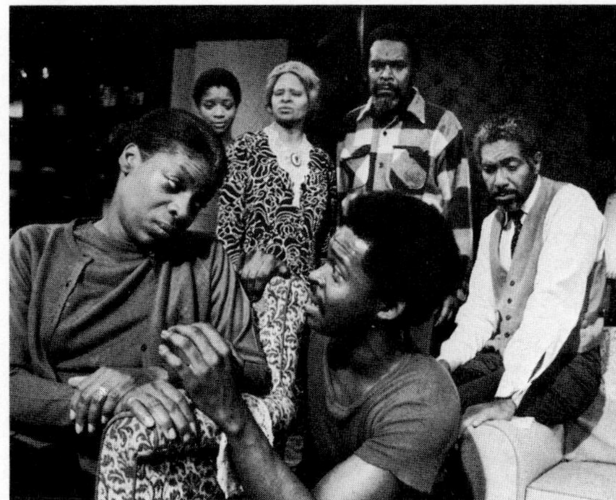

Scene from *The River Niger* by J. A. Walker, presented by the Negro Ensemble Company; Bert Andrews

Black American Drama of the 1960's and 1970's dealt realistically with life in the ghettos of large cities. Some black actors and writers formed theater companies to produce these plays.

which man tries to give a sense of purpose to otherwise nonsensical actions. Genet's principal successor has been the Spanish-born writer Fernando Arrabal. The characters in Arrabal's plays act with childish, thoughtless cruelty.

Later English Drama. In England after World War II, interest in verse drama was revived briefly by T. S. Eliot and Christopher Fry. Then, a new era in British drama started with John Osborne's realistic *Look Back in Anger* (1956). It expressed the rebellious mood of the time so well that the phrase "angry young man" became a rallying point for the discontented.

Since 1956, several important playwrights have emerged in England. The best known has been Harold Pinter. His plays create a menacing or sinister atmosphere out of apparently realistic dialogue and ordinary events. Other notable English dramatists today include Edward Bond, Tom Stoppard, and David Storey.

Later United States Drama. After World War II, Tennessee Williams and Arthur Miller became the leading American playwrights. Williams borrowed from earlier drama such devices as symbols, simplified settings, and compressed time. He combined these with penetrating analyses of character. Miller remained closer to the tradition of Ibsen with studies of moral values.

By the mid-1950's, American drama seemed to be at a standstill. Since then, only one dramatist, Edward Albee, has won acceptance. After some short plays in the absurdist style, Albee turned to dramas of hostile family relationships with philosophical overtones.

During the 1960's, a number of important black playwrights appeared. Most of them wrote plays about the black experience in the inner-city ghettos of American cities. The most notable of these dramatists included Ed Bullins, Lorraine Hansberry, and LeRoi Jones (who changed his name to Imamu Amiri Baraka).

Beginning in the early 1960's, many young playwrights living in New York City have presented their works in cafes, lofts, and other informal places instead of conventional theaters. Their plays form the basis of what has become known as the *off-off-Broadway* movement. Nearly all off-off-Broadway plays are short and organized around a single idea or theme. Characters are broad types rather than well-rounded human beings. Audio and visual effects generally play a greater role than language. The movement also deals with more controversial subject matter than Broadway plays, and obscene language and nudity are common elements. The best-known playwrights in the movement include Jean Claude Van Itallie, David Rabe, Sam Shepard, Megan Terry, and Lanford Wilson.

Recent Trends. Playwrights in several countries have experimented with the structure of plays and methods of staging. They have turned to new techniques to demonstrate their discontent with traditional ways of creating plays.

Some artists have tried to break down traditional barriers between the various art forms and between performers and spectators. The *happening* developed from this rejection of traditional dramatic and theatrical practices. Happenings achieved their greatest popularity in the early 1960's. They often combined improvised acting, motion pictures and slide projections, music, and painting. They emphasized spontaneous actions by everyone present, though the situation may have been planned in advance. Participants placed more value on the act of creating than on the completed work.

Some techniques of the happening have been adapted in *environmental theater.* Audiences and performers in environmental theater occupy the same playing area so that the spectators become part of the production. Often, different scenes are performed at different places in the theater at the same time. Most environmental theater groups believe they have a right to reshape a play, or to create a new play based on an older one.

OSCAR G. BROCKETT and LENYTH BROCKETT

Critically reviewed by HUBERT C. HEFFNER

DRAMA/*Study Aids*

Related Articles. See THEATER with its list of Related Articles. See also such literature articles as AMERICAN LITERATURE and the following articles:

AMERICAN PLAYWRIGHTS

Albee, Edward
Anderson, Maxwell
Barry, Philip
Behrman, S. N.
Belasco, David
Cohan, George M.
Connelly, Marc
Davis, Owen
Dunlap, William
Fitch, Clyde
Gillette, William
Glaspell, Susan
Green, Paul E.
Hart, Moss
Hecht, Ben
Hellman, Lillian
Herne, James A.
Howard, Bronson C.
Howard, Sidney
Inge, William
Kaufman, George S.
Kelly, George E.
Kingsley, Sidney
Lindsay, Howard
Logan, Joshua
Luce (Clare Boothe)
McCullers, Carson
Miller, Arthur
Moody, William Vaughn
Odets, Clifford
O'Neill, Eugene G.
Payne, John Howard
Rice, Elmer
Saroyan, William
Shaw, Irwin
Sherwood, Robert E.
Simon, Neil
Thomas, Augustus
Tyler, Royall
Van Druten, John W.
Wilder, Thornton N.
Williams, Tennessee

BRITISH PLAYWRIGHTS

Archer, William
Barrie, Sir James M.
Beaumont, Francis
Bulwer-Lytton, Edward
Chapman, George
Congreve, William
Coward, Sir Noel
Davenant, Sir William
Dekker, Thomas
Dryden, John
Eliot, T. S.
Etherege, Sir George
Farquhar, George
Fletcher, John
Ford, John
Fry, Christopher
Galsworthy, John
Gay, John
Gilbert and Sullivan
Goldsmith, Oliver
Granville-Barker, Harley
Greene, Robert
Heywood, Thomas
Jones, Henry Arthur
Jonson, Ben
Kyd, Thomas
Lyly, John
Marlowe, Christopher
Marston, John
Massinger, Philip
Maugham, W. Somerset
Osborne, John J.
Pinero, Sir Arthur Wing
Pinter, Harold
Priestley, J. B.
Shakespeare, William
Shaw, George Bernard
Sheridan, Richard Brinsley
Vanbrugh, Sir John
Webster, John
Wilde, Oscar
Williams, Emlyn
Wycherley, William

FRENCH PLAYWRIGHTS

Anouilh, Jean
Beaumarchais, Pierre
Beckett, Samuel
Brieux, Eugène
Camus, Albert
Claudel, Paul
Cocteau, Jean
Corneille, Pierre
Dumas, Alexandre
Genêt, Jean
Giraudoux, Jean
Hugo, Victor
Ionesco, Eugène
Marivaux, Pierre
Molière
Musset, Alfred de
Racine, Jean
Rostand, Edmond
Sardou, Victorien
Sartre, Jean-Paul
Scribe, Augustine Eugène
Voltaire

GERMAN LANGUAGE PLAYWRIGHTS

Brecht, Bertolt
Büchner, Georg
Dürrenmatt, Friedrich
Frisch, Max
Goethe, Johann W. von
Grillparzer, Franz
Hauptmann, Gerhart
Hebbel, Friedrich
Hofmannsthal, Hugo von
Kaiser, Georg
Kleist, Heinrich von
Lessing, Gotthold Ephraim
Schiller, Johann von
Schnitzler, Arthur
Sudermann, Hermann
Wedekind, Frank

IRISH PLAYWRIGHTS

Boucicault, Dion
Dunsany, Lord
Gregory, Lady Augusta
O'Casey, Sean
Synge, John Millington
Yeats, William Butler

ITALIAN PLAYWRIGHTS

Alfieri, Vittorio
Betti, Ugo
D'Annunzio, Gabriele
Goldoni, Carlo
Pirandello, Luigi

RUSSIAN PLAYWRIGHTS

Chekhov, Anton P.
Gogol, Nikolai V.
Gorki, Maxim
Pushkin, Alexander S.

SCANDINAVIAN PLAYWRIGHTS

Bjørnson, Bjørnstjerne
Holberg, Ludvig
Ibsen, Henrik
Lagerkvist, Pär F.
Strindberg, August

SPANISH PLAYWRIGHTS

Benavente, Jacinto
Calderón de la Barca, Pedro
García Lorca, Federico
Tirso de Molina
Vega, Lope de

ANCIENT GREEK AND ROMAN PLAYWRIGHTS

Aeschylus
Aristophanes
Euripides
Menander
Plautus
Seneca, Lucius A.
Sophocles
Terence
Thespis

OTHER PLAYWRIGHTS

Bhavabhuti
Čapek, Karel
Maeterlinck, Maurice
Molnár, Ferenc

OTHER RELATED ARTICLES

Burlesque
Comedy
Miracle Play
Morality Play
Musical Comedy
Opera
Pulitzer Prizes (table: Drama)
Tragedy

Outline

I. Forms of Drama
II. The Structure of Drama
III. Greek Drama
IV. Roman Drama
V. Medieval Drama
VI. Italian Renaissance Drama
VII. Elizabethan and Stuart Drama
VIII. The Golden Age of Spanish Drama
IX. French Neoclassical Drama
X. European Drama: 1660-1880
XI. Asian Drama
XII. Romanticism
XIII. Early Realism
XIV. Modern Drama

Questions

What are three leading theories about the origin of drama?

What was the influence of Thomas Kyd on Elizabethan drama?

What is the function of the plot of a play?

What contribution to theater was made by Sebastiano Serlio?

What were the major theories that shaped French neoclassicism?

What were some differences between Old Comedy and New Comedy?

What was the comedy of manners? Sentimental comedy?

What contribution did Sophocles make to dramatic form?

What role did the church play in the rebirth of drama during the Middle Ages?

What is the theme of most absurdist drama?

What are the three most important traditions in Japanese drama?

What were Victor Hugo's contributions to the rise of romanticism in drama?

Reading and Study Guide

See *Drama* in the RESEARCH GUIDE/INDEX, Volume 22, for a *Reading and Study Guide*.

DRAMAMINE is the G. D. Searle Company's trademark for a drug used to prevent motion sickness, and to control nausea and vomiting in certain illnesses. Dramamine, or *dimenhydrinate*, is one of the antihistaminic drugs. It acts as a mild sedative to reduce the activity of the central nervous system. Large doses may cause drowsiness. BENJAMIN F. MILLER

See also ANTIHISTAMINE; SEASICKNESS.

DRAMATIC POETRY. See Poetry (Types).

DRAMATIST. See DRAMA and its Related Articles.

DRAUGHTS. See CHECKERS.

DRAVIDIAN is a term that refers to the civilization of southern India. The origin of the first Dravidians is unknown, but their civilization is at least several thousand years old.

Most Dravidians are darker-skinned than the people of northern India. Dravidian clothing, houses, and food are different from those of the north. About 20 Dravidian languages, used by more than 100 million persons, form a separate language family. The government has created separate states for people speaking each of the four major Dravidian languages. Telugu is spoken in the state of Andhra Pradesh, Tamil in Tamil Nadu, Kannada in Karnataka, and Malayalam in Kerala.

About 1500 B.C., tribes from central Asia invaded India and drove the Dravidians south. Between A.D. 500 and 900, Dravidian kings adopted the Sanskrit language of northern India and welcomed the *Brahmans* (north Indian priests). The Brahmans eventually became one of the most powerful groups that lived in southern India.

But the Dravidians have also resisted influence from the north. For example, they used Sanskrit but wrote as much—or more—in the Dravidian languages. In the early 1900's, the Dravidians organized movements against the Brahmans, who had become regarded as "foreigners." Since about 1960, the Dravidians have fought the government's use of Hindi, a north Indian language, as India's official language. J. F. RICHARDS

See also INDIA (History).

DRAWBRIDGE. See BRIDGE (Movable Bridges); CASTLE.

DRAWEE, and DRAWER. See BILL OF EXCHANGE.

DRAWING is the act of making a design or image on any suitable surface. The design or image itself is also called a drawing. Drawings can be made for artistic or technical purposes. This article discusses drawing as a fine art. For information on technical drawing, see the WORLD BOOK article on MECHANICAL DRAWING.

Purposes. Artists create drawings for a variety of purposes. Many make preliminary drawings to help them develop the composition of a painting or sculpture. They also produce drawings as finished works of art. An artist may use drawings to record information for future use. For example, he may draw a detailed sketch of a tree and refer to it later when he incorporates the tree into a painting. Art students draw figures and objects to increase their skill with line and form.

Materials and Techniques. Artists draw with chalk, charcoal, crayon, or pencil. They may use a liquid, such as ink, applied with a brush or pen. Artists also scratch drawings into a surface. For example, a *silverpoint drawing* is made by scratching into specially coated paper with a silver instrument or silver wire.

Portrait of Isabella Brant (about 1625); The British Museum, London

A Chalk Drawing can be as delicate and realistic as a painting. The Flemish artist Peter Paul Rubens used black, red, and white chalk to draw this expressive portrait of his wife.

Color Intervals at Provincetown (1943); Addison Gallery of American Art, Phillips Academy, Andover, Mass.

A Crayon Drawing may have a forceful, dramatic quality. The German artist Hans Hofmann drew his forms in crayon and outlined them in ink to create this almost abstract picture of a town.

Manufacturers produce chalk and ink in a wide range of colors. Brushes, pencils, and pens are made in a variety of widths to create different kinds of lines. An artist can add tone to a drawing by applying a thin layer of liquid color called a *wash.* He also may combine several materials and techniques in one drawing.

Almost any surface can be used for a drawing. Pre-

Landscape with Satyr (early 1500's) attributed to Titian; © The Frick Collection, New York City

A Pen-and-Ink Drawing shows how forms can be developed by the combination of lines and blank areas. Artists often choose pen and ink to create a drawing with many details.

historic man drew on clay and stone, and the ancient Chinese used silk cloth. During the Middle Ages, many artists drew on parchment. Since the 1400's, paper has been the most popular drawing surface because it is inexpensive and easy to carry. Drawing paper is made in many colors and textures, and comes in various degrees of absorbency.

History. Man has made drawings since prehistoric times. This art form first gained widespread popularity among European artists during the 1400's, when paper became generally available. Since that time, each century has produced artists who have created great drawings.

Masters of drawing in the 1400's and 1500's included Leonardo da Vinci, Albrecht Dürer, Michelangelo, and Raphael. During the 1600's, Claude, Nicolas Poussin, Rembrandt, and Peter Paul Rubens created important drawings. In the 1700's, great drawings were produced by Jean Honoré Fragonard, Francisco Goya, Giovanni

Preliminary study for the portrait *Comtesse d'Haussonville* (1845); © The Frick Collection, New York City

A Pencil Drawing is often used as a preliminary study for a painting. The French artist Jean A. D. Ingres drew this pencil and chalk sketch to work out his ideas for a portrait. The finished painting appears in the WORLD BOOK article on PAINTING.

MAKING A DRAWING By following the steps shown below, an artist can create a drawing that is lifelike and has the proper proportions. This method can be used for a single figure or a complete composition.

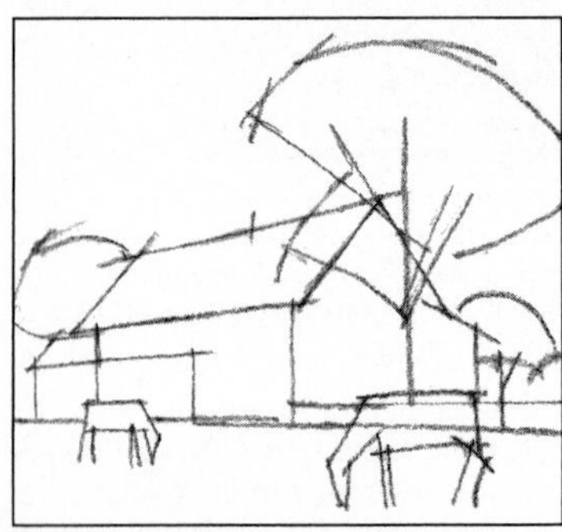

First, the artist sketches the chief elements of the drawing in a series of simple curved and straight lines.

Next, the artist refines his lines to make the drawing more realistic. He also adds details and shading to indicate solid forms.

WORLD BOOK illustrations by David Cunningham

Finally, the artist completes the drawing by adding textures and tones to the various figures. He also erases unwanted lines.

The Locomotive (1923); Philadelphia Museum of Art, the Harrison Fund

A Charcoal Drawing can effectively portray large, solid forms. The American artist Edward Hopper emphasized dark, heavy shapes to show a massive locomotive in front of a dark tunnel.

Battista Tiepolo, and Antoine Watteau. The masters of drawing during the 1800's included Paul Cézanne, Jacques Louis David, Edgar Degas, Théodore Géricault, Jean Ingres, Odilon Redon, Henri de Toulouse-Lautrec, and Vincent Van Gogh. Great drawings in the 1900's have been created by Max Beckmann, Willem De Kooning, Jean Dubuffet, Arshile Gorky, Paul Klee, Oscar Kokoschka, Henri Matisse, Jules Pascin, Pablo Picasso, and Jackson Pollock. Critically reviewed by REED KAY

See also DA VINCI, LEONARDO (pictures); DRAGON (picture); PAINTING (Water Color Painting); CARTOON; COMICS.

DRAWING, MECHANICAL. See BLUEPRINT; MECHANICAL DRAWING.

DRAYTON, MICHAEL (1563-1631), was an English poet who experimented with many literary forms. Some of his love sonnets rank close to Shakespeare's, but Drayton concentrated on English patriotic themes in his works.

Drayton was born in Warwickshire and settled in London in 1591 to pursue a literary career. His first works included the sonnets *Idea, the Shepherd's Garland* (1593) and *Idea, the Mirror* (1594). Drayton's favorite work was his long *Poly-Olbion* (1612-1622), a geographical and historical survey of England's counties. It was influenced by Spenser's poem *The Faerie Queene*. But his masterpiece was the poem *Nymphidia* (1627), which has a fairyland setting. This work shows the influence of Chaucer and Shakespeare, but yet it is highly individual. THOMAS A. ERHARD

DREADNOUGHT, or DREADNAUGHT, is a type of battleship first launched by the British Navy in 1906. It carried batteries of big guns in turrets, and had heavy armor plate. Shipbuilders later developed the more powerful superdreadnought. See also WARSHIP; NAVY (The Dreadnought Era).

DREAM is a story that a person "watches" or even takes part in during sleep. Dream events are imaginary, but they are related to real experiences and needs in the dreamer's life. They seem real while they are taking place. Some dreams are pleasant, others are annoying, and still others are frightening (see NIGHTMARE).

Everyone dreams, but some persons never recall dreaming. Others remember only a little about a dream they had just before awakening and nothing about earlier dreams. No one recalls all his dreams.

When Dreams Occur. Although scientists cannot see a person's dreams, they can tell when he is dreaming. Whether a person is awake or asleep, the brain continuously gives off electrical waves. Scientists measure these waves with an instrument called an *electroencephalograph* (see ELECTROENCEPHALOGRAPH). At most times during sleep, the brain waves are large and slow. But at some times, they become faster and smaller. During such periods of fast brain waves, the sleeper's eyes move rapidly as though he were watching a series of events. If awakened, he is likely to recall dreaming and remember details of the dream. Most adults dream about 100 minutes during about eight hours of sleep. From three to five dreams, each lasting from 10 to 30 minutes, occur during eight hours of sleep. The later dreams are longer than the early ones.

What Dreams Consist Of. The events of a dream form a story. In some dreams, the dreamer takes part in the story. In others, he merely "watches" the tale unfold. Dreams involve little logical thought. In most dreams, the dreamer cannot control what happens to him. The story may be confusing, and things happen that would not happen in real life.

People see in most dreams, but they may also hear, smell, touch, and taste in their dreams. Most dreams occur in color. But persons who have been blind since birth do not see at all in dreams.

Sources of Dreams. Dreams are a product of the sleeper's mind. They include events and feelings that he has experienced. Most dreams are related to (1) events of the day before the dream and (2) strong wishes of the dreamer. Many minor incidents of the hours before sleep appear in dreams. Few events more than two days old turn up. Deep wishes or fears—especially those held since childhood—often appear, and many dreams fulfill such wishes. Events in the sleeper's surroundings—a loud noise, for example—may become part of a dream, but they do not cause dreams.

Uses of Dreams. Some dreams involve deep feelings that a person may not realize he has. Psychiatrists often use material from a patient's dreams to help the person understand himself better.

Scientists have developed complicated theories on how to *interpret* (explain the meaning of) dreams. Sigmund Freud, an Austrian physician who originated psychoanalysis, developed one of the best-known theories of dream interpretation. Freud suggested that dreams are fulfillments of the dreamer's wishes, usually in disguised form. The disguise involves *condensation* (combining several ideas into one image), *displacement* (shifting a feeling from one idea or person to another), and the use of symbols to represent what cannot be pictured directly.

Dreaming may help maintain good learning ability, memory, and emotional adjustment. People who get plenty of sleep—but are awakened each time they begin to dream—become anxious and restless. ERNEST HARTMANN

DREBBEL, CORNELIUS VAN. See SUBMARINE (Development of the Submarine).

DRED SCOTT DECISION was an important ruling by the Supreme Court of the United States on the issue of slavery. The decision, made in 1857, declared that no Negro—free or slave—could claim United States citizenship. It also stated that Congress could not prohibit slavery in United States territories.

Missouri Historical Society

Dred Scott

The ruling aroused angry resentment in the North and led the nation a step closer to civil war. It also influenced the introduction and passage of the 14th Amendment to the U.S. Constitution after the Civil War (1861-1865). This amendment, adopted in 1868, extended citizenship to former slaves and gave them full civil rights.

The Background of the Case. Dred Scott was the slave of a U.S. Army surgeon, John Emerson of Missouri, a state that permitted slavery. In 1834, Scott went with Emerson to live in Illinois, which prohibited slavery. They later lived in the Wisconsin Territory, where slavery was forbidden by the Missouri Compromise (see MISSOURI COMPROMISE). In 1838, Scott returned to Missouri with Emerson. Emerson died there in 1843, and three years later Scott sued the surgeon's widow for his freedom.

Scott based his suit on the argument that his former residence in a free state and a free territory—Illinois and Wisconsin—made him a free man. A state circuit court ruled in Scott's favor, but the Missouri Supreme Court later reversed the decision. Meanwhile, Scott had become legally regarded as the property of John F. A. Sanford (spelled Sandford in the U.S. Supreme Court records) of New York. Because Sanford did not live in Missouri, Scott's lawyers were able to transfer the case to a federal court. This court ruled against Scott, and his lawyers then took the case to the Supreme Court.

The Supreme Court Ruling. By a majority of 7 to 2, the Supreme Court ruled that Scott could not bring a suit in a federal court. Chief Justice Roger B. Taney, speaking for the majority, declared that Scott could not do so because Negroes were not citizens of the United States.

The court could have simply dismissed the case after ruling on Scott's citizenship. But there was a growing national desire for a ruling on the constitutionality of such laws as the Missouri Compromise. Therefore, the court discussed this issue as part of its decision in the Dred Scott case. By a smaller majority, it ruled that the Missouri Compromise, which had been repealed in 1854, was unconstitutional. Taney argued that because slaves were property, Congress could not forbid slavery in the territories without violating a slaveowner's constitutional right to own property.

Dred Scott himself was sold shortly afterward. His new owner gave him his freedom two months after the Supreme Court decision. STANLEY I. KUTLER

See also TANEY, ROGER.

DREDGING, *DREHJ ing,* is the work of clearing out the bottom of rivers, harbors, and other bodies of water so that ships can use them. The machines which do the work are called *dredges.* They work somewhat as a *power shovel* does on land (see BUILDING AND WRECKING MACHINES). Dredges usually are run by steam or diesel engines.

The *dipper dredge* has a large scoop shovel, or *dipper,* shaped like a box which hangs on a chain from a long steel beam. The steel beam, or *derrick,* is attached to a strong mast which can swing the beam and dipper in a wide semicircle. The chain can be wound and unwound to raise and lower the dipper, and the derrick also can be raised and lowered.

When the dredging begins, the dipper is lowered to the bottom of the river or harbor. The derrick arm is swung in a semicircle to drag the dipper across the bottom so that it scoops up dirt and mud. Then the dipper is raised above the water and swung above a barge nearby. The bottom of the dipper has a door which is pulled open by a long cord to dump the dirt into the barge. Then the dipper is lowered again to dig more mud.

Great Lakes Dredge and Dock Co.

Dredging Requires Huge Equipment. This powerful dredging unit has a 150-foot (46-meter) hull and a 240-foot (73-meter) boom. The clamshell bucket that swings from the boom can scoop up from 6 to 12 cubic yards (5 to 9 cubic meters) of material from the bottom of a river. The operator runs the diesel-electric unit from a cab high above the hull's front end.

The first steam dredge was used in England in 1796. It had a long endless chain with several buckets hanging from the chain. One end of the chain was lowered to the bottom. The chain was revolved until one of the buckets caught in the mud and was filled. The chain was revolved again and the bucket was raised while other buckets were lowered on the chain to dig. The buckets were emptied into barges alongside the dredge.

The *hydraulic dredge* is the most efficient machine for moving large quantities of beach or river sand. The sand and water are sucked up through a suction pipe to a pump. A smaller discharge pipe leads from the pump to a barge or to a disposal area. Earth deposited by this process for dams, dikes, or building sites is called *hydraulic fill.* ROBERT G. HENNES

See also GOLD (The Dredge); MINING (picture).

DREISER, THEODORE (1871-1945), ranks as the foremost American writer in the *naturalism movement* (a somber and pessimistic form of realism). Dreiser's characters are victims of apparently meaningless incidents which result in pressures the characters can neither control nor understand. Dreiser based such novels as *Sister Carrie* and *An American Tragedy* on events from real life. He condemned not his villains, but the repressive, hypocritical society that produced them. His style lacks grace, but his best stories are powerful and sobering.

Dreiser was born in Terre Haute, Ind., on Aug. 27, 1871. His older brother was Paul Dresser, who wrote the song "On the Banks of the Wabash, Far Away." Dreiser's family was very poor, and he soon saw a profound difference between the promise and the reality of American life. This realization was a major source of his discontent and an important influence on his works.

Dreiser attended Indiana University for a year. In the 1890's, he worked as a newspaperman in Chicago and St. Louis. By 1907, he was the successful editor of the very sort of woman's magazine whose sentimentality and superficiality he despised.

Dreiser's first novel, *Sister Carrie*, was partly based on the experiences of one of his sisters. The novelist Frank Norris, an editor at Doubleday, Page, and Co., enthusiastically accepted the manuscript for publication. But Mrs. Doubleday, wife of the president of the company, was shocked by the manuscript's amorality, and the publisher tried to cancel the contract to publish the book. Dreiser insisted the agreement be honored. Doubleday printed the book in 1900, but did not advertise or distribute it. The novel became generally available in 1912, after another publisher issued it.

Sister Carrie is the story of Carrie Meeber, a poor girl alone in Chicago. She lives with a traveling salesman and then runs off to New York with George Hurstwood, a prosperous married man. Hurstwood's fortunes decline and he becomes a bum and commits suicide. Carrie finds success, but not happiness, as an actress.

Dreiser's reputation was assured with the publication of *The Financier* (1912), the most purely naturalistic of his works. It is the story of an industrial tycoon who claws his way to great power. Dreiser intended the novel as the beginning of a "Trilogy of Desire." But the second volume, *The Titan* (1914), was a failure, and the third volume, *The Stoic*, was not published until two years after Dreiser's death.

An American Tragedy (1925) is possibly the most impressive of Dreiser's books. It concerns a weak young man who is executed for the murder of his pregnant girl friend. Again, Dreiser did not condemn his villain, but the society that produced and destroyed him. See NATURALISM.

PHILIP YOUNG

DRENNAN, WILLIAM. See EMERALD ISLE.

DRESDEN, *DREHZ duhn* (pop. 501,508), lies on both sides of a broad curve of the Elbe River in East Germany (see GERMANY [political map]). It is a city of parks, gardens, and a center of the arts. Many visitors travel to Dresden to see its churches and other buildings, and to admire its paintings and sculpture. Dresden was founded in the 1200's.

Dresden is a manufacturing and trading city. Porcelain and pottery factories use the *kaolin* (porcelain clay) which lies in heavy deposits around the city. The city has given its name to the thin, delicate Dresden china, which has been made chiefly in Meissen, 14 miles (23 kilometers) outside of Dresden (see DRESDEN CHINA). Other products include beet sugar, chemicals, cotton and woolen materials, machinery, and pianos.

Schools include the Academy of Medicine and Surgery, Royal Music School, Technical High School, elementary schools, and art institutes.

Dresden's museums and theaters are well known to students of art, history, and the drama. The Museum of Zwinger has housed such famous paintings as Raphael's *Sistine Madonna*, Correggio's *Holy Night*, Titian's *The Tribute Money*, Rubens' *The Boar Hunt*, Cranach's *Adam and Eve*, and an altarpiece by Jan van Eyck. During World War II, the Germans hid their art treasures in underground caves and mines so that bombs would not damage them. The Russians seized many of the paintings in 1945 when Dresden was captured. They returned about 750 of them to Dresden in 1956.

Dresden was the scene of street fighting and unrest after World War I. During World War II, bombs and artillery fire damaged Dresden, but the city was one of the last German strongholds to surrender. Russia dismantled many of its industries. The city is now capital of the district of Dresden in Communist-controlled East Germany.

JAMES K. POLLOCK

DRESDEN CHINA is a delicate white glazed porcelain decorated in relief, bright color, and gold. It was first produced in Meissen, Germany. But it was named after Dresden, where Johann Friedrich Böttger discovered the secret of porcelain-making in 1708. Böttger

René von Schleinitz

A Dresden Clock of fine Meissen porcelain serves a useful purpose, but its chief value lies in its beautiful detail.

found that a white clay called *kaolin* could be used to produce porcelain like that made in China and Japan.

Augustus the Strong, Elector of Saxony and King of Poland, had ordered Böttger, an alchemist, to try to make gold from other metals. But Böttger's discovery of porcelain led the king to establish a factory in Meissen, near Dresden. He put Böttger in charge.

Böttger perfected his porcelain, and developed a glaze and various methods of decoration. From 1719 to 1870, the Meissen factory flourished, in spite of wars and changes in management, artists, and workmen. During that period, the factory enjoyed the patronage of kings. Its products won great popularity in Europe and elsewhere. Large and elaborately decorated porcelains commissioned by Augustus the Strong and Frederick the Great are preserved as national treasures in Dresden and Meissen museums. Also on display are figurines, vases, urns, plates, bowls, and candelabra, all of Dresden china. Examples of such porcelain can also be found in museums and private collections in many other parts of the world. EUGENE F. BUNKER, JR.

See also BÖTTGER, JOHANN FRIEDRICH; KAOLIN; PORCELAIN.

DRESS. See CLOTHING.

DRESSMAKING has regained popularity in recent years. But it was much more common 50 years ago, before the ready-to-wear industry developed. Many women and girls, and even men, still prefer to make their clothes. To some, designing and making clothes is a means of creative expression. Others may sew for reasons of economy. Still others sew because they are unable to find ready-made garments that fit as well as clothing they make for themselves. Others prefer to make their own clothes because they feel that ready-to-wear garments have too little individuality.

Garment Design. In order to design her own clothes successfully, a girl must understand the principles of art and their application to the human figure. She must understand body structure, and be able to interpret and select lines that emphasize good features and conceal imperfections. She must learn to modify an extreme fashion so that the proportions and lines of the design are becoming to her. In selecting a commercial pattern, or in creating her own pattern, she must learn to use the principles of design as guides, rather than as rigid laws.

Four elements of art are basic in costume selection or pattern designing. They are line, form and space, color, and fabric texture. Unity of line, proportion and scale, and appropriate use of color and texture all contribute to a harmonious costume. A girl can make her clothing attractive if she uses materials appropriate to the garments. But she should make sure that the dress will be appropriate for its intended use in her wardrobe.

The shape of a garment design is often called its *silhouette* or *background area.* There are only three basic silhouettes: the *tubular,* or straight, the *bouffant,* or bell-shaped, and the *bustle.* These shapes may vary, depending on how much the lines are exaggerated or minimized. The silhouette indicates whether or not the garment is in style with the prevailing fashion.

A good silhouette should be related to body structure, and should have emphasis at points of juncture, such as the shoulder, elbow, wrist, natural waistline, and knee. It should also provide a proper background for individual shapes or details. The background spacing for a pocket or ornament is as important as the shape of the pocket itself.

In any garment, the total areas are made up of parts

that must have individuality in themselves, but at the same time be in good relationship to each other. Four ways of achieving this relationship are proportion, scale, rhythm, and emphasis.

Proportion is the division of the total area into pleasing space relationships. Proportions of two to three or of three to five are usually considered pleasing. This principle may be applied to a decorative border design, or to the relationship of the length of a suit jacket to the length of a skirt.

Scale deals with the size relationships separate areas have to each other, as well as to the wearer. The size of the design in a printed fabric is one of the factors in scale.

Rhythm is the use of repeated design elements, as in the flowing lines of the classical Greek drapery or the vertical lines of a pleated skirt.

Emphasis is the selection of a major design factor. Minor points of interest should always support one main point. But there should not be so much emphasis that competition of interest results.

Color can either contribute to or detract from a costume's effectiveness. To use color successfully, a girl should judge its degree of brightness or intensity, its relative lightness or darkness, and the size of the area where the color will appear. She can use a strong color successfully if she does not use too much of it. Otherwise, it may seem too strong. There is no simple formula that can guarantee correct use of color. Individual color and figure-type charts are merely guides, not rules.

Fabric. A girl should select the fabric and pattern in relation to each other. She can create highly individual clothing if she chooses a fabric that emphasizes the pattern and a pattern that emphasizes the fabric. She should learn to judge the *hand* of a fabric, or the way it drapes. In some patterns, knowing the hand of the fabric is as important as knowing the structure of the design.

Fabrics vary greatly as to the degree of skill required in cutting, sewing, pressing, and handling. Extremely smooth, slippery fabrics or heavy, bulky fabrics are difficult to handle. Soft fabrics that drape easily, such as crepe, lend themselves to fullness, gathering, or draping. Crisp fabrics, such as taffeta, are better for a bouffant effect. A firm fabric is better for the structural details of a suit.

If the garment is one that will require frequent laundering, it is important to know whether or not the fabric is preshrunk and colorfast. Fiber content alone is no longer the major factor in how well a garment can be washed or dry-cleaned. Finishes applied to fabrics frequently alter their characteristic behavior. Many fabrics are made from blends of two or more fibers. The fabrics gain improved characteristics because, through blending, each fiber may supplement the least desirable characteristics of the other. There are countless types of fabrics on the market, and fabric selection has become increasingly complex. Fabrics should have labels that provide information on colorfastness, resistance to creasing or wear, shrinkage, stretching, and recommended method of care.

Construction. The girl who sews will find many commercial patterns available. Certain ones may fit better than others, and require less adjustment. She should be sure to choose the correct pattern size. She will find dressmaking more enjoyable if her pattern does not go too far beyond her skill and experience in sewing. Cutting charts and step-by-step directions will prove helpful in making the garment.

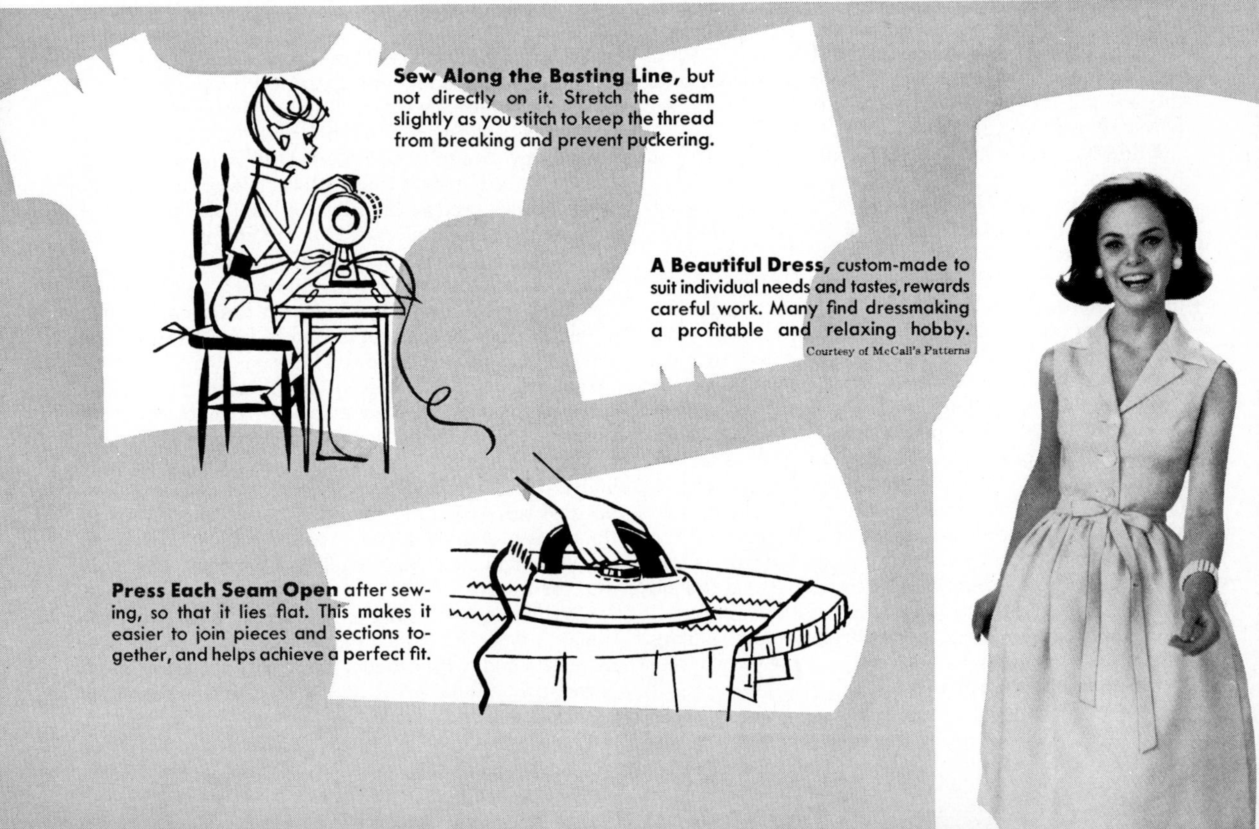

Sew Along the Basting Line, but not directly on it. Stretch the seam slightly as you stitch to keep the thread from breaking and prevent puckering.

A Beautiful Dress, custom-made to suit individual needs and tastes, rewards careful work. Many find dressmaking a profitable and relaxing hobby.

Courtesy of McCall's Patterns

Press Each Seam Open after sewing, so that it lies flat. This makes it easier to join pieces and sections together, and helps achieve a perfect fit.

Authorities often disagree on specific methods for construction processes. Some feel that simpler speed methods, such as basting with a sewing machine, are as good as traditional "custom" methods. The "custom" method is frequently slower, but it often produces a better appearance and fit. Both methods may produce satisfactory results. But the method that is most effective for one person is not necessarily the best method for another.

Methods in altering patterns and techniques of fitting are also controversial, but any one of a number of different methods may bring satisfying results.

Whether a girl uses a commercial pattern or drapes the fabric over a form, she must use and understand several basic factors. She must know which way the grain of her fabric runs. If she does not, the grain may spoil the appearance and fit of the finished garment. She must also make sure that the structural seam lines go in the proper directions, so they will not be subject to unnecessary strains, and so the fabric will lie smooth at the seams. HAZEL B. STRAHAN

See also CLOTHING; FASHION; SEWING; SEWING MACHINE; TEXTILE.

DREW, CHARLES RICHARD (1904-1950), a Negro surgeon, became known for research on blood preservation and for the organization of blood banks. He directed the blood plasma project for Great Britain in 1940 and then the American Red Cross blood program in New York City. He received the Spingarn medal in 1944 for his work. Drew served as professor and head of the Howard University surgery department and as chief surgeon at Freedman's Hospital, Washington, D.C., from 1941 until his death. He was born in Washington, D.C. HENRY H. FERTIG

DREW UNIVERSITY is a coeducational school in Madison, N.J. It is associated with the United Methodist Church, and has a college of liberal arts, a theological seminary, and a graduate school. It was founded in 1867, but operated only as a theological school until the college was founded in 1928. For enrollment, see UNIVERSITIES AND COLLEGES (table).

DREXEL, ANTHONY JOSEPH (1826-1893), was an American financier and philanthropist. In 1847, he became a partner in Drexel and Company, a Philadelphia banking firm founded by his father, Francis Martin Drexel (1792-1863). He became head of the firm in 1863. He and J. P. Morgan established the international bank of Drexel, Morgan & Company in 1871. Drexel was born in Philadelphia. He was a co-owner of the Philadelphia *Public Ledger*. JOHN B. MCFERRIN

DREXEL UNIVERSITY is a privately endowed coeducational school in Philadelphia, Pa. It offers daytime courses in its colleges of business administration, engineering, home economics, humanities and social science, and science. There is also a graduate school of library science. The evening college offers courses in architecture, engineering, and industrial administration. The university features the work-study plan in its day colleges. This plan combines classwork with on-the-job training. The school was founded in 1891 by Anthony J. Drexel. For enrollment, see UNIVERSITIES AND COLLEGES (table). W. W. HAGERTY

See also DREXEL, ANTHONY J.

DREYFUS, *DRAY fus,* **ALFRED** (1859-1935), was a Jewish French army officer who became the center of a bitter quarrel as a result of political injustice. He was arrested on Oct. 15, 1894, on suspicion of spying for Germany. In December, a military court found him guilty. It suspended him from the army and sentenced him to life imprisonment on Devils Island.

Throughout the trial, Dreyfus maintained that he was innocent. In 1896, a member of the French general staff, Georges Picquart, found documents that convinced him of Dreyfus' innocence. But his superiors ordered him to drop the matter. Many noted persons worked to get Dreyfus a new trial. Émile Zola wrote *J'accuse,* demanding justice (see ZOLA, ÉMILE).

He received a second trial in 1899, but it was a mockery, because feeling against Jews was so bitter in the army. Many officials felt that the case was closed and that the army's honor was at stake. Testimony favorable to Dreyfus was barred, and the court again found him guilty. He was sentenced to 10 years' imprisonment, but President Émile Loubet pardoned him after he had been confined for only a few days.

Culver

Alfred Dreyfus

Champions of justice, not only in France but throughout the world, protested the unfair trial. Finally, in 1906, the case was reviewed by the highest court in France, and Dreyfus was declared innocent.

In 1918, Dreyfus became a lieutenant colonel in the French army, and was enrolled in the Legion of Honor. At the outbreak of World War I, he commanded one of the forts defending Paris. He was born in Mulhouse, Alsace. ANDRÉ MAUROIS

DRIED FRUITS. See DATE AND DATE PALM; FIG; PRUNE; RAISIN; FOOD PRESERVATION (Drying).

DRIFT MINE. See COAL (Mining Methods).

DRILL is a strong cotton fabric with a diagonal weave, resembling denim (see DENIM). Drill may be used unbleached, although it is often bleached or dyed. Lightweight drill is used for blouses, suits, and play suits. *Khaki drill* is made into uniforms. *Boat-sail drill* is unbleached. It is used to make pocket linings as well as boat sails.

DRILL, or SEEDER, is a tractor-drawn machine used for planting seeds for farm crops. It has a narrow box, called a *hopper*, usually from 8 to 14 feet (2.4 to 4.3 meters) in length. It is mounted between two wheels connected by an axle. The seed to be planted is placed in the hopper, which has revolving *metering* devices at the bottom. The metering devices are spaced 6 to 8 inches (15 to 20 centimeters) apart, and are geared to the axle. These devices move the seed from the hopper to a row of tubes suspended beneath it. The seed drops through the tubes to shallow furrows made by hoe or disk openers. Wheels or short lengths of chain then push soil back into the furrow.

Grain drills are sometimes equipped with an additional hopper for spreading fertilizer. They are also manufactured with smaller hoppers for sowing grass, clover, and alfalfa seed. A. D. LONGHOUSE

DRILLING TOOLS are used to make round holes in metal, rock, wood, plastic, or other materials.

Metal Drills are usually made of hardened carbon or high-speed steel. Twist drills are the most commonly used metal drills. Some twist drills have straight cutting edges separated by *flutes* (grooves). However, most twist drills have spiraling cutting edges and flutes. The flutes carry chips out of the hole being drilled.

Twist drills can be used in hand-operated drills, in motor-driven hand drills, or in drilling machines or *drill presses*. The ordinary drill press has a platform similar to that on a butcher's scale. One or several drills are mounted above the platform. The operator pulls a lever to lower the drills to the metal placed on the platform. Some drill presses run automatically. They need an attendant only to supply material (see SOUND [picture: Ultrasound]).

Twist drills come in sizes based on the diameter of the holes they drill. The sizes are usually given in numbers, fractions, letters, or millimeters. The numbers range from No. 80 (.0135 inch) to No. 1 (.228 inch). The fractions increase by 64ths of an inch from $\frac{1}{64}$ to 2 inches. Fractions are also used for sizes up to $3\frac{1}{2}$ inches. Letters ranging from A (.234 inch) to Z (.413 inch) are used for sizes not covered by numbers or fractions. Drills sized in millimeters range from 0.20 to 100 millimeters.

Wood Drills are usually called *bits*. They resemble metal drills and can also be mounted on drill presses. Carpenters use bits chiefly to drill holes $\frac{3}{8}$ inch in diameter or less. Larger holes are drilled with special tools called *augers*. See BIT.

Reamers are drilling tools used to enlarge holes and to give them a smooth finish. Reamers may have straight or spiral cutting edges. *Solid reamers* come in various sizes to fit the hole being enlarged or finished. *Expansion* or *adjustable* reamers can be adjusted to fit the hole.

Rock Drills are usually run by compressed air that drives a chisel-shaped drill point. Some rock drills, such as those used to drill oil wells, have cutting edges like those on twist drills (see PETROLEUM [Drilling an Oil Well]; PNEUMATIC TOOL). FRED H. COLVIN

See also DENTISTRY (pictures).

DRINKING. See ALCOHOLISM.

DRINKWATER, JOHN (1882-1937), was an English playwright, poet, and biographer. He became known in the United States for his chronicle plays *Abraham Lincoln* and *Robert E. Lee*.

He wrote his most popular biography, *Pilgrim of Eternity*, about Lord Byron. In addition to writing plays, he also produced and acted in them. Drinkwater was born in Essex. LEO HUGHES

DRIVE SHAFT. See AUTOMOBILE (The Drive Train).

DRIVER, WILLIAM (1803-1886), a sea captain, gave the name *Old Glory* to the United States flag. When he was 21 years old, Driver became licensed to command his first ship. As a farewell gift, his mother and some friends gave him a United States flag. Driver called the flag *Old Glory*, and flew it on his ship, the *Charles Doggett*, during his voyages around the world. In 1837, Driver settled in Nashville, Tenn. During the Civil War, he kept the flag carefully hidden inside a quilt so it would not be harmed. The Driver family donated the flag to the Smithsonian Institution in 1922. Driver was born in Salem, Mass. WHITNEY SMITH, JR.

DRIVER EDUCATION. See AUTOMOBILE (Driving Safely).

DROGUE. See SPACE TRAVEL (Returning to Earth).

DROMEDARY, *DRAHM ih DAIR ee*, is a swift, slightly built camel used for travel in parts of India, Arabia, and Africa. It sometimes grows to be 7 feet (2 meters) tall. The dromedary has only one hump. It can live on small amounts of food and water, and requires only short periods of rest. The dromedary has a swinging trot, and travels at a rate of about 9 miles (14 kilometers) an hour. It can cover 100 miles (160 kilometers) in a day. It produces rich milk, and its hair is used for cloth. No true wild dromedaries exist.

Scientific Classification. The dromedary belongs to the camel family, *Camelidae*. It is genus *Camelus*, species *C. dromedarius*. DONALD F. HOFFMEISTER

See also ANIMAL (color picture: Animals of the Deserts); CAMEL.

DRILLING TOOLS

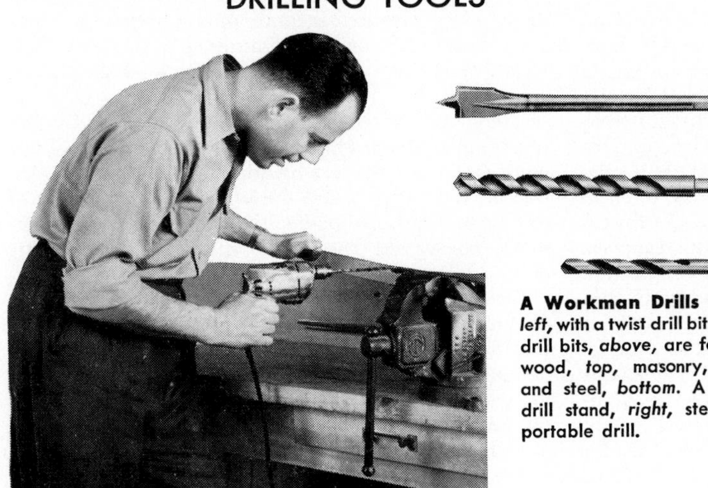

Black & Decker Mfg. Co.

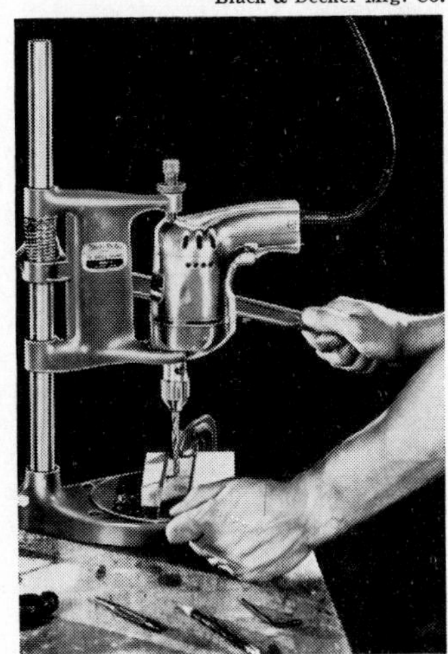

A Workman Drills in steel, *left*, with a twist drill bit. Special drill bits, *above*, are for use in wood, *top*, masonry, *center*, and steel, *bottom*. A vertical drill stand, *right*, steadies a portable drill.

DRONE. See BEE (Drones; picture); RADIO CONTROL.

DROP HAMMER. See FORGING.

DROPSIE UNIVERSITY. See UNIVERSITIES AND COLLEGES (table).

DROPSY is a condition in which a watery fluid gathers in the body cavities or tissues. It is sometimes called *edema* and occurs in diseases such as Bright's disease, cirrhosis of the liver, anemia, and some forms of heart disease. Disorders in blood circulation cause dropsy.

Dropsy may occur generally in almost all parts of the body, or it may be local, or present in one part of the body. General dropsy is called *anasarca*. Dropsy is most common in the abdomen, chest, brain, kidneys, legs, feet, and around the eyes. It can be recognized by the small cavity that lingers when the swollen part is pressed. Dropsy should be treated by a physician. JOHN B. MIALE

DROSOPHILA. See FRUIT FLY (Scientific Classification).

DROUGHT, *drowt*, or DROUTH, is a condition that results when the average rainfall for a fertile area drops far below the normal amount for a long period of time. In areas that are not irrigated, the lack of rain causes farm crops to wither and die. Higher than normal temperatures usually accompany periods of drought. They add to the crop damage. Forest fires start easily during droughts. Much valuable timberland has been burned during these dry periods. The soil of a drought area becomes dry and crumbles. Often the rich topsoil is blown away by the hot, dry winds (see DUST STORM). Streams, ponds, and wells often dry up during a drought, and animals suffer and may even die because of the lack of water.

Weather forecasters cannot predict with certainty just when a drought will occur. But they know that these drier-than-normal periods tend to alternate with wetter-than-normal periods in an irregular cycle. Droughts of the past can be read in the rings made by trees as they add new wood each year. In wet periods, the year's layer is thick, while in dry periods, the ring is thin (see TREE [illustration: How a Tree Reveals Its History]).

The Southwestern States of the United States suffered one of the worst droughts in their history from 1931 to 1938. The drought affected the entire country. Few food crops could be grown. Food became scarce, and prices went up throughout the nation. Hundreds of families in the Dust Bowl region had to be moved to farms in other areas with the help of the federal government (see DUST BOWL). In 1944, drought brought great damage to almost all Latin America. The drought moved to Australia and then to Europe, where it continued throughout the summer of 1945. From 1950 to 1954 in the United States, the South and Southwest suffered a severe drought. Hundreds of cattle ranchers had to ship their cattle to other regions because pasture lands had no grass. The federal government again conducted an emergency drought-relief program. It offered farmers emergency credit and seed grains at low prices.

In 1961, drought struck the northern Great Plains states and Canada's prairie provinces. The governments of both countries gave financial aid where needed. A severe drought also struck the Northeastern part of the United States in 1965. JAMES E. MILLER

See also ANIMAL (Animals and Climate).

DROWNING is death caused by suffocation in water or other liquid. A person who cannot swim can keep from drowning by floating upon the surface of the water. Floating is accomplished by rolling over on the back and extending the body in a relaxed position. Failure to float is usually the result of fear, which causes the body to stiffen and sink. A person becomes unconscious almost immediately after sinking. But death does not follow at once, for the heart continues to beat for several minutes. The popular belief that a person must come to the surface three times before finally sinking is false. He may not rise at all, depending upon circumstances, especially upon the position of his arms during his struggles. If they are held above the head, the body sinks deeper into the water. If they are held down at the sides, the body will probably rise to the surface.

Methods of Rescue. A drowning person should be rescued from a boat or with a life buoy whenever possible. This lessens the danger to the rescuer.

Rescue by Swimming. Approach the victim from the rear. Grasp his hair or coat collar, and swim vigorously with the free hand and both legs. The side stroke should provide sufficient power to move two people through the water. If the victim cannot be approached from the rear and starts to sink, grasp one of his hands and lie back in the water. Give a strong kick or two with the legs at the same time to keep from going under. A sharp pull with the right hand on that of the victim will turn him over on his back. Then the rescuer can swim with him and keep his head above water, using one of the following rescue methods:

In the *head carry* the rescuer swims on his back and holds the victim's head with both hands, at arms' length, in a floating position. In the *cross-chest carry* the rescuer holds the victim against his upper hip in a back-floating position, while swimming on his side. This position close to the rescuer means greater security. It is an excellent carry for panic-stricken victims.

Applying First Aid. Breathing, or respiration, should be restored as soon as the drowning person has been rescued. A person may apply artificial respiration himself or use such means as an inhalator. The person administering the artificial respiration must not give up easily. People have been saved after as many as eight hours. The person to person methods of applying artificial respiration include mouth-to-mouth, chest pressure-arm lift, or back pressure-arm lift. See ARTIFICIAL RESPIRATION; FIRST AID (Giving Artificial Respiration).

These methods can also be supplemented by the use of an *inhalator* (see RESUSCITATOR). The inhalator consists of a face mask, a breathing bag, and two tanks, one for the oxygen, and the other for the mixture of oxygen and carbon dioxide. Fire departments or public-utility companies can usually supply inhalators. But only a trained person should use one.

Drowning as a Form of Punishment. Drowning was a common form of punishment in most European countries from ancient times until the early 1600's. A condemned man sometimes received a choice of death by drowning or by hanging, or "by ditch or by gallows." He usually chose drowning, since that was considered more honorable. BENJAMIN F. MILLER

See also SAFETY (Water Safety); SWIMMING (Water Safety).

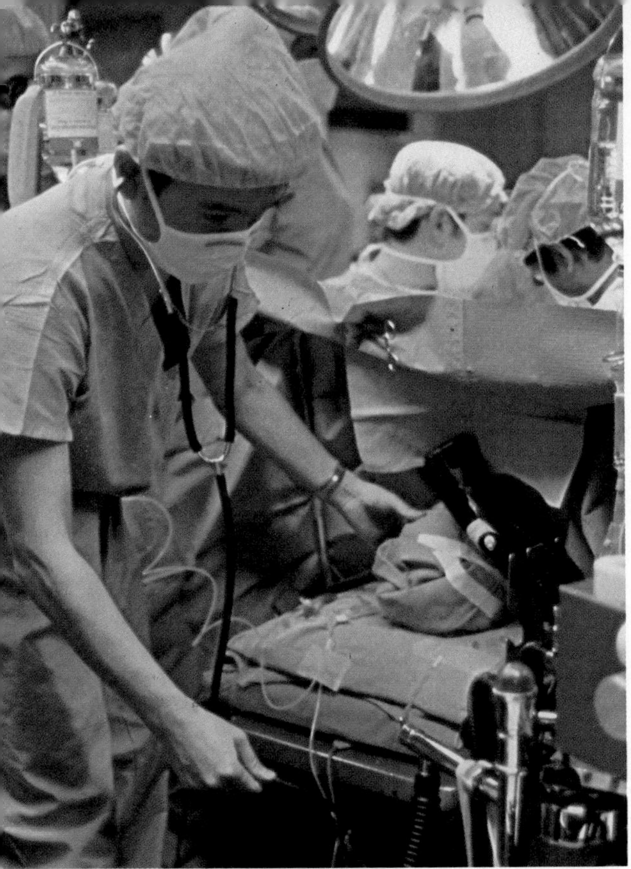

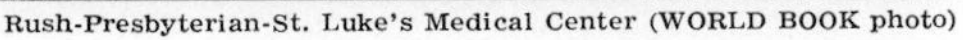

Rush-Presbyterian-St. Luke's Medical Center (WORLD BOOK photo)

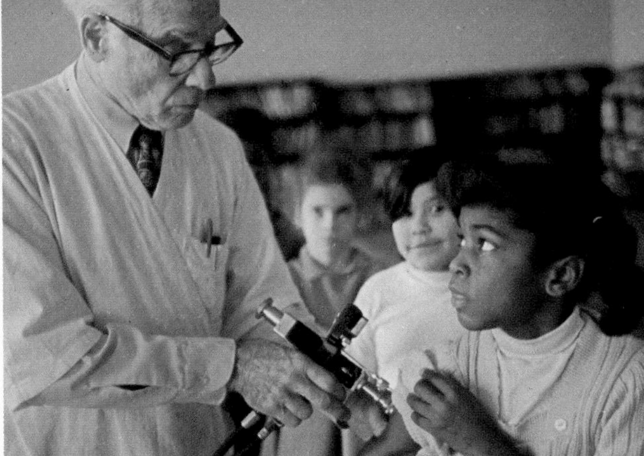

WORLD BOOK photo

WORLD BOOK photo

Modern Drugs help people live longer, healthier, and happier lives. Anesthetics, for example, enable doctors to perform lifesaving operations, *left.* Vaccines, *upper right,* protect people against many infectious diseases. The cold tablets, pain relievers, and similar remedies sold in drugstores, *lower right,* help ease the discomfort of many minor disorders.

DRUG

DRUG is one of the medical profession's most valuable tools. Doctors prescribe drugs to treat or prevent many diseases. Every year, penicillin and other germ-killing drugs save the lives of countless victims of meningitis, pneumonia, and other dangerous infectious diseases. Vaccines prevent attack by such diseases as measles, polio, and smallpox. Tranquilizers help in treating mental illness. The use of these and many other drugs has helped millions of people live longer, healthier lives than would otherwise have been possible.

Almost all our most important drugs, however, were unknown before the 1900's. For example, the sulfa drugs and antibiotics, our greatest germ-fighting drugs, did not come into use until the late 1930's and early 1940's. Before that time, about 25 per cent of all pneumonia victims in the United States died of the disease. The new drugs quickly reduced the death rate from pneumonia to less than 5 per cent. Polio vaccine was introduced in 1955. At that time, polio struck about 30,000 to 50,000 Americans each year. By 1960, use of the vaccine had reduced the number of new polio cases to about 3,000 a year. In 1900, most Americans did not live past the age of 47. Today, Americans live an average of more than 70 years, in great part because of the use of modern drugs.

But drugs can also cause sickness and death. Any drug, even a helpful one, may cause great harm if used improperly. Aspirin, for example, is one of the safest and most useful drugs. Yet every year, aspirin kills many children who mistake the pills for candy and eat too many of them. Any drug can kill if taken in a large enough dose. In addition, the widespread misuse of alcohol, narcotics, and certain other drugs has become a serious problem.

We generally use the word *drugs* to mean only medicines and certain other chemical substances that people use, such as alcohol or marijuana. But *pharmacologists,* the scientists who study drugs, consider all chemicals that affect living things to be drugs. For example, they classify insecticides, weedkillers, and a wide variety of other substances as drugs. Even the chemicals in automobile exhaust and other substances that pollute the environment are considered drugs because they affect living things. This article, however, deals chiefly with drugs used for medical purposes. Detailed information on the misuse of drugs can be found in the articles DRUG ABUSE and DRUG ADDICTION.

Edward J. Cafruny, the contributor of this article, is Adjunct Professor of Pharmacology at Cornell University Medical College and President of Sterling-Winthrop Research Institute, a private organization that conducts drug research.

The many kinds of drugs people use can be classified in several ways. For example, they can be grouped according to their form, such as a capsule, gas, or liquid. Or they can be classified according to the way they are taken, such as by swallowing, inhaling, or injection. Drugs can also be grouped by their chemical structure. But pharmacologists generally classify drugs according to the major beneficial effect they have on the body. Classified in this way, many of the most important and widely used drugs fall into one of four groups. These groups are (1) drugs that fight bacteria, (2) drugs that prevent disease, (3) drugs that affect the heart and blood vessels, and (4) drugs that affect the nervous system.

All drugs affect the body in more than one way. For example, some drugs taken to act on the nervous system also affect the heart. The drugs discussed in this section, however, are classified according to their chief effect on the body.

Drugs That Fight Bacteria

Two main types of drugs kill or help the body kill bacteria: (1) antibiotics and (2) sulfonamides, or sulfa drugs. Doctors prescribe these drugs in treating meningitis, pneumonia, and many other infectious diseases. A large dose of penicillin, streptomycin, or most other antibiotics kills bacteria. A smaller dose keeps the bacteria from multiplying and thus allows the body's natural defenses to kill them off. Other antibiotics and the sulfa drugs also prevent bacteria from multiplying in the body. But in most cases, these drugs do not kill the bacteria. See ANTIBIOTIC; SULFA DRUGS.

Drugs That Prevent Disease

Two main kinds of drugs prevent disease: (1) vaccines and (2) antiserums and globulins. Some of these drugs, such as polio and smallpox vaccines, are especially valuable because there is no known cure for the disease they prevent.

Vaccines. There are several kinds of vaccines. Each kind causes the body to produce substances, called *antibodies*, that fight a particular disease. The vaccine thus makes the body *immune* to the disease by providing resistance against attack by it. Vaccines have been developed against such infectious diseases as cholera, diphtheria, measles, and whooping cough, as well as polio and smallpox. See VACCINATION.

Antiserums and Globulins, like vaccines, prevent certain infectious diseases. But unlike vaccines, these drugs contain antibodies rather than substances that cause the body to produce antibodies. The antiserums and globulins thus act more quickly than vaccines to prevent infection. Physicians prescribe these drugs after a person who has not been vaccinated is exposed to an infectious disease. Antiserums are used against such diseases as diphtheria and *tetanus* (lockjaw). Diseases combated with globulins include hepatitis, measles, mumps, and whooping cough. See SERUM; GLOBULIN.

Drugs That Affect the Heart and Blood Vessels

Drugs that affect the heart and blood vessels are known as *cardiovascular drugs*. Doctors prescribe them in treating diseases of the heart and blood vessels. These diseases rank as the chief cause of death from disease in the United States, Canada, and many other countries. There are three major kinds of cardiovascular drugs: (1) antiarrhythmics, (2) cardiotonics, and (3) vasodilators.

Antiarrhythmics steady the heartbeat. People take these drugs to treat *fibrillation*, a condition in which the heart beats irregularly and usually at a rate much faster than normal.

Cardiotonics strengthen the heartbeat. These drugs cause the heart to beat more forcefully and thus increase circulation of the blood. Physicians prescribe the drugs to treat conditions in which the heart pumps too weakly. The most widely used cardiotonic drugs include digoxin and digitoxin.

Vasodilators enlarge, or *dilate*, the blood vessels. These drugs are taken mostly to treat narrowing of the coronary arteries, the vessels that carry blood to the heart. Drugs used to enlarge these arteries are called *coronary vasodilators*. Doctors prescribe them for people with such severe narrowing of the coronary arteries that they suffer chest pains while walking or exercising in some other way. Such persons are said to have *angina pectoris*. The most widely used coronary vasodilator is nitroglycerin.

Vasodilators also help in the treatment of *hypertension* (high blood pressure). The drugs lower blood pressure by enlarging blood vessels and thus allowing the

RULES FOR USING DRUGS

NO DRUG IS ABSOLUTELY SAFE. PROPER USE IS BENEFICIAL. IMPROPER USE IS HARMFUL.

1. **Do Not Take a Drug Prescribed for Someone Else.** Only a physician or dentist can determine which drug will help you. A drug that works for someone else may not work for you because of differences in age, weight, or other physical characteristics. In addition, you may not have the same disease or disorder as someone else, even though the symptoms appear to be the same.
2. **Do Not Save Prescription Drugs for Later Use.** Obtain a new prescription each time illness occurs. You may have an illness that seems the same as an earlier one but is actually different.
3. **Do Not Keep Nonprescription Drugs Too Long.** All drugs change chemically in time. Some become weaker than intended. Other drugs contain substances that evaporate, making the medicines stronger than intended. If a drug label does not tell how long a drug will remain safe and effective, ask your pharmacist.
4. **Follow All Instructions on Drug Labels.** The label tells how much of a drug to take and how often. It also tells under what conditions you should not take the drug. It may be dangerous to use more of a drug than the amount prescribed or recommended, or to ignore any other label instructions.
5. **Report Unpleasant or Unexpected Drug Effects** to your physician or dentist. Any drug may produce an unusual, unexpected effect.
6. **Keep All Drugs in a Safe Place** away from children and pets. An overdose of any drug can cause sickness or even death.

blood to circulate more freely. The vasodilators used to treat high blood pressure are called *antihypertensives*.

Drugs That Affect the Nervous System

Many of the most widely used drugs affect the brain and other parts of the nervous system. These drugs include alcohol; the caffeine in cocoa, coffee, and tea; marijuana; narcotics, such as heroin and morphine; and sleeping pills. Altogether, five major kinds of drugs affect the nervous system: (1) analgesics, (2) anesthetics, (3) hallucinogens, (4) stimulants, and (5) depressants.

Analgesics relieve pain without deadening any of the other senses, such as the sense of touch or taste. For example, an analgesic may relieve a person's headache, but it will not prevent that person from feeling heat or cold or from tasting food.

There are two main kinds of analgesics: (1) narcotics and (2) nonnarcotics. Both kinds relieve pain. But the narcotics also produce drowsiness, a dazed condition, and often a feeling of well-being. Aspirin is the most common nonnarcotic analgesic. The most widely used narcotics are *opiates*, which are obtained from the opium poppy, and certain related *synthetic* (man-made) drugs. Opiates include codeine, heroin, and morphine.

Physicians sometimes prescribe narcotics in treating certain disorders. For example, morphine is used to relieve the pain of severe injury and of some kinds of cancer. But excessive use of narcotics leads to drug addiction, a condition in which a person has become so dependent on the drug that illness results if use of the drug is stopped. For this reason, physicians prescribe narcotics only if other analgesics will not work. See NARCOTIC.

Anesthetics are drugs that eliminate sensation. *General anesthetics* eliminate all sensation throughout the body, thus causing unconsciousness. These drugs, which include halothane and sodium pentothal, are given to patients during many kinds of surgical operations. *Local anesthetics* deaden the senses only in the area of the body to which they are applied. Dentists often give such local anesthetics as lidocaine and procaine. Doctors use local anesthetics for eye surgery and other operations that do not require the patient to be unconscious. See ANESTHESIA.

Hallucinogens cause a person to *hallucinate*—that is, to see, hear, or otherwise sense something that exists only in the mind. These drugs are also called *psychedelic* (mind-revealing) drugs. They give people a distorted view of themselves and their surroundings. Hallucinogenic drugs include LSD, marijuana, and mescaline. Physicians have experimented with hallucinogens in treating mental illness, but no generally accepted medical use has been found for these drugs. See HALLUCINOGENIC DRUG.

Stimulants combat sleep and tiredness. These drugs *stimulate*, or increase the activity of, the nervous system. Stimulants include caffeine, cocaine, and synthetic drugs known as *amphetamines*. Common names for amphetamines include "speed," "uppers," and "wake-ups." See AMPHETAMINE.

Stimulants create a sense of well-being in most users, in addition to increasing mental and physical activity. But many people become sad and uneasy as the effects of a stimulant wear off. They may then take the drug again to feel better, and they thus become dependent on it. For this reason, doctors seldom prescribe stimulants for tiredness. See STIMULANT.

Depressants reduce tension and worry. These drugs *depress*, or decrease the activity of, the nervous system. They include tranquilizers, sedatives, and alcohol.

Tranquilizers calm a person without causing much drowsiness if taken in a small enough dose. Larger doses make the user sleepy as well as calmer. Psychiatrists prescribe powerful tranquilizers in treating severe mental illness. These drugs greatly reduce a patient's extreme fears and worries and thus improve the chances for successful treatment.

Many people who do not have severe mental illness but who have difficulty handling the stresses of everyday life take mild tranquilizers. However, use of these drugs over a long period of time may make the user dependent on them. See TRANQUILIZER.

Sedatives, like tranquilizers, have a calming effect. But sedatives have greater ability than tranquilizers to make a person sleepy. As a result, physicians generally prescribe sedatives for patients who suffer from *insomnia* (the inability to sleep naturally). The most widely used sedatives are a group of synthetic drugs called *barbiturates*. These drugs include pentobarbital and secobarbital. Barbiturates are sometimes called "barbs," "downers," or "goofballs." There are also nonbarbiturate sedatives, such as chloral hydrate and paraldehyde. People who use a sedative regularly may become dependent on it and have to increase the dose for the drug to be effective. See SEDATIVE; BARBITURATE.

Alcohol is the common name for ethyl alcohol, the drug found in alcoholic drinks. It relaxes most people and makes them drowsy. The use of alcohol, like the use of most other drugs that depress the nervous system, may make a person dependent on it. See ALCOHOLISM.

Other Kinds of Drugs

People also use many other kinds of drugs besides those discussed above. These drugs include (1) diuretics, (2) hormones, (3) vitamins, and (4) antitumor drugs.

Diuretics increase the formation of urine. In certain diseases, the kidneys do not produce enough urine. As a result, fluid, salts, and wastes build up in the body. Diuretics correct this condition by causing the kidneys to produce more urine. See DIURETIC.

Hormones are chemicals made by the glands of the body. The hormones control various body functions, such as growth and reproduction. Certain animal hormones are similar to those produced by human beings, and scientists have created synthetic hormones. These natural and man-made hormones are used as drugs in several ways.

Physicians prescribe hormones for patients whose glands produce too little of them. For example, people who have the disease diabetes mellitus do not produce enough of the hormone insulin. They must therefore receive injections of the hormone. Doctors also prescribe certain hormones to treat diseases that do not result from a *deficiency* (lack) of a hormone. The hormones

ACTH and cortisone, for example, are used in treating rheumatoid arthritis.

Hormones are also used to make *oral contraceptives*, or *birth control pills*, which prevent pregnancy. These drugs work by interfering with the normal reproductive processes in a woman's body. See HORMONE; BIRTH CONTROL (Methods of Birth Control).

Vitamins are essential to good health. Such diseases as rickets or scurvy develop if a person has a vitamin deficiency. The best way to obtain vitamins is to eat a well-balanced diet. But if necessary, a physician may prescribe vitamin pills or injections. See VITAMIN.

Antitumor Drugs destroy cancer cells. Although many such drugs have been developed, they all attack normal cells as well as cancer cells. But some antitumor drugs have been used to lengthen the life of patients with incurable cancer. Scientists hope to develop drugs that will destroy only cancer cells.

DRUG/*How Drugs Work*

Different drugs are *administered* (given) in different ways. But once in the body, almost all drugs work the same way—by altering the speed of cell activities.

Entrance into the Body. Most drugs are administered orally. But drugs may also be given in several other ways. For example, they may be injected, inhaled, or applied to the skin. The method of administration depends on the form and purpose of a drug. An anesthetic gas, for example, must be inhaled to produce unconsciousness. Ointments must be applied directly to the area being treated.

Each method of administration has advantages and disadvantages. For example, the easiest and safest way to take a drug is by swallowing it. But some drugs cannot be taken orally because stomach juices destroy them. Injected drugs act quickly in the body. But injection is somewhat painful, and it presents greater risk of infection than do other methods of administration.

Action in the Body. Most drugs that are swallowed, inhaled, or injected enter the blood stream and travel throughout the body before they act in cells. They pass from the blood into the cells of the tissues where the drug action occurs. Only a few kinds of drugs—such as eye drops, local anesthetics, and nasal sprays—act before entering the blood stream. When these drugs eventually enter the blood, the amount is usually too small to produce additional effects on the cells.

Almost all drugs create their effects by altering the speed of cell activities. To explain how drugs act on cells, pharmacologists developed the *receptor theory*. According to this theory, chemical reactions in every living cell control the cell's activities. Each controlling reaction causes a particular cell activity to begin, to speed up, or to slow down. A drug acts on a cell by interfering with one of these chemical reactions. It does so by attaching to *receptor molecules* in each

HOW A DRUG REACHES ITS SITE OF ACTION

These drawings show how three drugs, taken in different ways, reach the part of the body where they produce their chief effect. The arrows show the path each drug follows to its site of action. The red arrows in the second and third drawings indicate where a drug is carried by the blood stream.

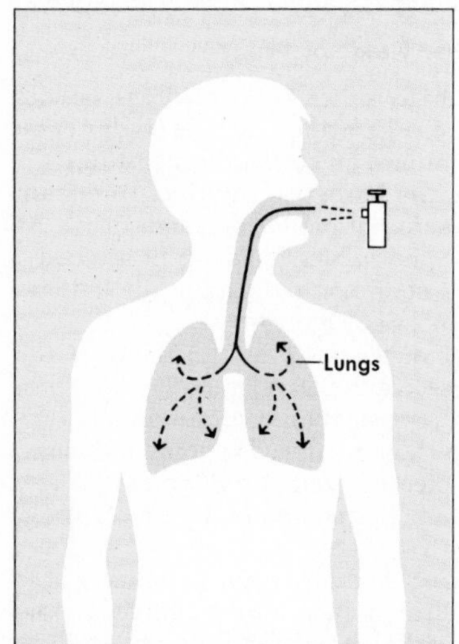

Epinephrine is used to treat asthma. When inhaled, the drug travels directly to the lungs, where it eases the difficulty in breathing that occurs with asthma.

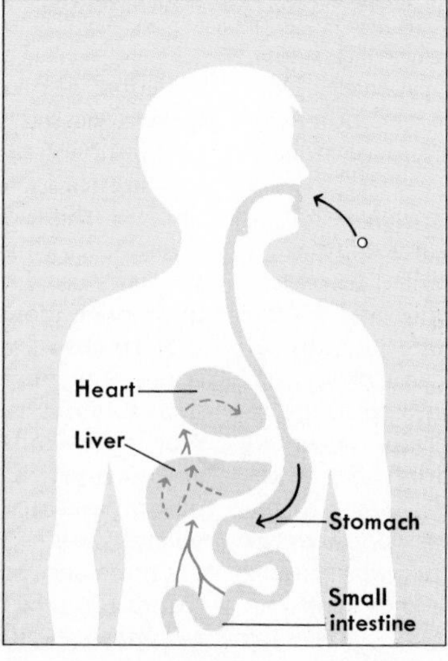

The drug digitoxin is used to strengthen a weak heartbeat. Taken orally, the drug passes through the digestive system and the liver to its site of action, the heart.

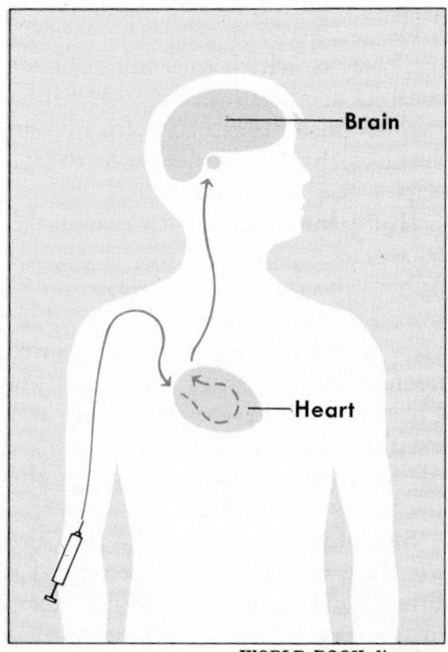

WORLD BOOK diagram

Morphine is administered to relieve severe pain. The injected drug quickly enters the blood stream and is carried to the brain, where it acts to ease the sense of pain.

HOW THE RECEPTOR THEORY EXPLAINS DRUG ACTION

According to the receptor theory, drugs produce their effects by attaching to *receptor molecules* in body cells. *Activator molecules* in every cell normally attach to each receptor molecule's cavities, *left*. This chemical reaction affects the body by causing a particular cell activity to begin, to speed up, or to slow down. A drug acts by attaching to receptor cavities, which prevents the activator from doing so, *right*. As a result, the particular cell activity does not begin, speed up, or slow down.

WORLD BOOK diagram

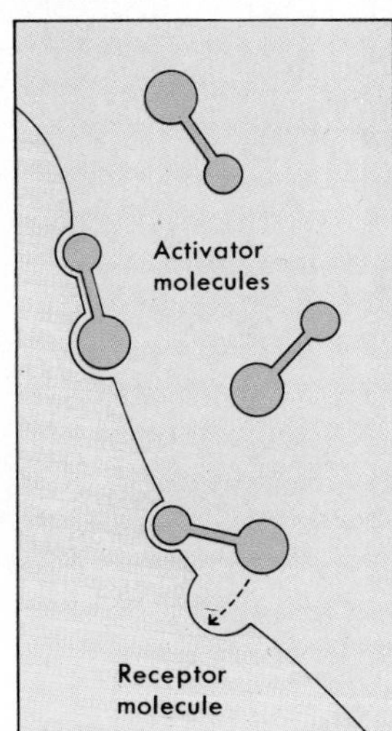

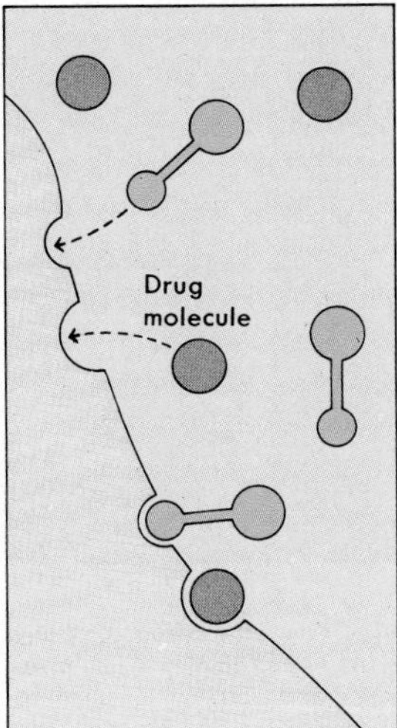

cell that are normally involved in the controlling chemical reaction. The drug thus prevents the chemical reaction from occurring.

The receptor theory not only explains how drugs work, but it also points up what drugs can and cannot do. Because they react with receptors that control cell activities, drugs can only alter the speed of those activities. They cannot create new cell activities.

In most cases, the chemical reaction between a drug and the body is not a one-way process. Drugs alter cell activity, but normal body processes also change most drugs. These processes transform a drug into one or more new substances, most of which are weaker than the original drug. This changing of drugs is called *biotransformation* or *drug metabolism*. It is one way in which the body protects itself against drugs. Most biotransformation occurs in the liver. A diseased liver takes longer than a healthy one to change a drug into a weaker substance. As a result, physicians generally reduce drug dosage for a patient with liver disease. Otherwise, the drug would have too great an effect on the body.

Effect on the Body. All drugs can affect the body in both helpful and harmful ways. For example, a particular drug may produce a stronger heartbeat, relief from pain, or some other desired effect. But that drug, like all drugs, can also cause undesired effects—especially if the dose is too large. Such effects might include fever, high blood pressure, or constipation.

Most drugs produce changes throughout the body because the drugs circulate through the blood stream. As a result, most drugs used to affect one part of the body also affect other parts. For example, physicians sometimes prescribe morphine to relieve pain. Morphine depresses the activities of cells in the brain and thus reduces the sensation of pain. But morphine also alters the function of cells elsewhere in the body. It may decrease the rate of breathing, cause vomiting, produce constipation, and create other undesired effects.

In general, a drug's effects are strengthened as the dose is increased and weakened as the dose is decreased. But all people do not react the same to a change in the dose of a drug. Doubling the dose, for example, may triple the strength of the drug effects in one person and not produce any increase in the effects in someone else.

The section *Kinds of Drugs* describes the chief desired effects of various drugs. Effects other than those desired are called *adverse reactions*. Drugs produce three main kinds of adverse reactions: (1) side reactions, (2) hypersensitivity reactions, and (3) toxic reactions. The repeated use of alcohol, narcotics, and certain other drugs may also create a condition called *drug dependence*.

Side Reactions, or *side effects*, occur with all drugs. Physicians can predict these reactions and tell a patient what to expect. For example, many of morphine's harmful effects are side reactions and should therefore be expected. Most drugs cause weak side reactions that do not prevent use of the drug. These reactions might include constipation or slight difficulty in breathing.

Hypersensitivity Reactions, also called *allergic reactions*, occur only in persons allergic to a particular drug. Many of these reactions are the same as side effects. But they occur unexpectedly the first time they strike a person. Any drug may cause an allergic reaction in people highly sensitive to that drug. For example, some people cannot take such common drugs as aspirin and penicillin because they are allergic to them.

Toxic Reactions result from drug poisoning. Such reactions damage body cells and may kill a person. All drugs can have at least a mild toxic effect, and a large enough overdose of any drug will produce a severe toxic reaction.

Drug Dependence. People who repeatedly take large amounts of such drugs as alcohol, amphetamines, barbiturates, or narcotics may become dependent on the drugs. These people have a great psychological or physical need for a drug's effects—or they may have both a psychological and a physical need. *Tolerance*, or resistance to a drug's effects, usually develops along with drug dependence. As drug use continues, tolerance increases. The drug user must thus take larger and larger doses to obtain the desired effects. The development of physical or psychological dependence, or both, is commonly called *drug addiction*. In most cases, a severe withdrawal illness occurs if a person stops taking the drug. See Drug Addiction; Drug Abuse.

Elimination from the Body. The body eliminates drugs with other waste materials. Most drugs travel from the cells through the blood stream to the kidneys and are eliminated in the urine. The body also eliminates drugs in such fluids as sweat and tears and in solid wastes. Some anesthetics are eliminated almost entirely in exhaled breath.

DRUG / How Drugs Are Produced and Sold

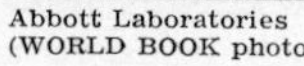

Abbott Laboratories (WORLD BOOK photo)

Nancy Palmer Photo Agency Inc.

Eli Lilly and Company

Abbott Laboratories (WORLD BOOK photo)

The Four Sources of Drugs. Most drugs are man-made compounds created in drug company laboratories, *far left.* Other drugs come from plants, animals, and minerals. For example, opium poppies, *second from left,* supply opium, used to make such narcotics as codeine and morphine. Ground-up hog pancreases, *second from right,* are used in producing insulin, which controls the disease diabetes. The mineral sodium chloride, or salt, and other substances are used in preparing *intravenous solutions, far right,* which are injected into the veins of patients who cannot eat or drink.

The production and sale of drugs used as medicines is a big business in many countries. The world's leading producers include France, Great Britain, Switzerland, the United States, and West Germany.

This section deals chiefly with the production and sale of drugs in the United States. The U.S. drug, or *pharmaceutical,* industry sells more than $8 billion worth of drugs a year. The industry includes over 1,000 drug companies and employs about 135,000 workers. New Jersey, New York, and Pennsylvania rank as the leading drug-producing states.

Sources of Drugs

The pharmaceutical industry produces mostly synthetic drugs. Chemists working in the laboratories of drug companies create these drugs from chemical elements. Other drugs produced by the industry are obtained from plants, animals, and minerals.

Chemical Laboratories. Chemists have created many of our most valuable medicines. A great number of these drugs, including aspirin, sulfa drugs, and many sedatives and tranquilizers, do not occur naturally. Other synthetic drugs duplicate or improve upon those obtained from plants, animals, or minerals. Pharmaceutical companies can produce many of these drugs at less cost and in greater quantity synthetically than by using the natural source. For example, the hormone cortisone, used to treat arthritis and many other ailments, can be obtained from the adrenal glands of cows and sheep. But drug companies can produce cortisone cheaper synthetically. In addition, the man-made product causes fewer adverse reactions than the natural form.

Plants. Drug companies make several important medicines from plants. These medicines include antibiotics, cardiotonics, and certain analgesics. For example, the antibiotic penicillin comes from a mold. The cardiotonic digitalis, used to stimulate the heart, is obtained from the leaves of the purple foxglove, a garden flower. The pain reliever morphine is taken from opium, which comes from the juice of the opium poppy. Plant drugs that pharmaceutical companies do not produce include such illegal drugs as marijuana and mescaline.

Animals supply a number of important drugs, including several of the hormones used to treat arthritis, hormone deficiencies, and various other ailments. For example, millions of diabetes victims use insulin obtained from the pancreas of cattle and hogs. Physicians prescribe the hormone thyroxine, obtained from the thyroid gland of cattle and hogs, for patients whose thyroid gland produces too little of the hormone.

Minerals. Pharmaceutical companies produce several common drugs from minerals. For example, the mineral iodine is used in making tincture of iodine, a liquid that helps prevent infection when applied to cuts and bruises. The mineral silver nitrate is manufactured in powder form and rubbed onto wounds to stop bleeding and help prevent infection. Physicians also use silver nitrate in mild solution to treat or prevent certain eye and skin infections.

Research and Development

Pharmaceutical firms are continually developing new drugs. Although company chemists discover some new drugs by accident, the creation of most new products begins with an idea. This idea may be for a new kind of drug or for one that works better than existing drugs. A pharmaceutical company must then obtain such a drug, test it, and develop it into a safe, easy-to-use form. The entire process takes at least five years for most drugs.

Creating a New Drug is the task of a company's research chemists. They may make a new chemical compound or obtain the drug from a natural source. This work may take many months or even years. For example, researchers for one U.S. drug company spent two years testing soil from all parts of the world in an effort to find new antibiotics. The tests involved more than 100,000 soil samples. The entire project resulted in the development of one antibiotic, Terramycin, used to treat such diseases as bronchitis, pneumonia, and whooping cough. The drug came from a mold in the soil of an Indiana farm.

In the process of creating a new drug, researchers perform tests with animals to see if the substance is safe and effective. They first give the substance to small animals, such as rats, mice, and guinea pigs. If the substance passes these tests, it is given to larger animals, such as dogs and monkeys. Researchers may test hundreds of substances before finding one that appears safe and effective. They then try to find out how this drug works, in what forms it can be given, how the animal body eliminates the drug, and what side effects it may have. The drug company then sends this and other information about the drug to the U.S. Food and Drug Administration (FDA) and asks for permission to conduct tests on people.

Abbott Laboratories (WORLD BOOK photo)

Tests with Animals help researchers determine if a new drug is safe and effective. As part of the tests, each animal is weighed, *above,* to see if the drug's effects differ among animals of different sizes.

Abbott Laboratories (WORLD BOOK photo)

Test Results for a new drug fill many volumes. The U.S. Food and Drug Administration (FDA) requires drug companies to submit this information when applying for approval to sell the drug.

Testing with People. After receiving FDA approval, a drug company performs two series of *clinical tests* with the new drug. The company first tests the drug for safety in healthy human volunteers. If the results of these tests are satisfactory, the company checks the drug further in patients who have the disorder the drug is designed to combat.

Most clinical tests are supervised by a *clinical investigator,* a physician employed by the drug firm's research department. Physicians on the staffs of university hospitals cooperate by arranging for volunteers to take part in the second series of clinical tests. The number of patients who receive the drug and the length of the tests depend on the disorder being treated and the kind of drug being tested. Most tests involve hundreds of patients and last from several months to a year. Some tests involve thousands of patients and last several years.

Careful testing is one of a pharmaceutical company's most important responsibilities. Drug companies and the FDA constantly guard against the possibility of a harmful drug being sold to the public. But even the most careful testing cannot always reveal the possibility that a drug might produce an unexpected harmful effect. A tragic example of such an unexpected effect occurred in Europe during the early 1960's. Thousands of pregnant women who took a new sedative, thalidomide, gave birth to babies with no arms or legs or with other deformities. The chances of such severe effects occurring unexpectedly are, however, very small.

The drug company's clinical investigator and other scientists evaluate the results of the clinical tests. They also compare the new drug with those already in use. Other physicians and scientists continue to study the effects of the drug in animals. If the company decides it has developed a safe, effective drug, it will submit a *new drug application* to the FDA requesting approval to sell the drug. The section *The New Drug Application* describes this step in drug production.

Developing the Finished Product. Before a company can sell a new drug, it must develop the product into a safe, easy-to-use form. Researchers determine what ingredients to add to the drug to make it into a capsule, liquid, pill, or other usable form. These ingredients, called *excipients,* must not interfere with the action of the drug. Researchers also determine how fast the drug will break down chemically and lose its effectiveness. The drug company can then include this information on the label if the chemical breakdown occurs quickly. After completing all these steps, the company is ready to plan mass production of the new drug.

Mass Production

During research and development, a company produces only small quantities of a drug. The firm must determine whether the process used to produce such small amounts will work for large-scale production. For this reason, the company usually conducts production tests in an experimental *pilot plant* before beginning mass production. The tests may indicate that small-scale methods have to be changed, or even that a new plant must be built to produce the drug.

A company has to plan its mass-production schedule carefully. If the firm produces too much of a drug, some of it might break down chemically and become worthless before it is sold. The company must also make certain that all batches of the drug have been made correctly. Samples of each batch are inspected. If such spot-checking reveals an error, the entire batch is either processed again or destroyed.

Distribution and Sale

A new drug may be distributed and sold in one of two ways, depending on whether it is an ethical or proprietary drug. *Ethical drugs* may be sold only by a pharmacist and only if prescribed by a physician or dentist. Ethical drugs are also called *prescription drugs. Proprietary drugs* need not be sold by pharmacists and

HOW A DRUG IS MASS-PRODUCED

Pharmaceutical companies manufacture drugs in a variety of forms, including capsules, liquids, and tablets. The pictures below show some of the steps in the mass production of tablets.

Drug Powder Poured into Stamping Machine

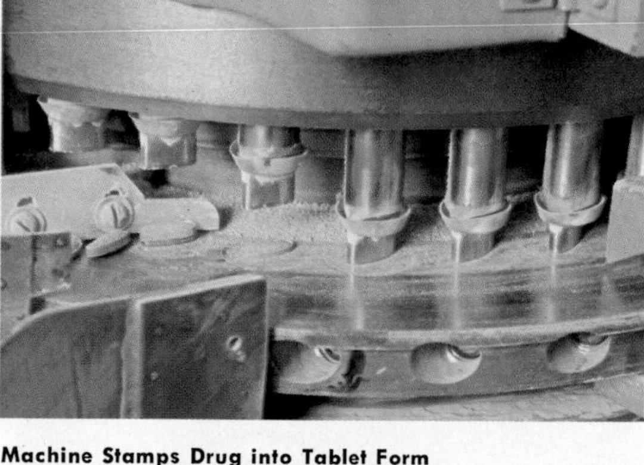

Machine Stamps Drug into Tablet Form

Tablets Receive Protective Coating

Abbott Laboratories (WORLD BOOK photos)

Tablets Bottled for Distribution

do not require a prescription. The Food and Drug Administration determines whether a drug may be sold as an ethical or proprietary drug.

Ethical Drugs include antibiotics, barbiturates, and certain tranquilizers. Because ethical drugs require a prescription, pharmaceutical companies aim their sales efforts for these drugs at physicians and dentists. The companies place advertisements in professional journals, mail out literature about the drugs, and set up advertising displays at medical and dental meetings. Most drug firms also employ *medical service representatives*, or *detail men*, who call on doctors to tell them about the firm's products.

Proprietary Drugs, such as aspirin and some cough medicines, are considered safe enough to be sold *over the counter*—that is, without a prescription. A drugstore, grocery store, department store, or any other establishment may sell such drugs. As a result, pharmaceutical companies advertise proprietary drugs widely to the public.

Drug Names

All drugs produced by the U.S. pharmaceutical industry are given at least three names: (1) a chemical name; (2) a United States Adopted Name (USAN); and (3) one or more trade names, or trademarks. For example, a certain diuretic has the chemical name 6-chloro-3,4-dihydro-7-sulfamyl-2H-1,2,4-benzothiadiazine, 1,1-dioxide. Its USAN is hydrochlorothiazide. The drug has more than 20 trade names, including Esidrex, HydroDiuril, and Oretic.

The Chemical Name of a drug describes its chemical structure. It is the only name that identifies a drug exactly. But because most drugs have long, difficult chemical names—such as the above example—these names are not commonly used.

The United States Adopted Name is sort of an abbreviated chemical name. It provides a hint about a drug's chemical structure, as the name *hydrochlorothiazide* does in the above example. But the USAN does not describe a drug completely. It is shorter than the chemical name, however, and thus easier to use. The USAN Council, made up of pharmacists and scientists in other fields, selects all United States Adopted Names.

The Trade Name is given to a drug by the company that sells it. A number of firms may sell a particular drug. Each company gives the drug a different trade name, and so the drug may have 10, 20, or more trade names. If a doctor prescribes a drug by its trade name, a pharmacist may not substitute another trademarked drug for the one prescribed. But if a drug is prescribed by its United States Adopted Name, a pharmacist may fill the prescription with a suitable drug sold by any company.

Drug Regulation

Almost all countries have laws regulating the manufacture, sale, and use of drugs. In the United States, every new drug sold must be approved by the Food and Drug Administration (FDA), an agency of the federal government. The FDA also inspects factories that produce drugs and checks the quality of drug samples taken from stores.

The U.S. Drug Enforcement Administration works to end the illegal use of narcotics and other drugs of abuse (see DRUG ENFORCEMENT ADMINISTRATION). In addition, many states have laws concerning the manufacture, sale, and use of drugs. In Canada, the manufacture and sale of drugs is regulated by the Health Protection Branch of the federal Department of National Health and Welfare.

U.S. Drug Laws. The Federal Food, Drug, and Cosmetic Act of 1938 outlaws the sale of impure and falsely labeled drugs. It also requires manufacturers to prove to the FDA that a new drug is safe before they may sell it. In addition, the law requires that drug labels list active ingredients, directions for use, and warnings of possible harmful effects. Under the Drug Amendments Act of 1962, drug companies must prove that a new product is effective as well as safe. This law also gives the FDA authority to withdraw from sale any drug introduced between 1938 and 1962 that is believed to be ineffective. The law further gives the FDA control over the advertising of prescription drugs. The Federal Trade Commission (FTC) has control over advertising for nonprescription drugs.

The Comprehensive Drug Abuse Prevention and Control Act of 1970 strengthened federal regulation of the manufacture, sale, possession, and use of narcotics and other drugs of abuse. The act also called for increased federal assistance in the treatment of drug-dependent persons.

The New Drug Application. In seeking FDA approval to sell a new drug, a drug company must submit a *new drug application*. The application must contain detailed information about the drug, including the following:

1. Records of tests that prove the drug is both safe and effective.
2. An account of the composition of the drug.
3. A description of the methods used to manufacture the drug.
4. The information to be included on the drug label.

The company must also provide the FDA with samples of the drug and of each ingredient in it.

FDA scientists study each new drug application and conduct tests, if necessary, with the samples. If they approve a drug, these scientists decide whether it will be sold as an ethical or proprietary drug.

Drug Standards. In the United States, standards of drug composition are set by two publications: *The Pharmacopeia of the United States of America* and *The National Formulary*. The Federal Food, Drug, and Cosmetic Act of 1938 recognizes both books as the official authorities on drug standards. *The National Formulary* and *The Pharmacopeia* are revised every five years by a committee of the United States Pharmacopeial Convention. Each convention includes representatives from schools of medicine and pharmacy; from various federal agencies; and from associations of physicians, dentists, and pharmacists. Other professionals qualified to help determine drug standards also attend the convention.

Prehistoric peoples probably used drugs long before the first civilizations arose. It is likely they discovered that their aches and pains disappeared after they ate certain plants. They may have also noticed that animals ate certain plants only when ill and then became better. Prehistoric people probably then ate the same plants when they felt sick.

Drugs in Ancient Times. The oldest known written record of drug use is a clay tablet from the ancient Sumerian civilization of the Middle East. This tablet, made in the 2000's B.C., lists about a dozen drug prescriptions. An Egyptian scroll from about 1550 B.C. names more than 800 prescriptions containing about 700 drugs. The ancient Chinese, Greeks, and Romans also used many drugs. In addition, the Romans opened the first drugstore and wrote the first prescriptions calling for definite amounts of drug ingredients.

Although ancient peoples used many drugs, most of the remedies were useless. An Egyptian physician, for example, tried to cure blindness by pouring a mixture of honey, pig's eye, and other ingredients into the patient's ear. But occasionally people who had taken useless remedies would recover naturally. As a result, they thought the drugs were responsible.

On the other hand, ancient peoples did discover some effective drugs. The Greeks and Romans, for example, used opium to relieve pain. They took squill, another plant drug, to strengthen a weak heartbeat. The Egyptians used castor oil as a laxative, and the Chinese ate liver to cure anemia.

Drugs in the Middle Ages. During the Middle Ages, which lasted from the A.D. 400's to the 1500's, interest in learning and science declined in Europe. As a result, Europeans produced little new information in the study of drugs. But in the Middle East, Arab physicians added many new discoveries to the knowledge of drugs they had acquired from the ancient Romans and Chinese. The Arabs later passed on their knowledge of drugs to Europeans.

Throughout the Middle Ages, the demand for drugs remained high, and pharmacies became increasingly common in Europe and the Arab world. But scientists had not yet learned how the human body functions, what causes infectious disease, or how drugs work. As a result, people continued to take many useless or harmful drugs, in addition to some effective ones.

Scientific Advances. During the 1500's and 1600's, doctors and scientists made important advances in *pharmacology* (the study of drugs) and in other fields of science. These advances laid the foundation for later revolutionary progress in the development of drugs.

In the early 1500's, the Swiss physician Philippus Paracelsus pioneered in the use of minerals as drugs. He introduced many compounds of lead, mercury, and other minerals in the treatment of various diseases. But further progress in the development of drugs required advances in knowledge of the structure and functioning of the human body.

In 1543, the Belgian physician Andreas Vesalius, known as the father of anatomy, published the first complete description of the body's structure. His work destroyed many false beliefs about human anatomy. In the early 1600's, the English physician William Harvey discovered how blood—pumped by the heart—circulates through the body. Later in the 1600's, Anton van Leeuwenhoek, an amateur Dutch scientist, discovered bacteria. He used crude microscopes to study the tiny organisms. But the role of germs as a cause of disease was not established until the 1800's.

The Drug Revolution began about 1800 and has continued to the present. During this period, scientists have discovered hundreds of drugs. They have also discovered the cause of many diseases, determined how drugs work, and learned much about how the body functions. In the process, the practice of medicine has been revolutionized, in large part by the use of drugs. Pharmacology has developed into an important science, and the manufacture of drugs has become a large industry.

Section of a Sumerian clay tablet from the 2000's B.C.; University Museums, University of Pennsylvania, Philadelphia

The Oldest Known Prescriptions, written on this ancient clay tablet, call mostly for the use of plant materials.

DRUG MILESTONES OF THE 1900'S

1903 The first barbiturate, barbital, was introduced.

1910 The German scientist Paul Ehrlich introduced *chemotherapy,* a method of treating infectious disease by using chemicals to attack the disease-causing bacteria.

1922 A research team led by Frederick Banting, a Canadian physician, announced the discovery of the hormone insulin, used to treat diabetes.

1928 The British scientist Alexander Fleming discovered the first antibiotic, penicillin.

1930's Amphetamines were first used medically.

1935 Gerhard Domagk, a German physician, discovered the first sulfa drug, Prontosil.

1950's Scientists developed several important *synthetic* (man-made) tranquilizers, which came into widespread use.

1960 Birth control pills were introduced.

1970's Drug researchers intensified their efforts to find drugs that will help cure cancer and many other diseases not yet conquered by medical science.

In 1796, an English physician named Edward Jenner developed the first successful vaccination in an effort to prevent the often deadly disease smallpox. He vaccinated a boy with pus from blisters on a woman infected with cowpox. The boy then caught cowpox, a minor disease related to smallpox. Jenner later injected smallpox matter into the boy. But the boy did not catch smallpox because his fight with cowpox had made his body *immune* (resistant) to the more dangerous disease. Jenner's discovery led to a search for vaccines against other diseases. This search gradually developed into the science of *immunology*.

Scientists learned how to *isolate* (separate) drugs from plants in the early 1800's. In 1806, morphine became the first plant drug to be isolated. Within a few years, scientists had isolated quinine and several other plant drugs. These advances enabled researchers and doctors to learn more about the composition and effects of plant drugs. Doctors could then prescribe the drugs more precisely and with greater confidence.

In the 1840's, the use of anesthetics during surgery was introduced by two Americans working independently—Crawford Long, a physician, and William T. G. Morton, a dentist. Later in the 1800's, the French scientist Louis Pasteur and the German physician Robert Koch established the *germ theory* of disease. Pasteur proved that germs cause infectious diseases and that the spread of such diseases can be stopped by killing the germs responsible. Koch developed a method for determining which bacteria cause particular diseases.

The pace of the drug revolution quickened in the 1900's. In fact, most of the major drugs used today, including the hormones, antibiotics, and sulfa drugs, have been discovered since 1900. Important developments in hormone research followed the first isolation of a hormone in 1898. That year, an American pharmacologist, John J. Abel, isolated the hormone epinephrine, used in treating cardiovascular disorders and asthma. Scientists isolated several other hormones during the next 20 years. Then in the early 1920's, a research team led by Frederick Banting, a Canadian physician, discovered the hormone insulin. This drug has saved the lives of millions of diabetics.

During the early 1900's, Paul Ehrlich, a German scientist, developed a new method of treating infectious diseases. This method, called *chemotherapy*, involves the use of chemicals that attack disease-causing bacteria in the body without harming body cells. Ehrlich announced the discovery of the first chemotherapeutic drug in 1910. This drug, arsphenamine (Salvarsan), kills the bacteria that cause the disease syphilis. Ehrlich's work led the way to the later discovery of the germ-fighting antibiotics and sulfa drugs.

The first antibiotic, penicillin, was discovered in 1928 by the British scientist Alexander Fleming. A German physician, Gerhard Domagk, discovered the first sulfa drug, Prontosil, in 1935. Scientists soon developed many other antibiotics and sulfa drugs. These "wonder drugs" proved to be remarkably effective against a variety of infectious diseases.

Many other important drugs have been discovered since 1900. The first barbiturate, barbital, was intro-

Leigh R. Marlatt

U.S. Drugstores of the 1800's sold many effective drugs that the pharmacists themselves prepared. They also sold such useless substances as Hamlin's Wizard Oil and Ayer's Sarsaparilla.

duced in 1903. Barbiturates have since become the most widely used sedatives. Amphetamines, which stimulate the nervous system, were first used medically in the early 1930's. Scientists developed several important tranquilizers in the 1950's, and birth control pills appeared in 1960.

Growth of the Drug Industry. Until about 1800, there were few drug companies. Pharmacists themselves made almost all the drugs they sold. Then two revolutions, one in drugs and the other in industrial development, gave birth to the modern drug industry. The discovery of more and more drugs that required great know-how to produce made it increasingly difficult for a pharmacist to prepare drugs. At the same time, the Industrial Revolution in Europe led to the development of manufacturing methods that could be used to mass-produce drugs. As a result, many drug companies were established in Europe, and European firms came to dominate the world drug market for many years.

The beginning of the United States drug industry can be traced back to the Revolutionary War in America (1775-1783). The chief pharmacist of the American army, Andrew Craigie, set up a laboratory in Carlisle, Pa., to supply drugs to the military. After the war, Craigie opened his own laboratory and began a wholesale drug business. Soon other pharmacists set up drug companies. These companies grew as they adopted the mass-production techniques developed in Europe.

The American Civil War (1861-1865)—like the Revolutionary War—created a great demand for drugs and so furthered the growth of the U.S. pharmaceutical industry. But European companies continued to dominate the world drug market until World War I (1914-1918). Before the war, the United States imported most of its drugs from Germany. But such imports stopped when the United States joined the war against Germany in 1917. The American pharmaceutical industry then expanded rapidly to meet the country's drug needs. The United States began to export drugs after World War I and became one of the world's leading producers.

Over the years, the worldwide demand for drugs has increased rapidly as more and more drugs have been developed. The drug industry has grown with this demand and, through its discoveries, helped create it. Today, the United States leads all countries in drug production.

Drugs Today benefit us tremendously. They also present us with some of our worst problems and greatest challenges. Drugs help cure and prevent many diseases. They also relieve pain and tension and help the body function properly. But the misuse of alcohol, narcotics, and other drugs has led to addiction for millions of people. In addition, the widespread illegal use of drugs has become a major crime problem.

The challenges that drugs offer lie in the discovery of medicines that will help cure cancer, cardiovascular diseases, and other crippling and deadly disorders. In the 1970's, drug researchers increased their efforts to find such cures. Someday, having controlled disease with drugs, scientists may develop drugs that lengthen life by slowing the aging process. EDWARD J. CAFRUNY

DRUG / *Study Aids*

Related Articles in WORLD BOOK include:

Outline

I. Kinds of Drugs
- A. Drugs That Fight Bacteria
- B. Drugs That Prevent Disease
- C. Drugs That Affect the Heart and Blood Vessels
- D. Drugs That Affect the Nervous System
- E. Other Kinds of Drugs

II. How Drugs Work
- A. Entrance into the Body
- B. Action in the Body
- C. Effect on the Body

D. Elimination from the Body

III. How Drugs Are Produced and Sold

A. Sources of Drugs
B. Research and Development
C. Mass Production
D. Distribution and Sale
E. Drug Names
F. Drug Regulation

IV. History

Questions

What are six important rules for the use of drugs?

What three main kinds of adverse reactions do drugs produce?

How did scientific advances of the 1500's and 1600's affect later development of drugs?

What is the difference between ethical and proprietary drugs?

How does the *receptor theory* explain drug action?

When was the first antibiotic discovered? The first sulfa drug?

How do drug companies test new drugs for safety and effectiveness?

What government agency determines whether a drug may be sold in the United States?

How do scientists generally classify drugs?

What three kinds of names are given to drugs produced by the U.S. pharmaceutical industry?

Reading and Study Guide

See *Drug Abuse* in the RESEARCH GUIDE/INDEX, Volume 22, for a *Reading and Study Guide*.

DRUG ABUSE is the harmful use of a drug. Many drugs can damage the body and the mind if taken for long periods of time or in large amounts. Most cases of drug abuse occur when people use drugs for nonmedical reasons.

Drug abuse can not only harm the person who uses the drug, but it also can destroy his relationships with other people. For example, the regular abuse of heroin, morphine, or other *opiates* (drugs made from opium) can lead to addiction to those drugs. An addict may lose interest in his family, and he may steal to get money to buy his drug.

It is not always easy to distinguish the normal use of drugs from drug abuse. For example, alcoholic beverages have been used by people in many societies for thousands of years. But alcohol ranks as one of the most widely abused drugs. Some people cannot control their drinking and in time become *alcoholic* (addicted to alcohol). Alcohol affects a person's judgment and reactions. It results in thousands of automobile accidents and other mishaps every year.

Commonly Abused Drugs include (1) alcohol; (2) *hallucinogenic* (vision-producing) drugs, such as LSD and mescaline; (3) marijuana; (4) nicotine, which is found in tobacco; (5) opiates, including most narcotics; (6) sedatives, including barbiturates and other kinds of sleeping pills; and (7) stimulants, such as cocaine and amphetamines and other "pep pills." *Inhalants*, which are fumes inhaled from such substances as cleaning fluids, gasoline, and model airplane glue, are sometimes classified as abused drugs.

Laws in the United States, Canada, and most other countries forbid the possession or sale of some commonly abused drugs. Others may be obtained legally only with a prescription from a physician. Still others, including alcohol and tobacco, can be purchased le everywhere.

Why People Abuse Drugs. Many people gain *euphoria* (a feeling of well-being). This feeling is also called a "high." Amphetamines, cocaine, and opiates can produce an especially intense "high." Alcohol, barbiturates, and marijuana usually cause a milder euphoria, and nicotine provides even less "lift." Hallucinogenic drugs distort a user's awareness of himself and his surroundings. Some users find such distortion a pleasant experience.

Many people experiment with drugs out of curiosity, for a thrill, or because their friends use drugs. Others do so to show their rejection of various standards and values of society. Much drug abuse results from depression, loneliness, or other personal problems. Some people develop an attitude toward society of being an outsider. Others feel they cannot meet the demands of life, and so they turn to drugs. Many drug abusers are people who easily become discouraged and require immediate satisfaction of their needs.

Effects of Drug Abuse. The regular use of many kinds of drugs results in *psychological dependence*—that is, the use of the drug becomes a hard-to-break habit. The regular use of alcohol, sedatives, and especially opiates can lead to *physical dependence* (addiction). An addict's body needs a drug so badly that he cannot stop using it without suffering pain or sickness. He also needs in-

WORLD BOOK photo

Drug Education Programs have been started in many schools to help prevent student drug abuse. Police officers often take part by visiting classrooms to talk about the drug problem.

creasingly larger doses to achieve the same effect. See DRUG ADDICTION.

The abuse of some drugs can seriously damage a person's health. An overdose of alcohol or sedatives can result in coma or even death. The use of alcohol and a sedative together can produce a stronger, more dangerous effect than a double dose of either of those drugs. Young people have suffocated while sniffing inhalants. Cigarette smoking can cause cancer, emphysema, and heart disease. Many drugs sold illegally are impure, and different batches have widely varying strengths. A mistaken overdose of a drug from a batch of great strength can cause death.

The use of hallucinogenic drugs or of some stimulants can cause *hallucinations* (seeing and hearing things that are not present). A user of these drugs may also develop *delusions* (false beliefs). He may think others want to harm him. Hallucinations and delusions can make a user extremely fearful, nervous, and suspicious. They also may cause panicky reactions in which the user could harm himself or others.

Alcohol, sedatives, and, to a lesser extent, marijuana decrease mental alertness and muscle coordination. Driving under the influence of drugs, especially alcohol, causes thousands of traffic deaths and injuries annually.

The combination of personality problems, withdrawal from society, and drug abuse itself leads many drug abusers to associate mostly with others who abuse drugs. Some members of such groups reject traditional values and lack interest in work and school.

The total cost of drug abuse in the United States may exceed $50 billion a year. This estimate includes hospitalization, time lost from work because of illness due to drug abuse, property damage in accidents resulting from drug abuse, and the cost of producing the drugs.

Signs of Drug Abuse. Even parents and friends cannot always tell if a person is abusing drugs. Many drug abusers try to keep their activities secret. Long absences from home, school, or work; or a sharp drop in performance at school or on the job may indicate drug abuse. A sudden change in personality, especially such changes as irritability or nervousness, may also be a clue. But such signs can also occur without drugs.

Most drugs that are abused can influence a person's behavior. Alcohol, inhalants, and sedatives produce drunkenness, poor muscle coordination, slurred speech, and sleepiness. Opiate users become sleepily absent-minded. Most people who use amphetamines or cocaine become restless and talkative. Marijuana users have a tendency to act silly. Hallucinogenic drugs may make users restless or confused. But in many cases, the effects of drugs cannot be noticed.

Prevention of Drug Abuse is easier than stopping it after it has started. Most people who abuse drugs begin doing so in their teens or early 20's. Young people are less likely to abuse drugs if their parents communicate with them, trust them, and try to understand them and help them with their problems. Parents of teen-agers should establish reasonable guidelines on behavior. In addition, parents themselves must set a good example for their children by not abusing drugs. If a young person does become involved in a drug abuse problem, his parents should seek help from a physician, a professional counselor, or a community organization set up to provide such assistance. DAVID C. LEWIS

Related Articles in WORLD BOOK include:

Alcoholism	Hallucinogenic Drug	Mescaline
Amphetamine	Hashish	Methamphetamine
Barbiturate	Heroin	Morphine
Cocaine	LSD	Narcotic
Drug Enforcement Administration	Marijuana	Opium
		Smoking

See also *Drug Abuse* in the RESEARCH GUIDE/INDEX, Volume 22, for a *Reading and Study Guide*.

DRUG ADDICTION is the inability of a person to control his use of a drug. Such a person is called a *drug addict*. For an addict, drug use is more than a habit. His craving for the drug also involves *physical dependence*. That is, an addict's body depends on a drug so greatly that he suffers a painful withdrawal illness if he stops using it. In addition, an addict also develops a *tolerance* to the drug, and so doses that once satisfied his craving no longer do so. As a result, the addict needs larger and larger doses to achieve the same effect.

For a discussion of some of the causes of drug addiction, see the WORLD BOOK article on DRUG ABUSE.

Addicting Drugs. Three major groups of drugs can cause addiction: (1) *narcotics*, such as heroin and morphine; (2) *sedatives*, including barbiturates and some sleeping pills and tranquilizers; and (3) alcohol.

Narcotics produce addiction faster than sedatives or alcohol do. Almost anyone who takes several doses of heroin daily for two weeks becomes addicted to the drug. But sedatives and alcohol, though less likely than heroin to cause addiction, can create even stronger addiction. Withdrawal from a narcotic causes aching muscles, chills, fever, runny nose and eyes, stomach cramps, and general body weakness. The symptoms resemble those of a bad cold. Withdrawal illness from sedatives or alcohol causes a high fever and convulsions. It also causes *delirium tremens*, a condition in which the victim becomes shaky and sees and hears things that are not present. Too swift a withdrawal from alcohol or sedatives can cause death.

The difference between addicting drugs and other habit-forming drugs is not clear in all cases. Some nonaddicting drugs—as well as the addicting drugs—cause a strong psychological craving that may make a drug habit as hard to break as physical dependence does. In addition, many nonaddicting drugs produce a tolerance in regular users. For such reasons, many experts use the term *drug dependence* rather than *addiction*.

Effects of Drug Addiction. Many addicts spend so much time under the influence of drugs that they neglect their health, work, family, and friends. They find it difficult to keep a job or to handle family responsibilities. They fail to eat well and to maintain personal cleanliness. As a result, many addicts suffer from malnutrition. Addicts who inject drugs may get such diseases as hepatitis or tetanus from an unsterile needle.

For most drug addicts, the chief goal in life is obtaining more drugs. Narcotics cannot be obtained legally without a physician's prescription, but they may be bought illegally at extremely high prices. Some addicts turn to crime, such as robbery and prostitution, to support their drug habit.

Treatment of Drug Addiction. An addict may withdraw from using a drug by slightly decreasing his daily dose over a period of weeks. Gradual withdrawal reduces the severity of withdrawal illness. But even after an addict has withdrawn completely, he feels irritable and restless for weeks or months. Some of his craving for the drug may remain for months or years. Many persons who have withdrawn eventually return to drugs—and to readdiction. They do so partly because they have not solved the problems that first led them to drugs.

Some people who treat addicts believe that the basic cause of addiction is that addicts have not learned to live with other people and to respect society's rules. A number of groups have been formed—some by former addicts—to help addicts adjust to society. One such group, Synanon, requires its members to obey Synanon's rules. In this way, the addict gradually learns to accept the rules of society. Alcoholics Anonymous has helped many persons formerly addicted to alcohol (see ALCOHOLICS ANONYMOUS.)

Physicians use drugs to treat some cases of addiction. For example, they may give heroin addicts a narcotic called *methadone*. Methadone develops physical dependence, but it satisfies the body's craving for heroin. Methadone users can live almost normal lives (see METHADONE). Other drugs, called *narcotic antagonists*, block the pleasant effects of heroin and prevent it from causing additional dependence. A drug called *Antabuse* is used to treat alcoholism. It makes a person sick if he drinks an alcoholic beverage (see ANTABUSE).

Control of Drug Addiction. Laws in the United States, Canada, and most other countries forbid the possession and sale of heroin. Other narcotics and addicting sedatives can be obtained legally only with a physician's prescription. Such laws, if they are fair and are rigorously enforced, probably limit addiction to certain drugs. They also probably decrease the total amount of drug addiction and drug abuse. But the strongest laws, which provide imprisonment and fines, have not eliminated either drug addiction or drug abuse. Other solutions to the problem must also be sought. WILLIAM R. MARTIN

See also DRUG ABUSE with its list of *Related Articles*.

DRUG DEPENDENCE. See DRUG ADDICTION.

DRUG ENFORCEMENT ADMINISTRATION (DEA), an agency of the United States government, enforces federal laws on drug abuse. The DEA has the responsibility for all investigation of drug abuse and arrest of suspected offenders.

The DEA investigates the smuggling of narcotics and dangerous drugs into the United States. It arrests suspected importers and distributors of drugs. It also cooperates with state and local officials in the fight against drug abuse. Agents of the DEA work abroad with agencies of other governments in collecting information about the production and shipment of drugs.

President Richard M. Nixon established the Drug Enforcement Administration in 1973 as part of the Department of Justice. He also created a new Narcotics Division in the department to give the DEA legal advice and to prosecute drug cases. The DEA's functions had previously been performed by three agencies of the Justice Department and by the Bureau of Customs (now the U.S. Customs Service). The DEA has headquarters in Washington, D.C.

Critically reviewed by the DRUG ENFORCEMENT ADMINISTRATION

DRUG THERAPY. See PSYCHIATRY (Drug Therapy).

DRUGGIST. See PHARMACY.

DRUID, *DROO ihd*, was a member of a priestly cult among ancient Celts in France, England, and Ireland. These priests worshiped some gods similar to those of the Greeks and Romans, but under different names. In forests and caves they gave instructions, foretold events, and administered justice.

People know little about Druid rites, because the priests handed down their doctrines by word of mouth, and swore their members to secrecy. The Druids held as sacred the hours of midnight and noon, the oak tree, and the mistletoe (see MISTLETOE). They forecast events by interpreting the flight of birds and the markings on the liver and other entrails of sacrificed animals. The folklore of early Ireland depicts Druids as offering human sacrifice. Some scholars think they used the structure at Stonehenge as a place of worship (see STONEHENGE). A group whose members call themselves Druids meet now at Stonehenge every year during the summer solstice. They conduct rites which they believe are like those of the ancient Druids.

The Druids urged their people to fight the Romans when Julius Caesar invaded Gaul and Britain. The Roman general Julius Agricola destroyed them in England in A.D. 78, but they were active in Ireland until the 400's, when Christianity displaced them. WILSON D. WALLIS

DRUM is any member of about 160 species of fishes. Some drums are also called *croakers*. Drums get their name from the sound some of them make during the mating season. These drums repeatedly tighten certain muscles in their abdomen to produce vibrations that sound like drumming. Many kinds of drums live in warm, shallow ocean water near the shores of most continents. Some of these fish spend part of their early life in fresh-water rivers or in bays where fresh and salt water are mixed. But only one species, the *freshwater drum*, spends its entire life in fresh water. The freshwater drum lives in large lakes and rivers from Canada to Central America.

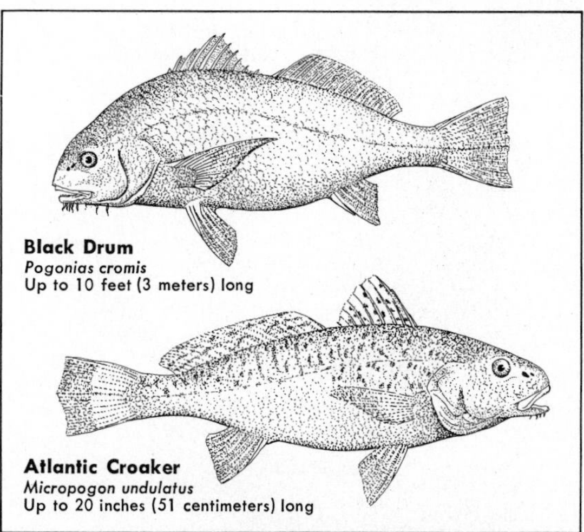

WORLD BOOK illustrations by Marion Pahl

Several Kinds of Drum are popular seafood. Commercial fishermen catch black drum and Atlantic croakers off the Atlantic coast of North America. These fish have firm, white flesh.

Drums range in size from species that weigh about 1 pound (0.45 kilogram) to those that weigh more than 100 pounds (45 kilograms). The *totuava*, which lives in the Gulf of California, is the heaviest drum. It weighs as much as 225 pounds (101 kilograms) and measures up to 6 feet (1.8 meters) long. Most drums have a scaly head; a blunt, rounded nose; and two upper fins separated by a deep notch.

Many drums, including the *red drum* and the *white croaker*, have teeth only in the rear of their mouth. These flat, grinding teeth enable the drums to eat clams, crabs, shrimp, and other shellfish that they find along the ocean floor. Other drums, including the *spotted seatrout* and the *weakfish*, have sharp front teeth that allow them to feed on such free-swimming animals as shrimp, squid, and small fish (see WEAKFISH).

Commercial fishermen in the United States use nets to catch several kinds of drums, including the *Atlantic croaker*, the *black drum*, and the red drum. The drum's firm, white flesh makes the fish a popular seafood.

Two drums of the tropical Atlantic, the *jackknife-fish* and the *high hat*, are favorites of aquarium owners. These small fish have an extremely high fin on their back, and interesting black-and-white markings.

Scientific Classification. Drums make up the drum family, *Sciaenidae*. WARREN J. WISBY

DRUM is a musical instrument that is played by *percussion* (striking sharply). It is made of an open cylinder or a kettle, with a skin called a *drumhead* stretched tightly across the opening. If it has an open cylinder, it has two drumheads. If it is built on a kettle, it has only one. When the drumhead is rapped sharply, it vibrates and produces a sound. This sound is *resonated* (increased) by the drum shell. Drumheads are usually made of stretched parchment or calfskin.

The drum is man's oldest musical instrument. It serves as a means of expressing his instinctive love of rhythm. It has also been used as a method of communication. The drum may be used as a center of ceremonial dances, as a call to battle, or as a requiem for the

Rie Gaddis

WORLD BOOK photo

The Snare Drum, *above,* provides rhythm in orchestras.

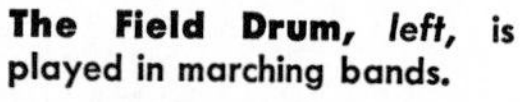

The Field Drum, *left,* is played in marching bands.

Courtesy of Jacob Jerger

The Bongo Drum, *above,* is used in folk and popular music.

The Conga Drum, *right,* is used in Latin-American music.

Am-Par Record Corp.

Rie Gaddis

The Timpani, or *kettledrums,* are the only drums that can be tuned to a definite pitch. They are used in symphony orchestras.

WORLD BOOK photo

The Bass Drum booms a deep, full tone. Marching bands that perform at football games usually include at least one bass drum.

dead. Much of the force and vitality of popular music would be lost without the rhythmic accent of drums.

Most drums do not produce definite musical notes. They are said to have *indefinite pitch.* A *bass drum* is made of wood, with metal tension rods holding the drumheads in place. The rods can be tightened to increase resonance. The drummer uses a *beater* covered with felt or sheep's wool. A *snare drum* measures 14 or 15 inches (36 to 38 centimeters) across and from 5 to 10 inches (13 to 25 centimeters) deep. It is built like a bass drum, except that it has *snares,* or strings of catgut or wire, across the underside. They vibrate against the drumhead, giving the drum its penetrating tone. The drummer uses two wooden sticks in alternate double strokes. A *field drum* resembles the snare drum, but is larger and deeper in proportion to its diameter. It is used chiefly in military and marching bands and in drum and bugle corps.

The *timpani,* or *kettledrums,* are the only drums that can be tuned to a definite pitch. They are hollow halves of globes with single drumheads. The globes are usually made of brass or copper. The drumheads are usually of calfskin. The player tunes timpani by adjusting screws that hold the head in place. This changes the tension and pitch. Some have pedals for rapid changes in tone. Timpani are usually used in pairs. The player makes single strokes with two padded sticks. Tone is affected by the kind of stick. Timpani may be muted by small pieces of cloth. CHARLES B. RIGHTER

See also MUSIC (Percussion Instruments); ORCHESTRA; SOUND (Musical Sounds).

DRUM BRAKE. See AUTOMOBILE (The Brake System).

DRUMFISH. See DRUM.

DRUMLIN. See GLACIER (Structure).

DRUMMOND, HENRY (1851-1897), a Scottish evangelist and author, became known for his books *Natural Law in the Spiritual World* and *The Ascent of Man.* He attempted to connect the theory of evolution with Christian belief. The religious movement he started spread through England, America, and Australia. He was born at Stirling, Scotland.

DRUMMOND, WILLIAM HENRY (1854-1907), was a Canadian poet and physician. He was called the *poet of the habitants.* French-Canadian farmers once called themselves *habitants.* Drummond was interested in their way of life, and that of the *voyageurs* (trappers and boatmen). Drummond turned their simple folk tales and legends into poems. He learned stories from farmers and backwoodsmen, after he became a country doctor at the age of 30. His books of poetry include *The Habitant* (1897) and *The Voyageur* (1905). Drummond was born in County Leitrim, Ireland. He moved to Canada with his parents when he was 10 years old. MICHEL BRUNET

DRUNKENNESS. See ALCOHOLISM.

DRUPE is a fleshy fruit containing a single seed, surrounded by a hard covering or *stone.* The pulp is not divided into segments like the pulp of an orange. The whole drupe is usually covered with a thin skin. Drupes include the olive, plum, cherry, and peach. See also FRUIT (pictures: Kinds of Fruits). ARTHUR W. GALSTON

DRURY, ALLEN (1918-), an American editor and writer, won the Pulitzer prize in 1960 for his novel *Advise and Consent.* The book, about Washington politics, was made into a motion picture. Other books by Drury include *A Shade of Difference* (1962) and *Senate Journal, 1943-1945* (1963). His editorials for the *Tulare* (Calif.) *Bee* won him the Sigma Delta Chi Editorial Award for 1941. Drury later reported national politics for the *Washington Evening Star* and *The New York Times.* He was born in Houston, Tex.

DRUSES, *DROOZ uz,* are an Arabic-speaking people of mixed origin, numbering about 400,000. About half of the Druses live in the Hauran districts of Syria, while most of the rest live in Lebanon. There are about 35,000 Druses in Israel who were recognized in 1957 as a separate religious colony. Some Druses have emigrated to the United States and Canada. Their religion is secret. It combines Christianity and Islam.

Hakim, sixth Fatimite caliph of Egypt, proclaimed himself the incarnation of God in the A.D. 1000's. When he was killed in a revolt, his confessor, Darazi, fled to the Syrian mountains, preaching the same religion. The name *Druse* is probably a corruption of Darazi (or Durusi). VERNON ROBERT DORJAHN

DRY CELL. See BATTERY (Open-Circuit Cells).

DRY CLEANING is a process that removes dirt and stains from fabrics. Dry cleaning uses little or no water. But the process is not really "dry" because it involves liquids called *solvents.*

Dry-cleaning plants handle mostly clothing, but they also clean such items as draperies and rugs. Certain garments, including many of those made of wool, should be dry-cleaned to prevent shrinkage, fading, or other damage. But some materials should not be dry-cleaned. For example, dry cleaning may cause vinyl or artificial leather to crack or split. Most garments have a label that tells how the fabric should be cleaned.

How Clothes Are Dry-Cleaned. At a dry-cleaning plant, each garment is handled with others of the same color and type of fabric. A worker called a *pre-spotter* removes any stains that could become permanent during the dry-cleaning process.

The clothing is put into a special washing machine that contains a movable drum filled with a cleaning fluid. Usually, this liquid is perchloroethylene or a petroleum solvent. A special soap or detergent may also be used in the solvent. After the cleaning stage, a machine called an *extractor* whirls the clothing to remove most of the fluid. Some dry-cleaning plants have a machine known as a *washer-extractor,* which performs both the washing and whirling functions. A machine called a *tumbler* finally dries the clothes by blowing warm air through them.

After drying, each garment goes to a worker called a *spotter,* who uses chemicals, water, and a steam gun and other devices to remove any remaining stains. The garment then goes to the *presser,* or *finisher.* This worker uses pressing, shaping, and steaming equipment to restore the shape, size, and style of the garment. The item is then inspected, and any necessary repairs are made. Finally, all of a customer's articles are assembled, and each piece of clothing is packaged.

Self-service dry-cleaning stores became widespread in the United States during the early 1960's. A coin-operated dry-cleaning machine automatically washes and dries the clothes. Some of these stores have equipment to remove wrinkles and especially deep stains.

Self-service dry cleaning costs less than the pro-

Artistic-Ruby Corporation (WORLD BOOK photo)

At a Professional Dry-Cleaning Plant, a worker sprays clothing and other items with chemicals to remove stains, *above.* The articles then go through machines that dry-clean them.

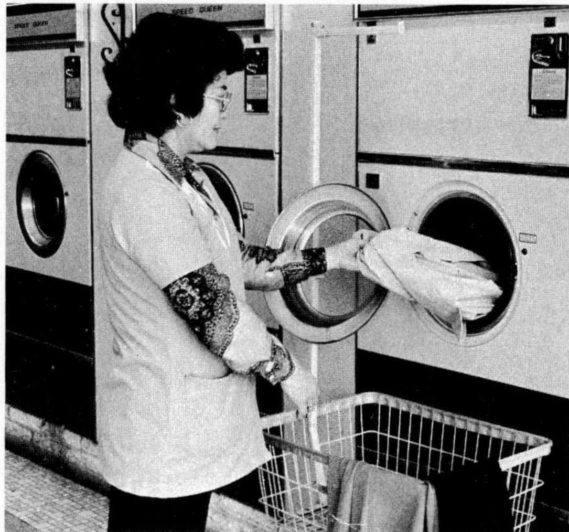

WORLD BOOK photo

At a Self-Service Dry Cleaner, people do their own cleaning in coin-operated machines, *above.* These machines clean various articles and tumble-dry them in a single operation.

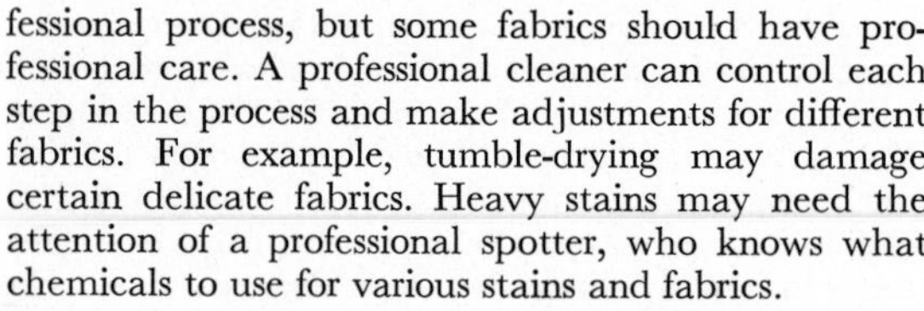

fessional process, but some fabrics should have professional care. A professional cleaner can control each step in the process and make adjustments for different fabrics. For example, tumble-drying may damage certain delicate fabrics. Heavy stains may need the attention of a professional spotter, who knows what chemicals to use for various stains and fabrics.

The Dry-Cleaning Industry ranks as one of the largest service industries in the United States. It employs about 250,000 persons. The nation has about 25,000 dry-cleaning plants. In addition, many thousands of laundries accept clothes for dry cleaning and send the clothes to a dry-cleaning plant. There are about 22,000 self-service dry-cleaning stores. PAUL T. GLAMAN

SOME COMMON STAINS AND THEIR TREATMENT

Professional dry cleaning is the best way to remove most large, stubborn stains. Certain small stains may be removed at home by either *dry* or *wet* treatment. Dry treatment involves the use of commercial dry-cleaning solvents that do not contain water. Wet treatment involves water. Some stains require both treatments. Stains should be removed promptly so they do not become permanent. The chart below lists some common stains and tells how to remove them.

Dry Treatment

Ballpoint ink
Candle wax
Carbon paper
Cooking grease and oil
Foundation makeup
Mascara
Motor oil
Road tar
Rouge
Rubber-base adhesive
Printing ink

1. Place a towel under the stained area.
2. Apply a dry-cleaning substance to the stain.
3. Rub the stain gently with the fingers. This action loosens the stain and transfers it to the towel. Continue rubbing until the stain disappears.
4. Remove the towel. Wet a cloth with the cleaning substance and wipe around the edges of the stain. Wipe toward the center to prevent a ring from forming.
5. Allow the area to dry.

Wet Treatment

Berry stains
*Blood
Catchup
*Coffee
*Egg
*Grass
Ice Cream
Milk
*Mustard
Soft drinks
Tea
Washable ink

*Removal especially difficult if dry.

1. Place a towel under the stained area.
2. Apply cool water to the stain.
3. Rub the stained area lightly with the fingertips to loosen the stain.
4. If the stain remains, gently rub a liquid detergent into the stained area.
5. Wet a cloth and squeeze water over the stain. This action rinses out the detergent so it does not leave a ring.
6. Remove the towel. Wipe around the edges of the area with a wet cloth.
7. Allow the area to dry.

Dry and Wet Treatment

Gravy
Lipstick
Paint
Salad dressing
Shoe polish

1. Follow the steps for dry treatment.
2. After the stained area has dried, use the wet treatment.

DRY DOCK is a dock in which a vessel can lie out of the water while repairs are being made below its water line (see DOCK). The two chief kinds of dry docks are graving docks and floating docks.

Graving Docks are used chiefly to repair large ships in shipyards. *Graving* was a term used in the days of wooden ships to mean cleaning a vessel's bottom and coating it with tar. A graving dock looks like a huge, concrete bathtub sunk into the ground. One end of the dock opens onto a harbor, river, or other waterway. When a ship enters the dock, shipyard workers place a huge floating or sliding *caisson*, or gate, against the open end. Pumps suck the water out and the vessel slowly sinks. Its *keel*, or bottom, comes to rest on wooden blocks placed on the floor of the dock. These blocks support the ship. *Spars*, or long pieces of wood wedged between the ship and the sides of the dock, also help support the vessel. When repairs are completed, workers flood the dock until the water reaches the same level as the water outside the gate. It is opened and the ship leaves.

Floating Docks can be self-propelled or towed from place to place. They are important in war to repair ships in forward battle areas. A floating dock looks like a shoebox with the top and ends removed. Some types are built in U-shaped sections that can be assembled to make one large dock. The *hull*, or bottom, and *wingwalls*, or sides, of a floating dock contain compartments. Water enters these compartments, making the dock sink low enough to allow a ship to enter. Pumps then suck the water out and the dock rises, lifting the ship out of the water. Wooden blocks and spars similar to those used on graving docks help support the vessel. When repairs are completed, the compartments are flooded again until the dock sinks enough to allow the ship to float. Such docks can raise an average-sized ship in from one to two hours. WILLIAM W. ROBINSON

U.S. Navy

Floating Dry Docks were used by the United States Navy during World War II to repair battle-damaged ships.

DRY FARMING is a method of farming without irrigation on land where little rain falls. Farmers use it in areas with a total of 8 to 20 inches (20 to 51 centimeters) of precipitation each year. Such a climate exists in many areas of the world. In the United States, the dry-farming area extends north from western Texas to the Canadian border, and west from the Dakotas and western Kansas to the Rocky Mountains. Other dry-farming areas include the Great Basin country between the Rockies and the Cascade and Sierra Nevada ranges, and the Central Valley in California.

In dry farming, farmers plow their land so that the soil helps hold the rain and snow where it falls. Furrows run across, instead of up and down, the hillsides. This forms a series of troughs in the land, one above the other, that hold the rain. If hills are plowed up and down, the furrows provide troughs that allow the water to run off. Tilling the soil keeps out weeds that take moisture and plant food from the soil. Other factors that affect the dry-farming methods in an area include the kind of soil, the amount of moisture different crops need, the rate of evaporation of moisture, the intensity of rainfall, and the season at which the rain comes. After the land has produced a crop, the farmer allows it to lie *fallow*, or idle, the next summer. This enables the land to store up moisture.

The use of dry-farming methods has enabled farmers in the West to produce a large share of the nation's food. Early settlers in the West brought with them the seeds and farming methods used in moist areas. Crop failures occurred until the farmers learned that many of the crops and practices were not suited to the drier climate. Critical problems arose because the settlers plowed up grasslands not suited for crops in areas of limited rainfall. When immigrants from eastern Europe settled in the Great Plains, they brought with them varieties of hard wheat from the Black Sea region, which has a similar climate. Other cereal grains and sorghums were also grown. Then farmers developed new techniques and methods of farming more suited to the dry climate of the West. A. D. LONGHOUSE

See also CONSERVATION (Soil Conservation).

DRY ICE is the name for solid carbon dioxide (chemical formula, CO_2), used as a refrigerant. The name comes from the fact that solid carbon dioxide does not return to liquid form when it melts. It changes directly into a gas. Dry ice is much colder than ordinary ice and sometimes reaches a temperature as low as −80° C (−112° F.). Because of this low temperature, it will cause death if taken into the body. Dry ice can be used to ship perishable foods by parcel post, because it cannot melt. Carloads of frozen fish packed with dry ice do not thaw during a five-day journey.

To make dry ice, the carbon-dioxide gas is compressed to a liquid and cooled. Some of the cold liquid is evaporated to make carbon-dioxide snow. Machines then compress the snow into blocks of solid dry ice.

DRY MEASURE. See WEIGHTS AND MEASURES.

DRY MILLING. See CORN (Milling).

DRY PAINTING. See SAND PAINTING.

DRY POINT. See ENGRAVING.

DRY ROT. See ROT.

DRY TORTUGAS, *tawr TOO guz*, are a group of low coral islands, or *keys*, which lie about 60 miles (97 kilometers) west of Key West, Fla. Ponce de León discovered them in 1513, and called them the Tortugas (Spanish for turtles), because of the many turtles in the nearby waters. Spain ceded the Tortugas to the United States in 1819 along with Florida. Fort Jefferson was built on Garden Key in the Tortugas in 1846. The Tortugas became a federal bird reservation in 1908, and Fort Jefferson became a national monument in 1935. The Carnegie Institute maintains Tortugas Marine Laboratory on Loggerhead Key. KATHRYN ABBEY HANNA

DRYAD, *DRY ad,* or HAMADRYAD, was a wood nymph in Greek mythology. The word *dryad* means *oak daughter.* Dryads lived in trees, and their lives were linked with the lives of their trees. They died when their trees died. These maidens are often associated in literature with gods and men. Eurydice, the wife of Orpheus, was a dryad. See also NYMPH. NATHAN DANE II

DRYDEN, JOHN (1631-1700), was the outstanding English writer of the *Restoration period* (about 1660 to 1700). He excelled as a poet, dramatist, and literary critic. Dryden believed that the individual is part of a society that has roots which go back to ancient Greece and Rome. He also believed that literature and the arts have value as civilizing forces. As a result, his writings deal with large social, political, and humanistic issues.

Dryden was born in Northamptonshire, and studied at Trinity College, Cambridge. He began writing after moving to London in the late 1650's. Dryden wrote only poetry at first, but later began writing plays to make a living. His finest play is *All for Love* (1677), an adaptation of Shakespeare's *Antony and Cleopatra.* Dryden simplified Shakespeare's story and concentrated on the tragic passions of the two famous lovers. *The Conquest of Granada* (1670, 1671), an imposing heroic drama, and *Marriage a la Mode* (1672), a gay, sophisticated comedy, rank among the best of Dryden's plays.

Dryden's best poems sprang from his involvement with political controversies of his time. In 1668, Dryden was appointed poet laureate, and in 1670 he received another government position as royal historiographer. He became involved in political disputes that developed between King Charles II and Parliament. A Tory, he was on the king's side against the Whigs. *Absalom and Achitophel* (1681), Dryden's most famous poem, is a brilliant, witty satire against the king's enemies. *The Medal* (1682) is an even more biting attack on the Whigs.

Dryden also wrote to defend his religious faith. *Religio Laici* (1682) is a poem that defends the Church of England against its enemies. Dryden became a Roman Catholic about 1686, and wrote *The Hind and the Panther* (1687) in defense of Catholicism. In *MacFlecknoe* (published in 1682 but written about 1678), he used humorous verse to attack a literary foe, Thomas Shadwell.

In 1688, King James II, a Catholic, lost his throne to William and Mary, who were Protestants. Dryden refused to swear allegiance to the new rulers, and he lost his government positions. He wrote a few plays and poems after 1688, but spent much of his time translating works into English to support himself. Dryden's most famous translations are the poems of Virgil (1697). "Alexander's Feast" (1697) is his best poem of the period.

Dryden also wrote much literary criticism. His best works include *An Essay of Dramatic Poesy* (1668), which expresses his admiration for Shakespeare; and his preface to a collection of fables published in 1700, in which he praised Chaucer. THOMAS H. FUJIMURA

For information on Dryden's influence and style, see ENGLISH LITERATURE (The Classical Age). See also POET LAUREATE.

DRYING FOOD. See DEHYDRATION.

DUAL MONARCHY. See AUSTRIA-HUNGARY.

DUALISM. See METAPHYSICS (Doctrines).

DU BARRY, *dyoo BAH REE,* **MADAME** (1746-1793), MARIE JEANNE BÉCU, COUNTESS DU BARRY, was the beautiful country girl who became the mistress of King Louis XV of France (see LOUIS [XV]). She had little education. Instead, the beauty of this blue-eyed blonde and her pleasant manner were her greatest assets. She was not meddlesome, but jealous rivals and the king's ministers hated her so much that she had to use her influence upon the king in self-defense. By the time Louis XV died in 1774, she counted many friends at court.

Detail of portrait by Madame Vigeè-Lebrun, private collection. Bulloz from Art Reference Bureau

Madame du Barry

She was born in Champagne, France. She first worked in a hat shop in Paris, but soon became the mistress of the Comte Jean du Barry. She met Louis in Du Barry's gambling rooms. She married William du Barry, Jean's brother, to gain enough social rank to be presented at court. This was required before she could become Louis XV's official mistress. In 1793, the French republicans accused her of aiding enemies of the French state. She was dragged to the guillotine just five weeks after Marie Antoinette's execution. RICHARD M. BRACE

DUBBING. See MOTION PICTURE (Steps in Making a Motion Picture).

DUBČEK, *DOOB check,* **ALEXANDER** (1921-), was first secretary of the Communist Party of Czechoslovakia in 1968 and 1969. He was the first Slovak ever to hold this top party position. Dubček began a program of liberal reforms which gave the Czech people increased freedom. But Russian party leaders viewed these reforms as threats to Soviet interests, and Russian troops invaded and occupied Czechoslovakia in August, 1968. Dubček was replaced as party leader in April, 1969, and formally expelled from the party in 1970.

Dubček was born in Uhrovec, near Topol'čany. His family moved to Russia in 1925, and Dubček lived there until 1938. He became a member of the Czechoslovak Communist Party in 1939. During World War II, Dubček worked in the resistance movement that fought the German forces occupying Czechoslovakia. After the war, he began to rise in the party ranks. In 1962, Dubček was elected to the Presidium of the Czechoslovak Communist Party. In 1963, he became first secretary of the Slovak Communist Party. WALTER C. CLEMENS, JR.

DU BELLAY, *doo buh LAY,* **JOACHIM** (1522-1560), was a French poet. With his friend Pierre de Ronsard, he founded a group of poets called the Pléiade. Du Bellay's essay *Defense and Glorification of the French Language* (1549) established the group's literary doctrines.

Du Bellay was born in Anjou of a noble, but poor, family. He lived in Rome from 1553 to 1557, and he wrote the major parts of two brilliant volumes of verse, *Antiquities of Rome* and *Regrets* (both 1558), while there. In *Antiquities,* he praises the virtues of ancient Rome. In

Regrets, written during a self-imposed exile from France, he deplores the corruption of modern Rome and speaks with both bitter disillusionment and longing of his native country. JOEL A. HUNT

See also FRENCH LITERATURE (The Pléiade).

DUBHE. See BIG AND LITTLE DIPPERS.

DUBINSKY, DAVID (1892-), an American labor leader, was president of the International Ladies' Garment Workers' Union from 1932 to 1966. He also helped found the Committee for Industrial Organization in 1935, which later became the Congress of Industrial Organizations (CIO), and became a founding vice-president of the American Federation of Labor-Congress of Industrial Organizations (AFL-CIO) in 1955. He became noted for work in collective bargaining, labor's international affairs, and anti-racketeering. Born in Brest-Litovsk, Poland, he was arrested for union activity there and was exiled to Siberia. He escaped and came to the United States in 1911. JACK BARBASH

DUBLIN (pop. 621,037; met. area pop. 778,127) is the capital and largest city of the Republic of Ireland. It lies on the east coast, at the mouth of the River Liffey. See IRELAND (color map).

The city has spacious squares and broad thoroughfares. O'Connell Street, which is 150 feet (46 meters) wide, ranks as one of the widest streets in Europe. Monuments honoring men famous in Irish history stand in the center of this street. The Nelson Pillar, a monument to Lord Horatio Nelson of Great Britain, stood there until 1966, when it was blown up by Irish Nationalists. Phoenix Park, which covers 1,760 acres (712 hectares), is one of the largest city parks in the world.

Dublin has many historic buildings. Dublin Castle was once the center of British rule. Leinster House, built in the 1700's, is the meeting place of the Dáil Éireann, the Irish House of Deputies. Dublin has a college of the National University, founded in 1854, and the University of Dublin, founded as Trinity College in 1591 by Queen Elizabeth I of England.

Trade and Manufacturing. Dublin serves as Ireland's chief port for trade with Great Britain, the country's biggest customer. Dublin's main products include biscuits, canned food, clothing, iron products, paper, processed tobacco, whiskey, and *stout,* a dark, heavy beer.

History. Viking settlers established a town on the present site of Dublin in the 800's. The city was later named *Dublin,* from the Gaelic words *dubh,* meaning *dark,* and *linn,* meaning *pool.* This name refers to the dark waters of the River Liffey which the vikings used as a harbor. Norman soldiers from England captured the city in 1170 and made it the capital of Ireland. They built Saint Patrick's Cathedral in 1190 and Dublin Castle about 1200. Dublin expanded greatly during the 1700's, when many of its present buildings, streets, and docks were built. In 1916, the city was the scene of the Easter Rebellion, which aroused the Irish to the final struggle that won their independence from Great Britain in 1921. T. W. FREEMAN

DUBLIN, UNIVERSITY OF, more generally known as Trinity College, Dublin, was founded in 1591 under a charter granted by Queen Elizabeth I. The financial support of this famous old Irish university came from funds and property given by James I. The university has faculties of arts and science, medicine, engineering, law, commerce, agriculture, divinity, music, and education. It has an enrollment of about 4,500. I. L. KANDEL

DU BOIS, *DYOO BWAH,* is the family name of an American artist and his son, a writer and illustrator.

Guy Pène du Bois (1884-1958) became well known for the witty and satirical style in his paintings. His works include *Bal des Quatre Arts* and *New Evidence.* He was born in Brooklyn, N.Y., and studied in New York and Paris.

William Pène du Bois (1916-), the son of Guy Pène du Bois, writes and illustrates children's books. He won the 1948 Newbery medal for his science fantasy, *The Twenty-One Balloons.* He also wrote *The Great Geppy, Peter Graves, The Three Policemen,* and *The Flying Locomotive.* He was born in Nutley, N.J., and was educated in France. JEAN THOMSON

DUBOIS, EUGÈNE (1858-1941), was a Dutch anatomist and physical anthropologist. While in Java in

Irish Tourist Board

O'Connell Street in Dublin is one of the widest streets in Europe. It is one of the most important streets in Dublin. The street and the statue, *foreground,* honor Daniel O'Connell, a noted Irish patriot and statesman of the early 1800's.

1891-1892, he discovered the fossilized bones which he later named *Pithecanthropus erectus*, or *the apeman that walked erect* (see JAVA MAN). His discovery led to the theory of a single "missing link" in the chain of evolution joining apes and man. Later discoveries have led scientists to believe that Pithecanthropus is only one form among many in the evolution of mankind. DAVID B. STOUT

DU BOIS, *doo BOYS*, **W. E. B.** (1868-1963), was one of the most important leaders of black protest in the United States. During the first half of the 1900's, he became the leading Negro spokesman against racial discrimination. He also won fame as a historian and sociologist. Historians still use Du Bois' research on Negroes in American society.

Du Bois was probably the first black American to express the idea of *Pan-Africanism*. Pan-Africanism is the belief that all people of African descent have common interests and should work together to conquer prejudice. In 1900, Du Bois predicted that man's chief problem of the new century would be "the color line." See SOUTH AFRICA (Opposition to Apartheid).

William Edward Burghardt Du Bois was born in Great Barrington, Mass. His ancestors were Dutch, French, Indian, and Negro. He graduated from Fisk University in 1888. In 1895, he became the first Negro to receive a Ph.D. degree at Harvard University.

From 1897 to 1910, Du Bois taught history and economics at Atlanta University. He attended the First Pan-African Conference in London in 1900. He later organized Pan-African conferences in Europe and the United States. Du Bois received the Spingarn Medal in 1920. See SPINGARN MEDAL.

Wide World

W. E. B. Du Bois

Du Bois strongly opposed the noted black educator Booker T. Washington. Washington believed that Negroes could advance themselves faster through hard work than by demands for equal rights (see WASHINGTON, BOOKER T.). But Du Bois declared that blacks must speak out constantly against discrimination. According to Du Bois, the best way to defeat prejudice was for college-educated Negroes to lead the fight. Many of his ideas appear in a collection of essays called *The Souls of Black Folk* (1903). Du Bois' other works include *Black Reconstruction in America* (1935) and *The Autobiography of W. E. B. Du Bois* (1968).

To fight racial discrimination, Du Bois founded the Niagara Movement in 1905 (see NIAGARA MOVEMENT). In 1909, he helped found the National Association for the Advancement of Colored People (NAACP). From 1910 to 1934, he was editor of the NAACP magazine *The Crisis*.

Du Bois left the NAACP in 1934 and returned to the faculty at Atlanta University. From 1944 to 1948, he again worked for the NAACP. After 1948, Du Bois became increasingly dissatisfied with the slow progress of race relations in the United States. He came to regard Communism as a solution to the problems of Negroes. In 1961, Du Bois joined the Communist Party and moved to Ghana in Africa. ELLIOTT RUDWICK

DUBOS, RENÉ JULES (1901-), a French-American microbiologist, pioneered in the development of antibiotics, a type of drug. In 1939, Dubos developed tyrothricin, the first commercially produced antibiotic, from a substance made by soil bacteria. Dubos' work led other researchers to develop the antibiotics penicillin and streptomycin for medical use.

Dubos also investigated and wrote about man's relationship to both his natural and social environment. He shared the 1969 Pulitzer Prize for general nonfiction for *So Human an Animal* (1968).

Dubos was born in Saint Brice, France, near Paris. In 1927, he earned a Ph.D. from Rutgers University and joined the Rockefeller Institute for Medical Research (now Rockefeller University). He became a United States citizen in 1938. ISAAC ASIMOV

See also GRAMICIDIN; TYROTHRICIN.

DUBUQUE, *duh BYUK*, Iowa (pop. 62,309; met. area 90,609), is a port city on the west bank of the Mississippi River, opposite the Illinois-Wisconsin border. For location, see IOWA (political map). Dubuque was named for Julien Dubuque, who began to mine lead here in 1788. Lead mining and fur trading have been replaced by lumber distributing, wood working, and meat processing as the chief industries. The city also manufactures plumbing supplies, tractors, combine power units, and fertilizers. Aquinas Institute of Theology, Clarke College, Loras College, and the University of Dubuque are located in the city. The settlement of Dubuque began in 1833. A town government was organized in 1837. The city was governed under a special charter from 1841 until 1920, when the council-manager plan was adopted. WILLIAM J. PETERSEN

DUBUQUE, JULIEN (1762-1810), a French-Canadian adventurer, was the first white man to settle in Iowa. He began mining lead ore in 1788 along the Mississippi River south of the present city of Dubuque. He had a Spanish title to his claim and named it "The Mine of Spain." He earned the friendship of his Indian neighbors by learning their language and trading with them. They gave him a chieftain's funeral when he died. He was born in Quebec province, Canada. THOMAS D. CLARK

DUBUQUE, UNIVERSITY OF. See UNIVERSITIES AND COLLEGES (table).

DUCAT, *DUCK ut*, is a coin first issued by Roger II of Sicily, Duke of Apulia, in the mid-1100's. It was called

Chase Manhattan Bank Money Museum

The Spanish Ducat, *above,* was used in the time of Ferdinand and Isabella. In the 1900's, ducats were used in Austria, Czechoslovakia, the East Indies, The Netherlands, and Yugoslavia.

Eliot Elisofon, *Life* © 1952 Time, Inc.

Nude Descending a Staircase, No. 2, ***right,*** **by Marcel Duchamp was completed in 1912. The painting caused a sensation when it appeared in the famous Armory Show of modern art in New York City in 1913. The painting shows the influence of cubism in its breakdown of the human figure into flat planes. It shows motion by blending a series of movements into one picture. The time-lapse photograph,** ***above,*** **shows Marcel Duchamp descending a staircase.**

Nude Descending a Staircase, No. 2, Philadelphia Museum of Art, Louise and Walter Arensberg Collection, Philadelphia

a ducat because it was issued by authority of a duchy. Later the coin was used in all southern European countries, either in silver or in gold. The silver ones were worth between 75 cents and $1.10, and the gold ones, $1.46 to $2.32. In Shakespeare's play *The Merchant of Venice* Antonio's debt to Shylock was 3,000 gold Venetian ducats. BURTON HOBSON

DUCCIO DI BUONINSEGNA, *DOO choh dee BWOHN een SEHN yah* (1250?-1319?), was the first great painter from Siena, Italy. He became noted for the graceful faces and the soft drapery of his figures. From 1308 to 1311, he painted *The Maestà*, the great altarpiece of the cathedral in Siena. It shows the Madonna enthroned, surrounded by many angels and saints, and is considered one of the masterpieces of Italian painting. Duccio also created miniature paintings for books. He was born in Siena. WOLFGANG LOTZ

DU CHAILLU, PAUL. See EXPLORATION AND DISCOVERY (table).

DUCHAMP, *dyoo shahn,* **MARCEL** (1887-1968), was a French painter. He first became noted about 1910, as a member of the cubist group of painters (see CUBISM). During and after World War I, he influenced the so-called Dada movement. This movement represented a pessimistic reaction against previously held ideas about the nature of art (see DADAISM).

Duchamp's best-known painting is *Nude Descending a Staircase, No. 2.* It caused great excitement when it was shown in the New York Armory Show of 1913.

Among Duchamp's unusual ideas was that of showing what he called "ready-mades." One of these, a rack for empty wine bottles, was exhibited as a work of art.

Duchamp was born in Blainville, France. He temporarily gave up art for chess in 1920. He lived and worked in New York in his later years. JOSEPH C. SLOANE

See also SURREALISM.

DUCHESS. See DUKE.

Dr. Paul A. Johnsgard

A Wood Duck and Her Ducklings stay close together so she can protect them from enemies. Most ducklings can swim on the day they are born, but they cannot fly for several weeks.

DUCK is a bird with a thick body covered with waterproof feathers. Ducks have webbed feet, and are related to geese and swans. But ducks have shorter necks and wings and flatter bills, and they quack or whistle rather than honk. Male ducks are called *drakes*, and females are called *ducks*.

Ducks live near rivers, lakes, and oceans; in muddy, tropical lowlands; and in prairie and mountain marshes. Every winter, flocks of ducks fly thousands of miles south from the Arctic Ocean to places where the water does not freeze.

William H. Drury, the contributor of this article, is Director of Scientific Staff of the Massachusetts Audubon Society. Illustrations throughout this article were prepared for WORLD BOOK *by Athos Menaboni, unless credited otherwise.*

Most ducks are good to eat, and some taste like fish. Farmers raise most of the ducks that man eats, but many wild ducks are also killed for food.

The Body of a Duck

Ducks spend most of the time in the water, and their webbed feet make them fine swimmers. Their thin legs are far back on their bodies, and the feet serve as paddles. Ducks spread their three toes and stretch out the webbing when they swim. But their legs and feet, which help ducks swim easily, make it hard for them to walk. The birds waddle clumsily on land.

The long necks of ducks allow them to dive or reach down through shallow water to pick food off the bottom. Ducks that get food from the water have large, broad bills with edges that let the water out. Some

Dabbling Duck *(Anatini)*

Mallard
Anas platyrhynchos
Found in Northern Hemisphere
(28 inches, or 71 centimeters)

Ruddy Duck *(Oxyurini)*

Ruddy Duck
Oxyura jamaicensis
Found in North and South America and West Indies
(17 inches, or 43 centimeters)

Wood Duck *(Cairinini)*

Mandarin Duck
Aix galericulata
Found in Eastern Asia and Japan
(20 inches, or 51 centimeters)

species have short bills that they use to pry snails and barnacles from rocks or to pull clams off the bottom. Others have long, narrow bills with rough edges for catching and holding fish.

Ducks protect themselves from cold water by waterproofing their feathers. They use their bills to rub the feathers with a waxy oil from a gland at the base of the tail. Under the oiled feathers is a layer of soft, curly feathers called *down*. The down keeps ducks warm by trapping air under the outside feathers.

Most drakes have bright-colored feathers in simple patterns. Their colors include green, chestnut, blue, black, white, and shiny, rainbow-colored patches. The female is plainly colored, and can easily hide when she is incubating eggs or taking care of her ducklings.

Ducks, especially those that dive under water, have short wings. If their wings were long enough to easily hold up their heavy bodies in flight, the birds would be clumsy in the water. Most diving ducks are heavier than those that stay on the surface. Most common wild ducks weigh from 2 to 4 pounds (0.9 to 1.8 kilograms), but some small ones weigh less than 1 pound (0.5 kilogram). Some ducks of the tropics or of ocean islands weigh from 5 to 10 pounds (2.3 to 4.5 kilograms).

Walter Chandoha

White Pekins are the most common ducks raised commercially in the United States. They weigh about 8 pounds (3.6 kilograms).

The Life of a Duck

Ducks seek mates at their winter feeding places. The bright colors of the drakes help make them attractive to the females. At the breeding grounds, each male has its own territory, generally a small pond. The drakes drive away other males or other pairs of their own species. When the ducks migrate north in spring, the male usually follows the female and they fly to a marsh near the place she was born.

FACTS IN BRIEF

Names: *Male*, drake; *female*, duck; *young*, duckling; *group*, flock.

Incubation Period: 23 to 30 days, depending on species.

Number of Eggs: 5 to 12.

Length of Life: 2 to 12 years (shoveler and mallard reported to 20 years).

Where Found: All parts of the world except Antarctica.

Scientific Classification: Ducks are in the class *Aves* and in the order *Anseres* or *Anseriformes*. They belong to the duck, goose, and swan family, *Anatidae*.

Ducklings. The female makes a nest, usually in a clump of grass, a hollow, or a hole in a tree. She lays from 5 to 12 eggs. After the female starts to sit on her eggs, the drake wanders off by himself. The ducklings are born from three weeks to a month later.

The females of some species, including the redhead duck of North America and the black-headed duck of South America, lay their eggs in the nests of other species. They depend on the other ducks to hatch the eggs and care for the young. Most ducklings look alike, and the new mother accepts them.

Most ducklings can run, swim, and find food by themselves on the day they hatch. They grow quickly and have most of their feathers in about a month. They

Eider *(Somateriini)*

Steller's Eider
Polysticta stelleri
Found in polar region, Northern Hemisphere
(18 inches, or 46 centimeters)

Diving Ducks *(Anthyni)*

Greater Scaup
Aythya marila
Found in Northern Hemisphere
(20 inches, or 51 centimeters)

Merganser *(Mergini)*

Red-Breasted Merganser
Mergus serrator
Found in polar region, Northern Hemisphere
(23 inches, or 58 centimeters)

learn to fly in five to eight weeks. A mother duck keeps her young together so she can protect them from other birds and animals. But sometimes when one female with ducklings meets another, some of her young shift to the other mother. The more a duck quacks and swims around the ducklings, the more youngsters she attracts to her. Some females end up with 20 to 40 ducklings, and others have only 2 or 3.

Food. Ducks that do not dive for their food are called *dabbling* ducks. They eat mostly marsh plants or water plants, including pond weeds, grasses, sedges, and rushes. They also eat floating plants and water animals that they can pry out of the water or mud. Fresh-water diving ducks eat plants and dive to the bottom for roots, seeds, snails, and newly hatched insects. In fresh water, divers and dabblers both eat insects, young beetles, bugs, dragonflies, may flies, stone flies, and caddis flies. In salt water, they feed on snails, barnacles, shrimp, and mussels. Wood ducks eat marsh plant fruits, and many nuts and fruits of water lilies.

Some ducks, called *mergansers*, eat almost nothing but fish. They catch fish in either salt water or fresh water. Other diving sea ducks pull crabs, barnacles, and shrimp off rocks and weeds. They dig snails, cockles, mussels, and clams off the bottom, and also catch fish. In fresh water, these ducks dive for mussels and young insects.

Habits. Most ducks live in flocks when they are migrating or at their wintering grounds. They usually travel with a group of ducks in the lead and a line of birds off to one side and behind. The other side of the "V" is seldom complete. In late summer, large flocks of young and old ducks gather on large lakes, marshes, or shallow places in the ocean. There they *molt* (lose their old feathers). The ducks lose all their flight feathers at once and cannot fly. The drakes lose their bright colors and turn a brown color, like that of the females.

After molting, the flocks migrate south to their winter feeding grounds. They use the same summer and winter marshes year after year. They even stop at the same marshes and bays along the way. Some ducks fly only a short distance. Others make long flights—from Alaska to Hawaii, from Canada to Chesapeake Bay in Maryland and Virginia, or across the Gulf of Mexico and the Caribbean Sea to South America.

THE TWO TYPES OF DUCK BILLS

Diving ducks have long, narrow bills, *top*, with toothlike edges to hold fish. Dabbling ducks have short, broad bills for prying.

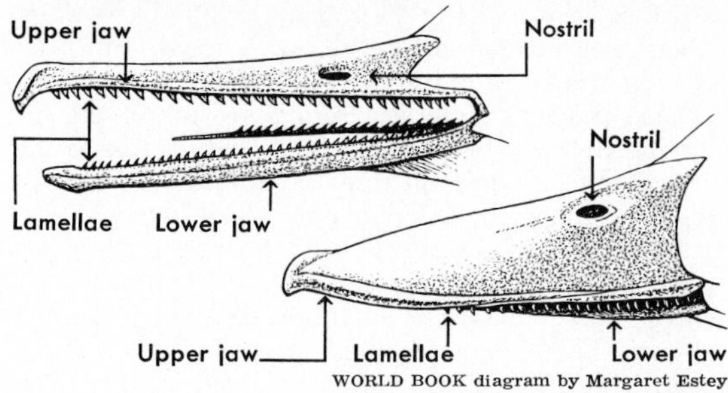

WORLD BOOK diagram by Margaret Estey

Kinds of Ducks

Scientists classify ducks into eight main groups. Most wild ducks of inland lakes and marshes are dabbling ducks or fresh-water diving ducks. They are found on the prairies of the north central United States and Canada.

Dabbling Ducks include the mallard, black duck, pintail, baldpate, gadwall, green-winged teal, blue-winged teal, cinnamon teal, and shoveler. These birds tip bottom up in shallow water, stretching their necks to feed on the bottom. They take off from the water by jumping and pushing down with their wings.

Fresh-water Diving Ducks include the canvasback, redhead, ring-neck, and greater and lesser scaup. They swim under water with their wings closed and their legs sticking out to the sides. Their bodies are heavy, and they run along the surface of the water to get airborne.

Wood Ducks include the wood duck, mandarin duck, and muscovy duck. They are especially colorful ducks of eastern North America and Asia.

Eiders have down that is valuable for use in sleeping bags, jackets, and bedding. Farmers in Iceland encourage eiders to nest in their fields, and some farms have as many as 10,000 nests.

Diving Sea Ducks include the merganser, scoter, old squaw, harlequin, bufflehead, and goldeneye. Mergansers have long, narrow bills with rough edges to hold fish. Most diving sea ducks have colorful feather patterns.

Almost All Kinds of Domestic Ducks developed from wild mallards. Common species besides the White Pekin include, *left to right*, the Indian Runner, the Rouen, the Khaki Campbell, and the Buff. Duck farms supply ducks to restaurants and homes in the United States.

Old squaws can dive deeper into the ocean—from 150 to 180 feet (46 to 55 meters)—than any other water bird.

Ruddy Ducks are common in eastern and northern North America. Although among the smallest ducks, they lay eggs about twice as large as chicken eggs.

Tree Ducks fly and feed mainly at night. The black-bellied tree duck usually avoids deep water. It finds food along the banks or shallow edges of rivers and ponds. It nests in trees, usually far from water.

Domestic Ducks nearly all developed originally from wild mallards. White Pekin ducks, which weigh about 8 pounds (3.6 kilograms), are the most common commercially raised ducks in the United States. Duck farming is a profitable business near such large metropolitan areas as Long Island, N.Y., and in the state of Washington. The sale of wild game is against the law in the United States, so ducks served in restaurants come from farms. Ducks are also raised in many parts of Europe, Australia, and New Zealand. WILLIAM H. DRURY

Related Articles in WORLD BOOK include:

Bird (Extinct Birds; pictures: Wild Ducks and Wild Geese)	Game (Game Laws)	Poultry
		Shoveler
	Goose	Swan
Baldpate	Hunting	Teal
Canvasback	Mallard	Wigeon
Eider Duck	Merganser	Wood Duck
Gadwall	Pintail	

DUCK is a lightweight canvas usually made of linen, cotton, or synthetic fibers in a plain weave. Duck is woven in many widths and weights. This stout, waterproof fabric is used for the aprons of cooks, waiters, and butchers; for the uniforms of dentists and surgeons; and for shower curtains, pressing cloths, and tennis shoes. The heaviest grades of duck are used to make machine aprons, machinery conveyor belts, boat sails, tarpaulins, tents, and mailbags. See also CANVAS. KENNETH R. FOX

DUCK HAWK is a name sometimes used in the United States for the *peregrine falcon*. This bird reportedly can reach speeds up to 180 miles (290 kilometers) per hour. See FALCON AND FALCONRY.

DUCKBILL. See PLATYPUS.

DUCKING STOOL was a form of punishment usually given to "witches and nagging women" in England and the American Colonies from the 1600's to the early 1800's. The ducking stool was a chair fastened to the end of a long plank extended from the bank of a pond or stream. The victim of the punishment was tied securely to the chair and *ducked* (plunged) into the water several times. See also COLONIAL LIFE IN AMERICA (picture: Public Disgrace). MARION F. LANSING

DUCKPINS. See BOWLING (Other Kinds of Bowling).

DUCKWEED is a tiny perennial water plant. It is the smallest flowering plant known. The duckweed floats on the surface of pools and ponds. It has no stems or true leaves. The plant consists of a *frond* (flat green structure) with a single hairlike root underneath. The flowers and fruits are so small they can barely be seen by the naked eye. Duckweed is sometimes grown for food for ducks and large goldfish. It has a healthful, laxative effect on some kinds of aquarium fish.

Scientific Classification. The duckweed belongs to the duckweed family, *Lemnaceae*. It is a member of the genus *Lemna*. One species is *L. minor*. EARL L. CORE

DUCOMMUN, ÉLIE. See NOBEL PRIZES (table: Nobel Prizes for Peace—1902).

DUCTED PROPELLER is a propeller that turns within a cylinderlike device called a *duct*. Ducted propellers are used on air-cushion vehicles and such aircraft as *VTOLs* (vertical take-off and landing aircraft). Putting a propeller inside a duct makes the propeller more efficient. The duct captures air normally thrown to the side by the propeller. This action increases the air pressure behind the propeller blades and increases the propeller's driving force.

The increased thrust provided by a ducted propeller permits the use of a smaller propeller than would be used on a similar aircraft without a duct. Ducted propellers also provide a quieter operation than propellers without ducts. ROBERT D. ROACH, JR.

See also AIR-CUSHION VEHICLE; CONVERTIPLANE.

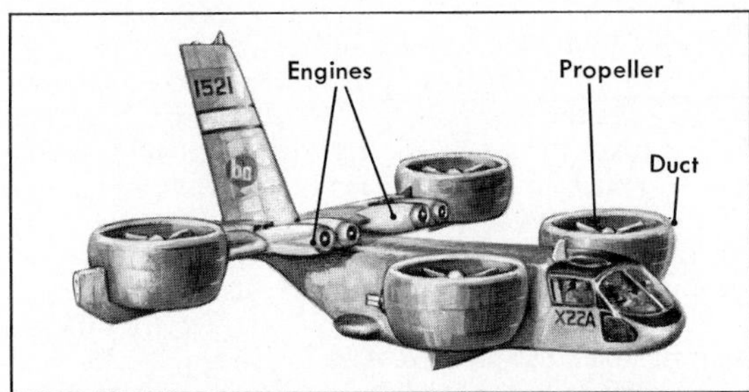

WORLD BOOK illustration

A Ducted Propeller Airplane uses propellers in *ducts* (circular wings) to lift it off the ground and propel it through the air. The above drawing shows the ducted propellers in a horizontal position so the plane can take off and land like a helicopter. In the air, the pilot rotates the ducted propellers into a vertical position for normal flight, as shown in the photograph below.

Bell Aerospace Company

DUCTILITY, *duck TIHL uh tee,* is the ability of certain solid substances to undergo permanent changes in shape without breaking. For example, a piece of copper can be drawn to make a thin wire. But the shape of a brick cannot be permanently changed except by breaking it.

Ductility is a valuable property of many metals, including aluminum, gold, iron, nickel, and silver. These metals can be drawn into wire, hammered into various shapes, or rolled into sheets. The term *malleability* is often used in place of ductility when describing the property of metals that allows them to be hammered into thin sheets. Metals are not the only ductile substances and not all metals are ductile. For example, modeling clay is a ductile nonmetallic substance and potassium is a nonductile metal.

DUCTLESS GLAND. See GLAND.

DUDE RANCH, *dood,* is a western-style ranch which receives paying guests who want a taste of life in the open. These guests are usually city dwellers who get little physical activity and contact with nature. Three brothers, Howard, Alden, and Willis Eaton, are believed to have established the West's first dude ranch near Sheridan, Wyo., in 1904.

Some dude ranches are regular cattle or sheep ranches that entertain a few guests as a sideline. But other ranches are devoted entirely to the business of entertaining *dudes* (guests). Most of the dude ranches are in the "cow country" of Montana, Wyoming, Arizona, California, Nevada, Colorado, New Mexico, and Oregon. Guests at a dude ranch go on horseback rides along mountain trails, hunt, fish, and in some cases help with the livestock. H. B. MEEK

DUDLEY, ROBERT. See LEICESTER, EARL OF.

DUDLEY, THOMAS (1576-1653), was a colonial governor of Massachusetts. Born in Northampton, England, he became steward to the powerful Earl of Lincoln, whose estates he managed. He sailed with John Winthrop on the *Arbella* in 1630 as deputy governor of the colony. He became governor four times, and served as deputy governor most of the other years until his death. A Puritan of the stern and harsh type, he often differed with the tolerant and kind Winthrop. He was a founder of First Church at Charlestown, Mass., and of Newtowne (now Cambridge, Mass.). He was an early promoter and overseer of Harvard College. BRADFORD SMITH

DUE PROCESS OF LAW is a basic principle in the American legal system that requires fairness in the government's dealing with persons. The term *due process of law* appears in the 5th and 14th amendments to the Constitution of the United States. These amendments forbid federal, state, and local governments from depriving a person of "life, liberty, or property, without due process of law." The Supreme Court of the United States has never clearly defined these words, and has applied them to a number of widely different situations.

The idea of due process of law dates from the English Magna Carta of 1215. One article in this document promises that no man shall be deprived of life, liberty, or property, except "by the lawful judgment of his peers or by the law of the land." Some early English *writs* (written legal orders) were designed to bring the government under a rule of law. For example, a writ of *habeas corpus* requires that the government show just cause before it can hold a person in custody. See MAGNA CARTA; HABEAS CORPUS.

Through law and custom, various safeguards have been developed in the United States to assure that persons accused of wrongdoing will be treated fairly. These safeguards are sometimes called *procedural due process.* Procedural due process includes the following requirements: (1) The law must be administered fairly. (2) A person must be informed of the charges against him and must be given a fair hearing. (3) The person bringing the charges must not be allowed to judge the case. (4) Criminal laws must be clearly worded so that they give adequate warning of the action prohibited.

Courts have also used the "due process" clauses of the 5th and 14th amendments to limit the content of laws, even though there was no procedural unfairness. For example, they have declared unconstitutional some laws restricting personal freedoms and business, on the ground that the laws violate due process of law. Because this practice involves the *substance* of public policy, it is called *substantive due process.* ROBERT G. DIXON, JR.

See also CIVIL RIGHTS; CONSTITUTION OF THE UNITED STATES (Amendments 5 and 14).

DUEL is a form of combat between two armed persons. It is conducted according to set rules or a code, and it is normally fought in the presence of witnesses. From early times through the 1800's, men of high rank settled personal quarrels with weapons. They generally used swords or pistols. Duels resulted from disputes over property, charges of cowardice, insults to family or personal honor, and cheating at cards or dice.

The duel probably originated in the custom of Germanic *judicial combat,* a method of administering justice. In judicial combat, the accused person challenged his accuser to a trial with weapons. The gods were supposed to give victory to the innocent man. Queen Elizabeth I of England was the first to abolish the duel as a form of justice. Later, all civilized countries abandoned the practice. But some private duels are still fought.

Some duels were more deadly than others. About 1800, French honor was satisfied by wounds, but the American dueling code at that time demanded death. The phrase *to give satisfaction* could mean either that blood must be drawn, or that one of the contestants must die. At other times it meant only that the challenged party had faced his enemy's fire.

The man challenged had his choice of weapons. The sword became the main dueling weapon in England and France. Duelists generally used pistols in America. Each duelist chose a friend who was called his *second,* and a surgeon usually attended. To avoid the police, the meeting usually took place in a forest clearing at daybreak. When duelists used pistols, they usually stood back to back, and marched an agreed number of steps in opposite directions. Then one of the seconds dropped a handkerchief. The fighters turned quickly and fired.

Dueling was common in the United States up to the mid-1800's. Many famous Americans fought duels. Aaron Burr fatally wounded Alexander Hamilton on July 11, 1804, in a pistol duel. Burr blamed Hamilton for his defeat in an election for governor of New York (see HAMILTON, ALEXANDER). General Andrew Jackson killed Charles Dickinson on May 30, 1806, in a pistol duel. Jackson challenged Dickinson because Dickinson denounced him in the press. The quarrel started in a dispute over a horse race. Commodore James Barron killed Commodore Stephen Decatur on Mar. 22, 1820, in a pistol duel. Barron claimed Decatur was persecuting him. Henry Clay fought John Randolph on Apr. 8, 1826, in a pistol duel, but neither was hurt. Clay challenged Randolph because Randolph made insulting remarks about him in the U.S. Senate (see RANDOLPH [John Randolph of Roanoke]).

Tennessee outlawed dueling in 1801, and the District of Columbia banned it in 1839. Several other states did so soon after that. Since then, one who kills an opponent in a duel can be tried for murder or manslaughter. Some German students still duel secretly with swords as a sport. They try only to inflict cheek wounds in duels with fellow members of the fencing fraternities in the German universities. HUGH M. COLE

DUERK, ALENE B. See NAVY, UNITED STATES (table: Important Dates in Navy History).

DUERO RIVER. See DOURO RIVER.

DU FAY, *DYOO FAY,* **CHARLES FRANÇOIS** (1698-1739). The ancient Greeks discovered that a piece of amber, when rubbed with fur, could pick up bits of cotton. We say the amber has an *electric charge.* Over 2,300 years later, Du Fay, a French scientist, found that a charge of electricity can be put on *any* object. He also discovered that there are two opposite kinds of electricity, later called *positive* and *negative.*

Du Fay also studied phosphorescence, and double refraction, which occurs when a ray of light bends and breaks into two rays (see PHOSPHORESCENCE; REFRACTION).

Du Fay was born in Paris. He served in the army for a time, then devoted himself to science. He became a member of the French Academy of Sciences in 1733. He also served as superintendent of gardens for King Louis XV. IRA M. FREEMAN

DUFF, SIR LYMAN POORE (1865-1955), served for 37 years on the Supreme Court of Canada from 1906 to 1944. During the last 11 years, he was Chief Justice. He wrote many Supreme Court decisions. He considered the most important of these the ruling that decisions of the Canadian Parliament were not to be appealed to London. He was also a member of the British Columbia Supreme Court. King George V knighted him in 1934. He was born in Meaford, Ont. J. E. HODGETTS

DUFFERIN AND AVA, MARQUIS OF (1826-1902), FREDERICK TEMPLE BLACKWOOD, was a British diplomat and statesman. As governor general of Canada from 1872 to 1878, he helped strengthen the bonds between Canada and Great Britain. After leaving Canada, he served as ambassador extraordinary and minister plenipotentiary to Russia from 1879 to 1881, to Constantinople in 1881, and to Egypt in 1882. He served as viceroy of India from 1884 to 1888. He was born in Florence, Italy. LUCIEN BRAULT

DUFY, *dyoo FEE,* **RAOUL** (1877-1953), was a French artist best known for his lively, decorative paintings. Dufy used bright colors and a simple style to portray a happy, carefree world. His subjects included landscapes, festivals, horse races, and figures in rooms.

Water color (1932); the Baltimore Museum of Art, Saidie A. May Collection

Dufy's *Le Haras du Pin* **shows the bright colors, sketchy details, and cheerful subject matter that typified his work.**

Dufy also illustrated books, designed fabrics and tapestries, designed theater costumes and sets, and made many lithographs and woodcuts.

Dufy was born in Le Havre. In 1900, he settled in Paris, where he painted briefly in the impressionist style. Dufy first attracted attention when he exhibited brightly colored pictures with the fauves (see FAUVES). He then came under the influence of cubism but found that style too severe. By 1920, Dufy had developed his own personal style. WILLARD E. MISFELDT

DU GARD, ROGER MARTIN. See MARTIN DU GARD, ROGER.

DUGGAR, B. M. See AUREOMYCIN.

DUGONG, *DOO gahng,* is a plant-eating mammal that lives in the shallow, warm coastal waters of the Red Sea and the Indian Ocean, as far south as Australia. The dugong has a blunt, rounded snout with a bristly upper lip. Its whalelike body has a notched tail. The dugong uses its flippers to swim and to push sea grass near its mouth. Most dugongs are brownish or grayish in color. The male has two long upper tusks, and the ends of the upper jaw bend downward. The female gives birth to one calf at a time. Dugongs may grow about 10 feet (3 meters) long and weigh up to 650 pounds (295 kilograms). Stories about mermaids may have started when seamen first saw this animal.

American Museum of Natural History

The Dugong, a sea mammal, lives in waters near shore. Some people use its flesh and blubber oil for food, and the animal has become rare throughout much of its range.

Scientific Classification. The dugong belongs to the order *Sirenia.* It is in the family *Dugongidae,* genus *Dugong,* species *D. dugon.* KARL W. KENYON

DUGOUT. See BOATING (Early Boats).

DUGWAY is the central proving ground of the United States Army Chemical Corps. Tests are conducted there on chemical, biological, and radiological weapons. Dugway is 100 miles (160 kilometers) southwest of Salt Lake City, Utah.

DUISBURG, *DYOOS boork* (pop. 457,900), is a trading and manufacturing city in West Germany. It is the largest inland port of western Europe. The city is built on the point where the Ruhr River flows into the Rhine and is connected with north German ports by the Rhine-Herne Canal. It is a gateway to the factories and mineral deposits of the Ruhr Valley. Duisburg has long been important in German industrial life. Its products include chemicals, furniture, silks and woolens, soap, and tobacco. JAMES K. POLLOCK

DUKAS, *DYOO KAH,* **PAUL ABRAHAM** (1865-1935), a French composer, won recognition for his *The Sorcerer's Apprentice* (1897), an orchestral scherzo. His opera *Ariadne and Bluebeard,* based upon Maurice Maeterlinck's play of the same name, is symphonic in form. It is second only to Debussy's *Pelléas et Mélisande* in importance among French operas of the 1900's. His last major work was a ballet, *The Peri* (1912). HALSEY STEVENS

DUKE. See CHERRY.

DUKE is a European title. It comes from the Latin word *dux* (leader), and is the title next highest to *prince.* In England, there are few dukes outside the royal family, where the sons have the title of Royal Duke. The wife of a duke is a *duchess,* the oldest son is a *lord* with the rank of *marquis,* and younger sons and daughters are called *lords* and *ladies.* A duke is addressed as "Your Grace."

In early days, a duke was a leader in battle, and sometimes a ruler as well. The first English duke was the Black Prince, oldest son of Edward III, who was made Duke of Cornwall in 1337.

Archduke was a title used by members of the royal family of Hapsburg from 1453 until the end of World War I. See also NOBILITY. MARION F. LANSING

DUKE, CHARLES MOSS, JR. (1935-), a United States astronaut, was the lunar module pilot on the Apollo 16 mission, from April 16 to April 27, 1972. Duke and astronaut John W. Young spent more than 71 hours on the moon. They explored the Descartes region of the moon, performed scientific experiments, and collected about 210 pounds (95 kilograms) of lunar rocks. While Duke and Young investigated the lunar surface, astronaut Thomas K. Mattingly II orbited the moon in the command module.

Duke was born in Charlotte, N.C., and entered the Air Force after graduating from the United States Naval Academy in 1957. He earned a master's degree from the Massachusetts Institute of Technology (M.I.T.) in 1964 and became an astronaut in 1966. WILLIAM J. CROMIE

DUKE, JAMES BUCHANAN (1856-1925), an American businessman and philanthropist, organized the American Tobacco Company (now American Brands, Inc.) in 1890. He established the Duke Endowment in 1924. He also gave funds to schools, hospitals, orphanages, and the Methodist Church. He was born near Durham, N.C. J. R. CRAF

See also DUKE ENDOWMENT; DUKE UNIVERSITY.

DUKE ENDOWMENT is a trust fund for education and charity set up in 1924 by James B. Duke. The purpose of the fund is "to make provision in some measure for the needs of mankind along physical, mental, and spiritual lines."

The original gift was approximately $40 million. Income of the endowment is distributed to specifically named beneficiaries in North and South Carolina. These include Duke University, three other educational institutions, hospitals, orphanages, rural Methodist churches, and retired Methodist clergymen. The endowment has offices in New York City, and in Charlotte and Durham, N.C. For assets, see FOUNDATIONS (table). Critically reviewed by DUKE ENDOWMENT

DUKE OF YORK ISLANDS. See BISMARCK ARCHIPELAGO.

DUKE UNIVERSITY is a private coeducational school in Durham, N.C. The university offers undergraduate programs in arts and sciences, engineering, and nursing. Duke also has a graduate school and professional schools of business administration, divinity, forestry, law, and medicine. Courses lead to bachelor's, master's, and doctor's degrees.

The university library contains more than 6 million books and manuscripts. Duke Hospital is a noted teaching and training institution. The 7,200-acre (2,910-hectare) Duke Forest serves as a laboratory for the School of Forestry. The marine laboratory near Beaufort, N.C., is used for training and research in marine biology and oceanography.

The school originated in 1838 as an academy. It became Union Institute in 1839, and in 1859 it was renamed Trinity College. The school is named for the family of James B. Duke, a tobacco millionaire. His endowment in 1924 helped the college become a leading university. For enrollment, see UNIVERSITIES AND COLLEGES (table). ROBERT L. DICKENS

DUKENFIELD, WILLIAM CLAUDE. See FIELDS, W. C.

DUKHOBORS. See DOUKHOBORS.

DULCIMER, *DUL suh mur,* is an ancient musical instrument. It was probably invented in Persia or Arabia. It consists of a flat box with metal wires stretched across the top. These wires are attached to adjustable tuning pegs on one side of the instrument. The player strikes the strings with small wooden or cork-covered mallets. A keyboard was later substituted for the hammers to produce the *clavichord* (see CLAVICHORD). The piano developed from this instrument. CHARLES B. RIGHTER

DU LHUT. See DULUTH, SIEUR.

The Dulcimer is used by many gypsy bands in Central Europe. The player produces harsh tones by striking wires with wooden mallets.

Arkansas Department of Parks and Tourism

DULLES, *DUHL uhs,* **JOHN FOSTER** (1888-1959), an American lawyer and diplomat, enjoyed a long and distinguished career in helping formulate the foreign policies of the United States. He won international acclaim in 1951 as the chief author of the Japanese peace treaty. He also negotiated the Australian, New Zealand, Philippine, and Japanese security treaties in 1950 and 1951. In 1953, he became the 52nd secretary of state of the United States, serving in the Cabinet of President Dwight D. Eisenhower.

Wide World
John Foster Dulles

Dulles was born in Washington, D.C. He was graduated from Princeton University, and received a law degree from George Washington University. His books include *War, Peace, and Change* (1939) and *War or Peace* (1950). Dulles helped form the UN, and later was a United States UN delegate. He served as a U.S. senator from New York in 1949. F. Jay Taylor

DULUTH, *duh LOOTH,* Minn. (pop. 100,578), extends for 26 miles (42 kilometers) along the west end of Lake Superior. The city lies on Saint Louis Bay, 156 miles (251 kilometers) northeast of Saint Paul (see Minnesota [political map]). Duluth and Superior, Wis., form a metropolitan area with a population of 265,350. Duluth lies on a bluff that rises from Lake Superior to a height of 600 to 800 feet (180 to 240 meters). An electrical lift bridge, one of the fastest of its kind in the world, passes over the Duluth ship canal. The canal was cut through a sand bar called Minnesota Point in 1871. The bridge can rise to its full height of 138 feet (42 meters) in 55 seconds.

Industry and Commerce. Duluth is a natural shipping center for products of the Northwest. The Duluth-Superior (Wis.) harbor is a Saint Lawrence Seaway terminal, and the volume of waterborne shipping at the harbor makes it one of the largest ports in the United States. Over 110 docks line the 49-mile (79-kilometer) harbor frontage. Facilities there include iron ore docks, coal docks, and grain elevators and storage sheds that can store more than 70 million bushels (2,500,000 cubic meters) of grain. Iron ore and grain are the principal exports and coal is the major import. Other industries include steel, ironworks, blast furnaces, machine shops, and meat packing. Four major freight railroads serve Duluth. No passenger trains stop there, but the city has bus and airline transportation.

Recreation and Cultural Life. Beautiful lakes nearby, a cool climate, and an excellent park and playground system make Duluth an attractive vacation center. It is the gateway to the scenic North Shore of Lake Superior and the great Superior National Forest. The Skyline Parkway along the heights of the city offers a picturesque view of Duluth and Lake Superior. The city has favorable conditions for summer and winter sports. The average summer temperature is 61° F. (16° C), and temperatures from December through March average 15° F. (−9° C). Duluth's location in the Minnesota Arrowhead Country puts it close to excellent hunting and fishing territory. The city is the home of the Duluth campus of the University of Minnesota. The College of Saint Scholastica is also located in Duluth. Duluth maintains its own symphony orchestra.

Government and History. Duluth is the seat of Saint Louis County. The city has a mayor-council form of government (see City Government).

Duluth was named in honor of Daniel Greysolon, Sieur Duluth, a French trader who visited the site about 1679. In the 1700's, British traders replaced the French. Fond du Lac, now a suburb of Duluth, became the first permanent white settlement in the area after John Jacob Astor's American Fur Company started a trading post there in 1817. Settlers began to come to the Duluth area in the 1850's. Duluth became a city in 1870. It grew rapidly after 1880, when lumbering and iron ore industries developed there. Harold T. Hagg

DULUTH, or **DU LHUT, SIEUR** (1636-1710), Daniel Greysolon, was a French explorer for whom Duluth, Minn., was named. Duluth moved to Canada about 1674, and decided to explore the West. He set out for Lake Superior in 1678, but he had to make peace between the Chippewa and Sioux Indians before he could work in that area. He negotiated with the Sioux near the site of the present city of Duluth. He claimed the area for King Louis XIV. Duluth later explored near the headwaters of the Mississippi River. He was born in St. Germain-en-Laye, France. He was a cousin of Henri de Tonti, who was an explorer and companion of Robert Cavelier, Sieur de la Salle. William P. Brandon

DUMA, *DOO mah,* was the name given to various legislative assemblies in Russia during the time when the czars ruled the country. *Duma* is a Russian word that can be translated as *a place for thinking.*

The most famous Duma was the lower house of an assembly that Czar Nicholas II established in 1906 as a result of the Russian Revolution of 1905. The czar had no use for elected assemblies, and did not wish to share his authority with one. But he feared another revolt if he did not give the people a chance to take part in the government. The people had some voting rights but were not allowed to vote directly for Duma members.

After Nicholas established the Duma, he did all he could to weaken it. He forced the Duma to share power with an upper house that he controlled. He forbade it to interfere in many important matters of government. The first Duma met only 40 times. Then the czar dismissed it because it disagreed with his policies.

The people elected a second Duma in 1907. But Nicholas dissolved it after a few months, because he thought it was too radical. Then he changed the electoral laws in an effort to obtain a conservative Duma that would follow his wishes. Nearly all men could still vote, but the voters were divided into four classes. Each class elected a certain number of members to the electoral colleges that chose members of the Duma. Property owners chose most of the electors. For this reason, the third Duma, which met between 1907 and 1912, and the fourth (1912-1917) were conservative.

None of the Dumas was truly representative of the Russian people. However, they were the closest approach the Russian Empire ever made toward establishing a national assembly elected by the people. The

Dumas gradually increased their influence, in spite of the restrictions the czar placed upon them. They urged farm reforms, the strengthening of Russia's armed forces, and more education for the people. But when the Russian Revolution of 1917 broke out, Nicholas was forced to give up his throne and the Duma came to an end (see NICHOLAS [of Russia]). WARREN B. WALSH

DUMAS, *du MAH,* **ALEXANDRE,** was the name of two French writers, father and son. The father is called Dumas *père* (the elder) and the son Dumas *fils* (the younger).

Alexandre Dumas père (1802-1870) wrote *The Three Musketeers* (1844) and *The Count of Monte Cristo* (1845), two of the most popular historical novels in literature. These exciting adventure stories have thrilled countless readers. But because of their careless style, unbelievable plots, and poor psychology, critics do not rank them highly.

Dumas' plays have the virtues and faults of his novels. They are usually exciting but have unbelievable plots. But they are more important than the novels in the history of French literature. *Henry III and His Court* (1829) and *Antony* (1831) were among the earliest and most successful plays of the French romantic movement. Both are stories of passion and murder.

Dumas was born in Villers-Cotterêts, the son of a general in Napoleon's army. His name came from his grandmother, a Negro from the Caribbean city of Santo Domingo. Dumas' works run into hundreds of volumes, but he wrote much with the assistance of hired writers. He earned a fortune and spent it carelessly. Dumas' romantic style became unfashionable during the French Second Empire (1852-1870), and he died poor.

Alexandre Dumas *fils* (1824-1895) was born in Paris, the illegitimate son of Dumas *père*. The shame of illegitimacy caused the younger Dumas much suffering. It helps to explain his concern for the victims of society and his emphasis on stable family life in his works.

Dumas wrote both novels and plays, but his fame rests chiefly on his plays. His first play, *The Lady of the Camellias* (often called *Camille*) was a great success when performed in 1852. Dumas based this tragic love story on one of his novels. Giuseppe Verdi used the story for his opera *La Traviata*.

Dumas came to believe that plays should teach social and moral lessons. He defended the family in *The Wife of Claude* (1873), *Denise* (1885), and *Francillon* (1887). Although he attacked wickedness, he also asked forgiveness for those who repent—as in *The Ideas of Madame Aubray* (1867). His plays, therefore, have a preaching tone, unpopular with many readers today. But the plays are well-constructed and often witty, and give a good picture of French upper-class society of his time. IRVING PUTTER

Chicago Hist. Soc.

Alexandre Dumas the Elder

Chicago Hist. Soc.

Alexandre Dumas the Younger

DU MAURIER, *dyu MAWH rih ay,* is the name of a family of English writers, artists, and actors.

George Louis Palmella Busson du Maurier (1834-1896) is known chiefly for his novels *Peter Ibbetson* (1892) and *Trilby* (1894). *Peter Ibbetson* is a tale of two lovers who could meet only in their dreams. *Trilby* is a story about artists in Paris. Trilby, the heroine, is an artist's model under the influence of Svengali, a hypnotist. Through hypnotism, she becomes a great singer. But she loses her power when Svengali dies.

Du Maurier was born in Paris. He became an accomplished artist in black-and-white. He illustrated his own stories and those of many notable authors.

Sir Gerald du Maurier (1873-1934), the son of George du Maurier, was born in London. Gerald was an actor-manager who specialized in playing gentleman criminals in plays such as *Raffles* and *Bulldog Drummond.* He starred in the popular dramatic adaptation of *Trilby* and also played Shakespearean roles.

Daphne du Maurier (1907-), the second daughter of Gerald du Maurier, wrote several popular romantic novels tinged with adventure or mystery. *Rebecca* (1938) is a suspense novel about a young wife's experiences in a strange mansion which is dominated by the spirit of her husband's first wife.

United Press Int.

Daphne du Maurier

Daphne du Maurier wrote two sea stories, *Jamaica Inn* (1936) and *Frenchman's Creek* (1941). Her other novels include *My Cousin Rachel* (1952), *The Glassblowers* (1963), and *The House on the Strand* (1969). Daphne du Maurier was born in London and was married to Lieutenant General Sir Frederick Browning. HARRY T. MOORE

DUMBARTON OAKS was the name of an international conference held in August-October, 1944, at Dumbarton Oaks, an estate in Washington, D.C. The name was also given to the proposals agreed upon at the conference. Thirty-nine delegates from the United States, Great Britain, and Russia met to discuss plans for the creation of an international organization to be called the *United Nations*. After six weeks of discussion, the Russian representatives, as agreed in advance, left, and delegates from Nationalist China replaced them.

The conference gave more attention to establishing ways to deal with "the maintenance of international peace and security" than it did to setting up agencies to handle economic and social problems. The delegates agreed that provision must be made for the peaceful settlement of international disputes and for the power to enforce the organization's decisions. The main achievement of the conference was the planning of a Security Council as the executive branch of the UN.

Most of the provisions of the Dumbarton Oaks Proposals were put into the UN charter. NORMAN D. PALMER

See also SAN FRANCISCO CONFERENCE; UNITED NATIONS (The Dumbarton Oaks Conference).

DUMBBELL, or BAR BELL, is a wooden or iron weight used for physical exercise. It consists of two balls or disks connected by a bar, which is used as a handle. When the handle is short, it is grasped with one hand, and called a *dumbbell*. When the handle is long, it can be grasped with two hands and is called a *bar bell*. Dumbbells and bar bells may be made heavier by attaching more balls and disks. The size of the balls and disks varies, depending on their weight. Today, when machines do most physical work, many people keep their bodies strong through exercise with dumbbells and bar bells. For weight lifters who enter competition, there are set systems of exercise, and competition. Weight lifting has long been an Olympic Games sport. See also WEIGHT LIFTING. T. K. CURETON, JR.

WORLD BOOK photo

Dumbbells Are Used in Weight-Lifting Exercises.

DUMONT, GABRIEL (1838-1906), served as military leader of the Saskatchewan Rebellion, a revolt against the Canadian government in 1885. He helped Louis Riel lead the *métis* (people of mixed French and Indian descent) in a fight for land privileges for the métis. Riel was the political head of the métis.

Dumont was born in Assiniboia, in what is now southern Manitoba. During the early 1870's, he and other métis moved to Saskatchewan. In 1873, Dumont became leader of a métis settlement in Saint Laurent, near Duck Lake. The métis surveyed their property according to the old French-Canadian system. In this system, settlers laid out lots in narrow strips so that almost every one bordered part of a river or a lake. However, the Canadian government surveyed land in square lots and refused to approve the métis surveys. This dispute became the chief cause of the 1885 revolt.

In March, 1885, Riel and Dumont formed a temporary government for the métis in Saskatchewan. Dumont's forces defeated mounted police who were sent to arrest him at Duck Lake. Fighting between the métis and Canadian forces ended in May, 1885, after Dumont's defeat at nearby Batoche. Dumont escaped to the United States but returned several years later after the Canadian government granted him amnesty. P. B. WAITE

Public Archives of Canada

Gabriel Dumont

See also SASKATCHEWAN REBELLION; RIEL, LOUIS.

DUMP. See ENVIRONMENTAL POLLUTION (Solid Wastes).

DUN. See MAYFLY.

DUN & BRADSTREET, INC., is a firm which furnishes businessmen with credit and marketing information about their customers and prospective customers. The firm publishes the famous *Dun and Bradstreet Reference Book*, which goes to its 80,000 subscribers. This book gives the names of about 2,900,000 companies and individuals in the United States and Canada, with the credit rating of each. There is a detailed, regularly revised report on file for each name. Dun & Bradstreet has thousands of reporters stationed in different parts of the country to gather this information. Correspondents in every business community forward information to the company. Its listings of business failures and key business ratios are among the most dependable of economic statistics.

The origins of the present Dun & Bradstreet, Inc., go back to 1841 when it was organized as The Mercantile Agency by Lewis Tappan. Abraham Lincoln, a friend of Tappan, served for a time as a Dun & Bradstreet correspondent. The firm now has more than 300 offices in the United States, Canada, and other countries. Dun & Bradstreet publishes a magazine, *Dun's*, and some reference books. Critically reviewed by DUN & BRADSTREET

DUNANT, *du NAHNG*, **JEAN HENRI** (1828-1910), a Swiss banker, was the founder of the International Red Cross. As a young businessman, he accidentally saw the battle of Solferino in 1859. He was shocked at the lack of care given the wounded. His book, *Recollections of Solferino* (1862), influenced the rulers of Europe tremendously, and in 1863 the Permanent International Committee was organized in Geneva. The next year, delegates of 16 countries agreed to the Geneva Convention for the treatment of wounded and prisoners (see GENEVA CONVENTIONS). The United States ratified this agreement in 1882.

Dunant himself went bankrupt and for 15 years his whereabouts was unknown. He was found in 1890, living in an almshouse, and in 1901 shared the first Nobel peace prize. He was born in Geneva. ALAN KEITH-LUCAS

See also RED CROSS (History).

DUNBAR, BATTLES OF. See SCOTLAND (History).

DUNBAR, PAUL LAURENCE (1872-1906), was an American novelist and poet. His father escaped from slavery in Kentucky before the Civil War and settled in Dayton, Ohio, where Dunbar was born. Dunbar was one of the first authors to picture black life with honesty and realism. For this reason, his works are historically important, though most critics do not consider him a major writer.

In much of his writing, Dunbar portrayed the lives, customs, and speech of Negro Americans. His best novel, *The Sport of the Gods* (1902), describes the hardships of Southern Negroes, but also their dignity and humor. Dunbar wrote many poems in the dialect of the former slave. They include "When Malindy Sings" and "When De Co'n Pone's Hot." CLARK GRIFFITH

DUNCAN I, *DUHNG kuhn* (? -1040), succeeded his grandfather, Malcolm II, as king of Scotland in 1034. William Shakespeare's play *Macbeth* portrays the events in his life in a distorted manner (see MACBETH). A series of unsuccessful efforts to expand his kingdom marked Duncan's reign. He also failed to rule all Scotland. Macbeth of Moray, who had a claim to the throne by right of his wife, killed Duncan in a battle near Elgin. Macbeth reigned until 1057. ROBERT S. HOYT

DUNCAN, ISADORA (1878-1927), an American dancer, greatly influenced dancing in the 1900's. She rebelled against the rigid, formal training of classical ballet and created an individual form of expression. Inspired by the art of Greece, she often danced barefoot in a loose, flowing Greek tunic. She found further inspiration in nature, and she used dance movements to mirror the waves of the sea, passing clouds, and the great thoughts of man.

The Dance Collection, New York Public Library

Isadora Duncan was strongly influenced by classical Greek culture. She usually danced barefoot in a flowing tunic.

Isadora Duncan was born in San Francisco. She gained great success in Europe, where she first performed in 1899. She lived abroad during most of her career and established schools of dance for children in France, Germany, and Russia. Miss Duncan did not succeed in teaching her very personal style to others, but her ideas inspired later generations to seek their own forms of dance expression. SELMA JEANNE COHEN

See also DANCING (Modern Dance).

DUNDEE, *duhn DEE* (pop. 181,842), is a Scottish seaport, 60 miles (97 kilometers) north of Edinburgh, on the Firth of Tay (see GREAT BRITAIN [political map]).

World-famous candy and marmalade come from Dundee. Industries produce ships, metal castings, textile machinery, electric appliances, and linen. Dundee is the center of the British jute trade. It is also the home of the University of Dundee. J. WREFORD WATSON

DUNE is a hill or mound of sand drifted by the wind. Dunes are common in all sandy regions. Many are found along coasts, near large bodies of water, and in deserts. A very large dune may grow to be 500 or 600 feet (150 to 180 meters) high, but most are much lower.

Michigan Tourist Council

The Sleeping Bear Dunes

A traveling dune may move across the desert as it loses sand on one side and gains it on the other. Some dunes make sounds as the grains of sand move across each other. They are called singing dunes. Dunes State Park in Indiana, at the southern end of Lake Michigan, has unusual dunes. Other noted dune areas are the eastern shore of Lake Michigan, Cape Cod in Massachusetts, and along the Gulf of California. ELDRED D. WILSON

See also DESERT (with pictures); SAHARA (picture: A Camel Caravan); NEBRASKA (Land Regions [The Great Plains]); NEW MEXICO (color picture: Shifting Dunes).

DUNFERMLINE, *duhn FURM lihn* (pop. 51,798), is a textile center in the Central Lowlands of Scotland. It lies near the Firth of Forth, about 13 miles (21 kilometers) northwest of Edinburgh. For location, see GREAT BRITAIN (political map).

Linen, silk, and nylon fabrics are produced in the mills of Dunfermline. Its factories manufacture textile machinery and electrical and rubber goods. Other industries include metal foundries and food-processing plants. Dunfermline was an important center of trade as early as the 1000's. Dunfermline Abbey, founded in 1072, is the burial place of several Scottish kings, including Robert Bruce. J. WREFORD WATSON

DUNG BEETLE. See TUMBLEBUG.

DUNHAM, KATHERINE (1909-), is an American dancer and *choreographer* (dance composer) noted for her interpretations of the dances of Negro peoples of the West Indies and the U.S. She made extensive studies of dances of Jamaica and other islands in the West Indies. In the late 1930's and early 1940's, Miss Dunham served as a dancer and choreographer in motion pictures and stage musicals. She organized her own dance company, touring the United States and Europe with ballets based on African and Caribbean ceremonial and folk dances. She operated her own school of dance.

Katherine Dunham was born in Chicago and received a master's degree in anthropology from the University of Chicago. She described her experiences in Jamaica in *Journey to Accompong* (1946). Her autobiography, *A Touch of Innocence*, was published in 1959. SELMA JEANNE COHEN

DUNIWAY, ABIGAIL JANE SCOTT. See OREGON (The Early 1900's).

DUNKER, or DUNKARD. See BRETHREN, CHURCH OF THE.

DUNKERQUE, *DUHN kurk* (pop. 27,504; met. area 143,425), is a seaport on the northern coast of France (see FRANCE [political map]). Dunkerque means *church among the dunes*. It is also spelled DUNKIRK or DUNQUERQUE. The beaches there are wide and sandy. Long bridges link the harbor to the town.

The harbor and town of Dunkerque were greatly damaged early in World War II, when German forces attacked retreating Allied troops. The British Expeditionary Force and other Allied soldiers withdrew into Dunkerque when the Belgian Army surrendered. Dunkerque made a natural spot for defense because it was cut off from the country by canals at the sides and back of the town, and by the sea at its front. German forces surrounded Dunkerque, and German ships lay out in the English Channel. A fleet of almost 1,000 British and French ships carried nearly 350,000 Allied soldiers from Dunkerque to England. All kinds of vessels took part, including destroyers, gunboats, minesweepers, yachts, cruisers, and rowboats. The withdrawal began late in May and ended on June 4, 1940. It was one of the best-ordered military movements in history. ROBERT E. DICKINSON

See also WORLD WAR II (Retreat to Dunkerque; picture: Dunkerque).

DUNLAP, WILLIAM (1766-1839), has been called the father of American drama. He was the first professional playwright in America, the first to produce his own plays, and the first to champion the cause of the native dramatist. He was also the first to adapt plays from the French and German, and his *History of the American Theater* (1832) is the earliest account of the American stage. Of the 56 plays attributed to him, 27 are originals and 29 translations or adaptations. Dunlap's best-known original plays include *André* (1798), *Leicester* (1806), and *A Trip to Niagara* (1828).

Dunlap also wrote biographies and a valuable source book, *History of the Arts of Design in the United States* (1834). He was also a successful painter. Dunlap was born in Perth Amboy, N.J. RICHARD MOODY

DUNLOP, JOHN BOYD (1840-1921), a Scottish veterinarian, developed the *pneumatic* (air-filled) *tire*. He made the first ones to replace solid rubber tires on his son's tricycle so it would ride more comfortably. Dunlop's tire was tested and patented in Great Britain in 1888 and in the United States in 1890. He sold his tire patent and company in 1896. SMITH HEMPSTONE OLIVER

DUNNE, FINLEY PETER (1867-1936), an American newspaperman and humorist, created the saloonkeeper-philosopher, Mr. Dooley. Dooley's criticism of the Spanish American War and its results made Dunne famous. He began his Mr. Dooley series with *Mr. Dooley in Peace and in War*. He was born in Chicago. EDWARD WAGENKNECHT

DUNNING, JOHN RAY (1907-), an American physicist, did research work important in developing the atomic bomb. He produced high-energy particles for changing atoms of one kind into atoms of another kind, by using a cyclotron (see CYCLOTRON). With the cooperation of Alfred O. Nier, who separated small quantities of U-235 and U-238 from uranium, Dunning, E. T. Booth, and A. V. Grosse proved that slowly moving neutrons can cause U-235, but not U-238, to *fission* (split) (see URANIUM [Fission]). Dunning also found that the neutron had magnetic properties.

Dunning pioneered in research on the discharge of neutrons from uranium fission. During World War II, he directed research in isotope separation which was put into large scale use at Oak Ridge, Tenn.

Dunning was born on Sept. 24, 1907, in Shelby, Nebr., and was graduated from Nebraska Wesleyan University. He received his Ph.D. degree at Columbia University. Dunning became assistant professor of physics at Columbia in 1935, and Dean of Engineering there in 1946. RALPH E. LAPP

DUNS SCOTUS, *dunz SKO tus*, **JOHN** (1265?-1308), was a Roman Catholic divine and one of the great thinkers of the Middle Ages. His birthplace is unknown. He entered the Franciscan order, studied at Oxford, and in 1301 became professor of theology there. He maintained the doctrine of the Immaculate Conception against the contrary opinion of Thomas Aquinas, a noted Dominican scholar. He is sometimes known by the title *Doctor Subtilis* (Subtle Doctor). His writings, which are only now being critically edited, combine full orthodoxy with a striking independence of thought. He wrote commentaries on the Bible and Aristotle, and also an *Opus Oxoniense* (Oxford Work). FULTON J. SHEEN

DUNS SCOTUS COLLEGE. See UNIVERSITIES AND COLLEGES (table).

DUNSANY, LORD (1878-1957), wrote more than 50 books, including collections of stories, a novel, and autobiography. He is remembered today for his tales, and for such plays as *The Gods of the Mountain* (1911) and *A Night at an Inn* (1916).

Dunsany's best work is in his short pieces and all his writings tend toward the form of the ironic fable. His writings often deal in the supernatural, and he invented his own mythology—"heavens and earths, and kings and peoples and customs, just as I need them." Nevertheless, his works show the influence of Oriental, Biblical, and classical literature.

Lord Dunsany was born EDWARD JOHN MORETON DRAX PLUNKETT in London of Irish parents. He was also a noted sportsman and soldier. MARTIN MEISEL

DUNSTAN, SAINT (925?-988), was a Roman Catholic archbishop and statesman. He was born and educated at Glastonbury, England, and later became abbot of the monastery there. Dunstan acted as adviser during the reigns of kings Edmund and Edred. Many wise religious and social reforms were begun under his direction, and he also aided in the conquest of the Danes.

He publicly criticized King Edwy, successor to King Edred. For this he was deprived of his offices and banished. But he returned to England in 957, and was made bishop of London the following year. In 960 he was elected archbishop of Canterbury. King Edgar, who followed Edwy, approved of Dunstan's reforms and gave him every assistance. Dunstan retired to Canterbury in 978 after the death of Edgar, and remained there until his death. He was considered a great scholar and statesman who worked for the unity and religious betterment of England. His feast day is May 19. FULTON J. SHEEN

DUODECIMAL NUMERALS, *DOO oh DES uh mul*, form a numeration system based on 12. The Romans, to whom the number 12 was sacred, used the duodecimal system in dividing the foot and pound into twelfths and the year into months. The words *inch* and *ounce* come from the Latin word *uncia*, which means *twelfth*. The system used by merchants in counting by the dozen and by the gross (12 dozen or 144) is a duodecimal system. The word *dozen* comes from *duodecim*, the Latin word for *twelve*. Some writers argue that a duodecimal system could be used more easily than the decimal system. See also NUMERATION SYSTEMS (The Duodecimal System). HOWARD F. FEHR

DUODENUM. See STOMACH.

DUPLICATOR is a machine that makes copies of typed, printed, or handwritten matter or of illustrations. Printing and the use of carbon paper may be considered forms of duplicating. But the term *duplicator* usually refers to office equipment that makes copies of letters, forms, and similar items quickly and inexpensively. Duplicators may also be called *duplicating machines* or *copiers*.

There are dozens of kinds of duplicators. Older types require the preparation of a *master*, a special form from which copies are made. Modern duplicators do not need a master. They duplicate originals—or even copies of originals—that have been typed or written on ordinary paper.

Duplicators differ in size, price, quality of reproduction, and the number of copies they can produce. Four of the most common duplicating machines are the offset duplicator, the spirit duplicator, the stencil duplicator, and the electrostatic copier.

The Offset Duplicator uses the principle of offset printing (see OFFSET). This duplicator requires the preparation of a master. A grease-base image is put on a master sheet by typing, printing, writing, or drawing. After the master has been made, it is placed on a drum in the duplicator. Water and a grease-base ink are applied to the master. The ink sticks only to the grease-base image. The inked image is transferred from the master to a rubber blanket. A roller presses paper against the rubber blanket, duplicating the image on the paper. Business offices use offset duplicators to produce thousands of high-quality copies inexpensively.

The Spirit Duplicator is a simple, inexpensive machine that makes from 30 to 300 copies of an original. Many schools and small firms use it. The spirit duplicator requires a master. The material to be copied is typed on a piece of paper that is backed up by another sheet of paper. The second sheet contains a waxy, dye-impregnated substance. The master sheet is placed face down on a drum on the duplicator. An alcohol-base fluid dissolves a portion of the dye in the image and transfers it to the copy paper in the form of the original typing. This duplicator got its name from the alcohol in the fluid.

The Stencil Duplicator is a small, simple machine that can make from 10 to 5,000 copies. The most widely used stencil duplicator is a machine called a *mimeograph*. A strong, coated tissue is used to make a master, and the typing cuts through the coating. The master is placed in the machine on an ink-filled cylinder covered with an ink pad. A roller presses a piece of paper against the master. The pressure squeezes ink from the pad, through the cuttings on the master, onto the paper.

Electrostatic Copiers use various processes involving static electricity (see ELECTRICITY [Static Electricity]). The best known of these processes is *xerography*. It uses a plate coated with a substance called *selenium*, which conducts electricity when exposed to light. The plate receives an electrostatic charge. The material to be copied is projected through a lens, and a positively charged image forms on the plate. The plate is dusted with negatively charged powder, which sticks to the image. Paper is placed on the plate and gets a positive charge. This charge attracts the powder image to the paper. The paper is heated briefly to melt the powder, forming a copy. Xerography uses the principles of photography, as do several other duplicating methods, including *contact copying* and *projection copying* (see PHOTOCOPYING).

JERRY EIMBINDER

See also HECTOGRAPH; OZALID PROCESS; EDISON, THOMAS A. (picture: Mimeograph Machine).

DU PONT COMPANY, officially the E. I. DU PONT DE NEMOURS & COMPANY, is the largest manufacturer of chemical products in the world. It has about 100 plants in the United States, and branches in Canada and other countries. These plants make cellophane, electrochemicals, explosives, paints, photographic film, plastics, dyes, and other synthetic organic chemicals. Other products include insecticides, fungicides, and such synthetic textile fibers as nylon and Dacron. Headquarters are in Wilmington, Del.

Éleuthère Irénée du Pont, a student of the famous French chemist Antoine Lavoisier, founded the company in 1802. At first the company made only black gunpowder, but in 1880 it began the production of high explosives. In 1890, Du Pont started producing a smokeless explosive based on nitrocellulose. It then became interested in the many useful applications of cellulose (see CELLULOSE). The company began manufacturing lacquers, adhesives, finishes, and plastics. Since the early 1900's, Du Pont has rapidly enlarged its list of products and product lines. Today, the company manufactures about 1,200 products.

During World War II, Du Pont designed, built, and operated the $350 million Hanford Engineer Works near Richland, Wash., for the manufacture of plutonium

WORLD BOOK photo

A Modern Duplicator, such as the machine shown above, can make dozens of copies in minutes. The operator sets an indicator to the number of copies desired and pushes a button.

(see PLUTONIUM). In 1950, Du Pont agreed to design, build, and operate the Savannah River plant in South Carolina for the Atomic Energy Commission.

Other developments since the war include Orlon fiber, Dacron fiber, and an industrial plastic called Teflon. The company makes annual grants of more than $1 million to about 140 universities and colleges in the United States. Critically reviewed by the DU PONT COMPANY

See also CHEMICAL INDUSTRY (table); DELAWARE (picture: Du Pont Experimental Plant); DU PONT DE NEMOURS; MANUFACTURING (table).

DU PONT DE NEMOURS is the name of a famous Delaware family that established the chemical firm of E. I. du Pont de Nemours & Company. Several members of the family have also been active in public affairs.

Pierre Samuel du Pont de Nemours (1739-1817) was a French economist and statesman who came to the United States in 1800. He studied medicine, but turned to economic affairs as a result of national pressures in France. He was a close associate of many well-known French economists of his time, and became a noted author in economics.

Du Pont was caught in the conflicts following the French Revolution, and fled to the United States. President Thomas Jefferson recognized his ability, and asked him to prepare a plan for national education. After affairs quieted in France, Du Pont went back to his home country. He was born in Paris.

Éleuthère Irénée du Pont (1771-1834), the son of Pierre Samuel du Pont, founded the powder works that formed the beginning of the present-day Du Pont Company. He was born in Paris, and ran his father's printing plant until the French Revolution. He fled from France to the United States with his father and older brother and their families. On his arrival, Du Pont saw the need for a powder plant in the new republic. He negotiated with Thomas Jefferson and others to establish it. In 1802, Du Pont selected a site along Brandywine Creek about 4 miles (6.4 kilometers) from Wilmington, Del. Du Pont founded the powder works on the site.

Samuel Francis du Pont (1803-1865), grandson of Pierre Samuel du Pont, served as a rear admiral in the Union Navy during the Civil War. He commanded the South Atlantic Blockading Squadron, and led an unsuccessful attack on Charleston, S.C. He was born at Bergen Point, N.J.

Henry Algernon du Pont (1838-1926), grandson of Éleuthère Irénée du Pont, served as an army officer for 14 years. He was graduated at the head of his class from the United States Military Academy. Du Pont served as a Republican United States senator from Delaware from 1906 to 1917, and was chairman of the Senate Military Committee from 1911 to 1913. He was born near Wilmington, Del.

Thomas Coleman du Pont (1863-1930), great-grandson of Éleuthère Irénée du Pont, made a fortune at an early age in the coal and iron business. He served as president of the Du Pont Company from 1902 to 1915. It was under his leadership that the wide business interests of the family were combined under the present corporate charter of the E. I. du Pont de Nemours Powder Company. Du Pont was active in politics both on the state and national level. A Republican, he was appointed U.S. senator from Delaware in 1921 to fill a vacancy. He served until the election of 1922. He was elected to a Senate term in 1924, but resigned in 1928. He was born in Louisville, Ky.

Pierre Samuel du Pont (1870-1954), great-grandson of Éleuthère Irénée du Pont, served as president of the Du Pont Company from 1915 to 1919 and as chairman of the board from 1919 to 1940. He gave money for schools, hospitals, and other public purposes. He was born in Wilmington. W. H. BAUGHN

See also DU PONT COMPANY.

DU PRÉ, JACQUELINE (1945-), an English cellist, made her debut in London at the age of 16. Before she was 25, she performed as soloist with many internationally famous symphony orchestras. In 1967, she married the Israeli pianist and conductor Daniel Barenboim. She gave many cello-piano recitals with him and appeared as soloist with orchestras he conducted.

David Hurn, Magnum
Jacqueline du Pré

Jacqueline du Pré was born in Surrey. She began studying the cello when she was 5 years old. Du Pré later studied with three famous cellists—William Pleeth in England, Paul Tortelier in Paris, and Mstislav Rostropovich in Moscow. She made her United States debut in New York City in 1965. In 1971, she became ill with multiple sclerosis, which ended her concert and recording activities. REINHARD G. PAULY

DUQUESNE UNIVERSITY, *doo KAYN,* is a coeducational Roman Catholic school in Pittsburgh. It is conducted by the Holy Ghost Fathers. The university has a college of liberal arts and sciences; schools of business and administration, education, law, music, nursing, and pharmacy; and a graduate school. Courses lead to bachelor's, master's, and doctor's degrees. The school was founded in 1878 as Pittsburgh Catholic College of the Holy Ghost and was renamed Duquesne University of the Holy Ghost in 1960. For enrollment, see UNIVERSITIES AND COLLEGES (table).

Critically reviewed by DUQUESNE UNIVERSITY

DURA MATER. See BRAIN (Brain Membranes).

DURALUMIN, *du RAL yuh muhn,* is a term for any one of a group of aluminum-copper alloys. A typical duralumin alloy contains about 95 per cent aluminum, 4 per cent copper, 0.5 per cent magnesium, and 0.5 per cent manganese. Some of these alloys include a small amount of silicon or iron. Duralumin alloys have both strength and lightness and are used in making aircraft parts and heavy-duty equipment such as railroad cars and truck frames. The term is obsolete in the United States but is used in other countries. SEROPE KALPAKJIAN

DURANGO, *doo RANG goh,* is a state of northwestern Mexico (see MEXICO [political map]). It has an area of 46,196 square miles (119,647 square kilometers) and a population of 939,208. Mountains of the Sierra Madre Occidental cover western Durango (see SIERRA MADRE). Silver, lead, copper, and iron ore are mined there.

The eastern part of the state is largely a dry plain

where ranchers raise cattle. Irrigation has aided farming in the Nazas River valley. The city of Durango is the capital and largest city of the state. Durango became a state in 1823. CHARLES C. CUMBERLAND

DURANT, WILL (1885-), is an American historian, philosopher, and educator. He first won recognition in 1926 for his *The Story of Philosophy.* He began his major historical series, *The Story of Civilization,* in 1935. Volumes in this series include *Our Oriental Heritage, The Life of Greece, Caesar and Christ, The Age of Faith, The Renaissance, The Reformation, The Age of Reason Begins, The Age of Louis XIV, The Age of Voltaire,* and *Rousseau and Revolution.* His wife, Ariel, was coauthor of the last four volumes. Durant presented a lively picture of the physical, mental, and spiritual developments of each period. His books are generally considered well documented and well written.

Wide World

Will Durant

Born William James Durant in North Adams, Mass., he was graduated from St. Peter's College, New Jersey. He taught at Columbia University and the University of California. EDWIN H. CADY

DURANT, WILLIAM CRAPO (1861-1947), an American manufacturer, became known as the *godfather of the automobile industry.* He outlined the principles of mass production, low costs, wide distribution, and increased profits. He organized General Motors Company in 1908 and lost control in 1910. He regained control in 1916, and the company was incorporated as General Motors Corporation. Durant was forced to resign in 1920. He organized the Chevrolet Motor Company in 1911, but lost control of it in 1920. He organized Durant Motors, Inc., in 1921, but it went bankrupt. Durant was born in Boston. R. E. WESTMEYER

DURANTE, *du RAN tee,* **JIMMY** (1893-), is an American entertainer. Born James Francis Durante in New York City, he began his career playing the piano. His comic singing and clowning won him fame in vaudeville, the theater, movies, radio, and television. He made his large nose the object of many jokes and became known as the *Schnozzle.* In 1951, he received a Peabody award for television entertainment. His biography, *Schnozzola; The Story of Jimmy Durante,* was written by Gene Fowler. BOSLEY CROWTHER

A. D. Cushman & Assoc.

Jimmy Durante

DURANTY, *du RAN tee,* **WALTER** (1884-1957), was a *New York Times* correspondent from 1913 to 1941. He also wrote novels, history, and books about his newspaper experiences. He covered the French army in World War I, and was the *Times* Moscow correspondent from 1921 to 1934. A series of articles on Russia earned him a Pulitzer prize in 1932. He was born in Liverpool, England. JOHN ELDRIDGE DREWRY

DURBAN, *DUR bun* (pop. 495,458; met. area 843,327), is the chief eastern seaport in South Africa. It is the largest city of Natal Province (see NATAL). For location, see SOUTH AFRICA (color map).

Durban is a trading and industrial center and the most important resort city of South Africa. The city's public buildings face Victoria Embankment, a fine highway along Bay Beach. The jewelry, fruit, and herb stalls of the Indian Market attract many tourists. Durban was founded in 1834. LEONARD M. THOMPSON

DÜRER, *DYOO rer,* **ALBRECHT** (1471-1528), a German painter, engraver, and designer, was one of the foremost artists of his country during the Renaissance. He was perhaps the most original creative German artist, and he influenced generations of artists in northern Europe. He learned much from the Italian painters, and combined their discoveries with the tradition of his German homeland. Dürer combined a love of the ancient world with a deep Christian spirit.

The Prado, Madrid

Albrecht Dürer (self-portrait)

His works include the engraving, *Knight, Death, and the Devil;* a woodcut series, *The Smaller Passion;* and the self-portrait in the Prado in Madrid. Two of his most notable paintings are *Martyrdom of the Ten Thousand* and *Adoration of the Magi.* His water color *Young Hare* appears in color in the PAINTING article.

As an engraver, Dürer developed the methods of Martin Schongauer, and combined them with the lessons of Andrea Mantegna to bring that art to its highest perfection in his century (see MANTEGNA, ANDREA; SCHONGAUER, MARTIN). He probably drew the designs for his woodcuts in the blocks, then carved away the wood to create wood engravings. They were widely copied. His woodcuts are inventive, exuberant, sometimes grim and grotesque.

Dürer was born in Nuremberg, where he probably learned how to engrave from his father, a goldsmith. For three years, he was apprenticed to Michel Wohlgemuth (1434-1519). At 19, he may have visited Italy.

After 1505, Dürer lived in Venice. From his contact with the Venetian painters, Dürer learned to simplify and strengthen his work. He learned further refinements from Flemish painters during a visit he made to The Netherlands. He returned to Nuremberg after 1512, and became the favorite painter of Emperor Maximilian I. He achieved his greatest works there. He was admired by Raphael and Erasmus. S. W. HAYTER

See also BOOKPLATE; ENGRAVING; JEROME, SAINT (picture); RELIGION (color picture: Praying Hands).

DURHAM, *DUR um* (pop. 27,550), is an ancient fortress town in northeastern England. It stands on a hill that is almost surrounded by the River Wear. Its cathedral is a fine example of Norman architecture. The University of Durham is nearby.

Allen Memorial Art Museum, Oberlin College, Oberlin, Ohio

Knight, Death, and the Devil **is one of the magnificent engravings of Albrecht Dürer. The fine details in both the figures and the background show Dürer's meticulous craftsmanship.**

DURHAM, N.C. (pop. 95,438), is a tobacco-manufacturing and textile center in the northeastern part of the state. With Raleigh, it forms a metropolitan area of 419,394 persons. Cigarettes, smoking tobacco, machinery, and cotton goods are manufactured in Durham. Durham is the home of Duke University and North Carolina Central University.

Durham was settled in the 1850's. In 1865, General Joseph E. Johnston surrendered his Confederate army to Union General William T. Sherman at the Bennett Place, just west of the city. Durham has a council-manager form of government. It is the seat of Durham County. HUGH T. LEFLER

DURHAM, COUNTY. See ENGLAND (political map).

DURHAM, *DUR uhm,* **EARL OF** (1792-1840), JOHN GEORGE LAMBTON, an English statesman, became one of the great radical Whig political leaders of his day. His *Report on the Affairs of British North America* was responsible for the union of Upper and Lower Canada, and became the basis of British colonial policy. It marked the peak of his short career as a diplomat. See CANADA, HISTORY OF (Struggle for Responsible Government).

Lambton entered the House of Commons in 1813, and advocated parliamentary reform. He became lord privy seal in 1830. He was one of the four men chosen to draft the Reform Bill in 1832. He resigned as lord privy seal in 1833, and received the title Earl of Durham.

Durham served as ambassador to Russia in 1836. He went to Canada in 1838 to settle matters after the rebellion of 1837 (see REBELLION OF 1837-1838). A special act of the British Parliament granted him special powers as high commissioner to Canada. He resigned this post in great anger in 1838 because the government would not support his highhanded policy toward the rebels. He returned to England in 1839, in failing health, and submitted his famous report. He lived only long enough to see the union of Canada become a reality. He was born in London, England. JAMES L. GODFREY

DURKHEIM, *DURK hym,* **ÉMILE** (1858-1917), was a French sociologist. His theories and writings helped establish the foundations of modern sociology. Durkheim disagreed with most sociologists of the late 1800's because they studied the individual as the basis of sociology. Durkheim regarded sociology as the study of the groups that surround the individual and influence him. Durkheim explained his theories of sociology in his book *The Rules of Sociological Method* (1895).

In *The Division of Labor* (1893), Durkheim developed the theory that societies are bound together by two sources of unity. He called these sources *mechanical solidarities* and *organic solidarities.* Mechanical solidarities are similarities that many people in the society share, such as values and religious beliefs. Organic solidarities result from the division of labor into specialized jobs. Durkheim believed that division of labor makes people depend on one another and thus helps create unity in a society.

Durkheim studied thousands of cases of suicide to demonstrate his theory that a person commits suicide because of the influence of society. He explained this theory in *Suicide* (1897).

Durkheim was born in Épinal, France. He studied at the École Normale Supérieure in Paris and taught sociology at the University of Bordeaux and at the Sorbonne. ROBERT NISBET

See also MYTHOLOGY (Mythology and Society).

DUROCHER, LEO (1906-   ), became one of the most colorful figures in baseball. Durocher was known for his fiery temper, both as a player and, later, as a manager. He managed three National League pennant winners, the Brooklyn Dodgers in 1941 and the New York Giants in 1951 and 1954. The 1954 Giants swept four straight games from the Cleveland Indians in the World Series.

Leo Ernest Durocher was born in West Springfield, Mass. From 1928 to the early 1940's, he played in the majors as a shortstop with the New York Yankees, Cincinnati Reds, St. Louis Cardinals, and Dodgers. He managed the Dodgers from 1939 to 1946 and for part of the 1948 season. He managed the Giants from 1948 to 1955, the Chicago Cubs from 1966 to 1972, and the Houston Astros in 1972 and 1973. HERMAN WEISKOPF

DURRA. See SORGHUM (Grain Sorghums).

DURRELL, LAWRENCE (1912-   ), an English writer, is best known for his series of four novels called *The Alexandria Quartet.* The novels in the series are *Justine* (1957), *Balthazar* (1958), *Mountolive* (1959), and *Clea* (1960). The novels are known for their rich language, unusual characters, and vivid descriptions of the Mediterranean Sea and the city of Alexandria, Egypt. The *Quartet* describes a series of love affairs as seen by the leading characters from different points of view. Durrell champions all forms of love in the *Quartet,* but seems to see love primarily as an emotion which leads to tragedy and despair. Durrell's two related novels *Tunc* (1968) and *Nunquam* (1970) are also filled with rich language and fantastic characters.

Durrell's first novel, *The Black Book* (1938), shows the influence of his close friend, American novelist Henry Miller. Durrell described his life on islands in and near Greece in *Prospero's Cell* (1945), *Reflections on a Marine Venus* (1953), and *Bitter Lemons* (1957). Durrell was born in India. FREDERICK R. KARL

DÜRRENMATT, *DOO ruhn maht,* **FRIEDRICH** (1921-), is a Swiss dramatist and novelist. Many of his plays are tragicomedies more notable for odd and arresting effects than for any single theme. His work shows a fascination with strange and horrible situations and characters. Dürrenmatt presents the world of his time in a state of decay and corruption. But some of his characters speak for his conviction that courage and goodness are possible, as in his best-known play *The Visit* (1956). He also wrote *Romulus the Great* (1949), *The Marriage of Mr. Mississippi* (1952), *The Physicists* (1962), and *The Meteor* (1966). His fiction includes *The Quarry* (1951), *Traps* (1956), and *The Pledge* (1958). Dürrenmatt was born near Bern. PETER GONTRUM

DURYEA is the family name of two brothers who were automobile pioneers. **Charles E.** (1861-1938) and **J. Frank** (1869-1967) built the first successful gasoline-powered automobile in America. Their one-cylinder model made a trial run in 1893 in Springfield, Mass. It is now on exhibition in the Smithsonian Institution in Washington, D.C. A second model won the $2,000 first prize in the Chicago-Evanston, Ill., Thanksgiving Day race in 1895. This was the first U.S. gasoline-automobile race. The two brothers organized the Duryea Motor Wagon Company in 1895, and produced 13 cars in 1896. In 1898, Frank Duryea joined the Stevens Arms Company. There, he designed the four- and six-cylinder Stevens-Duryea automobiles. Charles was born in Canton, Ill., and Frank in Washburn, Ill. See also AUTOMOBILE (picture: Parade of Famous Cars); AUTOMOBILE RACING (History). SMITH HEMPSTONE OLIVER

DU SABLE, *du SAH bul,* **JEAN BAPTISTE POINT** (1745-1818), an American pioneer, built the first house and opened the first trading post in what is now Chicago. Historians have also spelled his name Sable, De Sable, and De Saible.

Detail of an aquatint by an unknown artist. Courtesy of Chicago Historical Society

Jean du Sable

Du Sable, a Negro, was probably born in Haiti. He came to the Chicago area during the 1770's. He made friends with the Indians, and married a Potawatomi Indian girl. He had a farm near Peoria in 1773. Du Sable built a log cabin on the north bank of the Chicago River about 1779. He operated his trading post in part of the cabin, and became rich trading with the Indians. He sold his cabin and post in 1800. He died in St. Charles, Mo. EDGAR ALLAN TOPPIN

DUSE, *DOO zay,* **ELEONORA** (1859-1924), an Italian dramatic actress, has been called "the greatest actress of her time." She seemed to live her parts instead of act them. Critics praised her for her natural and sincere acting. Although shy, she felt at home on the stage.

Bettmann Archive

Eleonora Duse

Gabriele D'Annunzio wrote some of his best plays for her, including *La Gioconda* and *Francesca da Rimini* (see D'ANNUNZIO, GABRIELE). He also fell in love with her, and wrote a book, *The Flame of Life* (1900), based on their love story. She went into retirement for almost 20 years because of this book. She was one of the first major actresses to act in Henrik Ibsen's plays *Hedda Gabler* and *The Lady from the Sea.* She also acted in *Camille* and *Cavalleria Rusticana.*

Miss Duse was born on a train while her actor parents were traveling in Italy. At 14, she played Juliet in *Romeo and Juliet.* She made several successful tours in the United States and other countries. RICHARD MOODY

DUSHANBE, *dyoo shahn BEH* (pop. 388,000), is the capital of Tadzhikistan, a Russian republic. The city is an important transportation and industrial center. In 1929, the government changed the city's name to Stalinabad in honor of Joseph Stalin. During the "destalinization" campaign in 1961, the government renamed the city Dushanbe.

DÜSSELDORF, *DYOOS uhl dawrf* (pop. 680,800), is the capital of the state of North Rhine-Westphalia, in West Germany. It stands mainly on the right bank of the Rhine (see GERMANY [political map]).

Düsseldorf acts as the business and financial center of the great Ruhr industries. Products include chemicals, iron and steel, machinery, railroad equipment, and textiles. Railroads and air lines connect the city with all the important cities in western Europe. Düsseldorf has three important Rhine harbors. It is the home of an academy for medicine, an art school, and the Max-Planck Institute for Iron and Steel Research. The poet Heinrich Heine was born in Düsseldorf. At various times, Johannes Brahms, Robert Schumann, and Johann Wolfgang von Goethe lived there. The city received its first charter in 1288. Bombs severely damaged the city during World War II, but it was rebuilt after the war and again became a governmental and financial center. JAMES K. POLLOCK

DUST is made up of small particles of all kinds of solid matter. A speck of true dust is smaller than $\frac{1}{1000}$ of a millimeter ($\frac{4}{100,000}$ of an inch). Coarser dust may be as large as $\frac{5}{1000}$ of a millimeter ($\frac{2}{10,000}$ of an inch).

The greatest part of all ordinary dust in the atmosphere consists of mineral matter picked up by the wind. It comes from such places as bare soil, crumbling rock ledges, mud flats, and plowed fields.

Volcanic Dust is a special kind of dust that comes from volcanoes. Explosions of volcanoes change solid lava into powder and spray liquid lava into the air, forming tiny drops and shreds of glass. Volcanoes have spread large amounts of their dust over the earth.

Dust Deposits. True dust is repeatedly picked up by the wind or washed into streams. Coarser dust settles

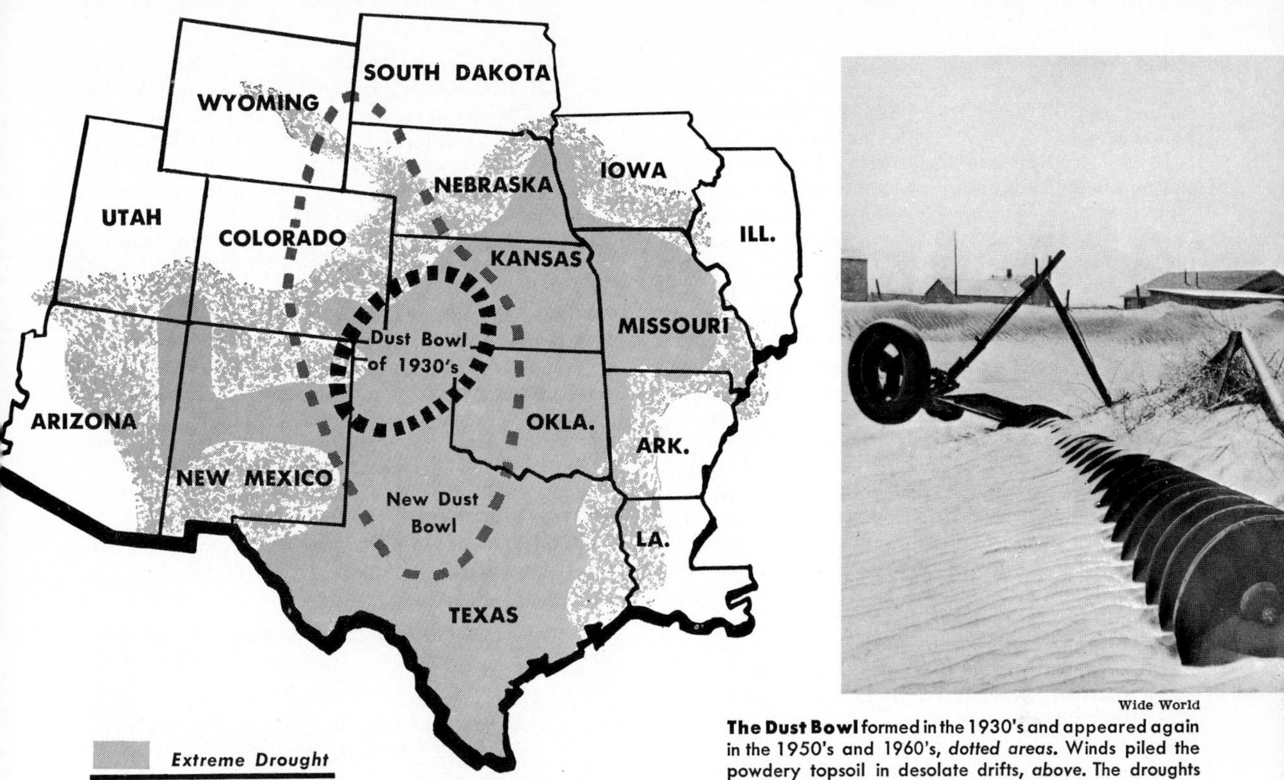

The Dust Bowl formed in the 1930's and appeared again in the 1950's and 1960's, *dotted areas.* Winds piled the powdery topsoil in desolate drifts, *above.* The droughts damaged crops in most of the Southwest and Great Plains, *shaded areas,* causing great hardship.

rapidly. Two kinds of dust deposits cover hills and valleys. One is volcanic dust. The other is ordinary mineral dust blown from the bare mud flats that once lay in front of the great ice sheets covering North America and Europe. The rich soil called *loess,* found in Europe, Asia, and North America, is made of such dust (see LOESS).

Importance to Man. Condensing water vapor settles on dust particles and forms water droplets. When these droplets unite with others, rain or snow may form (see RAIN). Dust also may keep many of the sun's rays from reaching the earth.

Large amounts of mineral dust are always in the air of some quarries, mines, and factories. This dust may collect in workmen's lungs and cause a disease called *silicosis* (see SILICOSIS). Dust also can serve as a carrier for disease bacteria. The spore stages of some disease bacteria can be thought of as dust particles themselves. The same is true of certain mold spores and the pollens which produce hay fever, asthma, and other allergies. ERNEST E. WAHLSTROM

See also DUST BOWL; DUST STORM; AIR (Particles in the Air); AIR CLEANER.

DUST BOWL was a name at one time applied to a part of the Great Plains region of the southwestern United States. Much of the soil there had been damaged by wind and rain, and many severe dust storms occurred. The soil in this area was subjected to water and wind damage because the protective cover of vegetation was impaired or destroyed through poor farming practices and the grazing of too many animals. The area covered some 50 million acres (20 million hectares) and included parts of Texas, New Mexico, Colorado, Kansas, and Oklahoma. Dust storms, however, have occurred in many other parts of the Great Plains, where the soil lacked sufficient vegetative cover to resist attacks by the wind. The Dust Bowl extended eastward from the Rocky Mountains to an irregular line where rainfall averaged only 20 inches (51 centimeters) a year.

Rainfall has often been scanty and scattered in this region. Rain may fall in large amounts at one point, while an area nearby remains dry. There may be a sprinkle of rain or a downpour. When rain does fall, it is usually accompanied by strong winds. Prevailing winds blow at rates from 8 miles (13 kilometers) an hour at the edge of the Great Plains to 16 miles (26 kilometers) an hour in this region and the eastern Dakotas. The temperature rises or falls rapidly. Wheat and sorghum grains are widely grown here and in other parts of the Great Plains. When contour cultivation is practiced, the yields frequently have been good even in years of scanty rainfall. The natural vegetation of the area is short grass, such as buffalo grass and grama. They furnish good grazing for animals, and they also help to keep the soil from washing or blowing away.

The first farmers in the Dust Bowl were settlers who came west after the Civil War and took up homesteads. These farms were often successful in wet years. But nearly all of them were too small to provide even a meager living for a family during periods of dry weather.

Much of the Dust Bowl was sown in wheat during World War I, to meet the great demand for this grain. The wheat, as it was grown then, did not adequately protect the ground against winds. As a result, the soil began to drift.

The most severe dust storms began in the Dust Bowl

in the early 1930's, but many local storms occurred before that where the soil became exposed to the wind.

In 1934, great curtains of dust were carried clear across the continent to the Atlantic Coast and far out into the Gulf of Mexico. During such a storm, it was impossible to see more than a short distance, and some persons in the area wore masks to protect throat and lungs. Farmhouses were sometimes nearly hidden behind drifts of dust. Many farm families left the region. *The Grapes of Wrath*, by John Steinbeck, is a story of some of these families on their migration to California. This novel also described the many hardships the farmers faced in the Dust Bowl. See STEINBECK, JOHN.

In the late 1930's and early 1940's, a fair amount of rain fell in the Dust Bowl and farmers were able to harvest good crops of grain. There were very few dust storms. However, in the 1950's, below-average rainfall and high winds again caused the soil to begin blowing away. Similar conditions occurred in the Dust Bowl area during the mid-1960's. GLENN K. RULE

See also DROUGHT; DUST; DUST STORM.

DUST EXPLOSION results from the rapid chemical union of oxygen with clouds of fine, inflammable dust in an enclosed area. Dust explosions are a hazard in such industrial operations as coal mines and flour mills, which create dust.

In the presence of oxygen, many substances undergo a chemical change called *oxidation*. During this process, molecules of oxygen collide with the surface of a substance and combine with atoms there. Large pieces of aluminum or iron oxidize only on the outside. But clouds of aluminum or iron dust have a huge surface area where oxidation reactions can take place. These reactions produce heat. As the temperature rises, oxidation occurs faster and faster. Finally, the dust explodes.

To help prevent dust explosions, the area around a dusty operation should be kept clean. Ventilating fans also reduce the danger by lowering temperatures and thinning out dust clouds. CHARLES F. SQUIRE

DUST STORM is a strong wind that moves across a region, picking up loose soil and carrying it long distances. This movement of soil, sometimes called *wind erosion*, may rob farmland of its rich topsoil. During a dust storm the air is usually very hot and dry. Sometimes the dust clouds are so thick it is impossible to see through them. Dust storms usually occur during a period of drought (see DROUGHT).

Dust storms are known to have occurred in the ancient world, for records have been found which describe clouds of volcanic ash which were carried for long distances by winds, and violent sand storms in the deserts. In 1902, dust clouds arose over Algeria, and were carried about 1,100 miles (1,770 kilometers) to the British Isles. In the southwestern United States, dust storms damaged valuable farmland during the 1930's.

Dust storms are most likely to occur in regions where there is little rainfall, and where the natural grasses and the farm crops are not deeply rooted in the soil. Areas where the soil is blown away are harmed, but the areas where the soil is deposited are improved. Geologists believe that the lower Mississippi Valley was made more fertile by soil from dust storms. JAMES E. MILLER

See also DUST BOWL; SHELTER BELT.

DUTCH. See NETHERLANDS.

DUTCH AUCTION is a type of public sale which originated in The Netherlands. In a Dutch auction, property is offered to the public at a price beyond its value. Then gradually the auctioneer lowers the price until someone buys the property. The opposite procedure is followed in a regular auction. See also AUCTION.

DUTCH EAST INDIA COMPANY was given a charter and Far Eastern trading privileges by the government of The Netherlands in 1602. This was to strengthen and protect Dutch trade in the East, and to prevent competition between Dutch companies. The headquarters of the company was at Batavia (now Jakarta), Java. Much of the trading was done in pepper and spices. Legislation passed by the Dutch government in 1798 caused the company to disband the following year. The government took over its property. See also EAST INDIA COMPANY; SOUTH AFRICA (History). J. SALWYN SCHAPIRO

DUTCH EAST INDIES. See INDONESIA (History).

DUTCH ELM DISEASE is a severe disease of the elm tree. It is caused by a fungus carried by the European bark beetle and the smaller American bark beetle. The disease can cause the death of a tree in four weeks.

Ewing Galloway

A Greatly Enlarged Photograph shows the tiny American bark beetle. This insect is one of the two kinds of beetles which spread Dutch elm disease from tree to tree.

Dutch elm disease usually begins with a wilting of the younger leaves in the upper part of the tree. Later, lower branches become infected. In about mid-summer, most of the leaves at the branch tips turn yellow, curl, and drop off. When diseased branches are cut, long brown streaks can be seen beneath the bark. Government agencies try to control Dutch elm disease by cutting and burning diseased trees.

Dutch elm disease is so called because the Dutch first observed it in Holland in 1919. It became known in America in 1930, and was limited to an area close to New York City. The disease has now spread over most of the United States. Dutch elm disease afflicts many trees. THEODORE W. BRETZ

DUTCH GUIANA. See SURINAM.

DUTCH HARBOR, Alaska, was the site of a United States naval air base during World War II. Planes flying from that base formed part of the continental air defense of the United States. The base was deactivated after the war. Dutch Harbor was one of several Alaskan towns bombed by the Japanese in 1942. The town lies on Dutch Harbor, a natural bay on the eastern side of Amaknak Island in Unalaska Bay. For location, see ALASKA (political map). LYMAN E. ALLEN

DUTCH LANGUAGE. See NETHERLANDS (People).

DUTCH LITERATURE. See NETHERLANDS (Arts).

DUTCH OVEN is a covered metal cooking pot. Modern Dutch ovens are usually made of aluminum. American pioneers used a cast-iron Dutch oven with a rimmed lid. The pot was set on hot coals, and coals were also placed on the lid. Brick ovens in fireplaces and chimneys are sometimes called Dutch ovens.

DUTCH REFORMED CHURCH. See REFORMED CHURCHES IN AMERICA.

DUTCH WEST INDIA COMPANY was formed by Dutch merchants and chartered by the government of The Netherlands in 1621. The company was given trading and colonizing privileges for a period of 24 years in North America, the West Indies, and Africa. The colony of New Netherland included parts of what are now the states of New York, New Jersey, Delaware, and Connecticut. The colony was founded by the Dutch West India Company, and had headquarters in New Amsterdam (now New York City). See also NEW NETHERLAND; PATROON SYSTEM. J. SALWYN SCHAPIRO

DUTCH WEST INDIES. See NETHERLANDS ANTILLES.

DUTCHMAN'S-BREECHES, also called WHITE HEART, is a small delicate plant with flattened, heart-shaped flowers. This perennial grows from Nova Scotia to Georgia and west to Nebraska. It is also found in Washington and Oregon. The plant has lacy, fernlike leaves, pale bluish-green in color. The stems of the plant are brittle and contain a watery sap. The stem grows from an underground tuber (see TUBER).

J. Horace McFarland
Dutchman's-Breeches

Dutchman's-breeches gets its name from the shape of its flowers. Each leafless flower stalk has four to ten nodding fragrant flowers that look like baggy trousers hanging upside down. The flowers are waxy white or pinkish-white with yellow tips.

Scientific Classification. Dutchman's-breeches is a member of the fumitory family, *Fumariaceae*. It is genus *Dicentra*, and species *D. cucullaria*. ROBERT W. HOSHAW

DUTY, in economics. See TARIFF.

DUVAL, WILLIAM P. See FLORIDA (History).

DUVALIER, *doo vah LYAY,* **FRANÇOIS** (1907-1971), was the president of Haiti from 1957 until his death in 1971. Duvalier ruled as a dictator and allowed no one to oppose or criticize him. He was elected to a seven-year term as president in 1957. In 1961, before his term ended, he declared himself re-elected. He was elected president for life in 1964 by the National Assembly, whose members he had selected.

Wide World
François Duvalier

Duvalier was a physician and an authority on voodoo, a kind of religion practiced by most Haitians. He used the Haitian peasants' fear of voodoo to maintain his power (see VOODOO). Many peasants believed he had magical powers. Duvalier also controlled the armed forces and a feared secret police force which the people call the *ton ton macoutes* (bogeymen).

Duvalier was born in Port-au-Prince, Haiti. He graduated from the National University of Haiti medical school in 1934. He was secretary of labor and public health in 1949 and 1950, and adviser to a public health commission from 1952 to 1954. THOMAS G. MATHEWS

DU VIGNEAUD, VINCENT. See NOBEL PRIZES (table: Nobel Prizes for Chemistry—1955).

DUVOISIN, *dyoo vwah ZAN,* **ROGER ANTOINE** (1904-), is an American artist and illustrator. He won the 1948 Caldecott medal for his illustrations in *White Snow, Bright Snow,* a children's book by Alvin Tresselt. He wrote and illustrated his first children's book, *A Little Boy Was Drawing,* for his son in 1932. He also wrote *And There Was America* and *Christmas Whale.* He illustrated many books by Tresselt and other authors, including Louise Fatio's *Happy Lion.* Duvoisin was born in Geneva, Switzerland, but became a United States citizen in 1938. RUTH HILL VIGUERS

DVINA RIVER, *dvee NAH,* is the name of two rivers in Russia. One, called the Western Dvina or Daugava, rises west of Moscow, and flows into the Gulf of Riga at Riga, Latvia. It is 633 miles (1,019 kilometers) long.

Another river, the Northern Dvina, is an important waterway in northwestern Russia. The Northern Dvina, formed by the Sukhona and Vychegda rivers, is 455 miles (732 kilometers) long. It flows into the White Sea at the port of Archangel. Steamboats travel on the Northern Dvina. It is connected to the Neva and Volga rivers by the Northern Dvina Canal. For the location of both of the rivers, see RUSSIA (map: European Russia). THEODORE SHABAD

DVOŘÁK, *DVAWR zhahk,* **ANTONÍN** (1841-1904), was a Czech composer. He and Bedřich Smetana are considered the founders of the Czech national school of music. Dvořák composed in a variety of musical forms, including songs, *chamber music* (compositions played by small groups), choral works, operas, symphonies, and dances. He is best known for his symphony *From the New World.* This symphony is a good example of the neoromantic music style of the late 1800's.

The folk music of the Czechs and other Slavic peoples was the main source of Dvořák's music. Dvořák's songs have passages of powerful dramatic expression and skillful use of melody. His best-known songs include *Moravian Duos* (1876), *Gypsy Melodies* (1880), and *Biblical Songs* (1894). His most famous chamber work is the piano trio *Dumky* (1891). The music in his chamber works, as well as in such orchestral works as the *Carnival* overture (1892), is lyrical and powerful. Dvořák's major choral works include the famous *Stabat Mater* (1876), composed after the death of two of his children; and the oratorio *St. Ludmila* (1886). *Rusalka* (*The Water-Nymph,* 1900) is the best of his several operas.

Dvořák was born in Nelahozeves, a small village near Prague. At the age of 16, he went to Prague to study music. The Czech National Theater was founded in 1862, and Dvořák became a viola player in its orchestra. Dvořák began composing at about the same time. He was his own greatest critic, and, in 1873, he burned the scores of most of the works he had composed.

A performance of the cantata *Hymnus* in 1873 marked the first public performance of a Dvořák work. The work received great acclaim. Dvořák soon applied for a *stipend* (grant) offered to musicians by the government. He submitted the score of a symphony to support his application. The judges, including Johannes Brahms, were so impressed by the power of Dvořák's music that they granted him a three-year stipend. This occasion also began a lifelong friendship with Brahms, who used his influence to help get Dvořák's works published.

In 1878, Dvořák composed the first set of his well-known *Slavonic Dances*. A performance of this work in 1879 in London made Dvořák known in England. Beginning in 1884, Dvořák visited England many times to conduct performances of his orchestral and his choral works.

In 1891, Dvořák became professor of musical composition at the Prague Conservatory. His growing fame and the success of his works in the United States brought him an offer to serve as director of the National Conservatory of Music in New York City. Dvořák held this position from 1892 to 1895. At the same time, he conducted, and visited Czech and other Slavic settlements in the Midwest. See Iowa (Places to Visit).

Dvořák composed *From the New World* while living in the United States. The work was his ninth and last symphony. But it is usually referred to as his fifth symphony, because he started numbering his symphonies only after 1880. Dvořák made use of Negro spiritual melodies in his last symphony. He never used folk song melodies note for note but transformed them, preserving their spirit. Miloš Velimirović

DWARF is an unusually small adult human being, animal, or plant. Human dwarfs are people who grow no more than 4½ feet (135 centimeters) tall. Those who have normal body proportions are often called *midgets*. Other human dwarfs have abnormal proportions. There are several kinds of dwarf animals, including dwarf cattle and toy dogs. Dwarf plants include ornamental fruit trees and several varieties of flowers, such as marigolds and dahlias.

Dwarfism occurs both in individual organisms and in entire groups of organisms. Such groups include African Pygmies, Shetland ponies, and the various kinds of dwarf trees. In general, dwarfism occurs as a result of defective cells, disease, or poor nutrition.

This article discusses human dwarfism, which occurs as the result of an underdeveloped skeleton. The growth of the skeleton depends on the formation of tissue called *cartilage* (see Cartilage; Bone [Development of the Bones]). Dwarfism results when the cartilage cells do not grow and divide properly. Such improper development may occur because of defective cartilage cells or interference with the growth of otherwise normal cartilage cells. Defective cartilage cells cause *chondrodystrophic dwarfism* or *chromosome-related dwarfism*, depending on whether the defect is restricted to the cartilage cells alone or is part of a more widespread cellular disorder. The interference with the growth of normal cartilage cells results in *hormonal dwarfism* or *nonhormonal dwarfism*, depending on what causes the interference.

Chondrodystrophic Dwarfism occurs when only certain cartilage cells are defective. The term *chondrodystrophic* means *underdeveloped cartilage*. Most chondrodystrophic dwarfs have abnormal body proportions. The defective cells occur only in the spine or only in the arms and legs. Consequently, either the *torso* (chest, abdomen, and hips) or the limbs grow unusually short.

Chromosome-Related Dwarfism results when all the cells of the body, including the cartilage cells, are defective. Such defects involve a disturbance in the number of *chromosomes* per cell. The chromosomes are the cell structures that contain *genes*. Genes provide the cell with information on how to grow and divide. Each body cell normally has 46 chromosomes. If a cell is missing one chromosome, it may lack genes essential for growth. One such disorder is *Turner's Syndrome*.

Hormonal Dwarfism may occur when a hormone deficiency interferes with the growth of normal cartilage cells. Hormones are chemical substances that are secreted by various glands. They circulate through the blood and influence the cells of the body to act in certain ways. The hormones that stimulate growth include growth hormone (GH) from the pituitary gland, insulin from the pancreas, and thyroxine from the thyroid gland.

An insufficient amount of a growth-promoting hor-

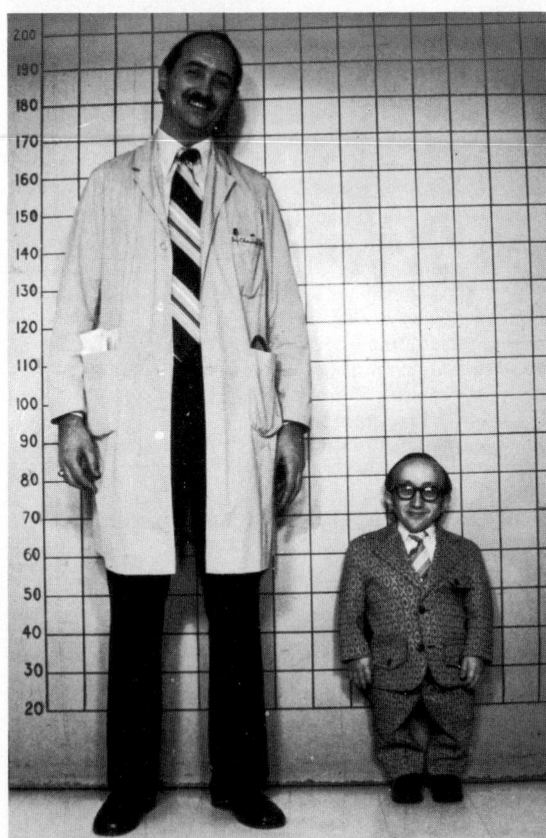

Charles I. Scott, Jr., The University of Texas Medical School at Houston

A Chondrodystrophic Dwarf has defects of the skeleton. The chondrodystrophic dwarf above stands about 2 feet 10 inches (85 centimeters) tall. His physician, shown for comparison, is nearly 6 feet 8 inches (200 centimeters) tall.

Bodger Seeds, Ltd.

Many Dwarf Plants, such as the dwarf zinnia above, are popular garden flowers. Most such plants have been bred by man. A flower from a full-sized zinnia is shown for comparison.

mone leads to stunted growth. For example, a shortage of GH results in a dwarf with normal proportions. Insufficient insulin leads to the disease *diabetes mellitus*, and a shortage from birth of thyroxine causes *cretinism*. Both these disorders interfere with growth and may lead to dwarfism. See DIABETES; CRETINISM.

Children who lack a certain growth-promoting hormone may be treated by a physician. Since the mid-1960's, doctors have given GH to children who lack this hormone. But only limited amounts of GH are available, and many youngsters remain untreated. Insulin and thyroxine, which are readily available, may be given to stimulate growth in children affected by diabetes or cretinism.

Nonhormonal Dwarfism occurs if disease or improper nourishment blocks the growth of cartilage cells. For example, a disease of the bowel or kidneys may interfere with growth. Many nonhormonal interferences can be corrected, with rapid "catch-up" growth taking place after treatment. DAVID RABINOWITZ

See also BONSAI; CATTLE (Dwarf Cattle); PYGMY; SHETLAND PONY; TOY DOG.

DWELLING. See HOUSE; HOUSING; SHELTER.

DWIGHT, JOHN (1637?-1703), an English potter, won fame for creating "Fulham figurines," a group of portrait busts and figurines in salt-glazed stoneware. The figurines are in the British Museum and Victoria and Albert Museum, both in London. Dwight may have been born in Oxfordshire. He founded the Fulham Pottery at Fulham, Middlesex, in 1671. EUGENE F. BUNKER, JR.

DYAK, *DIE ak*, or DAYAK, is a member of a tribe that lives on Borneo. There are two groups of Dyaks. *Sea Dyaks* (Iban) live along the seacoast and rivers of Borneo. *Land Dyaks*, a smaller group, live inland in Sarawak in northeastern Borneo. Dyaks are about 5 feet (1.5 meters) tall, and have brown skin, dark eyes, and broad faces with prominent cheekbones. They tie their long straight hair in a knot at the back of the head. Many Dyaks chew betel nuts, which make their mouths red and blacken their teeth (see BETEL).

Dyaks live in bamboo houses. The houses are built on poles, with floors from 6 to 10 feet (1.8 to 3 meters) above the ground. They may be from 30 to 1,000 feet (9 to 300 meters) long and may house as many as 50 families. Each family farms its own land. Rice is the chief crop. The leading industries are boat-building and weaving.

The Sea Dyaks once were aggressive hunters and pirates, and many were headhunters. The Land Dyaks were peaceful farmers. Now, most Dyaks are farmers or plantation workers. Some teach in schools. Others hold civil service or factory jobs. Many Dyaks are Christians, and others are Moslems. WILTON MARION KROGMAN

Visual Education Service

A Dyak Woman of Borneo spins the yarn for cloth on this crude wheel. She wears a metal corselet around the upper part of her body. Her necklace is made of betel nuts.

DYER, MARY (? -1660), a colonist from England, became a martyr to the Quaker faith. With her husband, William, she arrived in Massachusetts about 1635. Because of religious intolerance, they later moved to Rhode Island. In 1650 she returned to England, and joined the Society of Friends, or Quakers. Seven years later, she came back to America. She was arrested repeatedly for "bearing witness to her faith." Finally, in Boston, she was charged with sedition, convicted, and hanged. IAN C. C. GRAHAM

DYES AND DYEING. Dyes are coloring substances. They are used mainly to color clothing, draperies, carpets, and other *textiles* (woven or knit materials). Dyes are also used to color fur, hair, ink, leather, paper, wood, and many other materials. Dyeing is the process by which dyes are applied to materials.

Man has made clothing and other materials more attractive by dyeing them different colors for perhaps 5,000 years. Until the mid-1800's, all dyes were made from natural substances—usually from plants and animals. Natural dyes have been almost entirely replaced by *synthetic* (man-made) dyes since that time.

How Dyes Work

Dyes dissolve in water to form a solution. A dye's molecules are absorbed into the textile *fibers* (threads) from the solution. Dyes that become a fixed part of the fibers do not easily fade, even after many washings. Dyes that resist fading from ordinary conditions or use are called *fast* dyes. For example, dyes that do not wash out are *wash fast*. Dyes that are not faded by sunlight are *light fast*.

Fibers vary in their ability to absorb and hold dyes. Some fibers will readily absorb a wide variety of dyes, although many of the dyes may not be held fast. Other fibers have a very low *affinity* (chemical attraction) for some dyes. Substances called *mordants* help to improve the dyeability of both these types of fibers. Mordants are applied to the fibers to attract and hold the dyes permanently. Commonly used mordants include tannic acid, and salts of such metals as aluminum, chromium, copper, iron, lead, and tin.

Kinds of Dyes

Natural Dyes were the only dyes used until the mid-1800's. Natural dyes from vegetables were obtained from the bark, berries, flowers, leaves, and roots of a wide variety of plants. Indigo, a deep blue dye, was used on cotton and wool. It was made from the indigo plant, which grows chiefly in India. Bright red and brown dyes for cotton and wool were often made from the roots of the madder plant, which grows in Europe and Asia. Yellow, orange, brown, and black dyes came from the bark, leaves, and center wood of such trees as the oak, sumac, maple, and walnut. These dyes could be applied to leather, skins, and all natural fibers. Henna, an orange-red dye, came from a shrub grown in northern Africa and the Middle East. It was used for dyeing silk and wool, and for tinting or dyeing human hair.

Fred Fortess, the contributor of this article, is Manager of Consumer and Technical Services for the Celanese Fibers Marketing Company.

Animal dyes were used much less than vegetable dyes. Carmine, a bright red dye, was obtained from cochineal insects of Mexico and Central America. Tyrian purple was a scarce and expensive dye from certain shellfish found in the Aegean and eastern Mediterranean seas.

The salts of some metals were used as mordants to fix animal and vegetable dyes on fabrics. Many mineral *pigments* (powdered coloring matters) have been used since early times. Ancient peoples used pigments to color their bodies, decorate pottery, and make wall paintings. But pigments can be removed with soap and water. Therefore, they are not true dyes.

Synthetic Dyes have almost entirely replaced natural dyes for commercial dyeing. They are less expensive to produce than natural dyes. Thousands of synthetic dyes are available. They are much more colorfast than natural dyes. Most synthetic dyes are made from products distilled from coal tar. These products include aniline, anthracene, benzene, naphthalene, and toluene. See Coal Tar.

The first synthetic dye was made by William H. Perkin, an English chemist, in 1856. He accidentally produced a pale purple dye called mauve while he was trying to make quinine from aniline. Germany produced most of the world's supply of synthetic dyes before World War I. The war cut off this supply to the Allies, so the United States began developing its own dyes. Today, the United States is one of the world's leading manufacturers of synthetic dyes.

Synthetic dyes are often grouped according to the way they become *fixed* (attached and held) on fibers. *Vat dyes* and *sulfur dyes* are used on cotton and rayon. These dyes cannot be applied in their original forms, because they will not dissolve in water. When given certain chemical treatments, the insoluble dyes become pale or colorless solutions. Cotton and rayon fibers absorb these solutions. The fibers are then treated with oxygen to produce colored, wash-fast dyes. *Acid dyes* are applied to wool, silk, and nylon from an acid bath, and produce a wide range of bright, fast shades. Some acid dyes contain metals to help fix the dye on the fiber. *Disperse dyes* are used on acetate, nylon, polyester, and acrylic fibers. They are absorbed by the fibers from a mixture of the dye in very hot water.

Developed dyes are used on a wide variety of fibers. They are applied to the fibers as simple compounds that dissolve easily in water. The fibers are then treated with a solution that "develops" a new dye on the fiber. *Basic dyes* are applied to silk, wool, nylon, acetate, and acrylic fibers from slightly alkaline solutions. They produce many deep, brilliant colors. *Reactive dyes* chemically react with cotton, rayon, and nylon fibers to give bright, extremely wash-fast dyes.

Dyeing Textile Materials

Textile materials may be dyed at various stages in their manufacture. *Stock dyeing* is the dyeing of raw fibers before they are spun into yarn. Dyes may be applied to fibers after they have been spun into yarn and made into *skeins* (small coiled bundles). This is called *skein*, or *yarn, dyeing*. Fibers may also be dyed after being woven into cloth. This process is called *piece dyeing*.

Stock dyeing and skein dyeing are often done by soaking the fibers or yarn in large tubs. Piece dyeing may be done with several different types of machines. Machines either pull the fabric through the dye bath, or pump the hot dye through the material. Some continuous dyeing machines permit up to 50,000 yards (46,000 meters) of fabric to be dyed without stopping the machine.

Textile printing is done by applying colored patterns to the outer surface of fabrics. The patterns are transferred to the fabric from *etched* (engraved) rolls or from stencils placed on a silk screen. See Silk-Screen Printing.

Fred Fortess

Related Articles in World Book include:

Aniline	Coal Tar	Lake (dye)	Prussian Blue
Batik	Cobalt	Logwood	Purple
Buckthorn	Cochineal	Madder	Stain
Carmine	Color	Mauve	Tie Dyeing
Catechu	Henna	Mordant	Turmeric
Chrome	Indigo		

DYHRENFURTH, *DEER en furth,* **NORMAN GUNTHER** (1918-), organized the first United States expedition to reach the top of Mount Everest. Dyhrenfurth did not climb the summit himself, but he selected the six climbers who did. This expedition, in May, 1963, put more men on the 29,028-foot (8,848-meter) peak than any previous expedition. It was also the first to scale the summit by the difficult west ridge route. Dyhrenfurth worked on the preparations for this trip for $2\frac{1}{2}$ years.

Dyhrenfurth previously climbed in six other major expeditions and helped lead three of them. He was a member of four Himalayan climbing expeditions. Dyhrenfurth was born in Breslau, Germany (now Wrocław, Poland). He learned climbing from his parents in Switzerland. He moved to the United States in 1938 and became a citizen.

See also MOUNT EVEREST.

DYLAN, *DIHL ihn,* **BOB** (1941-), is an American folk singer, musician, and composer. He has written many songs about social problems. These songs made Dylan a symbol of protest by young people against what they considered the wrongs of society. His best-known compositions include "Blowin' in the Wind" (1962), "The Times They Are A-Changin' " (1963), "Like a Rolling Stone" (1965), and "John Wesley Harding" (1968).

Jim Marshall, Photon West

Bob Dylan

Dylan was born in Duluth, Minn. His real name was Robert Zimmerman. He played the guitar, harmonica, and piano by the time he was 15. In 1960, he traveled to New York City to visit Woody Guthrie, a famous folk singer and composer. Guthrie greatly influenced the musical style of Dylan, who remained in New York City and sang in folk music clubs. In 1963, Dylan met folk singer Joan Baez, who helped make him nationally famous. LEONARD FEATHER

DYNAMICS, *dy NAM iks,* in physics, is the study of force and motion. The name *dynamics* comes from the Greek word *dynamis,* meaning power. Forces cause an object to change its speed or the direction of its motion. Sir Isaac Newton stated the relationship between these forces and changes in motion in his second law of motion (see FORCE [Measuring Force]; MOTION [Newton's Laws]). According to this law, the larger the force on an object, the larger the change in its motion.

In music, dynamics indicates the degree of loudness or softness of a tone. Some dynamics terms include *piano* (soft), *forte* (loud), *crescendo* (gradually louder), and *diminuendo* (gradually softer). See MUSIC (Notation).

Psychologists use the term *group dynamics* to mean the study of how people work together in a group (see GROUP DYNAMICS). ROBERT L. WEBER

See also KINEMATICS; MECHANICS; STATICS.

DYNAMITE, *DIE nuh mite,* is the world's most valuable industrial explosive. It is used to blast out dam sites, canal beds, and the foundations for large buildings. Mines, quarries, and dredging and construction projects in the United States use about 2½ million pounds (1,130,000 kilograms) of dynamite every day.

Nitroglycerin is the principal explosive used in dynamite. It is mixed with other relatively inert materials, some explosive and some nonexplosive, to make an explosive charge. This charge is safe to handle until a *detonating cap,* also called a *blasting cap,* sets it off.

Dynamite may be packed in waxed paper cylinders called *cartridges.* These cartridges vary from ⅞-inch to 8 inches (22 millimeters to 200 millimeters) in diameter, and range in length from 4 to 30 inches (10 to 76 centimeters). There are nearly 200 kinds of dynamite, each of which is suited to some particular type of blasting.

The first dynamite was produced in 1867 by Alfred Nobel, Swedish chemist and donor of the five Nobel prizes. Nobel discovered that *kieselguhr,* a chalky earth, would absorb about three times its own weight of nitroglycerin. This mixture was less sensitive to shock than pure nitroglycerin. It could be packed into paper tubes and inserted into drilled holes for efficient blasting.

Nobel improved his original formula by first substituting wood pulp and sawdust for kieselguhr. He added potassium nitrate to furnish oxygen for the explosion. The present-day *straight dynamites* are made from the same ingredients, except that sodium nitrate has replaced the more expensive potassium nitrate. Straight dynamites are used chiefly for earth blasting. Other dynamites are less dangerous and less expensive. But straight dynamites still serve as the standard for determining the strength of dynamites.

In 1875, Nobel patented a dynamite called *blasting gelatin.* This was a plastic, rubberlike explosive made by adding 7 to 10 per cent of nitrocotton to nitroglycerin. This dynamite had the property of keeping its full blasting efficiency under water. Later, Nobel

Dynamite blows a column of smoke and dirt skyward, *above,* as it makes a test hole for oil-well drillers. It is set off from a safe distance by the worker, *right.* He presses a handle to turn a generator that sends a detonating electric current through a wire to the charge.

Sun Oil Company; DuPont

added wood pulp and sodium nitrate to a new formula for blasting gelatin, producing the type of dynamite now sold as *straight gelatin.*

Permissable dynamites were developed between 1900 and 1910. Low nitroglycerin and high ammonium-nitrate contents characterized these dynamites. They were designed to increase the safety of coal mining. They replaced black powder, which had been used as a mine explosive. The flame of a black-powder explosion has a tendency to ignite coal gas and coal dust. This had caused many mining disasters.

Today, ammonium nitrate is the major ingredient in most dynamite. This type of dynamite is manufactured in the form of *ammonia dynamite* and *ammonia gelatin.* These are just as strong as the straight types, but are less dangerous to handle and cheaper to manufacture. They cannot be used underwater, because the ammonium nitrate would dissolve. Many blasting operators use a mixture of ammonium nitrate and fuel oil as the main explosive charge. This mixture is cheaper to make and safer to use than dynamite, but it needs some dynamite to start it. JULIUS ROTH

Related Articles in WORLD BOOK include:

Blasting	Explosive	Nitroglycerin	TNT
Cellulose	Fuse	Nobel, Alfred B.	

DYNAMO. See ELECTRIC GENERATOR.

DYNAMOMETER. See HORSEPOWER.

DYNAMOTOR, *DIE nuh MOH ter,* is an electric machine that can be used as both a motor and a generator. It can change a direct current from high to lower voltage, or from low to higher voltage. Transformers usually handle only alternating current. The dynamotor might be called a direct-current transformer. Its armature has two windings, and each winding can be used as either a motor winding or a generator winding. Dynamotors are used to change low voltage into higher voltage to start a motor. They may also divide a high voltage into lower voltages. RAYMOND F. YATES

DYNE, *dine,* is a unit of the metric system which is used to measure force. A dyne is defined as the force which, acting upon one gram of matter, will give it an acceleration of one centimeter per second for every second the force acts. The dyne is the scientific, or absolute, unit in the centimeter-gram-second (C.G.S.) system of units, and corresponds to the *poundal* in the English system (see MECHANICAL UNIT). An *erg* of work is the work done by a force of one dyne acting through a distance of one centimeter. For large measurements it is customary to use the *megadyne,* which is equal to 1 million dynes. E. G. STRAUS

DYNEL, *DIE nul,* is a warm, strong, light-weight synthetic fiber (see FIBER [Synthetic Fibers]). It can be spun on the same machines as cotton, wool, or silk. Manufacturers use dynel, alone or in combination with other fabrics, to make clothing, blankets, draperies, and industrial products. Dynel fabrics launder easily and dry quickly. They resist moths, fungi, and mildew.

D'YOUVILLE COLLEGE. See UNIVERSITIES AND COLLEGES (table).

DYSENTERY, *DIHS un TER ih,* is a severe disease which affects the colon. There is inflammation of the colon with painful diarrhea. Blood and mucus are passed in the stool. In some cases there may be fever and delirium. The two most common kinds of dysentery are *amebic* dysentery and *bacillary* dysentery.

Amebic Dysentery is caused by a one-celled animal called an *ameba* (see AMEBA). It results in severe inflammation of the colon, bloody diarrhea, and sometimes formation of abscesses in the liver or brain. The disease is spread by taking the tiny amebas into the mouth on food and objects. Fresh vegetables and fruits which have been handled and those which have been grown in soil fertilized with human feces may be infected. The organism at this time is in a resting, or dormant, stage called the *cyst.* As it enters the intestinal tract, however, it becomes very active, growing and reproducing itself. The organism causes the formation of holes, or ulcers, in the bowel. Later, ulcers may also form in the liver.

Amebic dysentery is most common in warm and tropical countries. It may break out in cooler climates, however. A very severe epidemic of amebic dysentery occurred, for example, in Chicago in 1933.

Amebic dysentery can be prevented by cleanliness and sanitation, careful examination of food handlers, and purification of water and sewage. A person living in a region in which there is much amebic dysentery must be especially cautious about everything that is handled or eaten. Amebic dysentery can sometimes be cured by the drugs emetine and stovarsol.

Bacillary Dysentery is caused by bacteria. It occurs in all countries and climates, and is especially common during the summer. The disease occurs frequently in institutions and camps. The symptoms include severe, bloody diarrhea; abdominal cramps; fever; and loss of appetite. The disease is spread by eating contaminated foods. It can be prevented by cleanliness, sanitation, and the purification of water and food supplies. Treatment of bacillary dysentery includes complete bed rest, a liquid diet, and the use of sulfadiazine, one of the sulfa drugs. E. CLINTON TEXTER

DYSLEXIA. See ALEXIA.

DYSPEPSIA, *dis PEP shuh,* is a term which is loosely used to refer to a disorder in digestion. Dyspepsia usually has such symptoms as pain in the upper abdomen, heartburn, belching, fullness and heaviness in the stomach region, and spitting up food or sour-tasting liquid. Dyspepsia may be caused by ulcers of the stomach or duodenum, hyperacidity, cancer of the stomach, gallstones, infection of the gall bladder, colitis, constipation, adhesions, chronic appendicitis, and worry and nervousness. It can be treated only by treating the disorder which is causing it. In many cases, proper diet is part of the treatment. HYMAN S. RUBINSTEIN

DYSPROSIUM, *dihs PROH shih um* (chemical symbol, Dy), is one of the rare-earth metals. Its atomic number is 66, and its atomic weight is 162.50. The name comes from the Greek word *dysprositos,* meaning *hard to get.* French scientist Paul Émile Lecoq de Boisbaudran discovered dysprosium in 1886. It is found associated with erbium, holmium, and other rare earths in the minerals gadolinite, euxenite, xenotime, and others. Dysprosium is best separated from the other rare earths by ion-exchange processes (see ION AND IONIZATION). When cooled to low temperatures, dysprosium is strongly attracted by a magnet. FRANK H. SPEDDING

See also RARE EARTH.

DYSTROPHY, MUSCULAR. See MUSCULAR DYSTROPHY.